Principles of Economics

ECON 2105 & 2106

7th Edition

Robert L. Sexton

CENGAGE
Learning·

Australia • Brazil • Japan • Korea • Mexico • Singapore • Spain • United Kingdom • United States

Principles of Economics: ECON 2105 & 2106, 7th Edition

Exploring Microeconomics, 7th Edition
Robert L. Sexton

For product information and technology assistance, contact us at
Cengage Learning Customer & Sales Support, 1-800-354-9706

For permission to use material from this text or product,
submit all requests online at **cengage.com/permissions**
Further permissions questions can be emailed to
permissionrequest@cengage.com

This book contains select works from existing Cengage Learning resources and was produced by Cengage Learning Custom Solutions for collegiate use. As such, those adopting and/or contributing to this work are responsible for editorial content accuracy, continuity and completeness.

Compilation © 2015 Cengage Learning

ISBN: 978-1-305-74890-3

WCN: 01-100-101

Cengage Learning
20 Channel Center Street
Boston, MA 02210
USA

Cengage Learning is a leading provider of customized learning solutions with office locations around the globe, including Singapore, the United Kingdom, Australia, Mexico, Brazil, and Japan. Locate your local office at:
www.international.cengage.com/region.

Cengage Learning products are represented in Canada by Nelson Education, Ltd.

For your lifelong learning solutions, visit **www.cengage.com/custom.**

Visit our corporate website at **www.cengage.com.**

*To Teachers of Economics
Everywhere:*

*Opening Their Students'
Minds to the Wonders
of Economics*

BRIEF CONTENTS

TABLE OF CONTENTS

3 MARKET EFFICIENCY, MARKET FAILURE, AND THE PUBLIC SYSTEM

PREFACE

Exploring Microeconomics, 7th Edition, was written to not only be a student-friendly textbook, but one that was relevant, one that focused on those few principles and applications that demonstrate the enormous breadth of economics to everyday life. This text is lively, motivating, and exciting, and it helps students relate economics to their world.

The Section-by-Section Approach

Many students are not lacking in ability but, rather, are lacking a strategy. Information needs to be moved from short-term memory to long-term memory and then retrieved. Learning theory provides several methods for helping students do this.

Exploring Microeconomics uses a section-by-section approach in its presentation of economic ideas. Information is presented in small, self-contained sections rather than in large blocks of text. Learning theorists call this *chunking*. That is, more information can be stored in the working memory as a result of learning in smaller blocks of information. Also, by using shorter bite-sized pieces, students are not only more likely to read the material but also more likely to reread it, leading to better comprehension and test results. Learning theorists call this *rehearsal*.

Unlike standard textbook construction, this approach is distinctly more compatible with the modern communication style with which most students are familiar and comfortable: short, intense, and exciting bursts of information. Rather than being distracted and discouraged by the seeming enormity of the task before them, students are more likely to work through a short, self-contained section before getting up from their desks. More importantly, instructors benefit from having a student population that has actually read the textbook and prepared for class!

In executing the section-by-section approach in *Exploring Microeconomics*, every effort has been made to take the intimidation out of economics. The idea of sticking to the basics and reinforcing student mastery, concept by concept, has been done with the student in mind. But students aren't the only ones to benefit from this approach. The section-by-section presentation allows instructors greater flexibility in planning their courses.

Exploring Microeconomics was created with flexibility in mind in order to accommodate a variety of teaching styles. Many of the chapters are self-contained, allowing instructors to customize their course. For example, in Part 3, the theory of the firm chapters can be presented in any order. The theory of the firm chapters are introduced in the textbook from the most competitive market structure (perfect competition) to the least competitive market structure (monopoly). After all, almost all firms face a downward-sloping demand curve, not just monopolists. However, instructors who prefer can teach monopoly immediately following perfect competition because each chapter is self-contained. And for those who do not have sufficient time to cover the Aggregate expenditure model, the Fiscal Policy chapter has an extensive section on the multiplier.

Each chapter is comprised of approximately 6–10 short sections. These sections are self-contained learning units, typically presented in 3–6 pages that include these helpful learning features.

Key Questions

Each section begins with a list of questions that highlight the primary ideas that students should learn from the material. These questions are intended to serve as a preview and to pique interest in the material to come. They also serve as landmarks: if students can answer these questions after reading the material, they have prepared well.

Economics: A Brief Introduction   1.1

▸ What is economics?   ▸ What is the economic problem?
▸ What is scarcity?

Section Quizzes

It is also important that students learn to self-manage. They should ask themselves: How well am I doing? How does this relate to what I already know? The section-by-section approach provides continual self-testing along every step of the way. Each section ends with 4–10 multiple-choice questions emphasizing the important points in each section. It also includes 4–6 open-ended questions designed to test comprehension of the basic points of the section just covered. Answers for multiple-choice questions are provided in the Section Quiz box, and answers to the open-ended questions are provided at the end of each chapter so students can check their responses. If students can answer these Section Quiz questions correctly, they can feel confident about proceeding to the next topic.

SECTION QUIZ

1. Which of the following would reflect self-interested behavior to an economist?
   a. Worker pursuing a higher-paying job and better working conditions
   b. Consumer seeking a higher level of satisfaction with her current income
   c. Mother Teresa using her Nobel Prize money to care for the poor
   d. All of the above

2. When economists assume that people act rationally, it means they
   a. always make decisions based on complete and accurate information.
   b. make decisions that will not be regretted later.
   c. do the best they can based on their values and information under current and future circumstances.
   d. make decisions based solely on what is best for society.
   e. commit no errors in judgment.

3. Rational self-interest can include
   a. the welfare of our family.
   b. our friends.
   c. the poor people of the world.
   d. all of the above.

4. Rational self-interest means
   a. people never make mistakes.
   b. that our concerns for others does not involve costs.
   c. we are materialistic and selfish.
   d. people make decisions with some desired outcome in mind.

---

1. What do economists mean by self-interest?
2. What does rational self-interest involve?
3. How are self-interest and selfishness different?
4. What is rational behavior?

Answers: 1. d 2. c 3. d 4. d

Student Questions

Over the years, student questions have been tracked. These FAQs (Frequently Asked Questions) are highlighted in the margins and offset by an icon with students raising their hands in class.

What do economists mean when they say people are rational?

Economic Content Standards (ECS)

From the National Council of Economic Education are set in the margin where the content is introduced. This addition helps to establish clear learning objectives and ties the text to these objectives.

economic
content
standards

Effective decision making requires comparing the additional costs of alternatives with the additional benefits. Most choices involve doing a little more or a little less of something: few choices are "all or nothing" decisions.

Other End-of-Chapter Materials Include:

Interactive Summary

Each chapter ends with an interactive summary of the main ideas in the chapter. Students can fill in the blanks and check their answers against those provided at the end of the summary. It is a useful refresher before class or tests and a good starting point for studying.

Key Terms and Concepts

A list of key terms concludes each chapter. If students can define all these terms, they have a good head start on studying.

Problems

Each chapter provides a list of exercises to test students' comprehension and mastery of the material. Organized in chronological order to follow the chapter, students can easily refer back to the chapter content for review and support as they proceed through the exercises.

CHAPTER 5   Markets in Motion and Price Controls   **151**

INTERACTIVE SUMMARY

Fill in the blanks:

1. An increase in demand results in a(n) _____ equilibrium price and a(n) _____ equilibrium quantity.

2. A decrease in supply results in a(n) _____ equilibrium price and a(n) _____ equilibrium quantity.

3. If demand decreases and supply increases, but the decrease in demand is greater than the increase in supply, the equilibrium quantity will _____.

4. If supply decreases and demand increases, the equilibrium price will _____ and the equilibrium quantity will be _____.

5. A price _____ is a legally established maximum price; a price _____ is a legally established minimum price.

6. Rent controls distort market signals and lead to _____ of rent-controlled apartments.

7. The quality of rent-controlled apartments would tend to _____ over time.

8. An increase in the minimum wage would tend to create _____ unemployment for low-skilled workers.

9. The secondary effects of an action that may occur after the initial effects are called _____.

Answers: 1. greater; greater 2. higher; lower 3. decrease 4. increase; indeterminate 5. ceiling; floor 6. shortages 7. decline 8. additional 9. unintended consequences

KEY TERMS AND CONCEPTS

price ceiling 144   price floor 144   unintended consequences 148

SECTION QUIZ ANSWERS

5.1 Changes in Market Equilibrium

1. **Does an increase in demand create a shortage or surplus at the original price?**
   An increase in demand increases the quantity demanded at the original equilibrium price, but it does not change the quantity supplied at that price, meaning that it would create a shortage at the original equilibrium price.

2. **What happens to the equilibrium price and quantity as a result of a demand increase?**
   Frustrated buyers unable to buy all they would like at the original equilibrium price will compete the market price higher, and that higher price will induce suppliers to increase their quantity supplied. The result is a higher market price and a larger market output.

3. **Does an increase in supply create a shortage or surplus at the original price?**
   An increase in supply increases the quantity supplied at the original equilibrium price, but it does not change the quantity demanded at that price, meaning that it would create a surplus at the original equilibrium price.

4. **Assuming the market is already at equilibrium, what happens to the equilibrium price and quantity as a result of a supply increase?**
   Frustrated sellers unable to sell all they would like at the original equilibrium price will compete the market price lower, and that lower price will induce demanders to increase their quantity demanded. The result is a lower market price and a larger market output.

5. **Why do heating oil prices tend to be higher in the winter?**
   The demand for heating oil is higher in the cold winter months. The result of this higher winter heating oil demand, for a given supply curve, is higher prices for heating oil in the winter.

6. **What would have to be true for both supply and demand to shift in the same time period?**
   For both supply and demand to shift in the same time period, one or more of both the supply curve shifters and the demand curve shifters would have to change in that same time period.

Steps on How to Do Well in This (or any other) Course

1. Are you motivated to learn? Link your motivation to goals. I want an A in this class. I want to graduate. I want to go to medical school or law school. I want a college degree. Setting goals demonstrates an intention to achieve and activates learning. School is really about learning to learn and hopefully, learning to enjoy learning. Students must find satisfaction in learning based on the understanding that the goals are useful to them. Put yourself in the right mindset. In short, learning is most effective when an individual is ready to learn. If you are not ready for Step 1, the other nine steps are less useful.

2. Do you attend class and take good notes? Listen actively—think before you write but be careful not to fall behind. Try to capture the main points of the lecture. You cannot take down everything. Leave space in your notebook so you can fill in with greater clarity when reading or rereading text. This is also a good time to edit your notes. Review your notes within 24 hours of lecture. This way you will be reviewing rather than relearning!

3. Do you read before class? Stay current. If you are studying Chapter 3 when the lecture is on Chapter 6, it will harm your performance. While perfection is not necessary, do the best you can to read the material before it is covered in lecture. You don't need to reread. It is better to try to recall what you read the first time.

4. Do you just highlight when you read? Don't. It is too passive. Finish a section and summarize it in your own words. Afterward, compare it with the section checks and summary at the end of the chapter to see if you caught all the main points. Do NOT read something without learning anything. That's a waste of time. Train your mind to learn—questioning, reciting, and reviewing while you read will make you an active reader and a better student. Highlighting focuses on individual concepts, but is much less helpful when trying to make connections between concepts.

5. When do you study? Break up your study time to keep it fresh. Don't study when you are tired. Know when you function best. To many people, an hour of studying in the day is worth two at night! That is, reading in the morning after a good night's sleep may be much more productive than when you are tired late at night. Study in 20- to 50-minute chunks with 5- to 10-minute breaks. This has proven to be the most effective way to study. One of the most consistent findings of scholars of learning behavior is something called spacing effects, which means spacing your studies over time. That is, it is easier to retain information when you study 5 hours over 5 days than it is to study 5 hours in 1 day.

6. How do you study? Study actively. Study by doing. Work problems, like in physics, chemistry, or engineering. Go back and forth between problems, examples, and text. That is, practice, practice, and practice. There are many problems throughout the text and on the website. Do them. The late John Wooden (famous basketball coach at UCLA) would often quote Ben Franklin, "Failing to prepare is preparing to fail." Have you worked on your self-confidence? Before you look up the answer to a question, assign a "confidence factor" to your work. On a scale of 1–10, how confident are you that you are right? Be honest with yourself. The more often you prove yourself right, the less test anxiety you will have. Self-testing, or practice testing, is part of recalling. Practicing recall also involves writing down material to be learned. When you are reading a section or working on a practice exam, grab a pencil and a piece of paper and write it down.

7. Do you work for understanding? Can you explain the concepts to others? If you can explain it to others, perhaps in a study group, you will really know it. There is no better way to learn something than by teaching it to others.

8. Do you find a quiet place to study with few distractions? Music and TV are not conducive to quality study time. This will only impair concentration. If you find your mind wandering, get up and walk around for a couple of minutes. Try to relax before you start studying, and associate reading with relaxation, not anxiety. Set a goal of how much you want to accomplish in each session and try to increase it gradually.

9. Do you apply your reading and lectures to your daily life? Retention is always greater when you can make the connection between the course and your life. Read the *In the News* features and the real-world examples throughout the text and see how the economic principles apply to your everyday life. Economics should also help you better understand the events you read about in the newspaper and on the Internet.

10. Do you cram for tests? Don't. It will not work well in economics and perhaps not in any analytical field. Study regularly, with greater review being the only difference in your study habits prior to a test. Try to have all your material read two days prior to exam so the remaining time can be devoted to review. Cramming for tests leads to fatigue, test anxiety, and careless mistakes. Get plenty of sleep. Treat being in school as having a full-time job—put in your time regularly and you won't need or want to cram. In short, don't procrastinate!

VISUAL LEARNING FEATURES

Imagery is also important for learning. Visual stimulus helps the learning process. This text uses pictures and visual aids to reinforce valuable concepts and ideas. Information is often stored in visual form; thus, pictures are important in helping students retain important ideas and retrieve them from their long-term memory. Students want a welcoming, magazine-looking text; a brain-friendly environment. The most consistent remark we have received from *Exploring Microeconomics* adopters is that their students are reading their book, and reading the text leads to better test performance.

At every turn this text has been designed with interesting graphics so that visual cues help students learn and remember:

Photos

The text contains a number of colorful pictures. They are not, however, mere decoration; rather, these photos are an integral part of the book, for both learning and motivation purposes. The photos are carefully placed where they reinforce important concepts, and they are accompanied by captions designed to encourage students to extend their understanding of particular ideas.

How many workers could be added to this jackhammer and still be productive (not to mention safe)? If more workers were added, how much output would be derived from each additional worker? Slightly more total output might be realized from the second worker because the second worker would be using the jackhammer while the first worker was taking a break from "the shakes." However, the fifth or sixth worker would clearly not create any additional output, as workers would just be standing around for their turn. That is, the marginal product (additional output) would eventually fall because of diminishing marginal product.

BRUCE BURKHARDT/FLIRT/CORBIS

Exhibits

Graphs, tables, and charts are important economic tools. These tools are used throughout *Exploring Microeconomics* to illustrate, clarify, and reinforce economic principles. Text exhibits are designed to be as clear and simple as possible, and they are carefully coordinated with the text material.

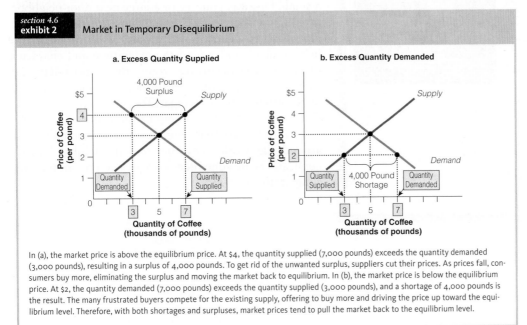

section 4.6 exhibit 2 Market in Temporary Disequilibrium

In (a), the market price is above the equilibrium price. At $4, the quantity supplied (7,000 pounds) exceeds the quantity demanded (3,000 pounds), resulting in a surplus of 4,000 pounds. To get rid of the unwanted surplus, suppliers cut their prices. As prices fall, consumers buy more, eliminating the surplus and moving the market back to equilibrium. In (b), the market price is below the equilibrium price. At $2, the quantity demanded (7,000 pounds) exceeds the quantity supplied (3,000 pounds), and a shortage of 4,000 pounds is the result. The many frustrated buyers compete for the existing supply, offering to buy more and driving the price up toward the equilibrium level. Therefore, with both shortages and surpluses, market prices tend to pull the market back to the equilibrium level.

APPLICATIONS

There are numerous applications to everyday life situations scattered throughout the text. These applications were chosen specifically with students in mind, and they are designed to help them find the connection between economics and their life. With that, economic principles are applied to everyday problems and issues, such as teen smoking, property rights and song swapping, crime, gift giving, and many others. There are also five special types of boxed applications scattered throughout each chapter:

IN THE NEWS

Gift Giving and Deadweight Loss

Only about 15 percent of gifts during the holidays are money. Money fits the description as an efficient gift. An efficient gift is one that the recipient values at least as much as it costs the giver.

There are a lot of unwanted gifts that recipients receive during the holidays. What do people do with their unwanted gifts? Many people exchange or repackage unwanted gifts. Gift cards are becoming more popular. While they provide less flexibility to recipients than cash, gift cards might be seen as less "tacky" than cash. So why don't more people give cash and gift cards?

Over the past 20 years, University of Minnesota Professor Joel Waldfogel has done numerous surveys asking gift recipients about the items they've received: Who bought it? What did the buyer pay? What's the most you would have been willing to pay for it? Based on these surveys, he's concluded that we value items we receive as gifts 20 percent less, per dollar spent, than items we buy for ourselves. Given the $65 billion in U.S. holiday spending per year, that means we get $13 billion less in satisfaction than we would receive if we spent that money the usual way on ourselves. That is, deadweight loss is about $13 billion a year, the difference between the price of the gifts and the value to their recipients. This is like the deadweight loss associated with subsidies; the recipient values the gift less than the cost to the giver who buys it.

That is, the marginal costs are greater than the marginal benefits.

Of course, people may derive satisfaction from trying to pick "the perfect gift." if that is the case, then the deadweight loss would be smaller. In addition, gift giving can provide a signal. If you really love a person, you will try to get enough information and spend enough time to get the right gift. This sends a strong signal that a gift card or money does not provide. If the recipients are adult children, they may already know of your affection for them so sending a gift card or cash might be less offensive.

NEWPORT NEWS DAILY PRESS/MCT/LANDOV

In the News

These applications focus primarily on current news stories that are relevant and thought provoking. These articles are placed strategically throughout the text to solidify particular concepts. In an effort to emphasize the breadth and diversity of the situations to which economic principles can be applied, these articles have been chosen from a wide range of sources.

GLOBAL WATCH

Chilean Bus Drivers Respond to Incentives

The problem with taking the bus is traffic congestion. Bad traffic gives people an incentive to take the bus, but slow buses give people an incentive to stick it out in the privacy of their own car—a vicious cycle. But there may be a solution. In Chile, bus drivers can be paid by the hour or by the passenger. Which of these do you think would lead to shorter delays? Think incentives. If you pay bus drivers by the passenger, they are looking for shortcuts when the traffic is bad. They also take shorter meal and bathroom breaks. They have an incentive to pick up the most passengers they can.

Bus drivers will also pay people known as *sapos* (frogs) for their information. Sapos will stand at bus stops, recording arrival times and selling their information to bus drivers who drive past. This depends significantly on the time interval (called headway in the transportation literature) between their bus and the bus immediately ahead on the same route. If the bus in front is far ahead, many passengers will have accumulated since the last bus came by, thus providing high profits for the driver. By contrast, if the bus in front is very close, then the driver can expect to be picking up few passengers and low profits. For their part, sapos provide valuable headway information to the drivers.

Each time a new bus arrives, a sapo marks the minute on his or her notepad, as well as tells the driver (for a fee) his or her headway, in minutes, with the immediately preceding bus. Given this information, the driver can choose to drive somewhat faster or slower in order to create more profitable spacing. For example, if the typical headway on a route is 10 minutes, but a driver has gone slowly enough to allow

PAUL KENNEDY/LONELY PLANET IMAGES/GETTY IMAGES

that headway to grow to 20 minutes, more passengers will be waiting and the driver will make more money. However, the bus behind that driver will then have a short headway, thus giving that second driver a strong incentive to change the spacing. Unlike drivers paid a fixed hourly wage, drivers receiving per-passenger compensation play a strategic game with each other, changing their driving in order to maximize profits given other drivers' behavior.

A study found that a typical bus passenger in Santiago waits roughly 10% longer for a bus on a paid-by-the-hour route relative to a paid-by-the-passenger route. However, paying by the passenger rather than by the hour leads to more aggressive driving and a lot more accidents. However, given the choice, over 90 percent of the routes in Santiago use the incentive plan—pay-by-the-passenger.

Global Watch

Whether we are concerned with understanding yesterday, today, or tomorrow, and whether we are looking at a small, far-away country or a large next door neighbor, economic principles can strengthen our grasp of many global issues. "Global Watch" articles were chosen to help students understand the magnitude and character of the changes occurring around the world today and to introduce them to some of the economic causes and implications of these changes. To gain a greater perspective on a particular economy or the planet as a whole, it is helpful to compare important economic indicators around the world. For this reason, "Global Watch" applications are sometimes also used to present relevant comparative statistics.

Using What You've Learned

Economic principles aren't just definitions to memorize; they are valuable tools that can help students analyze a whole host of issues and problems in the world around them. Part of learning economics is learning when and how to use new tools. These special boxes are scattered throughout the text as a way of reinforcing and checking students' true comprehension of important or more difficult concepts by assessing their ability to apply what they have learned to a real-world situation. Students can check their work against the answer given in the self-contained box, which provides them with immediate feedback and encouragement in the learning process.

USE WHAT YOU'VE LEARNED

Is That Really a Free Lunch, a Freeway, or a Free Beach?

The expression, "There's no such thing as a free lunch," clarifies the relationship between scarcity and opportunity cost. Suppose the school cafeteria is offering "free" lunches today. Although the lunch is free to you, is it really free from society's perspective? The answer is no, because some of society's scarce resources will have been used in the preparation of the lunch. The issue is whether the resources that went into creating that lunch could have been used to produce something else of value. Clearly, the scarce resources that went into the production of the lunch—the labor and materials (food-service workers, lettuce, meat, plows,

tractors, fertilizer, and so forth)—could have been used in other ways. They had an opportunity cost and thus were not free.

Do not confuse free with a zero money price. A number of goods—freeways, free beaches, and free libraries, for instance—do not cost consumers money, but they are still scarce. Few things are free in the sense that they use none of society's scarce resources. So what does a free lunch really mean? It is, technically speaking, a "subsidized" lunch—a lunch using society's scarce resources, but one that the person receiving it does not have to pay for personally.

Policy Application

These features focus primarily on news stories that involve a government policy decision based upon economic concepts. These applications are scattered throughout the text as a way of reinforcing important or more difficult concepts.

POLICY WATCH

Social Security: How Can We Save It?

What are the options for saving Social Security?

1. Increase the payroll taxes to a rate closer to 15 percent. It is currently 12.4 percent.

2. Increase the age of full-time benefits to age 70. The problem is that seniors already have a difficult time finding employment and may not be able to do the physical work expected of them.

3. Implement "means testing." Means testing would reduce the benefits to retirees who have "sufficient means" for retirement.

4. Increase the return to Social Security funds. The government might be interested in investing part of Social Security in the stock market. The historical returns are much greater in the stock market. The real rate of return (indexed for inflation) has been roughly 7 percent in the stock market compared with only 2 percent for government bonds. However, one of the drawbacks of government investment in the stock market is the potential for political abuse. With such a large amount

of funds, the temptation emerges for the government to favor some firms and punish others.

5. Put some of the payroll tax in an individual retirement plan and let individuals manage their own funds—perhaps choosing from a list of mutual funds.

6. Let individuals choose to continue with the current Social Security system or contribute a minimum of, say, 10 percent or 20 percent of their wages to a private investment fund. This option has been tried in a number of Central and South American countries. In Chile, almost 90 percent of workers choose to leave the government Social Security program to invest privately.

Critics of the private plan argue that it is risky, individuals might make poor investment decisions, and the government might ultimately have to pay for their mistakes. That is, the stock market may have a good long-term track record, but it is still inherently uncertain and risky because of economic fluctuations. This may not be consistent with a guaranteed stream of retirement income.

INSTRUCTOR RESOURCES

The 7th Edition offers an array of instructor resources designed to enhance teaching.

Instructor's Resource

The Instructor's Resource package includes electronic versions of the Instructor's Manual, Test Bank, and PowerPoint® slides, as well as Cognero, a Cloud-based testing software.

Instructor's Manual

Prepared by Gary Galles (Pepperdine University), the Instructor's Manual follows the textbook's concept-by-concept approach in two parts: chapter outlines and teaching tips. The Teaching Tips section provides analogies, illustrations, and examples to help instructors reinforce each section of the text. Answers to all of the end-of-chapter text questions can also be found in the Instructor's Manual.

Test Bank

Test bank questions, available online, have been thoroughly updated. The test bank includes approximately 150 test questions per chapter, consisting of multiple-choice, true-false, and short-answer questions.

Cognero Testing Software

Cognero is a Cloud-based, easy-to-use test creation software that allows instructors to add or edit questions, and select questions by previewing them on the screen, selecting them randomly, or selecting them by number.

Microsoft PowerPoint® Presentation Slides

- **Lecture Presentation in PowerPoint.** This PowerPoint presentation covers all the essential sections presented in each chapter of the book. Graphs, tables, lists, and concepts are animated sequentially to visually engage students. Additional examples and applications are used to reinforce major lessons. The slides are crisp, clear, and colorful. Instructors may adapt or add slides to customize their lectures.
- **Exhibits from the Text in PowerPoint.** Every graph and table within the text has been re-created in PowerPoint. These exhibits are available within the lecture presentation, but we have also made them available as a separate batch of slides for those instructors who don't want the lecture slides.

Both the Lecture and Exhibit PowerPoint presentations are available for downloading at the Sexton Companion Web site: **www.cengage.com**.

The 7th Edition offers an array of resources to help students test their understanding of chapter concepts and enhance their overall learning. Found at the student Companion Web site, these interactive resources provide exam preparation and help students get the most from their Principles of Economics course.

NEW! Graph Cards

Available on MindTap, Graph Cards allow students to learn how to work with graphs or prepare for examinations using Graph Cards. Just like flash cards, Graphs Cards present a graph and a question on one side and the answer on the opposite side.

Key Term Glossary and Flashcards

As a study aid, students may use the glossary terms as flashcards to test their knowledge. Students can state the definition of a term, then click on the term to check the correctness of their statement.

Adaptive Practice Test Generator

Adaptive Practice Test Generator helps students prepare for test success. The **Adaptive Practice Test Generator** on MindTap™ helps students gauge their understanding before taking an exam. The Adaptive Practice Test Generator offers a real testing scenario with multiple-choice questions similar to those in a test, as well as allows students to select multiple chapters.

Frequently Missed Test Questions (FMTQ)

Available on MindTap, FMTQs are short questions and videos that walk students step by step on the concepts and problems frequently missed in class or examinations.

MindTap

MindTap Exploring Microeconomics, 7th edition, is a personalized teaching experience with relevant assessments that guide students to analyze, apply, and improve thinking. The Learning Path lets professors create a personalized learning experience for their class, and students can take advantage of the resources created for their specific needs. Relevant readings and multimedia assets including Graph Cards, Adaptive Test Generator, Frequently Missed Test Questions (FMTQ), ConceptClips, Aplia, and more, are available with this platform. Analytics and reports provide a snapshot of class progress, time in course, and engagement.

APLIA™

Created by Paul Romer, one of the nation's leading economists, Aplia enhances teaching and learning by providing online interactive tools and experiments that help economics students become "active learners." This application allows a tight content correlation between Sexton's 7th Edition and Aplia's online tools.

Students Come to Class Prepared

It is a proven fact that students do better in their course work if they come to class prepared. Aplia's activities are engaging and based on discovery learning, requiring students to take an active role in the learning process. When assigned online homework, students are more apt to read the text, come to class better prepared to participate in discussions, and are more able to relate to the economic concepts and theories presented. Learning by doing helps students feel involved, gain confidence in the materials, and see important concepts come to life.

Assign Homework in an Effective and Efficient Way

Now you can assign homework without increasing your workload! Together, Sexton and Aplia provide the best text and technology resources to give you multiple teaching and learning solutions. Through Aplia, you can assign problem sets and online activities that automatically give feedback and are tracked and graded, all without requiring additional effort. Since Aplia's assignments are closely integrated with Sexton's 7th Edition, your students are applying what they have learned from the text to their homework.

Contact your local Cengage South-Western representative to find out how you can incorporate this exciting technology into your course. For more information, please visit: **www.aplia.com**.

Robert L. Sexton is Distinguished Professor of Economics at Pepperdine University. Professor Sexton has also been a Visiting Professor at the University of California at Los Angeles in the Anderson Graduate School of Management and the Department of Economics.

Professor Sexton's research ranges across many fields of economics: economics education, labor economics, environmental economics, law and economics, and economic history. He

has written several books and has published numerous articles, many in top economic journals such as *The American Economic Review, Southern Economic Journal, Economics Letters, Journal of Urban Economics*, and *The Journal of Economic Education*. Professor Sexton has also written more than 100 other articles that have appeared in books, magazines, and newspapers.

Professor Sexton received the Pepperdine Professor of the Year Award in 1991, a Harriet and Charles Luckman Teaching Fellow in 1994, Tyler Professor of the Year in 1997, and received the Howard A. White Award for Teaching Excellence in 2011.

ACKNOWLEDGMENTS

I would like to extend special thanks to the following colleagues for their valuable insight during the manuscript phase of this project. I owe a debt of gratitude to Edward Merkel, Troy University; Doug McNiel and Salvador Contreras, McNeese State University; David McClough, Ohio Northern University; Tim Bettner, University of La Verne; Inge O'Connor, Syracuse University; William Coomber, University of Maryland; Michael Marlow, Cal Poly; Nand Arora, Cleary University; Carlos F. Liard, Central Connecticut State University; Howard Cochran, Belmont University; Abdulhamid Sukar, Cameron University; Harry Karim, Los Angeles Community College; Maria DaCosta, University of Wisconsin-Eau Claire; Kelli Mayes-Denker, Carl Sandburg College; Elnora Farmer, Griffin Technical College; Robert Shoffner, Central Piedmont Community College; Mark Strazicich, Appalachian State University; Tanja Carter, El Camino College; and Jeffrey Phillips, SUNY Morrisville.

I also wish to thank Gary Galles of Pepperdine University for his help preparing the ancillaries that accompany the 7th Edition, and Mike Ryan of Gainesville State College for providing an invaluable verification of the text and updating the Test Bank.

I am truly indebted to the excellent team of professionals at Cengage Learning. My appreciation goes to Steve Scoble, Michael Parthenakis, Senior Product Managers; Daniel Noguera, Content Developer; Colleen Farmer, Senior Content Project Manager; and Michelle Kunkler, Senior Art Director. Also thanks to Mike Worls, Product Director; John Carey, Senior Marketing Manager; Erin Joyner, VP/GM Social Science and Qualitative Business, and the Cengage Sales Representatives. I sincerely appreciate your hard work and effort.

In addition, my family deserves special gratitude—my daughters, Elizabeth and Katherine; and my son, Tommy. They are an inspiration to my work. Also, special thanks to my brother Bill for all of his work that directly and indirectly helped this project come to fruition.

Thanks to all of my colleagues who reviewed this material for the 7th Edition. From very early on in the revision all the way up to publication, your comments were very important to me.

Robert L. Sexton

TECHNOTR/VETTA/GETTY IMAGES

PART 1

Introduction

The Role and Method of Economics

As you begin your first course in economics, you may be asking yourself why you're here. What does economics have to do with your life? Although we can list many good reasons to study economics, perhaps the best reason is that many issues in our lives are at least partly economic in character.

A good understanding of economics would allow you to answer such questions as, Why do 10:00 A.M. classes fill up more quickly than 8:00 A.M. classes during registration? Why is it so hard to find an apartment in cities such as San Francisco, Berkeley, and New York? Why is teenage unemployment higher than adult unemployment? Why is the price of your prescription drugs so high? Will higher taxes on cigarettes reduce the number of teenagers smoking? If so, by how much? Why do male basketball stars in the NBA make more than female basketball stars in the WNBA? Do houses with views necessarily sell faster than houses without views?

Why do people buy houses near noisy airports? Why do U.S. auto producers like tariffs (taxes) on imported cars? Is globalization good for the economy? The study of economics improves your understanding of these and many other concerns.

Economics is a unique way of analyzing many areas of human behavior. Indeed, the range of topics to which economic analysis can be applied is broad. Many researchers discover that the economic approach to human behavior sheds light on social problems that have been with us for a long time: discrimination, education, crime, divorce, political favoritism, and more. In fact, your daily newspaper is filled with economics. You can find economics on the domestic page, the international page, the business page, the sports page, the entertainment page, and even the weather page—economics is all around us.

However, before we delve into the details and models of economics, it is important that we present an overview of how economists approach problems—their methodology. How does an economist apply the logic of science to approach a problem? And what are the pitfalls that economists should avoid in economic thinking? We also discuss why economists disagree.

© NATA PUPO/SHUTTERSTOCK.COM

Why do female models make more money than male models?

Economics: A Brief Introduction   1.1

▶ What is economics?

▶ What is scarcity?

▶ What is the economic problem?

1.1a Economics—A Word with Many Different Meanings

Some people think economics involves the study of the stock market and corporate finance, and it does—in part. Others think that economics is concerned with the wise use of money and other matters of personal finance, and it is—in part. Still others think that economics involves forecasting or predicting what business conditions will be in the future, and again, it does—in part. The word *economics* is, after all, derived from the Greek *Oeconomicus*, which referred to the management of household affairs.

Precisely defined, **economics** is the study of the choices we make among our many wants and desires given our limited resources. What are resources? **Resources** are inputs—land, human effort, and skills, and machines and factories, for instance—used to produce goods and services. The problem is that our unlimited wants exceed our limited resources, a fact that we call **scarcity**. That is, scarcity exists because human wants for goods and services exceed the amount of goods and services that can be produced using all of our available resources. So scarcity forces us to decide how best to use our limited resources. This is **the economic problem**: Scarcity forces us to choose, and choices are costly because we must give up other opportunities that we value. Consumers must make choices on what to buy, how much to save, and how much to invest of their limited incomes. Workers must decide what types of jobs they want, when to enter the workforce, where they will work, and the number of hours they wish to work. Firms must

economics

the study of choices we make among our many wants and desires given our limited resources

resources

inputs used to produce goods and services

scarcity

exists because our unlimited wants exceed our limited resources

the economic problem

scarcity forces us to choose, and choices are costly because we must give up other opportunities that we value

Newspapers and websites are filled with articles related to economics—either directly or indirectly. News headlines may cover topics such as unemployment, deficits, financial markets, health care, Social Security, energy issues, war, global warming, and so on.

ECS

economic content standards

Productive resources are limited. Therefore, people cannot have all the goods and services they want. As a result, they must choose some things and give up others.

What is the relationship between scarcity and trade-offs?

decide what kinds of goods and services to produce, how much to produce, and how to produce those goods and services at the lowest cost. That is, consumers, workers, and firms all face choices because of scarcity, which is why economics is sometimes called the study of choice.

The economic problem is evident in every aspect of our lives. You may find that the choice between shopping for groceries and browsing at the mall, or between finishing a research paper and going to a movie, is easier to understand when you have a good handle on the "economic way of thinking."

1.1b **Economics Is All Around Us**

The tools of economics are far reaching. In fact, other social scientists have accused economists of being imperialistic because their tools have been used in so many fields outside the formal area of economics, like crime, education, marriage, divorce, addiction, finance, health, law, politics, and religion. Every individual, business, social, religious, and governmental organization faces the economic problem. Every society, whether it is capitalistic, socialistic, or totalitarian, must also face the economic problem of scarcity, choices, and costs.

Even time has an economic dimension. In fact, in modern culture, time has become perhaps the single most precious resource we have. Everyone has the same limited amount of time per day, and how we divide our time between work and leisure (including study, sleep, exercise, and so on) is a distinctly economic matter. If we choose more work, we must sacrifice leisure. If we choose to study, we must sacrifice time with friends or time spent sleeping or watching television. Virtually everything we decide to do, then, has an economic dimension.

Living in a world of scarcity involves trade-offs. As you are reading this text, you are giving up other things you value: shopping, spending time on Facebook, text messaging with friends, going to the movies, sleeping, or working out. When we know what the trade-offs are, we can make better choices from the options all around us, every day. George Bernard Shaw stated, "Economy is the art of making the most of life."

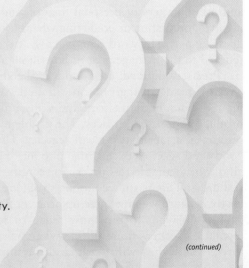

SECTION QUIZ

1. If a good is scarce,
   a. it only needs to be limited.
   b. it is not possible to produce any more of the good.
   c. our unlimited wants exceed our limited resources.
   d. our limited wants exceed our unlimited resources.

2. Which of the following is true of resources?
   a. Their availability is unlimited.
   b. They are the inputs used to produce goods and services.
   c. Increasing the amount of resources available could eliminate scarcity.
   d. Both b and c.

(continued)

SECTION QUIZ (cont.)

3. If scarcity were not a fact,

    a. people could have all the goods and services they wanted for free.

    b. it would no longer be necessary to make choices.

    c. poverty, defined as the lack of a minimum level of consumption, would also be eliminated.

    d. all of the above would be true.

4. Economics is concerned with

    a. the choices people must make because resources are scarce.

    b. human decision makers and the factors that influence their choices.

    c. the allocation of limited resources to satisfy unlimited wants.

    d. all of the above.

---

1. What is the definition of economics?
2. Why does scarcity force us to make choices?
3. Why are choices costly?
4. What is the economic problem?
5. Why do even "non-economic" issues have an economic dimension?

Answers: 1. c 2. b 3. d 4. d

© ZEED

Economic Behavior   1.2

▶ What is self-interest?

▶ Why is self-interest not the same as selfishness?

▶ What is rational behavior?

1.2a Self-Interest

Economists assume that most individuals act *as if* they are motivated by self-interest and respond in predictable ways to changing circumstances. In other words, self-interest is a good predictor of human behavior in most situations. For example, to a worker, self-interest means pursuing a higher-paying job and/or better working conditions. To a consumer, it means gaining a higher level of satisfaction from limited income and time.

Do people really pursue their self-interest? Do people really think that way?

We seldom observe employees asking employers to cut their wages and increase their workload to increase a company's profits. And how often do customers walk into a supermarket demanding to pay more for their groceries? In short, a great deal of human behavior can be explained and predicted by assuming that most people act *as if* they are motivated by their own self-interest in an effort to increase their *expected* personal satisfaction. When people make choices, they often do not know with certainty which choice is best. But they *expect* the best outcome from that decision—the one that will yield the greatest satisfaction.

Critics will say people don't think that way, and the critics might be right. But economists are arguing that people *act* that way. Economists are observing and studying what

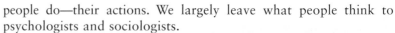

Enormous amounts of resources (time and money) were donated to the Hurricane Katrina victims. If individuals are acting to promote the things that interest them, are these self-interested acts necessarily selfish?

people do—their actions. We largely leave what people think to psychologists and sociologists.

Furthermore, when economists use the term *self-interest* they are not implying that people only seek to maximize their material consumption. Many acts of selfless behavior may be self-interested. For example, people may be kind to others in hopes that behavior will be returned. By establishing a reputation of honesty, it may send a signal of a willingness of commitment. This may make society a better place. So is it love, or self-interest, that keeps society together?

There is no question that self-interest is a powerful force that motivates people to produce goods and services. But self-interest can include benevolence. Think of the late Mother Teresa, who spent her life caring for others. One could say that her work was in her self-interest, but who would consider her actions selfish? Similarly, workers may be pursuing self-interest when they choose to work harder and longer to increase their charitable giving or saving for their children's education. That is, self-interest to an economist is not a narrow monetary self-interest. The enormous amount of money and time donated to victims of Hurricane Katrina is an example of self-interest too—the self-interest was to help others in need. However, our charitable actions for others are influenced by cost. We would predict that most people would be more charitable when the tax deductions are greater or that you may be more likely to offer a friend a ride to the airport when the freeway was less congested. In short, the lower the cost of helping others, the more help we would expect to be offered.

In the United States, people typically give more than $250 billion annually to charities. They also pay more money for environmentally friendly goods, "giving" a cleaner world to the future. Consumers can derive utility or satisfaction from these choices. It is clearly not selfish—it is in their best interest to care about the environment and those who are less fortunate than themselves.

What do economists mean when they say people are rational?

rational behavior

when people do the best they can, based on their values and information, under current and anticipated future circumstances

1.2b What Is Rational Behavior?

Economists assume that people, for the most part, engage in rational, or purposeful, behavior. And you might think that could not possibly apply to your brother, sister, or roommates. But the key is in the definition. To an economist, rational behavior merely means that people do the best they can, based on their values and information, under current and anticipated future circumstances. That is, people may not know with complete certainty which decisions will yield the most satisfaction and happiness, but they select the one that they expect to give them the best results among the alternatives. It is important to note that it is only the person making the choice that determines its rationality. You might like red sports cars while your friend might like black sports cars. So it would be rational for you to choose a red sports car and your friend to choose a black sports car.

Economists assume that people do not intentionally make decisions that will make them worse off. Most people act purposefully. They make decisions with some *expected* outcome in mind. Their actions are rational and purposeful, not random and chaotic. Individuals all take purposeful actions when they decide what to buy and produce. They make mistakes and are impacted by emotion, but the point is that they make their decisions with some expected results in mind. In short, rational self-interest means that individuals try to weigh the expected marginal (additional) benefits and marginal (additional) costs of their decisions, a topic we return to in Chapter 2.

GREAT ECONOMIC THINKERS

Adam Smith (1723–1790)

Adam Smith was born in a small fishing village just outside of Edinburgh, Scotland, in 1723. At age 4, gypsies (called *tinkers* in Scotland) kidnapped Smith, but he was rescued through the efforts of his uncle. He began studying at Glasgow College when he was just 14 and later continued his studies at Oxford University. He returned to Glasgow at age 28 as a professor of philosophy and logic. (Until the nineteenth century, economics was considered a branch of philosophy, thus Smith neither took nor taught a class in economics.) He later resigned that position to become the private tutor to the stepson of Charles Townshend.

Although known for his intelligence, warm hospitality, and charitable spirit, Smith was not without his eccentricities. Notorious for his absent-mindedness, there is a story about Smith taking a trip to a tanning factory and, while engaged in conversation with a friend, walking straight into a large tanning vat. Another tale features Smith walking 15 miles in his sleep, awakening from his sleepwalk to the ringing of church bells, and scurrying back home in his nightgown. Most astonishing and unfortunate, Smith, without explanation, had the majority of his unpublished writings destroyed before his death in 1790.

Adam Smith is considered the founder of modern economics. He addressed problems of both economic theory and policy in his famous book, *An Inquiry into the Nature and Causes of the Wealth of Nations*, published in 1776. The book was a success from the beginning, with its first edition selling out in just six months, and people have continued to read it for well over two centuries.

Smith believed that the wealth of a nation did not come from the accumulation of gold and silver—the prevailing thought of the day. Smith observed that people tend to pursue their own personal interests and that an "invisible hand" (the market) guides their self-interest, increasing social welfare and general economic well-being. Smith's most powerful and enduring contribution was this idea of an invisible hand of market incentives channeling individuals' efforts and promoting social welfare.

Smith also showed that through division of labor and specialization of tasks, producers could increase their

ROBERT L. SEXTON

Smith is buried in a small cemetery in Edinburgh, Scotland. The money left on the grave site is usually gone by morning; the homeless prey on the donations to use for food and spirits. Adam Smith is probably smiling somewhere. He had a reputation as a charitable man—"a scale much beyond what might have been expected from his fortunes."

output markedly. While Smith did not invent the market, he demonstrated that free markets, unfettered by monopoly and government regulation, and free trade were at the very foundation of the wealth of a nation. Many of Smith's insights are still central to economics today.

SECTION QUIZ

1. Which of the following would reflect self-interested behavior to an economist?

   a. Worker pursuing a higher-paying job and better working conditions

   b. Consumer seeking a higher level of satisfaction with her current income

   c. Mother Teresa using her Nobel Prize money to care for the poor

   d. All of the above

2. When economists assume that people act rationally, it means they

   a. always make decisions based on complete and accurate information.

   b. make decisions that will not be regretted later.

   c. do the best they can based on their values and information under current and future circumstances.

   d. make decisions based solely on what is best for society.

   e. commit no errors in judgment.

3. Rational self-interest can include

   a. the welfare of our family.

   b. our friends.

   c. the poor people of the world.

   d. all of the above.

4. Rational self-interest means

   a. people never make mistakes.

   b. that our concerns for others does not involve costs.

   c. we are materialistic and selfish.

   d. people make decisions with some desired outcome in mind.

---

1. What do economists mean by self-interest?

2. What does rational self-interest involve?

3. How are self-interest and selfishness different?

4. What is rational behavior?

Answers: 1. d 2. c 3. d 4. d

Economic Theories and Models 1.3

▶ What are economic theories and models?

▶ What can we expect from theories and models?

▶ Why do we need to abstract?

▶ What is a hypothesis?

▶ What is empirical analysis?

▶ What is the *ceteris paribus* assumption?

▶ What are microeconomics and macroeconomics?

1.3a Economic Theories and Models

Theories and models are explanations of how things work that help us understand and predict how and why economic agents like consumers, producers, firms, government, and so on behave the way they do. That is, we use the theories and models to observe how people really behave.

theories and models
simplified versions of the real world used to explain and predict behavior

1.3b Abstraction Is Important

Economic theories and models cannot realistically include every event that has ever occurred. A good economic theory or model weeds out the irrelevant facts from the relevant ones. We must abstract. Without abstraction or simplification, the world is too complex to analyze.

   Economic theories and models make some unrealistic assumptions. For example, we may assume there are only two countries in the world, producing two goods. Obviously, this is an abstraction from the real world. But if we can understand trade in a simplified world, it will help us understand trade in a more complex world. Similarly, sometimes economists make very strong assumptions, such as that all people seek self-betterment or all firms attempt to maximize profits. That is, economists use simplifying assumptions in their models to make the world more comprehendible. But only when we test our models using these assumptions can we find out if they are too simplified or too limiting.

   How are economic theories and models like a road map? Much like a road map, economic theories and models are more useful when they ignore details that are *not* relevant to the questions that are being investigated. Some maps, like some economic models, may be too detailed, while others may be too abstract. There is no single correct map or model. Suppose we wanted to drive from Chicago to Los Angeles. What kind of map would we need? All we would need is a map showing the interstate highways that ignores the details of individual streets within a city. However, if we were looking for a particular restaurant or a friend's house in Los Angeles, we would need a more detailed street map of Los Angeles.

hypothesis
a testable proposition

empirical analysis
the use of data to test a hypothesis

1.3c Developing a Testable Proposition

The beginning of any theory is a **hypothesis**, a testable proposition that makes some type of prediction about behavior in response to certain changes in conditions based on our assumptions. In economic theory, a hypothesis is a testable prediction about how people will behave or react to a change in economic circumstances. For example, if we notice an increase in the price of coffee beans (per pound), we might hypothesize that sales of coffee beans will fall, or if the price of coffee beans (per pound) decreases, our hypothesis might be that coffee bean sales will rise. Once we state our hypothesis, we test it by comparing what it predicts will happen to what actually happens.

Using Empirical Analysis

To determine whether our hypothesis is valid, we must engage in **empirical analysis**. That is, we must examine the data to see whether our hypothesis fits well with the facts. If the hypothesis is consistent

How is economic theory like a map? Much like a road map, economic theory is more useful when it ignores details that are not relevant to the questions that are being investigated.

with real-world observations, we can accept it; if it does not fit well with the facts, we must "go back to the drawing board."

Determining whether a hypothesis is acceptable is more difficult in economics than it is in the natural or physical sciences. Chemists, for example, can observe chemical reactions under laboratory conditions. They can alter the environment to meet the assumptions of the hypothesis and can readily manipulate the variables (chemicals, temperatures, and so on) crucial to the proposed relationship. Such controlled experimentation is seldom possible in economics. The laboratory of economists is usually the real world. Unlike chemists in their labs, economists cannot easily control all the variables that might influence human behavior.

From Hypothesis to Theory

After gathering their data, economic researchers must evaluate the results to determine whether their hypothesis is supported or refuted. If supported, the hypothesis can be tentatively accepted as an economic theory.

Every economic theory is on life-long probation; the hypothesis underlying an economic theory is constantly being tested against empirical findings. Do the observed findings support the prediction? When a hypothesis survives a number of tests, it is accepted until it no longer predicts well.

1.3d Science and Stories

How is scientific discovery like the stories presented by novelists?

Much of scientific discovery is expressed in terms of stories, not unlike the stories told by novelists. This similarity is not accidental. The novelist tries to persuade us that a story could almost be true; the scientist tries to persuade us that certain events fall into a certain meaningful pattern. The scientist does not (or is not supposed to) invent the underlying "facts" of the story, whereas the novelist is not so constrained. However, a scientist does select *certain* facts from among many facts that could have been chosen, just as the novelist chooses from an infinite number of possible characters and situations to make the story most persuasive. In both cases, the author "invents" the story. Therefore, we should not be surprised to find order in economic theory any more than we are surprised to find order in a good novel. Scientists would not bother to write about "life" if they were not convinced that they had stories worth telling.

What makes a story "worth telling"? When we look for order in nature, we cannot suppose that the "facts" are a sufficient basis for understanding observed events. The basic problem is that the facts of a complex world simply do not organize themselves. Understanding requires that a *conceptual order* be imposed on these "facts" to counteract the confusion that would otherwise result. For example, objects of different weights falling freely in the air do *not* travel at *precisely* the same rate (largely because of the different effects of air resistance). Yet this piece of information is generally much less significant than the fact that falling bodies do travel at *almost* the same rate (which presumably would be identical in a vacuum). By focusing on the most significant fact—the similarity, not the difference—Galileo was able to impose order on the story of gravity.

In the same way, to interpret the impact of rising housing prices on the amount of housing desired, economists must separate out the impact of increasing wealth, population, and other contributing factors. Failing to do so would obscure the central insight that people tend to buy less housing at higher prices. Without a story—a theory of causation—scientists could not sort out and understand the complex reality that surrounds us.

ceteris paribus

holding all other things constant

Why is the *ceteris paribus* so important?

1.3e The *Ceteris Paribus* Assumption

Virtually all economic theories share a condition usually expressed by the Latin phrase *ceteris paribus*. A rough translation of the phrase is "letting everything else be equal" or "holding everything else constant." When economists try to assess the effect of one variable on another, they must keep the relationship between the two variables isolated from other events that might also influence the situation that the theory tries to explain or predict. In other words, everything else freezes so we can see how one thing affects another. For example, if the price of tomatoes falls, we would expect to see more people buy tomatoes. But if the government recently recommended not buying tomatoes because they have been infected by a bug that causes intestinal problems, people would buy fewer, not more, at lower prices. Does that mean you throw out your theory that people buy more at lower prices? No, we just did not freeze the effects of news from the government, which had a greater impact on purchases than lower prices did.

Let's return to the gravity example. Suppose you drop a feather and a brick off the Eiffel Tower on a windy day. We would expect the brick to win the race. But if we could hold everything constant in a vacuum, then we would expect them to hit the ground at the same time. The law of gravity needs the *ceteris paribus* assumption, too.

1.3f Why Are Observation and Prediction Harder in the Social Sciences?

Working from observations, scientists try to make generalizations that will enable them to predict certain events. However, observation and prediction are more difficult in the social sciences than in physical sciences such as physics, chemistry, and astronomy. Why? The major reason for the difference is that social scientists, including economists, are concerned with *human* behavior. And human behavior is more variable and often less readily predictable than the behavior of experiments observed in a laboratory. However, by looking at the actions and the incentives faced by large groups of people, economists can still make many reliable predictions about human behavior.

1.3g Why Do Economists Predict on a Group Level?

Economists' predictions usually refer to the collective behavior of large groups rather than to that of specific individuals. Why is this? Looking at the behaviors of a large group allows economists to discern general patterns of actions. For example, consider what would happen if the price of air travel from the United States to Europe was reduced drastically, say from $1,000 to $400, because of the invention of a more fuel-efficient jet. What type of predictions could we make about the effect of this price reduction on the buying habits of typical consumers?

What Does Individual Behavior Tell Us?

Let's look first at the responses of individuals. As a result of the price drop, some people will greatly increase their intercontinental travel, taking theater weekends in London or week-long trips to France to indulge in French food. Some people, however, are terribly afraid to fly, and the price reduction will not influence their behavior in the slightest. Others might detest Europe and, despite the lowered airfares, prefer to spend a few days in Aspen, Colorado, instead. A few people might respond to the airfare reduction in precisely the opposite way: At the lower fare, they might make fewer trips to Europe, because they might believe (rightly or wrongly) that the price drop would be accompanied by a reduction in the quality of service, greater crowding, or reduced safety. In short, we cannot predict with any level of certainty how a given individual will respond to this airfare reduction.

What Does Group Behavior Tell Us?

Group behavior is often more predictable than individual behavior. When the weather gets colder, more firewood will be sold. Some individuals may not buy firewood, but we can predict with great accuracy that a group of individuals will establish a pattern of buying

If I study harder, I will perform better on the test. That sounds logical, right? Holding other things constant (*ceteris paribus*), your theory is likely to be true. However, what if you studied harder but inadvertently overslept the day of the exam? What if you were so sleepy during the test that you could not think clearly? Or what if you studied the wrong material? Although it might look like additional studying did not improve your performance, the real problem could be the impact of other variables, such as sleep deficiency or how you studied.

Why is group behavior more predictable than individual behavior?

Professors Oster and Jensen, by measuring revealed preferences rather than declared preferences, found that rural Indian families who had cable TV had lower birth rates than those with no television. Why? Television may provide information about family planning. Or it may expose rural families to the urban lifestyle, which is very different than their own. They may now begin to emulate the urban lifestyle.

more firewood. Similarly, while we cannot say what each individual will do, within a group of persons, we can predict with great accuracy that more flights to Europe from Los Angeles will be sold at lower prices than at higher prices, holding other things such as income and preferences constant. We cannot predict exactly how many more airline tickets will be sold at $400 than at $1,000, but we can predict the direction of the impact and approximate the extent of the impact. By observing the relationship between the price of goods and services and the quantities people purchase in different places and during different time periods, it is possible to make some reliable generalizations about how much people will react to changes in the prices of goods and services. Economists use this larger picture of the group for most of their theoretical analysis.

Economists and Survey Data

Economists do not typically use survey data. Economists prefer to look at revealed preferences (how people actually behave) rather than declared preferences (how they say they behave). Participants in surveys may consciously or subconsciously fib, especially when it costs almost nothing to fib. Measuring revealed preferences will generally give us more accurate results.

1.3h The Two Branches of Economics: Microeconomics and Macroeconomics

microeconomics

the study of household and firm behavior and how they interact in the marketplace

macroeconomics

the study of the whole economy, including the topics of inflation, unemployment, and economic growth

aggregate

the total amount—such as the *aggregate level of output*

Conventionally, we distinguish between two main branches of economics: microeconomics and macroeconomics. Microeconomics deals with the smaller units within the economy, attempting to understand the decision-making behavior of firms and households and their interaction in markets for particular goods or services. Microeconomic topics include discussions of health care, agricultural subsidies, the price of everyday items such as running shoes, the distribution of income, and the impact of labor unions on wages. Macroeconomics, in contrast, deals with the aggregate, or total, economy; it looks at economic problems as they influence the whole of society. Topics covered in macroeconomics include discussions of inflation, unemployment, business cycles, and economic growth. To put it simply, microeconomics looks at the trees while macroeconomics looks at the forest.

SECTION QUIZ

1. Economists use theories and models to

   a. abstract from the complexities of the world.

   b. understand economic behavior.

   c. explain and help predict human behavior.

   d. do all of the above.

   e. do none of the above.

2. The importance of the *ceteris paribus* assumption is that it

   a. allows one to separate subjective issues from objective ones.

   b. allows one to generalize from the whole to the individual.

   c. allows one to analyze the relationship between two variables apart from the influence of other variables.

   d. allows one to hold all variables constant so the economy can be carefully observed in a suspended state.

(continued)

SECTION QUIZ (cont.)

3. When we look at a particular segment of the economy, such as a given industry, we are studying

   a. macroeconomics.

   b. microeconomics.

   c. normative economics.

   d. positive economics.

4. Which of the following is most likely a topic of discussion in macroeconomics?

   a. An increase in the price of a pizza

   b. A decrease in the production of stereos by a consumer electronics company

   c. An increase in the wage rate paid to automobile workers

   d. A decrease in the unemployment rate

   e. The entry of new firms into the software industry

---

1. What are economic theories and models?

2. What is the purpose of a theory or a model?

3. Why must economic theories and models be abstract?

4. What is a hypothesis? How do we determine whether it is tentatively accepted?

5. Why do economists hold other things constant (*ceteris paribus*)?

6. Why are observation and prediction more difficult in the social sciences?

7. Why do economic predictions refer to the behavior of groups of people rather than individuals?

8. Why is revealed preference preferred over declared preference?

9. Why is the market for running shoes considered a microeconomic topic?

10. Why is inflation considered a macroeconomic topic?

Answers: 1. d 2. c 3. b 4. d

· ·

Pitfalls to Avoid in Scientific Thinking   1.4

▸ If two events usually occur together, does it mean one event caused the other to happen?

▸ What is the fallacy of composition?

In our discussion of economic theory we have not yet mentioned that there are certain pitfalls to avoid that may hinder scientific and logical thinking: confusing correlation and causation, and the fallacy of composition.

1.4a Confusing Correlation and Causation

Without a theory of causation, no scientist could sort out and understand the enormous complexity of the real world. But one must always be careful not to confuse correlation with causation. In other words, the fact that two events usually occur together (**correlation**) does not necessarily mean that one caused the other to occur (**causation**). For example, say a groundhog awakes after a long winter of hibernation, climbs out of his hole, and sees his

correlation
when two events occur together

causation
when one event brings about another event

In Europe, the stork population has fallen and so have birth rates. Does this mean that one event caused the other to occur?

shadow—then six weeks of bad weather ensue. Did the groundhog cause the bad weather?

Perhaps the causality runs in the opposite direction. A rooster may always crow before the sun rises, but it does not cause the sunrise; rather, the early light from the sunrise causes the rooster to crow.

Why Is the Correlation between Ice Cream Sales and Property Crime Positive?

Did you know that when ice cream sales rise, so do property crime rates? What do you think causes the two events to occur together? The explanation is that property crime peaks in the summer because of warmer weather, more people on vacations (leaving their homes vacant), teenagers out of school, and so on. It just happens that ice cream sales also peak in those months because of the weather. It is the case of a third variable causing both to occur. Or what if there were a positive correlation between sales of cigarette lighters and the incidence of cancer? The suspect might well turn out to be the omitted variable (the so-called "smoking gun"): the cigarette. Or what if research revealed that parents who bought parenting books were "better" parents. Does that prove the books work? Or is it possible that people who would buy books on parenting tend to be "better" parents? That is, it might be about the parents, not the book. Causality is tricky stuff. Be careful.

1.4b **The Fallacy of Composition**

fallacy of composition

the incorrect view that what is true for the individual is always true for the group

Economic thinking requires us to be aware of the problems associated with aggregation (adding up all the parts). One of the biggest problems is the fallacy of composition. This fallacy states that even if something is true for an individual, it is not necessarily true for many individuals as a group. For example, say you are at a football game and you decide to stand up to get a better view of the playing field. This works as long as the people seated around you don't stand up. But what happens if everyone stands up at the same time? Then your standing up does nothing to improve your view. Thus, what is true for an individual does not always hold true in the aggregate. The same can be said of getting to school early to get a better parking place—what if everyone arrived early? Or studying harder to get a better grade in a class that is graded on a curve—what if everyone studied harder?

SECTION QUIZ

1. Which of the following statements can explain why correlation between Event A and Event B may not imply causality from A to B?

   a. The observed correlation may be coincidental.

   b. A third variable may be responsible for causing both events.

   c. Causality may run from Event B to Event A instead of in the opposite direction.

   d. All of the above can explain why the correlation may not imply causality.

2. Ten-year-old Tommy observes that people who play football are larger than average and tells his mom that he's going to play football because it will make him big and strong. Tommy is

   a. committing the fallacy of composition.

   b. violating the *ceteris paribus* assumption.

   c. mistaking correlation for causation.

   d. committing the fallacy of decomposition.

(continued)

3. The fallacy of composition
   a. is a problem associated with aggregation.
   b. assumes that if something is true for an individual, then it is necessarily true for a group of individuals.
   c. is illustrated in the following statement: If I stand up at a football game, I will be able to see better; therefore, if we all stood up, we would all see better.
   d. all of the above are true.

---

1. What is the relationship between correlation and causation?
2. What types of misinterpretation result from confusing correlation and causation?
3. What is the fallacy of composition?
4. If you can sometimes get a high grade on an exam without studying, does it mean that additional studying does not lead to higher grades? Explain your answer.

Answers: 1. d 2. c 3. d

....

Positive Statements and Normative Statements   1.5

▶ What is a positive statement?   ▶ Why do economists disagree?

▶ What is a normative statement?

1.5a Positive Statement

Most economists view themselves as scientists seeking the truth about the way people behave. They make speculations about economic behavior, and then, ideally, they assess the validity of those predictions based on human experience. Their work emphasizes how people *do* behave, rather than how people *should* behave. In the role of scientist, an economist tries to observe patterns of behavior objectively, without reference to the appropriateness or inappropriateness of that behavior. This objective, value-free approach, based on the scientific method, is called positive analysis. In positive analysis, we want to know the impact of variable *A* on variable *B*. We want to be able to test a hypothesis. For example, the following is a **positive statement**: If rent controls are imposed, vacancy rates will fall. This statement is testable. A positive statement does not have to be a true statement, but it does have to be a testable statement.

Keep in mind, however, that it is doubtful that even the most objective scientist can be totally value free in his or her analysis. An economist may well emphasize data or evidence that supports a hypothesis, putting less weight on other evidence that might be contradictory. This tendency, alas, is human nature. But a good economist/scientist strives to be as fair and objective as possible in evaluating evidence and in stating conclusions based on the evidence. In some sense, economists are like engineers; they try to figure out how things work and then describe what would happen if you changed something.

positive statement
an objective, testable statement that describes what happens and why it happens

Does a positive statement have to be true, or just testable?

1.5b **Normative Statement**

normative statement
a subjective, contestable statement that attempts to describe what should be done

Economists, like anyone else, have opinions and make value judgments. And when economists, or anyone else for that matter, express opinions about an economic policy or statement, they are indicating in part how they believe things should be, not stating facts about the way things are. In other words, they are performing normative analysis. Normative statements involve judgments about what should be or what ought to happen. For example, normative questions might include: Should the government raise the minimum wage? Should the government increase spending in the space program? Should the government give "free" prescription drugs to senior citizens?

1.5c **Positive versus Normative Analysis**

The distinction between positive and normative analysis is important. It is one thing to say that everyone should have universal health care, an untestable normative statement, and quite another to say that universal health care would lead to greater worker productivity, a testable positive statement. It is important to distinguish between positive and normative analysis because many controversies in economics revolve around policy considerations that contain both. For example, what impact would a 3 percent reduction in income taxes across the board have on the economy? This question requires positive analysis. Whether we should have a 3 percent reduction in income taxes requires normative analysis as well. When economists are trying to explain the way the world works, they are scientists. When economists start talking about how the economy should work rather than how it does work, they have entered the normative world of the policy maker. Anytime you see the word *should*, that is a sign you are in the realm of normative economics. Positive statements are about *what is*, normative statements are about *what ought to* or *should* be. In short, positive statements are attempts to *describe* what happens and why it happens, while normative statements are attempts to *prescribe* what should be done. But sometimes the two are intertwined. For example, there are two different types of policies that are used to help low-income housing residents: rent controls, which control how much rent a landlord can charge, and rent subsidies, which provide low-income families with money to pay rent. While both are policies that engage normative analysis, most economists would favor the subsidy because it is more efficient—a conclusion derived from positive analysis.

Does positive analysis *prove* a policy is good?

1.5d **Disagreement Is Common in Most Disciplines**

Although economists do frequently have opposing views on economic policy questions, they probably disagree less than the media would have you believe. Disagreement is common in most disciplines: Seismologists differ over predictions of earthquakes or volcanic eruption; historians can be at odds over the interpretation of historical events; psychologists disagree on proper ways to raise children; and nutritionists debate the efficacy of particular vitamins and the quantities that should be taken.

The majority of disagreements in economics stem from normative issues; differences in values or policy beliefs result in conflict. For example, a policy might increase efficiency at the expense of a sense of fairness or equity, or it might help a current generation at the expense of a future generation. Because policy decisions involve trade-offs, they will always involve the potential for conflict.

Some economists are concerned about individual freedom and liberty, thinking that any encroachment on individual decision making is bad, other things being equal. People with this philosophic bent are inclined to be skeptical of any increased government involvement in the economy.

On the other hand, some economists are concerned with what they consider an unequal, "unfair," or unfortunate distribution of income, wealth, or power, and view governmental intervention as desirable in righting injustices that they believe exist in a market economy. To these persons, the threat to individual liberty alone is not sufficient to reject governmental intervention in the face of perceived economic injustice.

Aside from philosophic differences, a second reason helps explain why economists may differ on any given policy question. Specifically, they may disagree about the validity of a given economic theory for the policy in question—that is, they disagree over the positive analysis. Why would they disagree over positive analysis? For at least two reasons. One, a particular model may yield mixed results: some empirical evidence supporting it and some not. Two, the information available may be insufficient to make a compelling theory.

Currently, there are a number of well-respected economists who believe we should substitute a national sales tax (called a value-added tax) for the current income tax. A sales tax is the main source of revenue for many European countries. However, there are also many well-respected economists who think this is a bad idea. Why the differences? It might be because of fairness. But what is fairness? Some may think the tax would fall disproportionately on the poor and middle classes, so that it is not fair. Others might argue that the national tax is fair because everyone pays their fair share, based on what they spend rather than what they earn. Or they may disagree over the modeling. One model might focus on collection costs while the other might focus on its potential to increase savings and economic growth. Therefore the focus of different models may lead to different policy prescriptions.

1.5e **Often Economists Do Agree**

Although you may not believe it after reading the previous discussion, economists don't always disagree. In fact, according to a survey among members of the American Economic Association, most economists agree on a wide range of issues, including the effects of rent control, import tariffs, export restrictions, the use of wage and price controls to curb inflation, and the minimum wage.

It seems like economists always disagree on important issues. Is that true?

According to studies, most economists agree that these statements are correct:

1. A ceiling on rents (rent control) reduces the quantity and quality of rental housing available (93 percent agree).
2. Tariffs and import quotas usually reduce general economic welfare (93 percent agree).
3. The United States should not restrict employers from outsourcing work to foreign countries (90 percent agree).
4. Fiscal policy (e.g., tax cuts and/or increases in government expenditure) has significant stimulative impact on an economy that is less than fully employed (90 percent agree).
5. Flexible and floating exchange rates offer an effective international monetary arrangement (90 percent agree).
6. The gap between Social Security funds and expenditures will become unsustainably large within the next 50 years if the current policies remain unchanged (85 percent agree).
7. The United States should eliminate agricultural subsidies (85 percent agree).
8. Local and state governments in the United States should eliminate subsidies to professional sport franchises (85 percent agree).
9. A large budget deficit has an adverse effect on the economy (83 percent agree).
10. A minimum wage increases unemployment among the young and unskilled (79 percent agree).
11. Effluent taxes and marketable pollution permits represent a better approach to pollution control than imposition of pollution ceilings (78 percent agree).
12. Economists favor expanding competition and market forces in education (67 percent agree).[1]

---

[1]Richard M. Alston, J. R. Kearl, and Michael B. Vaughn, "Is there Consensus among Economists in the 1990s?" *American Economic Review* (May 1992): 203–09; Robert Whaples, "Do Economists Agree on Anything? Yes!" *Economists' Voice* (November 2006): 1–6.

SECTION QUIZ

1. Which of the following is a positive statement?

   a. New tax laws are needed to help the poor.

   b. Teenage unemployment should be reduced.

   c. We should increase Social Security payments to older adults.

   d. An increase in tax rates will reduce unemployment.

   e. It is only fair that firms protected from competition by government-granted monopolies pay higher corporate taxes.

2. Positive statements

   a. are testable.

   b. are attempts to describe what happens and why it happens.

   c. do not have to be a true statement.

   d. All of the above are true.

3. Normative statements

   a. attempt to describe what happens and why it happens.

   b. are objective and testable.

   c. attempt to describe the way the world works.

   d. are subjective and attempt to prescribe what should be done.

4. The statement "the government should increase spending for the space program" is

   a. objective and testable.

   b. a positive statement.

   c. subjective, prescriptive, and normative.

   d. a fact and very important for the defense of our country.

5. Which of the following statements is (are) true?

   a. Economists disagree but most often over normative issues.

   b. Economists do agree over a wide range of issues.

   c. Disagreement is also common in other disciplines.

   d. All of the above statements are true.

---

1. What is a positive statement? Must positive statements be testable?

2. What is a normative statement? Is a normative statement testable?

3. Why is the positive/normative distinction important?

4. Why do policy disagreements arise among economists?

Answers: 1. d 2. d 3. d 4. c 5. d

Fill in the blanks:

1. Economics is the study of the choices we make among our many wants and desires given our _____ resources.

2. _____ occurs because our unlimited wants exceed our limited resources.

3. Resources are _____ used to produce goods and services.

4. The economic problem is that _____ forces us to choose, and choices are costly because we must give up other opportunities that we _____.

5. Living in a world of scarcity means _____.

6. _____ deals with the aggregate (the forest), or total economy, while _____ deals with the smaller units (the trees) within the economy.

7. Economists assume that individuals act as if they are motivated by _____ and respond in _____ ways to changing circumstances.

8. Economists believe that it is _____ for people to anticipate the likely future consequences of their behavior.

9. Actions have _____.

10. Rational behavior implies that most people act _____.

11. Economic _____ and _____ are statements or

propositions used to _____ and _____ patterns of human economic behavior.

12. Because of the complexity of human behavior, economists must _____ to focus on the most important components of a particular problem.

13. A(n) _____ in economic theory is a testable prediction about how people will behave or react to a change in economic circumstances.

14. _____ analysis is the use of data to test a hypothesis.

15. In order to isolate the effects of one variable on another, we use the _____ assumption.

16. When two events usually occur together, it is called _____.

17. When one event brings on another event, it is called _____.

18. The _____ is the incorrect view that what is true for an individual is always true for the group.

19. The objective, value-free approach to economics, based on the scientific method, is called _____ analysis.

20. _____ analysis involves judgments about what should be or what ought to happen.

21. _____ analysis is descriptive; normative analysis is _____.

22. "A tax increase will lead to a lower rate of inflation" is a(n) _____ economic statement.

Answers: 1. limited 2. Scarcity 3. inputs 4. scarcity; value 5. trade-offs 6. Macroeconomics; microeconomics 7. self-interest; predictable 8. rational 9. consequences 10. purposefully 11. theories models; predict 12. abstract 13. hypothesis 14. Empirical 15. *ceteris paribus* 16. correlation 17. causation 18. fallacy of composition 19. positive 20. Normative 21. Positive; prescriptive 22. positive

economics 3
resources 3
scarcity 3
the economic problem 3
rational behavior 6
theories and models 9

hypothesis 9
empirical analysis 9
ceteris paribus 10
microeconomics 12
macroeconomics 12
aggregate 12

correlation 13
causation 13
fallacy of composition 14
positive statement 15
normative statement 16

SECTION QUIZ ANSWERS

1.1 Economics: A Brief Introduction

1. **What is the definition of economics?**
   Economics is the study of the choices we make among our many wants and desires given our limited resources.

2. **Why does scarcity force us to make choices?**
   Scarcity—the fact that our wants exceed what our resources can produce—means that we are forced to make choices on how best to use these limited resources.

3. **Why are choices costly?**
   In a world of scarcity, whenever we choose one option, we also choose to do without something else that we also desire. The want that we choose not to satisfy is the opportunity cost of that choice.

4. **What is the economic problem?**
   Scarcity forces us to choose, and choices are costly because we must give up other opportunities that we value. This is the economic problem. Every individual, business, social, religious, and governmental organization faces the economic problem. Every society, whether it is capitalistic, socialistic, or totalitarian, must also face the economic problem of scarcity, choices, and costs.

5. **Why do even "non-economic" issues have an economic dimension?**
   Even apparently non-economic issues have an economic dimension because economics concerns anything worthwhile to some human being (including love, friendship, charity, etc.) and the choices we make among those things we value.

1.2 Economic Behavior

1. **What do economists mean by self-interest?**
   By self-interest, economists simply mean that people try to improve their own situation (as they see it, not necessarily as others see it). Self-interest can also include benevolence.

2. **What does rational self-interest involve?**
   Economists consider individuals to be acting in their rational self-interest if they are striving to do their best to achieve their goals with their limited income, time, and knowledge, and given their expectations of the likely future consequences (both benefits and costs) of their behavior.

3. **How are self-interest and selfishness different?**
   Self-interest means people are striving to do their best to achieve their goals, which may or may not be selfish. Parents working more hours to give more to their children or a favorite charity can be self-interested but are not selfish.

4. **What is rational behavior?**
   Rational behavior is when people do the best they can based on their values and information, under current and anticipated future consequences. Rational individuals weigh the benefits and costs of their actions and they only pursue actions if they perceive their benefits to be greater than the costs.

1.3 Economic Theories and Models

1. **What are economic theories and models?**
   A theory, or model, is an established explanation that accounts for known facts or phenomena. Economic theories and models are statements or propositions about patterns of human behavior that are expected to take place under certain circumstances.

2. **What is the purpose of a theory?**
   The purpose of a theory is primarily to explain and predict well. Theories are necessary because the facts of a complex world do not organize themselves.

3. **Why must economic theories and models be abstract?**
   Economic theories and models must be abstract because they could not possibly include every possible event, circumstance, or factor that might affect behavior. Like a road map, economic theories and models abstract from some issues to focus more clearly and precisely on the central questions they are designed to understand.

4. **What is a hypothesis? How do we determine whether it is tentatively accepted?**
   A hypothesis is a testable proposal that makes some type of prediction about behavior in response to certain changed conditions. An economic hypothesis is a testable proposal about how people will behave or react to a change in economic circumstances. It is tentatively accepted if its predictions are consistent with what actually happens. In economics, testing involves empirical analysis to see whether the hypothesis is supported by the facts.

5. **Why do economists hold other things constant (*ceteris paribus*)?**
   The hold other things constant, or *ceteris paribus*, assumption is used in economics because in trying to

assess the effect of one variable on another, we must isolate their relationship from other important events or variables that might also influence the situation the theory tries to explain or predict.

6. Why are observation and prediction more difficult in the social sciences?

Observation and prediction are more difficult in the social sciences than in physical sciences because social sciences are concerned with human behavior, which is more variable and often less readily predictable than the behavior of experiments observed in a laboratory. Social scientists can seldom run truly "controlled" experiments like those of biological scientists.

7. Why do economic predictions refer to the behavior of groups of people rather than individuals?

Economists' predictions usually refer to the collective behavior of large groups rather than individuals because looking at the behaviors of a large group of individuals allows economists to discern general patterns of actions and therefore make more reliable generalizations.

8. Why is revealed preference preferred to declared preference?

Researchers find that their results are more accurate when they observe what people do (revealed preferences) rather that what they say they do (declared preferences).

9. Why is the market for running shoes considered a microeconomic topic?

Because a single industry is "small" relative to the economy as a whole, the market for running shoes (or the running-shoe industry) is a microeconomic topic.

10. Why is inflation considered a macroeconomic topic?

Inflation—a change in the overall price level—has effects throughout the entire economy, rather than just in certain small areas of the economy, which makes it a macroeconomic topic.

1.4 Pitfalls to Avoid in Scientific Thinking

1. What is the relationship between correlation and causation?

Correlation means that two things are related; causation means that one thing caused the other to occur. Even though causation implies correlation, correlation does not necessarily imply causation.

2. What types of misinterpretation result from confusing correlation and causation?

Confusing correlation between variables with causation can lead to misinterpretation where a person "sees"

causation between two variables or events where none exists or where a third variable or event is responsible for causing both of them.

3. What is the fallacy of composition?

The fallacy of composition is the incorrect idea that if something is true for an individual, it must also be true for many individuals as a group.

4. If you can sometimes get a high grade on an exam without studying, does it mean that additional studying does not lead to higher grades? Explain your answer.

In some instances a student can get a high grade on an exam without studying. However, because additional studying increases mastery of the material, additional studying would typically increase test performance and grades. That is, even though added studying would not raise grades in some unusual situations, as a generalization, additional studying does lead to higher grades.

1.5 Positive Statements and Normative Statements

1. What is a positive statement? Must positive statements be testable?

Positive statements focus on how people actually behave, rather than on how people should behave. They deal with how variable A impacts variable B. Positive statements must be testable to determine whether their predictions are borne out by the evidence.

2. What is a normative statement? Is a normative statement testable?

Normative statements focus on what should be or what ought to happen; they involve opinions about the desirability of various actions or results. Normative statements are not testable because it is not scientifically possible to establish whether one value judgment is better than another value judgment.

3. Why is the positive/normative distinction important?

It is important to distinguish between positive and normative statements because many controversies in economics revolve around policy considerations that contain both. Deciding whether a policy is good requires both positive analysis (what will happen) and normative analysis (is what happens good or bad).

4. Why do policy disagreements arise among economists?

As with most disciplines, economists do disagree. However, the majority of those disagreements stem from differences in normative analysis because the evidence cannot establish whether one set of value judgments is better or more appropriate than other sets of value judgments.

PROBLEMS

1. In most countries the birth rate has fallen as incomes and the economic opportunities for women have increased. Use economics to explain this pattern.

2. Write your own definition of economics. What are the main elements of the definition?

3. Are the following topics ones that would be covered in microeconomics or macroeconomics?
    a. The effects of an increase in the supply of lumber on the home-building industry
    b. Changes in the national unemployment rate
    c. Changes in the inflation rate
    d. Changes in the country's economic growth rate
    e. The price of concert tickets

4. Identify which of the following headlines represents a microeconomic topic and which represents a macroeconomic topic.
    a. "U.S. Unemployment Rate Reaches Historic Highs"
    b. "General Motors Closes Auto Plant in Wisconsin"
    c. "OPEC Action Results in a General Increase in Prices"
    d. "The Cost of Health Care Rises for Employees"
    e. "Lawmakers Worry about the Possibility of a U.S. Recession"
    f. "Los Angeles Dodgers Make Pitcher Highest Paid Ballplayer"

5. Suppose the Environmental Protection Agency asks you to help it understand the causes of urban pollution. Air pollution problems are worse the higher the Air Quality Index. You develop the following two hypotheses. Hypothesis I: Air pollution will be a greater problem as the average temperature increases in an urban area. Hypothesis II: Air pollution will be a greater problem as the population increases in an urban area.

    Test each hypothesis with the data given in the following table. Which hypothesis fits the facts better? Have you developed a theory?

Metropolitan Statistical Area	Days with Polluted Air	Average Maximum Temperature	Population (thousands)
Cincinnati, OH	30	64.0	1,979
El Paso, TX	13	77.1	680
Milwaukee, WI	12	55.9	1,690
Atlanta, GA	24	72.0	4,112
Philadelphia, PA	33	63.2	5,101
Albany, NY	8	57.6	876
San Diego, CA	20	70.8	2,814
Los Angeles, CA	80	70.6	9,519

6. Do any of the following statements involve fallacies? If so, which ones do they involve?
    a. Because sitting in the back of classrooms is correlated with getting lower grades in the class, students should always sit closer to the front of the classroom.
    b. Historically, the stock market rises in years an NFC team wins the Super Bowl and falls when the AFC wins the Super Bowl; I am rooting for an NFC team to win for the sake of my investment portfolio.
    c. When a basketball team spends more to get better players, it is more successful, which proves that all the teams should spend more to get better players.

7. In the 1940s, Dr. Melvin Page conducted a national campaign to stop people other than infants from drinking milk. According to Page, milk was a dangerous food and a leading cause of cancer. He pointed to the fact that more people died of cancer in Wisconsin, the nation's leading milk producer, than any other state as proof of his claim. How would you evaluate Dr. Page's claim?

8. Are the following statements normative or positive, or do they contain elements of both normative and positive statements?
    a. A higher income-tax rate would generate increased tax revenues. Those extra revenues should be used to give more government aid to the poor.
    b. The study of physics is more valuable than the study of sociology, but both should be studied by all college students.
    c. An increase in the price of corn will decrease the amount of corn purchased. However, it will increase the amount of wheat purchased.
    d. A decrease in the price of butter will increase the amount of butter purchased, but that would be bad because it would increase Americans' cholesterol levels.
    e. The birth rate is reduced as economies urbanize, but it also leads to a decreased average age of developing countries' populations.

9. In the debate about clean air standards we have often heard the statement, "A nation as rich as the United States should have no pollution." Why is this a normative statement? Would it help you make a decision on national air quality standards? Describe two positive statements that might be useful in determining the air *quality standards*.

10. Answer the following questions:
    a. What is the difference between self-interest and selfishness?
    b. Why does inaction have consequences?
    c. Why are observation and prediction more difficult in economics than in chemistry?
    d. Why do economists look at group behavior rather than individual behavior?

11. Using the map analogy from the chapter, talk about the importance of abstraction. How do you abstract when taking notes in class?

APPENDIX

Working with Graphs

Graphs are an important economic tool

Sometimes the use of visual aids, such as graphs, greatly enhances our understanding of a theory. It is much the same as finding your way to a friend's house with the aid of a map rather than with detailed verbal or written instructions. Graphs are important tools for economists. They allow us to understand better the workings of the economy. To economists, a graph can be worth a thousand words. This textbook will use graphs throughout to enhance the understanding of important economic relationships. This appendix provides a guide on how to read and create your own graphs.

The most useful graph for our purposes is one that merely connects a vertical line (the *y*-axis) with a horizontal line (the *x*-axis), as seen in Exhibit 1. The intersection of the two lines occurs at the *origin*, which is where the value of both variables is equal to zero. In Exhibit 1, the graph has four quadrants, or boxes. In this textbook, we will be primarily concerned with

y-axis
the vertical axis on a graph

x-axis
the horizontal axis on a graph

the shaded box in the upperright corner. This portion of the graph deals exclusively with positive numbers. Always keep in mind that moving out to the right on the horizontal axis and moving up along the vertical axis both lead to higher values.

Using Graphs and Charts

Exhibit 2 presents three common types of graphs. The pie chart in Exhibit 2(a) shows the revenues received from various taxes levied on households and corporations. Each slice in the pie chart represents the percentage of finances that are derived from different sources—for example, personal income taxes account for 46 percent of the federal government's tax revenues. Therefore, pie charts are used to show the relative size of various quantities that add up to 100 percent.

Exhibit 2(b) is a bar graph that shows the unemployment rate by age and sex in the United States. The height of the line represents the unemployment rate. Bar graphs are used to show a comparison of quantities.

Exhibit 2(c) is a time-series graph. This type of graph shows changes in the value of a variable over time. This visual tool allows us to observe important trends over a certain time period. In Exhibit 2(c) we see a graph that shows trends in the inflation rate over time. The horizontal axis shows us the passage of time, and the vertical axis shows us the inflation rate (annual percent change). From the graph, we can see the trends in the inflation rate from 1961 to 2013.

pie chart
visual display showing the relative size of various quantities that add up to 100 percent

bar graph
visual display showing the comparison of quantities

time-series graph
visual tool to show changes in a variable's value over time

variable
something that is measured by a number, such as your height

Using graphs to show the relationship between two variables

Even though the graphs and chart in Exhibit 2 are important, they do not allow us to show the relationship between two variables (a variable is something that is measured by a number, such as your height). To more closely examine the structures and functions of graphs, let's consider the story of Tony, an avid

---

appendix
exhibit 1   Plotting a Graph

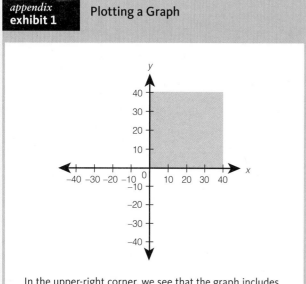

In the upper-right corner, we see that the graph includes a positive figure for the *y*-axis and the *x*-axis. As we move to the right along the horizontal axis, the numerical values increase. As we move up along the vertical axis, the numerical values increase.

24

appendix
exhibit 2   **Pie Chart, Bar Graph, and Time-Series Graph**

a. Pie Chart—Tax Revenues—Federal Government

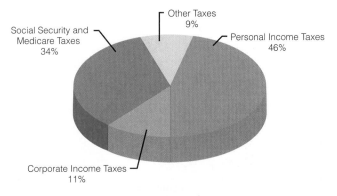

SOURCE: Economic Report of the President and Bureau of Economic Analysis, 2014.

b. Bar Graph—U.S. Unemployment, by Sex and Age

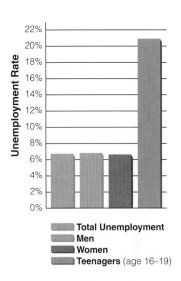

SOURCE: Bureau of Labor Statistics, March 2014.

c. Time-Series Graph—Inflation Rate

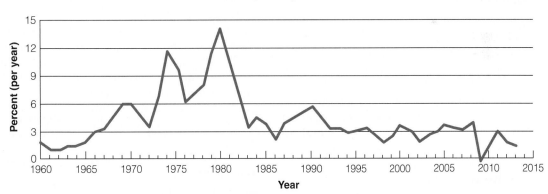

SOURCE: Bureau of Labor Statistics, March 2014.

skateboarder who has aspirations of winning the Z Games next year. He knows that to get there, he'll need to put in many hours of practice. But how many hours? In search of information about the practice habits of other skateboarders, he searches the Internet, where he finds the results of a study that looked at the score of each Z Games competitor in relation to the amount of practice time per week spent by each skateboarder. As Exhibit 3 shows, the results of the study indicate that skateboarders had to practice 10 hours per week to receive a score of 4, 20 hours per week to receive a score of 6, 30 hours per week to get a score of 8, and 40 hours per week to get a perfect score of 10. How does this information help Tony? By using a graph, he can more clearly understand the relationship between practice time and overall score.

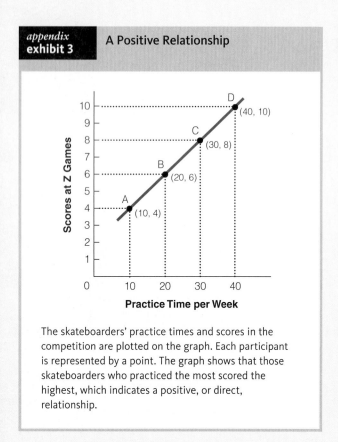

appendix exhibit 3   A Positive Relationship

The skateboarders' practice times and scores in the competition are plotted on the graph. Each participant is represented by a point. The graph shows that those skateboarders who practiced the most scored the highest, which indicates a positive, or direct, relationship.

appendix exhibit 4   A Negative Relationship

The downward slope of the curve means that price and quantity purchased are inversely, or negatively, related: When one increases, the other decreases. That is, moving down along the demand curve from point A to point E, we see that as the price falls, the quantity purchased increases. Moving up along the demand curve from point E to point A, we see that as the price increases, the quantity purchased falls.

A Positive Relationship

The study on scores and practice times reveals what is called a direct relationship, also called a positive relationship. A positive relationship means that the variables change in the same direction. That is, an increase in one variable (practice time) is accompanied by an increase in the other variable (overall score), or a decrease in one variable (practice time) is accompanied by a decrease in the other variable (overall score). In short, the variables change in the same direction.

A Negative Relationship

When two variables change in opposite directions, they have an inverse relationship, also called a negative relationship. That is, when one variable rises, the other variable falls, or when one variable decreases, the other variable increases.

The graph of a demand curve

Let's now examine one of the most important graphs in economics—the demand curve. In Exhibit 4, we see Emily's individual demand curve for pizzas per month. It shows the price of pizzas on the vertical axis and the quantity of pizzas purchased per month on the horizontal axis. Every point in the space shown represents

a price and quantity combination. The downward-sloping line, labeled "Demand curve," shows the different combinations of price and quantity purchased. Note that the higher the price of the pizzas (as shown on the vertical axis), the smaller the quantity purchased (as shown on the horizontal axis), and the lower the price (shown on the vertical axis), the greater the quantity purchased (shown on the horizontal axis).

In Exhibit 4, we see that moving up the vertical price axis from the origin, the price of pizzas increases from $5 to $25 in increments of $5. Moving out along the horizontal quantity axis, the quantity purchased increases from zero to five pizzas per month. Point A represents a price of $25 and a quantity of one pizza, point B represents a price of $20 and a quantity of two pizzas, point C a price of $15 and a quantity of three pizzas, and so on. When we connect all the points, we have what economists call a curve. As you can see, curves are sometimes drawn as straight lines for ease of illustration. Moving down along the curve, we see that as the price falls, a greater quantity is demanded; moving up the curve to higher prices, a smaller quantity is

positive relationship
when two variables change in the same direction

negative relationship
when two variables change in opposite directions

demanded. That is, when pizzas become less expensive, Emily buys more pizzas. When pizzas become more expensive, Emily buys fewer pizzas, perhaps choosing to go to the movies or buy downloadable music instead.

Using graphs to show the relationship among three variables

Although only two variables are shown on the axes, graphs can be used to show the relationship among three variables. For example, say we add a third variable—income—to our earlier example. Our three variables are now income, price, and quantity purchased. If Emily's income rises—say she gets a raise at work—she is now able and willing to buy more pizzas than before at each possible price. As a result, the whole demand curve shifts outward (to the right) compared with the old curve. That is, the new income gives her more money to use buying more pizzas. This shift

slope
the ratio of rise (change in the y variable) over run (change in the x variable)

is seen in the graph in Exhibit 5(a). On the other hand, if her income falls—say she quits her job to go back to school—she would have less income to buy pizzas. A decrease in this variable causes the whole demand curve to shift inward (to the left) compared with the old curve. This shift is seen in the graph in Exhibit 5(b).

The Difference between a Movement along and a Shift in the Curve

It is important to remember the difference between a movement between one point and another along a curve and a shift in the whole curve. A change in one of the variables on the graph, like price or quantity purchased, will cause a movement along the curve, say from point A to point B, as shown in Exhibit 6. A change in one of the variables not shown (held constant in order to show only the relationship between price and quantity), such as income in our example, will cause the whole curve to shift. The change from D_1 to D_2 in Exhibit 6 shows such a shift.

Slope

In economics, we sometimes refer to the steepness of a line or curve on a graph as the slope. A slope can be either positive (upward sloping) or negative (downward sloping). A curve that is downward sloping represents an inverse, or negative, relationship between the two variables and slants downward from left to right, as seen in Exhibit 7(a). A curve that is upward sloping represents a direct, or positive, relationship between the two variables and slants upward from left to right, as seen in Exhibit 7(b). The numeric value of the slope shows the number of units of change of the y-axis variable for each unit of change in the x-axis variable. Slope provides the direction (positive or negative) as well as the magnitude of the relationship between the two variables.

appendix
exhibit 5   Shifting a Curve

a. Demand Curve with Higher Income

Price of Pizzas (y-axis)
Quantity of Pizzas Purchased (x-axis)
D
D (with higher income)
0

b. Demand Curve with Lower Income

Price of Pizzas (y-axis)
Quantity of Pizzas Purchased (x-axis)
D (with lower income)
D
0

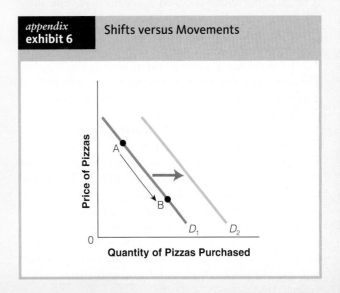

appendix
exhibit 6   Shifts versus Movements

Price of Pizzas (y-axis)
Quantity of Pizzas Purchased (x-axis)
A
B
D_1 D_2
0

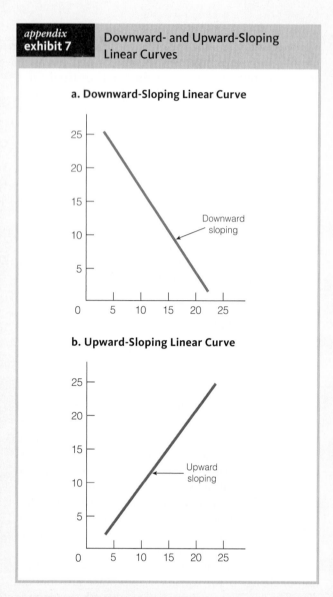

appendix **exhibit 7** Downward- and Upward-Sloping Linear Curves

a. Downward-Sloping Linear Curve

Downward sloping

b. Upward-Sloping Linear Curve

Upward sloping

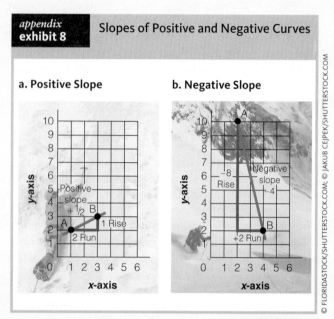

appendix **exhibit 8** Slopes of Positive and Negative Curves

a. Positive Slope

Positive slope +½

A B 1 Rise
2 Run

b. Negative Slope

−8 Rise

Negative slope −4

A B +2 Run

Finding the Slope of a Nonlinear Curve

In Exhibit 9, we show the slope of a nonlinear curve. A nonlinear curve is a line that actually curves. Here the slope varies from point to point along the curve. However, we can find the slope of this curve at any given point by drawing a straight line tangent to that point on the curve. A tangency is when a straight line just touches the curve without actually crossing it. At point A, we see that the positively sloped line that is tangent to the curve has a slope of 1: the line rises 1 and runs 1. At point B, the line is horizontal, so it has zero slope. At point C, we see a slope of −2 because the negatively sloped line has a rise of −2 (a fall of 2) for every run of 1.

Remember, many students have problems with economics simply because they fail to understand graphs, so make sure that you understand this material before going on to Chapter 2.

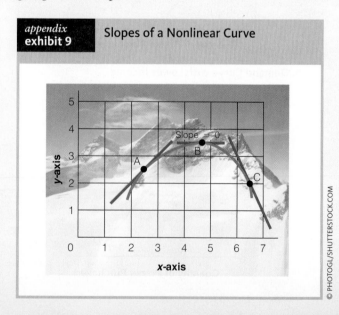

appendix **exhibit 9** Slopes of a Nonlinear Curve

A

Slope = 0 B

C

Measuring the Slope of a Linear Curve

A straight-line curve is called a linear curve. The slope of a linear curve between two points measures the relative rates of change of two variables. Specifically, the slope of a linear curve can be defined as the ratio of the change in the Y value to the change in the X value. The slope can also be expressed as the ratio of the rise over the run, where the rise is the vertical change and the run is the horizontal change.

Exhibit 8 shows two linear curves, one with a positive slope and one with a negative slope. In Exhibit 8(a), the slope of the positively sloped linear curve from point A to B is 1/2 because the rise is 1 (from 2 to 3) and the run is 2 (from 1 to 3). In Exhibit 8(b), the negatively sloped linear curve has a slope of −4: a rise of −8 (a fall of 8, from 10 to 2) and a run of 2 (from 2 to 4) gives us a slope of −8/2, or −4. Notice the appropriate signs on the slopes: the negatively sloped line carries a minus sign and the positively sloped line, a plus sign.

PROBLEMS

1. The following table gives the prices and quantity demanded of oranges (pounds) for the week of December 10–16.

Price ($/lb.)	Quantity Demanded (lbs.)
$0.80	0
0.70	3
0.60	4
0.50	5
0.40	7

a. Plot the data from the table into a graph.
b. Is it a positive or negative relationship? Explain.

Answer

We have created a negatively sloped demand curve. That is, the price and quantity demanded of oranges are inversely related:

$$\uparrow P \Rightarrow \downarrow Q_D \text{ and } \downarrow P \Rightarrow \uparrow Q_D$$

Individual demand curve of a customer for oranges of a certain grade, Week of December 10–16.
   The demand curve records the pounds of oranges a consumer desires at various prices in a given week, holding all other factors fixed. Because the individual desires more oranges at lower prices, the demand curve slopes downward.

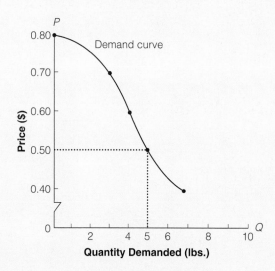

2. Which of the following will lead to a positive relationship? A negative relationship?
a. hours studied and grade in a course
b. the price of ice cream and the amount of ice cream purchased
c. the amount of seasonal snowfall and the sale of snow shovels

Answer

a. positive
b. negative
c. positive

3. Below is Emily's demand curve for pizza. How do we add income, a third variable, to price and quantity purchased on our graph? Using a graph, explain what would happen if Emily had an increase in income. What would happen if Emily had a decrease in income?

Answer

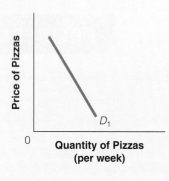 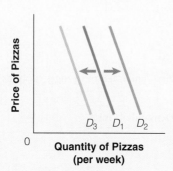

When income increases, Emily can purchase more pizzas at each and every price—a rightward shift from D_1 to D_2. If Emily's income falls, her demand will shift leftward from D_1 to D_3.

4. Use the information in the following table to plot a graph. Is it a positive or negative relationship? What is the slope?

x	y
1	2
2	4
3	6
4	8
5	10

Answer

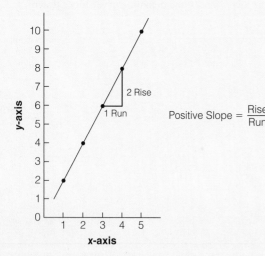

$$\text{Positive Slope} = \frac{\text{Rise}}{\text{Run}} = \frac{2}{1} = +2$$

5. What is a pie chart? Bar graph? Time-series graph?

Answer

Pie charts are used to show the relative size of various quantities that add up to 100 percent. Bar graphs are used to show a comparison of quantities of similar items. Time-series graphs allow us to see important trends over a period of time.

Economics: Eight Powerful Ideas

You're thinking about cutting class and going to the beach. Is the expected marginal benefit greater than the expected marginal cost? What if it is expected to be windy and rainy? What if your final exam is today? Do these scenarios affect your decision?

Studying economics may teach you how to "think better" because economics helps develop a disciplined method of thinking about problems. A student of economics becomes aware that, at a basic level, much of economic life involves choosing one course of action rather than another—making choices among our conflicting wants and desires in a world of scarcity. Economics provides insights about how to intelligently evaluate these options and determine the most appropriate choices in given situations.

ROBERT L. SEXTON

This chapter presents eight powerful ideas that will help you understand the economic way of thinking. The economic way of thinking provides a logical framework for organizing and analyzing your understanding of a broad set of issues, many of which do not even seem directly related to economics as you now know it.

The basic ideas that you learn in this chapter will occur repeatedly throughout the text. If you develop a good understanding of these principles and master the problem-solving skills inherent in them, they will serve you well for the rest of your life. Learning to think like an economist takes time. Like most disciplines, economics has its own specialized vocabulary, including such terms as *elasticity, comparative advantage, supply and demand, deadweight loss*, and *consumer surplus*. However, learning economics requires more than picking up this new terminology; it also involves using its powerful tools to improve your understanding of a whole host of issues in the world around you.

2.1   IDEA 1: People Face Scarcity and Costly Trade-offs

▶ What are goods and services?

▶ What are tangible and intangible goods?

▶ What are economic goods?

▶ Why do we have to make choices?

▶ What do we give up when we have to choose?

2.1a Introduction

This chapter presents eight powerful ideas that serve as the foundation of economics. Most of economics is really knowing certain principles well and knowing how and when to apply them. These few basic ideas will occur repeatedly throughout the text and are presented in this chapter as a preview of what is to come. If you develop a good understanding of these principles and master the problem-solving skills inherent in them, they will serve you well for the rest of your life.

The first three ideas focus on individual behavior: people face scarcity and costly trade-offs; people are rational decision makers and engage in marginal thinking; and people respond predictably to incentives. The next three ideas emphasize the interaction of people: specialization and trade makes people better off; markets can improve economic efficiency; and appropriate government policies can improve economic outcomes. The final two ideas are about how the economy as a whole interacts: government policies may help stabilize the economy, and increasing productivity leads to economic growth.

2.1b Human Wants Exceed Available Resources

scarcity
exists when human wants (material and nonmaterial) exceed available resources

Economics is concerned primarily with scarcity—how we satisfy our unlimited wants in a world of limited resources. We may want "essential" items such as food, clothing, schooling, and health care.

We may want many other items, such as vacations, cars, computers, and concert tickets. We may want more friendship, love, knowledge, and so on. We also may have many goals—perhaps an A in this class, a college education, and a great job. Unfortunately, people are not able to fulfill all their wants and desires, material and nonmaterial. Or, in the words of Mick Jagger, "You can't always get what you want." And as long as human wants exceed available resources, scarcity will exist.

2.1c **Scarcity and Resources**

Our desires and wants could all be met if we had unlimited resources. Unfortunately, resources are scarce: they are desirable and limited. Consequently, people have to make choices.

As we learned in the last chapter, a resource is anything that can be used to produce something else. Resources are costly because they have alternative uses. When we use land for a new football stadium that same land cannot be used for something else that is valuable like an office building or a hotel.

The scarce resources used in the production of goods and services can be grouped into four categories: labor, land, capital, and entrepreneurship.

Labor is the total of both physical and mental effort expended by people in the production of goods and services. The services of a teacher, nurse, cosmetic surgeon, professional golfer, and an electrician all fall under the general category of labor.

Land includes the "gifts of nature" or the natural resources used in the production of goods and services. Economists consider land to include trees, water, minerals, and so on, along with the physical space we normally think of as land.

Capital is the equipment and structures used to produce goods and services. Office buildings, tools, machines, and factories are all considered capital goods.

Entrepreneurship is a special human resource that is distinct from labor. The entrepreneur combines the resources of labor, land, and capital to produce goods and services. Entrepreneurs make the tough and risky decisions about what and how to produce goods and services. Entrepreneurs are always looking for new ways to improve production techniques or to create new products. They are lured by the chance of making a profit. It is this opportunity to make a profit that leads entrepreneurs to take risks.

Profits provide the financial incentive and income for entrepreneurs for their effort and risk if they are successful. Losses provide the financial incentive to let entrepreneurs know that resources are not being used efficiently.

Entrepreneurship is not just about new technology. It's also about the introduction of new goods, new production methods, new markets, new sources of raw materials, and new organizational structures.

However, not every entrepreneur is a Bill Gates or a Henry Ford. In some sense, we are all entrepreneurs when we try new products or when we find better ways to manage our households or our study time. Rather than money, then, our profits might take the form of greater enjoyment, additional time for recreation, or better grades.

labor
the physical and human effort used in the production of goods and services

land
the natural resources used in the production of goods and services

capital
the equipment and structures used to produce goods and services

entrepreneurship
the process of combining labor, land, and capital to produce goods and services

2.1d **What Are Goods and Services?**

Goods are the items that we value or desire to satisfy our wants. Goods tend to be **tangible**—objects that can be seen, held, tasted, or smelled, such as shirts, pizzas, and perfume.

Goods that we cannot reach out and touch are called **intangible goods**, which includes fairness for all, friendship, leisure, knowledge, security, prestige, respect, and health.

Services are intangible acts for which people are willing to pay, such as legal counsel, medical care, and education. Services are intangible because they are less overtly visible, but they are certainly no less valuable than goods.

All goods and services, whether tangible or intangible, are produced from scarce resources and can be subjected to economic analysis. Scarce goods created from scarce resources are called **economic goods**. These goods are *desirable but limited* in amount.

Oxygen to breathe is *not* scarce because it is desirable and abundant. Garbage is *not* scarce because it is abundant but not desirable. However, freedom, books, vacations, computers, cell phones, cars, houses, drinkable water, clean air, health, and even sunlight in December in Anchorage, Alaska, are all scarce. That is, for most people, all of these things are desirable but limited in amount—that is, scarce.

Without enough economic goods for all of us, we are forced to compete. That is, scarcity ultimately leads to competition for the available goods and services, a subject we return to often in the text.

goods
items we value or desire

tangible goods
items we value or desire that we can reach out and touch

intangible goods
goods that we cannot reach out and touch, such as friendship and knowledge

services
intangible items of value provided to consumers, such as education

economic goods
scarce goods created from scarce resources—goods that are desirable but limited in supply

2.1e **What Are Bads?**

bads
items that we do not desire or want, where less is preferred to more, like terrorism, smog, or poison oak

In contrast to goods, bads are those items that we do not desire or want. For most people, garbage, pollution, weeds, and crime are bads. People tend to eliminate or minimize bads, so they will often pay to have bads, like garbage, removed. The elimination of the bad—garbage removal, for example—is a good. A good to one person may be a bad to another. For example, the sound of a Harley-Davidson with its pipes revving might be a good to its owner, but a bad to the neighbors—especially at 5:00 on Saturday morning.

2.1f **Does Everyone Face Scarcity?**

We all face scarcity because we cannot have all the goods and services we desire. However, because we all have different wants and desires, scarcity affects everyone differently. For example, a child in a developing country may face a scarcity of food and clean drinking water, while a rich person may face a scarcity of garage space for his or her growing antique car collection. Likewise, a harried middle-class working mother may find time for exercise particularly scarce, while a pharmaceutical company may be concerned with the scarcity of the natural resources it uses in its production process. Its effects may vary, but no one can escape scarcity.

We often hear it said of rich people that "He has everything," or "She can buy anything she wants." Actually, even the richest person must live with scarcity and must, at some point, choose one want or desire over another. That is, even rich people have finite income. And of course, we all have only 24 hours in a day! The problem is that as we get more affluent, we learn of new luxuries to provide us with satisfaction. Wealth, then, creates a new set of wants to be satisfied. No evidence indicates that people would not find a valuable use for additional income, no matter how rich they became. Even the wealthy individual who decides to donate all her money to charity faces the constraints of scarcity. If she had greater resources, she could do still more for others.

Not even millionaire lottery winners can escape scarcity. They may become less content as the excitement wears off and they begin looking for new satisfactions. After winning his second $1 million scratch-off lottery, a 78-year-old man from Michigan said, "I am now going for three."

2.1g **Will Scarcity Ever Be Eradicated?**

It is probably clear by now that scarcity never has and never will be eradicated. The same creativity that develops new methods to produce goods and services in greater quantities also reveals new wants. Fashions are always changing. Clothes and shoes that are "in" one year will likely be "out" the next. New wants quickly replace old ones. It is also quite possible that over a period of time, a rising quantity of goods and services will not increase human happiness. Why? Because our wants may grow as fast—if not faster—than our ability to meet those wants.

2.1h **Wants versus Needs**

To an economist, the terms *wants* and *needs* are very different. In fact, it is difficult to objectively define a need. To most, a need is something you must have and don't currently possess. But it can be used to describe a trivial wish, a want, or something that is essential for survival. A need can be more or less urgent, depending on the circumstances. Whenever you hear somebody say, "I need a new car," "I need a vacation," or "I need new clothes," always be sure to ask: What does the person really mean?

KRISHNA MURARI KISHA/REUTERS

Scarcity even exists for billionaires Bill and Melinda Gates. If they had more resources at their disposal, they could do even more for others.

During rush hour, freeways can get very congested. Perhaps we should have an express lane for people who have urgent needs. What do you think of this idea? Imagine the number of people who would develop what they felt were urgent needs if the "urgent need" lane was much shorter than the other lanes. It would be inevitable that the system would fall apart. In fact, it would be fun to guess what might be defined as an urgent need when you are stopped by the urgent need police. It might include: "I am really in a hurry because I have to get home to clean my apartment," or "I need to get back to the dorm to type a term paper that is overdue." "Oh, shoot, I left the dog in the house." Many people would perceive their needs as more urgent than other people's urgent needs. This is a reason that the concept of need falls apart as a means of explaining behavior. It is impossible to make the concept of need useful when it is so hard to define or compare those "needs" among people.

What is the difference between a want and a need?

Need as a concept ignores scarcity and the fact that choices may change with circumstances and trade-offs. In a world of scarcity, we have unlimited wants in the face of limited resources. That is, we all must make choices because we have competing wants and limited resources. Whenever we choose, we can satisfy one want but we leave other wants not satisfied. We might satisfy our want for a new car but it may leave other wants, like a trip to Hawaii, tuition, or paying rent, unfilled.

2.1i **Scarcity Forces Us to Choose**

Each of us might want a nice home, two luxury cars, wholesome and good-tasting food, a personal trainer, and a therapist, all enjoyed in a pristine environment with zero pollution. If we had unlimited resources, and thus an ability to produce all the goods and services everyone wants, we would not have to choose among those desires. However, we all face scarcity, and as a consequence, we must make choices. If we did not have to make meaningful economic choices, the study of economics would not be necessary. The essence of economics is to understand fully the implications that scarcity has for wise decision making.

Doesn't the fact that we face scarcity mean we have to compete for the limited resources?

2.1j **Trade-Offs**

In a world of scarcity, we all face trade-offs. If you spend more time at work you might give up an opportunity to go shopping at the mall or watch your favorite television show. Time spent exercising means giving up something else that is valuable—perhaps relaxing with friends or studying for an upcoming exam. Or when you decide how to spend your income, buying a new car may mean you have to forgo a summer vacation. Businesses have tradeoffs, too. If a farmer chooses to plant his land in cotton this year, he gives up the opportunity to plant his land in wheat. If a firm decides to produce only cars, it gives up the opportunity to use those resources to produce refrigerators or something else that people value. Society, too, must make trade-offs. For example, the federal government faces trade-offs when it comes to spending tax revenues; additional resources used to enhance the environment may come at the expense of additional resources to provide health care, education, or national defense.

2.1k **To Choose Is to Lose**

Every choice involves a cost. Anytime you are doing something, you could be doing something else. The next highest or best forgone opportunity resulting from a decision is called the **opportunity cost**. Another way to put it is that "to choose is to lose," or, "An opportunity cost is the highest valued opportunity lost." It is important to remember that the opportunity cost involves the next highest valued alternative, not all alternatives not chosen. For example, what would you have been doing with your time if you were not reading this book? Or what if you were planning on going to the gym to work out, and then your best friend calls and invites you to sit in his courtside seats at the Los Angeles Lakers game (your favorite team). What

opportunity cost
the value of the best forgone alternative that was not chosen

just happened to the cost of going to the gym? The next best alternative is what you give up, not all the things you could have been doing. To get more of anything that is desirable, you must accept less of something else that you also value. The higher the opportunity cost of doing something, the less likely it will be done. So if the opportunity cost of going to class increases relative to its benefit, you will be less likely to go to class.

Every choice you make has a cost, an opportunity cost. All productive resources have alternative uses regardless of who owns them—individuals, firms, or government. For example, if a city uses land for a new school, the cost is the next-best alternative use of that land—perhaps, a park. To have a meaningful understanding of cost, you must be able to compare the alternative opportunities that are sacrificed in that choice.

Bill Gates, Tiger Woods, and Oprah Winfrey all quit college to pursue their dreams. Tiger Woods dropped out of Stanford (an economics major) to join the PGA golf tour. Bill Gates dropped out of Harvard to start a software company. Oprah Winfrey dropped out of Tennessee State to pursue a career in broadcasting. At the early age of 19, she became the co-anchor of the evening news. LeBron James (Cleveland Cavaliers), Kobe Bryant (LA Lakers), and Alex Rodriguez (New York Yankees) understood opportunity cost; they didn't even start college, and it worked out well for them. Staying in, or starting, college would have cost each of them millions of dollars. We cannot say it would have been the wrong decision to stay in or never start college, but it would have been costly. Their opportunity cost of staying in or going to or starting college was high.

Is an opportunity cost *all* the things you give up when you make a choice?

2.1| Money Costs and Non-money Costs

If you go to the store to buy groceries, you have to pay for the items you bought. This money cost is an opportunity cost because you could have used that money to purchase other goods or services. However, additional opportunity costs include the non-money costs incurred to acquire the groceries—time spent getting to the grocery store, finding a parking place, actual shopping, and waiting in the checkout line. The non-money costs are measured by assessing the sacrifice involved—the value you place on what you would have done with that time if you had not gone shopping. So the cost of grocery shopping is the price paid for the goods, plus the non-money costs incurred. Or your concert ticket may have only been $50. But what if you had to wait in line for six hours in the freezing cold to purchase your ticket? Waiting and enduring the cold are costs, too. Seldom are costs just dollars and cents. Shopping at a large discount store may save you on the money price, but cost you the value you place on your time waiting in long checkout lines. Also, buying food in bulk quantities may be less expensive per ounce, but cost inventory space in your pantry, or the food may spoil before it is eaten.

Remember that many costs do not involve money but are still costs. Do I major in economics or engineering? Do I go to Billy Madison University or Tech State University? Should I get an MBA now or work and wait a few years to go back to school?

Choices have present and future consequences. What if I decide *not* to study for my final exams? What future consequences will I bear? Flunk out of school? Not get into graduate school?

Policy makers are unavoidably faced with opportunity costs, too. Consider airline safety. Both money costs and time costs affect airline safety. New airline safety devices cost money (luggage inspection devices, smoke detectors, fuel tank safeguards, new radar equipment, and so on), and time costs are quite evident with the new security checks. Time waiting in line costs time doing something else that is valuable. New airline safety requirements could also actually cost lives. If the new safety equipment costs are passed on in the form of higher airline ticket prices, people may choose to travel by car, which is far more dangerous per mile traveled than by air. Opportunity costs are everywhere! And the real cost of anything is what you have to give up to get it.

The famous poet Robert Frost understood that choices have costs. In his poem, "The Road Not Taken," he writes, "two roads diverged in a yellow wood, and sorry I could not travel both."

© TIMOTHY EPP/SHUTTERSTOCK.COM

2.1m The Opportunity Cost of Going to College or Having a Child

The average person often does not correctly calculate opportunity costs. For example, the (opportunity) cost of going to college includes not just the direct expenses of tuition and books. Of course, those expenses do involve an opportunity cost because the money used for books and tuition could be used to buy other things that you value. But what about the non-money costs? That is, going to college also includes the opportunity cost of your time. Specifically, the time spent going to school is time that could have been spent on a job earning, say, $30,000 over the course of an academic year. What about room and board? That aspect is a little tricky because you would presumably have to pay room and board whether you went to college or not. The relevant question may be how much more it costs you to live at school rather than at home with your family (and living at home may have substantial non-money costs). Even if you stayed at home, your parents would sacrifice something; they could rent your room out or use the room for some other purpose such as storage, a guest room, a home office, a sibling's room, and so on.

How often do people consider the full opportunity of raising a child to age 18? The obvious money costs include food, visits to the doctor, clothes, piano lessons, time spent at soccer practices, and so on. According to the Department of Agriculture, a middle-income family with a child born in 2014 can expect to spend roughly $250,000 for food, shelter, and other necessities to raise that child through age 17. And that does not include college. Other substantial opportunity costs are incurred in raising a child as well. Consider the opportunity cost of one parent choosing to give up his or her job to stay at home. For a parent who makes that choice, the time spent in child raising is time that could have been used earning money and pursuing a career.

© ISTOCKPHOTO.COM/CARTERDAYNE

Economic questions are all around you. Take for instance the people who lined up to buy the latest Apple iPhone. Not only did it cost them money to purchase the item, but it also cost them the value of their time waiting in line—time that they might have spent doing other things. Choices like this one are all around us. By studying economics, we can better understand these choices and hopefully make better ones.

USE WHAT YOU'VE LEARNED

Is That Really a Free Lunch, a Freeway, or a Free Beach?

The expression, "There's no such thing as a free lunch," clarifies the relationship between scarcity and opportunity cost. Suppose the school cafeteria is offering "free" lunches today. Although the lunch is free to you, is it really free from society's perspective? The answer is no, because some of society's scarce resources will have been used in the preparation of the lunch. The issue is whether the resources that went into creating that lunch could have been used to produce something else of value. Clearly, the scarce resources that went into the production of the lunch—the labor and materials (food-service workers, lettuce, meat, plows,

tractors, fertilizer, and so forth)—could have been used in other ways. They had an opportunity cost and thus were not free.

Do not confuse free with a zero money price. A number of goods—freeways, free beaches, and free libraries, for instance—do not cost consumers money, but they are still scarce. Few things are free in the sense that they use none of society's scarce resources. So what does a free lunch really mean? It is, technically speaking, a "subsidized" lunch—a lunch using society's scarce resources, but one that the person receiving it does not have to pay for personally.

SECTION QUIZ

1. Scarcity occurs because our _____ wants exceed our _____ resources.

   a. limited; unlimited

   b. unlimited; limited

   c. limited; unlimited

   d. unlimited; unlimited

2. Scarce resources include

   a. labor—the human effort used in producing goods and services.

   b. land—the natural resources used in the production of goods and services.

   c. capital—the equipment and structures used to produce goods and services.

   d. entrepreneurship—the process of combining labor, land, and capital to produce goods and services.

   e. all of the above.

3. To economists, needs

   a. are difficult to define.

   b. can be more or less urgent, depending on the circumstances.

   c. are hard to compare among people.

   d. ignore scarcity and the fact that choices may change with circumstances and trade-offs.

   e. all of the above.

4. Which of the following statements is true?

   a. The opportunity cost of a decision is always expressed in monetary terms.

   b. The opportunity cost of a decision is the value of the best forgone alternative.

   c. Some economic decisions have zero opportunity cost.

   d. The opportunity cost of attending college is the same for all students at the same university but may differ among students at different universities.

   e. None of the above statements is true.

5. Money costs

   a. are not opportunity costs, since they involve money.

   b. are opportunity costs because you could have used that money to buy other goods and services.

   c. are always the only relevant opportunity costs.

   d. both (a) and (c).

6. Which of the following involve an opportunity cost?

   a. Choosing to go to law school rather than business school

   b. The money I used to pay for my new laptop

   c. New airline safety regulations

   d. All of the above

7. Which of the following are the opportunity costs of going to college?

   a. Tuition

   b. Books needed for classes

   c. The job I was going to take if I did not go to school

   d. All of the above

(continued)

1. What must be true for something to be an economic good?

2. Why does scarcity affect everyone?

3. How and why does scarcity affect each of us differently?

4. Why might daylight be scarce in Anchorage, Alaska, in the winter but not in the summer?

5. Would we have to make choices if we had unlimited resources?

6. What do we mean by opportunity cost?

7. Why was the opportunity cost of going to college higher for LeBron James (Miami Heat star) than for most undergraduates?

8. Why is the opportunity cost of time spent getting an MBA typically lower for a 22-year-old straight out of college than for a 45-year-old experienced manager?

Answers: 1. b 2. e 3. e 4. b 5. b 6. d 7. d

IDEA 2: People Engage in Rational Decision Making and Marginal Thinking   2.2

▶ What is rational decision making?

▶ What do we mean by marginal thinking?

▶ What is the rule of rational choice?

▶ Why do we use the word *expected* with marginal benefits and costs?

2.2a Do People Engage in Rational Decision Making?

Recall from Chapter 1 that economists assume that people, for the most part, engage in rational, or purposeful, behavior. That is, people systematically and purposefully do the best they can, based on their values and information, under current and anticipated future circumstances. In short, as rational individuals, we are influenced by an array of incentives, social norms, and past experiences. We act the way we do because we do not want to make ourselves worse off. Even if everyone does not behave rationally all the time, the assumption of rational decision making is still very useful in explaining most of the choices that individuals make.

rational decision making

people do the best they can, based on their values and information, under current and anticipated future circumstances.

economic content standards

Effective decision making requires comparing the additional costs of alternatives with the additional benefits. Most choices involve doing a little more or a little less of something: few choices are "all or nothing" decisions.

2.2b Many Choices We Face Involve Marginal Thinking

Some decisions are "all or nothing," like whether to start a new business or go to work for someone else, or whether to attend graduate school or take a job. But rational people know that many decisions are not black and white. Many choices we face involve how *much* of something to do rather than whether to do something. It is not *whether* you eat but *how much* will you eat? Or how many caffe lattes will I buy this week? Or how often do I change the oil in my car? Or how much of my check do I spend, and how much do I save? Your instructors hope that the question is not *whether* you study this semester but *how much* you study. You might think to yourself, "If I studied a little more, I might be able to improve my grade," or, "If I had a little better concentration when I was studying, I could improve my grade." That is, spending more time has an additional expected benefit (a higher grade) and an additional expected cost (giving up time to do something else that is valuable, such as watching TV or sleeping). These examples reflect what economists call **marginal thinking** because the focus is on the additional, or marginal, choices available to you. Or think of marginal as the edge—marginal decisions are made around the edge of what you are currently doing. Marginal choices involve the effects of adding or subtracting from the current situation. In short, they are the small (or large) incremental changes to a plan of action. It can be a small decision, like deciding whether to eat dessert; you must weigh the marginal benefits (the satisfaction gained from a piece of pie) versus the marginal cost (the extra money, time, and calories). Or it can be a large decision, like deciding to quit school and take a job.

marginal thinking
focusing on the additional, or marginal, choices; marginal choices involve the effects of adding or subtracting, from the current situation, the small (or large) incremental changes to a plan of action

Businesses are constantly engaged in marginal thinking. For example, firms have to decide whether the additional (marginal) revenue received from increasing production is greater than the marginal cost of that production. Or a firm might have to weigh the marginal benefits and marginal costs on a decision whether to build an additional new plant or relocate.

Always watch out for the difference between average and marginal costs. Suppose an airline had 10 unoccupied seats on a flight from Los Angeles to New York, and the average cost was $400 per seat (the total cost divided by the number of seats—$100,000/250). If 10 people are waiting on standby, each willing to pay $300, should the airline sell them the tickets? Yes! The unoccupied seats earn nothing for the airline. What are the additional (marginal) costs of a few more passengers? The marginal costs are minimal—slight wear and tear on the airplane, handling some extra baggage, and a few cans of soda. In this case, thinking at the margin can increase total profits, even if it means selling at less than the average cost of production.

rule of rational choice
individuals will pursue an activity if the expected marginal benefits are greater than the expected marginal costs

Another good example of marginal thinking is an auction. Prices are bid up marginally as the auctioneer calls out one price after another. When bidders view the new price (the marginal cost) to be greater than the value they place on the good (the marginal benefit), they withdraw from further bidding.

In trying to make themselves better off, people alter their behavior if the expected marginal benefits from doing so outweigh the expected marginal costs, which is the **rule of rational choice**. Economic theory is often called marginal analysis because it assumes that people are always weighing the expected marginal benefits against the expected marginal costs. The term *expected* is used with *marginal benefits* and *marginal costs* because the world is uncertain in many important respects, so the actual result of changing behavior may not always make people better off. However, as a matter of rationality, people are assumed to engage only in behavior that they think ahead of time will make them better off. That is, individuals will only pursue an activity if their expected marginal benefits are greater than their expected marginal costs of pursuing that activity one step further, $E(MB) > E(MC)$.

This fairly unrestrictive and realistic view of individuals seeking self-betterment can be used to analyze a variety of social phenomena.

Suppose that you have to get up for an 8:00 A.M. class but have been up very late. When the alarm goes off at 7:00 A.M. you are weighing the marginal benefits and marginal costs of an extra 15 minutes of sleep. If you perceive the marginal benefits of 15 additional minutes of sleep to be greater than the marginal costs of those extra minutes,

TARAS VYSHNYA/SHUTTERSTOCK.COM

During rush hour, some drivers will switch lanes if they perceive one lane is moving faster than another. This is purposeful behavior because drivers believe it will minimize their travel costs. These are also marginal adjustments. People are constantly weighing the marginal benefits of moving a little faster and the marginal costs of changing from their current lane to a new lane. Drivers do not have perfect information when they make their decisions. They may have selected a new lane that is now moving slower but when they made that choice, they thought it was optimal. Faced with an array of choices, consumers, workers, and firms rationally compare the expected marginal benefits and the expected marginal costs when making their decisions.

you may choose to hit the snooze button. Or perhaps you may decide to blow off class completely. But it's unlikely that you will choose that action if it's the day of the final exam—because it is now likely that the **net benefits** (the difference between the expected marginal benefits and the expected marginal costs) of skipping class have changed. When people have opportunities to make themselves better off they usually take them. And they will continue to seek those opportunities as long as they expect a net benefit from doing so.

To determine the optimal or best public policy program, voters and government officials must compare the expected marginal benefits against the expected marginal costs of providing a little more or a little less of the program's services.

Rational decision makers will follow the rule of rational choice. This is simply the rule of being sensible, and most economists believe that individuals act *as if* they are sensible and apply the rule of rational choice to their daily lives. It is a rule that can help us understand our decisions to study, walk, shop, exercise, clean house, cook, and perform just about every other action.

It is also a rule that we will continue to use throughout the text. Because whether it is consumers, producers, or policy makers, they all must compare the expected marginal benefits and the expected marginal cost to determine the best level to consume, produce, or provide public programs.

net benefit
the difference between the expected marginal benefits and the expected marginal costs

Do government policy makers have to weigh their expected marginal benefits against their expected marginal costs?

Zero Pollution Would Be Too Costly

Let's use the concept of marginal thinking to evaluate pollution levels. We all know the benefits of a cleaner environment, but what would we have to give up—that is, what marginal costs would we have to incur—to achieve zero pollution? A lot! You could not drive a car, fly in a plane, or even ride a bicycle, especially if everybody else were riding bikes, too (because congestion is a form of pollution). How would you get to school or work, or go to the movies or the grocery store? Everyone would have to grow their own food because transporting, storing, and producing food uses machinery and equipment that pollute. And even growing your own food would be a problem because many plants emit natural pollutants. We could go on and on. The point is *not* that we shouldn't be concerned about the environment; rather, we have to weigh the expected marginal benefits of a cleaner environment against the expected marginal costs of a cleaner environment. This discussion is not meant to say the environment should not be cleaner, only that zero pollution levels would be far too costly in terms of what we would have to give up.

Optimal (Best) Levels of Safety

Like pollution, crime and safety can have optimal (or best) levels that are greater than zero. Take crime. What would it cost society to have zero crime? It would be prohibitively costly to divert a tremendous amount of our valuable resources toward the complete elimination of crime. In fact, it would be impossible to eliminate crime totally. Even reducing crime significantly would be costly. Because lower crime rates are costly, society must decide how much it is willing to give up. The additional resources for crime prevention can only come from limited resources, which could be used to produce something else that people may value even more.

The same is true for safer products. Nobody wants defective tires on their cars, or cars that are unsafe and roll over at low speeds. The optimal amount of risk may not be zero. The issue is not safe versus unsafe products but rather, *how much* safety we want. It is not risk versus no-risk but rather, *how much* risk we are willing to take. Additional safety can only come at higher costs. To make all products perfectly safe would be impossible, so we must weigh the benefits and costs of safer products. In fact, according to one study by Sam Peltzman, a University of Chicago economist, additional safety regulations in cars (mandatory safety belts and padded dashboards) in the late 1960s may have had little impact on highway fatalities. Peltzman found that making cars safer led to more reckless driving and more accidents. Another study produced similar results with the introduction of airbags. That is, drivers with airbags engaged

© SERGGOD/SHUTTERSTOCK.COM

If you decide to buy a more expensive diamond ring for your fiancee, what are the expected marginal benefits? What are the expected marginal costs? What did you give up—part of a down payment for a house, a nicer honeymoon?

Shouldn't producers try to make products perfectly safe?

in enough additional reckless driving to offset the safety benefits of the airbags. People still benefitted from airbags, but took the benefits in the form of increased reckless driving. The real losers were those with no airbags and pedestrians; they had increased accidents without deriving any of the benefits from increased safety.

In short, reckless driving has a benefit in the form of getting somewhere more quickly, but it can also have a cost—an accident or even a fatality. Most people will compare the marginal benefits and marginal costs of safer driving, realizing that safer driving usually requires a driver to slow down and be more careful, also requiring more of a driver's time and energy. You would expect drivers to drive more slowly when the benefits of increased safety are high, such as driving on an icy, crowded road.

How recklessly would you drive if there were six sharp daggers sticking out of your steering wheel? Would that change the marginal benefits and costs of driving recklessly? Please don't try it, but the point is that sometimes the safer you make something, the more recklessly people behave.

SECTION QUIZ

1. Which of the following demonstrates marginal thinking?

   a. Deciding to never eat meat

   b. Deciding to spend one more hour studying economics tonight because you think the improvement on your next test will be large enough to make it worthwhile to you

   c. Working out an extra hour per week

   d. Both (b) and (c)

2. Which of the following best reflects rational decision-making behavior?

   a. Analyzing the total costs of a decision

   b. Analyzing the total benefits of a decision

   c. Undertaking an activity as long as the total benefits exceed the total costs

   d. Undertaking an activity whenever the marginal benefit exceeds the marginal cost

   e. Undertaking activities as long as the marginal benefit exceeds zero

3. Individual gallons of milk at a local grocery store are priced at $4, but two gallons purchased at the same time are priced at $6 for two. The marginal cost of buying a second gallon of milk on a shopping trip is

   a. $6.

   b. $4.

   c. $3.

   d. $2.

   e. none of the above.

4. The results of which of the following activities would marginal thinking help improve?

   a. Studying

   b. Driving

   c. Shopping

   d. Looking for a place to park your car

   e. All of the above

1. What are marginal choices? Why does economics focus on them?

2. What is the rule of rational choice?

(continued)

SECTION QUIZ (cont.)

3. How could the rule of rational choice be expressed in terms of net benefits?

4. Why does rational choice involve expectations?

5. What is rational decision making?

6. Why do students often stop taking lecture notes when a professor announces that the next few minutes of material will not be on any future test or assignment?

7. If you decide to speed to get to a doctor's appointment and then get in an accident due to speeding, does your decision to speed invalidate the rule of rational choice? Why or why not?

8. If pedestrians felt far safer using crosswalks to cross the street, how could adding crosswalks increase the number of pedestrian accidents?

9. Imagine driving a car with daggers sticking out of the steering wheel—pointing directly at your chest. Would you drive more safely? Why?

Answers: 1. d 2. d 3. d 4. e

IDEA 3: People Respond Predictably to Changes in Incentives **2.3**

▶ Can we predict how people will respond to changes in incentives?

▶ What are positive incentives?

▶ What are negative incentives?

positive incentive
an incentive that either reduces costs or increases benefits, resulting in an increase in an activity or behavior

2.3a Changes in Incentives Change Individual Behavior

Because most people are seeking opportunities to make themselves better off, they respond to changes in incentives. If you can figure out what people's incentives are, there is a good chance you can predict their behavior. That is, they are reacting to changes in expected marginal benefits and expected marginal costs. In fact, much of human behavior can be explained and predicted as a response to changing incentives. That is, changes in incentives cause people to change their behavior in predictable ways.

negative incentive
an incentive that either increases costs or reduces benefits, resulting in a decrease in the activity or behavior

2.3b Positive and Negative Incentives

Almost all of economics can be reduced to incentive stories, where consumers and producers are driven by incentives that affect expected costs or benefits. An incentive induces people to respond to a reward or a punishment. We just discussed that most rational people predictably respond to changes in incentives by weighing the expected marginal benefits against the expected marginal cost. Prices, wages, profits, taxes, and subsidies are all examples of economic incentives. Incentives can be classified into two types: positive and negative. **Positive incentives** are those that either increase benefits or reduce costs and thus result in an increased level of the related activity or behavior. **Negative incentives**, on the other hand, either reduce benefits or increase costs, resulting in a

© ZORAN KARAPANCEV/SHUTTERSTOCK.COM

A subsidy on hybrid electric vehicles would be a positive incentive that would encourage greater production and consumption of these vehicles. A wide variety of incentives are offered at the federal, state, and local levels to encourage the expanded use of alternative-fuel vehicles.

decreased level of the related activity or behavior. For example, a tax on cars that emit lots of pollution (an increase in costs) would be a negative incentive that would discourage the production and consumption of high pollution-emitting cars. On the other hand, a subsidy (the opposite of a tax) on hybrid cars—part electric, part internal combustion—would be a positive incentive that would encourage greater production and consumption of less-polluting hybrid cars. Human behavior is influenced in predictable ways by such changes in economic incentives, and economists use this information to predict what will happen when the benefits and costs of any choice are changed. In short, economists study the incentives and consequences of particular actions.

Because most people seek opportunities that make them better off, we can predict what will happen when incentives are changed. If salaries increase for engineers and decrease for MBAs, we would predict fewer people would go to graduate school in business and more would go into engineering. A permanent change to a much higher price of gasoline would lead us to expect fewer gas guzzlers on the highway. People who work on commission tend to work harder. If the price of downtown parking increased, we would predict that commuters would look for alternative methods to get to work that would save money. If households were taxed to conserve water, economists would expect people to use less water—and substantially less water than if they were simply asked to conserve water. Some people are charitable and some people are stingy, but if you change the tax code to give even greater deductions for charitable contributions, we can predict *more* people will be charitable, even some of those who are stingy. Incentives matter.

ECS

*economic
content
standards*

People respond predictably to positive and negative incentives.

GLOBAL WATCH

Chilean Bus Drivers Respond to Incentives

The problem with taking the bus is traffic congestion. Bad traffic gives people an incentive to take the bus, but slow buses give people an incentive to stick it out in the privacy of their own car—a vicious cycle. But there may be a solution. In Chile, bus drivers can be paid by the hour or by the passenger. Which of these do you think would lead to shorter delays? Think incentives. If you pay bus drivers by the passenger, they are looking for shortcuts when the traffic is bad. They also take shorter meal and bathroom breaks. They have an incentive to pick up the most passengers they can.

Bus drivers will also pay people known as *sapos* (frogs) for their information. Sapos will stand at bus stops, recording arrival times and selling their information to bus drivers who drive past. This depends significantly on the time interval (called headway in the transportation literature) between their bus and the bus immediately ahead on the same route. If the bus in front is far ahead, many passengers will have accumulated since the last bus came by, thus providing high profits for the driver. By contrast, if the bus in front is very close, then the driver can expect to be picking up few passengers and low profits. For their part, sapos provide valuable headway information to the drivers.

Each time a new bus arrives, a sapo marks the minute on his or her notepad, as well as tells the driver (for a fee) his or her headway, in minutes, with the immediately preceding bus. Given this information, the driver can choose to drive somewhat faster or slower in order to create more profitable spacing. For example, if the typical headway on a route is 10 minutes, but a driver has gone slowly enough to allow

PAUL KENNEDY/LONELY PLANET IMAGES/GETTY IMAGES

that headway to grow to 20 minutes, more passengers will be waiting and the driver will make more money. However, the bus behind that driver will then have a short headway, thus giving that second driver a strong incentive to change the spacing. Unlike drivers paid a fixed hourly wage, drivers receiving per-passenger compensation play a strategic game with each other, changing their driving in order to maximize profits given other drivers' behavior.

A study found that a typical bus passenger in Santiago waits roughly 10% longer for a bus on a paid-by-the-hour route relative to a paid-by-the-passenger route. However, paying by the passenger rather than by the hour leads to more aggressive driving and a lot more accidents. However, given the choice, over 90 percent of the routes in Santiago use the incentive plan—pay-by-the-passenger.

© INNA ASTAKHOVA/SHUTTERSTOCK.COM

In many countries of the world, the number of babies is on the decline. China has had a strict one-child-per-family policy since 1978. In a number of European countries and Japan, this poses a problem because fewer babies means an aging population and fewer people of working age to pay taxes to fund government pensions for older adults. What can the government do? They can subsidize those that have babies.

Estonia was one of the fastest-shrinking nations in the world. The government stepped in and provided pregnant women with monthly stipends. Without the subsidies women could not afford to take the time off of work to have children. In addition, they are planning to provide subsidized childcare centers. As you would expect, Estonia's fertility rate has increased. Russia, France, and Italy offer government subsidies to women who have a second child. Only time will tell if these policies will be effective in combating the social and economic forces that have lead to declining fertility rates.

SECTION QUIZ

1. Positive incentives make actions _____ likely; negative incentives make actions
   _____ likely.

   a. more; more

   b. more; less

   c. less; more

   d. less; less

2. A higher price is a _____ incentive to buyers and a _____ incentive to sellers.

   a. positive; positive

   b. positive; negative

   c. negative; positive

   d. negative; negative

3. Because most people seek opportunities that make people better off,

   a. it makes it more difficult to predict behavior.

   b. we can predict what will happen when incentives are changed.

   c. we cannot predict as well as we could if their behavior was random and chaotic.

   d. None of the above is true.

4. If household water usage was taxed, economists would expect

   a. people to use less water.

   b. people to use less water, but they would not reduce their consumption by as much as they would if they were asked to conserve water.

   c. they would not reduce their water consumption because people need water.

   d. none of the above.

(continued)

5. Who would be most likely to drop out of college before graduation?

    a. An economics major who wishes to go to graduate school

    b. A math major with a B+ average

    c. A chemistry major who has been reading about the great jobs available for people with chemistry degrees

    d. A star baseball player who has just received a multi million-dollar contract offer after his junior year

---

1. What is the difference between positive incentives and negative incentives?

2. According to the rule of rational choice, would you do more or less of something if its expected marginal benefits increased? Why?

3. According to the rule of rational choice, would you do more or less of something if its expected marginal costs increased? Why?

4. How does the rule of rational choice imply that young children are typically more likely to misbehave at a supermarket checkout counter than at home?

5. Why do many parents refuse to let their children have dessert before they eat the rest of their dinner?

Answers: 1. b 2. c 3. b 4. a 5. d

2.4 IDEA 4: Specialization and Trade Can Make Everyone Better Off

specializing

concentrating in the production of one, or a few, goods

comparative advantage

occurs when a person or country can produce a good or service at a lower opportunity cost than others

▶ What is the relationship between opportunity cost and specialization?

▶ What are the advantages of specialization in production?

2.4a Why Do People Specialize?

As you look around, you can see that people specialize in what they produce. They tend to dedicate their resources to one primary activity, whether it be performing brain surgery, driving a cab, or making bagels. Why? The answer, short and simple, is opportunity costs. By concentrating their energies on only one, or a few, activities, individuals are specializing. This focus allows them to make the best use of (and thus gain the most benefit from) their limited resources. A person, a region, or a country can gain by specializing in the production of the good in which they have a comparative advantage. That is, if they can produce a good or service at a lower opportunity cost than others, we say that they have a comparative advantage in the production of that good or service. Comparative advantage changes over time for many reasons, including changes in resources, prices, and events that occur in other countries. For example, the United States once had a comparative advantage in producing shoes, but now imports most of its shoes from

Without specialization and division of labor, this car and crew would not be as competitive. Imagine how much time would be lost if one person was changing four tires.

© ACTION SPORTS PHOTOGRAPHY/SHUTTERSTOCK.COM

foreign countries. Everyone has a comparative advantage in something, and everyone one has a comparative disadvantage in something.

2.4b Absolute versus Comparative Advantage

If one country can produce a good using fewer resources, then we say it has an absolute advantage over its competitor. Suppose U.S. workers can make both airplanes and auto parts in less time than Mexico. That is, the U.S. has an absolute advantage over Mexico in producing both goods. U.S. workers are more productive at producing auto parts and airplanes. But trade is based on comparative advantage, not absolute advantage. Individuals, firms, and countries are better off if they produce those goods where they have a comparative advantage, the ability to produce a good at a lower opportunity cost than other producers. That is, Mexico produces auto parts for the United States because Mexico has even lower productivity compared with U.S. workers in other industries, such as producing airplanes. Unless the two countries have identical opportunity costs of producing the goods, than one country will have a comparative advantage in producing one good and the other country will have a comparative advantage in producing the other good. Trade benefits everyone because it allows people to specialize in activities where they have a comparative advantage.

2.4c We All Specialize

We all specialize to some extent and rely on others to produce most of the goods and services we want. The work that we choose to do reflects our specialization. For example, we may specialize in selling or fixing automobiles. The wages from that work can then be used to buy goods from a farmer who has chosen to specialize in the production of food. Likewise, the farmer can use the money earned from selling his produce to get his tractor fixed by someone who specializes in that activity.

Specialization is evident not only among individuals but among regions and countries as well. In fact, the story of the economic development of the United States and the rest of the world involves specialization. Within the United States, the Midwest with its wheat, the coastal waters of the Northeast with its fishing fleets, and the Northwest with its timber are each examples of regional specialization.

2.4d The Advantages of Specialization

In a small business, every employee usually performs a wide variety of tasks—from hiring to word processing to marketing. As the size of the company increases, each employee can perform a more specialized job, with a consequent increase in output per worker. The primary advantages of specialization are that employees acquire greater skill from repetition, they avoid wasted time in shifting from one task to another, and they do the types of work for which they are best suited—and specialization promotes the use of specialized equipment for specialized tasks.

The advantages of specialization are seen throughout the workplace. For example, in larger firms, specialists conduct personnel relations, and accounting is in the hands of fulltime accountants instead of someone with half a dozen other tasks. Owners of small retail stores select the locations for their stores primarily through guesswork, placing them where they believe sales will be high or where empty low-rent buildings are available. In contrast, larger chains have store sites selected by experts who have experience in analyzing the factors that make different locations relatively more desirable, such as traffic patterns,

ANDREW BIRAJ/REUTERS/LANDOV

Bangladesh exports low-cost garments to mass-market retailers like Walmart. U.S. workers are a lot more productive in building airplanes and a little more productive in producing clothes than Bangladeshi workers. That is, the United States has an *absolute advantage*; they can produce planes and clothes using fewer resources than Bangladesh. However, If the two countries divide the work according to comparative advantage, then the U.S. workers would specialize in the tasks at which they are most productive, airplanes. And the Bangladeshi workers would concentrate on the tasks where their productivity is only slightly less, clothing. That is, the United States would have comparative disadvantage in producing cloth.

The entrepreneurs at Apple have learned how to combine almost 500 generic parts to make something of much greater value. The whole is greater than the sum of the parts. There is not one person at Apple or in the world who could put together an iPhone all alone. It takes many people, making many parts, living all over the world. In other words, specialization and exchange has given us the ability to do things we do not even understand.

income levels, demographics, and so on. In short, workers will earn more by specializing in doing the things that they do relatively well because that entails the least sacrifice in opportunities forgone. It is also important to remember that even if everyone had similar skills and resources, specialization could still lead to greater production because the concentration of production of some goods and services in one location can sometimes reduce the costs of production.

2.4e Specialization and Trade Lead to Greater Wealth and Prosperity

Trade, or voluntary exchange, directly increases wealth by making both parties better off (or they wouldn't trade). It is the prospect of wealth-increasing exchange that leads to productive specialization. That is, trade increases wealth by allowing a person, a region, or a nation to specialize in those products that it produces at a lower opportunity cost and to trade them for products that others produce at a lower opportunity cost. That is, we trade with others because it frees up time and resources to do other things that we do better.

In short, if we divide tasks and produce what we do *relatively* best and trade for the rest, we will be better off than if we were self-sufficient—that is, without trade. Imagine life without trade, where you were completely self-sufficient—growing your own food, making your own clothes, working on your own car, building your own house—do you think you would be better off?

Suppose the United States is better at producing wheat than is Brazil, and Brazil is better at producing coffee than is the United States. The United States and Brazil would each benefit if the United States produces wheat and trades some of it to Brazil for coffee. Coffee growers in the United States could grow coffee in expensive greenhouses, but it would result in higher coffee costs and prices, while leaving fewer resources available for employment in more beneficial jobs, such as wheat production.

In the words of growth theorist Paul Romer, "There are huge potential gains from trade. Poor countries can supply their natural and human resources. Rich countries can supply their know-how. When these are combined, everyone can be better off. The challenge is for a country to arrange its laws and institutions so that both sides can profitably engage in trade."

ECS
economic content standards

When individuals, regions, and nations specialize in what they can produce at lower costs and then trade with others, both production and consumption increase.

USE WHAT YOU'VE LEARNED

Comparative Advantage

Q Should an attorney who types 100 words per minute hire an administrative assistant to type her legal documents, even though he can only type 50 words per minute? If the attorney does the job, she can do it in five hours; if the administrative assistant does the job, it takes him 10 hours. The attorney makes $100 an hour, and the administrative assistant earns $10 an hour. Which one has the comparative advantage (the lowest opportunity cost) in typing documents?

A If the attorney types her own documents, it will cost $500 ($100 per hour × 5 hours). If she has the administrative assistant type her documents, it will cost $100 ($10 per hour × 10 hours). Clearly, then, the lawyer should hire the administrative assistant to type her documents, because the administrative assistant has the comparative advantage (lowest opportunity cost) in this case, despite being half as good in absolute terms.

Exchange, simultaneously swapping two different things, had to be invented. There is very little evidence of one animal giving an unrelated animal one thing in exchange for a different thing. As Adam Smith said, "No man ever saw a dog make a fair and deliberate exchange of a bone with another dog." But the beauty of trade is that it benefits both parties because each willing participant places a higher value on what they get from another than what they have to give up to get it. And the more individuals trade, the more they gain from specialization.

Standards of living can be increased through trade and exchange. In fact, the economy as a whole can create more wealth when each person specializes in a task that he or she does relatively best. And through specialization and trade, a country can gain a greater variety of goods and services at a lower cost. So while countries may be competitors in the global market, they are also partners.

SECTION QUIZ

1. The person, region, or country that can produce a good or service at a _____ opportunity cost than other producers has a _____ advantage in the production of that good or service.

   a. higher; comparative

   b. lower; absolute

   c. lower; comparative

   d. higher; absolute

2. Specialization is important for

   a. individuals.

   b. businesses.

   c. regions.

   d. nations.

   e. all of the above.

3. People can gain by specializing in the production of a good in which

   a. they have a comparative advantage.

   b. they have an absolute advantage.

   c. they have a lower opportunity cost.

   d. they have a higher opportunity cost.

   e. both (a) and (c).

(continued)

SECTION QUIZ (cont.)

4. If a country wants to maximize the value of its output, each job should be carried out by the person who

   a. has the highest opportunity cost.

   b. has a comparative advantage in that activity.

   c. can complete the particular job most rapidly.

   d. enjoys that job the least.

5. If resources and goods are free to move across states, and if Florida producers choose to specialize in growing grapefruit and Georgia producers choose to specialize in growing peaches, then we could reasonably conclude that

   a. Georgia has a comparative advantage in producing peaches.

   b. Florida has a comparative advantage in producing peaches.

   c. the opportunity cost of growing peaches is lower in Georgia than in Florida.

   d. the opportunity cost of growing grapefruit is lower in Florida than in Georgia.

   e. all of the above except (b) are true.

6. Kelly is an attorney and also an excellent typist. She can type 120 words per minute, but she is pressed for time because she has all the legal work she can handle at $75.00 per hour. Kelly's friend Todd works as a waiter and would like some typing work (provided that he can make at least his wage as a waiter, which is $25.00 per hour). Todd can type only 60 words per minute.

   a. Kelly should do all the typing because she is faster.

   b. Todd should do the typing as long as his earnings are more than $25.00 and less than $37.50 per hour.

   c. Unless Todd can match Kelly's typing speed, he should remain a waiter.

   d. Todd should do the typing, and Kelly should pay him $20.00 per hour.

   e. Both a and c are correct.

---

1. Why do people specialize?

2. What do we mean by comparative advantage?

3. Why does the combination of specialization and trade make us better off?

4. If you can mow your lawn in half the time it takes your spouse or housemate to do it, do you have a comparative advantage in mowing the lawn?

5. If you have a current comparative advantage in doing the dishes, and you then become far more productive than before in completing yard chores, could that eliminate your comparative advantage? Why or why not?

6. Could a student who gets a C in one class but a D or worse in everything else have a comparative advantage over someone who gets a B in that class but an A in everything else? Explain this concept using opportunity cost.

Answers: 1. c 2. e 3. e 4. b 5. e 6. b

· ·

2.5   IDEA 5: Markets Can Improve Economic Efficiency

▸ How does a market economy allocate scarce resources?

▸ What are the important signals that market prices communicate?

▸ What are the effects of price controls?

2.5a How Does the Market Work to Allocate Resources?

In a world of scarcity, competition is inescapable, and one method of allocating resources among competing uses is the market economy. The market economy provides a way for millions of producers and consumers to allocate scarce resources. For the most part, markets are efficient. To an economist, **efficiency** is achieved when the economy gets the most out of its scarce resources. In short, efficiency makes the economic pie as large as possible.

Competitive markets are powerful—they can make existing products better and/or less expensive, they can improve production processes, and they can create new products, from video games to life-saving drugs. Buyers and sellers indicate their wants through their action and inaction in the marketplace, and it is this collective "voice" that determines how resources are allocated. But how is this information communicated? Market prices serve as the language of the market system. By understanding what these market prices mean, you can get a better understanding of the vital function that the market economy performs.

Markets may not always lead to your desired tastes and preferences. You may think that markets produce too many pet rocks, chia pets, breast enhancements, and face lifts. Some markets are illegal—the market for cocaine, the market for stolen body parts, the market for child pornography, and the market for indecent radio announcers. Markets do not come with a moral compass; they simply provide what buyers are willing and able to pay for and what sellers are willing and able to produce.

2.5b Market Prices Provide Important Information

Market prices send signals and provide incentives to both buyers and sellers. These prices communicate information about the relative availability of products to buyers, and they provide sellers with critical information about the relative value that consumers place on those products. In short, buyers look at the price and decide how much they are willing and able to demand and sellers look at the price and decide how much they are able and willing to supply. The market price reflects the value a buyer places on a good and the cost to society of producing that good. Thus, market prices provide a way for both buyers and sellers to communicate about the relative value of resources. To paraphrase Adam Smith, prices adjust like an "invisible hand" to direct buyers and sellers to an outcome that is socially desirable. We will see how this works beginning in Chapter 4.

The basis of a market economy is voluntary exchange and the price system that guides people's choices and produces solutions to the questions of what goods to produce and how to produce and distribute them.

Take something as simple as the production of a pencil. Where did the wood come from? Perhaps the Northwest or Georgia. The graphite may have come from the mines in Michigan and the rubber may be from Malaysia. The paint, the glue, the metal piece that holds the eraser—who knows? The point is that market forces coordinated this production activity among literally thousands of people, some of whom live in different countries and speak different languages. The market brought these people together to make a pencil that sells for 25 cents at your bookstore. It all happened because the market economy provided the incentive for people to pursue activities that benefit others. This same process produces millions of goods and services around the world, from automobiles and computers to pencils and paper clips.

efficiency

when an economy gets the most out of its scarce resources

economic content standards

Markets exist when and where buyers and sellers interact. This interaction determines market prices and thereby allocates goods and services.

Prices provide incentives for buyers and sellers. Higher prices for a good or service provide incentives for buyers to purchase less of that good or service and for producers to make or sell more of it. Lower prices for a good or service provide incentives for buyers to purchase more of that good or service and for producers to make or sell less of it.

What is the invisible hand?

DESHAKALYAN CHOWDHURY/AFP/GETTY IMAGES

Economist Robert Jensen has found that the introduction of cell phones has made markets more efficient for Indian fisherman. Prior to the introduction of the cell phones, fishermen would have to guess to see which markets would have buyers. Buyers would also have to guess which markets had sellers. And without refrigeration, many unsold fish would be wasted by the end of the day. Cell phones made the market more efficient. Fishermen could now call ahead to see which markets would offer the best price. There soon was a better match between buyers and sellers and fewer wasted fish.

2.5c What Effect Do Price Controls Have on the Market System?

price controls
government-mandated minimum or maximum prices

Government policies called price controls sometimes force prices above or below what they would be in a market economy. Unfortunately, these controls often impose harm on the same people they are trying to help, in large part by short-circuiting the market's information-transmission function. That is, price controls effectively strip the market price of its meaning for both buyers and sellers (as we will see in Chapter 5). A sales tax also distorts price signals, leading to a misallocation of resources (as we will see in Chapter 6).

SECTION QUIZ

1. Markets

   a. for the most part are efficient.

   b. provide a way for millions of producers and consumers to allocate scarce resources.

   c. may not always lead to your desired tastes and preferences.

   d. All of the above statements are true.

2. Efficiency

   a. makes the size of the economic pie as large as possible.

   b. is achieved when the economy gets the most of its resources.

   c. Both (a) and (b) are true.

   d. None of the above is true.

3. Which of the following is (are) true statement(s)?

   a. Prices provide *incentives* for buyers and sellers.

   b. Higher prices for a good or service provide incentives for buyers to purchase less of that good or service and for producers to make or sell more of it.

   c. Lower prices for a good or service provide incentives for buyers to purchase more of that good or service and for producers to make or sell less of it.

   d. All of the above statements are correct.

4. Price controls

   a. ensure that society distributes its resources fairly.

   b. distort price signals.

   c. prevent the natural system of supply and demand from working.

   d. Both (b) and (c) are true.

1. Why must every society choose some manner in which to allocate its scarce resources?

2. How does a market system allocate resources?

3. What do market prices communicate to others in society?

4. How do price controls undermine the market as a communication device?

Answers: 1. d 2. c 3. d 4. d

IDEA 6: Appropriate Government Policies Can Improve Market Outcomes

2.6

▸ Why is it so important that the government protect our property rights?

▸ Why can't we rely exclusively on the "invisible hand" of the market to determine economic decisions?

▸ What are market failures?

▸ Does the market distribute income fairly?

2.6a Property Rights and the Legal System

In a market economy, private individuals and firms own most of the resources. For example, when consumers buy houses, cars, or pizzas, they have purchased the right to use these goods in ways they, not someone else, see fit. These rights are called property rights. Property rights are the rules of our economic game. If well defined, property rights give individuals the incentive to use their property efficiently. That is, owners with property rights have a greater incentive to maintain, improve, and conserve their property to preserve or increase its value.

The market system can only work if the government enforces the rules. That is, one of the key functions of government is to provide a legal framework that protects and enforces property rights and contracts. Markets, like baseball games, need umpires. It is the government that plays this role when it defines and protects the rights of people and their property through the legal system and police protection. That is, by providing rules and regulations, government can make markets work more efficiently. Private enforcement is possible, but as economic life becomes more complex, political institutions have become the major instrument for defining and enforcing property rights.

The government defines and protects property rights through the legal system and public policy. The legal system ensures the rights of private ownership, the enforcement of contracts, and the legal status for businesses. The legal system serves as the referee, imposing penalties on violators of our legal rules. Property rights also include intellectual property—the property rights that an owner receives through patents, copyrights, and trademarks. These rights give the owner long-term protection that encourages individuals to write books, music, and software programs and invent new products. In short, well-defined property rights encourage investment, innovation, exchange, conservation, and economic growth.

ECS

economic content standards

An important role for government in the economy is to define, establish, and enforce property rights. A property right to a good or service includes the right to exclude others from using the good or service and the right to transfer the ownership or use of the resource to others.

2.6b Market Failure

The market mechanism is a simple but effective and efficient general means of allocating resources among alternative uses. When the economy fails to allocate resources efficiently on its own, however, it is known as market failure. For example, a steel mill might put soot and other forms of "crud" into the air as a by-product of making steel. When it does, it imposes costs on others not connected with using or producing steel from the steel mill. The soot may require homeowners to paint their homes more often, entailing a cost. And studies show that respiratory diseases are greater in areas with more severe air pollution, imposing costs that may even include life itself. In addition, the steel mill might discharge chemicals into a stream, thus killing wildlife and spoiling recreational activities for the local population. In this case, the steel factory does not bear the costs of its polluting actions, and it continues to emit too much pollution. In other words, by transferring the pollution costs onto society, the firm lowers its costs of production and so produces more than the ideal output—which is inefficient because it is an overallocation of resources.

market failure

when the economy fails to allocate resources efficiently on its own

Am I sharing or stealing if I download a song from a site like Limewire or The Pirate Bay?

Markets sometimes produce too little of a good—research, for example. Therefore, the government might decide to subsidize promising scientific research that could benefit many people—such as cancer research. When one party prevents other parties from participating in mutually

IN THE NEWS

Song Swapping on the Net

A recent survey by the Institute for Policy Innovation concludes that the "piracy" of recorded music costs the U.S. recording industries billions of dollars annually in lost revenue and profits. In addition, the study states that recorded music piracy costs American workers significant losses in jobs and earnings, and lost tax revenues to the government.

Incentives play an important part in this story, too. If the price is zero, the probability of being caught is close to zero, and people do not view it as illegal, then you would expect many to download music illegally rather than purchase.

It is interesting to note that with the reduction in demand for CDs and legal downloadable music, more bands are taking their show on the road. That is, bands are more likely to tour now than before the era of file-sharing.

Piracy is not limited to music. The Business Software Alliance (BSA) reported that cost software companies about $53 billion a year worldwide.

On the short run, consumers may benefit from stealing or buying "bootlegged" copies. But most of the harm will occur in the long run. Because without copyright and patent protection, the incentives to create and innovate will be reduced.

SAMIR HUSSEIN/GETTY IMAGES

beneficial exchange, it also causes a market failure. This situation occurs in a monopoly, with its single seller of goods. Because the monopolist charges a price above the competitive price, some potential consumers are kept from buying the goods they would have bought at the lower price, and inefficiency occurs. Whether the market economy has produced too little (underallocation) or too much (overallocation), the government can improve society's well-being by intervening. The case of market failure will be taken up in more detail in Chapter 8.

We cannot depend on the market economy to always communicate accurately. Some firms may have market power to distort prices in their favor. For example, the only regional cement company in the area has the ability to charge a higher price and provide lowerquality services than if the company were in a highly competitive market. In this case, the lack of competition can lead to higher prices and reduced product quality. And without adequate information, unscrupulous producers may be able to misrepresent their products to the disadvantage of unwary consumers.

When such conditions of restricted competition arise, the communication system of the marketplace is disrupted, causing the market to function inefficiently, to the detriment of consumers. For this reason, since 1890, the federal government has engaged in antitrust activities designed to encourage competition and discourage monopoly conditions. Specifically, the Antitrust Division of the Department of Justice and the Federal Trade Commission attempt to increase competition by attacking monopolistic practices.

In sum, government *can* help promote efficiency when there is a market failure—making the economic pie larger.

Does the Market Distribute Income Fairly?

Sometimes a painful trade-off exists between how much an economy can produce efficiently and how that output is distributed—the degree of equality. An efficient market rewards those that produce goods and services that others are willing and able to buy. But this does not guarantee a "fair" or equal distribution of income. That is, how the economic pie is divided up. A market economy cannot guarantee everyone adequate amounts of food, shelter, and health care. That is, not only does the market determine what goods are going to be produced and in what quantities, but it also determines the distribution of output among members of society.

ROBERT L. SEXTON

Even though designating these parking spaces for disabled drivers may not be an efficient use of scarce parking spaces (because they are often not used), many believe it is fair to give these drivers a convenient spot. The debate between efficiency and equity is often heated.

As with other aspects of government intervention, the degree-of-equity argument can generate some sharp disagreements. What is "fair" for one person may seem highly "unfair" to someone else. One person may find it terribly unfair for some individuals to earn many times the amount earned by other individuals who work equally hard, and another person may find it highly unfair to ask one group, the relatively rich, to pay a much higher proportion of their income in taxes than another group pays. Government policy makers make decisions recognizing that there is a trade-off between efficiency (creating a bigger pie) and equality (dividing that pie). Some policies, like a progressive income tax system, unemployment compensation, and welfare programs, are aimed at redistributing the pie. While these programs aim to achieve a more equal distribution of income, they also may distort incentives for others to work hard and produce more goods and services. But that does not mean the poor should be ignored because helping them distorts incentives. We just need to recognize that there are trade-offs.

Can markets fail to allocate resources efficiently?

Government Is Not Always the Solution

However, just because the government could improve the situation does not mean it will. After all, the political process has its own set of problems, such as special interests, shortsightedness, and imperfect information. For example, government may reduce competition through tariffs and quotas, or it may impose inefficient regulations that restrict entry. Consequently, government, like markets, has shortcomings and imperfections; the cost of government policies can exceed the benefits. Citizens failing to understand the difference between actual and ideal government performance will find it difficult to decide the appropriate role for government.

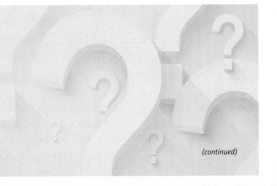

SECTION QUIZ

1. The government defines and protects property rights through
   a. the legal system.
   b. police protection.
   c. the military.
   d. all of the above.

(continued)

SECTION QUIZ (cont.)

2. Well-defined property rights encourage
   a. investment.
   b. innovation.
   c. conservation.
   d. exchange.
   e. economic growth.
   f. all of the above.

3. A market failure is said to occur
   a. when costs are imposed on some people without their consent.
   b. when the market economy fails to allocate resources efficiently.
   c. when one party prevents others from participating in mutually beneficial exchange.
   d. All of the above are examples of market failure.

4. The government redistributes income through
   a. taxes.
   b. subsidies.
   c. transfer payments.
   d. all of the above.

---

1. Why do owners with clear property rights have incentives to use their property efficiently?
2. When might the market fail to allocate resources efficiently?
3. Why would the government want to prevent market conditions of insufficient competition?
4. Why are policymakers often confronted with a trade-off between equality and efficiency?

Answers: 1. d 2. f 3. d 4. d

2.7 IDEA 7: Government Policies May Help Stabilize the Economy

▶ What can happen when total spending is insufficient?

▶ What can happen when total spending is excessive?

▶ What is inflation, and what causes it?

▶ Why is a stable monetary environment important?

▶ How can the government policies help stabilize the economy?

▶ Can government policies used to stabilize the economy be counterproductive?

The market mechanism does not always ensure fulfillment of macroeconomic goals, most notably full employment and stable prices. Sometimes total spending is insufficient, and unemployment occurs; sometimes total spending is excessive, and inflation occurs. Both inflation and unemployment affect economic growth and standards of living. Almost everyone is affected directly or indirectly by high rates of unemployment or high and variable rates of inflation.

2.7a **Inflation**

What is inflation, and what causes it? Inflation is an increase in the overall price level in the economy. Most economists believe that in the long run, sustained inflation is caused by the government printing too much money. When the government prints too much money, money loses its value. In its extreme form, inflation can lead to complete erosion in faith in the value of money. In Germany after both World Wars, prices increased so rapidly that people in some cases finally refused to take paper money, insisting instead on payment in goods or metals with some intrinsic worth.

A stable monetary environment can lead to price stability and enable producers and consumers to better coordinate their plans and decisions through the market. An increase in the overall price level increases burdens on people with fixed incomes when the inflation is not anticipated. It hurts savers, but helps those who have borrowed at a fixed rate. Moreover, inflation can raise one nation's prices relative to prices in other countries, which will either lead to difficulties in financing purchases of foreign goods or to a decline in the value of the national currency relative to that of other countries. Also, inflation imposes costs on people who devote resources to protecting themselves from expected inflation. The redistributional impact of inflation need not be the result of conscious public policy; it just happens.

economic content standards

Unemployment imposes costs on individuals and the overall economy. Inflation, both expected and unexpected, also imposes costs on individuals and the overall economy.

2.7b **Unemployment**

When the economy is producing at less than its capacity, there will be some unemployment. Unemployment will vary by age, sex, and race. It will also vary by work experience, years of schooling, and skill level.

Unemployment statistics do not always give us an accurate picture of the economy. There are discouraged workers who are so disillusioned by the economy they stop looking for work and are no longer counted as unemployed. There are also workers who take part-time jobs when they are looking for full-time jobs.

What causes unemployment? Some of it results from a downswing in a business cycle, the unpredictable fluctuations in the economy. Other unemployment occurs because people are changing jobs, different skills are needed by employers, or there are seasonal fluctuations in demand.

ECS

economic content standards

Federal government budgetary policy (fiscal policy) and the Federal Reserve System's monetary policy influence the overall levels of employment, output, and prices.

During the 1930s, the unemployment rate rose to more than 20 percent of the labor force, and among some groups, such as women and minority workers, unemployment rates were even higher. The concern over unemployment manifested itself in the passage of the Employment Act of 1946, committing the government to "promote maximum employment, production, and purchasing power." The act also implied that the government should respond to fluctuations in the economy through the use of stabilization policies.

More recently, as a result of a severe global recession, unemployment in many countries has remained high with many workers remaining unemployed for long periods of time. In 2009, 45 percent of unemployed workers had been without a job for at least 27 weeks. This is the longest downturn since World War II. The financial and psychological damage to the unemployed will last for years.

Government policies called fiscal policy use taxes and government spending to try to help stabilize the economy. If there is an unemployment problem, policy makers may lower taxes and/or increase government spending to stimulate demand. Alternatively, if there is a problem with persistent inflation, policy makers may raise taxes and/or reduce government spending.

Also, the Federal Reserve can use monetary policy to change the money supply and interest rates in an effort to achieve price stability, high employment, and economic growth. Many economists believe that these government policies play an important role in stabilizing the economy. In 2008 and 2009, the United States turned to both fiscal and monetary policy to respond to the economic downturn.

However, other economists believe the government policies can be ineffective and counterproductive. Because some government spending occurs for reasons other than macroeconomic stabilization—like money spent on defense and health care—government programs may have counterproductive effects on employment and inflation. And there are problems of time lags and the higher interest rate effect of expansionary fiscal policy, which can crowd out private investment and spending. This debate is important and is discussed in the macroeconomic portion of the text.

SECTION QUIZ

1. When total spending is insufficient, it can lead to
   a. economic growth.
   b. inflation.
   c. unemployment.
   d. none of the above.

2. When total spending is excessive it can lead to
   a. budget surpluses.
   b. inflation.
   c. unemployment.
   d. all of the above.

3. Inflation
   a. is when there is an increase in the overall price level in the economy.
   b. can be caused by the government printing too much money.
   c. can cause people to lose faith in the value of money.
   d. All of the above are true.

4. A stable monetary environment
   a. can lead to price stability.
   b. enables producers and consumers to better coordinate their plans and decisions.
   c. Both (a) and (b) are true.
   d. None of the above is true.

5. Unanticipated inflation
   a. redistributes income.
   b. increases burdens on people with fixed incomes when the inflation is not anticipated.
   c. hurts savers, but helps those who have borrowed at a fixed rate.
   d. can raise one nation's prices relative to prices in other countries.
   e. can cause all of the above.

6. The government may help stabilize the economy
   a. by providing a stable monetary environment.
   b. by using changes in government spending.
   c. by using changes in taxes.
   d. using any of the above.

---

1. What is inflation?
2. What causes inflation?
3. Why is a stable monetary environment so important?
4. What was the Employment Act of 1946?
5. What government policy changes might be effective in increasing employment in recessions?
6. What government policy changes might be effective in controlling inflation?

Answers: 1. c 2. b 3. d 4. c 5. e 6. d

IDEA 8: Increasing Productivity Leads to Economic Growth

▶ What is economic growth?

▶ Do differences in growth rates matter?

▶ What factors contribute to increases in productivity?

2.8a Defining Economic Growth

Economic growth is usually measured by the annual percentage change in real (indexed for inflation) output of goods and services per capita (real GDP per capita), reflecting the expansion of the economy over time. We focus on per capita measures because we want to adjust for the effect of increased population on economic well-being. An increase in population, *ceteris paribus*, will lower the standard of living because more people will be sharing a fixed real GDP. Long-run economic growth is a *sustained* increase in real output per capita. However, economic growth rates do not reveal anything about the distribution of output and income. For example, a country could have extraordinary growth in per capita output, and yet the poor might achieve little or no improvement in their standard of living.

From the year 1000 to 1820, the advance in per capita income was a slow crawl—the world average rose about 50 percent. Most of the growth went to accommodate a fourfold increase in population—stagnant economic growth rates mean little changes in the standard of living. The average Englishman was probably no better off in 1800 than he was in 1500. Life expectancy in England was less than 40 years in 1800. The effects of the Industrial Revolution had a huge impact beginning in the mid-1800s. Since then, world development has been much more dynamic. Per capita income rose more than eightfold, population more than fivefold.

Because of increased economic growth, the people of the world are better fed, better sheltered, and better protected against diseases. Global life expectancies have risen despite increases in population. This is not to say that millions of people do not still live in poverty. Admittedly, averages conceal a lot, but even the poorest countries of the world are better off than they were 60 years ago.

According to Stanford economist Paul Romer, "Economic growth springs from better recipes, not just from more cooking." Better recipes lead to permanent and continuing change. It is these better recipes that lead us down the path of innovation, the path of breakthroughs—organizational, intellectual, and technological. These are the ideas that can transform societies.

economic growth
the economy's abilities to produce more goods and services

Was the standard of living higher two hundred years ago, when we had fewer people?

Small Differences in Growth Rates Matter

If Nation A and Nation B start off with the same population and the same level of real GDP, will a slight difference in their growth rates over a long period of time make much of a difference? Yes. In the first year or two, the difference will be small. However, after a decade the difference will be large, and after 50 or 100 years, it will be huge. In the words of Nobel laureate Robert Lucas, "Once one starts to think about differences in growth rates among countries, it is hard to think about anything else."

Because of differences in growth rates, some countries will become richer than others over time. If they achieve relatively slower rates of economic growth, today's richest countries will not remain the richest over time. And with even slight improvements in economic growth, today's poorest countries will not remain poor for long. China and India have both experienced spectacular economic growth over the past 25 years. Because of this economic growth, much of the world is now poorer than these two heavily populated countries. Other countries, such as Ireland, once one of the poorest countries in Western Europe, is now one of the richest. Because of past economic growth, the "richest" or "most-developed" countries today have many times the market output of the "poorest" or "least-developed" countries.

2.8b Economic Growth, Productivity, and the Standard of Living

productivity
output per worker

The only way an economy can increase its rate of consumption in the long run is by increasing the amount it produces. Whether a country's standard of living rises, levels off, or declines over time depends for the most part on productivity growth. Productivity is the amount of goods and services a worker can produce per hour. Sustained economic growth occurs when workers' productivity rises. For example, slow growth of capital investment can lead to slower growth in labor productivity and, consequently, slower growth rates in real wages. On the other hand, increases in productivity and the associated higher real wages can be the result of carefully crafted economic policies, such as tax policies that stimulate investment or programs that encourage research and development. The only way an economy can increase its rate of consumption in the long run is by increasing the amount it produces. Will the standard of living in the United States rise, level off, or decline over time? For a large part, the answer depends on productivity growth. Productivity measures how efficiently resources are used. When productivity rises, more can be produced from a given amount of resources. A country's standard of living rises when it can produce goods and services more efficiently. All resources can become more productive—capital, labor, or natural resources. However, labor is the resource most often used to measure productivity because it accounts for roughly 70 percent of production costs.

2.8c What Factors Contribute to Increases in Productivity?

There are a number of major factors that contribute to productivity growth. These include physical capital, human capital, natural resources, technological change, as well as improvements in economic institutions and incentives. Today's workers generally produce more output than workers in the past. And workers in some countries, like the United States, generally produce more output than workers in most other countries. Workers with higher productivity usually have more physical capital to work with, like buildings and computers, are more educated, and have benefited from tremendous technological advancements.

Rate of productivity growth will be higher in countries that provide incentives for innovation, investment in research and development, and physical and human capital. So to increase living standards, policy makers could raise productivity by investing in education, by providing the tools needed to produce goods and services, and by providing access to better technology.

IN THE NEWS

Rockefeller and Carnegie

Is your standard of living greater than Rockefeller and Carnegie? John D. Rockefeller (left) and Andrew Carnegie (right) were the wealthiest Americans who ever lived. John D. Rockefeller had wealth valued at $340 billion in today's dollars (Bill Gates's estimated worth is about $136 billion), and Andrew Carnegie had wealth valued at $310 billion in today's dollars. But were they richer than you? Look what economic growth has done for you. Rockefeller and Carnegie could not travel by air, ride in a car, turn on an air conditioner on a hot and humid day, watch HDTV, text message their friends, download music, or use Facebook, Skype, or Twitter. And medicine was far less advanced. Improvements in medical technology and sanitation have increased life expectancies about 50 percent since their day.

Rockefeller (1839–1937)

PICTORIAL PRESS LTD/ALAMY

Carnegie (1835–1919)

ARCHIVE PICS/ALAMY

SECTION QUIZ

1. Economic growth is measured by

   a. the percentage change in nominal GDP.

   b. the percentage change in nominal GDP per capita.

   c. the percentage change in real GDP.

   d. the percentage change in real GDP per capita.

2. Growth in real per capita output

   a. says nothing about the distribution of output.

   b. has been far more common in the last 200 years than before.

   c. can make poorer countries richer over time.

   d. All of the above are true.

3. Productivity growth

   a. is a primary determinant of a country's standard of living.

   b. is a primary cause of growth in real wages.

   c. is the only way in the long run for an economy to increase its potential real consumption per capita over time.

   d. is crucially affected by saving and investment over time.

   e. All of the above are true.

4. Which of the following can add to productivity growth?

   a. Physical capital

   b. Human capital

   c. Discovery of new natural resources

   d. Technological advances

   e. All of the above can add to productivity growth.

---

1. What is long-run economic growth, and why do we use a per capita measure?

2. Why is economic growth important?

3. Do small differences in growth rates matter?

4. What is labor productivity?

5. What role do saving and investment have in economic growth?

6. What factors lead to increases in labor productivity?

Answers: 1. d 2. d 3. e 4. e

INTERACTIVE SUMMARY

Fill in the blanks:

1. As long as human _____ exceed available _____, scarcity will exist.

2. Something may be rare, but if it is not _____ it is not scarce.

3. The scarce resources that are used in the production of goods and services can be grouped into four categories: _____, _____, _____, and _____.

4. Capital includes human capital, the _____ people receive from _____.

5. Entrepreneurs are always looking for new ways to improve _____ or _____. They are lured by the chance of making a(n) _____.

6. _____ goods include fairness, friendship, knowledge, security, and health.

7. _____ are intangible items of value, such as education, provided to consumers.

8. Scarce goods created from scarce resources are called _____ goods.

9. Scarcity ultimately leads to _____ for the available goods and services.

10. Because we all have different _____, scarcity affects everyone differently.

11. Economics is the study of the choices we make among our many _____ and _____.

12. In a world of scarcity, we all face _____.

13. The highest or best forgone alternative resulting from a decision is called the _____.

14. The cost of grocery shopping is the _____ paid for the goods plus the _____ costs incurred.

15. Many choices involve _____ of something to do rather than whether to do something.

16. Economists emphasize _____ thinking because the focus is on additional, or _____, choices, which involve the effects of _____ or _____ the current situation.

17. The rule of rational choice is that in trying to make themselves better off, people alter their behavior if the _____ to them from doing so outweigh the _____ they will bear.

18. In acting rationally, people respond to _____.

19. If the benefits of some activity _____ and/ or if the costs _____, economists expect the amount of that activity to rise. Economists call these _____ incentives. Likewise, if the benefits of some activity _____ and/or if the costs _____, economists expect the amount of that activity to fall. Economists call these _____ incentives.

20. Because most people seek opportunities that make them better off, we can _____ what will happen when incentives are _____.

21. People _____ by concentrating their energies on the activity to which they are best suited because individuals incur _____ opportunity costs as a result.

22. If a person, a region, or a country can produce a good or service at a lower opportunity cost than others can, we say that they have a(n) _____ in the production of that good or service.

23. The primary advantages of specialization are that employees acquire greater _____ from repetition, they avoid _____ time in shifting from one task to another, and they do the types of work for which they are _____ suited.

24. We trade with others because it frees up time and resources to do other things we do _____.

25. Produce what we do _____ best and _____ for the _____.

26. Market prices serve as the _____ of the market system. They communicate information about the _____ to buyers, and they provide sellers with critical information about the _____ that buyers place on those products. This communication results in a shifting of resources from those uses that are _____ valued to those that are _____ valued.

27. The basis of a market economy is _____ exchange and the _____ system that guides people's choices regarding what goods to produce and how to produce those goods and distribute them.

28. _____ can lead the economy to fail to allocate resources efficiently, as in the cases of pollution and scientific research.

29. Sometimes a painful trade-off exists between how much an economy can produce _____ and how that output is _____.

30. In the case of market _____, appropriate government policies could improve on market outcomes.

31. Sometimes total spending is insufficient, and _____ occurs.

32. Sometimes total spending is excessive, and _____ occurs.

33. A stable _____ environment can lead to price stability.

34. Government policies called _____ policy use taxes and government spending to try to help stabilize the economy.

35. The Federal Reserve can use _____ policy to change the money supply and interest rates in an effort to achieve price stability, high employment, and economic growth.

36. The only way an economy can increase its rate of consumption in the long run is by increasing the amount it _____.

37. Whether a country's living standard of living rises, levels off, or declines over time depends for the most part on _____ growth.

38. _____ is the amount of goods and services a worker can produce per hour and _____ economic growth occurs when workers' productivity rises.

Answers: 1. wants; resources 2. desirable 3. land; labor; capital; entrepreneurship 4. knowledge and skill; education and on-the-job training 5. production techniques; products; profit 6. Intangible 7. Services 8. economic 9. competition 10. wants and desires 11. wants; desires 12. trade-offs 13. opportunity cost 14. money; non-money 15. how much 16. marginal; marginal; adding to; subtracting from 17. expected marginal benefits; expected marginal costs 18. incentives 19. rise; fall; positive; fall; rise; negative 20. predict; changed 21. specialize; lower 22. comparative advantage 23. skill; wasted; best 24. better 25. relatively; trade; rest 26. language; relative availability of products; relative value; less; more 27. voluntary; price 28. Market failure 29. efficiently; distributed 30. failure 31. unemployment 32. inflation 33. monetary 34. fiscal 35. monetary 36. produces 37. productivity 38. productivity; sustained

scarcity 32
labor 33
land 33
capital 33
human capital 33
entrepreneurship 33
goods 33
tangible goods 33
intangible goods 33

services 33
economic goods 33
bads 34
opportunity cost 35
rational decision making 39
marginal thinking 40
rule of rational choice 40
net benefit 41
positive incentive 43

negative incentive 43
specializing 46
comparative advantage 46
efficiency 51
price controls 52
market failure 53
economic growth 59
productivity 60

2.1 IDEA 1: People Face Scarcity and Costly Trade-offs

1. **What must be true for something to be an economic good?**
   An economic good, tangible or intangible, is any good or service that we value or desire. This definition includes the reduction of things we don't want—bads—as a good.

2. **Why does scarcity affect everyone?**
   Because no one can have all the goods and services that he or she desires, we all face scarcity as a fact of life.

3. **How and why does scarcity affect each of us differently?**
   Because our desires and the extent of the resources we have available to meet those desires vary, scarcity affects each of us differently.

4. **Why might daylight be scarce in Anchorage, Alaska, in the winter but not in the summer?**

   For a good to be scarce means we want more of it than we are able to have. Residents of Anchorage typically have all the daylight they wish in the summer, when the sun sets just before midnight, but they have only a few hours of daylight during the winter months. If daylight is desirable, it is limited in the winter.

5. **Would we have to make choices if we had unlimited resources?**

   We would not have to make choices if we had unlimited resources because we would then be able to produce all the goods and services anyone wanted, and having more of one thing would not require having less of other goods or services.

6. **What do we mean by opportunity cost?**

   The opportunity cost of a choice is the highest valued forgone opportunity resulting from a decision. It can usefully be thought of as the value of the opportunity a person would have chosen if his most preferred option was taken away from him.

7. **Why was the opportunity cost of going to college higher for LeBron James (Miami Heat star) than for most undergraduates?**

   The forgone alternative to LeBron James of going to college—starting a highly paid professional basketball career sooner than he could otherwise—was far more lucrative than the alternatives facing most undergraduates. Because his forgone alternative was more valuable for LeBron James, his opportunity cost of going to college was higher than for most.

8. **Why is the opportunity cost of time spent getting an MBA typically lower for a 22-year-old straight out of college than for a 45-year-old experienced manager?**

   The opportunity cost of time for a 45-year-old experienced manager—the earnings he would have to give up to spend a given period getting an MBA—is higher than that of a 22-year-old straight out of college, whose income earning alternatives are far less.

2.2 IDEA 2: People Engage in Rational Decision Making and Marginal Thinking

1. **What are marginal choices? Why does economics focus on them?**

   Marginal choices are choices of how much of something to do, rather than whether to do something. Economics focuses on marginal choices because those are the sorts of choices we usually face: Should I do a little more of this or a little less of that?

2. **What is the rule of rational choice?**

   The rule of rational choice is that in trying to make themselves better off, people alter their behavior if the expected marginal benefits from doing so outweigh the expected marginal costs they will bear. If the expected marginal benefits of an action exceed the expected marginal costs, a person will do more of that action; if the expected marginal benefits of an action are less than the expected marginal costs, a person will do less of that action.

3. **How could the rule of rational choice be expressed in terms of net benefits?**

   Because net benefits are expected to be positive when expected marginal benefits exceed expected marginal cost to the decision maker, the rule of rational choice could be restated as: People will make choices for which net benefits are expected to be positive.

4. **Why does rational choice involve expectations?**

   Because the world is uncertain in many important respects, we can seldom know for certain whether the marginal benefits of an action will in fact exceed the marginal costs. Therefore, the rule of rational choice deals with expectations decision makers hold at the time they make their decisions, recognizing that mistakes can be made.

5. **What is rational decision making?**

   Rational decision making is when people do the best they can based on their values and information, under current and anticipated future consequences. Rational individuals weigh the marginal benefits and marginal costs of their actions and they only pursue actions if they perceive the marginal benefits to be greater than the marginal costs.

6. **Why do students often stop taking lecture notes when a professor announces that the next few minutes of material will not be on any future test or assignment?**

   The benefit, in terms of grades, from taking notes in class falls when the material discussed will not be tested or "rewarded," and when the benefits of lecture note taking are smaller in this situation, students do less of it.

7. **If you decide to speed to get to a doctor's appointment and then get in an accident due to speeding, does your decision to speed invalidate the rule of rational choice? Why or why not?**

   No. Remember, the rule of rational choice deals with expectations at the time decisions were made. If you thought you would get in an accident due to speeding in this situation, you would not have decided to speed. The fact that you got in an accident doesn't invalidate the rule of rational choice; it only means your expectations at the time you decided to speed were incorrect.

8. **If pedestrians felt far safer using crosswalks to cross the street, how could adding crosswalks increase the number of pedestrian accidents?**

   Just like safer cars can lead people to drive less safely, if pedestrians felt safer in crosswalks, they might cross less safely, such as taking less care to look both ways. The result of pedestrians taking less care may well be an increase in the number of pedestrian accidents.

9. **Imagine driving a car with daggers sticking out of the steering wheel—pointing directly at your chest. Would you drive more safely? Why?**

   Because the cost to you of an accident would be so much higher in this case, you would drive far more safely as a result.

2.3 IDEA 3: People Respond Predictably to Changes in Incentives

1. **What is the difference between positive incentives and negative incentives?**

   Positive incentives are those that either increase benefits or decrease costs of an action, encouraging the action; negative incentives are those that either decrease benefits or increase costs of an action, discouraging the action.

2. **According to the rule of rational choice, would you do more or less of something if its expected marginal benefits increased? Why?**

   You would do more of something if its expected marginal benefits increased because then the marginal expected benefits would exceed the marginal expected costs for more "units" of the relevant action.

3. **According to the rule of rational choice, would you do more or less of something if its expected marginal costs increased? Why?**

   You would do less of something if its expected marginal costs increased because then the marginal expected benefits would exceed the marginal expected costs for fewer "units" of the relevant action.

4. **How does the rule of rational choice imply that young children are typically more likely to misbehave at a supermarket checkout counter than at home?**

   When a young child is at a supermarket checkout counter, the benefit of misbehaving—the potential payoff to pestering Mom or Dad for candy—is greater. Also, because his parents are less likely to punish him, or to punish him as severely, in public as in private when he pesters them, the costs are lower as well. The benefits of misbehavior are higher and the costs are lower at a supermarket checkout counter, so more child misbehavior is to be expected there.

5. **Why do many parents refuse to let their children have dessert before they eat the rest of their dinner?**

   Children often find that the costs of eating many foods at dinner exceed the benefits (e.g., "If it's green, it must be disgusting"), but that is seldom so of dessert. If parents let their children eat dessert first, children would often not eat the food that was "good for them." But by adding the benefit of getting dessert to the choice of eating their other food, parents can often get their children to eat the rest of their dinner, too.

2.4 IDEA 4: Specialization and Trade Can Make Everyone Better Off

1. **Why do people specialize?**

   People specialize because by concentrating their energies on the activities to which they are best suited, individuals incur lower opportunity costs. That is, they specialize in doing those things they can do at lower opportunity costs than others, and let others who can do other things at lower opportunity costs than they can specialize in doing them.

2. **What do we mean by comparative advantage?**

   A person, region, or country has a comparative advantage in producing a good or service when it can produce it at a lower opportunity cost than other persons, regions, or countries.

3. **Why does the combination of specialization and trade make us better off?**

   Trade increases wealth by allowing a person, region, or a nation to specialize in those products that it produces relatively better than others and to trade for those products that others produce relatively better than they do. Exploiting our comparative advantages, and then trading, allows us to produce, and therefore consume, more than we could otherwise from our scarce resources.

4. **If you can mow your lawn in half the time it takes your spouse or housemate to do it, do you have a comparative advantage in mowing the lawn?**

   Your faster speed at mowing the lawn does not establish that you have a comparative advantage in mowing. That can only be established relative to other tasks. The person with a comparative advantage in mowing lawns is the one with the lowest opportunity cost, and that could be your spouse or housemate in this case. For instance, if you could earn $12 an hour, mowing the lawn in half an hour implies an opportunity cost of $6 of forgone output elsewhere. If your spouse or housemate could only earn $5 per hour (because he or she was less than half as productive doing other things compared to you), the opportunity cost of that person mowing the lawn in an hour is $5. In this case, your spouse or housemate has a comparative advantage in mowing the lawn.

5. **If you have a current comparative advantage in doing the dishes, and you then become far more productive than before in completing yard chores, could that eliminate your comparative advantage? Why or why not?**

   The opportunity cost of you doing the dishes is the value of other chores you must give up to do the dishes. Therefore, an increase in your productivity doing yard chores would increase the opportunity cost of doing the dishes, and could well eliminate your current comparative advantage in doing the dishes compared to other members of your family.

6. **Could a student who gets a C in one class but a D or worse in everything else have a comparative advantage over someone who gets a B in that class but an A in everything else? Explain this concept using opportunity cost.**

   A student who gets a C in a class is less good, in an absolute sense, at that class than a student who gets a B in it. But if the C student gets Ds in other classes, he is relatively, or comparatively, better at the C class, while if the B student gets As in other classes, she is relatively, or comparatively, worse at that class.

2.5 IDEA 5: Markets Can Improve Economic Efficiency

1. **Why must every society choose some manner in which to allocate its scarce resources?**

   Every society must choose some manner in which to allocate its scarce resources because the collective wants of its members always far outweigh what the scarce resources nature has provided can produce.

2. **How does a market system allocate resources?**

   A market system allows individuals, both as producers and consumers, to indicate their wants and desires through their actions—how much they are willing to buy or sell at various prices. The market then acts to bring about that level of prices that allows buyers and sellers to coordinate their plans.

3. **What do market prices communicate to others in society?**

   The prices charged by suppliers communicate the relative availability of products to consumers; the prices consumers are willing to pay communicate the relative value consumers place on products to producers. That is, market prices provide a way for both consumers and suppliers to communicate about the relative value of resources.

4. **How do price controls undermine the market as a communication device?**

   Price controls—both price floors and price ceilings—prevent the market from communicating relevant information between consumers and suppliers. A price floor set above the market price prevents suppliers from communicating their willingness to sell for less to consumers. A price ceiling set below the market price prevents consumers from indicating their willingness to pay more to suppliers.

2.6 IDEA 6: Appropriate Government Policies Can Improve Market Outcomes

1. **Why do owners with clear property rights have incentives to use their property efficiently?**

   Private property rights mean that owners will capture the benefits and bear the cost of their choices with regard to their property, making it in their self-interest to use it efficiently, in ways in which the benefits are expected to exceed their costs. Owners with property rights have a greater incentive to maintain, improve and conserve their property to preserve or increase its value. When the government defines and protect property rights, it encourages investment, innovation, exchange, conservation, and economic growth.

2. **When might the market fail to allocate resources efficiently?**

   Markets can sometimes fail to allocate resources efficiently in what are called market failures. These can represent situations such as externalities, where costs can be imposed on some individuals without their consent (e.g., from dumping "crud" in their air or water), where information in the market may not be communicated honestly and accurately, and where firms may have market power to distort prices in their favor (against consumers' interests).

3. **Why would the government want to prevent market conditions of insufficient competition?**

   When there is insufficient or restricted competition, outputs are lower and prices paid by consumers are higher than they would be with more effective competition. By encouraging competition and discouraging monopoly, then, consumers can benefit.

4. **Why are policymakers often confronted with a trade-off between equality and efficiency?**

   Government policy makers make decisions recognizing that there is a trade-off between efficiency (creating a bigger pie) and equality (dividing that pie). Some policies, like a progressive income tax system, unemployment compensation, and welfare programs, are aimed at redistributing the pie. While these programs aim to achieve a more equal distribution of income, they also distort incentives for others to work hard and produce more goods and services (a shrinking pie).

2.7   IDEA 7: Government Policies May Help Stabilize the Economy

1. What is inflation?

Inflation is an increase in the overall price level in the economy.

2. What causes inflation?

Sustained inflation is usually caused by the government printing too much money. When the government prints too much money; money loses its value. The high inflation of the 1970s was associated with rapid growth in the quantity of money and the recent low inflation rates have been associated with slow growth in the quantity of money.

3. Why is a stable monetary environment so important?

A stable monetary environment can lead to price stability and enables producers and consumers to better coordinate their plans and decisions through the market. Inflation can redistribute income randomly. An increase in the overall price level increases burdens on people with fixed incomes when the inflation is not anticipated. Unanticipated inflation hurts savers, but helps those who have borrowed at a fixed rate. Also, inflation can raise one nation's prices relative to prices in other countries, which will either lead to difficulties in financing purchase of foreign goods or to a decline in the value of the national currency relative to that of other countries.

4. What was the Employment Act of 1946?

The passage of the Employment Act of 1946 committed the government to "promote maximum employment, production, and purchasing power." The act also implied that the government should respond to fluctuations in the economy through the use of stabilization policies.

5. What government policy changes be effective in increasing employment in recessions?

Government policies to stimulate the economy, such as decreasing taxes or increasing government purchases, could potentially increase employment in recessions.

6. What government policy changes might be effective in controlling inflation?

Government policies to control inflation can include increasing taxes, decreasing government purchases, and reducing the growth in the money supply through the banking system.

2.8   IDEA 8: Higher Productivity Growth Leads to Greater Long-Run Economic Growth

1. What is long-run economic growth and why do we use a per capita measure?

Economic growth is usually measured by the annual percentage change in real output of goods and services per capita (real GDP per capita), reflecting the expansion of the economy over time. We focus on per capita because we want to isolate the effect of increased population on economic growth.

2. Why is economic growth important?

Because of increases in economic growth, the people of the world are better fed, better sheltered, and better protected against disease. Global life expectancies have risen despite increases in population.

3. Do small differences in growth rates matter?

Because of differences in growth rates, over time some countries will become richer than others. With relatively slower economic growth, today's richest countries will not be the richest for very long. On the other hand, with even slight improvements in economic growth, today's poorest countries will not remain poor for long.

4. What is labor productivity?

Whether a country's living standard rises, levels off, or declines over time depends for the most part on productivity growth. For example, slow growth of capital investment can lead to lower labor productivity and, consequently, lower wages. On the other hand, increases in productivity and higher wages can occur as a result of carefully crafted economic policies, such as tax policies that stimulate investment or programs that encourage research and development. The only way an economy can increase its rate of consumption in the long run is by increasing the amount it produces.

5. What factors lead to increases in labor productivity?

Labor productivity increases as firms invest in new production techniques, acquire new capital (machines and factories), and incorporate new technology. This makes labor more productive, leading to increases in incomes and living standards. Of course, investing in new physical or human capital involves a trade-off—giving up consumption today in anticipation of greater future production and consumption. There are five major factors that contribute to growth in productivity: physical capital, human capital, natural resources, technological change, and improvements in economic institutions and incentives.

PROBLEMS

1. Which of the following goods are scarce?
    a. garbage
    b. salt water in the ocean
    c. clothes
    d. clean air in a big city
    e. dirty air in a big city
    f. a public library

2. Explain the difference between poverty and scarcity.

3. The automotive revolution after World War II reduced the time involved for travel and shipping goods. This innovation allowed the U.S. economy to produce more goods and services since it freed resources involved in transportation for other uses. The transportation revolution also increased wants. Identify two ways the car and truck revealed new wants.

4. The price of a one-way bus trip from Los Angeles to New York City is $150.00. Sarah, a school teacher, pays the same price in February (during the school year) as in July (during her vacation), so the cost is the same in February as in July. Do you agree?

5. McDonald's once ran a promotion that whenever St. Louis Cardinals' slugger Mark McGwire hit a home run into the upper deck at Busch Stadium, McDonald's gave anyone with a ticket to that day's game a free Big Mac. Is the Big Mac really "free"?

6. List some things that you need. Then ask yourself if you would still want some of those things if the price were five times higher. Would you still want them if the price were 10 times higher?

7. List the opportunity costs of the following:
    a. going to college
    b. missing a lecture
    c. withdrawing and spending $100 from your savings account, which earns 5 percent interest annually
    d. going snowboarding on the weekend before final examinations

8. Which of the following activities require marginal thinking, and why?
    a. studying
    b. eating
    c. driving
    d. shopping
    e. getting ready for a night out

9. Should you go to the movies this Friday? List the factors that affect the possible benefits and costs of this decision. Explain where uncertainty affects the benefits and costs.

10. Explain why following the rule of rational choice makes a person better off.

11. Which of the following are positive incentives? Negative incentives? Why?
    a. a fine for not cleaning up after your dog defecates in the park
    b. a trip to Hawaii paid for by your parents or significant other for earning an A in your economics course
    c. a higher tax on cigarettes and alcohol
    d. a subsidy for installing solar panels on your house

12. Modern medicine has made organ transplants a common occurrence, yet the number of organs that people want far exceeds the available supply. According to CNN, 10 people die each day because of a lack of transplantable organs like kidneys and livers. Some economists have recommended that an organ market be established through which doctors and others could pay people for the right to use their organs when they die. The law currently forbids the sale of organs. What do you think of such a proposal? What kind of incentives would an organ market provide for people to allow others to use their organs? What would happen to the supply of organs if, instead of relying on donated kidneys, livers, and retinas, doctors and hospitals could bid for them? What drawbacks would a free market in organs have? Have you made arrangements to leave your organs to your local organ bank? Would you do so if you could receive $50,000 for them?

13. Throughout history, many countries have chosen the path of autarky, choosing to not trade with other countries. Explain why this path would make a country poorer.

14. Farmer Fran can grow soybeans and corn. She can grow 50 bushels of soybeans or 100 bushels of corn on an acre of her land for the same cost. The price of soybeans is $1.50 per bushel and the price of corn is $0.60 per bushel. Show the benefits to Fran of specialization. What should she specialize in?

15. Which region has a comparative advantage in the following goods:
    a. wheat: Colombia or the United States?
    b. coffee: Colombia or the United States?
    c. timber: Iowa or Washington?
    d. corn: Iowa or Washington?

16. Why is it important that the country or region with the lower opportunity cost produce the good? How would you use the concept of comparative advantage to argue for reducing restrictions on trade between countries?

17. People communicate with each other in the market through the effect their decisions to buy or sell have on prices. Indicate how each of the following would affect prices by putting a check in the appropriate space.
    a. People who see an energetic and lovable Jack Russell Terrier in a popular TV series want Jack Russell Terriers as pets. The price of Jack Russell Terriers _____ Rises _____ Falls
    b. Aging retirees flock to Tampa, Florida, to live. The price of housing in Tampa _____ Rises _____ Falls
    c. Weather-related crop failures in Colombia and Costa Rica reduce coffee supplies. The price of coffee _____ Rises _____ Falls
    d. Sugarcane fields in Hawaii and Louisiana are replaced with housing. The price of sugar _____ Rises _____ Falls
    e. More and more students graduate from U.S. medical schools. The wages of U.S. doctors _____ Rise _____ Fall
    f. Americans are driving more, and they are driving bigger, gas-guzzling cars like sport utility vehicles. The price of gasoline _____ Rises _____ Falls

18. Prices communicate information about the relative value of resources. Which of the following would cause the relative value and, hence, the price of potatoes to rise?
    a. Fungus infestation wipes out half the Idaho potato crop.
    b. The price of potato chips rises.
    c. Scientists find that eating potato chips makes you better looking.
    d. The prices of wheat, rice, and other potato substitutes fall dramatically.

19. Imagine that you are trying to decide whether to cross a street without using the designated crosswalk at the traffic signal. What are the expected marginal benefits of crossing? The expected marginal costs? How would the following conditions change your benefit-cost equation?
    a. The street was busy.
    b. The street was empty, and it was 3:00 A.M.
    c. You were in a huge hurry.
    d. A police officer was standing 100 feet away.
    e. The closest crosswalk was a mile away.
    f. The closest crosswalk was 10 feet away.

Scarcity, Trade-Offs, and Production Possibilities

Goods and services can be distributed many different ways: prices, first come/first served, random selection (like a lottery), majority rule, according to need, equal shares, and so on. Each method has advantages and disadvantages. What are the benefits and costs of different allocative systems?

Some methods of resource allocation might seem bad and counterproductive; physical violence has been used since the beginning of time, as people, regions, and countries attacked one another to gain control over resources.

We could argue that government should allocate scarce resources on the basis of equal shares or according to need. However, this approach poses problems because of diverse individual preferences, the difficulty of ascertaining needs, and the negative work and investment incentives involved. In command economies,

resource allocation is determined by central planners rather than in the market. Consequently, the planners do not get market signals regarding consumers' preferences and producers' costs, and shortages and surpluses ensue. When prices are used to allocate resources, the seller produces something a consumer wants and takes the money from the sale and buys what she wants. If something other than price is used, say force, what incentive does a producer have to produce the good, if she knows it can be taken from her? People will not produce as much in this kind of world. Incentives matter. For many goods and services, consumers wait in line—called queuing. This is another way to distribute goods and services. People routinely queue at concerts or sporting events, to purchase groceries, to mail a parcel at the post office, to use a public toilet at a ball game, or to enter a congested highway. What are the costs of waiting in line?

Most queuing problems can be resolved by the market if people are willing to pay a higher price. For example, what if your grocery store charged you 5 percent to use the express lane, donating the express fee to charity? Or what if a store had a "discount line" that gave you coupons for waiting longer in line? However, the question remains, how do you create a system that simultaneously satisfies concerns about efficiency, time, money, and fairness?

This chapter builds on the foundations of the preceding chapters. We have learned that we have unlimited wants and limited resources—that is, we all face scarcity. And scarcity forces us to choose. To get one thing we like, we usually have to give up something else we want—that is, people face trade-offs. Recognizing these trade-offs will allow us to make better decisions.

Every economy must transform the resources that nature provides into goods and services. Economics is the study of that process. This chapter begins with a discussion of how every economy must respond to three fundamental questions: What goods and services will be produced? How will the goods and services be produced? Who will get the goods and services?

In this chapter, we also introduce our first economic models: the circular flow model and the production possibilities curve. In the circular flow model, we show how decisions made by households and firms interact with each other. Our second model, the production possibilities curve, illustrates many of the most important concepts in economics: scarcity, trade-offs, increasing opportunity costs, efficiency, investment in capital goods, and economic growth.

The Three Economic Questions Every Society Faces   3.1

▸ What goods and services will be produced?   ▸ Who will get the goods and services?

▸ How will the goods and services be produced?

3.1a The Three Economic Questions

Because of scarcity, certain economic questions must be answered, regardless of a society's level of affluence or its political structure. We consider three fundamental questions that every society inevitably faces: (1) What goods and services will be produced? (2) How will the goods and services be produced? (3) Who will get the goods and services produced? These questions are unavoidable in a world of scarcity.

How do we decide which colors and options to include with these cars?

Consumers say no to some new products. If consumers do not like a product, like the Ford Edsel above, it becomes unprofitable and will eventually disappear. Sometimes they become collector's items years later.

consumer sovereignty

consumers vote with their dollars in a market economy; this accounts for what is produced

command economy

an economy in which the government uses central planning to coordinate most economic activities

market economy

an economy that allocates goods and services through the private decisions of consumers, input suppliers, and firms

mixed economy

an economy where government and the private sector determine the allocation of resources

3.1b What Goods and Services Will Be Produced?

How do individuals control production decisions in market-oriented economies? Questions arise such as whether society should produce more baseball stadiums or more schools. Should Apple produce more iPhones or laptops? The government has a limited budget, too, and must make choices on how much to spend on defense, health care, highways, and education. In short, consumers, firms, and governments must all make choices about what goods and services will be produced and each one of those decisions has an opportunity cost—the highest valued alternative forgone. In the marketplace, the answer to these and other similar questions is that people "vote" in economic affairs with their dollars (or pounds or yen). This concept is called **consumer sovereignty**. Consumer sovereignty explains how individual consumers in market economies determine what continues to be produced.

High-definition televisions, DVD players, cell phones, iPods, camcorders, and computers, for example, became part of our lives because consumers "voted" hundreds of dollars apiece on these goods. Consumers "voted" fewer dollars on regular color televisions and more on high-definition televisions. Similarly, vinyl record albums gave way to tapes, CDs to streaming downloadable music, as consumers voted for these items with their dollars. If consumers vote for more fuel-efficient cars and healthier foods, then firms that wish to remain profitable must listen and respond.

How Different Types of Economic Systems Answer the Question "What Goods and Services Will Be Produced?"

Economies are organized in different ways to answer the question of what is to be produced. The dispute over the best way to answer this question has inflamed passions for centuries. Should a central planning board make the decisions, as in North Korea and Cuba? Sometimes this highly centralized economic system is referred to as a **command economy**. Under this type of regime, decisions about how many tractors or automobiles to produce are largely determined by a government official or committee associated with the central planning organization. That same group decides on the number and size of school buildings, refrigerators, shoes, and so on. Other countries, including the United States, much of Europe, and increasingly, Asia and elsewhere have largely adopted a decentralized decision-making process where literally millions of individual producers and consumers of goods and services determine what goods, and how many of them, will be produced. A country that uses such a decentralized decision-making process is often said to have a **market economy**. Actually, no nation has a pure market economy. The United States, along with most countries, is said to have a **mixed economy**. In such an economy, the government and the private sector together determine the allocation of resources.

3.1c How Will the Goods and Services Be Produced?

All economies, regardless of their political structure, must decide how to produce the goods and services that they want—because of scarcity. Goods and services can generally be produced in several ways. Firms may face a trade-off between using more machines or more workers. For example, a company might decide to move its production to a plant in another country that uses more workers and fewer machines.

A ditch can be dug by many workers using their hands, by a few workers with shovels, or by one person with a backhoe. Someone must decide which method is most appropriate. From this example, you might be tempted to conclude that it is desirable to use the biggest, most elaborate form of capital. But would you really want to plant your spring flowers with huge earthmoving machinery? That is, the most capital-intensive method of production may not always be the best. The best method is the least-cost method.

What Is the Best Form of Production?

The best or "optimal" form of production will usually vary from one economy to the next. For example, earth-moving machinery is used in digging large ditches in the United States and Europe, while in developing countries, shovels are often used. Why do these optimal forms of production vary? Compared with capital, labor is relatively inexpensive and plentiful in developing countries but relatively scarce and expensive in the United States. In contrast, capital (machines and tools, mainly) is comparatively plentiful and relatively inexpensive in the United States but scarcer and more costly in developing countries. That is, in developing countries, production tends to be more labor intensive, or labor driven. In the United States, production tends to be more capital intensive, or capital driven. Each nation tends to use the production processes that conserve its relatively scarce (and thus relatively more expensive) resources and use more of its relatively abundant resources.

labor intensive
production that uses a large amount of labor

capital intensive
production that uses a large amount of capital

3.1d Who Will Get the Goods and Services Produced?

In every society, some mechanism must exist to determine how goods and services are to be distributed among the population. Who gets what? Why do some people get to consume or use far more goods and services than others? This question of distribution is so important

---

USE WHAT YOU'VE LEARNED

Market Signals

Q Adam was a college graduate with a major in art. A few years ago, Adam decided that he wanted to pursue a vocation that utilized his talent. In response, he shut himself up in his studio and created a watercolor collection. With high hopes, Adam put his collection on display for buyers. After several years of displaying his art, however, the only one interested in the collection was his 18-year-old sister, who wanted the picture frames for her room. Recognizing that Adam was having trouble pursuing his chosen occupation, Adam's friend Karl told him that the market had failed. In the meantime, Adam turned to house painting (interior and exterior) and business was booming. Adam hired five workers and would often be painting all day and into the evenings and weekends. Do you think the market has failed?

A No. Markets provide important signals, and the signal being sent in this situation is that Adam should look for some other means of support—something that society values. Remember the function of consumer sovereignty in the marketplace. Clearly, consumers were not voting for Adam's art. The market seems to be telling Adam: less painting on canvas and more painting on walls, doors, and trim.

In a market economy, who decides what and how much to produce?

that wars and revolutions have been fought over it. Both the French and Russian revolutions were concerned fundamentally with the distribution of goods and services. Even in societies where political questions are usually settled peacefully, the question of the distribution of income is an issue that always arouses strong emotional responses. As we will see, in a market economy with private ownership and control of the means of production, the amounts of goods and services an individual can obtain depend on her or his income. Income, in turn, will depend on the quantity and quality of the scarce resources the individual controls. Income is also determined by the price others are willing and able to pay for what you have to sell. If you are a medical doctor and make $300,000 a year, that is income you will have available to buy goods and services. If you also own a condominium you rent out in Aspen, Colorado, you will have an even greater amount of income to spend on goods and services. Markets reward education, hard work, and training. Education (years of schooling) and earnings are highly (positively) correlated. Oprah Winfrey made a lot of money because she had unique and marketable skills as a talk show host. This basis for distribution may or may not be viewed as "fair," an issue we look at in detail later in this book.

Singer Beyonce gets paid a lot of money because she controls scarce resources: her talent and her name recognition. As we will see in Chapter 5, people's talents and other goods and services in limited supply relative to demand will command high prices.

Castaway and Resource Allocation

In the movie *Cast Away*, a plane crash leaves Chuck Noland (Tom Hanks) stranded on a deserted island, as in the classic 18th century novel *Robinson Crusoe*. In this simple island economy, Noland had to find a way to survive. His behavior was restricted by the resources that he salvaged from the crash and what he could find on the island. He was by himself, so property rights were not an issue. However, he still had to answer the *what, how,* and *for whom* questions. In this chapter, you will discover these are the three questions that every society must face—even the simplest island economy. To Noland, the *for whom* question, who gets the goods and services produced, was pretty easy: He was the only one on the island; he got what was produced. The *what* question, what goods and services would be produced, was pretty easy, too: He was trying to survive, so he was looking to produce food, shelter, and clothing. The *how* question, how will the goods and services be produced, was where this scene becomes interesting. How to best use his scarce resources? Noland salvaged several boxes from the plane crash. After a failed attempt to leave the island, he decided to open the boxes to see whether they contain anything useful. He first found a pair of ice skates. He uses the blade of the skate as a knife to open coconuts, to cut a dress to convert into a fishing net, and to sharpen a stick to use as a spear for catching fish. He uses the laces from the skate and the bubble wrap in the package to dress an injury. He uses the raft as a lean-to for his shelter. He builds a fire and even "makes" a friend out of a volleyball—Wilson. In short, Noland uses his entrepreneurial talents to try to make the best use of the scarce resources in order to survive on the island.

Chuck Noland (Tom Hanks) had to make the best use of his scarce resources to survive on the island.

SECTION QUIZ

1. Which of the following is not a question that all societies must answer?

    a. How can scarcity be eliminated?

    b. What goods and services will be produced?

    c. Who will get the goods and services?

    d. How will the goods and services be produced?

    e. All of the above are questions that all societies must answer.

2. Economic disputes over the distribution of income are generally associated with which economic question?

    a. Who should produce the goods?

    b. What goods and services will be produced?

    c. Who will get the goods and services?

    d. How will the goods and services be produced?

3. The private ownership of property and the use of the market system to direct and coordinate economic activity are most characteristic of

    a. a command economy.

    b. a mixed economy.

    c. a market economy.

    d. a traditional economy.

4. The degree of government involvement in the economy is greatest in

    a. a command economy.

    b. a mixed economy.

    c. a market economy.

    d. a traditional economy.

5. The best method of production is

    a. the capital-intensive method.

    b. the labor-intensive method.

    c. the same under all circumstances.

    d. the lowest cost method.

6. When _____ is relatively scarce, _____ methods of production will be relatively less expensive.

    a. capital; capital-intensive

    b. capital; labor-intensive

    c. labor; capital-intensive

    d. labor; labor-intensive

    e. Both (b) and (c) are true.

---

1. Why does scarcity force us to decide what to produce?

2. How is a command economy different from a market economy?

3. How does consumer sovereignty determine production decisions in a market economy?

4. Do you think that what and how much an economy produces depends on who will get the goods and services produced in that economy? Why or why not?

(continued)

3.2 The Circular Flow Model

▶ What are product markets?   ▶ What is the circular flow model?

▶ What are factor markets?

How do we explain how the millions of people in an economy interact when it comes to buying, selling, producing, working, hiring, and so on? A continuous flow of goods and services is bought and sold between the producers of goods and services (which we call firms) and the buyers of goods and services (which we call households). A continuous flow of income also moves from firms to households as firms buy inputs to produce the goods and services they sell. In our simple economy, these exchanges take place in product markets and factor markets.

A teacher's supply of labor generates personal income in the form of wages in the factor market, which she can use to buy automobiles, vacations, food, and other goods in the product market. Suppose she buys an automobile in the product market; the automobile dealer now has revenue to pay for his inputs in the factor market—wages to workers, payment for new cars to replenish his inventory, rent for his building, and so on.

© LAYLAND MASUDA/SHUTTERSTOCK.COM

3.2a Product Markets

product markets
markets where households are buyers and firms are sellers of goods and services

Product markets are the markets for consumer goods and services. In the product market, households are buyers and firms are sellers. Households buy the goods and services that firms produce and sell. The payments from the households to the firms, for the purchases of goods and services, flow to the firms at the same time as goods and services flow to the households.

3.2b Factor Markets

factor (or input) markets
markets where households sell the use of their inputs (capital, land, labor, and entrepreneurship) to firms

Factor or input markets are where households sell the use of their inputs (capital, land, labor, and entrepreneurship) to firms. In the factor market, households are the sellers and firms are the buyers. Households receive money payments from firms as compensation for the labor, land, capital, and entrepreneurship needed to produce goods and services. These payments take the form of wages (salaries), rent, interest payments, and profit.

3.2c The Simple Circular Flow Model

The **simple circular flow model** is illustrated in Exhibit 1. In the top half of the exhibit, the product markets, households purchase goods and services that firms have produced. In the lower half of the exhibit, the factor (or input) markets, households sell the inputs that firms use to produce goods and services. Households receive income (wages, rent, interest, and profit) from firms for the inputs used in production (capital, land, labor, and entrepreneurship).

So we see that in the simple circular flow model, income flows from firms to households (factor markets), and spending flows from households to firms (product markets). The simple circular flow model shows how households and firms interact in product markets and factor markets and how the two markets are interrelated.

simple circular flow model
an illustration of the continuous flow of goods, services, inputs, and payments between firms and households

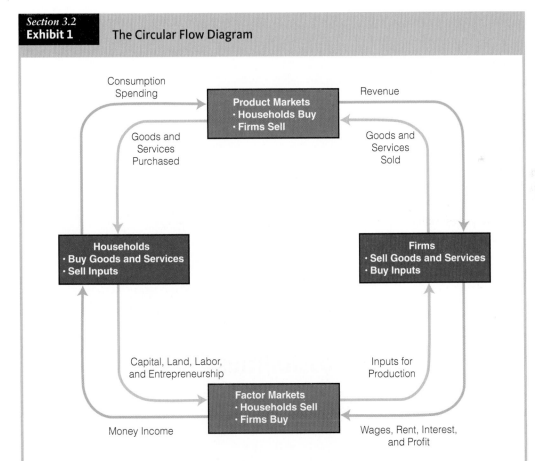

Section 3.2
Exhibit 1   **The Circular Flow Diagram**

The circular flow diagram is a visual model of the economy. Households and firms interact with each other in product markets (where households buy and firms sell) and factor markets (where households sell and firms buy). For example, households receive income from firms in exchange for working and providing other inputs. Households then recycle that income to firms in exchange for goods and services. Dollars flow clockwise, and goods and services flow counterclockwise.

Are households always buyers and firms always sellers?

SECTION QUIZ

1. In a circular flow diagram,

   a. goods and services flow in a clockwise direction.

   b. goods and services flow in a counterclockwise direction.

   c. product markets appear at the top of the diagram.

   d. factor markets appear at the left of the diagram.

   e. both (b) and (c) are true.

2. Which of the following is true?

   a. In the product markets, firms are buyers and households are sellers.

   b. In the factor markets, firms are sellers and households are buyers.

   c. Firms receive money payments from households for capital, land, labor, and entrepreneurship.

   d. All of the above are true.

   e. None of the above is true.

3. In the circular flow model,

   a. firms supply both products and resources.

   b. firms demand both products and resources.

   c. firms demand resources and supply products.

   d. firms supply resources and demand products.

4. The circular flow model

   a. traces the flow of goods and services among firms and households.

   b. traces the flow of payments among firms and households.

   c. includes both product markets and factor markets.

   d. All of the above are true.

---

1. Why does the circular flow of money move in the opposite direction from the flow of goods and services?

2. What is bought and sold in factor markets?

3. What is bought and sold in product markets?

Answers: 1. b 2. e 3. c 4. d

· ·

3.3   The Production Possibilities Curve

▶ What is a production possibilities curve?

▶ What are unemployed resources?

▶ What are underemployed resources?

▶ What is efficiency?

▶ What is the law of increasing opportunity costs?

3.3a The Production Possibilities Curve

production possibilities curve
the potential total output combinations of any two goods for an economy given the available factors of production and the available production technology that firms use to turn their inputs into outputs.

The economic concepts of scarcity, choice, and trade-offs can be illustrated visually by means of a simple graph called a production possibilities curve. The production possibilities curve represents the potential total output combinations of any two goods for an economy, given the available factors of production and the available production technology that firms use to turn their inputs into outputs. That is, it illustrates an economy's potential for allocating its limited resources in producing various combinations of goods, in a given time period.

The Production Possibilities Curve for Grades in Economics and History

What would the production possibilities curve look like if you were "producing" grades in two of your classes—say, economics and history? Exhibit 1 shows a hypothetical production possibilities curve for your expected grade in economics (on the vertical axis), and your expected grade in history (on the horizontal axis). Suppose you have a part-time restaurant job, so you choose to study 10 hours a week. You like both courses and are equally adept at studying for both.

Because Tia and Tamera only have so many hours a week to study, studying more for economics and less for history might hurt their grade in history, *ceteris paribus*. Life is full of trade-offs.

We see in Exhibit 1 that the production possibilities curve is a straight line. For example, if you spend the full 10 hours studying economics, your expected grade in economics is 95 percent (an A), and your expected grade in history is 55 percent (an F). Of course, this outcome assumes you can study zero hours a week and still get a 55 percent average or study the full 10 hours a week and get a 95 percent average. Moving down the production possibilities curve, we see that as you spend more of your time studying history and less on economics, you can raise your expected grade in history but only at the expense of lowering your expected grade in economics. Specifically, moving down along the straight-line production possibilities curve, the trade-off is one lower percentage point in economics for one higher percentage point in history. That is, with a straight-line production possibilities curve, the opportunity costs are constant.

The trade-offs between expected grades in economics and history are the result of holding study time constant (10 hours per week) and all other factors that could increase your ability to learn, such as software study packages. Of course, if you were to increase your overall study time, you would expect higher grades in both courses. But that would be on a different production possibilities curve. Along the production possibilities curve shown in Exhibit 1, we assume that technology and the number of study hours are given.

The Production Possibilities Curve for Food and Housing

To illustrate the production possibilities curve more clearly, imagine living in an economy that produces just two goods, food and housing. The fact that we have many goods in the real world makes actual decision making more complicated, but it does not alter the basic principles being illustrated. Each point on the production possibilities curve shown in Exhibit 2 represents the potential amounts of food and housing that we can produce in a given period, with a given quantity and quality of resources in the economy available for production.

Notice in Exhibit 2 that if we devote all our resources to making houses, we can produce 10 units of housing but no food (point A). If, on the other hand, we choose to devote all our resources to producing food, we end up with 80 units of food but no housing (point E).

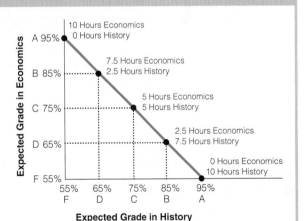

section 3.3 exhibit 1   Production Possibilities Curve: "Producing" Grades in Economics and History

The production possibilities curve highlights the concept of trade-offs. Assuming you choose to study a total of 10 hours a week, moving down the production possibilities curve shows that if you use your time to study history instead of economics, you can raise your expected grade in history but only at the expense of lowering your expected grade in economics. Note that, with a straight-line production possibilities curve, the opportunity costs are constant.

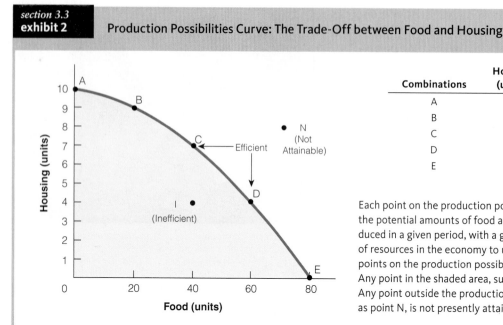

Production Possibilities Curve: The Trade-Off between Food and Housing

Combinations	Housing (units)	Food (units)
A	10	0
B	9	20
C	7	40
D	4	60
E	0	80

Each point on the production possibilities curve represents the potential amounts of food and housing that can be produced in a given period, with a given quantity and quality of resources in the economy to use for production. All the points on the production possibilities curve are efficient. Any point in the shaded area, such as point I, is inefficient. Any point outside the production possibilities curve, such as point N, is not presently attainable.

In reality, nations rarely opt for production possibility A or E, preferring instead to produce a mixture of goods. For example, our fictional economy might produce 9 units of housing and 20 units of food (point B) or perhaps 7 units of housing and 40 units of food (point C). Still other combinations along the curve, such as point D, are possible.

Off the Production Possibilities Curve

What causes the inefficiency that results when you operate inside a production possibilities curve?

The economy cannot operate at point N (not attainable) during the given period because not enough resources are currently available to produce that level of output. However, it is possible the economy can operate inside the production possibilities curve, at point I (inefficient). If the economy is operating at point I, or any other point inside the production possibilities curve, it is not at full capacity and is operating inefficiently. This inefficiency can be caused by unused resources, perhaps because of widespread unemployment or from machines that may lie idle in a factory. Inefficiency can also result from the missallocation of resources; perhaps we have very talented artists making frames and talented frame makers (but not good artists) making art. We could get more of both quality art and frames by reassigning theses workers to tasks that more closely match their skills. In short, the economy is not using all its scarce resources efficiently; as a result, actual output is less than potential output.

3.3b Inefficiency and Efficiency

Why can't a point inside the production possibilities curve be best?

Suppose for some reason employment is widespread or resources are not being put to their best uses. The economy would then be operating at a point inside the production possibilities curve, such as I in Exhibit 2, where the economy is operating inefficiently. At point I, 4 units of housing and 40 units of food are being produced. By putting unemployed resources to work or by putting already employed resources to better uses, we could expand the output of housing by 3 units (moving to point C) without giving up any units of food. Alternatively, we could boost food output by 20 units (moving to point D) without reducing housing production. We could even get more of both food and housing by moving to a point on the curve between C and D. Increasing or improving the utilization of resources, then, can lead to greater output of all goods. You may recall from Chapter 2, an efficient use of our resources means that more of everything we want can be available for our use. Thus, *efficiency* requires society to use its resources to the fullest extent—getting the most from our scarce resources and wasting none. If resources are being used efficiently—that is, at some point along a production possibilities curve—then more of one good or service requires the sacrifice of another good or service.

USE WHAT YOU'VE LEARNED

The Production Possibilities Curve

Q Imagine that you are the overseer on a small island that only produces two goods, cattle and wheat. About a quarter of the land is not fertile enough for growing wheat, so cattle graze on it. What would happen if you tried to produce more and more wheat, extending your planting even to the less fertile soil?

A Under the law of increasing opportunity cost, as you plant more and more of your acreage in wheat, you would move into some of the rocky, less fertile land, and, consequently, wheat yields on the additional acreage would fall. If you try to plant the entire island with wheat, you would find that some of the rocky, less fertile acreage would yield virtually no extra wheat. It would, however, have been great for cattle grazing—a large loss. Thus, the opportunity cost of using that marginal land for wheat rather than cattle grazing would be high. The law of increasing opportunity cost occurs because resources are not homogeneous (identical) and are not equally adaptable for producing cattle and wheat; some

acres are more suitable for cattle grazing, while others are more suitable for wheat growing. This relationship is shown in Exhibit 3, where the vertical lines represent the opportunity cost of growing 10 more bushels of wheat in terms of cattle production sacrificed. You can see that as wheat production increases, the opportunity cost in terms of lost cattle production rises.

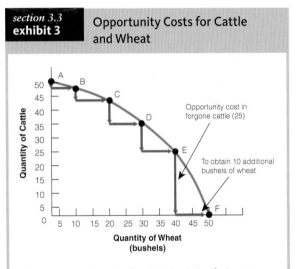

section 3.3 exhibit 3   **Opportunity Costs for Cattle and Wheat**

The opportunity cost of each 10 bushels of wheat in terms of forgone cattle is measured by the vertical distances. Moving from point A to point F, the opportunity cost of wheat in terms of forgone cattle rises.

Economists say that the economy is efficient when there are no opportunities for improvement left. This is the case when the economy is on the production possibilities curve. Notice that once the efficient points on the production possibilities curve are reached, there is no way to produce more of one good without producing less of the other. This is exactly the point we made in the last chapter: people face scarcity and costly trade-offs. Efficiency does not tell us which point along the production possibilities curve is *best*, but it does tell us that points inside the curve cannot be best because some resources are wasted.

3.3c The Law of Increasing Opportunity Cost

As in Exhibit 2, the production possibilities curve in Exhibit 4 is not a straight line like that in Exhibit 1. It is concave from below (that is, bowed outward from the origin). Looking at Exhibit 4, you can see that at low food output, an increase in the amount of food produced will lead to only a small reduction in the number of units of housing produced. For example, increasing food output from 0 to 20 (moving from point A to point B on the curve) requires the use of

Increasing Opportunity Cost and the Production Possibilities Curve

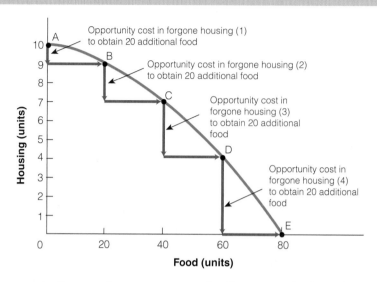

The production possibilities curve also illustrates the opportunity cost of producing more of a given product. For example, if we are to increase food output from 40 units to 60 units (moving from point C to point D), we must produce 3 fewer units of housing. The opportunity cost of those 20 additional units of food is the 3 units of housing we must forgo. We can see that, moving down the curve from A to E, each additional 20 units of food costs society more and more housing—the law of increasing opportunity cost.

---

resources capable of producing 1 unit of housing. In other words, for the first 20 units of food, 1 unit of housing must be given up. When food output is higher, however, more units of housing must be given up when switching additional resources from the production of housing to food. Moving from point D to point E, for example, an increase in food output of 20 (from 60 to 80) reduces the production of housing from 4 to 0. At this point, then, the cost of those 20 additional units of food is 4 units of housing, considerably more than the 1 unit of housing required in the earlier scenario. This difference shows us that opportunity costs do not remain constant but rise because more units of food and fewer units of housing are produced. It is this increasing opportunity cost, then, that is represented by the bowed production possibilities curve.

increasing opportunity cost
the opportunity cost of producing additional units of a good rises as society produces more of that good

What Is the Reason for the Law of Increasing Opportunity Cost?

The basic reason for the increasing opportunity cost is that some resources and skills cannot be easily adapted from their current uses to alternative uses. And, the more you produce of one good, the more you are forced to employ inputs that are relatively more suitable for producing other goods. For example, at low levels of food output, additional increases in food output can be obtained easily by switching relatively low-skilled carpenters from making houses to producing food. However, to get even more food output, workers who are less well suited or appropriate for producing food (i.e., they are better adapted to making houses) must be released from housing production to increase food output. For example, a skilled carpenter may be an expert at making houses but a very bad farmer because he lacks the training and skills necessary in that occupation. So using the skilled carpenter to farm results in a relatively greater opportunity cost than using the unskilled carpenter to farm. The production of additional units of food becomes increasingly costly as progressively lower-skilled farmers (but good carpenters) convert to farming.

In short, resources tend to be specialized. As a result, we lose some of their productivity when we transfer those resources from producing what they are relatively good at to producing something they are relatively bad at.

SECTION QUIZ

1. A point beyond the boundary of an economy's production possibilities curve is
   a. efficient.
   b. inefficient.
   c. attainable.
   d. unattainable.
   e. both attainable and efficient.

2. Which of the following is consistent with the implications of the production possibilities curve?
   a. If the resources in an economy are being used efficiently, scarcity will not be a problem.
   b. If the resources in an economy are being used efficiently, more of one good can be produced only if less of another good is produced.
   c. Producing more of any one good will require smaller and smaller sacrifices of other goods as more of that good is being produced in an economy.
   d. An economy will automatically attain that level of output at which all of its resources are fully employed.
   e. Both (b) and (c) are consistent with the implications of the production possibilities curve.

3. Consider a production possibilities curve for an economy producing bicycles and video game players. It is possible to increase the production of bicycles without sacrificing video game players if
   a. the production possibilities curve shifts outward due to technological progress.
   b. the production possibilities curve shifts outward due to increased immigration (which enlarges the labor force).
   c. the economy moves from a point inside the production possibilities curve to a point on the curve.
   d. any of the above occurs.
   e. either (a) or (b), but not (c), occurs.

4. What determines the position and shape of a society's production possibilities curve?
   a. the physical resources of that society
   b. the skills of the workforce
   c. the level of technology of the society
   d. the number of factories available to the society
   e. all of the above

5. Which of the following is the most accurate statement about a production possibilities curve?
   a. An economy can produce at any point inside or outside its production possibilities curve.
   b. An economy can produce only on its production possibilities curve.
   c. An economy can produce at any point on or inside its production possibilities curve, but not outside the curve.
   d. An economy can produce at any point inside its production possibilities curve, but not on or outside the curve.

6. A _____ production possibilities curve illustrates _____ costs of production.
   a. straight-line; constant
   b. straight-line; increasing
   c. bowed-outward; constant
   d. bowed-outward; increasing
   e. Both (a) and (d) are true.

(continued)

SECTION QUIZ (cont.)

7. Which statement(s) is/are true about the law of increasing opportunity cost?

   a. Some resources and skills cannot be easily adapted from their current uses to alternative uses.

   b. The more you produce of one good, the more you are forced to employ inputs that are relatively more suitable for producing other goods.

   c. Resources tend to be specialized so we lose some of their productivity when we transfer those resources from producing what they are relatively good at to producing something at which they are relatively bad.

   d. All of the above are true.

---

1. What does a production possibilities curve illustrate?

2. How are opportunity costs shown by the production possibilities curve?

3. Why do the opportunity costs of added production increase with output?

4. How does the production possibilities curve illustrate increasing opportunity costs?

5. Why are we concerned with widespread amounts of unemployed or underemployed resources in a society?

6. What do we mean by efficiency, and how is it related to underemployment of resources?

7. How are efficiency and inefficiency illustrated by a production possibilities curve?

8. Will a country that makes being unemployed illegal be more productive than one that does not? Why or why not?

9. If a 68-year-old worker in the United States chooses not to work at all, does that mean that the United States is functioning inside its production possibilities curve? Why or why not?

Answers: 1. d 2. b 3. d 4. e 5. c 6. c 7. d

. . . .

3.4 Economic Growth and the Production Possibilities Curve

▸ How much should we sacrifice today to get more in the future?

▸ How do we show economic growth on the production possibilities curve?

3.4a Generating Economic Growth

How have some nations been able to rapidly expand their outputs of goods and services over time, while others have been unable to increase their standards of living at all?

The economy can only grow with qualitative or quantitative changes in the factors of production—land, labor, capital, and entrepreneurship. Advancement in technology, improvements in labor productivity, or new sources of natural resources (such as previously undiscovered oil) could lead to outward shifts of the production possibilities curve.

In terms of the production possibilities curve, an outward shift in the possible combinations of goods and services produced leads to economic growth, as seen in Exhibit 1. With growth comes the possibility of having more of both goods than was previously available. Suppose we were producing at point C (7 units of housing, 40 units of food) on our original production possibilities curve. Additional resources and/or new methods of using them (technological progress) can lead to new production possibilities, creating the potential for more of all goods (or more of some with no less of others). These increases will push the production possibilities curve outward. That is, economic growth means an expansion of the economy's production possibilities. Notice that at point F (future) on the new curve, we can produce 9 units of housing and 70 units of food, more of both goods than we previously could produce, at point C.

3.4b Growth Does Not Eliminate Scarcity

With all of this discussion of growth, it is important to remember that growth, or increases in a society's output, does not make scarcity disappear. When output grows more rapidly than population, people are better off. But they still face trade-offs; at any point along the production possibilities curve, to get more of one thing, you must give up something else. There are no free lunches on the production possibilities curve.

Capital Goods versus Consumption Goods

Economies that choose to invest more of their resources for the future will grow faster than those that don't. To generate economic growth, a society must produce fewer consumer goods—video games, cameras, cell phones, cars, vacations, and so on—and produce more capital goods—machines, factories, tools, education, and the like—in the present. The society that devotes a larger share of its productive capacity to capital goods than to consumer goods will experience greater economic growth. It must sacrifice some present consumption of consumer goods and services to experience growth in the future. Why? Investing in capital goods, such as computers and other new technological equipment, as well as upgrading skills and knowledge, expands the ability to produce in the future. It shifts the economy's production possibilities curve outward, increasing the future production capacity of the economy. That is, the economy that invests more now (consumes less now) will be able to produce, and therefore consume, more in the future. In Exhibit 2, we see that Economy A invests more in

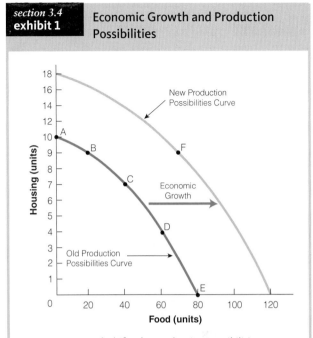

Economic Growth and Production Possibilities

Economic growth shifts the production possibilities curve outward, allowing increased output of both food and housing (compare point F with point C).

Can economic growth eliminate the problem of scarcity?

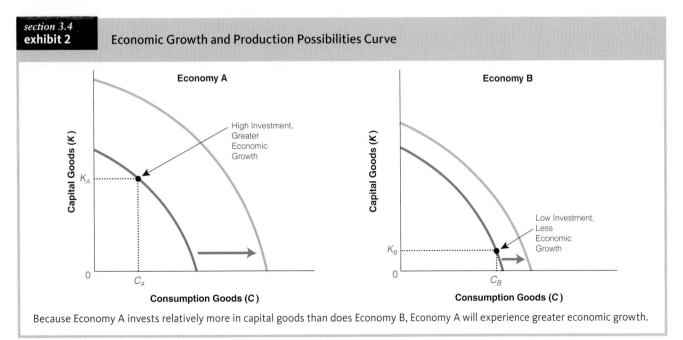

Economic Growth and Production Possibilities Curve

Economy A

Capital Goods (K)

K_A

High Investment, Greater Economic Growth

0   C_A

Consumption Goods (C)

Economy B

Capital Goods (K)

K_B

Low Investment, Less Economic Growth

0   C_B

Consumption Goods (C)

Because Economy A invests relatively more in capital goods than does Economy B, Economy A will experience greater economic growth.

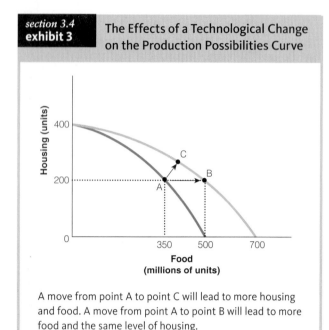

The Effects of a Technological Change on the Production Possibilities Curve

A move from point A to point C will lead to more housing and food. A move from point A to point B will lead to more food and the same level of housing.

capital goods than Economy B. Consequently, Economy A's production possibilities curve shifts outward further than does Economy B's over time.

3.4c The Effects of a Technological Change on the Production Possibilities Curve

In Exhibit 3, we see that a technological advance does not have to impact all sectors of the economy equally. There is a technological advance in food production but not in housing production. The technological advance in agriculture causes the production possibilities curve to extend out further on the horizontal axis, which measures food production. We can move to any point on the new production possibilities curve. For example, we could move from point A on the original production possibilities curve to point B on the new production possibilities curve. This would lead to 150 more units of food and the same amount of housing—200 units. Or, we could move from point A to point C, which would allow us to produce more units of both food and housing. How do we produce more housing, when the technological advance occurred in agriculture? The answer is that the technological advance in agriculture allows us to produce more from a given quantity of resources. That is, it allows us to shift some of our resources out of agriculture into housing. This is actually an ongoing story in U.S. economic history. In colonial days, about 90 percent of the population made a living in agriculture. Today it is less than 3 percent.

How can we produce more of two goods when there is a technology advance in only one of the goods?

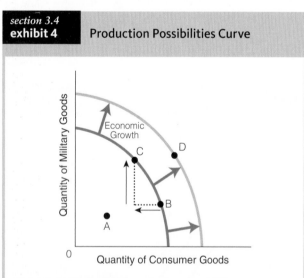

Production Possibilities Curve

Point A, inside the initial production possibilities curve, represents inefficiency. Points B and C, on the curve, are efficient points and represent two possible output combinations. Point D can only be attained with economic growth, illustrated by the outward shift in the production possibilities curve.

3.4d Summing up the Production Possibilities Curve

The production possibilities curve shown in Exhibit 4 illustrates the choices faced by an economy that makes military goods (guns) and consumer goods (butter). How are the economic concepts of scarcity, choice, opportunity cost, efficiency, and economic growth illustrated in the framework of this production possibilities curve?

In Exhibit 4, we can show scarcity because resource combinations outside the initial production possibilities curve, such as point D, are unattainable without economic growth. If the economy is operating efficiently, we are somewhere on that production possibilities curve, perhaps at point B or point C. However, if the economy is operating inefficiently, we are operating inside that production possibilities curve, at point A, for example. We can also see in this graph that to get more military goods, you must give up consumer goods, which represents the opportunity cost. Finally, we see that over time, with economic growth, the whole production possibilities curve can shift outward, making point D attainable.

SECTION QUIZ

1. Which of the following is most likely to shift the production possibilities curve outward?

   a. an increase in unemployment

   b. a decrease in the stock of physical or human capital

   c. a decrease in the labor force

   d. a technological advance

2. Suppose Country A produces few consumption goods and many investment goods while Country B produces few investment goods and many consumption goods. Other things being equal, you would expect

   a. per capita income to grow more rapidly in Country B.

   b. population to grow faster in Country B.

   c. the production possibilities curve for Country A to shift out more rapidly than that of Country B.

   d. that if both countries started with identical production possibilities curves, in 20 years, people in Country B will be able to produce more consumer goods than people in Country A can.

   e. that both (c) and (d) are true.

3. A virulent disease spreads throughout the population of an economy, causing death and disability. This event can be portrayed as

   a. a movement from a point on the production possibilities curve to a point inside the curve.

   b. a movement from a point on the production possibilities curve to the northeast.

   c. a movement along the production possibilities curve to the southeast.

   d. an outward shift of the production possibilities curve.

   e. an inward shift of the production possibilities curve.

---

1. What is the essential question behind issues of economic growth?

2. What is the connection between sacrifices and economic growth?

3. How is economic growth shown in terms of production possibilities curves?

4. Why doesn't economic growth eliminate scarcity?

5. If people reduced their saving (thus reducing the funds available for investment), what would that change do to society's production possibilities curve over time?

Answers: 1. d 2. c 3. e

INTERACTIVE SUMMARY

Fill in the blanks:

1. Because of scarcity, certain economic questions must be answered regardless of the level of affluence of the society or its political structure. Three fundamental questions that inevitably must be faced in a world of scarcity are (1) _____ will be produced? (2) _____ the goods and services be produced? (3) _____ the goods and services produced?

2. Market economies largely rely on a(n) _____ decision-making process, where literally millions of individual producers and consumers of goods and services determine what will be produced.

3. Most countries, including the United States, have _____ economies, in which the government and private sector determine the allocation of resources.

4. The _____ -cost method is the most appropriate method for producing a given product.

5. Methods of production used where capital is relatively scarce will be _____, and methods of production used where labor is relatively scarce will be _____.

6. In a market economy, the amount of goods and services one is able to obtain depends on one's _____, which depends on the quality and quantity of the scarce _____ he or she controls.

7. The markets where households are buyers and firms are sellers of goods and services are called _____ markets.

8. The markets where households sell the use of their _____ (capital, land, labor, and entrepreneurship) to _____ are called _____ or _____ markets.

9. The simple _____ model shows the continuous flow of goods, services, inputs, and payments through the _____ and _____ markets among households and _____.

10. A(n) _____ curve represents the potential total output combinations of any two goods for an economy.

11. On a production possibilities curve, we assume that the economy has a given quantity and quality of _____ and _____ available to use for production.

12. On a straight-line production possibilities curve, the _____ are constant.

13. If an economy is operating _____ its production possibilities curve, it is not at full capacity and is operating _____. Such an economy's actual output is less than _____ output.

14. By putting _____ resources to work or by putting already employed resources to _____ uses, we could expand output.

15. _____ requires society to use its resources to the fullest extent—getting the _____ we can out of our scarce resources.

16. If the production possibilities curve is concave from below (that is, bowed outward from the origin), it reflects _____ opportunity costs of producing additional amounts of a good.

17. On a bowed production possibilities curve (concave to the origin), the opportunity costs of producing additional units of a good rises as society produces more of that good. This relationship is called the law of _____.

18. Resources tend to be specialized, so we lose some of their productivity when we transfer those resources from what they are relatively _____ at producing to something they are relatively _____ at producing.

19. To generate economic growth, a society must produce _____ consumer goods and _____ capital goods in the present.

20. Advancements in _____, improvements in _____, or new _____ could all lead to outward shifts of the production possibilities curve.

21. Increases in a society's output do not make _____ disappear. Even when output has grown more rapidly than population so that people are made better off, they still face _____.

22. The production possibilities curve can be used to illustrate the economic concepts of _____ (resource combinations outside the production possibilities curve are unattainable), _____ (selecting among the alternative bundles available along the production possibilities curve), _____ (how much of one good you give up to get another unit of the second good as you move along the production possibilities curve), _____ (being on the production possibilities curve rather than inside it), and _____ (shifting the production possibilities curve outward).

PREFACE

This book presents economics as a serious, lively, and evolving science. Its goal is to open students' eyes to the "economic way of thinking" and to help them gain insights into how the economy works and how it might be made to work better. ◆ We provide a thorough and complete coverage of the subject, using a straightforward, precise, and clear writing style. ◆ We are conscious that many students find economics hard, so we place the student at centre stage and write for the student. We use language that doesn't intimidate and that allows the student to concentrate on the substance. ◆ We open each chapter with a clear statement of learning objectives, a real-world student-friendly vignette to grab attention, and a brief preview. We illustrate principles with examples that are selected to hold the student's interest and to make the subject lively. And we put principles to work by using them to illuminate current real-world problems and issues. ◆ We present some new ideas, such as dynamic comparative advantage, game theory, the modern theory of the firm, public choice theory, rational expectations, new growth theory, and real business cycle theory. But we explain these topics with familiar core ideas and tools. ◆ Today's course springs from today's issues—the information revolution, the impending global slowdown of 2003, the Kyoto debate, and the expansion of international trade and investment. But the principles that we use to understand these issues remain the core principles of our science. ◆ Governments and international agencies place renewed emphasis on long-term fundamentals as they seek to sustain economic growth. This book reflects this emphasis. ◆ To help promote a rich, active learning experience, we have developed a comprehensive online learning environment featuring diagnostic quizzes, a dynamic eText, eStudy Guide, interactive tutorials, practice exams, frequent news updates, and more.

The Fifth Edition Revision

ECONOMICS: CANADA IN THE GLOBAL ENVIRONMENT, Fifth Edition, retains all of the improvements achieved in its predecessor with its thorough and detailed presentation of modern economics, emphasis on real-world examples and critical thinking skills, diagrams renowned for pedagogy and precision, and path-breaking technology.

New to this edition are

■ New introductory chapter

■ All new chapter on global stock markets

■ Revised and updated microeconomics content

■ Revised and updated macroeconomics content

■ Vastly expanded Web site

New Introductory Chapter

Chapter 1 has been completely rewritten to emphasize the central role of tradeoffs in economics, setting the tone for the rest of the book.

All-New Chapter 35 on Global Stock Markets

This exciting addition provides a valuable framework for addressing students' questions about how the stock market works. *What is a stock? What determines stock prices? Why are stock prices volatile? Why is it rational to diversify? How does the stock market influence the economy, and vice versa?*

Revised and Updated Microeconomics Content

The four major revisions in the microeconomics chapters are

1. The Economic Problem (Chapter 2): A revised and more carefully paced explanation of the gains from specialization and exchange.

2. Monopolistic Competition and Oligopoly (Chapter 13): An expanded explanation of repeated games and sequential games. These traditionally advanced topics are explained with examples and illustrations that bring the ideas within the grasp of beginning students.

3. Economic Inequality (Chapter 15): Two chapters from the Fourth Edition have been combined, streamlined, and given a new focus to explain the sources of the trend in the distribution of income—the widening gap between the highest- and lowest-income households.

4. Externalities (Chapter 18): Reorganized to explain the full range of positive and negative production and consumption externalities.

Revised and Updated Macroeconomics Content

The five major revisions in the macroeconomics chapters are

1. Measuring GDP and Economic Growth (Chapter 20): A reorganized and more focused explanation of GDP and its measurement, along with a new and simplified explanation of the chain-weighted method of calculating real GDP.

2. Monitoring Cycles, Jobs, and the Price Level (Chapter 21): A much reorganized chapter that describes how we identify a recession and how Statistics Canada measures the labour market and the CPI. The chapter also explains the significance and interpretation of data on the labour market and price level.

3. Economic Growth (Chapter 30): A simplified and mainstreamed explanation and illustration of the classical, neoclassical, and new theories of economic growth.

4. Macroeconomic Policy Challenges (Chapter 32): Explanation of the Taylor rule and comparison of Bank of Canada interest rate decisions with such a rule.

5. Thorough and extensive updating to reflect the Canadian economy and the global economy of 2001 and 2002 and prospects for 2003 and beyond, as well as the response to the heightened security situation following the September 11 attacks on the United States.

Vastly Expanded Web Site

Our new Web site is the centrepiece of this Fifth Edition revision. The site is organized around "8 steps to success in economics." The 8 steps are

1. Diagnostic quizzes that provide feedback with hyperlinks to all the Web-based learning tools.

2. Online glossary with definitions, examples, and links to related terms.

3. Online eText—the entire textbook in electronic form with hyperlinks to all other components of the Web site and with Flash animations of every figure in the textbook.

4. Online eStudy Guide—the entire study guide in electronic form.

5. *Economics in Action*—our market-leading interactive tutorial software program now accessed on the Web. This Java-based learning tool has been expanded to cover each and every chapter in the textbook. Students manipulate figures from the textbook by changing the conditions that lie behind them and observing how the economy responds to events.

6. PowerPoint lecture notes for students to review.

7. Web-based exercises with links to data and other online sources.

8. Practice exams—students can select from five question types (fill-in-the-blank, true-or-false, multiple-choice, complete-the-graph, and numeric) to be worked with or without detailed feedback.

Features to Enhance Teaching and Learning

HERE, WE DESCRIBE THE CHAPTER FEATURES that are designed to enhance the learning process. Each chapter contains the following learning aids.

Chapter Opener

Each chapter opens with a one-page student-friendly, attention-grabbing vignette. The vignette raises questions that both motivate the student and focus the chapter. The Fifth Edition now carries this story into the main body of the chapter, and relates it to the chapter-ending *Reading Between the Lines* feature.

Chapter Objectives

A list of learning objectives enables students to see exactly where the chapter is going and to set their goals before they begin the chapter. We link these goals directly to the chapter's major headings.

After studying this chapter, you will be able to

- Describe a market and explain the link between price as an opportunity cost
- Explain the influences on demand
- Explain the influences on supply
- Explain how demand and supply determine prices and quantities bought and sold
- Use demand and supply to make predictions about changes in prices and quantities

In-Text Review Quizzes

A review quiz at the end of most major sections enables students to determine whether a topic needs further study before moving on.

REVIEW QUIZ

1 What is scarcity?
2 Give some examples of scarcity in today's world.
3 Define economics.
4 Use the headlines in today's news to illustrate the distinction between microeconomics and macroeconomics.

Key Terms

Highlighted terms within the text simplify the student's task of learning the vocabulary of economics. Each highlighted term appears in an end-of-chapter list with page numbers, in an end-of-book glossary, boldfaced in the index, and on the Parkin–Bade Web site.

.rve. The **marginal benefit** of a good or service is the .nefit received from consuming one more unit of it.

We measure the marginal benefit of rvice by what a person is *willing to pay* onal unit of it. The idea is that you are .y what the good is worth to you. It is v arginal benefit, and you're willing to pa nount up to the marginal benefit. So w .y measures marginal benefit.

The **marginal benefit curve** shows the tween marginal benefit of a good and that g e mor

KEY TERMS

Absolute advantage, 45
Allocative efficiency, 39
Capital accumulation, 40
Comparative advantage, 42
Dynamic comparative advantage, 45
Economic growth, 40
doing, 45
fit 39

Above full-employment equilibrium
A macroeconomic equilibrium in which real GDP exceeds potential GDP. (p. 510)

Absolute advantage A person has an absolute advantage if that person can produce more goods with amount of resources than son can; a country has an advantage if its output pe inputs of all goods is large of another country. (p. 45

After-tax income Total in tax na ments h househol

Topic: Capital

Definition   Examples   Related Terms

The tools, instruments, constructions that

Tom has a landscaping business. Tom's landscaping business owns some capital—lawn mowers, rakes, shovels,

Related Terms
Factor markets
Factors of production
Human capital
Interest

Diagrams That Show the Action

This book has set new standards of clarity in its diagrams. Our goal has always been to show "where the economic action is." The diagrams in this book continue to generate an enormously positive response, which confirms our view that graphical analysis is the most powerful tool available for teaching and learning economics. But many students find graphs hard to work with. For this reason, we have developed the entire art program with the study and review needs of the student in mind. The diagrams feature

■ Shifted curves, equilibrium points, and other important features highlighted in red

■ Colour-blended arrows to suggest movement

■ Graphs paired with data tables

■ Diagrams labelled with boxed notes

■ Extended captions that make each diagram and its caption a self-contained object for study and review

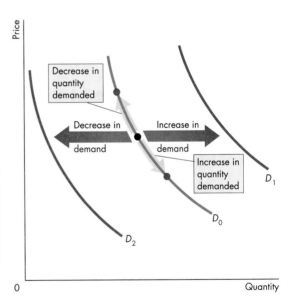

Reading Between the Lines

Each chapter ends with an economic analysis of a significant news article from the popular press together with a thorough economic analysis of the issues raised in the article. The Fifth Edition features all new *Reading Between the Lines* articles. We have chosen each article so that it sheds additional light on the questions first raised in the chapter opener.

Special "You're the Voter" sections in selected chapters invite students to analyze typical campaign topics and to probe their own stances on key public policy issues. Critical thinking questions about the article appear with the end-of-chapter questions and problems.

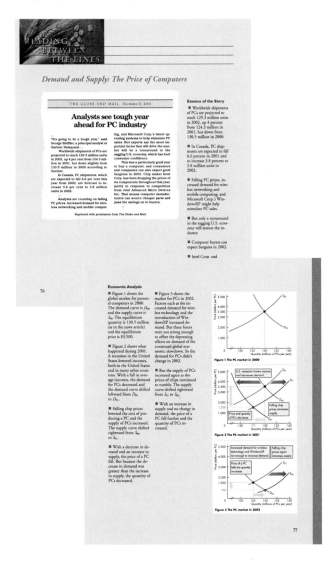

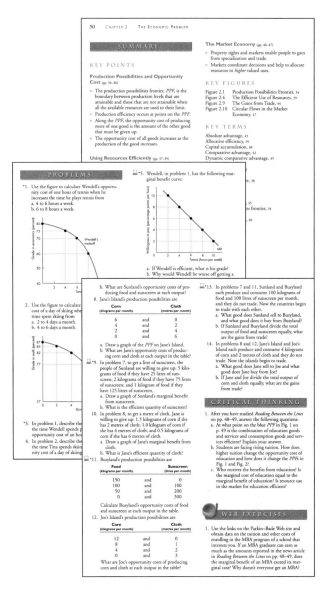

End-of-Chapter Study Material

Each chapter closes with a concise summary organized by major topics, lists of key terms (all with page references), problems, critical thinking questions, and Web exercises. The problems are arranged in parallel pairs with solutions to the odd-numbered problems provided on the Web site. Most of the even-numbered problems and the Web exercises are new for the Fifth Edition. We provide the links needed for the Web exercises on our Web site.

For the Instructor

THIS BOOK ENABLES YOU TO ACHIEVE THREE objectives in your principles course:

- Focus on the economic way of thinking
- Explain the issues and problems of our time
- Choose your own course structure

Focus on the Economic Way of Thinking

You know how hard it is to encourage a student to think like an economist. But that is your goal. Consistent with this goal, the text focuses on and repeatedly uses the central ideas: choice; tradeoff; opportunity cost; the margin; incentives; the gains from voluntary exchange; the forces of demand, supply, and equilibrium; the pursuit of economic rent; and the effects of government actions on the economy.

Explain the Issues and Problems of Our Time

Students must use the central ideas and tools if they are to begin to understand them. There is no better way to motivate students than by using the tools of economics to explain the issues that confront students in today's world. These issues include the anticipated 2003 global slow-down, environment, widening income gaps, energy deregulation, budget deficits or surpluses, restraining inflation, understanding the stock market, avoiding protectionism, and the long-term growth of output and incomes.

Choose Your Own Course Structure

You want to teach your own course. We have organized this book to enable you to do so. We demonstrate the book's flexibility in the flexibility chart and alternative sequences table that appear on pp. xvi–xvii. You can use this book to teach a traditional course that blends theory and policy or a current policy issues course. Your micro course can emphasize theory or policy. You can structure your macro course to emphasize long-term growth and supply-side fundamentals. Or you can follow a traditional macro sequence and emphasize short-term fluctuations. The choices are yours.

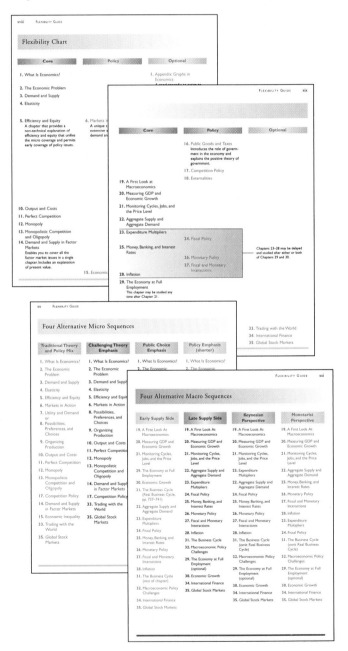

Instructor's Manual

The Instructor's Manual, written by Torben Drewes of Trent University, integrates the teaching and learning package and is a guide to all the supplements. Each chapter contains a chapter outline, what's new in the Fifth Edition, teaching suggestions, a look at where we have been and where we are going, lists of available overhead transparencies, descriptions of the electronic supplements, additional discussion questions, answers to the Review Quizzes, solutions to end-of-chapter problems, additional problems, and solutions to the additional problems. The chapter outline and teaching suggestions sections are keyed to the PowerPoint lecture notes.

Two Test Banks

To provide even greater choice when preparing tests and exams, we now offer two Test Banks with a total of more than 9,000 questions. Test Bank 1, prepared by Jane Waples and Saeed Moshiri of Memorial University, contains over 4,500 multiple-choice questions and is a thoroughly revised, upgraded, and improved version of our previous Test Bank. Test Bank 2, prepared by Glen Stirling of the University of Western Ontario and Ather Akbari of Saint Mary's University, contains about 4,300 *all new* multiple-choice, true-false, and short-answer questions.

PowerPoint Resources

We have developed a full-colour Microsoft PowerPoint Lecture Presentation for each chapter that includes all the figures from the text, animated graphs, and speaking notes. The slide outlines are based on the chapter outlines in the Instructor's Manual, and the speaking notes are based on the Instructor's Manual teaching suggestions. The presentations can be used electronically in the classroom or can be printed to create hard-copy transparency masters, and they can be accessed using Windows or Macintosh.

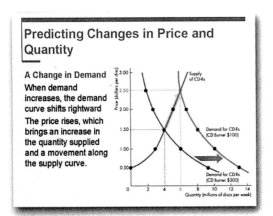

Overhead Transparencies

Full-colour transparencies of key figures from the text will improve the clarity of your lectures. They are available to qualified adopters of the text (contact your Pearson Education Canada sales representative).

Instructor's Resource CD with Computerized Test Banks

This CD contains Computerized Test Bank files, Instructor's Manual files in Microsoft Word, and PowerPoint files. Both test banks are available in Test Generator Software (TestGen-EQ with QuizMaster-EQ). Fully networkable, it is available for Windows and Macintosh. TestGen-EQ's new graphical interface enables instructors to view, edit, and add questions; transfer questions to tests; and print different forms of tests. Tests can be formatted with varying fonts and styles, margins, and headers and footers, as in any word-processing document. Search and sort features let the instructor quickly locate questions and arrange them in a preferred order. QuizMaster-EQ, working with your school's computer network, automatically grades the exams, stores the results on disk, and allows the instructor to view or print a variety of reports.

Course Management Systems

We offer three alternative course management systems—CourseCompass, Blackboard, and WebCT. Each system provides a dynamic, interactive, content-rich, and flexible online course management tool that enables instructors to easily and effectively customize online course materials to suit their needs. Instructors can track and analyze student performance on an array of Internet activities. Please contact your Pearson Education Canada representative for more details.

Economics in Action Software

Instructors can use *Economics in Action* interactive software in the classroom. Its many analytical graphs can be used as "electronic transparencies" for live graph manipulation in lectures. Its real-world data sets and graphing utility bring animated time-series graphs and scatter diagrams to the classroom.

The Parkin–Bade Web Site

The Fifth Edition of the textbook continues the tradition of path-breaking technology with *Parkin Online* at www.pearsoned.ca/parkin. The instructor side of *Parkin Online* includes all of the same resources as the student's side, but with the addition of speaking notes in the PowerPoint lecture notes, easy access to Instructor's Manual files, and an online "Consult the Authors" feature: Ask your questions or make your suggestions via e-mail, and we will answer you within 24 hours.

For the Student

Study Guide

The Fifth Edition Study Guide by Avi Cohen of York University and Harvey King of the University of Regina is carefully coordinated with the main text. For the first time, the Study Guide is available online. Print copies are also available.

Each chapter of the Study Guide contains

- Key concepts
- Helpful hints
- True/false questions that ask students to explain their answers
- Multiple-choice questions
- Short-answer questions

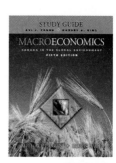

Each part allows students to test their cumulative understanding with questions that go across chapters and work a sample midterm examination.

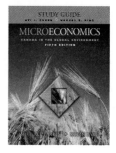

Economics in Action Interactive Software

With *Economics in Action* now available on the Web, students will have fun working the tutorials, answering questions that give instant explanations, and testing themselves ahead of their midterm tests. One of our students told us that using *Economics in Action* is like having a private professor in your dorm room! New modules now cover each and every chapter in the text.

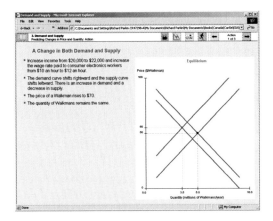

The Parkin–Bade Web Site

Parkin Online is the market-leading Web site for the principles of economics course. No other Web site comes close to matching the material offered on this site, on which students will find

■ Diagnostic quizzes with feedback hyperlinked to all the Web-based learning tools

■ The textbook—the *entire textbook in PDF format* with hyperlinks and Flash animated figures

■ *Economics in Action*—tutorials, quizzes, and graphing tools that make curves shift and graphs come to life with a click of the mouse

■ Study Guide—*the entire Study Guide, online*—with online quizzes

■ PowerPoint lecture notes

■ "Economics in the News" updated several times a week during the school year

■ Online "Office Hours": Ask your question via e-mail, and we will answer within 24 hours!

■ Economic links—links to Web sites that keep you up to date with what's going on in the economy and that enable you to work end-of-chapter Web exercises

■ Solutions to odd-numbered end-of-chapter problems

The power of *Parkin Online* lies not only in the breadth and depth of the learning tools available, but also in the way that we have linked the tools together and provided a mind map to show you these links. When a student submits a diagnostic quiz, he or she receives a report card with an explanation of why answers are correct or incorrect *and hyperlinks* to the part of the e-text that the student needs to read to better understand the concept, to the tutorial in *Economics in Action* that the student needs to work, and to related questions in the eStudy Guide and *Economics in Action*. The student is thus able to navigate easily through the site and to maximize the payoff from her or his study efforts.

Acknowledgments

WE THANK OUR CURRENT AND FORMER colleagues and friends at the University of Western Ontario who have taught us so much. They are Jim Davies, Jeremy Greenwood, Ig Horstmann, Peter Howitt, Greg Huffman, David Laidler, Phil Reny, Chris Robinson, John Whalley, and Ron Wonnacott. We also thank Doug McTaggart and Christopher Findlay, co-authors of the Australian edition, and Melanie Powell and Kent Matthews, co-authors of the European edition. Suggestions arising from their adaptations of earlier editions have been helpful to us in preparing this edition.

We thank the several thousand students whom we have been privileged to teach. The instant response that comes from the look of puzzlement or enlightenment has taught us how to teach economics.

It is an especial joy to thank the many outstanding managers, editors, and others at Pearson Education Canada who have contributed to the concerted publishing effort that brought this edition to completion. Tony Vander Woude, Chairman, and Allan Reynolds, President and CEO, have once again provided outstanding corporate direction. They have worked hard to ensure that Pearson evolves a culture that builds on the best of Addison Wesley and Prentice Hall, from which the new company has grown. Michael Young, Vice President and Editorial Director for Higher Education, has been a devoted contributor through his appointment and management of the outstanding editors with whom we've worked. When we began the revision, Dave Ward was our Acquisitions Editor. Dave has moved on to a new range of duties, but we want to place on the record the valuable contribution that he made to this revision in its early stages. Dave was succeeded by Gary Bennett as Acquisitions Editor. Gary played a major role in bringing this revision to completion and in finding and managing a team of outstanding supplements authors.

Suzanne Schaan brought her experience and dedicated professionalism to the development effort.

Toni Chahley, New Media Developmental Editor, provided direction and leadership in designing our new *Parkin Online* Web site. Deborah Meredith, Marketing Manager, provided inspired marketing direction. Her brochures and, more important, her timely questions and prodding for material had a significant impact on the shape of the text. Anthony Leung, Designer, designed the cover, text, and package and surpassed the challenge of ensuring that we meet the highest design standards. Marisa D'Andrea, our Production Editor, worked miracles on a tight production schedule and coped calmly with late-changing content. Laurel Sparrow copyedited the text manuscript. We thank all of these wonderful people. It has been inspiring to work with them and to share in creating what we believe is a truly outstanding educational tool.

We thank our supplements authors, Avi Cohen, Harvey King, Torben Drewes, Jane Waples, Saeed Moshiri, Glen Stirling, and Ather Akbari. And we thank Kit Pasula and Rosilyn Coulson for their extraordinarily careful accuracy review of near-final pages.

We thank the people who work directly with us. Jeannie Gillmore provided outstanding research assistance on many topics, including all the *Reading Between the Lines* news articles. Jane McAndrew provided excellent library help. Richard Parkin created the electronic art files and offered many ideas that improved the figures in this book. And Laurel Davies managed an ever-growing and more complex *Economics in Action* database.

As with the previous editions, this one owes an enormous debt to our students. We dedicate this book to them and again thank them for their careful reading and critical comments on the previous edition. We especially thank Chang Song and Johnathan Raiken, students at the University of Western Ontario in 2002, for finding errors and less-than-clear passages in the Fourth Edition.

Classroom experience will continue to test the value of this book. We would appreciate hearing from instructors and students about how we can continue to improve it in future editions.

Michael Parkin
Robin Bade
London, Ontario, Canada
michael.parkin@uwo.ca
robin@econ100.com

Reviewers

Ather H. Akbari, Saint Mary's University
Aurelia Best, Centennial College
Caroline Boivin, Université de Sherbrooke
Beverly Cameron, University of Manitoba
Scott Cawfield, Centennial College
Brian Coulter, University College of the Fraser Valley
Torben Drewes, Trent University
C.M. Fellows, Mount Royal College
Brian Ferguson, University of Guelph
Oliver Franke, Athabasca University
David Gray, University of Ottawa
Eric Kam, University of Western Ontario
Gordon Lee, University of Alberta
David Murrell, University of New Brunswick
Steve Rakoczy, Humber College
Kenneth Rea, University of Toronto
Jim Sentance, University of Prince Edward Island
Lance Shandler, Kwantlen University College
Lewis Soroka, Brock University
Glen Stirling, University of Western Ontario
Brian VanBlarcom, Acadia University
Joe Vieira, Confederation College
Graham Voss, University of Victoria
Baotai Wang, University of Northern British Columbia
Richard Watuwa, Saint Mary's University
Christopher Worswick, Carleton University
Emmanuel Yiridoe, Nova Scotia Agricultural College
Ayoub Yousefi, University of Western Ontario

Macroeconomics Flexibility Chart

Core	Policy	Optional

Core

1. What Is Economics?

2. The Economic Problem

3. Demand and Supply

19. A First Look At Macroeconomics

20. Measuring GDP and Economic Growth

21. Monitoring Cycles, Jobs, and the Price Level

22. Aggregate Supply and Aggregate Demand

23. Expenditure Multipliers

25. Money, Banking, and Interest Rates

28. Inflation

29. The Economy At Full Employment

30. Economic Growth
    The section on growth theory is optional.

31. The Business Cycle

Policy

24. Fiscal Policy

26. Monetary Policy

27. Fiscal and Monetary Interactions

Chapters 29 and 30 may be brought forward and studied after Chapter 22.

32. Macroeconomic Policy Challenges

Optional

23. Mathematical Note
    The Algebra of the Multiplier

24. Mathematical Note
    The Algebra of the Fiscal Policy Multipliers

33. Trading with the World

34. International Finance

35. Global Stock Markets

Four Alternative Macro Sequences

Early Supply Side	Late Supply Side	Keynesian Perspective	Monetarist Perspective
19. A First Look At Macroeconomics	19. A First Look At Macroeconomics	19. A First Look At Macroeconomics	19. A First Look At Macroeconomics
20. Measuring GDP and Economic Growth	20. Measuring GDP and Economic Growth	20. Measuring GDP and Economic Growth	20. Measuring GDP and Economic Growth
21. Monitoring Cycles, Jobs, and the Price Level	21. Monitoring Cycles, Jobs, and the Price Level	21. Monitoring Cycles, Jobs, and the Price Level	21. Monitoring Cycles, Jobs, and the Price Level
29. The Economy At Full Employment	22. Aggregate Supply and Aggregate Demand	23. Expenditure Multipliers	22. Aggregate Supply and Aggregate Demand
30. Economic Growth	23. Expenditure Multipliers	22. Aggregate Supply and Aggregate Demand	25. Money, Banking, and Interest Rates
31. The Business Cycle (Real Business Cycle, pp. 737–741)	24. Fiscal Policy	24. Fiscal Policy	26. Monetary Policy
22. Aggregate Supply and Aggregate Demand	25. Money, Banking, and Interest Rates	25. Money, Banking, and Interest Rates	27. Fiscal and Monetary Interactions
23. Expenditure Multipliers	26. Monetary Policy	26. Monetary Policy	28. Inflation
24. Fiscal Policy	27. Fiscal and Monetary Interactions	27. Fiscal and Monetary Interactions	23. Expenditure Multipliers
25. Money, Banking, and Interest Rates	28. Inflation	28. Inflation	24. Fiscal Policy
26. Monetary Policy	31. The Business Cycle	31. The Business Cycle (omit Real Business Cycle)	31. The Business Cycle (omit Real Business Cycle)
27. Fiscal and Monetary Interactions	32. Macroeconomic Policy Challenges	32. Macroeconomic Policy Challenges	32. Macroeconomic Policy Challenges
28. Inflation	29. The Economy At Full Employment (optional)	29. The Economy At Full Employment (optional)	29. The Economy At Full Employment (optional)
31. The Business Cycle (rest of chapter)	30. Economic Growth	30. Economic Growth	30. Economic Growth
32. Macroeconomic Policy Challenges	34. International Finance	34. International Finance	34. International Finance
34. International Finance	35. Global Stock Markets	35. Global Stock Markets	35. Global Stock Markets
35. Global Stock Markets			

BRIEF CONTENTS

CONTENTS

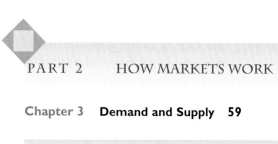

PART 10   THE GLOBAL ECONOMY

WHAT IS ECONOMICS? — CHAPTER 1

Choice, Change, Challenge, and Opportunity

You are studying economics, the science of choice, at a time of enormous change, challenge, and opportunity. Economics studies the choices that we make as we cope with the hard fact of life: we can't have everything we want. ◆ The engine of change is information technology, which has created the Internet and transformed our lives at both work and play. This transformation will continue, but in 2001 it was challenged by a U.S. recession and by the terrorist attacks of September 11. The events of September 11 have brought long-lasting changes to the political and security landscape and to the economic landscape. People now face choices not previously imagined. Some people are avoiding air travel, a choice that is sending shock waves through travel agencies, airports, airlines, airplane builders, and hotels and restaurants. Security at the Canada–U.S. border and at our airports and seaports is stepped up. Governments, airlines, and airport operators are buying more video and electronic surveillance equipment, which is creating new business and job opportunities. ◆ As 2003 began, people were wondering whether economic recovery and renewed expansion was just around the corner or whether there would be a second U.S. recession— a "double dip"—and worrying about how such a development might influence the Canadian economy.

◈ You've just glimpsed some of the economic issues in today's world. Your course in economics will help you to understand the powerful forces that are shaping this world. This chapter takes the first step. It describes the questions that economists try to answer, the way they think about choices, and the methods they use. An appendix provides a guide to the graphical methods that are widely used in economics.

After studying this chapter, you will be able to

- ■ **Define economics and distinguish between microeconomics and macroeconomics**
- ■ **Explain the three big questions of microeconomics**
- ■ **Explain the three big questions of macroeconomics**
- ■ **Explain the ideas that define the economic way of thinking**
- ■ **Explain how economists go about their work as social scientists**

Definition of Economics

ALL ECONOMIC QUESTIONS ARISE BECAUSE WE want more than we can get. We want a peaceful and secure world. We want clean air, lakes, and rivers. We want long and healthy lives. We want good schools, colleges, and universities. We want spacious and comfortable homes. We want an enormous range of sports and recreational gear, from running shoes to jet skis. We want the time to enjoy sports, games, novels, movies, music, travel, and hanging out with our friends.

Scarcity

What each one of us can get is limited by time, by the income we earn, and by the prices we must pay. Everyone ends up with some unsatisfied wants. What we can get as a society is limited by our productive resources. These resources include the gifts of nature, human labour and ingenuity, and tools and equipment that we have produced.

Our inability to satisfy all our wants is called **scarcity.** The poor and the rich alike face scarcity. A child wants a $1.00 can of pop and two 50¢ packs of gum but has only $1.00 in his pocket. He faces scarcity. A millionaire wants to spend the weekend playing golf *and* spend the same weekend at the office attending a business strategy meeting. She faces scarcity. A society wants to provide improved health care, install a computer in every classroom, explore space, clean polluted lakes and rivers, and so on. Even parrots face scarcity!

Not only do I want a cracker—we all want a cracker!

Faced with scarcity, we must make choices. We must *choose* among the available alternatives. The child must *choose* the pop *or* the gum. The millionaire must *choose* the golf game *or* the meeting. As a society, we must *choose* among health care, highways, peacekeeping, the environment, and so on.

Economics is the social science that studies the choices that we make as we cope with scarcity and the institutions that have evolved to influence and reconcile our choices. The subject divides into

- Microeconomics
- Macroeconomics

Microeconomics

Microeconomics is the study of the choices that individuals and businesses make, the way these choices interact, and the influence that governments exert on them. Some examples of microeconomic questions are: Why are more people buying SUVs and fewer people buying minivans? How will a decline in air travel affect the producers of airplanes? How would a tax on e-commerce affect the growth of the Internet? Who benefits from minimum wage laws?

Macroeconomics

Macroeconomics is the study of the effects on the national economy and the global economy of the choices that individuals, businesses, and governments make. Some examples of macroeconomic questions are: Why did production and jobs shrink in 2001? Why has Japan been in a long period of economic stagnation? Can the government bring prosperity by cutting interest rates? Will a tax cut increase the number of jobs and total production?

REVIEW QUIZ

1 What is scarcity?
2 Give some examples of scarcity in today's world.
3 Define economics.
4 Use the headlines in today's news to illustrate the distinction between microeconomics and macroeconomics.

Three Big Microeconomic Questions

LOOK AT THE WORLD AROUND YOU. YOU SEE AN enormous range of things that you might buy and jobs that you might do. You also see a huge range of incomes and wealth. Microeconomics explains much of what you see by addressing three big questions:

- What goods and services are produced?
- How are goods and services produced?
- For whom are goods and services produced?

What Goods and Services Are Produced?

The objects that people value and produce to satisfy wants are called **goods and services.** Goods are physical objects such as golf balls. Services are tasks performed for people such as haircuts.

FIGURE 1.1   What We Produce

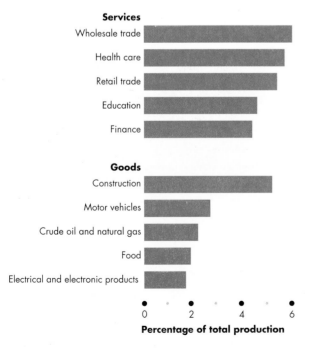

The production of wholesale trade and retail trade greatly exceeds the production of goods such as motor vehicles.

Source: Statistics Canada.

What *are* the goods and services that we produce in Canada today? Figure 1.1 shows the surprising answer. Canada is a service economy. Wholesale trade and retail trade are two of the three largest services. Between them, they represent nearly 12 percent of the value of total production. Health care, education, and financial services, such as banking and stock brokering, complete the five largest services. Among goods, only construction matches the size of the larger service items. Each of the other largest categories of goods—motor vehicles, crude oil and natural gas, food, and electrical and electronic products—accounts for less than 3 percent of the value of total production.

Figure 1.2 shows the trends in what we produce. Fifty years ago, almost 20 percent of Canadians worked on farms, 60 percent in mining, construction, and manufacturing, and 20 percent produced services. Today, more than 70 percent of working Canadians have service jobs. Mining, construction, and manufacturing jobs have shrunk to 25 percent, and farm jobs have almost disappeared.

You've reviewed some of the facts about *what* we produce. These facts raise the deeper question: What determines the quantities of retail services, new homes, DVD players, and wheat that we produce? Microeconomics provides some answers to these questions.

FIGURE 1.2   Trends in What We Produce

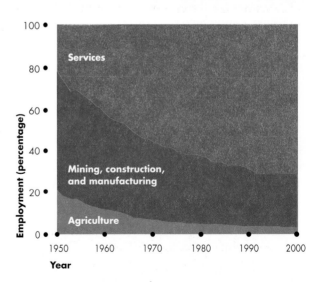

Services have expanded, and agriculture, mining, construction, and manufacturing have shrunk.

Source: Statistics Canada.

How Are Goods and Services Produced?

The range of jobs that you might do keeps changing. When Henry Ford built the world's first auto assembly line, he destroyed the jobs of the skilled craft workers who built cars using hand tools and created jobs for a new type of auto assembly worker. Every year, as businesses adopt new production technologies, similar changes occur. Today, it is information technology businesses that are producing new products, creating new jobs, and destroying old ones.

We call the resources that businesses use to produce goods and services **factors of production**. Factors of production are grouped into four categories:

- Land
- Labour
- Capital
- Entrepreneurship

Land   The "gifts of nature" that we use to produce goods and services are called **land.** In economics, land is what in everyday language we call natural resources. It includes land in the everyday sense, minerals, energy, water, and air.

Canada covers 9.9 billion square kilometres and we live on about 3.5 percent of this land. Almost 10 percent of Canada's land surface is water, about 30 percent is forest land, 50 percent is wild land, and 6.5 percent is farmland. Urban land is expanding and rural land is shrinking, but slowly.

Our land surface and water resources are renewable, and some of our mineral resources can be recycled. But many mineral resources, and all those that we use to create energy, are nonrenewable resources—they can be used only once.

Labour   The work time and work effort that people devote to producing goods and services is called **labour.** Labour includes the physical and mental efforts of all the people who work on farms and construction sites and in factories, shops, and offices.

In Canada in 2002, 16 million people had jobs or were available for work. An increasing population and an increasing percentage of women with jobs have increased the quantity of labour available.

The *quality* of labour depends on **human capital,** which is the knowledge and skill that people obtain from education, on-the-job training, and work experience. You are building your own human capital right now as you work on your economics course,

and your human capital will continue to grow as you become better at your job. Today, more than 80 percent of the Canadian population has completed high school and more than 40 percent has post-secondary certificates, diplomas, or university degrees. Figure 1.3 shows a measure of the growth of human capital in Canada over the past few decades.

Capital   The tools, instruments, machines, buildings, and other constructions that businesses now use to produce goods and services are called **capital.** The quantity of capital grows steadily over time.

Entrepreneurship   The human resource that organizes labour, land, and capital is called **entrepreneurship.** Entrepreneurs come up with new ideas about what and how to produce, make business decisions, and bear the risks that arise from these decisions.

You've reviewed some of the facts about *how* we produce in Canada. These facts raise deeper questions such as: What determines the quantities of labour and capital that get used? Microeconomics provides some answers to these questions.

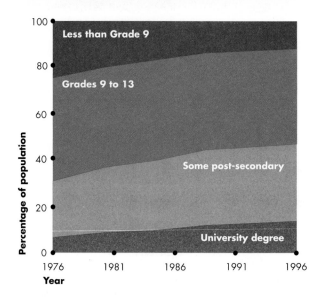

FIGURE 1.3   A Measure of Human Capital

Today, more than 40 percent of the Canadian population has post-secondary certificates, diplomas, or university degrees. A further 41 percent has completed high school.

Source: Statistics Canada.

For Whom Are Goods and Services Produced?

Who gets the goods and services that are produced depends on the incomes that people earn. The movie star who earns a few million dollars a year buys a large quantity of goods and services. A homeless unemployed person has few options and a small quantity of goods and services.

To earn an income, people sell the services of the factors of production they own:

- Land earns **rent**.
- Labour earns **wages**.
- Capital earns **interest**.
- Entrepreneurship earns **profit**.

Which factor of production earns the most income? The answer is labour. Total wages (including fringe benefits) were 69 percent of total income in 2000. Land, capital, and entrepreneurship share the remaining 31 percent. And over time, these percentages have been remarkably constant.

Knowing how income is shared among the factors of production doesn't tell us how it is shared among individuals. You know of lots of people who earn very large incomes. The average NHL player's salary in 2000 was about $3 million, and some stars, such as Mats Sundin of the Toronto Maple Leafs, earn almost $12 million a year. You know of even more people who earn very small incomes. Servers at McDonald's average around $7 an hour; checkout clerks, gas station attendants, and textile and leather workers earn less than $10 an hour.

You probably know about other persistent differences in incomes. Men, on the average, earn more than women. University and college graduates, on the average, earn more than high-school graduates. Canadians and Americans, on the average, earn more than Europeans, who in turn earn more, on the average, than Asians and Africans.

Figure 1.4 shows the incomes for five groups, each of which represents 20 percent of the population. If incomes were equal, each 20 percent group would earn 20 percent of total income. You know that incomes are unequal, and the figure provides a measure of just how unequal they are.

The 20 percent of individuals with the lowest incomes earn only 4 percent of total income. The 20 percent with the second lowest incomes earn 10 percent of total income. The next 20 percent—the middle 20 percent—earn 16 percent of total income.

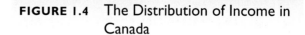

FIGURE 1.4   The Distribution of Income in Canada

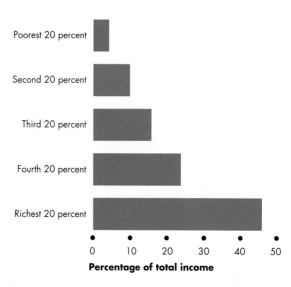

The richest 20 percent of the population earn 46 percent of total income. The poorest 20 percent earn only 4 percent of total income. (The data are for 1998.)

Source: Statistics Canada.

The 20 percent with the second highest incomes earn 24 percent of total income. And the 20 percent of individuals with the highest incomes earn 46 percent of total income.

You've reviewed some of the facts about *for whom* we produce in Canada. These facts raise deeper questions such as: Why do women earn less than men?

The three big microeconomic questions give you a sense of the *scope of microeconomics.* Next, we'll look at the big questions of macroeconomics.

REVIEW QUIZ

1 Does Canada produce more goods than services? What item accounts for the largest percent of the value of what we produce?
2 What are the trends in what we produce?
3 What are the factors of production and what are some of the changes in the way we produce goods and services?
4 Describe the distribution of income that shows for whom goods and services are produced.

Three Big Macroeconomic Questions

YOU'VE LIVED THROUGH A PERIOD OF DRAMATIC change in the way we work and play. The information age has created what has been called a "new economy" with rising living standards and new job opportunities. At the same time, prices have been remarkably stable. But you've also seen that our economy does not always expand. In 2001, economic slowdown brought job losses for millions of people. Macroeconomics explains these events by focusing on three big questions:

■ What determines the standard of living?

■ What determines the cost of living?

■ Why does our economy fluctuate?

What Determines the Standard of Living?

What is the standard of living? How do we measure it? How do we compare the standard of living in Africa with that in Canada and the United States?

The **standard of living** is the level of consumption that people enjoy, on the average, and is measured by average income per person. The greater the income per person, the higher is the standard of living, other things remaining the same.

Figure 1.5 shows the number of Canadian dollars per day earned on the average in different places. You can see that in the United States, the average is $148 a day. This number tells you that an average person in the United States can buy goods and services that cost $148—about five times the world average. Living standards fall off as we move down the figure, with average incomes in India and Africa of only $8 a day.

Most people live in the countries that have incomes below the world average. You can see this fact by looking at the population numbers shown in the figure. The poorest five countries or regions—China, Central Asia, Other Asia, India, and Africa—have a total population of 4 billion, which is two-thirds of the world's population.

What makes the standard of living rise? What can Indians and Africans do to increase their standard of living? Your study of macroeconomics will help you to understand some answers to questions like these.

FIGURE 1.5   Living Standards Around the World

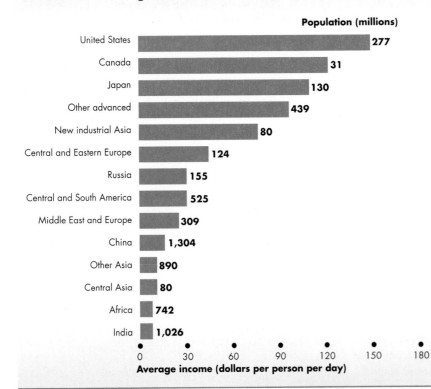

In 2000, average income per person ranged from $148 a day in the United States to $8 a day in Africa. The world average was $30 a day. Russia and Central and South America were close to the average.

Source: International Monetary Fund, *World Economic Outlook*, Washington, D.C., October 2001.

What Determines the Cost of Living?

In your great-grandparents' youth, when the electric light bulb was the latest big thing, the average Canadian earned $1 a day. But your great-grandparents' five cents would buy what you need a dollar to buy. The dollar of 2003 is worth only one-twentieth of the dollar of 1903. If the dollar continues to shrink in value at its average rate of loss, by the time you retire (sure, that's a long time in the future), you'll need almost $5 to buy what $1 buys today. The cost of living is rising.

The **cost of living** is the amount of money it takes to buy the goods and services that the average family consumes. In Canada, we measure money in dollars. So the cost of living in Canada is the number of dollars it takes to buy the goods and services that the average family buys. In the United Kingdom, it is the number of pounds; in Japan, it is the number of yen; and in Russia, it is the number of rubles.

Prices in Different Currencies To make this idea concrete, think about what a Big Mac costs. Table 1.1 shows some prices in 10 countries. The average price of a Big Mac in Canada is $3.00. In the United Kingdom, it is £2.00, and in Japan, it is ¥294. So in the United Kingdom, it costs a smaller number of money units to buy a Big Mac than it does in

Canada, and in Japan, it costs a larger number of money units. But a Big Mac costs more in the United Kingdom than in either Canada or Japan. The reason is that a pound is worth 2.40 Canadian dollars, so £2.00 is equivalent to $4.80. And a pound is worth 182 yen, so £2.00 is equivalent to ¥364.

The number of money units that something costs is not so important. But the rate at which the number is changing is very important. A rising cost of living is called **inflation** and a falling cost of living is called **deflation**. Inflation brings a shrinking value of the dollar and deflation brings a rising value of the dollar.

Inflation and Deflation Have we experienced inflation and a rising cost of living or deflation and a falling cost of living? If we look back over the past 100 years, we see that the cost of living has increased and the value of the dollar has shrunk.

In Canada, on the average between 1902 and 2002, the cost of living increased by 3 percent a year. Most people do not regard inflation at this rate as a big problem. But to place this inflation in perspective, it means that the dollar of 1902 was worth just 5 cents in 2002. At this inflation rate, a dollar earned in 2002 will be worth about 25 cents in 2052, a year in which you will probably be living on your pension!

Most of the advanced economies have low inflation. But the developing economies have higher inflation rates, some of them spectacularly so. In Central and South America, the average inflation rate during the 1980s and 1990s was 107 percent a year. A 100 percent change means a doubling. At this inflation rate, prices are rising by 6 percent a *month*. Inflation this rapid poses huge problems as people struggle to cope with an ever-falling value of money.

During the past few years, the cost of living has increased slowly. Can we count on it rising slowly in the future? What will the dollar buy next year? What will it buy in 10 years when you are paying off your student loan? And what will it buy in 50 years when you are spending your life's savings in retirement?

You've seen that over the years, our standard of living has increased. Why doesn't a rising *cost* of living mean that people must constantly cut back on their spending and endure a falling *standard* of living? Although the cost of living has increased steadily, incomes have increased more quickly. And because incomes have increased faster than the cost of living, the standard of living has increased.

What causes inflation? What can we do to avoid it? Your study of macroeconomics will help you to understand some answers to these questions.

TABLE 1.1 The Cost of a Big Mac in 10 Countries

Country	Name of currency	Price of a Big Mac
United Kingdom	Pound	2.00
United States	U.S. Dollar	2.50
Canada	Canadian Dollar	3.00
Brazil	Real	3.60
South Africa	Rand	9.70
Israel	Shekel	13.90
Russia	Ruble	35.00
Japan	Yen	294
South Korea	Won	3,000
Indonesia	Rupiah	14,700

Source: Economist.com

FIGURE 1.6   Business Cycle Phases and Turning Points

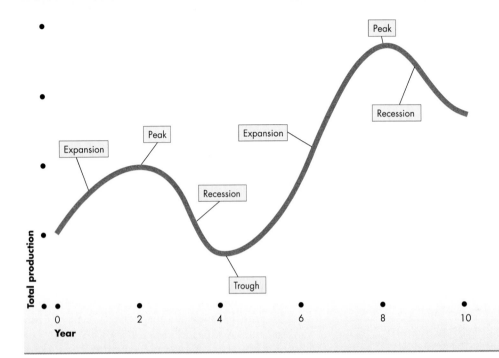

In a business cycle expansion, production and jobs increase more rapidly than normal. In a recession, production and jobs shrink. An expansion ends at a peak, and a recession ends at a trough.

Why Does Our Economy Fluctuate?

Over long periods, both the standard of living and the cost of living increase. But these increases are not smooth and continuous. During 2001, the number of Canadians who wanted a job increased by 330,000. But the Canadian economy created only 103,000 additional jobs. Our economy slowed. We call the periodic but irregular up-and-down movement in production and jobs the **business cycle.**

When production and jobs are increasing more rapidly than normal, the economy is in a business cycle expansion. When production and jobs are shrinking, the economy is in a recession.

Figure 1.6 illustrates the phases and turning points of a business cycle. A *recession* runs from year 2 to year 4, followed by an *expansion* from year 4 through year 8. Another recession runs from year 8 through year 10. A recession ends at a *trough*, and an expansion ends at a *peak*.

The most recent expansion in Canada began in 1991. The deepest recession of the 1990s was in Russia, where production fell by almost 30 percent between 1990 and 1994. The most persistent recession of recent years has been in Japan. The worst recession ever experienced occurred during the 1930s in an episode called the Great Depression. During this period, production in Canada shrank by 28 percent.

When a recession occurs, unemployment increases. During the Great Depression, almost 20 percent of the labour force in Canada was unable to find jobs. During the recession of the early 1990s, the unemployment rate climbed to 12 percent of the labour force.

What causes the business cycle? What can we do to smooth out the business cycle? Economists remain unsure about the answers to these questions. But in your study of macroeconomics, you will learn what economists have discovered about economic fluctuations.

REVIEW QUIZ

1 What are the three big issues that macroeconomics addresses?
2 What do we mean by the standard of living and what is its range from the richest to the poorest countries?
3 What do we mean by the cost of living? If the cost of living keeps rising, does the standard of living keep falling?
4 What are the phases of the business cycle?

The Economic Way of Thinking

THE DEFINITION OF ECONOMICS AND THE questions of microeconomics and macroeconomics tell you about the *scope of economics.* But they don't tell you how economists *think* about these questions and go about seeking answers to them.

You're now going to begin to see how economists approach economic questions. First, in this section, we'll look at the ideas that define the *economic way of thinking.* This way of thinking needs practice, but it is a powerful way of thinking and as you become more familiar with it, you'll begin to see the world around you with a new and sharp focus.

Choices and Tradeoffs

Because we face scarcity, we must make choices. And when we make a choice, we select from the available alternatives. For example, you can spend the weekend studying for your next economics test and having fun with your friends, but you can't do both of these activities at the same time. You must choose how much time to devote to each. Whatever choice you make, you could have chosen something else instead.

You can think about your choice as a tradeoff. A **tradeoff** is an exchange—giving up one thing to get something else. When you choose how to spend your weekend, you trade off between studying and hanging out with your friends.

Guns Versus Butter The classic tradeoff is guns versus butter. "Guns" and "butter" stand for any pair of goods and services. They might actually be guns and butter. Or they might be broader categories such as peacekeeping and food. Or they might be any pair of specific goods or services such as cola and bottled water, baseball bats and tennis racquets, colleges and hospitals, realty services and career counselling.

Regardless of the specific objects that guns and butter represent, the guns-versus-butter tradeoff captures a hard fact of life: If we want more of one thing, we must trade something else in exchange for it.

The idea of a tradeoff is central to the whole of economics. We can pose all the questions of microeconomics and macroeconomics in terms of tradeoffs. Let's return to these questions and view them in terms of tradeoffs.

Microeconomic Tradeoffs

The questions of what, how, and for whom goods and services are produced all involve tradeoffs that are similar to that of guns versus butter.

"What" Tradeoffs What goods and services get produced depends on choices made by each one of us, by our government, and by the businesses that produce the things we buy. Each of these choices involves a tradeoff.

Each one of us faces a tradeoff when we choose how to spend our income. You go to the movies this week, but you forgo a few cups of coffee to buy the ticket—you trade off coffee for a movie.

The federal government faces a tradeoff when it chooses how to spend our tax dollars. Parliament votes for more hospitals but cuts back on educational programs—Parliament trades off education for hospitals.

Businesses face a tradeoff when they decide what to produce. Nike hires Tiger Woods and allocates resources to designing and marketing a new golf ball but cuts back on its development of a new running shoe—Nike trades off running shoes for golf balls.

"How" Tradeoffs How goods and services get produced depends on choices made by the businesses that produce the things we buy. These choices involve a tradeoff. For example, Tim Hortons opens a new doughnut store with an automated production line and closes an older store with a traditional kitchen. Tim Hortons trades off labour for capital.

"For Whom" Tradeoffs For whom goods and services are produced depends on the distribution of buying power. Buying power can be redistributed—transferred from one person to another—in three ways: by voluntary payments, by theft, or through taxes and benefits organized by government. Redistribution brings tradeoffs.

Each of us faces a tradeoff when, for example, we choose how much to contribute to the United Nations famine relief fund. You donate $50 and cut your spending on other items by that amount. You trade off your own level of spending for a small increase in economic equality.

We make choices that influence redistribution by theft when we vote to make theft illegal and to devote resources to law enforcement. We trade off goods and services for an increase in the security of our property.

We also vote for taxes and social programs that redistribute buying power from the rich to the poor. Government redistribution confronts society with what has been called the **big tradeoff**—the tradeoff between equality and efficiency. Taxing the rich and making transfers to the poor bring greater economic equality. But taxing productive activities such as running a business, working hard, saving, and investing in capital discourages these activities. So taxing productive activities means producing less—it creates inefficiency.

You can think of the big tradeoff as being the problem of how to share a pie that everyone contributes to baking. If each person receives a share of the pie that reflects the size of her or his effort, everyone will work hard and the pie will be as large as possible. But if the pie is shared equally, regardless of contribution, some talented bakers will slacken off and the pie will shrink. The big tradeoff is one between the size of the pie and how equally it is shared. We trade off some efficiency for increased equality.

We've reviewed some microeconomic tradeoffs. Let's now look at some macroeconomic tradeoffs.

Macroeconomic Tradeoffs

The three macroeconomic questions about the standard of living, the cost of living, and the business cycle involve tradeoffs that are similar to that of guns versus butter.

Standard of Living Tradeoffs The standard of living is higher in Canada than in Africa. And the standard of living improves over time, so today it is higher than it was a generation ago. Our standard of living and its rate of improvement depend on the many choices made by each one of us, by governments, and by businesses. And these choices involve tradeoffs.

One choice is that of how much of our income to consume and how much to save. Our saving can be channelled through the financial system to finance businesses and to pay for new capital that increases productivity. The more we save and invest, the faster our productivity and our standard of living increase. When you decide to save an extra $1,000 and forgo a vacation, you trade off the vacation for a higher future income. If everyone saves an extra $1,000 and businesses invest in more equipment that increases productivity, the average income per person rises and the standard of living improves. As a society, we trade off current consumption for increased productivity and a higher future standard of living.

A second choice is how much effort to devote to education and training. By becoming better educated and more highly skilled, we become more productive and our standard of living rises. When you decide to remain in school for another two years to complete a professional degree and forgo a huge chunk of leisure time, you trade off leisure for a higher future income. If everyone becomes better educated, productivity increases, income per person rises, and the standard of living improves. As a society, we trade off current consumption and leisure time for increased productivity and a higher future standard of living.

A third choice, usually made by businesses, is how much effort to devote to research and the development of new products and production methods. Ford Motor Company can hire engineers to do research on a new robot assembly line or to operate the existing plant and produce cars. More research brings greater productivity in the future but means smaller current production—a tradeoff of current production for greater future production.

Output-Inflation Tradeoff When policy actions lower the interest rate and speed the pace at which money is created, spending, output, and employment increase. Higher spending brings rising inflation—the cost of living rises more rapidly. Eventually, output returns to its previous level. But the higher inflation rate has been accompanied by a temporary increase in output.

Similarly, when policy actions raise the interest rate and slow the pace at which money is created, spending, output, and employment decrease. Lower spending brings falling inflation—the cost of living rises more slowly. Again, output eventually returns to its previous level and the lower inflation rate has been accompanied by a temporary decrease in output.

When the inflation rate is too high, policy makers would like to lower inflation without lowering output. But they face an **output-inflation tradeoff** because the policy action that lowers inflation also lowers output and a policy action that boosts output increases inflation.

Seeing choices as tradeoffs emphasizes the idea that to get something, we must give up something. What we give up is the *cost* of what we get. Economists call this cost the *opportunity cost*.

Opportunity Cost

The highest-valued alternative that we give up to get something is the **opportunity cost** of the activity chosen. "There's no such thing as a free lunch" is not just a clever throwaway line. It expresses the central idea of economics: that every choice involves a cost.

You can quit school right now, or you can remain in school. If you quit school and take a job at Tim Hortons, you might earn enough to buy some CDs, go to the movies, and spend lots of free time with your friends. If you remain in school, you can't afford these things. You will be able to buy these things later, and that is one of the payoffs from being in school. But for now, when you've bought your books, you might have nothing left for CDs and movies. And doing assignments means that you've got less time for hanging around with your friends. The opportunity cost of being in school is the highest-valued alternative that you would have chosen if you had quit school.

All of the tradeoffs that we've just considered involve opportunity cost. The opportunity cost of some guns is the butter forgone; the opportunity cost of a movie ticket is the number of cups of coffee forgone; the opportunity cost of lower inflation is the output temporarily forgone.

Margins and Incentives

You can allocate the next hour between studying and e-mailing your friends. But the choice is not all or nothing. You must decide how many minutes to allocate to each activity. To make this decision, you compare the benefit of a little bit more study time with its cost—you make your choice at the **margin**.

The benefit that arises from an increase in an activity is called **marginal benefit**. For example, suppose that you're working four nights a week at your courses and your grade point average is 3.0. You decide that you want a higher grade and decide to study an extra night each week. Your grade now rises to 3.5. The marginal benefit from studying for one additional night a week is the 0.5 increase in your grade. It is *not* the 3.5 grade. The reason is that you already have the benefit from studying for four nights a week, so we don't count this benefit as resulting from the decision you are now making.

The cost of an increase in an activity is called **marginal cost**. For you, the marginal cost of increasing your study time by one night a week is the cost of the additional night not spent with your friends (if that is your best alternative use of the time). It does not include the cost of the four nights you are already studying.

To make your decision, you compare the marginal benefit from an extra night of study with its marginal cost. If the marginal benefit exceeds the marginal cost, you study the extra night. If the marginal cost exceeds the marginal benefit, you do not study the extra night.

By evaluating marginal benefits and marginal costs and choosing only those actions that bring greater benefit than cost, we use our scarce resources in the way that makes us as well off as possible.

Our choices respond to incentives. An **incentive** is an inducement to take a particular action. The inducement can be a benefit—a carrot—or a cost—a stick. A change in marginal cost and a change in marginal benefit change the incentives that we face and lead us to change our choices.

For example, suppose your economics instructor gives you some problem sets and tells you that all the problems will be on the next test. The marginal benefit from working these problems is large, so you diligently work them all. Suppose, in contrast, that your math instructor gives you some problem sets and tells you that none of the problems will be on the next test. The marginal benefit from working these problems is lower, so you skip most of them.

The central idea of economics is that we can predict the way choices will change by looking at changes in incentives. More of an activity is undertaken when its marginal cost falls or its marginal benefit rises; less of an activity is undertaken when its marginal cost rises or its marginal benefit falls.

REVIEW QUIZ

1 What is a tradeoff?
2 Provide three examples of microeconomic tradeoffs.
3 What is the big tradeoff and how does it arise?
4 Provide two examples of macroeconomic trade-offs.
5 What is the short-run tradeoff of macroeconomics?
6 What is opportunity cost?
7 How do economists predict changes in choices?

Economics: A Social Science

ECONOMICS IS A SOCIAL SCIENCE (ALONG WITH political science, psychology, and sociology). Economists try to discover how the economic world works, and in pursuit of this goal (like all scientists), they distinguish between two types of statements:

- What *is*
- What *ought to be*

Statements about what *is* are called *positive* statements and they might be right or wrong. We can test a positive statement by checking it against the facts. When a chemist does an experiment in a laboratory, she is attempting to check a positive statement against the facts.

Statements about what *ought to be* are called *normative* statements. These statements depend on values and cannot be tested. When Parliament debates a motion, it is ultimately trying to decide what ought to be. It is making a normative statement.

To see the distinction between positive and normative statements, consider the controversy over global warming. Some scientists believe that centuries of the burning of coal and oil are increasing the carbon dioxide content of the earth's atmosphere and leading to higher temperatures that eventually will have devastating consequences for life on this planet. "Our planet is warming because of an increased carbon dioxide buildup in the atmosphere" is a positive statement. It can (in principle and with sufficient data) be tested. "We ought to cut back on our use of carbon-based fuels such as coal and oil" is a normative statement. You can agree or disagree with this statement, but you can't test it. It is based on values. Health-care reform provides an economic example of the distinction. "Universal health care cuts the amount of work time lost to illness" is a positive statement. "All Canadians should have equal access to health care" is a normative statement.

The task of economic science is to discover positive statements that are consistent with what we observe and that help us to understand the economic world. This task can be broken into three steps:

- Observation and measurement
- Model building
- Testing models

Observation and Measurement

Economists observe and measure data on such things as natural and human resources, wages and work hours, the prices and quantities of the different goods and services produced, taxes and government spending, and the quantities of goods and services bought from and sold to other countries.

Model Building

The second step towards understanding how the economic world works is to build a model. An **economic model** is a description of some aspect of the economic world that includes only those features of the world that are needed for the purpose at hand. A model is simpler than the reality it describes. What a model includes and what it leaves out result from assumptions about what is essential and what are inessential details.

You can see how ignoring details is useful—even essential—to our understanding by thinking about a model that you see every day: the TV weather map. The weather map is a model that helps to predict the temperature, wind speed and direction, and precipitation over a future period. The weather map shows lines called isobars—lines of equal barometric pressure. It doesn't show the highways. The reason is that our theory of the weather tells us that the pattern of air pressure, not the location of the highways, determines the weather.

An economic model is similar to a weather map. It tells us how a number of variables are determined by a number of other variables. For example, an economic model of Vancouver's bid for the 2010 Winter Olympic Games might tell us the effects of the games on the number of houses and apartments, rents and prices, jobs, transportation facilities, and the outputs and profits of the businesses in the region.

Testing Models

The third step is testing the model. A model's predictions might correspond to the facts or be in conflict with them. By comparing the model's predictions with the facts, we can test a model and develop an economic theory. An **economic theory** is a generalization that summarizes what we think we understand about the economic choices that people make and the performance of industries and entire economies. It is a bridge between an economic model and the real economy.

The process of building and testing models creates theories. For example, meteorologists have a theory that if the isobars form a particular pattern at a particular time of the year (a model), then it will snow (reality). They have developed this theory by repeated observation and by carefully recording the weather that follows specific pressure patterns.

Economics is a young science. It was born in 1776 with the publication of Adam Smith's *Wealth of Nations* (see p. 54). Over the years since then, economists have discovered many useful theories. But in many areas, economists are still looking for answers. The gradual accumulation of economic knowledge gives most economists some faith that their methods will, eventually, provide usable answers to the big economic questions.

But progress in economics comes slowly. Let's look at some of the obstacles to progress in economics.

Obstacles and Pitfalls in Economics

We cannot easily do economic experiments. And most economic behaviour has many simultaneous causes. For these two reasons, it is difficult in economics to unscramble cause and effect.

Unscrambling Cause and Effect By changing one factor at a time and holding all the other relevant factors constant, we isolate the factor of interest and are able to investigate its effects in the clearest possible way. This logical device, which all scientists use to identify cause and effect, is called *ceteris paribus*. **Ceteris paribus** is a Latin term that means "other things being equal" or "if all other relevant things remain the same." Ensuring that other things are equal is crucial in many activities, and all successful attempts to make scientific progress use this device.

Economic models (like the models in all other sciences) enable the influence of one factor at a time to be isolated in the imaginary world of the model. When we use a model, we are able to imagine what would happen if only one factor changed. But *ceteris paribus* can be a problem in economics when we try to test a model.

Laboratory scientists, such as chemists and physicists, perform experiments by actually holding all the relevant factors constant except for the one under investigation. In non-experimental sciences such as economics (and astronomy), we usually observe the outcomes of the simultaneous operation of many factors. Consequently, it is hard to sort out the effects of each individual factor and to compare them with what a model predicts. To cope with this problem, economists take three complementary approaches.

First, they look for pairs of events in which other things were equal (or similar). An example might be to study the effects of unemployment benefits on the unemployment rate by comparing the United States with Canada on the presumption that the people in the two economies are sufficiently similar. Second, economists use statistical tools—called econometrics. Third, when they can, they perform experiments. This relatively new approach puts real subjects (usually students) in a decision-making situation and varies their incentives in some way to discover how they respond to a change in one factor at a time.

Economists try to avoid fallacies—errors of reasoning that lead to a wrong conclusion. But two fallacies are common, and you need to be on your guard to avoid them. They are the

- Fallacy of composition
- *Post hoc* fallacy

Fallacy of Composition The fallacy of composition is the (false) statement that what is true of the parts is true of the whole or that what is true of the whole is true of the parts. Think of the true statement "Speed kills" and its implication: Going more slowly saves lives. If an entire highway moves at a lower speed, everyone on the highway has a safer ride.

But suppose that only one driver slows down and all the other drivers try to maintain their original speed. In this situation, there will probably be more accidents because more cars will change lanes to overtake the slower vehicle. So in this example, what is true for the whole is not true for a part.

The fallacy of composition arises mainly in macroeconomics, and it stems from the fact that the parts interact with each other to produce an outcome for the whole that might differ from the intent of the parts. For example, a firm lays off some workers to cut costs and improve its profits. If all firms take similar actions, income falls and so does spending. The firm sells less, and its profits don't improve.

Post Hoc Fallacy Another Latin phrase—*post hoc, ergo propter hoc*—means "after this, therefore because of this." The *post hoc* fallacy is the error of reasoning that a first event *causes* a second event because the first occurred before the second. Suppose you are a visitor from a far-off world. You observe lots of people shopping in early December, and then you see them opening gifts and partying in the holiday season. You wonder, "Does the shopping cause the holiday season?" After a deeper study, you discover that the holiday season causes the shopping. A later event causes an earlier event.

Unravelling cause and effect is difficult in economics. And just looking at the timing of events often doesn't help. For example, the stock market booms, and some months later the economy expands—jobs and incomes grow. Did the stock market boom cause the economy to expand? Possibly, but perhaps businesses started to plan the expansion of production because a new technology that lowered costs had become available. As knowledge of the plans spread, the stock market reacted to *anticipate* the economic expansion. To disentangle cause and effect, economists use economic models and data and, to the extent that they can, perform experiments.

Economics is a challenging science. Does the difficulty of getting answers in economics mean that anything goes and that economists disagree on most questions? Perhaps you've heard the joke "If you laid all the economists in the world end to end, they still wouldn't reach agreement." Surprisingly, perhaps, the joke does not describe reality.

Agreement and Disagreement

Economists agree on a remarkably wide range of questions. And often the agreed-upon view of economists disagrees with the popular and sometimes politically correct view. When Bank of Canada Governor David Dodge testifies before Parliament, his words are rarely controversial among economists, even when they generate endless debate in the press and Parliament.

Here are 12 propositions with which at least 7 out of every 10 economists broadly agree:

- Tariffs and import restrictions make most people worse off.
- A large budget deficit has an adverse effect on the economy.
- A minimum wage increases unemployment among young workers and low-skilled workers.

- Cash payments to welfare recipients make them better off than do transfers-in-kind of equal cash value.
- A tax cut can help to lower unemployment when the unemployment rate is high.
- The distribution of income should be more equal.
- Inflation is primarily caused by a rapid rate of money creation.
- The government should restructure welfare along the lines of a "negative income tax."
- Rent ceilings cut the availability of housing.
- Pollution taxes are more effective than pollution limits.
- The redistribution of income is a legitimate role for the government.
- The federal budget should be balanced on the average over the business cycle but not every year.

Which of these propositions are positive and which are normative? Notice that economists are willing to offer their opinions on normative issues as well as their professional views on positive questions. Be on the lookout for normative propositions dressed up as positive propositions.

REVIEW QUIZ

1 What is the distinction between a positive statement and a normative statement? Provide an example (different from those in the chapter) of each type of statement.

2 What is a model? Can you think of a model that you might use (probably without thinking of it as a model) in your everyday life?

3 What is a theory? Why is the statement "It might work in theory, but it doesn't work in practice" a silly statement?

4 What is the *ceteris paribus* assumption and how is it used?

5 Try to think of some everyday examples of the fallacy of composition and the *post hoc* fallacy.

KEY POINTS

Definition of Economics (p. 2)

- All economic questions arise from scarcity—from the fact that wants exceed the resources available to satisfy them.
- Economics is the social science that studies the choices that people make as they cope with scarcity.
- The subject divides into microeconomics and macroeconomics.

Three Big Microeconomic Questions (pp. 3–5)

- Three big questions that summarize the scope of microeconomics are
  1. What goods and services are produced?
  2. How are goods and services produced?
  3. For whom are goods and services produced?

Three Big Macroeconomic Questions (pp. 6–8)

- Three big questions that summarize the scope of macroeconomics are
  1. What determines the standard of living?
  2. What determines the cost of living?
  3. Why does our economy fluctuate?

The Economic Way of Thinking (pp. 9–11)

- Every choice is a tradeoff—exchanging more of something for less of something else.
- The classic guns-versus-butter tradeoff represents all tradeoffs.
- All economic questions involve tradeoffs.
- The big social tradeoff is that between equality and efficiency.
- A macroeconomic tradeoff is the short-run tradeoff between output and inflation.
- The highest-valued alternative forgone is the opportunity cost of what is chosen.
- Choices are made at the margin and respond to incentives.

Economics: A Social Science (pp. 12–14)

- Economists distinguish between positive statements—what *is*—and normative statements—what *ought* to be.
- To explain the economic world, economists develop theories by building and testing economic models.
- Economists use the *ceteris paribus* assumption to try to disentangle cause and effect and are careful to avoid the fallacy of composition and the *post hoc* fallacy.
- Economists agree on a wide range of questions about how the economy works.

KEY TERMS

Big tradeoff, 10
Business cycle, 8
Capital, 4
Ceteris paribus, 13
Cost of living, 7
Deflation, 7
Economic model, 12
Economics, 2
Economic theory, 12
Entrepreneurship, 4
Factors of production, 4
Goods and services, 3
Human capital, 4
Incentive, 11
Inflation, 7
Interest, 5
Labour, 4
Land, 4
Macroeconomics, 2
Margin, 11
Marginal benefit, 11
Marginal cost, 11
Microeconomics, 2
Opportunity cost, 11
Output-inflation tradeoff, 10
Profit, 5
Rent, 5
Scarcity, 2
Standard of living, 6
Tradeoff, 9
Wages, 5

PROBLEMS

*1. Your friends go the movies one evening and you decide to stay home and do your economics assignment and practice test. You get 80 percent on your next economics exam compared with the 70 percent that you normally score. What is the opportunity cost of your extra points?

2. You go to the movies one evening instead of doing your economics assignment and practice test. You get 50 percent on your next economics exam compared with the 70 percent that you normally score. What is the opportunity cost of going to the movies?

*3. You plan to go to school this summer. If you do, you won't be able to take your usual job that pays $6,000 for the summer, and you won't be able to live at home for free. The cost of tuition is $2,000 and the cost of textbooks is $200, and living expenses are $1,400. What is the opportunity cost of going to summer school?

4. You plan to go skiing next weekend. If you do, you'll have to miss doing your usual weekend job that pays $100, you won't be able to study for 8 hours, and you won't be able to use your prepaid college meal plan. The cost of travel and accommodation will be $350, the cost of renting skis is $60, and your food will cost $40. What is the opportunity cost of the weekend ski trip?

*5. The local mall has free parking, but the mall is always very busy, and it usually takes 30 minutes to find a parking space. Today when you found a vacant spot, Harry also wanted it. Is parking really free at this mall? If not, what did it cost you to park today? When you parked your car today, did you impose any costs on Harry? Explain your answers.

6. The university has built a new movie theatre. Admission for students is free and there are always plenty of empty seats. But when the theatre screened *The Lord of the Rings*, the lines were long. So the theatre decided to charge $4 per student. Cadbury Schweppes offered students a free soft drink. Compare a student's opportunity cost of seeing the movie *The Lord of the Rings* with that of any other movie screened this year. Which is less costly and by how much?

*You can obtain the solutions to the odd-numbered problems on the Parkin–Bade Web site.

CRITICAL THINKING

1. Use the three big questions of microeconomics, the three big questions of macroeconomics, and the economic way of thinking to organize a short essay about the economic life of a homeless man. Does he face scarcity? Does he make choices? Can you interpret his choices as being in his own best interest? Can either his own choices or the choices of others make him better off? If so, how?

WEB EXERCISES

1. Use the link on the Parkin–Bade Web site to visit the CBC.
   a. What is the top economic news story today?
   b. With which of the big questions does it deal? (It must deal with at least one of them and might deal with more than one.)
   c. What tradeoffs does the news item discuss?
   d. Write a brief summary of the news item in a few bulleted points using as much as possible of the economic vocabulary that you have learned in this chapter and that is in the key terms list on p. 15.

2. Use the link on the Parkin–Bade Web site to visit *Resources For Economists on the Internet*. This site is a good place from which to search for economic information on the Internet.
   a. Scroll down the page and click on General Interest.
   b. Visit the "general interest" sites and become familiar with the types of information they contain.

3. Use the link on the Parkin–Bade Web site to visit Statistics Canada.
   a. What is the number of people employed (non-farm employment) in your area?
   b. Has employment increased or decreased?
   c. What is income per person (per capita income) in your area?

APPENDIX

Graphs in Economics

After studying this appendix, you will be able to

- Make and interpret a time-series graph, a cross-section graph, and a scatter diagram
- Distinguish between linear and nonlinear relationships and between relationships that have a maximum and a minimum
- Define and calculate the slope of a line
- Graph relationships among more than two variables

Graphing Data

A GRAPH REPRESENTS A QUANTITY AS A DISTANCE on a line. Figure A1.1 shows two examples. Here, a distance on the horizontal line represents temperature, measured in degrees Celsius. A movement from left to right shows an increase in temperature. The point marked 0 represents zero degrees Celsius. To the right of 0, the temperature is positive. To the left of 0 (as indicated by the minus sign), the temperature is negative. A distance on the vertical line represents altitude or height, measured in thousands of metres above sea level. The point marked 0 represents sea level. Points above 0 represent metres above sea level. Points below 0 (indicated by a minus sign) represent metres below sea level.

By setting two scales perpendicular to each other, as in Fig. A1.1, we can visualize the relationship between two variables. The scale lines are called *axes*. The vertical line is the *y-axis*, and the horizontal line is the *x-axis*. Each axis has a zero point, which is shared by the two axes. This zero point, common to both axes, is called the *origin*.

To show something in a two-variable graph, we need two pieces of information: the value of the *x*-variable and the value of the *y*-variable. For example, off the coast of British Columbia on a winter's day, the temperature is 10 degrees—the value of *x*. A fishing boat is located at 0 metres above sea level—the value of *y*. These two bits of information appear as point *A* in Fig. A1.1. A climber at the top of Mt. McKinley on a cold day is 6,194 metres above sea level in a zero-degree gale. These two pieces of information appear as point *B*. The position of the

FIGURE A1.1 Making a Graph

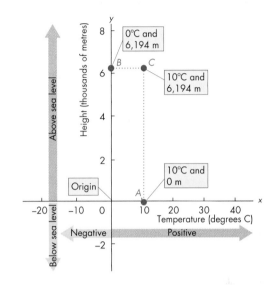

Graphs have axes that measure quantities as distances. Here, the horizontal axis (*x*-axis) measures temperature, and the vertical axis (*y*-axis) measures height. Point *A* represents a fishing boat at sea level (0 on the *y*-axis) on a day when the temperature is 10°C. Point *B* represents a climber on Mt. McKinley, 6,194 metres above sea level, at a temperature of 0°C. Point *C* represents a climber on Mt. McKinley, 6,194 metres above sea level, at a temperature of 10°C.

climber on a warmer day might be at the point marked *C*. This point represents the peak of Mt. McKinley at a temperature of 10 degrees.

We can draw two lines, called *coordinates*, from point *C*. One, called the *y*-coordinate, runs from *C* to the horizontal axis. Its length is the same as the value marked off on the *y*-axis. The other, called the *x*-coordinate, runs from *C* to the vertical axis. Its length is the same as the value marked off on the *x-axis*. We describe a point in a graph by the values of its *x*-coordinate and its *y*-coordinate.

Graphs like that in Fig. A1.1 can show any type of quantitative data on two variables. Economists use three types of graphs based on the principles in Fig. A1.1 to reveal and describe the relationships among variables. They are

- Time-series graphs
- Cross-section graphs
- Scatter diagrams

17

Time-Series Graphs

A **time-series graph** measures time (for example, months or years) on the *x*-axis and the variable or variables in which we are interested on the *y*-axis. Figures 1.2 and 1.3 on pp. 3 and 4 are examples of time-series graphs. So is Fig. A1.2, which provides some information about the price of coffee.

In Fig. A1.2, we measure time in years running from 1971 to 2001. We measure the price of coffee (the variable that we are interested in) on the *y*-axis.

The point of a time-series graph is to enable us to visualize how a variable has changed over time and how its value in one period relates to its value in another period.

A time-series graph conveys an enormous amount of information quickly and easily, as this example illustrates. It shows

- The *level* of the price of coffee—when it is *high* and *low*. When the line is a long way from the *x*-axis, the price is high. When the line is close to the *x*-axis, the price is low.

- How the price *changes*—whether it *rises* or *falls*. When the line slopes upward, as in 1976, the price is rising. When the line slopes downward, as in 1978, the price is falling.

- The *speed* with which the price changes—whether it rises or falls *quickly* or *slowly*. If the line is very steep, then the price rises or falls quickly. If the line is not steep, the price rises or falls slowly. For example, the price rose quickly in 1976 and 1977 and slowly in 1983. The price fell quickly in 1978 and slowly in 1984.

A time-series graph also reveals whether there is a trend. A **trend** is a general tendency for a variable to move in one direction. A trend might be upward or downward. In Fig. A1.2, you can see that the price of coffee had a general tendency to fall from the late 1970s to the early 1990s. That is, although the price rose and fell, the general tendency was for it to fall—the price had a downward trend.

A time-series graph also helps us detect cycles in variables. You can see some peaks and troughs in the price of coffee in Fig. A1.2. Figure 1.6 on p. 8 illustrates the business cycle. We rarely see a cycle as clear as the one shown in that figure.

Finally, a time-series graph also lets us compare the variable in different periods quickly. Figure A1.2 shows that the 1980s were different from the

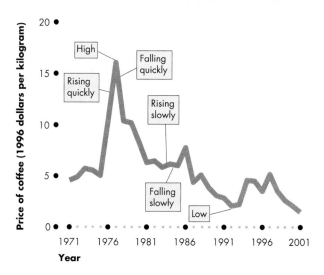

FIGURE A1.2   A Time-Series Graph

A time-series graph plots the level of a variable on the *y*-axis against time (day, week, month, or year) on the *x*-axis. This graph shows the price of coffee (in 1996 dollars per kilogram) each year from 1971 to 2001. It shows us when the price of coffee was *high* and when it was *low*, when the price *increased* and when it *decreased*, and when it changed *quickly* and when it changed *slowly*.

1970s. The price of coffee fluctuated more violently in the 1970s than it did in the 1980s.

You can see that a time-series graph conveys a wealth of information. And it does so in much less space than we have used to describe only some of its features. But you do have to "read" the graph to obtain all this information.

Cross-Section Graphs

A **cross-section graph** shows the values of an economic variable for different groups in a population at a point in time. Figure 1.4 on p. 5, called a *bar chart*, is an example of a cross-section graph. Figure A1.3 shows another example.

The bar chart in Fig. A1.3 shows the number of visitors to each province in 1999. The length of each bar indicates the number of visitors. This figure enables you to compare the number of visitors across the provinces. And you can do so much more quickly and clearly than you could by looking at a list of numbers.

FIGURE A1.3 A Cross-Section Graph

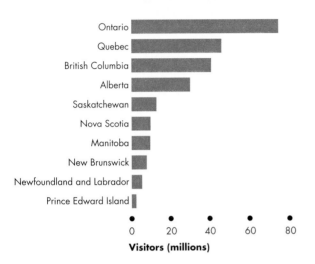

A cross-section graph shows the level of a variable across the members of a population. This bar chart shows the number of visitors to each province in 1999.

Scatter Diagrams

A **scatter diagram** plots the value of one variable against the value of another variable. Such a graph reveals whether a relationship exists between two variables and describes their relationship. Figure A1.4(a) shows the relationship between expenditure and income. Each point shows expenditure per person and income per person in a given year from 1984 to 2001. The points are "scattered" within the graph. The point labelled *A* tells us that in 1996, income per person was $18,095 and expenditure per person was $16,450. The dots in this graph form a pattern, which reveals that as income increases, expenditure increases.

Figure A1.4(b) shows the relationship between the number of international phone calls and the price of a call. This graph show that as the price per minute falls, the number of calls increases.

Figure A1.4(c) shows a scatter diagram of inflation and unemployment in Canada. Here, the dots show no clear relationship between these two variables. The dots in this graph reveal that there is no simple relationship between these variables.

FIGURE A1.4 Scatter Diagrams

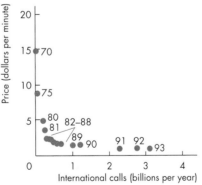
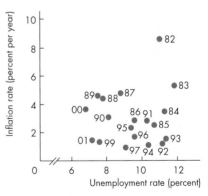

(a) Expenditure and income **(b) International phone calls and prices** **(c) Unemployment and inflation**

A scatter diagram reveals the relationship between two variables. Part (a) shows the relationship between expenditure and income. Each point shows the values of the two variables in a specific year. For example, point *A* shows that in 1996, average income was $18,095 and average expenditure was $16,450. The pattern formed by the points shows that as income increases, expenditure increases.

Part (b) shows the relationship between the price of an international phone call and the number of calls made. This graph shows that as the price of a phone call falls, the number of calls made increases. Part (c) shows a scatter diagram of the inflation rate and unemployment rate in Canada. This graph shows that the inflation rate and the unemployment rate are not closely related.

Breaks in the Axes Two of the graphs you've just looked at, Fig. A1.4(a) and Fig. A1.4(c), have breaks in their axes, as shown by the small gaps. The breaks indicate that there are jumps from the origin, 0, to the first values recorded.

In Fig. A1.4(a), the breaks are used because the lowest value of expenditure exceeds $13,000 and the lowest value of income exceeds $17,000. With no breaks in the axes of this graph, there would be a lot of empty space, all the points would be crowded into the top right corner, and we would not be able to see whether a relationship exists between these two variables. By breaking the axes, we are able to bring the relationship into view.

Putting a break in the axes is like using a zoom lens to bring the relationship into the centre of the graph and magnify it so that it fills the graph.

Misleading Graphs Breaks can be used to highlight a relationship. But they can also be used to mislead—to make a graph that lies. The most common way of making a graph lie is to use axis breaks and either to stretch or to compress a scale. For example, suppose that in Fig. A1.4(a), the *y*-axis ran from zero to $45,000 while the *x*-axis was the same as the one shown. The graph would now create the impression that despite a huge increase in income, expenditure had barely changed.

To avoid being misled, it is a good idea to get into the habit of always looking closely at the values and the labels on the axes of a graph before you start to interpret it.

Correlation and Causation A scatter diagram that shows a clear relationship between two variables, such as Fig. A1.4(a) or Fig. A1.4(b), tells us that the two variables have a high correlation. When a high correlation is present, we can predict the value of one variable from the value of the other variable. But correlation does not imply causation.

Sometimes a high correlation is a coincidence, but sometimes it does arise from a causal relationship. It is likely, for example, that rising income causes rising expenditure (Fig. A1.4a) and that the falling price of a phone call causes more calls to be made (Fig. A1.4b).

You've now seen how we can use graphs in economics to show economic data and to reveal relationships between variables. Next, we'll learn how economists use graphs to construct and display economic models.

Graphs Used in Economic Models

THE GRAPHS USED IN ECONOMICS ARE NOT always designed to show real-world data. Often they are used to show general relationships among the variables in an economic model.

An *economic model* is a stripped down, simplified description of an economy or of a component of an economy, such as a business or a household. It consists of statements about economic behaviour that can be expressed as equations or as curves in a graph. Economists use models to explore the effects of different policies or other influences on the economy in ways that are similar to the use of model airplanes in wind tunnels and models of the climate.

You will encounter many different kinds of graphs in economic models, but there are some repeating patterns. Once you've learned to recognize these patterns, you will instantly understand the meaning of a graph. Here, we'll look at the different types of curves that are used in economic models, and we'll see some everyday examples of each type of curve. The patterns to look for in graphs are the four cases:

- Variables that move in the same direction
- Variables that move in opposite directions
- Variables that have a maximum or a minimum
- Variables that are unrelated

Let's look at these four cases.

Variables That Move in the Same Direction

Figure A1.5 shows graphs of the relationships between two variables that move up and down together. A relationship between two variables that move in the same direction is called a **positive relationship** or a **direct relationship.** A line that slopes upward shows such a relationship.

Figure A1.5 shows three types of relationships: one that has a straight line and two that have curved lines. But all the lines in these three graphs are called curves. Any line on a graph—no matter whether it is straight or curved—is called a *curve.*

A relationship shown by a straight line is called a **linear relationship**. Figure A1.5(a) shows a linear rela-

FIGURE A1.5 Positive (Direct) Relationships

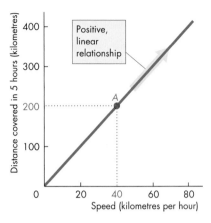

(a) Positive, linear relationship

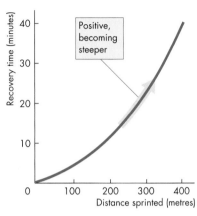

(b) Positive, becoming steeper

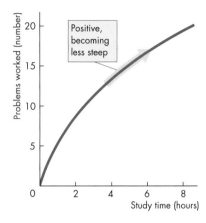

(c) Positive, becoming less steep

Each part of this figure shows a positive (direct) relationship between two variables. That is, as the value of the variable measured on the x-axis increases, so does the value of the variable measured on the y-axis. Part (a) shows a linear relationship—as the two variables increase together, we move along a straight line. Part (b) shows a positive relationship such that as the two variables increase together, we move along a curve that becomes steeper. Part (c) shows a positive relationship such that as the two variables increase together, we move along a curve that becomes less steep.

tionship between the number of kilometres travelled in 5 hours and speed. For example, point *A* shows that we will travel 200 kilometres in 5 hours if our speed is 40 kilometres an hour. If we double our speed to 80 kilometres an hour, we will travel 400 kilometres in 5 hours.

Figure A1.5(b) shows the relationship between distance sprinted and recovery time (the time it takes the heart rate to return to its normal resting value). This relationship is an upward-sloping one that starts out quite flat but then becomes steeper as we move along the curve away from the origin. The reason this curve slopes upward and becomes steeper is because the additional recovery time needed from sprinting an additional 100 metres increases. It takes less than 5 minutes to recover from the first 100 metres, but it takes more than 10 minutes to recover from the second 100 metres.

Figure A1.5(c) shows the relationship between the number of problems worked by a student and the amount of study time. This relationship is an upward-sloping one that starts out quite steep and becomes flatter as we move away from the origin. Study time becomes less productive as the student spends more hours studying and become more tired.

Variables That Move in Opposite Directions

Figure A1.6 shows relationships between things that move in opposite directions. A relationship between variables that move in opposite directions is called a **negative relationship** or an **inverse relationship**.

Figure A1.6(a) shows the relationship between the number of hours available for playing squash and the number of hours for playing tennis when the total is 5 hours. One extra hour spent playing tennis means one hour less playing squash and vice versa. This relationship is negative and linear.

Figure A1.6(b) shows the relationship between the cost per kilometre travelled and the length of a journey. The longer the journey, the lower is the cost per kilometre. But as the journey length increases, the cost per kilometre decreases, and the fall in the cost is smaller, the longer the journey. This feature of the relationship is shown by the fact that the curve slopes downward, starting out steep at a short journey length and then becoming flatter as the journey length increases. This relationship arises because some of the costs are fixed (such as auto insurance), and the fixed cost is spread over a longer journey.

FIGURE A1.6   Negative (Inverse) Relationships

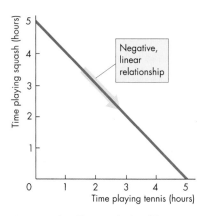

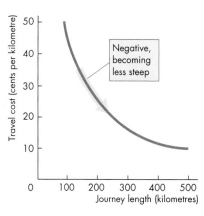

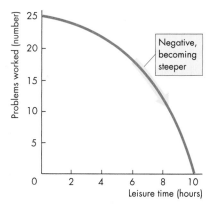

(a) Negative, linear relationship   **(b) Negative, becoming less steep**   **(c) Negative, becoming steeper**

Each part of this figure shows a negative (inverse) relationship between two variables. That is, as the value of the variable measured on the x-axis increases, the value of the variable measured on the y-axis decreases. Part (a) shows a linear relationship. The total time spent playing tennis and squash is 5 hours. As the time spent playing tennis increases, the time spent playing squash decreases, and we move along a straight line. Part (b) shows a negative relationship such that as the journey length increases, the curve becomes less steep. Part (c) shows a negative relationship such that as leisure time increases, the curve becomes steeper.

Figure A1.6(c) shows the relationship between the amount of leisure time and the number of problems worked by a student. Increasing leisure time produces an increasingly large reduction in the number of problems worked. This relationship is a negative one that starts out with a gentle slope at a small number of leisure hours and becomes steeper as the number of leisure hours increases. This relationship is a different view of the idea shown in Fig. A1.5(c).

Variables That Have a Maximum or a Minimum

Many relationships in economic models have a maximum or a minimum. For example, firms try to make the maximum possible profit and to produce at the lowest possible cost. Figure A1.7 shows relationships that have a maximum or a minimum.

Figure A1.7(a) shows the relationship between rainfall and wheat yield. When there is no rainfall, wheat will not grow, so the yield is zero. As the rainfall increases up to 10 days a month, the wheat yield increases. With 10 rainy days each month, the wheat

yield reaches its maximum at 2 tonnes per hectare (point A). Rain in excess of 10 days a month starts to lower the yield of wheat. If every day is rainy, the wheat suffers from a lack of sunshine and the yield decreases to zero. This relationship is one that starts out sloping upward, reaches a maximum, and then slopes downward.

Figure A1.7(b) shows the reverse case—a relationship that begins sloping downward, falls to a minimum, and then slopes upward. Most economic costs are like this relationship. An example is the relationship between the cost per kilometre and speed for a car trip. At low speeds, the car is creeping in a traffic jam. The number of kilometres per litre is low, so the cost per kilometre is high. At high speeds, the car is travelling faster than its efficient speed, using a large quantity of gasoline, and again the number of kilometres per litre is low and the cost per kilometre is high. At a speed of 100 kilometres an hour, the cost per kilometre is at its minimum (point B). This relationship is one that starts out sloping downward, reaches a minimum, and then slopes upward.

FIGURE A1.7 Maximum and Minimum Points

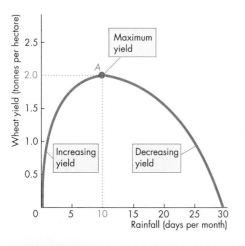

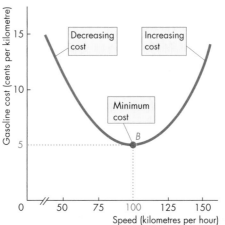

Part (a) shows a relationship that has a maximum point, A. The curve slopes upward as it rises to its maximum point, is flat at its maximum, and then slopes downward.

Part (b) shows a relationship with a minimum point, B. The curve slopes downward as it falls to its minimum, is flat at its minimum, and then slopes upward.

(a) Relationship with a maximum   **(b) Relationship with a minimum**

Variables That Are Unrelated

There are many situations in which no matter what happens to the value of one variable, the other variable remains constant. Sometimes we want to show the independence between two variables in a graph, and Fig. A1.8 shows two ways of achieving this.

In describing the graphs in Fig. A1.5 through A1.7, we have talked about curves that slope upward and downward, and curves that become less steep or steeper. Let's spend a little time discussing exactly what we mean by slope and how we measure the slope of a curve.

FIGURE A1.8 Variables That Are Unrelated

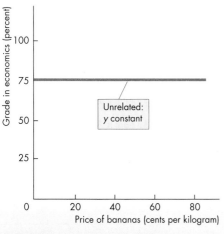

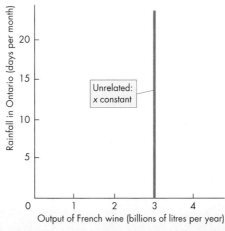

This figure shows how we can graph two variables that are unrelated. In part (a), a student's grade in economics is plotted at 75 percent on the *y*-axis regardless of the price of bananas on the *x*-axis. The curve is horizontal.

In part (b), the output of the vineyards of France on the *x*-axis does not vary with the rainfall in Ontario on the *y*-axis. The curve is vertical.

(a) Unrelated: *y* constant   **(b) Unrelated: *x* constant**

The Slope of a Relationship

WE CAN MEASURE THE INFLUENCE OF ONE variable on another by the slope of the relationship. The **slope** of a relationship is the change in the value of the variable measured on the y-axis divided by the change in the value of the variable measured on the x-axis. We use the Greek letter Δ (*delta*) to represent "change in." Thus Δy means the change in the value of the variable measured on the y-axis, and Δx means the change in the value of the variable measured on the x-axis. Therefore the slope of the relationship is

$$\Delta y/\Delta x$$

If a large change in the variable measured on the y-axis (Δy) is associated with a small change in the variable measured on the x-axis (Δx), the slope is large and the curve is steep. If a small change in the variable measured on the y-axis (Δy) is associated with a large change in the variable measured on the x-axis (Δx), the slope is small and the curve is flat.

We can make the idea of slope sharper by doing some calculations.

The Slope of a Straight Line

The slope of a straight line is the same regardless of where on the line you calculate it. The slope of a straight line is constant. Let's calculate the slopes of the lines in Fig. A1.9. In part (a), when x increases from 2 to 6, y increases from 3 to 6. The change in x

---

FIGURE A1.9   The Slope of a Straight Line

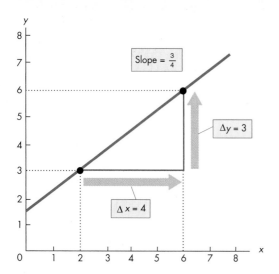

(a) Positive slope

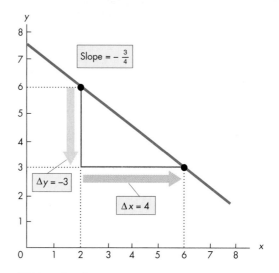

(b) Negative slope

To calculate the slope of a straight line, we divide the change in the value of the variable measured on the y-axis (Δy) by the change in the value of the variable measured on the x-axis (Δx), as we move along the curve. Part (a) shows the calculation of a positive slope. When x increases from 2 to 6, Δx equals 4. That change in x brings about an increase in y from 3 to 6, so Δy equals 3. The slope ($\Delta y/\Delta x$) equals 3/4. Part (b) shows the calculation of a negative slope. When x increases from 2 to 6, Δx equals 4. That increase in x brings about a decrease in y from 6 to 3, so Δy equals −3. The slope ($\Delta y/\Delta x$) equals −3/4.

is +4—that is, Δx is 4. The change in y is +3—that is, Δy is 3. The slope of that line is

$$\frac{\Delta y}{\Delta x} = \frac{3}{4}.$$

In part (b), when x increases from 2 to 6, y decreases from 6 to 3. The change in y is *minus* 3—that is, Δy is –3. The change in x is *plus* 4—that is, Δx is 4. The slope of the curve is

$$\frac{\Delta y}{\Delta x} = \frac{-3}{4}.$$

Notice that the two slopes have the same magnitude (3/4) but the slope of the line in part (a) is positive ($+3/+4 = 3/4$), while that in part (b) is negative ($-3/+4 = -3/4$). The slope of a positive relationship is positive; the slope of a negative relationship is negative.

The Slope of a Curved Line

The slope of a curved line is trickier. The slope of a curved line is not constant. Its slope depends on where on the line we calculate it. There are two ways to calculate the slope of a curved line: You can calculate the slope at a point, or you can calculate the slope across an arc of the curve. Let's look at the two alternatives.

Slope at a Point   To calculate the slope at a point on a curve, you need to construct a straight line that has the same slope as the curve at the point in question. Figure A1.10 shows how this is done. Suppose you want to calculate the slope of the curve at point A. Place a ruler on the graph so that it touches point A and no other point on the curve, then draw a straight line along the edge of the ruler. The straight red line is this line, and it is the tangent to the curve at point A. If the ruler touches the curve only at point A, then the slope of the curve at point A must be the same as the slope of the edge of the ruler. If the curve and the ruler do not have the same slope, the line along the edge of the ruler will cut the curve instead of just touching it.

Now that you have found a straight line with the same slope as the curve at point A, you can calculate the slope of the curve at point A by calculating the slope of the straight line. Along the straight line, as x

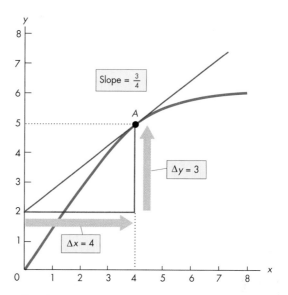

FIGURE A1.10   Slope at a Point

To calculate the slope of the curve at point A, draw the red line that just touches the curve at A—the tangent. The slope of this straight line is calculated by dividing the change in y by the change in x along the red line. When x increases from 0 to 4, Δx equals 4. That change in x is associated with an increase in y from 2 to 5, so Δy equals 3. The slope of the red line is 3/4. So the slope of the curve at point A is 3/4.

increases from 0 to 4 ($\Delta x = 4$) y increases from 2 to 5 ($\Delta y = 3$). Therefore the slope of the line is

$$\frac{\Delta y}{\Delta x} = \frac{3}{4}.$$

Thus the slope of the curve at point A is 3/4.

Slope Across an Arc   An arc of a curve is a piece of a curve. In Fig. A1.11, you are looking at the same curve as in Fig. A1.10. But instead of calculating the slope at point A, we are going to calculate the slope across the arc from B to C. You can see that the slope at B is greater than at C. When we calculate the slope across an arc, we are calculating the average slope between two points. As we move along the arc from B to C, x increases from 3 to 5 and y increases from 4 to 5.5. The change in x is 2 ($\Delta x = 2$), and the change

FIGURE A1.11   Slope Across an Arc

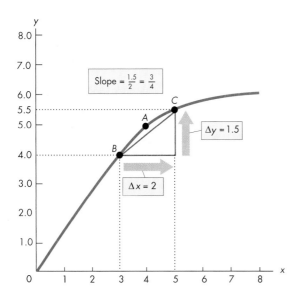

To calculate the average slope of the curve along the arc *BC*, draw a straight line from *B* to *C*. The slope of the line *BC* is calculated by dividing the change in *y* by the change in *x*. In moving from *B* to *C*, Δx equals 2 and Δy equals 1.5. The slope of the line *BC* is 1.5 divided by 2, or 3/4. So the slope of the curve across the arc *BC* is 3/4.

in *y* is 1.5 ($\Delta y = 1.5$). Therefore the slope of the line is

$$\frac{\Delta y}{\Delta x} = \frac{1.5}{2} = \frac{3}{4}.$$

Thus the slope of the curve across the arc *BC* is 3/4.

This calculation gives us the slope of the curve between points *B* and *C*. The actual slope calculated is the slope of the straight line from *B* to *C*. This slope approximates the average slope of the curve along the arc *BC*. In this particular example, the slope across the arc *BC* is identical to the slope of the curve at point *A*. But the calculation of the slope of a curve does not always work out so neatly. You might have some fun constructing some more examples and some counterexamples.

You now know how to make and interpret a graph. But so far, we've limited our attention to graphs of two variables. We're now going to learn how to graph more than two variables.

Graphing Relationships Among More Than Two Variables

WE HAVE SEEN THAT WE CAN GRAPH THE relationship between two variables as a point formed by the *x*- and *y*-coordinates in a two-dimensional graph. You may be thinking that although a two-dimensional graph is informative, most of the things in which you are likely to be interested involve relationships among many variables, not just two. For example, the amount of ice cream consumed depends on the price of ice cream and the temperature. If ice cream is expensive and the temperature is low, people eat much less ice cream than when ice cream is inexpensive and the temperature is high. For any given price of ice cream, the quantity consumed varies with the temperature; and for any given temperature, the quantity of ice cream consumed varies with its price.

Figure A1.12 shows a relationship among three variables. The table shows the number of litres of ice cream consumed each day at various temperatures and ice cream prices. How can we graph these numbers?

To graph a relationship that involves more than two variables, we use the *ceteris paribus* assumption.

Ceteris Paribus We noted in the chapter (see p. 13) that every laboratory experiment is an attempt to create *ceteris paribus* and isolate the relationship of interest. We use the same method to make a graph when more than two variables are involved.

Figure A1.12(a) shows an example. There, you can see what happens to the quantity of ice cream consumed when the price of ice cream varies and the temperature is held constant. The line labelled 21°C shows the relationship between ice cream consumption and the price of ice cream if the temperature remains at 21°C. The numbers used to plot that line are those in the third column of the table in Fig. A1.12. For example, if the temperature is 21°C, 10 litres are consumed when the price is 60¢ a scoop and 18 litres are consumed when the price is 30¢ a scoop. The curve labelled 32°C shows consumption as the price varies if the temperature remains 32°C.

We can also show the relationship between ice cream consumption and temperature when the price of ice cream remains constant, as shown in

FIGURE A1.12   Graphing a Relationship Among Three Variables

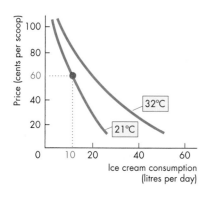

(a) Price and consumption at a given temperature

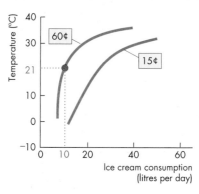

(b) Temperature and consumption at a given price

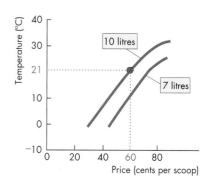

(c) Temperature and price at a given consumption

Price	Ice cream consumption (litres per day)			
(cents per scoop)	–10°C	10°C	21°C	32°C
15	12	18	25	50
30	10	12	18	37
45	7	10	13	27
60	5	7	10	20
75	3	5	7	14
90	2	3	5	10
105	1	2	3	6

The quantity of ice cream consumed depends on its price and the temperature. The table gives some hypothetical numbers that tell us how many litres of ice cream are consumed each day at different prices and different temperatures. For example, if the price is 60¢ a scoop and the temperature is 21°C, 10 litres of ice cream are consumed. This set of values is highlighted in the table and each part of the figure.

To graph a relationship among three variables, the value of one variable is held constant. Part (a) shows the relationship between price and consumption when temperature is held constant. One curve holds temperature at 32°C and the other at 21°C. Part (b) shows the relationship between temperature and consumption when price is held constant. One curve holds the price at 60¢ a scoop and the other at 15¢ a scoop. Part (c) shows the relationship between temperature and price when consumption is held constant. One curve holds consumption at 10 litres and the other at 7 litres.

Fig. A1.12(b). The curve labelled 60¢ shows how the consumption of ice cream varies with the temperature when ice cream costs 60¢ a scoop, and a second curve shows the relationship when ice cream costs 15¢ a scoop. For example, at 60¢ a scoop, 10 litres are consumed when the temperature is 21°C and 20 litres when the temperature is 32°C.

Figure A1.12(c) shows the combinations of temperature and price that result in a constant consumption of ice cream. One curve shows the combination that results in 10 litres a day being consumed, and the other shows the combination that results in 7

litres a day being consumed. A high price and a high temperature lead to the same consumption as a lower price and a lower temperature. For example, 10 litres of ice cream are consumed at 21°C and 60¢ a scoop, 32°C and 90¢ a scoop, and at 10°C and 45¢ a scoop.

◆ With what you have learned about graphs, you can move forward with your study of economics. There are no graphs in this book that are more complicated than those that have been explained in this appendix.

Mathematical Note:
Equations To Straight Lines

IF A STRAIGHT LINE IN A GRAPH DESCRIBES THE relationship between two variables, we call it a **linear relationship**. Figure 1 shows the linear relationship between a person's expenditure and income. This person spends $100 a week (by borrowing or spending previous savings) when income is zero. And out of each dollar earned, this person spends 50 cents (and saves 50 cents).

All linear relationships are described by the same general equation. We call the quantity that is measured on the horizontal (or x-axis) x and we call the quantity that is measured on the vertical (or y-axis) y. In the case of Fig. 1, x is income and y is expenditure.

A Linear Equation

The equation that describes a straight-line relationship between x and y is

$$y = a + bx.$$

In this equation, a and b are fixed numbers and they are called constants. The values of x and y vary so these numbers are called variables. Because the equation describes a straight line, it is called a **linear equation.**

The equation tells us that when the value of x is zero, the value of y is a. We call the constant a the y-axis intercept. The reason is that on the graph the straight line hits the y-axis at a value equal to a. Figure 1 illustrates the y-axis intercept.

For positive values of x, the value of y exceeds a. The constant b tells us by how much y increases above a as x increases. The constant b is the slope of the line.

Slope of Line

As we explain in the chapter, the **slope** of a relationship is the change in the value of y divided by the change in the value of x. We use the Greek letter Δ (delta) to represent "change in." Thus Δy means the change in the value of the variable measured on the y-axis, and Δx means the change in the value of the variable measured on the x-axis. Therefore the slope of the relationship is

$$\Delta y / \Delta x.$$

To see why the slope is b, suppose that initially the value of x is x_1, or $200 in Fig. 2. The corresponding value of y is y_1, also $200 in Fig. 2. The equation to the line tells us that

$$y_1 = a + bx_1. \qquad (1)$$

Now the value of x increases by Δx to $x_1 + \Delta x$ (or $400 in Fig. 2). And the value of y increases by Δy to $y_1 + \Delta y$ (or $300 in Fig. 2).

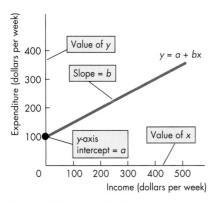

Figure 1 Linear relationship

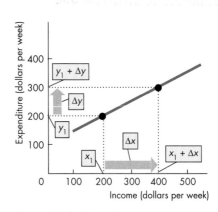

Figure 2 Calculating slope

The equation to the line now tells us that

$$y_1 + \Delta y = a + b(x_1 + \Delta x) \qquad (2)$$

To calculate the slope of the line, subtract equation (1) from equation (2) to obtain

$$\Delta y = b\Delta x \qquad (3)$$

and now divide equation (3) by Δx to obtain

$$\frac{\Delta y}{\Delta x} = b.$$

So, the slope of the line is b.

Position of Line

The y-axis intercept determines the position of the line on the graph. Figure 3 illustrates the relationship between the y-axis intercept and the position of the line on the graph. The y-axis measures saving and the x-axis measures income. When the y-axis intercept, a, is positive, the line hits the y-axis at a positive value of y—as the blue line does. When the y-axis intercept, a, is zero, the line hits the y-axis at the origin—as the purple line does. When the y-axis intercept, a, is negative, the line hits the y-axis at a negative value of y—as the red line does. As the equations to the three lines show, the value of the y-axis intercept does not influence the slope of the line.

Positive Relationships

Figure 1 shows a positive relationship—the two variables x and y move in the same direction. All positive relationships have a slope that is positive. In the equation to the line, the constant b is positive. In this example, the y-axis intercept, a, is 100. The slope b equals $\Delta y/\Delta x$, which is 100/200 or 0.5. The equation to the line is

$$y = 100 + 0.5x.$$

Negative Relationships

Figure 4 shows a negative relationship—the two variables x and y move in the opposite direction. All negative relationships have a slope that is negative. In the equation to the line, the constant b is negative. In the example in Fig. 4, the y-axis intercept, a, is 30. The slope, b, equals $\Delta y/\Delta x$, which is $-20/2$ or -10. The equation to the line is

$$y = 30 + (-10)x$$

or,

$$y = 30 - 10x.$$

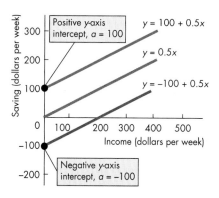

Figure 3 The *y*-axis intercept

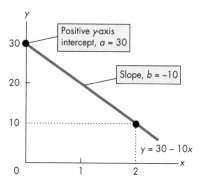

Figure 4 Negative relationship

SUMMARY

KEY POINTS

Graphing Data (pp. 17–20)

- A time-series graph shows the trend and fluctuations in a variable over time.
- A cross-section graph shows how variables change across the members of a population.
- A scatter diagram shows the relationship between two variables. It shows whether two variables are positively related, negatively related, or unrelated.

Graphs Used in Economic Models (pp. 20–23)

- Graphs are used to show relationships among variables in economic models.
- Relationships can be positive (an upward-sloping curve), negative (a downward-sloping curve), positive and then negative (have a maximum point), negative and then positive (have a minimum point), or unrelated (a horizontal or vertical curve).

The Slope of a Relationship (pp. 24–26)

- The slope of a relationship is calculated as the change in the value of the variable measured on the y-axis divided by the change in the value of the variable measured on the x-axis—that is, $\Delta y/\Delta x$.
- A straight line has a constant slope.
- A curved line has a varying slope. To calculate the slope of a curved line, we calculate the slope at a point or across an arc.

Graphing Relationships Among More Than Two Variables (pp. 26–27)

- To graph a relationship among more than two variables, we hold constant the values of all the variables except two.
- We then plot the value of one of the variables against the value of another.

KEY FIGURES

KEY TERMS

REVIEW QUIZ

1. What are the three types of graphs used to show economic data?
2. Give an example of a time-series graph.
3. List three things that a time-series graph shows quickly and easily.
4. Give three examples, different from those in the chapter, of scatter diagrams that show a positive relationship, a negative relationship, and no relationship.
5. Draw some graphs to show the relationships between two variables that
   a. Move in the same direction.
   b. Move in opposite directions.
   c. Have a maximum.
   d. Have a minimum.
6. Which of the relationships in question 5 is a positive relationship and which is a negative relationship?
7. What are the two ways of calculating the slope of a curved line?
8. How do we graph a relationship among more than two variables?

PROBLEMS

The spreadsheet provides data on the Canadian economy: Column A is the year, column B is the inflation rate, column C is the interest rate, column D is the growth rate, and column E is the unemployment rate. Use this spreadsheet to answer problems 1, 2, 3, and 4.

	A	B	C	D	E
1	1991	2.8	9.8	−2.1	10.3
2	1992	1.2	8.8	0.9	11.2
3	1993	1.5	7.8	2.3	11.4
4	1994	1.1	8.6	4.8	10.4
5	1995	2.3	8.3	2.8	9.4
6	1996	1.7	7.5	1.6	9.6
7	1997	0.9	6.4	4.2	9.1
8	1998	−0.5	5.5	4.1	8.3
9	1999	1.3	5.7	5.4	7.6
10	2000	3.6	5.9	4.5	6.8
11	2001	1.4	5.8	1.5	7.2

*1. a. Draw a time-series graph of the inflation rate.
   b. In which year(s) (i) was inflation highest, (ii) was inflation lowest, (iii) did it increase, (iv) did it decrease, (v) did it increase most, and (vi) did it decrease most?
   c. What was the main trend in inflation?

2. a. Draw a time-series graph of the interest rate.
   b. In which year(s) was the interest rate highest, (ii) was the interest rate lowest, (iii) did it increase, (iv) did it decrease, (v) did it increase most, and (vi) did it decrease most?
   c. What was the main trend in the interest rate?

*3. Draw a scatter diagram to show the relationship between the inflation rate and the interest rate. Describe the relationship.

4. Draw a scatter diagram to show the relationship between the growth rate and the unemployment rate. Describe the relationship.

*5. Draw a graph to show the relationship between the two variables x and y:

   x 0   1   2   3   4   5   6   7   8
   y 0   1   4   9   16 25 36 49 64

   a. Is the relationship positive or negative?
   b. Does the slope of the relationship increase or decrease as the value of x increases?
   c. Think of some economic relationships that might be similar to this one.

6. Draw a graph that shows the relationship between the two variables x and y:

   x 0   1   2   3   4   5
   y 25 24 22 16 8   0

   a. Is the relationship positive or negative?
   b. Does the slope of the relationship increase or decrease as the value of x increases?
   c. Think of some economic relationships that might be similar to this one.

*7. In problem 5, calculate the slope of the relationship between x and y when x equals 4.

8. In problem 6, calculate the slope of the relationship between x and y when x equals 3.

*9. In problem 5, calculate the slope of the relationship across the arc when x increases from 3 to 4.

10. In problem 6, calculate the slope of the relationship across the arc when x increases from 4 to 5.

*11. Calculate the slope of the relationship shown at point A in the following figure.

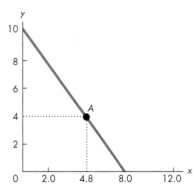

12. Calculate the slope of the relationship shown at point A in the following figure.

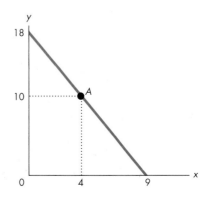

---

*You can obtain the solutions to the odd-numbered problems at *Parkin Online* (www.pearsoned.ca/parkin).

*13. Use the following figure to calculate the slope of the relationship:

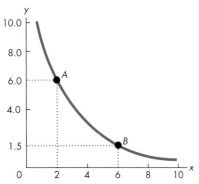

a. At points *A* and *B*.
b. Across the arc *AB*.

14. Use the following figure to calculate the slope of the relationship:

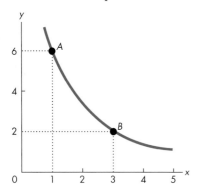

a. At points *A* and *B*.
b. Across the arc *AB*.

*15. The table gives the price of a balloon ride, the temperature, and the number of rides a day.

Price	Balloon rides (number per day)		
(dollars per ride)	10°C	20°C	30°C
5.00	32	40	50
10.00	27	32	40
15.00	18	27	32
20.00	10	18	27

Draw graphs to show the relationship between
a. The price and the number of rides, holding the temperature constant.
b. The number of rides and temperature, holding the price constant.
c. The temperature and price, holding the number of rides constant.

16. The table gives the price of an umbrella, the amount of rainfall, and the number of umbrellas purchased.

Price	Umbrellas (number per day)		
(dollars per umbrella)	0	2	10
	(mm of rainfall)		
10	7	8	12
20	4	7	8
30	2	4	7
40	1	2	4

Draw graphs to show the relationship between
a. The price and the number of umbrellas purchased, holding the amount of rainfall constant.
b. The number of umbrellas purchased and the amount of rainfall, holding the price constant.
c. The amount of rainfall and the price, holding the number of umbrellas purchased constant.

WEB EXERCISES

1. Use the link on the Parkin–Bade Web site and find the Consumer Price Index (CPI) for the latest 12 months. Make a graph of the CPI. During the most recent month, was the CPI rising or falling? Was the rate of rise or fall increasing or decreasing?

2. Use the link on the Parkin–Bade Web site and find the unemployment rate for the latest 12 months. Graph the unemployment rate. During the most recent month, was it rising or falling? Was the rate of rise or fall increasing or decreasing?

3. Use the data that you obtained in Web Exercises 1 and 2. Make a graph to show whether the CPI and the unemployment rate are related to each other.

4. Use the data that you obtained in Web Exercises 1 and 2. Calculate the percentage change in the CPI each month. Make a graph to show whether the percentage change in the CPI and the unemployment rate are related to each other.

THE ECONOMIC PROBLEM — CHAPTER 2

Good, Better, Best!

We live in a style that surprises our grandparents and would have astonished our great-grandparents. MP3s, video games, cell phones, gene splicing, and personal computers, which didn't exist even 25 years ago, have transformed our daily lives. For most of us, life is good, and getting better. But we still make choices and face costs. We still choose what we think is best for us. ◆ Perhaps the biggest choice that you will make is when to quit school and begin full-time work. When you've completed your current program, will you remain in school and work towards a postgraduate degree or a professional degree? What are the costs and consequences of this choice? We'll return to this question in *Reading Between the Lines* at the end of this chapter. ◆ We see an incredible amount of specialization and trade in the world. Each one of us specializes in a particular job—as a lawyer, a journalist, a home-maker. Why? How do we benefit from specialization and trade? ◆ Over many centuries, social institutions have evolved that we take for granted. One of them is property rights and a political and legal system that protects them. Another is markets. Why have these institutions evolved?

◆ These are the questions that we study in this chapter. We begin with the core economic problem—scarcity and choice—and the concept of the production possibilities frontier. We then learn about the central idea of economics: efficiency. We also discover how we can expand production by accumulating capital and by specializing and trading with each other. What you will learn in this chapter is the foundation on which all economics is built.

After studying this chapter, you will be able to

- Define the production possibilities frontier and calculate opportunity cost
- Distinguish between production possibilities and preferences and describe an efficient allocation of resources
- Explain how current production choices expand future production possibilities
- Explain how specialization and trade expand our production possibilities
- Explain why property rights and markets have evolved

33

Production Possibilities and Opportunity Cost

EVERY WORKING DAY, IN MINES, FACTORIES, shops, and offices and on farms and construction sites across Canada, 27 million people produce a vast variety of goods and services valued at more than $3 billion. But the quantities of goods and services that we can produce are limited by our available resources and by technology. And if we want to increase our production of one good, we must decrease our production of something else—we face tradeoffs. You are going to learn about the production possibilities frontier, which describes the limit to what we can produce and provides a neat way of thinking about and illustrating the idea of a tradeoff.

The **production possibilities frontier** (*PPF*) is the boundary between those combinations of goods and services that can be produced and those that cannot. To illustrate the *PPF*, we focus on two goods at a time and hold constant the quantities produced of all the other goods and services. That is, we look at a *model* economy in which everything remains the same (*ceteris paribus*) except for the production of the two goods we are considering.

Let's look at the production possibilities frontier for the classic general example of "guns" and "butter," which stand for *any* pair of goods or services.

Production Possibilities Frontier

The *production possibilities frontier* for guns and butter shows the limits to the production of these two goods, given the total resources available to produce them. Figure 2.1 shows this production possibilities frontier. The table lists some combinations of the quantities of butter and guns that can be produced in a month given the resources available. The figure graphs these combinations. The x-axis shows the quantity of butter produced, and the y-axis shows the quantity of guns produced.

Because the *PPF* shows the *limits* to production, we cannot attain the points outside the frontier. They are points that describe wants that can't be satisfied. We can produce at all the points *inside* the *PPF* and *on* the *PPF*. They are attainable points. Suppose that in a typical month, we produce 4 tonnes of butter and 5 guns. Figure 2.1 shows this combination as point *E* and as possibility *E* in the table. The figure also shows

FIGURE 2.1   Production Possibilities Frontier

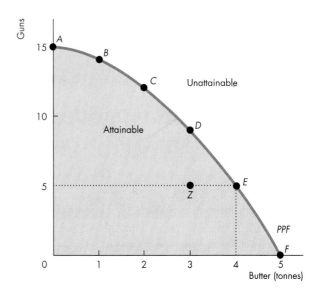

Possibility	Butter (tonnes)		Guns (units)
A	0	and	15
B	1	and	14
C	2	and	12
D	3	and	9
E	4	and	5
F	5	and	0

The table lists six points on the production possibilities frontier for guns and butter. Row A tells us that if we produce no butter, the maximum quantity of guns we can produce is 15. Points A, B, C, D, E, and F in the figure represent the rows of the table. The line passing through these points is the production possibilities frontier (PPF). It separates the attainable from the unattainable. Production is possible at any point inside the orange area or on the frontier. Points outside the frontier are unattainable. Points inside the frontier, such as point Z, are inefficient because resources are wasted or misallocated. At such points, it is possible to use the available resources to produce more of either or both goods.

other production possibilities. For example, we might stop producing butter and move all the people who produce it into producing guns. Point *A* in the figure and possibility *A* in the table show this case. The quantity of guns produced increases to 15, and butter production dries up. Alternatively, we might close the gun factories and switch all the resources into producing butter. In this situation, we produce 5 tonnes of butter. Point *F* in the figure and possibility *F* in the table show this case.

Production Efficiency

We achieve **production efficiency** if we cannot produce more of one good without producing less of some other good. When production is efficient, we are at a point *on* the *PPF*. If we are at a point *inside* the *PPF*, such as point *Z*, production is *inefficient* because we have some *unused* resources or we have some *misallocated* resources or both.

Resources are unused when they are idle but could be working. For example, we might leave some of the gun factories idle or some workers unemployed.

Resources are *misallocated* when they are assigned to tasks for which they are not the best match. For example, we might assign skilled butter-making machine operators to work in a gun factory and skilled gun makers to work in a dairy. We could get more butter *and* more guns from these same workers if we reassigned them to the tasks that more closely match their skills.

If we produce at a point inside the *PPF* such as *Z*, we can use our resources more efficiently to produce more butter, more guns, or more of *both* butter and guns. But if we produce at a point *on* the *PPF*, we are using our resources efficiently and we can produce more of one good only if we produce less of the other. That is, along the *PPF*, we face a *tradeoff*.

Tradeoff Along the *PPF*

Every choice *along* the *PPF* involves a *tradeoff*—we must give up something to get something else. On the *PPF* in Fig. 2.1, we must give up some guns to get more butter or give up some butter to get more guns.

Tradeoffs arise in every imaginable real-world situation, and you reviewed several of them in Chapter 1. At any given point in time, we have a fixed amount of labour, land, capital, and entrepreneurship. By using our available technologies, we can employ these resources to produce goods and services. But we are limited in what we can produce. This limit defines a boundary between what we can attain and what we cannot attain. This boundary is the real world's production possibilities frontier, and it defines the tradeoffs that we must make. On our real-world *PPF*, we can produce more of any one good or service only if we produce less of some other goods or services.

When doctors say that we must spend more on AIDS and cancer research, they are suggesting a tradeoff: more medical research for less of some other things. When the prime minister says that he wants to spend more on education and health care, he is suggesting a tradeoff: more education and health care for less peacekeeping and national security or less private spending (because of higher taxes). When an environmental group argues for less logging, it is suggesting a tradeoff: greater conservation of endangered wildlife for less paper. When your parents say that you should study more, they are suggesting a tradeoff: more study time for less leisure or sleep.

All tradeoffs involve a cost—an opportunity cost.

Opportunity Cost

The *opportunity cost* of an action is the highest-valued alternative forgone. The *PPF* helps us to make the concept of opportunity cost precise and enables us to calculate it. Along the *PPF*, there are only two goods, so there is only one alternative forgone: some quantity of the other good. Given our current resources and technology, we can produce more butter only if we produce fewer guns. The opportunity cost of producing an additional tonne of butter is the number of guns we must forgo. Similarly, the opportunity cost of producing an additional gun is the quantity of butter we must forgo.

For example, at point *C* in Fig. 2.1, we produce less butter and more guns than at point *D*. If we choose point *D* over point *C*, the additional tonne of butter *costs* 3 guns. One tonne of butter costs 3 guns.

We can also work out the opportunity cost of choosing point *C* over point *D* in Fig. 2.1. If we move from point *D* to point *C*, the quantity of guns produced increases by 3 and the quantity of butter produced decreases by 1 tonne. So if we choose point *C* over point *D*, the additional 3 guns *cost* 1 tonne of butter. One gun costs 1/3 of a tonne of butter.

Opportunity Cost Is a Ratio   Opportunity cost is a ratio. It is the decrease in the quantity produced of one good divided by the increase in the quantity produced of another good as we move along the production possibilities frontier.

Because opportunity cost is a ratio, the opportunity cost of producing an additional gun is equal to the *inverse* of the opportunity cost of producing an additional tonne of butter. Check this proposition by returning to the calculations we've just worked through. When we move along the *PPF* from *C* to *D*, the opportunity cost of a tonne of butter is 3 guns. The inverse of 3 is 1/3, so if we decrease the production of butter and increase the production of guns by moving from *D* to *C*, the opportunity cost of a gun must be 1/3 of a tonne of butter. You can check that this number is correct. If we move from *D* to *C*, we produce 3 more guns and 1 tonne less of butter. Because 3 guns cost 1 tonne of butter, the opportunity cost of 1 gun is 1/3 of a tonne of butter.

Increasing Opportunity Cost The opportunity cost of a tonne of butter increases as the quantity of butter produced increases. Also, the opportunity cost of a gun increases as the quantity of guns produced increases. This phenomenon of increasing opportunity cost is reflected in the shape of the *PPF*—it is bowed outward.

When a large quantity of guns and a small quantity of butter are produced—between points *A* and *B* in Fig. 2.1—the frontier has a gentle slope. A given increase in the quantity of butter *costs* a small decrease in the quantity of guns, so the opportunity cost of a tonne of butter is a small quantity of guns.

When a large quantity of butter and a small quantity of guns are produced—between points *E* and *F* in Fig. 2.1—the frontier is steep. A given increase in the quantity of butter *costs* a large decrease in the quantity of guns, so the opportunity cost of a tonne of butter is a large quantity of guns.

The *PPF* is bowed outward because resources are not all equally productive in all activities. People with many years of experience working for Smith & Wesson are very good at producing guns but not very good at making butter. So if we move some of these people from Smith & Wesson to Sealtest Dairies, we get a small increase in the quantity of butter but a large decrease in the quantity of guns.

Similarly, people who have spent years working at Sealtest Dairies are good at producing butter but not so good at producing guns. So if we move some of these people from Sealtest Dairies to Smith & Wesson, we get a small increase in the quantity of guns but a large decrease in the quantity of butter.

The more we try to produce of either good, the less productive are the additional resources we use to produce that good and the larger is the opportunity cost of a unit of that good.

Increasing Opportunity Costs Are Everywhere
Just about every activity that you can think of is one with an increasing opportunity cost. The most skilful farmers use the most fertile land to produce food. The best doctors use the least fertile land to produce health-care services. If hospitals buy fertile land, convert tractors into ambulances, and hire farmers as hospital porters, food production drops drastically and the production of health-care services increases by a tiny amount. The opportunity cost of a unit of health-care services rises. Similarly, if a farmer buys a hospital, converts it to a hydroponic tomato factory, and hires people who were previously doctors and nurses as farm workers, the decrease in the production of health-care services is large, but the increase in food production is small. The opportunity cost of a unit of food rises.

This example is extreme and unlikely, but these same considerations apply to any pair of goods that you can imagine.

REVIEW QUIZ

1 How does the production possibilities frontier illustrate scarcity?
2 How does the production possibilities frontier illustrate production efficiency?
3 How does the production possibilities frontier show that every choice involves a tradeoff?
4 How does the production possibilities frontier illustrate opportunity cost?
5 Why is opportunity cost a ratio?
6 Why does the *PPF* for most goods bow outward so that opportunity cost increases as the quantity produced of a good increases?

We've seen that what we can produce is limited by the production possibilities frontier. We've also seen that production on the *PPF* is efficient. But we can produce many different quantities on the *PPF*. How do we choose among them? How do we know which point on the *PPF* is the best one?

Using Resources Efficiently

You've seen that points inside the *PPF* waste resources or leave them unused and are inefficient. You've also seen that points *on* the *PPF* are efficient—we can't produce more of one good unless we forgo some units of another good. But there are many such points on the *PPF*. Each point on the *PPF* achieves production efficiency. Which point is the best? How can we choose among them? What are the efficient quantities of butter and guns to produce?

These questions are examples of real-world questions of enormous consequence such as: How much should we spend on treating AIDS and how much on cancer research? Should we expand education and health-care programs or cut taxes? Should we spend more on the environment and the conservation of endangered wildlife?

To determine the efficient quantities to produce, we must compare costs and benefits.

The *PPF* and Marginal Cost

The limits to production, which are summarized by the *PPF*, determine the marginal cost of each good or service. **Marginal cost** is the opportunity cost of producing *one more unit*. We can calculate marginal cost in a way that is similar to the way we calculate opportunity cost. *Marginal cost* is the opportunity cost of *one* additional tonne of butter—the quantity of guns that must be given up to get one more tonne of butter—as we move along the *PPF*.

Figure 2.2 illustrates the marginal cost of butter. If butter production increases from zero to 1 tonne—a move from *A* to *B*—the quantity of guns decreases from 15 to 14. So the opportunity cost of the first tonne of butter is 1 gun. If butter production increases from 1 tonne to 2 tonnes—a move from *B* to *C*—the quantity of guns decreases by 2. So the second tonne of butter costs 2 guns.

You can repeat this calculation for an increase in butter production from 2 to 3 tonnes, from 3 to 4 tonnes, and from 4 to 5 tonnes. Figure 2.2 shows the opportunity costs as a series of steps. Each extra tonne of butter costs more guns than the preceding tonne.

We've just calculated the opportunity cost of a tonne of butter and generated the steps in Fig. 2.2(a). The opportunity cost of a tonne of butter is also the *marginal cost* of producing a tonne of butter. In Fig. 2.2(b), the line labelled *MC* shows the marginal cost.

FIGURE 2.2   The *PPF* and Marginal Cost

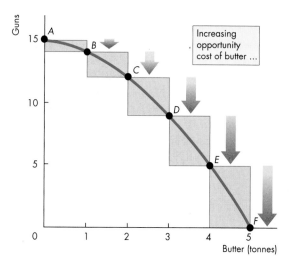

(a) *PPF* **and opportunity cost**

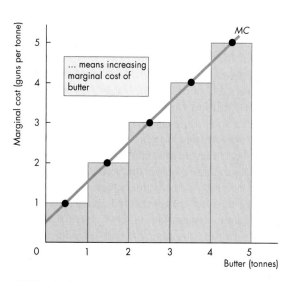

(b) Marginal cost

Opportunity cost is measured along the *PPF* in part (a). If the production of butter increases from zero to 1 tonne, the opportunity cost of a tonne of butter is 1 gun. If the production of butter increases from 1 to 2 tonnes, the opportunity cost of a tonne of butter is 2 guns. The opportunity cost of butter increases as the production of butter increases. Part (b) shows the marginal cost of a tonne of butter as the *MC* curve.

Preferences and Marginal Benefit

Look around your classroom and notice the wide variety of shirts, caps, pants, and shoes that you and your fellow students are wearing today. Why is there such a huge variety? Why don't you all wear the same styles and colours? The answer lies in what economists call preferences. **Preferences** are a description of a person's likes and dislikes.

You've seen that we have a concrete way of describing the limits to production: the *PPF*. We need a similarly concrete way of describing preferences. To describe preferences, economists use the concepts of marginal benefit and the marginal benefit curve. The **marginal benefit** of a good or service is the benefit received from consuming one more unit of it.

We measure the marginal benefit of a good or service by what a person is *willing to pay* for an additional unit of it. The idea is that you are willing to pay what the good is worth to you. It is worth its marginal benefit, and you're willing to pay an amount up to the marginal benefit. So willingness to pay measures marginal benefit.

The **marginal benefit curve** shows the relationship between marginal benefit of a good and the quantity of that good consumed. It is a general principle that the more we have of any good or service, the smaller is its marginal benefit and the less we are willing to pay for an additional unit of it. This tendency is so widespread and strong that we call it a principle—the *principle of decreasing marginal benefit*.

The basic reason why marginal benefit decreases as we consume more of any one item is that we like variety. The more we consume of one item, the more we can see of other things that we would like better.

Think about your willingness to pay for a coffee. You buy a bottomless cup. The first fill is important to you. You'd pay a lot more for it than what it costs. You can refill your cup as often as you wish. But you go back for only one more fill. You enjoy your second cup, but not as much as the first one. And you don't want a third cup, even though it is free.

In everyday life, we think of what we pay for something as the money that we give up—dollars. But you've learned to think about cost as opportunity cost, which is a cost in terms of other goods or services forgone, not a dollar cost. You can think about willingness to pay in the same terms. The price you are willing to pay for something is the quantity of other goods and services that you are willing to forgo. Let's illustrate preferences this way.

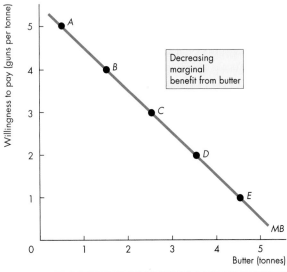

FIGURE 2.3   Preferences and the Marginal Benefit Curve

Possibility	Butter (tonnes)	Willingness to pay (guns per tonne)
A	0.5	5
B	1.5	4
C	2.5	3
D	3.5	2
E	4.5	1

The smaller the quantity of butter produced, the more guns people are willing to give up for an additional tonne of butter. If butter production is 0.5 tonnes, people are willing to pay 5 guns per tonne. But if butter production is 4.5 tonnes, people are willing to pay only 1 gun per tonne. Willingness to pay measures marginal benefit. And decreasing marginal benefit is a universal feature of people's preferences.

Figure 2.3 illustrates preferences in this way. In row *A*, butter production is 0.5 tonnes, and at that quantity, people are willing to pay 5 guns per tonne. As the quantity of butter produced increases, the amount that people are willing to pay for it falls. When butter production is 4.5 tonnes, people are willing to pay only 1 gun per tonne.

Let's now use the concepts of marginal cost and marginal benefit to describe the efficient quantity of butter to produce.

Efficient Use of Resources

When we cannot produce more of any one good without giving up some other good, we have achieved *production efficiency*, and we're producing at a point on the *PPF*. When we cannot produce more of any good without giving up some other good that we *value more highly*, we have achieved **allocative efficiency**, and we are producing at the point on the *PPF* that we prefer above all other points.

Suppose in Fig. 2.4, we produce 1.5 tonnes of butter. The marginal cost of butter is 2 guns per tonne, but the marginal benefit from butter is 4 guns per tonne. Because someone values an additional tonne of butter more highly than it costs to produce, resources get used more efficiently if butter production increases and gun production decreases.

Now suppose we produce 3.5 tonnes of butter. The marginal cost of butter is now 4 guns per tonne, but the marginal benefit from butter is only 2 guns per tonne. Because the additional butter costs more to produce than anyone thinks it is worth, we can get more value from our resources by moving some of them away from producing butter and into producing guns.

But suppose we produce 2.5 tonnes of butter. Marginal cost and marginal benefit are now equal at 3 guns per tonne. This allocation of resources between butter and guns is efficient. If more butter is produced, the forgone guns are worth more than the additional butter. If less butter is produced, the forgone butter is worth more than the additional guns.

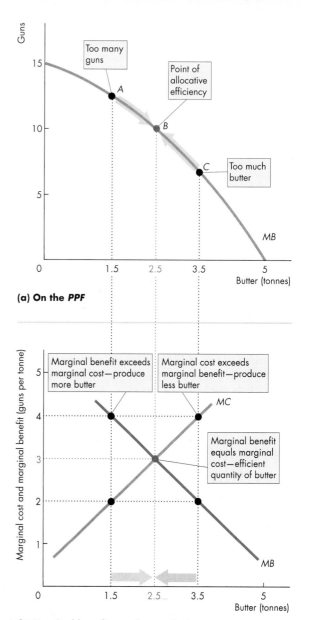

FIGURE 2.4 The Efficient Use of Resources

(a) On the PPF

(b) Marginal benefit equals marginal cost

The greater the quantity of butter produced, the smaller is the marginal benefit (*MB*) from it—the fewer guns people are willing to give up to get an additional tonne of butter. But the greater the quantity of butter produced, the greater is the marginal cost (*MC*) of butter—the more guns people must give up to get an additional tonne of butter. When marginal benefit equals marginal cost, resources are being used efficiently.

REVIEW QUIZ

1 What is marginal cost and how is it measured?
2 What is marginal benefit and how is it measured?
3 How does the marginal benefit from a good change as the quantity produced of that good increases?
4 What is production efficiency and how does it relate to the production possibilities frontier?
5 What conditions must be satisfied if resources are used efficiently?

You now understand the limits to production and the conditions under which resources are used efficiently. Your next task is to study the expansion of production possibilities.

Economic Growth

DURING THE PAST 30 YEARS, PRODUCTION PER person in Canada has doubled. Such an expansion of production is called **economic growth**. Economic growth increases our standard of living, but it doesn't overcome scarcity and avoid opportunity cost. To make our economy grow, we face a tradeoff—the standard of living tradeoff (p. 10)—and the faster we make production grow, the greater is the opportunity cost of economic growth.

The Cost of Economic Growth

Two key factors influence economic growth: technological change and capital accumulation. **Technological change** is the development of new goods and of better ways of producing goods and services. **Capital accumulation** is the growth of capital resources, which include *human capital.*

As a consequence of technological change and capital accumulation, we have an enormous quantity of cars that enable us to produce more transportation than was available when we had only horses and carriages; we have satellites that make global communications possible on a scale that is much larger than that produced by the earlier cable technology. But new technologies and new capital have an opportunity cost. To use resources in research and development and to produce new capital, we must decrease our production of consumption goods and services. Let's look at this opportunity cost.

Instead of studying the *PPF* of butter and guns, we'll hold the quantity of guns produced constant and examine the *PPF* for butter and butter-making machines. Figure 2.5 shows this *PPF* as the blue curve *ABC*. If we devote no resources to producing butter-making machines, we produce at point *A*. If we produce 3 tonnes of butter, we can produce 6 butter-making machines at point *B*. If we produce no butter, we can produce 10 machines at point *C*.

The amount by which our production possibilities expand depends on the resources we devote to technological change and capital accumulation. If we devote no resources to this activity (point *A*), our *PPF* remains at *ABC*—the blue curve in Fig. 2.5. If we cut the current production of butter and produce 6 machines (point *B*), then in the future, we'll have more capital and our *PPF* will rotate outward to the position shown by the red curve. The fewer resources

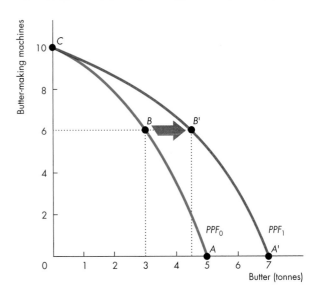

FIGURE 2.5   Economic Growth

PPF_0 shows the limits to the production of butter and butter-making machines, with the production of all other goods and services remaining the same. If we devote no resources to producing butter-making machines and produce 5 tonnes of butter, we remain at point A. But if we decrease butter production to 3 tonnes and produce 6 machines, at point B, our production possibilities expand. After one period, the PPF rotates outward to PPF_1 and we can produce at point B′, a point outside the original PPF. We can rotate the PPF outward, but we cannot avoid opportunity cost. The opportunity cost of producing more butter in the future is less butter today.

we devote to producing butter and the more resources we devote to producing machines, the greater is the expansion of our production possibilities.

Economic growth is not free. To make it happen, we devote resources to producing new machines and less to producing butter. In Fig. 2.5, we move from *A* to *B*. There is no free lunch. The opportunity cost of more butter in the future is less butter today. Also, economic growth is no magic formula for abolishing scarcity. On the new production possibilities frontier, we continue to face a tradeoff and opportunity cost.

The ideas about economic growth that we have explored in the setting of the dairy industry also apply to nations. Let's look at two examples.

Economic Growth in Canada and Hong Kong

If as a nation we devote all our resources to producing consumer goods and none to research and capital accumulation, production possibilities per person will be the same in the future as they are today. To expand our production possibilities in the future, we must devote fewer resources to producing consumption goods and some resources to accumulating capital and developing technologies so that we can produce more consumption goods in the future. The decrease in today's consumption is the opportunity cost of an increase in future consumption.

The experiences of Canada and Hong Kong make a striking example of the effects of our choices on the rate of economic growth. In 1960, the production possibilities per person in Canada were three times those in Hong Kong (see Fig. 2.6). Canada devoted one-fifth of its resources to accumulating capital and the other four-fifths to consumption. In 1960, Canada was at point A on its *PPF*. Hong Kong devoted one-third of its resources to accumulating capital and two-thirds to consumption. In 1960, Hong Kong was at point A on its *PPF*.

Since 1960, both countries have experienced economic growth, but growth in Hong Kong has been more rapid than that in Canada. Because Hong Kong devoted a bigger fraction of its resources to accumulating capital, its production possibilities have expanded more quickly.

By 2000, the production possibilities per person in Hong Kong and Canada were similar. If Hong Kong continues to devote more resources to accumulating capital than we do (at point B on its 2000 *PPF*), it will continue to grow more rapidly than Canada. But if Hong Kong increases consumption and decreases capital accumulation (moving to point D on its 2000 *PPF*), then its rate of economic growth will slow.

Canada is typical of the rich industrial countries, which include the United States, Western Europe, and Japan. Hong Kong is typical of the fast-growing Asian economies, which include Taiwan, Thailand, South Korea, and China. Growth in these countries slowed during the Asia Crisis of 1998 but quickly rebounded. Production possibilities expand in these countries by between 5 percent a year and almost 10 percent a year. If these high growth rates are maintained, these other Asian countries will eventually close the gap on Canada as Hong Kong has done.

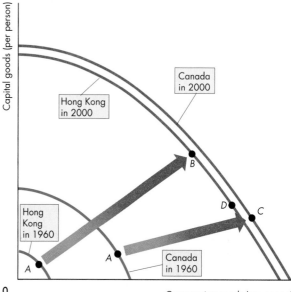

FIGURE 2.6 Economic Growth in Canada and Hong Kong

In 1960, the production possibilities per person in Canada were much larger than those in Hong Kong. But Hong Kong devoted more of its resources to accumulating capital than did Canada, so its production possibilities frontier has shifted outward more quickly than has that of Canada. In 2000, Hong Kong's production possibilities per person were similar to those in Canada.

REVIEW QUIZ

1 What are the two key factors that generate economic growth?
2 How does economic growth influence the production possibilities frontier?
3 What is the opportunity cost of economic growth?
4 Why has Hong Kong experienced faster economic growth than Canada has?

Next, we're going to study another way in which we expand our production possibilities—the amazing fact that *both* buyers and sellers gain from specialization and trade.

Gains from Trade

PEOPLE CAN PRODUCE FOR THEMSELVES ALL THE goods that they consume, or they can concentrate on producing one good (or perhaps a few goods) and then trade with others—exchange some of their own goods for those of others. Concentrating on the production of only one good or a few goods is called *specialization*. We are going to discover how people gain by specializing in the production of the good in which they have a *comparative advantage* and trading with each other.

Comparative Advantage

A person has a **comparative advantage** in an activity if that person can perform the activity at a lower opportunity cost than anyone else. Differences in opportunity costs arise from differences in individual abilities and from differences in the characteristics of other resources.

No one excels at everything. One person is an outstanding pitcher but a poor catcher; another person is a brilliant lawyer but a poor teacher. In almost all human endeavours, what one person does easily, someone else finds difficult. The same applies to land and capital. One plot of land is fertile but has no mineral deposits; another plot of land has outstanding views but is infertile. One machine has great precision but is difficult to operate; another is fast but often breaks down.

Although no one excels at everything, some people excel and can outperform others in many activities. But such a person does not have a *comparative* advantage in each of those activities. For example, Robertson Davies was a better actor than most people. But he was an even better writer. So his *comparative* advantage was in writing.

Because people's abilities and the quality of their resources differ, they have different opportunity costs of producing various goods. Such differences give rise to comparative advantage. Let's explore the idea of comparative advantage by looking at two CD factories: one operated by Tom and the other operated by Nancy.

Tom's Factory To simplify the story quite a lot, suppose that CDs have just two components: a disc and a plastic case. Tom has two production lines: one for discs and one for cases. Figure 2.7 shows Tom's

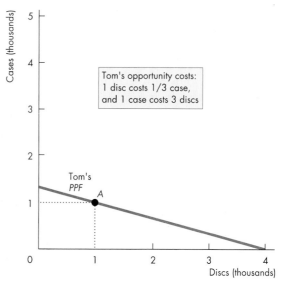

FIGURE 2.7   Production Possibilities in Tom's Factory

Tom's opportunity costs:
1 disc costs 1/3 case, and 1 case costs 3 discs

Tom can produce discs and cases along the production possibilities frontier *PPF*. For Tom, the opportunity cost of 1 disc is 1/3 of a case and the opportunity cost of 1 case is 3 discs. If Tom produces at point *A*, he can produce 1,000 cases and 1,000 discs an hour.

production possibilities frontier for discs and cases. It tells us that if Tom uses all his resources to make discs, he can produce 4,000 discs an hour. The *PPF* in Fig. 2.7 also tells us that if Tom uses all his resources to make cases, he can produce 1,333 cases an hour. But to produce cases, Tom must decrease his production of discs. For each case produced, he must decrease his production of discs by 3. So

Tom's opportunity cost of producing 1 case is 3 discs.

Similarly, if Tom wants to increase his production of discs, he must decrease his production of cases. And for each 1,000 discs produced, he must decrease his production of cases by 333. So

Tom's opportunity cost of producing 1 disc is 0.333 of a case.

Tom's *PPF* is linear because his workers have similar skills so if he reallocates them from one activity to another, he faces a constant opportunity cost.

Nancy's Factory The other factory, operated by Nancy, also produces cases and discs. But Nancy's factory has machines that are custom made for case production, so they are more suitable for producing cases than discs. Also, Nancy's work force is more skilled in making cases.

These differences between the two factories mean that Nancy's production possibilities frontier—shown along with Tom's *PPF* in Fig. 2.8—is different from Tom's. If Nancy uses all her resources to make discs, she can produce 1,333 an hour. If she uses all her resources to make cases, she can produce 4,000 an hour. To produce discs, Nancy must decrease her production of cases. For each 1,000 additional discs produced, she must decrease her production of cases by 3,000. So

Nancy's opportunity cost of producing 1 disc is 3 cases.

Similarly, if Nancy wants to increase her production of cases, she must decrease her production of discs. For each 1,000 additional cases produced, she must decrease her production of discs by 333. So

Nancy's opportunity cost of producing 1 case is 0.333 of a disc.

Suppose that Tom and Nancy produce both discs and cases and that each produces 1,000 discs and 1,000 cases—1,000 CDs—an hour. That is, each produces at point *A* on his or her *PPF*. Total production is 2,000 CDs an hour.

In which of the two goods does Nancy have a comparative advantage? Recall that comparative advantage is a situation in which one person's opportunity cost of producing a good is lower than another person's opportunity cost of producing that same good. Nancy has a comparative advantage in producing cases. Nancy's opportunity cost of producing a case is 0.333 of a disc, whereas Tom's is 3 discs.

You can see Nancy's comparative advantage by looking at the production possibilities frontiers for Nancy and Tom in Fig. 2.8. Nancy's production possibilities frontier is steeper than Tom's. To produce one more case, Nancy must give up fewer discs than Tom has to. Hence Nancy's opportunity cost of producing a case is less than Tom's. Nancy has a comparative advantage in producing cases.

Tom's comparative advantage is in producing discs. His production possibilities frontier is less steep than Nancy's. This means that to produce one more disc, Tom must give up fewer cases than Nancy has to.

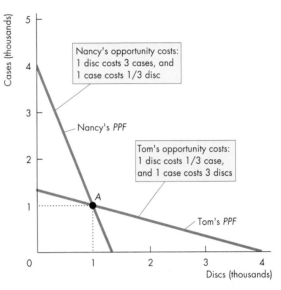

FIGURE 2.8 Comparative Advantage

Along Tom's *PPF*, the opportunity cost of 1 disc is 1/3 of a case and the opportunity cost of 1 case is 3 discs. Along Nancy's *PPF*, the opportunity cost of 1 disc is 3 cases and the opportunity cost of 1 case is 1/3 of a disc. Like Tom, Nancy produces 1,000 cases and 1,000 discs an hour at point *A*. Nancy's opportunity cost of a case is less than Tom's, so Nancy has a comparative advantage in cases. Tom's opportunity cost of a disc is less than Nancy's, so Tom has a comparative advantage in discs.

Tom's opportunity cost of producing a disc is 0.333 of a case, which is less than Nancy's 3 cases per disc. So Tom has a comparative advantage in producing discs.

Because Nancy has a comparative advantage in producing cases and Tom has a comparative advantage in producing discs, they can both gain from specialization and exchange.

Achieving the Gains from Trade

If Tom, who has a comparative advantage in producing discs, puts all his resources into that activity, he can produce 4,000 discs an hour—point *B* on his *PPF*. If Nancy, who has a comparative advantage in producing cases, puts all her resources into that activity, she can produce 4,000 cases an hour—point *B'* on her *PPF*. By specializing, Tom and Nancy together can produce 4,000 cases and 4,000 discs an hour, double the total production they can achieve without specialization.

By specialization and exchange, Tom and Nancy can get *outside* their individual production possibilities frontiers. To achieve the gains from specialization, Tom and Nancy must trade with each other.

Figure 2.9 shows how Tom and Nancy gain from trade. They make the following deal: Tom agrees to increase his production of discs from 1,000 an hour to 4,000 an hour—a move along his *PPF* from point A to point B in Fig. 2.9(a). Nancy agrees to increase her production of cases from 1,000 an hour to 4,000 an hour—a move along her *PPF* from point A to point B' in Fig. 2.9(b).

They also agree to exchange cases and discs at a "price" of one case for one disc. So Tom sells discs to Nancy for one case per disc, and Nancy sells cases to Tom for one disc per case.

With this deal in place, Tom and Nancy exchange along the red "Trade line." They exchange 2,000 cases and 2,000 discs, and each moves to point C (in both parts of the figure). At point C, each has 2,000 discs and 2,000 cases, or 2,000 CDs. So each

now produces 2,000 CDs an hour—double the previous output. This increase in production of 2,000 CDs an hour is the gain from specialization and trade.

Both parties to the trade share the gains. Nancy, who can produce discs at an opportunity cost of 3 cases per disc, can buy discs from Tom at a cost of 1 case per disc. Tom, who can produce cases at an opportunity cost of 3 discs per case, can buy cases from Nancy at a cost of 1 disc per case.

For Nancy, the cost of a disc falls from 3 cases to 1 case. So she gets her discs more cheaply than she can produce them herself. For Tom, the cost of a case falls from 3 discs to 1 disc. So he gets his cases more cheaply than he can produce them himself.

Because both Tom and Nancy obtain the items they buy from the other at a lower cost than that at which they can produce the items themselves, they both gain from specialization and trade.

The gains that Canada achieves from international trade are similar to those achieved by Tom and Nancy in this example. When Canadians buy T-shirts

---

FIGURE 2.9   The Gains from Trade

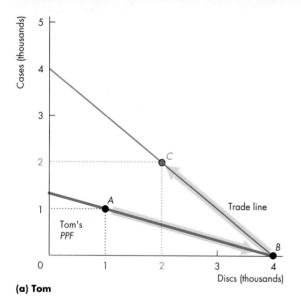

(a) Tom

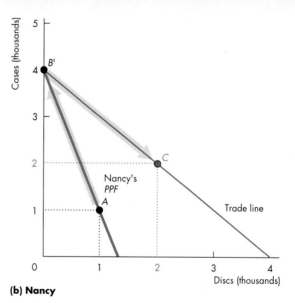

(b) Nancy

Tom and Nancy initially produce at point A on their respective *PPFs*. Tom has a comparative advantage in discs, and Nancy has a comparative advantage in cases. If Tom specializes in discs, he produces at point B on his *PPF*. If Nancy specializes in cases, she produces at point B' on her *PPF*. They exchange cases for discs along the red "Trade

line." Nancy buys discs from Tom for less than her opportunity cost of producing them, and Tom buys cases from Nancy for less than his opportunity cost of producing them. Each goes to point C—a point outside his or her *PPF*—where each produces 2,000 CDs an hour. Tom and Nancy increase production with no change in resources.

from China and when China buys regional jets from Canada, both countries gain. We get our shirts at a lower cost than that at which we can produce them, and China gets its regional jets at a lower cost than that at which it can produce them.

Tom and Nancy are equally productive. Tom can produce the same quantities of discs as Nancy can produce cases. But this equal productivity is not the source of the gains from specialization and trade. The gains arise from comparative advantage and would be available even if one of the trading partners was much more productive than the other. To see that comparative advantage is the source of the gains, let's look at Tom and Nancy when Nancy is much more productive than Tom.

Absolute Advantage

A person has an **absolute advantage** if that person can produce more goods with a given amount of resources than another person can. Absolute advantage arises from differences in productivity. A person who has a better technology or more capital or is more skilled than another person has an absolute advantage. (Absolute advantage also applies to nations.)

The gains from trade arise from *comparative* advantage, so people can gain from trade in the presence of *absolute* advantage. To see how, suppose that Nancy invents and patents a new production process that makes her *four* times as productive as she was before in the production of both cases and discs. With her new technology, Nancy can produce 16,000 cases an hour (4 times the original 4,000) if she puts all her resources into making cases. Alternatively, she can produce 5,332 discs (4 times the original 1,333) if she puts all her resources into making discs. Nancy now has an absolute advantage.

But Nancy's *opportunity cost* of 1 disc is still 3 cases. And this opportunity cost is higher than Tom's. So Nancy can still get discs at a lower cost by exchanging cases for discs with Tom.

In this example, Nancy will no longer produce only cases. With no trade, she would produce 4,000 discs and 4,000 cases. With trade, she will increase her production of cases to 7,000 and decrease her production of discs to 3,000. Tom will produce 4,000 discs and no cases. Tom will provide Nancy with 2,000 discs in exchange for 2,000 cases. So Tom's CD production will increase from 1,000 to 2,000 as before. Nancy's CD production will increase from 4,000 to 5,000.

Both Tom and Nancy have gained 1,000 CDs by taking advantage of comparative advantage, the same gains as before.

The key point to recognize is that even though someone (or some nation) has an absolute advantage, this fact does not destroy comparative advantage.

Dynamic Comparative Advantage

At any given point in time, the resources and technologies available determine the comparative advantages that individuals and nations have. But just by repeatedly producing a particular good or service, people become more productive in that activity, a phenomenon called **learning-by-doing**. Learning-by-doing is the basis of *dynamic* comparative advantage. **Dynamic comparative advantage** is a comparative advantage that a person (or country) possesses as a result of having specialized in a particular activity and, as a result of learning-by-doing, having become the producer with the lowest opportunity cost.

Hong Kong and Singapore are examples of countries that have pursued dynamic comparative advantage vigorously. They have developed industries in which initially they did not have a comparative advantage but, through learning-by-doing, became low opportunity cost producers in those industries. A specific example is the decision to develop a genetic engineering industry in Singapore. Singapore probably did not have a comparative advantage in genetic engineering initially. But it might develop one as its scientists and production workers become more skilled in this activity.

REVIEW QUIZ

1 What gives a person a comparative advantage?
2 Is production still efficient when people specialize?
3 Why do people specialize and trade?
4 What are the gains from specialization and trade?
5 What is the source of the gains from trade?
6 Distinguish between comparative advantage and absolute advantage.
7 How does dynamic comparative advantage arise?

The Market Economy

INDIVIDUALS AND COUNTRIES GAIN BY specializing in the production of those goods and services in which they have a comparative advantage and then trading with each other. Adam Smith identified this source of economic wealth in his *Wealth of Nations,* published in 1776—see p. 54.

To enable billions of people who specialize in producing millions of different goods and services to reap these gains, trade must be organized. But trade need not be *planned* or *managed* by a central authority. In fact, when such an arrangement has been tried, as it was for 60 years in Russia, the result has been less than dazzling.

Trade is organized by using social institutions. Two key social institutions are

- Property rights
- Markets

Property Rights

Property rights are social arrangements that govern the ownership, use, and disposal of resources, goods, and services. *Real property* includes land and buildings—the things we call property in ordinary speech—and durable goods such as factories and equipment. *Financial property* includes stocks and bonds and money in the bank. *Intellectual property* is the intangible product of creative effort. This type of property includes books, music, computer programs, and inventions of all kinds and is protected by copyrights and patents.

If property rights are not enforced, the incentive to specialize and produce the goods in which each person has a comparative advantage is weakened, and some of the potential gains from specialization and trade are lost. If people can easily steal the production of others, then time, energy, and resources are devoted not to production but to protecting possessions.

Property rights evolved because they enable societies to reap the gains from trade. If we had not developed property rights, we would still be hunting and gathering like our Stone Age ancestors.

Even in countries where property rights are well established, such as Canada, protecting intellectual property is proving to be a challenge in the face of modern technologies that make it relatively easy to copy audio and video material, computer programs, and books.

Markets

In ordinary speech, the word *market* means a place where people buy and sell goods such as fish, meat, fruits, and vegetables. In economics, a *market* has a more general meaning. A **market** is any arrangement that enables buyers and sellers to get information and to do business with each other. An example is the market in which oil is bought and sold—the world oil market. The world oil market is not a place. It is the network of oil producers, users, wholesalers, and brokers who buy and sell oil. In the world oil market, decision makers do not meet physically. They make deals throughout the world by telephone, fax, and direct computer link.

Nancy and Tom can get together and do a deal without markets. But for billions of individuals to specialize and trade millions of goods and services, markets are essential. Like property rights, markets have evolved because they facilitate trade. Without organized markets, we would miss out on a substantial part of the potential gains from trade. Enterprising individuals, each one pursuing his or her own goals, have profited from making markets, standing ready to buy or sell the items in which they specialize.

Circular Flows in the Market Economy

Figure 2.10 identifies two types of markets: goods markets and factor markets. *Goods markets* are those in which goods and services are bought and sold. *Factor markets* are those in which factors of production are bought and sold.

Households decide how much of their labour, land, capital, and entrepreneurship to sell or rent in factor markets. Households receive incomes in the form of wages, rent, interest, and profit. Households also decide how to spend their incomes on goods and services produced by firms. Firms decide the quantities of factors of production to hire, how to use them to produce goods and services, what goods and services to produce, and in what quantities to produce them.

Figure 2.10 shows the flows that result from these decisions by households and firms. The red flows are the factors that go from households through factor markets to firms and the goods and services that go from firms through goods markets to households. The green flows in the opposite direction are the payments made in exchange for these items.

How do markets coordinate all these decisions?

FIGURE 2.10 Circular Flows in the Market Economy

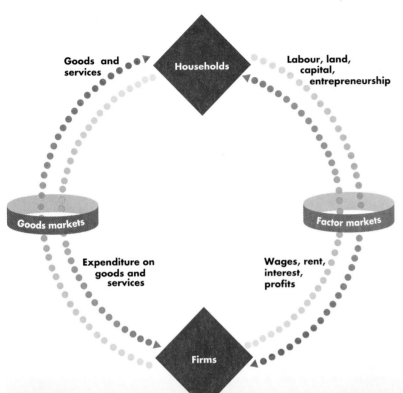

Households and firms make economic choices. Households choose the quantities of labour, land, capital, and entrepreneurship to sell or rent to firms in exchange for wages, rent, interest, and profit. Households also choose how to spend their incomes on the various types of goods and services available. Firms choose the quantities of factors of production to hire and the quantities of the various goods and services to produce. Goods markets and factor markets coordinate these choices of households and firms. Factors of production and goods flow clockwise (red), and money payments flow counterclockwise (green).

Coordinating Decisions

Markets coordinate individual decisions through price adjustments. To see how, think about your local market for hamburgers. Suppose that some people who want to buy hamburgers are not able to do so. To make the choices of buyers and sellers compatible, buyers must scale down their appetites or more hamburgers must be offered for sale (or both must happen). A rise in the price of a hamburger produces this outcome. A higher price encourages producers to offer more hamburgers for sale. It also encourages some people to change their lunch plans. Fewer people buy hamburgers, and more buy hot dogs. More hamburgers (and more hot dogs) are offered for sale.

Alternatively, suppose that more hamburgers are available than people want to buy. In this case, to make the choices of buyers and sellers compatible, more hamburgers must be bought or fewer hamburgers must be offered for sale (or both). A fall in the price of a hamburger achieves this outcome. A lower price encourages firms to produce a smaller quantity of hamburgers. It also encourages people to buy more hamburgers.

REVIEW QUIZ

1 Why are social arrangements such as markets and property rights necessary?
2 What are the main functions of markets?

◆ You have now begun to see how economists approach economic questions. Scarcity, choice, and divergent opportunity costs explain why we specialize and trade and why property rights and markets have developed. You can see all around you the lessons you've learned in this chapter. *Reading Between the Lines* on pp. 48–49 gives an example. It explores the *PPF* of a student like you and the choices that students must make that influence their own economic growth—the growth of their incomes.

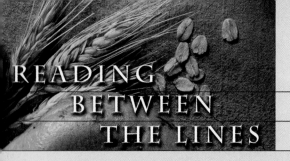

The Cost and Benefit of Education

THE GLOBE AND MAIL, AUGUST 28, 2002

Academics leap to defence of the MBA

They don't come with a guarantee, but business degrees offer students well-paying jobs with reputable companies, say many of Canada's top business schools, throwing cold water on a new study questioning the value of an MBA. ...

After surveying decades of research, Jeffrey Pfeffer and Christina Fong of Stanford's graduate school of business have concluded that, with the possible exception of the most elite programs, master's degrees in business administration teach little that would be of real use in the business world. ...

The salaries for these graduates are a telling story. At Queen's University's School of Business, for example, the average starting salary is $95,000. Before joining the program, the average salary of students is $59,750. And at the Rotman School of Management at the University of Toronto, students entering the two-year program have salaries in the $50,000 on average. But the average starting salary for this year's graduate was $89,000. ...

Brian Bemmels, associate dean for academic programs at the University of British Columbia's faculty of commerce, said the research article forces schools to evaluate their programs. He added that the article is based on a lot of opinion.

UBC's business school made a major change in 1995, restructuring its MBA program and reducing it to 15 months from two years to minimize losses of income to students. The average age of students in the program is 31.

Mr. Bemmels said the demand for an MBA degree speaks for itself. UBC had well over 700 applicants for 100 seats this year. Only 17 per cent of the incoming class has a business degree, he said. The rest are graduates of medicine, engineering and general arts.

"All these people wouldn't be doing it if they didn't think it was valuable," Mr. Bemmels said.

"I don't believe the notion that they have been fooled and tricked into something that's no good to them," he added.

Reprinted with permission from *The Globe and Mail.*

Essence of the Story

■ Jeffrey Pfeffer and Christina Fong of the Stanford Graduate School of Business say that MBA programs teach little of use in the business world.

■ The salaries earned by MBA graduates tell a different story.

■ The average starting salary for an MBA is $95,000, up from $59,750 before the MBA.

■ At the Rotman School of Management at the University of Toronto, students entering the two-year program have an average salary of $50,000 and an average starting salary of $89,000 after graduation.

■ Brian Bemmels said the UBC business school had over 700 applicants for 100 places and most were graduates of medicine, engineering, and general arts.

Economic Analysis

■ Education increases human capital and expands production possibilities.

■ The opportunity cost of a degree is forgone consumption. The payoff is an increase in lifetime production possibilities.

■ Figure 1 shows the choices facing a high school graduate who can consume education goods and services and consumption goods and services on the blue *PPF*.

■ Working full time, this person can consume at point *A* on the blue *PPF* in Fig. 1.

■ By attending university, the student moves from point *A* to point *B* along her *PPF*, forgoes current consumption (the opportunity cost of education), and increases the use of educational goods and services.

■ On graduating from university, earnings jump so production possibilities expand to the red *PPF* in Fig. 1.

■ Figure 2 shows a university graduate's choices. The blue curve is the same *PPF* as the red *PPF* in Fig. 1.

■ Working full time, this person earns enough to consume at point *C* on the blue *PPF* in Fig. 2.

■ By pursuing an MBA, the student moves from point *C* to point *D* along her *PPF*, forgoes current consumption (the opportunity cost of an MBA), and increases the use of educational goods and services.

■ With an MBA, a person's earnings jump again, so production possibilities expand to the red *PPF* in Fig. 2.

■ For people who have the required ability, the benefits of post-secondary and post-graduate education exceed the costs.

You're The Voter

■ The Canada Millennium Scholarship Foundation, funded by the federal government, provides $4,000 a year to 900 young Canadians.

■ Do you think the Canada Millennium Scholarship Foundation should be expanded so that more students can benefit from it?

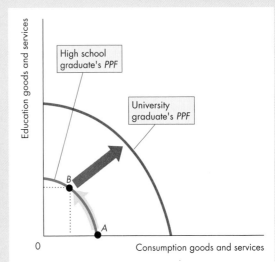

Figure 1 High school graduate's choices

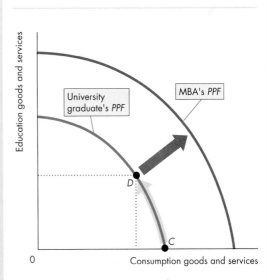

Figure 2 University graduate's choices

■ With the huge return from post-secondary and post-graduate education, why don't more people remain in school for longer?

■ Would you vote for or against a tax increase to provide greater funding for the Canada Millennium Scholarship Foundation? Why?

SUMMARY

KEY POINTS

Production Possibilities and Opportunity Cost (pp. 34–36)

- The production possibilities frontier, *PPF*, is the boundary between production levels that are attainable and those that are not attainable when all the available resources are used to their limit.
- Production efficiency occurs at points on the *PPF*.
- Along the *PPF*, the opportunity cost of producing more of one good is the amount of the other good that must be given up.
- The opportunity cost of all goods increases as the production of the good increases.

Using Resources Efficiently (pp. 37–39)

- The marginal cost of a good is the opportunity cost of producing one more unit.
- The marginal benefit from a good is the maximum amount of another good that a person is willing to forgo to obtain more of the first good.
- The marginal benefit of a good decreases as the amount available increases.
- Resources are used efficiently when the marginal cost of each good is equal to its marginal benefit.

Economic Growth (pp. 40–41)

- Economic growth, which is the expansion of production possibilities, results from capital accumulation and technological change.
- The opportunity cost of economic growth is forgone current consumption.

Gains from Trade (pp. 42–45)

- A person has a comparative advantage in producing a good if that person can produce the good at a lower opportunity cost than everyone else.
- People gain by specializing in the activity in which they have a comparative advantage and trading with others.
- Dynamic comparative advantage arises from learning-by-doing.

The Market Economy (pp. 46–47)

- Property rights and markets enable people to gain from specialization and trade.
- Markets coordinate decisions and help to allocate resources to *higher* valued uses.

KEY FIGURES

KEY TERMS

PROBLEMS

*1. Use the figure to calculate Wendell's opportunity cost of one hour of tennis when he increases the time he plays tennis from
a. 4 to 6 hours a week.
b. 6 to 8 hours a week.

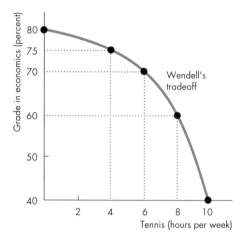

2. Use the figure to calculate Tina's opportunity cost of a day of skiing when she increases her time spent skiing from
a. 2 to 4 days a month.
b. 4 to 6 days a month.

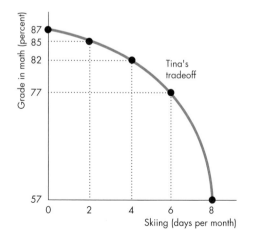

*3. In problem 1, describe the relationship between the time Wendell spends playing tennis and the opportunity cost of an hour of tennis.

4. In problem 2, describe the relationship between the time Tina spends skiing and the opportunity cost of a day of skiing.

*5. Wendell, in problem 1, has the following marginal benefit curve:

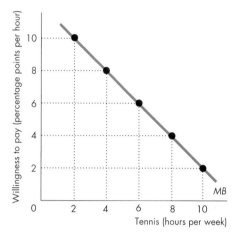

a. If Wendell is efficient, what is his grade?
b. Why would Wendell be worse off getting a higher grade?

6. Tina, in problem 2, has the following marginal benefit curve:

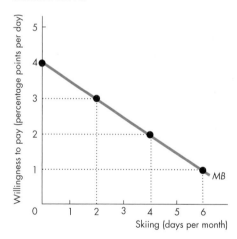

a. If Tina is efficient, how much does she ski?
b. Why would Tina be worse off spending more days a month skiing?

*7. Sunland's production possibilities are

Food (kilograms per month)		Sunscreen (litres per month)
300	and	0
200	and	50
100	and	100
0	and	150

a. Draw a graph of Sunland's production possibilities frontier.

b. What are Sunland's opportunity costs of producing food and sunscreen at each output?

8. Jane's Island's production possibilities are

Corn (kilograms per month)		Cloth (metres per month)
6	and	0
4	and	2
2	and	4
0	and	6

a. Draw a graph of the *PPF* on Jane's Island.
b. What are Jane's opportunity costs of producing corn and cloth at each output in the table?

*9. In problem 7, to get a litre of sunscreen, the people of Sunland are willing to give up: 5 kilograms of food if they have 25 litres of sunscreen; 2 kilograms of food if they have 75 litres of sunscreen; and 1 kilogram of food if they have 125 litres of sunscreen.
a. Draw a graph of Sunland's marginal benefit from sunscreen.
b. What is the efficient quantity of sunscreen?

10. In problem 8, to get a metre of cloth, Jane is willing to give up: 1.5 kilograms of corn if she has 2 metres of cloth; 1.0 kilogram of corn if she has 4 metres of cloth; and 0.5 kilograms of corn if she has 6 metres of cloth.
a. Draw a graph of Jane's marginal benefit from cloth.
b. What is Jane's efficient quantity of cloth?

*11. Busyland's production possibilities are

Food (kilograms per month)		Sunscreen (litres per month)
150	and	0
100	and	100
50	and	200
0	and	300

Calculate Busyland's opportunity costs of food and sunscreen at each output in the table.

12. Joe's Island's production possibilities are

Corn (kilograms per month)		Cloth (metres per month)
12	and	0
8	and	1
4	and	2
0	and	3

What are Joe's opportunity costs of producing corn and cloth at each output in the table?

*13. In problems 7 and 11, Sunland and Busyland each produce and consume 100 kilograms of food and 100 litres of sunscreen per month, and they do not trade. Now the countries begin to trade with each other.
a. What good does Sunland sell to Busyland, and what good does it buy from Busyland?
b. If Sunland and Busyland divide the total output of food and sunscreen equally, what are the gains from trade?

14. In problems 8 and 12, Jane's Island and Joe's Island each produce and consume 4 kilograms of corn and 2 metres of cloth and they do not trade. Now the islands begin to trade.
a. What good does Jane sell to Joe and what good does Jane buy from Joe?
b. If Jane and Joe divide the total output of corn and cloth equally, what are the gains from trade?

CRITICAL THINKING

1. After you have studied *Reading Between the Lines* on pp. 48–49, answer the following questions:
a. At what point on the blue *PPF* in Fig. 1 on p. 49 is the combination of education goods and services and consumption goods and services efficient? Explain your answer.
b. Students are facing rising tuition. How does higher tuition change the opportunity cost of education and how does it change the *PPF*s in Fig. 1 and Fig. 2?
c. Who receives the benefits from education? Is the marginal cost of education equal to the marginal benefit of education? Is resource use in the market for education efficient?

WEB EXERCISES

1. Use the links on the Parkin–Bade Web site and obtain data on the tuition and other costs of enrolling in the MBA program of a school that interests you. If an MBA graduate can earn as much as the amounts reported in the news article in *Reading Between the Lines* on pp. 48–49, does the marginal benefit of an MBA exceed its marginal cost? Why doesn't everyone get an MBA?

Your Economic Revolution

You are making progress in your study of economics. You've already encountered the big questions and big ideas of economics. And you've learned about the key insight of Adam Smith, the founder of economics: specialization and exchange create economic wealth. ◆ You are studying economics at a time that future historians will call the *Information Revolution*. We reserve the word "Revolution" for big events that influence all future generations. ◆ During the *Agricultural Revolution*, which occurred 10,000 years ago, people learned to domesticate animals and plant crops. They stopped roaming in search of food and settled in villages and eventually towns and cities, where they developed markets in which to exchange their products. ◆ During the *Industrial Revolution*, which began 240 years ago, people used science to create new technologies. This revolution brought extraordinary wealth for some but created conditions in which others were left behind. It brought social and political tensions that we still face today. ◆ During today's *Information Revolution*, people who embraced the new technologies prospered on an unimagined scale. But the incomes and living standards of the less educated are falling behind, and social and political tensions are increasing. Today's revolution has a global dimension. Some of the winners live in previously poor countries in Asia, and some of the losers live here in North America. ◆ So you are studying economics at an interesting time. Whatever *your* motivation is for studying economics, *our* objective is to help you do well in your course, to enjoy it, and to develop a deeper understanding of the economic world around you. ◆ There are three reasons why we hope that we both succeed: First, a decent understanding of economics will help you to become a full participant in the Information Revolution. Second, an understanding of economics will help you play a more effective role as a citizen and voter and enable you to add your voice to those who are looking for solutions to our social and political problems. Third, you will enjoy the sheer fun of *understanding* the forces at play and how they are shaping our world. ◆ If you are finding economics interesting, think seriously about majoring in the subject. A degree in economics gives the best training available in problem solving, offers lots of opportunities to develop conceptual skills, and opens doors to a wide range of graduate courses, including the MBA, and to a wide range of jobs. You can read more about the benefits of an economics degree in the essay by Robert Whaples and Harvey King in the *Study Guide*. ◆ Economics was born during the Industrial Revolution. We'll look at its birth and meet its founder, Adam Smith. Then we'll talk about the progress that economists have made and some of the outstanding policy problems of today with one of today's most distinguished economists, Lawrence H. Summers, President of Harvard University.

PROBING THE IDEAS
The Sources of Economic Wealth

ADAM SMITH *was a giant of a scholar who contributed to ethics and jurisprudence as well as economics. Born in 1723 in Kirkcaldy, a small fishing town near Edinburgh, Scotland, Smith was the only child of the town's customs officer (who died before Adam was born).*

His first academic appointment, at age 28, was as Professor of Logic at the University of Glasgow. He subsequently became tutor to a wealthy Scottish duke, whom he accompanied on a two-year grand European tour, following which he received a pension of £300 a year—ten times the average income at that time.

With the financial security of his pension, Smith devoted ten years to writing An Inquiry into the Nature and Causes of The Wealth of Nations, *which was published in 1776. Many people had written on economic issues before Adam Smith, but he made economics a science. Smith's account was so broad and authoritative that no subsequent writer on economics could advance ideas without tracing their connections to those of Adam Smith.*

"It is not from the benevolence of the butcher, the brewer, or the baker that we expect our dinner, but from their regard to their own interests."

ADAM SMITH
The Wealth of Nations

Why are some nations wealthy while others are poor? This question lies at the heart of economics. And it leads directly to a second question: What can poor nations do to become wealthy?

Adam Smith, who is regarded by many scholars as the founder of economics, attempted to answer these questions in his book *The Wealth of Nations*, published in 1776. Smith was pondering these questions at the height of the Industrial Revolution. During these years, new technologies were invented and applied to the manufacture of cotton and wool cloth, iron, transportation, and agriculture.

Smith wanted to understand the sources of economic wealth, and he brought his acute powers of observation and abstraction to bear on the question. His answer:

- The division of labour
- Free markets

The division of labour—breaking tasks down into simple tasks and becoming skilled in those tasks—is the source of "the greatest improvement in the productive powers of labour," said Smith. The division of labour became even more productive when it was applied to creating new technologies. Scientists and engineers, trained in extremely narrow fields, became specialists at inventing. Their powerful skills accelerated the advance of technology, so by the 1820s, machines could make consumer goods faster and more accurately than any craftsman could. And by the 1850s, machines could make other machines that labour alone could never have made.

But, said Smith, the fruits of the division of labour are limited by the extent of the market. To make the market as large as possible, there must be no impediments to free trade both within a country and among countries. Smith argued that when each person makes the best possible economic choice, that choice leads as if by "an invisible hand" to the best outcome for society as a whole. The butcher, the brewer, and the baker each pursue their own interests but, in doing so, also serve the interests of everyone else.

THEN

Adam Smith speculated that one person, working hard, using the hand tools available in the 1770s, might possibly make 20 pins a day. Yet, he observed, by using those same hand tools but breaking the process into a number of individually small operations in which people specialize—by the **division of labour**—ten people could make a staggering 48,000 pins a day. One draws out the wire, another straightens it, a third cuts it, a fourth points it, a fifth grinds it. Three specialists make the head, and a fourth attaches it. Finally, the pin is polished and packaged. But a large market is needed to support the division of labour: One factory employing ten workers would need to sell more that 15 million pins a year to stay in business.

NOW

If Adam Smith were here today, the computer chip would fascinate him. He would see it as an extraordinary example of the productivity of the division of labour and of the use of machines to make machines that make other machines. From a design of a chip's intricate circuits, cameras transfer an image to glass plates that work like stencils. Workers prepare silicon wafers on which the circuits are printed. Some slice the wafers, others polish them, others bake them, and yet others coat them with a light-sensitive chemical. Machines transfer a copy of the circuit onto the wafer. Chemicals then etch the design onto the wafer. Further processes deposit atom-sized transistors and aluminum connectors. Finally, a laser separates the hundreds of chips on the wafers. Every stage in the process of creating a computer chip uses other computer chips. And like the pin of the 1770s, the computer chip of today benefits from the large market—a global market—to buy chips in the huge quantities in which they are produced efficiently.

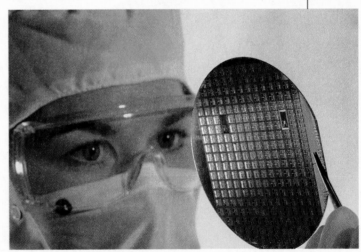

Many economists have worked on the big themes that Adam Smith began. One of these is Lawrence H. Summers, President of Harvard University and distinguished economist.

TALKING WITH

LAWRENCE H. SUMMERS

is President of Harvard University. Born in 1954 in New Haven, Connecticut, into a family of distinguished economists, he was an undergraduate at the Massachusetts Institute of Technology and a graduate student at Harvard University. While still in his 20s, he became one of the youngest tenured economics professors at Harvard University. In Washington, he has held a succession of public service jobs at the World Bank and in the U.S. government, culminating in 1999 with his appointment as Secretary of the Treasury—the chief financial officer of the United States and the president's highest-ranking adviser.

Lawrence H. Summers

Dr. Summers's research has covered an enormous range of macroeconomic and public policy issues that include capital taxation, unemployment, global financial crises, the transition to a market economy in Eastern Europe, and the problem of speeding progress in the developing countries.

Michael Parkin and Robin Bade talked with Lawrence Summers about his career and the progress that economists have made since the pioneering days of Adam Smith.

How does Adam Smith's assessment of the "nature and causes of the wealth of nations" look today in light of the lessons that economists have learned over the past two centuries?

Adam Smith is looking very good today. I think one of the most important insights of the social sciences of the last several centuries is Smith's idea that good things can come from the invisible hand—from decentralization rather than from central planning and direction. But Smith is also prescient in recognizing the various qualifications to the argument for the invisible hand, whether involving fairness, externalities, or monopoly.

What do we know today that Adam Smith didn't know?

We know today much more than Smith did about economic fluctuations and about the role of money—about what we today call macroeconomics. We know more today about economic situations that involve bargaining, whether between two individuals or between small numbers of firms in an industry, or between a buyer and a seller. We know much more today about markets without perfect information. I know how good my used car is when I sell it—you don't when you buy it. I know whether I'm sick when I buy medical insurance, but you the insurance company have to try to figure it out. The role of information in markets, which turns out to be quite profound, is something we understand much better today. And we also understand much better today the role of politics and governments in shaping the economy, which is far larger than it was in Smith's day.

Coincidentally, a few weeks before we're holding this conversation, a new nation was born—East Timor. What advice can economists offer a new and extremely poor nation as it takes its first steps?

Much of economic success involves strong rights to property. Has anyone ever washed a rented car or taken as good care of their hotel room as their home? When people own their farmlands, they're much more likely to farm them sustainably. When businesses own their machinery, they're much more likely to take care of it. When individuals own what they produce, they're much more likely to work hard.

Strong property rights and the framework of laws that support them are profoundly important to the market-based exchanges that are essential to economic success. So also is stable money that can be a basis for exchange. So also is an educated and capable population. But if there is a single lesson that is important for a starting economy, it is that strong property rights can motivate individuals.

One lesson that we've learned from your work at the World Bank is that the return to educating girls in developing countries is very high. What did you discover in that work?

Primary education, and especially for girls, may be the highest return investment available in the developing world. Those who read produce more and therefore earn more. Girls who are educated grow up to be better mothers who have smaller, happier, healthier families. Women who are educated are empowered with greater career options. They are less likely to fall into prostitution, and that reduces the spread of AIDS. Women who are educated are much more likely to take care of the environment. So it is in many respects that primary education, and especially that of girls, generates very large returns.

Are there any other activities that yield comparable returns for developing countries?

Maybe some investments in health care that generate very large returns—it's a difficult evaluation to make. The really crucial lesson is that a country's most precious assets are its people, and investments in people are likely to be the most important investments of all.

"The really crucial lesson is that a country's most precious assets are its people, and investments in people are likely to be the most important investments of all."

Some of your earliest research was on taxing the income from capital. Why isn't the income from capital just like the income from labour?

Think about it this way: two individuals both earn a hundred dollars. One spends it all this year; the other saves half of it and earns 10 percent interest next year. Who should pay more total taxes? Plausibly, for fairness, both should pay the same tax. A tax on income will lead to the same taxes in the first year for the two individuals; and higher taxes in the second year for the individual who saved.

In effect, taxes on capital income are taxes on future consumption, and it is far from clear why a society should want to tax future consumption more highly than present consumption.

On the other hand, very large fortunes often show up as capital income, and so designing a workable and fair tax system that doesn't tax investment income is something that is very difficult to do.

Would you say that we have not yet managed to figure this one out?

We'll all be working on finding the best tax systems for a long time to come. And it may mean that the income tax is, as Churchill said of democracy, terrible but the best alternative.

The United States has a large and persistent current account deficit, a low personal saving rate, and a projected deficit in the Social Security and Medicare trust funds. Are you concerned about these problems?

Herb Stein, who was a leading American policy economist, once said that the unsustainable cannot be sustained and must surely end!

This is a concern, given that U.S. national debt to foreigners is rising faster than U.S. income. And it's a concern in terms of the financing of Social Security and Medicare as our population ages. In a way, the solution to both these problems is more American saving, because that will put us in a stronger position as our population ages, and will allow us to have investments in the United States without incurring debts to foreigners.

Probably the most potent way of increasing a country's national savings is to improve the position of its budget. Whether to increase taxes or cut expenditures is a judgment for the congress to debate. My guess is that some combination would be appropriate. There are aspects of expenditures that are going to be hard to control. On the other hand, there are other aspects in terms of transfer payments and in terms of various subsidies where economies probably are possible. And one virtue of a strong fiscal position is that it reduces interest expense down the road.

Did you always want to be an economist? How did you choose economics?

I thought I would be a mathematician or a physicist, but found myself very interested in questions of public policy. I was very involved in debate when I was in college. So I found myself wanting very much to combine an interest in public policy issues with an analytical approach, and economics gave me a way to do that. I also found that I had some aptitude, relative to my aptitude for pure mathematics or physics, so I gravitated to economics.

What led a brilliant academic economist to Washington? What did you want to achieve?

I hoped to put to use some of what I had learned in my studies in a direct way and to enhance my understanding of the way actual economies work by seeing how the policy process operated. I had a great time in Washington and feel that my economics training made a huge difference in everything I did. Whether it was thinking about how to respond to the Mexican and Asian financial crises or working on financial deregulation. Whether it was choosing optimal investments for the Customs Department in protecting our borders or designing tax incentives to promote saving. Whether it was supporting the protection of the Social Security trust fund or thinking about enforcement policies against corporate tax shelters. Principles of economics—in terms of maximizing benefits relative to costs, in terms of always thinking of the margin, in terms of always recognizing the opportunity cost of choices taken, in terms of always needing to see things add up—was quite valuable.

And what insights does economics bring to the task of running a major university?

I came to Harvard because I thought after my time in government the two most important resources that were going to shape the economies of the future were leaders and new ideas, and those are the two things that a university produces.

Successful leadership in a university is all about what economists think about all the time—incentives—whether it's for professors to do a good job teaching, attracting the best scholars in a particular area, or motivating concern and research about the most important problems.

Leadership and management for the university are very much about economics because they're very much about incentives. Some of them are pecuniary and involve money, but other incentives come from people's feelings of being appreciated; they come from the teams in which people have an opportunity to work; they come from the way in which the university is organized. If working at the treasury was heavily about applied macroeconomics, leadership in the university is heavily about applied microeconomics.

What is your advice to a student who is just setting out to become an economist? What other subjects work well with economics?

The best advice to students is, don't be a commodity that's available in a perfectly competitive market. Stand out by developing your own distinctive expertise in something you care deeply about. It matters much less what it is and much more that it be yours and it not be a hundred other people's.

I think there is enormous potential in almost every area of economics, but I think that the people who will contribute the most to economics over the next quarter century will be those who have some keen understanding of the context in which economics is playing out—the international context, the technological context, and the political context. So my hope would be that those interested in economics would understand that economics is very different from physics in that it is tracking a changing reality and that in order to do the best economics in a given period, you have to be able to track that changing reality, and that means understanding international, technological, and political contexts.

DEMAND AND SUPPLY — CHAPTER 3

Slide, Rocket, and Roller Coaster

Slide, rocket, and roller coaster—Canada's Wonderland rides? No, they are commonly used descriptions of price changes. ◆ The price of a personal computer took a dramatic slide from around $3,000 in 2000 to around $700 in 2001. What caused this price slide? We'll answer this question in *Reading Between the Lines*. ◆ Occasionally, a price will rocket. But a price rocket, like a satellite-launching rocket, has a limited life. It eventually runs out of fuel. One spectacular price rocket occurred when the price of coffee shot skyward from $1.32 a kilogram in 1993 to $4.95 a kilogram in 1994. Why did the price of coffee rise so spectacularly? ◆ Over longer periods, the price of coffee, along with the prices of bananas and other agricultural commodities, rises and falls like a roller coaster ride. ◆ Economics is about the choices people make to cope with scarcity. These choices are guided by costs and benefits and are coordinated through markets. ◆ Demand and supply is the tool that explains how markets work. It is the main tool of economics. It is used to study the price of a CD, wage rates and jobs, rents and housing, pollution, crime, consumer protection, education, welfare, the value of money, and interest rates.

◆ Your careful study of this topic will bring big rewards both in your further study of economics and in your everyday life. When you have completed your study of demand and supply, you will be able to explain how prices are determined and make predictions about price slides, rockets, and roller coasters. Once you understand demand and supply, you will view the world through new eyes.

After studying this chapter, you will be able to

■ Describe a market and explain the link between price and opportunity cost

■ Explain the influences on demand

■ Explain the influences on supply

■ Explain how demand and supply determine prices and quantities bought and sold

■ Use demand and supply to make predictions about changes in prices and quantities

Markets and Prices

WHEN YOU NEED A NEW PAIR OF RUNNING shoes, want a bagel and a latte, plan to upgrade your stereo system, or fly to Florida for the winter break, you must find someone who is selling these items or offering these services. You will find them in a *market*. You learned in Chapter 2 (p. 46) that a market is any arrangement that enables buyers and sellers to get information and to do business with each other.

A market has two sides: buyers and sellers. There are markets for *goods* such as apples and hiking boots, for *services* such as haircuts and tennis lessons, for *factors of production* such as computer programmers and earthmovers, and for other manufactured *inputs* such as memory chips and auto parts. There are also markets for money such as Japanese yen and for financial securities such as Yahoo! stock. Only our imagination limits what can be traded in markets.

Some markets are physical places where buyers and sellers meet and where an auctioneer or a broker helps to determine the prices. Examples of this type of market are the New York Stock Exchange and the wholesale fish, meat, and produce markets.

Some markets are groups of people spread around the world who never meet and know little about each other but are connected through the Internet or by telephone and fax. Examples of this type of market are the e-commerce markets and currency markets.

But most markets are unorganized collections of buyers and sellers. You do most of your trading in this type of market. An example is the market for running shoes. The buyers in this vast international market are the millions of joggers (or those who want to make a fashion statement) who are looking for a new pair of shoes. The sellers are the tens of thousands of retail sports equipment and footwear stores. Each buyer can visit several different stores, and each seller knows that the buyer has a choice of stores.

Markets vary in the intensity of competition that buyers and sellers face. In this chapter, we're going to study a **competitive market**—a market that has many buyers and many sellers, so that no single buyer or seller can influence the price.

Producers offer items for sale only if the price is high enough to cover their opportunity cost. And consumers respond to changing opportunity cost by seeking cheaper alternatives to expensive items.

We are going to study the way people respond to *prices* and the forces that determine prices. But to pursue these tasks, we need to understand the relationship between a price and an opportunity cost.

In everyday life, the *price* of an object is the number of dollars that must be given up in exchange for it. Economists refer to this price as the *money price*.

The *opportunity cost* of an action is the highest-valued alternative forgone. If, when you buy a coffee, the highest-valued thing you forgo is some gum, then the opportunity cost of the coffee is the *quantity* of gum forgone. We can calculate the quantity of gum forgone from the money prices of coffee and gum.

If the money price of coffee is $1 a cup and the money price of gum is 50¢ a pack, then the opportunity cost of one cup of coffee is two packs of gum. To calculate this opportunity cost, we divide the price of a cup of coffee by the price of a pack of gum and find the *ratio* of one price to the other. The ratio of one price to another is called a **relative price,** and a *relative price is an opportunity cost.*

We can express the relative price of coffee in terms of gum or any other good. The normal way of expressing a relative price is in terms of a "basket" of all goods and services. To calculate this relative price, we divide the money price of a good by the money price of a "basket" of all goods (called a *price index*). The resulting relative price tells us the opportunity cost of an item in terms of how much of the "basket" we must give up to buy it.

The theory of demand and supply that we are about to study determines *relative prices,* and the word "price" means *relative* price. When we predict that a price will fall, we do not mean that its *money* price will fall—although it might. We mean that its *relative* price will fall. That is, its price will fall *relative* to the average price of other goods and services.

1   What is the distinction between a money price and a relative price?
2   Why is a relative price an opportunity cost?
3   Can you think of an example of a good whose money price and relative price have risen?
4   Can you think of an example of a good whose money price and relative price have fallen?

Let's begin our study of demand and supply, starting with demand.

Demand

IF YOU DEMAND SOMETHING, THEN YOU

1. Want it,
2. Can afford it, and
3. Have made a definite plan to buy it.

Wants are the unlimited desires or wishes that people have for goods and services. How many times have you thought that you would like something "if only you could afford it" or "if it weren't so expensive"? Scarcity guarantees that many—perhaps most—of our wants will never be satisfied. Demand reflects a decision about which wants to satisfy.

The **quantity demanded** of a good or service is the amount that consumers plan to buy during a given time period at a particular price. The quantity demanded is not necessarily the same as the quantity actually bought. Sometimes the quantity demanded exceeds the amount of goods available, so the quantity bought is less than the quantity demanded.

The quantity demanded is measured as an amount per unit of time. For example, suppose that you buy one cup of coffee a day. The quantity of coffee that you demand can be expressed as 1 cup per day, 7 cups per week, or 365 cups per year. Without a time dimension, we cannot tell whether the quantity demanded is large or small.

What Determines Buying Plans?

The amount of any particular good or service that consumers plan to buy depends on many factors. The main ones are

1. The price of the good
2. The prices of related goods
3. Expected future prices
4. Income
5. Population
6. Preferences

We first look at the relationship between the quantity demanded and the price of a good. To study this relationship, we keep all other influences on consumers' planned purchases the same and ask: How does the quantity demanded of the good vary as its price varies, other things remaining the same?

The Law of Demand

The **law of demand** states

Other things remaining the same, the higher the price of a good, the smaller is the quantity demanded.

Why does a higher price reduce the quantity demanded? For two reasons:

- Substitution effect
- Income effect

Substitution Effect When the price of a good rises, other things remaining the same, its *relative* price—its opportunity cost—rises. Although each good is unique, it has *substitutes*—other goods that can be used in its place. As the opportunity cost of a good rises, people buy less of that good and more of its substitutes.

Income Effect When a price rises and all other influences on buying plans remain unchanged, the price rises *relative* to people's incomes. So faced with a higher price and an unchanged income, people cannot afford to buy all the things they previously bought. They must decrease the quantities demanded of at least some goods and services, and normally, the good whose price has increased will be one of the goods that people buy less of.

To see the substitution effect and the income effect at work, think about the effects of a change in the price of a recordable compact disc—a CD-R. Several different goods are substitutes for a CD-R. For example, an audiotape and prerecorded CD provide services similar to those of a CD-R.

Suppose that a CD-R initially sells for $3 and then its price falls to $1.50. People now substitute CD-Rs for audiotapes and prerecorded CDs—the substitution effect. And with a budget that now has some slack from the lower price of a CD-R, people buy more CD-Rs—the income effect. The quantity of CD-Rs demanded increases for these two reasons.

Now suppose that a CD-R initially sells for $3 and then the price doubles to $6. People now substitute prerecorded CDs and audiotapes for CD-Rs—the substitution effect. And faced with a tighter budget, people buy fewer CD-Rs—the income effect. The quantity of CD-Rs demanded decreases for these two reasons.

Demand Curve and Demand Schedule

You are now about to study one of the two most used curves in economics: the demand curve. And you are going to encounter one of the most critical distinctions: the distinction between *demand* and *quantity demanded*.

The term **demand** refers to the entire relationship between the price of the good and the quantity demanded of the good. Demand is illustrated by the demand curve and the demand schedule. The term *quantity demanded* refers to a point on a demand curve—the quantity demanded at a particular price.

Figure 3.1 shows the demand curve for CD-Rs. A **demand curve** shows the relationship between the quantity demanded of a good and its price when all other influences on consumers' planned purchases remain the same.

The table in Fig. 3.1 is the demand schedule for CD-Rs. A *demand schedule* lists the quantities demanded at each price when all other influences on consumers' planned purchases—prices of related goods, expected future prices, income, population, and preferences—remain the same. For example, if the price of a CD-R is 50¢, the quantity demanded is 9 million a week. If the price is $2.50, the quantity demanded is 2 million a week. The other rows of the table show the quantities demanded at prices of $1.00, $1.50, and $2.00.

We graph the demand schedule as a demand curve with the quantity demanded of CD-Rs on the *x*-axis and the price of a CD-R on the *y*-axis. The points on the demand curve labelled *A* through *E* represent the rows of the demand schedule. For example, point *A* represents a quantity demanded of 9 million CD-Rs a week at a price of 50¢ a disc.

Willingness and Ability to Pay Another way of looking at the demand curve is as a willingness-and-ability-to-pay curve. And the willingness-and-ability-to-pay is a measure of *marginal benefit*.

If a small quantity is available, the highest price that someone is willing and able to pay for one more unit is high. But as the quantity available increases, the marginal benefit of each additional unit falls and the highest price that someone is willing and able to pay also falls along the demand curve.

In Fig. 3.1, if only 2 million CD-Rs are available each week, the highest price that someone is willing to pay for the 2 millionth CD-R is $2.50. But if 9 million CD-Rs are available each week, someone is willing to pay 50¢ for the last CD-R bought.

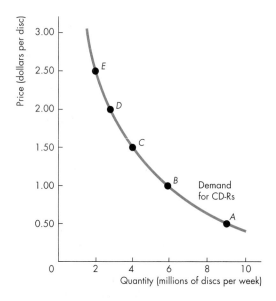

FIGURE 3.1   The Demand Curve

	Price (dollars per disc)	Quantity demanded (millions of discs per week)
A	0.50	9
B	1.00	6
C	1.50	4
D	2.00	3
E	2.50	2

The table shows a demand schedule for CD-Rs. At a price of 50¢ a disc, 9 million a week are demanded; at a price of $1.50 a disc, 4 million a week are demanded. The demand curve shows the relationship between quantity demanded and price, everything else remaining the same. The demand curve slopes downward: As price decreases, the quantity demanded increases.

The demand curve can be read in two ways. For a given price, the demand curve tells us the quantity that people plan to buy. For example, at a price of $1.50 a disc, the quantity demanded is 4 million discs a week. For a given quantity, the demand curve tells us the maximum price that consumers are willing and able to pay for the last disc available. For example, the maximum price that consumers will pay for the 6 millionth disc is $1.00.

A Change in Demand

When any factor that influences buying plans other than the price of the good changes, there is a **change in demand**. Figure 3.2 illustrates an increase in demand. When demand increases, the demand curve shifts rightward and the quantity demanded is greater at each and every price. For example, at $2.50 a disc, the quantity demanded on the original (blue) demand curve is 2 million discs a week. On the new (red) demand curve, the quantity demanded is 6 million discs a week. Look at the numbers in the table and check that the quantity demanded is greater at each price.

Let's look at the factors that bring a change in demand. There are five key factors to consider.

1. Prices of Related Goods The quantity of CD-Rs that consumers plan to buy depends in part on the prices of substitutes for CD-Rs. A **substitute** is a good that can be used in place of another good. For example, a bus ride is a substitute for a train ride; a hamburger is a substitute for a hot dog; and a prerecorded CD is a substitute for a CD-R. If the price of a substitute for a CD-R rises, people buy less of the substitute and more CD-Rs. For example, if the price of a prerecorded CD rises, people buy fewer CDs and more CD-Rs. The demand for CD-Rs increases.

The quantity of CD-Rs that people plan to buy also depends on the prices of complements with CD-Rs. A **complement** is a good that is used in conjunction with another good. Hamburgers and fries are complements. So are spaghetti and meat sauce, and so are CD-Rs and CD burners. If the price of a CD burner falls, people buy more CD burners *and more* CD-Rs. A fall in the price of a CD burner increases the demand for CD-Rs in Fig. 3.2.

2. Expected Future Prices If the price of a good is expected to rise in the future and if the good can be stored, the opportunity cost of obtaining the good for future use is lower today than it will be when the price has increased. So people retime their purchases—they substitute over time. They buy more of the good today before its price is expected to rise (and less after), so the current demand for the good increases.

For example, suppose that Florida is hit by a frost that damages the season's orange crop. You expect the price of orange juice to rise in the future. So you fill your freezer with enough frozen juice to get you through the next six months. Your current demand for frozen orange juice has increased and your future demand has decreased.

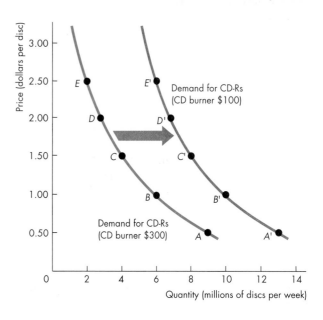

FIGURE 3.2 An Increase in Demand

A change in any influence on buyers' plans other than the price of the good itself results in a new demand schedule and a shift of the demand curve. A change in the price of a CD burner changes the demand for CD-Rs. At a price of $1.50 a disc, 4 million discs a week are demanded when the price of a CD burner is $300 (row *C* of the table) and 8 million CD-Rs a week are demanded when the price of a CD burner is $100. A *fall* in the price of a CD burner *increases* the demand for CD-Rs. The demand curve shifts *rightward*, as shown by the shift arrow and the resulting red curve.

	Original demand schedule CD burner $300			New demand schedule CD burner $100	
	Price (dollars per disc)	Quantity demanded (millions of discs per week)		Price (dollars per disc)	Quantity demanded (millions of discs per week)
A	0.50	9	A'	0.50	13
B	1.00	6	B'	1.00	10
C	1.50	4	C'	1.50	8
D	2.00	3	D'	2.00	7
E	2.50	2	E'	2.50	6

Similarly, if the price of a good is expected to fall in the future, the opportunity cost of buying the good today is high relative to what it is expected to be in the future. So again, people retime their purchases. They buy less of the good now before its price falls, so the demand for the good decreases today and increases in the future.

Computer prices are constantly falling, and this fact poses a dilemma. Will you buy a new computer now, in time for the start of the school year, or will you wait until the price has fallen some more? Because people expect computer prices to keep falling, the current demand for computers is less (the future demand is greater) than it otherwise would be.

3. Income Consumers' income influences demand. When income increases, consumers buy more of most goods, and when income decreases, consumers buy less of most goods. Although an increase in income leads to an increase in the demand for *most* goods, it does not lead to an increase in the demand for *all* goods. A **normal good** is one for which demand increases as income increases. An **inferior good** is one for which demand decreases as income increases. Long-distance transportation has examples of both normal goods and inferior goods. As incomes increase, the demand for air travel (a normal good) increases and the demand for long-distance bus trips (an inferior good) decreases.

4. Population Demand also depends on the size and the age structure of the population. The larger the population, the greater is the demand for all goods and services; the smaller the population, the smaller is the demand for all goods and services.

For example, the demand for parking spaces or movies or CD-Rs or just about anything that you can imagine is much greater in Ottawa than it is in North Bay.

Also, the larger the proportion of the population in a given age group, the greater is the demand for the types of goods and services used by that age group.

For example, in 2001, there were 2.1 million 20-24-year-olds in Canada compared with 2.5 million in 1981. As a result, the demand for college places decreased between 1981 and 2001. During those same years, the number of Canadians aged 85 years and over increased from 195,000 to 430,000. As a result, the demand for nursing home services increased.

TABLE 3.1   The Demand for CD-Rs

The Law of Demand

The quantity of CD-Rs demanded

Decreases if:	*Increases if:*
■ The price of a CD-R rises	■ The price of a CD-R falls

Changes in Demand

The demand for CD-Rs

Decreases if:	*Increases if:*
■ The price of a substitute falls	■ The price of a substitute rises
■ The price of a complement rises	■ The price of a complement falls
■ The price of a CD-R is expected to fall in the future	■ The price of a CD-R is expected to rise in the future
■ Income falls*	■ Income rises*
■ The population decreases	■ The population increases

*A CD-R is a normal good.

5. Preferences Demand depends on preferences. *Preferences* are an individual's attitudes towards goods and services. For example, a rock music fanatic has a much greater preference for CD-Rs than does a tone-deaf technophobe. As a consequence, even if they have the same incomes, their demands for CD-Rs will be very different.

Table 3.1 summarizes the influences on demand and the direction of those influences.

A Change in the Quantity Demanded Versus a Change in Demand

Changes in the factors that influence buyers' plans cause either a change in the quantity demanded or a change in demand. Equivalently, they cause either a movement along the demand curve or a shift of the demand curve.

The distinction between a change in the quantity demanded and a change in demand is the same as that between a movement along the demand curve and a shift of the demand curve.

A point on the demand curve shows the quantity demanded at a given price. So a movement along the demand curve shows a **change in the quantity demanded.** The entire demand curve shows demand. So a shift of the demand curve shows a *change in demand.* Figure 3.3 illustrates and summarizes these distinctions.

Movement Along the Demand Curve If the price of a good changes but everything else remains the same, there is a movement along the demand curve. Because the demand curve slopes downward, a fall in the price of a good or service increases the quantity demanded of it and a rise in the price of the good or service decreases the quantity demanded of it—the law of demand.

In Fig. 3.3, if the price of a good falls when everything else remains the same, the quantity demanded of that good increases and there is a movement down along the demand curve D_0. If the price rises when everything else remains the same, the quantity demanded of that good decreases and there is a movement up along the demand curve D_0.

A Shift of the Demand Curve If the price of a good remains constant but some other influence on buyers' plans changes, there is a change in the demand for that good. We illustrate a change in demand as a shift of the demand curve. For example, if the price of a CD burner falls, consumers buy more CD-Rs regardless of whether the price of a CD-R is high or low. That is what a rightward shift of the demand curve shows—more CD-Rs are bought at each and every price.

In Fig. 3.3, when any influence on buyers' planned purchases changes, other than the price of the good, there is a *change in demand* and the demand curve shifts. Demand *increases* and the demand curve *shifts rightward* (to the red demand curve D_1) if the price of a substitute rises, the price of a complement falls, the expected future price of the good rises, income increases (for a normal good), or the population increases. Demand *decreases* and the demand curve *shifts leftward* (to the red demand curve D_2) if the price of a substitute falls, the price of a complement rises, the expected future price of the good falls, income decreases (for a normal good), or the population decreases.(For an inferior good, the effects of changes in income are in the direction opposite to those described above.)

FIGURE 3.3   A Change in the Quantity Demanded Versus a Change in Demand

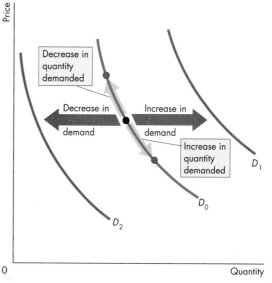

When the price of the good changes, there is a movement along the demand curve and *a change in the quantity demanded,* shown by the blue arrows on demand curve D_0. When any other influence on buyers' plans changes, there is a shift of the demand curve and a *change in demand.* An increase in demand shifts the demand curve rightward (from D_0 to D_1). A decrease in demand shifts the demand curve leftward (from D_0 to D_2).

REVIEW QUIZ

1 Define the quantity demanded of a good or service.
2 What is the law of demand and how do we illustrate it?
3 If a fixed amount of a good is available, what does the demand curve tell us about the price that consumers are willing to pay for that fixed quantity?
4 List all the influences on buying plans that change demand, and for each influence say whether it increases or decreases demand.
5 What happens to the quantity of Palm Pilots demanded and the demand for Palm Pilots if the price of a Palm Pilot falls and all other influences on buying plans remain the same?

Supply

IF A FIRM SUPPLIES A GOOD OR SERVICE, THE FIRM

1. Has the resources and technology to produce it,
2. Can profit from producing it, and
3. Has made a definite plan to produce it and sell it.

A supply is more that just having the *resources* and the *technology* to produce something. *Resources and technology* are the constraints that limit what is possible.

Many useful things can be produced, but they are not produced unless it is profitable to do so. Supply reflects a decision about which technologically feasible items to produce.

The **quantity supplied** of a good or service is the amount that producers plan to sell during a given time period at a particular price. The quantity supplied is not necessarily the same amount as the quantity actually sold. Sometimes the quantity supplied is greater than the quantity demanded, so the quantity bought is less than the quantity supplied.

Like the quantity demanded, the quantity supplied is measured as an amount per unit of time. For example, suppose that GM produces 1,000 cars a day. The quantity of cars supplied by GM can be expressed as 1,000 a day, 7,000 a week, or 365,000 a year. Without the time dimension, we cannot tell whether a particular number is large or small.

What Determines Selling Plans?

The amount of any particular good or service that producers plan to sell depends on many factors. The main ones are

1. The price of the good
2. The prices of resources used to produce the good
3. The prices of related goods produced
4. Expected future prices
5. The number of suppliers
6. Technology

Let's first look at the relationship between the price of a good and the quantity supplied. To study this relationship, we keep all other influences on the quantity supplied the same. We ask: How does the quantity supplied of a good vary as its price varies?

The Law of Supply

The **law of supply** states

Other things remaining the same, the higher the price of a good, the greater is the quantity supplied.

Why does a higher price increase the quantity supplied? It is because *marginal cost increases.* As the quantity produced of any good increases, the marginal cost of producing the good increases. (You can refresh your memory of increasing marginal cost in Chapter 2, p. 37.)

It is never worth producing a good if the price received for it does not at least cover the marginal cost of producing it. So when the price of a good rises, other things remaining the same, producers are willing to incur the higher marginal cost and increase production. The higher price brings forth an increase in the quantity supplied.

Let's now illustrate the law of supply with a supply curve and a supply schedule.

Supply Curve and Supply Schedule

You are now going to study the second of the two most used curves in economics: the supply curve. And you're going to learn about the critical distinction between *supply* and *quantity supplied.*

The term **supply** refers to the entire relationship between the quantity supplied and the price of a good. Supply is illustrated by the supply curve and the supply schedule. The term *quantity supplied* refers to a point on a supply curve—the quantity supplied at a particular price.

Figure 3.4 shows the supply curve of CD-Rs. A **supply curve** shows the relationship between the quantity supplied of a good and its price when all other influences on producers' planned sales remain the same. The supply curve is a graph of a supply schedule.

The table in Fig. 3.4 sets out the supply schedule for CD-Rs. A *supply schedule* lists the quantities supplied at each price when all the other influences on producers' planned sales remain the same. For example, if the price of a CD-R is 50¢, the quantity supplied is zero—in row *A* of the table. If the price of a CD-R is $1.00, the quantity supplied is 3 million CD-Rs a week—in row *B*. The other rows of the table show the quantities supplied at prices of $1.50, $2.00, and $2.50.

FIGURE 3.4   The Supply Curve

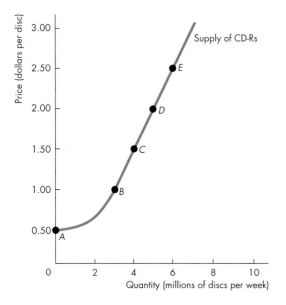

The table shows the supply schedule of CD-Rs. For example, at a price of $1.00, 3 million discs a week are supplied; at a price of $2.50, 6 million discs a week are supplied. The supply curve shows the relationship between the quantity supplied and price, everything else remaining the same. The supply curve usually slopes upward: As the price of a good increases, so does the quantity supplied.

A supply curve can be read in two ways. For a given price, it tells us the quantity that producers plan to sell. And for a given quantity, it tells us the minimum price that producers are willing to accept for that quantity.

	Price (dollars per disc)	Quantity supplied (millions of discs per week)
A	0.50	0
B	1.00	3
C	1.50	4
D	2.00	5
E	2.50	6

To make a supply curve, we graph the quantity supplied on the *x*-axis and the price on the *y*-axis, just as in the case of the demand curve. The points on the supply curve labelled *A* through *E* represent the rows of the supply schedule. For example, point *A* on the graph represents a quantity supplied of zero at a price of 50¢ a CD-R.

Minimum Supply Price   Just as the demand curve has two interpretations, so too does the supply curve. The demand curve can be interpreted as a willingness-and-ability-to-pay curve. The supply curve can be interpreted as a minimum-supply-price curve. It tells us the lowest price at which someone is willing to sell another unit.

If a small quantity is produced, the lowest price at which someone is willing to produce one more unit is low. But if a large quantity is produced, the lowest price at which someone is willing to sell one more unit is high.

In Fig. 3.4, if 6 million CD-Rs a week are produced, the lowest price that a producer is willing to accept for the 6 millionth disc is $2.50. But if only 4 million CD-Rs are produced each week, the lowest price that a producer is willing to accept for the 4 millionth disc is $1.50.

A Change in Supply

When any factor that influences selling plans other than the price of the good changes, there is a **change in supply.** Let's look at the five key factors that change supply.

1. Prices of Productive Resources   The prices of productive resources influence supply. The easiest way to see this influence is to think about the supply curve as a minimum-supply-price curve. If the price of a productive resource rises, the lowest price a producer is willing to accept rises, so supply decreases. For example, during 2001, the price of jet fuel increased and the supply of air transportation decreased. Similarly, a rise in the minimum wage decreases the supply of hamburgers. If the wages of disc producers rise, the supply of CD-Rs decreases.

2. Prices of Related Goods Produced   The prices of related goods and services that firms produce influence supply. For example, if the price of a prerecorded CD rises, the supply of CD-Rs decreases. CD-Rs and prerecorded CDs are *substitutes in production*—goods that can be produced by using the same resources.

If the price of beef rises, the supply of cowhide increases. Beef and cowhide are *complements in production*—goods that must be produced together.

3. Expected Future Prices If the price of a good is expected to rise, the return from selling the good in the future will be higher than it is today. So supply decreases today and increases in the future.

4. The Number of Suppliers The larger the number of firms that produce a good, the greater is the supply of the good. And as firms enter an industry, the supply in that industry increases. As firms leave an industry, the supply in that industry decreases. For example, over the past two years, there has been a huge increase in the number of firms that design and manage Web sites. As a result of this increase, the supply of Internet and World Wide Web services has increased enormously.

5. Technology New technologies create new products and lower the costs of producing existing products. As a result, they change supply. For example, the use of new technologies in the Taiwan factories that make CD-Rs for Imation Enterprises Corporation, a Minnesota based firm, have lowered the cost of producing a CD-R and increased its supply.

   Figure 3.5 illustrates an increase in supply. When supply increases, the supply curve shifts rightward and the quantity supplied is larger at each and every price. For example, at a price of $1.00, on the original (blue) supply curve, the quantity supplied is 3 million discs a week. On the new (red) supply curve, the quantity supplied is 6 million discs a week. Look closely at the numbers in the table in Fig. 3.5 and check that the quantity supplied is larger at each price.

   Table 3.2 summarizes the influences on supply and the directions of those influences.

A Change in the Quantity Supplied Versus a Change in Supply

Changes in the factors that influence producers' planned sales cause either a change in the quantity supplied or a change in supply. Equivalently, they cause either a movement along the supply curve or a shift of the supply curve.

   A point on the supply curve shows the quantity supplied at a given price. A movement along the supply curve shows a **change in the quantity supplied.** The entire supply curve shows supply. A shift of the supply curve shows a *change in supply*.

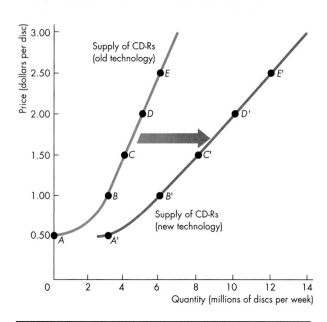

FIGURE 3.5   An Increase in Supply

Original supply schedule Old technology		New supply schedule New technology	
Price (dollars per disc)	Quantity supplied (millions of discs per week)	Price (dollars per disc)	Quantity supplied (millions of discs per week)
A 0.50	0	A' 0.50	3
B 1.00	3	B' 1.00	6
C 1.50	4	C' 1.50	8
D 2.00	5	D' 2.00	10
E 2.50	6	E' 2.50	12

A change in any influence on sellers' plans other than the price of the good itself results in a new supply schedule and a shift of the supply curve. For example, if Imation invents a new, cost-saving technology for producing CD-Rs, the supply of CD-Rs changes.

   At a price of $1.50 a disc, 4 million discs a week are supplied when producers use the old technology (row C of the table) and 8 million CD-Rs a week are supplied when producers use the new technology. An advance in technology *increases* the supply of CD-Rs. The supply curve shifts *rightward*, as shown by the shift arrow and the resulting red curve.

Figure 3.6 illustrates and summarizes these distinctions. If the price of a good falls and everything else remains the same, the quantity supplied of that good decreases and there is a movement down along the supply curve S_0. If the price of a good rises and everything else remains the same, the quantity supplied increases and there is a movement up along the supply curve S_0. When any other influence on selling plans changes, the supply curve shifts and there is a *change in supply*. If the supply curve is S_0 and if production costs fall, supply increases and the supply curve shifts to the red supply curve S_1. If production costs rise, supply decreases and the supply curve shifts to the red supply curve S_2.

TABLE 3.2   The Supply of CD-Rs

The Law of Supply

The quantity of CD-Rs supplied

Decreases if:	*Increases if:*
■ The price of a CD-R falls	■ The price of a CD-R rises

Changes in Supply

The supply of CD-Rs

Decreases if:	*Increases if:*
■ The price of a resource used to produce CD-Rs rises	■ The price of a resource used to produce CD-Rs falls
■ The price of a substitute in production rises	■ The price of a substitute in production falls
■ The price of a complement in production falls	■ The price of a complement in production rises
■ The price of a CD-R is expected to rise in the future	■ The price of a CD-R is expected to fall in the future
■ The number of CD-R producers decreases	■ The number of CD-R producers increases
	■ More efficient technologies for producing CD-Rs are discovered

FIGURE 3.6   A Change in the Quantity Supplied Versus a Change in Supply

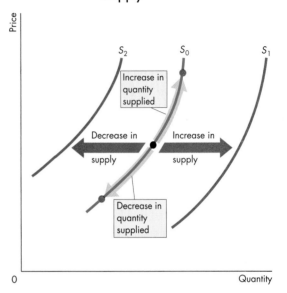

When the price of the good changes, there is a movement along the supply curve and *a change in the quantity supplied*, shown by the blue arrows on supply curve S_0. When any other influence on selling plans changes, there is a shift of the supply curve and a *change in supply*. An increase in supply shifts the supply curve rightward (from S_0 to S_1), and a decrease in supply shifts the supply curve leftward (from S_0 to S_2).

REVIEW QUIZ

1 Define the quantity supplied of a good or service.
2 What is the law of supply and how do we illustrate it?
3 What does the supply curve tell us about the price at which firms will supply a given quantity of a good?
4 List all the influences on selling plans, and for each influence say whether it changes supply.
5 What happens to the quantity of Palm Pilots supplied and the supply of Palm Pilots if the price of a Palm Pilot falls?

Your next task is to use what you've learned about demand and supply and learn how prices and quantities are determined.

Market Equilibrium

WE HAVE SEEN THAT WHEN THE PRICE OF A good rises, the quantity demanded *decreases* and the quantity supplied *increases*. We are now going to see how prices coordinate the plans of buyers and sellers and achieve an equilibrium.

An *equilibrium* is a situation in which opposing forces balance each other. Equilibrium in a market occurs when the price balances the plans of buyers and sellers. The **equilibrium price** is the price at which the quantity demanded equals the quantity supplied. The **equilibrium quantity** is the quantity bought and sold at the equilibrium price. A market moves towards its equilibrium because

■ Price regulates buying and selling plans.

■ Price adjusts when plans don't match.

Price as a Regulator

The price of a good regulates the quantities demanded and supplied. If the price is too high, the quantity supplied exceeds the quantity demanded. If the price is too low, the quantity demanded exceeds the quantity supplied. There is one price at which the quantity demanded equals the quantity supplied. Let's work out what that price is.

Figure 3.7 shows the market for CD-Rs. The table shows the demand schedule (from Fig. 3.1) and the supply schedule (from Fig. 3.4). If the price of a disc is 50¢, the quantity demanded is 9 million discs a week, but no discs are supplied. There is a shortage of 9 million discs a week. This shortage is shown in the final column of the table. At a price of $1.00 a disc, there is still a shortage, but only of 3 million discs a week. If the price of a disc is $2.50, the quantity supplied is 6 million discs a week, but the quantity demanded is only 2 million. There is a surplus of 4 million discs a week. The one price at which there is neither a shortage nor a surplus is $1.50 a disc. At that price, the quantity demanded is equal to the quantity supplied: 4 million discs a week. The equilibrium price is $1.50 a disc, and the equilibrium quantity is 4 million discs a week.

Figure 3.7 shows that the demand curve and the supply curve intersect at the equilibrium price of $1.50 a disc. At each price *above* $1.50 a disc, there is a surplus of discs. For example, at $2.00 a disc, the

FIGURE 3.7   Equilibrium

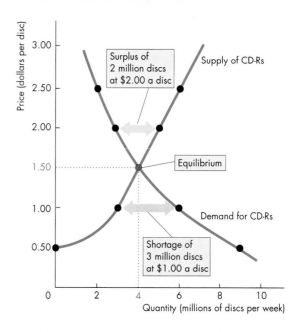

Price (dollars per disc)	Quantity demanded	Quantity supplied	Shortage (−) or surplus (+)
	(millions of discs per week)		
0.50	9	0	−9
1.00	6	3	−3
1.50	4	4	0
2.00	3	5	+2
2.50	2	6	+4

The table lists the quantities demanded and quantities supplied as well as the shortage or surplus of discs at each price. If the price is $1.00 a disc, 6 million discs a week are demanded and 3 million are supplied. There is a shortage of 3 million discs a week, and the price rises. If the price is $2.00 a disc, 3 million discs a week are demanded and 5 million are supplied. There is a surplus of 2 million discs a week, and the price falls. If the price is $1.50 a disc, 4 million discs a week are demanded and 4 million are supplied. There is neither a shortage nor a surplus. Neither buyers nor sellers have any incentive to change the price. The price at which the quantity demanded equals the quantity supplied is the equilibrium price.

surplus is 2 million discs a week, as shown by the blue arrow. At each price *below* $1.50 a disc, there is a shortage of discs. For example, at $1.00 a disc, the shortage is 3 million discs a week, as shown by the red arrow.

Price Adjustments

You've seen that if the price is below equilibrium, there is a shortage, and that if the price is above equilibrium, there is a surplus. But can we count on the price to change and eliminate a shortage or a surplus? We can, because such price changes are beneficial to both buyers and sellers. Let's see why the price changes when there is a shortage or a surplus.

A Shortage Forces the Price Up Suppose the price of a CD-R is $1. Consumers plan to buy 6 million discs a week, and producers plan to sell 3 million discs a week. Consumers can't force producers to sell more than they plan, so the quantity that is actually offered for sale is 3 million discs a week. In this situation, powerful forces operate to increase the price and move it towards the equilibrium price. Some producers, noticing lines of unsatisfied consumers, raise the price. Some producers increase their output. As producers push the price up, the price rises towards its equilibrium. The rising price reduces the shortage because it decreases the quantity demanded and increases the quantity supplied. When the price has increased to the point at which there is no longer a shortage, the forces moving the price stop operating and the price comes to rest at its equilibrium.

A Surplus Forces the Price Down Suppose the price of a CD-R is $2. Producers plan to sell 5 million discs a week, and consumers plan to buy 3 million discs a week. Producers cannot force consumers to buy more than they plan, so the quantity that is actually bought is 3 million discs a week. In this situation, powerful forces operate to lower the price and move it towards the equilibrium price. Some producers, unable to sell the quantities of CD-Rs they planned to sell, cut their prices. In addition, some producers scale back production. As producers cut prices, the price falls towards its equilibrium. The falling price decreases the surplus because it increases the quantity demanded and decreases the quantity supplied. When the price has fallen to the point at which there is no longer a surplus, the forces moving the price stop operating and the price comes to rest at its equilibrium.

The Best Deal Available for Buyers and Sellers
When the price is below equilibrium, it is forced up towards the equilibrium. Why don't buyers resist the increase and refuse to buy at the higher price? Because they value the good more highly than the current price and they cannot satisfy all their demands at the current price. In some markets—an example is the market for houses in Canada during 2001 and 2002—the buyers might even be the ones who force the price up by offering higher prices to divert the limited quantities away from other buyers.

When the price is above equilibrium, it is bid down towards the equilibrium. Why don't sellers resist this decrease and refuse to sell at the lower price? Because their minimum supply price is below the current price and they cannot sell all they would like to at the current price. Normally, it is the sellers who force the price down by offering lower prices to gain market share from their competitors.

At the price at which the quantity demanded and the quantity supplied are equal, neither buyers nor sellers can do business at a better price. Buyers pay the highest price they are willing to pay for the last unit bought, and sellers receive the lowest price at which they are willing to supply the last unit sold.

When people freely make offers to buy and sell and when demanders try to buy at the lowest possible price and suppliers try to sell at the highest possible price, the price at which trade takes place is the equilibrium price—the price at which the quantity demanded equals the quantity supplied. The price coordinates the plans of buyers and sellers.

REVIEW QUIZ

1 What is the equilibrium price of a good or service?
2 Over what range of prices does a shortage arise?
3 Over what range of prices does a surplus arise?
4 What happens to the price when there is a shortage?
5 What happens to the price when there is a surplus?
6 Why is the price at which the quantity demanded equals the quantity supplied the equilibrium price?
7 Why is the equilibrium price the best deal available for both buyers and sellers?

Predicting Changes in Price and Quantity

THE DEMAND AND SUPPLY THEORY THAT WE HAVE just studied provides us with a powerful way of analyzing influences on prices and the quantities bought and sold. According to the theory, a change in price stems from a change in demand, a change in supply, or a change in both demand and supply. Let's look first at the effects of a change in demand.

A Change in Demand

What happens to the price and quantity of CD-Rs if the demand for CD-Rs increases? We can answer this question with a specific example. Between 1998 and 2001, the price of a CD burner fell from $300 to $100. Because the CD burner and CD-R discs are complements, the demand for discs increased, as is shown in the table in Fig. 3.8. The original demand schedule and the new one are set out in the first three columns of the table. The table also shows the supply schedule for CD-Rs.

The original equilibrium price is $1.50 a disc. At that price, 4 million discs a week are demanded and supplied. When demand increases, the price that makes the quantity demanded equal the quantity supplied is $2.50 a disc. At this price, 6 million discs are bought and sold each week. When demand increases, both the price and the quantity increase.

Figure 3.8 shows these changes. The figure shows the original demand for and supply of CD-Rs. The original equilibrium price is $1.50 a CD-R, and the quantity is 4 million CD-Rs a week. When demand increases, the demand curve shifts rightward. The equilibrium price rises to $2.50 a CD-R, and the quantity supplied increases to 6 million CD-Rs a week, as highlighted in the figure. There is an *increase in the quantity supplied* but *no change in supply*—a movement along, but no shift of, the supply curve.

We can reverse this change in demand. Start at a price of $2.50 a disc with 6 million CD-Rs a week being bought and sold, and then work out what happens if demand decreases to its original level. Such a decrease in demand might arise from a fall in the price of an MP3 player (a substitute for CD-R technology). The decrease in demand shifts the demand curve leftward. The equilibrium price falls to $1.50 a disc, and the equilibrium quantity decreases to 4 million discs a week.

FIGURE 3.8   The Effects of a Change in Demand

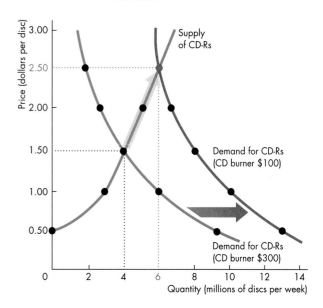

Price	Quantity demanded (millions of discs per week)		Quantity supplied
(dollars per disc)	CD burner $300	CD burner $100	(millions of discs per week)
0.50	9	13	0
1.00	6	10	3
1.50	**4**	8	**4**
2.00	3	7	5
2.50	2	6	**6**

With the price of a CD burner at $300, the demand for CD-Rs is shown by the blue demand curve. The equilibrium price is $1.50 a disc, and the equilibrium quantity is 4 million discs a week. When the price of a CD burner falls from $300 to $100, the demand for CD-Rs increases and the demand curve shifts rightward to become the red curve.

At $1.50 a disc, there is now a shortage of 4 million discs a week. The price of a disc rises to a new equilibrium of $2.50. As the price rises to $2.50, the quantity supplied increases—shown by the blue arrow on the supply curve—to the new equilibrium quantity of 6 million discs a week. Following an increase in demand, the quantity supplied increases but supply does not change—the supply curve does not shift.

We can now make our first two predictions:

1. When demand increases, both the price and the quantity increase.
2. When demand decreases, both the price and the quantity decrease.

A Change in Supply

When Imation and other producers introduce new cost-saving technologies in their CD-R production plants, the supply of CD-Rs increases. The new supply schedule (the same one that was shown in Fig. 3.5) is presented in the table in Fig. 3.9. What are the new equilibrium price and quantity? The answer is highlighted in the table: The price falls to $1.00 a disc, and the quantity increases to 6 million a week. You can see why by looking at the quantities demanded and supplied at the old price of $1.50 a disc. The quantity supplied at that price is 8 million discs a week, and there is a surplus of discs. The price falls. Only when the price is $1.00 a disc does the quantity supplied equal the quantity demanded.

Figure 3.9 illustrates the effect of an increase in supply. It shows the demand curve for CD-Rs and the original and new supply curves. The initial equilibrium price is $1.50 a disc, and the quantity is 4 million discs a week. When the supply increases, the supply curve shifts rightward. The equilibrium price falls to $1.00 a disc, and the quantity demanded increases to 6 million discs a week, highlighted in the figure. There is an *increase in the quantity demanded* but *no change in demand*—a movement along, but no shift of, the demand curve.

We can reverse this change in supply. If we start out at a price of $1.00 a disc with 6 million discs a week being bought and sold, we can work out what happens if supply decreases to its original level. Such a decrease in supply might arise from an increase in the cost of labour or raw materials. The decrease in supply shifts the supply curve leftward. The equilibrium price rises to $1.50 a disc, and the equilibrium quantity decreases to 4 million discs a week.

We can now make two more predictions:

1. When supply increases, the quantity increases and the price falls.
2. When supply decreases, the quantity decreases and the price rises.

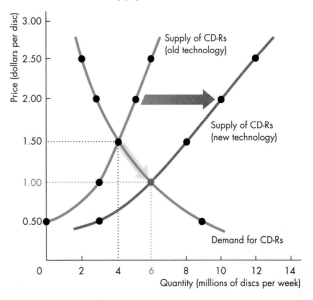

FIGURE 3.9   The Effects of a Change in Supply

Price (dollars per disc)	Quantity demanded (millions of discs per week)	Quantity supplied (millions of discs per week)	
		Old technology	New technology
0.50	9	0	3
1.00	6	3	6
1.50	4	4	8
2.00	3	5	10
2.50	2	6	12

With the old technology, the supply of CD-Rs is shown by the blue supply curve. The equilibrium price is $1.50 a disc, and the equilibrium quantity is 4 million discs a week. When the new technology is adopted, the supply of CD-Rs increases and the supply curve shifts rightward to become the red curve.

At $1.50 a disc, there is now a surplus of 4 million discs a week. The price of a CD-R falls to a new equilibrium of $1.00 a disc. As the price falls to $1.00, the quantity demanded increases—shown by the blue arrow on the demand curve—to the new equilibrium quantity of 6 million discs a week. Following an increase in supply, the quantity demanded increases but demand does not change—the demand curve does not shift.

A Change in Both Demand and Supply

You can now predict the effects of a change in either demand or supply on the price and the quantity. But what happens if *both* demand and supply change together? To answer this question, we look first at the case in which demand and supply move in the same direction—either both increase or both decrease. Then we look at the case in which they move in opposite directions—demand decreases and supply increases or demand increases and supply decreases.

Demand and Supply Change in the Same Direction We've seen that an increase in the demand for CD-Rs raises the price and increases the quantity bought and sold. And we've seen that an increase in the supply of CD-Rs lowers the price and increases the quantity bought and sold. Let's now examine what happens when both of these changes occur together.

The table in Fig. 3.10 brings together the numbers that describe the original quantities demanded and supplied and the new quantities demanded and supplied after the fall in the price of the CD burner and the improved CD-R production technology. These same numbers are illustrated in the graph. The original (blue) demand and supply curves intersect at a price of $1.50 a disc and a quantity of 4 million discs a week. The new (red) supply and demand curves also intersect at a price of $1.50 a disc but at a quantity of 8 million discs a week.

An increase in either demand or supply increases the quantity. So when both demand and supply increase, so does the quantity.

An increase in demand raises the price, and an increase in supply lowers the price, so we can't say whether the price will rise or fall when demand and supply increase together. In this example, the price does not change. But notice that if demand increases by slightly more than the amount shown in the figure, the price will rise. And if supply increases by slightly more than the amount shown in the figure, the price will fall.

We can now make two more predictions:

1. When *both* demand and supply increase, the quantity increases and the price might increase, decrease, or remain the same.
2. When *both* demand and supply decrease, the quantity decreases and the price might increase, decrease, or remain the same.

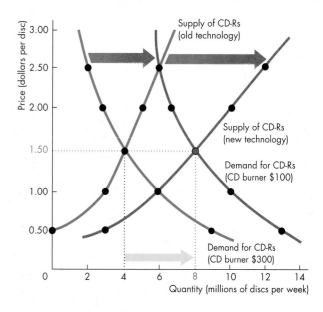

FIGURE 3.10   The Effects of an Increase in Both Demand and Supply

	Original quantities (millions of discs per week)		**New quantities** (millions of discs per week)	
Price (dollars per disc)	**Quantity demanded** CD burner $300	**Quantity supplied** old technology	**Quantity demanded** CD burner $100	**Quantity supplied** new technology
0.50	9	0	13	3
1.00	6	3	10	6
1.50	4	4	8	8
2.00	3	5	7	10
2.50	2	6	6	12

When a CD burner costs $300 and firms use the old technology to produce discs, the price of a disc is $1.50 and the quantity is 4 million discs a week. A fall in the price of the CD burner increases the demand for CD-Rs, and improved technology increases the supply of CD-Rs. The new supply curve intersects the new demand curve at $1.50 a disc, the same price as before, but the quantity increases to 8 million discs a week. These increases in demand and supply increase the quantity but leave the price unchanged.

Demand and Supply Change in Opposite Directions Let's now see what happens when demand and supply change together in *opposite* directions. A new production technology increases the supply of CD-Rs as before. But now the price of an MP3 download rises. An MP3 download is a *complement* of a CD-R. With more costly MP3 downloads, some people switch from buying CD-Rs to buying prerecorded CDs. The demand for CD-Rs decreases.

Figure 3.11 illustrates the original (blue) and new (red) demand and supply curves. The original equilibrium price is $2.50 a disc, and the quantity is 6 million discs a week. The new supply and demand curves intersect at a price of $1.00 a disc and at the original quantity of 6 million discs a week.

A decrease in demand or an increase in supply lowers the price. So when a decrease in demand and an increase in supply occur together, the price falls.

A decrease in demand decreases the quantity, and an increase in supply increases the quantity, so we can't say for sure which way the quantity will change when demand decreases and supply increases at the same time. In this example, the quantity doesn't change. But notice that if demand had decreased by slightly more than is shown in the figure, the quantity would have decreased. And if supply had increased by slightly more than is shown in the figure, the quantity would have increased.

We can now make two more predictions:

1. When demand decreases and supply increases, the price falls and the quantity might increase, decrease, or remain the same.

2. When demand increases and supply decreases, the price rises and the quantity might increase, decrease, or remain the same.

REVIEW QUIZ

1 What is the effect on the price of a CD-R and the quantity of CD-Rs if (a) the price of a PC falls or (b) the price of an MP3 download rises or (c) more firms produce CD-Rs or (d) CD-R producers' wages rise or (e) any two of these events occur at the same time? (Draw the diagrams!)

◆ To complete your study of demand and supply, take a look at *Reading Between the Lines* on pp. 76–77, which answers the question that we posed at the start of the chapter about falling prices.

FIGURE 3.11 The Effects of a Decrease in Demand and an Increase in Supply

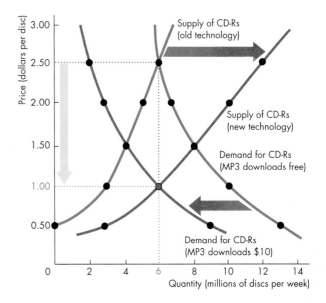

	Original quantities (millions of discs per week)		**New quantities** (millions of discs per week)	
Price (dollars per disc)	**Quantity demanded** MP3 download free	**Quantity supplied** old technology	**Quantity demanded** MP3 download $10	**Quantity supplied** new technology
0.50	13	0	9	3
1.00	10	3	6	6
1.50	8	4	4	8
2.00	7	5	3	10
2.50	6	6	2	12

When MP3 downloads are free and firms use the old technology to produce discs, the price of a CD-R is $2.50 and the quantity is 6 million discs a week. A rise in the price of an MP3 download decreases the demand for CD-Rs, and improved technology increases the supply of CD-Rs. The new equilibrium price is $1.00 a disc, a lower price, but in this case the quantity remains constant at 6 million discs a week. This decrease in demand and increase in supply lower the price but leave the quantity unchanged.

Demand and Supply: The Price of Computers

THE GLOBE AND MAIL, December 31, 2001

Analysts see tough year ahead for PC industry

...

"It's going to be a tough year," said George Shiffler, a principal analyst at Gartner Dataquest ...

Worldwide shipments of PCs are projected to reach 129.3 million units in 2002, up 4 per cent from 124.3 million in 2001, but down slightly from 130.5 million in 2000 according to Gartner.

In Canada, PC shipments, which are expected to fall 6.6 per cent this year from 2000, are forecast to increase 3.8 per cent to 3.8 million units in 2002.

...

Analysts are counting on falling PC prices, increased demand for wireless networking and mobile comput-

ing, and Microsoft Corp.'s latest operating systems to help stimulate PC sales. But experts say the most important factor that will drive the market will be a turnaround in the sagging U.S. economy, which has hurt consumer confidence.

This was a particularly good year to buy a computer, and consumers and companies can also expect good bargains in 2002. Chip maker Intel Corp. has been dropping the prices of its components throughout this year, partly in response to competition from rival Advanced Micro Devices Inc. That means computer manufacturers can source cheaper parts and pass the savings on to buyers.

...

Reprinted with permission from *The Globe and Mail.*

Essence of the Story

■ Worldwide shipments of PCs are projected to reach 129.3 million units in 2002, up 4 percent from 124.3 million in 2001, but down from 130.5 million in 2000.

■ In Canada, PC shipments are expected to fall 6.6 percent in 2001 and to increase 3.8 percent to 3.8 million units in 2002.

■ Falling PC prices, increased demand for wireless networking and mobile computing, and Microsoft Corp.'s WindowsXP might help stimulate PC sales.

■ But only a turnaround in the sagging U.S. economy will restore the industry.

■ Computer buyers can expect bargains in 2002.

■ Intel Corp. and Advanced Micro Devices Inc. have cut the prices of chips, which has lowered the costs of PC makers.

Economic Analysis

■ Figure 1 shows the global market for personal computers in 2000. The demand curve is D_{00} and the supply curve is S_{00}. The equilibrium quantity is 130.5 million (as in the news article) and the equilibrium price is $3,500.

■ Figure 2 shows what happened during 2001. A recession in the United States lowered incomes, both in the United States and in many other countries. With a fall in average incomes, the demand for PCs decreased and the demand curve shifted leftward from D_{00} to D_{01}.

■ Falling chip prices lowered the cost of producing a PC and the supply of PCs increased. The supply curve shifted rightward from S_{00} to S_{01}.

■ With a decrease in demand and an increase in supply, the price of a PC fell. But because the decrease in demand was greater than the increase in supply, the quantity of PCs decreased.

■ Figure 3 shows the market for PCs in 2002. Factors such as the increased demand for wireless technology and the introduction of WindowsXP increased demand. But these forces were not strong enough to offset the depressing effects on demand of the continued global economic slowdown. So the demand for PCs didn't change in 2002.

■ But the supply of PCs increased again as the prices of chips continued to tumble. The supply curve shifted rightward from S_{01} to S_{02}.

■ With an increase in supply and no change in demand, the price of a PC fell further and the quantity of PCs increased.

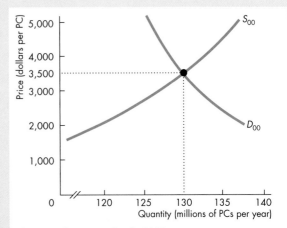

Figure 1 The PC market in 2000

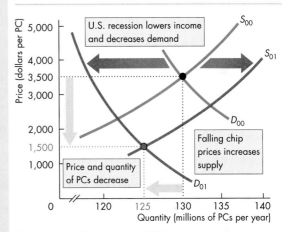

Figure 2 The PC market in 2001

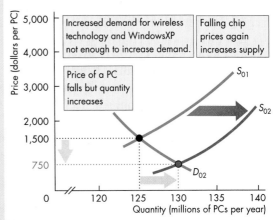

Figure 3 The PC market in 2002

Mathematical Note
Demand, Supply, and Equilibrium

Demand Curve

The law of demand says that as the price of a good or service falls, the quantity demanded of that good or service increases. We illustrate the law of demand by setting out a demand schedule, by drawing a graph of the demand curve, or by writing down an equation. When the demand curve is a straight line, the following linear equation describes it

$$P = a - bQ_D,$$

where P is the price and Q_D is the quantity demanded. The a and b are positive constants.

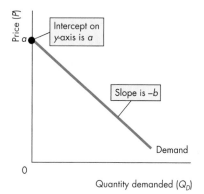

This equation tells us three things:

1. The price at which no one is willing to buy the good (Q_D is zero). That is, if the price is a, then the quantity demanded is zero. You can see the price a on the graph. It is the price at which the demand curve hits the y-axis—what we call the demand curve's "intercept on the y-axis."

2. As the price falls, the quantity demanded increases. If Q_D is a positive number, then the price P must be less than a. And as Q_D gets larger, the price P becomes smaller. That is, as the quantity increases, the maximum price that buyers are willing to pay for the good falls.

3. The constant b tells us how fast the maximum price that someone is willing to pay for the good falls as the quantity increases. That is, the constant b tells us about the steepness of the demand curve. The equation tells us that the slope of the demand curve is $-b$.

Supply Curve

The law of supply says that as the price of a good or service rises, the quantity supplied of that good increases. We illustrate the law of supply by setting out a supply schedule, by drawing a graph of the supply curve, or by writing down an equation. When the supply curve is a straight line, the following linear equation describes it

$$P = c + dQ_S,$$

where P is the price and Q_S is the quantity supplied. The c and d are positive constants.

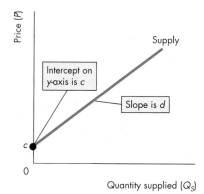

This equation tells us three things:

1. The price at which sellers are not willing to supply the good (Q_S is zero). That is, if the price is c, then no one is willing to sell the good. You can see the price c on the graph. It is the price at which the supply curve hits the y-axis—what we call the supply curve's "intercept on the y-axis."

2. As the price rises, the quantity supplied increases. If Q_S is a positive number, then the price P must be greater than c. And as Q_S increases, the price P gets larger. That is, as the quantity increases, the minimum price that sellers are willing to accept rises.

3. The constant d tells us how fast the minimum price at which someone is willing to sell the good rises as the quantity increases. That is, the constant d tells us about the steepness of the supply curve. The equation tells us that the slope of the supply curve is d.

Market Equilibrium

Demand and supply determine market equilibrium. The figure shows the equilibrium price (P^*) and equilibrium quantity (Q^*) at the intersection of the demand curve and the supply curve.

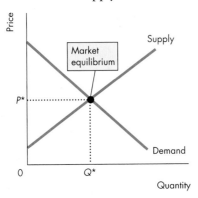

We can use the equations to find the equilibrium price and equilibrium quantity. The price of a good adjusts until the quantity demanded equals the quantity supplied. That is,

$$Q_D = Q_S.$$

So at the equilibrium price (P^*) and equilibrium quantity (Q^*),

$$Q_D = Q_S = Q^*.$$

To find the equilibrium price and equilibrium quantity, substitute Q^* for Q_D in the demand equation and Q^* for Q_S in the supply equation. Then the price is the equilibrium price (P^*), which gives

$$P^* = a - bQ^*$$

$$P^* = c + dQ^*.$$

Notice that

$$a - bQ^* = c + dQ^*.$$

Now solve for Q^*:

$$a - c = bQ^* + dQ^*$$

$$a - c = (b + d)Q^*$$

$$Q^* = \frac{a - c}{b + d}.$$

To find the equilibrium price, (P^*), substitute for Q^* in either the demand equation or the supply equation.

Using the demand equation, we have

$$P^* = a - b\left(\frac{a - c}{b + d}\right)$$

$$P^* = \frac{a(b + d) - b(a - c)}{b + d}$$

$$P^* = \frac{ad + bc}{b + d}.$$

Alternatively, using the supply equation, we have

$$P^* = c + d\left(\frac{a - c}{b + d}\right)$$

$$P^* = \frac{c(b + d) + d(a - c)}{b + d}$$

$$P^* = \frac{ad + bc}{b + d}.$$

An Example

The demand for ice-cream cones is

$$P = 800 - 2Q_D.$$

The supply of ice-cream cones is

$$P = 200 + 1Q_S.$$

The price of a cone is expressed in cents, and the quantities are expressed in cones per day.

To find the equilibrium price (P^*) and equilibrium quantity (Q^*), substitute Q^* for Q_D and Q_S and P^* for P in the demand and supply equations. That is,

$$P^* = 800 - 2Q^*$$

$$P^* = 200 + 1Q^*.$$

Now solve for Q^*:

$$800 - 2Q^* = 200 + 1Q^*$$

$$600 = 3Q^*$$

$$Q^* = 200.$$

And

$$P^* = 800 - 2(200)$$

$$= 400.$$

The equilibrium price is $4 a cone, and the equilibrium quantity is 200 cones per day.

SUMMARY

KEY POINTS

Markets and Prices (p. 60)

- A competitive market is one that has so many buyers and sellers that no one can influence the price.
- Opportunity cost is a relative price.
- Demand and supply determine relative prices.

Demand (pp. 61–65)

- Demand is the relationship between the quantity demanded of a good and its price when all other influences on buying plans remain the same.
- The higher the price of a good, other things remaining the same, the smaller is the quantity demanded—the law of demand.
- Demand depends on the prices of substitutes and complements, expected future prices, income, population, and preferences.

Supply (pp. 66–69)

- Supply is the relationship between the quantity supplied of a good and its price when all other influences on selling plans remain the same.
- The higher the price of a good, other things remaining the same, the greater is the quantity supplied—the law of supply.
- Supply depends on the prices of resources used to produce a good, the prices of related goods produced, expected future prices, the number of suppliers, and technology.

Market Equilibrium (pp. 70–71)

- At the equilibrium price, the quantity demanded equals the quantity supplied.
- At prices above equilibrium, there is a surplus and the price falls.
- At prices below equilibrium, there is a shortage and the price rises.

Predicting Changes in Price and Quantity (pp. 72–75)

- An increase in demand brings a rise in price and an increase in the quantity supplied. (A decrease in demand brings a fall in price and a decrease in the quantity supplied.)
- An increase in supply brings a fall in price and an increase in the quantity demanded. (A decrease in supply brings a rise in price and a decrease in the quantity demanded.)
- An increase in demand and an increase in supply bring an increased quantity, but the price might rise, fall, or remain the same. An increase in demand and a decrease in supply bring a higher price, but the quantity might increase, decrease, or remain the same.

KEY FIGURES

KEY TERMS

PROBLEMS

*1. What is the effect on the price of an audiotape and the quantity of audiotapes sold if
   a. The price of a CD rises?
   b. The price of a Walkman rises?
   c. The supply of CD players increases?
   d. Consumers' incomes increase?
   e. Workers who make audiotapes get a pay raise?
   f. The price of a Walkman rises at the same time as the workers who make audiotapes get a pay raise?

2. What is the effect on the price of a DVD player and the quantity of DVD players sold if
   a. The price of a DVD rises?
   b. The price of a DVD falls?
   c. The supply of DVD players increases?
   d. Consumers' incomes decrease?
   e. The wage rate of workers who produce DVD players increases?
   f. The wage rate of workers who produce DVD players rises and at the same time the price of a DVD falls?

*3. Suppose that the following events occur one at a time:
   (i)   The price of crude oil rises.
   (ii) The price of a car rises.
   (iii) All speed limits on highways are abolished.
   (iv) Robot technology cuts car production costs.
   Which of these events increases or decreases (state which):
   a. The demand for gasoline?
   b. The supply of gasoline?
   c. The quantity of gasoline demanded?
   d. The quantity of gasoline supplied?

4. Suppose that the following events occur one at a time:
   (i)   The price of airfares halves.
   (ii) The price of beef falls.
   (iii) A cheap new strong cloth, a close substitute for leather, is invented.
   (iv) A new high-speed technology for cutting leather is invented.
   Which of these events will increase or decrease (state which):
   a. The demand for leather bags?
   b. The supply of leather bags?
   c. The quantity of leather bags demanded?
   d. The quantity of leather bags supplied?

*5. The figure illustrates the market for pizza.
   a. Label the curves in the figure.
   b. What are the equilibrium price of a pizza and the equilibrium quantity of pizza?

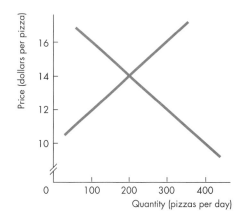

6. The figure illustrates the market for fish.
   a. Label the curves in the figure.
   b. What are the equilibrium price of a fish and the equilibrium quantity of fish?

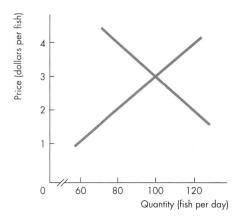

*7. The demand and supply schedules for gum are

Price (cents per pack)	Quantity demanded	Quantity supplied
	(millions of packs per week)	
20	180	60
30	160	80
40	140	100
50	120	120
60	100	140
70	80	160
80	60	180

   a. Draw a graph of the gum market and mark in the equilibrium price and quantity.

b. Suppose that gum is 70 cents a pack. Describe the situation in the gum market and explain how the price of gum adjusts.

8. The demand and supply schedules for potato chips are

Price (cents per bag)	Quantity demanded	Quantity supplied
	(millions of bag per week)	
50	160	130
60	150	140
70	140	150
80	130	160
90	120	170
100	110	180

a. Draw a graph of the potato chip market and mark in the equilibrium price and quantity.
b. Suppose that chips are 60 cents a bag. Describe the situation in the market for chips and explain how the price adjusts.

*9. In problem 7, suppose that a fire destroys some gum-producing factories and the supply of gum decreases by 40 million packs a week.
a. Has there been a shift of or a movement along the supply curve of gum?
b. Has there been a shift of or a movement along the demand curve for gum?
c. What are the new equilibrium price and equilibrium quantity of gum?

10. In problem 8, suppose a new dip comes onto the market and the demand for potato chips increases by 30 million bags per week.
a. Has there been a shift of or a movement along the supply curve of potato chips?
b. Has there been a shift of or a movement along the demand curve for potato chips?
c. What are the new equilibrium price and equilibrium quantity of potato chips?

*11. In problem 9, suppose an increase in the teenage population increases the demand for gum by 40 million packs per week at the same time as the fire occurs. What are the new equilibrium price and quantity of gum?

12. In problem 10, suppose that a virus destroys several potato farms with the result that the supply of potato chips decreases by 40 million bags a week at the same time as the dip comes onto the market. What are the new equilibrium price and quantity of potato chips?

CRITICAL THINKING

1. After you have studied *Reading Between the Lines* on pp. 76–77, answer the following questions:
a. What were the factors that changed the demand for and supply of PCs during 2001 and 2002?
b. How did competition between Intel and AMD influence the market for PCs?
c. How do you think the development of CD-R technology has changed the demand for PCs and the equilibrium price of a PC?

WEB EXERCISES

1. Use the links on the Parkin–Bade Web site and obtain data on the prices and quantities of wheat.
a. Make a figure similar to Fig. 3.7 on p. 70 to illustrate the market for wheat in 1999 and 2000.
b. Show the changes in demand and supply and the changes in the quantity demanded and the quantity supplied that are consistent with the price and quantity data.

2. Use the link on the Parkin–Bade Web site and obtain data on the price of oil.
a. Describe how the price of oil has changed over the past five years.
b. Draw a demand-supply diagram to explain what happens to the price when there is an increase or a decrease in supply and no change in demand.
c. What do you predict would happen to the price of oil if a new drilling technology permitted deeper ocean sources to be used?
d. What do you predict would happen to the price of oil if a clean and safe nuclear technology were developed?
e. What do you predict would happen to the price of oil if automobiles were powered by batteries instead of by internal combustion engines?

UNDERSTANDING HOW MARKETS WORK

PART 2

The Amazing Market

The four chapters that you've just studied explain how markets work. The market is an amazing instrument. It enables people who have never met and who know nothing about each other to interact and do business. It also enables us to allocate our scarce resources to the uses that we value most highly. Markets can be very simple or highly organized. ◆ A simple market is one that the American historian Daniel J. Boorstin describes in *The Discoverers* (p. 161). In the late fourteenth century,

> *The Muslim caravans that went southward from Morocco across the Atlas Mountains arrived after twenty days at the shores of the Senegal River. There the Moroccan traders laid out separate piles of salt, of beads from Ceutan coral, and cheap manufactured goods. Then they retreated out of sight. The local tribesmen, who lived in the strip mines where they dug their gold, came to the shore and put a heap of gold beside each pile of Moroccan goods. Then they, in turn, went out of view, leaving the Moroccan traders either to take the gold offered for a particular pile or to reduce the pile of their merchandise to suit the offered price in gold. Once again the Moroccan traders withdrew, and the process went on. By this system of commercial etiquette, the Moroccans collected their gold.*

An organized market is the Toronto Stock Exchange, which trades many millions of stocks each day. Another is an auction at which a government sells rights to broadcasters and cellular telephone companies for the use of the airwaves. ◆ All of these markets determine the prices at which exchanges take place and enable both buyers and sellers to benefit. ◆ Everything and anything that can be exchanged is traded in markets. There are markets for goods and services; for resources such as labour, capital, and raw materials; for dollars, pounds, and yen; for goods to be delivered now and for goods to be delivered in the future. Only the imagination places limits on what can be traded in markets. ◆ You've learned, in Chapter 3, about the laws of demand and supply. You've discovered the forces that determine buying plans and selling plans and you've seen how prices adjust to coordinate those plans. You've also used the laws of demand and supply to explain why some prices rise, some fall, and some rise and fall like a roller coaster ride. ◆ What you've learned about demand and supply is fundamental to your entire study of economics. It will help you to understand price movements in the world around you. And it will help you in your study of macroeconomics. ◆ The laws of demand and supply that you've learned and used in these four chapters were discovered during the nineteenth century by some remarkable economists. We conclude our study of demand and supply and markets by looking at the lives and times of some of these economists and by talking to one of today's most influential economists who studies and creates sophisticated auction markets.

PROBING THE IDEAS

Discovering the Laws of Demand and Supply

ALFRED MARSHALL *(1842–1924) grew up in an England that was being transformed by the railroad and by the expansion of manufacturing. Mary Paley was one of Marshall's students at Cambridge, and when Alfred and Mary married, in 1877, celibacy rules barred Alfred from continuing to teach at Cambridge. By 1884, with more liberal rules, the Marshalls returned to Cambridge, where Alfred became Professor of Political Economy.*

Many others had a hand in refining the theory of demand and supply, but the first thorough and complete statement of the theory as we know it today was set by Alfred Marshall, with the acknowledged help of Mary Paley Marshall. Published in 1890, this monumental treatise, The Principles of Economics, *became the textbook on economics on both sides of the Atlantic for almost half a century. Marshall was an outstanding mathematician, but he kept mathematics and even diagrams in the background. His supply and demand diagram appears only in a footnote.*

The laws of demand and supply that you studied in Chapter 3 were discovered during the 1830s by Antoine-Augustin Cournot (1801–1877), a professor of mathematics at the University of Lyon, France. Although Cournot was the first to use demand and supply, it was the development and expansion of the railroads during the 1850s that gave the newly emerging theory its first practical applications. Railroads then were at the cutting edge of technology just as airlines are today. And as in the airline industry today, competition among the railroads was fierce.

Dionysius Lardner (1793–1859), an Irish professor of philosophy at the University of London, used demand and supply to show railroad companies how they could increase their profits by cutting rates on long-distance business on which competition was fiercest and by raising rates on short-haul business on which they had less to fear from other transportation suppliers. Today, economists use the principles that Lardner worked out during the 1850s to calculate the freight rates and passenger fares that will give airlines the largest possible profit. And the rates calculated have a lot in common with the railroad rates of the nineteenth century. On local routes on which there is little competition, fares per kilometre are highest, and on long-distance routes on which the airlines compete fiercely, fares per kilometre are lowest.

Known satirically among scientists of the day as "Dionysius Diddler," Lardner worked on an amazing range of problems from astronomy to railway engineering to economics. A colourful character, he would have been a regular guest if late-night talk shows had been around in the 1850s. Lardner visited the École des Ponts et Chaussées (School of Bridges and Roads) in Paris and must have learned a great deal from Jules Dupuit.

In France, Jules Dupuit (1804–1866), a French engineer/economist, used demand to calculate the benefits from building a bridge and, once the bridge was built, for calculating the toll to charge for its use. His work was the forerunner of what is today called *cost-benefit analysis*. Working with the principles invented by Dupuit, economists today calculate the costs and benefits of highways and airports, dams, and power stations.

Today, using the same principles that Dupuit devised, economists calculate whether the benefits of expanding airports and air-traffic control facilities are sufficient to cover their costs. Airline companies use the principles developed by Lardner to set their prices and to decide when to offer "seat sales." Like the railroads before them, the airlines charge a high price per kilometre on short flights, for which they face little competition, and a low price per kilometre on long flights, for which competition is fierce.

Dupuit used the law of demand to determine whether a bridge or canal would be valued enough by its users to justify the cost of building it. Lardner first worked out the relationship between the cost of production and supply and used demand and supply theory to explain the costs, prices, and profits of railroad operations. He also used the theory to discover ways of increasing revenue by raising rates on short-haul business and lowering them on long-distance freight.

Markets do an amazing job. And the laws of demand and supply help us to understand how markets work. But in some situations, a market must be designed and institutions must be created to enable the market to operate. In recent years, economists have begun to use their tools to design and create markets. And one of the chief architects of new-style markets is John McMillan, whom you can meet on the following pages.

TALKING WITH

JOHN MCMILLAN *holds the Jonathan B. Lovelace Chair and teaches international management and economics in the Graduate School of Business at Stanford University. Born in Christchurch, New Zealand in 1951, he was an undergraduate at the University of Canterbury, where he studied first mathematics and then economics. For graduate school, he went to the University of New South Wales. John McMillan's research focuses on the way markets work. He wants to dig more deeply than demand and supply and explain how prices get determined, how markets are organized, why some use auctions and some don't, and why different types of auctions get used in different situations. His work has found practical application in the design of mechanisms for selling rights to the electromagnetic spectrum—the air waves that carry your cell-phone messages. His recent book,* Reinventing the Bazaar: A Natural History of Markets *(New York, W.W. Norton, 2002), provides a fascinating account of the rich diversity of market arrangements that have been used through the ages.*

Michael Parkin and Robin Bade talked with John McMillan about his career and the

John McMillan

progress that economists have made in understanding markets since the pioneering work of Alfred Marshall.

Professor McMillan, how does Alfred Marshall's assessment of how competitive markets work look today in the light of the progress that economists have made?

Supply and demand is still our basic tool of analysis, but modern microeconomics has dug deeper than Marshall was able to. The supply-demand diagram tells us what prices can do, but it sidesteps the question of where prices come from.

The main insight underlying much of modern microeconomics (and discussed in my book *Reinventing the Bazaar*) is that transaction costs can impede the smooth functioning of markets. Transaction costs include the time and money spent locating trading partners, assessing their reliability, negotiating an agreement, and monitoring performance.

Information is a major source of transaction costs. Often information is unevenly distributed: the seller knows more about the quality of the item for sale than the potential buyer; the buyer knows her willingness to pay but the seller doesn't. Informational asymmetries such as these can mean that transactions that would be mutually beneficial might fail to be realized.

The tools for analyzing the details of deal-making are game theory (as developed by John Nash, the hero of the motion picture *A Beautiful Mind*), and information economics (which was recognized by the Nobel committee in its 2001 economics award to George Akerlof, Michael Spence, and Joseph Stiglitz).

Marshall's economics is like physics without friction. For some questions, the assumption of a frictionless world is a useful short cut: for analyzing, say, the effects of rent controls or minimum-wage laws. For other questions, we need to examine the frictions explicitly. For example, to understand why financial markets are organized as they are we need to bring information asymmetries and transaction costs into the picture.

> *"The main insight underlying much of modern microeconomics... is that transaction costs can impede the smooth functioning of markets."*

The focus on the costs of transacting has brought a recognition that markets can't operate in thin air. A market is a social construction. To operate well, with transaction costs minimized, any market needs rules and procedures. Some of these rules, perhaps most of them, arise from the bottom up; that is, they evolve through the everyday trial and error of the market participants. Others are set from the top down: government-set laws and regulations can help foster efficient transacting.

Are there any contemporary or recent examples that illustrate the way markets get created, and that perhaps hold some lessons about what works and what doesn't?

Yes. An experiment in the creation of markets is offered to us by the ex-communist countries. In the early 1990s, a common view among those advising Russia, for example, was that the overriding objective was to get the government out. Russia's approach to reform was to abolish all the mechanisms that had run the planned economy and to start with a clean slate. Once the prohibitions on market activity were abolished, the reformers believed, the private sector would quickly take over. Later, in light of Russia's grim performance in the 1990s, this simple view was supplanted by recognition that building a market economy is exceedingly hard. Success requires a complex package of microeconomic reform, macroeconomic stability, and institution-building. Markets don't operate well in an institutional vacuum.

China provides a telling contrast to Russia. China's reforms consisted of leaving the old institutions of the planned economy in place and letting markets grow up around the plan. China boomed during reform; its spectacular economic growth lifted millions out of dire poverty. This growth resulted from the emergence and expansion of the scope of markets and the gradual erosion of the formerly planned economy.

Markets developed in China, paradoxically, in the absence of any laws of contract and of any formal recognition of property rights. In place of the usual market-economy institutions, the pre-existing mechanisms of the planned economy served as a transitional substitute. Highly imperfect as these institutions were, they were enough to support the rapid development of markets. The lesson from the Russia-China comparison is that, for markets to work well, some institutions are better than none.

What is the most remarkable market that you've encountered?

In the Dutch village of Aalsmeer, just outside Amsterdam, operates a flower market of almost unbelievable size and complexity. Its warehouses, full of flowers, cover an area the size of 125 soccer fields. Each morning, 2,000 or so buyers bid around US$5 million for the flowers. The flowers are flown in from far away, from places like Israel, Colombia, and Zimbabwe, and are later dispatched to buyers around the globe.

Sophisticated technology is needed to operate a global market in as perishable an item as cut flowers. The flower auctions are run via a giant clock at the front of the bidding hall, which winds down to successively lower prices. The bidders can stop the clock by pushing a button, meaning they have bought the flowers at the price shown on the clock. Computers then automatically organize the flowers' delivery to the buyer's address.

The auction that you've just described, appropriately called a Dutch auction, starts at a high price and goes down until someone accepts the price. It contrasts with a so-called English

151

auction, where the price starts low and rises until only one buyer is left. Which works best?

The Dutch auction is used at Aalsmeer because of its speed: a huge volume of flowers must be sold in a few hours. Both buyers and sellers value the speed of the Dutch auction. In other circumstances, the English auction works better from the seller's point of view, but not necessarily from the buyer's point of view.

Consider a situation where there is significant uncertainty about the value of the item for sale. The items has the same value whichever bidder ends up owning it, but at the time of bidding each of the bidders has a different estimate of the value. (This describes, for example, bidding for the right to drill for oil on a tract of land, and each of the bidders has an imperfect estimate of the amount of oil there.) In this situation, there is a risk of what is called the "winner's curse." The bidder who wins is the one with the highest value estimate, which might well be an overestimate. Winning thus conveys bad news: it tells the winner that everyone else believed the item was worth less than the winner believed.

Bidders who understand the winner's curse tend to bid cautiously. But they tend to bid less cautiously—that is, higher—in an English auction than in a Dutch auction. This is because they can see and react to each other's bids. The bids, as they ascend, convey some information about how highly the others value the item, mitigating the winner's curse and thereby usually inducing a higher price. The higher bids induced by the English auction than the other forms of auction are probably the reason that the English auction is the most commonly used auction form around the world.

What is special about selling airwaves that enables expensive economic consultants like you to show governments how to do it?

The spectrum auctions were unusually complex. Thousands of licences were offered. The sale procedure had to recognize complementarities among the licences: that is, the value to a bidder of a licence covering, say, New Jersey, was probably higher if that bidder was going to end up owning a New York licence as well (because the firm could spread its marketing costs across the wider region and in other ways offer more efficient service). None of the tried-and-true

auction forms allowed the bidding process to encompass such complementarities. As Vice President Al Gore said at the opening ceremony of one of the auctions, "They couldn't just go look it up in a book."

The auction form that we economists recommend and the government adopted was what came to be known as the "simultaneous ascending auction." Multiple licences were offered for sale at the same time. The ascending bids allowed the bidders to avoid the winner's curse, and the simultaneous bidding on multiple licences allowed the bidders to express their demands for packages of complementary licences. The new auction form has raised many billions of dollars.

What does the Internet mean for markets today? Is it creating gains from trade that were previously unattainable?

It certainly has. By lowering transaction costs—especially the cost of search—to close to zero, it has created global markets in goods that before, because of their lower value, previously had only a local sale. Before the Internet, if you wanted some obscure object, you had to hunt in antique shops, flea markets, and so on. Now you simply use your Internet search engine. Buyers and sellers can quickly and easily contact each other where before it would have been prohibitively expensive. The result is better matches of buyer and seller—and larger gains from trade.

You began your university life studying math. Why did you switch to economics?

I was intrigued that mathematics could be used to help understand how the world works. Of course, as I was to learn, any good piece of economic analysis contains much more than just mathematics, but the mathematics lends the study rigour and precision.

What other subjects work well with economics?

Almost any subject. Mathematics is essential; you can't get to the frontiers of economics research without it. But that's not the only discipline of relevance. Economics uses ideas from fields like biology (for example, natural selection), history (the origins of institutions), sociology (networks and social capital), and philosophy (what is meant by fairness).

A FIRST LOOK AT MACROECONOMICS

What Will Your World Be Like?

During the past 100 years, the quantity of goods and services produced in Canada's farms, factories, shops, and offices has expanded more than twentyfold. As a result, we have a much higher standard of living than our grandparents had. Will production always expand? ◆ For most of us, a high standard of living means finding a good job. What kind of job will you find when you graduate? Will you have lots of choice, or will you face a labour market with a high unemployment rate in which jobs are hard to find? ◆ A high standard of living means being able to afford to buy life's necessities and have some fun. If prices rise too quickly, some people get left behind and must trim what they buy. What will the dollar buy next year; in 10 years when you are paying off your student loan; and in 50 years when you are spending your life's savings in retirement? ◆ Every year between 1971 and 1997, the federal government spent more than it raised in taxes. And most years, we spend more on imports from the rest of the world than we earn on our exports. How will these deficits affect your future? ◆ To keep production expanding and prevent an economic slowdown, the federal government and the Bank of Canada—the nation's financial managers—take policy actions. How do their actions influence production, jobs, prices, and the ability of Canadians to compete in the global marketplace?

◆ These are the questions of macroeconomics that you are about to study. In *Reading Between the Lines* at the end of the chapter, we'll take a quick look at macroeconomic performance—inflation, deflation, and economic growth—around the world in 2002.

After studying this chapter, you will be able to

■ Describe the origins and issues of macroeconomics

■ Describe the trends and fluctuations in economic growth

■ Describe the trends and fluctuations in jobs and unemployment

■ Describe the trends and fluctuations in inflation

■ Describe the trends and fluctuations in government and international deficits

■ Identify the macroeconomic policy challenges and describe the tools available for meeting them

Origins and Issues of Macroeconomics

ECONOMISTS BEGAN TO STUDY ECONOMIC growth, inflation, and international payments as long ago as the 1750s, and this work was the origin of macroeconomics. But modern macroeconomics did not emerge until the **Great Depression**, a decade (1929–1939) of high unemployment and stagnant production throughout the world economy. In the Depression's worst year, 1933, the production of Canada's farms, factories, shops, and offices was only 70 percent of its 1929 level and 20 percent of the labour force was unemployed. These were years of human misery on a scale that is hard to imagine today. They were also years of extreme pessimism about the ability of the market economy to work properly. Many people believed that private ownership, free markets, and democratic political institutions could not survive.

The science of economics had no solutions to the Great Depression. The major alternative system of central planning and socialism seemed increasingly attractive to many people. It was in this climate of economic depression and political and intellectual turmoil that modern macroeconomics emerged with the publication in 1936 of John Maynard Keynes' *The General Theory of Employment, Interest, and Money* (see pp. 522–523).

Short-Term Versus Long-Term Goals

Keynes' theory was that depression and high unemployment result from insufficient private spending and that to cure these problems, the government must increase its spending. Keynes focused primarily on the *short term*. He wanted to cure an immediate problem almost regardless of the *long-term* consequences of the cure. "In the long run," said Keynes, "we're all dead."

But Keynes believed that after his cure for depression had restored the economy to a normal condition, the long-term problems of inflation and slow economic growth would return. And he suspected that his cure for depression, increased government spending, might trigger inflation and might lower the long-term growth rate of production. With a lower long-term growth rate, the economy would create fewer jobs. If this outcome did occur, a policy aimed at lowering unemployment in the short run might end up increasing it in the long run.

By the late 1960s and through the 1970s, Keynes' predictions became a reality. Inflation increased, economic growth slowed, and in some countries unemployment became persistently high. The causes of these developments are complex. But they point to an inescapable conclusion: The long-term problems of inflation, slow growth, and persistent unemployment and the short-term problems of depression and economic fluctuations intertwine and are most usefully studied together. So although macroeconomics was reborn during the Great Depression, it has now returned to its older tradition. Today, macroeconomics is a subject that tries to understand long-term economic growth and inflation as well as short-term business fluctuations and unemployment.

The Road Ahead

There is no unique way to study macroeconomics. Because its rebirth was a product of depression, the common practice for many years was to pay most attention to short-term output fluctuations and unemployment, but never to completely lose sight of the long-term issues. When a rapid inflation emerged during the 1970s, this topic returned to prominence. During the 1980s, when long-term growth slowed in Canada and other rich industrial countries but exploded in East Asia, economists redirected their energy towards economic growth. During the 1990s, as information technologies further shrank the globe, the international dimension of macroeconomics became more prominent. The result of these developments is that modern macroeconomics is a broad subject that studies all the issues we've just identified: economic growth and fluctuations, unemployment, inflation, and government and international deficits.

Over the past 40 years, economists have developed a clearer understanding of the forces that determine macroeconomic performance and have devised policies that they hope will improve this performance. Your main goal is to become familiar with the theories of macroeconomics and the policies that they make possible. To set you on your path towards this goal, we're going to take a first look at economic growth, jobs and unemployment, inflation, and surpluses and deficits, and learn why these macroeconomic phenomena merit our attention.

Economic Growth

YOUR PARENTS ARE RICHER THAN YOUR GRAND-parents were when they were young. But are you going to be richer than your parents are? And are your children going to be richer than you? The answers depend on the rate of economic growth.

Economic growth is the expansion of the economy's production possibilities. It can be pictured as an outward shift of the production possibilities frontier (*PPF*)—see Chapter 2, pp. 40–41.

We measure economic growth by the increase in real gross domestic product. **Real gross domestic product** (also called **real GDP**) is the value of the total production of all the nation's farms, factories, shops, and offices measured in the prices of a single year. Real GDP in Canada is currently measured in the prices of 1997 (called 1997 dollars). We use the dollar prices of a single year to eliminate the influence of *inflation*—the increase in the average level of prices—and determine how much production has grown from one year to another. (Real GDP is explained more fully in Chapter 20 on pp. 458–462.)

Real GDP is not a perfect measure of total production because it does not include everything that is produced. It excludes the things we produce for ourselves at home (preparing meals, doing laundry, house painting, gardening, and so on). It also excludes production that people hide to avoid taxes or because the activity is illegal—the underground economy. But despite its shortcomings, real GDP is the best measure of total production available. Let's see what it tells us about economic growth.

Economic Growth in Canada

Figure 19.1 shows real GDP in Canada since 1961 and highlights two features of economic growth:

- The growth of potential GDP
- Fluctuations of real GDP around potential GDP

The Growth of Potential GDP When all the economy's labour, capital, land, and entrepreneurial ability are fully employed, the value of production is called **potential GDP**. Real GDP fluctuates around potential GDP and the rate of long-term economic growth is measured by the growth rate of potential GDP. It is shown by the steepness of the potential GDP line (the black line) in Fig. 19.1.

From 1960 through 1974, potential GDP grew at an unusually rapid rate of 4.9 percent a year. But the growth rate slowed from the mid-1970s to the mid-1990s. The growth rate of output per person sagged during these years in a phenomenon called the **productivity growth slowdown**. The growth rate of potential GDP increased during the late 1990s and 2000s, but it is too soon to tell whether this increase is the beginning of a new phase of more rapid growth.

Why did the productivity growth slowdown occur? This question is controversial. We explore the causes of the productivity growth slowdown in Chapter 30. Whatever its cause, the slowdown means that we all have smaller incomes today than we would have had if the economy had continued to grow at its 1960s rate.

Let's now look at real GDP fluctuations around potential GDP.

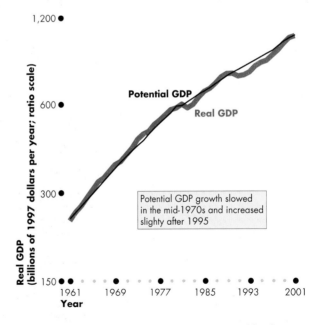

FIGURE 19.1 Economic Growth in Canada

The long-term economic growth rate, measured by the growth of potential GDP, was 4.9 percent a year from 1960 through 1974. Growth slowed from the mid-1970s to the mid-1990s but sped up slightly after 1995. Real GDP fluctuates around potential GDP.

Sources: Statistics Canada, CANSIM series v1992292 and International Monetary Fund, *World Economic Outlook* database, Output gap series.

Fluctuations of Real GDP Around Potential GDP
Real GDP fluctuates around potential GDP in a business cycle. A *business cycle* is the periodic but irregular up-and-down movement in production.

Business cycles are not regular, predictable, or repeating cycles like the phases of the moon. Their timing changes unpredictably. But cycles do have some things in common. Every business cycle has two phases:

1. A recession
2. An expansion

and two turning points:

1. A peak
2. A trough

Figure 19.2 shows these features of the most recent business cycle in Canada. A **recession** is a period during which real GDP decreases—the growth rate of real GDP is negative—for at least two successive quarters. The most recent recession, which is highlighted in the figure, began in the first quarter of

1990 and ended in the first quarter of 1991. This recession lasted for four quarters. An **expansion** is a period during which real GDP increases. The most recent expansion began in the second quarter of 1991. This expansion is the longest expansion on record. An earlier expansion ended in the first quarter of 1990.

When a business cycle expansion ends and a recession begins, the turning point is called a **peak**. The most recent peak occurred in the first quarter of 1990. When a business cycle recession ends and an expansion begins, the turning point is called a **trough**. The most recent trough occurred in the first quarter of 1991.

Sometimes, during a business cycle expansion phase, the growth rate slows down. A slowdown in the growth rate of real GDP but with the growth rate *not* becoming negative for two quarters is called a **growth recession**. Two growth recessions occurred during the long expansion of the 1990s and 2000s. The first of these ran from the beginning of 1995 to the first quarter of 1996 and the second one ran from mid 2000 to mid 2001. During a growth recession, real GDP dips below potential GDP.

FIGURE 19.2   The Most Recent Canadian Business Cycle

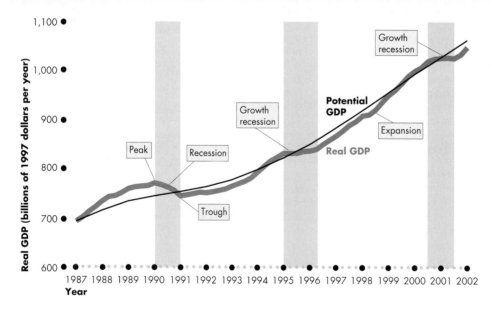

A business cycle has two phases: recession and expansion. The most recent recession (highlighted) ran from the first quarter of 1990 through the first quarter of 1991. Then a new expansion began in the second quarter of 1991. A business cycle has two turning points, a peak and a trough. In the most recent business cycle, the peak occurred in the first quarter of 1990 and the trough occurred in the first quarter of 1991. Growth recessions occurred in 1995–1996 and in 2000–2001.

Sources: Statistics Canada, CANSIM series v1992292 and International Monetary Fund, *World Economic Outlook* database, Output gap series.

The Most Recent Recession in Historical Perspective The recession of 1990–1991 seemed severe while we were passing through it, but compared with earlier recessions, it was mild. You can see how mild it was by looking at Fig. 19.3, which shows a longer history of Canadian economic growth. The biggest decrease in real GDP occurred during the Great Depression of the 1930s. A decrease also occurred in 1946 and 1947, after a huge World War II expansion. A serious recession also occurred during the early 1980s, when the Bank of Canada and the Federal Reserve Board in the United States hiked interest rates to previously unimagined levels.

Each of these economic downturns was more severe than that in 1990–1991. But you can see that the Great Depression was much more severe than anything that followed it. This episode was so extreme that we don't call it a recession. We call it a *depression.*

This last truly great depression occurred before governments started taking policy actions to stabilize the economy. It also occurred before the birth of modern macroeconomics. Is the absence of another great depression a sign that macroeconomics has contributed to economic stability? Some people believe it is. Others doubt it. We'll evaluate these opinions on a number of occasions in this book.

We've looked at real GDP growth and fluctuations in Canada. But is the Canadian experience typical? Do other countries share our experience? Let's see whether they do.

Economic Growth Around the World

A country might have a rapid growth rate of real GDP, but it might also have a rapid population growth rate. To compare growth rates over time and across countries, we use the growth rate of real GDP *per person*. Real GDP per person is real GDP divided by the population. For example, Canadian real GDP in the first quarter of 2002 was $1,048 billion a year. The population of Canada was 31.4 million. So Canadian real GDP per person was $1,048 billion divided by 31.4 million, which equals $33,376.

Figure 19.4 shows real GDP per person between 1960 and 2000 for Canada alongside the world's

---

FIGURE 19.3 Long-Term Economic Growth in Canada

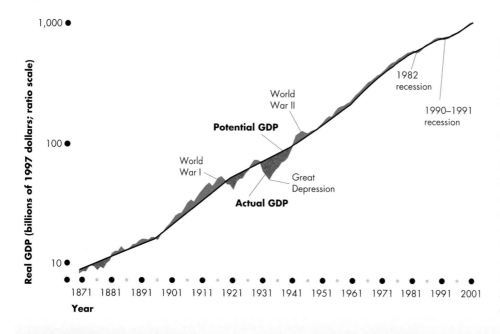

The thin black line shows potential GDP. Along this line, real GDP grew at an average rate of 3.7 percent a year between 1870 and 2001. The blue areas show when real GDP was above potential GDP, and the red areas show when it was below potential GDP. During some periods, such as World War II, real GDP expanded quickly. During other periods, such as the Great Depression and more recently in 1982 (following interest rate hikes) and 1990–1991, real GDP declined.

Sources: 1870–1925, Angus Maddison, *Dynamic Forces in Capitalist Development,* Oxford University Press, New York, 1991. 1926–2001, and Statistics Canada, *Historical Statistics of Canada,* series F 55 and CANSIM series v1992292.

three largest economies: the United States, Japan, and Germany. In these countries, four features of the paths of real GDP per person stand out:

- Similar business cycles before 1990
- Different business cycles in the 1990s
- Similar 1970s growth recessions
- Different long-term growth trends

Similar Business Cycles Before 1990 Each of the three big economies had an expansion running from the early or mid-1960s through 1973, a recession from 1973 to 1975, an expansion through 1979, another recession in the early 1980s, and a long expansion through the rest of the 1980s.

Different Business Cycles in the 1990s The 1990s saw Canada and the United States in a long and strong business cycle expansion. But the decade brought severe recession in Japan and only moderate expansion in Germany. This divergence of business cycles is relatively uncommon.

Similar 1970s Growth Recessions Canadian real GDP per person grew at 3.8 percent a year from 1960 through 1973, but slowed to 2.5 percent between 1974 and 1988 and to only 1.2 percent after 1988. Growth in the United States slowed from 2.9 percent to 1.7 percent and then to 1.8 percent, in Germany from 3.5 percent to 2.0 percent and then to 1.6 percent, and in Japan from 8.5 percent to 3.3 percent and then to 0.8 percent.

Different Long-Term Growth Trends In 1960, real GDP per person in Canada exceeded that in Germany, exceeded that in Japan by a large amount, but was less than that in the United States.

During the 1960s, Japan's real GDP streaked upward like a rocket departing Cape Canaveral. Canada and Germany grew quickly too, and all three countries closed the gap on the United States. Growth slowed in all four countries during the 1970s and Japan's growth rate more than halved. Even so, Japan's growth of real GDP per person equalled the U.S. rate *before* the slowdown. Because it achieved such a high growth rate, Japan narrowed the gap

---

FIGURE 19.4   Economic Growth in Canada and the Three Largest Economies

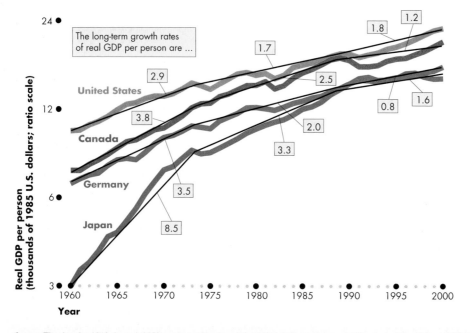

The long-term growth rates of real GDP per person are ...

Economic growth in Canada and the three large economies—the United States, Germany, and Japan—was the most rapid during the 1960s. The growth rate in all four countries slowed during the 1970s, and the countries had similar business cycles. The United States has grown slowest and Canada has narrowed the gap on the United States. Japan has grown fastest, and Germany too has grown faster than the United States. But in the mid-1990s, growth in Canada and in Japan had slowed to a crawl.

Sources: The data for 1960 through 1992 are from "The Penn World Table," *Quarterly Journal of Economics*, May 1991, pp. 327–368. New computer disk supplement (Mark 5.6a). The data use comparable international relative prices converted to 1985 U.S. dollars. The data for 1993–2000 are from the International Monetary Fund, *International Financial Statistics*, Washington, D.C., 2002.

between its own level of real GDP per person and those of Canada and the United States and overtook that of Germany.

During the 1990s, Japan's real GDP per person fell below Germany's and because the growth of Canada's real GDP per person slowed to a crawl, the gap between the levels of real GDP per person in Canada and the United States widened.

Figure 19.5 compares the growth of the Canadian economy with that of several other countries and regions since 1980. Among the industrial economies, the European Union has grown the slowest and the other industrial countries, mainly those of newly industrialized Asia, have grown the fastest. Among the developing economies the most rapid growth has occurred in Asia, where the average growth rate has exceeded 7 percent a year. The slowest growing developing countries are in Africa and the Western Hemisphere (Central and South America). The transition economies have grown the slowest. These are countries such as Russia and the other countries of Central Europe that are making a transition from a state-managed economy to a market economy. Production has been shrinking severely in these countries.

World average growth has been just over 3 percent a year. The Canadian growth rate is slightly below the world average and much below the growth rates that the developing economies of Asia have achieved.

Benefits and Costs of Economic Growth

What are the benefits and costs of economic growth? Does it matter if the long-term growth rate slows as it did during the 1970s?

The main benefit of long-term economic growth is expanded consumption possibilities, including more health care for the poor and elderly, more cancer and AIDS research, more space research and exploration, better roads, and more and better housing. We can even have cleaner lakes, more trees, and cleaner air by devoting more resources to environmental problems.

When the long-term growth rate slows, some of these benefits are lost, and the loss can be large. For example, if long-term growth had not slowed in Canada during the 1970s, real GDP in 2001 would have been about $1,700 billion, or $54,000 per person. Instead, real GDP was $1,035 billion, or $33,000 per person. So if the long-term trend of the 1960s had persisted, as a nation we would have had $665 billion more to spend. Each person (on the average) would have had $21,000 more each year. If the

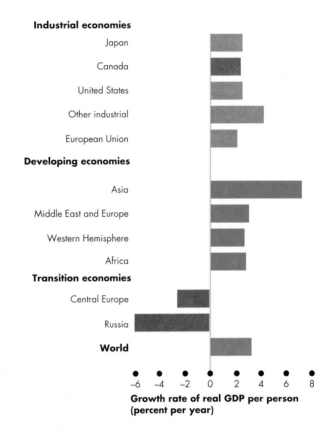

FIGURE 19.5   Growth Rates Around the World

Since 1980, the growth rate of real GDP per person has been lower in Canada than in some other industrial economies. The developing economies of Asia have had the most rapid growth rates and those of Central Europe and Russia have had the slowest growth.

Source: International Monetary Fund, *World Economic Outlook*, Washington D.C., October 1988, p.145.

government had taken one-third of this extra income, it could have provided more health care, more education, more day-care services, and more and better highways. All these items could have been obtained with no cut in the provision of other goods and services. At the same time, you might have had another $14,000 a year to spend on whatever pleased you.

The main cost of economic growth is forgone consumption. To sustain a high growth rate, resources must be devoted to advancing technology and accumulating capital rather than to producing goods and services for current consumption. This cost cannot be avoided. But it brings the benefit of greater consumption in the future.

Two other possible costs of faster growth are a more rapid depletion of exhaustible natural resources such as oil and natural gas and increased pollution of the air, rivers, and oceans. But neither of these two costs is inevitable. The technological advances that bring economic growth help us to economize on natural resources and to clean up the environment. For example, more efficient auto engines cut gasoline use and tailpipe emissions.

A fourth possible cost of faster growth is more frequent job changes and more frequent moves from one region of the country to another. For example, during the 1990s, the economy of central Canada expanded and people migrated there from the Maritimes and the Prairies.

The pace of economic growth is determined by the choices that people make to balance the benefits and costs of economic growth. You'll study these choices and their consequences in Chapter 30.

REVIEW QUIZ

1 What is economic growth and how is the long-term economic growth rate measured?

2 What is the distinction between real GDP and *potential* GDP?

3 What is a business cycle and what are its phases?

4 What is a *recession*?

5 In what phase of the business cycle was the Canadian economy during 2001?

6 What happened to economic growth in Canada and other countries during the 1970s?

7 What are the similarities and differences in growth among the major economies?

8 What are the benefits and the costs of long-term economic growth?

We've seen that real GDP grows and that it fluctuates over the business cycle. The business cycle brings fluctuations in the number of jobs available and in unemployment. Let's now examine these core macroeconomic problems.

Jobs and Unemployment

WHAT KIND OF LABOUR MARKET WILL YOU ENTER when you graduate? Will there be plenty of good jobs to choose from, or will there be so much unemployment that you will be forced to take a low-paying job that doesn't use your education? The answer depends, to a large degree, on the total number of jobs available and on the unemployment rate.

Jobs

Finance Minister Paul Martin introduced the 1995 federal budget with what seemed to be an astonishing fact: "Canada is enjoying a period of strong economic growth and job creation. In the past year, 433,000 jobs have been created."

The Canadian economy is an incredible job-creating machine. In 2001, 15.1 million Canadians had jobs. That number is 2.2 million more than in 1991 and 3.8 million more than in 1981. But a year in which we create 433,000 new jobs is unusual. Every year, on the average, the Canadian economy creates about 200,000 *additional* jobs.

The pace of job creation and destruction fluctuates over the business cycle. More jobs are destroyed than created during a recession, so the number of jobs decreases. But more jobs are created than destroyed during an expansion, so the number of jobs increases. For example, during the recession of 1990–1991, Canadian production shrank and 250,000 jobs disappeared. But through the expansion that followed, the number of jobs created expanded quickly.

Unemployment

Not everyone who wants a job can find one. On any one day in a normal or average year, more than 1 million people are unemployed, and during a recession or depression, unemployment rises above this level. For example, in November 1992, the worst month for unemployment in recent times, 1,740,000 people were looking for jobs.

Unemployment is defined as a state in which a person does not have a job but is available for work, willing to work, and has made some effort to find work within the previous four weeks. The total number of people who are employed and unemployed is called the **labour force**. The **unemployment rate** is the percentage of the people in the labour force who are unemployed. (The concepts of the labour force and unemployment are explained more fully in Chapter 21 on pp. 480–481.)

The unemployment rate is not a perfect measure of the underutilization of labour for two main reasons. First, the unemployment rate excludes discouraged workers. A **discouraged worker** is a person who does not have a job, is available for work, and is willing to work but who has given up the effort to find work. Many people switch between the unemployed and discouraged worker categories in both directions every month. Second, the unemployment rate measures unemployed people rather than unemployed labour hours. As a result, the unemployment rate excludes part-time workers who want full-time jobs.

Despite these two limitations, the unemployment rate is the best available measure of underused labour resources. Let's look at some facts about unemployment.

Unemployment in Canada

Figure 19.6 shows the unemployment rate in Canada from 1926 through 2001. Three features stand out. First, during the Great Depression of the 1930s, the unemployment rate climbed to an all-time high of almost 20 percent during 1933 and remained high throughout the 1930s.

Second, the unemployment rate reached an all-time low of 1.2 percent during World War II.

Third, although in recent years we have not experienced anything as devastating as the Great Depression, we have seen some high unemployment rates during recessions. The figure highlights two of them—the 1982 recession and the 1990–1991 recession.

Fourth, the unemployment rate never falls to zero. In the period since World War II, the average unemployment rate has been 6.7 percent.

How does Canadian unemployment compare with unemployment in other countries?

FIGURE 19.6   Unemployment in Canada

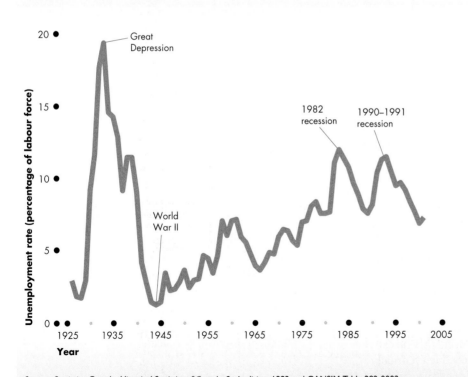

Unemployment is a persistent feature of economic life, but its rate varies. At its worst—during the Great Depression—20 percent of the labour force was unemployed. Even in recent recessions, the unemployment rate climbed towards 12 percent. Between the late 1960s and 1982, there was a general tendency for the unemployment rate to increase. Since 1982, the unemployment rate has remained below its 1982 peak and fell during the 1990s.

Sources: Statistics Canada, Historical Statistics of Canada, 2nd edition, 1983 and CANSIM Table 282-0002.

Unemployment Around the World

Figure 19.7 compares the unemployment rate in Canada with those in Western Europe, Japan, and the United States. Over the period shown in this figure, Canadian unemployment averaged 9.3 percent, much higher than Japanese unemployment (which averaged 3.0 percent), and higher than U.S. unemployment (which averaged 6.3 percent) and European unemployment (which averaged 8.6 percent).

Canadian unemployment fluctuates over the business cycle. It increases during a recession and decreases during an expansion. Like Canadian unemployment, U.S. and European unemployment increase during recessions and decrease during expansions. The cycles in Canadian unemployment are similar to those in U.S. unemployment, but the European cycle is out of phase with the North American cycle.

During the past 20 years, U.S. unemployment has been on a falling trend and during the past 10 years, Japanese unemployment has been on a rising trend. There have been no trends in the unemployment rates of Canada and Western Europe.

Let's now look at some of the consequences of unemployment that make it the serious problem that it is.

Why Unemployment Is a Problem

Unemployment is a serious economic, social, and personal problem for two main reasons:

■ Lost production and incomes
■ Lost human capital

Lost Production and Incomes The loss of a job brings an immediate loss of income and production. These losses are devastating for the people who bear them and make unemployment a frightening prospect for everyone. Employment insurance creates a safety net, but it does not provide the same living standard that having a job provides.

Lost Human Capital Prolonged unemployment can permanently damage a person's job prospects. For example, a manager loses his job when his employer downsizes. Short of income, he becomes a taxi driver. After a year in this work, he discovers that he can't compete with new MBA graduates. He eventually gets hired as a manager but in a small firm and at a low wage. He has lost some of his human capital.

The costs of unemployment are spread unequally,

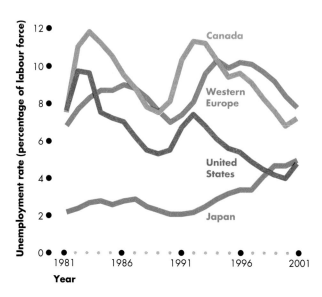

FIGURE 19.7 Unemployment in Industrial Economies

The unemployment rate in Canada has been higher, on the average, than the unemployment rates of the United States, Western Europe, and Japan. The cycles in Canadian unemployment are similar to those in the United States. Western European unemployment has a cycle that is out of phase with the North American unemployment cycle. Unemployment in Japan has drifted upward in recent years.

Source: International Monetary Fund, *World Economic Outlook,* September 2002, Washington, D.C.

which makes unemployment a highly charged political problem as well as a serious economic problem.

REVIEW QUIZ

1 What is unemployment?
2 What have been the main trends and cycles in the unemployment rate in Canada since 1926?
3 Compare unemployment in Canada, the United States, Western Europe, and Japan.
4 What are the main costs of unemployment that make it a serious problem?

Let's now turn to the third major macroeconomic issue: inflation.

Inflation

PRICES ON THE AVERAGE CAN BE RISING, FALLING, or stable. **Inflation** is a process of rising prices. We measure the *inflation rate* as the percentage change in the *average* level of prices or the **price level.** A common measure of the price level is the *Consumer Price Index* (CPI). The CPI tells us how the average price of all the goods and services bought by a typical urban household changes from month to month. (The CPI is explained in Chapter 21, p. 490.)

So that you can see how the inflation rate is measured, let's do a calculation. In December 2000, the CPI was 115.1, and in December 2001, it was 115.9, so the inflation rate during 2001 was

$$\text{Inflation rate} = \frac{115.9 - 115.1}{115.1} \times 100$$

$$= 0.7 \text{ percent.}$$

Inflation in Canada

Figure 19.8 shows the Canadian inflation rate from 1961 through 2001. During the early 1960s, the inflation rate was low. It began to increase during the late 1960s at the time of the Vietnam War. But the largest increases occurred in 1974 and 1980, years in which the actions of the Organization of Petroleum Exporting Countries (OPEC) resulted in exceptionally large increases in the price of oil. Inflation was brought under control in the early 1980s when Bank of Canada Governor Gerald Bouey and U.S. Federal Reserve Chairman Paul Volcker pushed interest rates up and people cut back on their spending. Since 1983, inflation has been relatively mild, and during the 1990s its rate continued to fall until 1998 when it began to increase again.

The inflation rate rises and falls over the years, but it rarely becomes negative. If the inflation rate is negative, the price *level* is falling and we have **deflation.** Since the 1930s, the price level has generally increased—the inflation rate has been positive.

FIGURE 19.8   Inflation in Canada

Inflation is a persistent feature of economic life in Canada. The inflation rate was low in the first half of the 1960s, but it increased during the late 1960s at the time of the Vietnam War. The inflation rate increased further with the OPEC oil price hikes but eventually declined in the early 1980s because of policy actions taken by the Bank of Canada. Since 1983, inflation has been mild, and during the 1990s it fell further. In the late 1990s, the inflation rate increased slightly and in 2001 was 2.6 percent.

Source: Statistics Canada CANSIM table 362-0002.

Inflation Around the World

Figure 19.9 shows inflation around the world since 1970. It also shows the Canadian inflation rate in a broader perspective. Part (a) shows that the other industrial countries shared Canada's burst of double-digit inflation during the 1970s and the decline in inflation during the 1980s and 1990s. But Canada has achieved a lower inflation rate than most countries. Part (b) shows that the average inflation rate of industrial countries has been very low compared with that of the developing counties. Among the developing countries, the most extreme inflation in recent times has occurred in the former Yugoslavia, where its rate has exceeded 6,000 percent per year.

Is Inflation a Problem?

A very low inflation rate is not much of a problem. But a high inflation rate is a serious problem. It makes inflation hard to predict, and unpredictable inflation makes the economy behave a bit like a casino in which some people gain and some lose and no one can predict where the gains and losses will fall. Gains and losses occur because of unpredictable changes in the value of money. Money is used as a measuring rod of value in the transactions that we undertake. Borrowers and lenders, workers and employers, all make contracts in terms of money. If the value of money varies unpredictably over time, then the amounts *really* paid and received—the quantity of goods that the money will buy—also fluctuate unpredictably. Measuring value with a measuring rod whose units vary is a bit like trying to measure a piece of cloth with an elastic ruler. The size of the cloth depends on how tightly the ruler is stretched.

In a period of rapid, unpredictable inflation, resources get diverted from productive activities to forecasting inflation. It becomes more profitable to forecast the inflation rate correctly than to invent a new product. Doctors, lawyers, accountants, farmers—just about everyone—can make themselves better off, not by specializing in the profession for which they have been trained but by spending more of their time dabbling as amateur economists and inflation forecasters and managing their investment portfolios.

From a social perspective, this diversion of talent resulting from inflation is like throwing scarce resources onto the garbage heap. This waste of resources is a cost of inflation.

FIGURE 19.9   Inflation Around the World

(a) Canada and other industrial countries

(b) Industrial countries and developing countries

Inflation in Canada is similar to that in the other industrial countries. Compared with the developing countries, inflation in Canada and the other industrial countries is low.

Sources: International Monetary Fund, *International Financial Statistics Yearbook,* Washington, D.C., 2001, and *World Economic Outlook,* October 2001.

The most serious type of inflation is called *hyperinflation*—an inflation rate that exceeds 50 percent a month. At the height of a hyperinflation, workers are often paid twice a day because money loses its value so quickly. As soon as workers are paid, they rush out to spend their wages before they lose too much value.

Hyperinflation is rare but there have been some spectacular examples of it. Several European countries experienced hyperinflation during the 1920s after World War I and again during the 1940s after World War II. But hyperinflation is more than just a historical curiosity. It occurs in today's world. In 1994, the African nation of Zaire had a hyperinflation that peaked at a *monthly* inflation rate of 76 percent, which is 88,000 percent a year! Brazil has also been close to the hyperinflation stratosphere with a monthly inflation rate of 40 percent. A cup of coffee that cost 15 cruzeiros in 1980 cost 22 *billion* cruzeiros in 1994.

Inflation imposes costs, but getting rid of inflation is also costly. Policies that lower the inflation rate increase the unemployment rate. Most economists think the increase in the unemployment rate that accompanies a fall in the inflation rate is temporary. But some economists say that higher unemployment is a permanent cost of low inflation. The cost of lowering inflation must be evaluated when an anti-inflation policy is pursued. You will learn more about inflation and the costs of curing it in Chapter 28.

REVIEW QUIZ

1 What is inflation and how does it influence the value of money?
2 How is inflation measured?
3 What has been Canada's inflation record since 1961?
4 How does inflation in Canada compare with inflation in other industrial countries and in developing countries?
5 What are some of the costs of inflation that make it a serious economic problem?

Now that you've studied economic growth and fluctuations, unemployment, and inflation, let's turn to the fourth macroeconomic issue: surpluses and deficits. What happens when a government spends more than it collects in taxes? And what happens when a nation buys more from other countries than it sells to them? Do governments and nations face the problem that you and I would face if we spent more than we earned? Do they run out of funds? Let's look at these questions.

Surpluses and Deficits

In 1998, for the first time in almost 30 years, the federal government had a budget surplus. For 28 years, it had a deficit. And most years, Canada has an international deficit. What is the government budget surplus and deficit? What is an international deficit?

Government Budget Surplus and Deficit

If a government collects more in taxes than it spends, it has a surplus—a **government budget surplus.** If a government spends more than it collects in taxes, it has a deficit—a **government budget deficit.** The federal government had a surplus in 2001.

Figure 19.10(a) shows the federal government and total government budget surplus and deficit from 1971 to 2001. (Total government is federal, provincial, and local government.) So that we can compare the surplus or deficit in one year with that in another year, we measure the surplus or deficit as a percentage of GDP. (The concept of GDP, which is explained more fully in Chapter 20, pp. 458–462, equals total income in the economy.) You can think of this measure as the number of cents of surplus or deficit per dollar of income earned by an average Canadian.

The total government had a budget deficit every year from 1975 through 1996. The government deficit fluctuated and swelled during recessions. From 1982 through 1996, the deficit was never less than 2 percent of GDP.

Since 1993, the federal government deficit has shrunk, and in 1998, a surplus emerged. Since 1998, the federal budget surplus has become larger. In 2001, the federal government surplus was 1.6 percent of GDP.

International Surplus and Deficit

When we import goods and services from the rest of the world, we make payments to foreigners. When we export goods and services to the rest of the world, we receive payments from foreigners. If our imports exceed our exports, we have an international deficit.

Figure 19.10(b) shows the history of Canada's international balance from 1971 to 2001. The figure shows the balance on the **current account,** which includes our exports minus our imports but also takes into account interest payments paid to and received from the rest of the world. To compare one year with

FIGURE 19.10 Government Budget and International Surpluses and Deficits

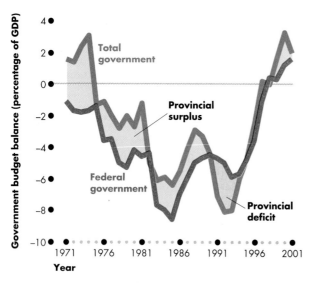

(a) Canadian government budget balance

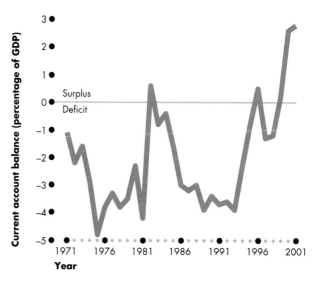

(b) Canadian international deficit

In part (a), the federal government had a large and persistent deficit between 1971 and the late-1990s. The provincial governments had a large deficit during the early 1990s. In part (b), the Canadian current account shows the balance of our exports minus our imports. In most years since

1970, Canada has had an international deficit. The deficit became large during the mid-1970s and early 1980s. It has persisted at around 3 to 4 percent of GDP through the mid-1990s. From 1999 to 2001, Canada had an international surplus.

Sources: Statistics Canada, CANSIM tables 376-0001, 380-0002, and 380-0007.

another, the figure shows the current account as a percentage of GDP. In 2001, Canada had a current account surplus of 2.8 percent of GDP. But in most years, Canada has had a current account deficit and it has fluctuated. From 1986 to 1995, the deficit was persistently around 3 percent to 4 percent of GDP. Our imports have exceeded our exports during these years. In 1996 and between 1999 and 2001, Canada had a current account surplus.

Do Surpluses and Deficits Matter?

Why do deficits cause anxiety? What happens when a government cannot cover its spending with taxes, or when a country buys more from other countries than it sells to them?

If you spend more than you earn, you have a deficit. And to cover your deficit, you go into debt. But when you borrow, you must pay interest on your debt. Just like you, if a government or a nation has a

deficit, it must borrow. And like you, the government and the nation must pay interest on their debts.

Whether borrowing and paying out huge amounts of interest is a good idea depends on what the borrowed funds are used for. If you borrow to finance a vacation, you must eventually tighten your belt, cut spending, and repay your debt as well as pay interest on the debt. But if you borrow to invest in a business that earns a large profit, you might be able to repay your debt and pay the interest on it while continuing to increase your spending. It is the same with a government and a nation. A government or a nation that borrows to increase its consumption might be heading for trouble later. But a government or a nation that borrows to buy assets that earn a profit might be making a sound investment.

You will learn more about the government's budget surplus in Chapter 24 and about the international current account in Chapter 34.

REVIEW QUIZ

1 What determines a government's budget deficit or budget surplus?
2 How have the budgets of the federal government and the provincial governments evolved since 1971?
3 What is a country's international deficit?
4 How has the Canadian international deficit changed since 1971?

Macroeconomic Policy Challenges and Tools

FROM THE TIME OF ADAM SMITH'S *Wealth of Nations* in 1776 until the publication of Keynes' *General Theory of Employment, Interest, and Money* in 1936, it was widely believed that the only economic role for government was to enforce property rights. The economy behaved best, it was believed, if the government left people free to pursue their own best interests. The macroeconomics of Keynes challenged this view. Keynes' central point was that the economy will not fix itself and that government actions are needed to achieve and maintain full employment. The Canadian government declared full employment as a policy goal soon after World War II ended.

Policy Challenges and Tools

Today, the five widely agreed challenges for macroeconomic policy are to

1. Reduce unemployment
2. Boost economic growth
3. Stabilize the business cycle
4. Keep inflation low
5. Reduce government and international deficits

But how can we do all these things? What are the tools available to pursue the macroeconomic policy challenges? Macroeconomic policy tools are divided into two broad categories:

■ Fiscal policy
■ Monetary policy

Fiscal Policy Making changes in tax rates and in government spending programs is called **fiscal policy**. This range of actions is under the control of the federal government. Fiscal policy can be used to try to boost long-term growth by creating incentives that encourage saving, investment, and technological change. Fiscal policy can also be used to try to smooth out the business cycle. When the economy is in a recession, the government might cut taxes or increase its spending. Conversely, when the economy is in a rapid expansion, the government might increase taxes or cut its spending in an attempt to slow real GDP growth and prevent inflation from increasing. Fiscal policy is discussed in Chapter 24.

Monetary Policy Changing interest rates and changing the amount of money in the economy is called **monetary policy**. These actions are under the control of the Bank of Canada. The principal aim of monetary policy is to keep inflation in check. To achieve this objective, the Bank prevents the quantity of money from expanding too rapidly. Monetary policy can also be used to smooth the business cycle. When the economy is in recession, the Bank might lower interest rates and inject money into the economy. And when the economy is in a rapid expansion, the Bank might increase interest rates in an attempt to slow real GDP growth and prevent inflation from increasing. We study monetary policy in Chapters 25 and 26.

REVIEW QUIZ

1 What are the main challenges of macroeconomic policy?
2 What are the main tools of macroeconomic policy?
3 Can you distinguish between fiscal policy and monetary policy?

◆ In your study of macroeconomics, you will learn what is currently known about the causes of unemployment, economic growth, business cycles, inflation, and government and international surpluses and deficits. You will also learn more about the policy choices and challenges that the government and the Bank of Canada face. *Reading Between the Lines* on pp. 452–453 examines inflation, deflation, and economic growth around the world in 2002.

Inflation, Deflation, and Economic Growth

NATIONAL POST, NOVEMBER 15, 2002

Buy technology stocks to hedge against deflation

Global economists are becoming worried about the risk of deflation. They are warning us of potential massive unemployment, terrible stock markets, economic collapse and widespread cannibalism. (OK... I made up the bit about cannibalism but economists tend to be a dry lot, and their pronouncements could use a little spicing up.)

Why the concern? Deflation is not a lowering of inflation rates; it is an absolute decline in prices. This creates a vicious cycle. Since goods get cheaper over time, why not wait and defer purchases?

If enough people do this, companies don't make money, nobody has jobs, prices go lower, and then even more people defer spending. Bad stuff. This spiral has crippled Japan for more than a decade. ...

In a recent newsletter, Toron Strategist Arthur Heinmaa talked about the possibility of deflation, the fact that the U.S. Federal Reserve is becoming increasingly aware of the dangers, and which kinds of companies are likely to do best if we do slip into deflation.

Mr. Heinmaa doesn't say that deflation is going to happen for sure, but says it is a big enough risk that as investors, we should at least partially deflation-proof our portfolios.

Investors should look for companies whose products are not commodities, with strong cash flows and minimal fixed debt. ...

Names like Microsoft, Cisco, Amgen and Intel (or Canada's Cognos, QLT or Dalsa) have good balance sheets and strong margins that reflect their considerable intellectual property.

Even after the bubble, Cisco is posting record gross margins (almost 70%), and over US$10-billion in cash. Software and drug makers routinely spend billions on research, but are still over 10 times as profitable as most industries.

Better yet, these companies already operate in a deflationary environment! The technology "industry has lived with deflation its entire existence," says University of British Columbia professor (and *Financial Post* columnist) Paul Kedrosky. ...

Reprinted by permission of Tera Capital.

Essence of the Story

■ Economists are warning about the risk of deflation—an absolute decline in the price level.

■ Deflation is said to bring unemployment, a fall in the stock market, and economic collapse.

■ Japan's economy is named as an example of the bad effects of deflation.

■ Investors can protect themselves against deflation by buying stock in companies such as Microsoft, Cisco, Amgen, Intel, Cognos, QLT, and Dalsa, which have strong cash flows and small fixed debt.

■ These companies already operate in a deflationary environment because the prices of their products have fallen every year.

Economic Analysis

■ Some economists fear the possibility of deflation in major economies such as the United States, but the consensus view is that deflation will not occur.

■ Deflation occurs when the quantity of money in the economy decreases. The opposite is happening in the United States and Canada today—we have inflation, not deflation.

■ It is true that Japan has had deflation and a poor economic performance.

■ But there is no simple and strong relationship between inflation and deflation on the one hand, and broader economic performance on the other hand.

■ Some countries have deflation and a strong economy, while others have deflation and a weak economy.

■ Also, some countries have inflation and a strong economy, while others have inflation and a weak economy.

■ Figure 1 shows the inflation and deflation rates in 2002 around the world. They ranged from an inflation rate of almost 140 percent per year in Zimbabwe to a deflation rate of 7 percent a year in Ethiopia.

■ Six countries (or territories) had deflation: Ethiopia, Hong Kong, Uganda, Bahrain, Japan, and China.

■ Compare these inflation and deflation rates with economic growth rates—a measure of the overall strength of the economy—shown in Fig. 2.

■ As the news article notes, Japan has deflation and a negative growth rate (a shrinking economy).

■ Angola, with the fastest growth rate, has a high inflation rate.

■ But high inflation and fast growth do not go together—neither do deflation and negative growth.

■ China, with the second-fastest growth rate, has a small deflation rate. Argentina, with the fastest shrinking rate, has one of the highest inflation rates. The biggest deflation occurred in Ethiopia—a country whose growth rate in 2002 was one of the highest.

■ The news article might be correct about the stocks that give the best protection against deflation. (We are not endorsing those recommendations!)

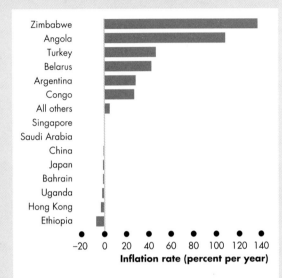

Figure 1 Inflation rates in 2002

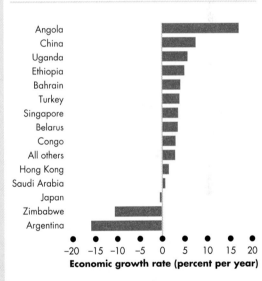

Figure 2 Economic growth rates in 2002

■ But the news article is incorrect when it says that these technology firms have experienced deflation. They have not—deflation is a falling price *level*, not a falling price of a particular group of goods.

453

SUMMARY

KEY POINTS

Origins and Issues of Macroeconomics (p. 438)

- Macroeconomics studies economic growth and fluctuations, jobs and unemployment, inflation, and surpluses and deficits.

Economic Growth (pp. 439–444)

- Economic growth is the expansion of potential GDP. Real GDP fluctuates around potential GDP in a business cycle.
- Countries have similar business cycles but different long-term trends in potential GDP.
- The main benefit of long-term economic growth is higher future consumption, and the main cost is lower current consumption.

Jobs and Unemployment (pp. 444–446)

- The Canadian economy creates about 200,000 jobs a year but unemployment persists.
- Canadian unemployment increases during a recession and decreases during an expansion.
- The Canadian unemployment rate is higher than that in the United States and Japan.
- Unemployment can permanently damage a person's job prospects.

Inflation (pp. 447–449)

- Inflation, a process of rising prices, is measured by the percentage change in the CPI.
- Inflation is a problem because it lowers the value of money and makes money less useful as a measuring rod of value.

Surpluses and Deficits (pp. 449–451)

- When the government collects more in taxes than it spends, the government has a budget surplus. When the government spends more than it collects in taxes, the government has a budget deficit.

- When imports exceed exports, a nation has an international deficit.
- Deficits are financed by borrowing.

Macroeconomic Policy Challenges and Tools (p. 451)

- The macroeconomic policy challenge is to use fiscal policy and monetary policy to boost long-term growth, stabilize the business cycle, lower unemployment, tame inflation, and prevent large deficits.

KEY FIGURES

KEY TERMS

PROBLEMS

*1. Use Data Graphing in Chapter 19 of *Economics in Action* to answer the following questions. In which country in 1992 was
  a. The growth rate of real GDP highest: Canada, Japan, or the United States?
  b. The unemployment rate highest: Canada, Japan, the United Kingdom, or the United States?
  c. The inflation rate lowest: Canada, Germany, the United Kingdom, or the United States?
  d. The government budget deficit (as a percentage of GDP) largest: Canada, Japan, the United Kingdom, or the United States?

2. Use Data Graphing in Chapter 19 of *Economics in Action* to answer the following questions. In which country in 2000 was
  a. The growth rate of real GDP highest: Canada, Japan, or the United States?
  b. The unemployment rate lowest: Canada, Japan, the United Kingdom, or the United States?
  c. The inflation rate lowest: Canada, the United Kingdom, Japan, or the United States?
  d. The government budget surplus (as a percentage of GDP) smallest: Canada, the United Kingdom, or the United States?
  e. Is it possible to say in which country consumption possibilities are growing fastest? Why or why not?

*3. The figure shows the real GDP growth rates in India and Pakistan from 1989 to 1996.

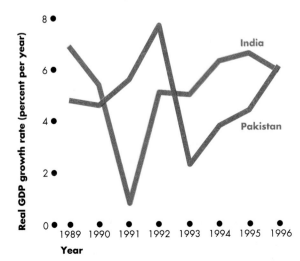

In which years did economic growth in
  a. India increase? And in which year was growth the fastest?
  b. Pakistan decrease? And in which year was growth the slowest?
  c. Compare the paths of economic growth in India and Pakistan during this period.

4. The figure shows real GDP per person in Australia and Japan from 1989 to 1996.

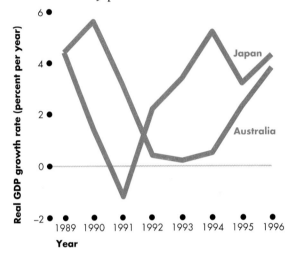

In which years did economic growth in
  a. Australia increase? And in which year was growth the fastest?
  b. Japan decrease? And in which year was growth the slowest?
  c. Compare the paths of economic growth in Australia and Japan during this period.

*5. The figure shows real GDP in Germany from the first quarter of 1991 to the fourth quarter of 1994.

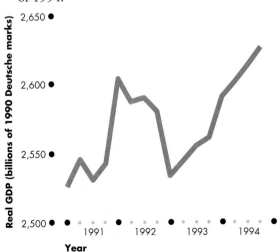

a. How many recessions did Germany experience during this period?

b. In which quarters, if any, did Germany experience a business cycle peak?

c. In which quarters, if any, did Germany experience a business cycle trough?

d. In which quarters, if any, did Germany experience an expansion?

6. The table shows Canada's rate of economic growth during 2001 and the first three quarters of 2002.

	2001	2002
First quarter	0.6	5.8
Second quarter	0.3	4.1
Third quarter	−0.5	3.0
Fourth quarter	2.9	

a. Did Canada experience a recession during this period?

b. Did the economic growth rate speed up or slow down during 2002?

c. Which of the two years had the highest average economic growth rate?

*7. Use Data Graphing in Chapter 19 of *Economics in Action* to answer the following questions. Which country, in 1998, had

a. The largest budget deficit: Canada, Japan, the United Kingdom, or the United States?

b. A current account surplus: Canada, Japan, Germany, or the United States?

8. Use Data Graphing in Chapter 19 of *Economics in Action* to answer the following questions. Which country, in 2002, had

a. The largest budget surplus: Canada, Japan, the United Kingdom, or the United States?

b. The largest current account deficit: Canada, Japan, Germany, or the United States?

*9. Use Data Graphing in Chapter 19 of *Economics in Action* to make a scatter diagram of the inflation rate and the unemployment rate in Canada.

a. Describe the relationship.

b. Do you think that low unemployment brings an increase in the inflation rate?

10. Use Data Graphing in Chapter 19 of *Economics in Action* to make a scatter diagram of the government budget deficit as a percentage of GDP and the unemployment rate in Canada.

a. Describe the relationship.

b Do you think that low unemployment brings a decrease in the budget deficit?

CRITICAL THINKING

1. Study *Reading Between the Lines* on pp. 452–453 and then answer the following questions:

a. Which countries experienced deflation during 2002?

b. Of the countries that experienced deflation, which experienced negative economic growth?

c. Which countries experienced high inflation rates during 2002?

d. Of the countries that experienced high inflation rates, which experienced negative economic growth?

e. What do you think the data presented in the figures on page 453 tell us about the effects of deflation?

WEB EXERCISES

1. Use the links on the Parkin–Bade Web site to obtain the latest data on real GDP, unemployment, and inflation in Canada

a. Update the figures on pages 440, 445, and 447.

b. What dangers does the Canadian economy face today?

c. What actions, if any, do you think might be needed to keep the economy strong?

2. Use the links on the Parkin–Bade Web site to obtain data on unemployment in your home province.

a. Compare unemployment in your home province with that in Canada as a whole.

b. Why do you think your province might have a higher or a lower unemployment rate than the Canadian average?

3. Use the links on the Parkin–Bade Web site to obtain data on the Consumer Price Index for the capital city in your home province.

a. Compare the inflation rate in your home province with that in Canada as a whole.

b. Compare the inflation rate in your home province with that of the capital cities in neighbouring provinces.

4. Use the links on the Parkin–Bade Web site to obtain data on the following variables for Canada for the most recent period. Describe how the following variables have changed over the last year.

a. The unemployment rate

b. The inflation rate

c. The government budget surplus or deficit

d. The international deficit

MEASURING GDP AND ECONOMIC GROWTH

CHAPTER 20

An Economic Barometer

Has our economy avoided the recession that in 2001 and 2002 hit the United States and several other parts of the world? In the fall of 2002, many Canadian and foreign corporations wanted to know the answer to this question. Nortel wanted to know whether to lay off more workers or delay the layoffs for a while in the hope that the economy might expand. Bombardier wanted to know whether to expand its capacity to build railroad engines. To assess the state of the economy and to make big decisions about business contraction and expansion, firms such as Nortel and Bombardier use forecasts of GDP. What exactly *is* GDP and how can we use it to tell us whether we are in a recession or how rapidly our economy is expanding? ◆ To reveal the growth or shrinkage of GDP, we must remove the effects of inflation and assess how *real* GDP is changing. How do we remove the inflation component of GDP to reveal *real* GDP? ◆ Some countries are rich while others are poor. How do we compare economic well-being in one country with that in another? How can we make international comparisons of GDP?

◆ In this chapter, you will find out how economic statisticians measure GDP, real GDP, and the economic growth rate. You will also learn about the limitations of these measures. In *Reading Between the Lines* at the end of the chapter, we'll look at Canadian real GDP during 2002.

After studying this chapter, you will be able to

- Define GDP and use the circular flow model to explain why GDP equals aggregate expenditure and aggregate income

- Explain the two ways of measuring GDP

- Explain how we measure *real* GDP and the GDP deflator

- Explain how we use real GDP to measure economic growth and describe the limitations of our measure

Gross Domestic Product

WHAT EXACTLY IS GDP, HOW IS IT CALCULATED, what does it mean, and why do we care about it? You are going to discover the answers to these questions in this chapter. First, what *is* GDP?

GDP Defined

GDP, or **gross domestic product**, is the market value of all the final goods and services produced within a country in a given time period. This definition has four parts:

- Market value
- Final goods and services
- Produced within a country
- In a given time period

We'll examine each in turn.

Market Value To measure total production, we must add together the production of apples and oranges, computers and popcorn. Just counting the items doesn't get us very far. For example, which is the greater total production: 100 apples and 50 oranges, or 50 apples and 100 oranges?

GDP answers this question by valuing items at their *market values*—at the prices at which each item is traded in markets. If the price of an apple is 10 cents, the market value of 50 apples is $5. If the price of an orange is 20 cents, the market value of 100 oranges is $20. By using market prices to value production, we can add the apples and oranges together. The market value of 50 apples and 100 oranges is $5 plus $20, or $25.

Final Goods and Services To calculate GDP, we value the *final goods and services* produced. A **final good** (or service) is an item that is bought by its final user during a specified time period. It contrasts with an **intermediate good** (or service), which is an item that is produced by one firm, bought by another firm, and used as a component of a final good or service.

For example, a Ford SUV is a final good, but a Firestone tire on the SUV is an intermediate good. A Dell computer is a final good, but an Intel Pentium chip inside it is an intermediate good.

If we were to add the value of intermediate goods and services produced to the value of final goods and services, we would count the same thing many times—a problem called *double counting*. The value of an SUV already includes the value of the tires, and the value of a Dell PC already includes the value of the Pentium chip inside it.

Some goods can be an intermediate good in some situations and a final good in other situations. For example, the ice cream that you buy on a hot summer day is a final good, but the ice cream that a café buys and uses to make sundaes is an intermediate good. The sundae is the final good. So whether a good is an intermediate good or a final good depends on what it is used for, not on what it is.

Produced Within a Country Only goods and services that are produced *within a country* count as part of that country's GDP. Bata Limited, a Canadian firm, produces shoes in Thailand, and the market value of those shoes is part of Thailand's GDP, not part of Canada's GDP. Toyota, a Japanese firm, produces automobiles in Cambridge, Ontario, and the value of this production is part of Canada's GDP, not part of Japan's GDP.

In a Given Time Period GDP measures the value of production *in a given time period*—normally either a quarter of a year (called the quarterly GDP data) or a year (called the annual GDP data). Some components of GDP are measured for a period as short as a month, but we have no reliable monthly GDP data.

Businesses such as Bell Canada and the Bank of Montreal and governments use the quarterly GDP data to keep track of the short-term evolution of the economy. They use the annual GDP data to examine long-term trends and changes in production and the standard of living.

GDP measures not only the value of total production but also total income and total expenditure. The equality between the value of total production and total income is important because it shows the direct link between productivity and living standards. Our standard of living rises when our incomes rise and we can afford to buy more goods and services. But we must produce more goods and services if we are to be able to buy more goods and services.

Rising incomes and a rising value of production go together. They are two aspects of the same phenomenon—increasing productivity. To see why, we study the circular flow of expenditure and income.

GDP and the Circular Flow of Expenditure and Income

Figure 20.1 illustrates the circular flow of expenditure and income. The economy consists of households, firms, governments, and the rest of the world (the diamonds), which trade in factor markets, goods (and services) markets, and financial markets. We focus first on households and firms.

Households and Firms Households sell and firms buy the services of labour, capital, and land in factor markets. For these factor services, firms pay income to households: wages for labour services, interest for the use of capital, and rent for the use of land. A fourth factor of production, entrepreneurship, receives profit.

Firms' retained earnings—profits that are not distributed to households—are part of the household sector's income. You can think of retained earnings as being income that households save and lend back to firms. Figure 20.1 shows the total income—*aggregate income*—received by households, including retained earnings, by the blue dots labelled *Y*.

Firms sell and households buy consumer goods and services—such as inline skates and haircuts—in the markets for goods and services. The total payment for these goods and services is **consumption expenditure,** shown by the red dots labelled *C*.

Firms buy and sell new capital equipment—such as computer systems, airplanes, trucks, and assembly line equipment—in the goods market. Some of what firms produce is not sold but is added to inventory. For example, if GM produces 1,000 cars and sells 950 of them, the other 50 cars remain in GM's inventory of unsold cars, which increases by 50 cars. When a firm adds unsold output to inventory, we can think of the firm as buying goods from itself. The

---

FIGURE 20.1   The Circular Flow of Expenditure and Income

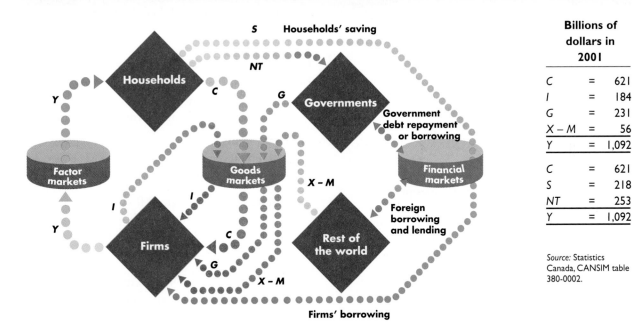

	Billions of dollars in 2001	
C	=	621
I	=	184
G	=	231
X – *M*	=	56
Y	=	1,092
C	=	621
S	=	218
NT	=	253
Y	=	1,092

Source: Statistics Canada, CANSIM table 380-0002.

In the circular flow of expenditure and income, households make consumption expenditures (*C*); firms make investment expenditures (*I*); governments purchase goods and services (*G*); and the rest of the world purchases net exports (*X* – *M*) —(red flows). Households receive incomes (*Y*) from firms (blue flow).

Aggregate income (blue flow) equals aggregate expenditure (red flows). Households use their income to consume (*C*), save (*S*), and pay net taxes (*NT*). Firms borrow to finance their investment expenditures, and governments and the rest of the world borrow to finance their deficits or lend their surpluses (green flows).

purchase of new plant, equipment, and buildings and the additions to inventories are **investment,** shown by the red dots labelled *I.*

Governments Governments buy goods and services, called **government expenditures,** from firms. In Fig. 20.1, government expenditures on goods and services are shown as the red flow *G.* Governments use taxes to pay for their purchases. Figure 20.1 shows taxes as net taxes by the green dots labelled *NT.* **Net taxes** are equal to taxes paid to governments minus transfer payments received from governments. *Transfer payments* are cash transfers from governments to households and firms, such as social security benefits, unemployment compensation, and subsidies, and interest payments on the governments' debt.

Rest of the World Firms sell goods and services to the rest of the world, **exports,** and buy goods and services from the rest of the world, **imports.** The value of exports minus the value of imports are called **net exports,** which Fig. 20.1 shows by the red flow $X - M.$

If net exports are positive, there is a net flow from the rest of the world to Canadian firms. If net exports are negative, there is net flow from Canadian firms to the rest of the world.

GDP Equals Expenditure Equals Income Gross domestic product can be determined in two ways: by the total expenditure on goods and services or by the total income earned producing goods and services.

The total expenditure—*aggregate expenditure*—is the sum of the red flows in Fig. 20.1. Aggregate expenditure equals consumption expenditure plus investment plus government expenditures plus net exports.

Aggregate income earned producing goods and services is equal to the total amount paid for the factors used—wages, interest, rent, and profit. This amount is shown by the blue flow in Fig. 20.1. Because firms pay out as incomes (including retained profits) everything they receive from the sale of their output, income (the blue flow) equals expenditure (the sum of the red flows). That is,

$$Y = C + I + G + X - M.$$

The table in Fig. 20.1 shows the numbers for 2001. You can see that the sum of the expenditures is $1,092 billion, which also equals aggregate income.

Because aggregate expenditure equals aggregate income, these two methods of valuing GDP give the same answer. So

GDP equals aggregate expenditure and equals aggregate income.

The circular flow model is the foundation on which the national economic accounts are built.

Financial Flows

The circular flow model also enables us to see the connection between the expenditure and income flows and flows through the financial markets that finance deficits and pay for investment. These flows are shown in green in Fig. 20.1. Household **saving** (*S*) is the amount that households have left after they have paid their net taxes and bought their consumption goods and services. Government borrowing finances a government budget deficit. (Government lending arises when the government has a budget surplus.) And foreign borrowing pays for a deficit with the rest of the world. These financial flows are the sources of the funds that firms use to pay for their investment in new capital. Let's look a bit more closely at how investment is financed.

How Investment Is Financed

Investment adds to the stock of capital and is one of the determinants of the rate at which production grows. Investment is financed from three sources:

1. Private saving
2. Government budget surplus
3. Borrowing from the rest of the world

Private saving is the green flow labelled *S* in Fig. 20.1. Notice that households' income is consumed, saved, or paid in net taxes. That is,

$$Y = C + S + NT.$$

But you've seen that *Y* also equals the sum of the components of aggregate expenditure. That is,

$$Y = C + I + G + X - M.$$

By using these two equations, you can see that

$$I + G + X - M = S + NT$$

Now subtract *G* and *X* from both sides of the last equation and add *M* to both sides to obtain

$$I = S + (NT - G) + (M - X).$$

In this equation, $(NT - G)$ is the government budget surplus and $(M - X)$ is borrowing from the rest of the world.

If net taxes (NT) exceed government expenditures (G), the government has a budget surplus equal to $(NT - G)$, and this surplus contributes towards paying for investment. If net taxes are less than government expenditures, the government has a budget deficit equal to $(NT - G)$, which is now negative. This deficit subtracts from the sources that finance investment.

If we import more than we export, we borrow an amount equal to $(M - X)$ from the rest of the world. So part of the rest of the world's saving finances investment in Canada. If we export more than we import, we lend an amount equal to $(X - M)$ to the rest of the world. So part of Canadian saving is used to finance investment in other countries.

The sum of private saving (S) and government saving $(NT - G)$ is called **national saving.** So investment is financed by national saving and foreign borrowing. In 2002, Canadian investment was $184 billion. National saving was $240 billion and $X - M$ was $56 billion. Canada lent $56 billion to the rest of the world.

Gross and Net Domestic Product

What does the "gross" in GDP mean? *Gross* means *before* accounting for the depreciation of capital. The opposite of gross is *net*, which means *after* accounting for the depreciation of capital. To understand what the depreciation of capital is and how it affects aggregate expenditure and income, we need to expand the accounting framework that we use and distinguish between flows and stocks.

Flows and Stocks in Macroeconomics A **flow** is a quantity per unit of time. The water that is running from an open faucet into a bathtub is a flow. So is the number of CDs you buy during a month and the amount of income that you earn during a month. GDP is a flow—the value of the goods and services produced in a country *during a given time period.* Saving and investment are also flows.

A **stock** is a quantity that exists at a point in time. The water in a bathtub is a stock. So are the number of CDs that you own and the amount of money in your savings account. The two key stocks in macroeconomics are wealth and capital. And the flows of saving and investment change these stocks.

Wealth and Saving The value of all the things that people own is called **wealth.** What people own (a stock) is related to what they earn (a flow). People earn an income, which is the amount they receive during a given time period from supplying the services of factors of production. Income that is left after paying net taxes is either consumed or saved. *Consumption expenditure* is the amount spent on consumption goods and services. *Saving* is the amount of income remaining after consumption expenditures are met. So saving adds to wealth.

For example, suppose that at the end of the school year, you have $250 in a savings account and some textbooks that are worth $300. That's all you own. Your wealth is $550. Suppose that you take a summer job and earn an income after taxes of $5,000. You are extremely careful and spend only $1,000 through the summer on consumption goods and services. At the end of the summer, when school starts again, you have $4,250 in your savings account. Your wealth is now $4,550. Your wealth has increased by $4,000, which equals your saving of $4,000. Your saving of $4,000 equals your income of $5,000 minus your consumption expenditure of $1,000.

National wealth and national saving work just like this personal example. The wealth of a nation at the start of a year equals its wealth at the start of the previous year plus its saving during the year. Its saving equals its income minus its consumption expenditure.

Capital and Investment *Capital* is the plant, equipment, buildings, and inventories of raw materials and semi-finished goods that are used to produce other goods and services. The amount of capital in the economy exerts a big influence on GDP.

Two flows change the stock of capital: investment and depreciation. *Investment,* the purchase of new capital, increases the stock of capital. (Investment includes additions to inventories.) **Depreciation** is the decrease in the stock of capital that results from wear and tear and obsolescence. Another name for depreciation is **capital consumption.** The total amount spent on purchases of new capital and on replacing depreciated capital is called **gross investment.** The amount by which the stock of capital increases is called **net investment.** Net investment equals gross investment minus depreciation.

Figure 20.2 illustrates these concepts. On January 1, 2003, Tom's Tapes, Inc., had 3 machines.

This quantity was its initial capital. During 2003, Tom's scrapped an older machine. This quantity is its depreciation. After depreciation, Tom's stock of capital was down to 2 machines. But also during 2003, Tom's bought 2 new machines. This amount is its gross investment. By December 31, 2003, Tom's Tapes had 4 machines, so its capital had increased by 1 machine. This amount is Tom's net investment. Tom's net investment equals its gross investment (the purchase of 2 new machines) minus its depreciation (1 machine scrapped).

The example of Tom's Tapes can be applied to the economy as a whole. The nation's capital stock decreases because capital depreciates and increases because of gross investment. The change in the nation's capital stock from one year to the next equals its net investment.

Back to the Gross in GDP We can now see the distinction between gross domestic product and net domestic product. On the income side of the flows that measure GDP, a firm's *gross* profit is its profit *before* subtracting *depreciation.* A firm's gross profit is part of aggregate income, so depreciation is counted as part of gross income and GDP. Similarly, on the expenditure side of the flows that measure GDP, *gross investment* includes depreciation, so depreciation is counted as part of aggregate expenditure, and total expenditure is a gross measure.

Net domestic product excludes depreciation. Like GDP, net domestic product can be viewed as the sum of incomes or expenditures. Net income includes firms' *net* profits—profits *after* subtracting depreciation. And net expenditure includes *net* investment, which also excludes depreciation.

The Short Term Meets the Long Term The flows and stocks that you've just studied influence GDP growth and fluctuations. One of the reasons why GDP grows is that the capital stock grows. Investment adds to capital, so GDP grows because of investment. But investment fluctuates, which brings fluctuations to GDP. So capital and investment along with wealth and saving are part of the key to understanding both the growth and the fluctuations of GDP.

Investment and saving interact with income and consumption expenditure in a circular flow of expenditure and income. In this circular flow, income equals expenditure, which also equals the value of production. This equality is the foundation on which a nation's economic accounts are built and from which its GDP is measured.

FIGURE 20.2   Capital and Investment

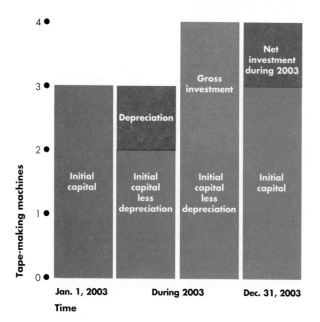

Tom's Tapes has a capital stock at the end of 2003 that equals its capital stock at the beginning of the year plus its net investment. Net investment is equal to gross investment less depreciation. Tom's gross investment is the 2 new machines bought during the year, and its depreciation is the 1 machine that Tom's scrapped during the year. Tom's net investment is 1 machine.

Let's now see how the ideas that you've just studied are used in practice. We'll see how GDP and its components are measured in Canada today.

Measuring Canada's GDP

STATISTICS CANADA USES THE CONCEPTS THAT you met in the circular flow model to measure GDP and its components in the *National Income and Expenditure Accounts*. Because the value of aggregate output equals aggregate expenditure and aggregate income, there are two approaches available for measuring GDP, and both are used. They are

- The expenditure approach
- The income approach

The Expenditure Approach

The *expenditure approach* measures GDP as the sum of consumption expenditure (C), investment (I), government expenditures on goods and services (G), and net exports of goods and services ($X - M$), corresponding to the red flows in the circular flow model in Fig. 20.1. Table 20.1 shows the result of this approach for 2001. The table uses the terms in the *National Income and Expenditure Accounts*.

Personal expenditures on consumer goods and services are the expenditures by households on goods and services produced in Canada and in the rest of the world. They include goods such as CDs and books and services such as banking and legal advice. They do *not* include the purchase of new homes, which is counted as part of investment. But they do include the purchase of consumer durable goods, which technically are capital like homes.

Business investment is expenditure on capital equipment and buildings by firms and expenditure on new homes by households. It also includes the change in business inventories.

Government expenditures on goods and services are the purchases of goods and services by all levels of government. This item includes expenditures on national defence and garbage collection. But it does *not* include *transfer payments* because they are not purchases of goods and services.

Net exports of goods and services are the value of exports minus the value of imports. This item includes telephone equipment that Nortel sells to AT&T in the United States (a Canadian export), and Japanese DVD players that Sears buys from Sony (a Canadian import).

Table 20.1 shows the relative magnitudes of the four items of aggregate expenditure.

TABLE 20.1 GDP: The Expenditure Approach

Item	Symbol	Amount in 2001 (billions of dollars)	Percentage of GDP
Personal expenditures on consumer goods and services	C	621	56.9
Business investment	I	184	16.8
Government expenditures on goods and services	G	231	21.2
Net exports of goods and services	$X - M$	56	5.1
Gross domestic product	Y	1,092	100.0

The expenditure approach measures GDP as the sum of personal expenditures on consumer goods and services (C), business investment (I), government expenditures on goods and services (G), and net exports ($X - M$). In 2001, GDP measured by the expenditure approach was $1,092 billion. Personal expenditures on consumer goods and services is the largest expenditure item.

Source: Statistics Canada, CANSIM table 380-0002.

The Income Approach

The *income approach* measures GDP by summing the incomes that firms pay households for the factors of production they hire—wages for labour, interest for capital, rent for land, and profits for entrepreneurship. Let's see how the income approach works.

The *National Income and Expenditure Accounts* divide incomes into five categories:

1. Wages, salaries, and supplementary labour income
2. Corporate profits
3. Interest and miscellaneous investment income
4. Farmers' income
5. Income from non-farm unincorporated businesses

Wages, salaries, and supplementary labour income is the payment for labour services. It includes net wages and salaries (called "take-home pay") plus taxes withheld plus benefits such as pension contributions.

Corporate profits are the profits of corporations, some of which are paid to households in the form of dividends and some of which are retained by corporations as undistributed profits. They are all income.

Interest and miscellaneous investment income is the interest households receive on loans they make minus the interest households pay on their own borrowing.

Farmers' income and *income from non-farm unincorporated businesses* are a mixture of the previous three items. They include compensation for labour, payment for the use of capital, and profit, lumped together in these two catch-all categories.

Table 20.2 shows these five incomes and their relative magnitudes.

The sum of the incomes is called *net domestic income at factor cost*. The term *factor cost* is used because it is the cost of the *factors of production* used to produce final goods and services. When we sum all the expenditures on final goods and services, we arrive at a total called *domestic product at market prices*. Market prices and factor cost would be the same except for indirect taxes and subsidies.

An *indirect tax* is a tax paid by consumers when they buy goods and services. (In contrast, a *direct tax* is a tax on income.) Provincial sales taxes, GST, and taxes on alcohol, gasoline, and tobacco products are indirect taxes. Because of indirect taxes, consumers pay more for some goods and services than producers receive. Market price exceeds factor cost. For example, if the sales tax is 7 percent, when you buy a $1 chocolate bar you pay $1.07. The factor cost of the chocolate bar including profit is $1. The market price is $1.07.

A *subsidy* is a payment by the government to a producer. Payments made to grain growers and dairy farmers are subsidies. Because of subsidies, consumers pay less for some goods and services than producers receive. Factor cost exceeds market price.

To get from factor cost to market price, we add indirect taxes and subtract subsidies. Making this adjustment brings us one step closer to GDP, but it does not quite get us there.

The final step is to add depreciation (or capital consumption). You can see the reason for this adjustment by recalling the distinction between gross and net profit and between gross and net investment. Total income is a net number because it includes firms' net profits, which exclude depreciation. Total expenditure is a gross number because it includes gross investment. So to get from total income to GDP, we must add depreciation to total income.

TABLE 20.2   GDP: The Income Approach

Item	Amount in 2001 (billions of dollars)	Percentage of GDP
Wages, salaries, and supplementary labour income	569	52.1
Corporate profits	128	11.7
Interest and miscellaneous investment income	53	4.9
Farmers' income	3	0.3
Income from non-farm unincorporated businesses	67	6.1
Indirect taxes *less* subsidies	128	11.7
Capital consumption (depreciation)	144	13.2
Gross domestic product	1,092	100.0

The sum of all incomes equals net domestic income at factor cost. GDP equals net domestic income at factor cost plus indirect taxes less subsidies plus capital consumption (depreciation). In 2001, GDP measured by the income approach was $1,092 billion. Wages, salaries, and supplementary labour income was by far the largest part of aggregate income.

Source: Statistics Canada, CANSIM table 380-0001.

REVIEW QUIZ

1 What is the expenditure approach to measuring GDP?
2 What is the income approach to measuring GDP?
3 What adjustments must be made to total income to make it equal GDP?

You now know how GDP is defined and measured. The dollar value of GDP can change because either prices change or the volume of goods and services produced changes. You are next going to learn how we unscramble these two sources of change in GDP to reveal changes in the volume of goods and services produced—changes in what we call *real* GDP.

Real GDP and the Price Level

YOU'VE SEEN THAT GDP MEASURES TOTAL expenditure on final goods and services in a given period. In 2001, GDP was $1,092 billion. The year before, in 2000, GDP was $1,065 billion. Because GDP in 2001 was greater than in 2000, we know that one or two things must have happened during 2001:

■ We produced more goods and services in 2001 than in 2000.

■ We paid higher prices for our goods and services in 2001 than we paid in 2000.

Producing more goods and services contributes to an improvement in our standard of living. Paying higher prices means that our cost of living has increased but our standard of living has not. So it matters a great deal why GDP has increased.

You're now going to learn how economists at Statistics Canada split GDP into two parts. One part tells us the change in production, and the other part tells us the change in prices. The method that is used has changed in recent years, and you are going to learn about the new method.

We measure the change in production by using a number that we call real GDP. **Real GDP** is the value of final goods and services produced in a given year when valued at constant prices. By comparing the value of the goods and services produced at constant prices, we can measure the change in the volume of production.

Calculating Real GDP

Table 20.3 shows the quantities produced and the prices in 2002 for an economy that produces only two goods: balls and bats. The first step towards calculating real GDP is to calculate **nominal GDP**, which is the value of the final goods and services produced in a given year valued at the prices that prevailed in that same year. Nominal GDP is just a more precise name for GDP that we use when we want to be emphatic that we are not talking about real GDP.

Nominal GDP Calculation   To calculate nominal GDP in 2002, sum the expenditures on balls and bats in 2002 as follows:

Expenditure on balls = 100 balls × $1 = $100.

Expenditure on bats = 20 bats × $5 = $100.

Nominal GDP in 2002 = $100 + $100 = $200.

Table 20.4 shows the quantities produced and the prices in 2003. The quantity of balls produced increased to 160, and the quantity of bats produced increased to 22. The price of a ball fell to 50¢, and the price of a bat increased to $22.50. To calculate nominal GDP in 2003, we sum the expenditures on balls and bats in 2003 as follows:

Expenditure on balls = 160 balls × $0.50 = $80.

Expenditure on bats = 22 bats × $22.50 = $495.

Nominal GDP in 2003 = $80 + $495 = $575.

To calculate real GDP, we choose one year, called the *base year*, against which to compare the other years. In Canada today, the base year is 1997. The choice of the base year is not important. It is just a common reference point. We'll use 2002 as the base year. By definition, real GDP equals nominal GDP in the base year. So real GDP in 2002 is $200.

Base-Year Prices Value of Real GDP   The base-year prices method of calculating real GDP, which is the traditional method, values the quantities produced in each year at the prices of the base year. Table 20.5 shows the prices in 2002 and the quantities in 2003 (based on the information in Tables 20.3

TABLE 20.3   GDP Data for 2002

Item	Quantity	Price
Balls	100	$1.00
Bats	20	$5.00

TABLE 20.4   GDP Data for 2003

Item	Quantity	Price
Balls	160	$ 0.50
Bats	22	$22.50

TABLE 20.5   2003 Quantities and 2002 Prices

Item	Quantity	Price
Balls	160	$1.00
Bats	22	$5.00

and 20.4). The value of the 2003 quantities at the 2002 prices is calculated as follows:

Expenditure on balls = 160 balls × $1.00 = $160.

Expenditure on bats = 22 bats × $5.00 = $110.

Value of the 2003 quantities at 2002 prices = $270.

Using the traditional base-year prices method, $270 would be recorded as real GDP in 2003.

Chain-Weighted Output Index Calculation The **chain-weighted output index** method, which is the new method of calculating real GDP, uses the prices of two adjacent years to calculate the real GDP growth rate. So to find the real GDP growth rate in 2003, we compare the quantities produced in 2002 and 2003 by using both the 2002 prices and the 2003 prices. We then average the two sets of numbers in a special way that we'll now describe.

To compare the quantities produced in 2002 and 2003 at 2003 prices, we need to calculate the value of 2002 quantities at 2003 prices. Table 20.6 summarizes these quantities and prices. The value of the 2002 quantities at the 2003 prices is calculated as follows:

Expenditure on balls = 100 balls × $0.50 = $50.

Expenditure on bats = 20 bats × $22.50 = $450.

Value of the 2002 quantities at 2003 prices = $500.

We now have two comparisons between 2002 and 2003. At the 2002 prices, the value of production increased from $200 in 2002 to $270 in 2003.

TABLE 20.6   2002 Quantities and 2003 Prices

Item	Quantity	Price
Balls	100	$ 0.50
Bats	20	$22.50

The increase in value is $70, and the percentage increase is ($70 ÷ $200) × 100, which is 35 percent.

At the 2003 prices, the value of production increased from $500 in 2002 to $575 in 2003. The increase in value is $75, and the percentage increase is ($75 ÷ $500) × 100, which is 15 percent.

The new method of calculating real GDP uses the average of these two percentage increases. The average of 35 percent and 15 percent is (35 + 15) ÷ 2, which equals 25 percent. Real GDP is 25 percent greater in 2003 than in 2002. Real GDP in 2002 is $200, so real GDP in 2003 is $250.

Chain Linking The calculation that we've just described is repeated each year. Each year is compared with its preceding year. So in 2004, the calculations are repeated but using the prices and quantities of 2003 and 2004. Real GDP in 2004 equals real GDP in 2003 increased by the calculated percentage change in real GDP for 2004. For example, suppose that real GDP for 2004 is calculated to be 20 percent greater than that in 2003. You know that real GDP in 2003 is $250. So real GDP in 2004 is 20 percent greater than this value and is $300. In every year, real GDP is valued in base-year (2002) dollars.

By applying the calculated percentage change to the real GDP of the preceding real GDP, each year is linked back to the dollars of the base year like the links in a chain.

Calculating the Price Level

You've seen how real GDP is used to reveal the change in the quantity of goods and services produced. We're now going to see how we can find the change in prices that increases our cost of living.

The average level of prices is called the **price level.** One measure of the price level is the **GDP deflator,** which is an average of current-year prices expressed as a percentage of base-year prices. We calculate the GDP deflator by using nominal GDP and real GDP in the formula:

GDP deflator = (Nominal GDP ÷ Real GDP) × 100.

You can see why the GDP deflator is a measure of the price level. If nominal GDP rises but real GDP remains unchanged, it must be that the price level has risen. The formula gives a higher value for the GDP deflator. The larger the nominal GDP for a given real GDP, the higher is the price level and the larger is the GDP deflator.

TABLE 20.7 Calculating the GDP Deflator

Year	Nominal GDP	Real GDP	GDP deflator
2002	$200	$200	100
2003	$575	$250	230

Table 20.7 shows how the GDP deflator is calculated. In 2002, the deflator is 100. In 2003, it is 230, which equals nominal GDP of $575 divided by real GDP of $250 and then multiplied by 100.

Deflating the GDP Balloon

You can think of GDP as a balloon that is blown up by growing production and rising prices. In Fig. 20.3, the GDP deflator lets the inflation air out of the nominal GDP balloon—the contribution of rising prices—so that we can see what has happened to *real* GDP. The red balloon for 1981 shows real GDP in that year. The green balloon shows *nominal* GDP in

2001. The red balloon for 2001 shows real GDP for that year. To see real GDP in 2001, we *deflate* nominal GDP using the GDP deflator.

REVIEW QUIZ

1 What is the distinction between nominal GDP and real GDP?
2 What is the traditional method of calculating real GDP?
3 What is the new method of calculating real GDP?
4 How is the GDP deflator calculated?

You now know how to calculate real GDP and the GDP deflator. Your next task is to learn how to use real GDP to calculate economic growth and to make economic welfare comparisons. We also look at some limitations of real GDP as a measure of economic welfare and as a tool for comparing living standards across countries.

FIGURE 20.3   The Canadian GDP Balloon

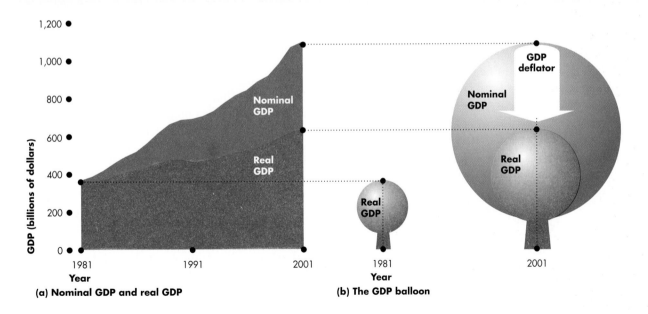

(a) Nominal GDP and real GDP

(b) The GDP balloon

Part of the rise in GDP comes from inflation and part from increased production—an increase in real GDP. The GDP deflator lets some air out of the GDP balloon so that we can see the extent to which production has increased.

Source: Statistics Canada, CANSIM table 380-0003.

Measuring Economic Growth

WE USE ESTIMATES OF REAL GDP TO CALCULATE the economic growth rate. The **economic growth rate** is the percentage change in the quantity of goods and services produced from one year to the next. To calculate the economic growth rate, we use the formula:

$$\text{Economic growth rate} = \frac{\text{Real GDP this year} - \text{Real GDP last year}}{\text{Real GDP last year}} \times 100.$$

For example, real GDP was $1,028 billion in 2001 and $1,012 billion in 2000. So the economic growth rate (percent per year) during 2001 was

$$\text{Economic growth rate} = \frac{(\$1,028 - \$1,012)}{\$1,012} \times 100$$

$$= 1.58 \text{ percent.}$$

We want to measure the economic growth rate so that we can make

- Economic welfare comparisons
- International comparisons
- Business cycle forecasts

Although the real GDP growth rate is used for these three purposes, it is not a perfect measure for any of them. Nor is it a totally misleading measure. We'll evaluate the limitations of real GDP and its growth rate in each of the three cases.

Economic Welfare Comparisons

Economic welfare is a comprehensive measure of the general state of economic well-being. Economic welfare improves when the production per person of *all* the goods and services grows. The goods and services that make up real GDP growth are only a part of all the items that influence economic welfare.

Today, because of real GDP growth, real GDP per person in Canada of $33,000 is 80 percent higher that it was in 1971. But are we 80 percent better off? Does this growth of real GDP provide a full and accurate measure of the change in economic welfare?

It does not. The reason is that economic welfare depends on many factors that are not measured by real GDP or that are not measured accurately by real GDP. Some of these factors are

- Overadjustment for inflation
- Household production
- Underground economic activity
- Health and life expectancy
- Leisure time
- Environment quality
- Political freedom and social justice

Overadjustment for Inflation   The price indexes that are used to measure inflation give an upward-biased estimate of true inflation. (You will learn about the sources of this bias on p. 493.) If we overestimate the rise in prices, we underestimate the growth of real GDP. When car prices rise because cars have gotten better (safer, more fuel efficient, more comfortable), the GDP deflator counts the price increase as inflation. So what is really an increase in production is counted as an increase in price rather than an increase in real GDP. It is deflated away by the wrongly measured higher price level. The magnitude of this bias is probably less than 1 percentage point a year, but its exact magnitude is not known.

Household Production   An enormous amount of production takes place every day in our homes. Preparing meals, cleaning the kitchen, changing a light bulb, cutting the grass, washing the car, and helping a high school student with homework are all examples of productive activities that do not involve market transactions and are not counted as part of GDP.

If these activities grew at the same rate as real GDP, then not measuring them would not be a problem. But it is likely that market production, which is part of GDP, is increasingly replacing household production, which is not part of GDP. Two trends point in this direction. One is the number of people who have jobs, which has increased from 58 percent in 1970 to 65 percent in 2001. The other is the trend in the purchase of traditionally home-produced goods and services in the market. For example, more and more families now eat in fast-food restaurants—one of the fastest-growing industries in Canada today—and use day-care services. This trend means that an increasing proportion of food preparation and child care that were part of household production are now measured as part of GDP. So real GDP grows more rapidly than does real GDP plus home production.

Underground Economic Activity   The *underground economy* is the part of the economy that is purposely hidden from the view of the government to avoid taxes and regulations or because the goods and services being produced are illegal. Because underground economic activity is unreported, it is omitted from GDP.

The underground economy is easy to describe, even if it is hard to measure. It includes the production and distribution of illegal drugs, production that uses illegal labour that is paid less than the minimum wage, and jobs done for cash to avoid paying income taxes. This last category might be quite large and includes tips earned by cab drivers, hairdressers, and hotel and restaurant workers.

Estimates of the scale of the underground economy range between 5 and 15 percent of GDP ($50 billion to $150 billion) in Canada and much more in some countries. It is particularly large in some Eastern European countries that are making a transition from communist economic planning to a market economy.

If the underground economy is a constant proportion of the total economy, the growth rate of real GDP provides a useful estimate of *changes* in economic welfare. But production can shift from the underground economy to the rest of the economy, and can shift the other way. The underground economy expands relative to the rest of the economy if taxes rise sharply or if regulations become especially restrictive. And the underground economy shrinks relative to the rest of the economy if the burdens of taxes and regulations ease.

During the 1980s, when tax rates were cut, there was an increase in the reporting of previously hidden income and tax revenues increased. So some part (but probably a small part) of the expansion of real GDP during the 1980s represented a shift from the underground economy rather than an increase in production.

Health and Life Expectancy Good health and a long life—the hopes of everyone—do not show up in real GDP, at least not directly. A larger real GDP does enable us to spend more on medical research, health care, a good diet, and exercise equipment. And as real GDP has increased, our life expectancy has lengthened—from 70 years at the end of World War II to approaching 80 years today. Infant deaths and death in childbirth, two fearful scourges of the nineteenth century, have almost been eliminated.

But we face new health and life expectancy problems every year. AIDS and drug abuse are taking young lives at a rate that causes serious concern.

When we take these negative influences into account, we see that real GDP growth overstates the improvements in economic welfare.

Leisure Time Leisure time is an economic good that adds to our economic welfare. Other things remaining the same, the more leisure we have, the better off we are. Our working time is valued as part of GDP, but our leisure time is not. Yet from the point of view of economic welfare, leisure time must be at least as valuable to us as the wage that we earn for the last hour worked. If it were not, we would work instead of taking the leisure. Over the years, leisure time has steadily increased. The workweek has become shorter, more people take early retirement, and the number of vacation days has increased. These improvements in economic well-being are not reflected in real GDP.

Environmental Quality Economic activity directly influences the quality of the environment. The burning of hydrocarbon fuels is the most visible activity that damages our environment. But it is not the only example. The depletion of exhaustible resources, the mass clearing of forests, and the pollution of lakes and rivers are other major environmental consequences of industrial production.

Resources that are used to protect the environment are valued as part of GDP. For example, the value of catalytic converters that help to protect the atmosphere from automobile emissions are part of GDP. But if we did not use such pieces of equipment and instead polluted the atmosphere, we would not count the deteriorating air that we were breathing as a negative part of GDP.

An industrial society possibly produces more atmospheric pollution than an agricultural society does. But pollution does not always increase as we become wealthier. Wealthy people value a clean environment and are willing to pay for one. Compare the pollution in East Germany in the late 1980s with pollution in Canada. East Germany, a poor country, polluted its rivers, lakes, and atmosphere in a way that is unimaginable in Canada or in wealthy West Germany.

Political Freedom and Social Justice Most people value political freedoms such as those provided by the Charter of Human Rights and the Constitution of Canada. And they value social justice or fairness—equality of opportunity and social security safety nets that protect people from the extremes of misfortune.

A country might have a very large real GDP per person but have limited political freedom and equity. For example, an elite might enjoy political liberty and extreme wealth while the vast majority are effectively enslaved and live in abject poverty. Such an economy would generally be regarded as having less economic welfare than one that had the same amount of real GDP but in which political freedoms were enjoyed by everyone. Today, China has rapid real GDP growth but limited political freedoms, while Russia has slow real GDP growth and an emerging democratic political system. Economists have no easy way to determine which of these countries is better off.

The Bottom Line   Do we get the wrong message about the growth in economic welfare by looking at the growth of real GDP? The influences that are omitted from real GDP are probably important and could be large. Developing countries have a larger underground economy and a larger amount of household production than do developed countries. So as an economy develops and grows, part of the apparent growth might reflect a switch from underground to regular production and from home production to market production. This measurement error overstates the rate of economic growth and the improvement in economic welfare.

Other influences on living standards include the amount of leisure time available, the quality of the environment, the security of jobs and homes, and the safety of city streets. It is possible to construct broader measures that combine the many influences that contribute to human happiness. Real GDP will be one element in those broader measures but by no means the whole of them.

International Comparisons

All the problems we've just reviewed affect economic welfare of every country, so to make international comparisons of economic welfare, factors additional to real GDP must be used. But real GDP comparisons are major components of international welfare comparisons, and two special problems arise in making these comparisons. First, the real GDP of one country must be converted into the same currency units as the real GDP of the other country. Second, the same prices must be used to value the goods and services in the countries being compared. Let's look at these two problems by using a striking example, a comparison of Canada and China.

In 1992 (the most recent year for which we can make this comparison), real GDP per person in Canada was $25,453. The official Chinese statistics published by the International Monetary Fund say that real GDP per person in China in 1992 was 2,028 yuan. (The yuan is the currency of China.) On the average, during 1992, a Canadian dollar was worth 4.768 yuan. If we use this exchange rate to convert Chinese yuan into Canadian dollars, we get a value of $425.

The official comparison of China and Canada makes China look extremely poor. In 1992, real GDP per person in Canada was 60 times that in China.

Figure 20.4 shows the official story of real GDP in China from 1980 to 1998. Figure 20.4 also shows another story based on an estimate of real GDP per person that is much larger than the official measure. Let's see how this alternative measurement is made.

GDP in Canada is measured by using prices that prevail in Canada. China's GDP is measured by using prices that prevail in China. But the relative prices in the two countries are very different. Some goods that are expensive in Canada cost very little in China. These items get a small weight in China's real GDP. If, instead of using China's prices, all the goods and services produced in China are valued at the prices prevailing in Canada, then a more valid comparison can be made of GDP in the two countries. Such a comparison uses prices called *purchasing power parity prices.*

Robert Summers and Alan Heston, economists in the Center for International Comparisons at the University of Pennsylvania, have used purchasing power parity prices to construct real GDP data for more than 100 countries. These data, which are published in the Penn World Table (PWT), tell a remarkable story about China. The PWT data use 1985 as the base year, so they are measured in 1985 dollars. According to the PWT, in 1992, real GDP per person in Canada was 11 times that of China, not the 60 times shown in the official data.

Figure 20.4 shows the PWT view of China's real GDP and compares it with the official view. The difference in the two views arises from the prices used. The official statistics use Chinese prices, while the PWT data use purchasing power parity prices.

Another China scholar, Thomas Rawski of the University of Pittsburgh, doubts both sets of data shown in Fig. 20.4. He believes that the growth rate

FIGURE 20.4   Two Views of Real GDP in China

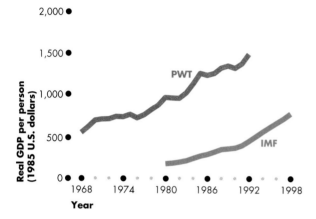

According to the official statistics of the International Monetary Fund (IMF) and the World Bank, China is a poor developing country. But according to an alternative view, Penn World Table (PWT), which is based on purchasing power parity prices, China's real GDP is more than 6 times the official view. Yet other China scholars think that even the official numbers are too big. So there is much uncertainty about China's real GDP.

Sources: International Monetary Fund, *World Economic Outlook* 2001 (Washington, DC, 2001) and "The Penn World Table" (Mark 5.6).

of China's real GDP has been exaggerated for some years and that even the official data overstate real GDP in China.

Canada's real GDP is measured pretty reliably. But China's is not. The alternative measures of China's real GDP are unreliable, and the truth about real GDP in China is not known. But China is growing, and many businesses are paying close attention to the prospects of expanding their activities in China and other fast-growing Asian economies.

Business Cycle Forecasts

If policymakers plan to raise interest rates to slow an expansion that they believe is too strong, they look at the latest estimates of real GDP. But suppose that for the reasons that we've just discussed, real GDP is mismeasured. Does this mismeasurement hamper our ability to identify the phases of the business cycle? It

does not. The reason is that although the omissions from real GDP do change over time, they probably do not change in a systematic way with the business cycle. So inaccurate measurement of real GDP does not necessarily cause a wrong assessment of the phase of the business cycle.

The fluctuations in economic activity measured by real GDP tell a reasonably accurate story about the phase of the business cycle that the economy is in. When real GDP grows, the economy is in a business cycle expansion; when real GDP shrinks (for two successive quarters), the economy is in a recession. Also, as real GDP fluctuates, so do production and jobs.

But real GDP fluctuations probably exaggerate or overstate the fluctuations in total production and economic welfare. The reason is that when business activity slows in a recession, household production increases and so does leisure time. When business activity speeds up in an expansion, household production and leisure time decrease. Because household production and leisure time increase in a recession and decrease in an expansion, real GDP fluctuations tend to overstate the fluctuations in total production and in economic welfare. But the directions of change of real GDP, total production, and economic welfare are probably the same.

REVIEW QUIZ

1 Does real GDP measure economic welfare? If not, why not?
2 Does real GDP measure total production of goods and services? If not, what are the main omissions?
3 How can we make valid international comparisons of real GDP?
4 Does the growth of real GDP measure the economic growth rate accurately?
5 Do the fluctuations in real GDP measure the business cycle accurately?

◆ You've now studied the methods used to measure GDP, economic growth, and the price level. And you've learned about some of the limitations of these measures. *Reading Between the Lines* on pp. 472–473 looks at Canadian real GDP during 2002.

Your next task is to learn how we measure employment and unemployment and inflation.

The Quarterly GDP Report

THE CANADIAN PRESS, AUGUST 30, 2002

Economy slowed in Q2 compared with Q1 but still showed healthy advance

The economy grew by 4.3 per cent on an annualized basis in the second quarter of this year, Statistics Canada said Friday. Second-quarter growth alone came in at 1.1 per cent, driven by domestic demand and a buildup of inventories.

That compared with 1.5 per cent growth in the first quarter and an annualized rate of 6.2 per cent. "GDP lost momentum towards the end of the (second) quarter, edging up in June," the agency said. "Canada's current account surplus with the rest of the world fell slightly, but remained strong at $4.9 billion."

Second-quarter growth in the gross domestic product "matched the average over the previous two quarters and was well above the flat showing of the first three quarters of 2001," Statistics Canada said.

Domestic demand, which gained 0.9 per cent and matched its first-quarter pace, "was boosted by strong consumer spending on services and a pick-up of business investment in machinery and equipment, which more than offset an easing of housing investment."

Manufacturers, wholesalers and retailers began to replenish inventory after drawing them down for three quarters.

"Corporate profits continued to recover from their tumble in 2001 and healthy gains in employment pushed up labour income," the agency said. "Imports were up strongly to satisfy domestic demand and the rebuilding of inventory."

Statistics Canada said that in the second quarter:

—Consumer spending was up a robust 0.7 per cent.

—Housing investment remained at historically high levels.

—Personal disposable income was up a healthy 1.5 per cent.

—Corporate profits advanced 9.8 per cent.

—Business plant and equipment spending recorded its strongest gain since the fourth quarter of 1999, boosted by a 4.8 per cent increase in spending on machinery and equipment.

—Imports jumped 4.0 per cent.

—Exports decelerated to 0.4 per cent from 1.3 per cent in the first quarter.

...

The Canadian Press

Essence of the Story

■ Statistics Canada reported that real GDP grew by 1.1 percent (a 4.3 percent annual rate) in the second quarter of 2002.

■ Real GDP had grown by 1.5 percent (a 6.2 percent annual rate) in the first quarter of 2002, so the growth rate slowed in the second quarter but was above the growth rate of the first three quarters of 2001.

■ The components of aggregate expenditure that grew quickly during the second quarter of 2002 were business inventories, consumer expenditure, and business fixed investment.

■ Exports slowed and imports jumped, so these components of aggregate expenditure contributed to the slowdown in the second quarter.

■ The components of aggregate income that grew quickly during the second quarter of 2002 were corporate profits and labour income.

Economic Analysis

■ Statistics Canada reports the nation's GDP numbers every three months.

■ To make the quarterly numbers easy to compare with annual numbers, growth rates are reported at annual rates.

■ An annual growth rate is calculated from quarterly data by using the formula:

$$g = [(x_t/x_{t-1})^4 - 1] \times 100,$$

where g is the annualized growth rate, x_t is the value of the variable in the current quarter, and x_{t-1} is the value of the variable in the preceding quarter.

■ The change in real GDP in a quarter is equal to

$$\Delta C + \Delta I + \Delta G + \Delta X - \Delta M$$

■ Figure 1 shows the composition of the change in real GDP in the second quarter of 2002 with the change in inventories, a component of investment, shown separately from the rest of investment.

■ You can see that consumption expenditure and the change in inventories were the items that changed most.

■ Notice that the increase in imports was large.

■ The news article compares the second quarter with the first quarter, and Fig. 2 shows the differences between the two quarters.

■ You can see that real GDP jumped by more in the first quarter of 2002 than it did in the second quarter.

■ In the first quarter, the change in inventories was much smaller than in the second quarter. Exports increased by more and imports by much less than in the second quarter.

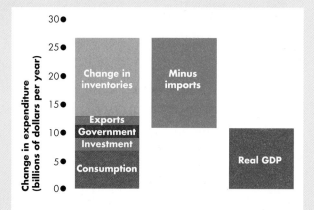

Figure 1 Changes in second quarter of 2002

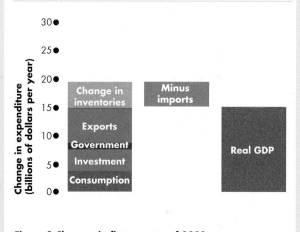

Figure 2 Changes in first quarter of 2002

SUMMARY

KEY POINTS

Gross Domestic Product (pp. 458–462)

- GDP, or gross domestic product, is the market value of all the final goods and services produced in a country during a given period.
- A final good is an item that is bought by its final user during a specified time period, and contrasts with an intermediate good, which is a component of a final good.
- GDP is calculated by using the expenditure and income totals in the circular flow of expenditure and income.
- Aggregate expenditure on goods and services equals aggregate income and GDP.

Measuring Canada's GDP (pp. 463–464)

- Because aggregate expenditure, aggregate income, and the value of aggregate production are equal, we can measure GDP by using the expenditure approach or the income approach.
- The expenditure approach sums consumption expenditure, investment, government expenditures on goods and services, and net exports.
- The income approach sums wages, interest, rent, and profit (and indirect taxes and depreciation).

Real GDP and the Price Level (pp. 465–467)

- Real GDP is measured by a chain-weighted output index that compares the value of production each year with its value at the previous year's prices.
- The GDP deflator measures the price level based on the prices of the items that make up GDP.

Measuring Economic Growth (pp. 468–471)

- We measure the economic growth rate as the percentage change in real GDP.

- Real GDP growth is not a perfect measure of economic growth because it excludes quality improvements, household production, the underground economy, environmental damage, health and life expectancy, leisure time, political freedom, and social justice.
- The growth rate of real GDP gives a good indication of the phases of the business cycle.

KEY FIGURES AND TABLES

KEY TERMS

PROBLEMS

*1. The figure at the bottom of the page shows the flows of expenditure and income on Lotus Island. During 2002, A was $20 million, B was $60 million, C was $24 million, D was $30 million, and E was $6 million. Calculate
   a. Aggregate expenditure.
   b. Aggregate income.
   c. GDP.
   d. Government budget deficit.
   e. Household saving.
   f. Government saving.
   g. National saving.
   h. Borrowing from the rest of the world.

2. In problem 1, during 2003, A was $25 million, B was $450 million, C was $30 million, D was $30 million, and E was –$10 million. Calculate the quantities in problem 1 during 2003.

*3. Martha owns a copy shop that has 10 copiers. One copier wears out each year and is replaced. In addition, this year Martha will expand her business to 14 copiers. Calculate Martha's initial capital stock, depreciation, gross investment, net investment, and final capital stock.

4. Wendy operates a weaving shop with 20 looms. One loom wears out each year and is replaced. But this year, Wendy will expand her business to 24 looms. Calculate Wendy's initial capital stock, depreciation, gross investment, net investment, and final capital stock.

*5. The transactions in Ecoland last year were

Item	Dollars
Wages paid to labour	800,000
Consumption expenditure	600,000
Taxes	250,000
Transfer payments	50,000
Profits	200,000
Investment	250,000
Government expenditures	200,000
Exports	300,000
Saving	300,000
Imports	250,000

   a. Calculate Ecoland's GDP.
   b. Did you use the expenditure approach or the income approach to make this calculation?
   c. How is investment financed?

6. The transactions in Highland last year were

Item	Dollars
Wages paid to labour	400,000
Consumption expenditure	350,000
Net taxes	125,000
Profits	140,000
Investment	150,000
Government expenditures	130,000
Exports	120,000
Saving	135,000
Imports	140,000

   a. Calculate Highland's GDP.
   b. What extra information do you need to calculate net domestic product at factor cost?
   c. Where does Highland get the funds to finance its investment?

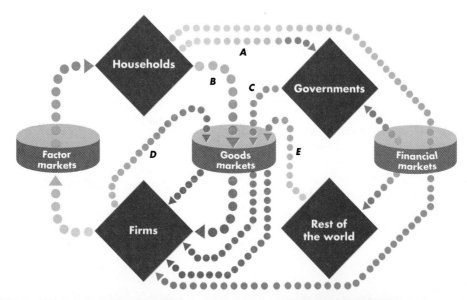

*7. Bananaland produces only bananas and sunscreen. The base year is 2002, and the tables give the quantities produced and prices.

| | Quantity | |
Good	2002	2003
Bananas	1,000 bunches	1,100 bunches
Sunscreen	500 bottles	525 bottles

| | Price | |
Good	2002	2003
Bananas	$2 a bunch	$3 a bunch
Sunscreen	$10 a bottle	$8 a bottle

a. Calculate nominal GDP in 2002 and 2003.
b. Calculate real GDP in 2003 using the base-year prices method.

8. Sea Island produces only lobsters and crabs. The base year is 2003, and the tables give the quantities produced and the prices.

| | Quantity | |
Good	2003	2004
Lobsters	1,000	1,450
Crabs	500	525

| | Price | |
Good	2003	2004
Lobsters	$20 each	$25 each
Crabs	$10 each	$12 each

a. Calculate nominal GDP in 2003 and 2004.
b. Calculate real GDP in 2004 using the base-year prices method.

*9. Bananaland (in problem 7) decides to use the chain-weighted output index method to calculate real GDP. Using this method,
a. Calculate the growth rate of real GDP in 2003.
b. Calculate the GDP deflator in 2003.
c. Compare and comment on the differences in real GDP using the base-year prices and chain-weighted output index methods.

10. Sea Island (in problem 8) decides to use the chain-weighted output index method to calculate real GDP. Using this method,
a. Calculate the growth rate of real GDP in 2004.
b. Calculate the GDP deflator in 2004.
c. Compare and comment on the differences in real GDP using the base-year prices and chain-weighted output index methods.

CRITICAL THINKING

1. Study *Reading Between the Lines* on pp. 472–473 and then answer the following questions:
   a. In the first and second quarters of 2002, which components of aggregate expenditure increased most?
   b. According to the news article, which components of aggregate income increased most during the first and second quarters of 2002?
   c. What happened to net exports during the first two quarters of 2002? Did they increase or decrease? Did Canada increase or decrease its net lending to the rest of the world during those two quarters?
   d. Was Canada in a recession, growth recession, or expansion during the first half of 2002?
   e. What happened to total investment during the first two quarters of 2002?
   f. Where, in the circular flow model, do changes in business inventories appear?

WEB EXERCISES

1. Use the link on the Parkin–Bade Web site to visit Statistics Canada. There you can obtain all the available data on GDP and the components of aggregate expenditure and aggregate income. You will find data in current prices (nominal GDP) and constant prices (real GDP).
   a. What is the value of nominal GDP in the current quarter?
   b. What is the value of real GDP in the current quarter using the chain-weighted index method?
   c. What is the GDP deflator in the current quarter?
   d. What was the value of real GDP in the same quarter of the previous year?
   e. By how much has real GDP changed over the past year? (Express your answer as a percentage.)
   f. Did real GDP increase or decrease and what does the change tell you about the state of the economy over the past year?

MONITORING CYCLES, JOBS, AND THE PRICE LEVEL

CHAPTER 21

Vital Signs

When the U.S. economy went into recession during 2001, Canada's economy slowed but avoided recession. What exactly is a recession, who decides when one begins and ends, and what criteria are used to make these decisions? ◆ Each month, we chart the unemployment rate as a measure of Canadian economic health. How do we measure the unemployment rate? What does it tell us? Is it a reliable vital sign for the economy? ◆ Every month, we also chart the number of people working, the number of hours they work, and the wages they receive. Are most new jobs full time or part time? And are they high-wage jobs or low-wage jobs? ◆ As the Canadian economy continued to slow in the first half of 2002, these questions about the health of the labour market became of vital importance to millions of Canadian families. We put the spotlight on the labour market during 2002 in *Reading Between the Lines* at the end of this chapter. ◆ Having a good job that pays a decent wage is only half of the equation that translates into a good standard of living. The other half is the cost of living. We track the cost of the items that we buy with another number that is published every month—the Consumer Price Index, or CPI. What is the CPI? How is it calculated? And does it provide a reliable guide to the changes in our cost of living?

◆ These are the questions we study in this chapter. We begin by looking at the way in which a recession is identified and dated. And we end, in *Reading Between the Lines,* by putting the spotlight on the CPI in 2002.

After studying this chapter, you will be able to

- Explain how we date business cycles

- Define the unemployment rate, the labour force participation rate, the employment-to-population ratio, and aggregate hours

- Describe the sources of unemployment, its duration, the groups most affected by it, and how it fluctuates over a business cycle

- Explain how we measure the price level and the inflation rate using the CPI

The Business Cycle

THE BUSINESS CYCLE IS A PERIODIC BUT IRREGU-lar up-and-down movement in production and jobs (see p. 440). There is no official, government-sponsored record of the dating of business cycles. Instead, business cycles are identified by two private agencies: the Economic Cycle Research Institute (ECRI) and the National Bureau of Economic Research (NBER). The ECRI identifies and dates the business cycles in Canada and 17 other countries and the NBER dates the U.S. business cycle. The working definition of the business cycle used by the ECRI is as follows:

> … pronounced, pervasive and persistent advances and declines in aggregate economic activity, which cannot be defined by any single variable, but by the consensus of key measures of output, income, employment and sales.[1]

A business cycle has two phases—expansion and recession—and two turning points—peak and trough. The NBER, whose methods the ECRI uses, defines the phases and turning points of the cycle as follows.

> A *recession* is a significant decline in activity spread across the economy, lasting more than a few months, visible in industrial production, employment, real income, and wholesale-retail trade. A recession begins just after the economy reaches a *peak* of activity and ends as the economy reaches its *trough*. Between trough and peak, the economy is in an *expansion*.[2]

Real GDP is the broadest measure of economic activity, and another popular working definition of a recession is a decrease in real GDP that lasts for at least two quarters. But we don't measure real GDP each month, so the ECRI and NBER do not use the real GDP numbers. Instead, they look at employment, which is the broadest *monthly* indicator of economic activity, along with other monthly measures that include personal income, sales of goods, and industrial production.

---

[1] You can find this definition and the dates of the business cycles in 18 countries at the ECRI Web site (www.businesscycle.com).

[2] "The NBER's Business-Cycle Dating Procedure," January 10, 2002, NBER Web site (www.nber.org). (Italicizing of key terms added.)

Business Cycle Dates

Figure 21.1(a) provides a quick summary of the Canadian business cycle since 1926. The figure shows the average per-year percentage change in real GDP during successive recessions and expansions.

The Great Depression, which began with a recession that ran from August 1929 to March 1933, was the most severe contraction of economic activity ever experienced. Over a 43-month period, real GDP shrank by 33 percent. Canada has had only four other recessions, at the end of World War II, 1954, 1982, and 1990–1991. The ECRI identified one other recession during 1957, but it was so mild that it doesn't show up in the real GDP data.

Expansion is the normal state of the economy, and the biggest expansion occurred during World War II. But the longest expansion ran from 1954 to 1982 (except for a mild stop in 1957). There is no correlation between the length of an expansion and the length of the preceding recession.

Growth Rate Cycles

Because recessions are rare, just looking at expansions and recessions misses a lot of the volatility in our economy. An alternative and more sensitive approach is to examine growth rate cycle downturns. A **growth rate cycle downturn** is a

> … pronounced, pervasive and persistent decline in the *growth rate* of aggregate economic activity. The procedures used to identify peaks and troughs in the growth rate cycle are analogous to those used to identify business cycle turning points, except that they are applied to the growth rates of the same time series, rather than their levels.[3]

Figure 21.1(b) shows the growth rate cycles since 1961 (the first year for which we have quarterly real GDP data).

REVIEW QUIZ

1 What are the phases of the business cycle?
2 Have recessions been getting worse?

---

[3] This definition is from the ECRI Web site (with small changes).

479

FIGURE 21.1   Two Views of Canadian Business Cycles

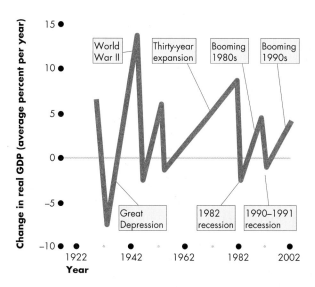

(a) Business cycle patterns

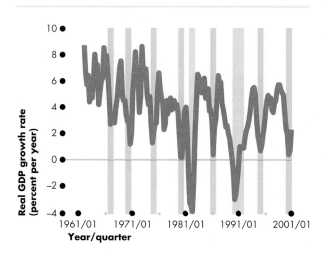

(b) Growth rate cycles

Part (a) shows the patterns of recession and expansion since the mid-1920s using real GDP as the measuring rod. Recessions have lasted from almost four years during the Great Depression, when real GDP fell by 33 percent, to a year in 1953–1954, when real GDP fell by 1.2 percent. Canada has had only four recessions since World War II.

Part (b) shows the higher frequency growth rate cycles since 1961, again using real GDP as the measuring rod of economic activity. The two deepest growth rate recessions occurred during 1982 and 1990–1991, the periods in which real GDP shrank and the economy was in recession in part (a). The other growth rate recessions identified by the shading in the figure were milder and did not take real GDP growth into negative territory.

Sources: Business cycle dates and growth rate cycle dates: the Economic Cycle Research Institute.
    Real GDP: Statistics Canada, CANSIM table 1992292.

Jobs and Wages

YOU HAVE SEEN THAT EMPLOYMENT IS ONE OF THE key features of the economy that helps the ECRI and NBER to determine the onset of recession. The state of the labour market has a large impact on our incomes and our lives. We become concerned when jobs are hard to find and more relaxed when they are plentiful. But we want a good job, which means that we want a well-paid and interesting job.

You are now going to learn how economists track the health of the labour market.

Labour Force

Every month, Statistics Canada surveys 59,000 households and asks a series of questions about the age and job market status of their members. This survey is called the Labour Force Survey. Statistics Canada uses the answers to describe the anatomy of the labour force.

Figure 21.2 shows the population categories used by Statistics Canada and the relationships among the categories. It divides the population into two groups: the working-age population and others who are too young to work. The **working-age population** is the total number of people aged 15 years and over. Statistics Canada divides the working-age population into two groups: those in the labour force and those not in the labour force. It also divides the labour force into two groups: the employed and the unemployed. So the **labour force** is the sum of the employed and the unemployed.

To be counted as employed in the Labour Force Survey, a person must have either a full-time job or a part-time job. To be counted as *un*employed, a person must be available for work and must be in one of three categories:

1. Without work but has made specific efforts to find a job within the previous four weeks
2. Waiting to be called back to a job from which he or she has been laid off
3. Waiting to start a new job within four weeks

Anyone surveyed who satisfies one of these three criteria is counted as unemployed. People in the working-age population who are neither employed nor unemployed are classified as not in the labour force.

In 2001, the population of Canada was 31.08

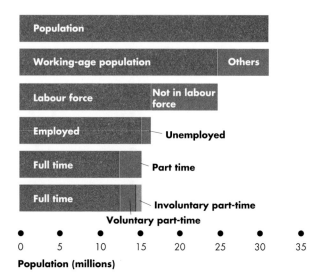

FIGURE 21.2 Population Labour Force Categories

Population (millions)

The population is divided into the working-age population and others. The working-age population is divided into those in the labour force and those not in the labour force. The labour force is divided into those employed and those unemployed. The people employed are divided into those with full-time jobs and those with part-time jobs. And part-time workers are divided into those who are voluntary and involuntary part-time workers.

Source: Statistics Canada, *Labour Force Historical Review*, CD-ROM 2001 and CANSIM tables 282-0002 and 051-0001.

million. There were 6.46 million people under 15 years of age. The working-age population was 24.62 million. Of this number, 8.37 million were not in the labour force. Most of these people were in school full time or had retired from work. The remaining 16.25 million people made up the Canadian labour force. Of these, 15.08 million were employed and 1.17 million were unemployed.

Four Labour Market Indicators

Statistics Canada calculates four indicators of the state of the labour market:

- The unemployment rate
- The involuntary part-time rate
- The labour force participation rate
- The employment-to-population ratio

The Unemployment Rate The amount of unemployment is an indicator of the extent to which people who want jobs can't find them. The **unemployment rate** is the percentage of the people in the labour force who are unemployed. That is,

$$\text{Unemployment rate} = \frac{\text{Number of people unemployed}}{\text{Labour force}} \times 100$$

and

$$\text{Labour force} = \text{Number of people employed} + \text{Number of people unemployed}.$$

In 2001, the number of people employed was 15.08 million and the number unemployed was 1.17 million. So the labour force was 16.25 million (15.08 million plus 1.17 million) and the unemployment rate was 7.2 percent (1.17 million divided by 16.25 million, multiplied by 100).

Figure 21.3 shows the unemployment rate (the orange line and plotted on the right-hand scale) and three other labour market indicators between 1961 and 2001. The average unemployment rate has been 7.7 percent, and it reached peak values at the ends of the 1982 and 1990–1991 recessions.

The Involuntary Part-Time Rate Part-time workers who want full-time work do not get counted as being unemployed. To measure the extent of this type of underemployment, Statistics Canada counts the number of involuntary part-time workers—part-time workers who want full-time jobs. The involuntary part-time rate is the percentage of the people in the labour force who have part-time jobs and want full-time jobs. That is,

$$\text{Involuntary part-time rate} = \frac{\text{Number of involuntary part-time workers}}{\text{Labour force}} \times 100.$$

In 2001, the number of involuntary part-time workers was 700,000, the labour force was 16.25 million, and the involuntary part-time rate was 4.3 percent.

Figure 21.3 shows the involuntary part-time rate (plotted on the right-hand scale) from 1976 to 1995 and then a new definition after 1997. You can see that an increasing percentage of the labour force wants full-time work but is not able to get full-time work. You can also see that the fluctuations in the involuntary part-time rate are like those in the unemployment rate.

FIGURE 21.3 Employment, Unemployment, and the Labour Force: 1961–2001

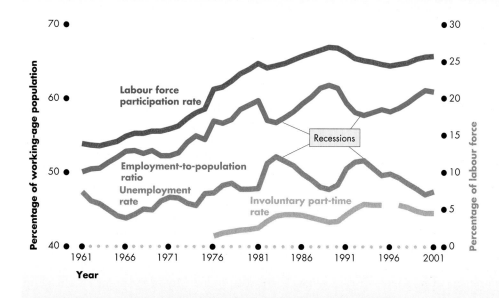

The unemployment rate increases in recessions and decreases in expansions. The labour force participation rate and the employment-to-population ratio have upward trends and fluctuate with the business cycle. The employment-to-population ratio fluctuates more than the labour force participation rate and reflects cyclical fluctuations in the unemployment rate. Fluctuations in the labour force participation rate arise mainly because of discouraged workers.

Source: Statistics Canada, *Labour Force Historical Review*, CD-ROM, 2001 and CANSIM table 282-0002.

The Labour Force Participation Rate The number of people who join the labour force is an indicator of the willingness of people of working age to take jobs. The **labour force participation rate** is the percentage of the working-age population who are members of the labour force. That is,

$$\text{Labour force participation rate} = \frac{\text{Labour force}}{\text{Working-age population}} \times 100.$$

In 2001, the labour force was 16.25 million and the working-age population was 24.62 million. By using the above equation, you can calculate the labour force participation rate. It was 66 percent (16.25 million divided by 24.62 million, multiplied by 100).

Figure 21.3 shows the labour force participation rate (graphed in red and plotted on the left-hand scale). It has followed an upward trend and has increased from 54 percent during the early 1960s to 66 percent in 2001. It has also had some mild fluctuations. They result from unsuccessful job seekers becoming discouraged workers. **Discouraged workers** are people who are available and willing to work but have not made specific efforts to find a job within the previous four weeks. These workers often temporarily leave the labour force during a recession and re-enter during an expansion and become active job seekers.

The Employment-to-Population Ratio The number of people of working age who have jobs is an indicator of both the availability of jobs and the degree of match between people's skills and jobs. The **employment-to-population ratio** is the percentage of people of working age who have jobs. That is,

$$\text{Employment-to-population ratio} = \frac{\text{Number of people employed}}{\text{Working-age population}} \times 100.$$

In 2001, the number of people employed was 15.08 million and the working-age population was 24.62 million. By using the above equation, you can calculate the employment-to-population ratio. It was 61.3 percent (15.08 million divided by 24.62 million, multiplied by 100).

Figure 21.3 shows the employment-to-population ratio (graphed in blue and plotted against the left-hand scale). It increased from 50 percent during the early 1960s to 61 percent in 2001. The increase

FIGURE 21.4   The Changing Face of the Labour Market

The upward trends in the labour force participation rate and the employment-to-population ratio are accounted for mainly by the increasing participation of women in the labour market. The male labour force participation rate and employment-to-population ratio have decreased.

Source: Statistics Canada, CANSIM table 282-0002.

in the employment-to-population ratio means that the Canadian economy has created jobs at a faster rate than the working-age population has grown. This labour market indicator also fluctuates, and its fluctuations coincide with but are opposite to those in the unemployment rate. The employment-to-population ratio falls during a recession and increases during an expansion.

Why have the labour force participation rate and the employment-to-population ratio increased? The main reason is an increase in the number of women in the labour force. Figure 21.4 shows this increase. Shorter work hours, higher productivity, and an increased emphasis on white-collar jobs have expanded the job opportunities and wages available to women. At the same time, technological advances have increased productivity in the home and freed up women's time to take jobs outside the home.

Figure 21.4 also shows another remarkable trend in the Canadian labour force: The labour force participation rate and the employment-to-population ratio for men have *decreased*. These indicators decreased because increasing numbers of men were remaining in school longer and because some were retiring earlier.

Aggregate Hours

The four labour market indicators that we've just examined are useful signs of the health of the economy and directly measure what matters to most people: jobs. But these four indicators don't tell us the quantity of labour used to produce real GDP, and we cannot use them to calculate the productivity of labour. The productivity of labour is significant because it influences the wages people earn.

The reason why the number of people employed does not measure the quantity of labour employed is that jobs are not all the same. People in part-time jobs might work just a few hours a week. People in full-time jobs work around 35 to 40 hours a week. And some people regularly work overtime. For example, a 7-11 store might hire six students who work for three hours a day each. Another 7-11 store might hire two full-time workers who work nine hours a day each. The number of people employed in these two stores is eight, but the total hours worked by six of the eight is the same as the total hours worked by the other two. To determine the total amount of labour used to produce real GDP, we measure labour in hours rather than in jobs. **Aggregate hours** are the total number of hours worked by all the people employed, both full time and part time, during a year.

Figure 21.5(a) shows aggregate hours in the Canadian economy from 1961 to 2001. Like the employment-to-population ratio, aggregate hours have an upward trend. But aggregate hours have not grown as quickly as has the number of people employed. Between 1961 and 2001, the number of people employed in the Canadian economy increased by 150 percent. During that same period, aggregate hours increased by a bit more than 110 percent. Why the difference? Because average hours per worker decreased.

Figure 21.5(b) shows average hours per worker. After hovering at a bit more than 40 hours a week during the early 1960s, average hours per worker decreased to about 34 hours a week during the 1990s. This shortening of the average workweek arose partly because of a decrease in the average hours worked by full-time workers, but mainly because the

FIGURE 21.5   Aggregate Hours: 1961–2001

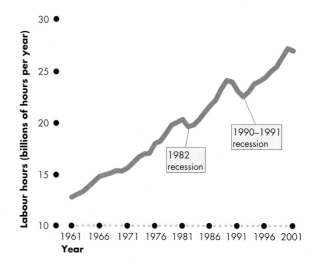

(a) Aggregate hours

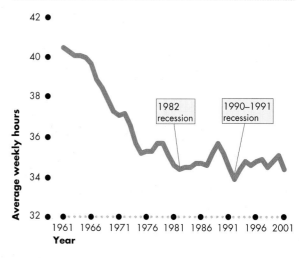

(b) Average weekly hours per person

Aggregate hours (part a) measure the total labour used to produce real GDP more accurately than does the number of people employed because an increasing proportion of jobs are part time. Between 1961 and 2001, aggregate hours increased by an average of 1.9 percent a year. Fluctuations in aggregate hours coincide with the business cycle. Aggregate hours have increased at a slower rate than the number of jobs because the average workweek has shortened (part b).

Source: Statistics Canada, CANSIM tables 282-0002 and 282-0022 and authors' calculations.

number of part-time jobs increased faster than the number of full-time jobs.

Fluctuations in aggregate hours and average hours per worker line up with the business cycle. Figure 21.5 highlights the past two recessions, during which aggregate hours decreased and average hours per worker decreased more quickly than the trend.

Real Wage Rate

The **real wage rate** is the quantity of goods and services that an hour's work can buy. It is equal to the money wage rate (dollars per hour) divided by the price level. If we use the GDP deflator to measure the price level, the real wage rate is expressed in 1997 dollars because the GDP deflator is 100 in 1997. The real wage rate is a significant economic variable because it measures the reward for labour.

FIGURE 21.6   Real Wage Rates: 1961–2001

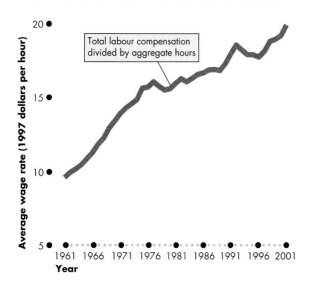

Total labour compensation divided by aggregate hours

The average hourly real wage rate follows an upward trend. But the trend growth rate of the real wage rate slowed during the 1970s and early 1980s. Occasionally, the real wage rate falls, as it did in the late 1970s and early 1990s.

Sources: Statistics Canada CANSIM tables 282-0002, 282-0022, and 380-0001, and the authors' calculations.

What has happened to the real wage rate in Canada? Figure 21.6 answers this question. Figure 21.6 shows the broadest measure of the average hourly real wage rate in the Canadian economy

The money wage rate is calculated from the national income accounts and aggregate hours. We know from the income side of the national income accounts the total amount of labour income. This total includes wages and salaries and all forms of supplementary labour income such as health and insurance benefits. It includes all labour income, not just that of people who are paid by the hour. If we divide this total by aggregate hours, we arrive at an estimate of the economy-wide average money wage rate. This average includes all types of labour in all parts of the economy.

The real wage rate follows an upward path. But the trend growth rate slowed during the 1970s and early 1980s in the *productivity growth slowdown*. This productivity growth slowdown is the main reason for this behaviour of the average real wage rate.

The average real wage rate usually increases but you can see in Fig. 21.6 that it sometimes decreases. The real wage rate decreased during the late 1970s, and it decreased again during the 1990s.

REVIEW QUIZ

1 What are the trends in the unemployment rate, the labour force participation rate, and the employment-to-population ratio?

2 How do the unemployment rate, the labour force participation rate, and the employment-to-population ratio fluctuate over the business cycle?

3 Has the female labour force participation rate been similar to or different from the male labour force participation rate?

4 How have aggregate hours changed since 1961?

5 How did the average hourly real wage rate change during the 1990s?

You've now seen how we measure employment, unemployment, and the real wage rate. Your next task is to study the anatomy of unemployment and see why it never disappears, even at full employment.

Unemployment and Full Employment

How do people become unemployed, and how does a period of unemployment end? How long do people remain unemployed on the average? Who is at greatest risk of becoming unemployed? Let's answer these questions by looking at the anatomy of unemployment.

The Anatomy of Unemployment

People become unemployed if they

1. Lose their jobs and search for another job.
2. Leave their jobs and search for another job.
3. Enter or re-enter the labour force to search for a job.

People end a spell of unemployment if they

1. Are hired or recalled.
2. Withdraw from the labour force.

People who are laid off from their jobs, either permanently or temporarily, are called **job losers.** Some job losers become unemployed, but some immediately withdraw from the labour force. People who voluntarily quit their jobs are called **job leavers.** Like job losers, some job leavers become unemployed and search for a better job, while others withdraw from the labour force temporarily or permanently retire from work. People who enter or re-enter the labour force are called **entrants** and **re-entrants.** Entrants are mainly people who have just left school. Some entrants get a job right away and are never unemployed, but many spend time searching for their first job, and during this period, they are unemployed. Re-entrants are people who have previously withdrawn from the labour force. Most of these people are formerly discouraged workers. Figure 21.7 shows these labour market flows.

The Sources of Unemployment Figure 21.8 shows unemployment by reason for becoming unemployed. Job losers are the biggest source of unemployment. On the average, they account for around half of total unemployment. Also, their number fluctuates a great deal. At the trough of the recession of 1990–1991, on any given day, almost 1 million of the 1.6 million unemployed were job losers. In con-

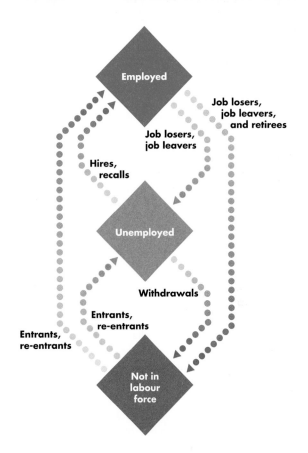

FIGURE 21.7 Labour Market Flows

Unemployment results from employed people losing or leaving their jobs (job losers and job leavers) and from people entering the labour force (entrants and re-entrants). Unemployment ends because people get hired or recalled or because they withdraw from the labour force.

trast, at the business cycle peak year of 1989, fewer than 600,000 of the 1 million unemployed were job losers.

Entrants and re-entrants also make up a large component of the unemployed, and their number fluctuates but more mildly than the fluctuations in the number of job losers.

Job leavers are the smallest and most stable source of unemployment. On any given day, less than 200,000 people are unemployed because they are job leavers. The number of job leavers is remarkably

FIGURE 21.8   Unemployment by Reason

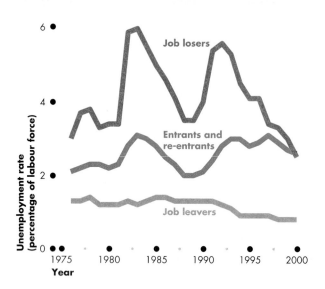

Everyone who is unemployed is a job loser, a job leaver, or an entrant or re-entrant into the labour force. Most unemployment results from job loss. The number of job losers fluctuates more closely with the business cycle than do the numbers of job leavers and entrants and re-entrants. Entrants and re-entrants are the second most common type of unemployed people. Their number fluctuates with the business cycle because of discouraged workers. Job leavers are the least common type of unemployed people.

Source: Statistics Canada, *Labour Force Historical Review* CD-ROM, 2001.

FIGURE 21.9   Unemployment by Duration

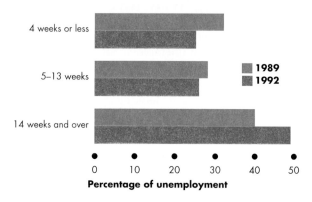

Close to a business cycle peak in 1989, when the unemployment rate was 7.5 percent, 32 percent of unemployment lasted for 4 weeks or less, 28 percent lasted for 5 to 13 weeks, and less than 40 percent lasted for 14 weeks or more. In a business cycle trough in 1992, when the unemployment rate was 11 percent, 25 percent of unemployment lasted for 4 weeks or less, 26 percent lasted for 5 to 13 weeks, and 49 percent lasted for 14 weeks or more.

Source: Statistics Canada, *Labour Force Historical Review* CD-ROM, 2001.

constant, although to the extent that it fluctuates, it does so in line with the business cycle: A slightly larger number of people leave their jobs in good times than in bad times.

The Duration of Unemployment   Some people are unemployed for a week or two, and others are unemployed for periods of a year or more. The longer the spell of unemployment, the greater the personal cost to the unemployed. The average duration of unemployment varies over the business cycle.

Figure 21.9 compares the duration of unemployment at a business cycle peak in 1989, when the unemployment rate was low, with that at a business cycle trough in 1992, when the unemployment rate

was high. In 1989, when the unemployment rate hit a low of 7.5 percent, 32 percent of the unemployed were in that situation for less than 4 weeks and less than 40 percent of the unemployed were jobless for longer than 13 weeks. In 1992, when the unemployment rate reached a high of 11 percent, only 25 percent of the unemployed found a new job in 4 weeks or less and 49 percent were unemployed for more than 13 weeks. At both low and high unemployment rates, about 27 percent of the unemployed take between 4 weeks and 13 weeks to find a job.

The Demographics of Unemployment   Figure 21.10 shows unemployment for different demographic groups. The figure shows that high unemployment rates occur among young workers. In the business cycle trough in 1992, the teenage unemployment rate was 20 percent. Even in 1989, when the national unemployment rate was 7.5 percent, the teenage unemployment rate was 13 percent.

FIGURE 21.10   Unemployment by Demographic Group

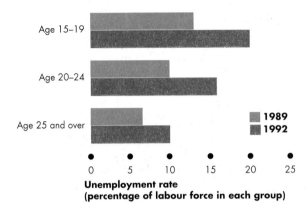

Teenagers experience the highest unemployment rates. In the 1992 business cycle trough (when unemployment was at its highest rate, 11 percent), the teenage unemployment rate was 20 percent. Even at the 1989 business cycle peak (when the unemployment rate was at its lowest, 7.5 percent), the teenage unemployment rate was 13 percent.

Source: Statistics Canada, CANSIM table 282-0002.

Why is the unemployment rate of young people so high? There are three reasons. First, young people are still in the process of discovering what they are good at and trying different lines of work. So they leave their jobs more frequently than do older workers. Second, firms sometimes hire teenagers on a short-term trial basis. So the rate of job loss is higher for teenagers than for other people. Third, most young persons are not in the labour force but are in school. This fact means that the percentage of the young adult population that is unemployed is much lower than the percentage of the young labour force that is unemployed. In 2001, for example, 340,000 15-to-24 year olds were unemployed and 2.3 million were employed. So the 15-to-24 year olds' unemployment rate was 12.9 percent. But 4 million were enrolled in post-secondary education. If we considered being in school as the equivalent of having a job and measured the unemployment rate as the percentage of the labour force plus the school population, we would record a 5.1 percent unemployment rate among 15-to-24 year olds.

Types of Unemployment

Unemployment is classified into four types that are based on its origins. They are

- Frictional
- Structural
- Seasonal
- Cyclical

Frictional Unemployment   The unemployment that arises from normal labour turnover—from people entering and leaving the labour force and from the ongoing creation and destruction of jobs—is called **frictional unemployment.** This type of unemployment is a permanent and healthy phenomenon in a dynamic, growing economy.

The unending flow of people into and out of the labour force and the processes of job creation and job destruction create the need for people to search for jobs and for businesses to search for workers. Always, there are businesses with unfilled jobs and people seeking jobs. Look in your local newspaper, and you will see that there are always some jobs being advertised. Businesses don't usually hire the first person who applies for a job, and unemployed people don't usually take the first job that comes their way. Instead, both firms and workers spend time searching out what they believe will be the best match available. By this search process, people can match their own skills and interests with the available jobs and find a satisfying job and income. While these unemployed people are searching, they are frictionally unemployed.

The amount of frictional unemployment depends on the rate at which people enter and re-enter the labour force and on the rate at which jobs are created and destroyed. During the 1970s, the amount of frictional unemployment increased as a consequence of the post-war baby boom that began during the 1940s. By the late 1970s, the baby boom created a bulge in the number of people leaving school. As these people entered the labour force, the amount of frictional unemployment increased.

The amount of frictional unemployment is influenced by unemployment compensation. The greater the number of unemployed people covered by employment insurance and the more generous the unemployment benefits they receive, the longer is the average time taken in job search and the greater is the amount of frictional unemployment. Canadian employment insurance is among the most comprehensive and generous in the world. It is much more comprehensive than that in the United States. This factor is one reason why the Canadian unemployment rate has exceeded the U.S. unemployment rate since the early 1980s. But there are other reasons. Canadian workers, especially young workers who make up the so-called Generation X, have shorter spells of employment and more frequent intervening spells of unemployment, supported by employment insurance, than do young U.S. workers.[4]

Structural Unemployment The unemployment that arises when changes in technology or international competition change the skills needed to perform jobs or change the locations of jobs is called **structural unemployment.** This type of unemployment usually lasts longer than frictional unemployment because workers must retrain and possibly relocate to find a job. For example, when a steel plant in Hamilton, Ontario, is automated, some jobs in that city are destroyed. Meanwhile, in the Ottawa valley and Vancouver, new jobs for security guards, life-insurance salespeople, and retail clerks are created. The unemployed former steelworkers remain unemployed for several months until they move, retrain, and get one of these jobs. Structural unemployment is painful, especially for older workers for whom the best available option might be to retire early but with a lower income than they had expected.

At some times the amount of structural unemployment is modest. At other times it is large, and at such times, structural unemployment can become a serious long-term problem. It was especially large during the late 1970s and early 1980s. During those years, oil price hikes and an increasingly competitive international environment destroyed jobs in traditional Canadian industries, such as auto and steel, and created jobs in new industries, such as electronics and bioengineering, as well as in banking and insurance. Structural unemployment was also present dur-

ing the early 1990s as many businesses and governments "downsized."

Seasonal Unemployment Many jobs are available only at certain times of the year. **Seasonal unemployment** is the unemployment that arises because the number of jobs available has decreased because of the season. Most seasonal unemployment in Canada occurs in the winter because construction and outdoor farming essentially close down for several months.

Cyclical Unemployment The unemployment that fluctuates over the business cycle is called **cyclical unemployment.** This type of unemployment increases during a recession and decreases during an expansion. An auto worker who is laid off because the economy is in a recession and who gets rehired some months later when the expansion begins has experienced cyclical unemployment.

Full Employment

There is always *some* unemployment. So what do we mean by *full employment?* **Full employment** occurs when there is no cyclical unemployment or, equivalently, when all the unemployment is frictional, structural, and seasonal. The unemployment rate at full employment is called the **natural rate of unemployment.** The divergence of the unemployment rate from the natural rate of unemployment is cyclical unemployment.

There can be a lot of unemployment at full employment, and the term "full employment" is an example of a technical economic term that does not correspond with everyday language. The term "natural rate of unemployment" is another technical economic term whose meaning does not correspond with everyday language. For most people—especially for unemployed workers—there is nothing *natural* about unemployment.

So why do economists call a situation with a lot of unemployment "full employment"? And why is the unemployment at full employment called "natural"?

The reason is that the economy is a complex mechanism that is always changing. Every day, some people retire, new workers enter the labour force, some businesses downsize or fail and others expand or start up. This process of change creates unavoidable frictions and dislocations, which create unemployment. Economists don't agree about the size of the natural rate of unemployment or the extent to which it fluctuates.

---

[4] These conclusions are based on the work of David Card and Craig W. Riddell, "A Comparative Analysis of Unemployment in Canada and the United States" *Small Differences that Matter: Labour Markets and Income Maintenance in Canada and the United States,* edited by Richard Freeman and David Card, Chicago: University of Chicago Press and NBER, 1993, pp. 149–189, and Audra J. Bowlus, "What Generation X Can Tell Us About the U.S.—Canadian Unemployment Rate Gap" University of Western Ontario, 1996.

FIGURE 21.11 Unemployment and Real GDP

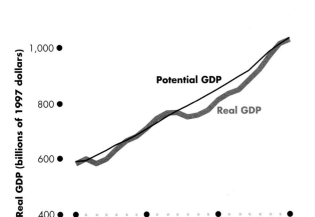

(a) Real GDP

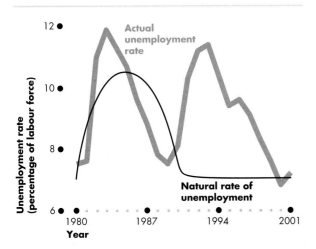

(b) Unemployment rate

As real GDP fluctuates around potential GDP (part a), the unemployment rate fluctuates around the natural rate of unemployment (part b). In the deep recession of 1982, the unemployment rate reached almost 12 percent. In the milder recession of 1990–1991, the unemployment rate peaked at about 11 percent. The natural rate of unemployment increased during the 1980s and decreased during the 1990s.

Sources: Statistics Canada, CANSIM tables 282-0002 and 380-0002, International Monetary Fund, *World Economic Outlook*, Output gap series, and the authors' assumptions.

Real GDP and Unemployment Over the Cycle

The quantity of real GDP at full employment is called **potential GDP.** You will study the forces that determine potential GDP in Chapter 29 (pp. 686–687). Over the business cycle, real GDP fluctuates around potential GDP and the unemployment rate fluctuates around the natural rate of unemployment. Figure 21.11 illustrates these fluctuations in Canada between 1980 and 2001—real GDP in part (a) and the unemployment rate in part (b).

When the economy is at full employment, the unemployment rate equals the natural rate of unemployment and real GDP equals potential GDP. When the unemployment rate is less than the natural rate of unemployment, real GDP is greater than potential GDP. And when the unemployment rate is greater than the natural rate of unemployment, real GDP is less than potential GDP.

Figure 21.11(b) shows one view of the natural rate of unemployment. Keep in mind that economists do not know the magnitude of the natural rate of unemployment and the natural rate shown in the figure is only one estimate. In Fig. 21.11(b), the natural rate of unemployment rose during the 1980s and then fell through the late 1980s and stabilized during the 1990s at around 7 percent. This estimate of the natural rate of unemployment in Canada is one that many, but not all, economists would accept.

REVIEW QUIZ

1 What are the categories of people who become unemployed?
2 Define frictional unemployment, structural unemployment, and cyclical unemployment and provide an example of each type of unemployment.
3 What is the natural rate of unemployment?
4 How might the natural rate of unemployment change and what factors might make it change?
5 How does the unemployment rate fluctuate over the business cycle?

Your final task in this chapter is to learn about another vital sign that gets monitored every month: the Consumer Price Index (CPI). What is the CPI, how do we measure it, and what does it mean?

The Consumer Price Index

STATISTICS CANADA CALCULATES THE CONSUMER Price Index every month. The **Consumer Price Index (CPI)** is a measure of the average of the prices paid by urban consumers for a fixed "basket" of consumer goods and services. What you learn in this section will help you to make sense of the CPI and relate it to your own economic life. The CPI tells you what has happened to the value of the money in your pocket.

Reading the CPI Numbers

The CPI is defined to equal 100 for a period called the **base period.** Currently, the base period is 1992. That is, for the average of the 12 months of 1992, the CPI equals 100.

In May 2002, the CPI was 118.6. This number tells us that the average of the prices paid by urban consumers for a fixed market basket of consumer goods and services was 18.6 percent higher in May 2002 than it was on the average during 1992.

In May 2001, the CPI was 117.4. Comparing the May 2002 CPI with the May 2001 CPI tells us that the index of the prices paid by urban consumers for a fixed basket of consumer goods and services increased during the year ended May 2002 by 1.2—from 117.4 to 118.6.

Constructing the CPI

Constructing the CPI is a huge operation that costs millions of dollars and involves three stages:

- Selecting the CPI basket
- Conducting the monthly price survey
- Calculating the CPI

Selecting the CPI Basket The first stage in constructing the CPI is to select what is called the CPI basket. This "basket" contains the goods and services represented in the index and the relative importance attached to each of them. The idea is to make the relative importance of the items in the CPI basket the same as that in the budget of an average urban household. For example, because people spend more on housing than on bus rides, the CPI places more weight on the price of housing than on the price of bus rides.

Statistics Canada uses several baskets and calculates several alternative CPIs. The goal of the alternatives is to omit items that are highly volatile and that mask the deeper changes in the index. Here, we'll look only at the main "All-Items" index.

To determine the spending patterns of households and to select the CPI basket, Statistics Canada conducts a Consumer Expenditure Survey. This survey is costly and so is undertaken only once every few years. Today's CPI basket is based on data gathered in a Consumer Expenditure Survey of 1996.

Figure 21.12 shows the CPI basket at the end of 2001. The basket contains thousands of individual goods and services arranged in the eight large groups shown in the figure. The most important item in a household's budget is shelter, which accounts for 27 percent of total expenditure. Transportation comes next at 19 percent. Third in relative importance is food at 18 percent. These three groups account for almost two-thirds of the average household budget.

FIGURE 21.12 The CPI Basket

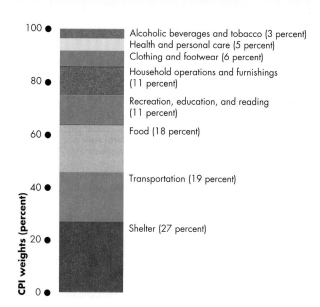

The CPI basket consists of the items that an average urban household buys. It consists mainly of shelter (27 percent), transportation (19 percent), and food (18 percent). All other items add up to 36 percent of the total.

Source: Statistics Canada, Catalogue 62-557-XIB.

Statistics Canada breaks down each of these categories into smaller ones. For example, the recreation, education, and reading category breaks down into textbooks and supplies, tuition, telephone services, and personal computer services.

As you look at the relative importance of the items in the CPI basket, remember that they apply to the *average* household. *Individual* households are spread around the average. Think about your own expenditure and compare the basket of goods and services you buy with the CPI basket.

Conducting the Monthly Price Survey   Each month, Statistics Canada employees check the prices of the goods and services in the CPI basket in 64 urban centres. Because the CPI aims to measure price *changes*, it is important that the prices recorded each month refer to exactly the same item. For example, suppose that the price of a box of jellybeans has increased, but a box now contains more beans. Has the price of jellybeans increased? Statistics Canada employees must record the details of changes in quality or packaging so that price changes can be isolated from other changes.

Once the raw price data are in hand, the next task is to calculate the CPI.

Calculating the CPI   The CPI calculation has three steps:

1. Find the cost of the CPI basket at base period prices.
2. Find the cost of the CPI basket at current period prices.
3. Calculate the CPI for the base period and the current period.

We'll work through these three steps for a simple example. Suppose the CPI basket contains only two goods and services: oranges and haircuts. We'll construct an annual CPI rather than a monthly CPI with the base period 2002 and the current period 2003.

Table 21.1 shows the quantities in the CPI basket and the prices in the base period and current period.

Part (a) contains the data for the base period. In that period, consumers bought 10 oranges at $1 each and 5 haircuts at $8 each. To find the cost of the CPI basket in the base period prices, multiply the quantities in the CPI basket by the base period prices. The cost of oranges is $10 (10 at $1 each), and the cost of haircuts is $40 (5 at $8 each). So total expenditure in the base period on the CPI basket is $50 ($10 + $40).

Part (b) contains the price data for the current period. The price of an orange increased from $1 to $2, which is a 100 percent increase ($1 ÷ $1 × 100 = 100). The price of a haircut increased from $8 to $10, which is a 25 percent increase ($2 ÷ $8 × 100 = 25).

The CPI provides a way of averaging these price increases by comparing the costs of the baskets rather than the prices of the items. To find the cost of the CPI basket in the current period, 2003, multiply the quantities in the basket by their 2003 prices. The cost of oranges is $20 (10 at $2 each), and the cost of haircuts is $50 (5 at $10 each) So total expenditure on the fixed CPI basket at current period prices is $70 ($20 + $50).

You've now taken the first two steps towards calculating the CPI: calculating the cost of the CPI basket in the base period and the cost in the current period. The third step uses the numbers you've just calculated to find the CPI for 2002 and 2003.

The formula for the CPI is

$$CPI = \frac{\text{Cost of CPI basket at current period prices}}{\text{Cost of CPI basket at base period prices}} \times 100.$$

TABLE 21.1   The CPI: A Simplified Calculation

(a) The cost of the CPI basket at base period prices: 2002

Item	Quantity	Price	Cost of CPI basket
Oranges	10	$1	$10
Haircuts	5	$8	$40
Cost of CPI basket at base period prices			$50

(b) The cost of the CPI basket at current period prices: 2003

Item	Quantity	Price	Cost of CPI basket
Oranges	10	$2	$20
Haircuts	5	$10	$50
Cost of CPI basket at current period prices			$70

In Table 21.1, you have established that in 2002, the cost of the CPI basket was $50 and in 2003, it was $70. You also know that the base period is 2002. So the cost of the CPI basket at base period prices is $50. If we use these numbers in the CPI formula, we can find the CPI for 2002 and 2003. For 2002, the CPI is

$$\text{CPI in 2002} = \frac{\$50}{\$50} \times 100 = 100.$$

For 2003, the CPI is

$$\text{CPI in 2003} = \frac{\$70}{\$50} \times 100 = 140.$$

The principles that you've applied in this simplified CPI calculation apply to the calculations performed every month by Statistics Canada.

Measuring Inflation

A major purpose of the CPI is to measure *changes* in the cost of living and in the value of money. To measure these changes, we calculate the **inflation rate,** which is the percentage change in the price level from one year to the next. To calculate the inflation rate, we use the formula:

$$\frac{\text{Inflation}}{\text{rate}} = \frac{(\text{CPI this year} - \text{CPI last year})}{\text{CPI last year}} \times 100.$$

We can use this formula to calculate the inflation rate. The CPI in May 2002 was 118.6, and the CPI in May 2001 was 117.4. So the inflation rate during the year to May 2002 was

$$\text{Inflation rate} = \frac{(118.6 - 117.4)}{117.4} \times 100 = 1.02.$$

Figure 21.13 shows the CPI and the inflation rate in Canada during the 30 years between 1971 and 2001. The two parts of the figure are related.

Figure 21.13 shows that when the price *level* in part (a) rises rapidly, the inflation rate in part (b) is high, and when the price level in part (a) rises slowly, the inflation rate in part (b) is low. Notice in part (a) that the CPI increased every year during this period.

During the late 1970s and early 1980s, the CPI increased rapidly, but its rate of increase slowed during the 1980s and 1990s.

FIGURE 21.13   The CPI and the Inflation Rate

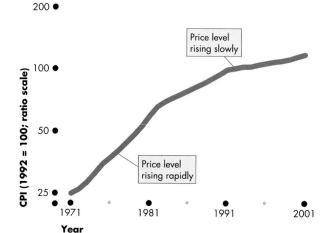

(a) CPI: 1971–2001

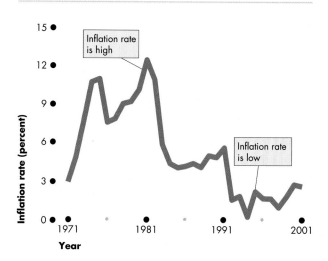

(b) Inflation rate: 1971–2001

In part (a), the CPI (the price level) has increased every year. In part (b), the inflation rate has averaged 5.25 percent a year. During the 1970s and early 1980s, the inflation rate was high and sometimes exceeded 10 percent a year. But after 1985, the inflation rate fell to an average of 3 percent a year.

Source: Statistics Canada, CANSIM table 326-0002.

The CPI is not a perfect measure of the price level, and changes in the CPI probably overstate the inflation rate. Let's look at the sources of bias.

The Biased CPI

The main sources of bias in the CPI are

- New goods bias
- Quality change bias
- Commodity substitution bias
- Outlet substitution bias

New Goods Bias If you want to compare the price level in 2003 with that in 1973, you must somehow compare the price of a computer today with that of a typewriter in 1973. Because a PC is more expensive than a typewriter was, the arrival of the PC puts an upward bias into the CPI and its inflation rate.

Quality Change Bias Cars, CD players, and many other items get better every year. Part of the rise in the prices of these items is a payment for improved quality and is not inflation. But the CPI counts the entire price rise as inflation and so overstates inflation.

Commodity Substitution Bias Changes in relative prices lead consumers to change the items they buy. For example, if the price of beef rises and the price of chicken remains unchanged, people buy more chicken and less beef. Suppose they switch from beef to chicken on a scale that provides the same amount of protein and the same enjoyment as before and their expenditure is the same as before. The price of protein has not changed. But because it ignores the substitution of chicken for beef, the CPI says the price of protein has increased.

Outlet Substitution Bias When confronted with higher prices, people use discount stores more frequently and convenience stores less frequently. This phenomenon is called *outlet substitution*. The CPI surveys do not monitor outlet substitutions.

The Magnitude of the Bias

How big is the bias in the measurement of the CPI? The answer varies from country to country. In the United States, the bias is believed to range between 1 percent and 2 percent a year. But in Canada, it is believed to be at most 1 percent a year and probably less than this amount.

To reduce the bias problems, Statistics Canada revises the basket used for calculating the CPI about every 10 years. Also, Statistics Canada tries to estimate the quantitative effects of the various sources of bias and eliminate them by statistical adjustments. It is these adjustments that make Canada's CPI a more reliable measure of the price level than the CPI in the United States is of the U.S. price level.

Some Consequences of the Bias

The bias in the CPI has three main consequences. It

- Distorts private contracts.
- Increases government outlays.
- Biases estimates of real earnings.

Many private agreements, such as wage contracts, are linked to the CPI. For example, a firm and its workers might agree to a three-year wage deal that increases the wage rate by 2 percent a year *plus* the percentage increase in the CPI. Such a deal ends up giving the workers more *real* income than the firm intended.

Close to a third of federal government outlays are linked directly to the CPI. And while a bias of 1 percent a year seems small, accumulated over a decade, it adds up to billions of dollars of additional expenditures.

Trade unions and businesses bargain over wages based in part on changes in the CPI. If the CPI is biased upwards, businesses might agree to wage increases that are larger than they would accept if the CPI were measured accurately.

REVIEW QUIZ

1 What is the CPI and how is it calculated?
2 How do we calculate the inflation rate and what is the relationship between the CPI and the inflation rate?
3 What are the four main ways in which the CPI is an upward-biased measure of the price level?
4 What problems arise from the CPI bias?

◆ *Readings Between the Lines* on pp. 494–495 looks at the CPI in 2002. You've now completed your study of the measurement of macroeconomic performance. Your task in the following chapters is to learn what determines that performance and how policy actions might improve it.

The Monthly CPI Report

THE GLOBE AND MAIL, SEPTEMBER 21, 2002

Ont. electricity jolts inflation

A huge jump in electricity prices in Ontario triggered by a heat wave that hit shortly after the province moved to open-market pricing drove the Canadian inflation rate in August to 2.6 per cent.

That was up from an annualized 2.1 per cent in July, Statistics Canada said yesterday. Some economists said the rise in the cost of living was steep enough to cause concern. ...

Electricity prices climbed 18.3 per cent in Ontario in August from a month earlier, Statscan said in its monthly inflation report. That followed a 9.2-per-cent increase in July from June. ...

Upward pressure on gasoline prices and car insurance also pushed up the cost of living in August as the cost of filling the gas tank climbed 2.5 per cent, and insurance premiums rose 2.6 per cent.

The core rate of inflation closely monitored by the Bank of Canada climbed 2.5 per cent in August from an annual rate of 2.1 per cent in July, the biggest advance since September of 1995. Without electricity, the core rate was 2.2 per cent in August.

The Bank of Canada's core measure excludes the eight most volatile items, such as food, energy and indirect taxes, but includes electricity prices. ...

The increase in gasoline, electricity and auto insurance premiums accounted for almost the entire upward movement in inflation in August—without those items, the rise was a tepid 0.6 per cent, ...

Some prices fell in August, including fresh vegetables, which dropped 13.8 per cent because of the increased availability as local crops came on the market.

Reprinted with permission from *The Globe and Mail*.

Essence of the Story

■ Statistics Canada reported that the inflation rate in August 2002 was 2.6 percent (annual rate) up from 2.1 percent in July 2002.

■ Ontario electricity prices increased by 18.3 percent in August and by 9.2 percent in July, and these increases are reported as the source of the jump in the inflation rate.

■ Gasoline and car insurance prices also increased at a faster pace in August.

■ The core inflation rate, which excludes food, energy, and indirect taxes but includes electricity, increased at an annual rate of 2.5 percent in August, up from 2.1 percent in July.

■ This jump in the core inflation rate in August 2002 was the biggest since September 1995.

■ Some prices fell in August, including those of fresh vegetables, which dropped 13.8 percent.

Economic Analysis

■ Statistics Canada reports the nation's Consumer Price Index (CPI) numbers every month.

■ The Consumer Price Index is an indicator of the changes in consumer prices experienced by Canadians.

■ The Consumer Price Index is obtained by comparing the price of a fixed basket of commodities purchased by Canadians over different time periods.

■ The fixed basket includes food, shelter, household operations and furnishings, clothing and footwear, transportation, health and personal care, recreation, education and reading, and alcoholic beverages and tobacco products.

■ Figure 1 shows the Consumer Price Index for each month from January 2000 through October 2002.

■ In August 2001, the Consumer Price Index was 116.7 and in August 2002, it was 119.2.

■ The annual inflation rate between August 2001 and August 2002 was 2.1 percent. This inflation rate is calculated as

$$\frac{(119.2 - 116.7)}{116.7} \times 100.$$

■ Figure 2 shows the inflation rate for each month between January 2000 and October 2002. You can see that the inflation rate was on a slightly rising trend through 2000 and the first half of 2001, fell in the second half of 2001, and increased during 2002.

■ In addition to reporting the Consumer Price Index, Statistics Canada also reports a monthly index for each component of the Consumer Price Index basket.

■ Figure 3 shows the percentage changes in each component of the Consumer Price Index basket between July and August 2002.

■ These price changes tell us about *relative prices*. They do not tell us anything about inflation. Nor do they tell us *why* the inflation rate changed.

■ It is a common mistake in the media to say that the inflation rate increased (or decreased) *because* a particular price increased (or decreased).

■ The price of Ontario electricity increased. But this change in relative prices provides no information about why the inflation rate changed. Lots of relative prices changed, as Fig. 3 shows.

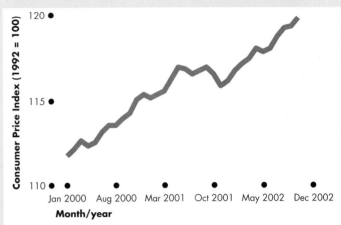

Figure 1 Consumer Price Index

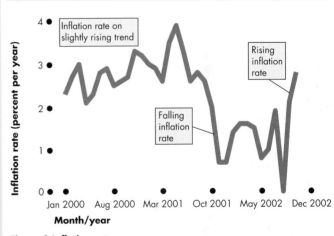

Figure 2 Inflation rate

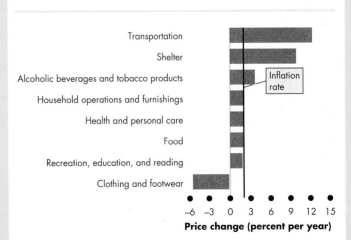

Figure 3 Relative price changes between July and August 2002

SUMMARY

KEY POINTS

The Business Cycle (pp. 478–479)

- A recession is a significant decline in activity spread across the economy and lasting more than a few months.
- Another definition of recession is a decrease in real GDP that lasts for at least two quarters.
- The ECRI has identified only 4 recessions and expansions in Canada since World War II.

Jobs and Wages (pp. 480–484)

- The unemployment rate averaged 7.7 percent between 1961 and 2001. It increases in recessions and decreases in expansions.
- The labour force participation rate and the employment-to-population ratio have an upward trend and fluctuate with the business cycle.
- The labour force participation rate has increased for females and decreased for males.
- Aggregate hours have an upward trend, and they fluctuate with the business cycle.
- Real hourly wage rates grow but their growth rates slowed during the 1970s.

Unemployment and Full Employment (pp. 485–489)

- People are constantly entering and leaving the state of unemployment.
- The duration of unemployment fluctuates over the business cycle. But the demographic patterns of unemployment are constant.
- Unemployment can be frictional, structural, seasonal, and cyclical.
- When all unemployment is frictional, structural, and seasonal, the unemployment rate equals the natural rate of unemployment, the economy is at full employment, and real GDP equals potential GDP.
- Over the business cycle, real GDP fluctuates around potential GDP and the unemployment rate fluctuates around the natural rate of unemployment.

The Consumer Price Index (pp. 490–493)

- The Consumer Price Index (CPI) measures the average of the prices paid by urban consumers for a fixed basket of consumer goods and services.
- The CPI is defined to equal 100 for the base period—currently 1992.
- The inflation rate is the percentage change in the CPI from one year to the next.
- Changes in the CPI probably overstate the inflation rate slightly.
- The bias in the CPI distorts private contracts and increases government outlays.

KEY FIGURES

KEY TERMS

PROBLEMS

💻 *1. Statistics Canada reported the following data for January 2000: Labour force: 15,537,700 Employment: 14,339,200 Working-age population: 24,137,100. Calculate for that month the
   a. Unemployment rate.
   b. Labour force participation rate.
   c. Employment-to-population ratio.

2. Statistics Canada reported the following data for January 2001: Labour force: 16,219,800 Employment: 14,990,400 Working-age population: 24,764,100. Calculate for that month the
   a. Unemployment rate.
   b. Labour force participation rate.
   c. Employment-to-population ratio.

💻 *3. During 2000, the working-age population in Canada increased by 327,100, employment increased by 280,900, and the labour force increased by 330,400. Use these numbers and the data in problem 1 to calculate the change in unemployment and the change in the number of people not in the labour force during 2000.

4. During 2001, the working-age population in Canada increased by 299,900, employment decreased by 16,600, and the labour force increased by 329,200. Use these numbers and the data in problem 2 to calculate the change in unemployment and the change in the number of people not in the labour force during 2001.

💻 *5. In August 2000, the unemployment rate was 7.2 percent. In August 2001, the unemployment rate was 7.5 percent. Use this information to predict what happened between August 2000 and August 2001 to the numbers of
   a. Job losers and job leavers.
   b. Labour force entrants and re-entrants.

6. In January 2001, the unemployment rate was 7.5 percent. In January 2002, the unemployment rate was 8.6 percent. Use these data to predict what happened between January 2001 and January 2002 to the numbers of
   a. Job losers and job leavers.
   b. Labour force entrants and re-entrants.

*7. In July 2002, on Sandy Island, 10,000 people were employed, 1,000 were unemployed, and 5,000 were not in the labour force. During August 2002, 80 people lost their jobs, 20 quit their jobs, 150 were hired or recalled, 50 withdrew from the labour force, and 40 entered or re-entered the labour force. Calculate for July 2002
   a. The labour force.
   b. The unemployment rate.
   c. The working-age population.
   d. The employment-to-population ratio.
   And calculate for the end of August 2002
   e. The number of people unemployed.
   f. The number of people employed.
   g. The labour force.
   h. The unemployment rate.

8. In July 2003 on Sandy Island, 11,000 people were employed, 900 were unemployed, and 5,000 were not in the labour force. During August 2003, 40 people lost their jobs, 10 quit their jobs, 180 were hired or recalled, 20 withdrew from the labour force, and 60 entered or re-entered the labour force. Calculate for July 2003
   a. The labour force.
   b. The unemployment rate.
   c. The working-age population.
   d. The employment-to-population ratio.
   And calculate for the end of August 2003
   e. The number of people unemployed.
   f. The number of people employed.
   g. The labour force.
   h. The unemployment rate.

9. A typical family on Sandy Island consumes only juice and cloth. Last year, which was the base year, the family spent $40 on juice and $25 on cloth. In the base year, juice was $4 a bottle and cloth was $5 a length. In the current year, juice is $4 a bottle and cloth is $6 a length. Calculate
   a. The basket used in the CPI.
   b. The CPI in the current year.
   c. The inflation rate in the current year.

10. A typical family on Lizard Island consumes only mangoes and nuts. In the base year, the family spent $60 on nuts and $10 on mangoes. In the base year, mangoes were $1 each and nuts were $3 a bag. In the current year, mangoes are $1.50 each and nuts are $4 a bag. Calculate
   a. The basket used in the CPI.
   b. The CPI in the current year.
   c. The inflation rate in the current year.

CRITICAL THINKING

1. Study *Reading Between the Lines* on pp. 494–495 and then answer the following questions:
   a. Describe the changes in the CPI that occurred during 2002.
   b. Explain the difference between a change in a relative price and inflation. Which relative prices increased most in August 2002 and which increased least or fell?
   c. Do you think the news article did a good job reporting the August CPI numbers? Write a brief report that does a better job and explain why it is better.

2. Thinking about the economy of Sandy Island in problems 7 and 8:
   a. In what phase of its business cycle was Sandy Island during 2003?
   b. What do you predict would be happening to real GDP on Sandy Island? Why?
   c. What do you predict would be happening to real GDP per person on Sandy Island? Why?

3. Describe the main features of the labour market at the peak of the business cycle.

4. Describe the main features of the labour market at the trough of the business cycle.

5. You've seen in this chapter that the average work-week has shortened over the years. Do you think that shorter work hours are a problem or a benefit? Do you expect the average workweek to keep getting shorter? Why or why not?

6. An increasing number of jobs are part-time jobs. Can you think of some reasons for this trend? Who benefits from part-time jobs: the employer, the worker, or both? Explain with examples.

7. You've seen that the CPI is biased and overstates the true inflation rate. It would be a simple matter to adjust the CPI for the known average bias. Yet we continue to keep a flawed measure of inflation in place. Why do you think we don't adjust the CPI for the known average bias so that its measure of the inflation rate is more accurate? Explain who gains from the biased measure and who loses from it. Try to think of reasons why those who lose have not persuaded those who win to adopt a more accurate measure.

WEB EXERCISES

1. Use the link on the Parkin–Bade Web site to review the Bank of Canada's latest Monetary Policy Report. In which phase of the business cycle is the economy in your region? How does your region compare to the nation as a whole?

2. Use the link on the Parkin–Bade Web site to visit the Web site of Statistics Canada and find labour market data for your own province.
   a. What have been the trends in employment, unemployment, and labour force participation in your province during the past two years?
   b. On the basis of what you know about your own province, how would you set about explaining these trends?
   c. Try to identify those industries that have expanded most and those that have shrunk.
   d. What are the problems with your own provincial labour market that you think need provincial government action to resolve?
   e. What actions do you think your provincial government must take to resolve these problems? Answer this question by using the demand and supply model of the labour market and predict the effects of the actions you prescribe.
   f. Compare the labour market performance of your own province with that of Canada.
   g. If your province is performing better than the national average, to what do you attribute the success? If your province is performing worse than the national average, to what do you attribute its problems? What federal actions are needed in your provincial labour market?

3. Use the link on the Parkin–Bade Web site to visit the Web site of Statistics Canada and find CPI data for your own province.
   a. What have been the trends in the CPI in your province during the past two years?
   b. Compare the CPI performance of your own province with that of Canada as a whole.
   c. On the basis of what you know about your own province, how would you set about explaining its deviation from the Canadian average?

AGGREGATE SUPPLY AND AGGREGATE DEMAND

CHAPTER 22

Production and Prices

During the 10 years from 1992 to 2002, Canadian real GDP increased by 40 percent. Expanding at this pace, real GDP doubles every 21 years. What forces bring persistent and rapid expansion of real GDP? ◆ Expanding real GDP brings a rising standard of living. Inflation brings a rising cost of living. Because of inflation, you need $2 today to buy what $1 bought in 1980. What causes inflation? ◆ Our economy does not expand at a constant pace. Instead, it ebbs and flows over the business cycle. For example, we had a recession during 1990 and early 1991. For half a year, real GDP decreased. Since that time, our economy has expanded, but at a variable rate. Why do we have a business cycle? ◆ Because our economy fluctuates, the government and the Bank of Canada try to smooth its path. How do the policy actions of the government and the Bank of Canada affect production and prices?

◆ To answer these questions, we need a *model* of real GDP and the price level. Our main task in this chapter is to study such a model: the *aggregate supply–aggregate demand model*. Our second task is to use the aggregate supply–aggregate demand (or *AS–AD*) model to answer the questions we've just posed. You'll discover that this model enables us to understand the forces that make our economy expand, that bring inflation, and that cause business cycle fluctuations. At the end of the chapter, in *Reading Between the Lines*, we'll put the *AS–AD* model to work to understand the macroeconomic effects of implementing the Kyoto agreement on climate control.

After studying this chapter, you will be able to

- Explain what determines aggregate supply
- Explain what determines aggregate demand
- Explain macroeconomic equilibrium
- Explain the effects of changes in aggregate supply and aggregate demand on economic growth, inflation, and the business cycle
- Explain Canadian economic growth, inflation, and the business cycle by using the *AS–AD* model

Aggregate Supply

THE AGGREGATE SUPPLY–AGGREGATE DEMAND model enables us to understand three features of macroeconomic performance:

- Growth of potential GDP
- Inflation
- Business cycle fluctuations

The model uses the concepts of *aggregate* supply and *aggregate* demand to determine *real GDP* and the *price level* (the GDP deflator). We begin by looking at the limits to production that influence aggregate supply.

Aggregate Supply Fundamentals

The *quantity of real GDP supplied* (Y) depends on

1. The quantity of labour (L)
2. The quantity of capital (K)
3. The state of technology (T)

The influence of these three factors on the quantity of real GDP supplied is described by the **aggregate production function,** which is written as the equation:

$$Y = F(L, K, T).$$

In words, the quantity of real GDP supplied is determined by (is a function F of) the quantities of labour and capital and the state of technology. The larger is L, K, or T, the greater is Y.

At any given time, the quantity of capital and the state of technology are fixed. They depend on decisions that were made in the past. The population is also fixed. But the quantity of labour is not fixed. It depends on decisions made by people and firms about the supply of and demand for labour.

The labour market can be in any one of three states: at full employment, above full employment, or below full employment.

Even at full employment, there are always some people looking for jobs and some firms looking for people to hire. The reason is that there is a constant churning of the labour market. Every day, some jobs are destroyed as businesses reorganize or fail. Some jobs are created as new businesses start up or existing ones expand. Some workers decide, for any of a thousand personal reasons, to quit their jobs. And other people decide to start looking for a job. This constant churning in the labour market prevents unemploy-

ment from ever disappearing. The unemployment rate at full employment is called the **natural rate of unemployment.**

Another way to think about full employment is as a state of the labour market in which the quantity of labour demanded equals the quantity supplied. Firms demand labour only if it is profitable to do so. And the lower the wage rate, which is the cost of labour, the greater is the quantity of labour demanded. People supply labour only if doing so is the most valuable use of their time. And the higher the wage rate, which is the return to labour, the greater is the quantity of labour supplied. The wage rate that makes the quantity of labour demanded equal to the quantity of labour supplied is the equilibrium wage rate. At this wage rate, there is full employment. (You can study the labour market at full employment in Chapter 29 on pp. 686–687.)

The quantity of real GDP at full employment is *potential GDP*, which depends on the full-employment quantity of labour, the quantity of capital, and the state of technology. Over the business cycle, employment fluctuates around full employment and real GDP fluctuates around potential GDP.

To study aggregate supply in different states of the labour market, we distinguish two time frames:

- Long-run aggregate supply
- Short-run aggregate supply

Long-Run Aggregate Supply

The economy is constantly bombarded by events that move real GDP away from potential GDP and, equivalently, that move employment away from full employment. Following such an event, forces operate to take real GDP back towards potential GDP and restore full employment. The **macroeconomic long run** is a time frame that is sufficiently long for these forces to have done their work so that real GDP equals potential GDP and full employment prevails.

The **long-run aggregate supply curve** is the relationship between the quantity of real GDP supplied and the price level in the long run when real GDP equals potential GDP. Figure 22.1 shows this relationship as the vertical line labelled *LAS*. Along the long-run aggregate supply curve, as the price level changes, real GDP remains at potential GDP, which in Fig. 22.1 is $1,000 billion. The long-run aggregate supply curve is always vertical and is located at potential GDP.

FIGURE 22.1   Long-Run Aggregate Supply

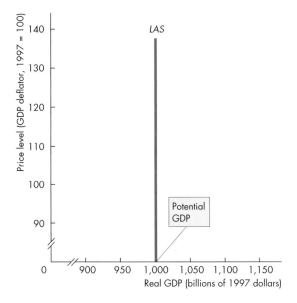

The long-run aggregate supply curve (*LAS*) shows the relationship between potential GDP and the price level. Potential GDP is independent of the price level, so the *LAS* curve is vertical at potential GDP.

The long-run aggregate supply curve is vertical because potential GDP is independent of the price level. The reason for this independence is that a movement along the *LAS* curve is accompanied by a change in *two* sets of prices: the prices of goods and services—the price level—and the prices of productive resources. A 10 percent increase in the prices of goods and services is matched by a 10 percent increase in the money wage rate and other resource prices. That is, the price level, money wage rate, and other resource prices all change by the same percentage, and *relative prices* and the *real wage rate* remain constant. When the price level changes but relative prices and the real wage rate remain constant, real GDP also remains constant.

Production at a Pepsi Plant You can see why real GDP remains constant when all prices change by the same percentage if you think about production decisions at a Pepsi bottling plant. The plant is producing the quantity of Pepsi that maximizes profit. The plant

can increase production but only by incurring a higher *marginal cost* (see Chapter 2, p. 37). So the firm has no incentive to change production.

Short-Run Aggregate Supply

The **macroeconomic short run** is a period during which real GDP has fallen below or risen above potential GDP. At the same time, the unemployment rate has risen above or fallen below the natural rate of unemployment.

The **short-run aggregate supply curve** is the relationship between the quantity of real GDP supplied and the price level in the short run when the money wage rate, the prices of other resources, and potential GDP remain constant. Figure 22.2 shows a short-run aggregate supply curve as the upward-sloping curve labelled *SAS*. This curve is based on the short-run aggregate supply schedule, and each point on the aggregate supply curve corresponds to a row of the aggregate supply schedule. For example, point *A* on the short-run aggregate supply curve and row *A* of the schedule tell us that if the price level is 100, the quantity of real GDP supplied is $900 billion.

At point *C*, the price level is 110 and the quantity of real GDP supplied is $1,000 billion, which equals potential GDP. If the price level is higher than 110, real GDP exceeds potential GDP; if the price level is below 110, real GDP is less than potential GDP.

Back at the Pepsi Plant You can see why the short-run aggregate supply curve slopes upward by returning to the Pepsi bottling plant. The plant produces the quantity that maximizes profit. If the price of Pepsi rises and the money wage rate and other costs don't change, the *relative price* of Pepsi rises and the firm has an incentive to increase its production. The higher relative price of Pepsi covers the higher marginal cost of producing more Pepsi, so the firm increases production.

Similarly, if the price of Pepsi falls and the money wage rate and other costs don't change, the lower relative price is not sufficient to cover the marginal cost of Pepsi, so the firm decreases production.

Again, what's true for Pepsi bottlers is true for the producers of all goods and services. So when the price level rises and the money wage rate and other resource prices remain constant, the quantity of real GDP supplied increases.

FIGURE 22.2   Short-Run Aggregate Supply

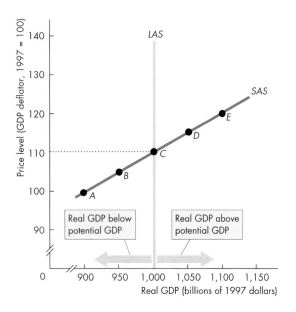

	Price level (GDP deflator)	Real GDP (billions of 1997 dollars)
A	100	900
B	105	950
C	110	1,000
D	115	1,050
E	120	1,100

The short-run aggregate supply curve shows the relationship between the quantity of real GDP supplied and the price level when the money wage rate, other resource prices, and potential GDP remain the same. The short-run aggregate supply curve, *SAS*, is based on the schedule in the table. This curve is upward-sloping because firms' marginal costs increase as output increases, so a higher price is needed, relative to the prices of productive resources, to bring forth an increase in the quantity produced. On the *SAS* curve, when the price level is 110, real GDP equals potential GDP. If the price level is greater than 110, real GDP exceeds potential GDP; if the price level is below 110, real GDP is less than potential GDP.

Movements Along the *LAS* and *SAS* Curves

Figure 21.3 summarizes what you've just learned about the *LAS* and *SAS* curves. When the price level, the money wage rate, and other resource prices rise by the same percentage, relative price remains constant and real GDP remains at potential GDP. There is a *movement along* the *LAS* curve.

When the price level rises but the money wage rate and other resource prices remain the same, the quantity of real GDP supplied increases and there is a *movement along* the *SAS* curve.

Let's next study the influences that bring changes in aggregate supply.

FIGURE 22.3   Movements Along the Aggregate Supply Curves

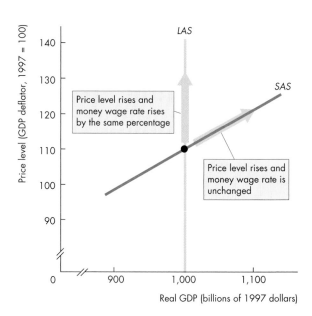

A rise in the price level with no change in the money wage rate and other resource prices brings an increase in the quantity of real GDP supplied and a movement along the short-run aggregate supply curve, *SAS*.

A rise in the price level with equal percentage increases in the money wage rate and other resource prices keeps the quantity of real GDP supplied constant at potential GDP and brings a movement along the long-run aggregate supply curve, *LAS*.

Changes in Aggregate Supply

You've just seen that a change in the price level brings a movement along the aggregate supply curves but does not change aggregate supply. Aggregate supply changes when influences on production plans other than the price level change. Let's begin by looking at factors that change potential GDP.

Changes in Potential GDP When potential GDP changes, both long-run aggregate supply and short-run aggregate supply change. Potential GDP changes for three reasons:

1. A change in the full-employment quantity of labour
2. A change in the quantity of capital
3. An advance in technology

An increase in the full-employment quantity of labour, an increase in the quantity of capital, or an advance in technology increases potential GDP. And an increase in potential GDP changes both the long-run aggregate supply and short-run aggregate supply.

Figure 22.4 shows these effects of a change in potential GDP. Initially, the long-run aggregate supply curve is LAS_0 and the short-run aggregate supply curve is SAS_0. If an increase in the quantity of capital or a technological advance increases potential GDP to $1,100 billion, long-run aggregate supply increases and the long-run aggregate supply curve shifts rightward to LAS_1. Short-run aggregate supply also increases, and the short-run aggregate supply curve shifts rightward to SAS_1.

Let's look more closely at the influences on potential GDP and the aggregate supply curves.

A Change in the Full-Employment Quantity of Labour A Pepsi bottling plant that employs 100 workers bottles more Pepsi than an otherwise identical plant that employs 10 workers. The same is true for the economy as a whole. The larger the quantity of labour employed, the greater is GDP.

Over time, potential GDP increases because the labour force increases. But (with constant capital and technology) *potential* GDP increases only if the full-employment quantity of labour increases. Fluctuations in employment over the business cycle bring fluctuations in real GDP. But these changes in real GDP are fluctuations around potential GDP. They are not changes in potential GDP and long-run aggregate supply.

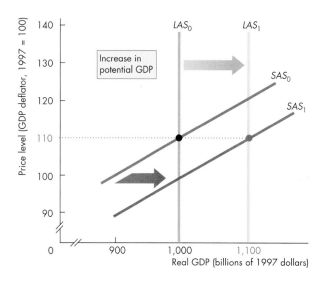

FIGURE 22.4 A Change in Potential GDP

An increase in potential GDP increases both long-run aggregate supply and short-run aggregate supply and shifts both aggregate supply curves rightward, from LAS_0 to LAS_1 and from SAS_0 to SAS_1.

A Change in the Quantity of Capital A Pepsi bottling plant with two production lines bottles more Pepsi than an otherwise identical plant that has only one production line. For the economy, the larger the quantity of capital, the more productive is the labour force and the greater is its potential GDP. Potential GDP per person in capital-rich Canada is vastly greater than that in capital-poor China and Russia.

Capital includes *human capital.* One Pepsi plant is managed by an economics major with an MBA and has a labour force with an average of 10 years of experience. This plant produces a much larger output than an otherwise identical plant that is managed by someone with no business training or experience and that has a young labour force that is new to bottling. The first plant has a greater amount of human capital than the second. For the economy as a whole, the larger the quantity of *human capital*—the skills that people have acquired in school and through on-the-job training—the greater is potential GDP.

An Advance in Technology A Pepsi plant that has pre-computer age machines produces less than one that uses the latest robot technology. Technological change enables firms to produce more from any given amount of inputs. So even with fixed quantities of labour and capital, improvements in technology increase potential GDP.

Technological advances are by far the most important source of increased production over the past two centuries. Because of technological advances, one farmer in Canada today can feed 100 people and one auto worker can produce almost 14 cars and trucks in a year.

Let's now look at the effects of changes in the money wage rate.

Changes in the Money Wage Rate and Other Resource Prices When the money wage rate or the money prices of other resources (such as the price of oil) change, short-run aggregate supply changes but long-run aggregate supply does not change.

Figure 22.5 shows the effect on aggregate supply of an increase in the money wage rate. Initially, the short-run aggregate supply curve is SAS_0. A rise in the money wage rate *decreases* short-run aggregate supply and shifts the short-run aggregate supply curve leftward to SAS_2.

The money wage rate (and resource prices) affect short-run aggregate supply because they influence firms' costs. The higher the money wage rate, the higher are firms' costs and the smaller is the quantity that firms are willing to supply at each price level. So an increase in the money wage rate decreases short-run aggregate supply.

A change in the money wage rate does not change long-run aggregate supply because on the *LAS* curve, a change in the money wage rate is accompanied by an equal percentage change in the price level. With no change in *relative* prices, firms have no incentive to change production and real GDP remains constant at potential GDP.

In Fig. 22.5, the vertical distance between the original *SAS* curve and the new *SAS* curve is determined by the percentage change in the money wage rate. That is, the percentage increase in the price level between point *A* and point *B* equals the percentage increase in the money wage rate.

Because potential GDP does not change when the money wage rate changes, long-run aggregate supply does not change. The long-run aggregate supply curve remains at *LAS*.

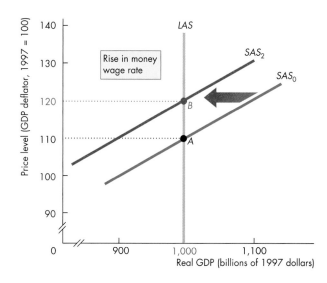

FIGURE 22.5 A Change in the Money Wage Rate

A rise in the money wage rate decreases short-run aggregate supply and shifts the short-run aggregate supply curve leftward from SAS_0 to SAS_2. A rise in the money wage rate does not change potential GDP, so the long-run aggregate supply curve does not shift.

REVIEW QUIZ

1 If the price level rises and if the money wage rate also rises by the same percentage, what happens to the quantity of real GDP supplied? Along which aggregate supply curve does the economy move?

2 If the price level rises and the money wage rate remains constant, what happens to the quantity of real GDP supplied? Along which aggregate supply curve does the economy move?

3 If potential GDP increases, what happens to aggregate supply? Is there a shift of or a movement along the *LAS* curve and the *SAS* curve?

4 If the money wage rate rises and potential GDP remains the same, what happens to aggregate supply? Is there a shift of or a movement along the *LAS* curve and the *SAS* curve?

Aggregate Demand

THE QUANTITY OF REAL GDP DEMANDED IS THE sum of the real consumption expenditure (C), investment (I), government expenditures (G), and exports (X) minus imports (M). That is,

$$Y = C + I + G + X - M.$$

The *quantity of real GDP demanded* is the total amount of final goods and services produced in Canada that people, businesses, governments, and foreigners plan to buy.

These buying plans depend on many factors. Some of the main ones are

- The price level
- Expectations
- Fiscal policy and monetary policy
- The world economy

We first focus on the relationship between the quantity of real GDP demanded and the price level. To study this relationship, we keep all other influences on buying plans the same and ask: How does the quantity of real GDP demanded vary as the price level varies?

The Aggregate Demand Curve

Other things remaining the same, the higher the price level, the smaller is the quantity of real GDP demanded. This relationship between the quantity of real GDP demanded and the price level is called **aggregate demand.** Aggregate demand is described by an aggregate demand schedule and an aggregate demand curve.

Figure 22.6 shows an aggregate demand curve (*AD*) and an aggregate demand schedule. Each point on the *AD* curve corresponds to a row of the schedule. For example, point *C'* on the *AD* curve and row *C'* of the schedule tell us that if the price level is 110, the quantity of real GDP demanded is $1,000 billion.

The aggregate demand curve slopes downward for two reasons:

- Wealth effect
- Substitution effects

Wealth Effect When the price level rises but other things remain the same, *real* wealth decreases. Real

FIGURE 22.6 Aggregate Demand

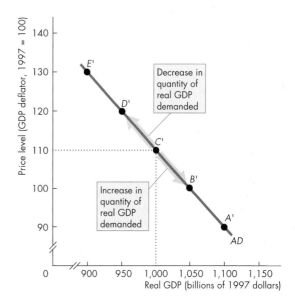

	Price level (GDP deflator)	Real GDP (billions of 1997 dollars)
A'	90	1,100
B'	100	1,050
C'	110	1,000
D'	120	950
E'	130	900

The aggregate demand curve (*AD*) shows the relationship between the quantity of real GDP demanded and the price level. The aggregate demand curve is based on the aggregate demand schedule in the table. Each point A' through E' on the curve corresponds to the row in the table identified by the same letter. Thus when the price level is 110, the quantity of real GDP demanded is $1,000 billion, shown by point *C'* in the figure. A change in the price level with all other influences on aggregate buying plans remaining the same brings a change in the quantity of real GDP demanded and a movement along the *AD* curve.

wealth is the amount of money in the bank, bonds, stocks, and other assets that people own, measured not in dollars but in terms of the goods and services that this money, bonds, and stocks will buy.

People save and hold money, bonds, and stocks for many reasons. One reason is to build up funds for education expenses. Another reason is to build up enough funds to meet possible medical or other big bills. But the biggest reason is to build up enough funds to provide a retirement income.

If the price level rises, real wealth decreases. People then try to restore their wealth. To do so, they must increase saving and, equivalently, decrease current consumption. Such a decrease in consumption is a decrease in aggregate demand.

Maria's Wealth Effect You can see how the wealth effect works by thinking about Maria's buying plans. Maria lives in Moscow, Russia. She has worked hard all summer and saved 20,000 rubles (the ruble is the currency of Russia), which she plans to spend attending graduate school when she has finished her economics degree. So Maria's wealth is 20,000 rubles. Maria has a part-time job, and her income from this job pays her current expenses. The price level in Russia rises by 100 percent, and now Maria needs 40,000 rubles to buy what 20,000 once bought. To try to make up some of the fall in value of her savings, Maria saves even more and cuts her current spending to the bare minimum.

Substitution Effects When the price level rises and other things remain the same, interest rates rise. The reason is related to the wealth effect that you've just studied. A rise in the price level decreases the real value of the money in people's pockets and bank accounts. With a smaller amount of real money around, banks and other lenders can get a higher interest rate on loans. But faced with higher interest rates, people and businesses delay plans to buy new capital and consumer durable goods and cut back on spending.

This substitution effect involves substituting goods in the future for goods in the present and is called an *intertemporal* substitution effect—a substitution across time. Saving increases to increase future consumption.

To see this intertemporal substitution effect more clearly, think about your own plan to buy a new computer. At an interest rate of 5 percent a year, you might borrow $2,000 and buy the new machine you've been researching. But at an interest rate of 10 percent a year, you might decide that the payments would be too high. You don't abandon your plan to buy the computer, but you decide to delay your purchase.

A second substitution effect works through international prices. When the Canadian price level rises and other things remain the same, Canadian-made goods and services become more expensive relative to foreign-made goods and services. This change in *relative prices* encourages people to spend less on Canadian-made items and more on foreign-made items. For example, if the Canadian price level rises relative to the U.S. price level, Americans buy fewer Canadian-made cars (Canadian exports decrease) and Canadians buy more U.S.-made cars (Canadian imports increase). Canadian GDP decreases.

Maria's Substitution Effects In Moscow, Russia, Maria makes some substitutions. She was planning to trade in her old motor scooter and get a new one. But with a higher price level and faced with higher interest rates, she decides to make her old scooter last one more year. Also, with the prices of Russian goods sharply increasing, Maria substitutes a low-cost dress made in Malaysia for the Russian-made dress she had originally planned to buy.

Changes in the Quantity of Real GDP Demanded When the price level rises and other things remain the same, the quantity of real GDP demanded decreases—a movement up the *AD* curve as shown by the arrow in Fig. 22.6. When the price level falls and other things remain the same, the quantity of real GDP demanded increases—a movement down the *AD* curve.

We've now seen how the quantity of real GDP demanded changes when the price level changes. How do other influences on buying plans affect aggregate demand?

Changes in Aggregate Demand

A change in any factor that influences buying plans other than the price level brings a change in aggregate demand. The main factors are

- Expectations
- Fiscal policy and monetary policy
- The world economy

Expectations An increase in expected future disposable income increases consumption goods (especially big-ticket items such as cars) that people plan to buy today and increases aggregate demand today.

An increase in the expected future inflation rate

increases aggregate demand today because people decide to buy more goods and services at today's relatively lower prices. An increase in expected future profit increases the investment that firms plan to undertake today and increases aggregate demand today.

Fiscal Policy and Monetary Policy The government's attempt to influence the economy by setting and changing taxes, making transfer payments, and purchasing goods and services is called **fiscal policy.** A tax cut or an increase in transfer payments—for example, unemployment benefits or welfare payments—increases aggregate demand. Both of these influences operate by increasing households' disposable income. **Disposable income** is aggregate income minus taxes plus transfer payments. The greater the disposable income, the greater is the quantity of consumption goods and services that households plan to buy and the greater is aggregate demand.

Government expenditures on goods and services are one component of aggregate demand. So if the government spends more on hospitals, schools, and highways, aggregate demand increases.

Monetary policy consists of changes in interest rates and in the quantity of money in the economy. The quantity of money is determined by the Bank of Canada and the banks (in a process described in Chapters 25 and 26). An increase in the quantity of money in the economy increases aggregate demand. To see why money affects aggregate demand, imagine that the Bank of Canada borrows the army's helicopters, loads them with millions of new $10 bills, and sprinkles these bills like confetti across the nation. People gather the newly available money and plan to spend some of it. So the quantity of goods and services demanded increases. But people don't plan to spend all the new money. They plan to save some of it and lend it to others through the banks. Interest rates fall, and with lower interest rates, people plan to buy more consumer durables and firms plan to increase their investment.

The World Economy Two main influences that the world economy has on aggregate demand are the foreign exchange rate and foreign income. The *foreign exchange rate* is the amount of a foreign currency that you can buy with a Canadian dollar. Other things remaining the same, a rise in the foreign exchange rate decreases aggregate demand. To see how the foreign exchange rate influences aggregate demand, suppose

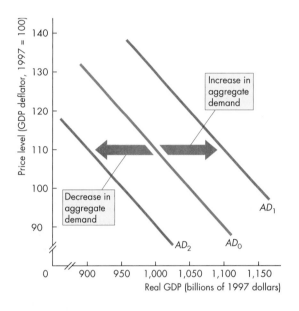

FIGURE 22.7 Changes in Aggregate Demand

Aggregate demand

Decreases if:	Increases if:
■ Expected future disposable income, inflation, or profits decrease	■ Expected future disposable income, inflation, or profits increase
■ Fiscal policy decreases government expenditures, increases taxes, or decreases transfer payments	■ Fiscal policy increases government expenditures, decreases taxes, or increases transfer payments
■ Monetary policy decreases the quantity of money and increases interest rates	■ Monetary policy increases the quantity of money and decreases interest rates
■ The exchange rate increases or foreign income decreases	■ The exchange rate decreases or foreign income increases

that $1 exchanges for 100 Japanese yen. A Fujitsu phone (made in Japan) costs 12,500 yen, and an equivalent Nortel phone (made in Canada) costs $110. In Canadian dollars, the Fujitsu phone costs $125, so people around the world buy the cheaper

Canadian phone. Now suppose the foreign exchange rate rises to 125 yen per dollar. At 125 yen per dollar, the Fujitsu phone costs $100 and is now cheaper than the Nortel phone. People will switch from the Canadian phone to the Japanese phone. Canadian exports will decrease and Canadian imports will increase, so Canadian aggregate demand will decrease.

An increase in foreign income increases Canadian exports and increases Canadian aggregate demand. For example, an increase in income in Japan and Germany increases Japanese and German consumers' and producers' planned expenditures on Canadian-made goods and services.

Shifts of the Aggregate Demand Curve When aggregate demand changes, the aggregate demand curve shifts. Figure 22.7 shows two changes in aggregate demand and summarizes the factors that bring about such changes.

Aggregate demand increases and the aggregate demand curve shifts rightward from AD_0 to AD_1 when expected future income, inflation, or profit increases; government expenditures on goods and services increase; taxes are cut; transfer payments increase; the quantity of money increases and interest rates fall; the foreign exchange rate falls; or foreign income increases.

Aggregate demand decreases and the aggregate demand curve shifts leftward from AD_0 to AD_2 when expected future income, inflation, or profit decreases; government expenditures on goods and services decrease; taxes increase; transfer payments decrease; the quantity of money decreases and interest rates rise; the foreign exchange rate rises; or foreign income decreases.

REVIEW QUIZ

1 What does the aggregate demand curve show? What factors change and what factors remain the same when there is a movement along the aggregate demand curve?
2 Why does the aggregate demand curve slope downward?
3 How do changes in expectations, fiscal policy and monetary policy, and the world economy change aggregate demand and shift the aggregate demand curve?

Macroeconomic Equilibrium

THE PURPOSE OF THE AGGREGATE SUPPLY–aggregate demand model is to explain changes in real GDP and the price level. To achieve this purpose, we combine aggregate supply and aggregate demand and determine macroeconomic equilibrium. There is a macroeconomic equilibrium for each of the time frames for aggregate supply: a long-run equilibrium and a short-run equilibrium. Long-run equilibrium is the state towards which the economy is heading. Short-run equilibrium is the normal state of the economy as it fluctuates around potential GDP.

We'll begin our study of macroeconomic equilibrium by looking first at the short run.

Short-Run Macroeconomic Equilibrium

The aggregate demand curve tells us the quantity of real GDP demanded at each price level, and the short-run aggregate supply curve tells us the quantity of real GDP supplied at each price level. **Short-run macroeconomic equilibrium** occurs when the quantity of real GDP demanded equals the quantity of real GDP supplied. That is, short-run equilibrium occurs at the point of intersection of the *AD* curve and the *SAS* curve. Figure 22.8 shows such an equilibrium at a price level of 110 and real GDP of $1,000 billion (points *C* and *C'*).

To see why this position is the equilibrium, think about what happens if the price level is something other than 110. Suppose, for example, that the price level is 120 and that real GDP is $1,100 billion (at point *E* on the *SAS* curve). The quantity of real GDP demanded is less than $1,100 billion, so firms are unable to sell all their output. Unwanted inventories pile up, and firms cut both production and prices. Production and prices are cut until firms can sell all their output. This situation occurs only when real GDP is $1,000 billion and the price level is 110.

Now suppose the price level is 100 and real GDP is $900 billion (at point *A* on the *SAS* curve). The quantity of real GDP demanded exceeds $900 billion, so firms are unable to meet the demand for their output. Inventories decrease, and customers clamour for goods and services. So firms increase production and raise prices. Production and prices increase until firms can meet demand. This situation

FIGURE 22.8 Short-Run Equilibrium

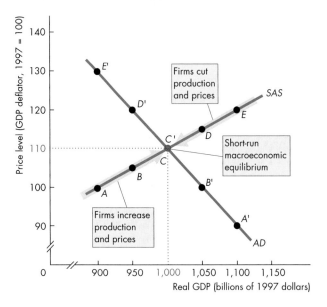

Short-run macroeconomic equilibrium occurs when real GDP demanded equals real GDP supplied—at the intersection of the aggregate demand curve (*AD*) and the short-run aggregate supply curve (*SAS*). Here, such an equilibrium occurs at points *C* and *C'*, where the price level is 110 and real GDP is $1,000 billion. If the price level is 120 and real GDP is $1,100 billion (point *E*), firms will not be able to sell all their output. They will decrease production and cut prices. If the price level is 100 and real GDP is $900 billion (point *A*), people will not be able to buy all the goods and services they demand. Firms will increase production and raise their prices. Only when the price level is 110 and real GDP is $1,000 billion can firms sell all that they produce and can people buy all that they demand. This is the short-run macroeconomic equilibrium.

occurs only when real GDP is $1,000 billion and the price level is 110.

In short-run equilibrium, the money wage rate is fixed. It does not adjust to bring full employment. So in the short run, real GDP can be greater than or less than potential GDP. But in the long run, the money wage rate does adjust and real GDP moves towards potential GDP. We are going to study this adjustment process. But first, let's look at the economy in long-run equilibrium.

Long-Run Macroeconomic Equilibrium

Long-run macroeconomic equilibrium occurs when real GDP equals potential GDP—equivalently, when the economy is on its *long-run* aggregate supply curve. Figure 22.9 shows *long-run* equilibrium, which occurs at the intersection of the aggregate demand curve and the long-run aggregate supply curve (the blue curves). Long-run equilibrium comes about because the money wage rate adjusts. Potential GDP and aggregate demand determine the price level, and the price level influences the money wage rate. In long-run equilibrium, the money wage rate has adjusted to put the (green) short-run aggregate supply curve through the long-run equilibrium point.

We'll look at this money wage adjustment process later in this chapter. But first, let's see how the *AS–AD* model helps us to understand economic growth and inflation.

FIGURE 22.9 Long-Run Equilibrium

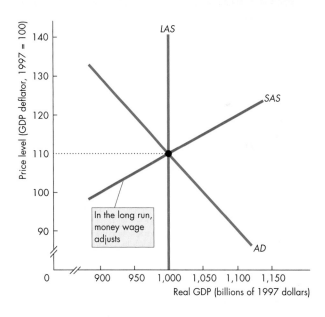

In long-run macroeconomic equilibrium, real GDP equals potential GDP. So long-run equilibrium occurs where the aggregate demand curve intersects the long-run aggregate supply curve. In the long run, aggregate demand determines the price level and has no effect on real GDP. The money wage rate adjusts in the long run, so the *SAS* curve intersects the *LAS* curve at the long-run equilibrium price level.

Economic Growth and Inflation

Economic growth occurs because over time, the quantity of labour grows, capital is accumulated, and technology advances. These changes increase potential GDP and shift the long-run aggregate supply curve rightward. Figure 22.10 shows such a shift. The growth rate of potential GDP is determined by the pace at which labour grows, capital is accumulated, and technology advances.

Inflation occurs when, over time, aggregate demand increases by more than long-run aggregate supply. That is, inflation occurs if the aggregate demand curve shifts rightward by more than the rightward shift in the long-run aggregate supply curve. Figure 22.10 shows such shifts.

If aggregate demand increased at the same pace as long-run aggregate supply, we would experience real GDP growth with no inflation.

In the long run, the main influence on aggregate demand is the growth rate of the quantity of money. At times when the quantity of money increases rapidly, aggregate demand increases quickly and the inflation rate is high. When the growth rate of the quantity of money slows, other things remaining the same, the inflation rate eventually decreases.

Our economy experiences growth and inflation, like that shown in Fig. 22.10. But it does not experience *steady* growth and *steady* inflation. Real GDP fluctuates around potential GDP in a business cycle, and inflation also fluctuates. When we study the business cycle, we ignore economic growth. By doing so, we can see the business cycle more clearly.

The Business Cycle

The business cycle occurs because aggregate demand and short-run aggregate supply fluctuate but the money wage rate does not adjust quickly enough to keep real GDP at potential GDP. Figure 22.11 shows three types of short-run equilibrium.

In part (a), there is a below full-employment equilibrium. A **below full-employment equilibrium** is a macroeconomic equilibrium in which potential GDP exceeds real GDP. The amount by which potential GDP exceeds real GDP is called a **recessionary gap.** This name reminds us that a gap has opened up between potential GDP and real GDP either because the economy has experienced a recession or because real GDP, while growing, has grown more slowly than potential GDP.

The below full-employment equilibrium shown in Fig. 22.11(a) occurs where the aggregate demand curve AD_0 intersects the short-run aggregate supply curve SAS_0 at a real GDP of $980 billion and a price level of 110. The recessionary gap is $20 billion. The Canadian economy was in a situation similar to that shown in Fig. 22.11(a) during the early 1980s, and again during the early 1990s. In those years, real GDP was less than potential GDP.

Figure 22.11(b) is an example of *long-run equilibrium*, in which real GDP equals potential GDP. In this example, the equilibrium occurs where the aggregate demand curve AD_1 intersects the short-run aggregate supply curve SAS_1 at an actual and potential GDP of $1,000 billion. The Canadian economy was in a situation such as that shown in Fig. 22.11(b) in 1999.

Figure 22.11(c) shows an above full-employment equilibrium. An **above full-employment equilibrium** is

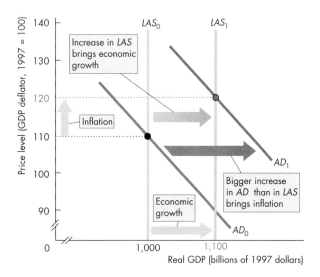

FIGURE 22.10   Economic Growth and Inflation

Economic growth is the persistent increase in potential GDP. Economic growth is shown as an ongoing rightward movement in the LAS curve. Inflation is the persistent rise in the price level. Inflation occurs when aggregate demand increases by more than the increase in long-run aggregate supply.

a macroeconomic equilibrium in which real GDP exceeds potential GDP. The amount by which real GDP exceeds potential GDP is called an **inflationary gap.** This name reminds us that a gap has opened up between real GDP and potential GDP and that this gap creates inflationary pressure.

The above full-employment equilibrium shown in Fig. 22.11(c) occurs where the aggregate demand curve AD_2 intersects the short-run aggregate supply curve SAS_2 at a real GDP of $1,020 billion and a price level of 110. There is an inflationary gap of $20

billion. The Canadian economy was last in a situation similar to that depicted in Fig. 22.11(c) in 2000.

The economy moves from one type of equilibrium to another as a result of fluctuations in aggregate demand and in short-run aggregate supply. These fluctuations produce fluctuations in real GDP and the price level. Figure 22.11(d) shows how real GDP fluctuates around potential GDP.

Let's now look at some of the sources of these fluctuations around potential GDP.

FIGURE 22.11   The Business Cycle

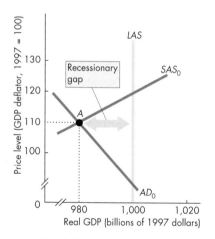

(a) Below full-employment equilibrium

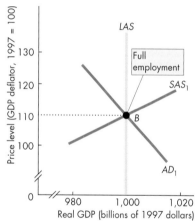

(b) Long-run equilibrium

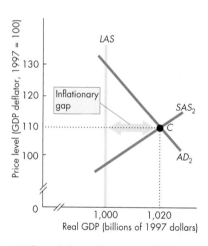

(c) Above full-employment equilibrium

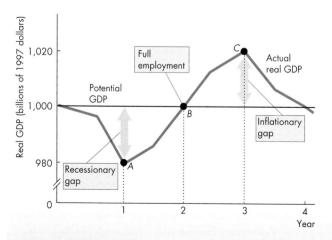

(d) Fluctuations in real GDP

Part (a) shows a below full-employment equilibrium in year 1; part (b) shows a long-run equilibrium in year 2; and part (c) shows an above full-employment equilibrium in year 3. Part (d) shows how real GDP fluctuates around potential GDP in a business cycle.

In year 1, a recessionary gap exists and the economy is at point A (in parts a and d). In year 2, the economy is in long-run equilibrium and the economy is at point B (in parts b and d). In year 3, an inflationary gap exists and the economy is at point C (in parts c and d).

Fluctuations in Aggregate Demand

One reason real GDP fluctuates around potential GDP is that aggregate demand fluctuates. Let's see what happens when aggregate demand increases.

Figure 22.12(a) shows an economy in long-run equilibrium. The aggregate demand curve is AD_0, the short-run aggregate supply curve is SAS_0, and the long-run aggregate supply curve is LAS. Real GDP equals potential GDP at $1,000 billion, and the price level is 110.

Now suppose that the world economy expands and that the demand for Canadian-made goods increases in Japan and Europe. The increase in Canadian exports increases aggregate demand, and the aggregate demand curve shifts rightward from AD_0 to AD_1 in Fig. 22.12(a).

Faced with an increase in demand, firms increase production and raise prices. Real GDP increases to $1,050 billion, and the price level rises to 115. The economy is now in an above full-employment equilibrium. Real GDP exceeds potential GDP, and there is an inflationary gap.

The increase in aggregate demand has increased the prices of all goods and services. Faced with higher prices, firms have increased their output rates. At this stage, prices of goods and services have increased but the money wage rate has not changed. (Recall that as we move along a short-run aggregate supply curve, the money wage rate is constant.)

The economy cannot produce in excess of potential GDP forever. Why not? What are the forces at work that bring real GDP back to potential GDP?

Because the price level has increased and the money wage rate is unchanged, workers have experienced a fall in the buying power of their wages and firms' profits have increased. In these circumstances, workers demand higher wages and firms, anxious to maintain their employment and output levels, meet those demands. If firms do not raise the money wage rate, they will either lose workers or have to hire less productive ones.

As the money wage rate rises, the short-run aggregate supply curve begins to shift leftward. In Fig. 22.12(b), the short-run aggregate supply curve moves

FIGURE 22.12   An Increase in Aggregate Demand

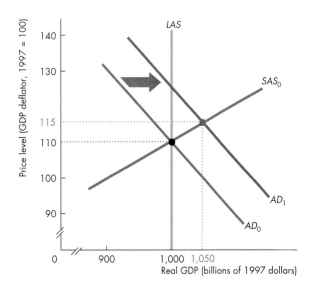

(a) Short-run effect

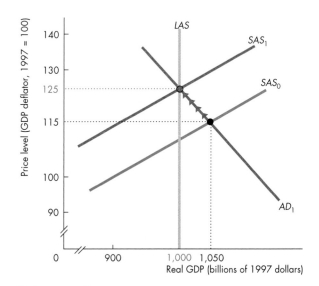

(b) Long-run effect

An increase in aggregate demand shifts the aggregate demand curve from AD_0 to AD_1. In short-run equilibrium, real GDP increases to $1,050 billion and the price level rises to 115. In this situation, an inflationary gap exists. In the long run, the money wage rate rises and the short-run

aggregate supply curve shifts leftward from SAS_0 to SAS_1 in part (b). As the SAS curve shifts leftward, it intersects the aggregate demand curve AD_1 at higher price levels and real GDP decreases. Eventually, the price level rises to 125 and real GDP decreases to $1,000 billion—potential GDP.

from SAS_0 towards SAS_1. The rise in the money wage rate and the shift in the SAS curve produce a sequence of new equilibrium positions. Along the adjustment path, real GDP decreases and the price level rises. The economy moves up along its aggregate demand curve as the arrowheads show.

Eventually, the money wage rate rises by the same percentage as the price level. At this time, the aggregate demand curve AD_1 intersects SAS_1 at a new long-run equilibrium. The price level has risen to 125, and real GDP is back where it started, at potential GDP.

A decrease in aggregate demand has similar but opposite effects to those of an increase in aggregate demand. That is, a decrease in aggregate demand shifts the aggregate demand curve leftward. Real GDP decreases to less than potential GDP, and a recessionary gap emerges. Firms cut prices. The lower price level increases the purchasing power of wages and increases firms' costs relative to their output prices because the money wage rate remains unchanged. Eventually, the money wage rate falls and the short-run aggregate supply curve shifts rightward. But the money wage rate changes slowly, so real GDP slowly returns to potential GDP and the price level falls slowly.

Let's now work out how real GDP and the price level change when aggregate supply changes.

Fluctuations in Aggregate Supply

Fluctuations in short-run aggregate supply can bring fluctuations in real GDP around potential GDP. Suppose that initially real GDP equals potential GDP. Then there is a large but temporary rise in the price of oil. What happens to real GDP and the price level?

Figure 22.13 answers this question. The aggregate demand curve is AD_0, the short-run aggregate supply curve is SAS_0, and the long-run aggregate supply curve is LAS. Real GDP is $1,000 billion, which equals potential GDP, and the price level is 110. Then the price of oil rises. Faced with higher energy and transportation costs, firms decrease production. Short-run aggregate supply decreases, and the short-run aggregate supply curve shifts leftward to SAS_1. The price level rises to 120, and real GDP decreases to $950 billion. Because real GDP decreases, the economy experiences recession. Because the price level increases, the economy experiences inflation. A combination of recession and inflation, called *stagflation*, actually occurred in the United States in the mid-1970s. But events like this are not common and Canada escaped the worst of that recession.

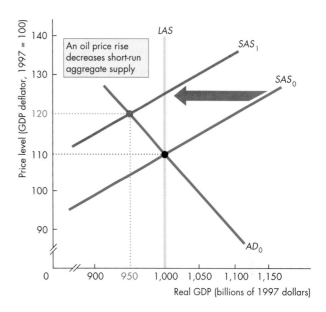

FIGURE 22.13 A Decrease in Aggregate Supply

An oil price rise decreases short-run aggregate supply

An increase in the price of oil decreases short-run aggregate supply and shifts the short-run aggregate supply curve from SAS_0 to SAS_1. Real GDP decreases from $1,000 billion to $950 billion, and the price level increases from 110 to 120. The economy experiences both recession and inflation—a situation known as stagflation.

REVIEW QUIZ

1 Does economic growth result from increases in aggregate demand, short-run aggregate supply, or long-run aggregate supply?
2 Does inflation result from increases in aggregate demand, short-run aggregate supply, or long-run aggregate supply?
3 Describe three types of short-run macroeconomic equilibrium.
4 How do fluctuations in aggregate demand and short-run aggregate supply bring fluctuations in real GDP around potential GDP?

Let's put our new knowledge of aggregate supply and aggregate demand to work and see how we can explain recent Canadian macroeconomic performance.

Canadian Economic Growth, Inflation, and Cycles

THE ECONOMY IS CONTINUALLY CHANGING. If you imagine the economy as a video, then an aggregate supply–aggregate demand figure such as Fig. 22.13 is a freeze-frame. We're going to run the video—an instant replay—but keep our finger on the freeze-frame button and look at some important parts of the previous action. Let's run the video from 1961.

Figure 22.14 shows the state of the economy in 1961 at the point of intersection of its aggregate demand curve, AD_{61}, and short-run aggregate supply curve, SAS_{61}. Real GDP was $240 billion, and the GDP deflator was 17 (less than one-fifth of its 2001 level). In 1961, real GDP equalled potential GDP—the economy was on its long-run aggregate supply curve, LAS_{61}.

By 2001, the economy had reached the point marked by the intersection of aggregate demand curve AD_{01} and short-run aggregate supply curve

SAS_{01}. Real GDP was $1,027 billion, and the GDP deflator was 106. The LAS curve assumes that potential GDP in 2001 was also $1,027 billion.

The path traced by the blue and red dots in Fig. 22.14 shows three key features:

- Economic growth
- Inflation
- Business cycles

Economic Growth

Over the years, real GDP grows—shown in Fig. 22.14 by the rightward movement of the points. The faster real GDP grows, the larger is the horizontal distance between successive dots in the figure. The forces that generate economic growth are those that increase potential GDP. Potential GDP grows because the quantity of labour grows, we accumulate physical capital and human capital, and our technologies advance.

These forces that bring economic growth were strongest during the early 1970s, mid-1980s, and late 1990s.

FIGURE 22.14 Aggregate Supply and Aggregate Demand: 1961–2001

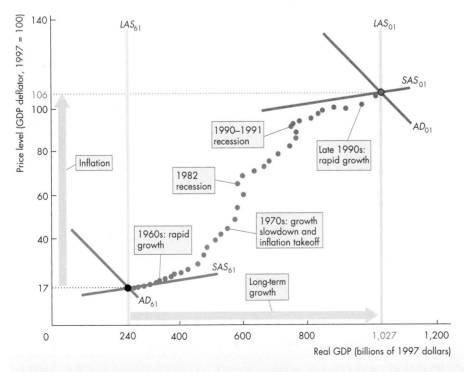

Each point shows the GDP deflator and real GDP in a given year. In 1961, the aggregate demand curve, AD_{61}, and the short-run aggregate supply curve, SAS_{61}, determined these variables. Each point is generated by the gradual shifting of the AD and SAS curves. By 2001, the curves were AD_{01} and SAS_{01}. Real GDP grew, and the price level increased. Real GDP grew quickly and inflation was moderate during the 1960s; real GDP growth sagged in 1974–1975 and again in 1982. Inflation was rapid during the 1970s but slowed after the 1982 recession. The period from 1982 to 1989 was one of strong, persistent expansion. A recession began in 1990, and a further strong and sustained expansion resumed in the late 1990s and through 2001.

Sources: Statistics Canada, CANSIM tables 326–0002 and 380–0003 and authors' assumptions.

Inflation

The price level rises over the years—shown in Fig. 22.14 by the upward movement of the points. The larger the rise in the price level, the larger is the vertical distance between successive dots in the figure. The main force generating the persistent increase in the price level is a tendency for aggregate demand to increase at a faster pace than the increase in long-run aggregate supply. All of the factors that increase aggregate demand and shift the aggregate demand curve influence the pace of inflation. But one factor—the growth of the quantity of money—is the main source of *persistent* increases in aggregate demand and persistent inflation.

Business Cycles

Over the years, the economy grows and shrinks in cycles—shown in Fig. 22.14 by the wavelike pattern made by the points, with the recessions highlighted. The cycles arise because both the expansion of short-run aggregate supply and the growth of aggregate demand do not proceed at a fixed, steady pace. Although the economy has cycles, recessions do not usually follow quickly on the heels of their predecessors; "double-dip" recessions like the one in the cartoon are rare.

The Evolving Economy: 1961–2001

During the 1960s, real GDP growth was rapid and inflation was low. This was a period of rapid increases in aggregate supply and of moderate increases in aggregate demand.

The mid-1970s were years of rapid inflation and slow growth. The major source of these developments was a series of massive oil price increases that slowed the rightward movement of the long-run aggregate supply curve and rapid increases in the quantity of money that speeded the rightward movement of the aggregate demand curve. The short-run aggregate supply curve shifted leftward at a faster pace than the aggregate demand curve shifted rightward.

The rest of the 1970s saw high inflation—the price level increased quickly—and only moderate growth in real GDP. By 1980, inflation was a major problem and the Bank of Canada decided to take strong action against it. It permitted interest rates to rise to previously unknown levels. Consequently, aggregate demand decreased. By 1982, the decrease in aggregate demand put the economy in a deep recession.

"Please stand by for a series of tones. The first indicates the official end of the recession, the second indicates prosperity, and the third the return of the recession."

During the years 1983–1990, capital accumulation and steady technological advance resulted in a sustained rightward shift of the long-run aggregate supply curve. Wage growth was moderate, and the short-run aggregate supply curve shifted rightward. Aggregate demand growth kept pace with the growth of aggregate supply. Sustained but steady growth in aggregate supply and aggregate demand kept real GDP growing and inflation steady. The economy moved from a recession with real GDP less than potential GDP in 1982 to above full employment in 1990. It was in this condition when a decrease in aggregate demand led to the 1990–1991 recession. The economy stagnated for a year and then began to expand again, expanding rapidly during the late 1990s. Growth slowed again in 2001.

◆ The *AS–AD* model explains economic growth, inflation, and the business cycle. The model is a useful one because it enables us to keep our eye on the big picture. But it lacks detail. It does not tell us as much as we need to know about the deeper forces that lie behind aggregate supply and aggregate demand. The chapters that follow begin to fill in the details on aggregate demand. But before you embark on this next stage, take a look at *Reading Between the Lines* on pp. 516–517, which looks at the effects of implementing the Kyoto agreement on climate control on aggregate supply and aggregate demand in the Canadian economy in 2010.

Kyoto in the AS–AD Model

FINANCIAL POST, OCTOBER 12, 2002

Kyoto could cost 244,000 jobs

The federal government conceded yesterday that implementing the Kyoto Protocol on climate change could cost the Canadian economy as many as a quarter of a million jobs, and $21-billion in output, by the end of the decade.

In a long awaited impact study of Kyoto, federal officials predicted the accord could mean between 61,000 and 244,000 fewer jobs by 2010. They also forecast the accord could mean gross domestic product would be between 0.4% ($5-billion) and 1.6% ($21-billion) lower than expected by the same year.

The federal document argued that the 244,000 job figure and 1.6% drop in GDP growth was a worst-case scenario. Officials said the lower figures were more likely. ...

Private-sector estimates place the cost of implementing Kyoto at 450,000 jobs by 2010, and $4.5-billion annually.

Pierre Alvarez, president of the Canadian Association of Petroleum Producers, called the federal calculations "empty numbers," adding that Ottawa's Kyoto plan remains a mystery.

"This is a model based on hypothetical assumptions, assumptions no one else has ever seen," he said.

"To extrapolate from that, they are simply empty numbers that are of little value to the current debate."

He added: "The assumptions are based on estimates we don't necessarily agree with—we've had inadequate information—they are based on assumptions that we don't understand and have only had one presentation on."

Nancy Hughes Anthony, president of the Canadian Chamber of Commerce, charged yesterday the government's economic model leaves a "false impression" about the impact of the Kyoto Protocol by presenting optimistic projections.

But she said it is even clear from the best and worst-case scenarios in the federal analysis that the prosperity of Canadians will suffer if Jean Chrétien, the Prime Minister, pushes ahead with ratification of Kyoto by the end of the year. ...

Reprinted by permission of the *National Post*.

Essence of the Story

■ The federal government predicts that ratifying the Kyoto accord will lower employment by between 61,000 and 244,000 persons by 2010.

■ The government also predicts that ratifying the Kyoto accord will lower real GDP by between 0.4 percent ($5 billion) and 1.6 percent ($21 billion) by 2010.

■ The government regards the higher numbers—244,000 jobs and $21 billion real GDP—as the worst-case scenario.

■ Private-sector estimates place the cost of implementing Kyoto at 450,000 jobs by 2010.

■ Private-sector estimates also place the cost of implementing Kyoto at $4.5 billion annually.

Economic Analysis

■ Implementing the Kyoto accord requires Canada to cut its emissions of "greenhouse" gasses, measured as carbon dioxide equivalent, from more than 700 million tonnes a year in 2002 to 540 million tonnes a year by 2010.

■ To achieve this large cut in emissions, we must generate electricity more cleanly and use technologies that are more costly and less productive.

■ We must also increase the fuel efficiency of automobiles and trucks.

■ These activities decrease the productivity of labour, slow the accumulation of productive capital, and slow the pace of productivity-enhancing technological change.

■ The overall consequence of this slowdown in productivity growth is a slower growth rate of potential GDP.

■ By not implementing the Kyoto accord and maintaining recent trends, real GDP will grow by 3 percent a year.

■ Maintaining the recent inflation trends (and the Bank of Canada's target for inflation), the annual inflation rate will be 2 percent a year.

■ Figure 1 shows where the economy will be by 2010 if these trends persist—the base line case.

■ Real GDP will be $1,240 billion, up by 27 percent from its 2002 level; and the price level will be 125, up by 17 percent from its 2002 level.

■ Figure 2 shows the difference that implementing Kyoto will make, using the numbers that the government describes as the worst-case scenario.

■ Relative to the base line case, long-run aggregate supply will be lower at LAS_1, and real GDP will be $21 billion less than it otherwise would have been.

■ If the Bank of Canada continues to pursue an inflation target of 2 percent a year, aggregate demand growth will slow to match the slower growth of potential GDP. The AD curve and SAS curve will be at AD_1 and SAS_1, and the price level will be unaffected by Kyoto.

■ If aggregate demand growth does not slow to match the slower growth rate of potential GDP, Kyoto will bring a higher price level and increased inflation.

■ The decrease in employment that results from Kyoto will either decrease the labour force or increase the natural rate of unemployment. It will not affect cyclical unemployment.

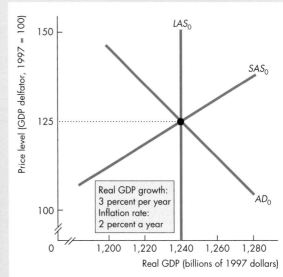

Figure 1 Base line case--no Kyoto

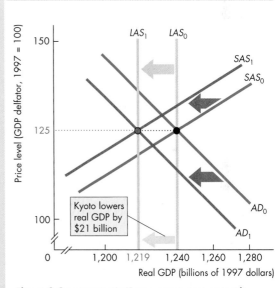

Figure 2 Government's Kyoto worst-case scenario

You're The Voter

■ Based just on its macroeconomic consequences, do you think that implementing Kyoto is a big deal?

■ What macroeconomic reasons would you give for supporting or opposing the implementation of Kyoto?

SUMMARY

KEY POINTS

Aggregate Supply (pp. 500–504)

- In the long run, the quantity of real GDP supplied is potential GDP, which is independent of the price level. The long-run aggregate supply curve is vertical.
- In the short run, the money wage rate is constant, so a rise in the price level increases the quantity of real GDP supplied. The short-run aggregate supply curve is upward sloping.
- A change in potential GDP changes both long-run and short-run aggregate supply. A change in the money wage rate or other resource prices changes only short-run aggregate supply.

Aggregate Demand (pp. 505–508)

- A rise in the price level decreases the quantity of real GDP demanded, other things remaining the same.
- The reason is that the higher price level decreases the quantity of *real* money, raises the interest rate, and raises the price of domestic goods compared with foreign goods.
- Changes in expected future disposable income, inflation, and profit; changes in fiscal policy and monetary policy; and changes in world real GDP and the foreign exchange rate change aggregate demand.

Macroeconomic Equilibrium (pp. 508–513)

- In the short run, real GDP and the price level are determined by aggregate demand and short-run aggregate supply.
- In the long run, real GDP equals potential GDP and aggregate demand determines the price level and the money wage rate.
- Economic growth occurs because potential GDP increases.
- Inflation occurs because aggregate demand grows more quickly than potential GDP.
- Business cycles occur because aggregate demand and aggregate supply fluctuate.

Canadian Economic Growth, Inflation, and Cycles (pp. 514–515)

- Potential GDP grew fastest during the early 1970s, mid-1980s, and late 1990s and slowest during the late 1970s and early 1990s.
- Inflation persists because aggregate demand grows faster than potential GDP.
- Business cycles occur because aggregate supply and aggregate demand change at an uneven pace.

KEY FIGURES

KEY TERMS

PROBLEMS

*1. The following events occur that influence the economy of Toughtimes:
   - A deep recession hits the world economy.
   - Oil prices rise sharply.
   - Businesses expect huge losses in the near future.
   a. Explain the separate effects of each of these events on real GDP and the price level in Toughtimes, starting from a position of long-run equilibrium.
   b. Explain the combined effects of these events on real GDP and the price level in Toughtimes, starting from a position of long-run equilibrium.
   c. Explain what the Toughtimes government and the Bank of Toughtimes can do to overcome the problems faced by the economy.

2. The following events occur that influence the economy of Coolland:
   - There is a strong expansion in the world economy.
   - Businesses expect huge profits in the near future.
   - The Coolland government cuts its expenditure.
   a. Explain the separate effects of each of these events on real GDP and the price level in Coolland, starting from a position of long-run equilibrium.
   b. Explain the combined effects of these events on real GDP and the price level in Coolland, starting from a position of long-run equilibrium.
   c. Explain why the Coolland government or the Bank of Coolland might want to take action to influence the Coolland economy.

*3. The economy of Mainland has the following aggregate demand and supply schedules:

Price level	Real GDP demanded	Real GDP supplied in the short run
	(billions of 1997 dollars)	
90	450	350
100	400	400
110	350	450
120	300	500
130	250	550
140	200	600

a. In a figure, plot the aggregate demand curve and the short-run aggregate supply curve.
b. What are the values of real GDP and the price level in Mainland in a short-run macroeconomic equilibrium?
c. Mainland's potential GDP is $500 billion. Plot the long-run aggregate supply curve in the same figure in which you answered part (a).

4. The economy of Miniland has the following aggregate demand and supply schedules:

Price level	Real GDP demanded	Real GDP supplied in the short run
	(billions of 1997 dollars)	
90	600	150
100	500	200
110	400	250
120	300	300
130	200	350
140	100	400

a. In a figure, plot the aggregate demand curve and the short-run aggregate supply curve.
b. What are the values of real GDP and the price level in Miniland in a short-run macroeconomic equilibrium?
c. Miniland's potential GDP is $250 billion. Plot the long-run aggregate supply curve in the same figure in which you answered part (a).

*5. In problem 3, aggregate demand increases by $100 billion. How do real GDP and the price level change in the short run?

6. In problem 4, aggregate demand decreases by $150 billion. How do real GDP and the price level change in the short run?

*7. In problem 3, aggregate supply decreases by $100 billion. What now is the short-run macroeconomic equilibrium?

8. In problem 4, aggregate supply increases by $150 billion. What now is the short-run macroeconomic equilibrium?

*9. In the economy shown in the figure on the next page, initially the short-run aggregate supply is SAS_0 and aggregate demand is AD_0. Then some events change aggregate demand, and the aggregate demand curve shifts rightward to AD_1. Later, some other events change aggregate supply, and the short-run aggregate supply curve shifts leftward to SAS_1.

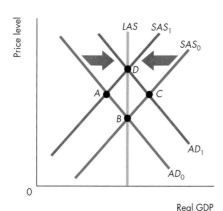

a. What is the short-run equilibrium point after the change in aggregate demand?
b. What is the equilibrium point after the change in aggregate supply?
c. What events could have changed aggregate demand from AD_0 to AD_1?
d. What events could have changed aggregate supply from SAS_0 to SAS_1?

10. In the economy shown in the figure, initially long-run aggregate supply is LAS_0, short-run aggregate supply is SAS_0, and aggregate demand is AD. Then some events change aggregate supply, and the aggregate supply curves shift right-ward to LAS_1 and SAS_1.

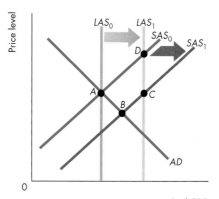

a. What is the short-run equilibrium point after the change in aggregate supply?
b. What events could have changed long-run aggregate supply from LAS_0 to LAS_1?
c. What events could have changed short-run aggregate supply from SAS_0 to SAS_1?
d. After the increase in aggregate supply, is real GDP greater than or less than potential GDP?
e. What change in aggregate demand will make real GDP equal to potential GDP?

CRITICAL THINKING

1. After you have studied the effects of implementing the Kyoto agreement on aggregate supply and aggregate demand in the Canadian economy in *Reading Between the Lines* on pp. 516–517:
   a. List the factors that influence long-run aggregate supply and explain how Kyoto might impact each of these factors.
   b. List the factors that influence short-run aggregate supply and explain how Kyoto might impact each of these factors.
   c. List the factors that influence aggregate demand and explain how Kyoto might impact each of these factors.
   d. Use the *AS–AD* model to illustrate and to explain why Kyoto need not increase the inflation rate, even if it brings a large decrease in potential GDP.

WEB EXERCISES

1. Use the links on the Parkin–Bade Web site to find data on recent changes in and forecasts of real GDP and the price level in Canada.
   a. What is your forecast of next year's real GDP?
   b. What is your forecast of next year's price level?
   c. What is your forecast of the inflation rate?
   d. What is your forecast of the growth rate of real GDP?
   e. Do you think there will be a recessionary gap or an inflationary gap next year?

2. Use the links on the Parkin–Bade Web site to find data on recent changes in and forecasts of real GDP and the price level in Japan.
   a. What is your forecast of next year's real GDP?
   b. What is your forecast of next year's price level?
   c. What is your forecast of the inflation rate?
   d. What is your forecast of the growth rate of real GDP?
   e. Compare and contrast the performance of the Canadian and Japanese economies.

UNDERSTANDING THE THEMES OF MACROECONOMICS

The Big Picture

Macroeconomics is a large and controversial subject that is interlaced with political ideological disputes. And it is a field in which charlatans as well as serious thinkers have much to say. This page is a map that looks back at the road you've just travelled and forward at the path you will take from here. ◆ You began your study of macroeconomics with the core questions of the subject. What are the causes of

- Economic growth?
- Business cycles?
- Unemployment?
- Inflation?

In Chapter 19, you took your first look at each of these questions. You learned some facts about economic growth, business cycles, unemployment, and inflation. In Chapter 20, you learned how we measure the economy's output and the price level. These measures are used to calculate the rate of economic growth, business cycle fluctuations, and inflation. You discovered that making these measurements is not straightforward and that small measurement errors can have a big effect on our perceptions about how we are doing. ◆ In Chapter 21, you learned how we measure the state of the labour market—the levels of employment and unemployment and wages. And in Chapter 22, you studied the macroeconomic version of supply and demand—*aggregate supply* and *aggregate demand*. You saw that the aggregate supply–aggregate

demand model is the big picture model. It explains both the long-term trends in economic growth and inflation and the short-term business cycle fluctuations in production, jobs, and inflation. ◆ The chapters that lie ahead of you look behind aggregate supply and aggregate demand, beginning on the demand side. In Chapters 23 through 28, you will study aggregate demand, inflation, and deflation and learn about the macroeconomics that Keynes developed as a response to the Great Depression. And you will learn about the effects of monetary and fiscal policies on aggregate demand. ◆ Then, in Chapters 29 through 32, you will study aggregate supply, economic growth and fluctuations, and policy challenges that we face in stabilizing our economy and speeding its growth. Here, you learn today's answer to the question posed by Adam Smith—what are the causes of differences in the wealth of nations? In Chapter 29, you study the economy at full employment and the forces that change potential GDP. In Chapter 30, you study the process of economic growth. In Chapter 31, you study the business cycle and in Chapter 32, the policy challenges. ◆ Before continuing your study of macroeconomics, spend a few minutes with John Maynard Keynes and Jean-Baptiste Say, the leading scholars who developed this subject. And spend a few minutes with one of today's leading macroeconomists, Robert Barro of Harvard University.

PROBING THE IDEAS

Macroeconomic Revolutions

"The ideas of economists and political philosophers, both when they are right and when they are wrong, are more powerful than is commonly understood. Indeed the world is ruled by little else."

JOHN MAYNARD
KEYNES
*The General
Theory of
Employment,
Interest, and
Money*

JOHN MAYNARD KEYNES, *born in England in 1883, was one of the outstanding minds of the twentieth century. He wrote on probability as well as economics, represented Britain at the Versailles peace conference at the end of World War I, was a master speculator on international financial markets (an activity he conducted from bed every morning and which made and lost him several fortunes), and played a prominent role in creating the International Monetary Fund. He was a member of the Bloomsbury Group, a circle of outstanding artists and writers that included E. M. Forster, Bertrand Russell, and Virginia Woolf. Keynes was a controversial and quick-witted figure. A critic once complained that Keynes had changed his opinion on some matters, to which Keynes retorted: "When I discover I am wrong, I change my mind. What do you do?"*

THE ISSUES

During the Industrial Revolution, as technological change created new jobs and destroyed old ones, people began to wonder whether the economy could create enough jobs and sufficient demand to buy all the things that the new industrial economy could produce.

Jean-Baptiste Say argues that production creates incomes that are sufficient to buy everything that is produced—supply creates its own demand—an idea that came to be called Say's Law.

Say and Keynes would have had a lot to disagree about. Jean-Baptiste Say, born in Lyon, France, in 1767 (he was 9 years old when Adam Smith's *Wealth of Nations* was published), suffered the wrath of Napoleon for his views on government and the economy. In today's world, Say would be leading a radical conservative charge for a smaller and leaner government. Say was the most famous economist of his era on both sides of the Atlantic. His book, *Traité d'économie politique* (*A Treatise in Political Economy*), published in 1803, became a best-selling university economics textbook in both Europe and North America.

As the Great Depression of the 1930s became more severe and more prolonged, Say's Law looked less and less relevant. John Maynard Keynes revolutionized macroeconomics thinking by turning Say's Law on its head, arguing that production does not depend on supply. Instead, it depends on what people are willing to buy—on demand. Or as Keynes put it, production depends on effective demand. It is possible, argued Keynes, for people to refuse to spend all of their incomes. If businesses fail to spend on new capital the amount that people plan to save, demand might be less than supply. In this situation, resources might go unemployed and remain unemployed indefinitely.

The influence of Keynes persists even today, more than 60 years after the publication of his main work. But during the past 20 years, Nobel Laureate Robert E. Lucas, Jr., with significant contributions from a list of outstanding macroeconomists too long to name, has further revolutionized macroeconomics. Today, we know a lot about economic growth, unemployment, inflation, and business cycles. And we know how to use fiscal policy and monetary policy to improve macroeconomic performance. But we don't yet have all the answers. Macroeconomics remains a field of lively controversy and exciting research.

Then

In 1776, James Hargreaves, an English weaver and carpenter, developed a simple hand-operated machine called a spinning jenny (pictured here). Using this machine, a person could spin 80 threads at once. Thousands of hand-wheel spinners, operators of machines that could spin only one thread, lost their jobs. They protested by wrecking spinning jennies. In the long run, the displaced hand-wheel spinners found work, often in factories that manufactured the machines that had destroyed their previous jobs. From the earliest days of the Industrial Revolution to the present day, people have lost their jobs as new technologies have automated what human effort had previously been needed to accomplish.

Now

Advances in computer technology have made it possible for us to dial our own telephone calls to any part of the world and get connected in a flash. A task that was once performed by telephone operators, who made connections along copper wires, is now performed faster and more reliably by computers along fibre-optic cables. Just as the Industrial Revolution transformed the textile industry, so today's Information Revolution is transforming the telecommunications industry. In the process, the mix of jobs is changing. There are fewer jobs for telephone operators but more jobs for telephone systems designers, builders, managers, and marketers. In the long run, as people spend the income they earn in their changing jobs, supply creates its own demand, just as Say predicted. But does supply create its own demand in the short run, when displaced workers are unemployed?

Robert Barro, whom you can meet on the following pages, is one of the most distinguished macroeconomists. He has contributed to our understanding of economic growth, inflation, and the business cycle and played a significant role in the contemporary macroeconomic revolution.

ROBERT J. BARRO *is Robert C. Waggoner Professor of Economics at Harvard University and a senior fellow at the Hoover Institution of Stanford University. Born in 1944 in New York City, he was a physics undergraduate at the California Institute of Technology and an economics graduate student at Harvard. Professor Barro is one of the world's leading economists and has done research on every aspect of macroeconomics, with a focus in recent years on economic growth. In addition to his many scholarly books and articles, he writes extensively for a wider audience. His book,* Getting it Right: Markets and Choices in a Free Society *(MIT Press, 1996) explains, in non-technical language,*

Robert J. Barro

the importance of property rights and free markets for achieving economic growth and a high standard of living. A new book, Nothing Is Sacred: Economic Ideas for the New Millennium *(MIT Press, 2002), expands on these ideas. And his regular articles in* Business Week *and the* Wall Street Journal *provide an accessible analysis of an incredible range of current economic issues.*

Michael Parkin and Robin Bade talked with Robert Barro about his work and the progress that economists have made in under-standing macroeconomic performance since the pioneering work of Keynes.

Professor Barro, your first degree was in physics. Why did you switch to economics when you went to graduate school?

For me, economics provided an ideal combination of technical analysis with applications to social problems and policies. Physics—or really mathematics—provided a strong background for economic theory and econometrics, but it was not until later in graduate school that I thought I acquired good economic insights. Overall, the transition from physics to economics was a relatively easy one for me, and I have never regretted the choice to switch fields. (Perhaps it also helped that, after taking courses from the great Richard Feynman at Caltech, I recognized that I would never be an outstanding theoretical physicist.)

Your recent research has focused on the determinants of economic growth. What do we know about the determinants of growth? And what do we still need to discover?

A lot of progress has been made over the last decade in attaining an empirical understanding of the determinants of economic growth. There are no "silver bullets" for growth, but there are a number of favourable policies, institutions, and national characteristics that have been identified.

For example, growth is stimulated by a strong rule of law, high levels of human capital in the forms of education and health, low levels of non-productive government spending (and associated taxes), international openness, low fertility rates, and macroeconomic stability (including low and stable inflation). Given these and other factors, growth tends to be higher if a country starts off poorer. That is, convergence—in the sense of the poor tending to grow faster than the rich—holds in a conditional sense, when one holds constant an array of policies and national characteristics. However, convergence does not apply in an absolute sense because the poorest countries tend to have the worst policies and characteristics (which explains why they are observed to be poor).

> *There are no "silver bullets" for growth, but there are a number of favourable policies, institutions, and national characteristics that have been identified.*

Is there anything that rich countries can do to help poor countries grow faster? Or does successful economic growth come only from self-help?

Mostly economic growth has to come from internal improvements in institutions and policies and from domestic accumulations of human and physical capital. There is no evidence that the rich countries can help through welfare programs, such as foreign aid and debt relief. On the contrary, there is some evidence that, because of the low quality of governance in most developing countries, foreign aid goes mainly to increased government spending and corruption. In the bad old days, the rich countries also provided governance (though not aimed especially at the interests of the governed). However, no one wants to return to the era of colonialism.

You've identified international openness as a characteristic that encourages growth. Is this an area in which the rich countries might do more by opening themselves to free trade with poor countries? Or is it enough for poor countries to just get on with opening their doors?

The rich countries could help to spur economic development by opening themselves more to trade in goods and services, technology, and financial transactions. Protectionist policies, notably in agriculture and textiles, are harmful to developing countries as well as to consumers in rich countries. President Bush's policies have been disgraceful in this area, notably in his protectionism during 2002 for steel and agriculture.

Inflation has been subdued in the United States for most of the 1990s and 2000s. Is this now a problem of the past that we can stop worrying about?

I am optimistic that the monetary authorities of the United States and many other countries have become committed to price stability and have learned that high inflation does not stimulate growth. Central banks seem also to have learned a lot about the mechanics of achieving price stability. One worry, however, is that U.S. monetary authorities—including the Federal Reserve—will become overconfident and will come to believe that they can fine-tune the real economy without losing price stability. For example, the Federal Reserve's interest rates reductions during the 2001 recession may have stimulated too much and could lead eventually to higher inflation.

> *I am optimistic that the monetary authorities of the United States and many other countries have become committed to price stability and have learned that high inflation does not stimulate growth.*

How do economic growth and inflation interact? Why can't a country grow faster by keeping demand growth strong and inflating?

Inflation is inversely related to economic growth over the medium term—for example, periods of five years or more. This relationship is particularly evident at high inflation rates—say, above 10–15% per year—but probably also applies for more moderate inflation. The likely reason for the inverse relation is that high and volatile inflation makes it difficult for the price system to operate efficiently. It is possible that unanticipated monetary stimulus expands the real economy in the short run. However, this short-term benefit is not worth the cost over the medium and long term. Moreover, the stimulus works mainly when it comes as a surprise, and it is hard to be surprising in a systematic way.

Some years ago, you worked on the business cycle. What is your current view on the nature and causes of aggregate fluctuations? Are they primarily an efficient response to the uneven pace of technical change, or are they primarily the consequence of market failure and demand fluctuations?

Many factors are sources of business cycles, and economists have not been very successful at isolating the precise causes. Influences that seem to matter include variations in the rate of technological progress, shifts in the terms of trade, fiscal effects (particularly important during wartime), and monetary fluctuations. In some countries, shifts in labour relations and in regulatory policies are important. Other countries are influenced by major changes in the quality of governance, such as the recent deterioration of public institutions in Argentina.

I do not think that we know what portion of fluctuations represents efficient responses to shocks as opposed to excess volatility associated with market failure. We do know that many observed fluctuations stem from failures of government policy and institutions, so it is inappropriate to think of governments as typically smoothing out the excesses of the private sector.

What remains in today's macroeconomics of the contribution of Keynes?

Probably Keynesian economics is most influential today in analyses that stress the real effects of monetary policy—either as sources of business fluctuations or as ways to smooth out the cycle. This situation is ironic because Keynes himself deemphasized monetary shocks as a source of fluctuations. He stressed the excesses of the private economy—including the amplifying effects of multipliers and the sensitivity of investment to shifting expectations—and the potentially beneficial role of offsetting fiscal policies.

Empirically, the multiplier seems to have existed only in the mind of Keynes.

What advice do you have for a student who is just starting to study economics? Is it a good subject in which to major? If so, what other subjects would you urge students to study alongside economics? Or is the path that you followed, starting with physics (or perhaps math) and then moving to economics for graduate school more effective?

Economics is an excellent field for an undergraduate to study whether one chooses to become an economist or—more likely—if one goes into other fields, such as business or law. Economists have found the framework or methodology that makes economics the core social science, and its impact has been felt greatly by other fields, such as political science, law, and history. These days, economic reasoning is being applied to the study of an array of social topics, including marriage and fertility, crime, democracy, and legal structure. As another example, I am currently participating in a project that involves the interactions between economics and religion. Partly this work is about how economic development and government policies affect religiosity and partly about how religious beliefs and participation influence economic and political outcomes. So perhaps in the future, economics will also be important for studies in theology. No doubt, many economists (including me) have

> *Economists have found the framework or methodology that makes economics the core social science ...*

imperialistic tendencies, but this is because they have a great product to sell. As to other complementary subjects to study, the most valuable one is probably mathematics, which provides many of the useful tools to carry out theoretical and empirical inquiries.

EXPENDITURE MULTIPLIERS

CHAPTER 23

Economic Amplifier or Shock Absorber?

Céline Dion sings into a microphone in a barely audible whisper. Increasing in volume, through the magic of electronic amplification, her voice fills Toronto's Molson Amphitheatre. ◆ Ralph Klein, the premier of Alberta, and his secretary are being driven to a business meeting along one of Edmonton's less well-repaired streets. The car's wheels bounce and vibrate over some of the worst potholes in the nation, but its passengers are completely undisturbed and the secretary's notes are written without a ripple, thanks to the car's efficient shock absorbers. ◆ Investment and exports fluctuate like the volume of Céline Dion's voice and the uneven surface of an Edmonton street. How does the economy react to those fluctuations? Does it react like a limousine, absorbing the shocks and providing a smooth ride for the economy's passengers? Or does it behave like an amplifier, blowing up the fluctuations and spreading them out to affect the many millions of participants in an economic rock concert?

◆ You will explore these questions in this chapter. You will learn how a recession or an expansion begins when a change in investment or exports induces an amplified change in aggregate expenditure and real GDP. And you'll learn the crucial role played by business inventories in the transition from expansion to recession and back to expansion. *Reading Between the Lines* at the end of the chapter looks at the multiplier at work during the first quarter of 2002, when real GDP grew by a near record 1.5 percent in three months.

After studying this chapter, you will be able to

■ **Explain how expenditure plans and real GDP are determined when the price level is fixed**

■ **Explain the expenditure multiplier**

■ **Explain how recessions and expansions begin**

■ **Explain the relationship between aggregate expenditure and aggregate demand**

■ **Explain how the multiplier gets smaller as the price level changes**

527

Expenditure Plans and GDP

THE COMPONENTS OF AGGREGATE EXPENDITURE are consumption expenditure (C), investment (I), government expenditures on goods and services (G), and net exports—exports (X) minus imports (M). The sum of these components is real GDP (Y). (See Chapter 20, p. 460). That is,

$$Y = C + I + G + X - M.$$

Two of these components—consumption expenditure and imports—depend on the level of real GDP. Because real GDP influences consumption expenditure and imports, and because consumption expenditure and imports are components of aggregate expenditure, there is a feedback loop between aggregate expenditure and GDP. You are going to learn how this feedback loop determines real GDP at a given price level.

The starting point is to consider the first piece of the feedback loop: the influence of real GDP on planned consumption expenditure and saving.

Consumption and Saving Plans

Several factors influence consumption expenditure and saving. The most direct influence, especially in the short term, is disposable income. **Disposable income** is real GDP or aggregate income (Y) minus net taxes (NT)—taxes minus transfer payments. And aggregate income equals real GDP. The equation for disposable income (YD) is

$$YD = Y - NT.$$

Disposable income is either spent on consumption goods and services—consumption expenditure (C)—or saved (S). So planned consumption expenditure plus planned saving equals disposable income. That is,

$$YD = C + S.$$

The table in Fig. 23.1 shows some examples of planned consumption expenditure and planned saving at different levels of disposable income. The greater the disposable income, the greater is consumption expenditure and the greater is saving. Also, at each level of disposable income, consumption expenditure plus saving equals disposable income.

The relationship between consumption expenditure and disposable income, with other things remaining the same, is called the **consumption function.** The relationship between saving and disposable income, with other things remaining the same, is called the **saving function.** Let's look at the consumption function and saving function in Fig. 23.1.

Consumption Function Figure 23.1(a) shows a consumption function. The y-axis measures consumption expenditure and the x-axis measures disposable income. Along the consumption function, the points labelled A through F correspond to the rows of the table. For example, point E shows that when disposable income is $800 billion, consumption expenditure is $750 billion. Along the consumption function, as disposable income increases, consumption expenditure also increases.

At point A on the consumption function, consumption expenditure is $150 billion even though disposable income is zero. This consumption expenditure is called *autonomous consumption*, and it is the amount of consumption expenditure that would take place in the short run even if people had no current income. You can think of this amount as the expenditure on the vital necessities of life.

When consumption expenditure exceeds disposable income, past savings are used to pay for current consumption. Such a situation cannot last forever, but it can occur temporarily.

Consumption expenditure in excess of autonomous consumption is called *induced consumption*—expenditure that is induced by an increase in disposable income.

45° Line Figure 23.1(a) also contains a 45° line, the height of which measures disposable income. At each point on this line, consumption expenditure equals disposable income. In the range over which the consumption function lies above the 45° line—between A and D—consumption expenditure exceeds disposable income. In the range over which the consumption function lies below the 45° line—between D and F—consumption expenditure is less than disposable income. And at the point at which the consumption function intersects the 45° line—at point D—consumption expenditure equals disposable income.

Saving Function Figure 23.1(b) shows a saving function. The x-axis is exactly the same as that in part (a). The y-axis measures saving. Again, the points marked A through F correspond to the rows of the table. For example, point *E* shows that when disposable income is $800 billion, saving is $50 billion. Along the saving function, as disposable income increases, saving also increases. At disposable incomes less than $600 billion (point *D*), saving is negative. Negative saving is called *dissaving*. At disposable incomes greater than $600 billion, saving is positive, and at $600 billion, saving is zero.

Notice the connection between the two parts of Fig. 23.1. When consumption expenditure exceeds

disposable income in part (a), saving is negative in part (b). When consumption expenditure is less than disposable income in part (a), saving is positive in part (b). And when consumption expenditure equals disposable income in part (a), saving is zero in part (b).

When saving is negative (when consumption expenditure exceeds disposable income), past savings are used to pay for current consumption. Such a situation cannot last forever, but it can occur if disposable income falls temporarily.

FIGURE 23.1   Consumption Function and Saving Function

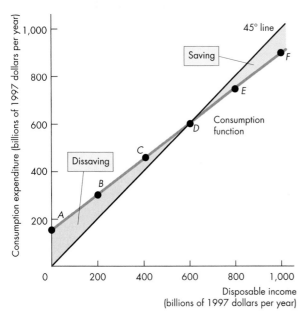

(a) Consumption function

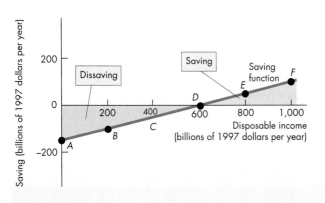

(b) Saving function

	Disposable income	Planned consumption expenditure	Planned saving
		(billions of 1997 dollars per year)	
A	0	150	−150
B	200	300	−100
C	400	450	−50
D	600	600	0
E	800	750	50
F	1,000	900	100

The table shows consumption expenditure and saving plans at various levels of disposable income. Part (a) of the figure shows the relationship between consumption expenditure and disposable income (the consumption function). The height of the consumption function measures consumption expenditure at each level of disposable income. Part (b) shows the relationship between saving and disposable income (the saving function). The height of the saving function measures saving at each level of disposable income. Points A through F on the consumption and saving functions correspond to the rows in the table. The height of the 45° line in part (a) measures disposable income. So along the 45° line, consumption expenditure equals disposable income. Consumption expenditure plus saving equals disposable income. When the consumption function is above the 45° line, saving is negative (dissaving occurs). When the consumption function is below the 45° line, saving is positive. At the point where the consumption function intersects the 45° line, all disposable income is consumed and saving is zero.

Marginal Propensity to Consume

The amount by which consumption expenditure changes when disposable income changes depends on the marginal propensity to consume. The **marginal propensity to consume** (*MPC*) is the fraction of a *change* in disposable income that is consumed. It is calculated as the *change* in consumption expenditure (Δ*C*) divided by the *change* in disposable income (Δ*YD*) that brought it about. That is,

$$MPC = \frac{\Delta C}{\Delta YD}.$$

In the table in Fig. 23.1, when disposable income increases from $600 billion to $800 billion, consumption expenditure increases from $600 billion to $750 billion. The $200 billion increase in disposable income increases consumption expenditure by $150 billion. The *MPC* is $150 billion divided by $200 billion, which equals 0.75.

The marginal propensity to consume is the slope of the consumption function. You can check this fact out in Fig. 23.2(a). Here, a $200 billion increase in disposable income from $600 billion to $800 billion is the base of the red triangle. The increase in consumption expenditure that results from this increase in disposable income is $150 billion and is the height of the triangle. The slope of the consumption function is given by the formula "slope equals rise over run" and is $150 billion divided by $200 billion, which equals 0.75—the *MPC*.

Marginal Propensity to Save

The amount by which saving changes when disposable income changes depends on the marginal propensity to save. The **marginal propensity to save** (*MPS*) is the fraction of a *change* in disposable income that is saved. It is calculated as the *change* in saving (Δ*S*) divided by the *change* in disposable income (Δ*YD*) that brought it about. That is,

$$MPS = \frac{\Delta S}{\Delta YD}.$$

In the table in Fig. 23.1, an increase in disposable income from $600 billion to $800 billion increases saving from zero to $50 billion. The $200 billion increase in disposable income increases saving by $50 billion. The *MPS* is $50 billion divided by $200 billion, which equals 0.25.

FIGURE 23.2 Marginal Propensities to Consume and Save

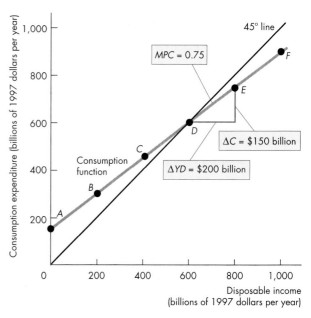

(a) Consumption function

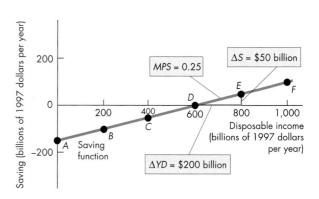

(b) Saving function

The marginal propensity to consume, *MPC*, is equal to the change in consumption expenditure divided by the change in disposable income, other things remaining the same. It is measured by the slope of the consumption function. In part (a), the *MPC* is 0.75.

The marginal propensity to save, *MPS*, is equal to the change in saving divided by the change in disposable income, other things remaining the same. It is measured by the slope of the saving function. In part (b), the *MPS* is 0.25.

The marginal propensity to save is the slope of the saving function. You can check this fact out in Fig. 23.2(b). Here, a $200 billion increase in disposable income from $600 billion to $800 billion (the base of the red triangle) increases saving by $50 billion (the height of the triangle). The slope of the saving function is $50 billion divided by $200 billion, which equals 0.25—the *MPS*.

The marginal propensity to consume plus the marginal propensity to save always equals 1. They sum to 1 because consumption expenditure and saving exhaust disposable income. Part of each dollar increase in disposable income is consumed, and the remaining part is saved. You can see that these two marginal propensities sum to 1 by using the equation:

$$\Delta C + \Delta S = \Delta YD.$$

Divide both sides of the equation by the change in disposable income to obtain

$$\frac{\Delta C}{\Delta YD} + \frac{\Delta S}{\Delta YD} = 1.$$

$\Delta C/\Delta YD$ is the *marginal propensity to consume* (*MPC*), and $\Delta S/\Delta YD$ is the *marginal propensity to save* (*MPS*), so

$$MPC + MPS = 1.$$

Other Influences on Consumption Expenditure and Saving

You've seen that a change in disposable income leads to changes in consumption expenditure and saving. A change in disposable income brings movements along the consumption function and saving function. A change in any other influence on consumption expenditure and saving shifts the consumption function and the saving function as shown in Fig. 23.3.

The main other influences are

1. Expected future disposable income
2. The real interest rate
3. Wealth

An increase in expected future disposable income makes people feel better off and leads to an increase in current consumption expenditure and a decrease in current saving. A fall in the real interest rate, other things remaining the same, encourages an increase in

FIGURE 23.3   Shifts in the Consumption and Saving Functions

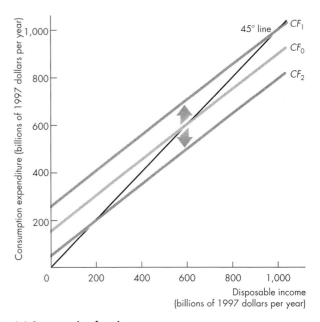

(a) Consumption function

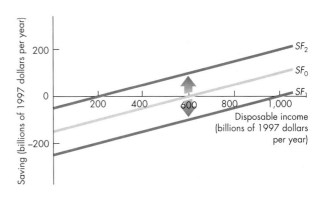

(b) Saving function

A fall in the real interest rate, an increase in wealth, or an increase in expected future disposable income shifts the consumption function upward from CF_0 to CF_1 and the saving function downward from SF_0 to SF_1.

A rise in the real interest rate, a decrease in wealth, or a decrease in expected future disposable income shifts the consumption function downward from CF_0 to CF_2 and shifts the saving function upward from SF_0 to SF_2.

borrowing and consumption expenditure and a decrease in saving. And an increase in wealth, other things remaining the same, stimulates consumption expenditure and decreases saving.

When expected future disposable income increases, the real interest rate falls, or when wealth increases, consumption expenditure increases and saving decreases. In Fig. 23.3 the consumption function shifts upward from CF_0 to CF_1, and the saving function shifts downward from SF_0 to SF_1.

When expected future disposable income decreases, the real interest rate rises, or when wealth decreases, consumption expenditure decreases and saving increases. The consumption function shifts downward from CF_0 to CF_2, and the saving function shifts upward from SF_0 to SF_2. Such shifts often occur when a recession begins because at such a time, expected future disposable income decreases.

We've studied the theory of the consumption function. Let's now see how that theory applies to the Canadian economy.

The Canadian Consumption Function

Figure 23.4 shows the Canadian consumption function. Each point identified by a blue dot represents consumption expenditure and disposable income for a particular year. (The dots are for the years 1961–2001. Five of the years are identified in the figure.) The line labelled CF_{61} is an estimate of the Canadian consumption function in 1961, and the line labelled CF_{01} is an estimate of the Canadian consumption function in 2001.

The slope of the consumption function in Fig. 23.4 is 0.7, which means that a $100 billion increase in disposable income brings a $70 billion increase in consumption expenditure. This slope, which is an estimate of the marginal propensity to consume, is an assumption that is at the middle of the range of values that economists have estimated for the marginal propensity to consume.

The consumption function shifts upward over time as other influences on consumption expenditure change. Of these other influences, expected future disposable income, the real interest rate, and wealth fluctuate and so bring upward *and* downward shifts in the consumption function. But rising wealth and rising expected future disposable income brings a steady upward shift in the consumption function. As the consumption function shifts upward, autonomous consumption expenditure increases.

FIGURE 23.4   The Canadian Consumption Function

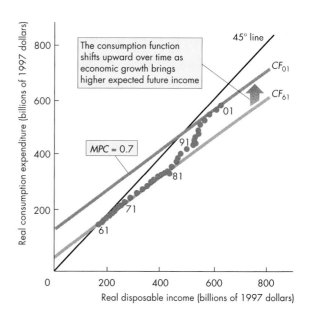

Each blue dot shows consumption expenditure and disposable income for a particular year. The lines CF_{61} and CF_{01} are estimates of the Canadian consumption function in 1961 and 2001, respectively. Here, the (assumed) marginal propensity to consume is 0.7.

Source: Statistics Canada, CANSIM tables 380-0002, 384-0013, 384-0035, and the authors' calculations.

Consumption as a Function of Real GDP

You've seen that consumption expenditure changes when disposable income changes. Disposable income changes when either real GDP changes or net taxes change. But net taxes—taxes minus transfer payments—are themselves related to real GDP. When real GDP increases, taxes increase and transfer payments decrease. Because net taxes depend on real GDP, disposable income depends on real GDP and so consumption expenditure depends not only on disposable income but also on real GDP. We use this link between consumption expenditure and real GDP to determine equilibrium expenditure. But before we do so, we need to look at one further component of aggregate expenditure: imports. Like consumption expenditure, imports also are influenced by real GDP.

Import Function

Canadian imports are determined by many factors, but in the short run, one factor dominates: Canadian real GDP. Other things remaining the same, the greater the Canadian real GDP, the larger is the quantity of Canadian imports.

The relationship between imports and real GDP is determined by the marginal propensity to import. The **marginal propensity to import** is the fraction of an increase in real GDP that is spent on imports. It is calculated as the change in imports divided by the change in real GDP that brought it about, other things remaining the same. For example, if a $100 billion increase in real GDP increases imports by $25 billion, the marginal propensity to import is 0.25.

In recent years, since the North American Free Trade Agreement (NAFTA) was implemented, Canadian imports have surged. For example, between 1991 and 2001, real GDP increased by $278 billion and imports increased by $167 billion. If no factors other than real GDP influenced imports during this period, these numbers would imply a marginal propensity to import of 0.6 ($167 billion divided by $278 billion). But other factors (such as NAFTA) increased imports, so the marginal propensity to import is smaller than 0.6. The marginal propensity to import might be as large as 0.3, and it has been increasing as the global economy has become more integrated.

REVIEW QUIZ

1   Which components of aggregate expenditure are influenced by real GDP?
2   Define the marginal propensity to consume. What is your estimate of your own marginal propensity to consume? After you graduate, will it change? Why or why not?
3   How do we calculate the effects of real GDP on consumption expenditure and imports?

Real GDP influences consumption and imports. But consumption and imports—along with investment, government expenditures, and exports—influence real GDP. Your next task is to study this second piece of the two-way link between aggregate expenditure and real GDP and see how all the components of aggregate planned expenditure interact to determine real GDP.

Equilibrium Expenditure at a Fixed Price Level

MOST FIRMS ARE LIKE YOUR LOCAL SUPERMARKET. They set their prices, advertise their products and services, and sell the quantities their customers are willing to buy. If they persistently sell a greater quantity than they plan to and are constantly running out of inventory, they eventually raise their prices. And if they persistently sell a smaller quantity than they plan to and have inventories piling up, they eventually cut their prices. But in the very short term, their prices are fixed. They hold the prices they have set, and the quantities they sell depend on demand, not supply.

The Aggregate Implications of Fixed Prices

Fixed prices have two immediate implications for the economy as a whole:

1. Because each firm's price is fixed, the *price level* is fixed.
2. Because demand determines the quantities that each firm sells, *aggregate demand* determines the aggregate quantity of goods and services sold, which equals real GDP.

So to understand how real GDP is determined when the price level is fixed, we must understand how aggregate demand is determined. Aggregate demand is determined by aggregate expenditure plans. We define **aggregate planned expenditure** as *planned* consumption expenditure plus *planned* investment plus *planned* government expenditures plus *planned* exports minus *planned* imports.

You've just studied planned consumption expenditure and planned imports and seen that these two components of aggregate planned expenditure are influenced by real GDP. The other components of aggregate expenditure—investment, government expenditures, and exports—are not influenced by real GDP. They fluctuate for many reasons but not because real GDP fluctuates.

You are now going to study a model called the *aggregate expenditure model*, which explains how consumption expenditure, imports, and real GDP are *simultaneously* determined by a feedback loop between expenditure plans and real GDP.

The Aggregate Expenditure Model

You are now going to discover how aggregate expenditure plans interact to determine real GDP when the price level is fixed. First, we will study the relationship between aggregate planned expenditure and real GDP. Second, we'll learn about the key distinction between *planned* expenditure and *actual* expenditure. And third, we'll study equilibrium expenditure, a situation in which aggregate planned expenditure and actual expenditure are equal.

The relationship between aggregate planned expenditure and real GDP can be described by either an aggregate expenditure schedule or an aggregate expenditure curve. The *aggregate expenditure schedule* lists aggregate planned expenditure generated at each level of real GDP. The *aggregate expenditure curve* is a graph of the aggregate expenditure schedule.

FIGURE 23.5   Aggregate Expenditure

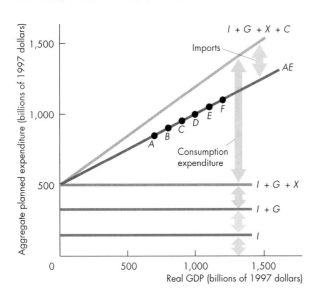

The aggregate expenditure schedule shows the relationship between aggregate planned expenditure and real GDP. Aggregate planned expenditure is the sum of planned consumption expenditure, investment, government expenditures, and exports minus imports. For example, in row B of the table, when real GDP is $800 billion, planned consumption expenditure is $560 billion, planned investment is $150 billion, planned government expenditures on goods and services are $180 billion, planned exports are $170 billion, and planned imports are $160 billion. So when real GDP is $800 billion, aggregate planned expenditure is $900 billion ($560 + $150 + $180 + $170 − $160). The schedule shows that aggregate planned expenditure increases as real GDP increases.

This relationship is graphed as the aggregate expenditure curve *AE*. The components of aggregate expenditure that increase with real GDP are consumption expenditure and imports. The other components—investment, government expenditures, and exports—do not vary with real GDP.

	Real GDP (Y)	Consumption expenditure (C)	Investment (I)	Government expenditures (G)	Exports (X)	Imports (M)	Aggregate planned expenditure (AE = C + I + G + X − M)
				(billions of 1997 dollars)			
	0	0	150	180	170	0	500
A	700	490	150	180	170	140	850
B	800	560	150	180	170	160	900
C	900	630	150	180	170	180	950
D	1,000	700	150	180	170	200	1,000
E	1,100	770	150	180	170	220	1,050
F	1,200	840	150	180	170	240	1,100

Aggregate Planned Expenditure and Real GDP

The table in Fig. 23.5 sets out an aggregate expenditure schedule together with the components of aggregate planned expenditure. To calculate aggregate planned expenditure at a given real GDP, we add the various components together. The first column of the table shows real GDP, and the second column shows the consumption expenditure generated by each level of real GDP. A $700 billion increase in real GDP generates a $490 billion increase in consumption expenditure—the *MPC* is 0.7.

The next two columns show investment and government expenditures on goods and services. Investment depends on such factors as the real interest rate and the expected future profit. But at a given point in time, these factors generate a particular level of investment. Suppose this level of investment is $150 billion. Also, suppose that government expenditures on goods and services is $180 billion.

The next two columns show exports and imports. Exports are influenced by income in the rest of the world, prices of foreign-made goods and services relative to the prices of similar Canadian-made goods and services, and foreign exchange rates. But exports are not directly affected by real GDP in Canada. Exports are a constant $170 billion no matter what real GDP in Canada is. Imports increase as real GDP increases. A $100 billion increase in real GDP generates a $20 billion increase in imports—the marginal propensity to import is 0.2.

The final column shows aggregate planned expenditure—the sum of planned consumption expenditure, investment, government expenditures on goods and services, and exports minus imports.

Figure 23.5 plots an aggregate expenditure curve. Real GDP is shown on the *x*-axis, and aggregate planned expenditure is shown on the *y*-axis. The aggregate expenditure curve is the red line *AE*. Points *A* through *F* on that curve correspond to the rows of the table. The *AE* curve is a graph of aggregate planned expenditure (the last column) plotted against real GDP (the first column).

Figure 23.5 also shows the components of aggregate expenditure. The constant components—investment (*I*), government expenditures on goods and services (*G*), and exports (*X*)—are shown by the horizontal lines in the figure. Consumption expenditure (*C*) is the vertical gap between the lines labelled *I + G + X* and *I + G + X + C*.

To construct the *AE* curve, subtract imports (*M*) from the line labelled *I + G + X + C*. Aggregate expenditure is expenditure on Canadian-made goods and services. But the components of aggregate expenditure—*C*, *I*, and *G*—include expenditure on imported goods and services. For example, if you buy a new cell phone, your expenditure is part of consumption expenditure. But if the cell phone is a Nokia made in Finland, your expenditure on it must be subtracted from consumption expenditure to find out how much is spent on goods and services produced in Canada—on Canadian real GDP. Money paid to Nokia for cell phone imports from Finland does not add to aggregate expenditure in Canada.

Because imports are only a part of aggregate expenditure, when we subtract imports from the other components of aggregate expenditure, aggregate planned expenditure still increases as real GDP increases, as you can see in Fig. 23.5.

Consumption expenditure minus imports, which varies with real GDP, is called **induced expenditure.** The sum of investment, government expenditures, and exports, which does not vary with real GDP, is called **autonomous expenditure.** Consumption expenditure and imports can also have an autonomous component—a component that does not vary with real GDP. Another way of thinking about autonomous expenditure is that it would be the level of aggregate planned expenditure if real GDP were zero.

In Fig. 23.5, autonomous expenditure is $500 billion—aggregate planned expenditure when real GDP is zero. For each $100 billion increase in real GDP, induced expenditure increases by $50 billion.

The aggregate expenditure curve summarizes the relationship between aggregate *planned* expenditure and real GDP. But what determines the point on the aggregate expenditure curve at which the economy operates? What determines *actual* aggregate expenditure?

Actual Expenditure, Planned Expenditure, and Real GDP

Actual aggregate expenditure is always equal to real GDP, as we saw in Chapter 20 (p. 460). But aggregate *planned* expenditure is not necessarily equal to actual aggregate expenditure and therefore is not necessarily equal to real GDP. How can actual expenditure and planned expenditure differ from each other? Why don't expenditure plans get implemented? The main reason is that firms might end up with greater inventories than planned or with smaller inventories than planned. People carry out their consumption expenditure plans, the government implements its planned purchases of goods and services, and net exports are as planned. Firms carry out their plans to purchase new buildings, plant, and equipment. But one component of investment is the change in firms' inventories. If aggregate planned expenditure is less than real GDP, firms don't sell all the goods they produce and they

end up with inventories they hadn't planned. If aggregate planned expenditure exceeds real GDP, firms sell more than they produce and inventories decrease below the level that firms had planned.

Equilibrium Expenditure

Equilibrium expenditure is the level of aggregate expenditure that occurs when aggregate *planned* expenditure equals real GDP. It is the level of aggregate

---

FIGURE 23.6   Equilibrium Expenditure

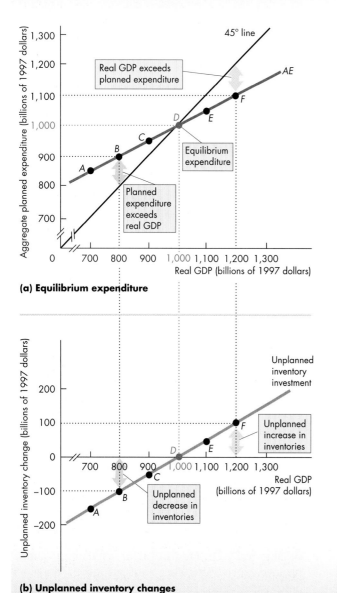

(a) Equilibrium expenditure

(b) Unplanned inventory changes

	Real GDP (Y)	Aggregate planned expenditure (AE)	Unplanned inventory change (Y – AE)
		(billions of 1997 dollars)	
A	700	850	–150
B	800	900	–100
C	900	950	–50
D	1,000	1,000	0
E	1,100	1,050	50
F	1,200	1,100	100

The table shows expenditure plans at different levels of real GDP. When real GDP is $1,000 billion, aggregate planned expenditure equals real GDP.

Part (a) of the figure illustrates equilibrium expenditure, which occurs when aggregate planned expenditure equals real GDP at the intersection of the 45° line and the AE curve. Part (b) of the figure shows the forces that bring about equilibrium expenditure. When aggregate planned expenditure exceeds real GDP, inventories decrease—for example, at point B in both parts of the figure. Firms increase production, and real GDP increases.

When aggregate planned expenditure is less than real GDP, inventories increase—for example, at point F in both parts of the figure. Firms decrease production, and real GDP decreases. When aggregate planned expenditure equals real GDP, there are no unplanned inventory changes and real GDP remains constant at equilibrium expenditure.

expenditure and real GDP at which everyone's spending plans are fulfilled. When the price level is fixed, equilibrium expenditure determines real GDP. When aggregate planned expenditure and actual aggregate expenditure are unequal, a process of convergence towards equilibrium expenditure occurs. And throughout this convergence process, real GDP adjusts. Let's examine equilibrium expenditure and the process that brings it about.

Figure 23.6(a) illustrates equilibrium expenditure. The table sets out aggregate planned expenditure at various levels of real GDP. These values are plotted as points *A* through *F* along the *AE* curve. The 45° line shows all the points at which aggregate planned expenditure equals real GDP. Thus where the *AE* curve lies above the 45° line, aggregate planned expenditure exceeds real GDP; where the *AE* curve lies below the 45° line, aggregate planned expenditure is less than real GDP; and where the *AE* curve intersects the 45° line, aggregate planned expenditure equals real GDP. Point *D* illustrates equilibrium expenditure. At this point, real GDP is $1,000 billion.

Convergence to Equilibrium

What are the forces that move aggregate expenditure towards its equilibrium level? To answer this question, we must look at a situation in which aggregate expenditure is away from its equilibrium level. Suppose that in Fig. 23.6, real GDP is $800 billion. With real GDP at $800 billion, actual aggregate expenditure is also $800 billion. But aggregate *planned* expenditure is $900 billion (point *B* in Fig. 23.6a). Aggregate planned expenditure exceeds *actual* expenditure. When people spend $900 billion and firms produce goods and services worth $800 billion, firms' inventories fall by $100 billion (point *B* in Fig. 23.6b). Recall that *investment* is the purchase of new plant, equipment and buildings and *additions to inventories*. Because the change in inventories is part of investment, *actual* investment is $100 billion less than *planned* investment.

Real GDP doesn't remain at $800 billion for very long. Firms have inventory targets based on their sales. When inventories fall below target, firms increase production to restore inventories to the target level. To increase inventories, firms hire additional labour and increase production. Suppose that they increase production in the next period by $100 billion. Real GDP increases by $100 billion to $900 billion. But again, aggregate planned expenditure

exceeds real GDP. When real GDP is $900 billion, aggregate planned expenditure is $950 billion (point *C* in Fig. 23.6a). Again, inventories decrease, but this time by less than before. With real GDP of $900 billion and aggregate planned expenditure of $950 billion, inventories decrease by $50 billion (point *C* in Fig. 23.6b). Again, firms hire additional labour, and production increases; real GDP increases yet further.

The process that we've just described—planned expenditure exceeds real GDP, inventories decrease, and production increases—ends when real GDP has reached $1,000 billion. At this real GDP, there is equilibrium. Unplanned inventory changes are zero. Firms do not change their production.

You can do an experiment similar to the one we've just done but starting with a level of real GDP greater than equilibrium expenditure. In this case, planned expenditure is less than actual expenditure, inventories pile up, and firms cut production. As before, real GDP keeps on changing (decreasing this time) until it reaches its equilibrium level of $1,000 billion.

REVIEW QUIZ

1 What is the relationship between aggregate planned expenditure and real GDP in expenditure equilibrium?

2 How does equilibrium expenditure come about? What adjusts to achieve equilibrium?

3 If real GDP and aggregate expenditure are less than their equilibrium levels, what happens to firms' inventories? How do firms change their production? And what happens to real GDP?

4 If real GDP and aggregate expenditure are greater than their equilibrium levels, what happens to firms' inventories? How do firms change their production? And what happens to real GDP?

We've learned that when the price level is fixed, real GDP is determined by equilibrium expenditure. And you have seen how unplanned changes in inventories and the production response that they generate brings a convergence towards equilibrium expenditure. We're now going to study *changes* in equilibrium expenditure and discover an economic amplifier called the *multiplier*.

The Multiplier

INVESTMENT AND EXPORTS CAN CHANGE FOR many reasons. A fall in the real interest rate might induce firms to increase their planned investment. A wave of innovation, such as occurred with the spread of multimedia computers in the 1990s, might increase expected future profits and lead firms to increase their planned investment. An economic boom in the United States and Western Europe might lead to a large increase in their expenditure on Canadian-produced goods and services—on Canadian exports. These are all examples of increases in autonomous expenditure.

When autonomous expenditure increases, aggregate expenditure increases, and so do equilibrium expenditure and real GDP. But the increase in real GDP is *larger* than the change in autonomous expenditure. The **multiplier** is the amount by which a change in autonomous expenditure is magnified or multiplied to determine the change in equilibrium expenditure and real GDP.

It is easiest to get the basic idea of the multiplier if we work with an example economy in which there are no income taxes and no imports. So we'll first assume that these factors are absent. Then, when you understand the basic idea, we'll bring these factors back into play and see what difference they make to the multiplier.

The Basic Idea of the Multiplier

Suppose that investment increases. The additional expenditure by businesses means that aggregate expenditure and real GDP increase. The increase in real GDP increases disposable income, and with no income taxes, real GDP and disposable income increase by the same amount. The increase in disposable income brings an increase in consumption expenditure. And the increased consumption expenditure adds even more to aggregate expenditure. Real GDP and disposable income increase further, and so does consumption expenditure. The initial increase in investment brings an even bigger increase in aggregate expenditure because it induces an increase in consumption expenditure. The magnitude of the increase in aggregate expenditure that results from an increase in autonomous expenditure is determined by the *multiplier*.

The table in Fig. 23.7 sets out aggregate planned expenditure. When real GDP is $900 billion, aggre-

gate planned expenditure is $925 billion. For each $100 billion increase in real GDP, aggregate planned expenditure increases by $75 billion. This aggregate expenditure schedule is shown in the figure as the aggregate expenditure curve AE_0. Initially, equilibrium expenditure is $1,000 billion. You can see this equilibrium in row B of the table and in the figure where the curve AE_0 intersects the 45° line at the point marked B.

Now suppose that autonomous expenditure increases by $50 billion. What happens to equilibrium expenditure? You can see the answer in Fig. 23.7. When this increase in autonomous expenditure is added to the original aggregate planned expenditure, aggregate planned expenditure increases by $50 billion at each level of real GDP. The new aggregate expenditure curve is AE_1. The new equilibrium expenditure, highlighted in the table (row D'), occurs where AE_1 intersects the 45° line and is $1,200 billion (point D'). At this real GDP, aggregate planned expenditure equals real GDP.

The Multiplier Effect

In Fig. 23.7, the increase in autonomous expenditure of $50 billion increases equilibrium expenditure by $200 billion. That is, the change in autonomous expenditure leads, like Céline Dion's electronic equipment, to an amplified change in equilibrium expenditure. This amplified change is the *multiplier effect*—equilibrium expenditure increases by *more than* the increase in autonomous expenditure. The multiplier is greater than 1.

Initially, when autonomous expenditure increases, aggregate planned expenditure exceeds real GDP. As a result, inventories decrease. Firms respond by increasing production so as to restore their inventories to the target level. As production increases, so does real GDP. With a higher level of real GDP, *induced expenditure* increases. Thus equilibrium expenditure increases by the sum of the initial increase in autonomous expenditure and the increase in induced expenditure. In this example, induced expenditure increases by $150 billion, so equilibrium expenditure increases by $200 billion.

Although we have just analyzed the effects of an *increase* in autonomous expenditure, the same analysis applies to a decrease in autonomous expenditure. If initially the aggregate expenditure curve is AE_1, equilibrium expenditure and real GDP are $1,200 billion. A decrease in autonomous expenditure of $50 billion shifts the aggregate expenditure

FIGURE 23.7   The Multiplier

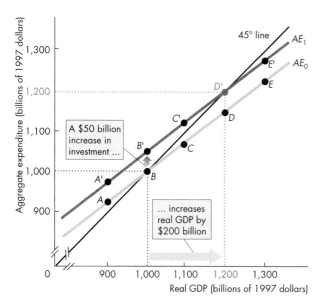

Real GDP (Y)	Aggregate planned expenditure			
	Original (AE₀)		New (AE₁)	
		(billions of 1997 dollars)		
900	A	925	A'	975
1,000	**B**	**1,000**	B'	1,050
1,100	C	1,075	C'	1,125
1,200	D	1,150	D'	1,200
1,300	E	1,225	E'	1,275

A $50 billion increase in autonomous expenditure shifts the AE curve upward by $50 billion from AE_0 to AE_1. Equilibrium expenditure increases by $200 billion from $1,000 billion to $1,200 billion. The increase in equilibrium expenditure is 4 times the increase in autonomous expenditure, so the multiplier is 4.

curve downward by $50 billion to AE_0. Equilibrium expenditure decreases from $1,200 billion to $1,000 billion. The decrease in equilibrium expenditure ($200 billion) is larger than the decrease in autonomous expenditure that brought it about ($50 billion).

Why Is the Multiplier Greater Than 1?

We've seen that equilibrium expenditure increases by more than the increase in autonomous expenditure. This makes the multiplier greater than 1. How come? Why does equilibrium expenditure increase by more than the increase in autonomous expenditure?

The multiplier is greater than 1 because of induced expenditure—an increase in autonomous expenditure *induces* further increases in expenditure. If Rogers Cablesystems spends $10 million on a new pay-per-view system, aggregate expenditure and real GDP immediately increase by $10 million. But that is not the end of the story. Video system designers and computer producers now have more income, and they spend part of the extra income on cars, microwave ovens, vacations, and a host of other goods and services. Real GDP now increases by the initial $10 million plus the extra consumption expenditure induced by the $10 million increase in income. The producers of cars, microwave ovens, vacations, and other goods and services now have increased incomes, and they, in turn, spend part of the increase in their incomes on consumption goods and services. Additional income induces additional expenditure, which creates additional income.

We have seen that a change in autonomous expenditure has a multiplier effect on real GDP. But how big is the multiplier effect?

The Size of the Multiplier

The *multiplier* is the amount by which a change in autonomous expenditure is multiplied to determine the change in equilibrium expenditure that it generates. To calculate the multiplier, we divide the change in equilibrium expenditure by the change in autonomous expenditure. Let's calculate the multiplier for the example in Fig. 23.7. Initially, equilibrium expenditure is $1,000 billion. Then autonomous expenditure increases by $50 billion, and equilibrium expenditure increases by $200 billion, to $1,200 billion. So

$$\text{Multiplier} = \frac{\text{Change in equilibrium expenditure}}{\text{Change in autonomous expenditure}}$$

$$= \frac{\$200 \text{ billion}}{\$50 \text{ billion}} = 4.$$

The Multiplier and the Slope of the *AE* Curve

What determines the magnitude of the multiplier? The answer is the slope of the *AE* curve. The steeper the slope of the *AE* curve, the larger is the multiplier. To see why, think about what the slope of the *AE* curve tells you. It tells you by how much induced expenditure increases when real GDP increases. The steeper the *AE* curve, the greater is the increase in induced expenditure that results from a given increase in real GDP. Let's do a calculation to show the relationship between the slope of the *AE* curve and the multiplier.

The change in real GDP (ΔY) equals the change in induced expenditure (ΔN) plus the change in autonomous expenditure (ΔA). That is,

$$\Delta Y = \Delta N + \Delta A.$$

The slope of the *AE* curve equals the "rise," ΔN, divided by the "run," ΔY. That is,

$$\text{Slope of } AE \text{ curve} = \Delta N \div \Delta Y.$$

So

$$\Delta N = \text{Slope of } AE \text{ curve} \times \Delta Y.$$

Now use this equation to replace ΔN in the first equation above to give

$$\Delta Y = (\text{Slope of } AE \text{ curve} \times \Delta Y) + \Delta A.$$

Now, solve for ΔY as

$$(1 - \text{Slope of } AE \text{ curve}) \times \Delta Y = \Delta A$$

and rearrange to give

$$\Delta Y = \frac{\Delta A}{1 - \text{Slope of the } AE \text{ curve}}.$$

Finally, divide both sides of the previous equation by ΔA to give

$$\text{Multiplier} = \frac{\Delta Y}{\Delta A} = \frac{1}{1 - \text{Slope of } AE \text{ curve}}.$$

Using the numbers for Fig. 23.7, the slope of the *AE* curve 0.75, so the multiplier is

$$\text{Multiplier} = \frac{1}{1 - 0.75} = \frac{1}{0.25} = 4.$$

When there are no income taxes and no imports, the slope of the *AE* curve equals the marginal propensity to consume (*MPC*). So the multiplier is

$$\text{Multiplier} = \frac{1}{1 - MPC}.$$

There is another formula for the multiplier in this special case. Because the marginal propensity to consume (*MPC*) plus the marginal propensity to save (*MPS*) sum to 1, the term $(1 - MPC)$ equals *MPS*. Therefore, another formula for the multiplier is

$$\text{Multiplier} = \frac{1}{MPS}.$$

Because the marginal propensity to save (*MPS*) is a number between 0 and 1, the multiplier is greater than 1.

Figure 23.8 illustrates the multiplier process. In round 1, autonomous expenditure increases by $50 billion (shown by the green bar). At this time, induced expenditure does not change, so aggregate expenditure and real GDP increase by $50 billion. In round 2, the larger real GDP induces more consumption expenditure. Induced expenditure increases by 0.75 times the increase in real GDP, so the increase in real GDP of $50 billion induces a further increase in expenditure of $37.5 billion. This change in induced expenditure (the green bar in round 2), when added to the previous increase in expenditure (the blue bar in round 2), increases aggregate expenditure and real GDP by $87.5 billion. The round 2 increase in real GDP induces a round 3 increase in expenditure. The process repeats through successive rounds. Each increase in real GDP is 0.75 times the previous increase. The cumulative increase in real GDP gradually approaches $200 billion.

So far, we've ignored imports and income taxes. Let's now see how these two factors influence the multiplier.

Imports and Income Taxes

The multiplier is determined, in general, not only by the marginal propensity to consume but also by the marginal propensity to import and by the marginal tax rate.

Imports make the multiplier smaller than it otherwise would be. To see why, think about what happens following an increase in investment. An increase in investment increases real GDP, which in

FIGURE 23.8   The Multiplier Process

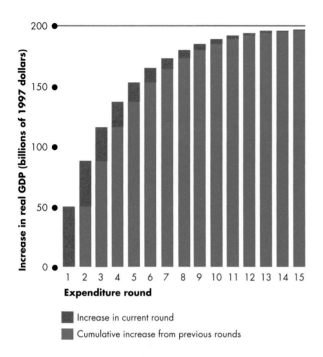

Increase in current round

Cumulative increase from previous rounds

Autonomous expenditure increases in round 1 by $50 billion. As a result, real GDP increases by the same amount. With a marginal propensity to consume of 0.75, each additional dollar of real GDP induces an additional 0.75 of a dollar of aggregate expenditure. The round 1 increase in real GDP induces an increase in consumption expenditure of $37.5 billion in round 2. At the end of round 2, real GDP has increased by $87.5 billion. The extra $37.5 billion of real GDP in round 2 induces a further increase in consumption expenditure of $28.1 billion in round 3. Real GDP increases yet further to $115.6 billion. This process continues with real GDP increasing by ever-smaller amounts. When the process comes to an end, real GDP has increased by a total of $200 billion.

turn increases consumption expenditure. But part of the increase in consumption expenditure is expenditure on imported goods and services, not Canadian-produced goods and services. Only expenditure on Canadian-produced goods and services increases Canadian real GDP. The larger is the marginal propensity to import, the smaller is the change in Canadian real GDP.

Income taxes also make the multiplier smaller

than it otherwise would be. Again, think about what happens following an increase in investment. An increase in investment increases real GDP. But because income taxes increase, disposable income increases by less than the increase in real GDP. Consequently, consumption expenditure increases by less than it would if taxes had not changed. The larger is the marginal tax rate, the smaller is the change in disposable income and real GDP.

The marginal propensity to import and the marginal tax rate together with the marginal propensity to consume determine the multiplier. And their combined influence determines the slope of the *AE* curve. The multiplier is equal to 1 divided by (1 minus the slope of the *AE* curve).

Figure 23.9 compares two situations. In Fig. 23.9(a), there are no imports and no taxes. The slope of the *AE* curve equals the marginal propensity to consume, which is 0.75, and the multiplier is 4. In Fig. 23.9(b), imports and income taxes decrease the slope of the *AE* curve to 0.5. In this case, the multiplier is 2.

Over time, the value of the multiplier changes as tax rates change and as the marginal propensity to consume and the marginal propensity to import change. These ongoing changes make the multiplier hard to predict. But they do not change the fundamental fact that an initial change in autonomous expenditure leads to a magnified change in aggregate expenditure and real GDP.

The math note on pp. 550–551 shows the effects of taxes, imports, and the *MPC* on the multiplier.

Now that we've studied the multiplier and the factors that influence its magnitude, let's use what we've learned to gain some insights into business cycle turning points.

Business Cycle Turning Points

At business cycle turning points, the economy moves from expansion to recession or from recession to expansion. Economists understand these turning points as seismologists understand earthquakes. They know quite a lot about the forces and mechanisms that produce them, but they can't predict them. The forces that bring business cycle turning points are the swings in autonomous expenditure such as investment and exports. The mechanism that gives momentum to the economy's new direction is the multiplier. Let's use what we've now learned to examine these turning points.

FIGURE 23.9   The Multiplier and the Slope of the *AE* Curve

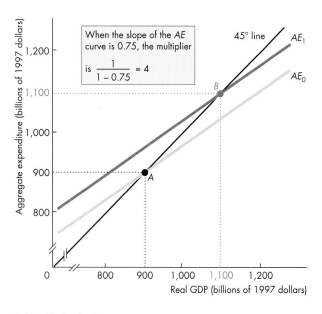

(a) Multiplier is 4

Imports and income taxes make the *AE* curve less steep and reduce the value of the multiplier. In part (a), with no imports and income taxes, the slope of the *AE* curve is 0.75 (the marginal propensity to consume) and the multi-

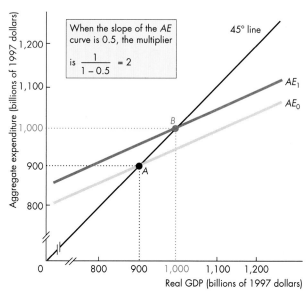

(b) Multiplier is 2

plier is 4. But with imports and income taxes, the slope of the *AE* curve is less than the marginal propensity to consume. In part (b), the slope of the *AE* curve is 0.5. In this case, the multiplier is 2.

An Expansion Begins   An expansion is triggered by an increase in autonomous expenditure that increases aggregate planned expenditure. At the moment the economy turns the corner into expansion, aggregate planned expenditure exceeds real GDP. In this situation, firms see their inventories taking an unplanned dive. The expansion now begins. To meet their inventory targets, firms increase production, and real GDP begins to increase. This initial increase in real GDP brings higher incomes that stimulate consumption expenditure. The multiplier process kicks in, and the expansion picks up speed.

A Recession Begins   The process we've just described works in reverse at a business cycle peak. A recession is triggered by a decrease in autonomous expenditure that decreases aggregate planned expenditure. At the moment the economy turns the corner into recession, real GDP exceeds aggregate planned expenditure. In this situation, firms see unplanned

inventories piling up. The recession now begins. To lower their inventories, firms cut production, and real GDP begins to decrease. This initial decrease in real GDP brings lower incomes that cut consumption expenditure. The multiplier process reinforces the initial cut in autonomous expenditure, and the recession takes hold.

The Next Canadian Recession?   Since 1991, the Canadian economy has been in a business cycle expansion. The last real GDP trough was in the first quarter of 1991. The science of macroeconomics cannot predict when the next recession will begin. A recession seemed possible in 1998 following a rapid buildup of inventories during 1997. But firms planned this inventory buildup. At the end of 2002, there was still no immediate prospect of the next recession. But it will surely come. And when it does, the mechanism you've just studied will operate.

REVIEW QUIZ

1 What is the multiplier? What does it determine? Why does it matter?
2 How do the marginal propensity to consume, the marginal propensity to import, and the marginal tax rate influence the multiplier?
3 If autonomous expenditure decreases, which phase of the business cycle does the economy enter?

The economy's potholes are changes in investment and exports. The economy does not operate like the shock absorbers on Ralph Klein's car. While the price level is fixed, the effects of the economic potholes are not smoothed out. Instead, they are amplified like Céline Dion's voice. But we've considered only the adjustments in spending that occur when the price level is fixed. What happens after a time lapse long enough for the price level to change? Let's answer this question.

The Multiplier and the Price Level

WHEN FIRMS CAN'T KEEP UP WITH SALES AND their inventories fall below target, they increase production, but at some point, they raise their prices. Similarly, when firms find unwanted inventories piling up, they decrease production, but eventually they cut their prices. So far, we've studied the macroeconomic consequences of firms changing their production levels when their sales change, but we haven't looked at the effects of price changes. When individual firms change their prices, the economy's price level changes.

To study the simultaneous determination of real GDP and the price level, we use the *aggregate supply–aggregate demand model*, which is explained in Chapter 22. But to understand how aggregate demand adjusts, we need to work out the connection between the aggregate supply–aggregate demand model and the equilibrium expenditure model that we've used in this chapter. The key to understanding the relationship between these two models is the distinction between the aggregate *expenditure* and aggregate *demand* and the related distinction between the aggregate *expenditure curve* and the aggregate *demand curve*.

Aggregate Expenditure and Aggregate Demand

The aggregate expenditure curve is the relationship between the aggregate planned expenditure and real GDP when all other influences on aggregate planned expenditure remain the same. The aggregate demand curve is the relationship between the aggregate quantity of goods and services demanded and the price level when all other influences on aggregate demand remain the same. Let's explore the links between these two relationships.

Aggregate Expenditure and the Price Level

When the price level changes, aggregate planned expenditure changes and the quantity of real GDP demanded changes. The aggregate demand curve slopes downward. Why? There are two main reasons:

- Wealth effect
- Substitution effects

Wealth Effect Other things remaining the same, the higher the price level, the smaller is the purchasing power of people's real wealth. For example suppose you have $100 in the bank and the price level is 110. If the price level rises to 130, your $100 buys fewer goods and services. You are less wealthy. With less wealth, you will probably want to try to spend a bit less and save a bit more. The higher the price level, other things remaining the same, the lower is aggregate planned expenditure.

Substitution Effects A rise in the price level today, other things remaining the same, makes current goods and services more costly relative to future goods and services and results in a delay in purchases—an *intertemporal substitution*. A rise in the price level, other things remaining the same, makes Canadian-produced goods more expensive relative to foreign-produced goods and services and increases imports and decreases exports—an *international substitution*.

When the price level rises, each of these effects reduces aggregate planned expenditure at each level of real GDP. As a result, when the price level *rises*, the *AE* curve shifts *downward*. A fall in the price level has the opposite effect. When the price level *falls*, the *AE* curve shifts *upward*.

Figure 23.10(a) shows the shifts of the *AE* curve.

When the price level is 110, the aggregate expenditure curve is AE_0, which intersects the 45° line at point B. Equilibrium expenditure is $1,000 billion. If the price level increases to 130, the aggregate expenditure curve shifts downward to AE_1, which intersects the 45° line at point A. Equilibrium expenditure is $900 billion. If the price level decreases to 90, the aggregate expenditure curve shifts upward to AE_2, which intersects the 45° line at point C. Equilibrium expenditure is $1,100 billion.

We've just seen that when the price level changes, other things remaining the same, the AE curve shifts and the equilibrium expenditure changes. And when the price level changes, other things remaining the same, there is a movement along the AD curve. Figure 23.10(b) shows these movements along the AD curve. At a price level of 110, the aggregate quantity of goods and services demanded is $1,000 billion—point B on the AD curve. If the price level rises to 130, the aggregate quantity of goods and services demanded decreases to $900 billion. There is a movement along the AD curve to point A. If the price level falls to 90, the aggregate quantity of goods and services demanded increases to $1,100 billion. There is a movement along the AD curve to point C.

Each point on the AD curve corresponds to a point of equilibrium expenditure. The equilibrium expenditure points A, B, and C in Fig. 23.10(a) correspond to the points A, B, and C on the AD curve in Fig. 23.10(b).

A change in the price level, other things remaining the same, shifts the AE curve and brings a movement along the AD curve. A change in any other influence on aggregate planned expenditure shifts *both* the AE curve and the AD curve. For example, an increase in investment or in exports increases both aggregate planned expenditure and aggregate demand and shifts both the AE curve and the AD curve. Figure 23.11 illustrates the effect of such an increase.

Initially, the aggregate expenditure curve is AE_0 in part (a) and the aggregate demand curve is AD_0 in part (b). The price level is 110, real GDP is $1,000 billion, and the economy is at point A in both parts of the figure. Now suppose that investment increases by $100 billion. At a constant price level of 110, the aggregate expenditure curve shifts upward to AE_1. This curve intersects the 45° line at an equilibrium expenditure of $1,200 billion (point B).

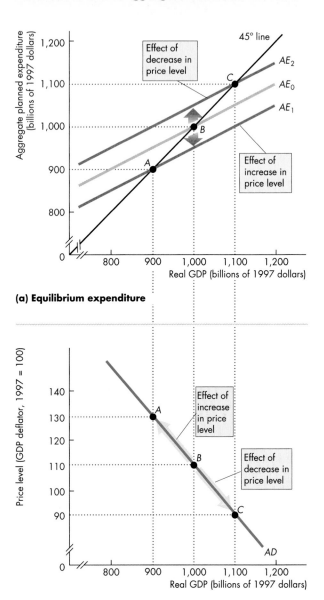

FIGURE 23.10   Aggregate Demand

(a) Equilibrium expenditure

(b) Aggregate demand

A change in the price level *shifts* the AE curve and results in a *movement along* the AD curve. When the price level is 110, the AE curve is AE_0 and equilibrium expenditure is $1,000 billion at point B. When the price level rises to 130, the AE curve is AE_1 and equilibrium expenditure is $900 billion at point A. When the price level falls to 90, the AE curve is AE_2 and equilibrium expenditure is $1,100 billion at point C. Points A, B, and C on the AD curve in part (b) correspond to the equilibrium expenditure points A, B, and C in part (a).

FIGURE 23.11 A Change in Aggregate Demand

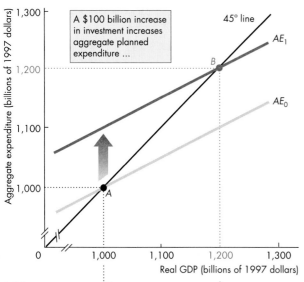

A $100 billion increase in investment increases aggregate planned expenditure ...

(a) Aggregate expenditure

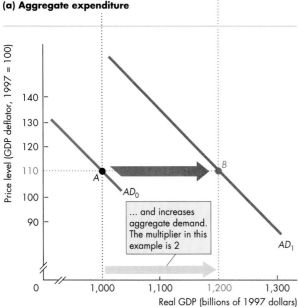

... and increases aggregate demand. The multiplier in this example is 2

(b) Aggregate demand

The price level is 110. When the aggregate expenditure curve is AE_0 (part a), the aggregate demand curve is AD_0 (part b). An increase in autonomous expenditure shifts the AE curve upward to AE_1. In the new equilibrium, real GDP is $1,200 billion (at point B). Because the quantity of real GDP demanded at a price level of 110 increases to $1,200 billion, the AD curve shifts rightward to AD_1.

This equilibrium expenditure of $1,200 billion is the aggregate quantity of goods and services demanded at a price level of 110, as shown by point B in part (b). Point B lies on a new aggregate demand curve. The aggregate demand curve has shifted rightward to AD_1.

But how do we know by how much the AD curve shifts? The multiplier determines the answer. The larger the multiplier, the larger is the shift in the AD curve that results from a given change in autonomous expenditure. In this example, the multiplier is 2. A $100 billion increase in investment produces a $200 billion increase in the aggregate quantity of goods and services demanded at each price level. That is, a $100 billion increase in autonomous expenditure shifts the AD curve rightward by $200 billion.

A decrease in autonomous expenditure shifts the AE curve downward and shifts the AD curve leftward. You can see these effects by reversing the change that we've just described. If the economy is initially at point B on the aggregate expenditure curve AE_1, the aggregate demand curve is AD_1. A decrease in autonomous expenditure shifts the aggregate planned expenditure curve downward to AE_0. The aggregate quantity of goods and services demanded decreases from $1,200 billion to $1,000 billion, and the aggregate demand curve shifts leftward to AD_0.

Let's summarize what we have just discovered:

If some factor other than a change in the price level increases autonomous expenditure, the AE curve shifts upward and the AD curve shifts rightward.

The size of the AD curve shift depends on the change in autonomous expenditure and the multiplier.

Equilibrium GDP and the Price Level

In Chapter 22, we learned that aggregate demand and short-run aggregate supply determine equilibrium real GDP and the price level. We've now put aggregate demand under a more powerful microscope and have discovered that a change in investment (or in any component of autonomous expenditure) changes aggregate demand and shifts the aggregate demand curve. The magnitude of the shift depends on the multiplier. But whether a change in autonomous expenditure results ultimately in a change in real GDP, a change in the price level, or a combination of the two depends on aggregate supply. There are two time frames to consider: the short run and the long run. First we'll see what happens in the short run.

An Increase in Aggregate Demand in the Short Run Figure 23.12 describes the economy. In part (a), the aggregate expenditure curve is AE_0 and equilibrium expenditure is $1,000 billion—point A. In part (b), aggregate demand is AD_0 and the short-run aggregate supply curve is SAS. (Chapter 22, pp. 501–502 explains the SAS curve.) Equilibrium is at point A, where the aggregate demand and short-run aggregate supply curves intersect. The price level is 110, and real GDP is $1,000 billion.

Now suppose that investment increases by $100 billion. With the price level fixed at 110, the aggregate expenditure curve shifts upward to AE_1. Equilibrium expenditure increases to $1,200 billion—point B in part (a). In part (b), the aggregate demand curve shifts rightward by $200 billion, from AD_0 to AD_1. How far the aggregate demand curve shifts is determined by the multiplier when the price level is fixed. But with this new aggregate demand curve, the price level does not remain fixed. The price level rises, and as it does so, the aggregate expenditure curve shifts downward. The short-run equilibrium occurs when the aggregate expenditure curve has shifted downward to AE_2 and the new aggregate demand curve, AD_1, intersects the short-run aggregate supply curve. Real GDP is $1,130 billion, and the price level is 123 (at point C).

When price level effects are taken into account, the increase in investment still has a multiplier effect on real GDP, but the multiplier effect is smaller than it would be if the price level were fixed. The steeper the slope of the short-run aggregate supply curve, the larger is the increase in the price level and the smaller is the multiplier effect on real GDP.

An Increase in Aggregate Demand in the Long Run Figure 23.13 illustrates the long-run effect of an increase in aggregate demand. In the long run, real GDP equals potential GDP and there is full employment. Potential GDP is $1,000 billion, and the long-run aggregate supply curve is LAS. Initially, the economy is at point A (parts a and b).

Investment increases by $100 billion. The aggregate expenditure curve shifts to AE_1, and the aggregate demand curve shifts to AD_1. With no change in the price level, the economy would move to point B and real GDP would increase to $1,200 billion. But in the short run, the price level rises to 123 and real GDP increases to only $1,130 billion. With the higher price level, the AE curve shifts from AE_1 to AE_2. The economy is now in a short-run equilibrium at point C.

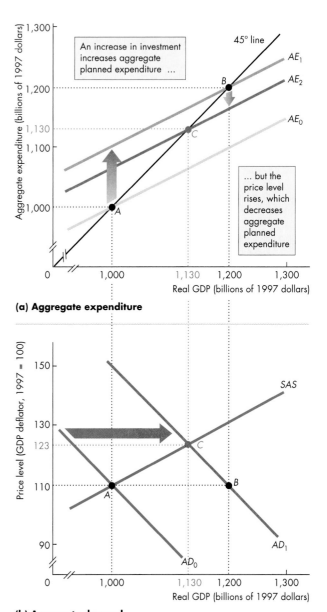

FIGURE 23.12   The Multiplier in the Short Run

(a) **Aggregate expenditure**

An increase in investment increases aggregate planned expenditure ...

... but the price level rises, which decreases aggregate planned expenditure

(b) **Aggregate demand**

An increase in investment shifts the AE curve from AE_0 to AE_1 (part a) and shifts the AD curve from AD_0 to AD_1 (part b). The price level does not remain at 110 but rises, and the higher price level shifts the AE curve downward from AE_1 to AE_2. The economy moves to point C in both parts. In the short run, when prices are flexible, the multiplier effect is smaller than when the price level is fixed.

FIGURE 23.13 The Multiplier in the Long Run

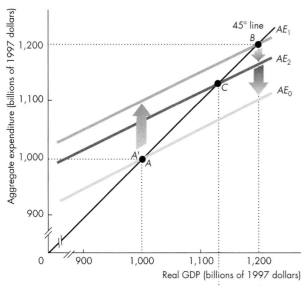

(a) Aggregate expenditure

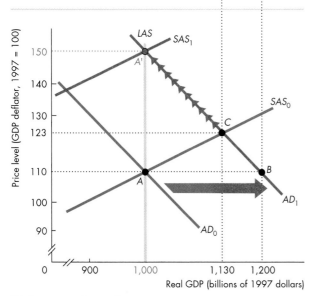

(b) Aggregate demand

Starting from point A, an increase in investment shifts the AE curve to AE_1 and shifts the AD curve to AD_1. In the short run, the economy moves to point C. In the long run, the money wage rate rises, the SAS curve shifts to SAS_1, the price level rises, the AE curve shifts back to AE_0, and real GDP decreases. The economy moves to point A', and in the long run, the multiplier is zero.

Real GDP is now above potential GDP. The labour force is more than fully employed, and shortages of labour increase the money wage rate. The higher money wage rate increases costs, which decreases short-run aggregate supply and shifts the SAS curve leftward to SAS_1. The price level rises further, and real GDP decreases. There is a movement along AD_1, and the AE curve shifts downward from AE_2 towards AE_0. When the money wage rate and the price level have increased by the same percentage, real GDP is again equal to potential GDP and the economy is at point A'. In the long run, the multiplier is zero.

REVIEW QUIZ

1 How does a change in the price level influence the AE curve and the AD curve?

2 If autonomous expenditure increases with no change in the price level, what happens to the AE curve and the AD curve? Which curve shifts by an amount that is determined by the multiplier and why?

3 How does real GDP change in the short run when there is an increase in autonomous expenditure? Does real GDP change by the same amount as the change in aggregate demand? Why or why not?

4 How does real GDP change in the long run when there is an increase in autonomous expenditure? Does real GDP change by the same amount as the change in aggregate demand? Why or why not?

◆ You are now ready to build on what you've learned about aggregate expenditure fluctuations and study the roles of fiscal policy and monetary policy in smoothing the business cycle. In Chapter 24, we study fiscal policy—government expenditures, taxes, and the deficit. In Chapters 25 and 26, we study monetary policy—interest rates and the quantity of money. But before you leave the current topic, look at *Reading Between the Lines* on pp. 548–549, which looks at the rapid expansion of real GDP that occurred in Canada during the first quarter of 2002.

The Aggregate Expenditure Multiplier in Action

THE VANCOUVER SUN, June 1, 2002

Canadian economy on fire in early 2002: hot housing market helped

Canada's economy had its best quarter of the new millennium in the first months of 2002 as a hot housing market and a rebound in manufacturing and exports buoyed the country's gross domestic product by 1.5 per cent, Statistics Canada said Friday.

Canada emerged from the post-Sept. 11 economic shock, which caused a short-term economic contraction in the third quarter of 2001 and a lacklustre fourth quarter, to post its best performance since the fourth quarter of 1999. ...

Virtually all of the economic growth came in the first two months of the year and was a result of inventory stocks having become depleted and manufacturing orders picking up. Statistics Canada said "economic activity paused late in the quarter as GDP leveled off in March ... ."

Record low interest rates led to a record high in new housing construction, which surged 10.5 per cent, smashing levels set in the late 1980s. Urban housing starts were up dramatically across the country, except in Atlantic Canada. At the same time, the cost of existing homes jumped 9.9 per cent, its largest single-quarter jump since 1996.

Statistics Canada said household furnishings, appliances and recreational equipment were the manufacturing sector's greatest strengths, while new automobiles continued to fly off the lots as consumers took advantage of sales and low loan rates. ...

"But this party won't last, or at least it won't be nearly as raucous in the quarters ahead," said economist Avery Shenfeld of CIBC World Markets.

Essence of the Story

■ During the first quarter of 2002, Canada's real GDP increased by 1.5 percent, the fastest quarterly expansion since the fourth quarter of 1999.

■ Virtually all of the economic growth was a result of inventories that became depleted and manufacturing orders that picked up in January and February.

■ Low interest rates stimulated housing construction, which increased by a record 10.5 percent.

■ Production of household furnishings, appliances, and recreational equipment increased most, while new automobile sales were strong.

■ Economist Avery Shenfeld of CIBC World Markets said "... this party won't last ..."

Economic Analysis

■ During the first quarter of 2002, real GDP increased by $16 billion, or 1.5 percent.

■ The table shows the amounts by which the components of aggregate expenditure increased.

■ On the average, an additional dollar of real GDP brings about 57 cents of additional consumption expenditure and about 32 cents of additional imports.

■ Using these two values, the slope of the AE curve is 0.25 and the multiplier, which equals $1/(1 - \text{Slope of } AE \text{ curve})$ equals $1/(1 - 0.25) = 1/0.75 = 1.33$.

■ The increase in consumption expenditure was $6 billion less than the amount that is normally induced by a $16 billion increase in real GDP. The consumption function shifted downward during the first quarter of 2002 by $6 billion.

■ The decrease in autonomous consumption decreased autonomous expenditure by $6 billion.

■ The increase in imports was $1 billion less than the amount that is normally induced by a $16 billion increase in real GDP. The import function shifted downward during the first quarter of 2002 by $1 billion.

■ The decrease in autonomous imports increased autonomous expenditure by $1 billion.

■ The increases in fixed investment (investment excluding the change in inventories), government expenditures, exports, and investment in inventories sum to $17 billion.

■ Subtracting the changes in autonomous consumption and imports from $17 billion gives an increase in autonomous expenditure of $12 billion.

■ Based on the assumptions just described, Fig. 1 shows the AE curve in the fourth quarter of 2001, AE_0, and in the first quarter of 2002, AE_1.

■ The AE curve shifted upward by $12 billion (the assumed increase in autonomous expenditure), and real GDP increased from $1,032 billion to $1,048 billion, an increase of $16 billion.

■ Check that the increase in real GDP equals the increase in autonomous expenditure, $12 billion, multiplied by 1.33, the multiplier.

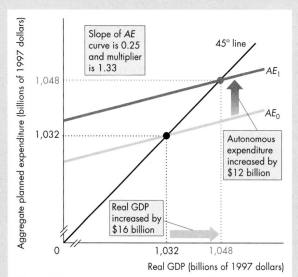

Figure 1 Increase in autonomous expenditure and multiplier

Item	Increase (billions of 1997 dollars)
Consumption expenditure	3
Fixed investment	4
Government expenditure	1
Exports	6
minus Imports	4
Investment in inventories	6
Real GDP	16

549

Mathematical Note
The Algebra of the Multiplier

THIS NOTE EXPLAINS THE MULTIPLIER IN GREATER detail than that presented on p. 540. We begin by defining the symbols we need:

- Aggregate planned expenditure, AE
- Real GDP, Y
- Consumption expenditure, C
- Investment, I
- Government expenditures, G
- Exports, X
- Imports, M
- Net taxes, NT
- Disposable income, YD
- Autonomous consumption expenditure, a
- Marginal propensity to consume, b
- Marginal propensity to import, m
- Marginal tax rate, t
- Autonomous expenditure, A

Aggregate Expenditure

Aggregate planned expenditure (AE) is the sum of the planned amounts of consumption expenditure (C), investment (I), government expenditures (G), and exports (X) minus the planned amount of imports (M). That is,

$$AE = C + I + G + X - M.$$

Consumption Function Consumption expenditure (C) depends on disposable income (YD), and we write the consumption function as

$$C = a + bYD.$$

Disposable income (YD) equals real GDP minus net taxes ($Y - NT$). So if we replace YD with ($Y - NT$), the consumption function becomes

$$C = a + b(Y - NT).$$

Net taxes equal real GDP (Y) multiplied by the marginal tax rate (t). That is,

$$NT = tY.$$

Use this equation in the previous one to obtain

$$C = a + b(1 - t)Y.$$

This equation describes consumption expenditure as a function of real GDP.

Import Function Imports depend on real GDP, and the import function is

$$M = mY.$$

Aggregate Expenditure Curve Use the consumption function and the import function to replace C and M in the aggregate planned expenditure equation. That is,

$$AE = a + b(1 - t)Y + I + G + X - mY.$$

Collect the terms on the right side of the equation that involve Y to obtain

$$AE = (a + I + G + X) + [b(1 - t) - m]Y.$$

Autonomous expenditure (A) is ($a + I + G + X$), and the slope of the AE curve is $[b(1 - t) - m]$. So the equation for the AE curve, which is shown in Fig. 1, is

$$AE = A + [b(1 - t) - m]Y.$$

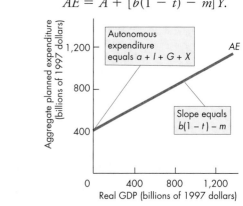

Figure 1 The AE curve

Equilibrium Expenditure

Equilibrium expenditure occurs when aggregate planned expenditure (*AE*) equals real GDP (*Y*). That is,

$$AE = Y.$$

In Fig. 2, the scales of the *x*-axis (real GDP) and the *y*-axis (aggregate planned expenditure) are identical, so the 45° line shows the points at which aggregate planned expenditure equals real GDP.

Figure 2 shows the point of equilibrium expenditure at the intersection of the *AE* curve and the 45° line.

To calculate equilibrium expenditure and real GDP, we solve the equations for the *AE* curve and the 45° line for the two unknown quantities *AE* and *Y*. So starting with

$$AE = A + [b(1 - t) - m] Y$$

$$AE = Y,$$

replace *AE* with *Y* in the *AE* equation to obtain

$$Y = A + [b(1 - t) - m] Y.$$

The solution for *Y* is

$$Y = \frac{1}{1 - [b(1 - t) - m]} A.$$

The Multiplier

The multiplier equals the change in equilibrium expenditure and real GDP (*Y*) that results from a change in autonomous expenditure (*A*) divided by the change in autonomous expenditure.

A change in autonomous expenditure (ΔA) changes equilibrium expenditure and real GDP (ΔY) by

$$\Delta Y = \frac{1}{1 - [b(1 - t) - m]} \Delta A.$$

So

$$\text{Multiplier} = \frac{1}{1 - [b(1 - t) - m]}.$$

The size of the multiplier depends on the slope of the *AE* curve, $b(1 - t) - m$. The larger the slope, the larger is the multiplier. So the multiplier is larger,

- The greater the marginal propensity to consume (*b*)
- The smaller the marginal tax rate (*t*)
- The smaller the marginal propensity to import (*m*)

An economy with no imports and no marginal taxes has $m = 0$ and $t = 0$. In this special case, the multiplier equals $1/(1 - b)$. If *b* is 0.75, then the multiplier is 4, as shown in Fig. 3.

In an economy with $b = 0.75$, $t = 0.2$, and $m = 0.1$, the multiplier is $1 \div [1 - 0.75(1 - 0.2) - 0.1]$, which equals 2. Make up some more examples to show the effects of *b*, *t*, and *m* on the multiplier.

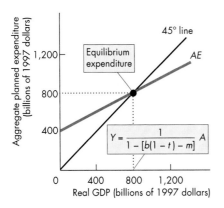

Figure 2 Equilibrium expenditure

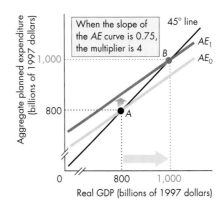

Figure 3 The multiplier

SUMMARY

KEY POINTS

Expenditure Plans and GDP (pp. 528–533)

- When the price level is fixed, expenditure plans determine real GDP.
- Consumption expenditure is determined by disposable income, and the marginal propensity to consume (*MPC*) determines the change in consumption expenditure brought about by a change in disposable income. Real GDP is the main influence on disposable income.
- Imports are determined by real GDP, and the marginal propensity to import determines the change in imports brought about by a change in real GDP.

Equilibrium Expenditure at a Fixed Price Level (pp. 533–537)

- Aggregate *planned* expenditure depends on real GDP.
- Equilibrium expenditure occurs when aggregate planned expenditure equals actual expenditure and real GDP.

The Multiplier (pp. 538–543)

- The multiplier is the magnified effect of a change in autonomous expenditure on real GDP.
- The multiplier equals 1 divided by (1 minus the slope of the *AE* curve).
- The multiplier is influenced by the marginal propensity to consume, the marginal propensity to import, and the marginal tax rate.

The Multiplier and the Price Level (pp. 543–547)

- The aggregate demand curve is the relationship between the quantity of real GDP demanded and the price level, other things remaining the same.
- The aggregate expenditure curve is the relationship between aggregate planned expenditure and real GDP, other things remaining the same.

- At a given price level, there is a given aggregate expenditure curve. A change in the price level changes aggregate planned expenditure and shifts the aggregate expenditure curve. A change in the price level also creates a movement along the aggregate demand curve.
- A change in autonomous expenditure that is not caused by a change in the price level shifts the aggregate expenditure curve and shifts the aggregate demand curve. The magnitude of the shift of the aggregate demand curve depends on the multiplier and on the change in autonomous expenditure.
- The multiplier decreases as the price level changes and the multiplier in the long run is zero.

KEY FIGURES

KEY TERMS

PROBLEMS

*1. You are given the following information about the economy of Heron Island:

Disposable income (millions of dollars per year)	Consumption expenditure (millions of dollars per year)
0	5
10	10
20	15
30	20
40	25

Calculate Heron Island's
a. Marginal propensity to consume.
b. Saving at each level of disposable income.
c. Marginal propensity to save.

2. You are given the following information about the economy of Spendthrift Island:

Disposable income (millions of dollars per year)	Saving (millions of dollars per year)
0	–10
50	–5
100	0
150	5
200	10
250	15
300	20

a. Calculate the marginal propensity to save.
b. Calculate consumption at each level of disposable income.
c. Calculate the marginal propensity to consume.
d. Why is the island called "spendthrift"?

*3. Turtle Island has no imports or exports, there are no income taxes, and the price level is fixed. The figure illustrates the components of aggregate planned expenditure.
a. What is autonomous expenditure?
b. What is the marginal propensity to consume?
c. What is aggregate planned expenditure when real GDP is $6 billion?
d. If real GDP is $4 billion, what is happening to inventories?
e. If real GDP is $6 billion, what is happening to inventories?

f. What is the multiplier?

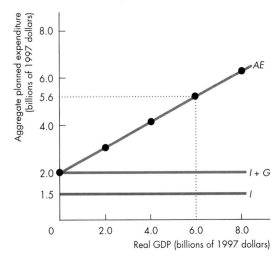

4. The spreadsheet lists the components of aggregate planned expenditure in Spice Bay. The numbers are in billions of cloves, the currency of Spice Bay.

	A	B	C	D	E	F	G
1		Y	C	I	G	X	M
2	A	100	110	50	60	60	15
3	B	200	170	50	60	60	30
4	C	300	230	50	60	60	45
5	D	400	290	50	60	60	60
6	E	500	350	50	60	60	75
7	F	600	410	50	60	60	90

In Spice Bay,
a. What is autonomous expenditure?
b. What is the marginal propensity to consume?
c. What is aggregate planned expenditure when real GDP is 200 billion cloves?
d. If real GDP is 200 billion cloves, what is happening to inventories?
e. If real GDP is 500 billion cloves, what is happening to inventories?
f. What is the multiplier in Spice Bay?

*5. You are given the following information about the economy of Zeeland: Autonomous consumption expenditure is $100 billion, and the marginal propensity to consume is 0.9. Investment is $460 billion, government expenditures on goods and services are $400 billion, and net taxes are a constant $400 billion—they do not vary with income.

a. What is the consumption function?
b. What is the equation that describes the aggregate expenditure curve?
c. Calculate equilibrium expenditure.
d. If investment falls to $360 billion, what is the change in equilibrium expenditure and what is the size of the multiplier?

6. You are given the following information about the economy of Antarctica: Autonomous consumption expenditure is $1 billion, and the marginal propensity to consume is 0.8. Investment is $5 billion, government expenditures on goods and services are $4 billion, and net taxes are a constant $4 billion—they do not vary with income.
a. What is the consumption function?
b. What is the equation that describes the aggregate expenditure curve?
c. Calculate equilibrium expenditure.
d. If investment falls to $3 billion, what is the change in equilibrium expenditure and what is the size of the multiplier?

*7. Suppose that in problem 5, the price level is 100 and real GDP equals potential GDP.
a. If investment increases by $100 billion, what happens to the quantity of real GDP demanded?
b. In the short run, does equilibrium real GDP increase by more than, less than, or the same amount as the increase in the quantity of real GDP demanded?
c. In the long run, does equilibrium real GDP increase by more than, less than, or the same amount as the increase in the quantity of real GDP demanded?
d. In the short run, does the price level in Zeeland rise, fall, or remain unchanged?
e. In the long run, does the price level in Zeeland rise, fall, or remain unchanged?

8. Suppose that in problem 6, the price level is 100 and real GDP equals potential GDP.
a. If investment increases by $1 billion, what happens to the quantity of real GDP demanded?
b. In the long run, does equilibrium real GDP increase by more than, less than, or the same amount as the increase in the quantity of real GDP demanded?
c. In the short run, does the price level in Antarctica rise, fall, or remain unchanged?

CRITICAL THINKING

1. Study *Reading Between the Lines* on pp. 548–549 and then:
a. Describe the changes in the components of aggregate expenditure during the first quarter of 2002.
b. Suppose that the assumptions about the extent to which a change in real GDP induces a change in consumption expenditure and imports on p. 549 are incorrect and that the slope of the *AE* curve is 0.3, not 0.25. What does this imply about the change in autonomous expenditure during the first quarter of 2002? What does it imply about the magnitude of the multiplier?
c. Draw the *AE* curves for the fourth quarter of 2001 and first quarter of 2002 on the assumption that the slope of the *AE* curve is 0.3.

WEB EXERCISES

1. Use the link on the Parkin–Bade Web site to visit the Penn World Table Web site and obtain data on real GDP per person and consumption as a percentage of real GDP for Canada, China, South Africa, and Mexico since 1960.
a. In a spreadsheet, multiply your real GDP data by the consumption percentage and divide by 100 to obtain data on real consumption expenditure per person.
b. Make graphs like Fig. 23.4 that show the relationship between consumption and real GDP for these four countries.
c. On the basis of the numbers you've obtained, in which country do you expect the multiplier to be largest (other things being equal)?
d. What other data would you need to be able to calculate the multipliers for these countries?

2. You are a research assistant in the office of the Prime Minister. Draft a note for the Prime Minister that explains the power and limitations of the multiplier. The Prime Minister wants only 250 words of crisp, clear, jargon-free explanation together with a lively example.

FISCAL POLICY — CHAPTER 24

Balancing Acts on Parliament Hill

In 2001, the federal government spent about 15 cents of every dollar that Canadians earned and collected almost 17 cents of every dollar earned in taxes. What are the effects of government spending and taxes on the economy? Does a dollar spent by the government have the same effect as a dollar spent by someone else? Does it create jobs, or does it destroy them? ◆ Do taxes harm employment and economic growth? ◆ For many years during the 1980s and 1990s, the government had a large budget deficit and ran up a debt. During the late 1990s, spending cuts brought the deficit under control and created a surplus. But in 2001, your share of government debt stood at $18,000. Does it matter if the government doesn't balance its books? What are the effects of an ongoing government deficit and accumulating debt? Do they slow economic growth? Do they impose a burden on future generations—on you and your children? Was the deficit-cutting exercise of the late 1990s beneficial to our economy?

◆ These are the fiscal policy issues that you will study in this chapter. We'll begin by describing the federal budget and the process of creating it. We'll also look at the recent history of the budget. We'll then use the multiplier analysis of Chapter 23 and the aggregate supply–aggregate demand model of Chapter 22 to study the effects of the budget on the economy. At the end of the chapter, in *Reading Between the Lines*, we'll look at the federal government's budget projections through 2008.

After studying this chapter, you will be able to

- Describe how federal and provincial budgets are created
- Describe the recent history of federal and provincial revenues, outlays, and budget deficits
- Distinguish between automatic and discretionary fiscal policy
- Define and explain the fiscal policy multipliers
- Explain the effects of fiscal policy in both the short run and the long run
- Distinguish between and explain the demand-side and supply-side effects of fiscal policy

Government Budgets

THE ANNUAL STATEMENT OF THE OUTLAYS AND revenues of the government of Canada, together with the laws and regulations that approve and support those outlays and revenues, make up the **federal budget**. Similarly, a **provincial budget** is an annual statement of the revenues and outlays of a provincial government, together with the laws and regulations that approve or support those revenues and outlays.

Before World War II, the federal budget had no purpose other than to finance the business of government. But since the late 1940s, the federal budget has assumed a second purpose, which is to pursue the government's fiscal policy. **Fiscal policy** is the use of the federal budget to achieve macroeconomic objectives such as full employment, sustained long-term economic growth, and price level stability. Our focus is this second purpose.

Budget Making

The federal government and Parliament make fiscal policy. The process begins with long drawn-out consultations between the Minister of Finance and Department of Finance officials and their counterparts in the provincial governments. These discussions deal with programs that are funded and operated jointly by the two levels of government. The Minister also consults with business and consumer groups on a wide range of issues.

After all these consultations, and using economic projections made by Department of Finance economists, the Minister develops a set of proposals, which are discussed in Cabinet and which become government policy. The Minister finally presents a budget plan to Parliament, which debates the plan and enacts the laws necessary to implement it.

Highlights of the 2002 Budget

Table 24.1 shows the main items in the federal budget. The numbers are projected amounts for the fiscal year beginning on April 1, 2002. The three main items shown are

- Revenues
- Outlays
- Budget balance

TABLE 24.1   The Federal Budget in 2002–03

Item	Projections (billions of dollars)	
Revenues	174	
Personal income taxes		82
Corporate income taxes		23
Indirect taxes		61
Investment income		8
Outlays	171	
Transfer payments		93
Expenditures on goods and services		42
Debt interest		36
Budget balance	**+3**	

Source: Department of Finance *Budget Plan* 2002.

Revenues Revenues are the federal government's receipts, which in the 2002–03 budget were projected at $174 billion. These revenues come from four sources:

1. Personal income taxes
2. Corporate income taxes
3. Indirect taxes
4. Investment income

The largest revenue source is *personal income taxes*, which in 2002–03 were projected to be $82 billion. These are the taxes paid by individuals on their incomes. The second largest source of revenue is *indirect taxes*, which in 2002–03 were projected to be $61 billion. These taxes include the Goods and Services Tax or GST and taxes on the sale of gasoline, alcoholic drinks, and a few other items. The smallest revenue sources are *corporate income taxes*, which are the taxes paid by companies on their profits, and *investment income*, which is the income from government enterprises and investments. In 2002–03, corporate income taxes were projected to raise $23 billion and investment income was projected at $8 billion. Total federal government revenue in 2002–03 was projected at $174 billion.

Outlays Outlays are classified in three categories:

1. Transfer payments
2. Expenditures on goods and services
3. Debt interest

The largest outlay, and by a big margin, is *transfer payments*. Transfer payments are payments to individuals, businesses, other levels of government, and the rest of the world. In 2002–03, this item was $93 billion. It includes unemployment cheques and welfare payments to individuals, farm subsidies, grants to provincial and local governments, aid to developing countries, and dues to international organizations such as the United Nations.

Expenditures on goods and services are expenditures on final goods and services, and in 2002–03 this item totalled $42 billion. These expenditures include those on national defence, computers for Canada Customs and Revenue Agency, government cars, and highways. This component of the federal budget is *government expenditures on goods and services* that appears in the circular flow of expenditure and income and in the national income and product accounts (see Chapter 20, pp. 459–460).

Debt interest is the interest on the government debt. In 2002–03, this item was $36 billion—almost as much as government expenditures on goods and services. This interest payment is large because the government has a large debt—$538 billion. This large debt has arisen because, until recently, the federal government has had a large and persistent budget deficit.

Budget Balance The government's budget balance is equal to its revenues minus its outlays. That is,

Budget balance = Revenues – Outlays.

If revenues exceed outlays, the government has a **budget surplus**. If outlays exceed revenues, the government has a **budget deficit**. If revenues equal outlays, the government has a **balanced budget**. In 2002–03, with projected outlays of $171 billion and revenues of $174 billion, the government projected a budget surplus of $3 billion.

How typical is the federal budget of 2002–03? Let's look at its recent history.

The Budget in Historical Perspective

Figure 24.1 shows the government's revenues, outlays, and budget balance since 1971. To get a better sense of the magnitudes of these items, they are shown as percentages of GDP. Expressing them in this way lets us see how large the government is rela-

---

FIGURE 24.1 Revenues, Outlays, and the Budget Balance

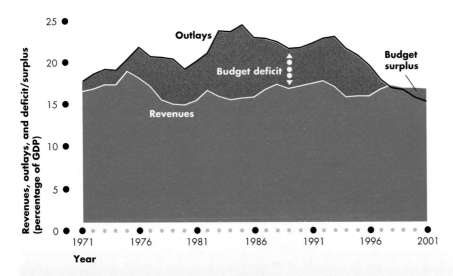

The figure records the federal government's revenues, outlays, and budget balance as percentages of GDP from 1971 to 2001. During the late 1970s, the budget deficit was small and decreasing, but during the 1980s, it became large and persisted. The budget deficit arose because revenues decreased and outlays increased as percentages of GDP. Spending cuts eliminated the deficit by 1997.

Source: Statistics Canada, CANSIM tables 380-0002 and 380-0007.

tive to the size of the economy, and also helps us to study *changes* in the scale of government over time. You can think of the percentages of GDP as telling you how many cents of each dollar that Canadians earn get paid to and spent by the government.

From 1971 through 1996, the federal budget was in deficit, and the average deficit over these years was 4.5 percent of GDP. The deficit climbed to a peak of 8.6 percent of GDP in 1985. It then decreased through the rest of the 1980s. During the recession of 1990–1991, the deficit increased again. The deficit remained above 4 percent of GDP for most of the 1980s and early 1990s.

Only in 1997 did the federal government finally eradicate its deficit. And it did so by cutting outlays, especially transfer payments to provincial governments.

Why did the government deficit grow during the early 1980s and remain high through the early 1990s? The immediate answer is that outlays increased while revenues remained relatively constant. But which components of outlays increased? And did all the sources of revenues remain constant?

To answer these questions, we need to examine each of the sources of revenues and outlays in detail. We'll begin by looking at the sources of revenues.

Revenues Figure 24.2 shows the components of government revenues (as percentages of GDP) since 1971. Total revenues have no strong trends. Throughout the 1980s, federal government revenues as a percentage of GDP increased slightly. The main source of this increase was an increase in personal income taxes. Corporate income taxes and indirect taxes decreased as a percentage of GDP.

The increase in personal income taxes resulted from increases in tax rates in successive budgets throughout the 1980s. The decrease in indirect taxes is mainly the result of replacing an old Federal Sales Tax with the current GST. This switch was intended to maintain revenues at a constant level, but this outcome was not realized.

Outlays Figure 24.3 shows the components of government outlays (as percentages of GDP) since 1971. Total outlays increased steadily from 1971 through 1985, were relatively flat through 1993, and then decreased sharply after 1993. The main source of the changing trends in outlays is transfer payments to provincial governments. These payments swelled during the 1980s and were cut drastically during the late 1990s.

FIGURE 24.2   Federal Government Revenues

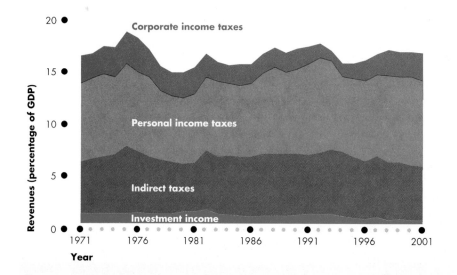

The figure shows four components of government revenues (as percentages of GDP): personal income taxes, corporate income taxes, indirect taxes, and investment income. Revenues from personal income taxes decreased during the late 1970s but trended upward during the 1980s and 1990s. Corporate income taxes decreased slightly. The other two components of revenues remained steady.

Source: Statistics Canada, CANSIM tables 380-0002 and 380-0007.

FIGURE 24.3 Federal Government Outlays

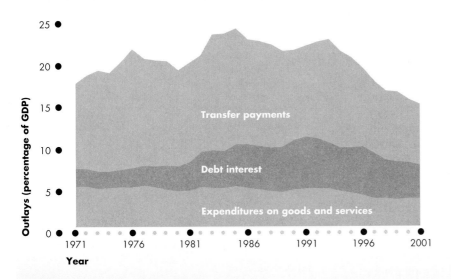

The figure shows three components of government outlays (as percentages of GDP): expenditures on goods and services, debt interest, and transfer payments. Expenditures on goods and services have been stable. Transfer payments increased during the 1970s and early 1980s, remained high through the early 1990s, and then decreased sharply during the 1990s. Debt interest increased steadily during the 1980s as the budget deficit fed on itself, but decreased during the late 1990s as surpluses began to lower the government's debt.

Source: Statistics Canada, CANSIM tables 380-0002 and 380-0007.

To understand the changes in debt interest, we need to see the connection between the budget deficit and government debt.

Deficit and Debt The government borrows to finance its deficit. And **government debt** is the total amount of government borrowing. It is the sum of past deficits minus the sum of past surpluses. When the government has a deficit, its debt increases. Once a persistent deficit emerged during the 1980s, the deficit began to feed on itself. The deficit led to increased borrowing; increased borrowing led to larger debt and larger interest payments; and larger interest payments led to a larger deficit and yet larger debt. That is the story of the increasing deficit of the 1980s.

Figure 24.4 shows the history of government debt since 1946. At the end of World War II, debt (as a percentage of GDP) was at an all-time high of 113 percent. Huge wartime deficits had increased debt to the point that it exceeded GDP. Postwar budget surpluses lowered the debt to GDP ratio through 1974, by which time it stood at 18 percent, its lowest point since World War II. Small deficits increased the debt to GDP ratio slightly through the 1970s, and large deficits increased it dramatically between 1981 and 1986. During the late 1980s, the ratio continued to

FIGURE 24.4 Federal Government Debt

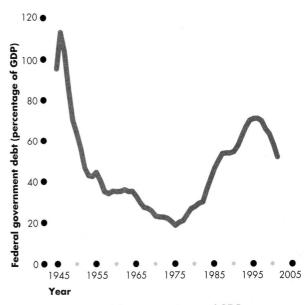

Federal government debt as a percentage of GDP decreased from 1946 through 1974, increased through 1997, and then began to decrease again.

Source: Statistics Canada, CANSIM tables 380-0002 and 385-0010.

increase but at a more moderate rate. It grew quickly again during the 1990–1991 recession, but its growth rate slowed after 1995 and debt interest decreased as a percentage of GDP.

Debt and Capital When individuals and businesses incur debts, they usually do so to buy capital—assets that yield a return. In fact, the main point of debt is to enable people to buy assets that will earn a return that exceeds the interest paid on the debt. The government is similar to individuals and businesses in this regard. Some government expenditure is investment—the purchase of public capital that yields a return. Highways, major irrigation schemes, public schools and universities, public libraries, and the stock of national defence capital all yield a social rate of return that probably far exceeds the interest rate the government pays on its debt.

But government debt, which is $538 billion, is much larger than the value of the public capital stock. This fact means that some government debt has been incurred to finance public consumption expenditure.

Provincial and Local Government Budgets

The *total government* sector of Canada includes provincial and local governments as well as the federal government. In 2001, when federal government outlays were $167 billion, provincial and local government outlays were $280 billion and total government outlays were $447 billion. Most provincial and local government outlays are on public hospitals and public schools, colleges, and universities.

Provincial government outlays and revenue sources vary a great deal across the provinces. Figure 24.5 shows the range of variation. Part (a) shows outlays as a percentage of provincial GDP. You can see that the outlays of Northern and Atlantic governments are the greatest, and those of the governments of Ontario, Alberta, and Saskatchewan are the least. Part (b) shows the sources of provincial revenues as a percentage of total outlays. The Northern and Atlantic provinces receive the largest transfers from the federal government, while Alberta, Ontario, and British Columbia receive the least.

Figure 24.6 shows the revenues, outlays, and deficits of the federal government and of total government between 1971 and 2001.

You can see that federal government outlays and revenues and total government outlays and revenues

FIGURE 24.5 Provincial Government Budgets

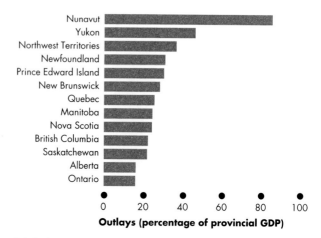

(a) Outlays

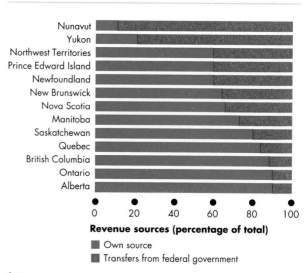

(b) Revenues

Provincial government budgets vary a lot across the provinces. As a percentage of provincial GDP, outlays (part a) are highest in Northern and Atlantic Canada and lowest in Ontario, Alberta, and Saskatchewan. The Northern and Atlantic regions receive the largest share of revenues from the federal government (part b) while Alberta, Ontario, and British Columbia receive the least.

Source: Statistics Canada, CANSIM tables 384-0002 and 385-0002.

FIGURE 24.6 Total Government Budgets

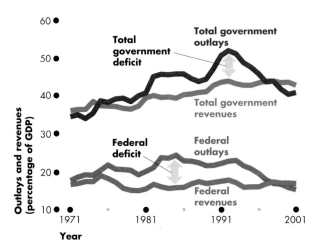

Total government is the sum of the federal, provincial, and local governments. Both the federal government deficit and the provincial government deficits increased from the early 1980s to the mid-1990s, so the total government deficit also increased. Both the federal government deficit and the provincial government deficits decreased after 1995 and turned to surpluses in the late 1990s, so the total government deficit also decreased and became a surplus.

Source: Statistics Canada, CANSIM tables 380-0002 and 380-0007.

FIGURE 24.7 Government Deficits Around the World in 2001

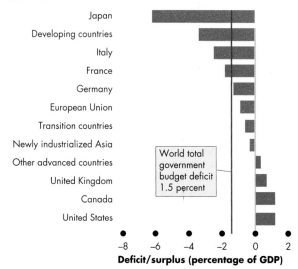

Governments in most countries had budget deficits in 2001. The largest ones were in Japan, the developing countries, Italy, and France. Canada, the United States, and a few other economies had surpluses.

Source: World Economic Outlook, October 2001 (Washington D.C.: International Monetary Fund), tables A15 and A20.

fluctuate in similar ways, but the total government is much larger than the federal government. In other words, the provincial and local governments are a large component of total government. You can also see that total government outlays fluctuate more than federal government outlays.

How does the Canadian government budget balance compare with budgets in other countries?

The Canadian Government Budget in Global Perspective

Is Canada unusual in having eliminated its budget deficit and now to be running a budget surplus? Do other countries have budget surpluses, or do they have budget deficits? Figure 24.7 answers these questions. In today's world, almost all countries have budget deficits. To compare countries, we measure the budget surplus or deficit as a percentage of GDP. The biggest deficit relative to GDP is found in Japan,

where the deficit exceeds 6 percent of GDP. The developing countries, along with Italy and France, have deficits greater than the world average. Canada, the United States, and a small group of other countries are relatively unusual in having budget surpluses.

REVIEW QUIZ

1 What are the main items of government revenues and outlays?
2 Under what circumstances does the government have a budget surplus?
3 Explain the connection between a government deficit and a government debt.

Your next task is to study the effects of the government's budget on the economy and learn about fiscal policy multipliers.

Fiscal Policy Multipliers

FISCAL POLICY ACTIONS CAN BE EITHER AUTOmatic or discretionary. **Automatic fiscal policy** is a change in fiscal policy that is triggered by the state of the economy. For example, an increase in unemployment triggers an automatic increase in payments to the unemployed. A fall in incomes triggers an automatic decrease in tax revenues. That is, this type of fiscal policy adjusts automatically. **Discretionary fiscal policy** is a policy action that is initiated by an act of Parliament. It requires a change in tax laws or in some spending program. For example, a cut in income tax rates and an increase in defence spending are discretionary fiscal policy actions. That is, discretionary fiscal policy is a deliberate policy action.

We begin by studying the effects of *discretionary* changes in government spending and taxes. To focus on the essentials, we'll initially study a model economy that is simpler than the one in which we live. In our model economy, there is no international trade and the taxes are autonomous. **Autonomous taxes** are taxes that do not vary with real GDP. The government fixes them, and they change when the government changes them. But they do not vary automatically with the state of the economy.

The main example of an autonomous tax is the *property tax*. This tax varies across individuals and depends on the value of the property a person occupies. But unlike the income tax, it does not change simply because a person's income changes.

We use autonomous taxes in our model economy because they make the principles we are studying easier to understand. Once we've grasped the principles, we'll explore our real economy with its international trade and income taxes—taxes that *do* vary with real GDP.

Like our real economy, the model economy we study is bombarded by spending fluctuations. Business investment in new buildings, plant and equipment, and inventories fluctuates because of swings in profit expectations and interest rates. These fluctuations set up multiplier effects that begin a recession or an expansion. If a recession takes hold, unemployment increases and incomes fall. If an expansion becomes too strong, inflationary pressures build up. To minimize the effects of these swings in spending, the government might change either its expenditures on goods and services or taxes. By changing either of these items, the government can influence aggregate expenditure and real GDP, but the government's budget deficit or surplus also changes. An alternative fiscal policy action is to change both expenditures and taxes together so that the budget balance does not change. We are going to study the initial effects of these discretionary fiscal policy actions in the very short run when the price level is fixed. Each of these actions creates a multiplier effect on real GDP. These multipliers are the

- Government expenditures multiplier
- Autonomous tax multiplier

Government Expenditures Multiplier

The **government expenditures multiplier** is the magnification effect of a change in government expenditures on goods and services on equilibrium aggregate expenditure and real GDP.

Government expenditures are a component of aggregate expenditure. So when government expenditures on goods and services change, aggregate expenditure and real GDP change. The change in real GDP induces a change in consumption expenditure, which brings a further change in aggregate expenditure. A multiplier process ensues. This multiplier process is like the one described in Chapter 23 (pp. 538–543). Let's look at an example.

A Mackenzie Valley Pipeline Multiplier Canada's Arctic region is rich in natural gas. But to get that gas to Canadian and U.S. markets, a huge $6 billion pipeline would have to be built. Although it is a controversial project because of its potential impact on the environment, building a pipeline in this region would have a large multiplier effect. Construction workers would be hired who would spend much of their income in the Arctic region. Retail stores, schools, health care centres, hotels and motels, and recreational facilities would open and hire yet more people. Some of the income earned by this second wave of workers would also be spent in the region. The Arctic economy would expand until aggregate planned expenditure again equalled aggregate income.

The Size of the Multiplier Table 24.2 illustrates the government expenditures multiplier with a numerical example. The first data column lists various possible levels of real GDP. Our task is to find equilibrium expenditure and the change in real GDP when government expenditures change. The second column shows taxes. They are fixed at $200 billion,

TABLE 24.2 The Government Expenditures Multiplier

Real GDP (Y)	Taxes (T)	Disposable income (Y − NT)	Consumption expenditure (C)	Investment (I)	Initial government expenditures (G)	Initial aggregate planned expenditure (AE = C + I + G)	New government expenditures (G')	New aggregate planned expenditure (AE' = C + I + G')
				(billions of dollars)				
A 900	200	700	525	200	200	925	250	975
B 1,000	**200**	**800**	**600**	**200**	**200**	**1,000**	250	1,050
C 1,100	200	900	675	200	200	1,075	250	1,125
D 1,200	200	1,000	750	200	200	1,150	**250**	**1,200**
E 1,300	200	1,100	825	200	200	1,225	250	1,275

regardless of the level of real GDP. (This is an assumption that keeps your attention on the key idea and makes the calculations easier to do.) The third column calculates disposable income. Because taxes are autonomous, disposable income equals real GDP minus the $200 billion of taxes. For example, in row *B*, real GDP is $1,000 billion and disposable income is $800 billion. The next column shows consumption expenditure. In this example, the *marginal propensity to consume* is 0.75. That is, a $1 increase in disposable income brings a 75-cent increase in consumption expenditure. Check this fact by calculating the increase in consumption expenditure when disposable income increases by $100 billion from row *B* to row *C*. Consumption expenditure increases by $75 billion. The next column shows investment, which is a constant of $200 billion. The next column shows the initial level of government expenditures, which is $200 billion. Aggregate planned expenditure is the sum of consumption expenditure, investment, and government expenditures.

Equilibrium expenditure and real GDP occur when aggregate planned expenditure equals actual expenditure. In this example, equilibrium expenditure is $1,000 billion (highlighted in row *B* of the table.)

The final two columns of the table show what happens when government expenditures increase by $50 billion, to $250 billion. Aggregate planned expenditure increases by $50 billion at each level of real GDP. At the initial real GDP of $1,000 billion

(row *B*), aggregate planned expenditure increases to $1,050 billion.

Because aggregate planned expenditure now exceeds real GDP, inventories decrease. So firms increase production. Output, incomes, and expenditure increase. Increased incomes induce a further increase in consumption expenditure, which is less than the increase in income. Aggregate planned expenditure increases and eventually, a new equilibrium is reached. The new equilibrium is at a real GDP of $1,200 billion (highlighted in row *D*).

A $50 billion increase in government expenditures has increased equilibrium expenditure and real GDP by $200 billion. So the government expenditures multiplier is 4. The size of the multiplier depends on the marginal propensity to consume, which in this example is 0.75. The following formula shows the connection between the government expenditures multiplier and the marginal propensity to consume (*MPC*):

$$\text{Government expenditures multiplier} = \frac{1}{1 - MPC}.$$

Let's check this formula by using the numbers in the above example. The marginal propensity to consume is 0.75, so the government expenditures multiplier is 4.

Figure 24.8 illustrates the government expenditures multiplier. Initially, aggregate planned expenditure is shown by the curve labelled AE_0. The points on this curve, labelled *A* through *E*, correspond with

FIGURE 24.8   Government Expenditures Multiplier

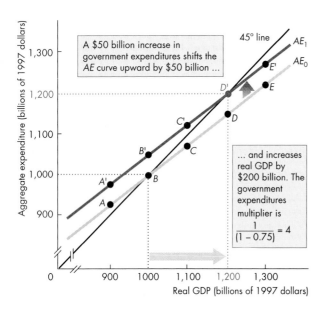

A $50 billion increase in government expenditures shifts the *AE* curve upward by $50 billion ...

... and increases real GDP by $200 billion. The government expenditures multiplier is

$$\frac{1}{(1 - 0.75)} = 4$$

Initially, the aggregate expenditure curve is AE_0, and real GDP is $1,000 billion (at point *B*). An increase in government expenditures of $50 billion increases aggregate planned expenditure at each level of real GDP by $50 billion. The aggregate expenditure curve shifts upward from AE_0 to AE_1—a parallel shift.

At the initial real GDP of $1,000 billion, aggregate planned expenditure is now $1,050 billion. Because aggregate planned expenditure is greater than real GDP, real GDP increases. The new equilibrium is reached when real GDP is $1,200 billion—the point at which the AE_1 curve intersects the 45° line (at point *D'*). In this example, the government expenditures multiplier is 4.

the rows of Table 24.2. This aggregate expenditure curve intersects the 45° line at the equilibrium level of real GDP, which is $1,000 billion.

When government expenditures increase by $50 billion, the aggregate expenditure curve shifts upward by that amount to AE_1. With this new aggregate expenditure curve, equilibrium real GDP increases by $200 billion to $1,200 billion. The increase in real GDP is 4 times the increase in government expenditures. The government expenditures multiplier is 4.

You've seen that in the very short term, when the

price level is fixed, an increase in government expenditures increases real GDP. But to produce more output, more people must be employed, so in the short term, an increase in government expenditures can create jobs.

Increasing its expenditures on goods and services is one way in which the government can try to stimulate the economy. A second way in which the government might act to increase real GDP in the very short run is by decreasing autonomous taxes. Let's see how this action works.

Autonomous Tax Multiplier

The **autonomous tax multiplier** is the magnification effect of a change in autonomous taxes on equilibrium aggregate expenditure and real GDP. An *increase* in taxes *decreases* disposable income, which *decreases* consumption expenditure. The amount by which consumption expenditure initially changes is determined by the marginal propensity to consume. In our example, the marginal propensity to consume is 0.75, so a $1 tax cut increases disposable income by $1 and increases aggregate expenditure initially by 75 cents.

This initial change in aggregate expenditure has a multiplier just like the government expenditures multiplier. We've seen that the government expenditures multiplier is $1/(1 - MPC)$. Because a tax *increase* leads to a *decrease* in expenditure, the autonomous tax multiplier is *negative*. And because a change in autonomous taxes changes aggregate expenditure initially by only MPC multiplied by the tax change, the

$$\text{Autonomous tax multiplier} = \frac{- MPC}{1 - MPC}.$$

In our example, the marginal propensity to consume is 0.75, so

$$\text{Autonomous tax multiplier} = \frac{- 0.75}{1 - 0.75} = -3.$$

Figure 24.9 illustrates the autonomous tax multiplier. Initially, the aggregate expenditure curve is AE_0 and equilibrium expenditure is $1,000 billion. Taxes increase by $100 billion, and disposable income falls by that amount. With a marginal propensity to consume of 0.75, aggregate expenditure decreases initially by $75 billion and the aggregate expenditure curve shifts downward by that amount to AE_1. Equilibrium expenditure and real GDP decrease by $300 billion, to $700 billion. The autonomous tax multiplier is –3.

FIGURE 24.9 Autonomous Tax Multiplier

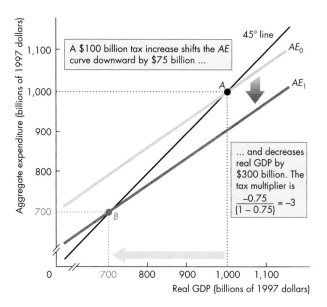

Initially, the aggregate expenditure curve is AE_0 and equilibrium expenditure is $1,000 billion. The marginal propensity to consume is 0.75. Autonomous taxes increase by $100 billion, so disposable income falls by $100 billion. The decrease in aggregate expenditure is found by multiplying this change in disposable income by the marginal propensity to consume and is $100 billion $\times$ 0.75 = $75 billion. The aggregate expenditure curve shifts *downward* by this amount to AE_1. Equilibrium expenditure decreases by $300 billion, from $1,000 billion to $700 billion. The autonomous tax multiplier is -3.

Autonomous Transfer Payments The autonomous tax multiplier also tells us the effects of a change in autonomous transfer payments. Transfer payments are like negative taxes, so an increase in transfer payments works like a decrease in taxes. Because the tax multiplier is negative, a decrease in taxes increases expenditure. An increase in transfer payments also increases expenditure. So the autonomous transfer payments multiplier is positive. It is

$$\text{Autonomous transfer} \atop \text{payments multiplier} = \frac{MPC}{1 - MPC}.$$

Induced Taxes and Transfer Payments

In the examples we've studied so far, taxes are autonomous. But in reality, net taxes (taxes minus transfer payments) vary with the state of the economy.

On the revenue side of the budget, tax laws define tax *rates* to be paid, not tax *dollars* to be paid. Tax *dollars* paid depend on tax *rates* and incomes. But incomes vary with real GDP, so tax *revenues* depend on real GDP. Taxes that vary with real GDP are called **induced taxes**. When the economy expands, induced taxes increase because real GDP increases. When the economy is in a recession, induced taxes decrease because real GDP decreases.

On the outlay side of the budget, the government creates programs that entitle suitably qualified people and businesses to receive benefits. The spending on such programs is not fixed in dollars and it results in transfer payments that depend on the economic state of individual citizens and businesses. When the economy is in a recession, unemployment is high, the number of people experiencing economic hardship increases, and a larger number of firms and farms experience hard times. Transfer payments increase. When the economy expands, transfer payments decrease.

Induced taxes and transfer payments decrease the multiplier effects of changes in government expenditures and autonomous taxes. The reason is that they weaken the link between real GDP and disposable income and so dampen the effect of a change in real GDP on consumption expenditure. When real GDP increases, induced taxes increase and transfer payments decrease, so disposable income does not increase by as much as the increase in real GDP. As a result, consumption expenditure does not increase by as much as it otherwise would have done and the multiplier effect is reduced.

The extent to which induced taxes and transfer payments decrease the multiplier depends on the *marginal tax rate*. The marginal tax rate is the proportion of an additional dollar of real GDP that flows to the government in net taxes (taxes minus transfer payments). The higher the marginal tax rate, the larger is the proportion of an additional dollar of real GDP that is paid to the government and the smaller is the induced change in consumption expenditure. The smaller the change in consumption expenditure induced by a change in real GDP, the smaller is the multiplier effect of a change in government expenditures or autonomous taxes.

International Trade and Fiscal Policy Multipliers

Not all expenditure in Canada is on Canadian-produced goods and services. Some of it is on imports—on foreign-produced goods and services. Imports affect the fiscal policy multipliers in the same way that they influence the investment multiplier, as explained in Chapter 23 (see pp. 540–541). The extent to which an additional dollar of real GDP is spent on imports is determined by the *marginal propensity to import*. Expenditure on imports does not generate Canadian real GDP and does not lead to an increase in Canadian consumption expenditure. The larger the marginal propensity to import, the smaller are the government expenditures and autonomous tax multipliers.

The math note on pp. 576–577 explains the details of the effects of induced taxes and transfer payments and imports on the fiscal policy multipliers.

So far, we've studied *discretionary* fiscal policy. Let's now look at *automatic* stabilizers.

Automatic Stabilizers

Automatic stabilizers are mechanisms that stabilize real GDP without explicit action by the government. Their name is borrowed from engineering and conjures up images of shock absorbers, thermostats, and sophisticated devices that keep airplanes and ships steady in turbulent air and seas. But automatic fiscal stabilizers do not actually stabilize. They just make the fluctuations less severe. These stabilizers operate because income taxes and transfer payments fluctuate with real GDP. If real GDP begins to decrease, tax revenues also fall and transfer payments rise and the government's budget deficit changes. Let's look at the budget deficit over the business cycle.

Budget Deficit Over the Business Cycle Figure 24.10 shows the business cycle and fluctuations in the budget deficit between 1981 and 2001. Part (a) shows the fluctuations of real GDP around potential GDP. Part (b) shows the federal budget deficit. Both parts highlight recessions by shading those periods. By comparing the two parts of the figure, you can see the relationship between the business cycle and the budget deficit. As a rule, when the economy is in the expansion phase of a business cycle, the budget deficit declines. (In the figure, a declining deficit means a deficit that is getting closer to zero.) As the expansion slows before the recession begins, the

FIGURE 24.10 The Business Cycle and the Budget Deficit

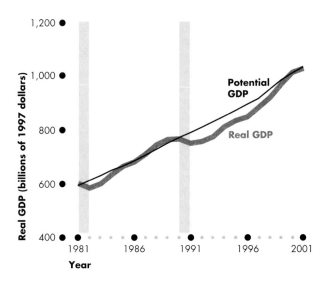

(a) Growth and recessions

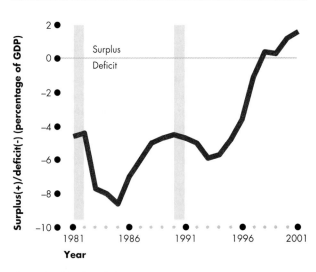

(b) Federal budget balance

As real GDP fluctuates around potential GDP (part a), the budget deficit fluctuates (part b). During a recession (shaded years), tax revenues decrease, transfer payments increase, and the budget deficit increases. The deficit also increases *before* a recession as real GDP growth slows and *after* a recession before real GDP growth speeds up.

Source: Statistics Canada, CANSIM tables 380-0002 and 380-0007.

budget deficit increases. It continues to increase during the recession and for a further period after the recession is over. Then, when the expansion is well underway, the budget deficit declines again.

The budget deficit fluctuates with the business cycle because both tax revenues and transfer payments fluctuate with real GDP. As real GDP increases during an expansion, tax revenues increase and transfer payments decrease, so the budget deficit automatically decreases. As real GDP decreases during a recession, tax revenues decrease and transfer payments increase, so the budget deficit automatically increases.

Fluctuations in investment and exports have a multiplier effect on real GDP. But fluctuations in tax revenues (and the budget deficit) act as an automatic stabilizer. They decrease the swings in disposable income and make the multiplier effect smaller. They dampen both expansions and recessions.

Cyclical and Structural Balances Because the government budget balance fluctuates with the business cycle, we need a method of measuring the balance that tells us whether it is a temporary cyclical phenomenon or a persistent phenomenon. A temporary and cyclical surplus or deficit vanishes when full employment returns. A persistent surplus or deficit requires government action to remove it.

To determine whether the budget balance is persistent or temporary and cyclical, economists have developed the concepts of the structural budget balance and the cyclical budget balance. The **structural surplus or deficit** is the budget balance that would occur if the economy were at full employment and real GDP were equal to potential GDP. The **cyclical surplus or deficit** is the actual surplus or deficit minus the structural surplus or deficit. That is, the cyclical surplus or deficit is the part of the budget balance that arises purely because real GDP does not equal potential GDP.

For example, suppose that the budget deficit is $10 billion. And suppose that economists have determined that there is a structural deficit of $2.5 billion. Then there is a cyclical deficit of $7.5 billion.

Figure 24.11 illustrates the concepts of the cyclical surplus or deficit and the structural surplus or deficit. The blue curve shows government outlays. The outlays curve slopes downward because transfer payments, a component of government outlays, decrease as real GDP increases. The green curve shows revenues. The revenues curve slopes upward

FIGURE 24.11 Cyclical and Structural Deficits and Surpluses

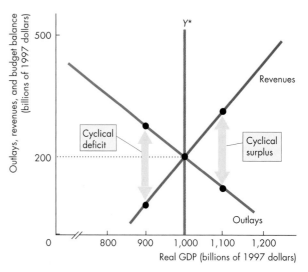

(a) Cyclical deficit and cyclical surplus

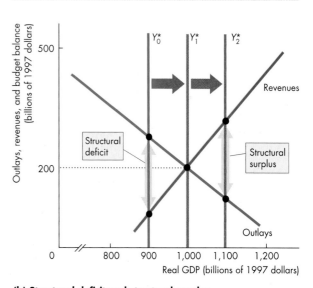

(b) Structural deficit and structural surplus

In part (a), potential GDP is $1,000 billion. When real GDP is less than potential GDP, the budget is in a *cyclical deficit*. When real GDP exceeds potential GDP, the budget is in a *cyclical surplus*. The government has a *balanced budget* when real GDP equals potential GDP. In part (b), when potential GDP is $900 billion, there is a *structural deficit*. But when potential GDP is $1,100 billion, there is a *structural surplus*.

because most components of tax revenues increase as incomes and real GDP increase.

In Fig. 24.11(a), potential GDP is $1,000 billion. If real GDP equals potential GDP, the government has a *balanced budget*. Outlays and revenues each equal $200 billion. If real GDP is less than potential GDP, outlays exceed revenues and there is a *cyclical deficit*. If real GDP is greater than potential GDP, outlays are less than revenues and there is a *cyclical surplus*.

In Fig. 24.11(b), potential GDP grows but the revenues curve and the outlays curve do not change. When potential GDP is $900 billion ($Y_0^*$), there is a *structural deficit*. When potential GDP grows to $1,000 billion ($Y_1^*$), there is a *structural balance* of zero. And when potential GDP grows to $1,100 billion ($Y_2^*$), there is a *structural surplus*.

The Canadian federal budget was in a structural deficit starting in the mid-1970s and continuing through the mid-1990s. That is, even if the economy had been at full employment, the budget would have been in deficit. Worse, the structural deficit was so large that even at the peak of a business cycle, the budget was in deficit. At the end of the 1990s, a budget surplus emerged. It is probable that this surplus was structural because the economy was close to full employment.

REVIEW QUIZ

1 What are the government expenditures multiplier and the autonomous tax multiplier? How do these multiplier effects work?
2 Which multiplier effect is larger: the multiplier effect of a change in government expenditures, or the multiplier effect of a change in autonomous taxes? Why is one larger than the other?
3 How do income taxes and imports influence the size of the fiscal policy multipliers?
4 How do income taxes and transfer payments work as automatic stabilizers to dampen the business cycle?
5 How do we tell whether a budget deficit needs government action to remove it?

Your next task is to see how, with the passage of more time and with some price level adjustments, these multiplier effects change.

Fiscal Policy Multipliers and the Price Level

WE'VE SEEN HOW REAL GDP RESPONDS TO changes in fiscal policy when the price level is fixed and all the adjustments that take place are in spending, income, and production. The period over which this response occurs is very short. Once production starts to change, regardless of whether it increases or decreases, prices also start to change. The price level and real GDP change together, and the economy moves to a new short-run equilibrium.

To study the simultaneous changes in real GDP and the price level, we use the *AS–AD* model of Chapter 22. In the long run, both the price level and the money wage rate respond to fiscal policy. As these further changes take place, the economy gradually moves towards a new long-run equilibrium. We also use the *AS–AD* model to study these adjustments.

We begin by looking at the effects of fiscal policy on aggregate demand and the aggregate demand curve.

Fiscal Policy and Aggregate Demand

You learned about the relationship between aggregate demand, aggregate expenditure, and equilibrium expenditure in Chapter 23 (pp. 543–545). You are now going to use what you learned there to work out what happens to aggregate demand, the price level, and real GDP when fiscal policy changes. We'll start by looking at the effects of a change in fiscal policy on aggregate demand.

Figure 24.12 shows the effects of an increase in government expenditures on aggregate demand. Initially, the aggregate expenditure curve is AE_0 in part (a), and the aggregate demand curve is AD_0 in part (b). The price level is 110, real GDP is $1,000 billion, and the economy is at point A in both parts of the figure. Now suppose that the government increases its expenditures by $50 billion. At a constant price level of 110, the aggregate expenditure curve shifts upward to AE_1. This curve intersects the 45° line at an equilibrium expenditure of $1,200 billion at point B. This amount is the aggregate quantity of goods and services demanded at a price level of 110, as shown by point B in part (b). Point B lies on a new aggregate demand curve. The aggregate demand curve has shifted rightward to AD_1.

The government expenditures multiplier determines the distance by which the aggregate demand

FIGURE 24.12 Government Expenditures and Aggregate Demand

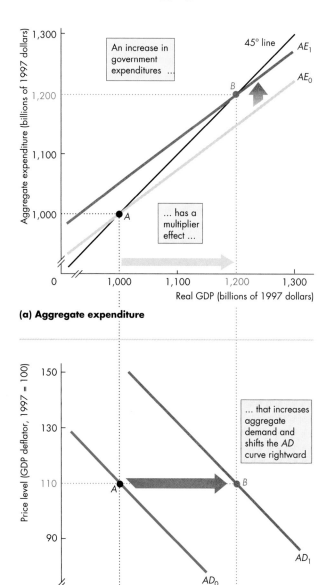

(a) Aggregate expenditure

(b) Aggregate demand

The price level is 110, aggregate planned expenditure is AE_0 (part a), and aggregate demand is AD_0 (part b). An increase in government expenditures shifts the AE curve to AE_1 and increases equilibrium real GDP to $1,200 billion. The aggregate demand curve shifts rightward to AD_1.

curve shifts rightward. The larger the multiplier, the larger is the shift in the aggregate demand curve resulting from a given change in government expenditures. In this example, a $50 billion increase in government expenditures produces a $200 billion increase in the aggregate quantity of goods and services demanded at each price level. The multiplier is 4. So the $50 billion increase in government expenditures shifts the aggregate demand curve rightward by $200 billion.

Figure 24.12 shows the effects of an increase in government expenditures. But a similar effect occurs for *any* expansionary fiscal policy. An **expansionary fiscal policy** is an increase in government expenditures or a decrease in taxes. But the distance that the aggregate demand curve shifts is smaller for a decrease in taxes than for an increase in government expenditures of the same size.

Figure 24.12 can also be used to illustrate the effects of a **contractionary fiscal policy**—a decrease in government expenditures or an increase in taxes. In this case, start at point *B* in each part of the figure and decrease government expenditures or increase taxes. Aggregate demand decreases and the aggregate demand curve shifts leftward from AD_1 to AD_0.

Equilibrium GDP and the Price Level in the Short Run We've seen how an increase in government expenditures increases aggregate demand. Let's now see how it changes real GDP and the price level. Figure 24.13(a) describes the economy. Aggregate demand is AD_0, and the short-run aggregate supply curve is *SAS*. (Check back to Chapter 22, pp. 501–502, to refresh your understanding of the *SAS* curve.) Equilibrium is at point *A*, where the aggregate demand and short-run aggregate supply curves intersect. The price level is 110, and real GDP is $1,000 billion.

An increase in government expenditures of $50 billion shifts the aggregate demand curve rightward from AD_0 to AD_1. While the price level is fixed at 110, the economy moves towards point *B* and real GDP increases towards $1,200 billion. But during the adjustment process, the price level does not remain constant. It gradually rises, and the economy moves along the short-run aggregate supply curve to the point of intersection of the short-run aggregate supply curve and the new aggregate demand curve—point *C*. The price level rises to 123, and real GDP increases to only $1,130 billion.

FIGURE 24.13 Fiscal Policy, Real GDP, and the Price Level

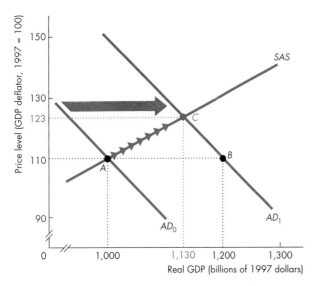

(a) Fiscal policy with unemployment

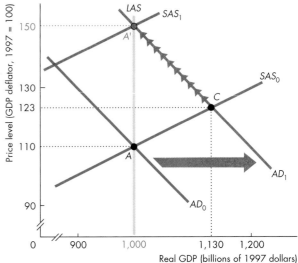

(b) Fiscal policy at full employment

An increase in government expenditures shifts the *AD* curve from AD_0 to AD_1 (part a). With a fixed price level, the economy would have moved to point *B*. But the price level rises, and in the short run, the economy moves to point *C*. The price level increases to 123, and real GDP increases to $1,130 billion.

At point *C*, real GDP exceeds potential GDP and unemployment is below the natural rate (part b). The money wage rate rises, and short-run aggregate supply decreases. The *SAS* curve shifts leftward to SAS_1, and in the long run, the economy moves to point *A'*. The price level rises to 150, and real GDP returns to $1,000 billion.

When we take the price level effect into account, the increase in government expenditures still has a multiplier effect on real GDP, but the effect is smaller than it would be if the price level remained constant. Also, the steeper the slope of the *SAS* curve, the larger is the increase in the price level, the smaller is the increase in real GDP, and the smaller is the government expenditures multiplier. But the multiplier is not zero.

In the long run, real GDP equals potential GDP—the economy is at full-employment equilibrium. When real GDP equals potential GDP, an increase in aggregate demand has the same short-run effect as we've just worked out, but its long-run effect is different. The increase in aggregate demand raises the price level but leaves real GDP unchanged at potential GDP.

To study this case, let's see what happens if the government embarks on an expansionary fiscal policy when real GDP equals potential GDP.

Fiscal Expansion at Potential GDP

Suppose that real GDP is equal to potential GDP, which means that unemployment is equal to the natural rate of unemployment. But suppose also that the unemployment rate and the natural rate are high and that most people, including the government, mistakenly think that unemployment is above the natural rate. In this situation, the government tries to lower the unemployment rate by using an expansionary fiscal policy.

Figure 24.13(b) shows the effect of an expansionary fiscal policy when real GDP equals potential GDP. In this example, potential GDP is $1,000 billion. Aggregate demand increases, and the aggregate demand curve shifts rightward from AD_0 to AD_1. The short-run equilibrium, point *C*, is an above full-employment equilibrium. Now the money wage rate begins to increase and short-run aggregate supply decreases. The *SAS* curve shifts leftward from SAS_0 to

SAS_1. The economy moves up the aggregate demand curve AD_1 towards point A'.

When all the wage and price adjustments have occurred, the price level is 150 and real GDP is again at potential GDP of $1,000 billion. The multiplier is zero. There has been only a temporary increase in real GDP but a permanent rise in the price level.

Limitations of Fiscal Policy

Because the short-run fiscal policy multipliers are not zero, expansionary fiscal policy can be used to increase real GDP and decrease the unemployment rate in a recession. Contractionary fiscal policy can also be used, if the economy is overheating, to decrease real GDP and help to keep inflation in check. But two factors limit the use of fiscal policy.

First, the legislative process is slow, which means that it is difficult to take fiscal policy actions in a timely way. The economy might be able to benefit from fiscal stimulation right now, but it will take Parliament many months, perhaps more than a year, to act. By the time the action is taken, the economy might need an entirely different fiscal medicine.

Second, it is not always easy to tell whether real GDP is below (or above) potential GDP. A change in aggregate demand can move real GDP away from potential GDP, or a change in aggregate supply can change real GDP and change potential GDP. This difficulty is a serious one because, as you've seen, fiscal stimulation might occur too close to full employment, in which case it will increase the price level and have no long-run effect on real GDP.

REVIEW QUIZ

1 How do changes in the price level influence the multiplier effects of fiscal policy on real GDP?
2 What are the long-run effects of fiscal policy on real GDP and the price level when real GDP equals potential GDP?

So far, we've ignored any potential effects of fiscal policy on aggregate supply. Yet many economists believe that the supply-side effects of fiscal policy are the biggest. Let's now look at these effects.

Supply-Side Effects of Fiscal Policy

TAX CUTS INCREASE DISPOSABLE INCOME AND increase aggregate demand. But tax cuts also strengthen incentives and increase aggregate supply. The strength of the supply-side effects of tax cuts is not known with certainty. Some economists believe that the supply-side effects are large and exceed the demand-side effects. Other economists, while agreeing that supply-side effects are present, believe that they are relatively small.

The controversy over the magnitude of the effects of taxes on aggregate supply is a political controversy. Generally speaking, people on the conservative or right wing of the political spectrum believe that supply-side effects are powerful, and people on the liberal or left wing of the political spectrum view supply-side effects as being small.

Regardless of which view is correct, we can study the supply-side effects of tax cuts by using the AS–AD model. Let's study the effects of taxes on potential GDP and then see how the supply-side effects and demand-side effects together influence real GDP and the price level.

Fiscal Policy and Potential GDP

Potential GDP depends on the full-employment quantity of labour, the quantity of capital, and the state of technology. Taxes can influence all three of these factors. The main tax to consider is the income tax. By taxing the incomes people earn when they work or save, the government weakens the incentives to work and save. The result is a smaller quantity of labour and capital and a smaller potential GDP. Also, the income tax weakens the incentive to develop new technologies that increase income. So the pace of technological change might be slowed, which slows the growth rate of potential GDP. Let's look at the effect of the income tax on both the quantity of labour and the quantity of capital.

Labour Market Taxes The quantity of labour is determined by demand and supply in the labour market. Figure 24.14(a) shows a labour market. The demand for labour is LD and the supply is LS. The equilibrium real wage rate is $15 an hour and 30 billion hours of labour per year are employed.

FIGURE 24.14 Supply-Side Effects of Taxes

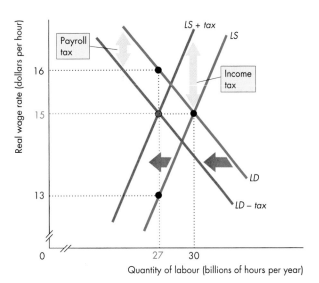

(a) The labour market

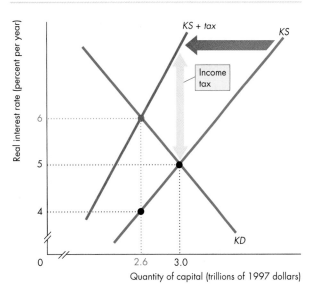

(b) The capital market

In part (a), an income tax decreases the supply of labour from *LS* to *LS* + *tax* and a payroll tax decreases the demand for labour from *LD* to *LD* – *tax*. The quantity of labour decreases. In part (b), the income tax decreases the supply of capital from *KS* to *KS* – *tax*. The quantity of capital decreases. With less labour and less capital, potential GDP decreases.

Now suppose that two taxes are introduced. An income tax weakens the incentive to work and decreases the supply of labour. The supply curve shifts leftward to *LS* + *tax*. A payroll tax makes it more costly to employ labour and decreases the demand for labour. The demand curve shifts leftward to *LD* – *tax*. With the new decreased supply and demand, the quantity of labour employed decreases to 27 billion hours a year. The *before-tax* real wage rate remains at $15 an hour (but it might rise or fall depending on whether demand or supply decreases more). The *after-tax* real wage rate falls to $13 an hour, and the cost of hiring labour rises to $16 an hour.

Capital and the Income Tax The quantity of capital is determined by demand and supply in the capital market. Figure 24.14(b) shows the capital market. The demand for capital is *KD* and the supply is *KS*. The equilibrium real interest rate is 5 percent a year and the quantity of capital is $3 trillion.

A tax on the income from capital weakens the incentive to save and decreases the supply of capital. The supply curve shifts leftward to *KS* + *tax*. With the new decreased supply, the quantity of capital decreases to $2.6 trillion. The *before-tax* interest rate rises to 6 percent a year, and the *after-tax* interest rate falls to 4 percent a year.

Potential GDP and *LAS* Because the income tax decreases the equilibrium quantities of labour and capital, it also decreases potential GDP. But potential GDP determines long-run aggregate supply. So the income tax decreases long-run aggregate supply and shifts the *LAS* curve leftward.

Supply Effects and Demand Effects

Let's now bring the supply-side effects and demand-side effects of fiscal policy together. Figure 24.15(a) shows the most likely effects of a tax cut. The tax cut increases aggregate demand and shifts the *AD* curve rightward, just as before. But a tax cut that increases the incentive to work and save also increases aggregate supply. It shifts the long-run and short-run aggregate supply curves rightward. Here we focus on the short run and show the effect on the *SAS* curve, which shifts rightward to *SAS*$_1$. In this example, the tax cut has a large effect on aggregate demand and a small effect on aggregate supply. The aggregate demand curve shifts rightward by a larger amount

FIGURE 24.15 Two Views of the Supply-Side Effects of Fiscal Policy

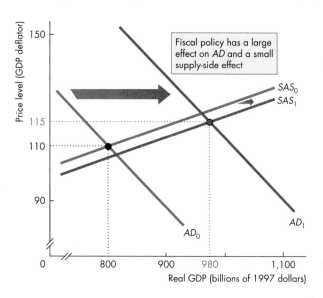

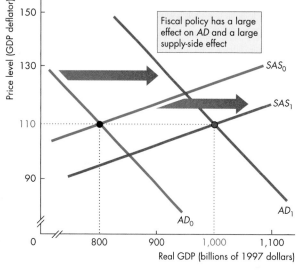

(a) The traditional view

A tax cut increases aggregate demand and shifts the *AD* curve rightward from AD_0 to AD_1 (both parts). Such a policy change also has a supply-side effect. If the supply-side effect is small, the *SAS* curve shifts rightward from SAS_0 to SAS_1 in part (a). The demand-side effect dominates the supply-side effect, real GDP increases, and the price level rises.

(b) The supply-side view

If the supply-side effect of a tax cut is large, the *SAS* curve shifts to SAS_1 in part (b). In this case, the supply-side effect is as large as the demand-side effect. Real GDP increases, and the price level remains constant. But if the supply-side effect were larger than the demand-side effect, the price level would actually fall.

than the rightward shift in the short-run aggregate supply curve. The outcome is a rise in the price level and an increase in real GDP. But notice that the price level rises by *less* and real GDP increases by *more* than would occur if there were no supply-side effects.

Figure 24.15(b) shows the effects that supply-siders believe occur. A tax cut still has a large effect on aggregate demand, but it has a similarly large effect on aggregate supply. The aggregate demand curve and the short-run aggregate supply curve shift rightward by similar amounts. In this particular case, the price level remains constant and real GDP increases. A slightly larger increase in aggregate supply would have brought a fall in the price level, a possibility that some supply-siders believe could occur.

The general point with which everyone agrees is that a tax cut that strengthens incentives increases real GDP by more and is less inflationary than an equal-size expansionary fiscal policy that does not change incentives or that weakens them.

REVIEW QUIZ

1 How do income taxes and payroll taxes influence the labour market, and how would a cut in these taxes influence real GDP?

2 How would an income tax cut influence aggregate supply and aggregate demand?

3 How would an income tax cut influence real GDP and the price level?

◆ You've seen how fiscal policy influences the way real GDP fluctuates around its trend and how it influences potential GDP. *Reading Between the Lines* on pp. 574–575 looks further at Finance Minister John Manley's fiscal policy projections through 2008.

Your next task is to study the other main arm of macroeconomic policy: monetary policy.

POLICY
WATCH

Fiscal Policy Projections

OTTAWA CITIZEN, October 31, 2002

Manley predicts $70B surplus by 2007

Finance Minister John Manley is projecting the government will have accumulated surpluses of more than $70 billion over this and the coming five years, money that will be used to continue transforming Canada into a "Northern tiger."

Even after setting aside about $30 billion over that time for unexpected emergencies or economic downturns, that if not needed will go to debt reduction, the federal government will still have more than $40 billion to fund promised improvements in health care, the child benefit, environmental cleanup and upgrades to city infrastructure, according to Mr. Manley's fiscal and economic update presented to the Commons finance committee yesterday.

The minister also hinted there will be more money for the military in his February budget to allow Canada to meet its defence and diplomatic responsibilities. ...

However, the update forecasts that this year there would be only $1 billion in surplus funds after setting aside $3 billion for unexpected emergencies.

And that's despite expected economic growth of 3.4 per cent this year, more than double the 1.5 per cent forecast in last year's budget, 3.4 per cent next year and an average of three per cent in each of the following five years....

TD Bank economist Don Drummond, a former associate deputy finance minister, said that while Mr. Manley "looks like he's awash in funds," he faces enormous spending pressures, noting that each of the major throne speech promises alone will cost billions.

He also noted that the big surpluses are well down the road.

The update projects annual surpluses of $1 billion this year, followed by $3.1 billion the year after, then $3.5 billion, $6.8 billion, $10.5 billion and $14.6 billion in 2007-08, not including about $30 billion that will be set aside for contingencies and prudence, including $7 billion in the last fiscal year of the forecast. ...

Essence of the Story

■ Finance Minister John Manley projects budget surpluses that will accumulate to more than $70 billion by 2007.

■ Of this amount, $30 billion will be spent on unexpected emergencies, be lost in economic downturns, or be used to pay down the national debt.

■ The projected annual surpluses, excluding $30 billion on contingencies, are

$1 billion in 2002–03, $3.1 billion in 2003–04, $3.5 billion in 2004–05, $6.8 billion in 2005–06, $10.5 billion in 2006–07, and $14.6 billion in 2007–08.

■ These surpluses will be spent on improvements in health care, the child benefit, environmental cleanup, upgrades to city infrastructure, and national defence.

■ The 2002–03 surplus is small despite the fact that economic growth in that year was strong.

Economic Analysis

- The table shows the federal government's budget projections through 2008.

- The "Planning surplus" numbers, which are the "surpluses" referred to in the news article, are actually amounts that the government intends to spend on improvements in health care, the child benefit, environmental cleanup, upgrades to city infrastructure, and national defence.

- The "Economic prudence" numbers are part of the $30 billion of "surplus" referred to in the news article. These amounts are expected to be spent or lost because of recession.

- The "Contingency reserve" numbers are also part of the $30 billion of "surplus" referred to in the news article. And these amounts are the actual surplus that will be used to pay down the federal government's debt.

- Figure 1 shows the rise and fall of government debt and the projected debt through 2008.

- Even if the government ran surpluses that totalled $70 billion by 2008, the debt would still be more than 30 percent of GDP in 2008 and would follow the lower path in the figure.

- The government says that its "Economic prudence" provision is to ensure that it never again has a deficit.

- Figure 2 shows that a deficit will most likely arise in a recession.

- In 2005, with real GDP at $1,250 billion and a structural surplus of $5 billion (the contingency reserve plus the economic prudence item for 2005), a recession that takes real GDP to 4 percent below potential GDP would create a deficit of around $3.5 billion.

You're The Voter

- Do you think the federal government's projected surplus is too big, too small, or about right? Provide your reasons.

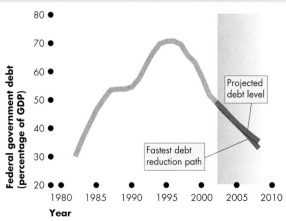

Figure 1 Paying off the federal government's debt

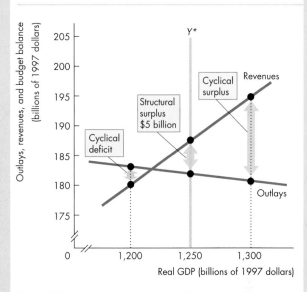

Figure 2 Cyclical and structural surpluses and deficits

Summary of Fiscal Projections: 2002–2008						
Financial year	**2002–03**	**2003–04**	**2004–05**	**2005–06**	**2006–07**	**2007–08**
Item	**Billions of dollars**					
Revenues	173.9	184.1	191.9	201.5	211.2	221.0
Program spending	134.3	140.7	146.6	152.4	158.0	163.6
Debt interest	35.6	36.3	36.8	36.3	36.2	35.8
Planning surplus (planned increase in spending)	1.0	3.1	3.5	6.8	10.5	14.6
Economic prudence (unplanned increase in spending or decrease in revenue)	0.0	1.0	2.0	3.0	3.5	4.0
Total planned spending	170.9	181.1	188.9	198.5	208.2	218.0
Contingency reserve (planned surplus for reducing debt)	3.0	3.0	3.0	3.0	3.0	3.0

Mathematical Note
The Algebra of the Fiscal Policy Multipliers

THIS MATHEMATICAL NOTE DERIVES FORMULAS FOR the fiscal policy multipliers. We begin by defining the symbols we need:

- Aggregate planned expenditure, AE
- Real GDP, Y
- Consumption expenditure, C
- Investment, I
- Government expenditures, G
- Exports, X
- Imports, M
- Net taxes, NT
- Autonomous consumption expenditure, a
- Autonomous taxes, T_a
- Autonomous transfer payments, T_r
- Marginal propensity to consume, b
- Marginal propensity to import, m
- Marginal tax rate, t
- Autonomous expenditure, A

Equilibrium Expenditure

Aggregate planned expenditure is

$$AE = C + I + G + X - M.$$

The consumption function is

$$C = a + b(Y - NT).$$

Net taxes equals autonomous taxes minus autonomous transfer payments plus induced taxes, which is

$$NT = T_a - T_r + tY.$$

Use the last equation in the consumption function to give consumption expenditure as a function of GDP:

$$C = a - bT_a + bT_r + b(1 - t)Y.$$

The import function is

$$M = mY.$$

Use the consumption function and the import function to replace C and M in the aggregate planned expenditure equation to obtain

$$AE = a - bT_a + bT_r + b(1 - t)Y + I + G + X - mY.$$

Collect the terms that involve Y on the right-side of the equation to obtain

$$AE = (a - bT_a + bT_r + I + G + X) + [b(1 - t) - m]Y.$$

Autonomous expenditure (A) is given by

$$A = a - bT_a + bT_r + I + G + X$$

and the slope of the AE curve is $[b(1 - t) - m]$, so

$$AE = A + [b(1 - t) - m]Y.$$

Equilibrium expenditure occurs when aggregate planned expenditure (AE) equals real GDP (Y). That is,

$$AE = Y.$$

To calculate equilibrium expenditure, we solve the equation:

$$Y = A + [b(1 - t) - m]Y$$

to obtain

$$Y = \frac{1}{1 - [b(1 - t) - m]}A.$$

Government Expenditures Multiplier

The government expenditures multiplier equals the change in equilibrium expenditure (Y) that results from a change in government expenditures (G) divided by the change in government expenditures. Because autonomous expenditure is equal to

$$A = a - bT_a + bT_r + I + G + X,$$

the change in autonomous expenditure equals the change in government expenditures. That is,

$$\Delta A = \Delta G.$$

The government expenditures multiplier is found by working out the change in Y that results from the change in A. You can see from the solution for Y that

$$\Delta Y = \frac{1}{1 - [b(1 - t) - m]}\Delta G.$$

The government expenditures multiplier equals

$$\frac{1}{1 - [b(1 - t) - m]}.$$

In an economy in which $t = 0$ and $m = 0$, the government expenditures multiplier is $1/(1 - b)$. With $b = 0.75$, the government expenditures multiplier equals 4, as part (a) of the figure shows. Make up some examples and use the above formula to show how b, m, and t influence the government expenditures multiplier.

Autonomous Tax Multiplier

The autonomous tax multiplier equals the change in equilibrium expenditure (Y) that results from a change in autonomous taxes (T_a) divided by the change in autonomous taxes. Because autonomous expenditure is equal to

$$A = a - bT_a + bT_r + I + G + X,$$

the change in autonomous expenditure equals *minus b* multiplied by the change in autonomous taxes. That is,

$$\Delta A = -b\Delta T_a.$$

You can see from the solution for equilibrium expenditure Y that

$$\Delta Y = \frac{-b}{1 - [b(1 - t) - m]}\Delta T_a.$$

The autonomous tax multiplier equals

$$\frac{-b}{1 - [b(1 - t) - m]}.$$

In an economy in which $t = 0$ and $m = 0$, the autonomous tax multiplier is $-b/(1 - b)$. With $b = 0.75$, the autonomous tax multiplier equals -3, as part (b) of the figure shows. Make up some

examples and use the above formula to show how b, m, and t influence the autonomous tax multiplier.

Autonomous Transfer Payments Multiplier

The autonomous transfer payments multiplier equals the change in equilibrium expenditure (Y) that results from a change in autonomous transfer payments (T_r) divided by the change in autonomous transfer payments. Because autonomous expenditure is equal to

$$A = a - bT_a + bT_r + I + G + X,$$

the change in autonomous transfer payments changes autonomous expenditure such that

$$\Delta A = b\Delta T_r.$$

Because transfer payments are like negative taxes, the autonomous transfer payments multiplier equals minus the autonomous tax multiplier. The autonomous transfer payments multiplier equals

$$\frac{b}{1 - [b(1 - t) - m]}.$$

In an economy in which $t = 0$ and $m = 0$, the autonomous transfer payments multiplier is $b/(1 - b)$. With $b = 0.75$, the autonomous transfer payments multiplier equals 3, as part (c) of the figure shows. Make up some examples and use the above formula to show how b, m, and t influence the autonomous transfer payments multiplier.

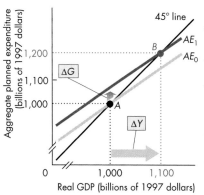

(a) Government expenditures multiplier

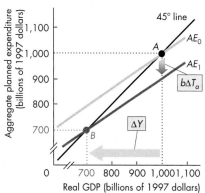

(b) Autonomous tax multiplier

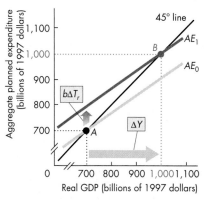

(c) Autonomous transfer payments multiplier

SUMMARY

KEY POINTS

Government Budgets (pp. 556–561)

- The federal budget finances the activities of the government and is used to stabilize real GDP.
- Federal revenues come from personal income taxes, corporate income taxes, indirect taxes, and investment income. Federal outlays include transfer payments, expenditures on goods and services, and debt interest.
- When government revenues exceed outlays, the government has a budget surplus.

Fiscal Policy Multipliers (pp. 562–568)

- Fiscal policy actions are discretionary or automatic.
- Government expenditures, taxes, and transfer payments have multiplier effects on real GDP.
- The government expenditures multiplier equals $1/(1 - MPC)$. The autonomous tax multiplier equals $-MPC/(1 - MPC)$.
- The transfer payments multiplier is equal to the magnitude of autonomous tax multiplier but is positive.
- Induced taxes and transfer payments and imports make the fiscal policy multipliers smaller.
- Income taxes and transfer payments act as automatic stabilizers.

Fiscal Policy Multipliers and the Price Level (pp. 568–571)

- An expansionary fiscal policy increases aggregate demand and shifts the aggregate demand curve rightward. It increases real GDP and raises the price level. (A contractionary fiscal policy has the opposite effects.)
- Price level changes dampen fiscal policy multiplier effects.
- At potential GDP, an expansionary fiscal policy raises the price level but leaves real GDP unchanged. The fiscal policy multipliers are zero.

Supply-Side Effects of Fiscal Policy (pp. 571–573)

- Fiscal policy has supply-side effects because increases in taxes weaken the incentives to work and save.
- A tax cut increases both aggregate demand and aggregate supply and increases real GDP, but the tax cut has an ambiguous effect on the price level.

KEY FIGURES

KEY TERMS

PROBLEMS

*1. In the economy of Zap, the marginal propensity to consume is 0.9. Investment is $50 billion, government expenditures on goods and services are $40 billion, and autonomous taxes are $40 billion. Zap has no exports and no imports.
   a. The government cuts its expenditures on goods and services to $30 billion. What is the change in equilibrium expenditure?
   b. What is the value of the government expenditures multiplier?
   c. The government continues to buy $40 billion worth of goods and services and cuts autonomous taxes to $30 billion. What is the change in equilibrium expenditure?
   d. What is the value of the autonomous tax multiplier?
   e. The government simultaneously cuts both its expenditures on goods and services and taxes to $30 billion. What is the change in equilibrium expenditure? Why does equilibrium expenditure decrease?

2. In the economy of Zip, the marginal propensity to consume is 0.8. Investment is $60 billion, government expenditures on goods and services are $50 billion, and autonomous taxes are $60 billion. Zip has no exports and no imports.
   a. The government increases its expenditures on goods and services to $60 billion. What is the change in equilibrium expenditure?
   b. What is the value of the government expenditures multiplier?
   c. The government continues to buy $60 billion worth of goods and services and increases autonomous taxes to $70 billion. What is the change in equilibrium expenditure?
   d. What is the value of the autonomous tax multiplier?
   e. The government simultaneously increases both its expenditures on goods and services and taxes by $10 billion. What is the change in equilibrium expenditure? Why does equilibrium expenditure increase?

*3. Suppose that the price level in the economy of Zap as described in problem 1 is 100. The economy is also at full employment.
   a. If the government of Zap increases its expenditures on goods and services by $10 billion, what happens to the quantity of real GDP demanded?
   b. How does Zap's aggregate demand curve change? Draw a two-part figure that is similar to Fig. 24.12 to illustrate the change in both the AE curve and the AD curve.
   c. In the short run, does equilibrium real GDP increase by more than, less than, or the same amount as the increase in the quantity of real GDP demanded?
   d. In the long run, does equilibrium real GDP increase by more than, less than, or the same amount as the increase in the quantity of real GDP demanded?
   e. In the short run, does the price level in Zap rise, fall, or remain unchanged?
   f. In the long run, does the price level in Zap rise, fall, or remain unchanged?

4. Suppose that the price level in the economy of Zip as described in problem 2 is 100. The economy is also at full employment.
   a. If the government of Zip decreases its expenditures on goods and services by $5 billion, what happens to the quantity of real GDP demanded?
   b. How does Zip's aggregate demand curve change? Draw a two-part figure that is similar to Fig. 24.12 to illustrate the change in both the AE curve and the AD curve.
   c. In the short run, does equilibrium real GDP decrease by more than, less than, or the same amount as the increase in the quantity of real GDP demanded?
   d. In the short run, does the price level in Zip rise, fall, or remain unchanged?
   e. Why does real GDP decrease by a smaller amount than the decrease in aggregate demand?

*5. The figure shows outlays and revenues of the government of Dreamland. Potential GDP is $40 million.

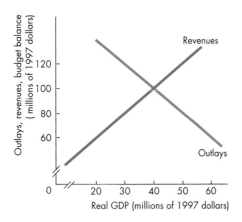

a. What is the government's budget balance if real GDP equals potential GDP?
b. Does Dreamland have a structural surplus or deficit if its real GDP is $40 million? What is the size of the structural surplus or deficit? Explain why.
c. What is the government's budget balance if real GDP is $30 million?
d. If Dreamland's real GDP is $30 million, does Dreamland have a structural surplus or deficit? What is its size? Explain why.
e. If Dreamland's real GDP is $50 million, does Dreamland have a structural surplus or deficit? What is its size? Explain why.

6. In problem 5, if Dreamland's real GDP is $50 million,
a. What is the government's budget balance?
b. Does Dreamland have a structural surplus? What is its size? Explain why.
c. What is the government's budget balance if potential GDP is $30 million?
d. If Dreamland's potential GDP is $30 million, does Dreamland have a structural surplus or deficit? What is its size? Explain why.
e. What would Dreamland's real GDP have to be for it to have neither a structural deficit or surplus nor a cyclical deficit or surplus if its potential GDP is $40 million?

CRITICAL THINKING

1. Study *Reading Between the Lines* on pp. 574–575 and then
a. Describe the overall plan for revenues and expenditures through 2008. Are government revenues and spending projected to increase as a percentage of GDP?
b. Do you think the government is planning a large enough budget surplus?
c. What do you predict would happen to aggregate demand if instead of spending, the government cut taxes to eliminate the "planning surplus"?
d. Suppose the government were to increase spending and turn its surplus into a deficit. What do you predict would be the short-run and long-run effects of such an action?

2. Thinking about the supply-side effects of the 2003 budget,
a. What would be the main effects of lower income tax rates on the level of potential GDP?
b. How would lower income taxes influence the real wage rate and the real interest rate?
c. What are the main costs of lower income taxes?

WEB EXERCISES

1. Use the link on the Parkin–Bade Web site to visit the Department of Finance and obtain data on the current federal budget. Use the information that you find, together with the fiscal policy multiplier analysis that you've learned about in this chapter, to predict the effects of the Canadian budget on real GDP and the price level. Explain reasons for your predictions.

2. Use the link on the Parkin–Bade Web site to visit Statistics Canada and obtain the most recent data you can find on the revenues, outlays, and budget surplus or deficit for Canada and for the province in which you live.
a. What are the main features of the two sets of budget data?
b. What are the main trends in the budget data?
c. Predict the effects of your province's budget on provincial GDP.

MONEY, BANKING, AND INTEREST RATES

CHAPTER 25

Money Makes the World Go Around

Money, like fire and the wheel, has been around for a long time. Wampum (beads made from shells) was used as money by the First Nations of North America, and tobacco was used by early American colonists. Today, we use coins, bills, cheques, and debit and credit cards. Tomorrow, we'll use "smart cards" that keep track of spending. Are all these things money? ◆ When we deposit some coins or notes into a bank, is that still money? ◆ There are enough coins and Bank of Canada notes circulating today for every Canadian to have a wallet stuffed with more than $1,000. In addition, there is enough money deposited in banks and other financial institutions for every Canadian to have a deposit of more than $20,000. Why do we hold all this money? During 2001 and 2002, interest rates fell. What determines interest rates and what makes them fall or rise?

◆ In this chapter, you'll study the functions of money, how banks and other financial institutions create money, and how interest rates are determined. At the end of the chapter, in *Reading Between the Lines*, we'll see how the growth in the use of debit cards and credit cards and the surprisingly small effect these electronic payment mehtods are having on the amount of currency we use.

After studying this chapter, you will be able to

- **Define money and describe its functions**
- **Explain the economic functions of banks and other depository institutions**
- **Describe some financial innovations that have changed the way we use money**
- **Explain how banks create money**
- **Explain what determines the demand for money**
- **Explain how interest rates are determined**
- **Explain how interest rates influence expenditure plans**

What Is Money?

WHAT DO WAMPUM, TOBACCO, AND NICKELS AND dimes have in common? Why are they all examples of money? To answer these questions, we need a definition of money. **Money** is any commodity or token that is generally acceptable as the means of payment. A **means of payment** is a method of settling a debt. When a payment has been made, there is no remaining obligation between the parties to a transaction. So what wampum, tobacco, and nickels and dimes have in common is that they have served (or still do serve) as the means of payment. But money has three other functions:

- Medium of exchange
- Unit of account
- Store of value

Medium of Exchange

A *medium of exchange* is an object that is generally accepted in exchange for goods and services. Money acts as such a medium. Without money, it would be necessary to exchange goods and services directly for other goods and services—an exchange called **barter.** For example, if you want to buy a hamburger, you offer the paperback novel you've just finished reading in exchange for it. Barter requires a *double coincidence of wants*, a situation that occurs when Erika wants to buy what Kazia wants to sell and Kazia wants to buy what Erika wants to sell. To get your hamburger, you must find someone who's selling hamburgers and who wants your paperback novel. Money guarantees that there is a double coincidence of wants because people with something to sell will always accept money in exchange for it. Money acts as a lubricant that smoothes the mechanism of exchange.

Unit of Account

A *unit of account* is an agreed measure for stating the prices of goods and services. To get the most out of your budget, you have to figure out whether seeing one more movie is worth its opportunity cost. But that cost is not dollars and cents. It is the number of ice-cream cones, cans of pop, or phone calls that you must give up. It's easy to do such calculations when all these goods have prices in terms of dollars and cents (see Table 25.1). If a movie costs $6 and a six-pack of pop costs $3, you know right away that seeing one more movie costs you 2 six-packs of pop. If jelly beans are

TABLE 25.1   The Unit of Account Function of Money Simplifies Price Comparisons

Good	Price in money units	Price in units of another good
Movie	$6.00 each	2 six-packs of pop
Pop	$3.00 per six-pack	2 ice-cream cones
Ice cream	$1.50 per cone	3 packs of jelly beans
Jelly beans	50¢ per pack	2 local phone calls
Phone call	25¢ per call	1/2 pack of jelly beans

Money as a unit of account: The price of a movie is $6 and the price of a local phone call is 25¢, so the opportunity cost of a movie is 24 local phone calls ($6.00 ÷ 25¢ = 24).

No unit of account: You go to a movie theatre and learn that the price of a movie is 2 six-packs of pop. You go to a candy store and learn that a pack of jelly beans costs 2 local phone calls. But how many phone calls does seeing a movie cost you? To answer that question, you go to the convenience store and find that a six-pack of pop costs 2 ice-cream cones. Now you head for the ice-cream shop, where an ice-cream cone costs 3 packs of jelly beans. Now you get out your pocket calculator: 1 movie costs 2 six-packs of pop, or 4 ice-cream cones, or 12 packs of jelly beans, or 24 phone calls!

50¢ a pack, one more movie costs 12 packs of jelly beans. You need only one calculation to figure out the opportunity cost of any pair of goods and services.

But imagine how troublesome it would be if your local movie theatre posted its price as 2 six-packs of pop, and if the convenience store posted the price of a six-pack of pop as 2 ice-cream cones, and if the ice-cream shop posted the price of a cone as 3 packs of jelly beans, and if the candy store priced a pack of jelly beans as 2 local phone calls! Now how much running around and calculating would you have to do to figure out how much that movie is going to cost you in terms of the pop, ice cream, jelly beans, or phone calls that you must give up to see it? You get the answer for pop right away from the sign posted at the movie theatre. But for all the other goods you'd have to visit many different stores to establish the price of each commodity in terms of another and then calculate prices in units that are relevant for your own decision. Cover up the column labelled "price in money units" in Table 25.1 and see how hard it is to figure out the number of local phone calls it costs to see one movie. It's enough to make a person swear off movies! How much simpler it is if all the prices are expressed in dollars and cents.

Store of Value

Any commodity or token that can be held and exchanged later for goods and services is called a *store of value*. Money acts as a store of value. If it did not, it would not be acceptable in exchange for goods and services. The more stable the value of a commodity or token, the better it can act as a store of value and the more useful it is as money. No store of value is completely safe. The value of a physical object—such as a house, a car, or a work of art—fluctuates over time. The values of commodities and tokens used as money also fluctuate, and when there is inflation, they persistently fall in value.

Money in Canada Today

In Canada today, money consists of

■ Currency

■ Deposits at banks and other financial institutions

Currency The coins and Bank of Canada notes that we use today are known as **currency.** Currency is money because the government declares it to be so. Look at a Bank of Canada note and notice the words

"CE BILLET A COURS LÉGAL—THIS NOTE IS LEGAL TENDER."

Currency is the most convenient type of money for settling small debts and buying low-priced items.

Deposits Deposits at banks and other financial institutions are also money. Deposits are money because they can be converted into currency and because they are used to settle debts. When you write a cheque or use a debit card, you are telling your bank to transfer money from your account to the account of the person from whom you are buying. Bank deposits are the most convenient type of money for settling large debts and buying big-ticket items.

Official Measures of Money There is no unique measure of money. The two main measures used in Canada today are M1 and M2+. Figure 25.1 shows the items that make up these two measures. **M1** con-

sists of currency held outside the banks plus demand deposits at chartered banks that are owned by individuals and businesses. M1 does *not* include currency held by banks, and it does not include currency and bank deposits owned by the government of Canada. **M2+** consists of M1 plus personal savings deposits and nonpersonal notice deposits at chartered banks plus all types of deposits at trust and mortgage loan companies, credit unions, caisses populaires, and other financial institutions.

FIGURE 25.1 Two Measures of Money

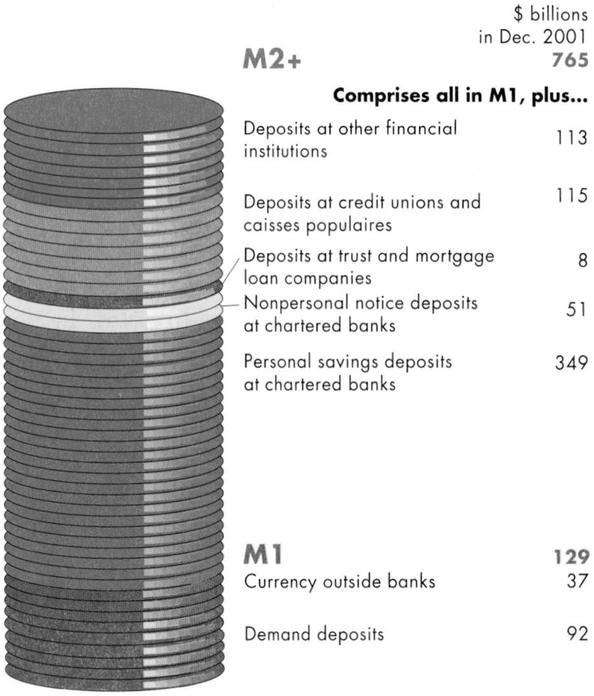

$ billions in Dec. 2001

M2+ 765

Comprises all in M1, plus...

Deposits at other financial institutions	113
Deposits at credit unions and caisses populaires	115
Deposits at trust and mortgage loan companies	8
Nonpersonal notice deposits at chartered banks	51
Personal savings deposits at chartered banks	349

M1	129
Currency outside banks	37
Demand deposits	92

M1 ■ Currency held outside banks

■ Demand deposits at chartered banks that are owned by individuals and businesses

M2+ ■ M1

■ Personal savings deposits at chartered banks

■ Nonpersonal notice deposits at chartered banks

■ Deposits at trust and mortgage loan companies

■ Deposits at credit unions and caisses populaires

■ Deposits at other financial institutions

Source: Bank of Canada, *Banking and Financial Statistics*, table E1.

Are M1 and M2+ Really Money? Money is the means of payment. So the test of whether an item is money is whether it serves as a means of payment. Currency passes the test. But what about deposits? Deposit accounts on which cheques can be written are money because they can be transferred from one person to another by writing a cheque. Transferring a deposit is equivalent to handing over currency. Because M1 consists of currency plus demand deposits and each of these is a means of payment, M1 *is money.*

But what about M2+? Some of the savings deposits in M2+ are just as much a means of payment as the demand deposits in M1. You can use the automated teller machine (ATM) at the grocery store checkout or gas station and transfer funds directly from your savings account to pay for your purchase. But other savings deposits are not means of payment. They are known as *liquid assets.* **Liquidity** is the property of being instantly convertible into a means of payment with little loss in value. Because most of the deposits in M2+ are quickly and easily converted into currency or demand deposits, they are operationally similar to M1, but they are not means of payment.

Deposits Are Money but Cheques Are Not In defining money, we include, along with currency, deposits at banks and other financial institutions. But we do not count the cheques that people write as money. Why are deposits money and cheques not?

To see why deposits are money but cheques are not, think about what happens when Colleen buys some roller blades for $200 from Rocky's Rollers. When Colleen goes to Rocky's shop, she has $500 in her deposit account at the Laser Bank. Rocky has $1,000 in his deposit account—at the same bank, as it happens. The total deposits of these two people are $1,500. Colleen writes a cheque for $200. Rocky takes the cheque to the bank and deposits it. Rocky's bank balance rises from $1,000 to $1,200 and Colleen's balance falls from $500 to $300. The total deposits of Colleen and Rocky are still the same as before: $1,500. Rocky now has $200 more and Colleen has $200 less.

This transaction has transferred money from Colleen to Rocky. The cheque itself was never money. There wasn't an extra $200 worth of money while the cheque was in circulation. The cheque instructs the bank to transfer money from Colleen to Rocky.

If Colleen and Rocky use different banks, there is an extra step. Rocky's bank credits the cheque to Rocky's account and then takes the cheque to a cheque-clearing centre. The cheque is then sent to Colleen's bank, which pays Rocky's bank $200 and debits Colleen's account $200. This process can take a few days, but the principles are the same as when two people use the same bank.

Debit Cards Are Not Money So cheques are not money. But what about debit cards? Isn't presenting a debit card to pay for your roller blades the same thing as using money? Why aren't debit cards counted as part of the quantity of money?

A debit card works just like a cheque, which, as you've seen, is not money. A debit card is like an electronic cheque. When you use a debit card, money leaves your bank account and is deposited into the account of the person from whom you are buying at the instant of the transaction.

Credit Cards Are Not Money Sometimes you need ID and you pull out your driver's licence. Your credit card is another type of ID card—a special ID card that enables you to take a loan at the instant you buy something. When you sign a credit card sales slip, you are saying: "I agree to pay for these goods when the credit card company bills me." Once you get your statement from the credit card company, you must make the minimum payment due (or clear your balance). To make that payment you need money—you need to have currency or a bank deposit to pay the credit card company. So although you use a credit card when you buy something, the credit card is not the *means of payment* and it is not money.

REVIEW QUIZ

1 What makes something money? What functions does money perform? Why do you think packs of chewing gum don't serve as money?
2 What problems arise when a commodity is used as money?
3 What are the main components of money in Canada today?
4 What are two official measures of money in Canada? Are all the measures really money?
5 Why are cheques, debit cards, and credit cards not money?

We've seen that the main component of money in Canada is deposits at banks and other depository institutions. Let's take a closer look at these institutions.

Depository Institutions

A FIRM THAT TAKES DEPOSITS FROM HOUSEHOLDS and firms and makes loans to other households and firms is called a **depository institution**. The deposits of three types of depository institution make up the nation's money:

■ Chartered banks
■ Credit unions and caisses populaires
■ Trust and mortgage loan companies

Chartered Banks

A **chartered bank** is a private firm, chartered under the Bank Act of 1992 to receive deposits and make loans. In 2001, there were 11 Canadian-owned banks and 43 foreign-owned banks chartered by Parliament. In 2001, total deposits at chartered banks were $617 billion. A chartered bank's business is summarized in its balance sheet.

A bank's *balance sheet* lists its assets, liabilities, and net worth. *Assets* are what the bank *owns*, *liabilities* are what the bank *owes*, and *net worth*, which is equal to assets minus liabilities, is the value of the bank to its stockholders—its owners. A bank's balance sheet is described by the equation

$$\text{Liabilities} + \text{Net worth} = \text{Assets}.$$

Among a bank's liabilities are the deposits that are part of the nation's money. Your deposit at the bank is a liability to your bank (and an asset to you) because the bank must repay your deposit (and sometimes interest on it too) whenever you decide to take your money out of the bank.

Profit and Prudence: A Balancing Act The aim of a bank is to maximize the net worth of its stockholders. To achieve this objective, the interest rate at which a bank lends exceeds the interest rate at which it borrows. But a bank must perform a delicate balancing act. Lending is risky, and the more a bank ties up its deposits in high-risk, high-interest rate loans, the bigger is its chance of not being able to repay its depositors. And if depositors perceive a high risk of not being repaid, they withdraw their funds and create a crisis for the bank. So a bank must be prudent in the way it uses its deposits, balancing security for the depositors against profit for its stockholders.

Reserves and Loans To achieve security for its depositors, a bank divides its funds into two parts: reserves and loans. **Reserves** are cash in a bank's vault plus its deposits at the Bank of Canada. (We'll study the Bank of Canada in Chapter 26.) The cash in a bank's vaults is a reserve to meet depositors' demand for currency. The bank replenishes the ATM every time you and your friends raid it for cash for a midnight pizza. The account of a bank at the Bank of Canada is similar to your own bank account. Chartered banks use these accounts to receive and make payments. A chartered bank deposits cash into or draws cash out of its account at the Bank of Canada and writes cheques on that account to settle debts with other banks.

If a bank kept all its deposits as reserves, it wouldn't make any profit. In fact, it keeps only a small fraction of its funds in reserves and lends the rest. A bank has three types of assets:

1. *Liquid assets* are Canadian government Treasury bills and commercial bills. These assets are the banks' first line of defence if they need cash. They can be sold and instantly converted into cash with virtually no risk of loss. Because liquid assets are virtually risk-free, they have a low interest rate.

2. *Investment securities* are longer-term Canadian government bonds and other bonds. These assets can be sold quickly and converted into cash but at prices that fluctuate. Because their prices fluctuate, these assets are riskier than liquid assets but they have a higher interest rate.

3. *Loans* are commitments of fixed amounts of money for agreed-upon periods of time. Most banks' loans are made to corporations to finance the purchase of capital equipment and inventories and to households—personal loans—to finance purchases of consumer durable goods, such as cars or boats. The outstanding balances on credit card accounts are also bank loans. Loans are the riskiest assets of a bank because they cannot be converted into cash until they are due to be repaid. And some borrowers default and never repay. Because they are the riskiest of a bank's assets, loans also carry the highest interest rate.

Chartered bank deposits are one component of the nation's money. But other depository institutions also take deposits that form part—an increasing part—of the nation's money. The largest of these other depository institutions are the credit unions and caisses populaires.

Credit Unions and Caisses Populaires

A **credit union** is a cooperative organization that operates under the Co-operative Credit Association Act of 1992 and that receives deposits from and makes loans to its members. A caisse populaire is a similar type of institution that operates in Quebec. In 2001, the deposits in these institutions were $115 billion.

Trust and Mortgage Loan Companies

A **trust and mortgage loan company** is a privately owned depository institution that operates under the Trust and Loan Companies Act of 1992. It receives deposits and makes loans and in addition acts as a trustee for pension funds and for estates. In 2001, deposits in trust and mortgage loan companies that are included in M2+ were $8 billion.

Financial Legislation

Canada has historically made a sharp legal distinction between banks and other depository institutions. But the economic functions of all depository institutions have grown increasingly similar. This fact is recognized in laws governing these institutions that became effective in 1992. Today, the deposits in other depository institutions approach the same magnitude as those of the chartered banks. For example, the deposits in depository institutions such as trust and mortgage loan companies, credit unions, and caisses populaires were 31 percent of the M2+ definition of money in 1970 but 37 percent in 2001.

Paul Martin's Reform Proposal Former Finance Minister Paul Martin has proposed a more competitive framework for Canada's depository institutions, foreign banks, and insurance companies. His proposal, outlined in *Reforming Canada's Financial Services Sector: A Framework for the Future,* seeks to promote a more competitive and less regulated Canadian banking and financial system.

If the proposal (or something like it) made headway, chartered banks would be able to form joint ventures and strategic alliances, broaden their investments, and face more streamlined regulation. And the process for reviewing bank mergers would become more open. But chartered banks would face tougher competition from trust companies, credit unions, and foreign banks.

The Economic Functions of Depository Institutions

All depository institutions make a profit from the spread between the interest rate they pay on deposits and the interest rate at which they lend. Why can depository institutions get deposits at a low interest rate and lend at a higher one? What services do they perform that makes their depositors willing to put up with a low interest rate and their borrowers willing to pay a higher one?

Depository institutions provide four main services for which people are willing to pay:

- Creating liquidity
- Minimizing the cost of borrowing
- Minimizing the cost of monitoring borrowers
- Pooling risk

Creating Liquidity Depository institutions create liquidity. *Liquid* assets are those that are easily and with certainty convertible into money. Some of the liabilities of depository institutions are themselves money; others are highly liquid assets.

Depository institutions create liquidity by borrowing short and lending long. Borrowing short means taking deposits but standing ready to repay them on short notice (and even on no notice in the case of demand deposits). Lending long means making loan commitments for a prearranged, and often quite long, period of time. For example, when a person makes a deposit with a trust company, that deposit can be withdrawn at any time. But the trust company makes a lending commitment for perhaps more than 20 years to a homebuyer.

Minimizing the Cost of Borrowing Finding someone from whom to borrow can be a costly business. Imagine how troublesome it would be if there were no depository institutions. A firm that was looking for $1 million to buy a new production plant would probably have to hunt around for several dozen people from whom to borrow in order to acquire enough funds for its capital project. Depository institutions lower those costs. The firm that needs $1 million can go to a single depository institution to obtain those funds. The depository institution has to borrow from a large number of people, but it's not doing that just for this one firm and the $1 million that it wants to borrow. The depository institution can establish an organization that is capable of raising funds from a large number of depositors and can spread the cost of this activity over a large number of borrowers.

Minimizing the Cost of Monitoring Borrowers

Lending money is a risky business. There is always a danger that the borrower may not repay. Firms are the biggest borrowers. They borrow to invest in projects that they hope will return a profit but sometimes those hopes are not fulfilled. Monitoring the activities of a borrower and ensuring that the best possible decisions are being taken to make a profit and to avoid a loss are costly and specialized activities. Imagine how costly it would be if each household that lent money to a firm had to incur the costs of monitoring that firm directly. By depositing funds with a depository institution, households avoid those costs. The depository institution performs the monitoring activity by using specialized resources that have a much lower cost than what each household would incur if it had to undertake the activity individually.

Pooling Risk

As we noted above, lending money is risky. There is always a chance of not being repaid—of default. Lending to a large number of different individuals can reduce the risk of default. In such a situation, if one person defaults on a loan, it is a nuisance but not a disaster. In contrast, if only one person borrows and that person defaults on the loan, the entire loan is a write-off. Depository institutions enable people to pool risk in an efficient way. Thousands of people lend money to any one depository institution, and, in turn, the depository institution re-lends the money to hundreds, perhaps thousands, of individuals and firms. If any one firm defaults on its loan, that default is spread across all the depositors and no individual depositor is left exposed to a high degree of risk.

REVIEW QUIZ

1. What are Canada's main depository institutions?
2. Why don't banks keep all the money that people place on deposit in their vaults?
3. What are the main economic functions of depository institutions?
4. How do depository institutions create liquidity?
5. How do depository institutions pool risk?

How Banks Create Money

BANKS CREATE MONEY.[1] BUT THIS DOESN'T MEAN that they have smoke-filled back rooms in which counterfeiters are busily working. Remember, most money is deposits, not currency. What banks create is deposits, and they do so by making loans. But the amount of deposits they can create is limited by their reserves.

Reserves: Actual and Desired

We've seen that banks don't have $100 in bills for every $100 that people have deposited with them. In fact, a typical bank today has reserves of $1.90 for every $100 of deposits. No need for panic. These reserve levels are adequate for ordinary business needs.

The fraction of a bank's total deposits that are held in reserves is called the **reserve ratio.** The reserve ratio changes when a bank's customers make a deposit or withdrawal. Making a deposit increases the reserve ratio, and making a withdrawal decreases the reserve ratio.

The **desired reserve ratio** is the ratio of reserves to deposits that banks wish to hold. A bank's *desired reserves* are equal to its deposits multiplied by the desired reserve ratio. Actual reserves minus desired reserves are **excess reserves.** Whenever banks have excess reserves, they are able to create money.

To see how banks create money, we'll look at two model banking systems. In the first, there is only one bank; in the second, there are many banks.

Creating Deposits by Making Loans in a One-Bank Economy

In the model banking system that we'll study first, there is only one bank, and its desired reserve ratio is 25 percent. That is, for each dollar deposited, the bank keeps 25¢ in reserves and lends the rest. The balance sheet of the One-and-Only Bank is shown in Fig. 25.2(a). On January 1, its deposits are $400 million and its reserves are 25 percent of this amount—$100 million. Its loans are equal to deposits minus reserves and are $300 million.

---

[1] In this section, we'll use the term *bank* to refer to any type of depository institution whose deposits are money—chartered banks, credit unions, caisses populaires, and trust and mortgage loan companies.

The story begins when Darth Vader retires and begins his quiet life in Winnipeg. He has been holding all his money in currency and has $1 million in Canadian money. On January 2, Darth puts his $1 million on deposit at the One-and-Only Bank. On the day that Darth makes his deposit, the One-and-Only Bank's balance sheet changes. The new situation is shown in Fig. 25.2(b). The bank now has $101 million in reserves and $401 million in deposits. It still has loans of $300 million.

FIGURE 25.2 Creating Money at the One-and-Only Bank

(a) Balance sheet on January 1

Assets (millions of dollars)		Liabilities (millions of dollars)	
Reserves	$100	Deposits	$400
Loans	$300		
Total	$400	Total	$400

(b) Balance sheet on January 2

Assets (millions of dollars)		Liabilities (millions of dollars)	
Reserves	$101	Deposits	$401
Loans	$300		
Total	$401	Total	$401

(c) Balance sheet on January 3

Assets (millions of dollars)		Liabilities (millions of dollars)	
Reserves	$101	Deposits	$404
Loans	$303		
Total	$404	Total	$404

In part (a) the One-and-Only Bank has deposits of $400 million, loans of $300 million, and reserves of $100 million. The bank's desired reserve ratio is 25 percent. When the bank receives a deposit of $1 million (part b), it has excess reserves. It lends $3 million and creates a further $3 million of deposits. Deposits increase by $3 million, and loans increase by $3 million (in part c). The bank has no excess reserves.

The bank now has *excess reserves*. With reserves of $101 million and a desired reserve ratio of 25 percent, the bank would like to have deposits of $404 million. Because the One-and-Only Bank is the only bank, the manager knows that the reserves will remain at $101 million. That is, she knows that when she makes a loan and creates a deposit, the amount lent remains on deposit at the One-and-Only Bank. She knows, for example, that all the suppliers of Sky's-the-Limit Construction are also depositors of One-and-Only. So she knows that if she makes the loan that Sky's-the-Limit has just requested, the deposit she creates will never leave One-and-Only. When Sky's-the-Limit uses part of its new loan to pay $100,000 to I-Dig-It Excavating Company for some excavations, the One-and-Only Bank simply moves the funds from Sky's-the-Limit's account to I-Dig-It's account.

So on January 3, the manager of One-and-Only calls Sky's-the-Limit's accountant and offers to lend the maximum that she can. How much does she lend? She lends $3 million. By lending $3 million, One-and-Only's balance sheet changes to the one shown in Fig. 25.2(c). Loans increase by $3 million to $303 million. The loan shows up in Sky's-the-Limit's deposit initially, and total deposits increase to $404 million—$400 million plus Darth Vader's deposit of $1 million plus the newly created deposit of $3 million. The bank now has no excess reserves and has reached the limit of its ability to create money.

The Deposit Multiplier

The **deposit multiplier** is the amount by which an increase in bank reserves is multiplied to calculate the increase in bank deposits. That is,

$$\text{Deposit multiplier} = \frac{\text{Change in deposits}}{\text{Change in reserves}}.$$

In the example we've just worked through, the deposit multiplier is 4. The $1 million increase in reserves created a $4 million increase in deposits.

The deposit multiplier is linked to the desired reserve ratio by the following equation:

$$\text{Deposit multiplier} = \frac{1}{\text{Desired reserve ratio}}.$$

In the example, the desired reserve ratio is 25 percent, or 0.25. That is,

$$\text{Deposit multiplier} = \frac{1}{0.25}$$

$$= 4.$$

Creating Deposits by Making Loans with Many Banks

If you told the loans officer at your own bank that she creates money, she wouldn't believe you. Bankers see themselves as lending the money they receive from others, not creating money. But in fact, even though each bank lends only what it receives, the banking *system* creates money. To see how, let's look at another example.

Figure 25.3 is going to keep track of what is happening in the process of money creation by a banking system in which each bank has a desired reserve ratio of 25 percent. The process begins when Art decides to decrease his currency holding and put $100,000 on deposit. Now Art's bank has $100,000 of new deposits and $100,000 of additional reserves. With a desired reserve ratio of 25 percent, the bank keeps $25,000 in reserves and lends $75,000 to Amy. Amy writes a cheque for $75,000 to buy a copy-shop franchise from Barb. At this point, Art's bank has a new deposit of $100,000, new loans of $75,000, and new reserves of $25,000. You can see this situation in Fig. 25.3 as the first row of the "running tally."

For Art's bank, that is the end of the story. But it's not the end of the story for the entire banking system. Barb deposits her cheque for $75,000 in another bank and its deposits and reserves increase by $75,000. This bank keeps 25 percent of its increase in deposits ($18,750) in reserves and lends $56,250 to Bob. And Bob writes a cheque to Carl to pay off a business loan. The current state of play is seen in the second row of the running tally in Fig. 25.3. Now total bank reserves have increased by $43,750 ($25,000 plus $18,750), total loans have increased by $131,250 ($75,000 plus $56,250), and total deposits have increased by $175,000 ($100,000 plus $75,000).

When Carl takes his cheque to his bank, its deposits and reserves increase by $56,250, $14,063 of which it keeps in reserve and $42,187 of which it lends. This process continues until there are no excess reserves in the banking system. But the process takes a lot of further steps. One additional step is shown in Fig. 25.3. The figure also shows the final tallies—

reserves increase by $100,000, loans increase by $300,000, and deposits increase by $400,000.

The sequence in Fig. 25.3 is the first four stages of the process. To figure out the entire process, look closely at the numbers in the figure. At each stage, the loan is 75 percent (0.75) of the previous loan and the deposit is 0.75 of the previous deposit. Call that proportion L ($L = 0.75$). The complete sequence is

$$1 + L + L^2 + L^3 + \dots .$$

Remember, L is a fraction, so at each stage in this sequence the amount of new loans gets smaller. The total number of loans made at the end of the process is the above sum, which is[2]

$$\frac{1}{(1 - L)}.$$

If we use the numbers from the example, the total increase in deposits is

$$\$100,000 + 75,000 + 56,250 + 42,187 + \dots$$

$$= \$100,000 \,(1 + 0.75 + 0.5625 + 0.42187 + \dots)$$

$$= \$100,000 \,(1 + 0.75 + 0.75^2 + 0.75^3 + \dots)$$

$$= \$100,000 \times \frac{1}{(1 - 0.75)}$$

$$= \$100,000 \times \frac{1}{(0.25)}$$

$$= \$100,000 \times 4$$

$$= \$400,000$$

By using the same method, you can check that the totals for reserves and loans are the ones shown in Fig. 25.3.

---

[2] Both here and in the expenditure multiplier process in Chapter 23, the sequence of values is called a convergent geometric series. To find the sum of a series such as this, begin by calling the sum S. Then write the sum as

$$S = 1 + L + L^2 + L^3 + \dots .$$

Multiply by L to get,

$$LS = L + L^2 + L^3 + \dots$$

and then subtract the second equation from the first to get

$$S(1 - L) = 1$$

or

$$S = \frac{1}{(1 - L)}.$$

FIGURE 25.3 The Multiple Creation of Bank Deposits

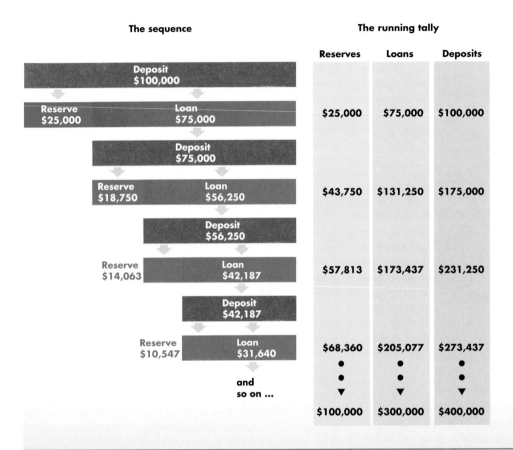

	Reserves	Loans	Deposits
	$25,000	$75,000	$100,000
	$43,750	$131,250	$175,000
	$57,813	$173,437	$231,250
	$68,360	$205,077	$273,437
	$100,000	$300,000	$400,000

When a bank receives a deposit, it keeps 25 percent of it in reserves and lends the other 75 percent. The amount lent becomes a new deposit at another bank. The next bank in the sequence keeps 25 percent and lends 75 percent, and the process continues until the banking system has created enough deposits to eliminate its excess reserves. The running tally tells us the total amounts of deposits and loans created at each stage. At the end of the process, an additional $100,000 of reserves creates an additional $400,000 of deposits.

So even though each bank lends only part of the money it receives, the banking system as a whole creates money by making loans. The amount created is exactly the same in a multibank system as in a one-bank system.

The Deposit Multiplier in Canada The deposit multiplier in Canada works like the deposit multiplier we've just worked out for a model economy. But the deposit multiplier in Canada differs from the one we've just calculated for two reasons. First, the desired reserve ratio of Canadian banks is smaller than the 25 percent we used here. Second, not all the loans made by banks return to them in the form of reserves. Some of the loans remain outside the banks and are held as currency. The smaller desired reserve ratio makes the Canadian multiplier larger than the multiplier in the above example. But the other factor makes the Canadian multiplier smaller.

REVIEW QUIZ

1 How do banks create deposits by making loans, and what are the factors that limit the amount of deposits and loans that banks can create?

2 A bank manager tells you that he doesn't create money. He just lends the money that people deposit in the bank. How do you explain to him that he's wrong and that he does create money?

3 If banks receive new deposits of $100 million, what determines the total change in deposits that the banking system can create?

We've now seen how banks create money. Money has a powerful influence on the economy and this influence begins with interest rates. To understand how money influences interest rates, we must study the demand for money.

The Demand for Money

THE AMOUNT OF MONEY WE RECEIVE EACH WEEK in payment for our labour is income—a flow. The amount of money that we hold in our wallet or in a deposit account at the bank is an inventory—a stock. There is no limit to how much income we would like to receive each week. But there is a limit to how big an inventory of money each of us would like to hold on to and not spend.

The Influences on Money Holding

The quantity of money that people choose to hold depends on four main factors:

■ The price level
■ The interest rate
■ Real GDP
■ Financial innovation

The Price Level The quantity of money measured in dollars is *nominal money*. The quantity of nominal money demanded is proportional to the price level, other things remaining the same. That is, if the price level rises by 10 percent, people hold 10 percent more nominal money than before, other things remaining the same. If you hold $20 to buy your weekly movies and pop, you will increase your money holding to $22 if the prices of movies and pop—and your wage rate—increase by 10 percent.

The quantity of money measured in constant dollars (for example, in 1997 dollars) is called *real money*. Real money is equal to nominal money divided by the price level. It is the quantity of money measured in terms of what it will buy. In the above example, when the price level rises by 10 percent and you increase the amount of money that you hold by 10 percent, you keep your *real* money constant. Your $22 at the new price level buys the same quantity of goods and is the same quantity of *real money* as your $20 at the original price level. The quantity of real money held does not depend on the price level.

The Interest Rate A fundamental principle of economics is that as the opportunity cost of something increases, people try to find substitutes for it. Money is no exception. The higher the opportunity cost of holding money, other things remaining the same, the smaller is the quantity of real money

demanded. But what is the opportunity cost of holding money? It is the interest rate that you must forgo on other assets that you could hold instead of money minus the interest rate that you can earn by holding money.

The interest rate that you earn on currency and demand deposits is zero. So the opportunity cost of holding these items is the interest rate on other assets such as a savings bond or Treasury bill. By holding money instead, you forgo the interest that you otherwise would have received. This forgone interest is the opportunity cost of holding money.

Money loses value because of inflation. So why isn't the inflation rate part of the cost of holding money? It is: Other things remaining the same, the higher the expected inflation rate, the higher are all interest rates and the higher, therefore, is the opportunity cost of holding money. The forces that make the interest rate change to reflect changes in the expected inflation rate are described in Chapter 28, pp. 666–667.)

Real GDP The quantity of money that households and firms plan to hold depends on the amount they are spending, and the quantity of money demanded in the economy as a whole depends on aggregate expenditure—real GDP.

Again, suppose that you hold an average of $20 to finance your weekly purchases of movies and pop. Now imagine that the prices of these goods and of all other goods remain constant but that your income increases. As a consequence you now spend more, and you keep a larger amount of money on hand to finance your higher volume of expenditure.

Financial Innovation Technological change and the arrival of new financial products—called **financial innovation**—change the quantity of money held. The major financial innovations are the widespread use of

1. Daily interest deposits
2. Automatic transfers between demand deposits and savings deposits
3. Automatic teller machines
4. Credit cards and debit cards

These innovations have occurred because the development of computing power has lowered the cost of calculations and record keeping.

We summarize the effects of the influences on money holding by using a demand for money curve.

The Demand for Money Curve

The **demand for money curve** is the relationship between the quantity of real money demanded and the interest rate when all other influences on the amount of money that people wish to hold remain the same.

Figure 25.4 shows a demand for money curve, *MD*. When the interest rate rises, everything else remaining the same, the opportunity cost of holding money rises and the quantity of real money demanded decreases—there is a movement along the demand for money curve. Similarly, when the interest rate falls, the opportunity cost of holding money falls, and the quantity of real money demanded increases—there is a movement down along the demand for money curve.

When any influence on the amount of money that people plan to hold changes, there is a change in the demand for money and the demand for money curve shifts. Let's study these shifts.

Shifts in the Demand for Money Curve

A change in real GDP or financial innovation changes the demand for money and shifts the demand for money curve. Figure 25.5 illustrates the change in the demand for money. A decrease in real GDP decreases the demand for money and shifts the demand curve leftward from MD_0 to MD_1. An increase in real GDP has the opposite effect. It increases the demand for money and shifts the demand curve rightward from MD_0 to MD_2.

The influence of financial innovation on the demand for money curve is more complicated. It might increase the demand for some types of deposits, decrease the demand for others, and decrease the demand for currency.

We'll look at the effects of changes in real GDP and financial innovation by studying the demand for money in Canada.

FIGURE 25.4 The Demand for Money

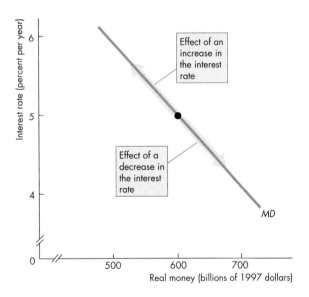

The demand for money curve, *MD*, shows the relationship between the quantity of real money that people plan to hold and the interest rate, other things remaining the same. The interest rate is the opportunity cost of holding money. A change in the interest rate brings a movement along the demand curve.

FIGURE 25.5 Changes in the Demand for Money

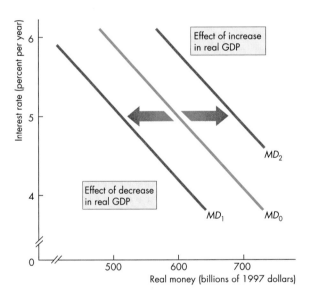

A decrease in real GDP decreases the demand for money. The demand curve shifts leftward from MD_0 to MD_1. An increase in real GDP increases the demand for money. The demand curve shifts rightward from MD_0 to MD_2. Financial innovation decreases the demand for some forms of money and increases the demand for other forms of money.

The Demand for Money in Canada

Figure 25.6 shows the relationship between the interest rate and the quantity of real money demanded in Canada between 1971 and 2001. Each dot shows the interest rate and the amount of real money held in a given year. In part (a), the measure of money is M1 and in part (b), it is M2+. In 1971, the demand for M1 (in part a) was MD_{71}. During the 1970s, real GDP increased by $200 billion, and this increase in real GDP increased the demand for M1 and shifted the demand for M1 curve rightward to MD_{81}. During the 1980s, real GDP increased by $150 billion, but the demand for M1 did not change. The reason is that during the 1980s the increased use of credit cards decreased the demand for M1. The increase in real GDP increased the demand for M1 and financial innovation decreased the demand for M1, so during the 1980s, the demand for M1 did not change. During the 1990s, real GDP increased by $280 billion and the demand for M1 increased again. The demand for M1 curve shifted rightward to MD_{01}.

In 1971, the demand for M2+ (in part b) was MD_{71}. The $200 billion increase in real GDP that occurred during the 1970s increased the demand for M2+ and the demand curve shifted rightward to MD_{81}. The $150 billion increase in real GDP that occurred during the 1980s increased the demand for M2+ and the demand curve shifted rightward. The further $280 billion increase in real GDP that occurred during the 1990s increased the demand for

FIGURE 25.6 The Demand for Money in Canada

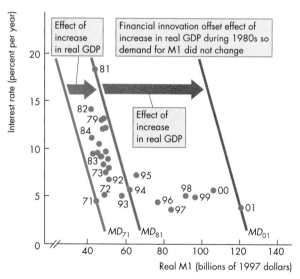

(a) Demand for M1

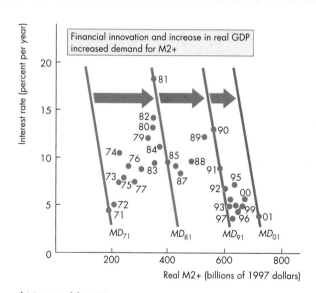

(b) Demand for M2+

The dots show the quantity of real money and the interest rate in each year between 1971 and 2001. In 1971, the demand for M1 was MD_{71} in part (a). The demand for M1 increased during the 1970s because real GDP grew and the demand curve shifted rightward to MD_{81}. The demand for M1 did not increase during the 1980s because financial innovation (mainly the spread of the use of credit cards) offset the effects of real GDP growth. The demand for M1

increased again during the 1990s.

In 1971, the demand for M2+ curve was MD_{71} in part (b). The growth of real GDP increased the demand for M2+ and by 1981 the demand curve had shifted rightward to MD_{81}. Real GDP growth and the development of interest-bearing accounts with cheque facilities further increased the demand for M2+ during the 1990s and the demand for M2+ curve shifted rightward to MD_{01}.

Source: Bank of Canada, *Banking and Financial Statistics*, tables E1 and F1, and authors' calculations and assumptions.

M2+ yet again. By 2001, the demand curve for M2+ had shifted rightward to MD_{01}.

You can see by comparing the two parts of Fig. 25.6 that the financial innovation that decreased the demand for M1 during the 1980s did not slow the growth of M2+. Because M1 is a component of M2+, the increased use of credit cards had the same effect on M2+ as it did on M1. But the development of new types of savings deposits with cheque facilities and the payment of more competitive interest rates on savings accounts increased the demand for M2+.

The opportunity cost of holding money is the interest forgone by not holding some other type of asset. But what is forgone depends partly on the interest that is paid on money itself. The interest rate on currency and demand deposits is zero. So for these components of money, the opportunity cost of holding money is the interest rate on non-money assets. But savings deposits and other types of deposits that are included in M2+ earn interest. So the opportunity cost of holding these forms of money is the interest rate on non-money assets minus the interest rate on these deposits.

REVIEW QUIZ

1 What are the main influences on the quantity of real money that people and businesses plan to hold?
2 What does the demand for money curve show?
3 How does an increase in the interest rate change the quantity of money demanded, and how would you use the demand for money curve to show the effects?
4 How does an increase in real GDP change the demand for money, and how would you use the demand for money curve to show the effects?
5 How have financial innovations changed the demand for M1 and the demand for M2+?

We now know what determines the demand for money. And we've seen that a key factor is the interest rate—the opportunity cost of holding money. But what determines the interest rate? Let's find out.

Interest Rate Determination

AN INTEREST RATE IS THE PERCENTAGE YIELD ON a financial security such as a *bond* or a *stock*. The **interest rate** is the amount received by a lender and paid by a borrower expressed as a percentage of the amount of the loan.

A bond is a promise to make a sequence of future payments. There are many different possible sequences but the simplest one is the case of a bond called a perpetuity. A *perpetuity* is a bond that promises to pay a specified fixed amount of money each year forever. The issuer of such a bond will never buy the bond back (redeem it); the bond will remain outstanding forever and will earn a fixed dollar payment each year. Because the payment each year is a fixed dollar amount, the interest rate on a bond varies as the price of the bond varies. In the case of a perpetuity, the formula that links the interest rate to the price of the bond is a particularly simple one. That formula is

$$\text{Interest rate} = \frac{\text{Dollar payment per year}}{\text{Price of bond}} \times 100.$$

This formula states that the higher the price of a bond, other things remaining the same, the lower is the interest rate. An example will make this relationship clear. Suppose the government of Canada sells a bond that promises to pay $10 a year. If the price of the bond is $100, the interest rate is 10 percent a year—$10 is 10 percent of $100. If the price of the bond is $50, the interest rate is 20 percent a year—$10 is 20 percent of $50. If the price of the bond is $200, the interest rate is 5 percent a year—$10 is 5 percent of $200.

You've just seen the link between the price of a bond and the interest rate. Because of this link, fluctuations in the interest rate bring fluctuations in the price of a bond. People try to anticipate these fluctuations and avoid holding bonds when they expect the price of a bond to fall. But they spread their risks. To do so, they divide their wealth between bonds (and other interest-bearing financial assets) and money, and the amount they hold as money depends on the interest rate. We can study the forces that determine the interest rate either in the market for bonds or the market for money. Because the Bank of Canada can influence the quantity of *money* (which we study in Chapter 26), we focus on the market for money.

Money Market Equilibrium

The supply of and the demand for money determine the interest rate. The actions of the Bank of Canada and the banking system determine the quantity of money supplied. On any given day, the quantity of money supplied is fixed. The quantity of *real* money supplied is equal to the nominal quantity supplied divided by the price level. At a given moment in time, there is a particular price level, and so the quantity of real money supplied is also a fixed amount. In Fig. 25.7, the quantity of real money supplied is $600 billion and the vertical line labelled *MS* is the supply of money curve.

On any given day, all the influences on the demand for money except for the interest rate are constant. But the lower the interest rate, the greater

is the quantity of money demanded. Figure 25.7 shows a demand for money curve, *MD*.

Equilibrium When the quantity of money supplied equals the quantity of money demanded, the money market is in equilibrium. Figure 25.7 illustrates equilibrium in the money market. Equilibrium is achieved by changes in the interest rate. If the interest rate is too high, people demand a smaller quantity of money than the quantity supplied. They are holding too much money. In this situation, they try to get rid of money by buying bonds. As they do so, the price of a bond rises and the interest rate falls to the equilibrium rate. Conversely, if the interest rate is too low, people demand a larger quantity of money than the quantity supplied. They are holding too little money. In this situation, they try to get more money by selling bonds. As they do so, the price of a bond falls and the interest rate rises to the equilibrium rate. Only when the interest rate is at the level at which people are holding the quantity of money supplied do they willingly hold the money and take no actions that change the interest rate.

Influencing the Interest Rate

Imagine that the economy is slowing down and the Bank of Canada wants to increase aggregate demand. To do so, it wants to lower the interest rate and encourage more borrowing and more expenditure on goods and services. What does the Bank of Canada do? How does it fiddle with the knobs to achieve a lower interest rate?

The answer is that the Bank of Canada changes the quantity of money in the economy. Chapter 26 (pp. 610–615) explains *how* the Bank of Canada changes the quantity of money. Here, we study the *effects* of a change in the quantity of money.

Suppose that initially, the quantity of real money is $600 billion. In Fig. 25.8, the supply of money curve is MS_0. With the demand for money given by the curve *MD*, the equilibrium interest rate is 5 percent a year.

Now suppose that the quantity of real money increases to $700 billion. The supply of money curve shifts rightward from MS_0 to MS_1. At an interest rate of 5 percent a year, people are now holding more money than they would like to hold. They attempt to decrease their money holding by buying bonds. As they do so, the price of a bond rises and the interest rate falls. When the interest rate has fallen to 3 percent

FIGURE 25.7 Money Market Equilibrium

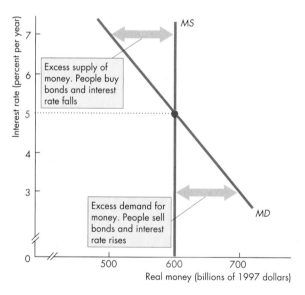

Money market equilibrium occurs when the interest rate has adjusted to make the quantity of money demanded equal to the quantity supplied. Here, equilibrium occurs at an interest rate of 5 percent a year. At interest rates above 5 percent a year, the quantity of money demanded is less than the quantity supplied, so people buy bonds, and the interest rate falls. At interest rates below 5 percent a year, the quantity of real money demanded exceeds the quantity supplied, so people sell bonds and the interest rate rises. Only at 5 percent a year is the quantity of real money in existence willingly held.

a year, people are willing to hold the greater $700 billion quantity of real money.

Conversely, suppose that the economy is overheating and the Bank of Canada fears inflation. The Bank decides to take action to decrease aggregate demand. In this case, the Bank decreases the quantity of real money. Suppose that the Bank decreases the quantity of real money from the initial quantity of $600 billion to $500 billion. Now, in Fig. 25.8, the supply of money curve shifts leftward from MS_0 to MS_2. At an interest rate of 5 percent a year, people are now holding less money than they would like to hold. They attempt to increase their money holding by selling bonds. As they do so, the price of a bond falls and the interest rate rises. When the interest rate has risen to 7 percent, people are willing to hold the smaller $500 billion quantity of real money.

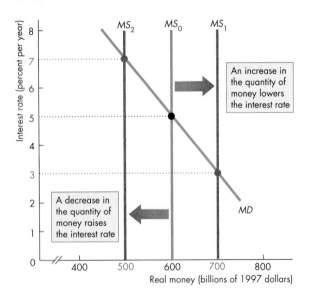

FIGURE 25.8 Interest Rate Changes

Initially, the quantity of real money is $600 billion and the interest rate is 5 percent a year. When the Bank of Canada increases the quantity of real money to $700 billion, the supply of money curve shifts rightward to MS_1 and the interest rate falls to 3 percent a year. When the Bank of Canada decreases the quantity of real money to $500 billion, the supply of money curve shifts leftward to MS_2 and the interest rate rises to 7 percent a year.

Influencing the Exchange Rate

The **exchange rate** is the price at which the Canadian dollar exchanges for another currency. For example, in October 2002, a Canadian dollar cost 63 U.S. cents. So the exchange rate at that time was 63 U.S. cents per Canadian dollar. The exchange rate is the price of the Canadian dollar determined by demand and supply in the global foreign exchange market. This market is described and studied in detail in Chapter 34 on pp. 815–823. Here, we'll look only at the influence of the interest rate on the exchange rate.

The interest rate that can be earned by moving funds into Canada is a key influence on the demand for Canadian dollars. People are constantly seeking the highest interest rate available, and when the interest rate that can be earned in one country rises with all other interest rates remaining the same, people move funds into that country. But to move funds into Canada, people must buy Canadian dollars in the foreign exchange market. And if more funds are moving into Canada, the demand for Canadian dollars increases.

An increase in the demand for Canadian dollars in the foreign exchange market raises the exchange rate. That is, the price of a Canadian dollar rises. So monetary policy actions that change the interest rate also change the exchange rate and in the same direction. Other things remaining the same, a rise in interest rates brings a rise in the exchange rate, and a fall in interest rates brings a fall in the exchange rate.

REVIEW QUIZ

1. What is a bond and what is the relationship between the price of a bond and the interest rate?
2. How is the interest rate determined?
3. What do people do if they are holding *less* money than they plan to hold and what happens to the interest rate?
4. What do people do if they are holding *more* money than they plan to hold and what happens to the interest rate?
5. What happens to the interest rate and the exchange rate if the quantity of money increases or decreases?

Your final task in this chapter is to study the influence of the interest rate on expenditure plans.

The Interest Rate and Expenditure Plans

YOU'VE SEEN THAT THE INTEREST RATE AFFECTS the quantity of money that people plan to hold. The interest rate also influences people's spending decisions. The reason is the same in both cases. The interest rate is an opportunity cost. But the interest rate that is relevant for the money holding decision is not quite the same as the interest rate that is relevant for a spending decision. Let's find out why.

Nominal Interest and Real Interest

We distinguish between two interest rates: the nominal interest rate and the real interest rate. The **nominal interest rate** is the percentage return on an asset such as a bond expressed in terms of money. It is the interest rate that is quoted in everyday transactions and news reports. The **real interest rate** is the percentage return on an asset expressed in terms of what money will buy. It is the nominal interest rate adjusted for inflation and is approximately equal to the nominal interest rate minus the inflation rate.

Suppose that the nominal interest rate is 10 percent a year and the inflation rate is 4 percent a year. The real interest rate is 6 percent a year—10 percent minus 4 percent.[3]

To see why the real interest rate is 6 percent, think about the following example. Jackie lends Joe $1,000 for one year. At the end of the year, Joe repays Jackie the $1,000 plus interest. At 10 percent a year, the interest is $100, so Jackie receives $1,100 from Joe.

Because of inflation, the money that Joe uses to repay Jackie is worth less than the money that Jackie originally lent to Joe. At an inflation rate of 4 percent a year, Jackie needs an extra $40 a year to compensate her for the fall in the value of money. So when Joe repays the loan, Jackie needs $1,040 to buy the same items that she could have bought for $1,000 when she made the loan. Because Joe pays Jackie $1,100, the interest that she *really* earns is $60, which is 6 percent of the $1,000 that she lent to Joe.

---

[3] The exact calculation allows for the change in the purchasing power of the interest as well as the amount of the loan. To calculate the *exact* real interest rate, use the formula: *real interest rate* = (*nominal interest rate* – *inflation rate*) divided by (1 + *inflation rate*/100). If the nominal interest rate is 10 percent and the inflation rate is 4 percent, the real interest rate is $(10 - 4) \div (1 + 0.04) = 5.77$ percent.

Interest Rate and Opportunity Cost

Now that you understand the distinction between the nominal interest rate and the real interest rate, let's think about the effects of interest rates on decisions.

The interest rate influences decisions because it is an opportunity cost. *The nominal interest rate is the opportunity cost of holding money.* And it is the nominal interest rate that is determined by the demand for real money and the supply of real money in the money market. To see why the nominal interest rate is the opportunity cost of holding money, think about the *real* interest rate on money compared with the real interest rate on other financial assets. Money loses value at the inflation rate. So the real interest rate on money equals *minus* the inflation rate. The real interest rate on other financial assets equals the nominal interest rate minus the inflation rate. So the difference between the real interest rate on money and the real interest rate on other financial assets is the nominal interest rate. By holding money rather than some other financial asset, we incur a *real* opportunity cost equal to the nominal interest rate.

The real interest rate is the opportunity cost of spending. Spending more today means spending less in the future. But spending one additional dollar today means cutting future spending by more than a dollar. And the real amount by which future spending must be cut is determined by the *real* interest rate.

A change in the real interest rate changes the opportunity cost of two components of aggregate expenditure:

■ Consumption expenditure
■ Investment

Consumption Expenditure

Other things remaining the same, the lower the real interest rate, the greater is the amount of consumption expenditure and the smaller is the amount of saving.

You can see why the real interest rate influences consumption expenditure and saving by thinking about the effect of the interest rate on a student loan. If the real interest rate on a student loan fell to 1 percent a year, students would be happy to take larger loans and spend more. But if the real interest rate on a student loan jumped to 20 percent a year, students would cut their expenditure, buying cheaper food and finding lower-rent accommodation for example, to pay off their loans as quickly as possible.

The effect of the real interest rate on consumption expenditure is probably not large. It is certainly not as powerful as the effect of disposable income that we studied in Chapter 23 (pp. 528–529). You can think of the real interest rate as influencing *autonomous consumption expenditure* (p. 532). The lower the real interest rate, the greater is autonomous consumption expenditure.

Investment

Other things remaining the same, the lower the real interest rate, the greater is the amount of investment.

The funds used to finance investment might be borrowed, or they might be the financial resources of the firm's owners (the firm's retained earnings). But regardless of the source of the funds, the opportunity cost of the funds is the real interest rate. The real interest paid on borrowed funds is an obvious cost. The real interest rate is also the cost of using retained earnings because these funds could be lent to another firm. The real interest rate forgone is the opportunity cost of using retained earnings to finance an investment project.

To decide whether to invest in new capital, firms compare the real interest rate with the expected profit rate from the investment. For example, suppose that Ford expects to earn 20 percent a year from a new car assembly plant. It is profitable for Ford to invest in this new plant as long as the real interest rate is less than 20 percent a year. That is, at a real interest rate below 20 percent a year, Ford will build this assembly plant; at a real interest rate in excess of 20 percent a year, Ford will not. Some projects are profitable at a high real interest rate, but other projects are profitable only at a low real interest rate. So the higher the real interest rate, the smaller is the number of projects that are worth undertaking and the smaller is the amount of investment.

The interest rate has another effect on expenditure plans—it changes net exports. Let's find out why.

Net Exports and the Interest Rate

Net exports change when the interest rate changes because, other things remaining the same, a change in the interest rate changes the exchange rate.

Net Exports and the Exchange Rate Let's first see why the exchange rate influences exports and imports. When a Canadian buys a Dell PC that is shipped from Texas, the price of the PC equals the U.S. dollar price converted into Canadian dollars. If the PC price is U.S.$2,000, and if the exchange rate is 66.67 U.S. cents per Canadian dollar, the PC price in Canada is $3,000. If the Canadian dollar rises to 75 U.S. cents per Canadian dollar, the PC price in Canada falls to $2,666.67. When the price of a U.S. PC falls, Canadians import more PCs.

Similarly, when a U.S. company buys a Nortel telephone system that is shipped from Ontario, the price of the system equals the Canadian dollar price converted into U.S. dollars. If the price of the telephone system is $6,000, and if the exchange rate is 66.67 U.S. cents per Canadian dollar, the price in the United States is U.S.$4,000. If the Canadian dollar rises to 75 U.S. cents per Canadian dollar, the price of the telephone system in the United States *rises* to $4,500. When the price of a Canadian telephone system rises, Americans buy fewer of them and Canada's exports decrease.

So when the Canadian dollar rises, imports increase, exports decrease, and net exports decrease. Similarly, when the Canadian dollar falls, imports decrease, exports increase, and net exports increase.

The Interest Rate and the Exchange Rate When the interest rate in Canada rises, and other things remain the same, the Canadian dollar exchange rate rises. The reason is that more people move funds into Canada to take advantage of the higher interest rate. But when money flows into Canada, the demand for Canadian dollars increases, so the Canadian dollar exchange rate (the price) rises. And when the interest rate in Canada falls, and other things remain the same, the Canadian dollar exchange rate falls.

Because the interest rate influences the exchange rate, it also influences net exports. A rise in the interest rate decreases net exports and a fall in the interest rate increases net exports, other things remaining the same.

Interest-Sensitive Expenditure Curve

Figure 25.9 illustrates the effects of the real interest rate on expenditure plans and summarizes those effects in the interest-sensitive expenditure curve. The **interest-sensitive expenditure curve** (the *IE* curve) shows the relationship between aggregate expenditure plans and the real interest rate when all other influences on expenditure plans remain the same.

FIGURE 25.9 The Interest Rate and Expenditure Plans

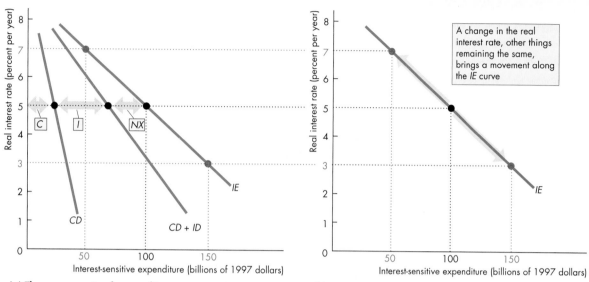

(a) The components of expenditure

(b) Aggregate expenditure plans

In part (a), when the interest rate is 5 percent a year, autonomous consumption expenditure is $20 billion, investment is $50 billion, net exports are $30 billion, and interest-sensitive expenditure is $100 billion. In part (b), when the real interest rate is 5 percent a year, interest-sensitive expen-

diture is $100 billion a year on the *IE* curve. Other things remaining the same, when the interest rate falls to 3 percent a year, interest-sensitive expenditure increases to $150 billion a year and when the interest rate rises to 7 percent a year, interest-sensitive expenditure decreases to $50 billion a year.

Figure 25.9(a) shows the components of interest-sensitive expenditure, autonomous consumption expenditure, investment, and net exports (*NX*). When the real interest rate is 5 percent a year, autonomous consumption expenditure is $20 billion on the curve *CD*. Investment is $50 billion, so when we add investment and autonomous consumption expenditure together, we get $70 billion on the curve *CD + ID*. Net exports are $30 billion, so when we add this amount to $70 billion, we obtain the sum of all the interest-sensitive components of aggregate expenditure, which is $100 billion on the *IE* curve.

In Fig. 25.9(b), as the real interest rate changes, interest-sensitive expenditure changes along the *IE* curve. Other things remaining the same, when the real interest rate falls to 3 percent a year, interest-sensitive expenditure increases to $150 billion. And when the real interest rate rises to 7 percent a year, interest-sensitive expenditure decreases to $50 billion.

REVIEW QUIZ

1. What is the real interest rate and how does it differ from the nominal interest rate?
2. Which interest rate influences the quantity of money that people plan to hold and why?
3. Which interest rate influences expenditure decisions and why?
4. How does the interest rate influence net exports?

◆ Take a look at some recent trends in the way we use currency in Canada in *Reading Between the Lines* on pp. 600–601. You've now seen how the quantity of money influences the interest rate and how the interest rate influences expenditure plans. In the next chapter, we're going to discover how the Bank of Canada can change the quantity of money and interest rates. Then, in Chapter 27, we see how fiscal policy and monetary policy interact to influence the course of the economy.

Canada's Changing Demand for Money

FINANCIAL POST, DECEMBER 3, 2002

Odds stacked against cash

From consumer demands for speed and convenience to banks' hunger for fatter returns, a collusion of forces is ensuring that the use of paper money is sliding into decline.

"Cash is a very inefficient system, physical bills don't last very long before they need replacing, if you lose it there is no recourse and it costs a lot to count and process," says Joseph D'Cruz a professor of strategy at the Rotman School of Management at the University of Toronto. "Couple that with the very high level of trust Canadians place in their national banks and the rise of electronic banking is sure to drive down the use of cash."

If Canadians have trust in their banks, they seem to have less trust in their national currency. Retailers from Dominion to Tim Hortons and Shoppers Drug Mart have refused to accept bills in $50 or $100 denominations out of counterfeiting fears. Some stores, including Loblaws, have even started to put lowly $5 bills through a security scan. It's just one more reason that cash and other paper transactions, including cheques, are giving way to debit and credit charges. ...

... Interac Direct Payment—which polls Canadians annually to establish their preferred mode of payment for goods and services—says the use of electronic payment outstripped cash transactions in 1999. ... In 1995 well over half of all transactions were made in cash, by last year cash accounted for roughly 30% of transactions, according to Interac. ...

One of the last industries to resist accepting credit and debit has been fast food—because consumers spend roughly $5 each and the merchant pays a fee for customers to pay electronically. In Canada, however, fast food joints including McDonald's, Burger King, and Wendy's introduced debit payment several years ago.

Essence of the Story

■ The use of paper money is decreasing, and the use of electronic credit and debit charges is increasing.

■ Joseph D'Cruz, a professor of strategy at the Rotman School of Management at the University of Toronto, says that cash is an inefficient system and because Canadians trust their banks, electronic systems will continue to decrease the use of cash.

■ Some retailers refuse to accept $50 bills or $100 bills because they fear counterfeiting, and some even put $5 bills through a security scan.

■ A survey shows that cash payments decreased from more than 50 percent of transactions in 1995 to 30 percent in 2001.

■ Because each transaction is small, the fast-food sector has been the most resistant to electronic transactions—but even in this sector, the use of cash is decreasing.

Economic Analysis

■ Figure 1 shows the amount of currency in Canada as a percentage of GDP since 1970. This percentage decreased during the 1970s and 1980s but increased during the early 1990s and was steady after 1994.

■ The news article emphasizes reasons why the amount of currency might have *decreased*. But why did currency increase during the 1990s?

■ Currency is one component of money, and the demand for money increases when real GDP increases.

■ In Figure 1, we graph currency *as a percentage of GDP* to remove the influence of GDP on the amount of currency held.

■ So Fig. 1 tells us that even holding real GDP constant, currency increased during the early 1990s and has not decreased during the 2000s.

■ The reason for the increase in currency is that the interest rate, which is the opportunity cost of holding currency, decreased during the 1990s.

■ Figure 2 shows the relationship between the amount of currency as a percentage of GDP against the interest rate on savings accounts at chartered banks.

■ You can see that, just as predicted by the theory of the demand for money, the lower the interest rate, the greater is the quantity of currency held.

■ As the opportunity cost of holding currency increased during the 1970s, the amount of currency held (as a percentage of GDP) decreased.

■ And as the opportunity cost of holding currency decreased during the 1990s, the amount of currency held (as a percentage of GDP) increased.

■ A change in the interest rate changes the quantity of currency demanded, but it does not change the demand for currency.

■ The demand for currency changes when some other influence on payment methods changes.

■ So what is left of the message in the news article? Are we using less currency as we switch increasingly to the use of debit cards?

■ Figure 2 provides part of the answer. The demand for currency has decreased. The demand curve of the 1990s is to the left of the demand curve of the 1970s.

■ But the demand for currency decreased during the early 1980s, not during the late 1990s when electronic payments technologies spread.

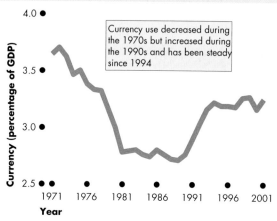

Figure 1 Trends in currency holding

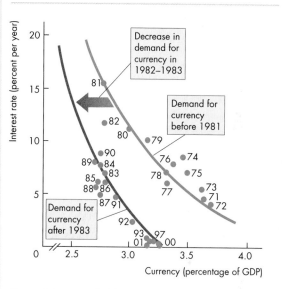

Figure 2 Currency holding and the interest rate

■ Most likely, the very high interest rate of 1981 made people think harder about how to be more economical in their use of currency, and the lesson was a permanent one.

■ Debit cards, which enable us to pay for purchases directly from our bank accounts, and credit cards, which enable us to buy on credit through the month and pay when we receive our own pay cheques, decrease our demand for currency.

■ As more and more businesses accept debit cards and credit cards and as more and more transactions are done by debit cards and credit cards, people will hold less cash.

■ But these changes are not visible in the aggregate data. Some other changes are working in the opposite direction to maintain the overall popularity of currency.

SUMMARY

KEY POINTS

What Is Money? (pp. 582–584)

- Money is the means of payment, a medium of exchange, a unit of account, and a store of value.
- M1 consists of currency and households' and businesses' demand deposits at chartered banks; M2+ consists of M1 plus savings deposits and other deposits at all types of depository institutions.

Depository Institutions (pp. 585–587)

- The depository institutions are the chartered banks, credit unions and caisses populaires, and trust and mortgage loan companies.
- Depository institutions provide four main economic services: They create liquidity, minimize the cost of obtaining funds, minimize the cost of monitoring borrowers, and pool risks.

How Banks Create Money (pp. 587–590)

- Banks create money by making loans.
- The total quantity of deposits that can be supported by a given amount of reserves (the deposit multiplier) is determined by the desired reserve ratio.

The Demand for Money (pp. 591–594)

- The quantity of money demanded is the amount of money that people plan to hold.
- The quantity of real money equals the quantity of nominal money divided by the price level.
- The quantity of real money demanded depends on the interest rate and real GDP. As the interest rate rises, the quantity of real money demanded decreases.

Interest Rate Determination (pp. 594–596)

- The interest rate adjusts to achieve equilibrium in the markets for money and financial assets.
- Money market equilibrium achieves an interest rate (and an asset price) that makes the quantity of real money available willingly held.
- If the quantity of real money increases, the interest rate falls and the prices of financial assets rise.

The Interest Rate and Expenditure Plans (pp. 597–599)

- The real interest rate (approximately) equals the nominal interest rate minus the inflation rate.
- The nominal interest rate is the opportunity cost of holding money. The real interest rate is the opportunity cost of consumption expenditure and investment.
- A fall in the interest rate increases interest-sensitive expenditure.

KEY FIGURES

KEY TERMS

PROBLEMS

*1. In Canada today, money includes which of the following items?
   a. Bank of Canada notes in the Bank of Montreal's cash machines
   b. Your Visa card
   c. The quarters inside public phones
   d. Canadian dollar coins in your pocket
   e. The cheque you have just written to pay for your rent
   f. The loan you took out last August to pay for your school fees

2. Which of the following items are money? Which are deposit money?
   a. Demand deposits at the CIBC
   b. Bell Canada stock held by individuals
   c. A "loonie"
   d. Canadian government securities

*3. Sara withdraws $1,000 from her savings account at the Lucky Trust and Mortgage Company, keeps $50 in cash, and deposits the balance in her demand deposit account at the Bank of Montreal. What is the immediate change in M1 and M2+?

4. Monica takes $10,000 from her savings account at Happy Credit Union and puts the funds into her demand deposit account at the Royal Bank. What is the immediate change in M1 and M2+?

*5. The banks in Zap have:

Reserves	$250 million
Loans	$1,000 million
Deposits	$2,000 million
Total assets	$2,500 million

   a. Construct the banks' balance sheet. If you are missing any assets, call them "other assets"; if you are missing any liabilities, call them "other liabilities."
   b. Calculate the banks' reserve ratio.
   c. If banks hold no excess reserves, calculate the deposit multiplier.

6. The banks in Zip have:

Reserves	$205 million
Loans	$3,750 million
Deposits	$4,000 million
Total assets	$4,200 million

   a. Construct the banks' balance sheet. If you are missing any assets, call them "other assets"; if you are missing any liabilities, call them "other liabilities."
   b. Calculate the banks' reserve ratio.
   c. If banks hold no excess reserves, calculate the deposit multiplier.

*7. The spreadsheet provides information about the demand for money in Minland. Column A is the interest rate, R. Columns B, C, and D show the quantity of money demanded at three different levels of real GDP: Y_0 is $10 billion, Y_1 is $20 billion, and Y_2 is $30 billion. The quantity of money supplied by the Minland central bank is $3.0 billion. Initially, real GDP is $20 billion.

	A	B	C	D
1	R	Y_0	Y_1	Y_2
2	7	1.0	1.5	2.0
3	6	1.5	2.0	2.5
4	5	2.0	2.5	3.0
5	4	2.5	3.0	3.5
6	3	3.0	3.5	4.0
7	2	3.5	4.0	4.5
8	1	4.0	4.5	5.0

   What happens in Minland if
   a. The interest rate exceeds 4 percent a year?
   b. The interest rate is less than 4 percent a year?
   c. The interest rate equals 4 percent a year?

8. The Minland economy in problem 7 experiences a severe recession. Real GDP falls to $10 billion. The Minland central bank takes no action to change the quantity of money.
   a. What happens in Minland if the interest rate is 4 percent a year?
   b. What is the equilibrium interest rate?
   c. Compared with the situation in problem 7, does the interest rate in Minland rise or fall? Why?

*9. The Minland economy in problem 7 experiences a severe business cycle. Real GDP rises to $30 billion and then falls to $10 billion. The Minland central bank takes no action to change the quantity of money. What happens to the interest rate in Minland
   a. During the expansion phase of the cycle?
   b. During the recession phase of the cycle?

10. Financial innovation in Minland changes the demand for money. People plan to hold $0.5 billion less than the numbers in the spreadsheet.
   a. What happens to the interest rate if the Minland central bank takes no actions?

b. What happens to the interest rate if the Minland central bank decreases the quantity of money by $0.5 billion? Explain

*11. The figure shows the demand for real money curve in Upland.

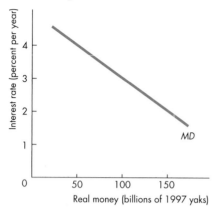

a. In the figure, draw the supply of money curve if the interest rate is 3 percent a year.
b. If the Upland central bank wants to lower the interest rate by 1 percentage point, by how much must it change the quantity of real money?

12. In problem 11, a new smart card replaces currency and the demand for money changes. Also, the new smart card causes business to boom and real GDP increases.
a. Use the figure for problem 11 and draw a new demand for real money curve.
b. If the Upland central bank wants to prevent the interest rate from changing, what must it do to the quantity of money?

*13. In problem 9, when Minland experiences a severe business cycle, what happens to autonomous consumption expenditure, investment, the exchange rate, and net exports
a. During the expansion phase of the cycle?
b. During the recession phase of the cycle?

14. In problem 10, what happens to autonomous consumption expenditure, investment, the exchange rate, and net exports in Minland if
a. The central bank takes no action?
b. The central bank decreases the quantity of money by $0.5 billion? Explain.

CRITICAL THINKING

1. Study *Reading Between the Lines* on pp. 600–601 and then answer the following questions:
a. What changes in the payments technology are described in the news article?
b. What does the news article imply has happened to the amount of currency held?
c. What are the trends in currency use?
d. Why did the use of currency increase during the 1990s?
e. Does the increased use of currency during the 1990s contradict the news article?
f. What do you expect the future trends in currency use to be and why?

2. Rapid inflation in Brazil caused the cruzeiro, the currency of Brazil, to lose its ability to function as money. People were unwilling to accept it because it lost value too fast. Which of the following commodities do you think would be most likely to take the place of the cruzeiro and act as money in the Brazilian economy?
a. Tractor parts
b. Packs of cigarettes
c. Loaves of bread
d. Impressionist paintings
e. Baseball trading cards

WEB EXERCISES

1. Use the link on the Parkin–Bade Web site to visit Mark Bernkopf's Central Banking Resource Centre and read the article on Electronic Cash. Also read "The End of Cash" by James Gleick (first published in the *New York Times Magazine* on June 16, 1996). Then answer the following questions:
a. What is e-cash?
b. Mark Bernkopf asks: "Will 'e-cash' enable private currencies to overturn the ability of governments to make monetary policy?" Will it?
c. When you buy an item on the Internet and pay by using a form of e-cash, are you using money? Explain why or why not.
d. In your opinion, is the concern about e-cash a real concern or hype?

MONETARY POLICY

CHAPTER 26

Fiddling with the Knobs

Almost every month, the financial news reports on the Bank of Canada's view about whether the time is near for a further fall or rise in interest rates. What *is* the Bank of Canada? Why would the Bank of Canada want to change interest rates—especially upward? And how can the Bank of Canada influence interest rates? ◆ For most of the 1990s and 2000s the Consumer Price Index has risen slowly—inflation has been low—because the quantity of money in our economy has grown slowly. But during the 1970s, inflation rocketed as the pace of money creation exploded. What makes the quantity of money increase quickly at some times and more slowly at others? What role does the Bank of Canada play in changing the quantity of money? How does the quantity of money in existence influence interest rates? ◆ And how do interest rates influence the economy? Can the Bank of Canada speed up economic growth and lower unemployment by lowering interest rates? And can the Bank of Canada keep inflation in check by raising interest rates?

◆ In this chapter, you will learn about the Bank of Canada and monetary policy. You will learn how the Bank of Canada influences interest rates and how interest rates influence the economy. You'll discover that interest rates depend, in part, on the amount of money in existence. You will also discover how the Bank of Canada changes the quantity of money to influence interest rates as it attempts to smooth the business cycle and keep inflation in check. In *Reading Between the Lines* at the end of the chapter, you will see the uncertainty that the Bank of Canada constantly faces as it tries to steer a steady course between inflation and recession.

After studying this chapter, you will be able to

- ■ Describe the structure of the Bank of Canada

- ■ Describe the tools used by the Bank of Canada to conduct monetary policy

- ■ Explain what an open market operation is and how it works

- ■ Explain how the Bank of Canada changes the quantity of money

- ■ Explain how the Bank of Canada influences interest rates

- ■ Explain how the Bank of Canada influences the economy

The Bank of Canada

THE BANK OF CANADA IS CANADA'S CENTRAL bank. A **central bank** is a public authority that supervises financial institutions and markets and conducts monetary policy. **Monetary policy** is the attempt to control inflation and moderate the business cycle by changing the quantity of money and adjusting interest rates and the exchange rate.

The **Bank of Canada** was established in 1935 and is directed by a governor who is appointed by the government of Canada. The seven people who have served as governor of the Bank of Canada are

- 1935–1954, Graham Towers
- 1955–1961, James Coyne
- 1961–1973, Louis Rasminsky
- 1973–1987, Gerald Bouey
- 1987–1994, John Crow
- 1994–2001, Gordon Thiessen
- 2001–   , David Dodge

Both the Bank of Canada and the government of Canada play a role in determining Canada's monetary policy. And the Bank of Canada Act regulates the balance between these two power centres. The Act embodies the practices that have evolved over 60 years of experience. There are two possible models for the relationship between a country's central bank and its central government, and Canada has evolved from one model to the other. The two models are

- Independent central bank
- Subordinate central bank

Independent Central Bank   An independent central bank is one that determines the nation's monetary policy without interference from the government. Public servants and politicians might comment on monetary policy but the Bank has no obligation to pay attention to these opinions.

The argument for an independent central bank is that it can pursue the long-term goal of price stability and can prevent monetary policy from being used for short-term, political advantage. This argument becomes more powerful when the government is running a budget deficit. One way of covering a deficit is for the central bank to buy government securities. But this action increases the quantity of money and creates inflation (see Chapter 27, p. 643 and Chapter 28, pp. 656–657). Another way of financing a government budget deficit is by selling securities to the general public. By taking a firm stand and being unwilling to print new money to pay for the government budget deficit, the central bank can force the government to face the higher interest rates that it brings upon itself by running a deficit.

Countries that have independent central banks today are Germany, the United States, and Switzerland. When the Bank of Canada was founded in 1935, it too was established as an independent central bank. Governors Towers and Coyne enjoyed substantial autonomy from the government of Canada. But in 1961, Governor James Coyne and Prime Minister John Diefenbaker clashed over who was in charge of monetary policy. Coyne resigned and for some time it was not clear whether the Bank of Canada was indeed independent (as the Act that established it proclaimed) or subordinate to the government (as the outcome of the Coyne–Diefenbaker clash seemed to imply).

The issue was resolved in 1967 when an amendment to the Bank of Canada Act redefined the relationship between the Bank and the government and made the Bank subordinate to the government.

Subordinate Central Bank   Many central banks are subordinate to their governments. In the event of a difference of opinion between the central bank and government, the government carries the day and, if necessary, the central bank governor resigns if he or she is unwilling to implement the policies directed by the government. The argument for a subordinate central bank is that monetary policy affects the lives of everyone and so must be subject to democratic control.

Although the government (through the minister of finance) has final responsibility for Canada's monetary policy, this fact does not mean that the Bank of Canada is impotent. Because of its expertise and authority in the field and because of the quality of the analysis done by the Bank's staff of senior economists and advisors, the Bank (through the governor) has considerable power. Only a sharp, deep, and wide-ranging disagreement would bring a government to the point of forcing a governor's resignation. Also, there are times when a government wants to pursue unpopular monetary policies and, at such times, it is convenient for the government to hide behind the authority of the Bank of Canada.

We are now going to study the policy actions that the Bank of Canada takes. To understand these actions, we first must describe the Bank's balance sheet.

The Bank of Canada's Balance Sheet

Table 26.1 shows the balance sheet of the Bank of Canada. The numbers are for December 31, 2001. The assets on the left side are what the Bank of Canada owns and the liabilities on the right side are what it owes. Most of the Bank of Canada's assets are government of Canada securities. A small asset item is loans to chartered banks.

The most significant aspect of the Bank of Canada's balance sheet is on the liabilities side. The largest liability is Bank of Canada notes outside the Bank. These are the bank notes that we use in our daily transactions. Some of these bank notes are held by households and firms and others are in the tills and vaults of banks and other financial institutions.

The other economically significant but numerically small liability of the Bank of Canada is the deposits by chartered banks. These deposits are reserves of the chartered banks. The liabilities of the Bank of Canada are the largest component of the monetary base. The **monetary base** is the sum of Bank of Canada notes outside the Bank, chartered banks' deposits at the Bank of Canada, and coins held by households, firms, and banks. The government of Canada issues coins, so they do not appear as a liability of the Bank of Canada. The government of Canada also has deposits with the Bank of Canada.

You now know what the Bank of Canada is and you can describe the Bank's assets and liabilities. Your next task is to learn how the Bank goes about its work of making monetary policy.

Making Monetary Policy

Making monetary policy is like driving a very strange car. The car has an accelerator (lower interest rates) and a brake (higher interest rates). The accelerator and the brake work, but not very predictably. The driver (the Bank of Canada) cannot be sure how strong or how delayed the response to its actions will be. Also, to make the ride more interesting, the driver has only a rear view. The road just travelled can be seen, but the road ahead is invisible.

The objective is to drive the car at a constant speed over a terrain that alternates between uphill (tough economic times with a falling real GDP growth rate and rising unemployment) and downhill (easy economic times with a rising real GDP growth rate and falling unemployment). So sometimes the accelerator must be applied, sometimes the brake, and sometimes neither. You can see that to have a smooth ride, the driver must read the current situation and try to predict what lies ahead.

So to make monetary policy, the Bank of Canada must anticipate the future course of the economy and it must try to read that course from current economic conditions. To study the Bank's challenging task, economists break the monetary policy process into three pieces:

■ Monetary policy objectives
■ Monetary policy indicators
■ Monetary policy tools

Monetary Policy Objectives

The objectives of monetary policy are ultimately political, and they stem from the mandate of the Bank that is set out in the Bank of Canada Act. These objectives are to

> regulate credit and currency in the best interests of the economic life of the nation... and to mitigate by its influence fluctuations in the general level of production, trade, prices and employment, so far as may be possible within the scope of monetary action...[1]

In simple language, these words have come to mean that the Bank's job is to control the quantity of money and interest rates in order to avoid inflation and, when possible, prevent excessive swings in real GDP growth and unemployment. In terms of the car

---

TABLE 26.1 The Bank of Canada's Balance Sheet, December 31, 2001

Assets (billions of dollars)		Liabilities (billions of dollars)	
Government securities	39	Bank of Canada notes	39
Loans to banks	1	Banks' deposits	2
		Government deposits	1
Other assets	2		—
Total assets	42	Total liabilities	42

[all the items are shown rounded to the nearest $1 billion].

Source: Bank of Canada, *Banking and Financial Statistics*, table B1.

---

[1] This quotation is from the preamble of the Bank of Canada Act, 1935.

analogy, the Bank sees its job as being cautious in applying the accelerator and more aggressive in applying the brake.

This modern interpretation of the Bank's objectives is controversial. Some people believe that the emphasis is wrong and that the Bank should pay less attention to inflation and use its influence to avoid low real GDP growth and high unemployment. Or, the Bank should put more pressure on the gas pedal and less on the brake.

Monetary Policy Indicators

If inflation is raging too rapidly or unemployment is too high, there is nothing the Bank of Canada can do that will bring immediate relief. Furthermore, if the Bank is doing a good job, it will already have taken the actions it believes are the best available for dealing with *today's* situation. The actions the Bank takes today are designed to influence the economy many months into the future. **Monetary policy indicators** are the *current* features of the economy that the Bank looks at to determine whether it needs to apply the brake or the accelerator to the economy to influence its *future* real GDP growth, unemployment, and inflation.

The best monetary policy indicators are variables that the Bank of Canada can observe accurately and frequently, that are good predictors of the future course of real GDP growth, unemployment, and inflation (the objectives of policy), and that the Bank can control quickly.

The Bank of Canada's monetary policy indicators change as more research is done and the Bank learns more about which indicators work well and which are faulty. Today, the main monetary policy indicator is an interest rate called the overnight loans rate. The **overnight loans rate** is the interest rate on large-scale loans that chartered banks make to each other and to dealers in financial markets. The Bank of Canada sets a range for the overnight loans rate of half a percentage point and takes actions to keep the rate inside its desired range.[2] The overnight loans rate is like the cruise control on the Bank's strange car.

Figure 26.1 shows the overnight loans rate. This interest rate climbed steeply after 1975 and reached a peak of 18 percent in 1981. At this time, Governor Gerald Bouey was wrestling with double-digit inflation. Since 1981, the overnight loans rate has fluctuated, but it has generally followed a downward trend. This downward trend was interrupted during the late 1980s when Governor John Crow put the Bank on its current course of aiming for low inflation. The overnight loans rate has remained low through the low-inflation era of the 1990s and 2000s.

Monetary Policy Tools

The Bank of Canada controls the overnight loans rate by adjusting the reserves of the banks. These adjustments then spread through the banks to change the quantity of money, other interest rates, and the

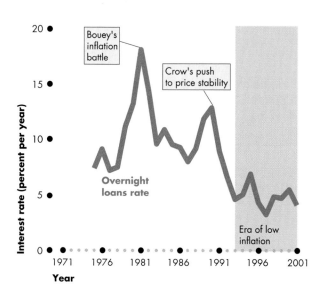

FIGURE 26.1   The Main Monetary Policy Indicator: The Overnight Loans Rate

The Bank of Canada sets a target range for the overnight loans rate and then takes actions to keep this monetary policy indicator inside its target range. When the Bank wants to slow inflation, it takes actions that raise the overnight loans rate. When the Bank wants to increase real GDP, it takes actions that lower the overnight loans rate.

Source: Bank of Canada, Banking and Financial Statistics, table F1.

---

[2] Half a percentage point is sometimes called 50 *basis points*. A basis point is one-hundredth of one percentage point. For example, the Bank might set the range at 3.5 to 4.0 percent or from 7.1 to 7.6 percent. In each case, the range is half a percentage point or 50 basis points.

exchange rate. Four policy tools impact on bank reserves and the quantity of money:

- Required reserve ratio
- Bank rate and bankers' deposit rate
- Open market operations
- Government deposit shifting

Required Reserve Ratio Banks hold reserves in the form of currency and deposits at the Bank of Canada so that they can meet the demands of their customers. If the Bank of Canada chooses to do so, it can require the chartered banks to hold larger reserves than the banks themselves desire. Since 1992, banks in Canada have not been required to hold reserves. The *required reserve ratio is zero*. Before 1992, the Bank of Canada imposed reserve requirements on the banks. Required reserves were 8 percent of deposits before 1967. They then decreased steadily through the 1970s and 1980s and were finally abolished in 1992.

By changing the required reserve ratio, the Bank of Canada changes the amount of lending the banks can do and therefore changes the quantity of money. It also changes the magnitude of the deposit multiplier. The higher the reserve ratio, the smaller is the deposit multiplier (see Chapter 25, p. 588).

Required reserves act like a tax on the banks. When banks are required to hold either currency or deposits at the Bank of Canada, the banks earn no interest on either of these assets. So the banks are taxed by the Bank of Canada by an amount equal to the interest that they could have earned by lending these funds rather than by holding them as reserves. The *opportunity cost* of reserves is the loan interest forgone. By abolishing required reserves, the Bank of Canada has made the banks more profitable.

Bank Rate and Bankers' Deposit Rate The chartered banks hold tiny reserves relative to their deposits. The key reason the banks can manage with such small reserves is that the Bank of Canada stands ready to lend reserves to them to ensure that they can always meet their depositors' demands for currency. **Bank rate** is the interest rate that the Bank of Canada charges the chartered banks on the reserves it lends them.

The Bank of Canada can set bank rate at any level it chooses. At one time, the Bank linked bank rate to the interest rate on 3-month government of Canada Treasury bills. But today, bank rate is set as the upper end of the range of the Bank's target for the overnight loans rate. Because the Bank is willing to lend funds to the chartered banks at this interest rate, bank rate

acts as a cap on the overnight loans rate. If the chartered banks can borrow from the Bank of Canada at bank rate, they will not borrow from another bank unless the rate is lower than or equal to bank rate.

The Bank of Canada pays the chartered banks interest at the *bankers' deposit rate* on their deposits at the Bank. The Bank of Canada sets this interest rate at bank rate minus half a percentage point, which also equals the low end of the Bank's target range for the overnight loans rate. If chartered banks can earn bank rate minus half a percentage point from the Bank of Canada, they will not make overnight loans to other banks unless they earn a higher interest rate than what the Bank of Canada is paying.

You can see now that the Bank of Canada can always make the overnight loans rate hit its target range by its setting of bank rate and bankers' deposit rate. But the Bank usually wants to keep the overnight loans rate inside its target range, not at one end of it. The other two policy tools are used to move the overnight loans rate around inside its target range.

Open Market Operations An **open market operation** is the purchase or sale of government of Canada securities—Treasury bills and government bonds—by the Bank of Canada from or to a chartered bank or the public. When the Bank of Canada buys securities, it pays for them with newly created monetary base. Its payment for the securities increases the chartered banks' deposits at the Bank of Canada. With extra reserves, the banks make new loans, the quantity of money increases, and interest rates fall. When the Bank of Canada sells securities, it receives payments that decrease the monetary base. Banks' reserves decrease, the banks cut lending, the quantity of money decreases, and interest rates rise.

Open market operations are the main method of controlling bank reserves and the quantity of money, and they are undertaken on a huge scale. In a typical week, the Bank of Canada might buy or sell government securities valued at several hundred million dollars. In some weeks, the Bank buys or sells more than a billion dollars worth of government securities. Some of these transactions occur to cope with seasonal fluctuations in the demand for money that arise from factors such as the timing of tax payments and Christmas shopping. Others occur because the Bank of Canada wants to raise or lower the overnight loans rate. Because open market operations are the main tool for controlling the quantity of money and influencing other interest rates, we study them in more detail later in this chapter (on pp. 611–615).

Government Deposit Shifting The government of Canada has deposits in accounts at chartered banks and the Bank of Canada. On a typical day, the government has about $2.5 billion in the bank and most of this money is on deposit at chartered banks. The government's deposit at the Bank of Canada is usually much smaller than the amount on deposit at the chartered banks.

Government deposit shifting is the transfer of government funds by the Bank of Canada from the government's account at the Bank of Canada to its accounts at the chartered banks, or from the government's accounts at the chartered banks to its account at the Bank of Canada. When the Bank of Canada shifts government funds from itself to the chartered banks, it increases chartered bank deposits and reserves. When the Bank shifts government funds from the chartered banks to itself, it decreases chartered bank deposits and reserves.

Table 26.2 shows the effects of government deposit shifting. Suppose the Bank of Canada writes cheques totalling $10 million on a government of Canada account and deposits those cheques into government of Canada accounts at the chartered banks. (To avoid benefiting or hurting an individual bank, these operations are spread across the banks according to an agreed-upon formula.)

Two sets of transactions now occur. First, government deposits decrease at the Bank of Canada and increase at the chartered banks. This transaction appears as –$10 million in government deposits in Bank of Canada liabilities and +$10 million in government deposits in chartered banks' liabilities. Second, chartered banks' reserves increase. This transaction appears as +$10 million in Bank of Canada liabilities and +$10 million in chartered banks' assets. The Bank of Canada has no net additional liabilities and the chartered banks have $10 million more assets and $10 million more liabilities.

The quantity of money has not changed because government deposits are not counted as money. But bank reserves have increased, so the banks can now increase their loans. And, when banks make loans they create money. The quantity of money increases.

By doing the transactions you've just seen in reverse, the Bank of Canada can decrease bank reserves and cause a contraction of loans, and the quantity of money decreases.

Government deposit shifting is done on a very small scale and is a way of fine-tuning the quantity of bank reserves from one day to another.

TABLE 26.2   The Effects of Government Deposit Shifting

(a) Bank of Canada's Balance Sheet

Change in assets		Change in liabilities	
		Government deposits	–$10 million
		Chartered bank deposits	+$10 million
Total assets	$0	Total liabilities	$0 million

(b) Chartered Banks' Balance Sheet

Change in assets		Change in liabilities	
Reserves (deposits at the Bank of Canada)	+$10 million	Government deposits	+$10 million
Total assets	+$10 million	Total liabilities	+$10 million

REVIEW QUIZ

1 What is the central bank of Canada?
2 What functions does a central bank perform?
3 What are the Bank of Canada's monetary policy objectives?
4 Why does the Bank of Canada need a monetary policy indicator and what is its main indicator?
5 What are the four policy tools that the Bank of Canada can use to attempt to achieve its monetary policy objectives?

We're now going to look in greater detail at the way the Bank of Canada influences the quantity of money and interest rates by using its main tool, the open market operation. We'll see first how the Bank changes the monetary base and second how the monetary base influences the quantity of money. We'll then see how the quantity of money influences interest rates and the exchange rate.

Controlling the Quantity of Money

THE BANK OF CANADA CONSTANTLY MONITORS and adjusts the quantity of money in the economy. When the Bank of Canada *buys* securities in an open market operation, the monetary base *increases*, banks increase their lending, and the quantity of money *increases*. When the Bank of Canada *sells* securities in an open market operation, the monetary base *decreases*, banks decrease their lending, and the quantity of money *decreases*.

Let's study these changes in the quantity of money, beginning with the effects of open market operations on the monetary base.

How an Open Market Operation Works

When the Bank of Canada conducts an open market operation, the reserves of the banking system—a part of the monetary base—change. To see why this outcome occurs, we'll trace the effects of an open market operation when the Bank of Canada buys securities.

Suppose the Bank of Canada buys $100 million of government securities in the open market. There are two cases to consider: when the Bank of Canada buys from a chartered bank, and when it buys from the public (a person or business that is not a chartered bank). The outcome is essentially the same in either case, but you need to be convinced of this fact. We'll start with the simpler case: the Bank of Canada buys securities from a chartered bank.

Buy from a Chartered Bank When the Bank of Canada buys $100 million of securities from the Royal Bank, two things happen:

1. The Royal Bank has $100 million less securities, and the Bank of Canada has $100 million more securities.
2. The Bank of Canada pays for the securities by crediting the Royal Bank's deposit account at the Bank of Canada with $100 million.

Figure 26.2(a) shows the effects of these actions on the balance sheets of the Bank of Canada and the Royal Bank. Ownership of the securities passes from the chartered bank to the Bank of Canada, so the Royal Bank's assets decrease by $100 million and the Bank of Canada's assets increase by $100 million, as shown by the blue arrow running from the Royal to

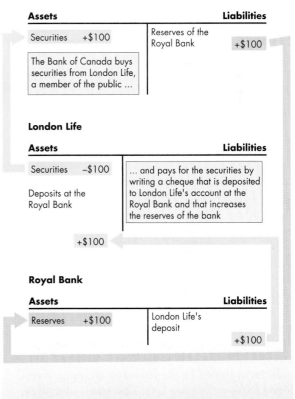

FIGURE 26.2 Bank of Canada Buys Securities in the Open Market

the Bank of Canada. The Bank of Canada pays for the securities by crediting the Royal Bank's deposit account at the Bank of Canada—its reserves—with $100 million, as shown by the green arrow running from the Bank of Canada to the Royal Bank. This action increases the monetary base and increases the reserves of the banking system.

The Bank of Canada's assets increase by $100 million, and its liabilities increase by $100 million. The chartered bank's total assets remain constant but their composition changes. Its deposit at the Bank of Canada increases by $100 million, and its holding of government securities decreases by $100 million. So the Royal Bank has additional reserves, which it can use to make loans.

We've just seen that when the Bank of Canada buys government securities from a bank, the bank's reserves increase. But what happens if the Bank of Canada buys government securities from the public—say from London Life, an insurance company?

Buy from the Public   When the Bank of Canada buys $100 million of securities from London Life, three things happen:

1. London Life has $100 million less securities, and the Bank of Canada has $100 million more securities.

2. The Bank of Canada pays for the securities with a cheque for $100 million drawn on itself, which London Life deposits in its account at the Royal Bank.

3. The Royal Bank collects payment of this cheque from the Bank of Canada, and $100 million is deposited in the Royal Bank's deposit account at the Bank of Canada.

Figure 26.2(b) shows the effects of these actions on the balance sheets of the Bank of Canada, London Life, and the Royal Bank. Ownership of the securities passes from London Life to the Bank of Canada, so London Life's assets decrease by $100 million and the Bank of Canada's assets increase by $100 million, as shown by the blue arrow running from London Life to the Bank of Canada.

The Bank of Canada pays for the securities with a cheque payable to London Life, which London Life deposits in the Royal Bank. This transaction increases London Life's deposit at the Royal Bank by $100 million, as shown by the red arrow running from the Royal Bank to London Life. This transaction also increases the Royal Bank's reserves by $100 million,

as shown by the green arrow running from the Bank of Canada to the Royal Bank. Just as when the Bank of Canada buys securities from a bank, this action increases the monetary base and increases the reserves of the banking system.

Again, the Bank of Canada's assets increase by $100 million, and its liabilities also increase by $100 million. London Life has the same total assets as before, but their composition has changed. It now has more money and less securities. The Royal Bank's total assets increase, and so do its liabilities. Its deposit at the Bank of Canada—its reserves—increases by $100 million, and its deposit liability to London Life increases by $100 million. Because its reserves have increased by the same amount as its deposits, the bank has excess reserves, which it can use to make loans.

We've now studied what happens when the Bank of Canada buys government securities from either a bank or from the public. If the Bank of Canada sells securities, all the events that you've just studied occur in reverse. Reserves decrease, and the banks are short of reserves.

The effects of an open market operation on the balance sheets of the Bank of Canada and the banks that we've just described are not the end of the story—they are just the beginning. With an increase in their reserves, the banks are able to make more loans, which increases the quantity of money. With a decrease in reserves, the banks must cut back on their loans, which decreases the quantity of money.

You learned how loans create deposits in Chapter 25. Here, we build on that basic idea but instead of studying the link between *bank reserves* and *bank deposits*, we examine the related broader link between the *monetary base* and the *quantity of money*.

Monetary Base and Bank Reserves

We've defined the monetary base as the sum of Bank of Canada notes outside the Bank, chartered banks' deposits at the Bank of Canada, and coins held by households, firms, and banks. The monetary base is held either by banks as reserves or by households and firms as currency.

When the monetary base increases, both bank reserves and currency held by households and firms increase. Banks can use the increase in bank reserves to make loans and create additional money. The increase in currency held by households and firms cannot be used to create additional money. An increase in currency held by households and firms is called a **currency drain**. A currency drain reduces the amount of additional money that can be created from a given increase in the monetary base.

The **money multiplier** is the amount by which a change in the monetary base is multiplied to determine the resulting change in the quantity of money. That is, the money multiplier is equal to the change in the quantity of money (M) divided by the change in the monetary base (MB):

$$\text{Money multiplier} = \frac{\Delta M}{\Delta MB}.$$

The money multiplier is related to but differs from the *deposit multiplier* that we studied in Chapter 25. The deposit multiplier is the amount by which a change in bank reserves is multiplied to determine the change in the bank deposits.

Let's now look at the money multiplier.

The Money Multiplier

Let's work out the money multiplier by studying the case in which the Bank of Canada *buys securities from the banks*. Figure 26.3 shows the events that follow this open market purchase by the Bank of Canada. These events are

1. Banks have excess reserves.
2. Banks lend excess reserves.
3. Bank deposits increase.
4. The quantity of money increases.
5. New money is used to make payments.
6. Some of the new money remains on deposit.
7. Some of the new money is a *currency drain*.
8. Desired reserves increase because deposits have increased.
9. Excess reserves decrease, but remain positive.

FIGURE 26.3   A Round in the Multiplier Process Following an Open Market Operation

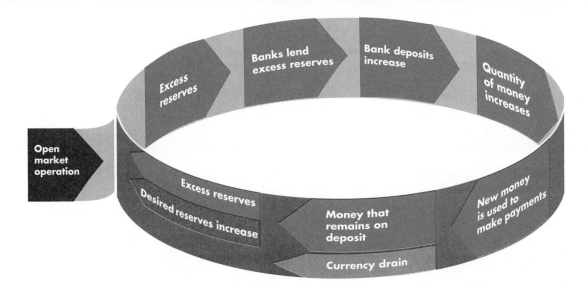

An open market operation increases bank reserves and creates excess reserves. Banks lend the excess reserves, new bank deposits are created, and the quantity of money increases. New money is used to make payments. Households and firms receiving payments keep some of the receipts as currency—a currency drain—and place the rest on deposit in banks. The increase in bank deposits increases banks' reserves but also increases banks' desired reserves. Desired reserves increase by less than the increase in actual reserves, so the banks still have some excess reserves, though less than before. The process repeats until excess reserves have been eliminated.

The sequence repeats in a series of rounds, but each round begins with a smaller quantity of excess reserves than did the previous one. The process continues until excess reserves have finally been eliminated.

You've seen that an open market operation creates excess reserves for the banks and that the reaction of the banks to this situation increases the quantity of money. But you've not yet seen the magnitude of the increase in the quantity of money.

Figure 26.4 illustrates the series of rounds and keeps track of the magnitudes of the increases in reserves, loans, deposits, currency, and money that result from an open market purchase of $100,000. In this figure, the *currency drain* is 33.33 percent of money and the *desired reserve ratio* is 10 percent of deposits.

The Bank of Canada buys $100,000 of securities from the banks. The banks' reserves increase by this amount, but deposits do not change. The banks have excess reserves of $100,000, and they lend those reserves. When the banks lend $100,000 of excess reserves, $66,667 remains in the banks as deposits and $33,333 drains off and is held outside the banks as currency. The quantity of money has now increased by $100,000—the increase in deposits plus the increase in currency holdings.

The increased bank deposits of $66,667 generate an increase in desired reserves of 10 percent of that amount, which is $6,667. Actual reserves have increased by the same amount as the increase in deposits—$66,667. So the banks now have excess reserves of $60,000. At this stage, we have gone around the circle shown in Fig. 26.3 once. The process we've just described repeats but begins with excess reserves of $60,000. Figure 26.4 shows the next two rounds. When the process comes to an end, the quantity of money has increased by $250,000.

FIGURE 26.4   The Multiplier Effect of an Open Market Operation

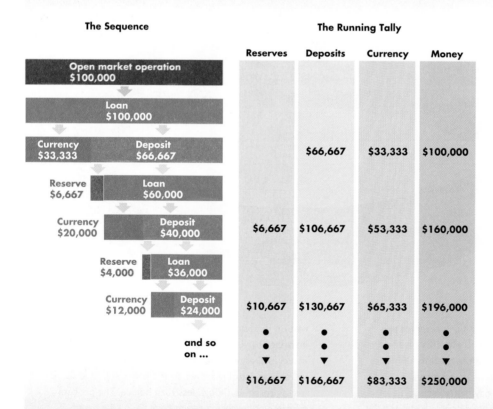

When a Bank of Canada open market operation gives the banks an additional $100,000 of reserves, the banks lend those reserves. Of the amount lent, $33,333 (33.33 percent) leaves the banks in a currency drain and $66,667 remains on deposit. With additional deposits, desired reserves increase by $6,667 (10 percent desired reserve ratio) and the banks lend $60,000. Of this amount, $20,000 leaves the banks in a currency drain and $40,000 remains on deposit. The process repeats until the banks have created enough deposits to eliminate their excess reserves. An additional $100,000 of reserves creates $250,000 of money.

The Canadian Money Multiplier

In the example you've just worked through, a $100,000 open market purchase increases the quantity of money by $250,000. The money multiplier is 2.5. What is the magnitude of the Canadian money multiplier? Let's look at some numbers.

The Canadian money multiplier is the change in the quantity of money divided by the change in the monetary base. Because there are two main definitions of money, there are two money multipliers: one for M1 and one for M2+. The M1 multiplier is about 2.2, and the M2+ multiplier is about 10. That is, a $1 million increase in the monetary base brings (approximately) a $2.2 million increase in M1 and a $10 million increase in M2+. These multipliers are based on a desired reserve ratio for M1 of 0.12 (12 percent) and for M2+ of 0.01 (1 percent). That is, a $100 increase in M1 increases desired reserves by $12, while a $100 increase in M2+ brings an increase in desired reserves of only $1. These multipliers are also based on a currency drain of 0.36 (or 36 percent) for M1 and 0.08 (or 8 percent) for M2+. That is, a $100 increase in M1 increases currency held by households and firms by $36, while a $100 increase in M2+ increases currency held by households and firms by $8.

REVIEW QUIZ

1 What happens when the Bank of Canada buys securities in the open market?
2 What happens when the Bank of Canada sells securities in the open market?
3 What do the banks do when they have excess reserves, and how do their actions influence the quantity of money?
4 What do the banks do when they are short of reserves, and how do their actions influence the quantity of money?

The Bank of Canada's objective in changing the quantity of money is to influence the course of the economy—especially unemployment, real GDP growth, and inflation. The immediate effects of a change in the quantity of money are changes in interest rate and the exchange rate. These changes create ripple effects that ultimately change the course of the economy. Let's now study these ripple effects.

Ripple Effects of Monetary Policy

YOU'VE SEEN HOW THE BANK OF CANADA CAN use its power in financial markets to change the quantity of money. And you learned in Chapter 25 that a change in the quantity of money changes the interest rate and the exchange rate.

We're now going to study the consequences of these changes in the interest rate and the exchange rate as they ripple through the economy.

When the Bank of Canada sells securities on the open market and decreases the monetary base, the quantity of money decreases, and the interest rate and the exchange rate rise. The higher interest rate decreases consumption expenditure and investment. And the higher exchange rate makes Canadian exports more expensive and imports cheaper. So net exports decrease. Tighter bank credit brings fewer loans, which reinforces the effects of higher interest rates on consumption expenditure and investment.

Similarly, when the Bank of Canada buys securities on the open market and increases the monetary base, the quantity of money increases, and the interest rate and the exchange rate fall. The lower interest rate increases consumption expenditure and investment. And the lower exchange rate makes Canadian exports cheaper and imports more costly. So net exports increase. Easier bank credit brings an expansion of loans, which reinforces the effects of lower interest rates on consumption expenditure and investment.

Figure 26.5 provides a schematic summary of these ripple effects. We're going to look at each stage in the transmission process. But before we do so, and so that we keep our eye on the ultimate objectives of monetary policy, we'll first use the *AS–AD* model and refresh our understanding of how a change in the quantity of money influences real GDP and the price level.

Monetary Policy to Lower Unemployment

Figure 26.6 shows an economy that is experiencing unemployment. Potential GDP is $1,000 billion, but actual real GDP is only $950 billion, at the intersection of the aggregate demand curve AD_0 and the short-run aggregate supply curve *SAS*. The price level is 105. With a large amount of unemployment,

FIGURE 26.5   The Channels for the Ripple Effects of Monetary Policy

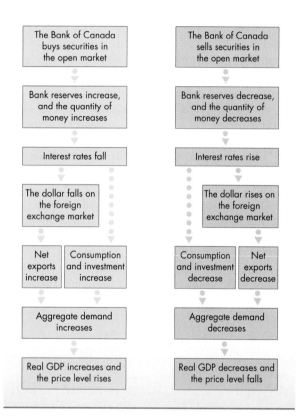

FIGURE 26.6   Monetary Policy to Lower Unemployment

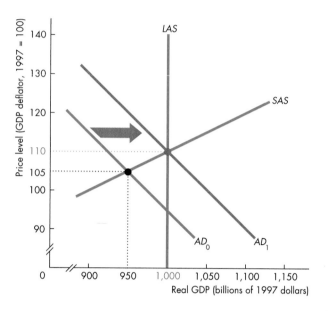

The aggregate demand curve is AD_0 and the short-run aggregate supply curve is SAS. The price level is 105, and real GDP is $950 billion. Long-run aggregate supply is LAS, and the economy is at a below full-employment equilibrium. An increase in the quantity of money shifts the aggregate demand curve rightward from AD_0 to AD_1. The price level rises to 110, and real GDP increases to $1,000 billion. Full employment is restored.

the money wage rate will eventually fall. As a result, the SAS curve will shift rightward, the price level will fall, and real GDP will increase, restoring full employment. But this automatic adjustment process is extremely slow.

To bring the economy to full employment more quickly, the Bank of Canada increases the quantity of money by conducting an open market operation in which it purchases government securities. Flush with excess reserves, banks make loans and the loans create money. With more money in their bank accounts, people increase their expenditure and aggregate demand increases.

In Fig. 26.6, the aggregate demand curve shifts rightward from AD_0 to AD_1. The new equilibrium is at the intersection point of AD_1 and SAS. The price level rises to 110, and real GDP increases to $1,000 billion. The economy is now at full employment.

Monetary Policy to Lower Inflation

Figure 26.7 shows an economy in which real GDP exceeds potential GDP and in which inflation is about to break out. Potential GDP is $1,000 billion and the long-run aggregate supply curve is LAS. Initially, the short-run aggregate supply curve is SAS_0, and the aggregate demand curve is AD_0. The price level is 115 and real GDP is $1,050 billion.

If the Bank of Canada does not take action, the money wage rate will begin to rise and the SAS curve will shift leftward to SAS_1. The price will rise to 125, and inflation will occur.

The Bank of Canada can prevent inflation by decreasing the quantity of money. By conducting an open market operation in which it sells securities, the Bank of Canada can decrease the quantity of money and shift the aggregate demand curve leftward to

FIGURE 26.7   Monetary Policy to Lower Inflation

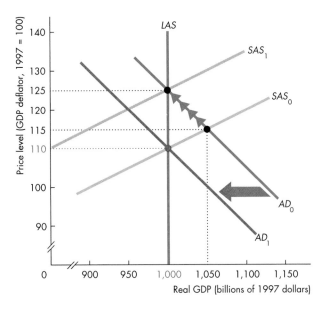

The economy is at an above full-employment equilibrium. The price level is 115, and real GDP is $1,050 billion. With no change in aggregate demand, the money wage rate rises and the short-run aggregate supply curve shifts to SAS_1. The price level rises to 125, and inflation occurs. If before the money wage rate rises, the Bank of Canada decreases the quantity of money so that the aggregate demand curve shifts to AD_1, the price level falls to 110 and the economy returns to full employment.

AD_1. If the Bank takes this action before the money wage rate has increased, the new equilibrium is at the intersection point of AD_1 and SAS_0. The price level falls to 110 and real GDP decreases to $1,000 billion. Inflation is avoided.

Time Lags in the Adjustment Process

To achieve its goal of full employment and the absence of inflation, the Bank of Canada needs a combination of good judgment and good luck. Too large an injection of money into an underemployed economy can bring inflation, as it did during the 1970s. And too large a decrease in the quantity of money in an inflationary economy can create unemployment, as it did in 1991.

The Bank is especially handicapped by the fact that the ripple effects of its policy actions are long and drawn out. Also, the economy does not always respond in exactly the same way to policy. Further, many factors other than policy are constantly changing and bringing a new situation for policy to respond to.

We'll look at each stage in the transmission process of monetary policy and see some of the problems that confront the Bank.

Interest Rate Fluctuations

The first effect of monetary policy is a change in the interest rate. This effect occurs quickly and relatively predictably. Figure 26.8 shows the fluctuations in three interest rates: the overnight loans rate, the 3-month Treasury bill rate, and the 10-year government bond rate (which is similar to the rate paid by big

FIGURE 26.8   Interest Rates

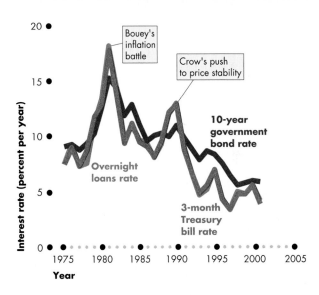

The short-term interest rates—the overnight loans rate and the 3-month Treasury bill rate—move closely together. The 10-year government bond rate moves in the same direction as the short-term rates but fluctuates less. The overnight loans rate climbed during the 1970s and peaked at 18 percent a year in 1981. The rate fell during the 1980s, but it increased again to peak at 13 percent a year in 1990. It fell again through the 1990s and remained low in the early 2000s.

Source: Bank of Canada, *Banking and Financial Statistics*, table F1.

corporations). The overnight loans rate is the one that the Bank of Canada targets directly and influences most closely. But notice how closely the 3-month Treasury bill rate follows the overnight loans rate. The 3-month Treasury bill rate is similar to the interest rate paid by Canadian businesses on short-term funds. These are short-term interest rates.

Notice also how the 10-year government bond rate moves with the short-term rates. It does not fluctuate as much as the short-term rates but its direction of change is the same.

Do the Bank of Canada's own actions make interest rates fluctuate? The answer is "yes." Figure 26.9 shows the relationship between the 3-month Treasury bill rate and the monetary base. Over time, the monetary base increases because the economy grows. So what matters for interest rates is not the absolute amount of monetary base, but the amount relative to GDP. The x-axis measures the monetary base as a percentage of GDP. During the 1970s and early 1980s, the Bank decreased the monetary base relative to GDP and interest rates rose. You can see the Bank at work as the movement up the line labelled MB_0. During the late 1990s and 2000s, the Bank increased the monetary base relative to GDP and interest rates fell. You can see the Bank at work as the movement down the line labelled MB_1.

But the relationship between monetary base and interest rates is not completely predictable. During the 1980s and early 1990s, the monetary base decreased relative to GDP and interest rates fell. The normal relationship broke down mainly because of ongoing decreases in the required reserve ratio.

Money Target Versus Interest Rate Target

Because the demand for money fluctuates, the Bank of Canada prefers to target the interest rate rather than the quantity of money. To target the interest rate, the Bank changes the quantity of money supplied in response to changes in the demand for money.

Figure 26.10 illustrates the difference between money targeting and interest rate targeting. In part (a), the Bank keeps the quantity of money at $600 billion. The money supply curve is MS. The demand for money fluctuates between a high of MD_H and a low of MD and averages MD_A. The interest rate averages 5 percent a year. But as the demand for money fluctuates, the interest rate fluctuates between 4 percent when the demand for money is MD_L and 6 per-

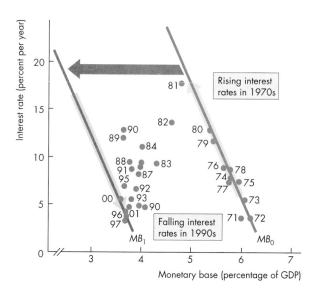

FIGURE 26.9 Monetary Base and the Interest Rate

To increase interest rates during the 1970s and early 1980s, the Bank of Canada decreased the monetary base relative to GDP. To decrease interest rates during the late 1990s and 2000s, the Bank of Canada increased the monetary base relative to GDP. During the 1980s and early 1990s, the relationship between the monetary base and the interest rate changed as reserve requirements and other factors changed.

Sources: Bank of Canada and *Monetary Base and the Interest Rate*; data calculated in part from the Statistics Canada CANSIM II database, table 380–0002.

cent when the demand for money is MD_H.

In Fig. 26.10(b), the Bank keeps the interest rate at 5 percent a year. To achieve its target the quantity of money is $600 billion on the average and the supply of money curve is MS_A. But when the demand for money changes, so does the quantity of money. When the demand for money increases to MD_H, the Bank increases the quantity of money to $610 billion and the supply of money curve becomes MS_H. When the demand for money decreases to MD_L, the Bank decreases the quantity of money to $590 billion and the supply of money curve becomes MS_L.

The decision by the Bank of Canada to target the interest rate does not mean that the Bank has abandoned control of the quantity of money. The Bank achieves its interest rate target by controlling the quantity of money. If the Bank wants to stop the

FIGURE 26.10 Money Target Versus Interest Rate Target

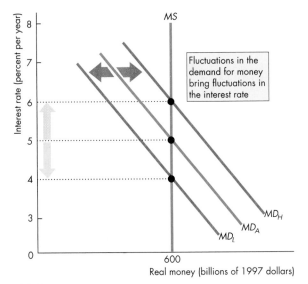

(a) Money target

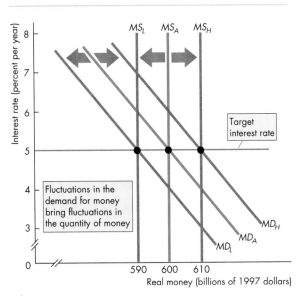

(b) Interest rate target

The demand for money fluctuates between MD_L and MD_H and on the average is MD_A. In part (a), the Bank of Canada keeps the quantity of money at $600 billion and the interest rate fluctuates between 4 percent and 6 percent a year and averages 5 percent a year. In part (b), the Bank of Canada keeps the interest rate at 5 percent a year and the quantity of money fluctuates between $590 billion ($MS_L$) and $610 billion ($MS_H$) and on the average is $600 billion ($MS_A$).

interest rate rising, it increases the quantity of money by increasing bank reserves. Flush with excess reserves, the banks increase the quantity of loans and bank deposits. And if the bank wants to stop the interest rate falling, it decreases the quantity of money by decreasing bank reserves. Short of reserves, banks decrease the quantity of loans and bank deposits.

The Exchange Rate

The exchange rate responds to changes in the interest rate in Canada relative to the interest rates in other countries. But other factors are also at work, which make the exchange rate hard to control and even harder to predict. The red line in Fig. 26.11 shows the gap between the Canadian and U.S. short-term interest

FIGURE 26.11 The Interest Rate and the Dollar

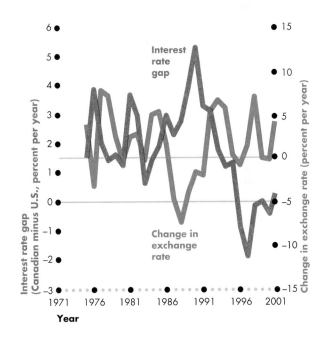

Other things remaining the same, when the gap between Canadian and U.S. short-term interest rates widens, the Canadian dollar rises in value or its value falls less quickly, and when the gap between Canadian and U.S. short-term interest rates narrows, the Canadian dollar falls in value or its value rises less quickly. Most of the time, other things do not remain the same, so the relationship between the interest rate gap and the exchange rate is weak.

Sources: Bank of Canada, *Banking and Financial Statistics*, tables F1 and 11, and authors' calculations.

rates. And the blue line shows the change in the Canadian dollar exchange rate against the U.S. dollar. You can see that sometimes when the interest rate gap widens (when the Canadian interest rate rises relative to the U.S. rate), the Canadian dollar rises or falls less quickly. Also, sometimes, when the interest rate gap narrows (when the Canadian interest rate falls relative to the U.S. rate), the Canadian dollar falls or rises less quickly. But the relationship between the interest rate gap and the exchange rate is weak. The exchange rate often changes independently of the interest rate gap.

Interest Rates, Aggregate Demand, and Real GDP Fluctuations

You've seen that the Bank of Canada's actions influence interest rates and the exchange rate. And you know that according to the *AS–AD* model, changes in the quantity of money, interest rates, and the exchange rate change aggregate demand and lead to changes in real GDP and the price level. But how powerful are the influences of money on real GDP? And how long does it take for these influences to occur?

Figure 26.12 answers these questions. The blue line shows the short-term interest rate minus the long-term interest rate. The Bank of Canada influences the short-term interest rate in the way that you studied earlier in this chapter. Changes in the short-term interest rate have some effect on the long-term interest rate, but this effect is small. The long-term interest rate is also influenced by saving and investment plans and by inflation expectations.

The red line in Fig. 26.12 is the real GDP growth rate *one year later.* You can see that when the short-term interest rate rises or the long-term interest rate falls, the real GDP growth rate slows down in the following year. The long-term interest rate fluctuates less than the short-term rate, so when the short-term rate rises above the long-term rate, it is because the Bank of Canada has pushed the short-term rate up. And when the short-term rate falls below the long-term rate, it is because the Bank of Canada has pushed the short-term rate down. So when the Bank of Canada stimulates aggregate demand (pushes the short-term rate down), the real GDP growth rate speeds up, and when the Bank of Canada lowers aggregate demand (pushes the short-term rate up), the real GDP growth rate slows. The inflation rate also increases and decreases in sympathy with these fluctuations in the real GDP growth rate. But the effects on the inflation rate take even longer.

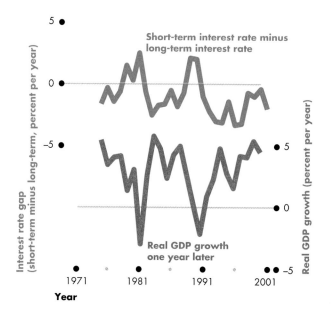

FIGURE 26.12 Interest Rates and Real GDP Growth

When the short-term interest rate rises relative to the long-term interest rate, the real GDP growth rate usually slows about one year later. Similarly, when the short-term interest rate falls relative to the long-term interest rate, the real GDP growth rate speeds up about one year later.

Sources: Bank of Canada and *Interest Rates and Real GDP Growth*; data calculated in part from the Statistics Canada CANSIM II database, table 380–0002.

REVIEW QUIZ

1 Describe the channels by which monetary policy ripples through the economy and explain why each channel operates.
2 Do interest rates fluctuate in response to the Bank of Canada's actions?
3 What change has occurred in the relationship between the monetary base and the interest rate?
4 How do the Bank of Canada's actions influence the exchange rate?
5 How do the Bank of Canada's actions influence real GDP and how long does it take for real GDP to respond to the Bank's policy actions?

We now look at the Bank of Canada in action.

The Bank of Canada in Action

YOU HAVE NOW LEARNED A GREAT DEAL ABOUT the Bank of Canada, the monetary policy actions it can take, and the effects of those actions on short-term interest rates. But you are possibly thinking: All this sounds nice in theory, but does it really happen? Does the Bank of Canada actually do the things we've learned about in this chapter? Indeed, it does happen, sometimes with dramatic effect, as two episodes in the life of the Bank of Canada show.

Gerald Bouey's Fight Against Inflation

Bank of Canada Governor Gerald Bouey eradicated a near double-digit inflation during the early 1980s. He did so by forcing interest rates sharply upward.

You know that to increase interest rates, the Bank must decrease the quantity of real money. In practice, because the economy is growing and because prices are rising, a slowdown in the growth rate of nominal money is enough to decrease the quantity of real money and increase interest rates.

In 1982, the quantity of money was held in check relative to the demand for money and interest rates increased sharply. The Treasury bill rate increased from 13 percent a year in 1980 to 18 percent a year in 1981. Mortgage rates—the rate at which house buyers borrow—increased to more than 20 percent a year. The economy went into severe recession. Real GDP shrank and the inflation rate slowed.

John Crow's Push for Price Stability

John Crow became governor of the Bank of Canada on February 1, 1987. Like his predecessor, Crow was a fierce inflation fighter and intent on holding the growth rate of money steady. But in October 1987, he was faced with one of the most severe crises that any central banker can face—a stock market crash. The Bank of Canada, in the company of other central banks around the world, feared the recession potential that might be signalled by the stock market crash. So to avoid any hint of financial tightness that might exacerbate a recessionary situation, the Bank of Canada permitted the quantity of money to grow quickly and short-term interest rates fell.

As the months passed, fears of recession were replaced by fears of a re-emergence of inflation. The Bank of Canada again slowed money growth and forced interest rates upward in a concerted attack on inflation. The Bank persisted in its focus on price stability despite a severe recession in 1990–1991.

Gordon Thiessen's and David Dodge's Balancing Acts

Gordon Thiessen succeeded John Crow in 1994 at a time of high unemployment. Many economists blamed the Bank for creating the 1990–1991 recession and for the absence of a strong recovery. Thiessen began the Bank's modern era of balancing the overriding goal of price stability with a strong secondary goal of trying to moderate the business cycle. Through 1995 and 1996, persistently high unemployment and slow economic growth combined with low inflation encouraged the Bank to lower interest rates and the economy embarked on what became a long and strong business cycle expansion. But inflation remained low.

This expansion was still underway but with increasing concern of a new recession when David Dodge succeeded Thiessen at the beginning of 2001. Soon thereafter, the United States went into recession and the U.S. slowdown, combined with the shock of September 11, brought ever lower interest rates both in the United States and Canada as the Bank sought to fight recession. As 2003 began, the Bank continued to walk a tightrope and began to consider raising interest rates again to hold back a possible upturn in the inflation rate.

REVIEW QUIZ

1 What were the policy challenges that Gerald Bouey and John Crow faced, and how did they respond to them?
2 What were the challenges that faced Gordon Thiessen during the 1990s and David Dodge during the 2000s, and how did they respond to them?

◆ In the next chapter, we're going to learn how monetary policy and fiscal policy interact. But first, take a look at *Reading Between the Lines* on pages 622–623 and see the Bank of Canada's challenge in 2002.

READING BETWEEN THE LINES

Monetary Policy in Action

FINANCIAL POST, OCTOBER 17, 2002

Strong growth, inflation spike not enough to send rates up: Bank of Canada stands pat

Bank of Canada said yesterday global economic, financial and political uncertainties persuaded it to keep interest rates steady for the second month in a row, despite a strong domestic expansion and a spike in inflation.

While the central bank left little doubt it would eventually drive rates higher, analysts detected a more dovish outlook in its statement that decreased the chances of a rise before the end of the year.

The bank kept its target for overnight lending rates between banks at 2.75% while the bank rate—the interest rate at which the central bank lends money to major financial institutions—was maintained at 3%.

"It remains the bank's view, going forward, that timely removal of monetary stimulus will be required to achieve the inflation target over the medium term," the bank said in a statement.

"The pace of monetary tightening will depend on unfolding economic, financial, and geopolitical developments and their implications for pressures on capacity and inflation in Canada."

David Dodge, the Bank of Canada governor, has now held interest rates steady since July after pushing them up from 40-year lows of 2% in three rate rises this spring.

While the bank's decision to keep interest rates on hold at its announcement in September caught many economists by surprise, yesterday's statement was widely anticipated as external conditions have become even more precarious since then.

The equity rally of the past few days has given investors heart, but the bear still has the market firmly in its claws, the U.S. recovery remains stubbornly weak, risk tolerance is wilting and the possibility of a U.S. attack on Iraq has cast a pall of uncertainty over everything.

"These uncertainties and the weaker global outlook may dampen growth in aggregate demand for Canadian output in the near term," the bank said. ...

Reprinted by permission of the *National Post.*

Essence of the Story

■ The Bank of Canada decided to leave its target for the overnight lending rate at 2.75 percent and the bank rate at 3 percent in October 2002.

■ Strong domestic expansion and a spike in inflation pointed to the need for an increase in the interest rate, but global economic, financial, and political uncertainties pointed in the opposite direction.

■ The Bank said that it would eventually raise interest rates to avoid inflation moving above its target range.

Economic Analysis

In the fall of 2002, Canada's inflation rate was rising and approaching 3 percent a year, the upper end of the Bank of Canada's target range.

In the absence of other considerations, the inflation situation would call for monetary policy to decrease aggregate demand and remove an inflationary gap.

But there were other considerations—global economic, financial, and political uncertainties—that pointed in the opposite direction.

Figures 1 and 2 illustrate that possible range of uncertainty about real GDP and the inflation rate through 2003.

If real GDP keeps growing rapidly, the small inflationary gap in late 2002 might become a large one in 2003. Or if real GDP growth slows, a recessionary gap might emerge.

Similarly, the inflation rate might keep rising and burst through the upper end of the target range, or the rise in the inflation rate might slow.

Figure 3 illustrates the possible developments during 2003 using the AS–AD model.

Potential GDP in 2003 is projected to be $1,084 billion and the short-run aggregate supply curve is SAS.

The Bank of Canada would like the aggregate demand curve to be AD_0 so that the economy attains full employment with real GDP at $1,084. The Bank would like the price level to rise by 2 percent to 115.

If aggregate demand continues to grow quickly, the aggregate demand curve would shift to AD_1. In this case, with no actions by the Bank of Canada, real GDP would be $1,095 and the price level would rise to 119. To prevent this outcome, the Bank would need to increase the interest rate.

Alternatively, if aggregate demand grows slowly, the aggregate demand curve would shift to AD_2. In this case, with no actions by the Bank of Canada, real GDP would be $1,073—below full employment—and the price level would rise to 111. To prevent this outcome, the Bank would need to *decrease* the interest rate.

The Bank of Canada must operate in a permanent state of uncertainty about the future course of the economy.

You're The Voter

Do you think the Bank of Canada should always err on the side of avoiding recession, even if that means risking rising inflation?

Do you think the Bank of Canada should always err on the side of avoiding inflation, even if that means risking recession?

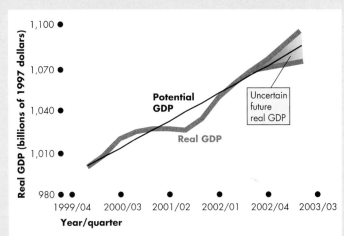

Figure 1 Real GDP and potential GDP

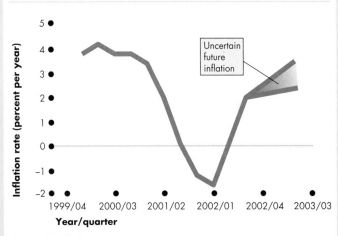

Figure 2 Inflation rate

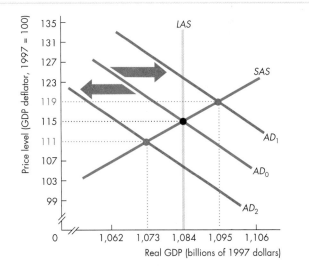

Figure 3 Aggregate supply and aggregate demand

SUMMARY

KEY POINTS

The Bank of Canada (pp. 606–610)

■ The Bank of Canada is the central bank of Canada.

■ The Bank of Canada's goals are to achieve low inflation, and as far as possible, to moderate the business cycle.

■ The Bank of Canada can influence the economy by setting the required reserve ratio for banks, by setting bank rate and bankers' deposit rate, by open market operations, and by government deposit shifting.

Controlling the Quantity of Money (pp. 611–615)

■ By buying government securities in the open market (an open market purchase), the Bank of Canada is able to increase the monetary base and the reserves available to banks.

■ There follows an expansion of bank lending and the quantity of money increases.

■ By selling government securities in the open market, the Bank of Canada is able to decrease the monetary base and bank reserves and decrease the quantity of money.

Ripple Effects of Monetary Policy (pp. 615–620)

■ An increase in the quantity of money lowers the interest rate and the exchange rate, increases aggregate demand, and eventually increases real GDP and the price level.

■ An increase in the quantity of money can fight unemployment, and a decrease in the quantity of money can fight inflation.

■ The Bank of Canada targets the short-term interest rate, but to change the interest rate, the Bank must change the quantity of money.

■ Changes in the short-term interest rate change real GDP about one year later and change the inflation rate with an even longer time lag.

The Bank of Canada in Action (p. 621)

■ Since the early 1980s the Bank of Canada has been fighting inflation.

■ Under Governor Gerald Bouey, the Bank increased the interest rate to a record level in 1981 and lowered the inflation rate, but at the cost of a severe recession.

■ Under Governor John Crow, the Bank increased the interest rate during the late 1980s and almost eliminated inflation, but again at the cost of a severe recession.

■ During the 1990s and 2000s, the Bank of Canada adjusted the interest rate to balance the primary goal of price stability with concerns for the business cycle.

KEY FIGURES

KEY TERMS

PROBLEMS

*1. You are given the following information about the economy of Nocoin: The banks have deposits of $300 billion. Their reserves are $15 billion, two-thirds of which is in deposits with the central bank. There is $30 billion in notes outside the banks. There are no coins!
   a. Calculate the monetary base.
   b. Calculate the quantity of money.
   c. Calculate the banks' reserve ratio.
   d. Calculate the currency drain as a percentage of the quantity of money.

2. You are given the following information about the economy of Freezone: The people and businesses in Freezone have bank deposits of $500 billion and hold $100 billion in notes and coins. The banks hold deposits at the Freezone central bank of $5 billion and they keep $5 billion in notes and coins in their vaults and ATMs. Calculate
   a. The monetary base.
   b. The quantity of money.
   c. The banks' reserve ratio.
   d. The currency drain as a percentage of the quantity of money.

*3. Suppose that in problem 1, the Bank of Nocoin, the central bank, undertakes an open market purchase of securities of $1 billion.
   a. What happens to the quantity of money?
   b. Explain why the change in the quantity of money is not equal to the change in the monetary base.
   c. Calculate the money multiplier.

4. Suppose that in problem 2, the Freezone central bank undertakes an open market sale of securities of $1 billion.
   a. What happens to the quantity of money?
   b. Explain why the change in the quantity of money is not equal to the change in the monetary base.
   c. Calculate the money multiplier.

*5. The figure shows the economy of Freezone. The aggregate demand curve is AD and the short-run aggregate supply curve is SAS_A. Potential GDP is $300 billion.
   a. What is the price level and real GDP?
   b. Does Freezone have an unemployment problem or an inflation problem? Why?
   c. What do you predict will happen in

Freezone if the central bank takes no monetary policy actions?
   d. What monetary policy action would you advise the central bank to take, and what do you predict will be the effect of that action?

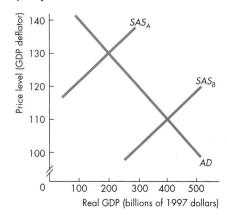

6. Suppose that in Freezone, shown in problem 5, the aggregate demand curve is AD and potential GDP is $300 billion, but the short-run aggregate supply curve is SAS_B.
   a. What is the price level and real GDP?
   b. Does Freezone have an unemployment problem or an inflation problem? Why?
   c. What do you predict will happen in Freezone if the central bank takes no monetary policy actions?
   d. What monetary policy action would you advise the central bank to take and what do you predict the effect of that action will be?

*7. Suppose that in Freezone, shown in problem 5, the short-run aggregate supply curve is SAS_B and potential GDP increases to $350 billion.
   a. What happens in Freezone if the central bank buys securities on the open market?
   b. What happens in Freezone if the central bank sells securities on the open market?
   c. Do you recommend that the central bank buy securities or sell securities? Why?

8. Suppose that in Freezone, shown in problem 5, the short-run aggregate supply curve is SAS_A and a drought decreases potential GDP to $250 billion.
   a. What happens in Freezone if the central bank buys securities on the open market?
   b. What happens in Freezone if the central bank sells securities on the open market?
   c. Do you recommend that the central bank buy securities or sell securities? Why?

*9. The figure shows that for a given real GDP, the demand for money in Minland fluctuates between MD_B and MD_C and on the average is MD_A.

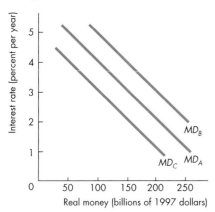

If the Minland central bank sets a target for the quantity of money at $150 billion,
a. What is the interest rate in Minland on the average?
b. What is the range of interest rates in Minland?
c. What do you expect to happen to aggregate demand, real GDP, and the price level when the demand for money changes but the quantity of money remains fixed?

10. Suppose that in Minland in problem 9, the central bank sets the interest rate target at 3 percent a year.
a. How does the Minland central bank prevent the interest rate from rising when the demand for money increases to MD_B?
b. How does the Minland central bank prevent the interest rate from falling when the demand for money decreases to MD_C?
c. Suppose that potential GDP decreases in Minland. Do you think that the Bank of Minland will maintain the 3 percent a year interest rate target? If not, do you think the Bank will try to raise the interest rate or lower it? What actions would the central bank have to take to change the interest rate?
d. If inflation breaks out in Minland, do you think that the Minland central bank will maintain its interest rate target? Why or why not?

1. Study *Reading Between the Lines* on pp. 622–623 and then answer the following questions:
a. Why did the Bank of Canada leave the interest rate unchanged in October 2002?
b. What were the major uncertainties facing the Canadian economy during 2002?
c. Was the Bank of Canada more concerned about inflation or recession during 2002?
d. Do you think the Bank of Canada got its monetary policy right during 2002, or do you think it should have either raised or lowered the interest rate? Provide reasons.

2. Could the Bank of Canada have brought inflation under control during the early 1990s without creating a recession? If you think the answer is "no," do you think it was wise to lower inflation? If you think the answer is "yes," what would the Bank of Canada have had to do differently?

1. Use the link on the Parkin–Bade Web site to visit the Web site of the Bank of Canada and obtain the latest data on M1, M2+, and some short-term interest rates. Then answer the following questions.
a. Is the Bank of Canada trying to slow the economy or speed it up? How can you tell?
b. What open market operations do you think the Bank of Canada has undertaken during the past month?
c. In the light of the Bank of Canada's recent actions, what ripple effects do you expect over the coming months?
d. What do you think the effects of the Bank of Canada's recent actions will be on bond prices and stock prices?

2. Use the link on the Parkin–Bade Web site to visit the Web site of Statistics Canada and look at the current economic conditions. On the basis of the current state of the Canadian economy, do you predict that the Bank of Canada will raise interest rates, lower interest rates, or hold interest rates steady? Write a brief summary of your predictions and reasons.

FISCAL AND MONETARY INTERACTIONS

CHAPTER 27

Sparks Fly in Ottawa

In 2002, the Parliament of Canada approved a federal government budget that showed a large surplus. Not far from Parliament Hill, on Sparks Street, the Bank of Canada pulls the nation's monetary policy levers that influence interest rates and the exchange rate. How does the government's fiscal policy interact with the Bank of Canada's monetary policy to influence interest rates, the exchange rate, and real GDP? ◆ Does it matter if fiscal and monetary policy come into conflict—creating sparks on Sparks Street? ◆ If a recession is looming on the horizon, is an interest rate cut by the Bank of Canada just as good as a tax cut by Parliament? If the economy is overheating, is an interest rate hike by the Bank of Canada just as good as a tax increase by Parliament?

◆ We are going to answer these questions in this chapter. You already know a lot about the effects of fiscal policy and monetary policy. And you know that their ultimate effects work through their influences on both aggregate demand and aggregate supply. This chapter gives you a deeper understanding of the aggregate demand side of the economy and how the combined actions of the federal government and the Bank of Canada affect aggregate demand. In *Reading Between the Lines* at the end of the chapter, we look at what David Dodge, governor of the Bank of Canada, thinks about the appropriate roles for monetary and fiscal policy today.

After studying this chapter, you will be able to

- ■ **Explain how fiscal policy and monetary policy interact to influence interest rates and aggregate demand**

- ■ **Explain the relative effectiveness of fiscal policy and monetary policy**

- ■ **Describe the Keynesian–monetarist controversy about policy and explain how the controversy was settled**

- ■ **Explain how the mix of fiscal and monetary policies influences the composition of aggregate expenditure**

- ■ **Explain how fiscal and monetary policy influence real GDP and the price level**

Macroeconomic Equilibrium

OUR GOAL IN THIS CHAPTER IS TO LEARN HOW changes in government expenditure and changes in the quantity of money interact to change real GDP, the price level, and the interest rate. But before we study the effects of *changes* in these policy variables, we must describe the state of the economy in which government expenditure and the quantity of money are given.

The Basic Idea

Aggregate demand and short-run aggregate supply determine real GDP and the price level. And the demand for and supply of real money determine the interest rate. But aggregate demand and the money market are linked together.

Other things remaining the same, the greater the level of aggregate demand, the higher are real GDP and the price level. A higher real GDP means a greater demand for money; a higher price level means a smaller supply of real money; so a greater level of aggregate demand means a higher interest rate.

Aggregate demand depends on the interest rate because consumption expenditure, investment, and net exports are influenced by the interest rate (see Chapter 25, pp. 597–599). So, other things remaining the same, the lower the interest rate, the greater is aggregate demand.

Only one level of aggregate demand and one interest rate are consistent with each other in macroeconomic equilibrium. Figure 27.1 describes this unique equilibrium.

AS–AD Equilibrium

In Fig. 27.1(a) the intersection of the aggregate demand curve, *AD*, and the short-run aggregate supply curve, *SAS*, determines real GDP at $1,000 billion and the price level at 110.

The equilibrium amounts of consumption expenditure, investment, government expenditures, and net exports lie behind the *AD* curve. But some components of these expenditures are influenced by the interest rate. And the interest rate, in turn, is determined by equilibrium in the money market. Assume that interest-sensitive expenditures total $100 billion, government expenditure is $100 billion, and the rest of real GDP totals $800 billion.

Money Market Equilibrium and Interest-Sensitive Expenditure

In Fig. 27.1(b) the intersection of the demand for money curve, *MD*, and the supply of money curve, *MS*, determines the interest rate at 5 percent a year.

The position of the *MD* curve depends on the level of real GDP. Suppose that the demand for money curve shown in the figure describes the demand for money when real GDP is $1,000 billion, which is equilibrium real GDP in Fig. 27.1(a).

The position of the *MS* curve depends on the quantity of nominal money and the price level. Suppose that the supply of money curve shown in the figure describes the quantity of real money when the price level is 110, which is the equilibrium price level in Fig. 27.1(a).

In Fig. 27.1(c), the *IE* curve determines the level of interest-sensitive expenditure at the equilibrium interest rate of 5 percent a year. Interest-sensitive expenditure is $100 billion, which is the level of this expenditure that lies behind the aggregate demand curve *AD* in Fig. 27.1(a).

Check the Equilibrium

The *AS–AD* equilibrium in Fig. 27.1(a), the money market equilibrium in Fig. 27.1(b), and interest-sensitive expenditure in Fig. 27.1(c) are consistent with each other. And there is no other equilibrium.

To check this claim, assume that aggregate demand is less than *AD* in Fig. 27.1(a) so that real GDP is less than $1,000 billion. If this assumption is correct, the demand for money curve lies to the left of *MD* in Fig. 27.1(b) and the equilibrium interest rate is less than 5 percent a year. With an interest rate less than 5 percent a year, interest-sensitive expenditure exceeds the $100 billion in Fig. 27.1(c). If interest-sensitive expenditure exceeds $100 billion, the *AD* curve lies to the right of the one we assumed and equilibrium real GDP exceeds $1,000 billion. So if we assume a real GDP of less than $1,000 billion, equilibrium real GDP is greater than $1,000 billion. There is an inconsistency. The assumed equilibrium real GDP is too small.

Now assume that aggregate demand is greater than *AD* in Fig. 27.1(a) so that real GDP exceeds $1,000 billion. If this assumption is correct, the demand for money curve lies to the right of *MD* in Fig. 27.1(b) and the equilibrium interest rate exceeds 5 percent a year. With an interest rate above 5 percent a year, interest-sensitive expenditure is less than the $100 billion in Fig. 27.1(c), in which case the

FIGURE 27.1   Equilibrium Real GDP, Price Level, Interest Rate, and Expenditure

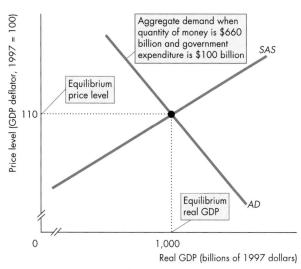

(a) Aggregate supply and aggregate demand

In part (a), the intersection of the aggregate demand curve, *AD*, and the short-run aggregate supply curve, *SAS*, determines real GDP at $1,000 billion and the price level at 110. Behind the *AD* curve, interest-sensitive expenditure is $100 billion, government expenditure is $100 billion, and the rest of real GDP is $800 billion. In part (b), when real GDP is $1,000 billion, the demand for money curve is *MD* and when the price level is 110, the supply of real money curve is *MS*. The intersection of the demand for money curve, *MD*, and the supply of money curve, *MS*, determines the interest rate at 5 percent a year. In part (c), on the *IE* curve, interest-sensitive expenditure is $100 billion at the equilibrium interest rate of 5 percent a year.

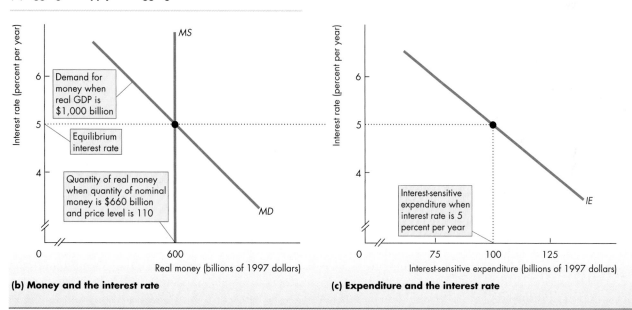

(b) Money and the interest rate   **(c) Expenditure and the interest rate**

AD curve must lie to the left of the one we assumed and equilibrium real GDP must be smaller than $1,000 billion. So if we assume that real GDP exceeds $1,000 billion, equilibrium real GDP is less than $1,000 billion. There is another inconsistency. The assumed equilibrium real GDP is too large.

Only one level of aggregate demand delivers the same money market equilibrium and *AS–AD* equilibrium. In this example, it is the aggregate demand

curve *AD* in Fig. 27.1(a). Assuming this level of aggregate demand implies this level of aggregate demand. Assuming a lower level of aggregate demand implies a higher level. And assuming a higher level of aggregate demand implies a lower level.

Now that you understand how aggregate demand and the interest rate are simultaneously determined, let's study the effects of a change in government expenditures.

Fiscal Policy in the Short Run

╿─── REAL GDP GROWTH IS SLOWING, AND THE Finance Minister is concerned that a recession is likely. So the government decides to try to head off the recession by using fiscal policy to stimulate aggregate demand. A fiscal policy that increases aggregate demand is called an *expansionary fiscal policy*.

The effects of an expansionary fiscal policy are similar to those of throwing a pebble into a pond. There's an initial splash followed by a series of ripples that become ever smaller. The initial splash is the "first round effect" of the fiscal policy action. The ripples are the "second round effects." You've already met the first round effects in Chapter 24, so here is a refresher.

First Round Effects of Fiscal Policy

The economy starts out in the position shown in Fig. 27.1. Real GDP is $1,000 billion, the price level is 110, the interest rate is 5 percent a year, and interest-sensitive expenditure is $100 billion. The government now increases its expenditures on goods and services by $100 billion.

Figure 27.2 shows the first round effects of this action. The increase in government expenditures has a multiplier effect because it induces an increase in consumption expenditure. (You can refresh your memory about the government expenditures multiplier on pp. 562–564.) Let's assume that the multiplier is 2, so a $100 billion increase in government expenditure increases aggregate demand at a given price level by $200 billion. The aggregate demand curve shifts rightward from AD_0 to AD_1. At a price level of 110, the quantity of real GDP demanded increases from $1,000 billion to $1,200 billion.

Real GDP now starts to increase and the price level starts to rise. These are the first round effects of expansionary fiscal policy.

Second Round Effects of Fiscal Policy

Through the second round, real GDP increases and the price level rises until a new macroeconomic equilibrium is reached. But to find that equilibrium and to describe the changes that result from the initial increase in government expenditures, we must keep

FIGURE 27.2　First Round Effects of an Expansionary Fiscal Policy

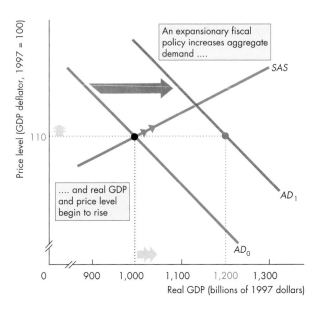

Initially, the aggregate demand curve is AD_0, real GDP is $1,000 billion, and the price level is 110. A $100 billion increase in government expenditures on goods and services has a multiplier effect and increases aggregate demand by $200 billion. The aggregate demand curve shifts rightward to AD_1. Real GDP begins to increase and the price level begins to rise. These are the first round effects of an expansionary fiscal policy.

track of further changes in the money market and in expenditure plans.

It is easier to keep track of the second round effects if we split them into two parts: one that results from the increasing real GDP, and the other that results from the rising price level. We follow these effects in Fig. 27.3.

First, the increasing real GDP increases the demand for money. In Fig. 27.3(b), the demand for money curve shifts rightward. Eventually, it shifts to MD_1 and the interest rate rises to 6 percent a year. At this interest rate, interest-sensitive expenditure decreases to $75 billion in Fig. 27.3(c). The decrease in planned expenditure decreases aggregate demand and the aggregate demand curve shifts leftward to AD_2 in Fig. 27.3(a).

FIGURE 27.3   Second Round Effects of an Expansionary Fiscal Policy

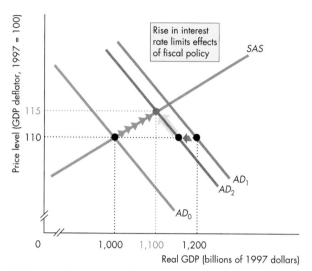

(a) **Aggregate supply and aggregate demand**

Initially, (part b), the money demand curve is MD_0, the real money supply curve is MS_0, and the interest rate is 5 percent a year. With an interest rate of 5 percent a year, interest-sensitive expenditure is $100 billion on the curve IE (part c). With increased government expenditures, the aggregate demand curve is AD_1 (part a). Real GDP is increasing, and the price level is rising. The increasing real GDP increases the demand for money and the money demand curve shifts rightward to MD_1. The higher interest rate decreases interest-sensitive expenditure, which decreases aggregate demand to AD_2. The rising price level brings a movement along the new AD curve. It does so because it decreases the quantity of real money. The money supply curve shifts leftward to MS_1, which in turn raises the interest rate further and decreases expenditure. The new equilibrium occurs when real GDP has increased to $1,100 billion and the price level has risen to 115.

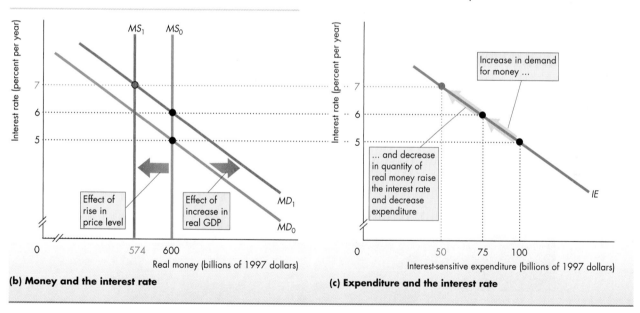

(b) **Money and the interest rate**

(c) **Expenditure and the interest rate**

Second, with a given quantity of nominal money, the rising price level decreases the quantity of real money. In Fig. 27.3(b), the money supply curve shifts leftward to MS_1. The decrease in the quantity of real money raises the interest rate further to 7 percent a year. In Fig. 27.3(c), the higher interest rate decreases interest-sensitive expenditure to $50 billion. Because this decrease in spending plans is induced by a rise in the price level, it decreases the quantity of real GDP

demanded and is shown as a movement up along the aggregate demand curve AD_2 in Fig. 27.3(a).

During this second round process, real GDP is increasing and the price level is rising in a gradual movement up along the short-run aggregate supply curve as indicated by the arrows. In the new equilibrium, real GDP is $1,100 billion, the price level is 115, the interest rate is 7 percent a year, and interest-sensitive expenditure is $50 billion.

FIGURE 27.4   How the Economy Adjusts to an Expansionary Fiscal Policy

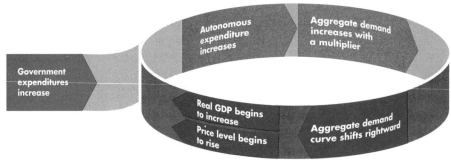

(a) First round effect of expansionary fiscal policy

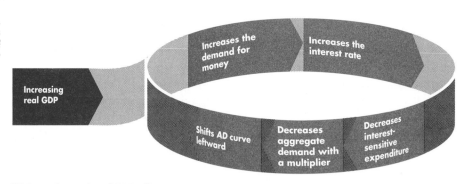

(b) Second round real GDP effect

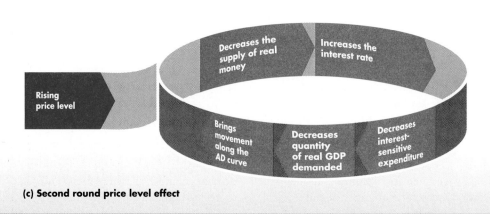

(c) Second round price level effect

Just as the initial equilibrium in Fig. 27.1 was consistent, so the new equilibrium is consistent. The *AS–AD* equilibrium in Fig. 27.3(a), the money market equilibrium in Fig. 27.3(b), and interest-sensitive expenditure in Fig. 27.3(c) are all consistent with each other. And there is no other equilibrium.

Figure 27.4(a) summarizes the first round effect of an expansionary fiscal policy action. Figure 27.4(b) summarizes the two parts of the second round adjustments as the economy responds.

Other Fiscal Policies

A change in government expenditures is only one possible fiscal policy action. Others are a change in transfer payments, such as an increase in unemployment compensation or an increase in social benefits and a change in taxes. All fiscal policy actions work by changing expenditure. But the magnitude of the initial change in expenditure differs for different fiscal actions. For example, changes in taxes and transfer payments change expenditure by smaller amounts than does a change in government expenditures on goods and services. But fiscal policies that change autonomous expenditure by a given amount and in a given direction have similar effects on equilibrium real GDP, the price level, and the interest rate regardless of the initial fiscal action. Let's take a closer look at the effect of the rise in the interest rate.

Crowding Out and Crowding In

Because an expansionary fiscal policy increases the interest rate, it decreases all the interest-sensitive components of aggregate expenditure. One of these components is investment, and the decrease in investment that results from an expansionary fiscal action is called **crowding out.**

Crowding out may be partial or complete. Partial crowding out occurs when the decrease in investment is less than the increase in government expenditures. This is the normal case—and the case we've just seen.

Complete crowding out occurs if the decrease in investment equals the initial increase in government expenditures. For complete crowding out to occur, a small change in the demand for real money must lead to a large change in the interest rate, and the change in the interest rate must lead to a large change in investment.

But another potential influence of government expenditures on investment works in the opposite direction to the crowding-out effect and is called "crowding in." **Crowding in** is the tendency for expansionary fiscal policy to *increase* investment. This effect works in three ways.

First, in a recession, an expansionary fiscal policy might create expectations of a more speedy recovery and bring an increase in expected profits. Higher expected profits might increase investment despite a higher interest rate.

Second, government expenditures might be productive and lead to more profitable business opportunities. For example, a new government-built highway might cut the cost of transporting a farmer's produce to a market and induce the farmer to invest in a new fleet of refrigerated trucks.

Third, if an expansionary fiscal policy takes the form of a cut in taxes on business profits, firms' after-tax profits increase and investment might increase.

The Exchange Rate and International Crowding Out

We've seen that an expansionary fiscal policy leads to higher interest rates. But a change in interest rates also affects the exchange rate. Higher interest rates make the dollar rise in value against other currencies. With interest rates higher in Canada than in the rest of the world, funds flow into Canada and people around the world demand more Canadian dollars. As the dollar rises in value, foreigners find Canadian-produced goods and services more expensive and Canadians find imports less expensive. Exports decrease and imports increase—net exports decrease. The tendency for an expansionary fiscal policy to decrease net exports is called **international crowding out.** The decrease in net exports offsets, to some degree, the initial increase in aggregate expenditure brought about by an expansionary fiscal policy.

REVIEW QUIZ

1 Describe macroeconomic equilibrium. What conditions are met in such an equilibrium? What are the links between aggregate demand, the money market, and investment?

2 What is an expansionary fiscal policy and what are its first round effects? What is happening at the end of the first round?

3 What are the second round effects of an expansionary fiscal policy action? Describe the forces at work and the changes that occur in the interest rate, investment, real GDP, and the price level.

4 What is crowding out? What is crowding in? How do they influence the outcome of a fiscal policy action?

5 How does an expansionary fiscal policy affect the exchange rate? What happens to imports and exports?

Monetary Policy in the Short Run

TO STUDY THE EFFECTS OF AN EXPANSIONARY monetary policy, we look at the first round effects and the second round effects, just as we did for fiscal policy. Figure 27.5 describes the economy, which is initially in the situation that we studied in Fig. 27.1. The quantity of money is $660 billion, the interest rate is 5 percent a year, interest-sensitive expenditure

is $100 billion, real GDP is $1,000 billion, and the price level is 110.

The Bank of Canada now increases the quantity of money to $1,155 billion. With a price level of 110, the quantity of real money increases to $1,050 billion. Figure 27.5(a) shows the immediate effect. The real money supply curve shifts rightward from MS_0 to MS_1, and the interest rate falls from 5 percent to 1 percent a year. The lower interest rate increases interest-sensitive expenditure to $200 billion (part b). The increase in interest-sensitive expenditure

---

FIGURE 27.5 First Round Effects of an Expansionary Monetary Policy

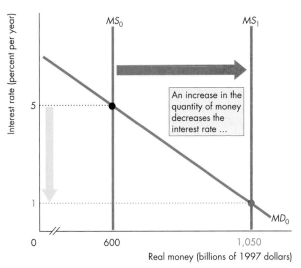

(a) Change in quantity of money

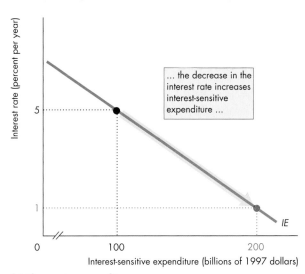

(b) Change in expenditure

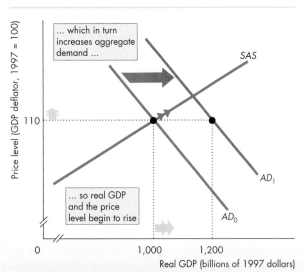

(c) Change in aggregate demand

Initially, the real money demand curve is MD_0, the real money supply curve is MS_0, and the interest rate is 5 percent a year (part a). With an interest rate of 5 percent a year, interest-sensitive expenditure is $100 billion on the IE curve (part b). The aggregate demand curve is AD_0. Equilibrium real GDP is $1,000 billion, and the price level is 110 (part c).

An increase in the quantity of money shifts the money supply curve rightward to MS_1 (part a). The interest rate falls to 1 percent a year and interest-sensitive expenditure increases to $200 billion (part b). The increase in expenditure increases aggregate demand and shifts the aggregate demand curve to AD_1 (in part c). Real GDP begins to increase and the price level begins to rise.

increases aggregate demand and shifts the *AD* curve rightward from AD_0 to AD_1 (part c). The increase in aggregate demand sets off a multiplier process in which real GDP and the price level begin to increase towards their equilibrium levels.

These are the first round effects of an expansionary monetary policy. An increase in the quantity of money lowers the interest rate and increases aggregate demand. Real GDP and the price level begin to increase.

Let's now look at the second round effects.

Second Round Effects

The increasing real GDP and rising price level set off the second round, which Fig. 27.6 illustrates. And as in the case of fiscal policy, it is best to break the second round into two parts: the consequence of increasing real GDP, and the consequence of the rising price level.

The increasing real GDP increases the demand for money from MD_0 to MD_1 in Fig. 27.6(a). The increased demand for money raises the interest rate to

FIGURE 27.6   Second Round Effects of an Expansionary Monetary Policy

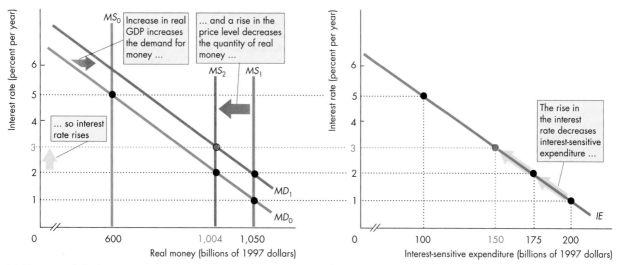

(a) Money and the interest rate

(b) Decrease in expenditure

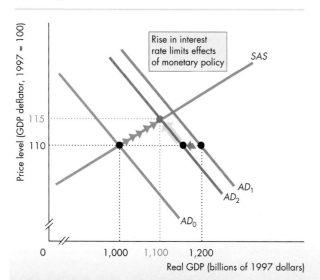

(c) Aggregate demand and aggregate supply

At the start of the second round, the money demand curve is still MD_0 (part a), the real money supply curve is MS_1, and the interest rate is 1 percent a year. With an interest rate of 1 percent a year, interest-sensitive expenditure is $200 billion on the curve *IE* (part b). With the increased quantity of money and expenditure level, the aggregate demand curve is AD_1 (part c). Real GDP is increasing, and the price level is rising. The increasing real GDP increases the demand for money and the money demand curve shifts rightward to MD_1. The higher interest rate decreases interest-sensitive expenditure, which decreases aggregate demand to AD_2. The rising price level brings a movement along the new *AD* curve. It does so because the rising price level decreases the quantity of real money and the money supply curve shifts to MS_2. The interest rate raises further and expenditure decreases. The new equilibrium occurs when real GDP has increased to $1,100 billion and the price level has risen to 115.

2 percent a year. The higher interest rate brings a decrease in interest-sensitive expenditure from $200 billion to $175 billion in Fig. 27.6(b). And the lower level of expenditure decreases aggregate demand and shifts the aggregate demand curve leftward from AD_1 to AD_2 in Fig. 27.6(c).

The rising price level brings a movement along the new aggregate demand curve in Fig. 27.6(c). This movement occurs because the rising price level decreases the quantity of real money. As the price

level rises, the quantity of real money decreases to $1,004 billion and the money supply curve shifts leftward from MS_1 to MS_2 (part a). The interest rate rises further to 3 percent a year. And interest-sensitive expenditure decreases to $150 billion (part b).

In the new short-run equilibrium, real GDP has increased to $1,100 billion, and the price level has risen to 115, where aggregate demand curve AD_2 intersects the short-run aggregate supply curve SAS.

FIGURE 27.7   How the Economy Adjusts to an Expansionary Monetary Policy

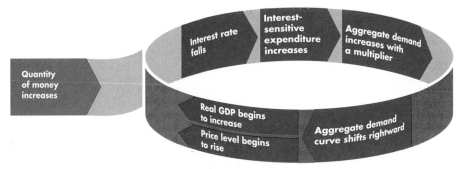

(a) First round effect of expansionary monetary policy

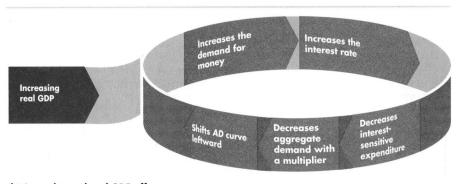

(b) Second round real GDP effect

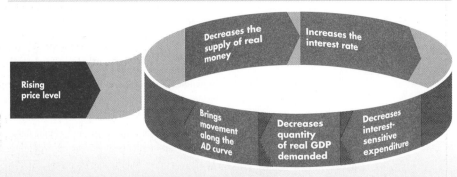

(c) Second round price level effect

The money demand curve is MD_1, the money supply curve is MS_2, and the interest rate is 3 percent a year in part (a). With an interest rate of 3 percent a year, interest-sensitive expenditure is $150 billion (part b).

The new equilibrium is the only consistent one and is like that of Fig. 27.1. Figure 27.7 summarizes the adjustments that occur to bring the economy to this new equilibrium.

Money and the Exchange Rate

An increase in the money supply lowers the interest rate. If the interest rate falls in Canada but does not fall in the United States, Japan, and Western Europe, international investors buy the now higher-yielding foreign assets and sell the relatively lower-yielding Canadian assets. As they make these transactions, they sell Canadian dollars. So the dollar depreciates against other currencies. (This mechanism is explained in greater detail in Chapter 26, pp. 619–620.)

With a cheaper Canadian dollar, foreigners face lower prices for Canadian-produced goods and services and Canadians face higher prices for foreign-produced goods and services. Foreigners increase their imports from Canada, and Canadians decrease their imports from the rest of the world. Canadian net exports increase, and real GDP and the price level increase further.

REVIEW QUIZ

1 What are the first round effects of an expansionary monetary policy? What happens to the interest rate, investment and other components of interest-sensitive expenditure, aggregate demand, the demand for money, real GDP, and the price level in the first round?
2 What are the second round effects of an expansionary monetary policy? What happens to the interest rate, investment and other components of interest-sensitive expenditure, aggregate demand, the demand for money, real GDP, and the price level in the second round?
3 How does an expansionary monetary policy influence the exchange rate, imports, and exports?

Relative Effectiveness of Policies

WE'VE SEEN THAT AGGREGATE DEMAND AND REAL GDP are influenced by both fiscal and monetary policy. But which policy is the more potent? This question was once at the centre of a controversy among macroeconomists. Later in this section we'll look at that controversy and see how it was settled. But we begin by discovering what determines the effectiveness of fiscal policy.

Effectiveness of Fiscal Policy

The effectiveness of fiscal policy is measured by the magnitude of the increase in aggregate demand that results from a given increase in government expenditures (or decrease in taxes). The effectiveness of fiscal policy depends on the strength of the crowding-out effect. Fiscal policy is most powerful if no crowding out occurs. Fiscal policy is impotent if there is complete crowding out. And the strength of the crowding-out effect depends on two things:

1. The responsiveness of expenditure to the interest rate
2. The responsiveness of the quantity of money demanded to the interest rate

If expenditure is not very responsive to a change in the interest rate, the crowding-out effect is small. But if expenditure is highly responsive to a change in the interest rate, the crowding-out effect is large. Other things remaining the same, the smaller the responsiveness of expenditure to the interest rate, the smaller is the crowding-out effect and the more effective is fiscal policy.

The responsiveness of the quantity of money demanded to the interest rate also affects the size of the crowding-out effect. An increase in real GDP increases the demand for money and with no change in the quantity of money, the interest rate rises. But the extent to which the interest rate rises depends on the responsiveness of the quantity of money demanded to the interest rate. Other things remaining the same, the greater the responsiveness of the quantity of money demanded to the interest rate, the smaller is the rise in the interest rate, the smaller is the crowding-out effect, and the more effective is fiscal policy.

Effectiveness of Monetary Policy

The effectiveness of monetary policy is measured by the magnitude of the increase in aggregate demand that results from a given increase in the quantity of money. The effectiveness of monetary policy depends on the same two factors that influence the effectiveness of fiscal policy:

1. The responsiveness of the quantity of money demanded to the interest rate
2. The responsiveness of expenditure to the interest rate

The starting point for monetary policy is a change in the quantity of money that changes the interest rate. A given change in the quantity of money might bring a small change or a large change in the interest rate. The less responsive the quantity of money demanded to the interest rate, the greater is the change in the interest rate. So other things remaining the same, the larger the initial change in the interest rate, the more effective is monetary policy.

But effectiveness of monetary policy also depends on how much expenditure changes. If expenditure is not very responsive to a change in the interest rate, monetary actions do not have much effect on expenditure. But if expenditure is highly responsive to a change in the interest rate, monetary actions have a large effect on aggregate expenditure. The greater the responsiveness of expenditure to the interest rate, the more effective is monetary policy.

The effectiveness of fiscal policy and monetary policy that you've just studied was once controversial. During the 1950s and 1960s, this issue lay at the heart of what was called the Keynesian–monetarist controversy. Let's look at the dispute and see how it was resolved.

Keynesian–Monetarist Controversy

The Keynesian–monetarist controversy was an ongoing dispute in macroeconomics between two broad groups of economists. A **Keynesian** is a macroeconomist who regards the economy as being inherently unstable and as requiring active government intervention to achieve stability. Keynesian views about the functioning of the economy are based on the theories of John Maynard Keynes, published in Keynes' *General Theory* (see pp. 522–523). Traditionally Keynesians assigned a low degree of importance to monetary policy and a high degree of importance to fiscal policy. Modern Keynesians

assign a high degree of importance to both types of policy. A **monetarist** is a macroeconomist who believes that most macroeconomic fluctuations are caused by fluctuations in the quantity of money and that the economy is inherently stable and requires no active government intervention. Monetarist views about the functioning of the economy are based on theories most forcefully set forth by Milton Friedman (see pp. 674–675). Traditionally monetarists assigned a low degree of importance to fiscal policy. But modern monetarists, like modern Keynesians, assign a high degree of importance to both types of policy.

The nature of the Keynesian–monetarist debate has changed over the years. During the 1950s and 1960s, it was a debate about the relative effectiveness of fiscal policy and monetary policy in changing aggregate demand. We can see the essence of that debate by distinguishing three views:

- Extreme Keynesianism
- Extreme monetarism
- Intermediate position

Extreme Keynesianism   The extreme Keynesian hypothesis is that a change in the quantity of money has no effect on aggregate demand and a change in government expenditures on goods and services or in taxes has a large effect on aggregate demand. The two circumstances in which a change in the quantity of money has no effect on aggregate demand are

1. Expenditure is completely insensitive to the interest rate
2. The quantity of money demanded is highly sensitive to the interest rate

If expenditure is completely insensitive to the interest rate (if the *IE* curve is vertical), a change in the quantity of money changes the interest rate, but the change does not affect aggregate planned expenditure. Monetary policy is impotent.

If the quantity of money demanded is highly sensitive to the interest rate (if the *MD* curve is horizontal), people are willing to hold any amount of money at a given interest rate—a situation called a *liquidity trap*. With a liquidity trap, a change in the quantity of money affects only the amount of money held. It does not affect the interest rate. With an unchanged interest rate, expenditure remains constant. Monetary policy is impotent. Some people believe that Japan was in a liquidity trap during the late 1990s.

RELATIVE EFFECTIVENESS OF POLICIES

Extreme Monetarism The extreme monetarist hypothesis is that a change in government expenditures on goods and services or in taxes has no effect on aggregate demand and that a change in the quantity of money has a large effect on aggregate demand. Two circumstances give rise to these predictions:

1. Expenditure is highly sensitive to the interest rate
2. The quantity of money demanded is completely insensitive to the interest rate

If an increase in government expenditures on goods and services induces an increase in the interest rate that is sufficiently large to reduce expenditure by the same amount as the initial increase in government expenditures, then fiscal policy has no effect on aggregate demand. This outcome is complete crowding out. For this result to occur, either the quantity of money demanded must be insensitive to the interest rate—a fixed amount of money is held regardless of the interest rate—or expenditure must be highly sensitive to the interest rate—any amount of expenditure will be undertaken at a given interest rate.

The Intermediate Position The intermediate position is that both fiscal and monetary policy affect aggregate demand. Crowding out is not complete, so fiscal policy does have an effect. There is no liquidity trap and expenditure responds to the interest rate, so monetary policy does indeed affect aggregate demand. This position is the one that now appears to be correct and is the one that we've spent most of this chapter exploring. Let's see how economists came to this conclusion.

Sorting Out the Competing Claims

The dispute between monetarists, Keynesians, and those taking an intermediate position was essentially a disagreement about the magnitudes of two economic parameters:

1. The responsiveness of expenditure to the interest rate
2. The responsiveness of the demand for real money to the interest rate

If expenditure is highly sensitive to the interest rate or the demand for real money is barely sensitive to the interest rate, then monetary policy is powerful and fiscal policy relatively ineffective. In this case, the world looks similar to the claims of extreme mone-

tarists. If expenditure is very insensitive to the interest rate, or the demand for real money is highly sensitive, then fiscal policy is powerful and monetary policy is relatively ineffective. In this case, the world looks similar to the claims of the extreme Keynesians.

By using statistical methods to study the demand for real money and expenditure and by using data from a wide variety of historical and national experiences, economists were able to settle this dispute. Neither extreme position turned out to be supported by the evidence and the intermediate position won. The demand curve for real money slopes downward. And expenditure *is* interest sensitive. Neither the money demand curve nor the interest-sensitive expenditure curve is vertical or horizontal, so the extreme Keynesian and extreme monetarist hypotheses are rejected.

Interest Rate and Exchange Rate Effectiveness

Although fiscal policy and monetary policy are alternative ways of changing aggregate demand, they have opposing effects on the interest rate and the exchange rate. A fiscal policy action that increases aggregate demand raises the interest rate and increases the exchange rate. A monetary policy action that increases aggregate demand lowers the interest rate and decreases the exchange rate. Because of these opposing effects on interest rates and the exchange rate, if the two policies are combined to increase aggregate demand, their separate effects on the interest rate and the exchange rate can be minimized.

REVIEW QUIZ

1 What two macroeconomic parameters influence the relative effectiveness of fiscal policy and monetary policy?
2 Under what circumstances is the Keynesian view correct and under what circumstances is the monetarist view correct?
3 How can fiscal policy and monetary policy be combined to increase aggregate demand yet at the same time keep the interest rate constant?

We're now going to look at expansionary fiscal and monetary policy at full employment.

Policy Actions at Full Employment

AN EXPANSIONARY FISCAL POLICY OR MONETARY policy can bring the economy to full employment. But it is often difficult to determine whether the economy is below full employment. So an expansionary fiscal policy or monetary policy might be undertaken when the economy is at full employment. What happens then? Let's answer this question starting with an expansionary fiscal policy.

Expansionary Fiscal Policy at Full Employment

Suppose the economy is at full employment and the government increases expenditure. All the effects that we worked out earlier in this chapter occur. Except that these effects determine only a *short-run equilibrium*. That is, the first round and second round effects of policy both occur in the short run. There is a third round, which is the long-run adjustment.

Starting out at full employment, an expansionary fiscal policy will create an above full-employment equilibrium in which there is an *inflationary gap*. The money wage rate begins to rise, short-run aggregate supply decreases, and a long-run adjustment occurs in which real GDP decreases to potential GDP and the price level rises.

Figure 27.8 illustrates the combined first and second round short-run effects and the third round long-run adjustment.

In Fig. 27.8, potential GDP is $1,000 billion. Real GDP equals potential GDP on aggregate demand curve AD_0 and short-run aggregate supply curve SAS_0. An expansionary fiscal action increases aggregate demand. The combined first round and second round effect increases aggregate demand to AD_1. Real GDP increases to $1,100 billion and the price level rises to 115. There is an inflationary gap of $100 billion.

With the economy above full employment, a shortage of labour puts upward pressure on the money wage rate, which now begins to rise. And a third round of adjustment begins. The rising money wage rate decreases short-run aggregate supply and the *SAS* curve starts moving leftward towards SAS_1.

As short-run aggregate supply decreases, real GDP decreases and the price level rises. This process

FIGURE 27.8   Fiscal Policy at Full Employment

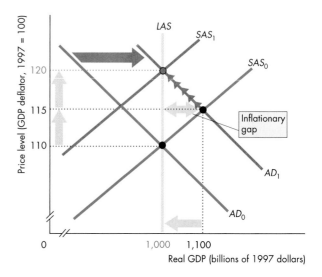

The long-run aggregate supply curve is *LAS* and initially the aggregate demand curve is AD_0 and the short-run aggregate supply curve is SAS_0. Real GDP is $1,000 billion and the GDP deflator is 110. Fiscal and monetary policy changes shift the aggregate demand curve to AD_1. At the new short-run equilibrium, real GDP is $1,100 billion and the GDP deflator is 115. Because real GDP exceeds potential GDP, the money wage rate begins to rise and the short-run aggregate supply curve begins to shift leftward to SAS_1. At the new long-run equilibrium, the GDP deflator is 120 and real GDP is back at its original level.

continues until the inflationary gap has been eliminated at full employment. At long-run equilibrium, real GDP is $1,000, which is potential GDP, and the price level is 120.

Crowding Out at Full Employment

You've just seen that when government expenditures increase at full employment, the long-run change in real GDP is zero. The entire effect of the increase in aggregate demand is to increase the price level. This outcome implies that at full employment, an increase in government expenditures *completely crowds out private expenditure* or *creates an international (net exports) deficit*, or results in a combination of the two.

The easiest way to see why is to recall that aggregate expenditure, which equals consumption expenditure, C, plus investment, I, plus government expenditures, G, plus net exports, NX, equals real GDP. That is,

$$Y = C + I + G + NX.$$

Comparing the initial situation with the outcome, real GDP has not changed. So aggregate expenditure, $C + I + G + NX$, is constant between the two situations.

But government expenditures have increased, so the sum of consumption, investment, and net exports must have decreased. If net exports don't change, consumption plus investment decreases by the full amount of the increase in government expenditures. If consumption and investment don't change, net exports decrease by an amount equal to the increase in government expenditures. A decrease in net exports is an increase in our international deficit.

You've now seen that the effects of expansionary fiscal policy are extremely sensitive to the state of the economy when the policy action is taken. At less than full employment, an expansionary fiscal policy can move the economy towards full employment. At full employment, an expansionary fiscal policy raises the price level, crowds out private expenditure, and creates an international deficit.

Expansionary Monetary Policy at Full Employment

Now suppose the economy is at full employment and the Bank of Canada increases the quantity of money. Again, all the effects that we worked out earlier in this chapter occur. But again, these effects determine only a *short-run equilibrium*. That is, the first round and second round effects of monetary policy both occur in the short run. And again, there is a third round, which is the long-run adjustment.

Starting out at full employment, an expansionary monetary policy will create an above full-employment equilibrium in which there is an *inflationary gap*. The money wage rate begins to rise, short-run aggregate supply decreases, and a long-run adjustment occurs in which real GDP decreases to potential GDP and the price level rises.

Figure 27.8, which illustrates the effects of an expansionary fiscal policy at full employment, also

illustrates the effects of an expansionary monetary policy at full employment.

In the short run, an expansionary monetary policy increases real GDP and the price level. But in the long run, it increases only the price level and leaves real GDP unchanged at potential GDP.

Long-Run Neutrality

In the long run, a change in the quantity of money changes only the price level and leaves real GDP unchanged. The independence of real GDP from the quantity of money is an example of the long-run neutrality of money.

But long-run neutrality applies not only to real GDP but also to all real variables. The so-called **long-run neutrality** proposition is that in the long run, a change in the quantity of money changes the price level and leaves all real variables unchanged.

You can see this outcome in the case of real GDP in Fig. 27.8. With no change in real GDP, the demand for money does not change. The price level rises by the same percentage as the increase in the quantity of money, so the quantity of real money does not change. With no change in the demand for money and no change in the quantity of real money, the interest rate does not change. And with no change in the interest rate, expenditure remains the same. Finally, with no change in real GDP or the real interest rate, consumption expenditure, investment, government expenditures, and net exports are unchanged.

REVIEW QUIZ

1 Contrast the short-run effects of an expansionary fiscal policy on real GDP and the price level with its long-run effects when the policy action occurs at full employment.
2 Contrast the short-run effects of an expansionary monetary policy on real GDP and the price level with its long-run effects when the policy action occurs at full employment.
3 Explain crowding out at full employment.
4 Explain the long-run neutrality of money.

Policy Coordination and Conflict

SO FAR, WE'VE STUDIED FISCAL POLICY AND monetary policy in isolation from each other. We are now going to consider what happens if the two branches of policy are coordinated and if they come into conflict.

Policy coordination occurs when the government and the Bank of Canada work together to achieve a common set of goals. **Policy conflict** occurs when the government and the Bank of Canada pursue different goals and the actions of one make it harder (perhaps impossible) for the other to achieve its goals.

Policy Coordination

The basis for policy coordination is the fact that either fiscal policy or monetary policy can be used to increase aggregate demand. Starting from a *below full-employment equilibrium*, an increase in aggregate demand increases real GDP and decreases unemployment. If the size of the policy action is well judged, it can restore full employment. Similarly, starting from an *above full-employment equilibrium*, a decrease in aggregate demand decreases real GDP and can, if the size of the policy action is well judged, eliminate an *inflationary gap*. Because either a fiscal policy or a monetary policy action can achieve these objectives, the two policies can (in principle) be combined to also achieve the same outcome.

If either or both policies can restore full employment and eliminate inflation, why does it matter which policy is used? It matters because the two policies have different side effects—different effects on other variables about which people care. These side effects work through the influence of policy on two key variables:

- The interest rate
- The exchange rate

Interest Rate Effects An expansionary fiscal policy *raises* the interest rate, while an expansionary monetary policy *lowers* the interest rate. When the interest rate changes, investment changes, so an expansionary fiscal policy lowers investment (crowding out) while an expansionary monetary policy increases investment. So if an expansionary fiscal policy increases aggregate demand, consumption expenditure

increases and investment decreases. But if an expansionary monetary policy increases aggregate demand, consumption expenditure and investment increase.

By coordinating fiscal policy and monetary policy and increasing aggregate demand with an appropriate combination of the two, it is possible to increase real GDP and lower unemployment with either no change in the interest rate or any desired change in the interest rate. A big dose of fiscal expansion and a small dose of monetary expansion raises the interest rate and decreases investment, while a small dose of fiscal expansion and a big dose of monetary expansion lowers the interest rate and increases investment.

The interest rate affects our long-term growth prospects because the growth rate of potential GDP depends on the level of investment. The connection between investment, capital, and growth is explained in Chapters 29 and 30.

Exchange Rate Effects An expansionary fiscal policy raises not only the interest rate but also the exchange rate. In contrast, an expansionary monetary policy *lowers* the exchange rate. When the exchange rate changes, net exports change. An expansionary fiscal policy lowers net exports (international crowding out) while an expansionary monetary policy increases net exports. So if full employment is restored by expansionary policy, net exports decrease with fiscal expansion and increase with monetary expansion.

Policy Conflict

Policy conflicts are not planned. But they sometimes happen. When they arise, it is usually because of a divergence of the political priorities of the government and the objectives of the Bank of Canada.

Governments (both federal and provincial) pay a lot of attention to employment and production over a short time horizon. They look for policies that make their re-election chances high. The Bank of Canada pays a lot of attention to price level stability and has a long time horizon. It doesn't have an election to worry about.

So a situation might arise in which the government wants the Bank to pursue an expansionary monetary policy but the Bank wants to keep its foot on the monetary brake. The government says that an increase in the quantity of money is essential to lower interest rates and the exchange rate and to boost investment and exports. The Bank says that the problem is with fiscal policy. Spending is too high and revenues too low. With fiscal policy too expansionary, interest rates and the exchange rate are high and they cannot be lowered permanently by monetary policy. To lower interest rates and give investment and exports a boost, fiscal policy must become contractionary. Only then can an expansionary monetary policy be pursued.

A further potential conflict between the government and the Bank of Canada concerns the financing of the government deficit. A government deficit can be financed either by borrowing from the general public or by borrowing from the Bank. If the government borrows from the general public, it must pay interest on its debt. If it borrows from the Bank, it pays interest to the Bank. But the government owns the Bank, so the interest comes back to the government. Financing a deficit by selling debt to the central bank costs the government no interest. So the temptation to sell debt to the central bank is strong.

But when the Bank of Canada buys government debt, it pays for the debt with newly created monetary base. The quantity of money increases. And such finance leads to inflation. In many countries—for example in Eastern Europe, Latin America, and Africa—government deficits are financed by the central bank. In Canada, they are not. Despite huge government deficits in the 1980s and early 1990s, the Bank of Canada has stood firm in its purchase of government debt. Only tiny amounts have been bought by the Bank to keep the monetary base growing at a rate that keeps up with real GDP growth and sustains a modest inflation rate. Figure 27.9 shows the Bank's contribution to financing the government of Canada's deficits since those deficits emerged in 1975. You can see that the Bank has been able to pursue its primary objective of price level stability despite the huge debts incurred by the government.

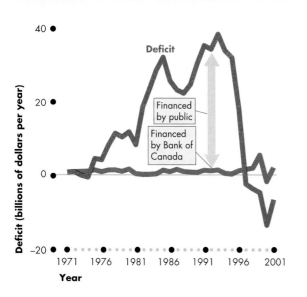

FIGURE 27.9   Debt Financing

The federal government's budget deficit mushroomed after 1975. The deficit was financed mostly by selling bonds to the public. The Bank of Canada's monetary policy has created little new money to finance the deficit.

Source: Bank of Canada, *Banking and Financial Statistics*, table G4.

REVIEW QUIZ

1 What are the main things that can be achieved by coordinating fiscal policy and monetary policy?
2 What are the main sources of conflict in policy between the Bank of Canada and the government of Canada?
3 What are the main consequences of the government and the Bank of Canada pursuing conflicting policies? Are all the consequences bad?

◆ You have now studied the interaction of fiscal policy and monetary policy. *Reading Between the Lines* on pp. 644–645 examines the views of David Dodge, governor of the Bank of Canada, on the appropriate roles for monetary and fiscal policy today.

You've seen that monetary and fiscal policy policies are alternative ways of changing aggregate demand and real GDP. But they have different effects on the interest rate and the exchange rate. You've seen what determines the relative effectiveness of fiscal and monetary policies and how the mix of these policies can influence the composition of aggregate expenditure. But you've also seen that the ultimate effects of these policies on real GDP and the price level depend not only on the behaviour of aggregate demand but also on aggregate supply and the state of the labour market. You will turn to the aggregate supply side of the economy in the next part. But first, in Chapter 28, we complete our study of aggregate demand by learning about inflation.

READING BETWEEN THE LINES

POLICY WATCH

Monetary and Fiscal Tensions

CALGARY HERALD, SEPTEMBER 4, 2002

Central bank boss warns against big spending

The head of the Bank of Canada has warned the Chrétien government against eroding the country's hard-earned anti-inflation credibility.

The not-so-veiled warning by governor David Dodge came amid rising speculation that the prime minister is about to go on a social policy spending spree in advance of his retirement in 18 months.

It also came on the eve of what many analysts expect will be another interest rate increase aimed at reducing the stimulus that is already in the economy. Earlier this year, the bank rate was the lowest in more than four decades.

In a speech to other central bankers in Jackson Hole, Wyo., last weekend Dodge stressed the importance of the credibility that the bank and government have earned with "joint agreements on inflation-control targets" and "a framework that greatly reduces the probability of running a fiscal deficit and thus puts the debt-to-GDP ratio on a clear downward track."

"Fiscal and monetary credibility is high," Dodge said, noting that markets, businesses and individuals "trust" that the central bank will meet its inflation target and that the government will not start spending more than it takes in.

"Initially, the credibility of these policies was not high," Dodge noted. "So it was essential to demonstrate clearly our resolve to achieve greater fiscal prudence and lower inflation until credibility was gained."

To do that, he said, it meant that the bank at times had to keep interest rates higher, and that the government had to keep a tighter rein on spending than otherwise necessary.

Dodge also said it was fortunate the government in its last budget did not inject a lot of new spending into the economy.

"I say fortunately because... there was more underlying strength in the economy than we expected," Dodge explained.

He went on to note that the bank had already injected a lot of stimulus into the economy by cutting interest rates.

"Therefore, added fiscal stimulus was not necessary to get the economy going and the monetary stimulus provided is proving much easier to turn around."

Material reprinted with the express permission of Calgary Herald Company, a CanWest Partnership.

Essence of the Story

■ In a speech at a conference of central bankers, Bank of Canada governor David Dodge said that the joint agreements on inflation-control targets between the Bank and government have created a high degree of trust that inflation targets will be met.

■ He warned against increasing government spending and said it was fortunate that in its last budget, the government did not inject a lot of new spending into the economy because the economy was already expanding strongly.

■ He noted that the Bank of Canada had injected a lot of stimulus into the economy by cutting interest rates and that added fiscal stimulus was neither necessary nor as easy to reverse as monetary policy actions.

Economic Analysis

■ David Dodge wants to maintain the credibility that the Bank of Canada has established and keep the inflation rate below 3 percent a year.

■ He thinks that macroeconomic stability—low inflation *and* full employment—can best be achieved by using monetary policy alone.

■ He fears that if fiscal policy were to become too expansionary, inflation could take off.

■ Figure 1 illustrates David Dodge's concern.

■ In Fig. 1, potential GDP is $1,084, but aggregate demand, AD_0, and short-run aggregate supply, SAS_0, intersect at a below-full employment equilibrium so there is a recessionary gap.

■ If the Bank of Canada cuts the interest rate to stimulate demand, and if the government increases its expenditure, which also stimulates demand, the AD curve shifts rightward to AD_1.

■ This expansionary fiscal and monetary policy brings an inflationary gap.

■ With an inflationary gap, the money wage rate begins to rise and the SAS curve starts to shift leftward towards SAS_1.

■ Real GDP falls back towards potential GDP, but inflation takes off as the price level rises to 127.

■ Figure 2 shows what David Dodge would like to achieve.

■ With the same initial recessionary gap, the Bank of Canada takes action to stimulate demand by cutting the interest rate.

■ The government holds expenditure steady so that fiscal policy does not increase aggregate demand.

■ The AD curve shifts rightward to AD_2 and full employment is achieved while the inflation rate remains low.

■ If the Bank of Canada sees an inflationary gap, it can take quick action in the opposite direction—raise the interest rate—to decrease aggregate demand.

■ In contrast, if increased government spending brings an inflationary gap, it is difficult to cut spending.

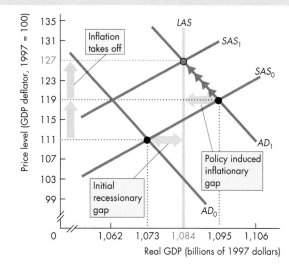

Figure 1 Fiscal and monetary stimulus

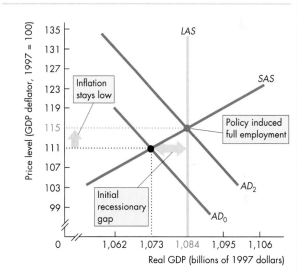

Figure 2 Monetary stimulus alone

You're The Voter

■ Do you agree with David Dodge that monetary policy alone is the appropriate tool for achieving low inflation and full employment?

■ Do you think there is ever a role for fiscal policy?

645

SUMMARY

KEY POINTS

Macroeconomic Equilibrium (pp. 628–629)

- Equilibrium real GDP, the price level, and the interest rate are determined simultaneously by equilibrium in the money market and equality of aggregate demand and aggregate supply.

Fiscal Policy in the Short Run (pp. 630–633)

- The first round effects of an expansionary fiscal policy are an increase in aggregate demand, increasing real GDP, and a rising price level.
- The second round effects are an increasing demand for money and a decreasing quantity of real money that increase the interest rate and limit the increase in real GDP and the rise in the price level.
- Interest-sensitive expenditure, which includes investment and net exports, decreases.

Monetary Policy in the Short Run (pp. 634–637)

- The first round effects of an expansionary monetary policy are a fall in the interest rate, an increase in aggregate demand, an increasing real GDP, and a rising price level.
- The second round effects are an increasing demand for money and a decreasing quantity of real money that increase the interest rate and limit the increase in real GDP and the rise in the price level.
- Interest-sensitive expenditure, which includes investment and net exports, increases.

Relative Effectiveness of Policies (pp. 637–639)

- The relative effectiveness of fiscal and monetary policy depends on the interest-sensitivity of both expenditure and the quantity of money demanded.
- The extreme Keynesian position is that only fiscal policy affects aggregate demand. The extreme monetarist position is that only monetary policy affects aggregate demand. Neither extreme is correct.

- The mix of fiscal and monetary policy influences the composition of aggregate demand.

Policy Actions at Full Employment (pp. 640–641)

- An expansionary fiscal policy at full employment increases real GDP and the price level in the short run but increases only the price level in the long run. Complete crowding out of investment occurs or the international deficit increases.
- An expansionary monetary policy at full employment increases real GDP and the price level in the short run but increases only the price level in the long run. Money is neutral—has no real effects—in the long run.

Policy Coordination and Conflict (pp. 642–643)

- Policy coordination can make changes in the interest rate and the exchange rate small.
- Policy conflict can avoid inflation in the face of a government deficit.

KEY FIGURES

KEY TERMS

PROBLEMS

*1. In the economy described in Fig. 27.1, suppose the government decreases its expenditures on goods and services.
   a. Work out the first round effects.
   b. Explain how real GDP and the interest rate change.
   c. Explain the second round effects that take the economy to a new equilibrium.

2. In the economy described in Fig. 27.1, suppose the government increases its expenditures on goods and services by $25 billion.
   a. Work out the first round effects.
   b. Explain how real GDP and the interest rate change.
   c. Explain the second round effects that take the economy to a new equilibrium.
   d. Compare the equilibrium in this case with the one described in the chapter on pp. 630–632. In which case does real GDP change most? In which case does the interest rate change most? Why?

*3. In the economy described in Fig. 27.1, suppose the Bank of Canada decreases the quantity of money.
   a. Work out the first round effects.
   b. Explain how real GDP and the interest rate change.
   c. Explain the second round effects that take the economy to a new equilibrium.

4. In the economy described in Fig. 27.1, suppose the Bank of Canada increases the quantity of money by $250 billion.
   a. Work out the first round effects.
   b. Explain how real GDP and the interest rate change.
   c. Explain the second round effects that take the economy to a new equilibrium.
   d. Compare the equilibrium in this case with the one described in the chapter on pp. 634–636. In which case does real GDP change most? In which case does the interest rate change most? Why?

*5. The economies of two countries, Alpha and Beta, are identical in every way except the following: in Alpha, a change in the interest rate of 1 percentage point (for example, from 5 percent to 6 percent) results in a $1 billion change in the quantity of real money demanded. In

Beta, a change in the interest rate of 1 percentage point results in a $0.1 billion change in the quantity of real money demanded.
   a. In which economy does an increase in government expenditures on goods and services have a larger effect on real GDP?
   b. In which economy is the crowding-out effect weaker?
   c. In which economy does a change in the quantity of money have a larger effect on equilibrium real GDP?
   d. Which economy, if either, is closer to the Keynesian extreme and which is closer to the monetarist extreme?

6. The economies of two countries, Gamma and Delta, are identical in every way except the following: in Gamma, a change in the interest rate of 1 percentage point (for example, from 5 percent to 6 percent) results in a $0.1 billion change in interest-sensitive expenditure. In Delta, a change in the interest rate of 1 percentage point results in a $10 billion change in interest-sensitive expenditure.
   a. In which economy does an increase in government expenditures on goods and services have a larger effect on real GDP?
   b. In which economy is the crowding-out effect weaker?
   c. In which economy does a change in the quantity of money have a larger effect on equilibrium real GDP?
   d. Which economy, if either, is closer to the Keynesian extreme and which is closer to the monetarist extreme?

*7. The economy is in a recession and the government wants to increase aggregate demand, stimulate exports, and increase investment. It has three policy options: increase government expenditures on goods and services, decrease taxes, and increase the quantity of money.
   a. Explain the mechanisms at work under each alternative policy.
   b. What is the effect of each policy on the composition of aggregate demand?
   c. What are the short-run effects of each policy on real GDP and the price level?
   d. Which policy would you recommend that the government adopt? Why?

8. The economy has an inflationary gap and the government wants to decrease aggregate demand, cut exports, and decrease investment.

It has three policy options: decrease government expenditures on goods and services, increase taxes, and decrease the quantity of money.
   a. Explain the mechanisms at work under each alternative policy.
   b. What is the effect of each policy on the composition of aggregate demand?
   c. What are the short-run effects of each policy on real GDP and the price level?
   d. Which policy would you recommend that the government adopt? Why?

*9. The economy is at full employment, but the government is disappointed with the growth rate of real GDP. It wants to increase real GDP growth by stimulating investment. At the same time, it wants to avoid an increase in the price level.
   a. Suggest a combination of fiscal and monetary policies that will achieve the government's objective.
   b. Which policy would you recommend that the government adopt?
   c. Explain the mechanisms at work under your recommended policy.
   d. What is the effect of your recommended policy on the composition of aggregate demand?
   e. What are the short-run and long-run effects of your recommended policy on real GDP and the price level?

10. The economy is at full employment, and the government is worried that the growth rate of real GDP is too high because it is depleting the country's natural resources. The government wants to lower real GDP growth by lowering investment. At the same time it wants to avoid a fall in the price level.
   a. Suggest a combination of fiscal and monetary policies that will achieve the government's objective.
   b. Which policy would you recommend that the government adopt?
   c. Explain the mechanisms at work under your recommended policy.
   d. What is the effect of your recommended policy on the composition of aggregate demand?
   e. What are the short-run and long-run effects of your recommended policy on real GDP and the price level?

CRITICAL THINKING

1. Study *Reading Between the Lines* on pp. 644–645 and then answer the following questions:
   a. What does David Dodge think the government's fiscal policy should do?
   b. What are your predictions about the effects of a large increase in government expenditure on real GDP, the price level, interest rates, investment, the exchange rate, and net exports?
   c. What actions do you think that the Bank of Canada would need to take to ensure that an increase in government expenditure doesn't bring an increase in the inflation rate?
   d. What would happen if the Bank of Canada decided to raise interest rates at the same time that the government increased its expenditure? Explain the likely effects on real GDP, the price level, investment, the exchange rate, and net exports.

WEB EXERCISES

1. Use the link on the Parkin–Bade Web site to visit Statistics Canada and look at the current economic conditions. On the basis of the current state of the Canadian economy, and in light of what you now know about fiscal and monetary policy interaction, what do you predict would happen to real GDP and the price level
   a. If the Bank of Canada conducted an expansionary monetary policy?
   b. If the Bank of Canada conducted a contractionary monetary policy?
   c. If the government of Canada conducted an expansionary fiscal policy?
   d. If the government of Canada conducted a contractionary fiscal policy?
   e. If the Bank of Canada conducted an expansionary monetary policy and the government of Canada conducted a contractionary fiscal policy?
   f. If the Bank of Canada conducted a contractionary monetary policy and the government of Canada conducted an expansionary fiscal policy?

2. What do you think the government of Canada should do with its fiscal surplus? Should it cut taxes, increase spending, or do some of both? How would your recommended actions influence real GDP, the price level, the interest rate, the exchange rate, and net exports?

CHAPTER 28

INFLATION

From Rome to Rio de Janeiro

At the end of the third century A.D., Roman Emperor Diocletian struggled to contain an inflation that raised prices by more than 300 percent a year. At the end of the twentieth century, Brazil's president, Fernando Henrique Cardoso, struggled to contain an inflation that hit a rate of 40 percent *per month*—or 5,600 percent a year. ◆ Today, Canada has remarkable price stability, but during the 1970s, the Canadian price level more than doubled—an inflation of more than 100 percent over the decade. Why do inflation rates vary? And why do serious inflations break out from time to time? ◆ Will inflation increase so our savings buy less? Or will inflation decrease so our debts are harder to repay? To make good decisions, we need good forecasts of inflation, and not for just next year but for many years into the future. How do people try to forecast inflation? And how do expectations of inflation influence the economy? ◆ Does the Bank of Canada face a tradeoff between inflation and unemployment? And does a low unemployment rate signal a rising inflation rate? How does inflation affect the interest rate?

◇ We'll answer these questions in this chapter. We'll begin by reviewing what inflation is and how it is measured. And we'll end, in *Reading Between the Lines*, by looking at the views of Nobel Laureate George Akerlof on the links between inflation and unemployment in Canada.

After studying this chapter, you will be able to

- ■ **Distinguish between inflation and a one-time rise in the price level**
- ■ **Explain how demand-pull inflation is generated**
- ■ **Explain how cost-push inflation is generated**
- ■ **Describe the effects of inflation**
- ■ **Explain the quantity theory of money**
- ■ **Explain the short-run and long-run relationships between inflation and unemployment**
- ■ **Explain the short-run and long-run relationships between inflation and interest rates**

649

Inflation and the Price Level

WE DON'T HAVE MUCH INFLATION TODAY, BUT during the 1970s, inflation was a major problem. **Inflation** is a process in which the *price level is rising* and *money is losing value.*

If the price level rises persistently, then people need more and more money to make transactions. Incomes rise, so firms must pay out more in wages and other payments to owners of factors of production. And prices rise, so consumers must take more money with them when they go shopping. But the value of money gets smaller and smaller.

A change in one price is not inflation. For example, if the price of a hot dog jumps to $25 and all other money prices fall slightly so that the price level remains constant, there is no inflation. Instead, the relative price of a hot dog has increased. If the price of a hot dog and all other prices rise by a similar percentage, there is inflation.

But a one-time jump in the price level is not inflation. Instead, inflation is an ongoing *process.* Figure 28.1 illustrates this distinction. The red line shows the price level rising continuously. That is inflation. The blue line shows a one-time jump in the price level. This economy is not experiencing inflation. Its price level is constant most of the time.

Inflation is a serious problem, and preventing inflation is the main task of monetary policy and the actions of the Bank of Canada. We are going to learn how inflation arises and see how we can avoid the situation shown in the cartoon. But first, let's see how we calculate the inflation rate.

"I told you the Fed should have tightened."

FIGURE 28.1   Inflation Versus a One-Time Rise in the Price Level

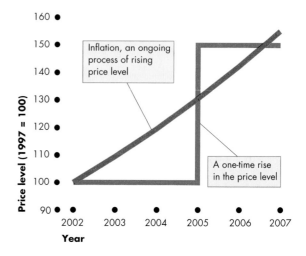

Along the red line, an economy experiences inflation because the price level is rising persistently. Along the blue line, an economy experiences a one-time rise in the price level.

To measure the inflation *rate,* we calculate the annual percentage change in the price level. For example, if this year's price level is 126 and last year's price level was 120, the inflation rate is 5 percent per year. That is,

$$\text{Inflation rate} = \frac{126 - 120}{120} \times 100$$

$$= 5 \text{ percent per year.}$$

This equation shows the connection between the *inflation rate* and the *price level.* For a given price level last year, the higher the price level in the current year, the higher is the inflation rate. If the price level is *rising,* the inflation rate is *positive.* If the price level rises at a *faster* rate, the inflation rate *increases.* Also, the higher the new price level, the lower is the value of money and the higher is the inflation rate.

Inflation can result from either an increase in aggregate demand or a decrease in aggregate supply. These two sources of impulses are called

1. Demand-pull inflation
2. Cost-push inflation

We'll first study a demand-pull inflation.

Demand-Pull Inflation

AN INFLATION THAT RESULTS FROM AN INITIAL increase in aggregate demand is called **demand-pull inflation.** Demand-pull inflation can arise from *any* factor that increases aggregate demand, such as an

1. Increase in the quantity of money
2. Increase in government expenditures
3. Increase in exports

Initial Effect of an Increase in Aggregate Demand

Suppose that last year the price level was 110 and real GDP was $1,000 billion. Potential GDP was also $1,000 billion. Figure 28.2(a) illustrates this situation. The aggregate demand curve is AD_0, the short-run aggregate supply curve is SAS_0, and the long-run aggregate supply curve is LAS.

In the current year, aggregate demand increases to AD_1. Such a situation arises if, for example, the

Bank of Canada loosens its grip on the quantity of money, or the government increases its expenditures on goods and services, or exports increase.

With no change in potential GDP, and with no change in the money wage rate, the long-run aggregate supply curve and the short-run aggregate supply curve remain at LAS and SAS_0, respectively.

The price level and real GDP are determined at the point where the aggregate demand curve AD_1 intersects the short-run aggregate supply curve. The price level rises to 113, and real GDP increases above potential GDP to $1,050 billion. The economy experiences a 2.7 percent rise in the price level (a price level of 113 compared with 110 in the previous year) and a rapid expansion of real GDP. Unemployment falls below its natural rate. The next step in the unfolding story is a rise in the money wage rate.

Money Wage Rate Response

Real GDP cannot remain above potential GDP forever. With unemployment below its natural rate, there is a shortage of labour. In this situation, the

---

FIGURE 28.2   A Demand-Pull Rise in the Price Level

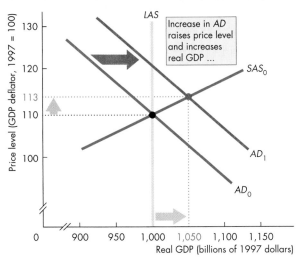

(a) Initial effect

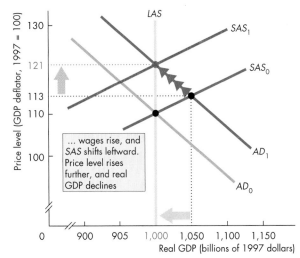

(b) Wages adjust

In part (a), the aggregate demand curve is AD_0, the short-run aggregate supply curve is SAS_0, and the long-run aggregate supply curve is LAS. The price level is 110, and real GDP is $1,000 billion, which equals potential GDP. Aggregate demand increases to AD_1. The price level rises

to 113, and real GDP increases to $1,050 billion. In part (b), starting from above full employment, the money wage rate begins to rise and the short-run aggregate supply curve shifts leftward towards SAS_1. The price level rises further, and real GDP returns to potential GDP.

money wage rate begins to rise. As it does so, short-run aggregate supply decreases and the *SAS* curve starts to shift leftward. The price level rises further, and real GDP begins to decrease.

With no further change in aggregate demand—that is, the aggregate demand curve remains at AD_1—this process ends when the short-run aggregate supply curve has shifted to SAS_1 in Fig. 28.2(b). At this time, the price level has increased to 121 and real GDP has returned to potential GDP of $1,000 billion, the level from which it started.

A Demand-Pull Inflation Process

The process we've just studied eventually ends when, for a given increase in aggregate demand, the money wage rate has adjusted enough to restore the real wage rate to its full-employment level. We've studied a one-time rise in the price level like that described in Fig. 28.1. For inflation to proceed, aggregate demand must persistently increase.

The only way in which aggregate demand can persistently increase is if the quantity of money persistently increases. Suppose the government has a budget deficit that it finances by selling bonds. Also suppose that the Bank of Canada buys some of these bonds. When the Bank of Canada buys bonds, it creates more money. In this situation, aggregate demand increases year after year. The aggregate demand curve keeps shifting rightward. This persistent increase in aggregate demand puts continual upward pressure on the price level. The economy now experiences demand-pull inflation.

Figure 28.3 illustrates the process of demand-pull inflation. The starting point is the same as that shown in Fig. 28.2. The aggregate demand curve is AD_0, the short-run aggregate supply curve is SAS_0, and the long-run aggregate supply curve is *LAS*. Real GDP is $1,000 billion, and the price level is 110. Aggregate demand increases, shifting the aggregate demand curve to AD_1. Real GDP increases to $1,050 billion, and the price level rises to 113. The economy is at an above full-employment equilibrium. There is a shortage of labour, and the money wage rate rises. The short-run aggregate supply curve shifts to SAS_1. The price level rises to 121, and real GDP returns to potential GDP.

But the Bank of Canada increases the quantity of money again, and aggregate demand continues to increase. The aggregate demand curve shifts rightward to AD_2. The price level rises further to 125, and

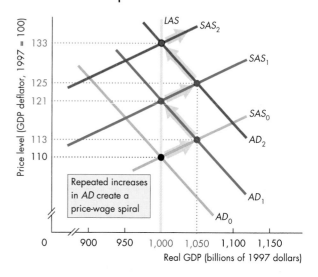

FIGURE 28.3   A Demand-Pull Inflation Spiral

Each time the quantity of money increases, aggregate demand increases, and the aggregate demand curve shifts rightward from AD_0 to AD_1 to AD_2, and so on. Each time real GDP goes above potential GDP, the money wage rate rises and the short-run aggregate supply curve shifts leftward from SAS_0 to SAS_1 to SAS_2, and so on. The price level rises from 110 to 113, 121, 125, 133, and so on. There is a perpetual demand-pull inflation. Real GDP fluctuates between $1,000 billion and $1,050 billion.

real GDP again exceeds potential GDP at $1,050 billion. Yet again, the money wage rate rises and decreases short-run aggregate supply. The *SAS* curve shifts to SAS_2, and the price level rises further, to 133. As the quantity of money continues to grow, aggregate demand increases and the price level rises in an ongoing demand-pull inflation process.

The process you have just studied generates inflation—an ongoing process of a rising price level.

Demand-Pull Inflation in Chatham   You may better understand the inflation process that we've just described by considering what is going on in an individual part of the economy, such as a Chatham ketchup-bottling plant. Initially, when aggregate demand increases, the demand for ketchup increases and the price of ketchup rises. Faced with a higher price, the ketchup plant works overtime and increases production. Conditions are good for workers in Chatham, and the ketchup factory finds it hard to hang onto its best people. To do so, it has to offer a higher money wage rate. As the wage rate rises, so do the ketchup factory's costs.

What happens next depends on what happens to aggregate demand. If aggregate demand remains constant (as in Fig. 28.2b), the firm's costs are increasing, but the price of ketchup is not increasing as quickly as its costs. Production is scaled back. Eventually, the money wage rate and costs increase by the same percentage as the rise in the price of ketchup. In real terms, the ketchup factory is in the same situation as it was initially—before the increase in aggregate demand. The plant produces the same amount of ketchup and employs the same amount of labour as before the increase in demand.

But if aggregate demand continues to increase, so does the demand for ketchup and the price of ketchup rises at the same rate as wages. The ketchup factory continues to operate above full employment, and there is a persistent shortage of labour. Prices and wages chase each other upward in an unending spiral.

Demand-Pull Inflation in Canada A demand-pull inflation like the one you've just studied occurred in Canada during the late 1960s and early 1970s. In 1960, inflation was a moderate 2 percent a year, but its rate increased slowly through the mid-1960s. Then, between 1966 and 1969, the inflation rate surged upward. Inflation then decreased slightly during 1970 and 1971, but it took off again in 1972. By 1973, the inflation rate was approaching 10 percent a year.

These increases in inflation resulted from increases in aggregate demand that had two main sources. The first was from the United States, where large increases in government expenditures and in the quantity of money increased aggregate demand in the entire world economy. The second source was an increase in Canadian government expenditures and the quantity of money.

With the economy above full employment, the money wage rate started to rise more quickly and the *SAS* curve shifted leftward. The Bank of Canada responded with a further increase in the money growth rate, and a demand-pull inflation spiral unfolded. By 1974, the inflation rate had reached double digits.

Next, let's see how shocks to aggregate supply can create cost-push inflation.

Cost-Push Inflation

AN INFLATION THAT RESULTS FROM AN INITIAL increase in costs is called **cost-push inflation**. The two main sources of increases in costs are

1. An increase in money wage rates
2. An increase in the money prices of raw materials

At a given price level, the higher the cost of production, the smaller is the amount that firms are willing to produce. So if money wage rates rise or if the prices of raw materials (for example, oil) rise, firms decrease their supply of goods and services. Aggregate supply decreases, and the short-run aggregate supply curve shifts leftward.[1] Let's trace the effects of such a decrease in short-run aggregate supply on the price level and real GDP.

Initial Effect of a Decrease in Aggregate Supply

Suppose that last year the price level was 110 and real GDP was $1,000 billion. Potential real GDP was also $1,000 billion. Figure 28.4 illustrates this situation. The aggregate demand curve was AD_0, the short-run aggregate supply curve was SAS_0, and the long-run aggregate supply curve was LAS. In the current year,

---

[1] Some cost-push forces, such as an increase in the price of oil accompanied by a decrease in the availability of oil, can also decrease long-run aggregate supply. We'll ignore such effects here and examine cost-push factors that change only short-run aggregate supply.

FIGURE 28.4   A Cost-Push Rise in the Price Level

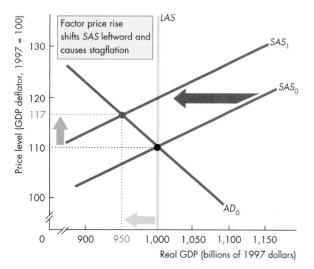

Initially, the aggregate demand curve is AD_0, the short-run aggregate supply curve is SAS_0, and the long-run aggregate supply curve is LAS. A decrease in aggregate supply (for example, resulting from a rise in the world price of oil) shifts the short-run aggregate supply curve to SAS_1. The economy moves to the point where the short-run aggregate supply curve SAS_1 intersects the aggregate demand curve AD_0. The price level rises to 117, and real GDP decreases to $950 billion.

the world's oil producers form a price-fixing organization that strengthens their market power and increases the relative price of oil. They raise the price of oil, and this action decreases short-run aggregate supply. The short-run aggregate supply curve shifts leftward to SAS_1. The price level rises to 117, and real GDP decreases to $950 billion. The combination of a rise in the price level and a fall in real GDP is called *stagflation*.

This event is a one-time rise in the price level, like that in Fig. 28.1. It is not inflation. In fact, a supply shock on its own cannot cause inflation. Something more must happen to enable a one-time supply shock, which causes a one-time rise in the price level, to be converted into a process of money growth and ongoing inflation. The quantity of money must persistently increase. And it often does increase, as you will now see.

Aggregate Demand Response

When real GDP falls, the unemployment rate rises above its natural rate. In such a situation, there is usually an outcry of concern and a call for action to restore full employment. Suppose that the Bank of Canada increases the quantity of money. Aggregate demand increases. In Fig. 28.5, the aggregate demand curve shifts rightward to AD_1. The increase in aggregate demand has restored full employment. But the price level rises to 121, a 10 percent increase over the initial price level.

A Cost-Push Inflation Process

The oil producers now see the prices of everything that they buy increase by 10 percent. So they increase the price of oil again to restore its new high relative price. Figure 28.6 continues the story.

The short-run aggregate supply curve now shifts to SAS_2, and another bout of stagflation ensues. The

FIGURE 28.5   Aggregate Demand Response to Cost Push

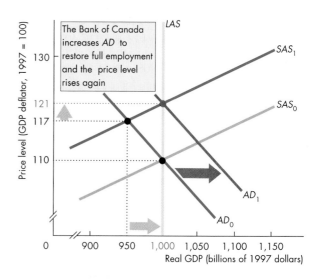

Following a cost-push increase in the price level, real GDP is below potential GDP and unemployment is above its natural rate. If the Bank of Canada responds by increasing aggregate demand to restore full employment, the aggregate demand curve shifts rightward to AD_1. The economy returns to full employment but the price level rises to 121.

price level rises further, to 129, and real GDP falls to $950 billion. Unemployment increases above its natural rate. If the Bank of Canada responds yet again with an increase in the quantity of money, aggregate demand increases and the aggregate demand curve shifts to AD_2. The price level rises even higher—to 133—and full employment is again restored. A cost-push inflation spiral results. But if the Bank of Canada does not respond, the economy remains below full employment until the price of oil falls.

You can see that the Bank of Canada has a dilemma. If it increases the quantity of money to restore full employment, the Bank invites another oil price hike that will call forth yet a further increase in the quantity of money. Inflation will rage along at a rate decided by the oil-exporting nations. If the Bank of Canada keeps the lid on money growth, the economy operates with a high level of unemployment.

FIGURE 28.6   A Cost-Push Inflation Spiral

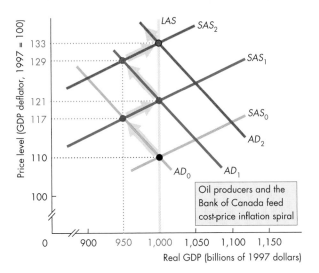

When a cost increase decreases short-run aggregate supply from SAS_0 to SAS_1, the price level rises to 117 and real GDP decreases to $950 billion. The Bank of Canada responds with an increase in the quantity of money. The aggregate demand curve shifts from AD_0 to AD_1, the price level rises to 121, and real GDP returns to $1,000 billion. A further cost increase occurs, which shifts the short-run aggregate supply curve again, this time to SAS_2. Stagflation is repeated, and the price level rises to 129. The Bank of Canada responds again, and the cost-price inflation spiral continues.

Cost-Push Inflation in Chatham What is going on in the Chatham ketchup-bottling plant when the economy is experiencing cost-push inflation? When the oil price increases, so do the costs of bottling ketchup. These higher costs decrease the supply of ketchup, increasing its price and decreasing the quantity produced. The ketchup plant lays off some workers. This situation will persist until either the Bank of Canada increases aggregate demand or the price of oil falls. If the Bank of Canada increases aggregate demand, as it did in the mid-1970s, the demand for ketchup increases and so does its price. The higher price of ketchup brings higher profits, and the bottling plant increases its production. The ketchup factory rehires the laid-off workers.

Cost-Push Inflation in Canada A cost-push inflation like the one you've just studied occurred in Canada during the 1970s. It began in 1974 when the Organization of the Petroleum Exporting Countries (OPEC) raised the price of oil fourfold. The higher oil price decreased aggregate supply, which caused the price level to rise more quickly and real GDP to shrink. The Bank of Canada then faced a dilemma: Would it increase the quantity of money and accommodate the cost-push forces, or would it keep aggregate demand growth in check by limiting money growth? In 1975, 1976, and 1977, the Bank of Canada repeatedly allowed the quantity of money to grow quickly and inflation proceeded at a rapid rate. In 1979 and 1980, OPEC was again able to push oil prices higher. On that occasion, the Bank of Canada decided not to respond to the oil price hike with an increase in the quantity of money. The result was a recession but also, eventually, a fall in inflation.

REVIEW QUIZ

1 How does cost-push inflation begin? What are the initial effects of a cost-push rise in the price level?

2 What is *stagflation* and why does cost-push inflation cause stagflation?

3 What must the Bank of Canada do to convert a one-time rise in the price level into a freewheeling cost-push inflation?

The Quantity Theory of Money

YOU'VE SEEN THAT REGARDLESS OF WHETHER IT originates in a demand-pull or a cost-push, to convert a one-time rise in the price level into an ongoing inflation, aggregate demand must increase. And although many factors can and do influence aggregate demand, only one factor can persistently increase in the long run: the quantity of money. This special place of money gives rise to a special long-run theory of inflation, called the quantity theory of money.

The **quantity theory of money** is the proposition that in the long run, an increase in the quantity of money brings an equal percentage increase in the price level. The basis of the quantity theory of money is a concept known as *the velocity of circulation* and an equation called *the equation of exchange*.

The **velocity of circulation** is the average number of times a dollar of money is used annually to buy the goods and services that make up GDP. GDP equals the price level (P) multiplied by real GDP (Y). That is,

$$GDP = PY.$$

Call the quantity of money M. The velocity of circulation, V, is determined by the equation

$$V = PY/M.$$

For example, if GDP is $1,000 billion ($PY = $1,000 billion) and the quantity of money is $250 billion, the velocity of circulation is 4. ($1,000 billion divided by $250 billion equals 4.)

The **equation of exchange** states that the quantity of money (M) multiplied by the velocity of circulation (V) equals GDP, or

$$MV = PY.$$

Given the definition of the velocity of circulation, this equation is always true—it is true by definition. With M equal to $250 billion and V equal to 4, MV is equal to $1,000 billion, the value of GDP.

The equation of exchange becomes the quantity theory of money by making two assumptions:

1. The velocity of circulation is not influenced by the quantity of money.
2. Potential GDP is not influenced by the quantity of money.

If these two assumptions are true, then the equation of exchange tells us that a change in the quantity of money brings about an equal proportional change in the price level. You can see why by solving the equation of exchange for the price level. Dividing both sides of the equation by real GDP (Y) gives

$$P = (V/Y) \times M.$$

In the long run, real GDP equals potential GDP, so if potential GDP and velocity are not influenced by the quantity of money, then the relationship between the change in the price level (ΔP) and the change in the quantity of money (ΔM) is

$$(\Delta P = (V/Y) \times \Delta M.$$

Divide this equation by $P = (V/Y) \times M$, and multiply by 100 to get

$$(\Delta P/P) \times 100 = (\Delta M/M) \times 100.$$

$(\Delta P/P) \times 100$ is the inflation rate and $(\Delta M/M) \times 100$ is the growth rate of the quantity of money. So this equation is the quantity theory of money: The percentage increase in the price level and the percentage increase in the quantity of money are equal.

Evidence on the Quantity Theory

Figure 28.7 summarizes some Canadian evidence on the quantity theory of money. The figure reveals that

1. On the average, the money growth rate exceeds the inflation rate.
2. The money growth rate is correlated with the inflation rate.

Money growth exceeds inflation because real GDP grows. Money growth that matches real GDP growth does not create inflation. But money growth in excess of real GDP growth does create inflation.

Money growth and inflation are correlated—move up and down together. For example, the rise in the inflation rate during the 1970s and the slight rebound in inflation during the late 1980s were accompanied by a rise in the money growth rate. The decreases in the inflation rate during the 1980s and 1990s were accompanied by decreases in the money growth rate. But the correlation is not perfect. Nor does it tell us that money growth *causes* inflation. Money growth might cause inflation; inflation might cause money growth; or some third variable might simultaneously cause inflation and money growth.

Figure 28.8 summarizes some international evidence on the quantity theory of money. It shows the inflation rate and the money growth rate for 60 countries. There is a clear tendency for high money

FIGURE 28.7 Money Growth and Inflation in Canada

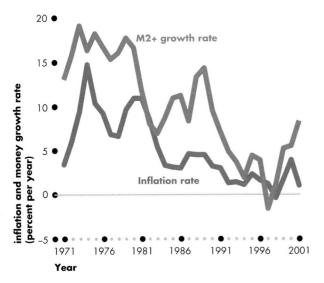

On the average, the money growth rate exceeds the inflation rate because real GDP grows. Money growth and inflation are correlated—they rise and fall together.

Source: Statistics Canada, CANSIM tables 176-0020, 380-0056, and authors' calculations.

FIGURE 28.8 Money Growth and Inflation in the World Economy

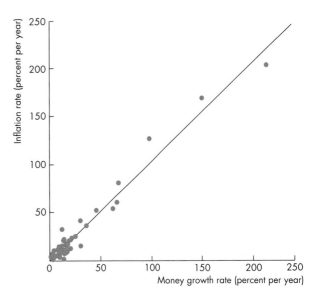

(a) 60 countries during the 1980s

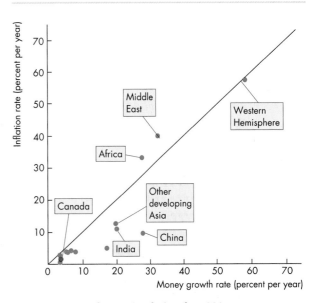

(b) 13 regions and countries during the 1990s

Inflation and money growth in 60 countries (in part a) and low-inflation countries (in part b) show a clear positive relationship between money growth and inflation.

Source: Federal Reserve Bank of St. Louis, *Review*, May/June 1988, p. 15.

growth to be associated with high inflation. The evidence is strongest for the high-inflation countries shown in Fig. 28.8(a), but it is also present for low-inflation countries, which are shown in Fig. 28.8(b).

REVIEW QUIZ

1 What is the quantity theory of money?
2 What is the velocity of circulation of money and how is it calculated?
3 What is the equation of exchange? Can the equation of exchange be wrong?
4 What does the long-run historical evidence and international evidence on the relationship between money growth and inflation tell us about the quantity theory of money?

We next turn to an examination of the effects of inflation.

Effects of Inflation

REGARDLESS OF WHETHER INFLATION IS DEMAND pull or cost push, the failure to correctly *anticipate* it results in unintended consequences. These unintended consequences impose costs in both labour markets and capital markets. Let's examine these costs.

Unanticipated Inflation in the Labour Market

Unanticipated inflation has two main consequences for the operation of the labour market:

- Redistribution of income
- Departure from full employment

Redistribution of Income Unanticipated inflation redistributes income between employers and workers. Sometimes employers gain at the expense of workers, and sometimes they lose. If an unexpected increase in aggregate demand increases the inflation rate, then the money wage rate will not have been set high enough. Profits will be higher than expected, and real wages will buy fewer goods than expected. In this case, employers gain at the expense of workers. But if aggregate demand is expected to increase at a rapid rate and it fails to do so, workers gain at the expense of employers. With a high inflation rate anticipated, the money wage rate is set too high and profits are squeezed. Redistribution between employers and workers creates an incentive for both firms and workers to try to forecast inflation correctly.

Departures from Full Employment Redistribution brings gains to some and losses to others. But departures from full employment impose costs on everyone. To see why, let's return to the ketchup-bottling plant in Chatham.

If the bottling plant and its workers do not anticipate inflation but inflation occurs, the money wage rate does not rise to keep up with inflation. The real wage rate falls, and the firm tries to hire more labour and increase production. But because the real wage rate has fallen, the firm has a hard time attracting the labour it wants to employ. It pays overtime rates to its existing work force, and because it runs its plant at a faster pace, it incurs higher plant maintenance and parts replacement costs. But also, because the real

wage rate has fallen, workers begin to quit the bottling plant to find jobs that pay a real wage rate that is closer to one that prevailed before the outbreak of inflation. This labour turnover imposes additional costs on the firm. So even though its production increases, the firm incurs additional costs and its profits do not increase as much as they otherwise would. The workers incur additional costs of job search, and those who remain at the bottling plant wind up feeling cheated. They've worked overtime to produce the extra output, and when they come to spend their wages, they discover that prices have increased so their wages buy a smaller quantity of goods and services than expected.

If the bottling plant and its workers anticipate a high inflation rate that does not occur, they increase the money wage rate by too much and the real wage rate rises. At the higher real wage rate, the firm lays off some workers and the unemployment rate increases. The workers who keep their jobs gain, but those who become unemployed lose. Also, the bottling plant loses because its output and profits fall.

Unanticipated Inflation in the Market for Financial Capital

Unanticipated inflation has two consequences for the operation of the market for financial capital:

- Redistribution of income
- Too much or too little lending and borrowing

Redistribution of Income Unanticipated inflation redistributes income between borrowers and lenders. Sometimes borrowers gain at the expense of lenders, and sometimes they lose. When inflation is unexpected, interest rates are not set high enough to compensate lenders for the falling value of money. In this case, borrowers gain at the expense of lenders. But if inflation is expected and then fails to occur, interest rates are set too high. In this case, lenders gain at the expense of borrowers. Redistributions of income between borrowers and lenders create an incentive for both groups to try to forecast inflation correctly.

Too Much or Too Little Lending and Borrowing If the inflation rate turns out to be either higher or lower than expected, the interest rate does not incorporate a correct allowance for the falling value of money and the real interest rate is either lower or higher than it otherwise would be. When the real interest rate turns out to be too low, which occurs when inflation is *higher* than expected, borrowers wish they had borrowed more and lenders wish they had lent less. Both groups would have made different lending and borrowing decisions with greater foresight about the inflation rate. When the real interest rate turns out to be too high, which occurs when inflation is lower than expected, borrowers wish they had borrowed less and lenders wish they had lent more. Again, both groups would have made different lending and borrowing decisions with greater foresight about the inflation rate.

So unanticipated inflation imposes costs regardless of whether the inflation turns out to be higher or lower than anticipated. The presence of these costs gives everyone an incentive to forecast inflation correctly. Let's see how people go about this task.

Forecasting Inflation

Inflation is difficult to forecast for two reasons. First, there are several sources of inflation—the demand-pull and cost-push sources you've just studied. Second, the speed with which a change in either aggregate demand or aggregate supply translates into a change in the price level varies. This speed of response also depends, as you will see below, on the extent to which the inflation is anticipated.

Because inflation is costly and difficult to forecast, people devote considerable resources to improving inflation forecasts. Some people specialize in forecasting, and others buy forecasts from specialists. The specialist forecasters are economists who work for public and private macroeconomic forecasting agencies and for banks, insurance companies, labour unions, and large corporations. The returns these specialists make depend on the quality of their forecasts, so they have a strong incentive to forecast as accurately as possible. The most accurate forecast possible is the one that is based on all the relevant information available and is called a **rational expectation.**

A rational expectation is not necessarily a correct forecast. It is simply the best forecast available. It will often turn out to be wrong, but no other forecast that could have been made with the information available could be predicted to be better.

You've seen the effects of inflation when people fail to anticipate it. And you've seen why it pays to try to anticipate inflation. Let's now see what happens if inflation is correctly anticipated.

Anticipated Inflation

In the demand-pull and cost-push inflations that we studied in this chapter, the money wage rate is sticky. When aggregate demand increases, either to set off a demand-pull inflation or to accommodate a cost-push inflation, the money wage rate does not change immediately. But if people correctly anticipate increases in aggregate demand, they will adjust the money wage rate so as to keep up with anticipated inflation.

In this case, inflation proceeds with real GDP equal to potential GDP and unemployment equal to its natural rate. Figure 28.9 explains why. Suppose that last year the price level was 110 and real GDP was $1,000 billion, which is also potential GDP. The aggregate demand curve was AD_0, the aggregate supply curve was SAS_0, and the long-run aggregate supply curve was LAS.

Suppose that potential GDP does not change, so the LAS curve does not shift. Also suppose that aggregate demand is expected to increase and that the expected aggregate demand curve for this year is AD_1. In anticipation of this increase in aggregate demand, the money wage rate rises and the short-run aggregate supply curve shifts leftward. If the money wage rate rises by the same percentage as the price level rises, the short-run aggregate supply curve for next year is SAS_1.

If aggregate demand turns out to be the same as expected, the aggregate demand curve is AD_1. The short-run aggregate supply curve SAS_1 and AD_1 determine the actual price level at 121. Between last year and this year, the price level increased from 110 to 121 and the economy experienced an inflation rate of 10 percent, the same as the inflation rate that was anticipated. If this anticipated inflation is ongoing, in the following year aggregate demand increases (as anticipated) and the aggregate demand curve shifts to AD_2. The money wage rate rises to reflect the anticipated inflation, and the short-run aggregate supply curve shifts to SAS_2. The price level rises by a further 10 percent to 133.

What has caused this inflation? The immediate answer is that because people expected inflation, the money wage rate increased and the price level increased. But the expectation was correct. Aggregate demand was expected to increase, and it did increase. Because aggregate demand was *expected* to increase from AD_0 to AD_1, the short-run aggregate supply curve shifted from SAS_0 to SAS_1. Because aggregate demand actually did increase by the amount that was expected, the actual aggregate demand curve shifted from AD_0 to AD_1. The combination of the anticipated and actual shifts of the aggregate demand curve rightward produced an increase in the price level that was anticipated.

Only if aggregate demand growth is correctly forecasted does the economy follow the course described in Fig. 28.9. If the expected growth rate of aggregate demand is different from its actual growth rate, the expected aggregate demand curve shifts by an amount that is different from the actual aggregate demand curve. The inflation rate departs from its expected level, and to some extent, there is unanticipated inflation.

FIGURE 28.9   Anticipated Inflation

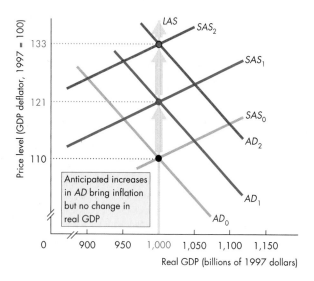

Potential real GDP is $1,000 billion. Last year, the aggregate demand curve was AD_0, and the short-run aggregate supply curve was SAS_0. The actual price level was the same as the expected price level—110. This year, aggregate demand is expected to increase to AD_1. The rational expectation of the price level changes from 110 to 121. As a result, the money wage rate rises and the short-run aggregate supply curve shifts to SAS_1. If aggregate demand actually increases as expected, the actual aggregate demand curve AD_1 is the same as the expected aggregate demand curve. Real GDP is $1,000 billion and the actual price level is 121. The inflation is correctly anticipated. Next year, the process continues with aggregate demand increasing as expected to AD_2 and the money wage rate rising to shift the short-run aggregate supply curve to SAS_2. Again, real GDP remains at $1,000 billion, and the price level rises, as anticipated, to 133.

Unanticipated Inflation

When aggregate demand increases by *more* than expected, there is some unanticipated inflation that looks just like the demand-pull inflation that you studied earlier. Some inflation is expected, and the money wage rate is set to reflect that expectation. The *SAS* curve intersects the *LAS* curve at the expected price level. Aggregate demand then increases but by more than expected. So the *AD* curve intersects the *SAS* curve at a level of real GDP that exceeds potential GDP. With real GDP above potential GDP and unemployment below its natural rate, the money wage rate rises. So the price level rises further. If aggregate demand increases again, a demand-pull inflation spiral unwinds.

When aggregate demand increases by *less* than expected, there is some unanticipated inflation that looks like the cost-push inflation that you studied earlier. Again, some inflation is expected, and the money wage rate is set to reflect that expectation. The *SAS* curve intersects the *LAS* curve at the expected price level. Aggregate demand then increases but by less than expected. So the *AD* curve intersects the *SAS* curve at a level of real GDP below potential GDP. Aggregate demand increases to restore full employment. But if aggregate demand is expected to increase by more than it actually does, the money wage rate again rises, short-run aggregate supply again decreases, and a cost-push spiral unwinds.

We've seen that only when inflation is unanticipated does real GDP depart from potential GDP. When inflation is anticipated, real GDP remains at potential GDP. Does this mean that an anticipated inflation has no costs?

The Costs of Anticipated Inflation

The costs of an anticipated inflation depend on its rate. At a moderate rate of 2 or 3 percent a year, the cost is probably small. But as the anticipated inflation rate rises, so does its cost, and an anticipated inflation at a rapid rate can be extremely costly.

Anticipated inflation decreases potential GDP and slows economic growth. These adverse consequences arise for three major reasons:

■ Transactions costs
■ Tax effects
■ Increased uncertainty

Transactions Costs The first transactions costs are known as the "boot leather costs." These are costs that arise from an increase in the velocity of circulation of money and an increase in the amount of running around that people do to try to avoid incurring losses from the falling value of money.

When money loses value at a rapid anticipated rate, it does not function well as a store of value and people try to avoid holding money. They spend their incomes as soon as they receive them, and firms pay out incomes—wages and dividends—as soon as they receive revenue from their sales. The velocity of circulation increases. During the 1920s in Germany, when inflation reached *hyperinflation* levels (rates more than 50 percent a month), wages were paid and spent twice in a single day!

The range of estimates of the boot leather costs is large. Some economists put them at close to zero. Others estimate them to be as much as 2 percent of GDP for a 10 percent inflation. For a rapid inflation, these costs are much more.

The boot leather costs of inflation are just one of several transactions costs that are influenced by the inflation rate. At high anticipated inflation rates, people seek alternatives to money as means of payment and use tokens and commodities or even barter, all of which are less efficient than money as a means of payment. For example, in Russia during the 1990s, when inflation reached 1,000 percent a year, the U.S. dollar started to replace the increasingly worthless Russian ruble. Consequently, people had to keep track of the exchange rate between the ruble and the dollar hour by hour and had to engage in many additional and costly transactions in the foreign exchange market.

Because anticipated inflation increases transactions costs, it diverts resources from producing goods and services and it decreases potential GDP. The faster the anticipated inflation rate, the greater is the decrease in potential GDP and the farther leftward does the *LAS* curve shift.

Tax Effects Anticipated inflation interacts with the tax system and creates serious distortions in incentives. Its major effect is on real interest rates.

Anticipated inflation swells the dollar returns on investments. But dollar returns are taxed, so the effective tax rate rises. This effect becomes serious at even modest inflation rates. Let's consider an example.

Suppose the real interest rate is 4 percent a year and the tax rate is 50 percent. With no inflation, the nominal interest rate is also 4 percent a year and 50 percent of this rate is taxable. The real *after-tax* interest rate is 2 percent a year (50 percent of 4 percent). Now suppose the inflation rate is 4 percent a year, and the nominal interest rate is 8 percent a year. The *after-tax* nominal rate is 4 percent a year (50 percent of 8 percent). Now subtract the 4 percent inflation rate from this amount, and you see that the *after-tax real interest rate* is zero! The true tax rate on interest income is 100 percent.

The higher the inflation rate, the higher is the effective tax rate on income from capital. And the higher the tax rate, the higher is the interest rate paid by borrowers and the lower is the after-tax interest rate received by lenders.

With a low after-tax real interest rate, the incentive to save is weakened and the saving rate falls. With a high cost of borrowing, the amount of investment decreases. And with a fall in saving and investment, the pace of capital accumulation slows and so does the long-term growth rate of real GDP.

Increased Uncertainty When the inflation rate is high, there is increased uncertainty about the long-term inflation rate. Will inflation remain high for a long time, or will price stability be restored? This increased uncertainty makes long-term planning difficult and gives people a shorter-term focus. Investment falls, and so the growth rate slows.

But this increased uncertainty also misallocates resources. Instead of concentrating on the activities at which they have a comparative advantage, people find it more profitable to search for ways of avoiding the losses that inflation inflicts. As a result, inventive talent that might otherwise work on productive innovations works on finding ways of profiting from the inflation instead.

The implications of inflation for economic growth have been estimated to be enormous. Peter Howitt of Brown University, building on work by Robert Barro of Harvard University, has estimated that if inflation is lowered from 3 percent a year to zero, the growth rate of real GDP will rise by between 0.06 and 0.09 percentage points a year. These numbers might seem small, but they are growth rates. After 30 years, real GDP would be 2.3 percent higher and the present value of all the future output would be 85 percent of current GDP—$850 billion! In the rapid anticipated inflations of Brazil and Russia, the costs are much greater than the numbers given here.

You've seen that an increase in aggregate demand that is not fully anticipated increases both the price level and real GDP. It also decreases unemployment. Similarly, a decrease in aggregate demand that is not fully anticipated decreases the price level and real GDP. It also increases unemployment. Do these relationships mean that there is a tradeoff between inflation and unemployment? Does low unemployment always bring inflation and does low inflation bring high unemployment? We explore these questions.

Inflation and Unemployment: The Phillips Curve

THE AGGREGATE SUPPLY–AGGREGATE DEMAND model focuses on the price level and real GDP. Knowing how these two variables change, we can work out what happens to the inflation rate and the unemployment rate. But the model does not place inflation and unemployment at the centre of the stage.

A more direct way of studying inflation and unemployment uses a relationship called the Phillips curve. The Phillips curve approach uses the same basic ideas as the *AS–AD* model, but it focuses directly on inflation and unemployment. The Phillips curve is so named because New Zealand economist A.W. Phillips popularized it. A **Phillips curve** is a curve that shows a relationship between inflation and unemployment. There are two time frames for Phillips curves:

■ The short-run Phillips curve
■ The long-run Phillips curve

The Short-Run Phillips Curve

The **short-run Phillips curve** is a curve that shows the tradeoff between inflation and unemployment, holding constant

1. The expected inflation rate
2. The natural rate of unemployment

You've just seen what determines the expected inflation rate. The natural rate of unemployment and the factors that influence it are explained in Chapter 21, pp. 488–489 and Chapter 29, pp. 693–695.

Figure 28.10 shows a short-run Phillips curve, *SRPC*. Suppose that the expected inflation rate is 10 percent a year and the natural rate of unemployment is 6 percent, point *A* in the figure. A short-run Phillips curve passes through this point. If inflation

---

FIGURE 28.10   A Short-Run Phillips Curve

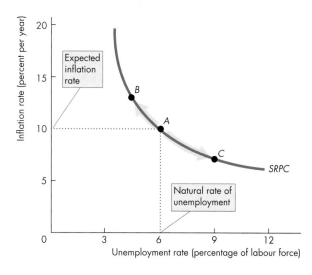

The short-run Phillips curve (*SRPC*) shows the relationship between inflation and unemployment at a given expected inflation rate and a given natural rate of unemployment. With an expected inflation rate of 10 percent a year and a natural rate of unemployment of 6 percent, the short-run Phillips curve passes through point *A*. An unanticipated increase in aggregate demand lowers unemployment and increases inflation—a movement up along the short-run Phillips curve. An unanticipated decrease in aggregate demand increases unemployment and lowers inflation—a movement down along the short-run Phillips curve.

rises above its expected rate, unemployment falls below its natural rate. This joint movement in the inflation rate and the unemployment rate is illustrated as a movement up along the short-run Phillips curve from point A to point B in the figure. Similarly, if inflation falls below its expected rate, unemployment rises above its natural rate. In this case, there is movement down along the short-run Phillips curve from point A to point C.

This negative relationship between inflation and unemployment along the short-run Phillips curve is explained by the aggregate supply–aggregate demand model. Figure 28.11 shows the connection between the two approaches. Initially, the aggregate demand curve is AD_0, the short-run aggregate supply curve is SAS_0, and the long-run aggregate supply curve is LAS. Real GDP is $1,000 billion, and the price level is 100. Aggregate demand is expected to increase, and the aggregate demand curve is expected to shift rightward to AD_1. Anticipating this increase in aggregate demand, the money wage rate rises, which shifts the short-run aggregate supply curve to SAS_1. What happens to actual inflation and real GDP depends on the *actual* change in aggregate demand.

First, suppose that aggregate demand actually increases by the amount expected, so the aggregate demand curve shifts to AD_1. The price level rises from 100 to 110, and the inflation rate is an anticipated 10 percent a year. Real GDP remains at potential GDP, and unemployment remains at its natural rate—6 percent. The economy moves to point A in Fig. 28.11, and it can equivalently be described as being at point A on the short-run Phillips curve in Fig. 28.10.

Alternatively, suppose that aggregate demand is expected to increase to AD_1 but actually increases by more than expected, to AD_2. The price level now rises to 113, a 13 percent inflation rate. Real GDP increases above potential GDP, and unemployment falls below its natural rate. We can now describe the economy as moving to point B in Fig. 28.11 or as being at point B on the short-run Phillips curve in Fig. 28.10.

Finally, suppose that aggregate demand is expected to increase to AD_1 but actually remains at AD_0. The price level now rises to 107, a 7 percent inflation rate. Real GDP falls below potential GDP, and unemployment rises above its natural rate. We can now describe the economy as moving to point C in Fig. 28.11 or as being at point C on the short-run Phillips curve in Fig. 28.10.

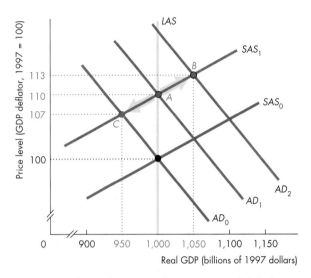

FIGURE 28.11   AS–AD and the Short-Run Phillips Curve

If aggregate demand is expected to increase and shift the aggregate demand curve from AD_0 to AD_1, then the money wage rate rises by an amount that shifts the short-run aggregate supply curve from SAS_0 to SAS_1. If aggregate demand increases as expected, the price level rises to 110, a 10 percent rise, and the economy is at point A in this figure and at point A on the short-run Phillips curve in Fig. 28.10. If, with the same expectations, aggregate demand increases and shifts the aggregate demand curve from AD_0 to AD_2, the price level rises to 113, a 13 percent rise, and the economy is at point B in this figure and at point B on the short-run Phillips curve in Fig. 28.10. If, with the same expectations, aggregate demand does not change, the price level rises to 107, a 7 percent rise, and the economy is at point C in this figure and at point C on the short-run Phillips curve in Fig. 28.10.

The short-run Phillips curve is like the short-run aggregate supply curve. A movement along the *SAS* curve that brings a higher price level and an increase in real GDP is equivalent to a movement along the short-run Phillips curve that brings an increase in the inflation rate and a decrease in the unemployment rate. (Similarly, a movement along the *SAS* curve that brings a lower price level and a decrease in real GDP is equivalent to a movement along the short-run Phillips curve that brings a decrease in the inflation rate and an increase in the unemployment rate.)

The Long-Run Phillips Curve

The **long-run Phillips curve** shows the relationship between inflation and unemployment when the actual inflation rate equals the expected inflation rate. The long-run Phillips curve is vertical at the natural rate of unemployment. In Fig. 28.12, it is the vertical line *LRPC*. The long-run Phillips curve tells us that any anticipated inflation rate is possible at the natural rate of unemployment. This proposition is consistent with the *AS–AD* model, which predicts that when inflation is anticipated, real GDP equals potential GDP and unemployment is at its natural rate.

When the expected inflation rate changes, the short-run Phillips curve shifts but the long-run Phillips curve does not shift. If the expected inflation rate is 10 percent a year, the short-run Phillips curve is $SRPC_0$. If the expected inflation rate falls to 7 per-

cent a year, the short-run Phillips curve shifts downward to $SRPC_1$. The distance by which the short-run Phillips curve shifts downward when the expected inflation rate falls is equal to the change in the expected inflation rate.

To see why the short-run Phillips curve shifts when the expected inflation rate changes, let's do a thought experiment. There is full employment, and a 10 percent a year anticipated inflation is raging. The Bank of Canada now begins an attack on inflation by slowing money growth. Aggregate demand growth slows, and the inflation rate falls to 7 percent a year. At first, this decrease in inflation is *un*anticipated, so the money wage rate continues to rise at its original rate. The short-run aggregate supply curve shifts leftward at the same pace as before. Real GDP decreases, and unemployment increases. In Fig. 28.12, the economy moves from point *A* to point *C* on $SRPC_0$.

If the actual inflation rate remains steady at 7 percent a year, this rate eventually comes to be expected. As this happens, wage growth slows and the short-run aggregate supply curve shifts leftward less quickly. Eventually, it shifts leftward at the same pace at which the aggregate demand curve is shifting rightward. The actual inflation rate equals the expected inflation rate, and full employment is restored. Unemployment is back at its natural rate. In Fig. 28.12, the short-run Phillips curve has shifted from $SRPC_0$ to $SRPC_1$ and the economy is at point *D*.

An increase in the expected inflation rate has the opposite effect to that shown in Fig. 28.12. Another important source of shifts in the Phillips curve is a change in the natural rate of unemployment.

Changes in the Natural Rate of Unemployment

The natural rate of unemployment changes for many reasons (see Chapter 29, pp. 693–695). A change in the natural rate of unemployment shifts both the short-run and long-run Phillips curves. Figure 28.13 illustrates such shifts. If the natural rate of unemployment increases from 6 percent to 9 percent, the long-run Phillips curve shifts from $LRPC_0$ to $LRPC_1$, and if expected inflation is constant at 10 percent a year, the short-run Phillips curve shifts from $SRPC_0$ to $SRPC_1$. Because the expected inflation rate is constant, the short-run Phillips curve $SRPC_1$ intersects the long-run curve $LRPC_1$ (point *E*) at the same inflation rate at which the short-run Phillips curve $SRPC_0$ intersects the long-run curve $LRPC_0$ (point *A*).

FIGURE 28.12   Short-Run and Long-Run Phillips Curves

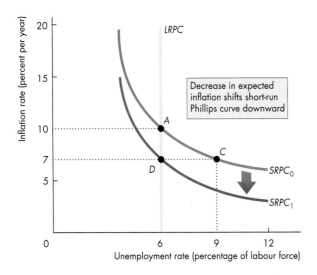

The long-run Phillips curve is *LRPC*. A fall in the expected inflation rate from 10 percent a year to 7 percent a year shifts the short-run Phillips curve downward from $SRPC_0$ and $SRPC_1$. The new short-run Phillips curve intersects the long-run Phillips curve at the new expected inflation rate—point *D*. With the original expected inflation rate (of 10 percent), a fall in the actual inflation rate to 7 percent a year increases the unemployment rate from 6 percent to 9 percent, at point *C*.

FIGURE 28.13   A Change in the Natural Rate of Unemployment

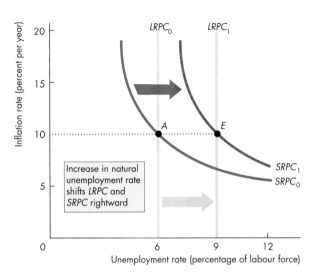

A change in the natural rate of unemployment shifts both the short-run and long-run Phillips curves. Here, the natural rate of unemployment increases from 6 percent to 9 percent, and the two Phillips curves shift right to $SRPC_1$ and $LRPC_1$. The new long-run Phillips curve intersects the new short-run Phillips curve at the expected inflation rate—point E.

The Canadian Phillips Curve

Figure 28.14(a) is a scatter diagram of inflation and unemployment since 1960. The data follow a course like a Formula 1 race track with 2001 almost at the same spot as 1961. Figure 28.14(b) interprets the data in terms of the Phillips curve. In 1960, the natural rate of unemployment was 5 percent so the long-run Phillips curve was $LRPC_1$. The expected inflation rate was 3 percent a year so the short-run Phillips curve, $SRPC_1$, intersects $LRPC_1$ at point A. During the 1970s and through 1982, the expected inflation rate and the natural rate of unemployment increased. The long-run curve shifted to $LRPC_2$ and the short-run curve shifted to $SRPC_2$. During the 1980s and 1990s, the expected inflation rate and the natural rate of unemployment decreased. The long-run curve shifted to $LRPC_3$ and the short-run curve shifted back to $SRPC_1$. The $SRPC$ of 2001 is the same as that of 1960, but in 2001, the natural rate of unemployment is higher and the expected inflation rate is lower than in 1960.

FIGURE 28.14   Phillips Curves in Canada

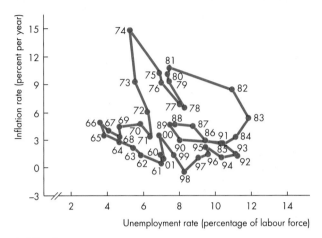

(a) The time sequence

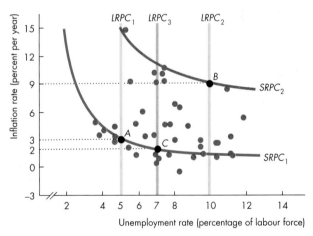

(b) Shifting Phillips curves

In part (a), each dot represents the combination of inflation and unemployment for a particular year in Canada.

Part (b) interprets the data with a shifting short-run Phillips curve. The black dots A, B, and C show the combination of the natural rate of unemployment and the expected inflation rate in different periods. The short-run Phillips curve was $SRPC_1$ during the 1960s and the late 1990s and early 2000s. It was $SRPC_2$ during the early 1970s and early 1980s. The long-run Phillips curve was $LRPC_1$ during the 1960s, $LRPC_2$ during the 1970s and early 1980s, and $LRPC_3$ during the 1990s.

Sources: Statistics Canada, CANSIM tables 380-0002 and 380-0056, and authors' calculations and assumptions.

REVIEW QUIZ

1 How would you use the Phillips curve to illustrate an unanticipated change in the inflation rate?
2 What are the effects of an unanticipated increase in the inflation rate on the unemployment rate?
3 If the expected inflation rate increases by 10 percentage points, how do the short-run Phillips curve and the long-run Phillips curve change?
4 If the natural rate of unemployment increases, what happens to the short-run Phillips curve and the long-run Phillips?
5 Does Canada have a stable short-run Phillips curve? Explain why or why not.
6 Does Canada have a stable long-run Phillips curve?

So far, we've studied the effects of inflation on real GDP, real wages, employment, and unemployment. But inflation lowers the value of money and changes the real value of the amounts borrowed and repaid. As a result, interest rates are influenced by inflation. Let's see how.

Interest Rates and Inflation

TODAY, BUSINESSES IN CANADA CAN BORROW AT interest rates of around 6 percent a year. Businesses in Russia pay interest rates of 60 percent a year, and those in Turkey pay 80 percent a year. Although Canadian interest rates have never been as high as these two cases, Canadian businesses faced interest rates of 20 percent or higher during the early 1980s. Why do interest rates vary so much both across countries and over time? Part of the answer is because risk differences make *real interest rates* vary across countries. Borrowers in high-risk countries pay higher interest rates than do those in low-risk countries. But another part of the answer is that the inflation rate varies.

Figure 28.15 shows that the higher the inflation rate, the higher is the nominal interest rate. This proposition is true for Canada over time in part (a) and the world in 2000 in part (b).

FIGURE 28.15   Inflation and the Interest Rate

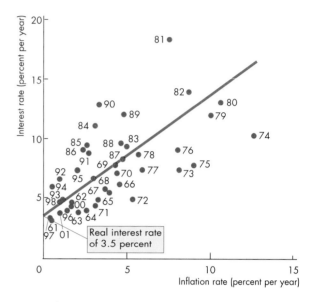

(a) Canada

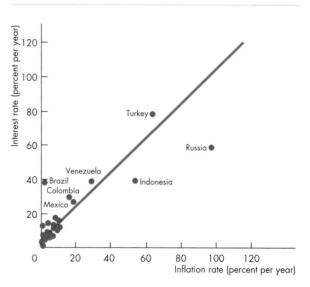

(b) Around the world

Other things remaining the same, the higher the inflation rate, the higher is the nominal interest rate. Part (a) shows this relationship between nominal interest rates and the inflation rate in Canada, and part (b) shows the relationship across a number of countries in 2000.

Sources: Statistics Canada, CANSIM tables 176-0043 and 380-0056 and International Monetary Fund, *International Financial Statistics Yearbook 2001.*

How Interest Rates Are Determined

The *real* interest rate is determined by investment demand and saving supply in the global market for financial capital. Investment demand and saving supply depend on the real interest rate. And the real interest rate adjusts to make investment plans and saving plans equal. You can think of the forces that determine the equilibrium real interest rate by using the standard demand and supply model. National real interest rates vary around the world-average real interest rate because of national differences in risk.

A *nominal* interest rate is determined by the demand for money and the quantity of money in each nation's money market. The demand for money depends on the nominal interest rate, and the quantity of money is determined by the central bank's monetary policy—the Bank of Canada's monetary policy in Canada. The nominal interest rate adjusts to make the quantity of money demanded equal to the quantity supplied. (Chapter 25, p. 595–596, explains the forces that determine the equilibrium nominal interest rate.)

Why Inflation Influences the Nominal Interest Rate

Because the real interest rate is determined in the global capital market and nominal interest rates are determined in each nation's money market, there is no tight and mechanical link between the two interest rates. But on the average, and other things remaining the same, a 1 percentage point rise in the inflation rate leads to a 1 percentage point rise in the nominal interest rate. Why? The answer is that the capital market and the money market are closely interconnected. The investment, saving, and demand for money decisions that people make are connected and the result is that the equilibrium nominal interest rate approximately equals the real interest rate plus the expected inflation rate.

To see why this relationship between the real interest rate and the nominal interest rate arises, think about the investment, saving, and demand for money decisions that people make. Imagine first that there is no inflation. Investment equals saving at a real interest rate of 6 percent a year. The demand for money equals the supply of money at a nominal interest rate of 6 percent a year. Teleglobe Canada is willing to pay an interest rate of 6 percent a year to get the funds it needs to pay for its global investment in new satellites. Sue and thousands of people like her are willing to save and lend Teleglobe Canada the amount it needs for its satellites if

they can get a *real* return of 6 percent a year. (Sue is saving to buy a new car.) And Teleglobe Canada, Sue, and everyone else are willingly holding the quantity of (real) money supplied by the Bank of Canada.

Now imagine that the inflation rate is a steady and expected 4 percent a year. All dollar amounts, including satellite service profits and car prices, are rising by 4 percent a year. If Teleglobe Canada was willing to pay a 6 percent interest rate when there was no inflation, it is now willing to pay 10 percent interest. Its profits are rising by 4 percent a year, so it is *really* paying only 6 percent. Similarly, if Sue was willing to lend at a 6 percent interest rate when there was no inflation, she is now willing to lend only if she gets 10 percent interest. The price of the car Sue is planning to buy is rising by 4 percent a year, so she is *really* getting only a 6 percent interest rate.

Because borrowers are willing to pay the higher rate and lenders are willing to lend only if they get the higher rate when inflation is anticipated, the *nominal interest rate* increases by an amount equal to the expected inflation rate. The *real interest rate* remains constant.

At a nominal interest rate of 10 percent a year, people are willingly holding the quantity of (real) money supplied by the Bank of Canada. This quantity is less than that with zero inflation. The price level rises by more than the quantity of money, and the real quantity of money decreases because of the increase in inflation.

REVIEW QUIZ

1 What is the relationship between the real interest rate, the nominal interest rate, and the inflation rate?
2 Why does inflation change the nominal interest rate?

◆ *Reading Between the Lines* on pp. 668–669 looks at the views of an economist who believes there is a long-run tradeoff between inflation and unemployment.

You have now completed your study of the aggregate demand side of the economy. Your task in the following chapters is to probe the supply side more deeply. We study the forces that determine aggregate supply in the short run and the long run and that bring economic growth and cycles.

Inflation–Unemployment Tradeoff

THE VANCOUVER SUN, JUNE 18, 2002

High jobless rate avoidable

Canada could have done more to stimulate employment through the 1990s without risking inflation, the winner of the 2001 Nobel Prize in Economics said Monday.

Dr. George Akerlof said during a meeting of the Canadian Institute for Advanced Research that the chairman of the U.S. Federal Reserve Board, Edward Greenspan, went against the advice of his staff and traditional economic theory and kept stimulating the economy with low interest rates as unemployment hit historic lows.

Canada took a more conservative and ideological approach.

The result was Canada had an unemployment rate much higher than that in the United States, where inflation stayed low even when unemployment fell below five per cent as a result of the investment generated by the economic stimulus program.

"The Canadian economy serves up a sober lesson," said Akerlof, who is a professor of economics at the University of California at Berkeley.

As the economy stalled in the past couple of years, the Bank of Canada lowered interest rates, but unemployment rates have been held high by the global recession, Akerlof said.

"You can't expect that Canada wouldn't have the same repercussions that are happening in the rest of the world," he said.

Akerlof recommended that in future, Canada adopt a policy similar to that employed in the U.S.

"I sincerely hope the Canadian unemployment of the 1990s is not going to repeat itself," he said.

...

Akerlof won the Nobel prize for work he did more than 30 years ago, describing how markets break down when buyers and sellers have conflicting needs and expectations.

Essence of the Story

■ George Akerlof, a professor of economics at the University of California at Berkeley and a Nobel Laureate, says that Canada could have had higher employment (lower unemployment) with no higher inflation rate during the 1990s.

■ He contrasted Canada with the United States and said that as the unemployment rate hit historic lows, the U.S. kept stimulating the economy with low interest rates.

■ U.S. inflation stayed low even when unemployment fell below five percent because of the investment generated by the economic stimulus program.

■ Canada took a more conservative and ideological approach and had an unemployment rate much higher than that in the United States.

Economic Analysis

- It is difficult to recognize the Canada portrayed by George Akerlof.

- Canada's unemployment rate was indeed higher than the U.S. unemployment rate.

- But the gap between the Canadian and U.S. unemployment rates, which opened up during the early 1980s (not the 1990s), was persistent and not cyclical.

- Figure 1 shows the unemployment rates in the two countries.

- Because the unemployment gap was persistent, it is likely that it represents an increase in the natural rate of unemployment in Canada.

- If Canada's natural rate of unemployment is higher than the U.S. rate, lowering interest rates to stimulate aggregate demand will bring no improvement in the unemployment situation, but will bring greater inflation.

- Canada had a more severe inflation problem than the United States during the early 1980s.

- But Canada brought its inflation under control and had lower inflation than the United States during the 1990s and 2000s.

- Figure 2 shows the inflation records in the two countries.

- George Akerlof says that U.S. unemployment fell because low interest rates brought a high investment rate.

- He implies that Canada's investment rate was too low and could have been boosted by lower interest rates.

- Figure 3 shows that generally Canada has invested a larger percentage of its GDP than the United States has invested.

- It is true that U.S. investment increased during the 1990s. But it increased from a very low level and began to catch up to Canada's higher investment rate.

- Canada chose to fight inflation and accept a temporarily higher unemployment rate. But the persistently higher unemployment rate in Canada is a natural phenomenon that cannot be changed with demand stimulation.

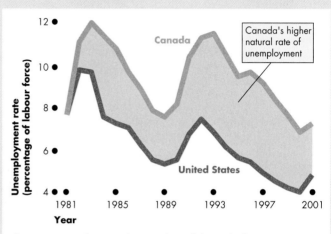

Figure 1 Unemployment in Canada and the United States

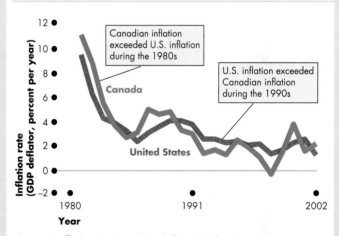

Figure 2 Inflation in Canada and the United States

Figure 3 Investment in Canada and the United States

669

SUMMARY

KEY POINTS

Inflation and the Price Level (p. 650)

- Inflation is a process of persistently rising prices and falling value of money.

Demand-Pull Inflation (pp. 651–653)

- Demand-pull inflation arises from increasing aggregate demand.
- Its main sources are increases in the quantity of money, government expenditures, or exports.

Cost-Push Inflation (pp. 653–655)

- Cost-push inflation can result from any factor that decreases aggregate supply.
- Its main sources are increasing money wage rates and increasing prices of key raw materials.

Quantity Theory of Money (pp. 656–657)

- The quantity theory of money is the proposition that money growth and inflation move up and down together in the long run.
- The Canadian and international evidence is consistent with the quantity theory on the average.

Effects of Inflation (pp. 658–662)

- Inflation is costly when it is unanticipated because it creates inefficiencies and redistributes income and wealth.
- People try to anticipate inflation to avoid its costs.
- Forecasts of inflation based on all the available relevant information are called rational expectations.
- A moderate anticipated inflation has a small cost. A rapid anticipated inflation is costly because it decreases potential GDP and slows economic growth.

Inflation and Unemployment: The Phillips Curve (pp. 662–666)

- The short-run Phillips curve shows the tradeoff between inflation and unemployment when the expected inflation rate and the natural rate of unemployment are constant.
- The long-run Phillips curve, which is vertical, shows that when the actual inflation rate equals the expected inflation rate, the unemployment rate equals the natural rate of unemployment.
- Unexpected changes in the inflation rate bring movements along the short-run Phillips curve.
- Changes in expected inflation shift the short-run Phillips curve.
- Changes in the natural rate of unemployment shift both the short-run and long-run Phillips curves.

Interest Rates and Inflation (pp. 666–667)

- The higher the expected inflation rate, the higher is the nominal interest rate.
- As the expected inflation rate rises, borrowers willingly pay a higher interest rate and lenders successfully demand a higher interest rate.
- The nominal interest rate adjusts to equal the real interest rate plus the expected inflation rate.

KEY FIGURES

KEY TERMS

PROBLEMS

*1. The figure shows an economy's long-run aggregate supply curve *LAS*; three aggregate demand curves AD_0, AD_1, and AD_2; and three short-run aggregate supply curves SAS_0, SAS_1, and SAS_2. The economy starts out on the curves AD_0 and SAS_0.

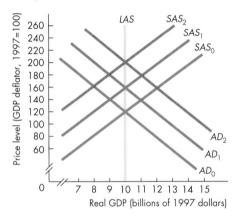

Some events occur that generate a demand-pull inflation.
a. List the events that might cause a demand-pull inflation.
b. Using the figure, describe the initial effects of a demand-pull inflation.
c. Using the figure, describe what happens as a demand-pull inflation spiral unwinds.

2. In the economy described in problem 1, some events then occur that generate a cost-push inflation.
a. List the events that might cause a cost-push inflation.
b. Using the figure, describe the initial effects of a cost-push inflation.
c. Using the figure, describe what happens as a cost-push inflation spiral unwinds.

*3. Quantecon is a country in which the quantity theory of money operates. The country has a constant population, capital stock, and technology. In year 1, real GDP was $400 million, the price level was 200, and the velocity of circulation of money was 20. In year 2, the quantity of money was 20 percent higher than in year 1.
a. What was the quantity of money in year 1?
b. What was the quantity of money in year 2?

c. What was the price level in year 2?
d. What was the level of real GDP in year 2?
e. What was the velocity of circulation in year 2?

4. In Quantecon described in problem 3, in year 3, the quantity of money falls to one-fifth of its year 2 level.
a. What is the quantity of money in year 3?
b. What is the price level in year 3?
c. What is the level of real GDP in year 3?
d. What is the velocity of circulation in year 3?
e. If it takes more than one year for the full quantity theory effect to occur, what do you predict happens to real GDP in Quantecon in year 3? Why?

*5. The economy described in problem 1 starts out on the curves AD_o and SAS_0. Some events now occur that generate a perfectly anticipated inflation.
a. List the events that might cause a perfectly anticipated inflation.
b. Using the figure, describe the initial effects of an anticipated inflation.
c. Using the figure, describe what happens as an anticipated inflation proceeds.

6. In the economy described in problem 1, suppose that people anticipate deflation (a falling price level) but aggregate demand turns out not to change.
a. What happens to the short-run and long-run aggregate supply curves? (Draw some new curves if you need to.)
b. Using the figure, describe the initial effects of an anticipated deflation.
c. Using the figure, describe what happens as it becomes obvious to everyone that the anticipated deflation is not going to occur.

*7. An economy has an unemployment rate of 4 percent and an inflation rate of 5 percent at point *A* in the figure. Some events then occur that move the economy to point *D*.
a. Describe the events that could move the economy from point *A* to point *D*.
b. Draw in the figure the economy's short-run and long-run Phillips curves when the economy is at point *A*.
c. Draw in the figure the economy's short-run and long-run Phillips curves when the economy is at point *D*.

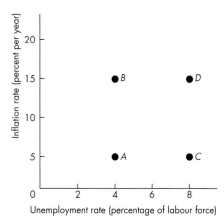

Inflation rate (percent per year)

Unemployment rate (percentage of labour force)

8. In the economy described in problem 7, some events occur that move the economy from point *B* to point *C*.
   a. Describe the events that could move the economy from point *B* to point *C*.
   b. Draw in the diagram the economy's short-run and long-run Phillips curves when the economy is at point *B*.
   c. Draw in the diagram the economy's short-run and long-run Phillips curves when the economy is at point *C*.
*9. An economy with a natural rate of unemployment of 4 percent and an expected inflation rate of 6 percent a year has the following inflation and unemployment history:

Year	Inflation rate (percent per year)	Unemployment rate (percentage of labour force)
1999	10	2
2000	8	3
2001	6	4
2002	4	5
2003	2	6

   a. Draw a graph of the economy's short-run and long-run Phillips curves.
   b. If the actual inflation rate rises from 6 percent a year to 8 percent a year, what is the change in the unemployment rate? Explain why it occurs.
10. For the economy described in problem 9, the natural rate of unemployment increases to 5 percent and the expected inflation rate falls to 5 percent a year. Draw the new short-run and long-run Phillips curves in the graph.

CRITICAL THINKING

1. Study *Reading Between the Lines* on pp. 668–669 and then answer the following questions:
   a. What does George Akerlof believe about the tradeoff between inflation and unemployment?
   b. Why, according to Akerlof, did the United States have a better unemployment performance than Canada?
   c. Do you think the data on inflation and unemployment are consistent with the view that the natural rate of unemployment is 7 percent? Explain why or why not.

WEB EXERCISES

1. Use the links on the Parkin–Bade Web site to obtain data on the growth rate of the quantity of money and the inflation rate in Canada since 2000.
   a. Calculate the average growth rate of the quantity of money since 2000.
   b. Calculate the average inflation rate since 2000.
   c. Make a graph of the growth rate of the quantity of money and the inflation rate since 2000.
   d. Interpret your graph and explain what it tells you about the forces that generate inflation and the relationship between money growth and inflation.
2. Use the links on the Parkin–Bade Web site to obtain data on the inflation rate and the unemployment rate in the United States during the 1990s and 2000s.
   a. Make a graph using the data you've obtained that is similar to Fig. 28.14.
   b. Describe the similarities and the differences in relationship between inflation and unemployment found in the United States and in Canada.

UNDERSTANDING AGGREGATE DEMAND AND INFLATION

PART 8

Money Chasing Goods

Aggregate demand fluctuations bring recessions and expansions. If aggregate demand expands more rapidly than long-run aggregate supply, we get inflation. So understanding the forces that determine aggregate demand helps us to understand both the business cycle and inflation. ◆ It took economists a long time to achieve this knowledge, and we still don't know enough about aggregate demand to be able to forecast it more than a few months ahead. But we do know the basic factors that influence aggregate demand. And we know a lot about how those factors interact to send shock waves rippling through the economy. ◆ Fundamentally, aggregate demand is a monetary phenomenon. The quantity of money is the single most significant influence on aggregate demand. This insight was first outlined more than 200 years ago by David Hume, a Scottish philosopher and close friend of Adam Smith. Said Hume, "In every Kingdom into which money begins to flow in greater abundance than formerly, everything takes a new face: labour and industry gain life; the merchant becomes more enterprising, the manufacturer more diligent and skilful, and even the farmer follows his plough with greater alacrity and attention." Milton Friedman and other economists known as monetarists also emphasize the central role of money. Money lies at the centre of Keynes' theory of aggregate demand as well. But Keynes also called attention to the power of independent changes in government expenditures, taxes, and business investment to influence aggregate demand. In the modern world, we also recognize the effect of changes in exports on aggregate demand. ◆ The chapters in this part explain the factors that influence aggregate demand and help you to understand how they interact to bring multiplier effects on aggregate expenditure. Chapter 23 explained the effects of changes in business investment and the multiplier effect they have on consumption expenditure and aggregate expenditure. This chapter also explained how changes in business inventories trigger changes in production and incomes. Chapter 24 looked at fiscal policy and applied the model of Chapter 23 to study the effects of changes in government expenditures and taxes. Chapter 25 brought money into the picture and explained what money is, how banks create it, and what determines the interest rate. Chapter 26 showed how the Bank of Canada controls the quantity of money and influences interest rates and expenditure. Chapter 27 returned to the aggregate supply–aggregate demand framework and explained how fiscal policy and monetary policy interact. Chapter 28 explained inflation and showed how the trend in money growth determines the trend in inflation and how fluctuations in aggregate demand bring fluctuations in inflation, employment, and unemployment. ◆ Many economists have developed the insights you've learned in these chapters. One of the truly outstanding ones is Milton Friedman, whom you can meet on the next page. You can also meet one of today's leading macroeconomists, Michael Woodford of Princeton University.

673

Understanding Inflation

"Inflation is always and everywhere a monetary phenomenon."

MILTON
FRIEDMAN
*The Counter-
Revolution in
Monetary
Theory*

THE ECONOMIST

MILTON FRIEDMAN *was born into a poor immigrant family in New York City in 1912. He was an undergraduate at Rutgers and graduate student at Columbia University during the Great Depression. Today, Professor Friedman is a Senior Fellow at the Hoover Institution at Stanford University. But his reputation was built between 1946 and 1983, when he was a leading member of the "Chicago School," an approach to economics developed at the University of Chicago and based on the views that free markets allocate resources efficiently and that stable and low money supply growth delivers macroeconomic stability.*

Friedman has advanced our understanding of the forces that determine aggregate demand and clarified the effects of the quantity of money and for this work, he was awarded the (much overdue, in the opinion of his many admirers) 1977 Nobel Prize for Economic Science.

By reasoning from basic economic principles, Friedman predicted that persistent demand stimulation would not increase output but would cause inflation. When output growth slowed and inflation broke out in the 1970s, Friedman seemed like a prophet, and for a time, his policy prescription, known as monetarism, was embraced around the world.

THE ISSUES

The combination of history and economics has taught us a lot about the causes of inflation. Severe inflation—hyperinflation—arises from a breakdown of the normal fiscal policy processes at times of war or political upheaval. Tax revenues fall short of government spending, and newly printed money fills the gap between them. As inflation increases, the quantity of money that is needed to make payments increases, and a shortage of money can even result. So the rate of money growth increases yet further, and prices rise yet faster. Eventually, the monetary system collapses. Such was the experience of Germany during the 1920s and Brazil during the 1990s.

In earlier times, when commodities were used as money, inflation resulted from the discovery of new sources of money. The most recent occurrence of this type of inflation was at the end of the nineteenth century when gold, then used as money, was discovered in Australia, the Klondike, and South Africa.

In modern times, inflation has resulted from increases in the quantity of money that has accommodated increases in costs. The most dramatic such inflations occurred during the 1970s when the Bank of Canada, the Federal Reserve, and other central banks around the world accommodated oil price increases.

To avoid inflation, money growth must be held in check. But at times of severe cost pressure, central banks feel a strong tug in the direction of avoiding recession and accommodating the cost pressure.

Yet some countries have avoided inflation more effectively than others have. One source of success is central bank independence. In low-inflation countries, such as Germany and Japan, the central bank decides how much money to create and at what level to set interest rates, and does not take instructions from the government. In high-inflation countries, such as Angola and Zimbabwe, the central bank takes direct orders from the government about interest rates and money growth. The architects of the new monetary system for the European Community based on the euro noticed this connection between central bank independence and inflation and modelled the constitution for the European Central Bank on the independent German central bank.

THEN

When inflation is especially rapid, as it was in Germany in 1923, money becomes almost worthless. In Germany at that time, bank notes were more valuable as fire kindling than as money, and the sight of people burning Reichmarks was a common one. To avoid having to hold money for too long, wages were paid and spent twice a day. Banks took deposits and made loans, but at interest rates that compensated both depositors and the bank for the falling value of money—interest rates that could exceed 100 percent a month. The price of a dinner would increase during the course of an evening, making lingering over coffee a very expensive pastime.

Now

In 1994, Brazil had a computer-age hyperinflation, an inflation rate that was close to 50 percent a month. Banks installed ATMs on almost every street corner and refilled them several times an hour. Brazilians tried to avoid holding currency. As soon as they were paid, they went shopping and bought enough food to get them through to the next payday. Some shoppers filled as many as six carts on a single monthly trip to the supermarket. Also, instead of using currency, Brazilians used credit cards whenever possible. But they paid their card balances off quickly because the interest rate on unpaid balances was 50 percent a month. Only at such a high interest rate did it pay banks to lend to cardholders, because banks themselves were paying interest rates of 40 percent a month to induce depositors to keep their money in the bank.

Many economists today are working on aggregate demand and inflation. One distinguished contributor, whom you can meet on the following pages, is Michael Woodford of Princeton University.

675

MICHAEL WOODFORD *is Harold H. Helm '20 Professor of Economics and Banking at Princeton University. Born in 1955 in Chicopee, Massachusetts, he was an undergraduate at the University of Chicago and a doctoral student at the Yale Law School before pursuing his doctorate in economics at the Massachusetts Institute of Technology. Professor Woodford's research on money and monetary policy has challenged much traditional thinking, and his ideas about a (future) world without money are attracting a great deal of interest. His advanced text,* Interest and Prices: Foundations of a Theory of Monetary Policy, *is being published by Princeton University Press.*

Michael Parkin and Robin Bade talked with Michael Woodford about his work and the progress that economists have made in designing effective monetary policy rules.

Michael Woodford

Why, after completing law school, did you decide to become an economist?

Almost every class in law school was full of economic reasoning. I became fascinated by economic analysis, and thought that I would have to get a better foundation in economics in order to think clearly about legal issues. In the end I found that I liked economics enough to become an economist.

I am able to address questions of public policy, which is what had originally drawn me to law, but in a way that also allows me to indulge a taste for thinking about what

the world might be like or should be like, and not simply the way that it already is.

In a world as rapidly changing as ours is, I think that the perspective provided by economics is essential for understanding which kinds of laws and rules make sense.

You are a supporter of rules for monetary policy. Why are rules so important?

In my view, rules are important not because central bankers can't be relied upon to take the public interest to heart, or because they don't know what they're doing, but because the effects of monetary policy depend critically upon what the private sector expects about future policy, and hence about the future course of the economy. Thus effective monetary policy depends more on the successful *management of expectations* than on any direct consequences of the current level of interest rates.

In order to steer people's expectations about future monetary policy in the way that it would like, a central bank needs to communicate details about how policy will be conducted in the future. The best way to do this is by being explicit about the rule that guides its decision making. The central bank also needs to establish a reputation for actually following the rule.

Following the rule means not always doing what might seem best in given current conditions. What is best for the economy now will be independent of what people may have expected in the past. But if the central bank doesn't feel bound to follow through on its prior commitments, people will learn that they don't mean anything. Then those commitments will not shape people's expectations in the desired way.

There is actually a strong parallel between monetary policy rules and the law, and the desirability of rules is an example of the perspective that I gained from the study of law. A judge doesn't simply seek to determine, in each individual case, what outcomes would do the most good, given the individual circumstances. Instead, the judge makes a decision based on rules established either by precedent or by statute. Because the law is rule-based, people are able to forecast more accurately the consequences of their contemplated actions.

A central banker is often portrayed as the captain of the economic ship, steering it skillfully between the rocks of inflation and unemployment in a choppy sea. But a ship's captain doesn't need to care about how the ocean will interpret his actions. So the parallel isn't a good one. In my view, the role of a central banker is more similar to that of a judge than to that of a ship's captain. Both central bankers and judges care enormously about the effects of their decisions on the expectations of people whose behaviour depends on expected future decisions.

> *"Following the rule means not always doing what might seem best in given current conditions."*

The rule that you favour is different from that suggested by Milton Friedman. What is wrong with the Friedman rule?

Friedman's rule involves a target for the growth rate of some definition of the quantity of money. I don't think that the best monetary rule involves a target of any kind for the growth rate of a monetary aggregate. Friedman's rule is not the worst sort of rule, as simple rules go, but we can do better.

Just a century ago, no one had any idea how to establish a reasonably predictable monetary standard except by guaranteeing the convertibility of money into a precious metal such as gold. We didn't have the surprisingly modern concept of index numbers and today's routinely calculated price indexes like the CPI that enable us to measure, to a decent approximation, the purchasing power of the dollar.

We now understand that pegging the value of money to something like gold is a cruder solution to the problem than is necessary. We don't need to leave the value of money hostage to the vagaries of the gold

market simply in order to maintain confidence that a dollar means *something*.

Friedman recognizes the value of a well-managed fiat currency, but supposes that there is unlikely to be much predictability to the value of money unless the central bank is committed to a fixed target growth path for the quantity of money. But that again is a more indirect solution to the problem of maintaining a stable and predictable value for money than is necessary.

And there is a potentially large cost of such a crude approach when the relation between one's favourite monetary aggregate and the value of money shifts over time. A focus on stabilizing a monetary aggregate means less stability than would otherwise have been possible in the purchasing power of money.

So what would be a good monetary rule?

First, there should be a clearly defined target in terms of variables that policymakers actually care about, such as the inflation rate, rather than an "intermediate target" such as a monetary aggregate. Second, the central bank should be as clear as possible about the decision making process through which it determines the level of interest rates that is believed to be consistent with achieving the target.

"Inflation targeting," as currently practised in the United Kingdom, Canada, and New Zealand, is an example of the general approach that I would advocate. But I think that central banks of the inflation-targeting countries could do a better job of explaining the procedures used to determine the interest rate that is judged to be consistent with the inflation target—they could be more transparent.

And all of these countries could better explain to the public the ways in which variables other than inflation are also taken into consideration. I'm not sure that inflation targeting needs to be *stricter*, in the sense that considerations other than inflation should be more scrupulously ruled out. But I think that it is desirable to make it more of a *rule*.

One of the most intriguing issues that you've worked on is the question of what determines the price level in a "cashless economy." How would we control inflation in such a world?

One advantage of the approach the monetary policy that I've just mentioned is that the form of policy rule that is appropriate need not change much at all if we were to progress to a "cashless economy." As long as the central bank can still control the overnight interest rate—the overnight loans rate in Canada—the *rule* for adjusting the interest rate need not change. Yet there might no longer be any meaning to a target path for a monetary aggregate in such a world.

The critical question is whether a central bank would still be able to control the overnight interest rate in such a world. Some argue that central banks only control interest rates in the interbank market for reserves because the private sector cannot supply a good substitute for reserves and the central bank is therefore a monopoly supplier. They then worry that if private substitutes for reserves were available, central banks would lose control of the interest rate.

But this line of reasoning assumes, as do most textbooks (even the good ones!), that central banks can change the interest rate *only* by changing the *opportunity cost* of holding reserves, which should only be possible in the presence of market power. But central banks can change the overnight interest rate *without* changing the opportunity cost of holding reserves. Indeed, the Bank of Canada already does so. It pays interest on reserves and maintains a fixed difference between the interest rate on reserves and the discount rate—the rate at which it stands willing to lend reserves to the banks. The overnight rate fluctuates inside the range of these two rates, so by changing the interest rate on reserves, the Bank of Canada controls the overnight rate but doesn't change the opportunity cost of holding reserves.

Every central bank, including the Federal Reserve, would have to adjust the interest rate in a way similar to this in a "cashless economy."

Where do you stand on the sources of aggregate fluctuations? Are they primarily an efficient response to the uneven pace of technical change, or are they primarily the consequence of market failure and demand fluctuations?

I don't think that they are primarily an *efficient* response to variations in technical progress or to other real disturbances of that kind. I think that there are important distortions that often result in *inefficient* responses of the economy to real disturbances, and this is why monetary policy matters. But I do think that real disturbances are important—for example, I don't think that exogenous variations in monetary policy have been responsible for too much of the economic instability in the U.S. economy in recent decades—and I think that their supply-side effects are important, too.

The important issue, to my mind, is not whether the disturbances are thought to have more to do with supply or demand factors; it is whether the economy can be relied upon to respond efficiently to them, regardless of the nature of monetary policy. I don't think that that occurs automatically. The goal of good monetary policy is to bring about such a world: one in which monetary policy is not itself a source of disturbances, and in which the responses to real disturbances are efficient ones. The first part simply requires that monetary policy be systematic, but the second part depends upon the choice of a monetary policy rule of the right sort.

What advice do you have for a student who is just starting to study economics? Is it a good subject in which to major? What other subjects would you urge students to study alongside economics?

I think economics is an excellent major for students with many different interests. Most people who study economics are probably looking for an edge in the business world, and economics is valuable for that. But it's also all extremely valuable background for people interested in careers in law, government, or public policy. And of course, to some of us, the subject is interesting in its own right. I find that the challenges just get deeper the farther I get into the subject.

Probably the most important other subject for someone thinking of actually becoming an economist is mathematics. This is often the determining factor as to how well a student will do in graduate study, because the research literature is a good deal more mathematical than many people suspect from their undergraduate economics courses. But economics is not a branch of mathematics. It's a subject that seeks to understand people and social institutions, and so all sorts of other subjects—history, politics, sociology, psychology, moral and political philosophy—are useful background for an economist, too. I don't at all regret the amount of time I spent in liberal arts courses as an undergraduate.

THE ECONOMY AT FULL EMPLOYMENT

CHAPTER 29

Production and Jobs

Over time, we become more productive and our incomes grow. For each hour we worked in 2001, we earned twice what we earned in 1961. What makes production and incomes grow? Why did productivity grow during a recession? ◆ Our population also grows every year. How does population size influence employment, wage rates, and potential GDP? ◆ We hear a lot about the need to increase our national saving to invest in new capital, the importance of education, and the need to support science and technology. How do capital accumulation, education, and advances in technology influence employment, wage rates, and potential GDP? ◆ You know that when we talk about full employment, we don't mean there is *no* unemployment. But what determines the amount of unemployment when the economy is at full employment?

◆ We'll answer these questions in this chapter. We'll discover how changes in population, capital, and technology influence production, jobs, and incomes over long periods of time. We'll learn about the forces that create unemployment when the economy is at full employment. And in *Reading Between the Lines* at the end of this chapter, we'll compare productivity in Canada with that in the United States.

After studying this chapter, you will be able to

■ Describe the relationship between the quantity of labour employed and real GDP

■ Explain what determines the demand for labour and the supply of labour and how labour market equilibrium determines employment, the real wage rate, and potential GDP

■ Explain how an increase in the population, an increase in capital, and an advance in technology change employment, the real wage rate, and potential GDP

■ Explain what determines unemployment when the economy is at full employment

Real GDP and Employment

To produce more output, we must use more inputs. We can increase real GDP by employing more labour, increasing the quantity of capital, or developing technologies that are more productive. In the short term, the quantity of capital and the state of technology are fixed. So to increase real GDP in the short term, we must increase the quantity of labour employed. Let's look at the relationship between real GDP and the quantity of labour employed.

Production Possibilities

When you studied the limits to production in Chapter 2 (see p. 34), you learned about the *production possibilities frontier*, which is the boundary between those combinations of goods and services that can be produced and those that cannot. We can think about the production possibilities frontier for any pair of goods or services when we hold the quantities of all other goods and services constant. Let's think about the production possibilities frontier for two special items: real GDP and the quantity of leisure time.

Real GDP is a measure of the final goods and services produced in the economy in a given time period (see Chapter 20, p. 458). We measure real GDP as a number of 1997 dollars, but the measure is a *real* one. Real GDP is not a pile of dollars. It is a pile of goods and services. Think of it as a number of big shopping carts filled with goods and services. Each cart contains some of each kind of different goods and services produced, and one cartload of items costs $100 billion. To say that real GDP is $1,000 billion means that real GDP is 10 very big shopping carts of goods and services.

The quantity of leisure time is the number of hours we spend not working. It is the time we spend playing or watching sports, seeing movies, and hanging out with friends. Leisure time is a special type of good or service.

Each hour that we spent pursuing fun could have been an hour that we spent working. So when the quantity of leisure time increases by one hour, the quantity of labour employed decreases by one hour. If we spent all our time having fun rather than working, we would not produce anything. Real GDP would be zero. The more leisure time we forgo to work, the

greater is the quantity of labour employed and the greater is real GDP.

The relationship between leisure time and real GDP is a *production possibilities frontier* (*PPF*). Figure 29.1(a) shows an example of this frontier. The economy has 45 billion hours of leisure time available. If people use all these hours to pursue leisure, no labour is employed and real GDP is zero. As people forgo leisure and work more, real GDP increases. If people spent 20 billion hours working and took 25 billion hours in leisure, real GDP would be $1,000 billion at point *A*. If people spent all the available hours working, real GDP would be $1,500 billion.

The bowed-out *PPF* displays increasing opportunity cost. In this case, the opportunity cost of a given amount of real GDP is the amount of leisure time forgone to produce it. As real GDP increases, each additional unit of real GDP costs an increasing amount of forgone leisure. The reason is that we use the most productive labour first, and as we use more labour, we use increasingly less productive labour.

The Production Function

The **production function** is the relationship between real GDP and the quantity of labour employed when all other influences on production remain the same. The production function shows how real GDP varies as the quantity of labour employed varies, other things remaining the same.

Because one more hour of labour employed means one less hour of leisure, the production function is like a mirror image of the leisure time–real GDP *PPF*. Figure 29.1(b) shows the production function for the economy whose *PPF* is shown in Fig. 29.1(a). You can see that when the quantity of labour employed is zero, real GDP is also zero. And as the quantity of labour employed increases, so does real GDP. When 20 billion labour hours are employed, real GDP is $1,000 billion (at point *A*).

A decrease in leisure hours and the corresponding increases in the quantity of labour employed and real GDP bring a movement along the production possibilities frontier and along the production function (*PF*). The arrows along the *PPF* and the *PF* in Fig. 29.1 show these movements. Such movements occurred when employment and real GDP surged during World War II.

But the increase in real GDP during World War II changed for an additional reason. Labour became more productive. Let's study the influences on the productivity of labour.

FIGURE 29.1 Production Possibilities and the Production Function

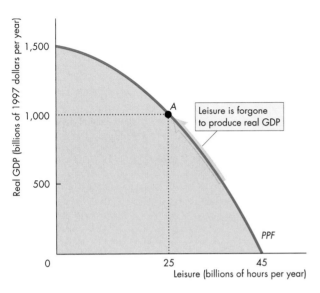

(a) Production possibility frontier

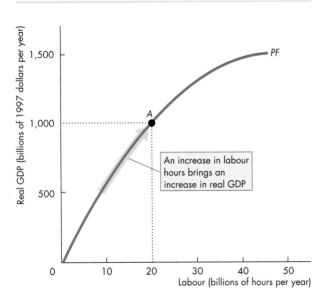

(b) Production function

On the production possibilities frontier in part (a), if we enjoy 45 billion hours of leisure, we produce no real GDP. If we forgo 20 billion hours of leisure time to work and spend 25 billion hours of leisure time, we produce a real GDP of $1,000 billion, at point A. At point A on the production function in part (b), we use 20 billion hours of labour to produce $1,000 billion of real GDP.

Changes in Productivity

When we talk about *productivity*, we usually mean labour productivity. **Labour productivity** is real GDP per hour of labour. Three factors influence labour productivity:

- Physical capital
- Human capital
- Technology

Physical Capital A farm worker equipped with only a stick and primitive tools can cultivate almost no land and grow barely enough food to feed a single family. A farmer equipped with a steel plow pulled by an animal can cultivate more land and produce enough food to feed a small village. A farmer equipped with a modern tractor, plow, and harvester can cultivate thousands of hectares and produce enough food to feed hundreds of people.

By using physical capital on our farms and in our factories, shops, and offices, we enormously increase labour productivity. And the more physical capital we use, the greater is our labour productivity, other things remaining the same.

Human Capital An economy's **human capital** is the knowledge and skill that people have obtained from education and on-the-job training.

The average university graduate has a greater amount of human capital than the average high school graduate possesses. Consequently, the university graduate is able to perform some tasks that are beyond the ability of the high school graduate. The university graduate is more productive. For the nation as a whole, the greater the amount of schooling its citizens complete, the greater is its real GDP, other things remaining the same.

Regardless of how much schooling a person has completed, not much production is accomplished on the first day at work. Learning about the new work environment consumes the newly hired worker. But as time passes and experience accumulates, the worker becomes more productive. We call this on-the-job education activity **learning-by-doing**.

Learning-by-doing can bring incredible increases in labour productivity. The more experienced the labour force, the greater is its labour productivity, and other things remaining the same, the greater is real GDP.

World War II provides a carefully documented example of the importance of this source of increase in labour productivity. In the shipyards that produced the transport vessels called Liberty ships, labour productivity increased by an astonishing 30 percent purely as a result of learning-by-doing.

Technology A student equipped with a pen can complete a readable page of writing in perhaps 10 minutes. This same task takes 5 minutes with a typewriter and 2 minutes with a computer. Travelling on foot from Toronto to Vancouver takes a person (a fit person!) more than 100 days. In a car, the trip takes a comfortable 5 days. And in an airplane, the trip takes 5 hours. These are examples of the enormous impact of technology on productivity. Imagine the profound effect of these advances in technology on the productivity of a movie director who works in both Toronto and Vancouver!

Shifts in the Production Function

Any influence on production that increases labour productivity shifts the production function upward. Real GDP increases at each level of labour hours. In Fig. 29.2(a), the production function is initially PF_0. Then an increase in physical capital and human capital or an advance in technology occurs. The production function shifts upward to PF_1.

At each quantity of labour employed, real GDP is greater on the new production function than it was on the original one. For example, at 20 billion hours, real GDP increases from $1,000 billion (point A) to $1,100 billion (point B).

Figure 29.2(b) shows how the production function in Canada shifted upward between 1981 and 2001. Along the production function PF_{01}, labour productivity is 42 percent greater than that on PF_{81}. Labour productivity in Canada increased by 1.8 percent a year.

R E V I E W   Q U I Z

1 What is the relationship between the leisure hours–real GDP *PPF* and the production function?

2 What does the outward-bowed shape of the leisure hours–real GDP *PPF* imply about the opportunity cost of real GDP and why is the *PPF* bowed outward?

3 Why does the production function shift upward when capital increases and/or technology advances?

FIGURE 29.2   An Increase in Labour Productivity

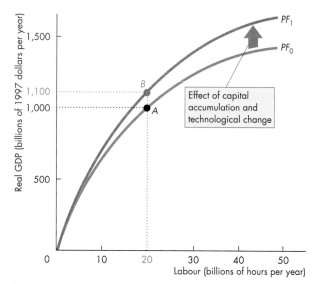

(a) An increase in labour productivity

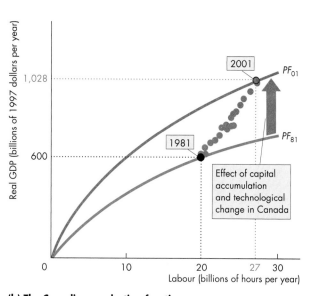

(b) The Canadian production function

On PF_0 in part (a), 20 billion labour hours produce a real GDP of $1,000 billion (point A). An increase in capital or an advance in technology increases labour productivity and shifts the production function upward to PF_1. Now, 20 billion labour hours produce a real GDP of $1,100 billion (point B). Canadian real GDP has increased (part b) because labour has become more productive and the quantity of labour has increased.

The Labour Market and Aggregate Supply

YOU'VE SEEN THAT IN A GIVEN YEAR, WITH A given amount of physical and human capital and given technology, real GDP depends on the quantity of labour hours employed. To produce more real GDP, we must employ more labour hours. The labour market determines the quantity of labour hours employed and the quantity of real GDP supplied. We'll learn how by studying

- The demand for labour
- The supply of labour
- Labour market equilibrium and potential GDP
- Aggregate supply

The Demand for Labour

The **quantity of labour demanded** is the number of labour hours hired by all the firms in the economy. The **demand for labour** is the relationship between the quantity of labour demanded and the real wage rate when all other influences on firms' hiring plans remain the same. The **real wage rate** is the quantity of goods and services that an hour of labour earns. In contrast, the **money wage rate** is the number of dollars that an hour of labour earns. A real wage rate is equal to a money wage rate divided by the price of a good. For the economy as a whole, the average real wage rate equals the average money wage rate divided by the price level multiplied by 100. So we express the real wage rate in constant dollars. (Today, we express this real wage rate in 1997 dollars.)

The *real* wage rate influences the quantity of labour demanded because what matters to firms is how much output they must sell to earn the number of dollars they pay (the money wage rate).

We can represent the demand for labour as either a demand schedule or a demand curve. The table in Fig. 29.3 shows part of a demand for labour schedule. It tells us the quantity of labour demanded at three different real wage rates. For example, if the real wage rate falls from $40 an hour to $35 an hour, the quantity of labour demanded increases from 15 billion hours a year to 20 billion hours a year. (You can find these numbers in rows *A* and *B* of the table.) The demand for labour curve is *LD*. Points *A*, *B*, and *C* on the curve correspond to rows *A*, *B*, and *C* of the demand schedule.

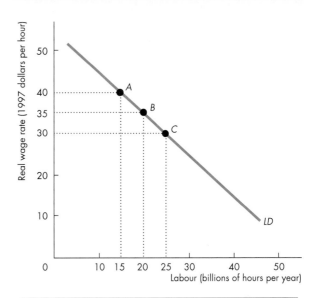

FIGURE 29.3   The Demand for Labour

	Real wage rate (1997 dollars per hour)	Quantity of labour demanded (billions of hours per year)
A	40	15
B	35	20
C	30	25

The table shows part of a demand for labour schedule. Points *A, B,* and *C* on the demand for labour curve correspond to the rows of the table. The lower the real wage rate, the greater is the quantity of labour demanded.

Why does the quantity of labour demanded *increase* as the real wage rate *decreases*? That is, why does the demand for labour curve slope downward? To answer these questions, we must learn about the marginal product of labour.

The Marginal Product of Labour The **marginal product of labour** is the additional real GDP produced by an additional hour of labour when all other influences on production remain the same. The marginal product of labour is governed by the **law of diminishing returns,** which states that as the quantity of labour increases, other things remaining the same, the marginal product of labour decreases.

The Law of Diminishing Returns Diminishing returns arise because the amount of capital is fixed. Two people operating one machine are not twice as productive as one person operating one machine. Eventually, as more labour hours are hired, workers get in each other's way and output barely increases.

Marginal Product Calculation We calculate the marginal product of labour as the change in real GDP divided by the change in the quantity of labour employed. Figure 29.4(a) shows some calculations, and Fig. 29.4(b) shows the marginal product curve.

In Fig. 29.4(a), when the quantity of labour employed increases from 10 billion hours to 20 billion hours, an increase of 10 billion hours, real GDP increases from $600 billion to $1,000 billion, an increase of $400 billion. The marginal product of labour equals the increase in real GDP ($400 billion) divided by the increase in the quantity of labour employed (10 billion hours), which is $40 an hour.

When the quantity of labour employed increases from 20 billion hours to 30 billion hours, an increase of 10 billion hours, real GDP increases from $1,000 billion to $1,300 billion, an increase of $300 billion. The marginal product of labour equals $300 billion divided by 10 billion hours, which is $30 an hour.

In Fig. 29.4(b), as the quantity of labour employed increases, the marginal product of labour diminishes. Between 10 billion and 20 billion hours (at 15 billion hours), marginal product is $40 an hour. And between 20 billion and 30 billion hours (at 25 billion hours), marginal product is $30 an hour.

The diminishing marginal product of labour limits the demand for labour.

Diminishing Marginal Product and the Demand for Labour Firms are in business to maximize profits. Each hour of labour that a firm hires increases output and adds to costs. Initially, an extra hour of labour produces more output than the real wage that the labour costs. Marginal product exceeds the real wage rate. But each additional hour of labour produces less additional output than the previous hour—the marginal product of labour diminishes.

As a firm hires more labour, eventually the extra output from an extra hour of labour is exactly what that hour of labour costs. At this point, marginal product equals the real wage rate. Hire one less hour and marginal product exceeds the real wage rate. Hire one more hour and the real wage rate exceeds marginal product. In either case, profit is less.

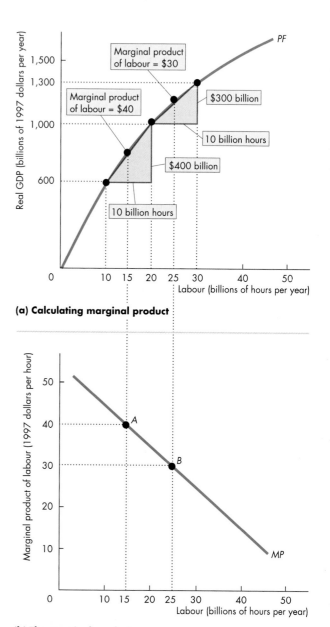

FIGURE 29.4 Marginal Product and the Demand for Labour

(a) Calculating marginal product

(b) The marginal product curve

Between 10 billion and 20 billion hours, the marginal product of labour is $40 an hour. Between 20 billion and 30 billion hours, the marginal product of labour is $30 an hour. At 15 billion hours (midway between 10 billion and 20 billion), the marginal product of labour is $40 an hour at point A on the MP curve. The MP curve is the demand for labour curve.

Because marginal product diminishes as the quantity of labour employed increases, the lower the real wage rate, the greater is the quantity of labour that a firm can profitably hire. The marginal product curve is the same as the demand for labour curve.

You might gain a clearer understanding of the demand for labour by looking at an example.

Demand for Labour in a Ketchup Factory

Suppose that when a ketchup factory employs one additional hour of labour, output increases by 11 bottles. Marginal product is 11 bottles an hour. If the money wage rate is $5.50 an hour and ketchup sells for 50¢ a bottle, the real wage rate is 11 bottles an hour. (We calculate the factory's real wage rate as the money wage rate of $5.50 an hour divided by a price of 50¢ a bottle, which equals a real wage rate of 11 bottles an hour.) Because marginal product diminishes, we know that if the firm did not hire this hour of labour, marginal product would exceed 11 bottles. Because the firm can hire the hour of labour for a real wage rate of 11 bottles, it just pays it to do so.

If the price of ketchup remains at 50¢ a bottle and the money wage rate falls to $5.00 an hour, the real wage rate falls to 10 bottles an hour and the firm increases the quantity of labour demanded.

Similarly, if the money wage rate remains at $5.50 an hour and the price of ketchup rises to 55¢ a bottle, the real wage rate falls to 10 bottles an hour and the firm increases the quantity of labour demanded.

When the firm pays a real wage rate equal to the marginal product of labour, it is maximizing profit.

Changes in the Demand for Labour

When the marginal product of labour changes, the demand for labour changes and the demand for labour curve shifts. You've seen that an increase in capital (both physical and human) and an advance in technology that increases productivity shift the production function upward. These same forces increase the demand for labour and shift the demand for labour curve rightward.

The Supply of Labour

The **quantity of labour supplied** is the number of labour hours that all the households in the economy plan to work. The **supply of labour** is the relationship between the quantity of labour supplied and the real wage rate when all other influences on work plans remain the same.

We can represent the supply of labour as either a supply schedule or a supply curve. The table in Fig. 29.5 shows a supply of labour schedule. It tells us the quantity of labour supplied at three different real wage rates. For example, if the real wage rate rises from $15 an hour (row A) to $35 an hour (row B), the quantity of labour supplied increases from 15 billion hours a year to 20 billion hours a year. The curve LS is a supply of labour curve. Points A, B, and C on the curve correspond to rows A, B, and C of the supply schedule.

The *real* wage rate influences the quantity of labour supplied because what matters to people is not the number of dollars they earn (the money wage rate) but what those dollars will buy.

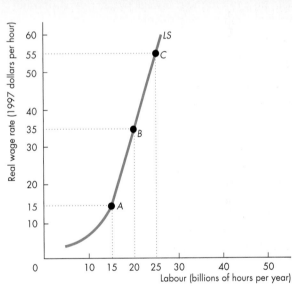

FIGURE 29.5   The Supply of Labour

	Real wage rate (1997 dollars per hour)	Quantity of labour supplied (billions of hours per year)
A	15	15
B	35	20
C	55	25

The table shows part of a supply of labour schedule. Points A, B, and C on the supply of labour curve correspond to the rows of the table. The higher the real wage rate, the greater is the quantity of labour supplied.

The quantity of labour supplied increases as the real wage rate increases for two reasons:

- Hours per person increase
- Labour force participation increases

Hours per Person In choosing how many hours to work, a household considers the opportunity cost of not working. This opportunity cost is the real wage rate. The higher the real wage rate, the greater is the opportunity cost of taking leisure and not working. And as the opportunity cost of taking leisure rises, so the more the household chooses to work, other things remaining the same.

But other things don't remain the same. The higher the real wage rate, the greater is the household's income. And the higher the household's income, the more it wants to consume. One item that it wants to consume more of is leisure.

So a rise in the real wage rate has two opposing effects. By increasing the opportunity cost of leisure, it makes the household want to consume less leisure and to work more. And by increasing the household's income, it makes the household want to consume more leisure and to work fewer hours. For most households, the opportunity cost effect is stronger than the income effect. So the higher the real wage rate, the greater is the amount of work that the household chooses to do.

Labour Force Participation Some people have productive opportunities outside the labour force. These people choose to work only if the real wage rate exceeds the value of these other productive activities. For example, a parent might spend time caring for her or his child. The alternative is day care. The parent will choose to work only if he or she can earn enough per hour to pay the cost of child care and have enough left to make the work effort worthwhile. The higher the real wage rate, the more likely it is that a parent will choose to work and so the greater is the labour force participation rate.

Labour Supply Response The quantity of labour supplied increases as the real wage rate rises. But the quantity of labour supplied is not highly responsive to the real wage rate. A large percentage change in the real wage rate brings a small percentage change in the quantity of labour supplied.

Let's now see how the labour market determines employment, the real wage rate, and potential GDP.

Labour Market Equilibrium and Potential GDP

The forces of supply and demand operate in labour markets just as they do in the markets for goods and services. The price of labour is the real wage rate. A rise in the real wage rate eliminates a shortage of labour by decreasing the quantity demanded and increasing the quantity supplied. A fall in the real wage rate eliminates a surplus of labour by increasing the quantity demanded and decreasing the quantity supplied. If there is neither a shortage nor a surplus, the labour market is in equilibrium.

In macroeconomics, we study the economy-wide labour market to determine the total quantity of labour employed and the average real wage rate.

Labour Market Equilibrium Figure 29.6(a) shows a labour market in equilibrium. The demand curve *LD* and the supply curve *LS* are the same as those in Fig. 29.3 and Fig. 29.5, respectively.

If the real wage rate exceeds $35 an hour, the quantity of labour supplied exceeds the quantity demanded and there is a surplus of labour. In this situation, the real wage rate falls.

If the real wage rate is less than $35 an hour, the quantity of labour demanded exceeds the quantity supplied and there is a shortage of labour. In this situation, the real wage rate rises.

If the real wage rate is $35 an hour, the quantity of labour demanded equals the quantity supplied and there is neither a shortage nor a surplus of labour. In this situation, the labour market is in equilibrium and the real wage rate remains constant. The equilibrium level of employment is 20 billion hours a year. This equilibrium is a *full-employment equilibrium*.

Potential GDP You've seen that the quantity of real GDP depends on the quantity of labour employed. The production function tells us how much real GDP a given amount of employment can produce. At the equilibrium level of employment, there is full employment. And the level of real GDP at full employment is *potential GDP*. So the equilibrium level of employment produces potential GDP.

Figure 29.6(b) shows potential GDP. The equilibrium level of employment in Fig. 29.6(a) is 20 billion hours. The production function in Fig. 29.6(b) tells us that 20 billion hours of labour can produce a real GDP of $1,000 billion. This amount is potential GDP.

FIGURE 29.6   The Labour Market and Potential GDP

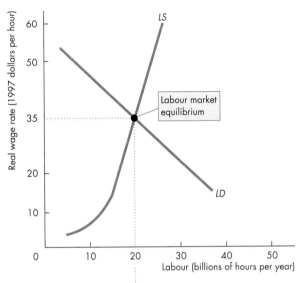

(a) The labour market

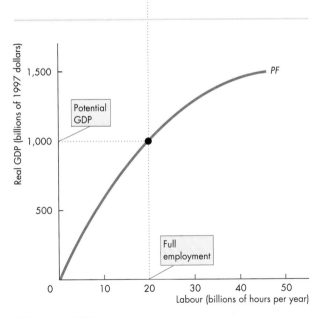

(b) Potential GDP

Full employment occurs (part a) when the quantity of labour demanded equals the quantity of labour supplied. The real wage rate is $35 an hour, and employment is 20 billion hours a year. Part (b) shows how potential GDP is determined. It is the quantity of real GDP determined by the production function and the full-employment quantity of labour.

Aggregate Supply

The **long-run aggregate supply curve** is the relationship between the quantity of real GDP supplied and the price level when real GDP equals potential GDP. Figure 29.7 shows this relationship as the vertical *LAS* curve. Along the long-run aggregate supply curve, as the price level changes, the money wage rate also changes to keep the real wage rate at the full-employment equilibrium level in Fig. 29.6(a). With no change in the real wage rate and no change in employment, real GDP remains at potential GDP.

The **short-run aggregate supply curve** is the relationship between the quantity of real GDP supplied and the price level when the money wage rate and potential GDP remain constant. Figure 29.7 shows a short-run aggregate supply curve as the upward-sloping *SAS* curve. Along the short-run aggregate supply curve, as the price level rises, the money wage rate remains fixed, so the real wage rate *falls*. In Fig. 29.6,

FIGURE 29.7   The Aggregate Supply Curves

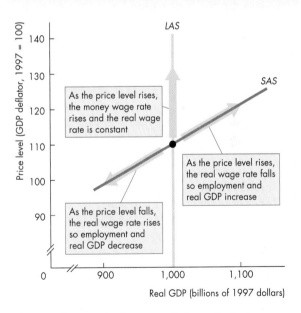

A rise in the price level accompanied by a rise in the money wage rate that keeps the real wage rate at its full-employment equilibrium level keeps the quantity of real GDP supplied constant at potential GDP. There is a movement along the *LAS* curve. A rise in the price level with no change in the money wage rate lowers the real wage rate and brings an increase in employment and in the quantity of real GDP supplied. There is a movement up along the *SAS* curve.

when the real wage rate falls, the quantity of labour demanded increases and real GDP increases.

When the economy is at a point on its short-run aggregate supply curve above potential GDP, the real wage rate is below the full-employment equilibrium level. And when the economy is at a point on the short-run aggregate supply curve below potential GDP, the real wage rate is above the full-employment equilibrium level. In both cases, the quantity of labour that firms employ departs from the quantity that households would like to supply.

Production is efficient in the sense that the economy operates on its production possibilities frontier. But production is inefficient in the sense that the economy operates at the wrong point on the frontier. When the real wage rate is below the full-employment equilibrium, people do too much work and produce too much real GDP. When the real wage rate is above the full-employment equilibrium, people do too little work and produce too little real GDP.

When the real wage rate departs from its full-employment equilibrium level, the resulting shortage or surplus of labour brings market forces into play that move the real wage rate and quantity of labour employed back towards their full-employment levels.

The appendix on pp. 698–703 explains in detail how to derive the *LAS* and *SAS* curves.

REVIEW QUIZ

1 Why does a rise in the real wage rate bring a decrease in the quantity of labour demanded, other things remaining the same?

2 Why does a rise in the real wage rate bring an increase in the quantity of labour supplied, other things remaining the same?

3 What happens in the labour market if the real wage rate is above or below the full-employment level?

4 How is potential GDP determined?

5 What is the relationship between full-employment equilibrium in the labour market and long-run aggregate supply?

6 What is the relationship between the labour market and short-run aggregate supply?

You have studied the forces that determine full-employment real wages, employment, and potential GDP. Let's now look at *changes* in full-employment equilibrium.

Changes in Potential GDP

REAL GDP WILL INCREASE IF

1. The economy recovers from recession.
2. Potential GDP increases.

Recovery from recession means that the economy moves along the real GDP–leisure *PPF* from a point at which real GDP and employment are too low relative to the full-employment equilibrium point. Equivalently, the economy moves along the short-run aggregate supply curve. Economists have a lot to say about such a move. Chapters 23–28 explain this type of short-term change in real GDP.

Increasing potential GDP means expanding production possibilities. We're going to study such an expansion in the rest of this chapter and in Chapter 30. We begin this process here by examining two influences on potential GDP:

■ An increase in population
■ An increase in labour productivity

An Increase in Population

As the population increases and the additional people reach working age, the supply of labour increases. With more labour available, the economy's production possibilities expand. But does the expansion of production possibilities mean that potential GDP increases? And does it mean that potential GDP *per person* increases?

The answers to these questions have intrigued economists for many years. And they cause heated political debate today. In China, for example, families are under enormous pressure to limit the number of children they have. In some other countries, such as France, the government encourages large families. We can study the effects of an increase in population by using the model of the full-employment economy in Fig. 29.8.

In Fig. 29.8(a), the demand for labour is *LD* and initially the supply of labour is LS_0. At full employment, the real wage rate is $35 an hour and the level of employment is 20 billion hours a year. In Fig. 29.8(b), the production function (*PF*) shows that with 20 billion hours of labour employed, potential GDP is $1,000 billion. We're now going to work out what happens when the population increases.

FIGURE 29.8 The Effects of an Increase in Population

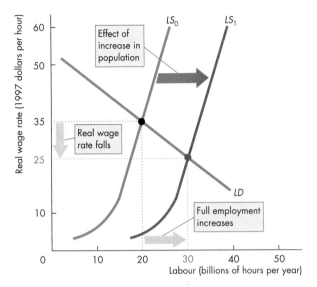

(a) The labour market

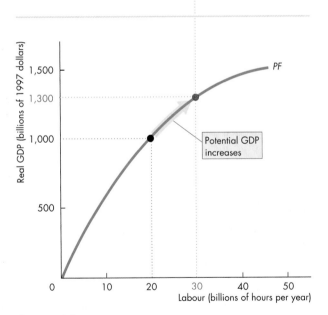

(b) Potential GDP

An increase in population increases the supply of labour. In part (a), the real wage rate falls, and the full-employment quantity of labour increases. In part (b), the increase in full employment increases potential GDP. Because the marginal product of labour diminishes, the increased population increases potential GDP but potential GDP per hour of work decreases.

An increase in the population increases the number of people of working age, and the supply of labour increases. The labour supply curve shifts rightward to LS_1. At a real wage rate of $35 an hour, there is now a surplus of labour. So the real wage rate falls. In this example, it falls until it reaches $25 an hour. At $25 an hour, the quantity of labour demanded equals the quantity of labour supplied. Equilibrium employment increases to 30 billion hours a year.

Figure 29.8(b) shows the effect of the increase in equilibrium employment on real GDP. As the full-employment quantity of labour increases from 20 billion hours to 30 billion hours, potential GDP increases from $1,000 billion to $1,300 billion.

So at full employment, an increase in population increases full employment, increases potential GDP, and lowers the real wage rate.

An increase in population also decreases potential GDP per hour of work. You can see this decrease by dividing potential GDP by total labour hours. Initially, with potential GDP at $1,000 billion and labour hours at 20 billion, potential GDP per hour of work was $50. With the increase in population, potential GDP is $1,300 billion and labour hours are 30 billion. Potential GDP per hour of work is $43.33. Diminishing returns are the source of the decrease in potential GDP per hour of work.

You've seen that an increase in population increases potential GDP and decreases potential GDP per work hour. Some people challenge this conclusion and argue that people are the ultimate economic resource. They claim that a larger population brings forth a greater amount of scientific discovery and technological advance. Consequently, they argue that an increase in population never takes place in isolation. It is always accompanied by an increase in labour productivity. Let's now look at the effects of this influence on potential GDP.

An Increase in Labour Productivity

We've seen that three factors increase labour productivity:

- An increase in physical capital
- An increase in human capital
- An advance in technology

Saving and investment increase the quantity of physical capital over time. Education and on-the-job training and experience increase human capital. Research and development efforts bring advances in technology. In Chapter 30, we study how all these forces interact to determine the growth rate of potential GDP.

Here, we study the *effects* of an increase in physical capital, an increase in human capital, or an advance in technology on the labour market and potential GDP. We'll see how potential GDP, employment, and the real wage rate change when any of these three influences on labour productivity changes.

An Increase in Physical Capital If the quantity of physical capital increases, labour productivity increases. With labour being more productive, the economy's production possibilities expand. How does such an expansion of production possibilities change the real wage rate, employment, and potential GDP?

The additional capital increases the real GDP that each quantity of labour can produce. It also increases the marginal product of labour and so increases the demand for labour. Some physical capital replaces some types of labour, so the demand for those types of labour decreases when capital increases. But an increase in physical capital creates a demand for the types of labour that build, sell, and maintain the additional capital. The increases in demand for labour are always larger than the decreases in demand, and the economy-wide demand for labour increases.

With an increase in the economy-wide demand for labour, the real wage rate rises and the quantity of labour supplied increases. Equilibrium employment increases.

Potential GDP now increases for two reasons. First, a given level of employment produces more real GDP. Second, full employment increases.

An Increase in Human Capital If the quantity of human capital increases, labour productivity increases. Again, with labour being more productive, the economy's production possibilities expand. And this expansion of production possibilities changes the equilibrium real wage rate, full employment, and potential GDP in a similar manner to the effects of a change in physical capital.

An Advance in Technology As technology advances, labour productivity increases. And exactly as in the case of an increase in capital, the economy's production possibilities expand. Again, just as in the case of an increase in capital, the new technology increases the real GDP that each quantity of labour

can produce and increases the marginal product of labour and the demand for labour.

With an increase in the demand for labour, the real wage rate rises, the quantity of labour supplied increases, and equilibrium employment increases. And again, potential GDP increases because a given level of employment produces more real GDP and because full employment increases.

Illustrating the Effects of an Increase in Labour Productivity Figure 29.9 shows the effects of an increase in labour productivity that results from an increase in capital or an advance in technology. In part (a), the demand for labour initially is LD_0 and the supply of labour is LS. The real wage rate is $35 an hour, and full employment is 20 billion hours a year.

In part (b), the production function initially is PF_0. With 20 billion hours of labour employed, potential GDP is $1,000 billion.

Now an increase in capital or an advance in technology increases the productivity of labour. In Fig. 29.9(a), the demand for labour increases and the demand curve shifts rightward to LD_1. In Fig. 29.9(b), the productivity of labour increases and the production function shifts upward to PF_1.

In Fig. 29.9(a), at the original real wage rate of $35 an hour, there is now a shortage of labour. So the real wage rate rises. In this example, it keeps rising until it reaches $45 an hour. At $45 an hour, the quantity of labour demanded equals the quantity of labour supplied and full employment increases to 22.5 billion hours a year.

Figure 29.9(b) shows the effects of the increase in full employment combined with the new production function on potential GDP. As full employment increases from 20 billion hours to 22.5 billion hours, potential GDP increases from $1,000 billion to $1,500 billion.

Potential GDP per hour of work also increases. You can see this increase by dividing potential GDP by total labour hours. Initially, with potential GDP at $1,000 billion and labour hours at 20 billion, potential GDP per hour of work was $50. With the increase in labour productivity, potential GDP is $1,500 billion and labour hours are 22.5 billion, so potential GDP per hour of work is $66.67.

We've just studied the effects of an increase in population and an increase in labour productivity separately. In reality, these changes occur together. We can see the combined effects by examining an episode in the life of the Canadian economy.

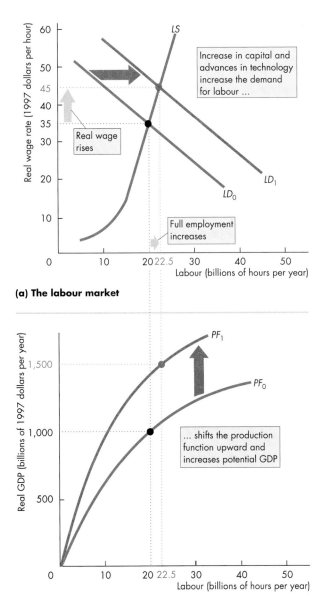

FIGURE 29.9   The Effects of an Increase in Labour Productivity

(a) The labour market

(b) Potential GDP

An increase in labour productivity shifts the demand for labour curve rightward from LD_0 to LD_1 (part a) and the production function upward from PF_0 to PF_1 (part b). The real wage rate rises from $35 to $45 an hour, and full employment increases from 20 billion to 22.5 billion hours. Potential GDP increases from $1,000 billion to $1,500 billion. Potential GDP increases because labour becomes more productive and full employment increases.

Population and Productivity in Canada

The Canadian economy was close to full employment in 1998. It was also close to full employment in 1980. We're going to compare these two years and look at the forces that moved the economy from one full-employment equilibrium to another.

In 1980, real GDP in Canada was $582 billion, employment was 20 billion hours, and the real wage rate was $15.77 an hour. (We are using 1997 dollars.)

By 1998, real GDP had increased to $919 billion, labour hours had increased to 25 billion, and the real wage rate had risen to $19.66 an hour. (Again, we are using 1997 dollars.)

The factors that you've just studied—an increase in population, increases in physical and human capital, and advances in technology—brought these changes.

Population Increase In 1980, the working-age population of Canada was 18.7 million. By 1998, this number had increased to 23.2 million. The 1998 working-age population was 24 percent larger than the 1980 working-age population. Recall that labour hours were 20 billion in 1980. A 24 percent increase would take labour hours in 1998 to 24.8 billion. But labour hours actually increased to 25 billion. Why? The increased labour productivity increased the real wage rate, which increased the quantity of labour supplied by increasing the labour force participation rate.

Capital Increase In 1980, the capital stock in Canada was estimated to be $1.4 trillion (in 1997 dollars). By 1998, the capital stock had increased to $2.4 trillion. This increase in capital increased labour productivity. But the increase in capital was not the only influence on labour productivity. Technological advances also occurred.

Technological Advances In 1980, we were just getting into the information revolution. Personal computers had just arrived. They were slow, had little memory, and had no hard drive, much less the CD-ROM and DVD drives of today. The Internet existed as a tool used by academic researchers for e-mail and file transfers, but no one had imagined the World Wide Web. Telephones couldn't remember numbers or record messages. Communication was slower and more costly than it was to become by 1998.

Production processes were beginning to be computerized but on a limited scale. Banks equipped with ATMs were in the future. Supermarkets with laser scanners were only a dream. Robots in car facto-

FIGURE 29.10   Full Employment in Canada: 1980 and 1998

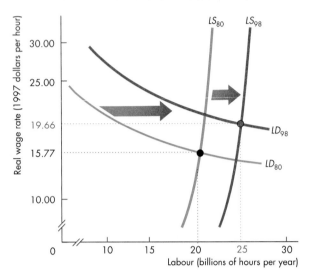

(a) The Canadian labour market in 1980 and 1998

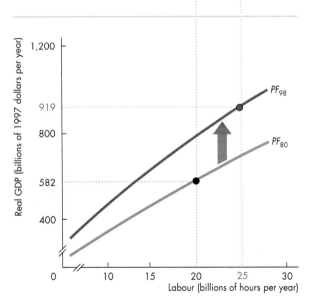

(b) The Canadian production function in 1980 and 1998

In 1980, the real wage rate was $15.77 an hour and the quantity of labour employed was 20 billion hours at the intersection of LD_{80} and LS_{80} (part a). Potential GDP was $582 billion on PF_{80} (part b). By 1998, the real wage rate had increased to $19.66 an hour and the quantity of labour employed had increased to 25 billion hours at the intersection of LD_{98} and LS_{98} (part a). Potential GDP had increased to $919 billion on PF_{98} (part b).

ries and coal mines were still unknown. The biotechnology sector had yet to be developed. The combined effects of capital accumulation and technological advance have made our farms and factories, shops and offices more productive.

Figure 29.10 shows these effects along with the effects of the increase in population that occurred. In 1980, the demand for labour curve was LD_{80}, the supply of labour curve was LS_{80}, the full-employment real wage rate was $15.77 an hour, and 20 billion hours of labour were employed. The production function in 1980 was PF_{80}. With 20 billion hours of labour employed, real GDP (and potential GDP) was $582 billion.

By 1998, the increase in population had increased the working-age population by 24 percent. This increase in population increased the supply of labour and shifted the labour supply curve rightward to LS_{98}.

The accumulation of capital and advances in technology increased labour productivity. The demand for labour increased, and the demand for labour curve shifted rightward to LD_{98}. And the production function shifted upward to PF_{98}.

The real wage rate increased to $19.66 an hour, and employment increased to 25 billion hours. At this quantity of labour, real GDP (and potential GDP) increased to $919 billion.

So in Canada, the effects of an increase in capital and advances in technology have been larger than the effects of increases in population. The forces that increase labour productivity have been strong enough to overcome the effects of an increase in population.

REVIEW QUIZ

1 When the population increases but nothing else changes, why does real GDP per hour of work decrease?

2 How does an increase in capital change the real wage rate, full employment, and potential GDP?

3 How do advances in technology change the real wage rate, full employment, and potential GDP?

4 If, as some people suggest, capital accumulation and technological change always accompany an increase in population, is it possible for potential GDP per hour of work to decrease?

Unemployment at Full Employment

SO FAR, WE'VE FOCUSED ON THE FORCES THAT determine the real wage rate, the quantity of labour employed, and potential GDP. And we've studied the effects of changes in population, capital, and technology on these variables. We're now going to bring unemployment into the picture.

In Chapter 21 (p. 480), we learned how unemployment is measured. We described how people become unemployed—they lose jobs, leave jobs, and enter or re-enter the labour force—and we classified unemployment—it can be frictional, structural, seasonal, and cyclical. We also learned that we call the unemployment rate at full employment the *natural rate of unemployment.*

But measuring, describing, and classifying unemployment do not *explain* it. Why is there always some unemployment? Why does its rate fluctuate? Why was the unemployment rate lower during the 1960s and the late 1990s than during the 1980s and early 1990s?

The forces that make the unemployment rate fluctuate around the natural rate take some time to explain, and we study these forces in Chapters 27–32. Here, we look at the churning economy and the reasons why we have unemployment at full employment.

Unemployment is ever present for two broad reasons:

- Job search
- Job rationing

Job Search

Job search is the activity of looking for an acceptable vacant job. There are always some people who have not yet found a suitable job and who are actively searching for one. The reason is that the labour market is in a constant state of change. The failure of existing businesses destroys jobs. The expansion of existing businesses and the startup of new businesses that use new technologies and develop new markets create jobs. As people pass through different stages of life, some enter or re-enter the labour market. Others leave their jobs to look for better ones, and still others retire. This constant churning in the labour mar-

ket means that there are always some people looking for jobs, and these people are the unemployed.

The amount of job search depends on a number of factors, one of which is the real wage rate. In Figure 29.11, when the real wage rate is $35 an hour, the economy is at a full-employment equilibrium. The amount of job search that takes place at this wage rate generates unemployment at the natural rate. If the real wage rate is above the full-employment equilibrium—for example, at $45 an hour—there is a surplus of labour. At this higher real wage rate, more job search takes place and the unemployment rate rises above the natural rate. If the real wage rate is below the full-employment equilibrium—for example, at $25 an hour—there is a shortage of labour. At this real wage rate, less job search takes place and the unemployment rate falls below the natural rate.

The market forces of supply and demand move

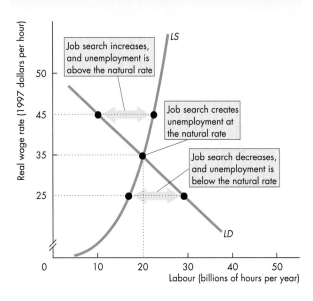

FIGURE 29.11   Job Search Unemployment

When the real wage rate is at its full-employment level—$35 an hour in this example—job search puts unemployment at the natural rate. If the real wage rate is above the full-employment level, there is a surplus of labour. Job search increases, and unemployment rises above the natural rate. If the real wage rate is below the full-employment level, there is a shortage of labour. Job search decreases, and unemployment falls below the natural rate.

the real wage rate towards the full-employment equilibrium. And these same forces move the amount of job search towards the level that creates unemployment at the natural rate.

But other influences on the amount of job search bring changes, over time, in the natural rate of unemployment. The main sources of these changes are

■ Demographic change
■ Unemployment compensation
■ Structural change

Demographic Change An increase in the proportion of the population that is of working age brings an increase in the entry rate into the labour force and an increase in the unemployment rate. This factor has been important in the Canadian labour market in recent years. The bulge in the birth rate that occurred from the late 1940s through the late 1950s increased the proportion of new entrants into the labour force during the 1970s and brought an increase in the natural rate of unemployment.

As the birth rate declined, the bulge moved into higher age groups, and the proportion of new entrants declined during the 1980s. During this period, the natural rate of unemployment decreased.

Another demographic trend is an increase in the number of households with two paid workers. When one of these workers becomes unemployed, it is possible, with income still flowing in, to take longer to find a new job. This factor might have increased frictional unemployment.

Unemployment Compensation The length of time that an unemployed person spends searching for a job depends, in part, on the opportunity cost of job search. An unemployed person who receives no unemployment compensation faces a high opportunity cost of job search. In this situation, search is likely to be short and the person is likely to accept a less attractive job rather than continue a costly search process. An unemployed person who receives generous unemployment compensation faces a low opportunity cost of job search. In this situation, search is likely to be prolonged. The unemployed worker will continue to search for an ideal job.

The extension of unemployment compensation to larger groups of workers during the late 1960s and 1970s lowered the opportunity cost of job search. Consequently, the amount of job search and the natural rate of unemployment increased during those years.

Structural Change Labour market flows and unemployment are influenced by the pace and direction of technological change. Sometimes, technological change brings a *structural slump*, a condition in which some industries die and some regions suffer while other industries are born and other regions flourish. When these events occur, labour turnover is high—the flows between employment and unemployment increase and the number of unemployed people increases. The decline of industries in the Maritimes and the rapid expansion of industries in the Ottawa Valley illustrate the effects of technological change and were a source of the increase in unemployment during the 1970s and early 1980s. While these changes were taking place, the natural rate of unemployment increased.

Job Rationing

You've learned that markets *allocate* scarce resources by adjusting the market price to make buying plans and selling plans agree. Another word that has a meaning similar to "allocate" is "ration." Markets *ration* scarce resources by adjusting prices. In the labour market, the real wage rate rations employment and therefore rations jobs. Changes in the real wage rate keep the number of people seeking work and the number of jobs available in balance.

But the real wage rate is not the only possible instrument for rationing jobs. And in some industries, the real wage rate is set above the market equilibrium level. **Job rationing** is the practice of paying a real wage rate above the equilibrium level and then rationing jobs by some method.

Two reasons why the real wage rate might be set above the equilibrium level are

■ Efficiency wage
■ Minimum wage

Efficiency Wage It is costly for a firm to pay its workers more than the market wage rate. But doing so also brings benefits. An **efficiency wage** is a real wage rate that is set above the full-employment equilibrium wage rate that balances the costs and benefits of this higher wage rate to maximize the firm's profit.

The cost of paying a higher wage is direct. It is the addition to the firm's wage bill. The benefits of paying a higher wage rate are indirect.

First, a firm that pays a high wage rate can attract the most productive workers. Second, the firm can get greater productivity from its work force if it threatens to fire those who do not perform at the desired standard. The threat of losing a well-paid job stimulates greater work effort. Third, workers are less likely to quit their jobs, so the firm faces a lower rate of labour turnover and lower training costs. Fourth, the firm's recruiting costs are lower. The firm always faces a steady stream of available new workers.

Faced with benefits and costs, a firm offers a wage rate that balances productivity gains from the higher wage rate against its additional cost. This wage rate maximizes the firm's profit and is the efficiency wage.

Minimum Wage A **minimum wage** law determines the lowest wage rate at which a firm may legally hire labour. If the minimum wage is set *below* the equilibrium wage, the minimum wage has no effect. The minimum wage law and market forces are not in conflict. But if a minimum wage is set *above* the equilibrium wage, the minimum wage is in conflict with the market forces and does have some effects on the labour market.

In Canada, provincial governments set the minimum wages. In 2003, the minimum wage ranged from lows of $5.90 an hour in Alberta and $6.00 an hour in Newfoundland and Nova Scotia to highs of $7.30 an hour in Quebec and the Yukon and $8.00 an hour in British Columbia. The minimum wage increases from time to time and has fluctuated relative to the average wage of all workers.

Job Rationing and Unemployment Regardless of the reason, if the real wage rate is set above the equilibrium level, the natural rate of unemployment increases. The above-equilibrium real wage rate decreases the quantity of labour demanded and increases the quantity of labour supplied. So even at full employment, the quantity of labour supplied exceeds the quantity of labour demanded.

The surplus of labour is an addition to the amount of unemployment. The unemployment that results from a non-market wage rate and job rationing increases the natural rate of unemployment because it is added to the job search that takes place at full-employment equilibrium.

Economists broadly agree that efficiency wages can create persistent unemployment. And most economists believe that the minimum wage contributes to unemployment, especially among low-skilled young workers. But David Card of the University of

California at Berkeley and Alan Krueger of Princeton University have challenged this view. And the challenge has been rebutted.

Card and Krueger say that an increase in the minimum wage works like an efficiency wage. It makes workers more productive and less likely to quit. Most economists remain skeptical about this suggestion. If higher wages make workers more productive and reduce labour turnover, why don't firms freely pay the wage rates that encourage the correct work habits? Daniel Hamermesh of the University of Texas at Austin says that firms anticipate increases in the minimum wage and cut employment *before* they occur. Looking for the effects of an increase in the minimum wage *after* it has occurred misses its effects. Finis Welch of Texas A&M University and Kevin Murphy of the University of Chicago say that regional differences in economic growth and not changes in the minimum wage explain the facts that Card and Krueger found.

REVIEW QUIZ

1 Why does the economy experience unemployment at full employment?
2 Why does the natural rate of unemployment fluctuate?
3 What is job rationing and why does it occur?
4 How does an efficiency wage influence the real wage rate, employment, and unemployment?
5 How does the minimum wage create unemployment?

◆ In this chapter, you've seen how the economy operates at full employment. *Reading Between the Lines* on pp. 696–697 compares productivity in Canada with that in the United States.

In the next chapter, we study the rate of growth of the full-employment economy. We study the interactions of capital accumulation, technological change, and population growth in the process of economic growth.

Canada–U.S. Productivity Gap

NATIONAL POST, OCTOBER 8, 2002

Bank CEOs fear Canada falling further behind U.S.

Productivity gap grows

The leaders of two major banks warned yesterday about the widening gap in productivity between Canada and the United States, with one saying it could be this country's main economic threat.

Gordon Nixon, chief executive of the Royal Bank of Canada, said Canada's future prosperity is "far from guaranteed" because our productivity, regulatory efficiency and innovation lag those of many other countries.

"Our failure to achieve better productivity growth, and the widening gap with the United States, may well be the single biggest threat to our long-term prosperity," he said in a speech at Queen's University in Kingston.

"Our competitive performance is Canada's only lasting source of economic vitality and the wealth creation that we need to sustain our way of life."

Though Canada's economy is growing at an envious rate compared to other G7 countries, our standard of living has fallen 20% relative to the U.S., he said. "Clearly, we need a strategy that will help Canadians catch up to Americans in terms of per capita income. And in time, even surpass them."

Charles Baillie, chairman of TD Financial Group, warned Canada will find it harder to maintain top jobs and keep creative young people without a sustained effort to reach a standard of living similar to that in the United States.

Mr. Baillie and TD Group are sponsoring a forum today in Ottawa on how to restore the country's competitive edge with the United States.

While closing the gap on individual incomes is the goal, the larger objective is to improve the quality of life for Canadians, Mr. Baillie said in an interview. ...

Reprinted by permission of the *National Post*.

Essence of the Story

◾ Gordon Nixon, chief executive of the Royal Bank of Canada, believes that the widening gap between Canadian and U.S. productivity is a serious problem.

◾ He noted that although Canada's real GDP growth was rapid during 2002, our standard of living has fallen 20 percent relative to that in the United States and we need a strategy for catching up to or even surpassing U.S. per capita income.

◾ Charles Baillie, chairman of TD Financial Group, said that if we don't achieve the same standard of living as that in the United States, we will find it hard to keep creative young people in Canada.

Economic Analysis

■ Comparisons of Canada and the United States reveal a widening gap in production per person and incomes.

■ Different methods of making the comparison lead to slightly different numbers, but the picture that Fig. 1 presents is reasonably accurate.

■ Figure 1 shows the ratio of real GDP per person in Canada to real GDP per person in the United States, with the values converted to a common currency using the OECD's estimates of the purchasing power parity exchange rate between the Canadian and U.S. dollars in 1997, the base year for the comparison.

■ The figure illustrates Gordon Nixon's and Charles Baillie's concerns.

■ The productivity gap widened from 10 percent in the late 1970s to almost 20 percent in the late 1990s.

■ Because income per person equals the value of production per person, the income gap between Canada and the United States has widened in the same way as the productivity gap.

■ Figure 2 illustrates the production functions in Canada and the United States. With more productive capital and technologies, the U.S. production function, PF_{US}, is above the Canadian production function, PF_C.

■ Figure 3 illustrates the implications of the greater productivity for the labour market.

■ The U.S. demand for labour curve, LD_{US}, is above the Canadian demand for labour curve, LD_C.

■ The supply of labour (per person) is assumed to be the same in both countries—a reasonable assumption—and the labour supply curve in both countries is LS.

■ The equilibrium real wage rate and employment level are higher in the United States than in Canada.

■ But the gap in real wage rates is smaller than the gap in production per employed person because the higher real wage rate in the United States induces a greater number of hours per person.

■ Figure 3 implies that Canadians enjoy more leisure time than Americans, so the productivity gap overstates the difference in overall economic well-being.

You're The Voter

■ Do you agree with Gordon Nixon and Charles Baillie that Canada's low productivity is a major problem?

■ Can you suggest some actions that the government of Canada might take to close the productivity gap?

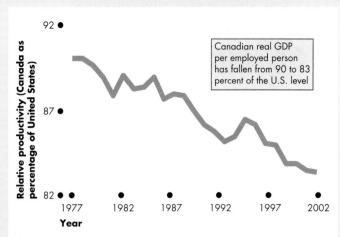

Figure 1 Canadian versus U.S. productivity

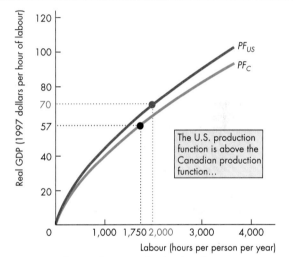

Figure 2 Canadian and U.S. production functions

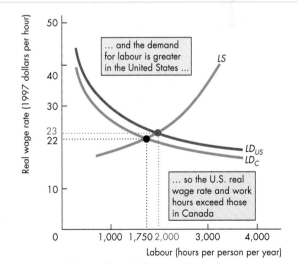

Figure 3 Canadian and U.S. labour markets

697

APPENDIX

Deriving the Aggregate Supply Curves

THIS APPENDIX EXPLAINS HOW TO DERIVE THE long-run aggregate supply curve and the short-run aggregate supply curve. It shows the links between the labour market, the production function, and the aggregate supply curves and fills in the steps from Figure 29.6 to Figure 29.7 on p. 687 in this chapter.

Deriving the Long-Run Aggregate Supply Curve

FIGURE A29.1 SHOWS HOW TO DERIVE THE LONG-run aggregate supply curve. Part (a) shows the labour market. The demand and supply curves shown are similar to those in Fig. 29.6(a) on p. 687. The equilibrium, a real wage of $35 an hour and employment of 20 billion hours, is exactly the same equilibrium that was determined in that figure.

Figure A29.1(b) shows the production function. This production function is similar to that in Fig. 29.1(b) on p. 687. We know from the labour market (part a) that 20 billion hours of labour are employed. Part (b) tells us that when 20 million hours of labour are employed, real GDP is $1,000 billion.

Figure A29.1(c) shows the long-run aggregate supply curve. That curve tells us that real GDP is $1,000 billion regardless of the price level. To see why, look at what happens when the price level changes.

Start with a GDP deflator of 100. The economy is at point *J* in part (c) of the figure. That is, the GDP deflator is 100 and real GDP is $1,000 billion. We've determined, in part (a), that the real wage rate is $35 an hour. With a GDP deflator of 100, the money wage rate (the wage rate in current dollars) is also $35 an hour.

What happens to real GDP if the GDP deflator falls from 100 to 80 (a 20 percent decrease in the price level)? If the money wage rate remains at $35 an hour, the real wage rate rises and the quantity of labour supplied exceeds the quantity demanded. In the long run, the money wage rate will fall. It falls to $28 an hour. With a money wage rate of $28 an hour and a GDP deflator of 80, the real wage rate is still $35 an hour ($28 divided by 80 and multiplied by 100 equals $35). With the lower money wage rate but a constant real wage rate, employment remains at 20 billion hours and real GDP remains at $1,000 billion. The economy is at point *K* in Fig. A29.1(c).

What happens to real GDP if the GDP deflator rises from 100 to 120 (a 20 percent increase in the price level)? If the money wage rate stays at $35 an hour, the real wage rate falls and the quantity of labour demanded exceeds the quantity supplied. In the long run, the money wage rate rises. It keeps rising until it reaches $42 an hour. At that money wage rate, the real wage rate is $35 an hour ($42 divided by 120 and multiplied by 100 equals $35) and the quantity of labour demanded equals the quantity supplied. Employment remains at 20 billion hours and real GDP remains at $1,000 billion. The economy is at point *I* in Fig. A29.1(c).

Points *J*, *K*, and *I* in part (c) all lie on the long-run aggregate supply curve. We have considered only three price levels. We can consider any price level and we will reach the same conclusion: a change in the price level generates a proportionate change in the money wage rate and leaves the real wage rate unchanged. Employment and real GDP are also unchanged.

Because in the long run the price level *and the money wage rate* adjust to achieve full employment, the real wage rate, employment, and real GDP remain constant as the price level changes. In the long run, one level of real GDP—potential GDP—occurs at any price level and the *LAS* curve is vertical.

FIGURE A29.1   The Labour Market and Long-Run Aggregate Supply

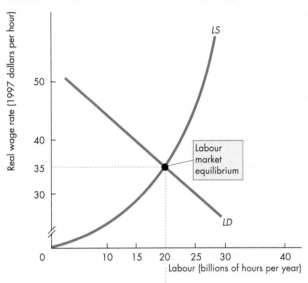

(a) The labour market

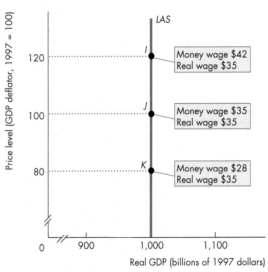

(c) Long-run aggregate supply curve

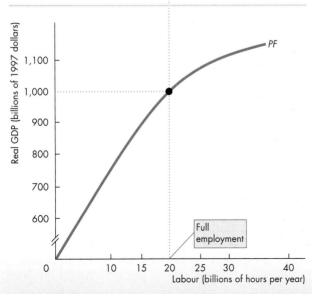

(b) Potential GDP

Equilibrium in the labour market determines the real wage rate and employment. The demand for labour curve (*LD*) intersects the supply of labour curve (*LS*) at a real wage rate of $35 an hour and 20 billion hours of employment (part a). The production function (*PF*) and employment of 20 billion hours determine real GDP at $1,000 billion (part b). Potential GDP is $1,000 billion and in the long run, real GDP supplied is $1,000 billion regardless of the price level. The long-run aggregate supply curve (*LAS*) is the vertical line in part (c). If the GDP deflator is 100, the economy is at point *J*. If the GDP deflator is 120, the money wage rate rises to keep the real wage rate constant at $35 an hour, employment remains at 20 billion hours, and real GDP is $1,000 billion. The economy is at point *I*. If the GDP deflator is 80, the money wage rate falls to keep the real wage rate constant at $35 an hour, employment remains at 20 billion hours, and real GDP is $1,000 billion. The economy is at point *K*.

Changes in Long-Run Aggregate Supply

Long-run aggregate supply can change for two reasons:

■ Change in labour supply
■ Change in labour productivity

Change in Labour Supply The supply of labour can change for many reasons, but the biggest one is a change in the population. Over time, the population grows and the supply of labour increases.

We study and illustrate the effects of these labour market changes and their effects on potential GDP on pp. 688–689. An increase in the supply of labour means the supply of labour curve shifts rightward. The real wage rate falls and full employment increases. Potential GDP increases.

Now that we've derived the long-run aggregate supply curve, you can see when potential GDP changes, long-run aggregate supply also changes and the long-run aggregate supply curve shifts. Because an increase in the supply of labour increases potential GDP, it also increases long-run aggregate supply and shifts the long-run aggregate supply curve rightward. The new (vertical) long-run aggregate supply curve is located at the increased level of potential GDP.

Change in Labour Productivity An increase in labour productivity means that a given amount of labour can produce a larger quantity of real GDP. The production function shifts upward and the demand for labour curve shifts rightward. The real wage rate rises, full employment increases. Potential GDP increases.

We study and illustrate the effects of an increase in productivity on the quantity of labour, the real wage rate, and potential GDP on pp. 689–691.

Again, because an increase in labour productivity increases potential GDP, it also increases long-run aggregate supply and shifts the long-run aggregate supply curve rightward. The new (vertical) long-run aggregate supply curve is located at the increased level of potential GDP.

Whether the real wage rate increases when long-run aggregate supply increases depends on the source of the increase in potential GDP. If the source is an increase in the supply of labour, the real wage rate falls. If the source is an increase in labour productivity, the real wage rate rises.

Short-Run Aggregate Supply

SHORT-RUN AGGREGATE SUPPLY IS THE RELATIONship between the quantity of real GDP supplied and the price level when the money wage rate and all other influences on production plans remain the same. We are now going to learn about the connection between short-run aggregate supply and the labour market. Before we can derive the short-run aggregate supply curve, we must understand how the labour market works when the money wage rate is fixed.

Short-Run Equilibrium in the Labour Market

When the money wage rate is fixed, a change in the price level changes the real wage rate. Suppose the money wage rate is $35 an hour and the GDP deflator is 100. Then the real wage rate is also $35 an hour.

Now suppose that the money wage rate remains at $35 an hour but the GDP deflator rises to 116.7. In this case, the real wage rate falls to $30 an hour. A money wage rate of $35 an hour and a GDP deflator of 116.3 enables people to buy the same goods and services that a money wage rate of $30 an hour buys when the GDP deflator is 100.

Alternatively, suppose that the GDP deflator falls to 87.5. In this case, the real wage rate rises to $40 an hour. A money wage rate of $35 an hour with a GDP deflator of 87.5 buys the same quantity of goods and services that a money wage rate of $40 an hour buys when the GDP deflator is 100.

Figure A29.2 shows the labour market in the short run at the three different price levels we've just considered. As before, the demand for labour is LD and the supply of labour is LS. The money wage rate is constant at $35 an hour and the higher the price level, the lower is the real wage rate. The three points B, C, and D in Fig. A29.2 tell us the quantities of labour demanded at the three different real wage rates. If the price level is 87.5, the real wage rate is $40 an hour and the quantity of labour demanded is 15 billion hours a year, (indicated by point B). If the price level is 100, the real wage rate is $35 an hour and the quantity of labour demanded is 20 billion hours a year, (indicated by point C). And if the price level is 116.7, the real wage rate is $30 an hour and

FIGURE A29.2   The Labour Market in the Short Run

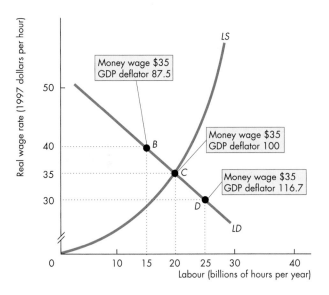

The labour demand curve is *LD* and the labour supply curve is *LS*. The money wage rate is fixed at $35 an hour. If the GDP deflator is 100, the *real* wage rate is $35 an hour and 20 billion hours of labour are employed. The economy operates at point *C*. If the GDP deflator is 87.5, the real wage rate is $40 an hour and 15 billion hours of labour are employed. The economy operates at point *B*. If the GDP deflator is 116.7, the real wage rate is $30 an hour and 25 billion hours of labour are employed. The economy operates at point *D*.

the quantity of labour demanded is 25 billion hours a year (indicated by point *D*).

You can see that when the money wage rate is fixed and the price level rises, the real wage rate falls, and the quantity of labour *demanded* increases. But what determines the quantity of labour *employed*?

Employment with Sticky Wages When the real wage rate is not at its long-run equilibrium level, there are many possible ways in which the level of employment could be determined. It is assumed that when the labour market is not at full employment, firms decide the level of employment and households supply whatever quantity firms demand. Provided that firms pay the agreed money wage rate, house-

holds supply whatever quantity of labour firms demand. In the short run, households are willing to be "off" their labour supply curves.

In Fig. A29.2, with a money wage rate of $35 an hour and a price level of 87.5 (point *B* in the figure) the actual level of employment is 15 billion hours. In this situation, people supply less labour than they would like to. If the GDP deflator is 116.7, the real wage rate is $30 an hour and employment is 25 billion hours (point *D* in the figure). In this case, people supply more labour than they would like to.

It is easy to understand why people might supply less labour than they would like to. But why would people supply *more* labour than they would like to? In the long run, they would not. But in the short run, during the life of an existing wage contract, it is quite likely that people will agree to supply whatever quantity of labour their employer demands. The employer gives the employee an "all-or-nothing" choice. The employee must either work the hours requested or find another job.

Deriving the Short-Run Aggregate Supply Curve

The short-run aggregate supply curve is the relationship between the quantity of real GDP supplied and the price level when the money wage rate and all other influences on production plans remain the same. Along the short-run aggregate supply curve, when the price level changes, the *real wage rate also changes*, which means that employment and real GDP also change. The short-run aggregate supply curve is upward sloping.

Figure A29.3 shows the derivation of the short-run aggregate supply curve. Part (a) shows the aggregate labour market. The demand and supply curves are the same as those in Fig. A29.2. The long-run equilibrium, a real wage of $35 an hour and employment of 20 billion hours, is exactly the same equilibrium that was determined in that figure.

Focus first on part (a). It shows the three short-run equilibrium levels of the real wage rate and employment that we discovered in Fig. A29.2. The money wage rate is fixed at $35 an hour. If the price level is 100, the real wage rate is also $35 an hour and 20 billion hours of labour are employed—point *C*. If the price level is 87.5, the real wage rate is $40 an hour and employment is 15 billion hours—point *B*. If the price level is 116.7, the real wage rate is $30 an hour and employment is 25 billion hours—point *D*.

FIGURE A29.3   The Labour Market and Short-Run Aggregate Supply

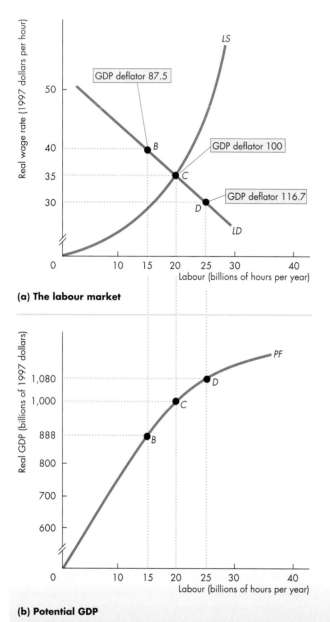

(a) The labour market

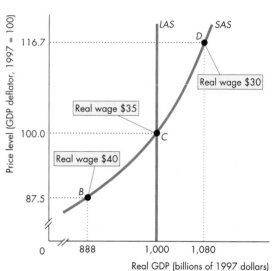

(c) Aggregate supply curves

(b) Potential GDP

The money wage rate is fixed at $35 an hour. In part (a), the demand for labour curve (*LD*) intersects the supply of labour curve (*LS*) at a real wage rate of $35 an hour and 20 billion hours of employment. If the GDP deflator is 100, the economy operates at point *C*. In part (b), the production function (*PF*) determines real GDP at $1,000 billion. The economy is at point *C* on its long-run aggregate supply curve (*LAS*), in part (c). If the GDP deflator is 87.5, the real wage rate is $40 an hour and the economy is at point *B*. Employment is 15 billion hours (part a) and real GDP is $888 billion (part b). The economy is at point *B* on its short-run aggregate supply curve (*SAS*) in part (c). If the GDP deflator is 116.7, the real wage rate is $30 an hour and the economy is at point *D*. Employment is 25 billion hours (part a) and real GDP is $1,080 billion (part b). The economy is at point *D* on its short-run aggregate supply curve in part (c).

Figure A29.3(b) shows the production function. We know from the labour market (part a) that at different price levels, different quantities of labour are employed. Part (b) shows the real GDP produced by these employment levels. For example, when employment is 15 billion hours, real GDP is $888 billion—point *B*. When employment is 20 billion hours, real GDP is $1,000 billion—point *C*. And when employ-

ment is 25 billion hours, real GDP is $1,080 billion—point *D*.

Figure A29.3(c) shows the short-run aggregate supply curve. It also shows the long-run aggregate supply curve, *LAS*, that we derived in Fig. A29.1. The short-run aggregate supply curve, *SAS*, is derived from the labour market and production function. To see how, first focus on point *B* in all three parts of the figure. At point *B*, the price level is 87.5. From the labour market (part a) we know that when the price level is 87.5, the real wage is $40 an hour, and 15 billion hours of labour are employed. At this employment level, we know from the production function (part b) that real GDP is $888 billion. That's what point *B* on the *SAS* curve in part (c) tells us—when the price level is 87.5, the quantity of real GDP supplied is $888 billion. The other two points on the *SAS* curve, *C* and *D*, are derived in the same way. At point *D*, the price level is 116.7 so the real wage rate is $30 an hour and 25 billion hours of labour are employed (part a). This employment level produces a real GDP of $1,080 billion (part b).

The short-run aggregate supply curve intersects the long-run aggregate supply curve at the price level that delivers the equilibrium real wage rate in the labour market. In this example, that price level is 100. At labour market equilibrium, the economy is at full employment and real GDP equals potential GDP. At price levels above 100, the quantity of real GDP supplied in the short run exceeds potential GDP; at price levels below 100, the quantity of real GDP supplied in the short run falls short of potential GDP.

Changes in Short-Run Aggregate Supply

Short-run aggregate supply can change for two reasons:

- Change in long-run aggregate supply
- Change in money wage rate

Change in Long-Run Aggregate Supply Anything that changes long-run aggregate supply also changes short-run aggregate supply. That is, anything that increases potential GDP increases the quantity of real GDP supplied at each and every price level. Both long-run aggregate supply and short-run aggregate supply increase and both curves shift rightward.

A key feature of the *SAS* curve is that it intersects the *LAS* curve at the price level that puts the real wage rate at its full-employment level. That is, the real wage rate at which the labour market is in equilibrium. So if long-run aggregate supply changes and the *LAS* curve shifts, the short-run aggregate supply curve also shifts. And the new *SAS* curve intersects the new *LAS* curve at the price level that makes the real wage rate equal to its *new* full-employment level.

Change in Money Wage Rate Short-run aggregate supply changes and long-run aggregate supply remains unchanged if the money wage rate changes and all other influences on production plans remain the same. A rise in the money wage rate with a given price level means that the real wage rate has increased. Faced with a higher real wage rate, firms decrease the quantity of labour demanded. Employment decreases and firms produce less output, so the quantity of real GDP supplied decreases.

But the changes that we've just described would occur at any given price level. So short-run aggregate supply decreases. The *SAS* curve shifts leftward.

Short-Run Changes in the Quantity of Real GDP Supplied

Even if short-run aggregate supply does not change, real GDP can change in the short run. The reason is that there can be a *change in the quantity of real GDP supplied*, which appears as a *movement along the SAS curve*. These changes in real GDP are brought about by changes in aggregate demand. All the factors that can change aggregate demand result in a shift of the aggregate demand curve and movement along the *SAS* curve. Real GDP changes and so does the price level. They both change in the same direction. An increase in aggregate demand brings an increase in real GDP and a rise in the price level; a decrease in aggregate demand brings a decrease in real GDP and a fall in the price level.

The Shape of the Short-Run Aggregate Supply Curve

The short-run aggregate supply curve that we've derived in Fig. A29.3(c) is *curved*. Along this *SAS* curve, as the price level rises, real GDP increases. But for given increments in the price level, the increments in real GDP become successively smaller. In contrast, the *SAS* curve in Fig. 29.7 on p. 687, like that in Chapter 22, is linear—a curve that graphs as a straight line. Along a linear *SAS* curve, as the price level rises, real GDP increases. You can regard the linear *SAS* curve as an approximation over a small range of real GDP in the neighbourhood of potential GDP. The farther the economy moves away from potential GDP, the less close is the approximation.

SUMMARY

KEY POINTS

Real GDP and Employment (pp. 680–682)

- To produce real GDP, we must forgo leisure time.
- As the quantity of labour increases, real GDP increases.
- Labour productivity increases if the amount of physical capital or human capital increases or if technology advances.

The Labour Market and Aggregate Supply (pp. 683–688)

- The quantity of labour demanded increases as the real wage rate falls, other things remaining the same.
- The diminishing marginal product of labour is the reason the quantity of labour demanded increases as the real wage rate falls.
- The quantity of labour supplied increases as the real wage rate rises, other things remaining the same.
- At full-employment equilibrium, the quantity of labour demanded equals the quantity of labour supplied.
- Potential GDP is real GDP produced by the full-employment quantity of labour.
- Along the long-run aggregate supply curve, the real wage rate is constant at its full-employment level. Along the short-run aggregate supply curve, the real wage rate, employment, and real GDP change.

Changes in Potential GDP (pp. 688–692)

- An increase in population increases the supply of labour, lowers the real wage rate, increases the quantity of labour employed, and increases potential GDP. It decreases potential GDP per hour of work.
- An increase in capital or an advance in technology increases labour productivity. It shifts the production function upward and the demand for labour curve rightward. The real wage rate rises, full employment increases, and potential GDP increases.

Unemployment at Full Employment (pp. 693–695)

- The unemployment rate at full employment is the natural rate of unemployment.
- Unemployment is ever present because of job search and job rationing.
- Job-search unemployment is influenced by demographic change, unemployment compensation, and structural change.
- Job-rationing unemployment arises from efficiency wages and the minimum wage.

KEY FIGURES

KEY TERMS

PROBLEMS

*1. Robinson Crusoe lives on a desert island on the equator. He has 12 hours of daylight every day to allocate between leisure and work. The table shows seven alternative combinations of leisure and real GDP in Crusoe's economy:

Possibility	Leisure (hours per day)	Real GDP (dollars per day)
A	12	0
B	10	10
C	8	18
D	6	24
E	4	28
F	2	30
G	0	30

a. Make a graph of Crusoe's *PPF* for leisure and real GDP.
b. Make a table and a graph of Crusoe's production function.
c. Find the marginal product of labour for Crusoe at different quantities of labour.

2. The people of Nautica have a total of 100 hours every day to allocate between leisure and work. The table shows the opportunity cost of real GDP in terms of leisure time forgone in the economy of Nautica:

Possibility	Leisure (hours per day)	Opportunity cost of leisure (dollars of real GDP per hour)
A	0	0
B	20	5
C	40	10
D	60	15
E	80	20
F	100	25

a. Make a table and a graph of Nautica's *PPF* for leisure and real GDP.
b. Make a table and a graph of Nautica's production function.
c. Find the marginal product of labour for Nautica at different quantities of labour.

*3. Use the information provided in problem 1 about Robinson Crusoe's economy. Also, use

the information that Crusoe must earn $4.50 an hour. If he earns less than this amount, he does not have enough food on which to live. He has no interest in earning more than $4.50 an hour. At a real wage rate of $4.50 an hour, he is willing to work any number of hours between zero and the total available to him.
a. Make a table that shows Crusoe's demand for labour schedule and draw Crusoe's demand for labour curve.
b. Make a table that shows Crusoe's supply of labour schedule and draw Crusoe's supply of labour curve.
c. What are the full-employment equilibrium real wage rate and quantity of labour in Crusoe's economy?
d. Find Crusoe's potential GDP.

4. Use the information provided in problem 2 about the economy of Nautica. Also, use the information that the people of Nautica are willing to work 20 hours a day for a real wage rate of $10 an hour. And for each 50¢ an hour *increase* in the real wage, they are willing to work an *additional* hour a day.
a. Make a table that shows Nautica's demand for labour schedule and draw Nautica's demand for labour curve.
b. Make a table that shows Nautica's supply of labour schedule and draw Nautica's supply of labour curve.
c. Find the full-employment equilibrium real wage rate and quantity of labour in Nautica's economy.
d. Find Nautica's potential GDP.

*5. Robinson Crusoe, whose economy is described in problems 1 and 3, gets a bright idea. He diverts a stream and increases his food production by 50 percent. That is, each hour that he works produces 50 percent more real GDP than before.
a. Make a table that shows Crusoe's new production function and new demand for labour schedule.
b. Find the new full-employment equilibrium real wage rate and quantity of labour in Crusoe's economy.
c. Find Crusoe's new potential GDP.
d. Explain and interpret the results you obtained in parts (a), (b), and (c).

6. Nautica's economy, described in problems 2 and 4, experiences a surge in its population. The supply of labour increases, and 50 percent more hours are supplied at each real wage rate.
   a. Make a table that shows Nautica's new supply of labour schedule.
   b. Find the new full-employment equilibrium real wage rate and quantity of labour in Nautica's economy.
   c. Find Nautica's new potential GDP.
   d. Explain and interpret the results you obtained parts in (a), (b), and (c).

*7. The figure describes the labour market on Cocoa Island. In addition (not shown in the figure), a survey tells us that when Cocoa Island is at full employment, people spend 1,000 hours a day in job search.

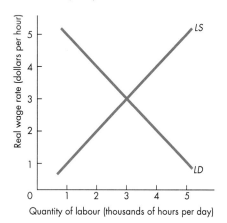

a. Find the full-employment equilibrium real wage rate and quantity of labour employed.
b. Find potential GDP on Cocoa Island. (*Hint*: The demand for labour curve tells you the *marginal* product of labour. How do we calculate the marginal product of labour?)
c. Calculate the natural rate of unemployment on Cocoa Island.

8. On Cocoa Island described in the figure and in problem 7, the government introduces a minimum wage of $4 an hour.
   a. Find the new equilibrium real wage rate and quantity of labour employed.
   b. What now is potential GDP on Cocoa Island?
   c. Calculate the new natural rate of unemployment on Cocoa Island.
   d. How much of the unemployment results from the minimum wage?

CRITICAL THINKING

1. Study the news article about the productivity gap between Canada and the United States in *Reading Between the Lines* on pp. 696–697 and then
   a. Describe the productivity difference between Canada and the United States.
   b. List the factors that influence a nation's production function that might explain why there is a gap between U.S. and Canadian productivity.
   c. List the factors that influence a nation's production function that might explain why the gap between U.S. and Canadian productivity has widened.
   d. List the factors that influence a nation's production function that might be manipulated by Canadian economic policy to narrow the gap between U.S. and Canadian productivity.

2. You are working for the Finance Minister and must write a memo for the minister that provides a checklist of policy initiatives that will increase potential GDP. Be as imaginative as possible, but justify each of your suggestions with reference to the concepts and tools that you have learned about in this chapter.

WEB EXERCISES

1. Use the links on the Parkin–Bade Web site to obtain information about the economy of Russia during the 1990s. Try to figure out what happened to the production possibilities frontier and production function and to the demand for labour and supply of labour in Russia during the 1990s. Tell a story about the Russian economy during those years using only the concepts and tools that you have learned about in this chapter.

2. Use the links on the Parkin–Bade Web site to obtain information about the economy of China during the 1990s. Try to figure out what happened to the production possibilities frontier and production function and to the demand for labour and supply of labour in China during the 1990s. Tell a story about the Chinese economy during those years using only the concepts and tools that you have learned about in this chapter.

Transforming People's Lives

Real GDP *per person* in Canada more than doubled between 1961 and 2001. If you live in a dorm, chances are it was built during the 1960s and equipped with two electrical outlets: one for a desk lamp and one for a bedside lamp. Today, with the help of a power bar (or two), your room bulges with a personal computer, television and VCR or DVD player, stereo system, microwave, refrigerator, coffee maker, and toaster—the list goes on. What has brought about this growth in production, incomes, and living standards? ◆ We see even greater economic growth if we look at modern Asia. On the banks of the Li River in Southern China, Songman Yang breeds cormorants, amazing birds that he trains to fish and to deliver their catch to a basket on his simple bamboo raft. Songman's work, the capital equipment and technology he uses, and the income he earns are similar to those of his ancestors going back some 2,000 years. Yet all around Songman, in China's bustling cities, people are participating in an economic miracle. They are creating businesses, investing in new technologies, developing local and global markets, and transforming their lives. Why are incomes in China growing so rapidly?

◆ In this chapter, we study the forces that make real GDP grow, that make some countries grow faster than others, and that make our own growth rate sometimes slow down and sometimes speed up. And at the end of the chapter, in *Reading Between the Lines*, we examine Canada's recent growth performance and compare it with that of other major industrial countries.

After studying this chapter, you will be able to

■ Describe the long-term growth trends in Canada and other countries and regions

■ Identify the main sources of long-term real **GDP** growth

■ Explain the productivity growth slowdown in Canada during the 1970s and the speedup during the 1990s

■ Explain the rapid economic growth rates being achieved in Asia

■ Explain the theories of economic growth

Long-Term Growth Trends

The long-term growth trends that we study in this chapter are the trends in *potential GDP*. We are interested in long-term growth primarily because it brings rising incomes *per person*. So we begin by looking at some facts about the level and the growth rate of real GDP per person in Canada and around the world. Let's look first at real GDP per person in Canada over the past 75 years.

Growth in the Canadian Economy

Figure 30.1 shows real GDP *per person* in Canada for the 75 years from 1926 to 2001. The average growth rate over this period is 2.2 percent a year.

The earliest years in the graph are dominated by two extraordinary events: the Great Depression of the 1930s and World War II of the 1940s. The fall in real GDP during the depression and the bulge during the war obscure the changes in the long-term growth trend that occurred within these years. Averaging out the depression and the war, the long-term growth rate was close to its 75-year average of 2.2 percent a year.

The 1950s had slow growth but then, during the 1960s, the growth rate speeded and averaged 3.6 percent a year. The 1970s growth slowed to 2.8 percent a year and in the 1980s the growth rate slowed to a crawl of 1.0 percent a year. After 1996, the growth rate increased again and for the five years between 1996 and 2001, the growth rate was back at its 75-year average.

A major goal of this chapter is to explain why our economy grows and why the long-term growth rate varies. Why did growth speed up during the 1960s, slow through the 1970s and 1980s, and then speed up again during the late 1990s and 2000s? Another goal is to explain variations in the growth rate across countries. Let's look at some facts about the growth rates of other nations and compare them with Canada's growth rate.

FIGURE 30.1 Economic Growth in Canada: 1926–2001

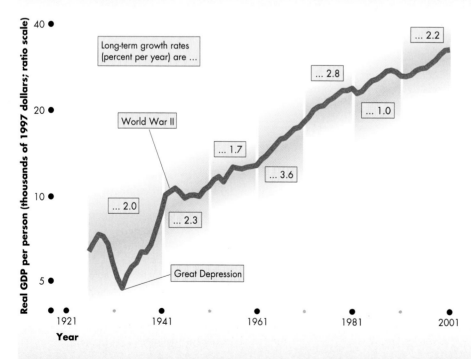

During the 75 years from 1926 to 2001, real GDP per person in Canada grew by 2.2 percent a year, on the average. Growth was the most rapid during the 1960s and slowest during the 1980s.

Sources: F.H. Leacy (ed.), *Historical Statistics of Canada*, 2nd ed., catalogue 11-516, series A1, F32, F55, Statistics Canada, Ottawa, 1983; Statistics Canada, CANSIM tables 380-0002 and 051-0005, and authors' calculations.

Real GDP Growth in the World Economy

Figure 30.2 shows real GDP per person in Canada and in other countries between 1961 and 2001. (The data shown in this figure are in 1985 U.S. dollars.) Part (a) looks at the seven richest countries—known as the G7 nations. Among these nations, the United States has the highest real GDP per person.

In 2001, Canada had the second-highest real GDP per person and Japan the third. Before the 1990s, Canada and Japan grew faster than the United States and were catching up. Japan also grew faster than the Europe Big 4 (France, Germany, Italy, and the United Kingdom) and overtook Europe in the mid-1980s. But during the 1990s, the Japanese economy stagnated while Europe's continued to expand,

so by 2001, these nations had similar levels of real GDP per person.

Not all countries are growing faster than, and catching up with, Canada. Figure 30.2(b) looks at some of these. Western Europe (other than the Big 4) grew faster than Canada before 1975, slowed to the Canadian growth rate during the 1980s, and fell farther behind during the 1990s. After a brief period of catch-up, the former Communist countries of Central Europe have fallen increasingly behind Canada, and by 2001, they were as far behind as they had been 30 years earlier.

Africa and Central and South America have grown more slowly than Canada. Real GDP per person in Central and South America slipped from a comparative high of 35 percent of the Canadian level of real GDP per person in 1980 to 25 percent in 2001. Africa

---

FIGURE 30.2   Economic Growth Around the World: Catch-Up or Not?

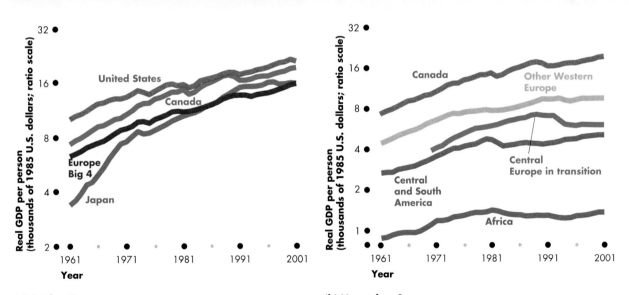

(a) Catch-up?

(b) No catch-up?

Real GDP per person has grown throughout the world economy. Among the rich industrial countries (part a), real GDP growth has been faster in Canada, the Europe Big 4 (France, Germany, Italy, and the United Kingdom), and Japan than in the United States, and these countries have narrowed the gap. The most spectacular growth was in Japan during the 1960s. Real GDP per person in Canada

became close to the U.S. level during the 1980s but slipped back during the 1990s. Among a wider range of countries (part b), there is little sign of catch-up. The gap between real GDP per person in Canada and other Western European countries has remained constant. The gaps between Canada and Central Europe, Central and South America, and Africa have widened.

Sources: 1960–1992: Robert Summers and Alan Heston, New Computer Diskette, January 15, 1995, distributed by the National Bureau of Economic Research to update "The Penn World Table: An Expanded Set of International Comparisons, 1950–1988," *Quarterly Journal of Economics,* May 1991, 327–368. 1993–2001: *World Economic Outlook* (Washington, DC: International Monetary Fund, October 2001).

slipped from 11 percent of the Canadian level of real GDP per person in 1960 to 7 percent in 2001.

Taking both parts of Fig. 30.2 together, we can see that the catch-up in real GDP per person that is visible in part (a) is not a global phenomenon.

Hong Kong, Korea, Singapore, and Taiwan have experienced spectacular growth, which you can see in Fig. 30.3. During the 1960s, real GDP per person in these economies ranged from 10 to 25 percent of that in Canada. But by 2001, two of them, Hong Kong and Singapore, had caught up with Canada and the other two were close behind.

Figure 30.3 shows that China is also catching up, but more slowly and from a very long way behind.

China's real GDP per person increased from 5 percent of Canada's level in 1961 to 15 percent in 2001.

The four small Asian economies shown in Fig. 30.3 are like fast trains running on the same track at similar speeds and with a roughly constant gap between them. Hong Kong is the lead train and runs about 15 years in front of Korea, which is the last train. Real GDP per person in Korea in 2001 was similar to that in Hong Kong in 1986, 15 years earlier. Between 1961 and 2001, Hong Kong transformed itself from a poor developing economy into one of the world's richest economies.

China is now doing what Hong Kong has done. If China continues its rapid growth, the world economy will become a dramatically different place, because China is equivalent to more than 200 countries of the size of Hong Kong. Whether China will continue on its current path of rapid growth is impossible to predict.

FIGURE 30.3   Catch-Up in Asia

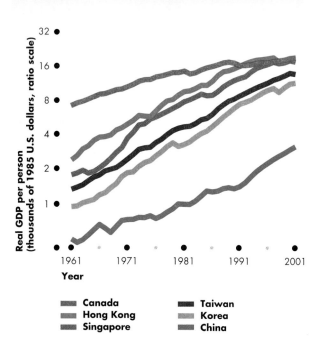

Catch-up has occurred in five economies in Asia. After starting out in 1960 with real GDP per person as low as 10 percent of that in Canada, Hong Kong, Korea, Singapore, and Taiwan have substantially narrowed the gap between them and Canada. And from being a very poor developing country in 1960, China now has a real GDP per person that equals that of Hong Kong in 1960. China is growing at a rate that is enabling it to continue to catch up with Canada.

Sources: See Fig. 30.2.

> ### R E V I E W   Q U I Z
>
> 1 What has been the average economic growth rate in Canada over the past 75 years? In which periods was growth the most rapid and in which periods was it the slowest?
>
> 2 Describe the gaps between the levels of real GDP per person in Canada and other countries. For which countries are the gaps narrowing? For which countries are the gaps widening? And for which countries are the gaps remaining unchanged?
>
> 3 Compare the growth rates and levels of real GDP per person in Hong Kong, Korea, Singapore, Taiwan, China, and Canada. How far is China behind the other Asian economies?

The facts about economic growth in Canada and around the world raise some big questions that we're now going to answer. We'll study the causes of economic growth in three stages. First, we'll look at the preconditions for growth and the activities that sustain it. Second, we'll learn how economists measure the relative contributions of the sources of growth—an activity called *growth accounting*. And third, we'll study three theories of economic growth that seek to explain how the influences on growth interact to determine the growth rate. Let's take our first look at the causes of economic growth.

The Causes of Economic Growth: A First Look

MOST HUMAN SOCIETIES HAVE LIVED FOR centuries and even thousands of years, like Songman Yang and his ancestors, with no economic growth. The key reason is that they have lacked some fundamental social institutions and arrangements that are essential preconditions for economic growth. Let's see what these preconditions are.

Preconditions for Economic Growth

The most basic precondition for economic growth is an appropriate *incentive* system. Three institutions are crucial to the creation of incentives:

1. Markets
2. Property rights
3. Monetary exchange

Markets enable buyers and sellers to get information and to do business with each other, and market prices send signals to buyers and sellers that create incentives to increase or decrease the quantities demanded and supplied. Markets enable people to specialize and trade and to save and invest. But markets need property rights and monetary exchange.

Property rights are the social arrangements that govern the ownership, use, and disposal of factors of production and goods and services. They include the rights to physical property (land, buildings, and capital equipment), to financial property (claims by one person against another), and to intellectual property (such as inventions). Clearly established and enforced property rights give people an assurance that a capricious government will not confiscate their income or savings.

Monetary exchange facilitates transactions of all kinds, including the orderly transfer of private property from one person to another. Property rights and monetary exchange create incentives for people to specialize and trade, to save and invest, and to discover new technologies.

No unique political system is necessary to deliver the preconditions for economic growth. Liberal democracy, founded on the fundamental principle of the rule of law, is the system that does the best job. It provides a solid base on which property rights can be established and enforced. But authoritarian political systems have sometimes provided an environment in which economic growth has occurred.

Early human societies, based on hunting and gathering, did not experience economic growth because they lacked these preconditions. Economic growth began when societies evolved the three key institutions that create incentives. But the presence of an incentive system and the institutions that create it does not guarantee that economic growth will occur. It permits economic growth but does not make that growth inevitable.

The simplest way in which growth happens when the appropriate incentive system exists is that people begin to specialize in the activities at which they have a comparative advantage and trade with each other. You saw in Chapter 2 how everyone can gain from such activity. By specializing and trading, everyone can acquire goods and services at the lowest possible cost. Equivalently, people can obtain a greater volume of goods and services from their labour.

As an economy moves from one with little specialization to one that reaps the gains from specialization and exchange, its production and consumption grow. Real GDP per person increases, and the standard of living rises.

But for growth to be persistent, people must face incentives that encourage them to pursue three activities that generate ongoing economic growth:

- Saving and investment in new capital
- Investment in human capital
- Discovery of new technologies

These three sources of growth, which interact with each other, are the primary sources of the extraordinary growth in productivity during the past 200 years. Let's look at each in turn.

Saving and Investment in New Capital

Saving and investment in new capital increase the amount of capital per worker and increase real GDP per hour of labour—labour productivity. Labour productivity took the most dramatic upturn when the amount of capital per worker increased during the Industrial Revolution. Production processes that use hand tools can create beautiful objects, but production methods that use large amounts of capital per worker, such as auto plant assembly lines, are much more productive. The accumulation of capital on farms, in textile factories, in iron foundries and steel mills, in coal mines, on building sites, in chemical plants, in auto plants, in banks and insurance companies, and in shopping malls has added incredibly to the productivity of our economy. The next time you see a movie set in the Old West or colonial times, look carefully at the small amount of capital around. Try to imagine how productive you would be in such circumstances compared with your productivity today.

Investment in Human Capital

Human capital—the accumulated skill and knowledge of human beings—is the most fundamental source of economic growth. It is a source of both increased productivity and technological advance.

The development of one of the most basic human skills—writing—was the source of some of the earliest major gains in productivity. The ability to keep written records made it possible to reap ever-larger gains from specialization and exchange. Imagine how hard it would be to do any kind of business if all the accounts, invoices, and agreements existed only in people's memories.

Later, the development of mathematics laid the foundation for the eventual extension of knowledge about physical forces and chemical and biological processes. This base of scientific knowledge was the foundation for the technological advances of the Industrial Revolution 200 years ago and of today's information revolution.

But much human capital that is extremely productive is much more humble. It takes the form of millions of individuals learning and repetitively doing simple production tasks and becoming remarkably more productive in the tasks.

One carefully studied example illustrates the importance of this kind of human capital. Between 1941 and 1944 (during World War II), U.S. shipyards produced some 2,500 units of a cargo ship, called the Liberty Ship, to a standardized design. In 1941, it took 1.2 million person-hours to build one ship. By 1942, it took 600,000 person-hours, and by 1943, it took only 500,000. Not much change occurred in the capital employed during these years. But an enormous amount of human capital was accumulated. Thousands of workers and managers learned from experience and accumulated human capital that more than doubled their productivity in two years.

Discovery of New Technologies

Saving and investment in new capital and the accumulation of human capital have made a large contribution to economic growth. But technological change—the discovery and the application of new technologies and new goods—has made an even greater contribution.

People are many times more productive today than they were a hundred years ago. We are not more productive because we have more steam engines per person and more horse-drawn carriages per person. Rather, it is because we have engines and transportation equipment that use technologies that were unknown a hundred years ago and that are more productive than the old technologies were. Technological change makes an enormous contribution to our increased productivity. It arises from formal research and development programs and from informal trial and error, and it involves discovering new ways of getting more out of our resources.

To reap the benefits of technological change, capital must increase. Some of the most powerful and far-reaching fundamental technologies are embodied in human capital—for example, language, writing, and mathematics. But most technologies are embodied in physical capital. For example, to reap the benefits of the internal combustion engine, millions of horse-drawn carriages and horses had to be replaced by automobiles; more recently, to reap the benefits of computerized word processing, millions of typewriters had to be replaced by PCs and printers.

REVIEW QUIZ

1 What economic activities that lead to economic growth do markets, property rights, and monetary exchange facilitate?
2 What are the roles of saving and investment in new capital, the growth of human capital, and the discovery of new technologies in economic growth?
3 Provide some examples of how human capital has created new technologies that are embodied in both human and physical capital.

What is the quantitative contribution of the sources of economic growth? To answer this question, economists use growth accounting.

Growth Accounting

THE QUANTITY OF REAL GDP SUPPLIED (Y) depends on three factors:

1. The quantity of labour (L)
2. The quantity of capital (K)
3. The state of technology (T)

The purpose of **growth accounting** is to calculate how much real GDP growth results from growth of labour and capital and how much is attributable to technological change.

The key tool of growth accounting is the **aggregate production function,** which we write as

$$Y = F(L, K, T).$$

In words, the quantity of real GDP supplied is determined by (is a function F of) the quantities of labour and capital and of the state of technology. The larger L, K, or T, the greater is Y. And the faster L and K grow and T advances, the faster Y grows.

So understanding what makes labour and capital grow and technology advance is the key to understanding economic growth. Labour growth depends primarily on population growth. And the growth rate of capital and the pace of technological advance determine the growth rate of labour productivity.

Labour Productivity

Labour productivity is real GDP per hour of labour. Labour productivity is calculated by dividing real GDP Y by aggregate labour hours L.

Labour productivity determines how much income an hour of labour generates. Figure 30.4 shows labour productivity for the period 1961–2001. Productivity growth was most rapid during the 1960s. It slowed down in 1973 and remained low for about 10 years. Productivity growth then speeded up again in what has been called the new economy of the 1990s.

Why did productivity grow fastest during the 1960s and late 1990s? Why did it slow down in 1973 and then speed up again during the 1990s?

Growth accounting answers these questions by dividing the growth in labour productivity into two components and then measuring the contribution of each. The components are

■ Growth in capital per hour of labour
■ Technological change

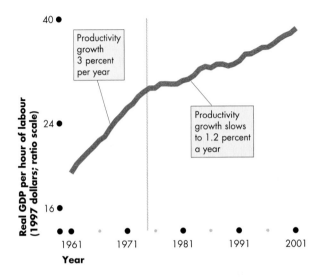

FIGURE 30.4 Real GDP per Hour of Labour

Real GDP divided by aggregate hours equals real GDP per hour of labour, which is a broad measure of productivity. During the 1960s and late 1990s, the productivity growth rate was high. It slowed between 1973 and 1983.

Sources: Statistics Canada, CANSIM tables 282-0022 and 380-0002, and authors' calculations.

Capital is physical capital. Technological change includes everything that contributes to labour productivity growth that is not included in the growth in capital per hour. In particular, it includes human capital growth. Human capital growth and technological change are intimately related. Technology advances because knowledge advances. And knowledge is part of human capital. So "technological change" is a broad catchall concept.

The analytical engine of growth accounting is a relationship called the productivity curve. Let's learn about this relationship and see how it is used.

The Productivity Curve

The **productivity curve** is a relationship that shows how real GDP per hour of labour changes as the amount of capital per hour of labour changes with a given state of technology. Figure 30.5 illustrates the productivity curve. Capital per hour of labour is measured on the *x*-axis, and real GDP per hour of labour is measured on the *y*-axis. The figure shows *two* productivity curves. One is the curve labelled PC_0, and the other is the curve labelled PC_1.

An increase in the quantity of capital per hour of labour increases real GDP per hour of labour, which is shown by a movement along a productivity curve. For example, on PC_0, when capital per hour of labour is $30, real GDP per hour of labour is $20. If capital per hour of labour increases to $60, real GDP per hour of labour increases to $25.

Technological change increases the amount of GDP per hour of labour that can be produced by a given amount of capital per hour of labour. Technological change shifts the productivity curve upward. For example, if capital per hour of labour is $30 and a technological change increases real GDP per hour of labour from $20 to $25, the productivity curve shifts upward from PC_0 to PC_1 in Fig. 30.5. Similarly, if capital per hour of labour is $60, the same technological change increases real GDP per hour of labour from $25 to $32 and shifts the productivity curve upward from PC_0 to PC_1.

To calculate the contributions of capital growth and technological change to productivity growth, we need to know the shape of the productivity curve. The shape of the productivity curve reflects a fundamental economic law—the law of diminishing returns. The **law of diminishing returns** states that as the quantity of one input increases with the quantities of all other inputs remaining the same, output increases but by ever smaller increments. For example, in a factory that has a given amount of capital, as more labour is hired, production increases. But each *additional* hour of labour produces less *additional* output than the previous hour produced. Two typists working with one computer type fewer than twice as many pages per day as one typist working with one computer.

Applied to capital, the law of diminishing returns states that if a given number of hours of labour use more capital (with the same technology), the *additional* output that results from the *additional* capital gets smaller as the amount of capital increases. One typist working with two computers types fewer than twice as many pages per day as one typist working with one computer. More generally, one hour of labour working with $40 of capital produces less than twice the output of one hour of labour working with $20 of capital. But how much less? The answer is given by the *one-third rule*.

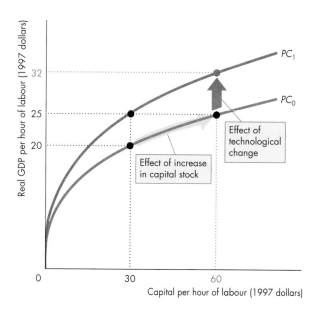

FIGURE 30.5   How Productivity Grows

Productivity is measured by real GDP per hour of labour, and it can grow for two reasons: (1) Capital per hour of labour increases, and (2) technological advances occur. The productivity curve, PC_0, shows the effects of an increase in capital per hour of labour on productivity. Here, when capital per hour of labour increases from $30 to $60, real GDP per hour of labour increases from $20 to $25 along the productivity curve PC_0. Technological advance shifts the productivity curve upward. Here, an advance in technology shifts the productivity curve from PC_0 to PC_1. When capital per hour of labour is $60, real GDP per hour of labour increases from $25 to $32.

The One-Third Rule   Robert Solow of MIT estimated a U.S. productivity curve and discovered the **one-third rule** that, on the average, with no change in technology, a 1 percent increase in capital per hour of labour brings a *one-third of 1 percent* increase in real GDP per hour of labour. This one-third rule is used to calculate the contributions of an increase in capital per hour of labour and technological change to the growth of real GDP. Let's do such a calculation.

Suppose that capital per hour of labour grows by 3 percent a year and real GDP per hour of labour grows by 2.5 percent a year. The one-third rule tells us that capital growth has contributed one-third of

3 percent, which is 1 percent, to the growth of real GDP per hour of labour. The rest of the 2.5 percent growth of real GDP per hour of labour comes from technological change. That is, technological change has contributed 1.5 percent, which is the 2.5 percent growth of real GDP per hour of labour minus the estimated 1 percent contribution of capital growth.

Accounting for the Productivity Growth Slowdown and Speedup

We can use the one-third rule to study Canadian productivity growth and the productivity growth slowdown. Figure 30.6 tells the story, starting in 1961.

Booming Sixties and Early Seventies In 1961, capital per hour of labour was $48 and real GDP per hour of labour was $19 at the point marked 61 on PC_{61} in Fig. 30.6. By 1973, real GDP per hour of labour had expanded by 47 percent, to $28, and capital per hour of labour had increased by 36 percent, to $65. With no change in technology, the economy would have moved to point A on PC_{61}, where real GDP per hour of labour has increased by 12 percent (1/3 of 36 percent). But rapid technological change shifted the productivity curve upward to PC_{73}, and the economy moved to the point marked 73 on that curve.

Slowdown During the 23 years from 1973 to 1996, real GDP per hour of labour expanded by only 25 percent, to $35. At the same time, capital per hour of labour increased by 43 percent, to $93. With no change in technology, the economy would have moved to point B on PC_{73} in Fig. 30.6, where real GDP per hour of labour has increased by 14 percent (1/3 of 43 percent). But a small amount of technological change shifted the productivity curve upward to PC_{96}, and the economy moved to the point marked 96 on that curve. So the productivity growth slowdown occurred because the contribution of technological change to real GDP growth slowed.

Growth Again During the 5 years from 1996 to 2001, real GDP per hour of labour expanded by 8.5 percent, to $38. At the same time, capital per hour of labour increased by 4.5 percent, to $97. With no change in technology, the economy would have moved to point C on PC_{96} in Fig. 30.6, where real GDP per hour of labour has increased by 1.5 percent (1/3 of 4.5 percent). But a speedup in the pace of technological change shifted the productivity curve

FIGURE 30.6 Growth Accounting and the Productivity Growth Slowdown

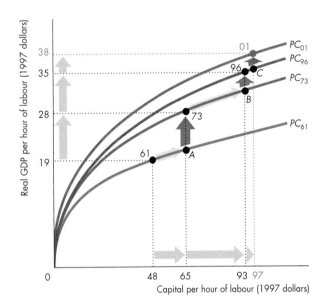

Between 1961 and 1973, a period in which productivity growth was rapid, capital per hour of labour increased from $48 to $65 and technological progress shifted the productivity curve upward from PC_{61} to PC_{73}. Between 1973 and 1996, a period in which productivity growth was slow, capital per hour of labour increased from $65 to $93 and technological progress shifted the productivity curve upward from PC_{73} to PC_{96}. Between 1996 and 2001, a period in which productivity growth speeded, capital per hour of labour increased from $93 to $97 and technological progress shifted the productivity curve upward from PC_{96} to PC_{01}. Although productivity growth increased after 1996, its pace was slower than that of the 1960s and early 1970s.

Sources: Statistics Canada, CANSIM tables 282-0022, 378-0004, and 380-0002, and authors' calculations.

upward to PC_{01}, and the economy moved to the point marked 01 on that curve. Although technological change speeded, its pace was slower than that during the 1960s.

The growth accounting exercise that we've just worked through suggests that the so-called new economy of the late 1990s was not such a spectacular or unusual growth phenomenon.

Technological Change During the Productivity Growth Slowdown

Technological change did not stop during the productivity growth slowdown. But its focus changed from increasing productivity to coping with

- Energy price shocks
- The environment

Energy Price Shocks Energy price increases that occurred in 1973–1974 and in 1979–1980 diverted research efforts towards saving energy rather than increasing productivity. Airplanes became more fuel efficient, but they didn't operate with smaller crews. Real GDP per litre of fuel increased faster, but real GDP per hour of labour increased more slowly.

The Environment The 1970s saw an expansion of laws and resources devoted to protecting the environment and improving the quality of the workplace. The benefits of these actions—cleaner air and water and safer factories—are not counted as part of real GDP. So the growth of these benefits is not measured as part of productivity growth.

Achieving Faster Growth

Growth accounting tells us that to achieve faster economic growth, we must either increase the growth rate of capital per hour of labour or increase the pace of technological advance (which includes improving human capital). The main suggestions for achieving these objectives are

- Stimulate saving
- Stimulate research and development
- Target high-technology industries
- Encourage international trade
- Improve the quality of education

Stimulate Saving Saving finances investment, which brings capital accumulation. So stimulating saving can stimulate economic growth. The East Asian economies have the highest growth rates and the highest saving rates. Some African economies have the lowest growth rates and the lowest saving rates.

Tax incentives can increase saving. Registered Retirement Savings Plans (RRSPs) are a tax incentive to save. Economists claim that a tax on consumption rather than income provides the best saving incentive.

Stimulate Research and Development Everyone can use the fruits of *basic* research and development efforts. For example, all biotechnology firms can use advances in gene-splicing technology. Because basic inventions can be copied, the inventor's profit is limited, and the market allocates too few resources to this activity.

Governments can use public funds to finance basic research, but this solution is not foolproof. It requires a mechanism for allocating the public funds to their highest-valued use. The National Science and Engineering Research Council of Canada is one possibly efficient channel for allocating public funds to universities to finance and stimulate basic research.

Target High-Technology Industries Some people say that by providing public funds to high-technology firms and industries, a country can become the first to exploit a new technology and can earn above-average profits for a period while others are busy catching up. This strategy is risky and just as likely to use resources inefficiently as to speed growth.

Encourage International Trade Free international trade stimulates growth by extracting all the available gains from specialization and exchange. The fastest-growing nations today are those with the fastest-growing exports and imports.

Improve the Quality of Education The free market produces too little education because it brings benefits beyond those valued by the people who receive the education. By funding basic education and by ensuring high standards in basic skills such as language, mathematics, and science, governments can contribute to a nation's growth potential. Education can also be stimulated and improved by using tax incentives to encourage improved private provision.

REVIEW QUIZ

1 Explain how the one-third rule isolates the contributions of capital growth and technological change to productivity growth.
2 Explain how growth accounting gives us information about the factors that contributed to the productivity growth slowdown of the 1970s. Why did the slowdown occur?

Growth Theories

WE'VE SEEN THAT REAL GDP GROWS WHEN THE quantities of labour and capital (which includes human capital) grow and when technology advances. Does this mean that the growth of labour and capital and technological advances *cause* economic growth? It might mean that. But there are other possibilities. *One of these factors might be the cause of real GDP growth, and the others might be the effect.* We must try to discover how the influences on economic growth interact with each other to make some economies grow quickly and others grow slowly. And we must probe the reasons why a country's long-term growth rate sometimes speeds up and sometimes slows down.

Growth theories are designed to study the interactions among the several factors that contribute to growth and to disentangle cause and effect. They are also designed to enable us to study the way the different factors influence each other.

Growth theories are also designed to be universal. They are not theories about the growth of poor countries only or rich countries only. They are theories about why and how poor countries become rich and rich countries continue to get richer.

We're going to study three theories of economic growth, each one of which gives some insights into the process of economic growth. But none provides a definite answer to the basic questions: What causes economic growth and why do growth rates vary? Economics has some way to go before it can provide a definite answer to these most important of questions. The three growth theories we study are

- Classical growth theory
- Neoclassical growth theory
- New growth theory

Classical Growth Theory

Classical growth theory is the view that real GDP growth is temporary and that when real GDP per person rises above the subsistence level, a population explosion eventually brings real GDP per person back to the subsistence level. Adam Smith, Thomas Robert Malthus, and David Ricardo, the leading economists of the late eighteenth century and early nineteenth century, proposed this theory, but the view is most closely associated with the name of Malthus and is sometimes called the *Malthusian theory*.

Many people today are Malthusians! They say that if today's global population of 6.2 billion explodes to 11 billion by 2200, we will run out of resources and return to a primitive standard of living. We must act, say the Malthusians, to contain the population growth.

The Basic Classical Idea To understand classical growth theory, let's transport ourselves back to the world of 1776, when Adam Smith is first explaining the idea. Most of the 2.5 million people who live in the newly emerging nations of North America work on farms or on their own land and perform their tasks using simple tools and animal power. They earn an average of 2 shillings (a bit less than $12 in today's money) for working a 10-hour day.

Then advances in farming technology bring new types of plows and seeds that increase farm productivity. As farm productivity increases, farm production increases and some farm workers move from the land to the cities, where they get work producing and selling the expanding range of farm equipment. Incomes rise, and the people seem to be prospering. But will the prosperity last? Classical growth theory says it will not.

Advances in technology—in both agriculture and industry—lead to an investment in new capital, which makes labour more productive. More and more businesses start up and hire the now more productive labour. The greater demand for labour raises the real wage rate and increases employment.

At this stage, economic growth has occurred and everyone has benefited from it. Real GDP has increased, and the real wage rate has increased. But the classical economists believe that this new situation can't last because it will induce a population explosion.

Classical Theory of Population Growth When the classical economists were developing their ideas about population growth, an unprecedented population explosion was underway. In Britain and other Western European countries, improvements in diet and hygiene had lowered the death rate while the birth rate remained high. For several decades, population growth was extremely rapid. For example, after being relatively stable for several centuries, the population of Britain increased by 40 percent between 1750 and 1800 and by a further 50 percent between 1800 and 1830. Meanwhile, an estimated 1 million people (about 20 percent of the 1750 population) left Britain for North

America and Australia before 1800, and outward migration continued on a similar scale through the nineteenth century. These facts are the empirical basis for the classical theory of population growth.

To explain the high rate of population growth, the classical economists used the idea of a **subsistence real wage rate,** which is the minimum real wage rate needed to maintain life. If the actual real wage rate is less than the subsistence real wage rate, some people cannot survive and the population decreases. In classical theory, when the real wage rate exceeds the subsistence real wage rate, the population grows. But a rising population brings diminishing returns to labour. So labour productivity eventually decreases. This implication led to economics being called the *dismal science.* The dismal implication is that no matter how much technological change occurs, real wage rates are always pushed back towards the subsistence level.

Classical Theory and the Productivity Curve

Figure 30.7 illustrates the classical growth theory using the productivity curve. Initially, the productivity curve is PC_0. Subsistence real GDP is $20 an hour, shown by the horizontal line in the graph. The economy starts out at point A, with $60 of capital per hour of labour and $20 of real GDP per hour of labour, the subsistence level. Because real GDP is at the subsistence level, the population is constant.

Then a technological advance occurs, which shifts the productivity curve upward to PC_1. The economy now moves to point B on PC_1, and real GDP per hour of labour rises to $30. Now earning more than the subsistence wage, people have more children and live longer. The population grows.

A growing population means that labour hours grow, so capital per hour of labour falls. As capital per hour of labour falls, there is a movement down along the productivity curve PC_1. Real GDP per hour of labour falls and keeps falling as long as the population grows and capital per hour of labour falls.

This process ends when real GDP per hour of labour is back at the subsistence level at point C on productivity curve PC_1. The population stops growing and capital per hour of labour stops falling.

Repeated advances in technology play out in the same way as the advance that we've just studied. No matter how productive our economy becomes, population growth lowers capital per hour of labour and drives real GDP per hour of labour towards the subsistence level. Living standards temporarily improve

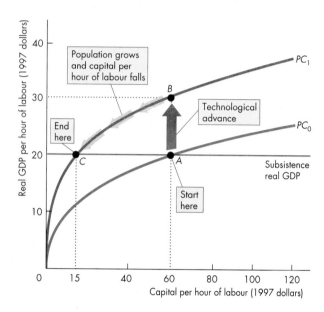

FIGURE 30.7   Classical Growth Theory

The economy starts out at point A with capital per hour of labour of $60 and real GDP per hour of labour of $20—the subsistence level—on productivity curve PC_0. A technological advance shifts the productivity curve upward to PC_1 and the economy moves to point B. The population grows, and both capital and real GDP per hour of labour decrease. The process ends at point C when real GDP per hour of labour is back at its subsistence level.

while the population is expanding, but when the population expansion ends, the standard of living is back at the subsistence level.

Classical Theory and Capital Accumulation In the story you've just worked through, the total quantity of capital didn't change. Suppose that people save and invest, so capital grows. Doesn't a growing quantity of capital prevent the dismal conclusion of classical theory? It does not. *Anything* that raises real GDP per hour of labour above the subsistence level triggers a population explosion that eventually wipes out the gains from greater productivity.

The dismal conclusion of classical growth theory is a direct consequence of the assumption that the population explodes if real GDP per hour of labour exceeds the subsistence level. To avoid this conclusion, we need a different view of population growth.

The neoclassical growth theory that we'll now study provides a different view.

Neoclassical Growth Theory

Neoclassical growth theory is the proposition that real GDP per person grows because technological change induces a level of saving and investment that makes capital per hour of labour grow. Growth ends only if technological change stops.

Robert Solow of MIT suggested the most popular version of neoclassical growth theory in the 1950s. But Frank Ramsey of Cambridge University in England first developed this theory in the 1920s.

Neoclassical theory's big break with its classical predecessor is its view about population growth. So we'll begin our account of neoclassical theory by examining its views about population growth.

The Neoclassical Economics of Population Growth
The population explosion of eighteenth-century Europe that created the classical theory of population eventually ended. The birth rate fell, and while the population continued to increase, its rate of increase became moderate. This slowdown in population growth seemed to make the classical theory less relevant. It also eventually led to the development of a modern economic theory of population growth.

The modern view is that although the population growth rate is influenced by economic factors, the influence is not a simple and mechanical one like that proposed by the classical economists. Key among the economic influences on population growth is the opportunity cost of a woman's time. As women's wage rates increase and their job opportunities expand, the opportunity cost of having children increases. Faced with a higher opportunity cost, families choose to have fewer children and the birth rate falls.

A second economic influence works on the death rate. The technological advance that brings increased productivity and increased incomes brings advances in health care that extend lives.

These two opposing economic forces influence the population growth rate. As incomes increase, both the birth rate and the death rate decrease. It turns out that these opposing forces almost offset each other, so the rate of population growth is independent of the rate of economic growth.

This modern view of population growth and the historical trends that support it contradict the views of the classical economists and call into question the

modern doomsday conclusion that the planet will one day be swamped with too many people to feed.

Neoclassical growth theory adopts this modern view of population growth. Forces other than real GDP and its growth rate determine population growth.

Technological Change In the neoclassical theory, the rate of technological change influences the rate of economic growth but economic growth does not influence the pace of technological change. It is assumed that technological change results from chance. When we get lucky, we have rapid technological change, and when bad luck strikes, the pace of technological advance slows.

Target Rate of Return and Saving The key assumption in the neoclassical growth theory concerns saving. Other things remaining the same, the higher the real interest rate, the greater is the amount that people save. To decide how much to save, people compare the rate of return with a *target rate of return*. If the rate of return exceeds the target rate of return, saving is sufficient to make capital per hour of labour grow. If the target rate of return exceeds the rate of return, saving is not sufficient to maintain the current level of capital per hour of labour, so capital per hour of labour shrinks. And if the rate of return equals a target rate of return, saving is just sufficient to maintain the quantity of capital per hour of labour at its current level.

The Basic Neoclassical Idea To understand neoclassical growth theory, imagine the world of the mid-1950s, when Robert Solow is explaining his idea. Canadians are enjoying post–World War II prosperity. Income per person is around $12,000 a year in today's money. The population is growing at about 1 percent a year. People are saving and investing about 20 percent of their incomes, enough to keep the quantity of capital per hour of labour constant. Income per person is growing, but not by much.

Then technology begins to advance at a more rapid pace across a range of activities. The transistor revolutionizes an emerging electronics industry. New plastics revolutionize the manufacture of household appliances. The national highway system revolutionizes road transportation. Jet airliners start to replace piston-engine airplanes and speed air transportation.

These technological advances bring new profit opportunities. Businesses expand, and new businesses are created to exploit the newly available profitable technologies. Investment and saving increase. The economy enjoys new levels of prosperity and growth. But will the prosperity last? And will the growth last? Neoclassical growth theory says that the *prosperity* will last but the *growth* will not last unless technology keeps advancing.

According to the neoclassical growth theory, the prosperity will persist because there is no classical population growth to induce lower wages.

But growth will stop if technology stops advancing, for two related reasons. First, high profit rates that result from technological change bring increased saving and capital accumulation. But second, capital accumulation eventually results in diminishing returns that lower the rate of return, and that eventually decrease saving and slow the rate of capital accumulation.

Neoclassical Theory and the Productivity Curve

Figure 30.8 illustrates the neoclassical growth theory using the productivity curve. Initially, the productivity curve is PC_0 and the economy is at point A, with $60 of capital per hour of labour and real GDP of $20 an hour.

The slope of the productivity curve measures the additional output that results from an additional unit of capital—the marginal product of capital or rate of return on capital. People have a target rate of return that can be illustrated by a straight line with a slope equal to the target rate of return.

At point A on productivity curve PC_0, the slope of the PC curve equals the slope of the target rate of return line. If the quantity of capital per hour of labour were less than $60, the real interest rate would exceed the target rate of return and capital per hour of labour would grow. If the quantity of capital per hour of labour were greater than $60, the rate of return would be less than the target rate of return and capital per hour of labour would shrink. But when the quantity of capital per hour of labour is $60, the rate of return equals the target rate of return and capital per hour of labour is constant.

Now a technological advance occurs that shifts the productivity curve upward to PC_1. The economy now moves to point B on PC_1, and real GDP per hour of labour rises to $30. It is at this point in the classical theory that forces kick in to drive real GDP per hour of labour back to the subsistence level. But in the neoclassical theory, no such forces operate. Instead, at point B, the rate of return exceeds the target rate of return. (You can see why by comparing the

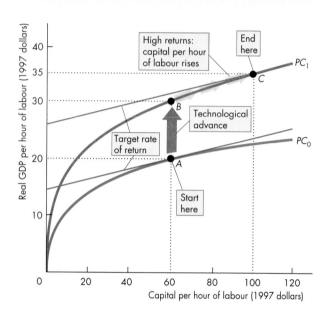

FIGURE 30.8   Neoclassical Growth Theory

The economy starts on productivity curve PC_0 at point A. The slope of the productivity curve measures the rate of return, so at point A the rate of return equals the target rate of return. A technological advance shifts the productivity curve upward to PC_1 and the economy moves to point B. The rate of return exceeds the target rate of return, and the quantity of capital per hour of labour increases—a movement up along the productivity curve PC_1. Growth ends when the rate of return again equals the target rate of return at point C.

slopes of PC_1 at point B and the target rate of return line.)

With a high rate of return available, saving and investment increase and the quantity of capital per hour of labour increases. There is a movement up along the productivity curve PC_1, and real GDP per hour of labour increases.

This growth process eventually ends because, as the quantity of capital per hour of labour increases, the rate of return falls. At point C, where the process ends, the real interest rate again equals the target rate of return.

Throughout the process you've just studied, real GDP per hour of labour grows but the growth rate gradually decreases and eventually growth ends.

But if another advance in technology occurs, the process you've just seen repeats. Ongoing advances in technology constantly increase the rate of return, inducing the saving that increases capital per hour of labour. The growth process persists as long as technology advances. And the growth rate fluctuates because technological progress occurs at a variable rate.

A Problem with Neoclassical Growth Theory All economies have access to the same technologies, and capital is free to roam the globe seeking the highest available rate of return. Given these facts, neoclassical growth theory implies that growth rates and income levels per person around the globe will converge. While there is some sign of convergence among the rich countries, as Fig. 30.2(a) shows, convergence is slow, and it does not appear to be imminent for all countries, as Fig. 30.2(b) shows.

New growth theory attempts to overcome this shortcoming of neoclassical growth theory. It also attempts to explain how the rate of technological change is determined.

New Growth Theory

New growth theory holds that real GDP per person grows because of the choices people make in the pursuit of profit and that growth can persist indefinitely. Paul Romer of Stanford University developed this theory during the 1980s, but the ideas go back to work by Joseph Schumpeter during the 1930s and 1940s.

The theory begins with two facts about market economies:

■ Discoveries result from choices.
■ Discoveries bring profit and competition destroys profit.

Discoveries and Choices When people discover a new product or technique, they think of themselves as being lucky. They are right. But the pace at which new discoveries are made—and at which technology advances—is not determined by chance. It depends on how many people are looking for a new technology and how intensively they are looking.

Discoveries and Profits Profit is the spur to technological change. The forces of competition squeeze profits, so to increase profit, people constantly seek either lower-cost methods of production or new and better

products for which people are willing to pay a higher price. Inventors can maintain a profit for several years by taking out a patent or copyright. But eventually, a new discovery is copied, and profits disappear.

Two further facts play a key role in the new growth theory:

■ Discoveries are a public capital good.
■ Knowledge is capital that is not subject to the law of diminishing returns.

Discoveries Are a Public Capital Good
Economists call a good a *public good* when no one can be excluded from using it and when one person's use does not prevent others from using it. National defence is one example of a public good. Knowledge is another.

When in 1992, Marc Andreesen and his friend Eric Bina developed a browser they called Mosaic, they laid the foundation for Netscape Navigator and Internet Explorer, two pieces of capital that have increased productivity unimaginably.

While patents and copyrights protect the inventors or creators of new products and production processes and enable them to reap the returns from their innovative ideas, once a new discovery has been made, everyone can benefit from its use. And one person's use of a new discovery does not prevent others from using it. Your use of a Web browser doesn't prevent someone else from using that same browser simultaneously.

Because knowledge is a public good, as the benefits of a new discovery spread, free resources become available. These resources are free because nothing is given up when they are used. They have a zero opportunity cost. Knowledge is even more special because it is not subject to diminishing returns.

Knowledge Capital Not Subject to Diminishing Returns Production is subject to diminishing returns when one resource is fixed and the quantity of another resource changes. Adding labour to a fixed amount of equipment or adding equipment to a fixed amount of labour both bring diminishing marginal product—diminishing returns.

But increasing the stock of knowledge makes labour and machines more productive. Knowledge capital does not bring diminishing returns.

The fact that knowledge capital does *not* experience diminishing returns is the central novel proposition of the new growth theory. And the implication of this simple and appealing idea is astonishing. The new growth theory has no growth-stopping mechanism like those of the other two theories. As physical capital accumulates, the rate of return falls. But the incentive to innovate and earn a higher profit becomes stronger. So innovation occurs, which increases the rate of return. Real GDP per hour of labour grows indefinitely as people find new technologies that yield a higher real interest rate.

The growth rate depends on people's ability to innovate and the rate of return. Over the years, the ability to innovate has changed. The invention of language and writing (the two most basic human capital tools) and later the development of the scientific method and the establishment of universities and research institutions brought huge increases in the rate of return. Today, a deeper understanding of genes is bringing profit in a growing biotechnology industry. And astonishing advances in computer technology are creating an explosion of profit opportunities in a wide range of information-age industries.

New Growth Theory and the Productivity Curve
Figure 30.9 illustrates new growth theory. Like Fig. 30.8, which illustrates neoclassical growth theory, Fig. 30.9 contains a productivity curve and a target rate of return curve.

But unlike in neoclassical theory, the productivity curve in the new growth theory never stands still. The pursuit of profit means that technology is always advancing and human capital is always growing. The result is an ever upward-shifting PC curve. As physical capital is accumulated, diminishing returns lower its rate of return. But ever-advancing productivity counteracts this tendency and keeps the rate of return above the target rate of return curve.

Advancing technology and human capital growth keep the PC curve shifting upward in Fig. 30.9 from PC_0 to PC_1 to PC_2 and beyond. As the productivity curve shifts upward, capital per hour of labour and real GDP per hour of labour increase together along the line labelled "Ak line."

The new growth theory implies that although the productivity curve shows diminishing returns, if capital is interpreted more broadly as physical capital, human capital, and the technologies they embody, then real GDP per hour of labour grows at the same rate as the growth in capital per hour of labour. Real GDP per hour of labour is proportional to capital per hour of labour.

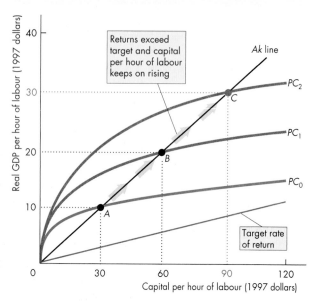

FIGURE 30.9   New Growth Theory

In new growth theory, economic growth results from incentives to innovate and from capital that does not experience diminishing returns. The productivity curve, PC, keeps shifting upward, and real GDP per hour of labour and capital per hour of labour grow along the Ak line.

Real GDP per hour of labour y is related to capital per hour of labour k by the equation:

$$y = Ak.$$

In Fig 30.9, $A = (1/3)$. When capital per hour of labour is $30, real GDP per hour of labour is $10 at point A. People look for yet more profit and accumulate yet more capital. The economy expands to point B, with capital per hour of labour of $60 and real GDP per hour of labour of $20. In pursuit of further profit, technology keeps advancing and capital per hour of labour rises to $90 with real GDP per hour of labour of $30, at point C. Real GDP per hour of labour and capital per hour of labour increase without limit.

A Perpetual Motion Economy   The new growth theory sees the economy as a perpetual motion machine, which Fig. 30.10 illustrates. Insatiable wants lead us to pursue profit, innovate, and create new and better products. New firms start up and old firms go out of business. As firms start up and die, jobs are created and destroyed. New and better jobs

FIGURE 30.10   A Perpetual Motion Machine

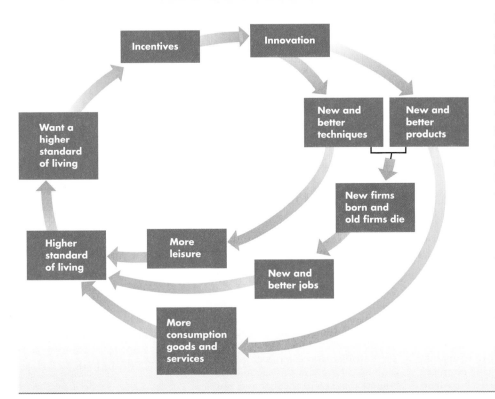

People want a higher standard of living and are spurred by profit incentives to make the innovations that lead to new and better techniques and new and better products, which in turn lead to the birth of new firms and the death of some old firms, new and better jobs, and more leisure and more consumption goods and services. The result is a higher standard of living. But people want a still higher standard of living, and the growth process continues.

Source: Based on a similar figure in *These Are the Good Old Days: A Report on U.S. Living Standards*, Federal Reserve Bank of Dallas 1993 Annual Report.

lead to more leisure and more consumption. But our insatiable wants are still there, so the process continues, going around and around a circle of wants, profits, innovation, and new products.

Sorting Out the Theories

Which theory is correct? Probably none, but they all teach us something of value. The classical theory reminds us that our physical resources are limited and that with no advances in technology, we must eventually hit diminishing returns. Neoclassical theory reaches essentially the same conclusion, but not because of a population explosion. Instead, it emphasizes diminishing returns to capital and reminds us that we cannot keep growth going just by accumulating physical capital. We must also advance technology and accumulate human capital. We must become more creative in our use of scarce resources. New growth theory emphasizes the possible capacity of human resources to innovate at a pace that offsets diminishing returns.

REVIEW QUIZ

1 What is the key idea of classical growth theory that leads to the dismal outcome?
2 What, according to the neoclassical growth theory, is the fundamental cause of economic growth?
3 What is the key proposition of the new growth theory that makes growth persist?

◆ Economic growth is the single most decisive factor influencing a country's living standard. But another is the extent to which the country fully employs its scarce resources. In the next part, we study economic fluctuations and recessions. But before embarking on this new topic, take a look at *Reading Between the Lines* on pp. 724–725 and compare Canada's recent economic growth with that of other major industrial countries.

READING BETWEEN THE LINES

Forecasting Economic Growth

THE GLOBE AND MAIL, SEPTEMBER 21, 2002

Economists cut back estimates

Forecasters are growing pessimistic about the outlook for growth in the major industrial countries, according to a survey.

In its latest poll, Consensus Economics Inc. found that economists have marked down their growth forecasts for most European countries for this year and 2003. Canadian forecasters trimmed their estimates slightly from what they were expecting in August while their counterparts in the United States raised their hopes a bit.

Each month, London-based Consensus Economics surveys about 240 forecasts in more than 20 countries on where their own economies are heading. The latest survey was conducted Sept. 9.

The consensus among the 13 Canadians in the poll was that Canada's economy will grow 3.4 per cent this year and 3.5 per cent in 2003. That compares with the August predictions of 3.5 per cent for this year and 3.7 per cent for 2003.

Canada grew much faster in the second quarter than all the other Group of Seven leading industrialized countries, the company said in its report, but "questions remain over whether the second-quarter results are a sign of Canadian economic resilience or of an economy lagging the U.S. downturn."

Canadian forecasters said growth will slow sharply in the second half from its robust 5-per-cent annual rate expansion in the first half.

U.S. forecasters lifted their expectations for 2002 growth to 2.4 per cent this month from the 2.3-per-cent expansion they anticipated in August, but left their 2003 prediction of 3.1-per-cent growth unchanged. The outlook for German growth this year has slipped to 0.5 per cent from 1 per cent in the June survey, while forecasters in Britain are now expecting only 1.6-per-cent growth, compared with 1.8 per cent in June.

Reprinted with permission from *The Globe and Mail*.

Essence of the Story

■ Each month, Consensus Economics Inc. surveys about 240 economists in more than 20 countries on where their own economies are heading.

■ In September 2002, economists lowered their growth forecasts for most European countries for 2002 and 2003.

■ Canadian forecasters lowered their estimates slightly while U.S. forecasters increased their estimates.

■ Canada grew much faster in the second quarter of 2002 than all the other G7 countries.

Economic Analysis

■ The G7 is the seven industrial countries: Canada, France, Germany, Italy, Japan, the United Kingdom, and the United States.

■ Consensus Economics Inc. says that Canada was the fastest growing G7 economy in 2002.

■ Most reports on economic growth (including this one) do not distinguish between short-term growth of real GDP at different phases of the business cycle and the growth rate of *potential* GDP, which excludes the effects of the business cycle.

■ The fact that Canada was the fastest-growing G7 economy in 2002 was a consequence of Canada's current business cycle expansion, which remained strong while other economies slowed.

■ The ranking of countries in the growth league table depends on the time period over which we measure growth.

■ Figure 1 shows the growth rate of real GDP in the G7 countries between 1972 and 2002. (The data for 2002 are forecasts by the International Monetary Fund made in October 2002.)

■ Over this thirty-year period, Japan has grown much more than Canada, the European members of the G7 (Europe Big 4), and the United States, all of which have grown by similar amounts.

■ Figure 2 shows growth during the decade 1992–2002. Over this period, Canada tops the table and the United States places second. But the United States was top until 2000. Over this time frame, Japan comes in last.

■ Figure 3 looks at the International Monetary Fund (IMF) growth forecast for 2002. Over this very short period, Canada is first and the United States is second, followed by the United Kingdom, France, and Italy, with Germany and Japan coming last.

■ Growth rates differ across countries because of differences in saving rates and differences in the pace of technological change.

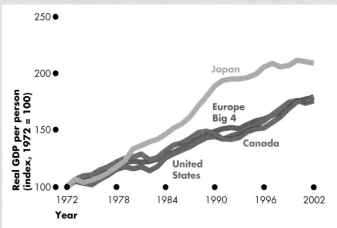

Figure 1 Growth since 1972

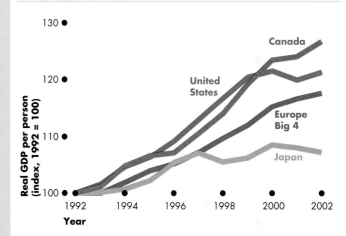

Figure 2 Growth since 1992

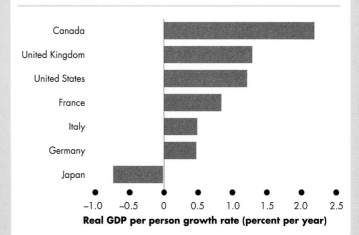

Figure 3 Growth in 2002

725

SUMMARY

KEY POINTS

Long-Term Growth Trends (pp. 708–710)

- Between 1926 and 2001, real GDP per person in Canada grew at an average rate of 2.2 percent a year. Growth was most rapid during the 1960s and slowest during the 1980s.
- The real GDP per person gaps between Canada and Hong Kong, Korea, Taiwan, and China have narrowed. The gaps between Canada and Central and South America, Africa, and Central Europe have widened.

The Causes of Economic Growth: A First Look (pp. 711–712)

- Economic growth requires an *incentive* system created by markets, property rights, and monetary exchange.
- Economic growth occurs when people save, invest in physical and human capital, and discover new technologies.

Growth Accounting (pp. 713–716)

- Growth accounting measures the contributions of capital accumulation and technological change to productivity growth.
- Growth accounting uses the productivity curve and the one-third rule: A 1 percent increase in capital per hour of labour brings a one-third of 1 percent increase in real GDP per hour of labour.
- During the productivity growth slowdown of the 1970s, technological change made no contribution to real GDP growth.
- It might be possible to achieve faster growth by stimulating saving, stimulating research and development, targeting high-technology industries, encouraging more international trade, and improving the quality of education.

Growth Theories (pp. 717–723)

- In classical theory, when technological advances increase real GDP per person above the *subsistence* level, a population explosion brings diminishing returns to labour and real GDP per person returns to the subsistence level.
- In neoclassical growth theory, when technological advances increase saving and investment, an increase in the capital stock brings diminishing returns to capital and eventually, without further technological change, the capital stock and real GDP per person stop growing.
- In new growth theory, when technological advances increase saving and investment, an increase in the capital stock *does not* bring diminishing returns to capital and growth persists indefinitely.

KEY FIGURES

KEY TERMS

PROBLEMS

*1. The following information has been discovered about the economy of Longland. The economy's productivity curve is

Capital per hour of labour (1997 dollars per hour)	Real GDP per hour of labour (1997 dollars per hour)
10	3.80
20	5.70
30	7.13
40	8.31
50	9.35
60	10.29
70	11.14
80	11.94

Does this economy conform to the one-third rule? If so, explain why. If not, explain why not and explain what rule, if any, it does conform to. Explain how you would do the growth accounting for this economy.

2. The following information has been discovered about the economy of Flatland. The economy's productivity curve is

Capital per hour of labour (1997 dollars per hour)	Real GDP per hour of labour (1997 dollars per hour)
20	6.00
40	7.50
60	8.44
80	9.14
100	9.72
120	10.20
140	10.62
160	11.00

Does this economy conform to the one-third rule? If so, explain why. If not, explain why not and explain what rule, if any, it does conform to. Explain how you would do the growth accounting for this economy.

*3. In Longland, described in problem 1, capital per hour of labour in 1999 was $40 and real GDP per hour of labour was $8.31. In 2001, capital per hour of labour was $50 and real GDP per hour of labour was $10.29 an hour.
   a. Does Longland experience diminishing returns? Explain why or why not.

   b. Use growth accounting to find the contribution of the change in capital between 1999 and 2001 to the growth of productivity in Longland.
   c. Use growth accounting to find the contribution of technological change between 1999 and 2001 to the growth of productivity in Longland.

4. In Flatland, described in problem 2, capital per hour of labour in 1999 was $60 and real GDP per hour of labour was $8.44. In 2001, capital per hour of labour was $120 and real GDP per hour of labour was $12.74 an hour.
   a. Does Flatland experience diminishing returns? Explain why or why not.
   b. Use growth accounting to find the contribution of the change in capital between 1999 and 2001 to the growth of productivity in Flatland.
   c. Use growth accounting to find the contribution of technological change between 1999 and 2001 to the growth of productivity in Flatland.

*5. The following information has been discovered about the economy of Cape Despair. Subsistence real GDP is $15 an hour. Whenever real GDP per hour rises above this level, the population grows, and when real GDP per hour of labour falls below this level, the population falls. The productivity curve in Cape Despair is as follows:

Capital per hour of labour (1997 dollars per hour)	Real GDP per hour of labour (1997 dollars per hour)
20	8
40	15
60	21
80	26
100	30
120	33
140	35
160	36

Initially, the population of Cape Despair is constant, and real GDP is at its subsistence level. Then a technological advance shifts the productivity curve upward by $7 at each level of capital per hour of labour.
   a. What are the initial capital per hour of labour and real GDP per hour of labour?

b. What happens to real GDP per hour of labour immediately following the technological advance?

c. What happens to the population growth rate following the technological advance?

d. What is the eventual quantity of capital per hour of labour in Cape Despair?

6. Martha's Island is an economy that behaves according to the neoclassical growth model. The economy has no growth, a target rate of return of 10 percent a year, and the following productivity curve:

Capital per hour of labour (1997 dollars per hour)	Real GDP per hour of labour (1997 dollars per hour)
40	16
80	30
120	42
160	52
200	60
240	66
280	70
320	72

A technological advance shifts the productivity curve upward.

a. What is the initial capital per hour of labour on Martha's Island?

b. What is the initial real GDP per hour of labour?

c. What happens to the return from capital immediately following the technological advance?

d. What happens to the return on capital and the quantity of capital per hour of labour?

 *7. Romeria is a country that behaves according to the predictions of new growth theory. The target rate is 3 percent a year. A technological advance increases the demand for capital and raises the rate of return to 5 percent a year. Describe the events that happen in Romeria and contrast them with the events in Martha's Island in problem 6.

8. Suppose that in Romeria, described in problem 7, technological advance slows and the rate of return falls to 3 percent a year. Describe what happens in Romeria.

CRITICAL THINKING

1. After studying *Reading Between the Lines* on pp. 724–725, answer the following questions:

a. How does the growth rate of real GDP in Canada compare with that of the other G7 nations over the past 30 years, 10 years, and 1 year?

b. Do you think Canada's real GDP growth is faster than other countries because Canada's potential GDP growth is faster or because Canada has moved from below full employment to above full employment in the comparisons?

c. Explain why faster real GDP growth does not necessarily mean faster improvements in the standard of living.

2. Is faster economic growth always a good thing? Argue the case for faster growth and the case for slower growth and then reach a conclusion on whether growth should be increased or decreased.

WEB EXERCISES

1. Use the links on the Parkin–Bade Web site to obtain data on real GDP per person for Canada, China, South Africa, and Mexico since 1960.

a. Draw a graph of the data.

b. Which country has the lowest real GDP per person and which has the highest?

c. Which country has experienced the fastest growth rate since 1960 and which the slowest?

d. Explain why the growth rates in these four countries are ranked in the order you have discovered.

e. Return to the Penn World Table Web site and obtain data for any four other countries that interest you. Describe and explain the patterns that you find for these countries.

2. Write a memo to your member of Parliament in which you set out the policies you believe the Canadian government must follow to speed up the growth rate of real GDP in Canada.

THE BUSINESS CYCLE — CHAPTER 31

Must What Goes Up Always Come Down?

The 1920s were years of unprecedented prosperity for Canadians. After the horrors of World War I (1914–1918), the economic machine was back at work, producing such technological marvels as cars and airplanes, telephones and vacuum cleaners. Houses and apartments were being built at a frantic pace. Then, almost without warning, in October 1929 came a devastating stock market crash. Overnight, the values of stocks trading on Wall Street and Bay Street fell by 30 percent. During the four succeeding years, there followed the most severe economic contraction in recorded history. By 1933, real GDP had fallen by 30 percent and unemployment had increased to 20 percent of the labour force. What caused the Great Depression? ◆ By the standard of the Great Depression, recent recessions have been mild. But recessions have not gone away. Our economy has experienced 15 recessions since 1920, 10 of which have occurred since the end of World War II in 1945. In 1981, real GDP fell by 3.2 percent. It fell again in 1990 and 1991 by more than 2 percent. It was not until mid-1992 that real GDP returned to its 1989 level. Since the 1990–1991 recession, real GDP has soared. By the end of 2002, it was some 42 percent higher than it had been in the 1990–1991 recession and 39 percent higher than its peak before the 1990–1991 recession. What causes a repeating sequence of recessions and expansions in our economy? Must what goes up always come down? Will we have another recession? When? *Reading Between the Lines* at the end of the chapter explores this question in the context of the state of the Canadian economy at the end of 2002.

◆ We are going to explore the business cycle in this chapter. You will see how all the strands of macroeconomics that you've been following come together and weave a complete picture of the forces and mechanisms that generate economic growth and fluctuations in production, employment and unemployment, and inflation.

After studying this chapter, you will be able to

- Distinguish among the different theories of the business cycle
- Explain the Keynesian and monetarist theories of the business cycle
- Explain the new classical and new Keynesian theories of the business cycle
- Explain real business cycle theory
- Describe the origins of and the mechanisms at work during recessions in the 1990s
- Describe the origins of and the mechanisms at work during the Great Depression

729

Cycle Patterns, Impulses, and Mechanisms

CYCLES ARE A WIDESPREAD PHYSICAL PHENOMENON. In a tennis match, the ball cycles from one side of the court to the other and back again. Every day, the earth cycles from day to night and back to day. A child on a rocking horse creates a cycle as the horse swings back and forth.

The tennis ball cycle is the simplest. It is caused by the actions of the players. Each time the ball changes direction (at each turning point), the racquet (an outside force) is applied. The day-night-day cycle is the most subtle. The rotation of the earth causes this cycle. No new force is applied each day to make the sun rise and set. It happens because of the design of the objects that interact to create the cycle. Nothing happens at a turning point (sunrise and sunset) that is any different from what is happening at other points except that the sun comes into or goes out of view. The child's rocking horse cycle is a combination of these two cases. To start the horse rocking, some outside force must be exerted (as in the tennis ball cycle). But once the horse is rocking, the to-and-fro cycle continues for some time with no further force being applied (as in the day-night-day cycle). The rocking horse cycle eventually dies out unless the horse is pushed again, and each time the horse is pushed, the cycle temporarily becomes more severe.

The economy is a bit like all three of these examples. It can be hit by shocks (like a tennis ball) that send it in one direction or another, it can cycle indefinitely (like the turning of day into night), and it can cycle in swings that get milder until another shock sets off a new burst of bigger swings (like a rocking horse). While none of these analogies is perfect, they all contain some insights into the business cycle. Different theories of the cycle emphasize different impulses (different tennis racquets) and different cycle mechanisms (different solar system and rocking horse designs).

Although there are several different theories of the business cycle, they all agree about one aspect of the cycle: the central role played by investment and the accumulation of capital.

The Role of Investment and Capital

Whatever the shocks are that hit the economy, they hit one crucial variable: investment. Recessions begin when investment in new capital slows down, and they turn into expansions when investment speeds up. Investment and capital interact like the spinning earth and the sun to create an ongoing cycle.

In an expansion, investment proceeds at a rapid rate and the capital stock grows quickly. But rapid capital growth means that the amount of capital per hour of labour is growing. Equipped with more capital, labour becomes more productive. But the *law of diminishing returns* begins to operate. The law of diminishing returns states that as the quantity of capital increases, with the quantity of labour remaining the same, the gain in productivity from an additional unit of capital eventually diminishes. Diminishing returns to capital bring a fall in the profit rate and with a lower profit rate, the incentive to invest weakens. As a result, investment eventually falls. When it falls by a large amount, recession begins.

In a recession, investment is low and the capital stock grows slowly. In a deep recession, the capital stock might actually decrease. Slow capital growth (or even a decreasing capital stock) means that the amount of capital per hour of labour is decreasing. With a low amount of capital per hour of labour, businesses begin to see opportunities for profitable investment and the pace of investment eventually picks up. As it does so, recession turns into expansion.

The *AS–AD* Model

Investment and capital are a crucial part of the business cycle mechanism, but they are just one part. To study the broader business cycle mechanism, we need a broader framework—the *AS–AD* model. We can use the *AS–AD* model to describe all theories of the business cycle. The theories differ in what they identify as the impulse and in the cycle mechanism. But all theories can be thought of as making assumptions about the factors that make either aggregate supply or aggregate demand fluctuate and about how those assumptions interact to create a business cycle. Business cycle impulses can affect either the supply side or the demand side of the economy or both. There are no pure supply-side theories, so we classify the theories as either

1. Aggregate demand theories
2. Real business cycle theory

We'll study the aggregate demand theories first. Then we'll study real business cycle theory, which is a more recent approach that isolates a shock that has both aggregate supply and aggregate demand effects.

Aggregate Demand Theories of the Business Cycle

THREE TYPES OF AGGREGATE DEMAND THEORY OF the business cycle have been proposed. They are

- Keynesian theory
- Monetarist theory
- Rational expectations theories

Keynesian Theory

The **Keynesian theory of the business cycle** regards volatile expectations as the main source of economic fluctuations. This theory is distilled from Keynes' *General Theory of Employment, Interest, and Money.* We'll explore the Keynesian theory by looking at its main impulse and the mechanism that converts that impulse into a real GDP cycle.

Keynesian Impulse The impulse in the Keynesian theory of the business cycle is *expected future sales and profits.* A change in expected future sales and profits changes the demand for new capital and changes the level of investment.

Keynes reasoned that profit expectations would be volatile because most of the events that shape the future are unknown and impossible to forecast. So, he reasoned, news or even rumours about future influences on profit (such as tax rate changes, interest rate changes, advances in technology, global economic and political events, or any of the thousands of other relevant factors) have large effects on the expected profit rate.

To emphasize the volatility and diversity of sources of changes in expected sales and profits, Keynes described these expectations as *animal spirits*.

Keynesian Cycle Mechanism In the Keynesian theory, once a change in animal spirits has changed investment, a cycle mechanism begins to operate that has two key elements. First, the initial change in investment has a multiplier effect. The change in investment changes *aggregate* expenditure, real GDP, and disposable income. The change in disposable income changes consumption expenditure, and aggregate demand changes by a multiple of the initial change in investment. (This mechanism is described

in detail in Chapter 23, p. 538 and pp. 544–545.) The aggregate demand curve shifts leftward in a recession and rightward in an expansion.

The second element of the Keynesian cycle mechanism is a sticky money wage rate together with a horizontal *SAS* curve. With a horizontal *SAS* curve, swings in aggregate demand translate into swings in real GDP with no changes in the price level.

Figure 31.1 illustrates the Keynesian cycle. The long-run aggregate supply curve is *LAS*, the short-run aggregate supply curve is *SAS*, and the aggregate demand curve is AD_0. Initially, the economy is at full employment (point *A*) with real GDP at $1,000 billion and the price level at 110.

A fall in animal spirits decreases investment and a multiplier process decreases aggregate demand. The aggregate demand curve shifts leftward to AD_1. With

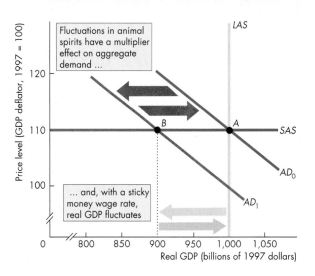

FIGURE 31.1   The Keynesian Cycle

The economy is operating at point *A* at the intersection of the long-run aggregate supply curve (*LAS*), the short-run aggregate supply curve (*SAS*), and the aggregate demand curve (AD_0). A Keynesian recession begins when a fall in animal spirits decreases investment. Aggregate demand decreases and the *AD* curve shifts leftward to AD_1. With a sticky money wage rate, real GDP decreases to $900 billion and the price level does not change. The economy moves to point *B*. An increase in animal spirits has the opposite effect and takes the economy back to point *A*. The economy cycles by bouncing between point *A* and point *B*.

a fixed money wage rate, real GDP decreases to $900 billion and the economy moves to point *B*.

Unemployment has increased and there is a surplus of labour, but the money wage rate does not fall and the economy remains at point *B* until some force moves it away.

That force is a rise in animal spirits, which increases investment. The multiplier process kicks in again and aggregate demand increases. The *AD* curve shifts back to AD_0 and real GDP increases in an expansion to $1,000 billion again.

As long as real GDP remains below potential GDP ($1,000 billion in this example), the money wage rate and the price level remain constant. And real GDP cycles between points *A* and *B*.

Keynes at Above-Full Employment If animal spirits increase investment at full employment, an inflationary gap arises. Real GDP increases temporarily, but soon returns to potential GDP at a higher price level. Figure 31.2 shows this case.

Starting from full employment, at point *A*, an increase in aggregate demand shifts the aggregate demand curve rightward from AD_0 to AD_1. Real GDP increases to $1,100 billion at point *C*. There is now an inflationary gap. Once real GDP exceeds potential GDP and unemployment falls below the natural rate, the money wage rate begins to rise. As it does so, the short-run aggregate supply curve begins to shift from SAS_0 towards SAS_1. Real GDP now begins to decrease and the price level rises. The economy follows the arrows from point *C* to point *D*, the eventual long-run equilibrium.

The Keynesian business cycle is like a tennis match. It is caused by outside forces—animal spirits—that change direction and set off a process that ends at an equilibrium that must be hit again by the outside forces to disturb it.

On the downside, when aggregate demand decreases and unemployment rises, the money wage rate does not change. It is completely rigid in the downward direction. With a decrease in aggregate demand and no change in the money wage rate, the economy gets stuck in a below full-employment equilibrium. There are no natural forces operating to restore full employment. The economy remains in that situation until animal spirits are lifted and investment increases again.

On the upside, if an increase in aggregate demand creates an inflationary gap, the money wage rate rises and the price level also rises. Real GDP returns to potential GDP.

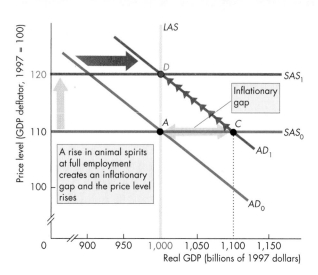

FIGURE 31.2   A Keynesian Inflationary Gap

The economy is initially at full employment at point *A*. A Keynesian expansion begins when a rise in animal spirits increases investment. Aggregate demand increases and the *AD* curve shifts rightward from AD_0 to AD_1. With a sticky money wage rate, real GDP increases to $1,100 billion at point *C*. There is now an inflationary gap. The money wage rate rises and the *SAS* curve shifts from SAS_0 towards SAS_1. Real GDP decreases and the price level rises as the economy heads towards point *D*.

Monetarist Theory

The **monetarist theory of the business cycle** regards fluctuations in the quantity of money as the main source of economic fluctuations. This theory is distilled from the writings of Milton Friedman and several other economists. We'll explore the monetarist theory as we did the Keynesian theory, by looking first at its main impulse and second at the mechanism that creates a cycle in real GDP.

Monetarist Impulse The impulse in the monetarist theory of the business cycle is the *growth rate of the quantity of money*. A speedup in money growth brings expansion, and a slowdown in money growth brings recession. The source of the change in the growth rate of the quantity of money is the monetary policy actions of the Bank of Canada.

Monetarist Cycle Mechanism In the monetarist theory, once the Bank of Canada has changed the money growth rate, a cycle mechanism begins to operate that, like the Keynesian mechanism, first affects aggregate demand. When the money growth rate increases, the quantity of real money in the economy increases. Interest rates fall. The foreign exchange rate also falls—the dollar loses value on the foreign exchange market. These initial financial market effects begin to spill over into other markets. Investment and exports increase, and consumers spend more on durable goods. These initial changes in expenditure have a multiplier effect, just as investment has in the Keynesian theory. Through these mechanisms a speedup in money growth shifts the aggregate demand curve rightward and brings an expansion. Similarly, a slowdown in money growth shifts the aggregate demand curve leftward and brings a recession.

The second element of the monetarist cycle mechanism is the response of aggregate supply to a change in aggregate demand. The short-run aggregate supply curve is upward sloping. With an upward-sloping *SAS* curve, swings in aggregate demand translate into swings in both real GDP and the price level. But monetarists believe that real GDP deviations from full employment are temporary.

In monetarist theory, the money wage rate is only *temporarily sticky*. When aggregate demand decreases and unemployment rises above the natural rate, the money wage rate eventually begins to fall. As the money wage rate falls, so does the price level. And through a period of adjustment, real GDP returns to potential GDP and the unemployment rate returns to the natural rate. When aggregate demand increases and unemployment falls below the natural rate, the money wage rate begins to rise. As the money wage rate rises, so does the price level. And through a period of adjustment, real GDP returns to potential GDP and the unemployment rate returns to the natural rate.

Figure 31.3 illustrates a monetarist recession and recovery. The economy is initially at full employment (point *A*) on the long-run aggregate supply curve (*LAS*), the aggregate demand curve (*AD₀*), and the short-run aggregate supply curve (*SAS₀*). A slowdown in the money growth rate decreases aggregate demand, and the aggregate demand curve shifts leftward to AD_1. Real GDP decreases to $950 billion, and the economy goes into recession (point *B*).

Unemployment increases and there is a surplus of labour. The money wage rate begins to fall. As the money wage rate falls, the short-run aggregate supply curve starts to shift rightward towards SAS_1. The price level falls, and real GDP begins to expand as the economy moves to point *C*, its new full-employment equilibrium.

The monetarist business cycle is like a rocking horse. It needs an outside force to get it going, but once going, it rocks back and forth (but just once). Starting from full employment, when the quantity of money decreases (or its growth rate slows), the economy cycles with a recession followed by expansion. And if the quantity of money increases (or its growth rate speeds) the economy also cycles but with an expansion followed by recession.

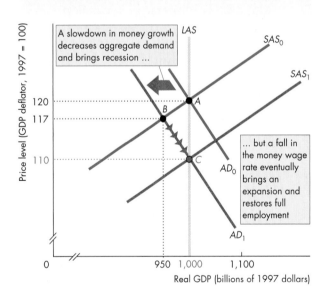

FIGURE 31.3   A Monetarist Recession

The economy is initially at full employment at point A. Real GDP is $1,000 billion and the price level is 120. A monetarist recession begins when a slowdown in money growth decreases aggregate demand. The AD curve shifts leftward from AD_0 to AD_1. With a sticky money wage rate, real GDP decreases to $950 billion and the price level falls to 117 as the economy moves from point A to point B. With a surplus of labour, the money wage rate falls and the SAS curve shifts rightward to SAS_1. The price level falls further, and real GDP returns to potential GDP at point C.

Figure 31.4 shows the effects of this opposite case in which the quantity of money increases. Here, starting out at point *C*, an increase in the quantity of money increases aggregate demand and shifts the *AD* curve to *AD₂*. Both real GDP and the price level increase as the economy moves to point *D*, where *SAS₁* and *AD₂* intersect. With real GDP above potential GDP and unemployment below the natural rate, the money wage rate begins to rise and the *SAS* curve starts to shift leftward towards *SAS₂*. As the money wage rate rises, the price level also rises and real GDP decreases. The economy moves from point *D* to point *E*, its new full-employment equilibrium.

Although monetarists think that the money wage rate will fall when real GDP is less than potential GDP—when there is a recessionary gap—they do not see this process as being a rapid one.

FIGURE 31.4   A Monetarist Expansion

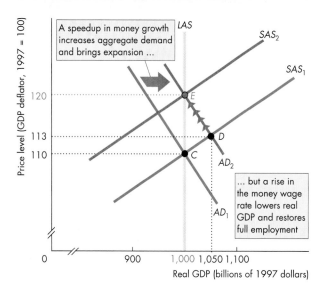

Starting at point *C*, a monetarist expansion begins when an increase in money growth increases aggregate demand and shifts the *AD* curve rightward to *AD₂*. With a sticky money wage rate, real GDP rises to $1,050 billion, the price level rises to 113, and the economy moves to point *D*. With a shortage of labour, the money wage rate rises and the *SAS* curve shifts towards *SAS₂*. The price level rises and real GDP decreases to potential GDP as the economy heads towards point *E*.

Rational Expectations Theories

A **rational expectation** is a forecast that is based on all the available relevant information. Rational expectations theories of the business cycle are theories based on the view that the money wage rate is determined by a rational expectation of the price level. Two distinctly different rational expectations theories of the cycle have been proposed. A **new classical theory of the business cycle** regards *unanticipated* fluctuations in aggregate demand as the main source of economic fluctuations. This theory is based on the work of Robert E. Lucas, Jr. and several other economists, including Thomas J. Sargent and Robert J. Barro (see pp. 524–526). A different **new Keynesian theory of the business cycle** also regards *unanticipated* fluctuations in aggregate demand as the main source of economic fluctuations but also leaves room for *anticipated* demand fluctuations to play a role. We'll explore these theories as we did the Keynesian and monetarist theories, by looking first at the main impulse and second at the cycle mechanism.

Rational Expectations Impulse   The impulse that distinguishes the rational expectations theories from the other aggregate demand theories of the business cycle is the *unanticipated change in aggregate demand*. A larger than anticipated increase in aggregate demand brings an expansion, and a smaller than anticipated increase in aggregate demand brings a recession. Any factor that influences aggregate demand—for example, fiscal policy, monetary policy, or developments in the world economy that influence exports—whose change is not anticipated, can bring a change in real GDP.

Rational Expectations Cycle Mechanisms   To describe the rational expectations cycle mechanisms, we'll deal first with the new classical version. When aggregate demand decreases, if the money wage rate doesn't change, short-run aggregate supply remains unchanged, so real GDP and the price level both decrease. The fall in the price level increases the *real* wage rate, and employment decreases and unemployment rises. In the new classical theory, these events occur only if the decrease in aggregate demand is not anticipated. If the decrease in aggregate demand *is* anticipated, the price level is expected to fall and both firms and workers will agree to a lower money wage rate. By doing so, they can prevent the real wage from rising and avoid a rise in the unemployment rate.

Similarly, if firms and workers anticipate an increase in aggregate demand, they expect the price level to rise and will agree to a higher money wage rate. By doing so, they can prevent the real wage rate from falling and avoid a fall in the unemployment rate below the natural rate.

Only fluctuations in aggregate demand that are unanticipated and not taken into account in wage agreements bring changes in real GDP. *Anticipated* changes in aggregate demand change the price level but they leave real GDP and unemployment unchanged and do not create a business cycle.

New Keynesian economists, like new classical economists, believe that the money wage rate is influenced by rational expectations of the price level. But new Keynesians emphasize the long-term nature of most wage contracts. They say that *today's* money wage rate is influenced by *yesterday's* rational expectations. These expectations, which were formed in the past, are based on old information that might now be known to be incorrect. After they have made a long-term wage agreement, both firms and workers might anticipate a change in aggregate demand, which they expect will change the price level. But because they are locked into their agreement, they are unable to change the money wage rate. So the money wage rate is sticky in the new Keynesian theory and with a sticky money wage rate, even an *anticipated* change in aggregate demand changes real GDP.

New classical economists believe that long-term contracts are renegotiated when conditions change to make them outdated. So they do not regard long-term contracts as an obstacle to money wage flexibility, provided both parties to an agreement recognize the changed conditions. If both firms and workers expect the price level to change, they will change the agreed money wage rate to reflect that shared expectation. In this situation, anticipated changes in aggregate demand change the money wage rate and the price level and leave real GDP unchanged.

The distinctive feature of both versions of the rational expectations theory of the business cycle is the role of *unanticipated* changes in aggregate demand. Figure 31.5 illustrates their effect on real GDP and the price level.

Potential GDP is $1,000 billion and the long-run aggregate supply curve is *LAS*. Aggregate demand is expected to be *EAD*. Given potential GDP and *EAD*, the money wage rate is set at the level that is expected to bring full employment. At this money wage rate, the short-run aggregate supply curve is *SAS*.

Imagine that initially aggregate demand equals expected aggregate demand, so there is full employment. Real GDP is $1,000 billion and the price level is 110, at point *A*. Then, unexpectedly, aggregate demand turns out to be less than expected and the aggregate demand curve shift leftward to AD_0. Many different aggregate demand shocks, such as a slow-down in the money growth rate or a collapse of exports, could have caused this shift. A recession begins. But aggregate demand is expected to be at *EAD*, so the money wage rate doesn't change and the short-run aggregate supply curve remains at *SAS*. Real GDP decreases to $950 billion and the price level falls to 107. The economy moves to point *B*. Unemployment increases and there is a surplus of labour.

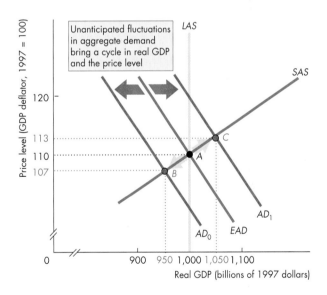

FIGURE 31.5   A Rational Expectations Business Cycle

The economy is expected to be at point A. As long as aggregate demand is *expected* to be EAD, there is no change in the money wage rate and the SAS curve does not shift. A rational expectations recession begins when an unanticipated decrease in aggregate demand shifts the AD curve leftward to AD_0. Real GDP decreases to $950 billion and the price level falls to 107, at point B. A rational expectations expansion begins when an unanticipated increase in aggregate demand shifts the AD curve rightward to AD_1. Real GDP increases to $1,050 billion and the price level rises to 113, at point C.

A shock that takes aggregate demand to a level that exceeds EAD brings an expansion. The aggregate demand curve shifts rightward to AD_1. A speedup in the money growth rate or an export boom might have increased aggregate demand. But aggregate demand is expected to be at EAD, so the money wage rate doesn't change and the short-run aggregate supply curve remains at SAS. Real GDP increases to $1,050 billion and the price level rises to 113. The economy moves to point C. Unemployment is below the natural rate.

Fluctuations in aggregate demand between AD_0 and AD_1 around expected aggregate demand EAD bring fluctuations in real GDP and the price level between points B and C.

The two versions of the rational expectations theory differ in their predictions about the effects of a change in expected aggregate demand. The new classical theory predicts that as soon as expected aggregate demand changes, the money wage rate also changes so the SAS curve shifts. The new Keynesian theory predicts that the money wage rate changes only gradually when new contracts are made so that the SAS curve moves only slowly. This difference between the two theories is crucial for policy. According to the new classical theory, anticipated policy actions change the price level only and have no effect on real GDP and unemployment. The reason is that when policy is expected to change, the money wage rate changes so the SAS curve shifts and offsets the effects of the policy action on real GDP. In contrast, in the new Keynesian theory, because the money wage rate changes only when new contracts are made, even anticipated policy actions change real GDP and can be used in an attempt to stabilize the cycle.

Like the monetarist business cycle, these rational expectations cycles are similar to rocking horses. They need an outside force to get going, but once going the economy rocks around its full employment point. The new classical horse rocks faster and comes to rest more quickly than does the new Keynesian horse.

AS–AD General Theory

All the theories of the business cycle that we've considered can be viewed as particular cases of the more general AS–AD theory. In this more general theory, the impulses of both the Keynesian and monetarist theories can change aggregate demand. A multiplier effect makes aggregate demand change by more than any initial change in one of its components. The

money wage rate can be viewed as responding to changes in the expected price level. Even if the money wage is flexible, it will change only to the extent that price level expectations change. As a result, the money wage rate will adjust gradually.

Although in all three business cycle theories that we've considered, the cycle is caused by fluctuations in aggregate demand, the possibility that an occasional aggregate supply shock might occur is not ruled out by the aggregate demand theories.

A recession could occur because aggregate supply decreases. For example, a widespread drought that cuts agricultural production could create a recession in an economy that has a large agricultural sector. But these aggregate demand theories of the business cycle regard aggregate supply shocks as rare rather than normal events. Aggregate demand fluctuations are the normal ongoing sources of fluctuations.

REVIEW QUIZ

1 What, according to Keynesian theory, is the main business cycle impulse?

2 What, according to Keynesian theory, are the main business cycle mechanisms? Describe the roles of *animal spirits*, the multiplier, and a sticky money wage rate in this theory.

3 What, according to monetarist theory, is the main business cycle impulse?

4 What, according to monetarist theory, are the business cycle mechanisms? Describe the roles of the Bank of Canada and the quantity of money in this theory.

5 What, according to new classical theory and new Keynesian theory, causes the business cycle? What are the roles of rational expectations and unanticipated fluctuations in aggregate demand in these theories?

6 What are the differences between the new classical theory and the new Keynesian theory concerning the money wage rate over the business cycle?

A new theory of the business cycle challenges the mainstream and traditional aggregate demand theories that you've just studied. It is called the real business cycle theory. Let's look at this new theory of the business cycle.

Real Business Cycle Theory

THE NEWEST THEORY OF THE BUSINESS CYCLE, known as **real business cycle theory** (or RBC theory), regards random fluctuations in productivity as the main source of economic fluctuations. These productivity fluctuations are assumed to result mainly from fluctuations in the pace of technological change, but they might also have other sources such as international disturbances, climate fluctuations, or natural disasters. The origins of real business cycle theory can be traced to the rational expectations revolution set off by Robert E. Lucas, Jr., but the first demonstration of the power of this theory was given by Edward Prescott and Finn Kydland and by John Long and Charles Plosser. Today, real business cycle theory is part of a broad research agenda called *dynamic general equilibrium analysis,* and hundreds of young macroeconomists do research on this topic.

We'll explore RBC theory by looking first at its impulse and second at the mechanism that converts that impulse into a cycle in real GDP.

The RBC Impulse

The impulse in RBC theory is the *growth rate of productivity that results from technological change.* Real business cycle theorists believe this impulse to be generated mainly by the process of research and development that leads to the creation and use of new technologies.

Most of the time, technological change is steady and productivity grows at a moderate pace. But sometimes productivity growth speeds up and occasionally productivity *decreases*—labour becomes less productive, on the average.

A period of rapid productivity growth brings a strong business cycle expansion, and a *decrease* in productivity triggers a recession.

It is easy to understand why technological change brings productivity growth. But how does it *decrease* productivity? All technological change eventually increases productivity. But if, initially, technological change makes a sufficient amount of existing capital (especially human capital) obsolete, productivity temporarily decreases. At such a time, more jobs are destroyed than created and more businesses fail than start up.

FIGURE 31.6   The Real Business Cycle Impulse

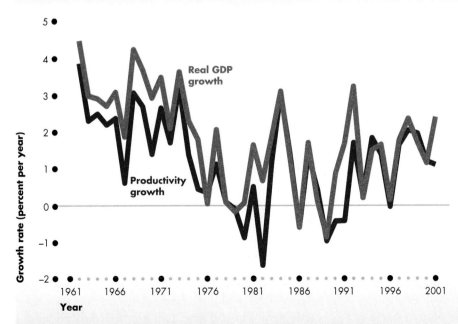

The real business cycle impulse is fluctuations in the growth rate of productivity that are caused by changes in technology. The fluctuations in productivity growth shown here are calculated by using growth accounting (the one-third rule) to remove the contribution of capital accumulation to productivity growth. Productivity fluctuations are correlated with real GDP fluctuations. Economists are not sure what the productivity variable actually measures or what causes it to fluctuate.

Sources: Statistics Canada, CANSIM tables 282-0002, 378–0004, and 380-0002, and authors' calculations.

To isolate the RBC theory impulse, economists use growth accounting, which is explained in Chapter 30, pp. 713–716. Figure 31.6 shows the RBC impulse for Canada from 1961 to 2001. You can see that fluctuations in productivity growth are correlated with real GDP fluctuations. But this RBC impulse is a catchall variable and no one knows what it actually measures or what causes it to fluctuate.

The RBC Mechanism

According to RBC theory, two immediate effects follow from a change in productivity that get an expansion or a contraction going. They are

1. Investment demand changes.
2. The demand for labour changes.

We'll study these effects and their consequences during a recession. In an expansion, they work in the direction opposite to what is described here.

Technological change makes some existing capital obsolete and temporarily decreases productivity. Firms expect the future profits to fall and see their labour productivity falling. With lower profit expectations, they cut back their purchases of new capital, and with lower labour productivity, they plan to lay off some workers. So the initial effect of a temporary fall in productivity is a decrease in investment demand and a decrease in the demand for labour.

Figure 31.7 illustrates these two initial effects of a decrease in productivity. Part (a) shows investment demand, ID, and saving supply, SS. (In real business cycle theory, saving depends on the real interest rate.) Initially, investment demand is ID_0, and the equilibrium investment and saving are $100 billion at a real interest rate of 6 percent a year. A decrease in productivity decreases investment demand and the ID curve shifts leftward to ID_1. The real interest rate falls to 4 percent a year, and investment and saving decrease to $70 billion.

Part (b) shows the demand for labour, LD, and the supply of labour, LS (which are explained in Chapter 29, pp. 683–686). Initially, the demand for labour is LD_0, and equilibrium employment is 20 billion hours a year at a real wage rate of $15 an hour. The decrease in productivity decreases the demand for labour, and the LD curve shifts leftward to LD_1.

Before we can determine the new level of employment and real wage rate, we need to take a ripple effect into account—the key ripple effect in RBC theory.

The Key Decision: When to Work? According to RBC theory, people decide when to work by doing a cost–benefit calculation. They compare the return from working in the current period with the *expected* return from working in a later period. You make such a comparison every day in school. Suppose your goal in this course is to get an A. To achieve this goal, you work pretty hard most of the time. But during the few days before the midterm and final exams, you work especially hard. Why? Because you believe that the return from studying just prior to the exam is greater than the return from studying when the exam is a long time away. So during the term, you take time off for the movies and other leisure pursuits, but at exam time, you work every evening and weekend.

Real business cycle theory says that workers behave like you. They work fewer hours, sometimes zero hours, when the real wage rate is temporarily low, and they work more hours when the real wage rate is temporarily high. But to properly compare the current wage rate with the expected future wage rate, workers must use the real interest rate. If the real interest rate is 6 percent a year, a real wage of $1 an hour earned this week will become $1.06 a year from now. If the real wage rate is expected to be $1.05 an hour next year, today's real wage of $1 looks good. By working longer hours now and shorter hours a year from now, a person can get a 1 percent higher real wage. But suppose the real interest rate is 4 percent a year. In this case, $1 earned now is worth $1.04 next year. Working fewer hours now and more next year is the way to get a 1 percent higher real wage.

So the when-to-work decision depends on the real interest rate. The lower the real interest rate, other things remaining the same, the smaller is the supply of labour. Many economists believe this *intertemporal substitution* effect to be of negligible size. RBC theorists believe that the effect is large, and it is the key element in the RBC mechanism.

You've seen in Fig. 31.7(a) that the decrease in investment demand lowers the real interest rate. This fall in the real interest rate lowers the return to current work and decreases the supply of labour. In Fig. 31.7(b) the labour supply curve shifts leftward to LS_1. The effect of a productivity shock on the demand for labour is larger than the effect of the fall in the real interest rate on the supply of labour. That is, the LD curve shifts farther leftward than does the LS curve. The real wage rate falls to $14.50 an hour and employment decreases to 19.5 billion hours. A recession has begun, and it is intensifying.

FIGURE 31.7   Capital and Labour Markets in a Real Business Cycle

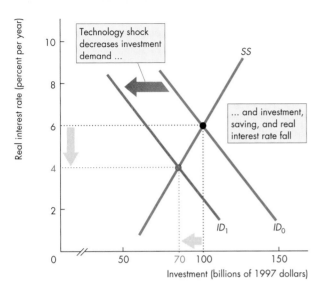

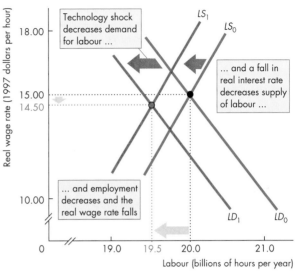

(a) Investment, saving, and interest rate

(b) Labour and wage rate

Saving supply is SS and, initially, investment demand is ID_0 (part a). The real interest rate is 6 percent a year, and saving and investment are $100 billion. In the labour market (part b) the demand for labour is LD_0 and the supply of labour is LS_0. The real wage rate is $15 an hour, and employment is 20 billion hours.

A technological change temporarily decreases productivity, and both investment demand and the demand for labour decrease. The two demand curves shift leftward to ID_1 and LD_1. In part (a), the real interest rate falls to 4 percent a year and investment and saving decrease. In part (b) the fall in the real interest rate decreases the supply of labour (the when-to-work decision) and the supply curve shifts leftward to LS_1. Employment decreases to 19.5 billion hours, and the real wage rate falls to $14.50 an hour. A recession is underway.

Real GDP and the Price Level The next part of the RBC story traces the consequences of the changes you've just seen for real GDP and the price level. With a decrease in employment, aggregate supply decreases, and with a decrease in investment demand, aggregate demand decreases. Figure 31.8 illustrates these effects, using the *AS–AD* framework. Initially, the long-run aggregate supply curve is LAS_0, and the aggregate demand curve is AD_0. The price level is 110, and real GDP is $1,000 billion. There is no short-run aggregate supply curve in this figure because the *SAS* curve has no meaning in RBC theory. The labour market moves relentlessly towards its equilibrium, and the money wage rate adjusts freely (either increases or decreases) to ensure that the real wage rate keeps the quantity of labour demanded equal to the quantity supplied. In RBC theory,

unemployment is always at the natural rate, and the natural rate fluctuates over the business cycle because the amount of job search fluctuates.

The decrease in employment decreases total production, and aggregate supply decreases. The *LAS* curve shifts leftward to LAS_1. The decrease in investment demand decreases aggregate demand, and the *AD* curve shifts leftward to AD_1. The price level falls to 107, and real GDP decreases to $950 billion. The economy is in a recession.

What Happened to Money? The name *real* business cycle theory is no accident. It reflects the central prediction of the theory. Real things, not nominal or monetary things, cause the business cycle. If the quantity of money changes, aggregate demand changes. But if there is no real change—with

FIGURE 31.8   *AS–AD* in a Real
Business Cycle

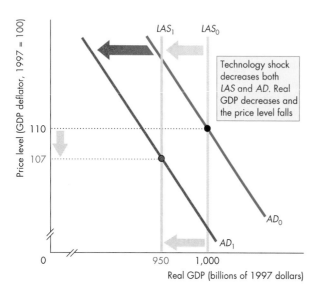

Initially, the long-run aggregate supply curve is *LAS*₀ and the aggregate demand curve is *AD*₀. Real GDP is $1,000 billion (which equals potential GDP), and the price level is 110. There is no *SAS* curve in the real business cycle theory because the money wage rate is flexible. The technological change described in Fig. 31.7 temporarily decreases potential GDP, and the *LAS* curve shifts leftward to *LAS*₁. The fall in investment decreases aggregate demand, and the *AD* curve shifts leftward to *AD*₁. Real GDP decreases to $950 billion, and the price level falls to 107. The economy has gone into recession.

no change in the use of resources and no change in potential GDP—the change in the quantity of money changes only the price level. In real business cycle theory, this outcome occurs because the aggregate supply curve is the *LAS* curve, which pins real GDP down at potential GDP. So a change in aggregate demand changes only the price level.

Cycles and Growth   The shock that drives the business cycle of RBC theory is the same as the force that generates economic growth: technological change. On the average, as technology advances, productivity grows. But it grows at an uneven pace. You saw this

fact when you studied growth accounting in Chapter 30. There, we focused on slow-changing trends in productivity growth. Real business cycle theory uses the same idea but says that there are frequent shocks to productivity that are mostly positive but that are occasionally negative.

Criticisms of Real Business Cycle Theory

RBC theory is controversial, and when economists discuss it, they often generate more heat than light. Its detractors claim that its basic assumptions are just too incredible. The money wage rate *is* sticky, they claim, so to assume otherwise is at odds with a clear fact. Intertemporal substitution is too weak, they say, to account for large fluctuations in labour supply and employment with small changes in the real wage rate.

But what really kills the RBC story, say most economists, is an implausible impulse. Technology shocks are not capable of creating the swings in productivity that growth accounting reveals. These swings in productivity are caused by something, they concede, but they are as likely to be caused by *changes in aggregate demand* as by technology. If the fluctuations in productivity are caused by aggregate demand fluctuations, then the traditional demand theories are needed to explain them. Fluctuations in productivity do not cause the cycle but are caused by it!

Building on this theme, the critics point out that the so-called productivity fluctuations that growth accounting measures are correlated with changes in the growth rate of money and other indicators of changes in aggregate demand.

Defence of Real Business Cycle Theory

The defenders of RBC theory claim that the theory works. It explains the macroeconomic facts about the business cycle and is consistent with the facts about economic growth. In effect, a single theory explains *both economic growth and business cycles*. The growth accounting exercise that explains slowly changing trends also explains the more frequent business cycle swings. Its defenders also claim that RBC theory is consistent with a wide range of *micro*economic evidence about labour supply decisions, labour demand and investment demand decisions, and information on the distribution of income between labour and capital.

RBC theorists acknowledge that money growth and the business cycle are correlated. That is, rapid money growth and expansion go together, and slow money growth and recession go together. But, they argue, causation does not run from money to real GDP as the traditional aggregate demand theories state. Instead, RBC theorists view causation as running from real GDP to money—so-called reverse causation. In a recession, the initial fall in investment demand that lowers the real interest rate decreases the demand for bank loans and lowers the profitability of banking. So banks increase their reserves and decrease their loans. The quantity of bank deposits and hence the quantity of money decreases. This reverse causation is responsible for the correlation between money growth and real GDP according to real business cycle theory.

Its defenders also argue that the RBC view is significant because it at least raises the possibility that the business cycle is efficient. The business cycle does not signal an economy that is misbehaving; it is business as usual. If this view is correct, it means that policy designed to smooth the business cycle is misguided. Only by taking out the peaks can the troughs be smoothed out. But peaks are bursts of investment to take advantage of new technologies in a timely way. So smoothing the business cycle means delaying the benefits of new technologies.

REVIEW QUIZ

1 What, according to real business cycle theory, causes the business cycle? What is the role of fluctuations in the rate of technological change?

2 How, according to real business cycle theory, does a fall in productivity growth influence investment demand, the real interest rate, the demand for labour, the supply of labour, employment, and the real wage rate?

3 How, according to real business cycle theory, does a fall in productivity growth influence long-run aggregate supply, aggregate demand, real GDP, and the price level?

You've now reviewed the main theories of the business cycle. Your next task is to examine some actual business cycles. In pursuing this task, we'll focus on two episodes of recession during the 1990s and on the Great Depression of the 1930s.

Recessions During the 1990s

THE 1990s HAVE BROUGHT SOME INTERESTING business cycle experience. In Canada, we had a recession during 1990–1991 followed by a period of sustained expansion. In contrast, Japan experienced a decade of slow growth and ended the decade in serious recession. In 1999, while the three-fifths of the global economy that includes Canada, the United States, and Western Europe continued to expand vigorously, the other two-fifths that includes Japan, some other East Asian countries, and Central Europe were in recession.

In the theories of the business cycle that you've studied, recessions and expansions can be triggered by a variety of forces, some on the aggregate demand side and some on the aggregate supply side. We'll study the shocks that triggered some of these 1990s episodes and the processes at work during them. We'll focus on two cases:

■ The recession of 1990–1991
■ Japanese stagnation

The Recession of 1990–1991

Three forces were at work in Canada during 1990 that appear to have contributed to the recession and subsequent sluggish growth. They were

■ The Bank of Canada's anti-inflation policy
■ A slowdown in economic expansion in the United States
■ The Canada–United States Free Trade Agreement

The Bank of Canada's Anti-Inflation Policy The Bank of Canada began to pursue low inflation targets in 1988. But because of the time lags involved in the operation of monetary policy, the policy began to bite in 1989 and to bite hard in 1990. The best evidence available suggests that the long-term effects of price stability will be extremely beneficial to Canadians. But its short-term effects are costly.

To achieve price stability, the Bank of Canada must slow the growth rate of money. The extent to which the Bank did slow money growth can be seen in Fig. 31.9. The growth rate of the narrow definition of money, M1, slowed in 1989 to almost zero during 1990. The growth rate of the M2+ definition of money also slowed, but more gently.

FIGURE 31.9   Money Growth: 1989–1995

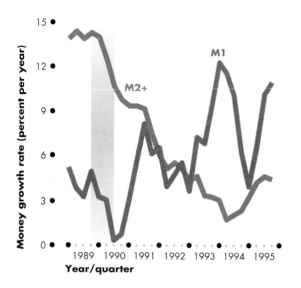

The Bank of Canada began to pursue the goal of low infla-tion in 1988 and the growth rate of the M2+ money began to slow during 1989. It slowed even further during 1990. The narrow definition of money, M1, barely grew during 1990.

Source: Bank of Canada, *Banking and Financial Statistics,* table E1.

FIGURE 31.10   U.S. and Canadian Real GDP Growth: 1989–1995

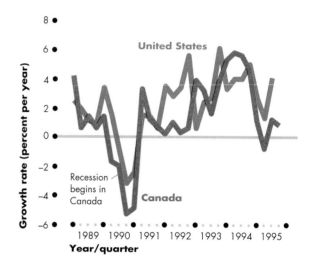

The United States had a recession in 1990, but Canada's recession preceded that in the United States by one quar-ter. The Canadian recession was deeper than the U.S. recession and with the exception of the first quarter of 1991, Canadian real GDP growth rate was below that of the United States throughout the recession.

Sources: Statistics Canada, CANSIM table 380-0002 and Bureau of Economic Analysis.

A Slowdown in Economic Expansion in the United States After its longest ever period of peace-time expansion, U.S. real GDP growth began to slow in 1989 and 1990 and the United States went into recession in mid-1990, a quarter of a year behind Canada. You can see the performance of real GDP growth in the United States (and Canada) by looking at Fig. 31.10. You can see that the U.S. recession not only lagged behind Canada's recession but was also less severe than Canada's. Also, the U.S. recovery dur-ing 1991 and 1992 was more rapid than Canada's.

The slowdown of the U.S. economy brought slower growth in the demand for Canada's exports, which resulted in lower export prices and smaller export volumes.

The Canada–United States Free Trade Agreement The first tariff cuts under the Free Trade Agreement with the United States occurred on January 1, 1989, and the second phase of cuts came a year later. The gradual elimination of tariffs on most

of Canada's trade with the United States will result in a rationalization of production activities on both sides of the border. The long-term effects of this rationalization are expected to be beneficial to Canada (and the United States). But like the Bank of Canada's price stability policy, tariff cuts impose costs in the short term. These costs arise because initially, tariff cuts destroy more jobs than they create. Production cutbacks in sectors that must contract precede production increases in sectors that must expand. The result is a temporary decrease in both short-run and long-run aggregate supply as structural unemployment increases.

The elimination of tariffs changes the profitabil-ity of businesses, bringing gains to some industries and firms and losses to others. It is easy to see who the immediate winners and losers are. But it is diffi-cult to predict where the gains and losses will ulti-mately be when the new tariff structure has been in place for some time. As a result, tariff cuts bring an increase in uncertainty that decreases investment in new buildings, plant, and equipment. This decrease in investment decreases aggregate demand.

Let's see how the events we've just described influenced the Canadian economy in 1990–1991.

Aggregate Demand and Aggregate Supply in the 1990–1991 Recession The Canadian economy in the first quarter of 1990, on the eve of the 1990–1991 recession, is shown in Fig. 31.11. The aggregate demand curve was AD_0, the short-run aggregate supply curve was SAS_0, real GDP was $767 billion, and the price level was 89.

The 1990–1991 recession was caused by a decrease in both aggregate demand and aggregate supply. Aggregate demand decreased, initially, because of the slowdown in the growth rate of the quantity of money. This initial source was soon reinforced by the slowdown in the U.S. economy that

brought a decline in the growth of exports. These two factors, together with increased uncertainty arising from tariff cuts, triggered a massive decline in investment. The resulting decrease in aggregate demand is shown in Fig. 31.11 by the shift of the aggregate demand curve leftward to AD_1. Aggregate supply decreased partly because of the effects of the Free Trade Agreement and partly because the money wage rate continued to increase throughout 1990 at a rate similar to that in 1989. This decrease in aggregate supply is shown as the shift in the short-run aggregate supply curve leftward to SAS_1. (The figure does not show the long-run aggregate supply curve.)

The combined effect of the decreases in aggregate supply and aggregate demand was a decrease in real GDP to $741 billion—a 3.4 percent decrease—and a rise in the price level to 92—a 3.4 percent rise.

What happened in the labour market during this recession?

The Labour Market in the 1990s The unemployment rate increased persistently from the beginning of 1990 to the end of 1992. Figure 31.12 shows two

FIGURE 31.11 The 1990–1991 Recession

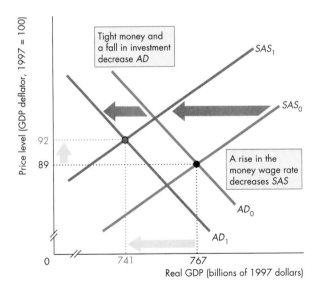

At the beginning of 1990, real GDP was $767 billion and the GDP deflator was 89. Sectoral reallocations resulting from the Canada–U.S. Free Trade Agreement together with increases in the money wage rate decreased aggregate supply, and the short-run aggregate supply curve shifted leftward to SAS_1. Tight monetary policy, a slowdown in the U.S. economy, and increased uncertainty shifted the aggregate demand curve leftward to AD_1. Real GDP decreased to $741 billion, and the economy went into recession.

FIGURE 31.12 Employment and Real Wages

During 1990–1991, the economy was in a recession. Employment decreased, and the real wage rate increased. During the expansion that followed, employment increased and the real wage rate decreased.

Sources: Statistics Canada, CANSIM tables 282-0002, 282-0022, and 380-0001 and authors' calculations.

other facts about the labour market during this period—facts about employment and the real wage rate. As employment decreased through 1990 and 1991, the real wage rate increased. During the recovery, employment increased and the real wage rate decreased. These movements in employment and the real wage rate suggest that the forces of supply and demand do not operate smoothly in the labour market. The money wage rate rose because people didn't anticipate the slowdown in inflation. When inflation did slow down, the real wage increased and the quantity of labour demanded decreased.

Japanese Stagnation

Between 1992 and 2002, when real GDP in Canada expanded by more than 40 percent, Japan's real GDP expanded by a mere 10 percent—a growth rate of less than 1 percent per year. Between 1997 and 2002, Japan's real GDP barely changed.

Why has Japan experienced such a low rate of economic growth during the 1990s and stagnation since 1997? Several factors seem to have combined to produce Japan's problems. And these factors together with the fiscal policies and monetary policies that Japan has pursued provide valuable information about the validity of the alternative theories of the business cycle that you studied earlier in this chapter.

The main factors that have contributed to Japan's weak economy and ultimate recession are

- Collapse of asset prices
- Fiscal policy
- Monetary policy
- Structural rigidities

Collapse of Asset Prices During the second half of the 1980s, land prices and stock prices in Japan increased *threefold*. This increase was much larger than that in Canada, the United States, and Europe. Asset prices increased for three main reasons.

First, investors believed Japan's medium-term and long-term prospects were bright. Second, financial deregulation brought an increase of foreign investment into Japan. Japan's banks expanded loans to finance the purchase of assets whose prices were rising. Third, the Bank of Japan (the nation's central bank) lowered interest rates between 1985 and 1987 and permitted a rapid growth rate of money. The motivation for rapid monetary expansion was to prevent the yen from rising and the U.S. dollar from falling in the foreign exchange market. (See Chapter

34, pp. 822–823 for an explanation of how monetary policy influences the foreign exchange rate.)

Asset prices collapsed in 1990. And the collapse created a wealth effect. Saving and consumption were not much affected by the decrease in wealth. But investment expenditure decreased sharply and so did aggregate demand. And with a lower investment rate, the capital stock and potential GDP grew more slowly.

Fiscal Policy From 1991 through 1996, Japan pursued ambitious and substantial fiscal policies to stimulate the economy. In 1991, the government of Japan had a budget surplus equal to 3 percent of GDP. By 1996, this surplus had been transformed into a deficit equal to more than 7 percent of GDP. Six major *discretionary* actions occurred, which are detailed in Table 31.1, that added 12.9 percent to aggregate expenditure. With its associated multiplier effects, this represents an enormous increase in aggregate demand relative to what it would have been in the absence of stimulation. But the stimulation was not persistent during the 1990s.

The removal of temporary tax cuts and cuts in government investment expenditures *lowered* aggregate expenditure by 3 percent of real GDP in 1996–1997. This fiscal policy tightening decreased aggregate demand and contributed to the recession of 1998.

Monetary Policy The Bank of Japan lowered its official interest rate (called the official discount rate or ODR) from 6 percent in 1991 to 1.75 percent by the end of 1993 and to 0.5 percent by 1995. The ODR

TABLE 31.1 Fiscal Stimulation in Japan

Date proposed	Total stimulation (percent of GDP)
August 1992	2.3
April 1993	2.8
September 1993	1.3
February 1994	3.2
September 1995	3.0
Mid-1996–mid-1997	−3.0
April 1998	3.3
Total	**12.9**

Source: Bank of Japan.

FIGURE 31.13   Japan's Sliding Growth Rate

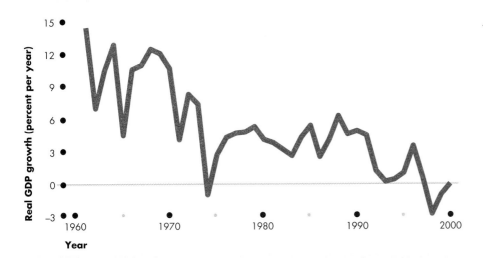

Japan's economic growth rate has been on a slide for many years. Growth of 10 percent a year on the average during the 1960s was followed by growth of 4 percent a year on the average during the 1970s and 1980s and by less than 1 percent a year on the average during the 1990s.

Sources: The Penn World Table: An Expanded Set of International Comparisons, 1950–1988, *Quarterly Journal of Economics*, May 1991, 327–368. 1993–2001, *World Economic Outlook*, International Monetary Fund, Washington D.C., October 2002.

has remained at this level since 1995. Despite these large cuts in the interest rate, a lower inflation rate meant that the real interest rate did not fall as much and so did not act as a stimulus to investment. Also, a strong yen limited the growth of export demand.

Since 1996, a weaker yen and lower real short-term interest rates have had a small but positive effect on aggregate demand in Japan.

Structural Problems Market distortions in agriculture, transportation, retail and wholesale trades, and construction that protect inefficient farms and firms create a lack of competition and low productivity growth. Rich countries such as the United States, Canada, and those in Western Europe have experienced a process of de-industrialization as manufacturing processes have migrated to poorer countries and have been replaced by rapid expansion in the service sector. Japan has not shared this experience.

Japan's structural problems are real, supply-side problems. These problems have brought a gradually falling growth rate of real GDP over many years. Figure 31.13 shows this steadily falling growth rate.

This aspect of Japan's business cycle is an example of a real business cycle. It is a slowdown in productivity growth that slows the rate of increase in long-run aggregate supply. Slower productivity growth works through the real business cycle mecha-

nism described earlier in this chapter. It reduces the demand for capital and labour and decreases potential GDP.

If this explanation for Japan's problems is the correct one, no amount of fiscal and monetary stimulation will end the recession.

You've now seen how business cycle theory can be used to interpret Canada's recession of 1990–1991 and Japan's stagnation of the 1990s. We're now going to use business cycle theory to explain the greatest of recessions—the Great Depression that engulfed the global economy during the 1930s.

The Great Depression

THE LATE 1920S WERE YEARS OF ECONOMIC boom. New houses and apartments were built on an unprecedented scale, new firms were created, and the capital stock of the nation expanded. At the beginning of 1929, Canadian real GDP equalled potential GDP and the unemployment rate was only 2.9 percent.

But as that eventful year unfolded, increasing signs of economic weakness began to appear. The most dramatic events occurred in October when the stock market collapsed. Stocks lost more than one-third of their value in two weeks. The four years that followed were a period of monstrous economic depression.

We'll describe the recession by using the *AS–AD* model and identify the forces that made aggregate demand and aggregate supply change.

Figure 31.14 shows the dimensions of the Great Depression and the changes in aggregate demand and aggregate supply that occurred. On the eve of the Great Depression in 1929, the economy was on aggregate demand curve AD_{29} and short-run aggregate supply curve SAS_{29}. Real GDP was $87 billion (1997 dollars) and the GDP deflator was 7.1.

In 1930, there was a widespread expectation that the price level would fall, and the money wage rate fell. With a lower money wage rate, short-run aggregate supply increased. But increased pessimism and uncertainty decreased investment and the demand for consumer durables. Aggregate demand decreased. In 1930, the economy went into recession as real GDP decreased by about 7 percent. The price level also fell by a similar amount.

In a normal recession, the economy might have remained below full employment for a year or so and then started an expansion. But the recession of 1930 was not a normal one. In 1930 and for the next two years, the economy was further bombarded with huge negative aggregate demand shocks (the sources of which we'll look at in a moment). The aggregate demand curve shifted leftward all the way to AD_{33}. With a depressed economy, the price level was expected to fall and the money wage rate fell in line with those expectations. As a result, the aggregate supply curve shifted rightward to SAS_{33}. But the size of the shift of the short-run aggregate supply curve was much less than the decrease in aggregate demand. As a result, the aggregate demand curve and the short-run aggregate supply curve intersected in

FIGURE 31.14   The Great Depression

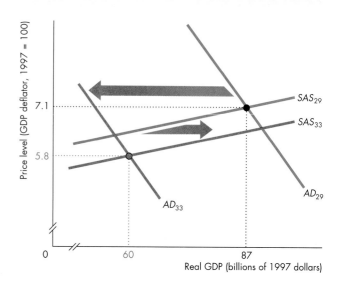

In 1929, real GDP was $87 billion and the GDP deflator was 7.1—at the intersection of AD_{29} and SAS_{29}. In 1930, increased pessimism and uncertainty decreased aggregate demand. Real GDP and the price level fell, and the economy went into recession. In the next three years, decreases in money growth and investment decreased aggregate demand and shifted the aggregate demand curve to AD_{33}. With the price level expected to fall, the money wage rate fell and the short-run aggregate supply curve shifted to SAS_{33}. By 1933, real GDP had decreased to $60 billion (69 percent of its 1929 level) and the price level had fallen to 5.8 (82 percent of its 1929 level).

1933 at a real GDP of $60 billion (a decrease of 31 percent from 1929) and a GDP deflator of 5.8 (a fall of 18 percent from 1929).

Although the Great Depression brought enormous hardship, the distribution of that hardship was uneven. Twenty percent of the work force had no jobs at all. Also at that time, there were virtually no organized social assistance and unemployment programs in place. So many families had virtually no income. But the pocketbooks of those who kept their jobs barely noticed the Great Depression. It is true that the money wage rate fell. But at the same time, the price level fell by almost exactly the same percentage, so the real wage rate remained constant. So those who had jobs continued to be paid a wage rate that had roughly the same buying power at the depth of the Great Depression as in 1929.

You can begin to appreciate the magnitude of the Great Depression if you compare it with the 1990–1991 recession. In 1990, real GDP fell by 3.4 percent. In comparison, from 1929 to 1933, it fell by 31 percent. A 1999 Great Depression of the same magnitude would lower income per person to its level of more than 20 years earlier.

Why the Great Depression Happened

The late 1920s were years of economic boom, but they were also years of increasing uncertainty. The main source of increased uncertainty was international. The world economy was going through tumultuous times. The patterns of world trade were changing as Britain, the traditional economic powerhouse of the world, began its period of relative economic decline and new economic powers such as Japan began to emerge. International currency fluctuations and the introduction of restrictive trade policies by many countries (see Chapter 33) further increased the uncertainty faced by firms. There was also domestic uncertainty arising from the fact that there had been such a strong boom in recent years, especially in the capital goods sector and housing. No one believed that this boom could continue, but there was great uncertainty as to when it would end and how the pattern of demand would change.

This environment of uncertainty led to a slow-down in consumer spending, especially on new homes and household appliances. By the fall of 1929, the uncertainty had reached a critical level and contributed to the stock market crash. The stock market crash, in turn, heightened people's fears about economic prospects in the foreseeable future. Fear fed fear. Investment collapsed. The building industry almost disappeared. An industry that had been operating flat out just two years earlier was now building virtually no new houses and apartments. It was this drop in investment and a drop in consumer spending on durables that led to the initial decrease in aggregate demand.

At this stage, what became the Great Depression was no worse than many previous recessions had been. What distinguishes the Great Depression from previous recessions are the events that followed between 1930 and 1933. But economists, even to this day, have not come to agreement on how to interpret those events. One view, argued by Peter Temin, is that spending continued to fall for a wide variety of reasons—including a continuation of increasing pessimism and uncertainty.[1] According to Temin's view, the continued contraction resulted from a collapse of expenditure that was independent of the decrease in the quantity of money. The investment demand curve shifted leftward. Milton Friedman and Anna J. Schwartz have argued that the continuation of the contraction was almost exclusively the result of the subsequent worsening of financial and monetary conditions in the United States.[2] According to Friedman and Schwartz, it was a severe cut in the quantity of U.S. money that lowered U.S. aggregate demand and that prolonged the contraction and deepened the depression. Recently, Ben Bernanke, Barry Eichengreen, and James Hamilton have added further to our understanding of the Great Depression by explaining how it was transmitted among countries by the attempts of central banks to increase their gold reserves.[3]

As a result of these recent efforts to probe more deeply into the causes of the Great Depression, the range of disagreement has narrowed. Everyone now agrees that increased pessimism and uncertainty lowered investment demand, and that there was a massive contraction of the quantity of real money. Temin and his supporters assign primary importance to the fall in autonomous expenditure and secondary importance to the fall in the quantity of money. Friedman and Schwartz and their supporters assign primary responsibility to the quantity of money and regard the other factors as being of limited importance.

Let's look at the contraction of U.S. money a bit more closely. Between 1929 and 1933, the nominal quantity of money in the United States decreased by 20 percent. This decrease in money was not directly induced by the Federal Reserve's actions. The *monetary base* (currency in circulation and bank reserves) hardly fell at all. But the bank deposits component of money suffered an enormous collapse. It did so primarily because a large number of banks failed. Before

[1]Peter Temin, *Did Monetary Forces Cause the Great Depression?* (New York: W. W. Norton, 1976).

[2]This explanation was developed by Milton Friedman and Anna J. Schwartz in *A Monetary History of the United States 1867–1960* (Princeton: Princeton University Press, 1963), Chapter 7.

[3]Ben Bernanke, "The Macroeconomics of the Great Depression: A Comparative Approach," *Journal of Money, Credit, and Banking,* 28 (1995), pp. 1–28; Barry Eichengreen, *Golden Fetters: The Gold Standard and the Great Depression, 1919–1939* (New York: Oxford University Press, 1992); and James Hamilton, "The Role of the International Gold Standard in Propagating the Great Depression," *Contemporary Policy Issues,* 6 (1988), pp. 67–89.

the Great Depression, fuelled by increasing stock prices and booming business conditions, bank loans expanded. But after the stock market crash and the downturn, many borrowers found themselves in hard economic times. They could not pay the interest on their loans, and they could not meet the agreed repayment schedules. Banks had deposits that exceeded the realistic value of the loans that they had made. When depositors withdrew funds from the banks, the banks lost reserves and many of them simply couldn't meet their depositors' demands to be repaid.

Bank failures feed on themselves and create additional failures. Seeing banks fail, people become anxious to protect themselves and so take their money out of the banks. Such were the events in the United States in 1930. The quantity of notes and coins in circulation increased and the volume of bank deposits declined. But the very action of taking money out of the bank to protect one's wealth accelerated the process of banking failure. Banks were increasingly short of cash and unable to meet their obligations.

Monetary contraction also occurred in Canada, although on a less serious scale than in the United States. In Canada, the quantity of money declined during 1929 to 1933 but at a steady 5 percent a year in contrast to the whopping 20 percent in the United States. Also, we had much less severe problems with bank failures than Americans did.

What role did the stock market crash of 1929 play in producing the Great Depression? It certainly created an atmosphere of fear and panic, and probably also contributed to the overall air of uncertainty that dampened investment spending. It also reduced the wealth of stockholders, encouraging them to cut back on their consumption spending. But the direct effect of the stock market crash on consumption, although a contributory factor to the Great Depression, was not the major source of the drop in aggregate demand. It was the collapse in investment arising from increased uncertainty that brought the 1930 decline in aggregate demand.

But the stock market crash was a predictor of severe recession. It reflected the expectations of stockholders concerning future profit prospects. As those expectations became pessimistic, people sold their stocks. There were more sellers than buyers and the prices of stocks were bid lower and lower. That is, the behaviour of the stock market was a consequence of expectations about future profitability and those expectations were lowered as a result of increased uncertainty.

Can It Happen Again?

Since, even today, we have an incomplete understanding of the causes of the Great Depression, we are not able to predict such an event or to be sure that it cannot occur again. But there are some significant differences between the economy of the 2000s and that of the 1930s that make a severe depression much less likely today than it was 60 years ago. The most significant features of the economy that make severe depression less likely today are

- Bank deposit insurance
- Bank of Canada's role as lender of last resort
- Taxes and government spending
- Multi-income families

Let's examine these in turn.

Bank Deposit Insurance In 1967, the government of Canada established the Canada Deposit Insurance Corporation (CDIC). The CDIC insures bank deposits for up to $60,000 per deposit so that most depositors need no longer fear bank failure. If a bank fails, the CDIC pays the deposit holders.

Similar arrangements have been introduced in the United States, where deposits up to $100,000 are insured by the Federal Deposit Insurance Corporation. With government-insured bank deposits, the key event that turned a fairly ordinary recession into the Great Depression is most unlikely to occur. It was the fear of bank failure that caused people to withdraw their deposits from banks. The aggregate consequence of these individually rational acts was to cause the very bank failures that were feared. With deposit insurance, most depositors have nothing to lose if a bank fails and so have no incentive to take actions that are likely to give rise to that failure.

Although bank failure was not a severe problem in Canada during the Great Depression, it clearly was an important factor in intensifying the depression in the United States. And the severity of the U.S. depression had an impact on Canada and the rest of the world.

Bank of Canada's Role as Lender of Last Resort
The Bank of Canada is the lender of last resort in the Canadian economy. If a single bank is short of reserves, it can borrow reserves from other banks. If the entire banking system is short of reserves, banks can borrow from the Bank of Canada. By making reserves available (at a suitable interest rate), the Bank

of Canada is able to make the quantity of reserves in the banking system respond flexibly to the demand for those reserves. Bank failure can be prevented, or at least contained, to cases where bad management practices are the source of the problem. Widespread failures of the type that occurred in the Great Depression can be prevented.

It is interesting to note, in this regard, that during the weeks following the October 1987 stock market crash, Bank of Canada Governor John Crow and Federal Reserve Chairman Alan Greenspan used every opportunity available to remind the world banking and financial community of their ability and readiness to maintain calm financial conditions and to supply sufficient reserves to ensure that the banking system did not begin to contract.

Taxes and Government Spending   The government sector was a much smaller part of the economy in 1929 than it has become today. On the eve of that earlier recession, government expenditures on goods and services were less than 11 percent of GDP. Today, government expenditures exceed 20 percent of GDP. Government transfer payments were about 5 percent of GDP in 1929. Today, they are 20 percent of GDP.

A larger level of government expenditures on goods and services means that when recession hits, a large component of aggregate demand does not decline. But it is government transfer payments that are the most sensitive economic stabilizer. When the economy goes into recession and depression, more people qualify for unemployment benefits and social assistance. As a consequence, although disposable income decreases, the extent of the decrease is moderated by the existence of such programs. Consumption expenditure, in turn, does not decline by as much as it would in the absence of such government programs. The limited decline in consumption spending further limits the overall decrease in aggregate expenditure, thereby limiting the magnitude of an economic downturn.

Multi-Income Families   At the time of the Great Depression, families with more than one wage earner were much less common than they are today. The labour force participation rate in 1929 was 58 percent. Today, it is 66 percent. Thus even if the unemployment rate increased to around 20 percent today, close to 53 percent of the adult population would actually have jobs. During the Great Depression, only

46 percent of the adult population had work. Multi-income families have greater security than single-income families. The chance of both (or all) income earners in a family losing their jobs simultaneously is much lower than the chance of a single earner losing work. With greater family income security, family consumption is likely to be less sensitive to fluctuations in family income that are seen as temporary. Thus when aggregate income falls, it does not induce a cut in consumption. For example, during the 1982 and 1990–1991 recessions, as real GDP fell personal consumption expenditure actually increased.

For the four reasons we have just reviewed, it appears the economy has better shock-absorbing characteristics today than it had in the 1920s and 1930s. Even if there is a collapse of confidence leading to a decrease in investment, the recession mechanism that is now in place will not translate that initial shock into the large and prolonged decrease in real GDP and increase in unemployment that occurred more than 60 years ago.

Because the economy is now more immune to severe recession than it was in the 1930s, even a stock market crash of the magnitude that occurred in 1987 had barely noticeable effects on spending. A crash of a similar magnitude in 1929 resulted in the near collapse of housing investment and consumer durable purchases. In the period following the 1987 stock market crash, investment and spending on durable goods hardly changed.

None of this is to say that there might not be a deep recession or even a Great Depression in the future. But it would take a very severe shock to trigger one.

◆   We have now completed our study of the business cycle. You can put what you've learned to work examining the prospects for expansion and recession in the United States and Canada in *Reading Between the Lines* on pp. 750–751.

We have also completed our study of the science of macroeconomics and learned about the influences on long-term economic growth and inflation as well as the business cycle. We have discovered that these issues pose huge policy challenges. How can we speed up the rate of economic growth while at the same time keeping inflation low and avoiding big swings of the business cycle? Our task in the next chapter is to study these macroeconomic policy challenges.

Fighting a North American Recession

OTTAWA CITIZEN, NOVEMBER 7, 2002

U.S. Fed battles prospect of double-dip

Increasingly worried that U.S. economic growth is close to stalling, Federal Reserve officials cut a key short-term interest rate yesterday to its lowest level in more than four decades to help lift the economy over what they called "this current soft spot."

The Fed's top policy-making group, the Federal Open Market Committee, cut its target for overnight interest rates by a half-percentage point to 1.25 per cent. Separately, the Fed reduced a companion rate governing what banks pay when they borrow from a regional Federal Reserve bank to only 0.75 per cent, the lowest in the Fed's 89-year history.

Those extraordinarily low rates are a sign of how seriously Fed Chairman Alan Greenspan and other Fed officials regard the failure of the U.S. economy to sustain a stronger recovery this year.

In Ottawa last night, Finance Minister John Manley said the lack of confidence in the U.S. economy shown in yesterday's steeper-than-expected interest-rate cut makes the Canadian government more cautious about risks in its fiscal forecasts. "If the U.S. economy goes back into recession, it will definitely affect us," he told business executives and financial workers at a budget-consultation meeting. ...

The half-point rate cut is seen as good news for the Canadian economy, which itself emitted further symptoms of weakness yesterday with news that builders have cut construction plans and that bankruptcies have edged up.

"With this kind of a shot in the arm, maybe the U.S. economy will improve in '03 and that will help Canada," said Patti Croft, economist at Sceptre Investment Counsel Ltd.

Statistics Canada said the value of building permits fell in September for the second straight month in both residential and the non-residential sectors, and Industry Canada said there were 7,347 business and consumer bankruptcies in September, up six per cent from 6,920 a year earlier. ...

Southam News/Southam Publications.

Essence of the Story

■ The U.S. economy was in a weak expansion from recession in November 2002 and the Federal Reserve (the Fed) wanted to avoid a slip into a second recession.

■ To prevent recession, the Fed cut overnight interest rates by a half-percentage point to 1.25 percent and cut the discount rate (like Canada's bank rate) to 0.75 percent, the lowest in the Fed's 89-year history.

■ The Canadian economy also showed symptoms of slower growth with the value of building permits falling for a second straight month and bankruptcies increasing.

■ The cut in the U.S. interest rate was seen as good news for Canada.

■ Finance Minister John Manley said that a U.S. recession would place a strain on the Canadian government's budget.

Economic Analysis

- The United States went into recession in March 2001 and a new expansion probably began before the end of 2001.

- But the expansion was slow and real GDP remained below potential GDP through 2002.

- Figure 1 shows the path of potential GDP and real GDP in the United States from the first quarter of 2000 to the third quarter of 2002.

- In mid-2001, the U.S. economy moved from above-full employment equilibrium with an inflationary gap to below-full employment equilibrium with a recessionary gap.

- Figure 2 illustrates the situation in the United States at the end of 2002 using the *AS–AD* model.

- Potential GDP was $9,600 billion on long-run aggregate supply curve *LAS*. Short-run aggregate supply was *SAS* and aggregate demand was AD_0.

- Equilibrium real GDP was $9,550 billion, the price level was 111, and there was a recessionary gap of $50 billion.

- The Federal Reserve feared that aggregate demand might decrease towards AD_1, which would bring recession.

- To try to avoid recession, the Federal Reserve cut the interest rate. The

hope was that the lower interest rate would increase aggregate demand towards AD_2 and restore full employment.

- Figure 3 illustrates the situation in Canada at the end of 2002 using the *AS–AD* model.

- Potential GDP was $1,065 billion on long-run aggregate supply curve *LAS*. Short-run aggregate supply was *SAS* and aggregate demand was AD_0.

- Equilibrium real GDP was $1,065 billion, the price level was 108, and there was full employment.

- A recession in the United States would decrease Canadian aggregate demand towards AD_1, and bring recession in Canada.

- Signs of a decrease in Canadian aggregate demand—falling building permits and increasing bankruptcies—were already present in the fourth quarter of 2002.

- The forces leading to a decrease in Canadian aggregate demand might be countered by a higher real GDP in the United States.

- If U.S. aggregate demand increased to AD_2 (in Fig. 2), U.S. demand for Canadian-produced goods and services would increase, so Canadian aggregate demand might remain close to AD_0 (in Fig. 3) with the economy at full employment.

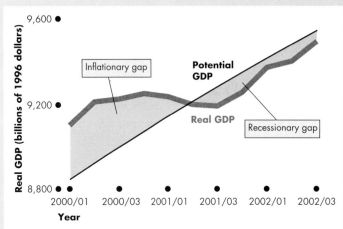

Figure 1 U.S. real GDP and potential GDP: 2000–2002

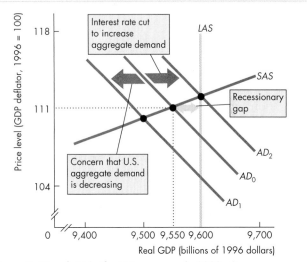

Figure 2 *AS* and *AD* in the U.S. economy in 2002

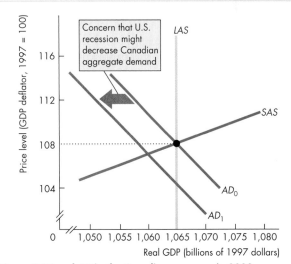

Figure 3 *AS* and *AD* in the Canadian economy in 2002

SUMMARY

KEY POINTS

Cycle Patterns, Impulses, and Mechanisms (pp. 730)

- The economy can be hit (like a tennis ball), cycle indefinitely (like the turning of day into night), and cycle in swings that get milder until another shock hits (like a rocking horse).

Aggregate Demand Theories of the Business Cycle (pp. 731–736)

- Keynesian business cycle theory identifies volatile expectations about future sales and profits as the main source of economic fluctuations.
- Monetarist business cycle theory identifies fluctuations in the quantity of money as the main source of economic fluctuations.
- Rational expectations theory identifies unanticipated fluctuations in aggregate demand as the main source of economic fluctuations.

Real Business Cycle Theory (pp. 737–741)

- In real business cycle (RBC) theory, economic fluctuations are caused by fluctuations in the influence of technological change on productivity growth.
- A temporary slowdown in the pace of technological change decreases investment demand and both the demand for labour and supply of labour.

Recessions During the 1990s (pp. 741–745)

- The 1990–1991 recession resulted from tight monetary policy, a slowdown in the United States, and adjustments to the Canada–United States Free Trade Agreement.
- The Japanese slowdown and recession of the 1990s was triggered by an asset price collapse combined with structural problems. Policy stimulation occurred but it was not sufficient to prevent recession, and a tightening of fiscal policy in 1996 and 1997 contributed to the 1998 recession.

The Great Depression (pp. 746–749)

- The Great Depression started with increased uncertainty, which brought a decrease in investment (especially in housing) and spending on consumer durables.
- There then followed a near total collapse of the financial system. Banks failed and the quantity of money decreased, resulting in a continued decrease in aggregate demand.
- The Great Depression itself produced a series of reforms that make a repeat of such a depression much less likely.

KEY FIGURES

Figure 31.1   The Keynesian Cycle, 731
Figure 31.2   A Keynesian Inflationary Gap, 732
Figure 31.3   A Monetarist Recession, 733
Figure 31.5   A Rational Expectations Business Cycle, 735
Figure 31.7   Capital and Labour Markets in a Real Business Cycle, 739
Figure 31.8   *AS–AD* in a Real Business Cycle, 740
Figure 31.11   The 1990–1991 Recession, 743

KEY TERMS

Keynesian theory of the business cycle, 731
Monetarist theory of the business cycle, 732
New classical theory of the business cycle, 734
New Keynesian theory of the business cycle, 734
Rational expectation, 734
Real business cycle theory, 737

PROBLEMS

*1. The figure shows the economy of Virtual Reality. When the economy is in a long-run equilibrium, it is at points *B, F,* and *J.* When a recession occurs in Virtual Reality, the economy moves away from these points to one of the three other points identified in each part of the figure.

   a. If the Keynesian theory is the correct explanation for the recession, to which points does the economy move?

   b. If the monetarist theory is the correct explanation for the recession, to which points does the economy move?

   c. If the new classical rational expectations theory is the correct explanation for the recession, to which points does the economy move?

   d. If the new Keynesian rational expectations theory is the correct explanation for the recession, to which points does the economy move?

   e. If real business cycle theory is the correct explanation for the recession, to which points does the economy move?

2. The figure shows the economy of Vital Signs. When the economy is in a long-run equilibrium, it is at points *A, E,* and *I.* When an expansion occurs in Vital Signs, the economy moves away from these points to one of the three other points identified in each part of the figure.

   a. If the Keynesian theory is the correct explanation for the expansion, to which points does the economy move?

   b. If the monetarist theory is the correct explanation for the expansion, to which points does the economy move?

   c. If the new classical rational expectations theory is the correct explanation for the expansion, to which points does the economy move?

   d. If the new Keynesian rational expectations theory is the correct explanation for the expansion, to which points does the economy move?

   e. If real business cycle theory is the correct explanation for the expansion, to which points does the economy move?

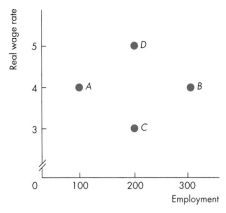

(a) Labour market

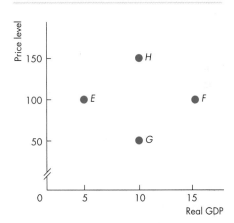

(b) AS–AD

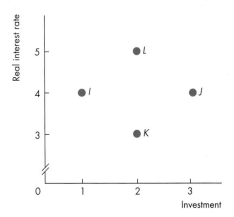

(c) Investment

*3. Suppose that when the recession occurs in Virtual Reality, the economy moves to *D*, *G*, and *K*. Which theory of the business cycle, if any, explains this outcome?

4. Suppose that when the expansion occurs in Vital Signs, the economy moves to *D*, *H*, and *L*. Which theory of the business cycle, if any, explains this outcome?

*5. Suppose that when the recession occurs in Virtual Reality, the economy moves to *C*, *G*, and *K*. Which theory of the business cycle, if any, explains this outcome?

6. Suppose that when the expansion occurs in Vital Signs, the economy moves to *C*, *H*, and *L*. Which theory of the business cycle, if any, explains this outcome?

*7. Suppose that when the recession occurs in Virtual Reality, the economy moves to *D*, *H*, and *K*. Which theory of the business cycle, if any, explains this outcome?

8. Suppose that when the expansion occurs in Vital Signs, the economy moves to *D*, *G*, and *L*. Which theory of the business cycle, if any, explains this outcome?

*9. Suppose that when the recession occurs in Virtual Reality, the economy moves to *C*, *H*, and *K*. Which theory of the business cycle, if any, explains this outcome?

10. Suppose that when the expansion occurs in Vital Signs, the economy moves to *C*, *G*, and *L*. Which theory of the business cycle, if any, explains this outcome?

*11. Suppose that when the recession occurs in Virtual Reality, the economy moves to *D*, *G*, and *L*. Which theory of the business cycle, if any, explains this outcome?

12. Suppose that when the expansion occurs in Vital Signs, the economy moves to *C*, *H*, and *K*. Which theory of the business cycle, if any, explains this outcome?

*13. Suppose that when the recession occurs in Virtual Reality, the economy moves to *C*, *G*, and *L*. Which theory of the business cycle, if any, explains this outcome?

14. Suppose that when the expansion occurs in Vital Signs, the economy moves to *D*, *H*, and *K*. Which theory of the business cycle, if any, explains this outcome?

CRITICAL THINKING

1. Study *Reading Between the Lines* on pp. 750–751 and then answer the following questions:
   a. What does this news article see as the uncertainties for the Canadian economy in 2003?
   b. What does the article regard as symptoms that slower growth might be ahead?
   c. How would a U.S. recession affect John Manley's budget problems?
   d. What policy actions, if any, do you think the Bank of Canada or Parliament of Canada needs to take in 2003 and 2004 to keep the economy growing and to prevent a new recession?
   e. Do you think any policy actions the Bank of Canada or Parliament of Canada might take can work if the U.S. economy goes into recession?
   f. What is the main danger facing Canada in 2003, inflation or recession?

2. Describe the changes in real GDP, employment and unemployment, and the price level that occurred during the Great Depression years of 1929–1933.

WEB EXERCISES

1. Use the links on the Parkin–Bade Web site to obtain information on the current state of the Canadian economy. Then
   a. List all of the features of the economy during the current year that you can think of that are consistent with a pessimistic outlook for the next two years.
   b. List all of the features of the economy during the current year that you can think of that are consistent with an optimistic outlook for the next two years.
   c. Drawing on the pessimistic and optimistic factors that you have listed in parts (a) and (b) and on your knowledge of macroeconomic theory, explain how you think the Canadian economy is going to evolve over the next year or two.

MACROECONOMIC POLICY CHALLENGES

What Can Policy Do?

From 1995 through 2000, the Canadian economy performed well. Real GDP expanded, unemployment fell, the inflation rate was steady, and a federal government budget deficit was turned into a surplus. ◆ But by 2001, growth was slowing, and in 2002 unemployment turned upward. ◆ Canada was not alone in facing a growth slowdown. Every other major country in the so-called Group of Seven saw its economy slow. ◆ Prime ministers and finance ministers began to talk of stimulus packages. And some people talked about a concerted global stimulus package. But not everyone agreed that the economy needed government stimulation. ◆ What can and should policymakers do to achieve a desirable macroeconomic performance?

◆ In this chapter, we're going to study the challenges of achieving sustainable long-term growth and low unemployment, and of avoiding inflation. We're also going to review the alternative views on these issues. At the end of the chapter, in *Reading Between the Lines*, you can examine the macroeconomic policy problems facing the Canadian economy and the global economy today.

After studying this chapter, you will be able to

■ Describe the goals of macro-economic policy

■ Describe the main features of fiscal policy and monetary policy since 1971

■ Explain how fiscal policy and monetary policy influence long-term economic growth

■ Distinguish between and evaluate fixed-rule and feedback-rule policies to stabilize the business cycle

■ Evaluate fixed-rule and feedback-rule policies to contain inflation and explain why lowering inflation usually brings recession

Policy Goals

MACROECONOMIC POLICY GOALS FALL INTO TWO big categories: domestic and international. We will study international macroeconomic policy issues in Chapters 33 and 34. Here, we focus on domestic policy. The four main domestic macroeconomic policy goals are to

- Achieve the highest sustainable rate of potential GDP growth
- Smooth out avoidable business cycle fluctuations
- Maintain low unemployment
- Maintain low inflation

Potential GDP Growth

Rapid sustained real GDP growth can make a profound contribution to economic well-being. With a growth rate of 2 percent a year, it takes more than 30 years for production to double. With a growth rate of 5 percent a year, production more than doubles in just 15 years. And with a growth rate of 10 percent a year, as some Asian countries are achieving, production doubles in just 7 years. The limits to *sustainable* growth are determined by the availability of natural resources, by environmental considerations, and by the willingness of people to save and invest in new capital and new technologies rather than consume everything they produce.

How fast can the economy grow over the long term? Between 1988 and 2001, through a complete business cycle, potential GDP grew at a rate of 2.7 percent a year in Canada. But the Canadian population grew at a rate of 1.1 percent a year, so the growth rate of real GDP per person was about 1.6 percent a year. A growth rate of real GDP per person of 1.6 percent a year means that output per person would double every 45 years. Most economists believe that the Canadian economy can maintain a long-term growth rate of potential GDP of more than 2.7 percent a year. A few economists believe that with the right policies, sustainable growth of 5 percent a year is possible. This growth rate would double output per person every 18 years, increase it more than sixfold over 48 years, and increase it more than twelvefold in 65 years. So increasing the long-term growth rate is of critical importance.

The Business Cycle

Potential GDP probably does not grow at a constant rate. Fluctuations in the pace of technological advance and in the pace of investment in new capital bring fluctuations in potential GDP. So some fluctuations in real GDP represent fluctuations in potential GDP. But when real GDP grows less quickly than potential GDP, output is lost, and when real GDP grows more quickly than potential GDP, bottlenecks arise. Keeping real GDP growth steady and equal to potential GDP growth avoids these problems.

It is not known how smooth real GDP growth can be made. Real business cycle theory regards all the fluctuations in real GDP as fluctuations in potential GDP. The aggregate demand theories regard most of the fluctuations in real GDP as being avoidable deviations from potential GDP.

Unemployment

When real GDP grows more slowly than potential GDP, unemployment rises above the natural rate of unemployment. The higher the unemployment rate, the longer is the time taken by unemployed people to find jobs. Productive labour is wasted, and there is a slowdown in the accumulation of human capital. If high unemployment persists, serious psychological and social problems arise for the unemployed workers and their families.

When real GDP grows more quickly than potential GDP, unemployment decreases and falls below the natural rate of unemployment. The lower the unemployment rate, the harder it becomes for expanding industries to get the labour they need to keep growing. If extremely low unemployment persists, serious bottlenecks and production dislocations occur.

Keeping unemployment at the natural rate avoids both of these problems. But just what is the natural rate of unemployment? Assessments vary. The actual average unemployment rate over the most recent business cycle—1988 to 2001—was 8.9 percent. Few economists would think the natural rate to be as high as this number. And most believe that the natural rate has fallen in recent years. Real business cycle theorists believe that the natural rate fluctuates and always equals the actual unemployment rate.

If the natural rate of unemployment becomes high, then a goal of policy becomes lowering the natural rate itself. This goal is independent of smoothing the business cycle.

Inflation

When inflation fluctuates unpredictably, money becomes less useful as a measuring rod for conducting transactions. In extreme cases, it becomes useless and is abandoned as the means of payment. Borrowers and lenders and employers and workers must take on extra risks. Keeping the inflation rate steady and predictable avoids these problems.

What is the most desirable inflation rate? Some economists say that the *rate* of inflation doesn't matter much as long as the rate is *predictable*. But most economists believe that price stability, which they translate as an inflation rate of between 0 and 3 percent a year, is desirable. The reason why zero is not the target is that some price increases are due to quality improvements—a measurement bias in the price index—so a *measured* inflation rate of between 0 and 3 percent a year is equivalent to price stability.

The Two Core Policy Indicators: Real GDP Growth and Inflation

Although macroeconomic policy pursues the four goals we've just considered, the goals are not independent ones. Three of these goals—increasing the real GDP growth rate, smoothing the business cycle, and maintaining low unemployment—are linked together. Real GDP growth tells us directly about the long-term goal of high sustainable growth and the business cycle. It also has a strong link to unemployment. If growth becomes too rapid, unemployment falls below the natural rate, and if growth becomes too slow, unemployment rises above the natural rate. So keeping real GDP growing steadily at its maximum sustainable rate is equivalent to avoiding business fluctuations and keeping unemployment at the natural rate.

There are some connections between real GDP growth and inflation, but over the long run, these two variables are largely independent. So two variables, real GDP growth and inflation, are the core policy targets.

Policy performance, judged by the two core policy targets—real GDP growth and inflation—is shown in Fig. 32.1. Here the red line shows real GDP growth. As we've noted, real GDP growth has averaged 3.3 percent a year. But the growth rate has fluctuated between a high of 7.2 percent in 1973 and a low of −2.9 percent in 1982. The height of the green shaded area shows inflation. The inflation rate exploded during the 1970s, and then fell through the 1980s. During the 1990s, inflation has been low.

FIGURE 32.1 Macroeconomic Performance: Real GDP and Inflation

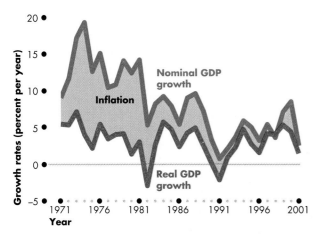

Real GDP growth and inflation fluctuate a great deal, and during the 1970s, inflation (the height of the green shaded area) mushroomed and real GDP growth slowed. This macroeconomic performance falls far short of the goals of a high and stable real GDP growth rate and low and predictable inflation.

Sources: Statistics Canada, CANSIM table 380-0002 and authors' calculations.

REVIEW QUIZ

1 Why does macroeconomic stabilization policy try to achieve the highest sustainable rate of potential GDP growth, small business cycle fluctuations, low unemployment, and low inflation?
2 Can stabilization policy keep the unemployment rate below the natural rate?
3 Why are real GDP growth and inflation the two core policy indicators?

We've examined the policy goals. Let's now look at the policy tools and the way they have been used.

Policy Tools and Performance

THE TOOLS THAT ARE USED TO TRY TO ACHIEVE macroeconomic performance objectives are fiscal policy and monetary policy.

Fiscal policy, which is described in Chapter 24, is the use of the federal budget to achieve macroeconomic objectives. The detailed fiscal policy tools are tax rates, benefit rates, and government expenditures on goods and services. These tools work by influencing aggregate supply and aggregate demand in the ways explained in Chapter 22.

Monetary policy, which is described in Chapter 26, is the adjustment of the quantity of money and interest rates by the Bank of Canada to achieve macroeconomic objectives. These tools work by changing aggregate demand.

How have these policy tools been used in Canada? Let's answer this question by summarizing the main directions of fiscal and monetary policy in recent years.

Fiscal Policy Since 1971

Figure 32.2 gives a broad summary of fiscal policy from 1971 to 2001. It shows the levels of government revenues and outlays and the budget balance (each as a percentage of GDP). So that you can see the political context of fiscal policy, the figure also shows the election years and the names of the incumbent prime ministers.

Fiscal policy was neutral during the early 1970s, when Pierre Trudeau was prime minister. It then became expansionary before the 1976 election. Trudeau won that election, and during his next term as prime minister, spending exploded and so did the deficit. At this time, fiscal policy was strongly expansionary.

The Progressive Conservatives replaced the Liberals, and Brian Mulroney became prime minister in 1984. The Mulroney years were a period of spending cuts and modest tax increases and overall fiscal policy was contractionary during these years.

The Liberals returned to power in the election of 1993, and during 1994 through 1998, Prime Minister Jean Chrétien and Finance Minister Paul

---

FIGURE 32.2   The Fiscal Policy Record: A Summary

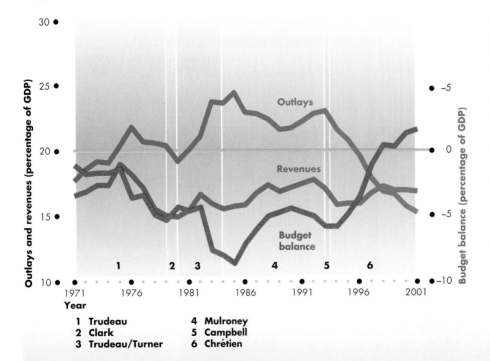

When Pierre Trudeau was prime minister, fiscal policy was expansionary—outlays and the deficit increased. When Brian Mulroney was prime minister, fiscal policy was contractionary—outlays were cut, revenues increased, and deficit decreased. When Jean Chrétien was prime minister, fiscal policy continued to be contractionary—outlays were cut further and the deficit was eventually eliminated. Cyclical fluctuations in outlays, revenues, and the deficit followed the business cycle.

1 Trudeau
2 Clark
3 Trudeau/Turner
4 Mulroney
5 Campbell
6 Chrétien

Source: Statistics Canada, CANSIM tables 380-0002 and 380-0007.

Martin cut outlays and reduced the deficit. By 1998, aided by strong real GDP growth, the deficit was finally eliminated and a surplus was achieved for the first time since 1970.

Recall that the Canadian economy experienced a recession during 1982 and again during 1990–1991. You can see, in Fig. 32.2, that in these two recessions, outlays increased, revenues decreased, and the deficit increased. But when the economy expanded after the recessions, outlays decreased, revenues increased, and the deficit decreased.

Let's now look at monetary policy.

Monetary Policy Since 1971

Figure 32.3 shows three broad measures of monetary policy. They are the growth rate of M2+, the overnight loans rate, and the real overnight loans rate.

The M2+ growth rate provides a broad indication of the influence of monetary policy on aggregate demand.

The overnight loans rate is the interest rate on large-scale loans that chartered banks make to each other and to dealers in financial markets. The Bank of Canada sets a target range for the overnight loans rate and takes actions to keep the rate inside its target range (see Chapter 26, p. 608). Movements in the overnight loans rate tell us how the Bank is acting to change money growth. When the overnight loans rate rises, the Bank is tightening; and when it falls, the Bank is loosening its grip on money growth.

The real overnight rate tells us how the Bank of Canada's actions eventually ripple through the economy to influence spending plans. It is the real interest rate, not the nominal rate, to which expenditure plans respond.

Figure 32.3 also identifies the election years, the prime ministers, and the Bank of Canada governors. The Bank has had four governors during this period. Notice that the term of a governor does not coincide with the term of a government, and the governor's term extends across the terms of several governments.

There are four distinct phases of monetary policy. In the first phase, between 1971 and 1980, inflation was rapid and so was money growth. During this

---

FIGURE 32.3   The Monetary Policy Record: A Summary

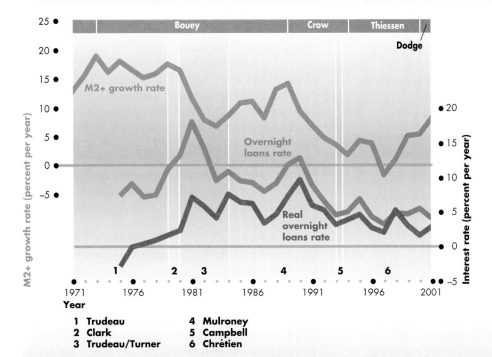

Monetary policy is summarized here by the growth rate of M2+ and by the overnight loans rate. The M2+ growth rate was extremely high during the first Trudeau term but slowed during Trudeau's second term. It increased and then decreased again during Mulroney's term. M2+ growth remained low during most of Chrétien's term but began to increase in the late 1990s and 2000s.

1 Trudeau   4 Mulroney
2 Clark   5 Campbell
3 Trudeau/Turner   6 Chrétien

Sources: Bank of Canada and *The Monetary Summary Record: A Summary;* data calculated in part from the Statistics Canada CANSIM II database, table 380-0031.

period, the nominal interest rate was not much higher than the inflation rate, so the real interest rate was close to zero.

In the second phase, during the early 1980s, Bank of Canada governor Gerald Bouey embarked on a concerted anti-inflation policy. The money growth rate fell, and interest rates increased. As a result of these actions, the inflation rate fell from around 10 percent a year to less than 5 percent a year.

In the third phase, which began in 1989 when John Crow was governor of the Bank of Canada, a further attack on inflation was launched to achieve price stability. The money growth rate fell again, and interest rates increased.

In the fourth phase, which began in 1994 when Gordon Thiessen became governor of the Bank of Canada and which has continued into David Dodge's term as governor, the challenge has been to keep inflation at its new low level but to pursue a monetary policy that permits the economy to expand and to bring lower unemployment. The M2+ growth trend has been downward, and falling inflation has lowered the nominal interest rate and achieved a remarkably steady real interest rate.

You can see that monetary policy has had a long-term anti-inflation focus rather than a short-term business cycle focus. You can also see that there is no tendency for monetary policy to be linked to the timing of elections. The Bank of Canada has pursued its monetary policy to achieve its economic objectives and has been immune from political pressures to change the course of monetary policy for short-term political gains.

REVIEW QUIZ

1 What were the main features and effects of fiscal policy during the terms of the various prime ministers during the 1980s and 1990s?
2 What were the main features and effects of monetary policy during the 1980s and 1990s? In which periods was monetary policy inflationary? In which periods was it used to fight inflation?

Now that we've examined the goals of policy and the policy actions of the past, we're going to look at ways in which policy might be used better to achieve its goals.

Long-Term Growth Policy

THE SOURCES OF THE LONG-TERM GROWTH OF potential GDP, which are explained in Chapter 30 (pp. 711–712), are the accumulation of physical and human capital and the advance of technology. Chapter 30 briefly examines the range of policies that might achieve faster growth. Here, we probe more deeply into the problem of boosting the long-term growth rate.

Monetary policy can contribute to long-term growth by keeping the inflation rate low. (Chapter 28, pp. 660–661, explains some connections between inflation and growth.) Fiscal policy and other policies can also contribute to growth by influencing the private decisions on which long-term growth depends in three areas. All growth policies increase

- National saving
- Investment in human capital
- Investment in new technologies

National Saving

National saving equals private saving plus government saving. Figure 32.4 shows the private and government components of national saving between 1971 and 2001. Over this period, national saving (the green line) fluctuated around an average of 20 percent of GDP. It ranged between a low of 17 percent in 1993 and a high of 27 percent in 1974.

Private saving (the blue line) increased to 25 percent of GDP in 1975 and remained fairly steady until 1993 when it began to decrease. By 2001, private saving had decreased to 15 percent of GDP. Government saving (the vertical gap between the blue line and the green line) was positive before 1976, became negative (government dissaving) during the 1980s and early 1990s, and returned to positive in 1997.

The data you have just examined are for *gross* saving. Each year, national wealth grows by the amount of *net* saving, which equals gross saving minus the value of capital that is scrapped during the year. Figure 32.4 shows net saving as a percentage of GDP. You can see that net national saving (the red line) has had a downward trend through the period 1971 to 2001. Gross national saving minus net national saving is the average depreciation of capital. In 1971, depreciation was about 11 percent of GDP. Over the period from 1971 to 2001, depreciation gradually increased to 13 percent of GDP. Because depreciation has gradually increased, the fluctuations in net national saving are similar to those in gross national saving.

Canadian investment, which is one of the engines of real GDP growth, is not limited by Canadian saving. The reason is that Canadians can borrow abroad to finance domestic investment. And foreigners can invest some of their saving directly in Canadian businesses. Either way, the foreign saving boosts Canadian real GDP growth. Also, because all investment, regardless of how it is financed, creates jobs, the boost in Canadian incomes leads to an increase in national saving. Further, by using foreign saving along with domestic saving, Canadians can invest in a wider range of potentially profitable business enterprises and can better spread their risks across traditional and high-return new technologies.

FIGURE 32.4   Saving Rates in Canada: 1971–2001

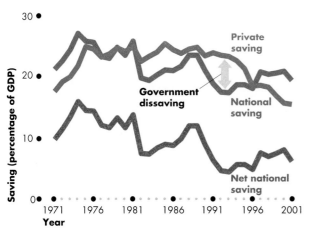

Gross national saving (green line) ranged between 17 percent in 1993 and 27 percent in 1974. Private saving (blue line) increased to 25 percent of GDP in 1975, remained steady until 1993, then decreased. Government saving (the vertical gap between the blue line and the green line) was positive before 1975, became negative during the 1980s and early 1990s, and positive again in the late 1990s. Net national saving (red line) has fluctuated, but it has had a downward trend.

Source: Statistics Canada, CANSIM table 380–0031.

How can national saving be increased? The two points of attack are

- Increasing government saving
- Increasing private saving

Increasing Government Saving   Government saving was negative between 1976 and 1997, and its average during the 1990s was –0.7 percent of GDP. But government saving increased after 1993 as the federal budget deficit was gradually eliminated and replaced by a surplus. Maintaining a federal budget surplus will be hard work and will be achieved only by resisting increases in social programs and educational and health-care expenditures.

Increasing Private Saving   Private saving has fallen from its average of 24 percent of GDP in the period 1975 to 1993. Private saving in 2001 was the lowest it has been since 1971. The main way in which government actions can boost private saving is by increasing the after-tax rate of return on saving. This is what government policy has sought to do, but on only one type of asset: Registered Retirement Savings Plans (RRSPs) and pension funds. By putting their savings into RRSPs and pension funds, people can avoid income tax on their interest income. But they cannot use their RRSPs (without a tax penalty) until they retire. Also, there are limits to the amount that can be accumulated tax-free in an RRSP and a pension fund each year.

Private saving probably could be stimulated more effectively by cutting taxes on interest income and capital gains and by replacing the lost government revenue from such a tax cut with an increase in the Goods and Services Tax (GST) or an increase in the tax on labour income. But such a move would be regarded as inequitable and probably not politically feasible. So governments are limited to making minor changes to the taxation of interest income, and these changes will have negligible effects on the saving rate.

Private Saving and Inflation   Inflation erodes the value of money and other financial assets such as bonds, and uncertainty about future inflation discourages saving. So a monetary policy that preserves stable prices and minimizes uncertainty about the future value of money stimulates saving. Chapter 28 (pp. 660–661) spells out the broader connection between inflation and real GDP and explains why low inflation brings greater output and faster growth.

Investment in Human Capital

The accumulation of human capital plays a crucial role in economic growth, and three areas are relevant: education, on-the-job experience, and health care. Economic research shows that education, on-the-job training, and good health yield high rates of return.

On the average, the greater the number of years a person remains in school, the higher are that person's earnings. A university graduate earns more, on the average, than does a college graduate, who in turn earns more than does a high school graduate. Again on the average, a person with ten years of work experience earns more than an otherwise identical person who has no work experience. Similarly, and again on the average, the better a person's health, the more productive is that person.

So, by providing subsidized education, governments can increase the rate of investment in human capital and boost the rate of real GDP growth. By keeping unemployment low, the government can increase the number of people who have work experience and again increase the rate of investment in human capital. And by providing comprehensive high-quality health-care services, the government can help to build a more productive labour force.

But if education, on-the-job experience, and good health yield higher earnings, why, you might be wondering, does the government need a policy that increases the rate of investment in human capital? Why can't people simply be left to get on with making their own decisions about how much human capital to acquire?

The answer is that the *social* returns to human capital probably exceed the *private* returns. Some of the productivity of human capital comes from the *interactions* of people who are well endowed with human capital. The greater the number of well-educated, experienced, and healthy people, the greater is the productivity of each person. The design and production of just about every good and service benefits from team efforts.

When each person makes a decision about how much education or on-the-job training to get, the benefits that will accrue to others are ignored. So, left to ourselves, we would probably accumulate too little human capital. For this reason, free schooling and heavily subsidized college and university education is efficient. Tax deductibility of interest on student loans is also efficient. Countries that provide a good basic education and health care for everyone have a better economic growth performance, on the average, than countries that do not.

Investment in New Technologies

Investment in new technologies is the third area in which policy can influence economic growth. As Chapter 30 explains, investment in new technologies is special for two reasons. First, it appears not to run into the problem of diminishing returns that plague the other types of capital and the other factors of production. Second, the benefits of new technologies spill over to influence all parts of the economy, not just the firms undertaking the investment. For these reasons, increasing the rate of investment in new technologies is a promising way of boosting long-term growth. But how can government policy influence the pace of technological change?

The government can fund and provide tax incentives for research and development activities. Through the Natural Sciences Research Council, the universities, and various research establishments, the government funds a large amount of basic research.

Considering the payoff from faster growth and the payoff, therefore, from improved knowledge about the forces that create growth, it is surprising that more is not spent, both on research and development and on economic research on the causes of growth.

REVIEW QUIZ

1 Why do long-term growth policies focus on increasing saving and increasing investment in human capital and new technologies?
2 What has been the trend in the net national saving rate in Canada since 1971?
3 What actions can the government take that might increase the saving rate?
4 What actions can the government take that might increase the rate of investment in human capital?
5 What actions can the government take that might increase investment in new technologies?

We've seen how government might use its fiscal and monetary policies to influence long-term growth. How can it influence the business cycle and unemployment? Let's now address this question.

Business Cycle and Unemployment Policy

MANY DIFFERENT FISCAL AND MONETARY POLICIES can be pursued to stabilize the business cycle and cyclical unemployment. But all these policies fall into three broad categories:

- Fixed-rule policies
- Feedback-rule policies
- Discretionary policies

Fixed-Rule Policies

A **fixed-rule policy** specifies an action to be pursued independently of the state of the economy. An everyday life example of a fixed rule is a stop sign. It says, "Stop regardless of the state of the road ahead—even if no other vehicle is trying to use the road." One fixed-rule policy, proposed by Milton Friedman, is to keep the quantity of money growing at a constant rate year in and year out, regardless of the state of the economy, to make the *average* inflation rate zero. Another fixed-rule policy is to balance the federal budget. Fixed rules are rarely followed in practice, but they have some merits in principle. Later in this chapter, we will study how they would work if they were pursued.

Feedback-Rule Policies

A **feedback-rule policy** specifies how policy actions respond to changes in the state of the economy. A yield sign is an everyday feedback rule. It says, "Stop if another vehicle is attempting to use the road ahead, but otherwise, proceed." A macroeconomic feedback-rule policy is one that changes the quantity of money, interest rates, or even tax rates in response to the state of the economy. Some feedback rules guide the actions of policymakers. For example, the Bank of Canada used a feedback rule when it kept pushing interest rates ever higher through 1994 in response to persistently falling unemployment and strong real GDP growth. Other feedback-rule policies are automatic. Examples are the automatic increase in tax revenues and decrease in transfer payments during an expansion and the automatic decrease in tax revenues and increase in transfer payments during a recession.

Discretionary Policies

A **discretionary policy** responds to the state of the economy in a possibly unique way that uses all the information available, including perceived lessons from past "mistakes." An everyday discretionary policy occurs at an unmarked intersection. Each driver uses discretion in deciding whether to stop and how slowly to approach the intersection. Most macroeconomic policy actions have an element of discretion because every situation is to some degree unique. For example, through 1994, the Bank of Canada raised interest rates several times but by small increments. The Bank might have delayed cutting rates until it was sure that lower rates were needed and then cut them in larger increments. The Bank used discretion based on lessons it had learned from earlier expansions. But despite the fact that all policy actions have an element of discretion, they can be regarded as modifications of a basic feedback-rule policy.

We'll study the effects of business cycle policy by comparing the performance of real GDP and the price level under a fixed rule and a feedback rule. Because the business cycle can result from demand shocks or supply shocks, we need to consider these two cases. We'll begin by studying demand shocks.

Stabilizing Aggregate Demand Shocks

We'll study an economy that starts out at full employment and has no inflation. Figure 32.5 illustrates this situation. The economy is on aggregate demand curve AD_0 and short-run aggregate supply curve SAS. These curves intersect at point A on the long-run aggregate supply curve, LAS. The GDP deflator is 110, and real GDP is $1,000 billion. Now suppose that there is an unexpected and temporary decrease in aggregate demand. Let's see what happens.

Perhaps investment decreases because of a wave of pessimism about the future, or perhaps exports decrease because of a recession in the rest of the world. Regardless of the origin of the decrease in aggregate demand, the aggregate demand curve shifts leftward, to AD_1 in Fig. 32.5. Aggregate demand curve AD_1 intersects the short-run aggregate supply curve, SAS, at point B where the GDP deflator is 105 and real GDP is $950 billion. The economy is in a recession. Real GDP is less than potential GDP, and unemployment is above its natural rate.

FIGURE 32.5 A Decrease in Aggregate Demand

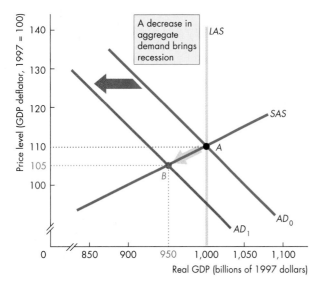

The economy starts out at full employment on aggregate demand curve AD_0 and short-run aggregate supply curve SAS, the two curves intersecting on the long-run aggregate supply curve, LAS, at point A. Real GDP is $1,000 billion, and the GDP deflator is 110. A fall in aggregate demand (due to pessimism about future profits, for example) unexpectedly shifts the aggregate demand curve to AD_1. Real GDP falls to $950 billion, and the GDP deflator falls to 105. The economy is in a recession at point B.

Suppose that the decrease in aggregate demand from AD_0 to AD_1 is temporary. As confidence in the future improves, firms' investment picks up, or as economic expansion proceeds in the rest of the world, exports gradually increase. As a result, the aggregate demand curve gradually returns to AD_0, but it takes some time to do so.

We are going to work out how the economy responds under two alternative policies during the period in which aggregate demand gradually increases to its original level: a fixed rule and a feedback rule.

Fixed Rule: Monetarism The fixed rule that we'll study here is one in which government expenditures on goods and services, taxes, and the quantity of money remain constant. Neither fiscal policy nor monetary policy responds to the depressed economy.

This rule is advocated by monetarists. A **monetarist** is an economist who believes that fluctuations in the quantity of money are the main source of economic fluctuations—the monetarist theory of the business cycle (see Chapter 31, pp. 732–734).

Figure 32.6(a) illustrates the response of the economy under a fixed rule when the decrease in aggregate demand to AD_1 is *temporary*. Starting from the recession at point B, aggregate demand gradually returns to its original level and the aggregate demand curve shifts rightward to AD_0. Real GDP and the GDP deflator gradually increase as the economy returns to point A in Fig. 32.6(a). Throughout this process, real GDP growth is more rapid than usual but beginning from below potential GDP. Throughout the adjustment, unemployment remains above the natural rate.

Figure 32.6(b) illustrates the response of the economy under a fixed rule when the decrease in aggregate demand to AD_1 is *permanent*. Again starting from the recession at point B and with unemployment above the natural rate, the money wage rate falls. Short-run aggregate supply increases and the SAS curve shifts rightward to SAS_1. Real GDP gradually increases towards $1,000 billion and the GDP deflator falls towards 95, at point C. Throughout the adjustment, real GDP is less than potential GDP and unemployment exceeds the natural rate.

Let's contrast the adjustment under a fixed-rule policy with that under a feedback-rule policy.

Feedback Rule: Keynesian Activism The feedback rule that we'll study is one in which government expenditures on goods and services increase, tax rates decrease, and the quantity of money increases when real GDP falls below potential GDP. In other words, both fiscal policy and monetary policy become expansionary when real GDP is less than potential GDP. When real GDP exceeds potential GDP, both policies operate in reverse, becoming contractionary. This rule is advocated by Keynesian activists. A **Keynesian activist** is an economist who believes that fluctuations in aggregate demand combined with sticky wages (and/or sticky prices) are the main source of economic fluctuations—the Keynesian and new Keynesian theories of the business cycle (see Chapter 31, pp. 731–732 and pp. 734–735).

Figure 32.6(c) illustrates the response of the economy under this feedback-rule policy. Starting from the recession at point B, the expansionary fiscal and monetary policies shift the aggregate

FIGURE 32.6   Two Stabilization Policies: Aggregate Demand Shock

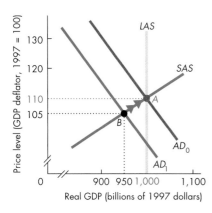

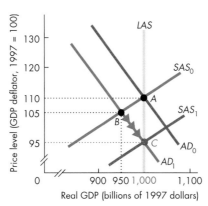

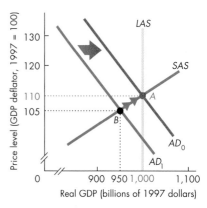

(a) Fixed rule: temporary demand shock   **(b) Fixed rule: permanent demand shock**   **(c) Feedback rule**

Aggregate demand is AD_1 and the economy is in a recession at point B. Real GDP is $950 billion, and the GDP deflator is 105. In part (a) the aggregate demand shock is temporary and a fixed-rule policy is pursued. Aggregate demand gradually increases to AD_0. Real GDP increases to $1,000 billion, and the GDP deflator increases to 110 at point A. In part (b), the demand shock is permanent and a fixed-rule policy is pursued. Aggregate demand remains at

AD_1. Eventually the money wage rate falls and the SAS curve shifts to SAS_1. The price level falls to 95, and real GDP increases to $1,000 billion at point C. In part (c), a feedback rule is pursued. With the economy in recession, expansionary fiscal and monetary policies increase aggregate demand and shift the aggregate demand curve from AD_1 to AD_0. Real GDP increases to $1,000 billion, and the GDP deflator increases to 110 at point A.

demand curve immediately to AD_0 and the economy moves back to point A. As other influences increase aggregate demand, fiscal and monetary policies become contractionary to hold the aggregate demand curve steady at AD_0. Real GDP is held steady at $1,000 billion, and the GDP deflator remains at 110.

The Two Rules Compared Under a fixed-rule policy, the economy goes into a recession and stays there for as long as it takes for aggregate demand to increase again under its own steam. Only gradually does the aggregate demand curve return to its original position and the recession come to an end.

Under a feedback-rule policy, the policy action pulls the economy out of its recession. Once back at potential GDP, real GDP is held there by a gradual, policy-induced decrease in aggregate demand that exactly offsets the increase in aggregate demand coming from private spending decisions.

The price level and real GDP decrease and increase by exactly the same amounts under the two policies, but real GDP stays below potential GDP for longer with a fixed rule than it does with a feedback rule.

So Feedback Rules Are Better? Isn't it obvious that a feedback rule is better than a fixed rule? Can't the government and the Bank of Canada use feedback rules to keep the economy close to full employment with a stable price level? Of course, unforecasted events—such as a collapse in business confidence—will hit the economy from time to time. But by responding with a change in tax rates, spending, interest rates, and the quantity of money, can't the government and the Bank minimize the damage from such a shock? It appears to be so from our analysis, and the Bank did a pretty good job through the late 1990s and into the 2000s.

Despite the apparent superiority of a feedback rule, many economists remain convinced that a fixed rule stabilizes aggregate demand more effectively than a feedback rule does. These economists assert that fixed rules are better than feedback rules because

- Potential GDP is not known.
- Policy lags are longer than the forecast horizon.
- Feedback-rule policies are less predictable than fixed-rule policies.

Let's look at these assertions.

Knowledge of Potential GDP To decide whether a feedback policy needs to stimulate or retard aggregate demand, it is necessary to determine whether real GDP is currently above or below potential GDP. But potential GDP is not known with certainty. It depends on a large number of factors, one of which is the level of employment when unemployment is at its natural rate. But uncertainty and disagreement exist about how the labour market works, so we can only estimate the natural rate of unemployment. As a result, there is uncertainty about the *direction* in which a feedback policy should be pushing the level of aggregate demand.

Policy Lags and the Forecast Horizon The effects of policy actions taken today are spread out over the next two years or even more. But no one is able to forecast accurately that far ahead. The forecast horizon of the policymakers is less than one year. Further, it is not possible to predict the precise timing and magnitude of the effects of policy actions. So a feedback policy that reacts to today's economy may be inappropriate for the state of the economy at that uncertain future date when the policy's effects are felt.

For example, suppose that today the economy is in recession. The Bank of Canada reacts with an increase in the money growth rate. When the Bank steps on the monetary accelerator, the first reaction is a fall in interest rates. Some time later, lower interest rates produce an increase in investment and the purchases of consumer durable goods. Some time still later, this increase in expenditure increases income; higher income in turn induces higher consumption expenditure. Later yet, the higher expenditure increases the demand for labour, and eventually, money wage rates and prices rise. The industries and regions in which spending increases occur vary, and so does the impact on employment. It can take from nine months to two years for an initial action by the Bank to cause a change in real GDP, employment, and the inflation rate.

By the time the Bank's actions are having their maximum effect, the economy has moved on to a new situation. Perhaps a world economic slowdown has added a new negative effect on aggregate demand that is offsetting the Bank's expansionary actions. Or perhaps a boost in business confidence has increased aggregate demand yet further, adding to the Bank's own expansionary policy. Whatever the situation, the Bank can take the appropriate actions today only if it can forecast those future shocks to aggregate demand.

To smooth the fluctuations in aggregate demand, the Bank of Canada needs to take actions today that are based on a forecast of what will be happening over a period stretching two or more years into the future. It is no use taking actions a year from today to influence the situation that then prevails. By then it will be too late.

If the Bank is good at economic forecasting and bases its policy actions on its forecasts, then the Bank can deliver the type of aggregate demand-smoothing performance that we assumed in the model economy that we studied earlier in this chapter. But if the Bank takes policy actions that are based on today's economy rather than on the forecasted economy a year into the future, then those actions will often be inappropriate ones.

When unemployment is high and the Bank puts its foot on the accelerator, it speeds the economy back to full employment. But the Bank might not be able to see far enough ahead to know when to ease off the accelerator and gently tap the brake, holding the economy at its full-employment point. Usually, the Bank keeps its foot on the accelerator for too long, and after the Bank has taken its foot off the accelerator pedal, the economy races through the full-employment point and starts to experience shortages and inflationary pressures. Eventually, when inflation increases and unemployment falls below its natural rate, the Bank steps on the brake and pushes the economy back below full employment.

According to advocates of fixed rules, the Bank's own reactions to the current state of the economy are one of the major sources of fluctuations in aggregate demand and the major factor that people have to forecast to make their own economic choices.

During 1994, the Bank of Canada tried hard to avoid the problems just described. It increased interest rates early in the expansion and by small increments. In 1995, after real GDP growth slowed but before any serious signs of recession were on the horizon, it began to cut interest rates. And in 1997, before inflation turned seriously upward, the Bank squeezed the monetary brake. Whether the Bank now knows enough to avoid some of the mistakes of the past is too early to tell. But its actions during the period 1992 to 2001 were gentler and better timed than those in previous cycles.

The problems with feedback rules for fiscal policy are more severe than those for monetary policy because of the lags in the implementation of fiscal policy. The Bank of Canada can take actions relatively quickly, but before a fiscal policy action can be taken, the entire legislative process must be completed. So even before a fiscal policy action is implemented, the economy may have moved on to a new situation that calls for a different feedback policy from the one that is in the legislative pipeline.

Predictability of Policies   To make decisions about long-term contracts for employment (wage contracts) and for borrowing and lending, people have to anticipate the future course of prices—the future inflation rate. To forecast the inflation rate, it is necessary to forecast aggregate demand. And to forecast aggregate demand, it is necessary to forecast the policy actions of the government and the Bank of Canada.

If the government and the Bank of Canada stick to rock-steady, fixed rules for tax rates, spending programs, and money growth, then policy itself cannot be a contributor to unexpected fluctuations in aggregate demand.

In contrast, when a feedback rule is being pursued, there is more scope for the policy actions to be unpredictable. The main reason is that feedback rules are not written down for all to see. Rather, they have to be inferred from the behaviour of the government and the Bank of Canada.

So with a feedback policy, it is necessary to predict the variables to which the government and Bank of Canada react and the extent to which they react. Consequently, a feedback rule for fiscal and monetary policies can create more unpredictable fluctuations in aggregate demand than a fixed rule can.

Economists disagree about whether those bigger fluctuations offset the potential stabilizing influence of the predictable changes the Bank of Canada makes. No agreed measurements have been made to settle this dispute. Nevertheless, the unpredictability of the Bank in its pursuit of feedback policies is an important fact of economic life. And the Bank does not always go out of its way to make its reactions clear. Even in parliamentary testimony, Bank of Canada governors are reluctant to make the Bank's actions and intentions entirely plain. Rather they like to create a degree of mystery about what they are doing and place a smokescreen between themselves and the rest of the government economic policy-making machine.

It is not surprising that the Bank of Canada seeks to keep *some* of its actions behind a smokescreen. First, the Bank wants to maintain as much freedom of action as possible and so does not want to state

with too great a precision the feedback rules that it will follow in any given circumstances. Second, the Bank is part of a political process and, although legally independent of the federal government, is not immune to subtle influence. For at least these two reasons, the Bank does not specify feedback rules as precisely as the one we've analyzed in this chapter. As a result, the Bank cannot deliver an economic performance that has the stability that we generated in the model economy.

To the extent to which the Bank's actions are discretionary and unpredictable, they lead to unpredictable fluctuations in aggregate demand. These fluctuations, in turn, produce fluctuations in real GDP, employment, and unemployment.

If it is difficult for the Bank to pursue a predictable feedback stabilization policy, it is probably impossible for Parliament to do so. The stabilization policy of Parliament is formulated in terms of spending programs and tax laws. Because these programs and laws are the outcome of a political process that is constrained only by the Constitution, there can be no effective way in which a predictable feedback fiscal policy can be adhered to.

We reviewed three reasons why feedback-rule policies might not be more effective than fixed-rule policies in controlling aggregate demand. But there is a fourth reason why some economists prefer fixed rules: Not all shocks to the economy are on the demand side. Let's now see how aggregate supply fluctuations affect the economy under a fixed rule and a feedback rule. We will also see why the economists who believe that aggregate supply fluctuations are the dominant ones also favour a fixed rule rather than a feedback rule.

Stabilizing Aggregate Supply Shocks

Real business cycle theorists believe that fluctuations in real GDP (and in employment and unemployment) are caused not by fluctuations in aggregate demand but by fluctuations in productivity growth. According to real business cycle theory, there is no useful distinction between long-run aggregate supply and short-run aggregate supply. Because money wage rates are flexible, the labour market is always in equilibrium and unemployment is always at its natural rate. The vertical long-run aggregate supply curve is also the short-run aggregate supply curve. Fluctuations occur because of shifts in the long-run aggregate supply curve. Normally, the long-run aggregate supply curve shifts to the right—the economy expands. But the pace at which the long-run aggregate supply curve shifts to the right varies. Also, on occasion, the long-run aggregate supply curve shifts leftward, bringing a decrease in aggregate supply and a decrease in real GDP.

If real business cycle theory is correct, economic policy that influences the aggregate demand curve has no effect on real GDP. But it does affect the price level. If a feedback-rule policy is used to increase aggregate demand every time real GDP decreases, and if real business cycle theory is correct, the feedback-rule policy will make price level fluctuations more severe than they otherwise would be.

Figure 32.7 illustrates these alternative policy responses to a decrease in aggregate supply. The economy starts out at point A on aggregate demand curve AD_0 and long-run aggregate supply curve LAS_0 at a GDP deflator of 110 and with real GDP equal to $1,000 billion. Now suppose that the long-run aggregate supply curve shifts to LAS_1. A decrease in long-run aggregate supply can occur as a result of a severe drought or other natural catastrophe or perhaps as the result of a disruption of international trade such as the OPEC embargo of the 1970s.

Fixed Rule With a fixed rule, the fall in the long-run aggregate supply has no effect on the policies of the Bank of Canada or the government and no effect on aggregate demand. The aggregate demand curve remains AD_0. Real GDP decreases to $950 billion, and the price level increases to 120 at point B.

Feedback Rule Now suppose that the Bank of Canada and the government use feedback rules. In particular, suppose that when real GDP decreases, the Bank increases the quantity of money and Parliament enacts a tax cut to increase aggregate demand. In this example, aggregate demand increases and the aggregate demand curve shifts to AD_1. The policy goal is to bring real GDP back to $1,000 billion. But the long-run aggregate supply curve has shifted, and so potential GDP has decreased to $950 billion. The increase in aggregate demand cannot bring forth an increase in output if the economy does not have the capacity to produce that output. So real GDP stays at $950 billion, but the price level rises further—to 130 at point C. You can see that in this case the attempt to stabilize real GDP using a feedback-rule policy has no effect on real GDP but generates a substantial price level increase.

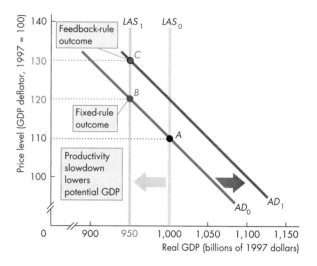

FIGURE 32.7   Responding to a Productivity Growth Slowdown

Initially the economy is at point A. A productivity growth slowdown shifts the long-run aggregate supply curve from LAS_0 to LAS_1. Real GDP decreases to $950 billion, and the price level rises to 120 at point B. With a fixed rule, there is no change in the quantity of money, taxes, or government expenditures; aggregate demand stays at AD_0 and that is the end of the matter. With a feedback rule, the Bank increases the quantity of money and Parliament cuts taxes or increases expenditures, intending to increase real GDP. Aggregate demand shifts to AD_1, but the result is an increase in the price level—to 130—with no change in real GDP, at point C.

We've now seen some of the shortcomings of using feedback rules for stabilization policy. Some economists believe that these shortcomings are serious and want to constrain Parliament and the Bank of Canada so that they use fixed rules. Others, regarding the potential advantages of feedback rules as greater than their costs, advocate the continued use of such policies but with an important modification that we'll now look at.

Natural Rate Policies

The business cycle and unemployment policies we've considered have been directed at smoothing the business cycle and minimizing *cyclical unemployment*. It is also possible to pursue policies aimed at lowering the natural rate of unemployment. But there are no costless ways of lowering the natural rate of unemployment. Let's look at two possible ways.

One policy tool is unemployment compensation. To lower the natural rate of unemployment, the government might lower the unemployment compensation rate, or shorten the period for which compensation is paid, or restrict compensation to people who undertake training programs that increase the likelihood of their finding jobs. With lower compensation, an unemployed person would spend less time looking for a job and would accept a job even it was not a good match for the person's skills. But such a policy might create hardship and have a cost that exceeds the cost of a high natural rate of unemployment.

The government might lower the minimum real wage rate. It could achieve a cut in the minimum wage either by holding the minimum money wage rate constant and letting inflation cut the minimum real wage rate or by cutting the minimum money wage rate. A lower minimum wage increases the quantity of labour demanded and lowers unemployment. Again, the government faces the trade-off.

REVIEW QUIZ

1 What is a fixed-rule fiscal policy and what is a fixed-rule monetary policy? Can you provide two examples of fixed rules in everyday life (other than those in the text)?

2 What is a feedback fiscal policy and what is a feedback monetary policy? When might a feedback policy be used? Can you provide two examples of feedback rules in everyday life (other than those in the text)?

3 Why do some economists say that feedback rules do not necessarily deliver a better macroeconomic performance than fixed rules? Do you agree or disagree with them? Why?

We've studied growth policy and business cycle and unemployment policy. Let's now study anti-inflation policy.

Anti-Inflation Policy

THERE ARE TWO INFLATION POLICY PROBLEMS. In times of price level stability, the problem is to prevent inflation from breaking out. In times of inflation, the problem is to reduce its rate and restore price stability. Preventing inflation from breaking out means avoiding both demand-pull and cost-push forces. Avoiding demand-pull inflation is the flip side of avoiding demand-driven recession and is achieved by stabilizing aggregate demand. So the business cycle and unemployment policy we've just studied is also an anti-inflation policy. But avoiding cost-push inflation raises some special issues that we need to consider. So we will look at two issues for inflation policy:

■ Avoiding cost-push inflation
■ Slowing inflation

Avoiding Cost-Push Inflation

Cost-push inflation is inflation that has its origins in cost increases (see Chapter 28, pp. 653–655). In 1973–1974 and again in 1979, the world oil price exploded. Cost shocks such as these become inflationary if they are accommodated by an increase in the quantity of money. Such an increase in the quantity of money can occur if a monetary policy feedback rule is used. A fixed-rule policy for the quantity of money makes cost-push inflation impossible. Let's see why.

Figure 32.8 shows the economy at full employment. Aggregate demand is AD_0, short-run aggregate supply is SAS_0, and long-run aggregate supply is LAS. Real GDP is $1,000 billion, and the price level is 110 at point A. Now suppose that OPEC tries to gain a temporary advantage by increasing the price of oil. The short-run aggregate supply curve shifts leftward from SAS_0 to SAS_1.

Monetarist Fixed Rule Figure 32.8(a) shows what happens if the Bank of Canada follows a fixed rule for monetary policy and the government follows a fixed rule for fiscal policy. Suppose that the fixed rule is for zero money growth and no change in taxes or government expenditures on goods and services. With these fixed rules, the Bank and the government pay no attention to the fact that there has been an increase in the price of oil. No policy actions are taken. The short-run aggregate supply curve has shifted to SAS_1, but the aggregate demand curve remains at AD_0. The price level rises to 120, and real

FIGURE 32.8   Responding to an OPEC Oil Price Increase

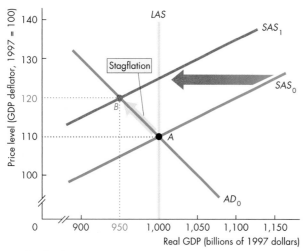

(a) Fixed rule

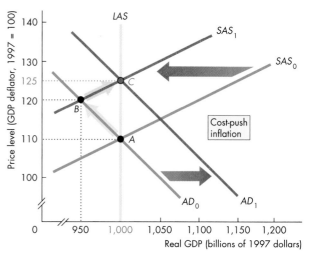

(b) Feedback rule

The economy starts out at point A on AD_0 and SAS_0, with a price level of 110 and real GDP of $1,000 billion. OPEC forces up the price of oil, and the short-run aggregate supply curve shifts to SAS_1. Real GDP decreases to $950 billion, and the price level increases to 120 at point B. With a fixed-rule policy (part a), aggregate demand remains at AD_0. The economy stays in a recession at point B until the price

of oil falls and the economy returns to its original position. With a feedback-rule policy (part b), the Bank injects additional money and the government increases spending. The aggregate demand curve shifts to AD_1. Real GDP returns to $1,000 billion (potential GDP), but the price level increases to 125 at point C. The economy is set for another round of cost-push inflation.

GDP falls to $950 billion at point *B*. The economy has experienced *stagflation*. With unemployment above the natural rate, the money wage rate will eventually fall. The low level of real GDP and low sales will probably also bring a fall in the price of oil. These events shift the short-run aggregate supply curve back to SAS_0. The price level will fall to 110, and real GDP will increase to $1,000 billion. But this adjustment might take a long time.

Keynesian Feedback Rule   Figure 32.8(b) shows what happens if the Bank and government operate a feedback rule. The starting point *A* is the same as before—the economy is on SAS_0 and AD_0 with a price level of 110 and real GDP of $1,000 billion. OPEC raises the price of oil, and the short-run aggregate supply curve shifts to SAS_1. Real GDP decreases to $950 billion, and the price level rises to 120 at point *B*.

A feedback rule is followed. With potential GDP perceived to be $1,000 billion and with actual real

GDP at $950 billion, the Bank pumps money into the economy and the government increases its spending and lowers taxes. Aggregate demand increases, and the aggregate demand curve shifts rightward to AD_1. The price level rises to 125, and real GDP returns to $1,000 billion at point *C*. The economy moves back to full employment but at a higher price level. The economy has experienced *cost-push inflation*.

The Bank of Canada responded in the way we've just described to the first wave of OPEC price rises in the mid-1970s. OPEC saw the same advantage in forcing up the price of oil again. A new rise in the price of oil decreased aggregate supply, and the short-run aggregate supply curve shifted leftward once more. If the Bank had chased it with an increase in aggregate demand, the economy would have been in a freewheeling inflation. Realizing this danger, the Bank did *not* respond to the second wave of OPEC price increases in the early 1980s as it had done before. Instead, the Bank held firm and even slowed the growth of aggregate demand to further dampen the inflation consequences of OPEC's actions.

Incentives to Push Up Costs You can see that there are no checks on the incentives to push up *nominal* costs if the Bank accommodates price hikes. If some group sees a temporary gain from pushing up the price at which it is selling its resources and if the Bank always accommodates the increase to prevent unemployment and slack business conditions from emerging, then cost-push elements will have a free rein. But when the Bank pursues a fixed-rule policy, the incentive to attempt to steal a temporary advantage from a price increase is severely weakened. The cost of higher unemployment and lower output is a consequence that each group will have to face and recognize.

So a fixed rule can deliver steady inflation, while a feedback rule, in the face of cost-push pressures, leaves inflation free to rise at the whim of whichever group believes a temporary advantage to be available from pushing up its price.

Slowing Inflation

So far, we've concentrated on *avoiding* inflation. But often the problem is not to avoid inflation but to tame it. Canada was in such a situation during the late 1970s and early 1980s. How can inflation, once it has set in, be cured? We'll look at two cases:

- A surprise inflation reduction
- A credible announced inflation reduction

A Surprise Inflation Reduction We'll use two equivalent approaches to study the problem of lowering inflation: the aggregate supply–aggregate demand model and the Phillips curve. The *AS–AD* model tells us about real GDP and the price level, while the Phillips curve, which is explained in Chapter 28 (pp. 662–664), lets us keep track of inflation and unemployment.

Figure 32.9 illustrates the economy at full employment with inflation raging at 10 percent a year. In part (a), the economy is on aggregate demand curve AD_0 and short-run aggregate supply curve SAS_0. Real GDP is $1,000 billion, and the price level is 110. With real GDP equal to potential GDP on the *LAS* curve, the economy is at full employment. Equivalently, in part (b), the economy is on its long-run Phillips curve, *LRPC*, and short-run Phillips curve, $SRPC_0$. The inflation rate of 10 percent a year

is anticipated, so unemployment is at its natural rate, 6 percent of the labour force.

Next year, aggregate demand is *expected* to increase and the aggregate demand curve in Fig. 32.9(a) is expected to shift rightward from AD_0 to AD_1. In expectation of this increase in aggregate demand, the money wage rate increases and shifts the short-run aggregate supply curve from SAS_0 to SAS_1. If expectations are fulfilled, the price level rises to 121—a 10 percent inflation—and real GDP remains at potential GDP. In part (b), the economy remains at its original position—unemployment is at the natural rate, and the inflation rate is 10 percent a year.

Now suppose that people expect the Bank not to change its policy, but the Bank actually tries to slow inflation. It raises interest rates and slows money growth. Aggregate demand growth slows, and the aggregate demand curve (in part a) shifts rightward from AD_0 not to AD_1 as people expect but only to AD_2.

With no change in the expected inflation rate, the money wage rate rises by the same amount as before and the short-run aggregate supply curve shifts leftward from SAS_0 to SAS_1. Real GDP decreases to $950 billion, and the price level rises to 118.8—an inflation rate of 8 percent a year. In Fig. 32.9(b), the economy moves along the short-run Phillips curve $SRPC_0$ as unemployment rises to 9 percent and inflation falls to 8 percent a year. The Bank's policy has succeeded in slowing inflation, but at the cost of recession. Real GDP is below potential GDP, and unemployment is above its natural rate.

A Credible Announced Inflation Reduction
Suppose that instead of simply slowing down the growth of aggregate demand, the Bank announces its intention ahead of its action and in a credible and convincing way so that its announcement is believed. That is, the Bank's policy is anticipated. Because the lower level of aggregate demand is expected, the money wage rate increases at a pace that is consistent with the lower level of aggregate demand. The short-run aggregate supply curve (in Fig. 32.9a) shifts leftward from SAS_0 but only to SAS_2. Aggregate demand increases by the amount expected, and the aggregate demand curve shifts from AD_0 to AD_2. The price level rises to 115.5—an inflation rate of 5 percent a year—and real GDP remains at potential GDP.

In Fig. 32.9(b), the lower expected inflation rate shifts the short-run Phillips curve downward to $SRPC_1$, and inflation falls to 5 percent a year, while unemployment remains at its natural rate of 6 percent.

FIGURE 32.9   Lowering Inflation

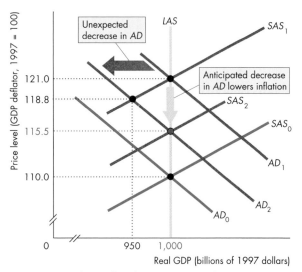

(a) Aggregate demand and aggregate supply

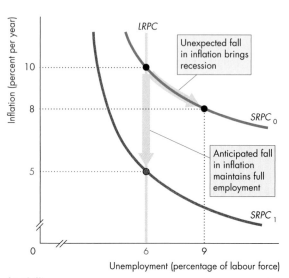

(b) Phillips curves

In part (a), aggregate demand is AD_0, short-run aggregate supply is SAS_0, and real GDP and potential GDP are \$1,000 billion on the long-run aggregate supply curve LAS. The aggregate demand curve is expected to shift and actually shifts to AD_1. The short-run aggregate supply curve shifts to SAS_1. The price level rises to 121, but real GDP remains at \$1,000 billion. Inflation is proceeding at 10 percent a year, and this inflation rate is anticipated. In part (b), which shows this same situation, the economy is on the short-run Phillips curve $SRPC_0$ and on the long-run Phillips curve $LRPC$. Unemployment is at the natural rate of 6 percent, and inflation is 10 percent a year.

An unexpected slowdown in aggregate demand growth means that the aggregate demand curve shifts from AD_0 to AD_2, real GDP decreases to \$950 billion, and inflation slows to 8 percent (price level is 118.8). Unemployment rises to 9 percent as the economy slides down $SRPC_0$. An anticipated, credible, announced slowdown in aggregate demand growth means that when the aggregate demand curve shifts from AD_0 to AD_2, the short-run aggregate supply curve shifts from SAS_0 to SAS_2. The short-run Phillips curve shifts to $SRPC_1$. Inflation slows to 5 percent, real GDP remains at \$1,000 billion, and unemployment remains at its natural rate of 6 percent.

A credible announced inflation reduction lowers inflation but with no accompanying loss of output or increase in unemployment.

Inflation Reduction in Practice

When the Bank of Canada slowed inflation in 1981, we paid a high price. The Bank's policy action was unpredicted. It occurred in the face of wages that had been set at too high a level to be consistent with the growth of aggregate demand that the Bank subsequently allowed. The consequence was recession—a decrease in real GDP and a rise in unemployment. Could the Bank have lowered inflation without causing recession by telling people far enough ahead of time that it did indeed plan to lower inflation?

The answer appears to be no. The main reason is that people expect the Bank to behave in line with its record, not with its stated intentions. How many times have you told yourself that it is your firm intention to take off 5 unwanted kilograms or to keep within your budget and put a few dollars away for a rainy day, only to discover that, despite your very best intentions, your old habits win out in the end?

To form expectations of the Bank's actions, people look at the Bank's past *actions*, not its stated intentions. On the basis of such observations—called Bank-watching—they try to work out what the Bank's policy is, to forecast its future actions, and to forecast the effects of those actions on aggregate demand and inflation. The Bank of Canada has built a reputation for being anti-inflationary. That reputation is valuable because it helps the Bank to contain inflation and lowers the cost of eliminating inflation if it temporarily returns. The reason is that with a low expected inflation rate, the short-run Phillips curve is in a favourable position (like $SRPC_1$ in Fig. 32.9b). The Bank's actions during the 1990s were designed to keep inflation expectations low and prevent the gains made during the 1980s recession from being eroded.

Balancing the Inflation and Real GDP Objective: The Taylor Rule

John Taylor, formerly an economics professor at Stanford University and now Undersecretary of the Treasury for International Affairs in the Bush administration, has suggested a policy feedback rule that he says would deliver a better performance than what central banks have achieved.

The idea is to target inflation but also to be explicit about the extent to which the interest rate will be changed in response to both inflation and deviations of real GDP from potential GDP. By being explicit and always following the same rule, central bank watching becomes a simpler task and smaller forecasting errors might be made, which translates into smaller deviations of real GDP from potential GDP and smaller deviations of the unemployment rate from the natural rate.

If the Bank of Canada followed the Taylor rule with a target inflation rate of 2 percent a year and an average real overnight loans rate of 3 percent a year, it would set a target for the overnight loans rate equal to 5 percent plus one-half of the amount by which the inflation rate exceeds 2 percent a year, plus one-half of the percentage gap between real GDP and potential GDP. And the Bank would move the actual overnight loans rate gradually towards the target rate.

Figure 32.10 shows the overnight loans rate and the target rate if the Taylor rule were followed. You can see that the Bank of Canada's actual policy is similar to the Taylor rule. So if the Bank announced that it were using the Taylor rule, it would not be changing the way it acts, but by being explicit about the formula that determines the overnight loans rate, it would take the mystery and unpredictability out of its policy actions.

But you can also see that the Bank of Canada's actions have not exactly followed the Taylor rule. During the recessions of the early 1980s and early 1990s, the Bank set the overnight loans rate higher than the Taylor rule. The reason could be that the Bank has a lower target inflation rate or places less weight on real GDP fluctuations than does the Taylor rule.

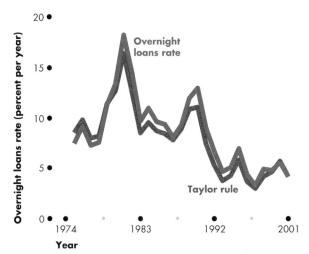

FIGURE 32.10   The Overnight Loans Rate and the Taylor Rule

The green line shows the overnight loans interest rate between 1975 and 2001. The orange line shows what the overnight rate would have been if the Bank of Canada had followed the Taylor rule and adjusted the overnight loans rate to place equal emphasis on achieving low inflation and full employment.

Sources: Bank of Canada, *Banking and Financial Statistics*, table F1, and authors' calculations.

REVIEW QUIZ

1 Why does a fixed rule provide more effective protection against cost-push inflation than does a feedback rule?
2 Why does a recession usually result as inflation is being tamed?
3 How does establishing a reputation of being an inflation fighter improve the Bank of Canada's ability to maintain low inflation and to lower the cost of fighting inflation?

◆ *Reading Between the Lines* on pp. 774–775 looks Canada's stabilization challenge at the end of 2002 as the world economy appeared to be slowing.

You've now completed your study of macroeconomics. In the remaining chapters, we shift our focus to the international economy.

The Stabilization Policy Balancing Act

NATIONAL POST, OCTOBER 12, 2002

Canadian job growth surges ahead:

Best 9-months in 15 years: 'emerging cracks' enough to prevent near-term rate hike

The Canadian economy blasted through forecasts to pump out another 40,700 jobs in September, but analysts said the labour market showed signs of tiring and that, combined with a minefield of global uncertainties, should keep the Bank of Canada from raising interest rates next week. ...

The economy has created almost as many jobs so far this year as in all of 1999, when the world economy was roaring. That year, 433,000 jobs were generated.

Despite September's employment gain, the unemployment rate jumped to 7.7%, from 7.5%, because more people felt confident enough to start looking for work—another sign of a strength—analysts said. The participation rate rose to a 12-year high of 67.2%. But analysts spotted weaknesses concealed in the strong headline numbers. ...

Among the cracks:
• All the gains were part-time. Full-time jobs fell by 5,000 in the month, the first drop in a year.
• the manufacturing sector lost 16,900 jobs.
• almost half the gains were in self-employment;
• the private sector generated gains of only 8,600;
• for the third quarter as a whole, total hours worked fell 0.9% at annual rates.
• the rise in the unemployment rate could be psychologically damaging ...

Many analysts said that, if anything, the world has become a more uncertain place ... with banking concerns brewing in Japan and Germany and corporate credit concerns adding to an ugly outlook for the world economy. ...

Reprinted by permission of the *National Post*.

Essence of the Story

■ The Canadian economy created 40,700 jobs in September 2002.

■ Despite September's increase in employment, the unemployment rate increased because the labour force participation rate increased.

■ Most of the jobs created were part-time and aggregate hours decreased. Only one job in five was in the private sector (four in five were in the public sector).

■ The global economic outlook appeared uncertain.

Economic Analysis

■ Figure 1 illustrates the Canadian economy at the start of 2002. Potential GDP was $1,045 billion, long-run aggregate supply was LAS_0, short-run aggregate supply was SAS_0, and aggregate demand was AD_0. Equilibrium real GDP was $1,030 billion, so there was a recessionary gap of $15 billion.

■ Potential GDP increased to $1,065 billion by the third quarter of 2002, and the long-run aggregate supply curve shifted rightward to LAS_1.

■ During 2002, short-run aggregate supply increased slightly to SAS_1 and aggregate demand increased strongly to AD_1.

■ Equilibrium real GDP increased to $1,065 billion, and the economy was at a full-employment equilibrium.

■ Figure 2 illustrates the uncertain outlook for 2003 that confronts the Bank of Canada as it makes decisions about monetary policy.

■ By the third quarter of 2003, potential GDP will be around $1,095 billion so the long-run aggregate supply curve will be LAS in Fig. 2.

■ The SAS curve in 2003 will depend on the change in LAS and the change in the money wage rate. The SAS curve for 2003 in Fig. 2 assumes that these two influences exactly offset each other.

■ If aggregate demand increases to AD_0 in Fig. 2, real GDP will increase to $1,095—potential GDP—and the price level will rise to 110—an inflation rate of less than 2 percent a year. The Bank of Canada would like to deliver this outcome.

■ But if aggregate demand continues to increase as strongly as it did in 2002, by the third quarter of 2003, the AD curve will be at AD_1 in Fig. 2. Real GDP will exceed potential GDP and the inflation rate will be increasing.

■ To try to avoid such an inflation, the Bank of Canada would increase the interest rate, hoping to keep aggregate demand at AD_0 and achieve full employment.

■ A global recession will decrease Canadian aggregate demand towards AD_2, and bring recession in Canada.

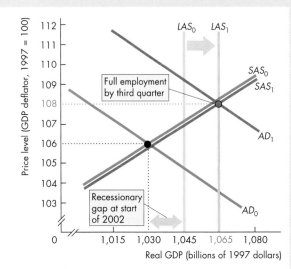

Figure 1 The Canadian economy in 2002

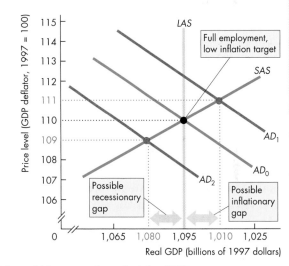

Figure 2 The uncertain outlook for 2003

SUMMARY

KEY POINTS

Policy Goals (pp. 756–757)

■ The goals of macroeconomic policy are to achieve the highest sustainable rate of potential GDP growth, smooth the business cycle, maintain low unemployment, and avoid inflation.

■ The two core policy indicators are real GDP growth and inflation.

Policy Tools and Performance (pp. 758–760)

■ Fiscal policy was expansionary during the Trudeau years and contractionary during the Mulroney and Chrétien years.

■ There have been four phases of monetary policy since 1971: (1) permit inflation to rise, (2) bring inflation down, (3) eliminate inflation, and (4) keep inflation low and encourage expansion.

Long-Term Growth Policy (pp. 760–762)

■ Policies to increase the long-term growth rate focus on increasing saving and investment in human capital and new technologies.

■ To increase the saving rate, government saving must increase or incentives for private saving must be strengthened by increasing after-tax returns.

■ Human capital investment might be increased with improved education and by improving on-the-job training programs and health care.

■ Investment in new technologies can be encouraged by tax incentives.

Business Cycle and Unemployment Policy (pp. 763–769)

■ In the face of an aggregate demand shock, a fixed-rule policy takes no action. Real GDP and the price level fluctuate.

■ In the face of an aggregate demand shock, a feedback-rule policy takes offsetting fiscal and monetary action. An ideal feedback rule keeps the economy at full employment, with stable prices.

■ Some economists say that a feedback rule creates fluctuations because it requires greater knowledge of the economy than we have, operates with time lags that extend beyond the forecast horizon, and introduces unpredictability about policy reactions.

■ In the face of a productivity growth slowdown, both rules have the same effect on output. A feedback rule brings a higher inflation rate than does a fixed rule.

Anti-Inflation Policy (pp. 769–773)

■ A fixed rule minimizes the threat of cost-push inflation. A feedback rule validates cost-push inflation and leaves the price level and inflation rate free to move to wherever they are pushed.

■ Inflation can be tamed, at little or no cost in terms of lost output or excessive unemployment, by slowing the growth of aggregate demand in a credible and predictable way. But usually, when inflation is slowed down, a recession occurs.

KEY FIGURES

KEY TERMS

PROBLEMS

*1. A productivity growth slowdown has occurred. Explain its possible origins and describe a policy package that is designed to speed up growth again.

2. A nation is experiencing a falling saving rate. Explain its possible origins and describe a policy package that is designed to increase the saving rate.

*3. The economy shown in the figure is initially on aggregate demand curve AD_0 and short-run aggregate supply curve SAS. Then aggregate demand decreases, and the aggregate demand curve shifts leftward to AD_1.

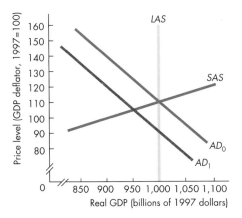

a. What is the initial equilibrium real GDP and price level?
b. If the decrease in aggregate demand is temporary and the government follows a fixed-rule fiscal policy, what happens to real GDP and the price level? Trace the immediate effects and the adjustment as aggregate demand returns to its original level.
c. If the decrease in aggregate demand is temporary and the government follows a feedback-rule fiscal policy, what happens to real GDP and the price level? Trace the immediate effects and the adjustment as aggregate demand returns to its original level.
d. If the decrease in aggregate demand is permanent and the government follows a fixed-rule fiscal policy, what happens to real GDP and the price level?
e. If the decrease in aggregate demand is permanent and the government follows a feed-

back-rule fiscal policy, what happens to real GDP and the price level?

4. The economy shown in the figure is initially on aggregate demand curve AD and short-run aggregate supply curve SAS_0. Then short-run aggregate supply decreases, and the short-run aggregate supply curve shifts leftward to SAS_1.

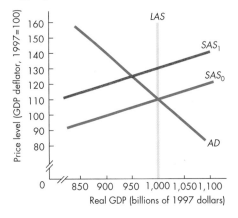

a. What is the initial equilibrium real GDP and price level?
b. What type of event could have caused the decrease in short-run aggregate supply?
c. If the Bank of Canada follows a fixed-rule monetary policy, what happens to real GDP and the price level? Trace the immediate effects and the adjustment as aggregate demand and short-run aggregate supply return to their original level.
d. If the Bank of Canada follows a feedback-rule monetary policy, what happens to real GDP and the price level? Trace the immediate effects and the adjustment as aggregate demand and short-run aggregate supply respond to the policy action.

*5. The economy is experiencing 10 percent inflation and 7 percent unemployment. Real GDP growth has sagged to 1 percent a year. The stock market has crashed.
a. Explain how the economy might have got into its current state.
b. Set out policies for the Bank of Canada and Parliament to pursue that will lower inflation, lower unemployment, and speed real GDP growth.
c. Explain how and why your proposed policies will work.

6. The inflation rate has fallen to less than 1 percent a year, and the unemployment rate has fallen to less than 4 percent. Real GDP is growing at almost 5 percent a year. The stock market is at a record high.
   a. Explain how the economy might have got into its current state.
   b. Set out policies for the Bank of Canada and Parliament to pursue that will maintain low inflation, low unemployment, and rapid real GDP growth.
   c. Explain how and why your proposed policies will work.

*7. When the economies of Indonesia, Korea, Thailand, Malaysia, and the Philippines entered into recession in 1997, the International Monetary Fund (IMF) made loans but only on the condition that the recipients of the loans increase interest rates, raise taxes, and cut government expenditures.
   a. Would you describe the IMF prescription as a feedback-rule policy or a fixed-rule policy?
   b. What do you predict the effects of the IMF policies would be?
   c. Do you have any criticisms of the IMF policies? What would you have required these countries to do? Why?

8. As the Canadian economy continued to expand and its stock market soared to new record levels during 1998, the Bank of Canada cut interest rates.
   a. Would you describe the Bank's actions as a feedback-rule policy or a fixed-rule policy?
   b. What do you predict the effects of the Bank's policies would be?
   c. Do you have any criticisms of the Bank's policies? What monetary policy would you have pursued? Why?

CRITICAL THINKING

1. Study *Reading Between the Lines* on pp. 774–775 and then
   a. Do you think the labour market indicators reported in the news article indicate expansion or recession? Explain your answer.
   b. Describe the cracks that were appearing in the Canadian economy that suggested a slower growth rate in 2003.
   c. What are David Dodge's views on the appropriate fiscal policy reported in the news article? Do you agree with those views? Why or why not?
   d. What was the likely influence of the United States, Japan, and Germany on the Canadian economy during 2003?

2. Suppose the economy is booming and inflation is beginning to rise, but it is widely agreed that a massive recession is just around the corner. Weigh the advantages and disadvantages of the government pursuing a fixed rule and a feedback rule for *fiscal* policy.

3. Suppose the economy is in a recession and inflation is falling. It is widely agreed that a strong recovery is just around the corner. Weigh the advantages and disadvantages of the Bank of Canada pursuing a fixed-rule policy and a feedback-rule policy.

WEB EXERCISES

1. Use the links on the Parkin–Bade Web site to review the Bank of Canada's latest *Monetary Policy Report* and the latest *Annual Financial Report of the Government of Canada*. Write a summary and critique of these reports.

2. Use the link on the Parkin–Bade Web site to review the latest *World Economic Outlook*.
   a. What are the major macroeconomic stabilization policy problems in the world today?
   b. What is the general direction in which policy actions are pushing the global economy?

UNDERSTANDING AGGREGATE SUPPLY AND ECONOMIC GROWTH

PART 9

Expanding the Frontier

Economics is about how we cope with scarcity. We cope by making choices that balance marginal benefits and marginal costs so that we use our scarce resources efficiently. ◆ These choices determine how much work we do; how hard we work at school to learn the mental skills that form our human capital and that determine the kinds of jobs we get and the incomes we earn; and how much we save for future big-ticket expenditures. These choices also determine how much businesses and governments spend on new capital—on auto assembly lines, computers and fibre cables for improved Internet services, shopping malls, highways, bridges, and tunnels; and how intensively existing capital and natural resources are used and therefore how quickly they wear out or are used up. Most significant of all, these choices determine the problems that scientists, engineers, and other inventors work on to develop new technologies. ◆ All the choices we've just described determine two vital measures of economic performance:

■ Real GDP
■ Economic growth

Real GDP is determined by the quantity of labour, the quantity of capital, and the state of technological knowledge. And economic growth—the growth rate of real GDP—is determined by growth in the quantity of labour, capital accumulation, and technological advances. ◆ Economic growth, maintained at a steady rate over a number of decades, is the single most powerful influence on any society. It brings a transformation that continues to amaze thoughtful people. Economic growth that is maintained at a rapid rate can transform a society in years, not decades. Such transformations are taking place right now in many Asian countries. These transformations are economic miracles. ◆ The four chapters in this part studied the miracle of rapid economic growth, the forces that shape our capacity to produce goods and services, and the forces that from time to time interrupt the growth process. ◆ Chapter 29 explains how labour market equilibrium determines potential GDP. Chapter 30 studies the process of economic growth in the fast-growing economies of Asia and Canada. It explains how growth is influenced by technological change and the incentives that stimulate it. Chapter 31 studies the business cycle that interrupts growth, and Chapter 32 reviews the policy debate and looks at alternative approaches to speeding growth, smoothing the business cycle, and containing inflation. ◆ Modern ideas about economic growth owe much to two economists, Joseph Schumpeter and Paul Romer, whom you can meet on the following pages.

Incentives to Innovate

"Economic progress, in capitalist society, means turmoil."

JOSEPH
SCHUMPETER
Capitalism, Socialism, and Democracy

JOSEPH SCHUMPETER, *the son of a textile factory owner, was born in Austria in 1883. He moved from Austria to Germany during the tumultuous 1920s when those two countries experienced hyperinflation. In 1932, in the depths of the Great Depression, he came to the United States and became a professor of economics at Harvard University.*

This creative economic thinker wrote about economic growth and development, business cycles, political systems, and economic biography. He was a person of strong opinions who expressed them strongly and delighted in verbal battles.

Schumpeter has become the unwitting founder of modern growth theory. He saw the development and diffusion of new technologies by profit-seeking entrepreneurs as the source of economic progress. But he saw economic progress as a process of creative destruction—the creation of new profit opportunities and the destruction of currently profitable businesses. For Schumpeter, economic growth and the business cycle were a single phenomenon.

When Schumpeter died, in 1950, he had achieved his self-expressed life ambition: He was regarded as the world's greatest economist.

Technological change, capital accumulation, and population growth all interact to produce economic growth. But what is cause and what is effect? And can we expect productivity and income per person to keep growing?

The classical economists of the eighteenth and nineteenth centuries believed that technological advances and capital accumulation were the engines of growth. But they also believed that no matter how successful people were at inventing more productive technologies and investing in new capital, they were destined to live at the subsistence level. These economists based their conclusion on the belief that productivity growth causes population growth, which in turn causes productivity to decline. These classical economists believed that whenever economic growth raises incomes above the subsistence level, the population will increase. They went on to reason that the increase in population brings diminishing returns that lower productivity. As a result, incomes must always return to the subsistence level. Only when incomes are at the subsistence level is population growth held in check.

A new approach, called neoclassical growth theory, was developed by Robert Solow of MIT, during the 1950s. Solow, who was one of Schumpeter's students, received the Nobel Prize for Economic Science for this work.

Solow challenged the conclusions of the classical economists. But the new theories of economic growth developed during the 1980s and 1990s went further. They stand the classical belief on its head. Today's theory of population growth is that rising income slows the population growth rate because it increases the opportunity cost of having children and lowers the opportunity cost of investing in children and equipping them with more human capital, which makes them more productive. Productivity and income grow because technology advances, and the scope for further productivity growth, which is stimulated by the search for profit, is practically unlimited.

THEN

In 1830, a strong and experienced farm worker could harvest three acres of wheat in a day. The only capital employed was a scythe to cut the wheat, which had been used since Roman times, and a cradle on which the stalks were laid, which had been invented by Flemish farmers in the fifteenth century. With newly developed horse-drawn plows, harrows, and planters, farmers could plant more wheat than they could harvest. But despite big efforts, no one had been able to make a machine that could replicate the swing of a scythe. Then in 1831, 22-year-old Cyrus McCormick built a machine that worked. It scared the horse that pulled it, but it did in a matter of hours what three men could accomplish in a day. Technological change has increased productivity on farms and brought economic growth. Do the facts about productivity growth mean that the classical economists, who believed that diminishing returns would push us relentlessly back to a subsistence living standard, were wrong?

NOW

Today's technologies are expanding our horizons beyond the confines of our planet and are expanding our minds. Geosynchronous satellites bring us global television, voice and data communication, and more accurate weather forecasts, which, incidentally, increase agricultural productivity. In the foreseeable future, we might have superconductors that revolutionize the use of electric power, virtual reality theme parks and training facilities, pollution-free hydrogen cars, wristwatch telephones, and optical computers that we can talk to. Equipped with these new technologies, our ability to create yet more dazzling technologies increases. Technological change begets technological change in an (apparently) unending process and makes us ever more productive and brings ever higher incomes.

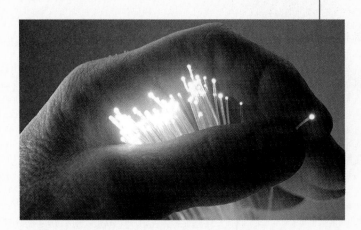

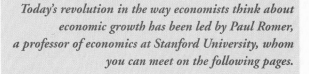

Today's revolution in the way economists think about economic growth has been led by Paul Romer, a professor of economics at Stanford University, whom you can meet on the following pages.

TALKING WITH

Paul Romer

PAUL ROMER *is Professor of Economics at the Graduate School of Business at Stanford University and the Royal Bank Fellow of the Canadian Institute for Advanced Research. Born in 1955 in Denver, Colorado, he earned his B.S. in Mathematics (1977) and his Ph.D. in Economics (1983) from the University of Chicago.*

Professor Romer has transformed the way economists think about economic growth. He believes that sustained economic growth arises from competition among firms. Firms try to increase their profits by devoting resources to creating new products and developing new ways of making existing products.

Michael Parkin and Robin Bade talked with Professor Romer about his work, how he was influenced by Joseph Schumpeter and Robert Solow, and the insights economic growth offers us.

Professor Romer, why did you decide to become an economist?

As an undergraduate, I studied math and physics and was interested in becoming a cosmologist. During my senior year, I concluded that job prospects in physics were not very promising, so I decided to go to law school. I was an undergraduate at the University of Chicago, where the law and economics movement first emerged. In the fall of my senior year, I took my first economics course to prepare for law school. My economics pro-

fessor, Sam Peltzman presented a simple piece of economic analysis that changed my life. He argued that the demand for economists was likely to grow for decades. The government, which employs economists, would grow in size. Businesses that deal with the government would want their own economists. The legal profession that serves businesses would also need more economists. Because of all these demands, many students would want to take economics courses. This meant that there would be many job openings for economists at universities. Moreover, he claimed, being a professor of economics was a lot like being a cosmologist and far more fun than being a lawyer. I could take fragmentary bits of evidence and try to make sense of them using mathematical equations. So I tore up my law school applications, applied to graduate school in economics, and never looked back.

What are the truly important lessons about the causes economic growth?

As a physics major, I felt that the description economists used for growth violated a basic law of physics: the conservation of mass. Economists seemed to be saying that GDP, the output of a nation, was a bunch of stuff that was "produced" and that the quantity of stuff produced has grown steadily over time and will continue to do so. But this can't be right. We have the same amount of stuff, or elements from the periodic table, that we had 100,000 years ago. Because there are many more people now, in terms of kilograms of matter per person, we know that we are vastly poorer than our ancestors were 100,000 years ago. Yet we clearly have a higher standard of living. How could this be? This basic question indicates that thinking about growth as a production process that generates stuff is a dead-end. Instead, economic growth has to be about rearranging the fixed amount of matter that we have to work with and making new combinations that seem a lot more valuable. The key insight is that economic growth comes from increases in value, not increases in the amount of matter.

Can you give us an example of an increase in value?

For tens of thousands of years, we treated iron oxide, ordinary rust, like dirt. When we lived in caves, we learned how to use it as a pigment for decorating cave walls. We took the low-value dirt and put it to the higher-valued use of making cave paintings. Later, we learned how to extract the iron from iron ore to make bridges and rails. Later still, we learned how to arrange the iron atoms together with carbon atoms and make steel. Recently, we learned how to take iron oxide and put it on magnetic tape and use it to store sound and pictures. The iron, oxygen, and carbon atoms have always been here. We have a higher standard of living because we have learned how to arrange these atoms in ways that we find more valuable.

What kind of policy implications does this kind of thinking lead to?

Policy makers must encourage institutions to become more efficient at discovering new recipes to rearrange matter. Consider the transistor as an example. We take silicon and mix it with a few impurities and some metal in just the right way, and we get a computer chip worth thousands of times what the raw ingredients were worth. Research grants, subsidies for education, and institutions like the nonprofit private

> *We take silicon and mix it with a few impurities and some metal in just the right way, and we get a computer chip worth thousands of times what the raw ingredients were worth.*

university encourage the production of new recipes or ideas. But so do venture capitalists who help new-technology startups, competitive markets that allow the firms with better instructions or ideas to quickly displace existing firms, and labour laws that let ineffi-

cient firms lay off workers when more efficient new firms come on the scene. We must let firms like Digital Electronics or Wang Computers shrink, maybe even fail, if we want to make room for new firms like Intel to enter the scene and thrive.

Were the classical economists wrong in their view that population growth and diminishing returns are the dominant long-term influences on production and incomes? Or is the current global population explosion part of a process that will ultimately prove them correct?

Classical economists like Malthus and Ricardo were right when they argued that we have a fixed amount of natural resources to work with. Malthus pointed out that resource scarcity will lead to falling standards of living if we continue to work with the same set of recipes or instructions for using our resources. Where he went wrong was in assuming that there was little scope for us to find new recipes for taking resources such as land, water, carbon dioxide, nitrogen, and sunshine and converting them into carbohydrates and proteins that we can eat.

The classical economists got half of the story right. We do live in a world with scarce resources. They missed the other half. There is an incomprehensibly large number of different formulas we can use to recombine these scarce resources into things we value, such as protein or entertainment.

Scarcity is a very important part of economics and our lives. For example, we know that there is an absolute limit on the number of people who can live on the earth. One way or another, we know that the rate of population growth will slow down. It's only a question of how and when. But will this ultimately lead to a period when standards of living fall as Malthus predicted? I doubt it. As countries get rich, population growth slows. As a larger fraction of the worldwide population becomes educated, these people will help us to discover new things, like plants that are more efficient at taking carbon dioxide out of the atmosphere, and more efficient distribution systems. Thus standards of living for all humans will continue to improve.

During the past decade, China and several other economies in East Asia have experienced rapid, unheralded growth rates. Why?

These countries took some of the recipes, formulas, and instructions for generating value that already existed in the advanced countries of the world and put them to use within their borders. It's the same process that the Japanese followed after the Meiji restoration at the end of the last century. These countries noticed that other people in the world knew a lot about how to create value and realized that by trading with these people, they could share in the gains.

What lessons from East Asia can, in principle, be applied in Africa and Central Europe?

The basic insight is that there are huge potential gains from trade. Poor countries can supply their natural and human resources. Rich countries can supply their know-how. When these are combined, everyone can be better off. The challenge is for a country to arrange its laws and institutions so that both sides can profitably engage in trade. If there are barriers to trade or if the government cannot protect basic property rights and prevent crime, trade can't take place. For example, the Japanese have been able to borrow many ideas about manufacturing and design and even to improve on some of these ideas. But because they have barriers that limit entry of foreign firms into the retail sector, they still waste vast quantities of resources on a very inefficient distribution system.

What does today's thinking about economic growth owe to Joseph Schumpeter and Robert Solow?

Schumpeter worked at a time before most economists had learned to work with equations. He coined the phrase "creative destruction," which describes the process by which companies like Wang shrink or go out of business when new firms come in. He also described in words how important monopoly profits are in the process of innovation. There were many other economists, including Alfred Marshall, who described these same issues in verbal terms and also struggled to express these ideas in terms of equations.

Robert Solow was part of the post-World War II generation of economists who truly mastered the use of equations and wrote eloquently using both words and equations. As a result, his ideas have been far more influential than Schumpeter's. Many economists in the 1950s were trying to get a grasp on the economic effects of knowledge, formulas, recipes, and instructions. Solow called these things "technology" and gave us a wonderfully concise and workable way to think about how technology interacts with other economic inputs such as capital and labour. He also linked the methods that he and several economists were using to measure technology with this framework for thinking about the behaviour of the economy as a whole. His work on growth was a masterful piece of invention, synthesis, and exposition.

Recent economists have taken Solow's mathematical framework and extended it to bring in some of the elements that Schumpeter described in words, like creative destruction and monopoly power. One of the great things about ideas is that they build on each other. In Isaac Newton's famous phrase, those of us working on growth today are "able to see farther because we stand on the shoulders of giants." Newton was another person who was pretty good with equations and could turn a good phrase.

Is economics a worthwhile subject to major in? What can one do with an economics degree?

Economics is an excellent training ground for developing mathematical and verbal skills. But students should supplement the courses in economics with courses in mathematics and science that force them to practise working with equations, graphs, and numbers. There is no substitute for such practice. Innate ability is far less important than most students think.

> *If you can learn how to write readable prose and use the basic tools of mathematics, you can do almost anything.*

They should also take courses that force them to write, revise, and edit. I took an English course in college that taught me the basics of how to edit, and it is one of the best investments I made. You can't tell what you will end up doing or what skills you will need later in life. But if you can learn how to write readable prose and use the basic tools of mathematics, you can do almost anything.

TRADING WITH THE WORLD

CHAPTER

33

Silk Routes and Sucking Sounds

Since ancient times, people have expanded their trading as far as technology allowed. Marco Polo opened up the silk route between Europe and China in the thirteenth century. Today, container ships laden with cars and electronics and Boeing 747s stuffed with farm-fresh foods ply sea and air routes, carrying billions of dollars' worth of goods. Why do people go to such great lengths to trade with those in other nations? ◆ In 1994, Canada entered into a free trade agreement with the United States and Mexico—the North American Free Trade Agreement, or NAFTA. Some people predicted a "giant sucking sound" as jobs were transferred from high-wage Michigan and Ontario to low-wage Mexico. Can we compete with a country that pays its workers a fraction of Canadian wages? Are there any industries, besides perhaps the software and movie industries, in which we have an advantage? ◆ Canada exports lumber to the United States for homebuilding. But U.S. lumber producers say that Canadian producers receive an unfair subsidy from their government, so the United States has imposed a tariff on Canadian lumber imports. Do tariffs benefit the importing country? We examine this question in *Reading Between the Lines*.

◆ In this chapter, we're going to learn about international trade and discover how *all* nations can gain from trading with other nations. We'll discover that all nations can compete, no matter how high their wages. We'll also explain why, despite the fact that international trade brings benefits to all, governments restrict trade.

After studying this chapter, you will be able to

- ■ **Describe the trends and patterns in international trade**

- ■ **Explain comparative advantage and explain why all countries can gain from international trade**

- ■ **Explain why international trade restrictions reduce the volume of imports and exports and reduce our consumption possibilities**

- ■ **Explain the arguments that are used to justify international trade restrictions and show how they are flawed**

- ■ **Explain why we have international trade restrictions**

Patterns and Trends in International Trade

THE GOODS AND SERVICES THAT WE BUY FROM people in other countries are called **imports.** The goods and services that we sell to people in other countries are called **exports.** What are the most important things that we import and export? Most people would probably guess that a rich nation such as Canada imports raw materials and exports manufactured goods. Although that is one feature of Canadian international trade, it is not its most important feature. The vast bulk of our exports *and* imports is manufactured goods. We sell foreigners earth-moving equipment, airplanes, telecommunications equipment, and scientific equipment. We buy televisions, VCRs, blue jeans, and T-shirts from foreigners. Also, we are a major exporter of agricultural products and raw materials. We also import and export a huge volume of services.

Trade in Goods

Of the goods that we trade, manufactured goods account for 50 percent of our exports and 70 percent of our imports. Industrial materials (raw materials and semimanufactured items) account for 40 percent of our exports and 15 percent of our imports, and agricultural products account for only 5 percent of our exports and 2 percent of our imports. Our largest individual export and import items are capital goods and automobiles.

But goods account for only 80 percent of our exports and imports. The rest of our international trade is in services.

Trade in Services

You may be wondering how a country can "export" and "import" services. Here are some examples.

If you take a vacation in France and travel there on an Air France flight from Montreal, you import transportation services from France. The money you spend in France on hotel bills and restaurant meals is also classified as the import of services. Similarly, the money spent by a French student on vacation in Canada is a Canadian export of services to France.

When we import TV sets from South Korea, the owner of the ship that transports them might be

Greek and the company that insures them might be British. The payments that we make for the transportation and insurance are Canadian imports of services. Similarly, when a Canadian shipping company transports timber from British Columbia to Tokyo, the transportation cost is a Canadian export of a service to Japan. Our international trade in these types of services is large and growing.

Geographical Patterns of International Trade

Canada has trading links with every part of the world, but the United States is our biggest trading partner. In 2001, 82 percent of our exports went to the United States and 71 percent of our imports came from the United States. Our trade with the European Union is also large—7 percent of our exports and 11 percent of our imports in 2001. Other major trading partners include the countries of Latin America and Japan. But our trade with Japan is only 2 percent of exports and 3 percent of imports.

Trends in the Volume of Trade

In 1978, we exported 25 percent of total output and imported 25 percent of the goods and services that we bought. In 2001, we exported 43 percent of total output and imported 38 percent of the goods and services that we bought.

On the export side, capital goods, automobiles, food, and raw materials have remained large items and held a roughly constant share of total exports. But the composition of imports has changed. Food and raw material imports have fallen steadily. Imports of fuel increased during the 1970s but decreased during the 1980s. Imports of machinery have grown and today approach 30 percent of total imports.

Net Exports and International Borrowing

The value of exports minus the value of imports is called **net exports.** In 2001, Canadian net exports were $57 billion. Our exports were $57 billion more than our imports. When we export more than we import, as we did in 2001, we lend to foreigners or buy some of their assets. When we import more than we export, we borrow from foreigners or sell some of our assets to them.

The Gains from International Trade

THE FUNDAMENTAL FORCE THAT GENERATES international trade is *comparative advantage*. And the basis of comparative advantage is divergent *opportunity costs*. You met these ideas in Chapter 2, when we learned about the gains from specialization and exchange between Tom and Nancy.

Tom and Nancy each specialize in producing just one good and then trade with each other. Most nations do not go to the extreme of specializing in a single good and importing everything else. But nations can increase the consumption of all goods if they redirect their scarce resources towards the production of those goods and services in which they have a comparative advantage.

To see how this outcome occurs, we'll apply the same basic ideas that we learned in the case of Tom and Nancy to trade among nations. We'll begin by recalling how we can use the production possibilities frontier to measure opportunity cost. Then we'll see how divergent opportunity costs bring comparative advantage and gains from trade for countries as well as for individuals even though no country completely specializes in the production of just one good.

Opportunity Cost in Farmland

Farmland (a fictitious country) can produce grain and cars at any point inside or along its production possibilities frontier, *PPF*, shown in Fig. 33.1. (We're holding constant the output of all the other goods that Farmland produces.) The Farmers (the people of Farmland) are consuming all the grain and cars that they produce, and they are operating at point *A* in the figure. That is, Farmland is producing and consuming 15 million tonnes of grain and 8 million cars each year. What is the opportunity cost of a car in Farmland?

We can answer that question by calculating the slope of the production possibilities frontier at point *A*. The magnitude of the slope of the frontier measures the opportunity cost of one good in terms of the other. To measure the slope of the frontier at point *A*, place a straight line tangential to the frontier at point *A* and calculate the slope of that straight line. Recall that the formula for the slope of a line is the change in the value of the variable measured on the *y*-axis divided by the change in the value of the variable

measured on the *x*-axis as we move along the line. Here, the variable measured on the *y*-axis is millions of tonnes of grain, and the variable measured on the *x*-axis is millions of cars. So the slope is the change in the number of tonnes of grain divided by the change in the number of cars.

As you can see from the red triangle at point *A* in the figure, if the number of cars produced increases by 2 million, grain production decreases by 18 million tonnes. Therefore the magnitude of the slope is 18 million divided by 2 million, which equals 9. To get one more car, the people of Farmland must give up 9 tonnes of grain. So the opportunity cost of 1 car is 9 tonnes of grain. Equivalently, 9 tonnes of grain cost 1 car. For the people of Farmland, these opportunity costs are the prices they face. The price of a car is 9 tonnes of grain, and the price of 9 tonnes of grain is 1 car.

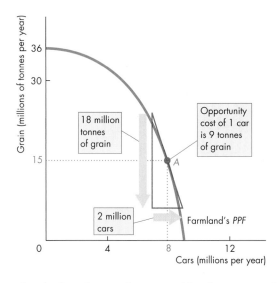

FIGURE 33.1   Opportunity Cost in Farmland

Farmland produces and consumes 15 million tonnes of grain and 8 million cars a year. That is, it produces and consumes at point A on its production possibilities frontier. Opportunity cost is equal to the magnitude of the slope of the production possibilities frontier. The red triangle tells us that at point A, 18 million tonnes of grain must be forgone to get 2 million cars. That is, at point A, 2 million cars cost 18 million tonnes of grain. Equivalently, 1 car costs 9 tonnes of grain or 9 tonnes of grain cost 1 car.

Opportunity Cost in Mobilia

Figure 33.2 shows the production possibilities frontier of Mobilia (another fictitious country). Like the Farmers, the Mobilians consume all the grain and cars that they produce. Mobilia consumes 18 million tonnes of grain a year and 4 million cars, at point A'.

Let's calculate the opportunity costs in Mobilia. At point A', the opportunity cost of a car is equal to the magnitude of the slope of the red line tangential to the production possibilities frontier, *PPF*. You can see from the red triangle that the magnitude of the slope of Mobilia's production possibilities frontier is 6 million tonnes of grain divided by 6 million cars, which equals 1 tonne of grain per car. To get one more car, the Mobilians must give up 1 tonne of grain. So the opportunity cost of 1 car is 1 tonne of grain, or equivalently, the opportunity cost of 1 tonne of grain is 1 car. These are the prices faced in Mobilia.

Comparative Advantage

Cars are cheaper in Mobilia than in Farmland. One car costs 9 tonnes of grain in Farmland but only 1 tonne of grain in Mobilia. But grain is cheaper in Farmland than in Mobilia—9 tonnes of grain cost only 1 car in Farmland, while that same amount of grain costs 9 cars in Mobilia.

Mobilia has a comparative advantage in car production. Farmland has a comparative advantage in grain production. A country has a comparative advantage in producing a good if it can produce that good at a lower opportunity cost than any other country. Let's see how opportunity cost differences and comparative advantage generate gains from international trade.

The Gains from Trade: Cheaper to Buy Than to Produce

If Mobilia bought grain for what it costs Farmland to produce it, then Mobilia could buy 9 tonnes of grain for 1 car. That is much lower than the cost of growing grain in Mobilia, for there it costs 9 cars to produce 9 tonnes of grain. If the Mobilians can buy grain at the low Farmland price, they will reap some gains.

If the Farmers can buy cars for what it costs Mobilia to produce them, they will be able to obtain a car for 1 tonne of grain. Because it costs 9 tonnes of grain to produce a car in Farmland, the Farmers would gain from such an opportunity.

In this situation, it makes sense for Mobilians to buy their grain from Farmers and for Farmers to buy their cars from Mobilians. But at what price will Farmland and Mobilia engage in mutually beneficial international trade?

The Terms of Trade

The quantity of grain that Farmland must pay Mobilia for a car is Farmland's **terms of trade** with Mobilia. Because Canada exports and imports many different goods and services, we measure the terms of trade in the real world as an index number that averages the terms of trade over all the items we trade.

The forces of international supply and demand determine the terms of trade. Figure 33.3 illustrates these forces in the Farmland-Mobilia international car market. The quantity of cars *traded internationally* is measured on the *x*-axis. On the *y*-axis, we measure the price of a car. This price is expressed as the *terms of trade*: tonnes of grain per car. If no international trade takes place, the price of a car in Farmland is 9 tonnes of grain, its opportunity cost, indicated by point *A* in

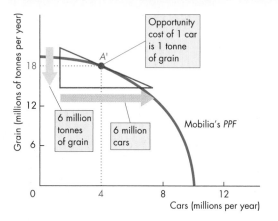

FIGURE 33.2   Opportunity Cost in Mobilia

Mobilia produces and consumes 18 million tonnes of grain and 4 million cars a year. That is, it produces and consumes at point A' on its production possibilities frontier. Opportunity cost is equal to the magnitude of the slope of the production possibilities frontier. The red triangle tells us that at point A', 6 million tonnes of grain must be forgone to get 6 million cars. That is, at point A', 6 million cars cost 6 million tonnes of grain. Equivalently, 1 car costs 1 tonne of grain or 1 tonne of grain costs 1 car.

FIGURE 33.3   International Trade in Cars

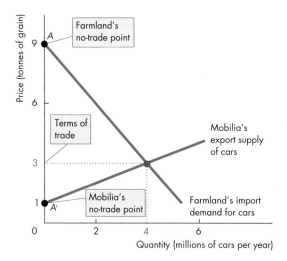

Farmland's import demand curve for cars is downward sloping, and Mobilia's export supply curve of cars is upward sloping. Without international trade, the price of a car is 9 tonnes of grain in Farmland (point A) and 1 tonne of grain in Mobilia (point A').

With free international trade, the price (terms of trade) is determined where the export supply curve intersects the import demand curve: 3 tonnes of grain per car. At that price, 4 million cars a year are imported by Farmland and exported by Mobilia. The value of grain exported by Farmland and imported by Mobilia is 12 million tonnes a year, the quantity required to pay for the cars imported.

the figure. Again, if no trade takes place, the price of a car in Mobilia is 1 tonne of grain, its opportunity cost, indicated by point A' in the figure. The no-trade points A and A' in Fig. 33.3 correspond to the points identified by those same letters in Figs. 33.1 and 33.2. The lower the price of a car (terms of trade), the greater is the quantity of cars that the Farmers are willing to import from the Mobilians. This fact is illustrated by the downward-sloping curve, which shows Farmland's import demand for cars.

The Mobilians respond in the opposite direction. The higher the price of a car (terms of trade), the greater is the quantity of cars that Mobilians are willing to export to Farmers. This fact is reflected in Mobilia's export supply of cars—the upward-sloping line in Fig. 33.3.

The international market in cars determines the equilibrium terms of trade (price) and quantity traded. This equilibrium occurs where the import demand curve intersects the export supply curve. In this case, the equilibrium terms of trade are 3 tonnes of grain per car. Mobilia exports and Farmland imports 4 million cars a year. Notice that the terms of trade are lower than the initial price in Farmland but higher than the initial price in Mobilia.

Balanced Trade

The number of cars exported by Mobilia—4 million a year—is exactly equal to the number of cars imported by Farmland. How does Farmland pay for its cars? The answer is by exporting grain. How much grain does Farmland export? You can find the answer by noticing that for 1 car, Farmland must pay 3 tonnes of grain. So for 4 million cars, Farmland pays 12 million tonnes of grain. Farmland's exports of grain are 12 million tonnes a year, and Mobilia imports this same quantity of grain.

Mobilia is exchanging 4 million cars for 12 million tonnes of grain each year, and Farmland is doing the opposite: exchanging 12 million tonnes of grain for 4 million cars. Trade is balanced between these two countries. The value received from exports equals the value paid out for imports.

Changes in Production and Consumption

We've seen that international trade makes it possible for Farmers to buy cars at a lower price than they can produce them and sell their grain for a higher price. International trade also enables Mobilians to sell their cars for a higher price and buy grain for a lower price. Everyone gains. How is it possible for *everyone* to gain? What are the changes in production and consumption that accompany these gains?

An economy that does not trade with other economies has identical production and consumption possibilities. Without trade, the economy can consume only what it produces. But with international trade, an economy can consume different quantities of goods from those that it produces. The production possibilities frontier describes the limit of what a country can produce, but it does not describe the limits to what it can consume. Figure 33.4 will help you to see the distinction between production possibilities and consumption possibilities when a country trades with other countries.

FIGURE 33.4 Expanding Consumption Possibilities

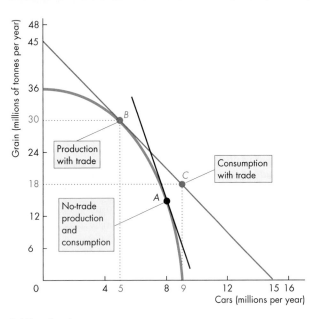

(a) Farmland

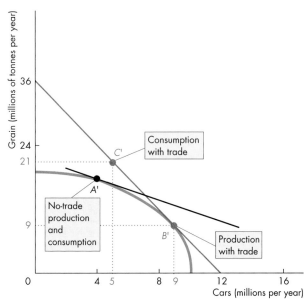

(b) Mobilia

With no international trade, the Farmers produce and consume at point *A* and the opportunity cost of a car is 9 tonnes of grain (the slope of the black line in part a). Also, with no international trade, the Mobilians produce and consume at point *A'* and the opportunity cost of 1 tonne of grain is 1 car (the slope of the black line in part b). Goods can be exchanged internationally at a price of 3 tonnes of grain for 1 car along the red line in each part of the figure. In part (a), Farmland decreases its production of cars and increases its production of grain, moving from *A*

to *B*. It exports grain and imports cars, and it consumes at point *C*. The Farmers have more of both cars and grain than they would if they produced all their own consumption goods—at point *A*. In part (b), Mobilia increases car production and decreases grain production, moving from *A'* to *B'*. Mobilia exports cars and imports grain, and it consumes at point *C'*. The Mobilians have more of both cars and grain than they would if they produced all their own consumption goods—at point *A'*.

First of all, notice that the figure has two parts: part (a) for Farmland and part (b) for Mobilia. The production possibilities frontiers that you saw in Figs. 33.1 and 33.2 are reproduced here. The slopes of the two black lines in the figure represent the opportunity costs in the two countries when there is no international trade. Farmland produces and consumes at point *A*, and Mobilia produces and consumes at *A'*. Cars cost 9 tonnes of grain in Farmland and 1 tonne of grain in Mobilia.

Consumption Possibilities The red line in each part of Fig. 33.4 shows the country's consumption possibilities with international trade. These two red

lines have the same slope, and the magnitude of that slope is the opportunity cost of a car in terms of grain on the world market: 3 tonnes per car. The *slope* of the consumption possibilities line is common to both countries because its magnitude equals the *world* price. But the position of a country's consumption possibilities line depends on the country's production possibilities. A country cannot produce outside its production possibilities curve, so its consumption possibilities curve touches its production possibilities curve. So Farmland could choose to consume at point *B* with no international trade or, with international trade, at any point on its red consumption possibilities line.

Free Trade Equilibrium With international trade, the producers of cars in Mobilia can get a higher price for their output. As a result, they increase the quantity of car production. At the same time, grain producers in Mobilia get a lower price for their grain, and so they reduce production. Producers in Mobilia adjust their output by moving along their production possibilities frontier until the opportunity cost in Mobilia equals the world price (the opportunity cost in the world market). This situation arises when Mobilia is producing at point B' in Fig. 33.4(b).

But the Mobilians do not consume at point B'. That is, they do not increase their consumption of cars and decrease their consumption of grain. Instead, they sell some of their car production to Farmland in exchange for some of Farmland's grain. They trade internationally. But to see how that works out, we first need to check in with Farmland to see what's happening there.

In Farmland, producers of cars now get a lower price and producers of grain get a higher price. As a consequence, producers in Farmland decrease car production and increase grain production. They adjust their outputs by moving along the production possibilities frontier until the opportunity cost of a car in terms of grain equals the world price (the opportunity cost on the world market). They move to point B in part (a). But the Farmers do not consume at point B. Instead, they trade some of their additional grain production for the now cheaper cars from Mobilia.

The figure shows us the quantities consumed in the two countries. We saw in Fig. 33.3 that Mobilia exports 4 million cars a year and Farmland imports those cars. We also saw that Farmland exports 12 million tonnes of grain a year and Mobilia imports that grain. So Farmland's consumption of grain is 12 million tonnes a year less than it produces, and its consumption of cars is 4 million a year more than it produces. Farmland consumes at point C in Fig. 33.4(a).

Similarly, we know that Mobilia consumes 12 million tonnes of grain more than it produces and 4 million cars fewer than it produces. Mobilia consumes at point C' in Fig. 33.4(b).

Calculating the Gains from Trade

You can now literally see the gains from trade in Fig. 33.4. Without trade, Farmers produce and consume at A (part a)—a point on Farmland's production possibilities frontier. With international trade, Farmers

consume at point C in part (a)—a point *outside* the production possibilities frontier. At point C, Farmers are consuming 3 million tonnes of grain a year and 1 million cars a year more than before. These increases in consumption of both cars and grain, beyond the limits of the production possibilities frontier, are the Farmers' gains from international trade.

Mobilians also gain. Without trade, they consume at point A' in part (b)—a point on Mobilia's production possibilities frontier. With international trade, they consume at point C'—a point outside their production possibilities frontier. With international trade, Mobilia consumes 3 million tonnes of grain a year and 1 million cars a year more than it would without trade. These are the gains from international trade for Mobilia.

Gains for All

Trade between the Farmers and the Mobilians does not create winners and losers. It creates only winners. Farmers selling grain and Mobilians selling cars face an increased demand for their products because the net demand by foreigners is added to domestic demand. With an increase in demand, the price rises.

Farmers buying cars and Mobilians buying grain face an increased supply of these products because the net foreign supply is added to domestic supply. With an increase in supply, the price falls.

Gains from Trade in Reality

The gains from trade that we have just studied between Farmland and Mobilia in grain and cars occur in a model economy—in a world economy that we have imagined. But these same phenomena occur every day in the real global economy.

Comparative Advantage in the Global Economy We buy TVs and VCRs from Korea, machinery from Europe, and fashion goods from Hong Kong. In exchange, we sell machinery, grain and lumber, airplanes, computers, and financial services. All this international trade is generated by comparative advantage, just like the international trade between Farmland and Mobilia in our model economy. All international trade arises from comparative advantage, even when trade is in similar goods such as tools and machines. At first thought, it seems puzzling that countries exchange manufactured goods. Why doesn't each developed country produce all the manufactured goods its citizens want to buy?

Trade in Similar Goods Why does Canada produce automobiles for export and at the same time import large quantities of automobiles from the United States, Japan, Korea, and Western Europe? Wouldn't it make more sense to produce all the cars that we buy here in Canada? After all, we have access to the best technology available for producing cars. Auto workers in Canada are surely as productive as their fellow workers in the United States, Western Europe, and Asian countries. So why does Canada have a comparative advantage in some types of cars and Japan and Europe in others?

Diversity of Taste and Economies of Scale The first part of the answer is that people have a tremendous diversity of taste. Let's stick with the example of cars. Some people prefer a sports car, some prefer a limousine, some prefer a regular, full-size car, some prefer a sport utility vehicle, and some prefer a mini-van. In addition to size and type of car, there are many other dimensions in which cars vary. Some have low fuel consumption, some have high performance, some are spacious and comfortable, some have a large trunk, some have four-wheel drive, some have front-wheel drive, some have a radiator grille that looks like a Greek temple, others resemble a wedge. People's preferences across these many dimensions vary. The tremendous diversity in tastes for cars means that people value variety and are willing to pay for it in the marketplace.

The second part of the answer to the puzzle is *economies of scale*—the tendency for the average cost to be lower, the larger the scale of production. In such situations, larger and larger production runs lead to ever lower average costs. Production of many goods, including cars, involves economies of scale. For example, if a car producer makes only a few hundred (or perhaps a few thousand) cars of a particular type and design, the producer must use production techniques that are much more labour-intensive and much less automated than those employed to make hundreds of thousands of cars in a particular model. With short production runs and labour-intensive production techniques, costs are high. With very large production runs and automated assembly lines, production costs are much lower. But to obtain lower costs, the automated assembly lines have to produce a large number of cars.

It is the combination of diversity of taste and economies of scale that determines opportunity cost, produces comparative advantages, and generates such

a large amount of international trade in similar commodities. With international trade, each car manufacturer has the whole world market to serve. Each producer can specialize in a limited range of products and then sell its output to the entire world market. This arrangement enables large production runs on the most popular cars and feasible production runs even on the most customized cars demanded by only a handful of people in each country.

The situation in the market for cars is also present in many other industries, especially those producing specialized equipment and parts. For example, Canada exports illustration software but imports database software, exports telecommunications systems but imports PCs, exports specialized video equipment but imports VCRs. International trade in similar but slightly different manufactured products is profitable.

REVIEW QUIZ

1 What is the fundamental source of the gains from international trade?
2 In what circumstances can countries gain from international trade?
3 What determines the goods and services that a country will export?
4 What determines the goods and services that a country will import?
5 What is comparative advantage and what role does it play in determining the amount and type of international trade that occurs?
6 How can it be that all countries gain from international trade and that there are no losers?
7 Provide some examples of comparative advantage in today's world.
8 Why does Canada both export and import automobiles?

You've now seen how free international trade brings gains for all. But trade is not free in our world. We'll now take a brief look at the history of international trade restrictions and also work out the effects of international trade restrictions. We'll see that free trade brings the greatest possible benefits and that international trade restrictions are costly.

International Trade Restrictions

GOVERNMENTS RESTRICT INTERNATIONAL TRADE to protect domestic industries from foreign competition by using two main tools:

1. Tariffs
2. Nontariff barriers

A **tariff** is a tax that is imposed by the importing country when an imported good crosses its international boundary. A **nontariff barrier** is any action other than a tariff that restricts international trade. Examples of nontariff barriers are quantitative restrictions and licensing regulations limiting imports. First, let's look at tariffs.

The History of Tariffs

The Canadian economy has always been protected by a tariff. Figure 33.5 shows the history of that tariff, from Confederation through 2001. The figure shows tariffs as a percentage of total imports—the average tariff rate. As you can see, the average tariff rate climbed from the early 1870s to exceed 20 percent by

the late 1880s. The rate fluctuated but gradually decreased through the early 1920s. It increased again during the Great Depression years of the early 1930s. During these years, most countries increased their tariff rates in what became a "beggar-my-neighbour" policy. The average tariff then decreased through the late 1930s and continued its decrease throughout the years after World War II. Today, the average tariff rate is less than 1 percent.

The reduction in tariffs after World War II followed the signing in 1947 of the **General Agreement on Tariffs and Trade** (GATT). From its formation, GATT organized a series of "rounds" of negotiations that resulted in a steady process of tariff reduction. One of these, the Kennedy Round that began in the early 1960s, resulted in large tariff cuts starting in 1967. Another, the Tokyo Round, resulted in further tariff cuts in 1979. The final round, the Uruguay Round, started in 1986 and was completed in 1994.

The Uruguay Round was the most ambitious and comprehensive of the rounds and led to the creation of the **World Trade Organization** (WTO). Membership of the WTO brings greater obligations for countries to observe the GATT rules. Canada signed the Uruguay Round agreements, and Parliament ratified them in 1994.

In addition to the agreements under the GATT

FIGURE 33.5 Canadian Tariffs: 1867–2001

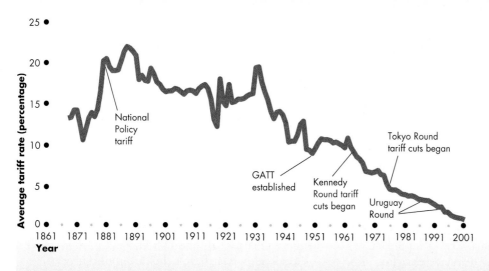

Canadian tariffs were in place before Confederation. Tariffs increased sharply in the 1870s and remained high until the 1930s. Since the establishment of the GATT in 1947, tariffs have steadily declined in a series of negotiating rounds, the most significant of which are identified in the figure. Tariffs are now as low as they have ever been.

Sources: Statistics Canada, *Historial Statistics of Canada*, Series G485, CANSIM tables 380-0002 and 380-0007, and authors' calculations.

and the WTO, Canada is a party to the **North American Free Trade Agreement** (NAFTA), which became effective on January 1, 1994, and under which barriers to international trade between the United States, Canada, and Mexico will be virtually eliminated after a 15-year phasing-in period.

In other parts of the world, trade barriers have virtually been eliminated among the member countries of the European Union, which has created the largest unified tariff-free market in the world. In 1994, discussions among the Asia-Pacific Economic Cooperation (APEC) led to an agreement in principle to work towards a free-trade area that embraces China, all the economies of East Asia and the South Pacific, and the United States and Canada. These countries include the fastest-growing economies and hold the promise of heralding a global free-trade area.

The effort to achieve freer trade underlines the fact that trade in some goods is still subject to a high tariff. Textiles and footwear are among the goods that face the highest tariffs, and rates on these items average more than 10 percent. Some individual items face a tariff much higher than the average. For example, when you buy a pair of blue jeans for $20, you pay about $5 more than you would if there were no tariffs on textiles. Other goods that are protected by tariffs are agricultural products, energy and chemicals, minerals, and metals. The meat, cheese, and sugar that you consume cost significantly more because of protection than they would with free international trade.

The temptation for governments to impose tariffs is a strong one. First, tariffs provide revenue to the government. Second, they enable the government to satisfy special interest groups in import-competing industries. But, as we'll see, free international trade brings enormous benefits that are reduced when tariffs are imposed. Let's see how.

How Tariffs Work

To see how tariffs work, let's return to the example of trade between Farmland and Mobilia. Figure 33.6 shows the international market for cars in which these two countries are the only traders. The volume of trade and the price of a car are determined at the point of intersection of Mobilia's export supply curve of cars and Farmland's import demand curve for cars.

In Fig. 33.6, these two countries trade cars and grain in exactly the same way that we saw in Fig. 33.3.

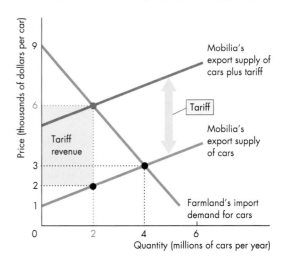

FIGURE 33.6   The Effects of a Tariff

Farmland imposes a tariff on car imports from Mobilia. The tariff increases the price that Farmers have to pay for cars. It shifts the supply curve of cars in Farmland leftward. The vertical distance between the original supply curve and the new one is the amount of the tariff, $4,000 per car. The price of cars in Farmland increases, and the quantity of cars imported decreases. The government of Farmland collects a tariff revenue of $4,000 per car—a total of $8 billion on the 2 million cars imported. Farmland's exports of grain decrease because Mobilia now has a lower income from its exports of cars.

Mobilia exports cars, and Farmland exports grain. The volume of car imports into Farmland is 4 million a year, and the world market price of a car is 3 tonnes of grain. Figure 33.6 expresses prices in dollars rather than in units of grain and is based on a money price of grain of $1 a tonne. With grain costing $1,000 a tonne, the money price of a car is $3,000.

Now suppose that the government of Farmland, perhaps under pressure from car producers, decides to impose a tariff on imported cars. In particular, suppose that a tariff of $4,000 per car is imposed. (This is a huge tariff, but the car producers of Farmland are pretty fed up with competition from Mobilia.) What happens?

- The supply of cars in Farmland decreases.
- The price of cars in Farmland rises.
- The quantity of cars imported by Farmland decreases.
- The government of Farmland collects the tariff revenue.
- Resource use is inefficient.
- The *value* of exports changes by the same amount as the *value* of imports, and trade remains balanced.

Change in the Supply of Cars Farmland cannot buy cars at Mobilia's export supply price. It must pay that price plus the $4,000 tariff. So the supply curve in Farmland shifts leftward. The new supply curve is that labelled "Mobilia's export supply of cars plus tariff." The vertical distance between Mobilia's original export supply curve and the new supply curve is the tariff of $4,000 a car.

Rise in Price of Cars A new equilibrium occurs where the new supply curve intersects Farmland's import demand curve for cars. That equilibrium is at a price of $6,000 a car, up from $3,000 with free trade.

Fall in Imports Car imports fall from 4 million to 2 million cars a year. At the higher price of $6,000 a car, domestic car producers increase their production. Domestic grain production decreases as resources are moved into the expanding car industry.

Tariff Revenue Total expenditure on imported cars by the Farmers is $6,000 a car multiplied by the 2 million cars imported ($12 billion). But not all of that money goes to the Mobilians. They receive $2,000 a car, or $4 billion for the 2 million cars. The difference—$4,000 a car, or a total of $8 billion for the 2 million cars—is collected by the government of Farmland as tariff revenue.

Inefficiency The people of Farmland are willing to pay $6,000 for the marginal car imported. But the opportunity cost of that car is $2,000. So there is a gain from trading an extra car. In fact, there are gains—willingness to pay exceeds opportunity cost— all the way up to 4 million cars a year. Only when 4 million cars are being traded is the maximum price that a Farmer is willing to pay equal to the minimum price that is acceptable to a Mobilian. Restricting trade reduces the gains from trade.

Trade Remains Balanced With free trade, Farmland was paying $3,000 a car and buying 4 million cars a year from Mobilia. The total amount paid to Mobilia for imports was $12 billion a year. With a tariff, Farmland's imports have been cut to 2 million cars a year and the price paid to Mobilia has also been cut to only $2,000 a car. The total amount paid to Mobilia for imports has been cut to $4 billion a year. Doesn't this fact mean that Farmland now has a balance of trade surplus? It does not.

The price of cars in Mobilia has fallen. But the price of grain remains at $1 a tonne. So the relative price of cars has fallen, and the relative price of grain has increased. With free trade, the Mobilians could buy 3,000 tonnes of grain for the price of one car. Now they can buy only 2,000 tonnes for the price of a car. With a higher relative price of grain, the quantity demanded by the Mobilians decreases and Mobilia imports less grain. But because Mobilia imports less grain, Farmland exports less grain. In fact, Farmland's grain industry suffers from two sources. First, there is a decrease in the quantity of grain sold to Mobilia. Second, there is increased competition for inputs from the now-expanded car industry. The tariff leads to a contraction in the scale of the grain industry in Farmland.

It seems paradoxical at first that a country imposing a tariff on cars hurts its own export industry, lowering its exports of grain. It may help to think of it this way: Mobilians buy grain with the money they make from exporting cars to Farmland. If they export fewer cars, they cannot afford to buy as much grain. In fact, in the absence of any international borrowing and lending, Mobilia must cut its imports of grain by exactly the same amount as the loss in revenue from its export of cars. Grain imports into Mobilia are cut back to a value of $4 billion, the amount that can be paid for by the new lower revenue from Mobilia's car exports. Trade is still balanced. The tariff cuts imports and exports by the same amount. The tariff has no effect on the *balance* of trade, but it reduces the *volume* of trade.

The result that we have just derived is perhaps one of the most misunderstood aspects of international economics. On countless occasions, politicians and others call for tariffs to remove a balance of trade deficit or argue that lowering tariffs would produce a balance of trade deficit. They reach this conclusion by failing to work out all the implications of a tariff.

Let's now look at nontariff barriers.

Nontariff Barriers

The two main forms of nontariff barriers are

1. Quotas
2. Voluntary export restraints

A **quota** is a quantitative restriction on the import of a particular good, which specifies the maximum amount of the good that may be imported in a given period of time. A **voluntary export restraint** (VER) is an agreement between two governments in which the government of the exporting country agrees to restrain the volume of its own exports.

Quotas are especially prominent in textiles and agriculture. Voluntary export restraints are used to regulate trade between Japan and Canada.

How Quotas and VERs Work

To see how a quota works, suppose that Farmland imposes a quota that restricts its car imports to 2 million cars a year. Figure 33.7 shows the effects of this action. The quota is shown by the vertical red line at 2 million cars a year. Because it is illegal to exceed the quota, car importers buy only that quantity from Mobilia, for which they pay $2,000 a car. But because the import supply of cars is restricted to 2 million cars a year, people are willing to pay $6,000 per car. This is the price of a car in Farmland.

The value of imports falls to $4 billion, exactly the same as in the case of the tariff in Fig. 33.6. So with lower incomes from car exports and with a higher relative price of grain, Mobilians cut back on their imports of grain in exactly the same way that they did under a tariff.

The key difference between a quota and a tariff lies in who collects the gap between the import supply price and the domestic price. In the case of a tariff, it is the government of the importing country. In the case of a quota, it goes to the person who has the right to import under the import quota regulations.

A VER is like a quota arrangement in which quotas are allocated to each exporting country. The effects of VERs are similar to those of quotas but differ from them in that the gap between the domestic price and the export price is captured not by domestic importers but by the foreign exporter. The government of the exporting country has to establish procedures for allocating the restricted volume of exports among its producers.

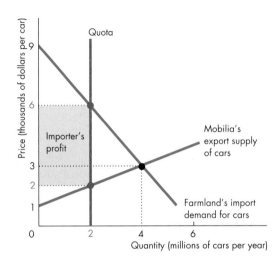

FIGURE 33.7   The Effects of a Quota

Farmland imposes a quota of 2 million cars a year on car imports from Mobilia. That quantity appears as the vertical line labelled "Quota." Because the quantity of cars supplied by Mobilia is restricted to 2 million, the price at which those cars will be traded increases to $6,000. Importing cars is profitable because Mobilia is willing to supply cars at $2,000 each. There is competition for import quotas.

REVIEW QUIZ

1 What are the tools that a country can use to restrict international trade?
2 What do international trade restrictions do to the gains from international trade?
3 Which is best for a country: restricted trade, no trade, or free trade? Why?
4 What does a tariff on imports do to the volume of imports and the volume of exports?
5 In the absence of international borrowing and lending, how do tariffs and other international trade restrictions influence the total value of imports and exports and the balance of trade—the value of exports minus the value of imports?

We're now going to look at some commonly heard arguments for restricting international trade and see why they are almost never correct.

The Case Against Protection

FOR AS LONG AS NATIONS AND INTERNATIONAL trade have existed, people have debated whether a country is better off with free international trade or with protection from foreign competition. The debate continues, but for most economists, a verdict has been delivered and is the one you have just seen. Free trade promotes prosperity for all; protection is inefficient. We've seen the most powerful case for free trade in the example of how Farmland and Mobilia both benefit from their comparative advantage. But there is a broader range of issues in the free trade versus protection debate. Let's review these issues.

Three arguments for restricting international trade are

- The employment argument
- The infant-industry argument
- The dumping argument

Let's look at each in turn.

The Employment Argument

The argument that protection saves jobs goes as follows: When we buy shoes from Brazil or shirts from Taiwan, Canadian workers in these industries lose their jobs. With no earnings and poor prospects, these workers become a drain on welfare and spend less, causing a ripple effect of further job losses. The proposed solution to this problem is to ban imports of cheap foreign goods and protect Canadian jobs. This argument for protection does not withstand scrutiny for three reasons.

First, free trade does cost some jobs, but it also creates other jobs. It brings about a global rationalization of labour and allocates labour resources to their highest-valued activities. Because of international trade in textiles, tens of thousands of workers in Canada have lost their jobs because textile mills and other factories have closed. But tens of thousands of workers in other countries have gotten jobs because textile mills have opened there. And tens of thousands of Canadian workers have gotten better-paying jobs than those of textile workers because other export industries have expanded and created more jobs than have been destroyed.

Second, imports create jobs. They create jobs for retailers that sell imported goods and firms that service those goods. They also create jobs by creating incomes in the rest of the world, some of which are spent on imports of Canadian-made goods and services.

Although protection does save particular jobs, it does so at inordinate cost. A striking example of the cost of quotas is that of the quotas on the import of textiles. Quotas imposed under an international agreement called the Multifiber Arrangement (that is being phased out) have protected textile jobs, especially in the United States. The U.S. International Trade Commission (ITC) has estimated that because of quotas, 72,000 jobs exist in textiles that would otherwise disappear and annual clothing expenditure in the United States is $U.S. 15.9 billion or $U.S. 160 per family higher than it would be with free trade. Equivalently, the ITC estimates that each textile job saved costs $U.S. 221,000 a year.

The Infant-Industry Argument

The so-called **infant-industry argument** for protection is that it is necessary to protect a new industry to enable it to grow into a mature industry that can compete in world markets. The argument is based on the idea of *dynamic comparative advantage*, which can arise from *learning-by-doing* (see Chapter 2).

Learning-by-doing is a powerful engine of productivity growth, and comparative advantage does evolve and change because of on-the-job experience. But these facts do not justify protection.

First, the infant-industry argument is valid only if the benefits of learning-by-doing *not only* accrue to the owners and workers of the firms in the infant industry but also *spill over* to other industries and parts of the economy. For example, there are huge productivity gains from learning-by-doing in the manufacture of aircraft. But almost all of these gains benefit the stockholders and workers of Boeing and other aircraft producers. Because the people making the decisions, bearing the risk, and doing the work are the ones who benefit, they take the dynamic gains into account when they decide on the scale of their activities. In this case, almost no benefits spill over to other parts of the economy, so there is no need for government assistance to achieve an efficient outcome.

Second, even if the case is made for protecting an infant industry, it is more efficient to do so by a subsidy to the firms in the industry, with the subsidy out of taxes.

The Dumping Argument

Dumping occurs when a foreign firm sells its exports at a price below its cost of production. Dumping might be used by a firm that wants to gain a global monopoly. In this case, the foreign firm sells its output at a price below its cost to drive domestic firms out of business. When the domestic firms have gone, the foreign firm takes advantage of its monopoly position and charges a higher price for its product. Dumping is usually regarded as a justification for temporary countervailing tariffs.

But there are powerful reasons to resist the dumping argument for protection. First, it is virtually impossible to detect dumping because it is hard to determine a firm's costs. As a result, the test for dumping is whether a firm's export price is below its domestic price. But this test is a weak one because it can be rational for a firm to charge a low price in markets in which the quantity demanded is highly sensitive to price and a higher price in a market in which demand is less price-sensitive.

Second, it is hard to think of a good that is produced by a natural *global* monopoly. So even if all the domestic firms were driven out of business in some industry, it would always be possible to find several and usually many alternative foreign sources of supply and to buy at prices determined in competitive markets.

Third, if a good or service were a truly global natural monopoly, the best way of dealing with it would be by regulation—just as in the case of domestic monopolies. Such regulation would require international cooperation.

The three arguments for protection that we've just examined have an element of credibility. The counterarguments are in general stronger, however, so these arguments do not make the case for protection. But they are not the only arguments that you might encounter. The many other arguments that are commonly heard are quite simply wrong. They are fatally flawed. The most common of them are that protection

- Maintains national security
- Allows us to compete with cheap foreign labour
- Brings diversity and stability
- Penalizes lax environmental standards
- Protects national culture
- Prevents rich countries from exploiting developing countries

Maintains National Security

The national security argument for protection is that a country must protect industries that produce defence equipment and armaments and industries on which the defence industries rely for their raw materials and other intermediate inputs. This argument for protection does not withstand close scrutiny.

First, it is an argument for international isolation, for in a time of war, there is no industry that does not contribute to national defence. Second, if the case is made for boosting the output of a strategic industry, it is more efficient to achieve this outcome with a subsidy to the firms in the industry that is financed out of taxes. Such a subsidy would keep the industry operating at the scale judged appropriate, and free international trade would keep the prices faced by consumers at their world market levels.

Allows Us to Compete with Cheap Foreign Labour

With the removal of tariffs in Canadian trade with Mexico, people said we would hear a "giant sucking sound" as jobs rushed to Mexico (shown in the cartoon). Let's see what's wrong with this view.

The labour cost of a unit of output equals the wage rate divided by labour productivity. For example, if a Canadian auto worker earns $30 an hour and produces 15 units of output an hour, the average labour cost of a unit of output is $2. If a Mexican auto assembly worker earns $3 an hour and produces 1 unit of output an hour, the average labour cost of a unit of output is $3. Other things remaining the same, the higher a worker's productivity, the higher is the worker's wage rate. High-wage workers have high productivity. Low-wage workers have low productivity.

Although high-wage Canadian workers are more productive, on the average, than low-wage Mexican workers, there are differences across industries. Canadian labour is relatively more productive in some activities than in others. For example, the productivity of Canadian workers in producing financial services and telephone systems is relatively higher than their productivity in the production of metals and some standardized machine parts. The activities in which Canadian workers are relatively more productive than their Mexican counterparts are those in which Canada has a *comparative advantage*. By engaging in free trade, increasing our production and exports of the goods and services in which we have a comparative advantage and decreasing our produc-

"I don't know what the hell happened—one minute I'm at work in Flint, Michigan, then there's a giant sucking sound and suddenly here I am in Mexico."

tion and increasing our imports of the goods and services in which our trading partners have a comparative advantage, we can make ourselves and the citizens of other countries better off.

Brings Diversity and Stability

A diversified investment portfolio is less risky than one that has all the eggs in one basket. The same is true for an economy's production. A diversified economy fluctuates less than an economy that produces only one or two goods.

But big, rich, diversified economies such as those of Canada, the United States, Japan, and Europe do not have this type of stability problem. Even a country such as Saudi Arabia that produces only one good (in this case, oil) can benefit from specializing in the activity at which it has a comparative advantage and then investing in a wide range of other countries to bring greater stability to its income and consumption.

Penalizes Lax Environmental Standards

Another argument for protection is that many poorer countries, such as Mexico, do not have the same environmental policies that we have and, because they are willing to pollute and we are not, we cannot compete with them without tariffs. So if they want free trade with the richer and "greener" countries, they must clean up their environments to our standards.

This argument for international trade restrictions is weak. First, not all poorer countries have significantly lower environmental standards than Canada has. Many poor countries and the former communist countries of Eastern Europe do have bad environment records. But some countries enforce strict laws. Second, a poor country cannot afford to be as concerned about its environment as a rich country can. The best hope for a better environment in Mexico and in other developing countries is rapid income growth through free trade. As their incomes grow, developing countries will have the *means* to match their desires to improve their environment. Third, poor countries have a comparative advantage at doing "dirty" work, which helps rich countries achieve higher environmental standards than they otherwise could.

Protects National Culture

The national culture argument for protection is one of the most commonly heard argument in Canada and Europe.

The expressed fear is that free trade in books, magazines, movies, and television programs means U.S. domination and the end of local culture. So, the reasoning continues, it is necessary to protect domestic "culture" industries from free international trade to ensure the survival of a national cultural identity.

Protection of these industries is common and takes the form of nontariff barriers. For example, local content regulations on radio and television broadcasting and in magazines is often required.

The cultural identity argument for protection has no merit. Writers, publishers, and broadcasters want to limit foreign competition so that they can earn larger economic profits. There is no actual danger to national culture. In fact, many of the creators of so-called American cultural products are not Americans but the talented citizens of other countries, ensuring the survival of their national cultural identities in Hollywood! Also, if national culture is in danger, there is no surer way of helping it on its way out than by impoverishing the nation whose culture it is. And protection is an effective way of doing just that.

Prevents Rich Countries from Exploiting Developing Countries

Another argument for protection is that international trade must be restricted to prevent the people of the rich industrial world from exploiting the poorer people of the developing countries, forcing them to work for slave wages.

Wage rates in some developing countries are indeed very low. But by trading with developing countries, we increase the demand for the goods that these countries produce and, more significantly, we increase the demand for their labour. When the demand for labour in developing countries increases, the wage rate also increases. So, far from exploiting people in developing countries, trade improves their opportunities and increases their incomes.

We have reviewed the arguments that are commonly heard in favour of protection and the counterarguments against them. There is one counterargument to protection that is general and quite overwhelming: Protection invites retaliation and can trigger a trade war. The best example of a trade war occurred during the Great Depression of the 1930s when the United States introduced the Smoot-Hawley tariff. Country after country retaliated with its own tariff, and in a short period, world trade had almost disappeared. The costs to all countries were large and led to a renewed international resolve to avoid such self-defeating moves in the future. They also led to the creation of GATT and are the impetus behind NAFTA, APEC, and the European Union.

REVIEW QUIZ

1 Can we save jobs, stimulate the growth of new industries, or to restrain foreign monopoly by restricting international trade?
2 Can we achieve national security goals, compensate for low foreign wages, make the economy more diversified, compensate for costly environmental policies, protect national culture, or to protect developing countries from being exploited by restricting international trade?
3 Is there any merit to the view that we should restrict international trade for any reason? What is the main argument against international trade restrictions?

Why Is International Trade Restricted?

WHY, DESPITE ALL THE ARGUMENTS AGAINST PROtection, is trade restricted? There are two key reasons:

- Tariff revenue
- Rent seeking

Tariff Revenue

Government revenue is costly to collect. In the developed countries such as Canada, a well-organized tax collection system is in place that can generate billions of dollars of income tax and sales tax revenues. This tax collection system is made possible by the fact that most economic transactions are done by firms that must keep properly audited financial records. Without such records, the revenue collection agencies (for example, Canada Customs and Revenue Agency) would be severely hampered in the work. Even with audited financial accounts, some proportion of potential tax revenue is lost. Nonetheless, for the industrialized countries, income taxes and sales taxes are the major sources of revenue and the tariff plays a very small role.

But governments in developing countries have a difficult time collecting taxes from their citizens. Much economic activity takes place in an informal economy with few financial records. So only a small amount of revenue is collected from income taxes and sales taxes in these countries. The one area in which economic transactions are well recorded and audited is in international trade. So this activity is an attractive base for tax collection in these countries and is used much more extensively than in the developed countries.

Rent Seeking

Rent seeking is the major reason why international trade is restricted. **Rent seeking** is lobbying and other political activity that seeks to capture the gains from trade. Free trade increases consumption possibilities *on the average*, but not everyone shares in the gain and some people even lose. Free trade brings benefits to some and imposes costs on others, with total benefits exceeding total costs. It is the uneven distribution of costs and benefits that is the principal source of impediment to achieving more liberal international trade.

Let's return to our example of trade in cars and grain between Farmland and Mobilia. In Farmland, the benefits from free trade accrue to all the producers of grain and to those producers of cars who would not have to bear the costs of adjusting to a smaller car industry. Those costs are transition costs, not permanent costs. The costs of moving to free trade are borne by those car producers and their employees who have to become grain producers.

The number of people who gain will, in general, be enormous in comparison with the number who lose. The gain per person will therefore be rather small. The loss per person to those who bear the loss will be large. Because the loss that falls on those who bear it is large, it will pay those people to incur considerable expense to lobby against free trade. On the other hand, it will not pay those who gain to organize to achieve free trade. The gain from trade for any one individual is too small for that individual to spend much time or money on a political organization to achieve free trade. The loss from free trade will be seen as being so great by those bearing that loss that they *will* find it profitable to join a political organization to prevent free trade. Each group is optimizing—weighing benefits against costs and choosing the best action for itself. The anti-free trade group will, however, undertake a larger quantity of political lobbying than the pro-free trade group.

Compensating Losers

If, in total, the gains from free international trade exceed the losses, why don't those who stand to gain from free trade offer to compensate those who stand to lose so that everyone votes for free trade?

The main answer is that there are serious obstacles to providing direct and correctly calculated compensation. First, the cost of identifying the losers from free trade and of estimating the value of their losses would be enormous.

Second, it would never be clear whether a person who has fallen on hard times is suffering because of free trade or for other reasons, perhaps reasons that are largely under the control of the individual.

Third, some people who look like losers at one point in time may, in fact, end up gaining. The young auto worker that loses her job in Windsor and becomes a computer assembly worker in Ottawa resents the loss of work and the need to move. But a year or two later, looking back on events, she counts herself fortunate. She has made a move that has increased her income and given her greater job security.

Despite the absence of explicit compensation, those who lose from a change in protection do receive some compensation. But compensation is not restricted to the losers from changes in trade policy. In Canada (and in all the other rich industrial countries) elaborate schemes are in place to ensure that people who suffer from economic change receive help during their transition to new activities.

Two major forms of compensation in Canada arise from interprovincial fiscal transfers and employment insurance. Interprovincial fiscal transfers result in tax dollars collected in the rich and expanding regions of the country being spent in the poorer regions. Employment insurance provides substantial compensation for workers who lose their jobs regardless of the reason for the job loss. Jobs lost because of changes in international protection are included among those for which benefits are paid.

But because we do not explicitly compensate the losers from free international trade, protectionism remains a popular and permanent feature of our national economic and political life.

Compensating Losers from Protection

There is no general presumption that it is the ones who lose from a tariff cut that should be compensated. Protection brings losses to the consumer and the view might be taken that the winners from protection should compensate the losers from protection. When this perspective is taken, the removal of protection would mean the removal of the compensation of the losers by the winners and no further adjustments would be needed. What is fair is a tricky matter (see Chapter 5, pp. 114–117).

REVIEW QUIZ

1 What are the two main reasons for imposing tariffs on imports?

2 What type of country most benefits from the revenue from tariffs? Provide some examples of such countries.

3 If international trade restrictions are costly, why do we use them? Why don't the people who gain from trade organize a political force that is strong enough to ensure that their interests are protected?

The North American Free Trade Agreement

THE NORTH AMERICAN FREE TRADE AGREE-ment came into effect on January 1, 1994. It was the outgrowth of an earlier Canada–United States Free Trade Agreement, which was signed in October 1987. Both agreements were struck only after several years of intense negotiations and, on the Canadian side of the border, an intense political debate. First, let's look at the terms of the Canada–United States agreement of 1987 and at the progress made in achieving freer trade between two of the world's largest trading partners.

The Terms of the Canada–United States Agreement

The main terms of the Canada–United States Free Trade Agreement are:

- Tariffs to be phased out through 1999
- Nontariff barriers to be reduced
- Free trade in energy products, with energy resource sharing in times of national shortage
- More freedom of trade in services
- Future negotiations to eliminate subsidies
- Creation of dispute-settling mechanisms

Removal of Tariffs Scheduled tariff cuts began on January 1, 1989 and were completed on January 1, 1998. But tariff protection remains in place and an atmosphere of tension prevails in many areas. Agriculture remains effectively protected with new tariffs that have replaced old quotas. And a series of so-called *countervailing duties* has been introduced to offset the effects of domestic subsidies. Further, several so-called *antidumping duties* have also been introduced in cases in which it is alleged that products are being exported at a price below the cost of production.

Nontariff Barriers Nontariff barriers such as government procurement policies of buying local products are removed by the agreement. Subsequent to entering into the free trade agreement, Canada and the United States took on additional obligations as members of the WTO that require the removal of agricultural quotas. Many agricultural quotas have been removed but they have been replaced with tariffs. So despite the free trade agreement, we remain a long way from achieving free trade in agricultural products.

Energy Products Free trade in energy products existed before the free trade agreement but the agreement ratified the intent to maintain that arrangement. The agreement that scarce energy resources will be shared in times of national shortage became a controversial one. In effect, what the energy sharing clause amounts to is an agreement that governments will not intervene in energy markets to prevent firms from selling their energy to the other country.

Trade in Services International trade in services has been expanding more quickly than trade in manufactured goods in recent years. The free trade agreement, recognizing this factor and seeking to facilitate further expansion of trade in services between the United States and Canada, incorporates two principles: the *right of establishment* and *national treatment*. The right of establishment means that American firms have the right to set up branches in Canada and Canadian firms have the right to set up operations in the United States. National treatment means that each country will treat the goods and firms and investors of the other country as if they were operating within its own borders.

Future Negotiations on Subsidies In both the United States and Canada, there are many subsidies, especially on agricultural products. The presence of subsidies causes problems and makes it legitimate under the agreement for the country importing subsidized goods to impose countervailing duties. As we have just noted, several such duties have been imposed.

Dispute-Settling Mechanisms The Free Trade Agreement included two dispute-settling mechanisms: one to settle disputes relating to all aspects of the agreement, and the other to deal with applications of countervailing duties and antidumping laws in either country. For example, the United States has applied for and received permission to impose countervailing duties on Canadian exports of durum wheat, lumber products, poultry, and live hogs. In each case, the United States accuses Canada of subsidizing these industries unfairly so that Canadian exports are cheaper than U.S. producers can supply these goods.

The Extension of the Agreement: NAFTA

The North American Free Trade Agreement (NAFTA) is an agreement between Canada, the United States, and Mexico that has six objectives. They are to

1. Eliminate trade barriers
2. Promote conditions of fair competition
3. Increase investment opportunities
4. Protect intellectual property rights
5. Create an effective dispute resolution mechanism
6. Establish a framework for the expansion of the agreement to include other nations in the hemisphere

Effects of the Free Trade Agreement

Working out the effects of an agreement as complex as NAFTA is difficult, and there is no general consensus on what the effects have been. The theory that you have studied in this chapter predicts that the removal of tariffs will produce an increase in the *volume* of international trade. That is, the theory predicts that Canadians will increasingly specialize in those activities at which they have a comparative advantage and Mexicans and Americans will specialize in a different range of activities and that the three countries will exchange a larger volume of goods and services.

As predicted, trade among the three countries has increased. During the first five years of NAFTA, Canada's trade with the United States increased by 80 percent and Canada's trade with Mexico doubled.

The trade expansion that followed the entry of Mexico in 1995 was especially dramatic. Mexico's exports increased by 31 percent (in U.S. dollar value) in 1995 and by 21 percent in 1996, compared with increases that averaged less than 15 percent a year during the two years before the agreement. But trade expansion with Mexico has not been in one direction. Mexico's imports also increased following the agreement by 23 percent in both 1996 and 1997.

During the 1990s, Canada's exports expanded from less than 30 percent of total production to 36 percent, and Canada's imports have increased from 27 percent to 34 percent of total expenditure.

Canada greatly increased its exports of advertising services, office and telecommunications equipment, paper, and transportation services. And its imports of meat and dairy products, communications services, clothing, furniture, and processed foods and beverages also increased by a large percentage.

These huge changes in exports and imports brought gains from increased specialization and exchange. But they also brought a heavy toll of adjustment. Thousands of jobs were lost in the declining sectors and new jobs were created in the expanding sectors. The amount of job destruction in the years following the free trade agreement was historically high and the unemployment rate rose for three successive years. Only during the Great Depression did the rate of job destruction exceed that in the late 1980s and early 1990s. To what extent a high rate of labour market turnover was caused by the free trade agreement is unclear and controversial. But the net outcome of NAFTA appears to be strongly positive. More than a million new Canadian jobs were created between 1994 and 1999.

REVIEW QUIZ

1 By when, under the Canada–United States Free Trade Agreement, were all tariffs on trade between Canada and the United States intended to be phased out? What progress and setbacks have we experienced?
2 What effect has NAFTA had on nontariff barriers?
3 What effect has NAFTA had on trade in services?
4 How has the volume of trade among Canada, the United States, and Mexico changed during the period since NAFTA was established?

◆ You've now seen how free international trade enables all nations to gain from specialization and trade. By producing goods in which we have a comparative advantage and trading some of our production for that of others, we expand our consumption possibilities. Placing impediments on that trade decreases the gains from specialization and trade. By opening our country up to free international trade, the market for the things that we sell expands and the relative price rises. The market for the things that we buy also expands, and the relative price falls.

Reading Between the Lines on pp. 804–805 looks at a recent example of an international trade dispute between the United States and Canada—the lumber dispute. This dispute provides a clear example of the economic cost of restricting international trade.

Tariffs in Action: Lumber

THE GLOBE AND MAIL, July 27, 2002

Officials applaud softwood victory

Canadian forestry officials applauded a first-round victory in the bitter softwood dispute, but warned there is no quick relief for an industry still facing crippling duties.

The punitive duties, which have shut dozens of sawmills across Canada and cost thousands of forestry workers their jobs, were imposed to support allegations by the U.S. industry that Canadian lumber is unfairly subsidized.

The World Trade Organization said yesterday the United States was not justified in using cross-border pricing comparisons for calculating duties on lumber imports.

While the WTO accepted the U.S. argument that Canada's stumpage system does violate WTO subsidy rules, Frank Dottori, president of Montreal-based lumber producer Tembec Inc., said he was "ecstatic" with the ruling. "We hope the Ameri-

cans respect this third-party ruling and see it as an opportunity to stop persecuting us and move forward," he said. ...

Mr. De Jong said the decision will not bestow immediate benefits on the lumber industry, which is currently paying a 27-per-cent duty on about $10-billion worth of lumber shipments into the key U.S. market. ...

"The American lumber lobby will probably try to minimize the importance of the decision and stick to their guns," said Carl Grenier, president of the Free Trade Lumber Council, whose members account for about 40 per cent of Canadian lumber exports to the United States.

Mr. Grenier said the U.S. trade position is driven by a powerful industry lobby, not by government, and that he expects that lobby to continue to forcefully argue its case. ...

Reprinted with permission from *The Globe and Mail.*

Essence of the Story

■ A 27-percent duty on Canadian lumber exports to the United States has shut dozens of sawmills across Canada and cost thousands of forestry workers their jobs.

■ The U.S. lumber industry claims that Canadian lumber is unfairly subsidized.

■ The World Trade Organization agrees that Canadian lumber is subsidized but says that the United States is not justified in calculating duties on lumber imports by comparing the Canadian and U.S. prices.

■ While Canadian lumber producers hope that this ruling paves the way for tariff cuts, U.S. lumber producers are a powerful lobby and one that will be hard to overcome.

Economic Analysis

■ The U.S. tariff on Canadian lumber damages Canada, but it also damages the United States.

■ Figure 1 shows the U.S. market for lumber.

■ The demand curve of U.S. buyers of lumber is D.

■ There are two supply curves: the supply curve of the Canadian producers, S_C, and the supply curve of U.S. producers, S_{US}. We'll assume that Canada can supply any quantity at a price of $100 per load.

■ With no tariff, the quantity of lumber bought in the United States is QC_0. Of this amount, QP_0 is produced in the United States and the rest is imported from Canada, as shown by the arrow in Fig. 1.

■ Now the United States puts a 27-percent tariff on the import of lumber. Canadian lumber is now supplied to the U.S. market at the original supply price, $100, plus the tariff, $27, so the supply curve of lumber from Canada shifts to become S_C + *tariff*.

■ With the tariff, the quantity of lumber bought in the United States is QC_1. Of this amount, QP_1 is produced in the United States and the rest is imported from Canada, as shown by the arrow in Fig. 1.

■ The tariff decreases U.S. consumption and imports and increases U.S. production.

■ Figure 2 shows the winners and the losers in the United States.

■ The winners include U.S lumber producers, who gain additional producer surplus, which is shown by the blue area in Fig. 2.

■ Another winner is the U.S. government, which collects additional revenue, shown by the purple area in Fig. 2.

■ The sum of the blue, red, purple, and gray areas is the loss of consumer surplus that results from the tariff.

■ The Canadian subsidy has no influence on the effects of the tariff. A deadweight loss arises—the decrease in consumer surplus exceeds the increase in producer surplus—regardless of whether Canadian lumber producers receive a subsidy.

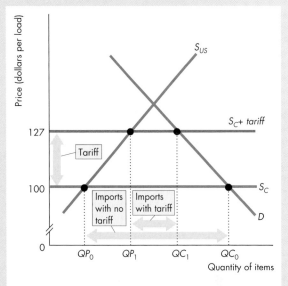

Figure 1 Tariffs and imports

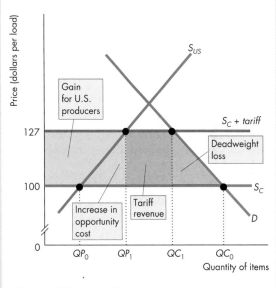

Figure 2 Winners and losers

805

SUMMARY

KEY POINTS

Patterns and Trends in International Trade
(p. 786)

- Large flows of trade take place between countries, most of which is in manufactured goods exchanged among rich industrialized countries.
- Since 1978, the volume of Canadian international trade has increased to more than one-third of total production.

The Gains from International Trade (pp. 787–792)

- Comparative advantage is the fundamental source of the gains from trade.
- Comparative advantage exists when opportunity costs between countries diverge.
- By increasing its production of goods in which it has a comparative advantage and then trading some of the increased output, a country can consume at points outside its production possibilities frontier.
- In the absence of international borrowing and lending, trade is balanced as prices adjust to reflect the international supply of and demand for goods.
- The world price balances the production and consumption plans of the trading parties. At the equilibrium price, trade is balanced.
- Comparative advantage explains the international trade that takes place in the world.
- But trade in similar goods arises from economies of scale in the face of diversified tastes.

International Trade Restrictions (pp. 793–796)

- Countries restrict international trade by imposing tariffs and nontariffs, such as quotas and VERS.
- International trade restrictions raise the domestic price of imported goods, lower the volume of imports, and reduce the total value of imports.
- They also reduce the total value of exports by the same amount as the reduction in the value of imports.

The Case Against Protection (pp. 797–800)

- Arguments that protection is necessary to save jobs, to protect infant industries, and to prevent dumping are weak.
- Arguments that protection is necessary for national security, allows us to compete with cheap foreign labour, makes the economy diversified and stable, penalizes lax environmental standards, protects national culture, and prevents exploitation of developing countries are fatally flawed.

Why Is International Trade Restricted?
(pp. 800–801)

- Trade is restricted because tariffs raise government revenue and because protection brings a small loss to a large number of people and a large gain per person to a small number of people.

The North American Free Trade Agreement
(pp. 802–803)

- NAFTA is an agreement between Canada, the United States, and Mexico, which began in 1995 and grew from a previous Canada–U.S. agreement.
- Under NAFTA, trade has expanded more rapidly than before the agreement.

KEY FIGURES

KEY TERMS

PROBLEMS

*1. The table provides information about Virtual Reality's production possibilities.

TV sets (per day)		Computers (per day)
0	and	36
10	and	35
20	and	33
30	and	30
40	and	26
50	and	21
60	and	15
70	and	8
80	and	0

a. Calculate Virtual Reality's opportunity cost of a TV set when it produces 10 sets a day.

b. Calculate Virtual Reality's opportunity cost of a TV set when it produces 40 sets a day.

c. Calculate Virtual Reality's opportunity cost of a TV set when it produces 70 sets a day.

d. Using the answers to parts (a), (b), and (c), sketch the relationship between the opportunity cost of a TV set and the quantity of TV sets produced in Virtual Reality.

2. The table provides information about Vital Sign's production possibilities.

TV sets (per day)		Computers (per day)
0	and	18.0
10	and	17.5
20	and	16.5
30	and	15.0
40	and	13.0
50	and	10.5
60	and	7.5
70	and	4.0
80	and	0

a. Calculate Vital Sign's opportunity cost of a TV set when it produces 10 sets a day.

b. Calculate Vital Sign's opportunity cost of a TV set when it produces 40 sets a day.

c. Calculate Vital Sign's opportunity cost of a TV set when it produces 70 sets a day.

d. Using the answers to parts (a), (b), and (c), sketch the relationship between the opportu-nity cost of a TV set and the quantity of TV sets produced in Vital Sign.

*3. Suppose that with no international trade, Virtual Reality in problem 1 produces and con-sumes 10 TV sets a day and Vital Sign produces and consumes 60 TV sets a day. Now suppose that the two countries begin to trade with each other.

a. Which country exports TV sets?

b. What adjustments are made to the amount of each good produced by each country?

c. What adjustments are made to the amount of each good consumed by each country?

d. What can you say about the terms of trade (the price of a TV set expressed as computers per TV set) under free trade?

4. Suppose that with no international trade, Virtual Reality in problem 1 produces and con-sumes 50 TV sets a day and Vital Sign produces and consumes 20 TV sets a day. Now suppose that the two countries begin to trade with each other.

a. Which country exports TV sets?

b. What adjustments are made to the amount of each good produced by each country?

c. What adjustments are made to the amount of each good consumed by each country?

d. What can you say about the terms of trade (the price of a TV set expressed as computers per TV set) under free trade?

*5. Compare the total quantities of each good pro-duced in problems 1 and 2 with the total quanti-ties of each good produced in problems 3 and 4.

a. Does free trade increase or decrease the total quantities of TV sets and computers pro-duced in both cases? Why?

b. What happens to the price of a TV set in Virtual Reality in the two cases? Why does it rise in one case and fall in the other?

c. What happens to the price of a computer in Vital Sign in the two cases? Why does it rise in one case and fall in the other?

6. Compare the international trade in problem 3 with that in problem 4.

a. Why does Virtual Reality export TV sets in one of the cases and import them in the other case?

b. Do the TV producers or the computer pro-ducers gain in each case?

c. Do consumers gain in each case?

*7. The figure depicts the international market for soybeans.

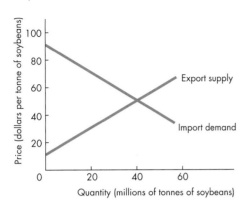

a. If the two countries did not engage in international trade, what would be the prices of soybeans in the two countries? Show the prices on the graph.
b. What is the world price of soybeans if there is free trade between these countries?
c. What quantities of soybeans are exported and imported?
d. What is the balance of trade?

8. If the country in problem 7 that imports soybeans imposes a tariff of $20 per tonne, what is the world price of soybeans and what quantity of soybeans gets traded internationally? What is the price of soybeans in the importing country? Calculate the tariff revenue.

*9. The importing country in problem 7 imposes a quota of 30 million tonnes on imports of soybeans.
a. What is the price of soybeans in the importing country?
b. What is the revenue from the quota?
c. Who gets this revenue?

10. The exporting country in problem 7 imposes a VER of 30 million tonnes on its exports of soybeans.
a. What is the world price of soybeans now?
b. What is the revenue of soybean growers in the exporting country?
c. Which country gains from the VER?

CRITICAL THINKING

1. Study *Reading Between the Lines* on pp. 804–805 and then answer the following questions:
a. Why did the United States impose a tariff on lumber imports from Canada?
b. What are the effects of the tariff on lumber?
c. Who are the winners and who are the losers from the tariff on lumber?
d. Modify the figures on page 805 to show the effects of a Canadian subsidy to lumber producers on the consumer surplus, producer surplus, and deadweight loss in the United States.

WEB EXERCISES

1. Visit the Parkin–Bade Web site and study the Web *Reading Between the Lines* on steel dumping, and then answer the following questions.
a. What is the argument in the news article for limiting steel imports?
b. Evaluate the argument. Is it correct or incorrect in your opinion? Why?
c. Would you vote to eliminate steel imports? Why or why not?
d. Would you vote differently if you lived in another steel-producing country? Why or why not?

2. Use the links on the Parkin–Bade Web site to view a NAFTA report card on agriculture. Then answer the following questions:
a. What does NAFTA seek to achieve in agriculture trade?
b. What has NAFTA achieved to date?
c. What are the obstacles to greater gains for North American trade in agricultural products?
d. Would you vote to maintain NAFTA? Why or why not?
e. Would you vote to expand NAFTA to include other countries? Why or why not?

INTERNATIONAL FINANCE

¥€$!

Yes! The yen (¥), the euro (€), and the U.S. dollar ($) are the world's three big currencies. The yen (the currency of Japan) and the dollar (the currency of the United States) have been around for a long time. The euro is new. It was launched on January 1, 1999, as the fledgling currency of 11 members of the European Union. But it is already an international currency. Most of the world's international trade and finance is conducted using these three currencies. ◆ In 1976, an American needed 1.01 U.S. dollars to buy a Canadian dollar. But in 2002, 63 U.S. cents was sufficient to buy a Canadian dollar. Many currencies have fallen by much more than the Canadian dollar. In 1997 and 1998, during the Asian financial crisis, the currency of Indonesia fell against our dollar to less than one-third of its pre-crisis value. ◆ Why do currency values fluctuate? Is there anything we can do or should do to stabilize the value of the dollar? ◆ In 2001, Canadian receipts from the rest of the world for exports and debt interest exceeded the amount paid by Canadians for imports by $30 billion. But during most of the 1990s, imports and debt interest exceeded exports. Through those years, foreigners bought Canadian assets on a grand scale. Cadbury Schweppes (a British firm) bought George Weston's chocolate company and foreign companies now own Canada's four biggest makers of chocolate bars. Why have foreigners bought so many Canadian businesses?

◆ In this chapter, we're going to discover what determines the amount of international borrowing and lending, and why the dollar fluctuates against other currencies. At the end of the chapter, in *Reading Between the Lines*, we'll look at a projection of the Canadian dollar exchange rate through 2026.

After studying this chapter, you will be able to:

- Explain how international trade is financed
- Describe a country's balance of payments accounts
- Explain what determines the amount of international borrowing and lending
- Explain why Canada is an international borrower
- Explain how the foreign exchange value of the dollar is determined
- Explain why the foreign exchange value of the dollar fluctuates

Financing International Trade

WHEN A SONY STORE IN CANADA IMPORTS CD players from Japan, it does not pay for them with Canadian dollars—it uses Japanese yen. And when an Irish railroad company buys a locomotive from GM in London, Ontario, it pays in Canadian dollars. Whenever we buy things from another country, we use the currency of that country to make the transaction. It doesn't make any difference what the item being traded is; it might be a consumption good or a capital good, a building, or even a firm.

We're going to study the markets in which money—different types of currency—is bought and sold. But first we're going to look at the scale of international trading and borrowing and lending and at the way in which we keep our records of these transactions. Such records are called the balance of payments accounts.

Balance of Payments Accounts

A country's **balance of payments accounts** record its international trading, borrowing, and lending. There are in fact three balance of payments accounts:

1. Current account
2. Capital account
3. Official settlements account

The **current account** records payments for imports of goods and services from abroad, receipts from exports of goods and services sold abroad, net interest paid abroad, and net transfers (such as foreign aid payments). The *current account balance* equals exports minus imports, net interest payments, and net transfers. The **capital account** records foreign investment in Canada minus Canadian investment abroad. The **official settlements account** records the change in official Canadian reserves. **Official Canadian reserves** are the government's holdings of foreign currency. If Canadian official reserves increase, the *official settlements account balance* is negative. The reason is that holding foreign money is like investing abroad. Canadian investment abroad is a minus item in the capital account and in the official settlements account. (By the same reasoning, if official Canadian reserves decrease, the *official settlements account balance* is positive.)

The sum of the balances on the three accounts always equals zero. That is, to pay for a current account deficit, we must either borrow more from abroad than we lend abroad or use our official reserves to cover the shortfall.

Table 34.1 shows the Canadian balance of payments accounts in 2001. Items in the current account and capital account that provide foreign currency to Canada have a plus sign; items that cost Canada foreign currency have a minus sign. The table shows that in 2001, exports plus net transfers exceeded imports plus net interest payments and the current account had a surplus of $30 billion.

What do we do with our current account surplus? We lend it to the rest of the world. The capital account tells us by how much. We borrowed $90 billion (foreign investment in Canada) but made loans of $108 billion (Canadian investment abroad). Thus our net foreign lending was $18 billion. A statistical discrepancy arises because of illegal and hidden transactions, which in 2001 was $9 billion.

Our current account surplus minus our net foreign lending and the statistical discrepancy is the

TABLE 34.1   Canadian Balance of Payments Accounts in 2001

Current account	Billions of dollars
Imports of goods and services	−416
Exports of goods and services	+471
Net interest payments	−27
Net transfers	+2
Current account balance	+30

Capital account	
Foreign investment in Canada	+90
Canadian investment abroad	−108
Capital account balance	−18
Statistical discrepancy	−9

Official settlements account	
Increase in official Canadian reserves	−3

Source: Statistics Canada, CANSIM tables 376-0001 and 376-0002.

change in official Canadian reserves. In 2001, reserves increased because our current account surplus of $30 billion exceeded our net foreign lending of $18 billion plus the statistical discrepancy of $9 billion by $3 billion. When our reserves change, we record an *increase* in reserves as a negative number in our international accounts. Why? Because an increase in our reserves is like making a loan to the rest of the world.

The numbers in Table 34.1 give a snapshot of the balance of payments accounts in 2001. Figure 34.1 puts that snapshot into perspective by showing the balance of payments between 1981 and 2001. Because the economy grows and the price level rises, changes in the dollar value of the balance of payments do not convey much information. To remove the influences of growth and inflation, Fig. 34.1 shows the balance of payments as a percentage of nominal GDP.

As you can see, the capital account balance is almost a mirror image of the current account balance. The official settlements balance is very small in comparison with the balances of these other two accounts. A large current account deficit (and capital account surplus) emerged during the 1980s but declined after 1993. By 1996 we had a small surplus and after two more years of deficit, the early 2000s saw an increasing surplus.

You can understand the balance of payments and the way the accounts are linked together if you think about the income and expenditure, borrowing and lending, and bank account of an individual.

Individual Analogy An individual's current account records the income from supplying the services of productive resources and the expenditure on goods and services. Consider, for example, Joanne. She worked in 2002 and earned an income of $25,000. Joanne has $10,000 worth of investments that earned her an interest income of $1,000. Joanne's current account shows an income of $26,000. Joanne spent $18,000 buying goods and services for consumption. She also bought a new house, which cost her $60,000. So Joanne's total expenditure was $78,000. The difference between her expenditure and income is $52,000 ($78,000 minus $26,000). This amount is Joanne's current account deficit.

To pay for expenditure of $52,000 in excess of her income, Joanne has to use the money that she has in the bank or has to take out a loan. In fact, Joanne took a mortgage of $50,000 to help buy her house. This mortgage was the only borrowing that Joanne did, so her capital account surplus was $50,000. With a current account deficit of $52,000 and a capi-

---

FIGURE 34.1   The Balance of Payments: 1981–2001

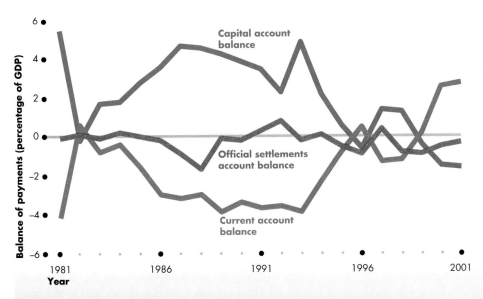

During the 1980s, a large current account deficit arose. That deficit decreased after 1993 and by the early 2000s an increasing surplus arose. The capital account balance mirrors the current account balance. When the current account balance is negative, the capital account balance is positive— we borrow from the rest of the world. Fluctuations in the official settlements account balance are small in comparison with fluctuations in the current account balance and the capital account balance.

Source: Statistics Canada, CANSIM tables 376-0001 and 376-0002.

tal account surplus of $50,000, Joanne is still $2,000 short. She got that $2,000 from her own bank account. Her cash holdings decreased by $2,000.

Joanne's income from her work is analogous to a country's income from its exports. Her income from her investments is analogous to a country's interest income from foreigners. Her purchases of goods and services, including her purchase of a house, are analogous to a country's imports. Joanne's mortgage—borrowing from someone else—is analogous to a country's borrowing from the rest of the world. The change in her own bank account is analogous to the change in the country's official reserves.

Borrowers and Lenders, Debtors and Creditors

A country that has a current account deficit and that borrows more from the rest of the world than it lends to it is called a **net borrower**. Similarly, a **net lender** is a country that lends more to the rest of the world than it borrows from it.

From 1999 through 2001, Canada was a net lender. But most years, Canada has been a net borrower. During the 57 years between the end of World War II and 2001, Canada was a net lender in only 15 years, and most of those were in the 1940s. During the 1990s alone, Canada borrowed $140 billion (net) from the rest of the world. Canada's cumulative borrowing since the end of World War II is $265 billion. Only in the past few years has Canada been a net lender in recent memory. The year of greatest foreign borrowing was 1993, when Canada borrowed (net) almost $30 billion from the rest of the world.

Most countries are net borrowers. But like Canada today, a small number of countries, including Japan and oil-rich Saudi Arabia, are net lenders. For the world as a whole, net foreign borrowing equals net foreign lending.

A net borrower might be going deeper into debt or might simply be reducing its net assets held in the rest of the world. The total stock of foreign investment determines whether a country is a debtor or creditor. A **debtor nation** is a country that during its entire history has borrowed more from the rest of the world than it has lent to it. It has a stock of outstanding debt to the rest of the world that exceeds the stock of its own claims on the rest of the world. A **creditor nation** is a country that has invested more in

the rest of the world than other countries have invested in it.

At the heart of the distinction between a net borrower/net lender and a debtor/creditor nation is the distinction between flows and stocks, which you have encountered many times in your study of macroeconomics. Borrowing and lending are flows—amounts borrowed or lent per unit of time. Debts are stocks—amounts owed at a point in time. The flow of borrowing and lending changes the stock of debt. But the outstanding stock of debt depends mainly on past flows of borrowing and lending, not on the current period's flows. The current period's flows determine the *change* in the stock of debt outstanding.

Canada is a debtor nation. In 2001, the net international debt of Canadians was $203 billion. To put this number in perspective, it is $6,500 per person, or 20 percent of total income. Other debtor nations are a diverse group. They include the United States as well as the poor capital-hungry nations of the developing regions of Central and South America, Asia, and Africa. The international debt of the developing countries grew from less than one-third to more than half of their gross domestic product during the 1980s and 1990s and created what was called the "Third World debt crisis."

Should we be concerned that Canada is a net borrower and debtor nation? The answer to this question depends on what we do with the funds that we borrow. If borrowing finances investment that in turn generates economic growth and higher income, borrowing is not a problem. If borrowing finances consumption, then higher interest payments are being incurred, and as a consequence, consumption will eventually have to be reduced. In this case, the more the borrowing and the longer it goes on, the greater is the reduction in consumption that will eventually be necessary.

Has Canada Borrowed for Consumption or Investment?

In 1998, the last time we had a current account deficit, we borrowed $12 billion from abroad. Did we borrow for consumption or investment? In 1998, private investment in buildings, plant, and equipment was $176 billion. Government investment in a wide range of public buildings and structures such as highways was around $20 billion. All this investment added to the nation's capital and much of it increased productivity. Government also spends on education and health-care services, which increase *human capital*. Our international borrowing has financed private and public investment, not consumption.

Current Account Balance

What determines a country's current account balance and net foreign borrowing? You've seen that net exports (*NX*) is the main item in the current account. We can define the current account balance (*CAB*) as

$$CAB = NX + \text{Net interest income} + \text{Net transfers}.$$

Fluctuations in net exports are the main source of fluctuations in the current account balance. The other two items have trends but they do not fluctuate much. So we can study the current account balance by looking at what determines net exports.

Net Exports

Net exports are determined by the government budget and private saving and investment. To see how net exports are determined, we need to recall some of the things that we learned about the National Income Accounts in Chapter 20. Table 34.2 will refresh your memory and summarize some calculations.

Part (a) lists the national income variables that are needed, with their symbols. Part (b) defines three balances. **Net exports** is the value of exports of goods and services minus the value of imports of goods and services.

The **government sector balance** is equal to net taxes minus government expenditures on goods and services. If that number is positive, the government sector has a surplus and it is lent to other sectors; if that number is negative, the government sector has a deficit that must be financed by borrowing from other sectors. The government sector balance is the sum of the balances of the federal, provincial, and municipal governments.

The **private sector balance** is equal to saving minus investment. If saving exceeds investment, a private sector has a surplus and it is lent to other sectors. If investment exceeds saving, borrowing from other sectors finances a private sector deficit.

Part (b) also shows the values of these balances for Canada in 2001. As you can see, net exports were

TABLE 34.2   Net Exports, the Government Budget, Saving, and Investment

	Symbols and equations	Canada in 2001 (billions of dollars)
(a) Variables		
Exports*	X	473
Imports*	M	416
Government expenditures	G	231
Net taxes	NT	280
Investment	I	184
Saving	S	192
(b) Balances		
Net exports	X – M	473 – 416 = 57
Government sector	NT – G	280 – 231 = 49
Private sector	S – I	192 – 184 = 8
(c) Relationship among balances		
National accounts	Y = C + I + G + X – M	
	= C + S + NT	
Rearranging:	X – M = S – I + NT – G	
Net exports	X – M	57
Equals:		
Government sector	NT – G	49
Plus		
Private sector	S – I	8

Source: Statistics Canada, CANSIM tables 380-0002 and 380-0034.

* The national income accounts' measures of exports and imports are different from the balance of payments' accounts measures by small amounts.

$57 billion, a surplus of $57 billion. The government sector's revenue from net taxes was $280 billion and it purchased $231 billion worth of goods and services. The government sector surplus was $49 billion. The private sector saved $192 billion and invested $184 billion, so it had a surplus of $8 billion.

Part (c) shows the relationship among the three balances. From the national income accounts, we know that real GDP (Y) is the sum of consumption expenditure (C), investment (I), government expenditures (G), and net exports (X – M). It also equals the sum of consumption expenditure (C), saving (S), and net taxes (NT). Rearranging these equations tells us that net exports (X – M) is the sum of the government sector surplus (NT – G) and the private sector surplus (S – I). In Canada in 2001, the government sector had a surplus of $49 billion and the private sector had a surplus of $8 billion. The government sector surplus plus the private sector surplus equals net exports of $57 billion.

The Twin Deficits

You've seen that net exports equals the sum of the government surplus and the private surplus. And net exports plus debt interest (and other small transfers) equals the current account balance. What is the relationship over time between the current account balance and the government budget balance? How do these balances fluctuate over time? Figure 34.2 answers this question. It shows the government budget (the red line) and the current account balance (the blue line).

You can see that, with an important exception during the early 1980s, there is a tendency for the current account to go into a deeper deficit when the government budget goes into a deeper deficit. Because of the tendency for the government budget deficit and the current account deficit to move in the same direction they have been called the **twin deficits.**

Why are the two deficits linked? They are linked because capital is highly mobile in today's world. If the Canadian government increases expenditure or lowers taxes, total spending in Canada rises. But with the economy at or near full employment, the extra goods and services demanded are sucked in from the rest of the world. Imports increase. Capital flows in to pay for those imports. Saving and investment don't change. This relationship broke down during the early 1980s because we were in recession and investment decreased relative to saving.

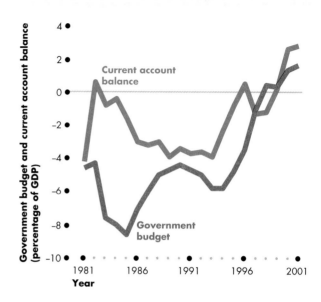

FIGURE 34.2   The Twin Deficits

The current account balance and the government budget balance move in similar ways and look like twin deficits. But this relationship broke down during the early 1980s when the private sector surplus swelled.

Source: Statistics Canada, CANSIM tables 376-0001 and 380-0007.

R E V I E W   Q U I Z

1 When a Canadian art dealer buys a painting from a French gallery, which currency gets used to make the transaction?
2 When a German car maker buys parts from a Windsor car maker, which currency gets used to make the transaction?
3 What types of transactions do we record in the balance of payments accounts?
4 What transactions does the current account record? What transactions does the capital account record? What transactions does the official settlements account record?
5 How are the current account balance, the government sector balance, and the private sector balance related?

The Exchange Rate

WHEN WE BUY FOREIGN GOODS OR INVEST IN another country, we have to obtain some of that country's currency to make the transaction. When foreigners buy Canadian-produced goods or invest in Canada, they have to obtain some Canadian dollars. We get foreign currency, and foreigners get Canadian dollars in the foreign exchange market. The **foreign exchange market** is the market in which the currency of one country is exchanged for the currency of another. The foreign exchange market is not a place like a downtown flea market or produce market. The market is made up of thousands of people—importers and exporters, banks, and specialists in the buying and selling of foreign exchange—called foreign exchange brokers. The foreign exchange market opens on Monday morning in Hong Kong, which is still Sunday evening in Montreal and Toronto. As the day advances, markets open in Singapore, Tokyo, Bahrain, Frankfurt, London, New York, Montreal, Toronto, and Vancouver. As the West Coast markets close, Hong Kong is only an hour away from opening for the next day of business. The sun barely sets on the foreign exchange market. Dealers around the world are in continual contact by telephone and on a typical day in 2001, $1.5 trillion changed hands.

The price at which one currency exchanges for another is called a **foreign exchange rate.** For example, in October 2002, one Canadian dollar bought 63 U.S. cents. The exchange rate was 63 U.S. cents per dollar.

Figure 34.3 shows the exchange rate of the Canadian dollar in terms of the U.S. dollar between 1971 and 2001. On the average over this period, the Canadian dollar has depreciated against the U.S. dollar.

Currency depreciation is a fall in the value of one currency in terms of another currency. For example when the Canadian dollar fell from 101 U.S. cents in 1976 to 94 U.S. cents in 1977, the Canadian dollar depreciated by 7 percent.

Currency appreciation is the rise in the value of one currency in terms of another currency. From 1986 to 1991, the value of the Canadian dollar increased against the U.S. dollar—the Canadian dollar appreciated.

We've just expressed the value of the Canadian dollar in terms of the U.S. dollar. But we can express the value of the dollar in terms of any currency. Also, we can express the exchange rate of the U.S. dollar in terms of the Canadian dollar as a number of Canadian dollars per U.S. dollar.

When the Canadian dollar depreciates against the U.S. dollar, the U.S. dollar appreciates against the Canadian dollar.

Why does the Canadian dollar fluctuate in value? Why does it sometimes depreciate and sometimes appreciate? What happened between 1976 and 1986 and again between 1992 and 2001 to make the Canadian dollar depreciate? And what happened between 1986 and 1991 to make the Canadian dollar appreciate against the U.S. dollar? To answer these questions, we need to understand the forces that determine the exchange rate.

The exchange rate is the price of one country's money in terms of another country's money. And like all prices, the exchange rate is determined by demand and supply.

FIGURE 34.3 The Exchange Rate

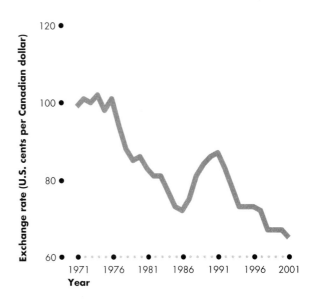

The Canadian dollar exchange rate, expressed as U.S. cents per Canadian dollar, shows that the Canadian dollar fell in value—depreciated—against the U.S. dollar from 1976 through 1986. The Canadian dollar rose in value against the U.S. dollar—appreciated—from 1986 through 1991 and then depreciated again.

Source: Bank of Canada, *Banking and Financial Statistics*, table J1.

Demand in the Foreign Exchange Market

The quantity of Canadian dollars demanded in the foreign exchange market is the amount that traders plan to buy during a given time period at a given exchange rate. This quantity depends on many factors but the main ones are

- The exchange rate
- Interest rates in Canada and other countries
- The expected future exchange rate

Let's look first at the relationship between the quantity of Canadian dollars demanded in the foreign exchange market and the exchange rate.

The Law of Demand for Foreign Exchange

People do not buy dollars because they enjoy them. The demand for dollars is a *derived demand*. People demand Canadian dollars so that they can buy Canadian-made goods and services (Canadian exports). They also demand dollars so they can buy Canadian assets such as bank accounts, bonds, stocks, businesses, and real estate. Nevertheless, the law of demand applies to dollars just as it does to anything else that people value.

Other things remaining the same, the higher the exchange rate, the smaller is the quantity of Canadian dollars demanded in the foreign exchange market. For example, if the price of the Canadian dollar rose from 68 U.S. cents to 75 U.S. cents but nothing else changed, the quantity of Canadian dollars that people plan to buy in the foreign exchange market would decrease. The exchange rate influences the quantity of dollars demanded for two reasons:

- Exports effect
- Expected profit effect

Exports Effect   The larger the value of Canadian exports, the larger is the quantity of Canadian dollars demanded on the foreign exchange market. But the value of Canadian exports depends on the exchange rate. The lower the exchange rate, with other things remaining the same, the cheaper are Canadian-produced goods and services and the more Canada exports. So the quantity of Canadian dollars demanded on the foreign exchange market increases.

Expected Profit Effect   The larger the expected profit from holding Canadian dollars, the greater is the quantity of Canadian dollars demanded. But expected profit depends on the exchange rate. The lower the exchange rate, other things remaining the same, the larger is the expected profit from buying Canadian dollars and the greater is the quantity of Canadian dollars demanded.

To understand this effect, suppose that today, a Canadian dollar costs 68 U.S. cents. Tina thinks the dollar will be worth 70 U.S. cents by the end of the month and Jack thinks it will be worth 67 U.S. cents. In this situation, Tina buys Canadian dollars but Jack does not. Now suppose that expectations remain the same, but that today a Canadian dollar costs 65 U.S. cents. Now both Tina and Jack buy Canadian dollars. So the quantity of dollars demanded increases.

For the two reasons we've just reviewed, other things remaining the same, when the foreign exchange rate rises, the quantity of Canadian dollars demanded decreases and when the foreign exchange rate falls, the quantity of Canadian dollars demanded increases.

Figure 34.4 shows the demand curve for Canadian dollars in the foreign exchange market. When the foreign exchange rate rises, other things remaining the same, there is a decrease in the quantity of Canadian dollars demanded and a movement up along the demand curve as shown by the arrow. When the exchange rate falls, other things remaining the same, there is an increase in the quantity of Canadian dollars demanded and a movement down along the demand curve as shown by the arrow.

Changes in the Demand for Dollars

A change in any other influence on the quantity of Canadian dollars that people plan to buy brings a change in the demand for dollars and a shift in the demand curve for dollars. Demand either increases or decreases. These other influences are

- Interest rates in Canada and other countries
- The expected future exchange rate

Interest Rates in Canada and Other Countries
People and businesses buy financial assets to make a return. The higher the interest rate that people can make on Canadian assets compared with foreign assets, the more Canadian assets they buy. What matters is not the level of Canadian interest rates, but the

FIGURE 34.4   The Demand for Dollars

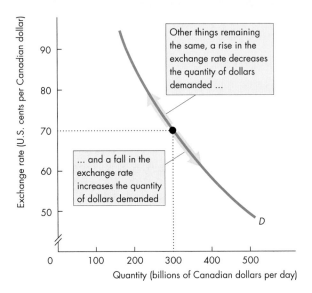

Other things remaining the same, a rise in the exchange rate decreases the quantity of dollars demanded ...

... and a fall in the exchange rate increases the quantity of dollars demanded

The quantity of Canadian dollars that people plan to buy depends on the exchange rate. Other things remaining the same, if the exchange rate rises, the quantity of dollars demanded decreases and there is a movement up along the demand curve for dollars. If the exchange rate falls, the quantity of dollars demanded increases and there is a movement down along the demand curve for dollars.

Canadian interest rate minus the foreign interest rate, a gap that is called the **Canadian interest rate differential.** If the Canadian interest rate rises and the foreign interest rate remains constant, the Canadian interest rate differential increases. The larger the Canadian interest rate differential, the greater is the demand for Canadian assets and the greater is the demand for Canadian dollars on the foreign exchange market.

The Expected Future Exchange Rate Other things remaining the same, the higher the expected future exchange rate, the greater is the demand for Canadian dollars. To see why, suppose you are American Express's finance manager. The exchange rate is 70 U.S cents per dollar and you think that by the end of the month, it will be 75 U.S. cents per dollar. You spend $U.S.700,000 today and buy $C1,000,000. At the end of the month, the Canadian dollar is 75 U.S. cents, as you predicted it would be, and you sell the $C1,000,000. You get $U.S.750,000.

You've made a profit of $U.S.50,000. The higher the expected future exchange rate, other things remaining the same, the greater is the expected profit and the greater is the demand for Canadian dollars.

Figure 34.5 summarizes the influences on the demand for dollars. A rise in the Canadian interest rate differential or a rise in the expected future exchange rate increases the demand for Canadian dollars and shifts the demand curve rightward from D_0 to D_1. A fall in the Canadian interest rate differential or a fall in the expected future exchange rate decreases the demand for Canadian dollars and shifts the demand curve leftward from D_0 to D_2.

FIGURE 34.5   Changes in the Demand for Dollars

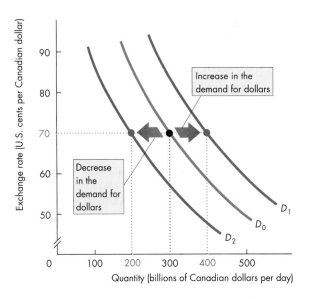

Increase in the demand for dollars

Decrease in the demand for dollars

A change in any influence on the quantity of Canadian dollars that people plan to buy, other than today's exchange rate, brings a change in the demand for Canadian dollars.

The demand for Canadian dollars

Increases if:	Decreases if:
■ The Canadian interest rate differential increases	■ The Canadian interest rate differential decreases
■ The expected future exchange rate rises	■ The expected future exchange rate falls

Supply in the Foreign Exchange Market

The quantity of Canadian dollars supplied in the foreign exchange market is the amount that traders plan to sell during a given time period at a given exchange rate. This quantity depends on many factors but the main ones are

- The exchange rate
- Interest rates in Canada and other countries
- The expected future exchange rate

Let's look first at the relationship between the quantity of Canadian dollars supplied in the foreign exchange market and the exchange rate.

The Law of Supply of Foreign Exchange

People supply dollars in the foreign exchange market when they buy other currencies. And they buy other currencies so they can buy foreign-made goods and services (Canadian imports). People also supply dollars and buy foreign currencies so they can buy foreign assets such as bank accounts, bonds, stocks, businesses, and real estate. The law of supply applies to dollars just as it does to anything else that people plan to sell.

Other things remaining the same, the higher the exchange rate, the greater is the quantity of dollars supplied in the foreign exchange market. For example, if the price of the Canadian dollar rose from 68 U.S. cents to 75 U.S. cents but nothing else changed, the quantity of Canadian dollars that people plan to sell in the foreign exchange market would increase. Why does the exchange rate influence the quantity of dollars supplied?

The exchange rate influences the quantity of dollars supplied for two reasons:

- Imports effect
- Expected profit effect

Imports Effect The larger the value of Canadian imports, the larger is the quantity of foreign currency demanded to pay for these imports. And when people buy foreign currency, they supply Canadian dollars. So the larger the value of Canadian imports, the greater is the quantity of Canadian dollars supplied on the foreign exchange market. But the value of Canadian imports depends on the exchange rate. The

higher the exchange rate, with other things remaining the same, the cheaper are foreign-produced goods and services to Canadians, and the more Canada imports. So the greater is the quantity of Canadian dollars supplied.

Expected Profit Effect The larger the expected profit from holding a foreign currency, the greater is the quantity of that currency demanded and the greater is the quantity of Canadian dollars supplied in the foreign exchange market. But the expected profit from holding a foreign currency depends on the exchange rate. The higher the exchange rate, other things remaining the same, the larger is the expected profit from selling Canadian dollars and the greater is the quantity of Canadian dollars supplied.

For the two reasons we've just reviewed, other things remaining the same, when the foreign

FIGURE 34.6   The Supply of Dollars

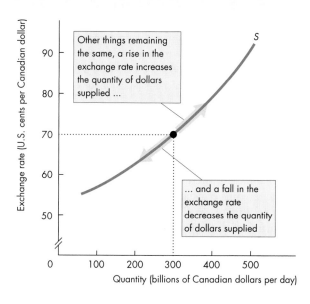

The quantity of Canadian dollars that people plan to sell depends on the exchange rate. Other things remaining the same, if the exchange rate rises, the quantity of Canadian dollars supplied increases and there is a movement up along the supply curve of dollars. If the exchange rate falls, the quantity of Canadian dollars supplied decreases and there is a movement down along the supply curve of dollars.

exchange rate rises, the quantity of dollars supplied increases and when the foreign exchange rate falls, the quantity of Canadian dollars supplied decreases. Figure 34.6 shows the supply curve for Canadian dollars in the foreign exchange market. In this figure, when the foreign exchange rate rises, other things remaining the same, there is an increase in the quantity of Canadian dollars supplied and a movement up along the supply curve as shown by the arrow. When the exchange rate falls, other things remaining the same, there is a decrease in the quantity of Canadian dollars supplied and a movement down along the supply curve as shown by the arrow.

Changes in the Supply of Dollars

A change in any other influence on the quantity of Canadian dollars that people plan to sell in the foreign exchange market brings a change in the supply of dollars and a shift in the supply curve of dollars. Supply either increases or decreases. These other influences parallel the other influences on demand but have exactly the opposite effects. These influences are

- Interest rates in Canada and other countries
- The expected future exchange rate

Interest Rates in Canada and Other Countries
The larger the Canadian interest rate differential, the smaller is the demand for foreign assets, and the smaller is the supply of Canadian dollars on the foreign exchange market.

The Expected Future Exchange Rate
Other things remaining the same, the higher the expected future exchange rate, the smaller is the supply of dollars. To see why, suppose the Canadian dollar is trading at 70 U.S. cents per dollar today and you think that by the end of the month, the dollar will be worth 75 U.S. cents per dollar. You were planning on selling Canadian dollars today, but you decide to hold off and wait until the end of the month. If you supply dollars today, you get only 70 U.S. cents. But at the end of the month, if the dollar is worth 75 U.S. cents as you predict, you'll get 75 U.S. cents for each dollar you supply. You'll make a profit of 5 U.S. cents per dollar. So the higher the expected future exchange rate, other things remaining the same, the smaller is the expected profit from selling Canadian

dollars today and the smaller is the supply of Canadian dollars today.

Figure 34.7 summarizes the influences on the supply of Canadian dollars. A rise in the Canadian interest rate differential or a rise in the expected future exchange rate decreases the supply of Canadian dollars and shifts the demand curve leftward from S_0 to S_1. A fall in the Canadian interest rate differential or a fall in the expected future exchange rate increases the supply of Canadian dollars and shifts the supply curve rightward from S_0 to S_2.

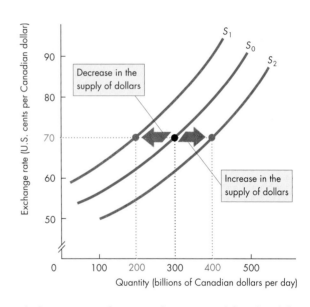

FIGURE 34.7   Changes in the Supply of Dollars

A change in any influence on the quantity of Canadian dollars that people plan to sell, other than today's exchange rate, brings a change in the supply of Canadian dollars.

The supply of Canadian dollars

Increases if:	Decreases if:
■ The Canadian interest rate differential decreases	■ The Canadian interest rate differential increases
■ The expected future exchange rate falls	■ The expected future exchange rate rises

Market Equilibrium

Figure 34.8 shows how demand and supply in the foreign exchange market determine the exchange rate. The demand curve is *D* and the supply curve is *S*. As in other markets you've studied, price (the exchange rate) acts as a regulator. If the exchange rate is too high, there is a surplus—the quantity supplied exceeds the quantity demanded. For example, in Fig. 34.8, if the exchange rate is 80 U.S. cents per Canadian dollar, there is a surplus of Canadian dollars.

If the exchange rate is too low, there is a shortage—the quantity supplied is less than the quantity demanded. For example, in Fig. 34.8, if the exchange rate is 60 U.S. cents per Canadian dollar, there is a shortage of Canadian dollars.

At the equilibrium exchange rate, there is neither a shortage nor a surplus. The quantity supplied equals the quantity demanded. In Fig. 34.8, the equilibrium exchange rate is 70 U.S. cents per Canadian dollar. At this exchange rate, the quantity demanded and the quantity supplied are each $300 billion a day.

The foreign exchange market is constantly pulled to its equilibrium by the forces of supply and demand. Foreign exchange dealers are constantly looking for the best price they can get. If they are selling, they want the highest price available. If they are buying, they want the lowest price available. Information flows from dealer to dealer through the worldwide computer network and the price adjusts second by second to keep buying plans and selling plans in balance. That is, price adjusts minute by minute to keep the market at its equilibrium.

Changes in the Exchange Rate

If the demand for dollars increases and the supply of dollars does not change, the exchange rate rises. If the demand for dollars decreases and the supply of dollars does not change, the exchange rate falls. Similarly, if the supply of dollars decreases and the demand for dollars does not change, the exchange rate rises. If the supply of dollars increases and the demand for dollars does not change, the exchange rate falls.

These predictions about the effects of changes in demand and supply are exactly the same as for any other market.

Why the Exchange Rate Is Volatile   Sometimes the dollar depreciates and at other times it appreciates but the quantity of dollars traded each day barely changes. Why? The main reason is that supply and demand are not independent of each other in the foreign exchange market.

When we studied the demand for dollars and the supply of dollars, we saw that the demand side and the supply side of the market have some common influences. A change in the expected future exchange rate or a change in the Canadian interest rate differential changes both demand and supply and in opposite directions. These common influences explain why the exchange rate can be volatile at times even though the quantity of dollars traded does not change.

Everyone in the market is potentially either a demander or a supplier. Each has a price above which he or she will sell and below which he or she will buy. Let's see how these common supply and demand effects work by looking at two episodes: one in which the dollar appreciated and one in which it depreciated.

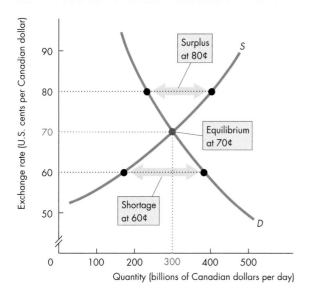

FIGURE 34.8   Equilibrium Exchange Rate

The demand curve for dollars is *D* and the supply curve is *S*. If the exchange rate is 80 U.S. cents per dollar, there is a surplus of dollars and the exchange rate falls. If the exchange rate is 60 U.S. cents per dollar, there is a shortage of dollars and the exchange rate rises. If the exchange rate is 70 U.S. cents per dollar, there is neither a shortage nor a surplus of dollars and the exchange rate remains constant. The market is in equilibrium.

An Appreciating Dollar: 1986–1991 Between 1986 and 1991 the Canadian dollar appreciated. It rose from 72 U.S. cents in 1986 to 87 U.S. cents in 1991. Figure 34.9(a) explains why this happened. In 1986, the demand and supply curves were those labelled D_{86} and S_{86}. The exchange rate was 72 U.S. cents per dollar—where the supply and demand curves intersect. During the next five years, people expected the Canadian dollar to appreciate. They expected a higher future exchange rate. As a result, the demand for dollars increased and the supply of dollars decreased. The demand curve shifted from D_{86} to D_{91} and the supply curve shifted from S_{86} to S_{91}. These two shifts reinforced each other and the exchange rate increased to 87 U.S. cents per dollar.

A Depreciating Dollar: 1991–2001 Between 1991 and 2001, the dollar fell from 87 U.S. cents to 65 U.S. cents per dollar. Figure 34.9(b) explains this fall. In 1991, the demand and supply curves were those labelled D_{91} and S_{91}. The exchange rate was 87 U.S. cents per dollar. During the 1990s, traders expected the Canadian dollar to depreciate. They expected a lower exchange rate. As a result, the demand for dollars decreased and the supply of dollars increased. The demand curve shifted leftward to D_{01} and the supply curve shifted rightward to S_{01}. The exchange rate fell to 65 U.S. cents per dollar.

Exchange Rate Expectations

The changes in the exchange rate that we've just examined occurred mainly because the exchange rate was *expected to change.* This explanation sounds a bit like a self-fulfilling forecast. But what makes expectations change? The answer is new information about the deeper forces that influence the value of money. Two such forces are

- Purchasing power parity
- Interest rate parity

FIGURE 34.9   Exchange Rate Fluctuations

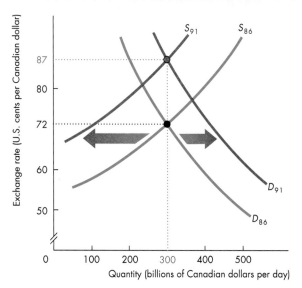

(a) 1986 to 1991

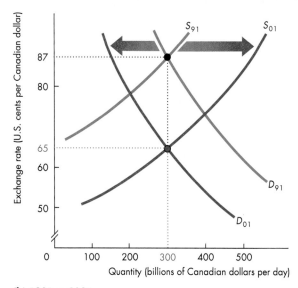

(b) 1991 to 2001

The exchange rate fluctuates because changes in demand and supply are not independent of each other. Between 1986 and 1991 (part a), the Canadian dollar appreciated from 72 U.S. cents to 87 U.S. cents per dollar. This appreciation occurred because an increase in the expected future exchange rate increased the demand for dollars and decreased the supply. Between 1991 and 2001 (in part b), the exchange rate fell from 87 U.S. cents to 65 U.S. cents per dollar. This depreciation occurred because a decrease in the expected future exchange rate decreased the demand for dollars and increased the supply.

Purchasing Power Parity Money is worth what it will buy. But two kinds of money, Canadian dollars and U.S. dollars for example, might buy different amounts of goods and services. Suppose a Big Mac costs $4 (Canadian) in Toronto and $3 (U.S.) in New York. If the Canadian dollar exchange rate is 75 U.S. cents per Canadian dollar, the two monies have the same value. You can buy a Big Mac in either Toronto or New York for either $4 Canadian or $3 U.S.

The situation we've just described is called **purchasing power parity,** which means *equal value of money.* If purchasing power parity does not prevail, some powerful forces go to work. To understand these forces, let's suppose that the price of a Big Mac in New York rises to $4 U.S. but in Toronto it remains at $4 Canadian. Suppose the exchange rate remains at 75 U.S. cents per Canadian dollar. In this case, a Big Mac in Toronto still costs $4 Canadian or $3 U.S. But in New York, it costs $4 U.S. or $5.33 Canadian. Money buys more in Canada than in the United States. Money is not of equal value in both countries.

If all (or most) prices have increased in the United States and have not increased in Canada, then people will generally expect that the value of the Canadian dollar on the foreign exchange market must rise. In this situation, the exchange rate is expected to rise. The demand for Canadian dollars increases and the supply of Canadian dollars decreases. The exchange rate rises, as expected. If the exchange rate rises to $1.00 U.S. per Canadian dollar and there are no further price changes, purchasing power parity is restored. A Big Mac now costs $4 in either Canadian or U.S. dollars in both New York and Toronto.

If prices increase in Canada but remain constant in other countries, then people will generally expect that the value of the Canadian dollar on the foreign exchange market is too high and that it is going to fall. In this situation, the exchange rate is expected to fall. The demand for Canadian dollars decreases and the supply of Canadian dollars increases. The exchange rate falls, as expected.

Ultimately, the value of money is determined by the price level, which in turn is determined by aggregate supply and aggregate demand (see Chapter 22) So the deeper forces that influence the exchange rate have tentacles that spread throughout the economy. If the price level rises more quickly in Canada than in other countries, the exchange rate falls. And if the price level rises more slowly in Canada than in other countries, the exchange rate rises.

Interest Rate Parity Money is worth what it can earn. Again two kinds of money, Canadian dollars and U.S. dollars for example, might earn different amounts. For example, suppose a Canadian dollar bank deposit in Toronto earns 4 percent a year and a U.S. dollar bank deposit in New York earns 5 percent a year. In this situation, why does anyone deposit money in Toronto? Why doesn't all the money flow to New York? The answer is: because of exchange rate expectations. Suppose people expect the Canadian dollar to appreciate by 1 percent a year. This 1 percent appreciation must be added to the 4 percent interest to obtain a return of 5 percent a year that an American can earn by depositing funds in a Toronto bank. The two returns are equal. This situation is one of **interest rate parity,** which means *equal interest rates.*

Adjusted for risk, interest rate parity always prevails. Funds move to get the highest return available. If for a few seconds a higher return is available in Toronto than in New York, the demand for Canadian dollars rises and the exchange rate rises until the expected interest rates are equal.

The Bank of Canada in the Foreign Exchange Market

The Bank of Canada influences the quantity of money and the Canadian interest rate (see Chapter 25, pp. 594–595). So the Bank of Canada influences the exchange rate through its monetary policy. When interest rates in Canada rise relative to those in other countries, the demand for Canadian dollars increases, the supply decreases, and the exchange rate rises. (Similarly, when interest rates in Canada fall relative to those in other countries, the demand for Canadian dollars decreases, the supply increases, and the exchange rate falls.)

But the Bank of Canada can intervene directly in the foreign exchange market. It can buy or sell dollars and try to smooth out fluctuations in the exchange rate. Let's look at the foreign exchange interventions that the Bank can make.

Suppose the Bank of Canada wants the exchange rate to be steady at 70 U.S. cents per dollar. If the exchange rate rises above 70 U.S. cents, the Bank sells dollars. If the exchange rate falls below 70 U.S. cents, the Bank buys dollars. By these actions, it changes the supply of dollars and keeps the exchange rate close to its target rate of 70 U.S. cents per Canadian dollar.

Figure 34.10 shows the Bank of Canada's intervention in the foreign exchange market. The supply

FIGURE 34.10   Foreign Exchange Market Intervention

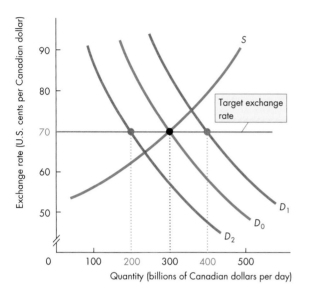

Initially, the demand for dollars is D_0, the supply of dollars is S, and the exchange rate is 70 U.S. cents per dollar. The Bank of Canada can intervene in the foreign exchange market to keep the exchange rate close to its target rate (70 U.S. cents in this example). If demand increases from D_0 to D_1, the Bank sells dollars to increase supply. If demand decreases from D_0 to D_2, the Bank buys dollars to decrease supply. Persistent intervention on one side of the market cannot be sustained.

of dollars is S and initially the demand for dollars is D_0. The equilibrium exchange rate is 70 U.S. cents per dollar. This exchange rate is the Bank's target rate, shown by the horizontal red line.

When the demand for dollars increases and the demand curve shifts rightward to D_1, the Bank of Canada sells $100 billion. This action increases the supply of dollars by $100 billion and prevents the exchange rate from rising. When the demand for dollars decreases and the demand curve shifts leftward to D_2, the Bank buys $100 billion. This action decreases the supply of dollars by $100 billion and prevents the exchange rate from falling.

If the demand for dollars fluctuates between D_1 and D_2 and on the average is D_0, the Bank of Canada can repeatedly intervene in the way we've just seen. Sometimes the Bank buys and sometimes it sells but, on the average, it neither buys nor sells.

But suppose the demand for dollars increases permanently from D_0 to D_1. The Bank cannot now maintain the exchange rate at 70 U.S. cents indefinitely. For to do so, the Bank would have to sell dollars every day. When the Bank sells dollars in the foreign exchange market, it buys foreign currency. So the Bank would be piling up foreign currency.

Now suppose the demand for dollars decreases permanently from D_0 to D_2. Again the Bank cannot maintain the exchange rate at 70 U.S. cents indefinitely. In this situation, to hold the exchange rate at 70 U.S. cents per dollar the Bank would have to buy dollars every day. When the Bank buys dollars in the foreign exchange market, it uses its holdings of foreign currency. So the Bank would be losing foreign currency. Eventually, it would run out of foreign currency and would then have to abandon its attempt to fix the exchange rate.

REVIEW QUIZ

1 What is the exchange rate and how is it determined?
2 What are the influences of interest rates and the expected future exchange rate on the demand for and supply of dollars in the foreign exchange market?
3 How do changes in the expected future exchange rate influence the actual exchange rate?
4 How do purchasing power parity and interest rate parity affect exchange rate expectations?
5 How can the Bank of Canada influence the foreign exchange market?

◆ *Reading Between the Lines* on pages 824–825 looks at a projection of the Canadian dollar through 2026.

In the final chapter, we expand our view of the global economy and study global stock markets. These are the markets in which firms borrow the funds that finance their investment in new capital. Those funds often cross national borders, and when they do so, they move through the foreign exchange markets and show up in the balance of payments capital accounts that you've studied in this chapter. Keep what you've learned about the balance of payments and the foreign exchange market in mind as you work through the stock markets chapter.

Exchange Rate Projections

FINANCIAL POST, NOVEMBER 5, 2002

Loonie to rise above US80 cents: climb to take 15 years

The Canadian dollar, now worth just over US64 cents, is heading back up to more than US80 cents, a level not seen since the early 1990s and then only briefly, a major economic think-tank is forecasting.

But that increase in the exchange rate will take more than 15 years, according to the new DRI-WEFA forecast.

Still, the loonie's worst days are now behind it, thanks to higher interest rates here than in the U.S., relatively low and stable inflation, and healthy trade and budget surpluses, it says.

"These factors combined are expected to impart modest upward pressure on the Canadian dollar, moving it... through the US70 cents barrier in 2004 and to the US80 cents level by 2018," says the Canadian arm of the international economic research firm.

And that's not the peak.

The loonie will continue to rise steadily after 2018, reaching a peak of US84.5 cents sometime between 2021 and 2026, which is the outer limit of the near quarter-century forecast.

"DRI-WEFA has been forecasting slight upward pressures on the Canadian dollar for several years now," it notes. "This is the obvious forecast given the strong fundamentals, in spite of the fact that history has not been kind."

The think-tank assumes "a reasonably healthy spread will be maintained over U.S. interest rates."

And that's despite what it says will be lower inflation here, averaging close to two per cent compared with 2.4% in the U.S. ...

With permission of Southam Publications.

Essence of the Story

■ DRI-WEFA, an international economy forecasting firm, says that the Canadian dollar will rise from US64 cents in 2002 to more than US70 cents during 2004, to US80 cents by 2018, and to US84.5 cents sometime between 2021 and 2026.

■ Higher interest rates and a lower inflation rate in Canada than in the U.S. and healthy trade and budget surpluses will be the sources of the strength of the Canadian dollar.

■ The Canadian inflation rate will average 2 percent a year compared with 2.4 percent a year in the United States.

Economic Analysis

■ Exchange rate forecasting over a 25-year horizon is impossible, and the DRI-WEFA projections are not worth much.

■ Despite the fact that we can't forecast the exchange rate, we can predict that it is unlikely that a currency will remain either undervalued or overvalued relative to purchasing power parity (PPP) for two decades.

■ The DRI-WEFA projection implies that the Canadian dollar will remain undervalued for the next 25 years and is almost certainly going to be incorrect.

■ Figure 1 shows the history of the Canadian dollar since 1970 with the DRI-WEFA projection through 2026.

■ Figure 2 shows the path that the Canadian dollar would have followed since 1970 and would follow through 2026 based on the DRI-WEFA projection of the inflation differential between Canada and the United States—Canadian inflation rate minus U.S. inflation rate.

■ Figure 3 shows the fluctuations of the Canadian dollar around PPP. It shows an overvalued Canadian dollar during the 1970s, early 1980s, and around 1990 and an undervalued dollar in the mid 1980s, late 1990s, and 2000s.

■ The DRI-WEFA projects another 25 years of undervaluation. More likely, the dollar will alternate between undervaluation and overvaluation, but at unpredictable times.

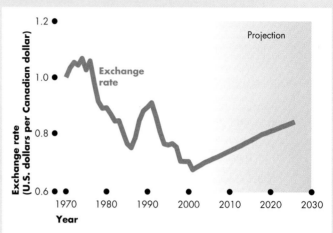

Figure 1 The Canadian dollar: 1970 to 2026

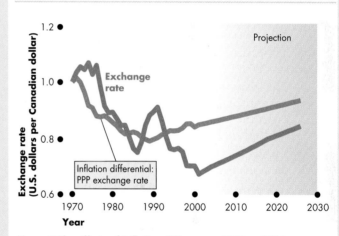

Figure 2 The effects of inflation differences: 1970 to 2026

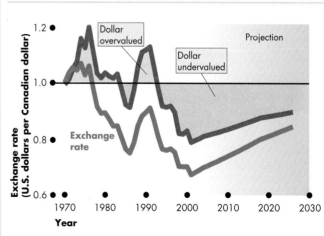

Figure 3 Departures from PPP: 1970 to 2026

SUMMARY

KEY POINTS

Financing International Trade (pp. 810–814)

- International trade, borrowing, and lending are financed by using foreign currency.
- A country's international transactions are recorded in its balance of payments accounts.
- Canada is a net borrower and a debtor nation.
- The net exports surplus is equal to the government sector surplus plus the private sector surplus.

The Exchange Rate (pp. 815–823)

- Foreign currency is obtained in exchange for domestic currency in the foreign exchange market.
- The exchange rate is determined by demand and supply in the foreign exchange market.
- The lower the exchange rate, the greater is the quantity of dollars demanded. A change in the exchange rate brings a movement along the demand curve for dollars.
- Changes in the expected future exchange rate and the Canadian interest rate differential change the demand for Canadian dollars and shift the demand curve.
- The lower the exchange rate, the smaller is the quantity of dollars supplied. A change in the exchange rate brings a movement along the supply curve of dollars.
- Changes in the expected future exchange rate and the Canadian interest rate differential change the supply of Canadian dollars and shift the supply curve.
- Fluctuations in the exchange rate occur because fluctuations in the demand for and supply of dollars are not independent.
- The Bank of Canada can intervene in the foreign exchange market to smooth fluctuations in the dollar.

KEY FIGURES AND TABLE

KEY TERMS

PROBLEMS

*1. The citizens of Silecon, whose currency is the grain, conducted the following transactions in 2002:

Item	Billions of grains
Imports of goods and services	350
Exports of goods and services	500
Borrowing from the rest of the world	60
Lending to the rest of the world	200
Increase in official holdings of foreign currency	10

   a. Set out the three balance of payments accounts for Silecon.
   b. Does the Silecon central bank intervene in the foreign exchange market?

2. The citizens of Spin, whose currency is the wheel, conducted the following transactions in 2002:

Item	Billions of wheels
Imports of goods and services	100
Exports of goods and services	120
Borrowing from the rest of the world	4
Lending to the rest of the world	24
Increase in official holdings of foreign currency	0

   a. Set out the three balance of payments accounts for Spin.
   b. Does the central bank intervene in the foreign exchange market?

*3. The figure at the bottom of the page shows the flows of income and expenditure in Dream Land in 2000. The amounts are in millions of dollars. GDP in Dream Land is $120 million.
   a. Calculate Dream Land's net exports.
   b. Calculate saving in Dream Land.
   c. How is Dream Land's investment financed?

4. The figure shows the flows of income and expenditure in Dream Land in 2001. The amounts are in millions of dollars. Dream Land's GDP has increased to $130 million but all the other items whose values are provided in the figure remain the same as they were in 2000.
   a. Calculate Dream Land's net exports in 2001.
   b. Calculate saving in Dream Land in 2001.
   c. How is Dream Land's investment financed?

*5. The table on the next page tells you about Ecflex, a country whose currency is the band. The official settlements balance is zero. Net interest income and net transfers from abroad are zero.

   Calculate for Ecflex its
   a. Imports of goods and services
   b. Current account balance
   c. Capital account balance
   d. Net taxes
   e. Private sector balance

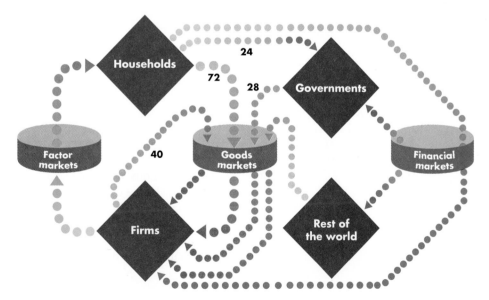

Item	Billions of bands
GDP	100
Consumption expenditure	60
Government expenditures on goods and services	24
Investment	22
Exports of goods and services	20
Government budget deficit	4

6. The following table tells you about Ecfix, a country whose currency is the rock:

Item	Billions of rocks
GDP	400
Consumption expenditure	240
Government expenditures on goods and services	100
Investment	100
Exports of goods and services	80
Saving	90

   Calculate for Ecfix its
   a. Imports of goods and services
   b. Current account balance
   c. Government sector balance
   d. Net taxes
   e. Private sector balance

*7. A country's currency appreciates, and its official reserves increase. What can you say about
   a. Intervention in the foreign exchange market by the country's central bank?
   b. The possible central bank sources of the currency appreciation?
   c. The possible private actions behind the appreciation?

8. A country has a lower inflation rate than all other countries. It has more rapid economic growth. The central bank does not intervene in the foreign exchange market. What can you say about each of the following (and why)?
   a. The exchange rate
   b. The current account balance
   c. The expected exchange rate
   d. The interest rate differential
   e. Interest rate parity
   f. Purchasing power parity

CRITICAL THINKING

1. Study *Reading Between the Lines* on pp. 824–825 and then answer the following questions:
   a. What does DRI-WEFA predict will happen to the Canadian dollar exchange rate during the next 25 years?
   b. Are the projections consistent with purchasing power parity?
   c. Are the projections consistent with interest rate parity?
   d. What could happen over the next 25 years to make the Canadian dollar either rise much faster than the DRI-WEFA projection, or fall rather than rise?

WEB EXERCISES

1. Use the link on the Parkin–Bade Web site to visit Statistics Canada and find data on the exchange rate and international trade.
   a. When did Canada last have a current account surplus?
   b. When did official Canadian reserves last increase?
   c. Does Canada have a surplus or a deficit in its trade in services?
   d. What has happened to foreign investment in Canada during the past ten years?
   e. Do you think that Canada's balance of payments record is a matter for concern? Why or why not?

2. Use the link on the Parkin–Bade Web site to visit PACIFIC (an exchange rate service) and read the page on purchasing power parity.
   a. What is purchasing power parity?
   b. Which currencies are the most overvalued relative to the U.S. dollar today?
   c. Which currencies are the most undervalued relative to the U.S. dollar today?
   d. Can you offer some suggestions as to why some currencies are overvalued and some are undervalued?
   e. Do you think that the information on overvaluation and undervaluation is useful to currency speculators? Why or why not?

GLOBAL STOCK MARKETS

CHAPTER 35

Irrational Exuberance?

On December 5, 1996, Alan Greenspan, chairman of the U.S. Federal Reserve, said that stock market investors were suffering from *irrational exuberance*. It appeared that some people agreed with Mr. Greenspan, for when the New York Stock Exchange opened the next morning, the Dow Jones Industrial Average immediately dropped by 2.3 percent. During the American night, stock prices in Japan, Hong Kong, Germany, and Britain had dropped an average of almost 4 percent. ◆ Alan Greenspan's remark was prompted by an extraordinary rise in stock prices in the United States and around the world that began in 1994 and was to continue through 1999. During these years, the Dow (as the Dow Jones Industrial Average is known) tripled! It then stopped climbing and eventually nose-dived following September 11, 2001, but only temporarily. By January 2002, prices were back at the pre-September 11 levels. ◆ How are stock prices determined? Do investors suffer from "irrational exuberance" or are their buying and selling decisions rational? Do Canadian stock prices behave like those in the United States? How does the economy influence the stock market? And how does the stock market influence the economy?

◆ You are going to probe some interesting questions in this chapter. But first, a warning: You will not learn in this chapter which stocks to buy and how to get rich. You will, though, learn some important lessons about traps to avoid that could easily make you poor. And you will see in *Reading Between the Lines* at the end of the chapter how it is impossible to predict when a falling stock market will turn the corner and start rising.

After studying this chapter, you will be able to

- ■ Explain what a firm's stock is and how its rate of return and price are related

- ■ Describe the global markets in which stocks are traded and the stock price indexes

- ■ Describe the long-term performance of stock prices and earnings

- ■ Explain what determines the price of stock and why stock prices are volatile

- ■ Explain why it is rational to diversify a stock portfolio rather than to hold the one stock that has the highest expected return

- ■ Explain how the stock market influences the economy and how the economy influences the stock market

Stock Market Basics

ALL FIRMS GET SOME OF THEIR FINANCIAL capital from the people who own the firm. A large firm has possibly millions of owners from whom it raises billions of dollars in financial capital. These owners are the firm's stockholders—the holders of stock issued by the firm.

What Is Stock?

Stock is a tradable security that a firm issues to certify that the stockholder owns a share of the firm. Figure 35.1 shows a famous stock certificate that has become a collector's item—a Walt Disney Company stock certificate. The value of a firm's stock is called the firm's **equity capital** (or just equity). The terms "stock" and "equity" are often used interchangeably.

A stockholder has *limited liability*, which means that if the firm can't pay all its debts, a stockholder's liability for the firm's debts is limited to the amount invested in the firm by that stockholder. For example, when Enron collapsed, its stockholders lost everything they had invested in the firm's stock, but they weren't forced to contribute anything to make up for Enron's remaining debts.

FIGURE 35.1   A Stock Certificate

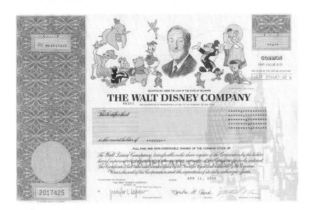

The Walt Disney Company issues a colourful stock certificate to record the ownership of its common stock. Attractive share certificates, like postage stamps and coins, become collectors' items.

Source: © Disney Enterprises Inc.

Stockholders receive a **dividend,** which is a share of the firm's profit, in proportion to their stock holdings. For example, holders of stock in PepsiCo received a dividend of 58 cents per share during 2002.

Firms issue two types of stock:

- Preferred stock
- Common stock

Preferred stock entitles its owner to a pre-agreed dividend before common stock dividends are paid and to first claim on the firm's assets in the event that it is liquidated.

Common stock holders are entitled to a share of the firm's assets and earnings and to a vote (one vote per share held) in the selection of the firm's directors.

When a firm issues stock, the buyer of the stock invests directly in the firm. For example, in March 1986, Microsoft Corporation issued 161 million shares of common stock for $21 a share and raised a total of $3.4 billion. The buyers of those shares paid Microsoft Corporation.

Most stockholders buy stock not from the firm that issues it but from other holders who bought the stock from yet other holders. People buy and sell stock on a stock exchange. For example, on an average day during the past ten years, 14 million Microsoft shares have changed hands. Microsoft doesn't receive anything from these transactions and doesn't even keep track of who owns its stock. It hires another firm, Mellon Investor Services, to do that job and to issue stock certificates.

What Is a Stock Exchange?

A **stock exchange** is an organized market on which people can buy and sell stock. The stocks of major Canadian corporations are traded on the Toronto Stock Exchange, which is the centre of Canada's major stock market. Canadian stocks are also traded, along with the stocks of global and U.S. corporations, in the United States on the New York Stock Exchange (NYSE). High-tech stocks are traded on the National Association of Securities Dealers Automated Quotation (NASDAQ) system.

Some stock exchanges—the New York Stock Exchange is one of them—are physical trading arenas. Traders shout and signal their buy and sell orders on the trading floor of the exchange. In the case of the New York Stock Exchange, trades take place on the trading floor on Wall Street in New York City.

Other stock exchanges—the Toronto Stock Exchange is one of them—do not have a trading floor. These more recently upgraded stock exchanges trade through a computer and telecommunications network that links together buyers and sellers from all parts of the world. For example, the NASDAQ computer system enables more than 1.3 million traders in 83 countries to trade more than 4,000 (mainly high-tech) stocks.

NASDAQ is a global stock exchange with large operations in Canada, Japan, and Europe as well as the United States. The other major stock exchanges in the global economy are those in London, Frankfurt, Tokyo, and Hong Kong.

Stock Prices and Returns

You can find the price and other information about the stocks of most of the large firms in the daily newspaper. You can also find the same information (and much more) on a newspaper's Web site. The Web sites of the stock exchanges and of major stock dealers also provide a wealth of data on stocks. You can also install software such as MarketBrowser that provides an easy way of viewing stock prices and making graphs of the recent price history. (The Parkin–Bade Web site provides the links that will get you to these Web resources.)

To read the stock market reports, you need to know the meaning of a few technical terms that we'll now review.

The point of buying stock is to earn an income from it. A **stock price** is the price at which one share of a stock trades on a stock exchange. The price is expressed like any other price: in dollars and cents. For example, on October 11, 2002, the price of a share of Bombardier stock was $3.83. The price can change from minute to minute and almost certainly will change over the trading day, and it can be tracked on the Internet (with a short time delay). Because the price keeps changing, in addition to tracking the current price, people also pay attention to the high and low prices during the previous year and the change from day to day.

The annual **return** on a stock consists of the stock's dividend plus its capital gain (or minus its capital loss) during the year. A stock's **capital gain** is the increase in its price, and a stock's **capital loss** is the decrease in its price. For example, between October 2001 and October 2002, the price of

Bombardier stock fell from $17.37 to $3.83, a capital loss of $13.54.

The absolute return—the number of dollars returned by the stock—is not very informative because the stock might be cheap or costly. More informative is the return per dollar invested. So we express the return, or its components, as a percentage of the stock price. The dividend expressed as a percentage of the stock price is called the stock's **dividend yield.** For example, during the year from October 2001 to October 2002, Bombardier paid dividends of 18¢. Expressed as a percentage of the price of the stock in October 2002, the dividend yield was 4.7 percent.

The return on a stock expressed as a percentage of the stock price is called the stock's **rate of return.** For example, the return of a Bombardier share in the year from October 2001 to October 2002 was a dividend of 18¢ minus a capital loss of $13.54, or a loss of $13.36. The rate of return was –$13.36 as a percentage of $17.37, the price of a share in October 2001, which is –76.9 percent—a loss of almost 77 percent.

Earnings and the Price-Earnings Ratio

A firm's accounting profit is called the firm's **earnings.** A firm's directors decide how much of the earnings to pay out as dividends and how much to retain—called *retained earnings*—to invest in new capital and expand the firm.

Because they are the ultimate source of income for stockholders, a lot of attention is paid to a firm's earnings. And those earnings must be calculated and reported to meet standards of accuracy determined by government regulations and accounting standards. Following the Enron debacle in the United States, these standards have been reviewed and will be the object of an ongoing review for some time.

Earnings are the source of stockholder returns, but it is the relationship between a stock's price and earnings that matters most to the stockholder. So another number that is routinely calculated for each stock is its **price-earnings ratio**—the stock price divided by the most recent year's earnings. For example during 2001, Bombardier reported earnings of 11¢ per share, so its price-earnings ratio was $3.83 divided by 11¢, which equals 34.8.

The price-earnings ratio is the inverse of earnings per dollar invested. For example, because in October 2002 the price of a share of Bombardier stock was

$3.83 and the earnings per share during 2002 were 11¢, earnings per dollar invested were 11¢ ÷ $3.83 = 0.0287, or 2.87 percent. Check that 0.0287, earnings per dollar invested, equals the inverse of the price-earnings ratio and equals 1/34.8.

Now that you've reviewed some of the key vocabulary of the stock market, let's look at the stock market report.

Reading the Stock Market Report

Figure 35.2 shows part of a *Financial Post* stock market page. (The format varies from one newspaper to another, but the content is similar in all of them.) You can see some numbers for Bombardier that might seem familiar. They are some of the numbers that we've just used to illustrate the technical terms used in the report. Figure 35.2 also provides the CHUM (radio and television company line of the report).

The first two columns show the range of prices for the stock (expressed in dollars) over the preceding year. This information is useful because it tells you about the volatility of the stock. Some stocks fluctuate a lot more than others. By glancing at the numbers in these two columns, you can get a quick sense of how volatile the price is. In this example, the price of CHUM stock ranged from a high of $64.50 to a low of $40.00 (its current price), a range of $24.50 and more than 50 percent of its current price.

Following the firm's name is the ticker symbol, BBD for Bombardier and CHM for CHUM. This symbol appears on real-time reports of the stock price. You need to know the symbol for any stocks that you own so that you can easily check their prices during the trading day.

The dividend paid expressed in dollars comes next. In this example, Bombardier paid 0.18 or 18¢ a share and CHUM paid 0.08 or 8¢ a share. The dividend yield—the dividend as a percentage of the stock's closing price—comes next, followed by the price-earnings ratio. The next column records the volume of trades in hundreds during the day. This number is the actual number of shares bought and sold. In this example, 287,800 Bombardier shares and 252,200 CHUM shares changed hands during the day.

The next three columns show the range of prices over the day and the closing price, and the final column shows the change in price from the previous day.

Stock Price Indexes

Because thousands of different stocks are traded on the world's stock markets every business day, we need a handy way of summarizing the thousands of different stock prices. Investors want to know not only how their own stocks have performed, but also how they have performed relative to other stocks on the average.

To make these comparisons and to indicate the general movements in the market, index numbers of the average stock prices are calculated and published. You will encounter hundreds of different stock price indexes. The three main U.S. stock price indexes are

---

FIGURE 35.2   Reading the Stock Market Report

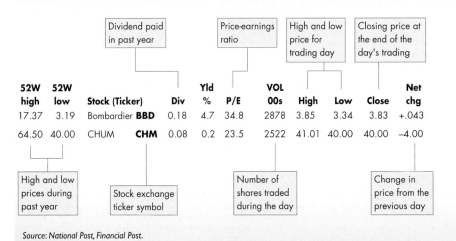

52W high	52W low	Stock (Ticker)	Div	Yld %	P/E	VOL 00s	High	Low	Close	Net chg
17.37	3.19	Bombardier **BBD**	0.18	4.7	34.8	2878	3.85	3.34	3.83	+.043
64.50	40.00	CHUM **CHM**	0.08	0.2	23.5	2522	41.01	40.00	40.00	–4.00

The stock market report provides information each day on the high and low prices over the previous year, dividend, price-earnings ratio, volume of shares traded, the price range over the day, the day's closing price, and price change from the previous day.

Source: National Post, Financial Post.

- S&P Composite Index
- Dow Jones Industrial Average (DJIA)
- NASDAQ Index

S&P Composite Index The S&P Composite Index is an average of the prices of 500 stocks traded on the New York Stock Exchange, the NASDAQ, and the American Stock Exchange. The index is calculated and published by Standard & Poor's (S&P), a New York financial information and services company. Figure 35.3 shows the breadth of coverage of this index, which provides one of the most comprehensive guides to the state of the stock market. Notice in Fig. 35.3 the importance of consumer products in the index.

DJIA The DJIA, or "the Dow," as it is often called, is perhaps the best-known stock price index. The Dow Jones Company is the owner of the *Wall Street Journal*, and because of this link, the Dow is the most widely and rapidly reported barometer of the state of the New York stock market.

Although the DJIA is widely quoted, it is not as broadly representative as the S&P Composite Index. It is an average of the prices of just 30 stocks of major U.S. corporations traded on the New York Stock Exchange. In 2002, these corporations are: Philip Morris Companies, Inc.; Eastman Kodak Co.; J.P. Morgan Chase & Co.; General Motors Corp.; E.I. DuPont de Nemours & Co.; SBC Communications, Inc.; Caterpillar, Inc.; Merck & Co., Inc.; International Paper Co.; Minnesota Mining & Manufacturing Co.; Exxon Mobil Corp.; Honeywell International, Inc.; General Electric Co.; Hewlett-Packard Co.; Procter & Gamble Co.; Alcoa, Inc.; Coca-Cola Co.; Boeing Co.; Citigroup, Inc.; United Technologies Corp.; Johnson & Johnson; AT&T Corp.; Walt Disney Co.; McDonald's Corp.; American Express Co.; International Business Machines Corp.; Wal-Mart Stores, Inc.; Home Depot, Inc.; Intel Corp.; and Microsoft Corp.

NASDAQ The NASDAQ Index is the average price of the stocks traded on this global electronic stock exchange. Like the Dow, this index looks at only part of the market—in this case, the high-tech part.

Four indexes track the state of the world's other major stock markets. They are the

- S&P/TSX
- FTSE 100
- DAX
- Nikkei

S&P/TSX The S&P/TSX is an index of the stock prices of the 300 largest Canadian corporations traded on the Toronto Stock Exchange. It is Canada's main stock price index and is comparable to the S&P 500 for the United States.

FTSE 100 The FTSE 100 (pronounced "footsie") is an index calculated by FTSE, a financial information services firm owned by the *Financial Times* (FT) and the London Stock Exchange (SE). (The *Financial Times* is Europe's leading business and financial daily newspaper and rivals the *Wall Street Journal* outside the United States.)

DAX The DAX index is an average of prices on the Frankfurt stock exchange in Germany.

Nikkei The Nikkei index is the average of prices on the Tokyo stock exchange.

FIGURE 35.3   The Scope of the S&P Composite

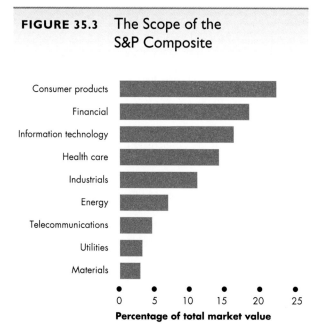

Percentage of total market value

The 500 stocks in the S&P Composite Index cover all parts of the economy. Consumer products are the largest component of the index.

Source: www.spglobal.com.

Stock Price Performance

How has the stock market performed in recent years and over the longer term? Do stock prices generally rise? How much do they fluctuate? To answer these questions, we'll look at some actual stock price data, using the S&P/TSX and the S&P 500 (composite). But first, we need to make two technical points.

Inflation Adjustments Stock prices, like all prices, need to be corrected for inflation. So rather than looking at the actual index numbers, we deflate them to remove the effects of inflation and examine *real* stock price indexes.

Ratio Scale Graphs Stock prices rise and fall, but over the long term, they rise. The interesting question about stock price changes is not the absolute change but the percentage change. For example a ten-point change in the S&P was a 1 percent change in 2002, but it was a 10 percent change in 1982. To reveal percentage changes, we graph stock prices using a ratio scale (or logarithmic scale). On a ratio scale, the distance between 1 and 10 equals that between 10 and 100 and between 100 and 1000. Each distance represents a tenfold increase.

Stock Prices

Figure 35.4 shows the real S&P/TSX for the period since 1956 when the index begins, and the S&P 500 over the past 130 years, both placed on a base of 1975 = 1,000 and measured on a ratio scale.

Both indexes move together, but the S&P 500 climbs more than the S&P/TSX. Notice the general upward trend of the real stock price index. In 2001, the S&P was 33 times its 1871 value. This increase translates to a 2.7 percent per year increase on the average.

This average rate of increase masks some subperiods of spectacular increases and spectacular decreases in stock prices. The largest increases occurred during the "roaring twenties" and the "booming nineties." Between 1920 and 1929, on the eve of the Great Depression, stock prices increased by almost 19 percent a year. Between 1991 and 2000, they increased by 15 percent a year, and between 1995 and 2000, the rate of increase hit 24 percent a year.

FIGURE 35.4 Stock Prices

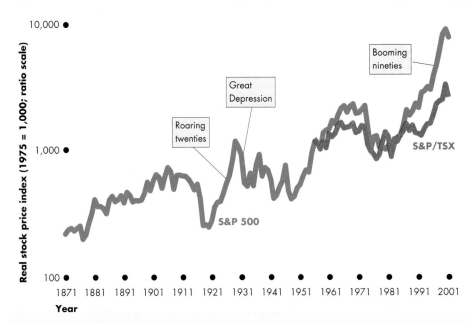

In 2001, average stock prices stood at 33 times their 1871 level (after adjusting for the effects of inflation). This increase translates to an average increase of 2.7 percent a year. Earnings per share stood at 14 times their 1871 level (after adjusting for the effects of inflation). This increase translates to an average increase of 2.7 percent a year. Stock prices increased fastest during the "roaring twenties" and the "booming nineties."

Sources: Reprinted by permission of Robert J. Shiller, Professor of Economics, Yale University (www.econ.yale.edu/~shiller) and adapted in part by the Statistics Canada CANSIM II database, table 176–0047.

The most spectacular period of falling stock prices occurred during World War I (1914–1918), the opening years of the Great Depression (the early 1930s), and the mid-1970s.

Earnings Per Share

Stocks are worth owning because of what they earn. Like stock prices, earnings per share have increased over the long term. But the rate of increase in earnings per share is less than the rate of increase in stock prices. Earnings per share in 2001 were 14 times their 1871 level, which translates to a growth rate of 2 percent per year on the average.

Figure 35.5 looks at the price-earnings ratio for the S&P/TSX over the years since 1956 and for the S&P 500 over the 130 years from 1871 to 2001. The average S&P price-earnings ratio has been 13.9. But there is a lot of variation around this average value. The low values of around 6 occurred in 1916, 1950, and 1979. The high values of around 27 occurred in 1894, 1921, 1931, and the period from 1998 into 2001.

Figure 35.5 is important for the perspective in which it places the stock market's recent performance. Stock prices were high and increased rapidly during the late 1990s and into 2001. And the price-earnings ratio increased to a level not seen since the opening years of the Great Depression.

Figure 35.5 also provides a reminder that in all previous periods when the price-earnings ratio was above average, it eventually fell below the average.

Being a ratio of stock prices and earnings, the price-earnings ratio can change either because stock prices change or because earnings change. The price-earnings ratio can fall sharply either because stock prices fall sharply or because earnings rise sharply. But all the cases in which the price-earnings ratio has fallen sharply are ones in which stock prices have fallen sharply. For this reason, some people are concerned that the stock market of the 1990s and 2000 increased by too much and that a sharp fall is coming some time in the future.

What does it mean to say that stock prices have increased by too much? To answer this question, we need to understand the forces that determine stock prices and the relationship between prices and earnings. That is the task of the next section.

FIGURE 35.5   The Price-Earnings Ratio

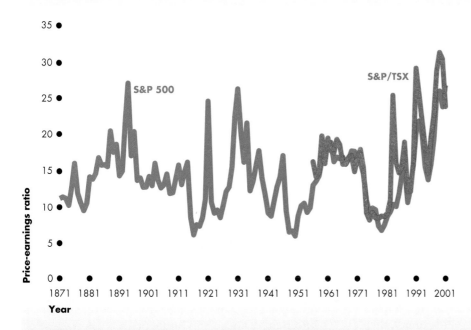

The S&P price-earnings ratio has swung between a low of around 6 in 1916, 1950, and 1979 and a high of around 27 in 1894, 1921, 1931, and 1998–2001. The S&P average price-earnings ratio is 13.9. When the price-earnings ratio exceeds the average, it eventually falls below the average. The S&P/TSX price-earnings ratio follows a similar path to that of the S&P.

Sources: Reprinted by permission of Robert J. Shiller, Professor of Economics, Yale University (www.econ.yale.edu/~shiller) and adapted in part by the Statistics Canada CANSIM II database, table 176–0047.

1 What is a stock and what is the distinction between a preferred stock and a common stock?

2 What are the two sources of return from a stock?

3 What is a stock market and what are the leading stock exchanges in the United States, Canada, and around the world?

4 What is a price-earnings ratio and how is it calculated?

5 What is the most comprehensive stock price index for the United States? How does it differ from some other major indexes?

6 Describe the major trends and fluctuations in stock prices, earnings per share, and the price-earnings ratio.

How Are Stock Prices Determined?

YOU'VE SEEN THAT STOCK PRICES GENERALLY RISE over long periods but fluctuate a lot over shorter periods. What determines the price of a stock? Why is the long-term trend upward? Why do stock prices fluctuate so much?

There is no firm and universally agreed-upon answer to these questions. Instead, there are two possible types of answers. They are that prices are determined by

■ Market fundamentals
■ Speculative bubbles

Market Fundamentals

The price of a stock is the amount that people *on the average* are willing to pay for the opportunity that the stock provides to earn a dividend and a capital gain. If a stock price exceeds what people are willing to pay, they sell the stock and its price falls. If a stock price is less than what people are willing to pay, they

buy and the stock price rises. The price always settles down at the amount that people are willing to pay.

The *market fundamentals* price that people are willing to pay is a price that is based on the deep sources of value that make a stock worth holding. These sources of value are

1. The activities of the firm that issued the stock
2. The stream of profits that these activities generate
3. The stream of dividend payments to stockholders
4. The degree of uncertainty surrounding profits and dividends
5. The attitudes of stockholders towards the timing and uncertainty of the stream of dividends

We're now going to discover how these deep sources of value of a firm's stock combine to determine the market fundamentals price of the stock. To do so, we're going to figure out how much you would be willing to pay for a stock or be willing to accept to sell it.

Price, Value, and Willingness to Pay The market fundamentals value of a stock is the price that people *on the average* are willing to pay for the opportunity that the stock provides to earn a dividend and a capital gain. To figure out how this price is determined, let's look at your decision to buy or sell a stock.

Suppose the price of a stock that you own is $1. You're trying to figure out whether to buy 50 more units of this stock or to sell the 50 units you own. If you sell, you have $50 more to spend, and if you buy, you have $50 less to spend—a $100 difference. You can spend $100 today on something that you will enjoy. In the language of the economist, you will get some utility from what you buy—the marginal utility of $100 worth of consumption. Alternatively, you can buy more stock and sell it later, say, after a year. If you buy the stock, you'll receive the dividend plus the stock's market price at the end of the year.

For it to be worth buying, you must believe that the utility you will receive from owning the stock is going to be worth at least the $1 a share you must pay for it.

But comparing what you must pay with what you'll gain is a difficult exercise for two main reasons. First, you must compare an amount paid in the present with an amount received in the future. And second, you must compare a definite price today with an uncertain dividend and future price.

Present Versus Future People are impatient. We prefer good things to happen sooner rather than later, other things remaining the same. Suppose that you're offered the chance to take an exotic trip that really excites you and are told that you can go right away or after a year. Which would you choose (other things remaining the same)? Most of us would take the trip right away. Because we prefer good things now more than later, we must be compensated for delaying consumption.

Certainty Versus Uncertainty People prefer certainty to uncertainty, other things remaining the same. Suppose you're offered the opportunity to pay $50 for a chance to win $100 on the flip of a coin. Would you accept the offer? Most people would not. Accepting the offer would give you a 50 percent chance of gaining $50 and a 50 percent chance of losing $50. On the average, you get nothing from this offer. Your *expected return* is zero. Most people need to be compensated for taking risks, and the bigger the risk, the bigger is the compensation that must be offered to make bearing the risk worthwhile.

In figuring out what you're willing to pay for a stock, you can see that, for two reasons, you will not be willing to pay as much as the amount that you expect to receive in dividends and from selling the stock. You're going to get the returns later and you're going to face uncertainty, and you must be compensated for both of these consequences of buying a stock.

Discounting Future Uncertain Returns Another way of expressing the relationship between the price you're willing to pay and what you expect to get back is to *discount* the uncertain future amount. You get a discount when a shop lowers the price of an item. And you will insist on a discount if you buy a stock.

To determine the discounted price, we multiply the original price by a **discount factor.** If you get a 20 percent discount on something, you pay 80 percent, or 0.8, of the original price. The discount factor is 0.8.

We can use the idea of a discount factor to link the highest price you're willing to pay for a stock to the amount you'll get back from the stock a year later. Let's call this price P. Suppose that your discount factor is 0.8, and suppose that you believe that the stock will pay a dividend of 5¢ and that its price next year will be $1.20. Then the highest price that you're willing to pay for a stock is

$$P = 0.8 \times (\$0.05 + \$1.20) = \$1.$$

In this example, you would be on the fence. If the price were a bit less than $1, you'd buy, and if the price were a bit more than $1, you'd sell the stock that you already own.

Because people buy if the price is less than the price they are willing to pay and sell if the price is greater than the price they are willing to pay, the market price moves towards the average of what people are willing to pay. If the price exceeded the average of what people are willing to pay, there would be more sellers than buyers and the price would fall. If the price was less than the average of what people are willing to pay, there would be more buyers than sellers and the price would rise. Only if the price equals the average of what people are willing to pay is there no tendency for it to rise or fall.

The Stock Price Equation Call the price of a stock P_1, the dividend D_1, the price at the end of a year P_2, and the discount factor b_1. Then the stock price is the expected value of the discounted uncertain future dividend and stock price. That is,

$$P_1 = \text{Expected value of } [b_1(D_1 + P_2)].$$

Expected Future Stock Price You've seen that the stock price depends on expectations about the future stock price. That is, to figure out what you're willing to pay for a stock today, you must forecast next period's stock price.

The market fundamentals method assumes that an investor's forecast of a future stock price is a rational expectation. A **rational expectation** is a forecast that uses all the available information, including knowledge of the relevant economic forces that influence the variable being forecasted.

But the stock price equation tells us how the price at one time depends on the expected price a year later. This same stock price equation relationship applies to the current period and all future periods. So if we call next period's discount factor b_2, next period's dividend D_2, and the price at the end of next period P_3, you can see that the stock price equation next year will be

$$P_2 = \text{Expected value of } [b_2(D_2 + P_3)].$$

That is, the price next period depends on the expected dividend next period and the price at the end of the next period.

This relationship repeats period after period into the future. And each period's expected future price depends on the dividend expected in that period along with the price at the end of the period.

Table 35.1 illustrates the link between the current price and the expected future price, dividend, and discount factor. In period 1, the price depends on expectations about the price in period 2. In period 2, the price depends on expectations about the price in period 3. And in period 3, the price depends on expectations about the price in period 4. This relationship repeats indefinitely to period N.

Because each period's price depends on the expected price in the following period, the dividend stream, D_1, D_2, D_3, ... D_N, is the only fundamental that determines the price of a stock.

Market Fundamental Price The market fundamental stock price depends only on the stream of expected future dividend payments. If the expected dividend rises, so does the stock price. And starting from a given dividend, if the dividend is expected to grow at a faster rate, the stock price rises.

But dividends depend on profit, or earnings, so if earnings are expected to increase, dividends will also be expected to increase—if not right away, then at some point in the future. So if earnings increase, the stock price increases. And starting from a given level of earnings, if earnings are expected to grow more quickly, the stock price rises.

TABLE 35.1   Rational Expectations

P_1 = Expected value of $[b_1(D_1 + P_2)]$

P_2 = Expected value of $[b_2(D_2 + P_3)]$

P_3 = Expected value of $[b_3(D_3 + P_4)]$

P_N = Expected value of $[b_N(D_N + P_{N+1})]$

The market fundamentals are the expected dividends that will be earned out into the indefinite future. Rational expectations of future prices and future discount factors are driven by this one fundamental.

Notice that it is changes in expected future earnings and dividends that drive changes in stock price, not changes in actual earnings or dividends. But expectations about the future don't change without reason. And when earnings change, investors project those changes into the future. So fluctuations in earnings might be expected to bring similar fluctuations in stock prices.

In reality, the link between earnings and stock prices is a loose one. You can see just how loose by glancing back at Fig. 35.5 and noting the large swings that range between 6 and 27 in the price-earnings ratio. The booming stock prices of the late 1990s, for example, outpaced the growth of earnings during that same period by a huge margin.

For this reason, some economists believe that stock prices can be understood only as speculative bubbles. Let's now look at this approach.

Speculative Bubbles

A **speculative bubble** is a price increase followed by a price plunge, both of which occur because people expect them to occur and act on that expectation.

Suppose that most people believe that stock prices are going to rise by 30 percent next year. With such a huge price rise, stocks provide the best available rate of return. The demand for stocks increases, and stock prices rise by the expected amount immediately.

Conversely, suppose that most people believe that stock prices are going to *fall* by 30 percent next year. With such a huge price fall, stockholders will earn less than people who simply sit on cash. In this situation, the demand for stocks collapses and a selling spree brings stock prices tumbling by the expected amount.

Why might either of these events occur? And why would a bubble burst? Why would a price collapse follow a price rise?

Guessing Other People's Guesses Part of the answer to the questions just posed arises from the fact that forecasting future stock prices means forecasting other people's forecasts—or, more accurately, guessing other people's guesses.

The most famous English economist of the twentieth century, John Maynard Keynes, described the challenge of the stock market investor as being like that of trying to win the prize in a "select the most beautiful person" contest. Each entrant must pick the most beautiful person from a group of ten photographs. The winner is selected at random from all those who chose the photograph that most other entrants chose. So the challenge is not to pick the most beautiful person, but to pick the one that most people will pick. Or is it to pick the one that most people think that most people will pick? Or is it to pick the one that most people think that most people think that most people will pick? And so on!

Because no one knows the correct choice and because everyone faces the same challenge and shares the same sources of information, people are likely to use similar rules of thumb and theories to guide them. So people might behave in a herdlike way and form and act upon similar expectations.

The booming stock market of the 1990s provides an example of the possibility of a speculative bubble.

The Booming Nineties: A Bubble?

Some economists believe that the booming stock market of the 1990s occurred because the market fundamentals changed. They see the stock price rise as the consequence of a "new economy" in which the rational expectation is that earnings will grow in the future at a more rapid rate than in the past.

Other economists believe that the market of the booming nineties was a speculative bubble. Prominent among those who take this view is Robert Shiller, a professor at Yale University, who explains his view in a popular and readable book, *Irrational Exuberance.*

According to Robert Shiller, the late 1990s stock price rise was a bubble encouraged by 12 "precipitating factors":

1. The arrival of the Internet at a time of solid earnings growth
2. A sense that the United States had triumphed over its former rivals
3. A cultural change that favours business and profit
4. A Republican Congress and cuts in capital gains taxes
5. The baby boom and its perceived effects on the stock market
6. An expansion of media reporting of business news
7. Increasingly optimistic forecasts by "experts"
8. The expansion of pension plans with fixed contributions
9. The growth of mutual funds

10. The fall in inflation
11. The expansion of stock trading opportunities
12. A rise of gambling opportunities

Many of these factors directly influence stockholder expectations, and all of them encouraged an optimistic outlook for stock prices during the late 1990s. Probably no one investor thought that all of these factors would bring rising stock prices, but almost every investor believed that more than one of the factors would bring rising prices.

According to the speculative bubble view, the factors that encourage rising stock prices eventually weaken, prices stop rising and possibly crash. Some people see the falling stock prices of 2001 and 2002 as the bursting of a bubble.

But through 2002, the Internet and the information age remained a strong force for rising prices. So did the expansion of trading opportunities, especially on-line opportunities. The major new factor was the long-term campaign against terrorism. But the effects of this campaign on average stock prices were not clear at the end of 2002. The global economy was still adjusting to a new situation by reallocating resources away from travel and tourism and towards security and defence goods and services. Some sectors were expanding, and some were shrinking. The impact on average stock prices might be positive or negative.

REVIEW QUIZ

1 What is the market fundamentals view of the forces that determine stock prices?

2 What is the speculative bubble view of the forces that determine stock prices?

3 List five factors that you think might have encouraged the booming stock market of the 1990s.

You've seen that there are two views about the forces that determine stock prices. No one knows which view is correct. And no one can predict stock prices. For these reasons, rational stockholders diversify their holdings across a number of stocks. Let's see how diversification spreads risks.

Risk and Return

STOCK PRICES FLUCTUATE IN UNPREDICTABLE ways, and stockholders might receive a large capital gain or incur a large capital loss. But stocks differ in both their expected return and risk, and generally, the greater the risk, the higher is the expected return from a stock. We call the additional return that is earned for bearing an additional risk a **risk premium.** Let's see why a risk premium arises.

Risk Premium

Recall the stock price equation:

$$P_1 = \text{Expected value of } [b_1(D_1 + P_2)].$$

Suppose that two stocks have the same expected dividend, D_1, and the same expected future price, P_2, but one is riskier than the other. Because people dislike risk and must be compensated for bearing it, a riskier return is discounted more than a safe return—the discount factor, b_1, is smaller for the riskier return. Because b_1 is smaller, the price of a stock, P_1, is lower for the riskier stock. But if the price of the riskier stock is lower, the expected return from holding it is greater than the expected return from the safer stock.

Because expected return increases with risk, a person earns the highest expected return by holding only the one stock that has the highest expected return.

But this investment strategy is not usually the best one. The reason is that by diversifying stock holdings across a number of different stocks, an investor can lower the risk. To do so, the investor must accept a lower expected return. There is a trade-off between risk and expected return.

Let's see how and why diversification lowers risk. To do so, we'll look at some actual stock purchases that you could have made in January 2001 and see what your investments would have been worth in 2002 with different degrees of diversification.

Portfolio Diversification

Table 35.2 shows the prices of five stocks in January 2001 and January 2002. Suppose that in January 2001, you had $1,000 to invest and put it all into just one of these five stocks.

You might have been lucky and chosen Procter & Gamble (P&G), in which case your $1,000 grew to $1,139 over the year. But you might have been very unlucky and chosen Enron, in which case you lost your entire investment.

Now suppose that instead of investing in only one of these stocks, you had put $500 into each of Enron and Procter & Gamble. In this case, your investment would have been worth $569.50 at the end of the year—a loss, but not as big as if you'd gone for only Enron.

Now imagine that you diversified even more, putting $200 each into Enron, Microsoft, Procter & Gamble, McDonald's, and Wal-Mart. In this case, your investment would have been worth $834 at the beginning of 2002.

You could spread your risks even more by investing in a mutual fund—a fund that is managed by investment specialists and that is diversified across a large number of stocks.

You can see from this example that lowering risk means accepting a lower return. The highest return across the five stocks in Table 35.2 comes from buying only Procter & Gamble. But at the beginning of 2001, you might equally have thought that buying Enron would provide the highest return. Because you can't predict which individual stock is going to perform best, it pays to diversify and take a lower expected return in return for a lower risk.

TABLE 35.2	Five Stock Prices in January 2001 and January 2002		
	Price in January 2001	**Price in January 2002**	**Value in 2002 of $1,000 in 2001**
Enron	60	0	0
McDonald's	29	27	931
Microsoft	61	64	1,049
P&G	72	82	1,139
Wal-Mart	57	60	1,053

REVIEW QUIZ

1 Why do stocks' returns include a risk premium?
2 How does diversification across a number of stocks lower the risk that a stockholder faces?

We next look at the links between the stock market and the rest of the economy.

The Stock Market and the Economy

THE LINKS BETWEEN THE STOCK MARKET AND THE rest of the economy that we're now going to look at run in two directions: effects from the rest of the economy *on* the stock market and effects on the rest of the economy *from* the stock market. We'll look first at influences *on* the stock market, which fall into three broad groups:

- Trends and cycles in earnings growth
- Central bank monetary policy
- Taxes

Trends and Cycles in Earnings Growth

You've seen that expected future earnings are the fundamental influence on stock prices. Current earnings are known, but future earnings can only be forecasted. And the central question on which investors must take a position is the *expected growth rate* of earnings.

If earnings are expected to grow more rapidly, the fundamental value of a stock rises relative to current earnings—its price-earnings ratio rises. Conversely, if earnings are expected to grow more slowly, the fundamental value of a stock falls relative to current earnings—its price-earnings ratio falls.

The nature and pace of technological change and the state of the business cycle are the main influences on earnings growth. And expectations about future earnings growth are based on the best information that people can obtain about future technological change and business cycle developments.

The long-term trend in earnings growth has been remarkably constant at about 2 percent a year (after the effects of inflation are removed). But earnings growth has fluctuated a great deal around its trend. Figure 35.6 shows these fluctuations. The figure highlights the interesting fact that there have been only three main periods during which earnings have grown rapidly to reach a new higher level: the 1890s, 1950s and 1960s, and 1990s. There was only one other period of rapid earnings growth, from 1921 to 1931, but this episode was a temporary burst of growth from an extremely low level that did not take earnings back to their previous peak of 1918.

Each period during which earnings grew rapidly to a new level was one in which far-reaching new technologies spread. During the 1890s, it was the

---

FIGURE 35.6 Three Bursts of Earnings Growth

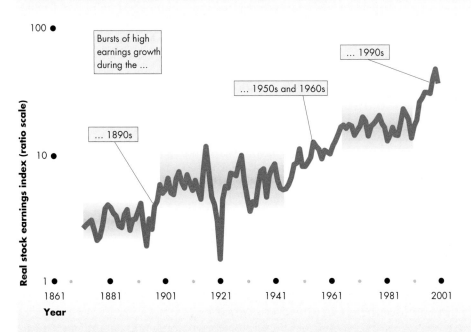

Earnings grew rapidly during three periods of rapid technological change: the 1890s (railroad, telegraph, electricity); 1950s and 1960s (highway system, plastics, transistor, and television); and 1990s (Internet and information technologies).

Source: Reprinted by permission of Robert J. Shiller, Professor of Economics, Yale University (www.econ.yale.edu/~schiller).

railroad, telegraph, and electricity. During the 1950s and 1960s, it was the highway system, plastics, the transistor, and television. And during the 1990s, it was the Internet and associated information technologies.

Although earnings are the fundamental source of value for stocks, the connection between earnings growth and stock prices cannot be used to make reliable predictions of stock prices. Stock prices did increase more rapidly than usual during the periods of rapid earnings growth. But they outpaced earnings growth—increased by more than was justified by the growth of earnings. And during the 1920s, stock prices grew beyond the levels that were supported by the underlying earnings fundamentals.

Some people have argued that the 1990s were special—unique—and marked a new era for permanently faster earnings growth arising from the information technologies that brought the exploding Internet. Does the earnings growth rate change permanently when a major new technology spreads? And are we living today in a "new economy"?

A New Economy? It is a well-documented fact that the spread of the Internet was unusually rapid. Not since the spread of television during the 1950s has there been such a rapid penetration of a new technology.

It is also a solid fact that the pace of earnings growth was unusually rapid during the 1990s—13 percent a year compared to the long-term average of 2 percent a year. But as you can see in Fig. 35.6, earnings growth was similarly rapid in earlier periods, only to return to its long-term average growth rate.

The only exception to this tendency to return to the preceding long-term average growth rate occurred more than 200 years ago, in an event called the Industrial Revolution. The Industrial Revolution was possibly unique, not because it saw the introduction of powerful new technologies but because it was a period in which for the first time in human history, research and the development of new technologies became commercially viable activities. People began to make a living by inventing new technologies rather than merely by producing goods and services. Before this period, invention and innovation had been a spasmodic and relatively rare event. The last really big invention had been the chronometer, a reliable method of keeping time on ships that improved the reliability of navigation.

It is still too soon to be sure, but more and more people are coming to the view that the "new economy" is just another stage in the evolution of the old economy. If this view is correct, the stock market of the early 2000s remains overvalued relative to its fundamentals. If the "new economy" view is correct, the stock market has correctly incorporated the future earnings growth that the new economy will bring.

Central Bank Monetary Policy

The U.S. Federal Reserve (Fed) and the European Central Bank (ECB) are the most powerful central banks in today's world. Their actions influence global stock markets. Whether you've studied monetary policy or not, you can understand how a central bank influences the stock market by seeing how interest rates affect stock prices.

If the Fed or ECB take actions that raise interest rates, stock prices usually fall. Conversely, if monetary policy lowers interest rates, stock prices usually rise. But policy influences on stock prices are short lived, and the timing of the influences depends on whether the policy actions are anticipated or they surprise the market.

Interest Rates and Stock Prices When the economy is expanding too rapidly and the policy goal is to slow down the growth of spending, interest rates are pushed upward. Higher interest rates make borrowing more costly and lending more rewarding. People who are borrowing to finance their expenditure face higher costs, and some of them cut back on spending.

Lower spending and higher saving translate into a smaller demand for the output of firms and smaller profits. With smaller profits expected, the prices of stocks fall.

Higher interest rates also encourage some stockholders to sell risky stocks and put their funds into lower-risk, lower-return bonds and other securities that now yield a higher return. This action increases the supply of stocks and lowers stock prices further.

Similarly, lower interest rates make borrowing less costly and lending less rewarding. People who are borrowing to finance their expenditure face lower costs, and some of them increase their spending.

Greater spending and lower saving translate into a greater demand for the output of the nation's firms, and larger profits. With larger profits expected, the prices of stocks rise.

Lower interest rates on bonds and other securities also encourage some bond holders to sell bonds and put their funds into higher-risk, higher-return stocks. This action increases the demand for stocks and raises stock prices still further.

Anticipating Policy Because monetary policy actions influence stock prices in the way we've just seen, it is profitable to anticipate future policy actions. If interest rates are expected to rise in the near future, then stock prices are expected to fall in the near future. Selling stocks before the price falls and buying them back after the price has fallen is profitable. So if a large number of people expect a rise in interest rates, they will sell stock. The selling action increases supply and lowers the stock price before the interest rate rises. Monetary policy has caused the stock price to fall, but the stock price falls *before* the policy action occurs. (This timing relationship is an example of the *post hoc* fallacy— see pp. 13–14.)

Taxes

Taxes can influence stock prices in a number of ways, some direct and some indirect. Three types of tax can affect stock markets:

- Capital gains tax
- Corporate profits tax
- Transactions (Tobin) tax

Capital Gains Tax The capital gains tax is a tax on the income that people earn when they *realize* a capital gain. A **realized capital gain** is a capital gain that is obtained when a stock is sold for a higher price than the price paid for it. People who hold onto stocks that have increased in value also enjoy a capital gain, but they do not pay a tax on that gain until they sell the stock and realize the gain.

When a capital gains tax is introduced or when the rate of capital gains tax is increased, stock prices fall, other things remaining the same. The reason is that the capital gains tax lowers the after-tax return on stocks and so lowers the price that people are willing to pay for stocks.

The lowering of the capital gains tax rate in the United States during the 1980s and 1990s probably contributed to the booming stock prices of the 1990s.

Corporate Profits Tax The corporate profits tax is an income tax on the profits of corporations. If this

tax is increased, corporate after-tax profits fall. The firm has smaller earnings from which to pay dividends and invest in new capital. So the market fundamentals value of a firm falls, and so do stock prices.

Transactions (Tobin) Tax Transactions on the stock market are not taxed. But their value is enormous, and a tax set at a tiny rate would raise a huge amount of tax revenue for the government.

James Tobin, an economist at Yale University (who died in 2002), proposed that stock market transactions be taxed—hence the name "the Tobin tax." Tobin believed that such a tax would discourage speculative buying and selling of stocks and make the stock market more efficient. The evidence on transactions taxes in other markets, notably real estate markets, does not support the view that a transactions tax lowers speculation.

Let's now change directions and look at influences *from* the stock market to the rest of the economy. We'll look at the influences of stock prices on

- Wealth, consumption expenditure, and saving
- The distribution of wealth

Wealth, Consumption Expenditure, and Saving

Wealth is the market value of assets. The influence of wealth on consumption expenditure and saving is called the **wealth effect**. *Disposable income* equals income minus taxes. A household can do only two things with its disposable income: spend it on consumption goods and services or save it. The **saving rate** is saving as a percentage of disposable income. The greater is wealth, the smaller is the saving rate.

How do stock prices influence the saving rate? The answer depends on how we measure saving (and, related, how we measure disposable income).

There are two definitions of saving that are equivalent, provided that we measure everything in a consistent way. The first definition is

$$\text{Saving} = \frac{\text{Disposable}}{\text{income}} - \frac{\text{Consumption}}{\text{expenditure.}}$$

The second definition arises from the fact that saving adds to wealth. That is,

$$\frac{\text{Wealth at}}{\text{end of year}} = \frac{\text{Wealth at}}{\text{start of year}} + \frac{\text{Saving during}}{\text{the year,}}$$

or

$$\text{Saving} = \text{Change in wealth.}$$

The first definition of saving focuses on the fact that saving is what is left over after buying consumer goods and services. The second definition focuses on the fact that saving adds to wealth.

Because the two definitions of saving are equivalent, it must be the case that

$$\frac{\text{Disposable}}{\text{income}} = \frac{\text{Consumption}}{\text{expenditure}} + \frac{\text{Change in}}{\text{wealth.}}$$

In the data on income and wealth, disposable income does not include capital gains and losses. In the data on wealth, capital gains and losses *are* included. So there is a measurement discrepancy between saving measured using the first definition, which excludes capital gains, and saving measured using the second definition, which includes capital gains.

Figure 35.7 shows you what has happened to the saving rate based on the first measure and excluding capital gains. The saving rate was on an upward trend in Canada during the 1960s and 1970s. It was roughly constant in the United States. But during the 1990s, the saving rate collapsed in both countries. By 2000, the U.S. personal saving rate was less than 1 percent.

This collapse of the personal saving rate coincided with the explosion of stock prices through the 1990s.

You might expect that if people are enjoying capital gains on the stock market, they will think of these gains as being part of their saving. So they will not be concerned if their saving rate *excluding* capital gains falls. So what happened to the saving rate defined to include capital gains? Figure 35.8 answers this question for the period 1981–2001. While the saving rate excluding capital gains was collapsing, the saving rate including capital gains increased from about 7 percent in the early 1980s to around 20 percent in the late 1990s.

Which measure of saving is the correct one?

FIGURE 35.7   The Personal Saving Rate

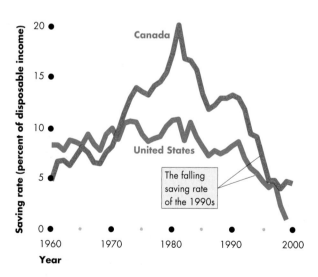

The personal saving rate increased in Canada and was flat in the United States before 1980. The saving rate fell in both countries during the 1980s and 1990s.

Sources: U.S. Bureau of Economic Analysis and adapted in part from the Statistics Canada CANSIM II database, table 380-0031.

FIGURE 35.8   Two Views of the Personal Saving Rate

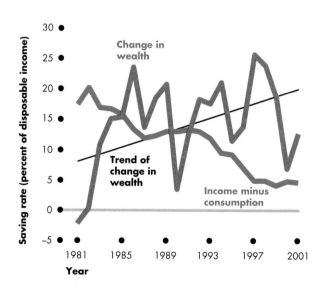

The personal saving rate including capital gains—the change in wealth—increased, while the saving rate excluding capital gains—disposable income minus consumption—collapsed.

Sources: Statistics Canada, CANSIM tables 378–0004 and 380–0031.

Neither! The rate that excludes capital gains is incorrect because it omits an important source of changes in wealth. But the rate that includes capital gains is incorrect because those gains are not realized. And if everyone attempted to realize their gains, the stock market would almost surely crash, thereby wiping out some unknown proportion of the gains. So the truth lies at some unknown place between the two available measures.

The Distribution of Wealth

When stock prices are rising as rapidly as they did from 1995 to 2000, stockholders enjoy spectacular increases in their wealth. Do all income groups share in these increases in wealth? Or are the increases concentrated among the already wealthy?

The answer to this question depends on the distribution of stockholdings. It turns out that the wealthier households are those that tend to hold stocks. So the wealthiest have gained the most.

The only wealth distribution data available is for the United States, and it ends in 1998. But these data tell an amazing story. You can see the data in Fig. 35.9. Here, we plot the mean wealth in 1992, 1995, and 1998 of households in five income groups ranging from those who earn less than $10,000 a year to those who earn more than $100,000 a year. The wealth data are in 1998 dollars, which means that they are adjusted to remove the effects of inflation.

Notice that the wealth of the four lowest-income groups barely changes. In contrast, the wealth of the highest-income group increases. In fact, the increase in wealth of the highest-income group exceeds the level of wealth of the next highest group. Between 1995 and 1998, households that have an income of $100,000 or more a year enjoyed an increase in average wealth of more than $300,000. The average wealth of households that earn between $50,000 and $99,999 was only $275,000 in 1998.

While we cannot be sure that all the wealth changes shown in Fig. 35.9 resulted from the rising stock prices, much of the change must have come from that source. Whether the changes in the distribution of wealth will be permanent depends on the future of stock prices. If stock prices collapse, much of the gain in wealth by the highest-income group will be reversed. And many families will wish that they had not lowered their saving rate.

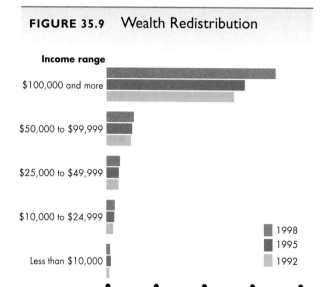

FIGURE 35.9 Wealth Redistribution

Income range

$100,000 and more

$50,000 to $99,999

$25,000 to $49,999

$10,000 to $24,999

Less than $10,000

■ 1998
■ 1995
■ 1992

0   500   1,000   1,500   2,000

Mean wealth (thousands of 1998 dollars)

The wealth of the highest-income households increased between 1995 and 1998 by more than the level of wealth of other households.

Source: Board of Governors of the Federal Reserve System.

REVIEW QUIZ

1 What are the main trends in earnings growth?
2 What events are associated with the three periods of rapid earnings growth?
3 How does monetary policy influence the stock market?
4 How do taxes influence the stock market?
5 How does the stock market influence saving?
6 How does the stock market influence the distribution of wealth?

◆ You've learned the two main approaches to understanding stock prices, seen why portfolio diversification is a good idea, and seen how the stock market and the economy interact. To reinforce your appreciation of the impossibility of predicting stock prices, we look at the stock market at the end of 2002 in *Reading Between the Lines* on pp. 846–847.

Stock Price Uncertainties

THE GLOBE AND MAIL, DECEMBER 3, 2002

Analysts just can't agree: recovery or bear respite?

The stock markets have been rallying for the better part of seven weeks, but analysts continue to disagree over whether this is a full-fledged recovery or just a bear market taking a breather.

"I think, so far, that is the $64-million question, or the $8-trillion question," said Ross Healy, president of Strategic Analysis Corp.

The S&P/TSX composite index rose 5.2 per cent last month, and is up 17 per cent from its Oct. 9 low. Over the same period, the S&P 500 in the United States is up 20.3 per cent. However, that hasn't convinced many experts that the 2½-year bear market is at an end.

"Unfortunately, I think no matter how adamant that the born-again bulls are, or I suppose, for that matter, how adamant the unrepentant bears are, things are murky … they are not cut and dried," Mr. Healy said.

What is cut and dried is that as a bear market bottoms, valuations become so attractive that they tend to draw investors into the market, he said. He doesn't see that yet.

He said the U.S. market is trading at about three times or more book value, far above the 1.6 times of the 1990 bear market. The dividend yield was far higher in 1990 than in today's market. Moreover, he pointed out, the price/earnings multiple on the Standard & Poor's 500-stock index stands at a relatively high 30 times trailing earnings.

Many market watchers zero in on the multiple on next year's earnings, which is significantly lower than the trailing multiple, but that is based on expectations that earnings will grow sharply next year. "I don't see 20- or 25-per-cent increase in earnings year over year next year," he said. …

Reprinted with permission from *The Globe and Mail*.

Essence of the Story

■ Stock prices fell for two and a half years to October 2002—a bear market.

■ The S&P/TSX composite index increased by 5.2 percent in November 2002 and by 17 percent over its October 9 low.

■ Over the same period, the S&P 500 in the United States increased by 20.3 percent.

■ Uncertainty persisted over whether price increase would continue—whether the bear market was gone and a rising bull market had begun.

■ Reasons to believe that the market was not ready to begin a new long period of rising prices were: a high ratio of stock prices to the book value of firms, a low dividend yield, and a high price-earnings ratio.

■ Earnings would need to grow by an unlikely 20 percent to 25 percent to support a rising market.

Economic Analysis

■ This news article reports the rising stock prices of November 2002 and notes the uncertainty about the continuation of the increase.

■ Figure 1 shows the stock market of the 1990s and 2000s. The graph shows the S&P/TSX composite index.

■ The bull market—rising prices—began in the early 1990s and, with a brief pause in 1998, continued until August 2000.

■ A bear market—falling prices—began in September 2000.

■ The stock market never moves relentlessly in one direction. It is constantly fluctuating around its general trend and in November 2002, prices increased. They had also increased during November 2001.

■ Figure 2 expands our view of November and December 2002.

■ Stock prices increased for about a month and then fell before returning in mid-December to their previous peak of December 2, the date of the news article.

■ If stock prices are determined by market fundamentals, it is unlikely that a new bull market began at the end of 2002.

■ Uncertainty about continued economic growth in the United States, Japan, and Germany made Canada's continued strong expansion equally uncertain.

■ If in early 2003, real GDP growth slows and business profits are weak, stock prices will reflect these fundamentals and fall further.

■ If real GDP growth speeds up and business profits are strong, stock prices will reflect these more encouraging fundamentals and a bull market will begin.

■ At the end of 2002 (the date of the news article), slow growth and weak profits appeared more likely than fast growth and high profits.

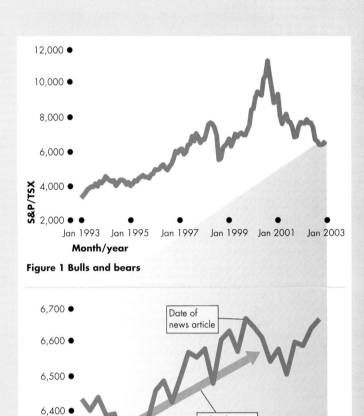

Figure 1 Bulls and bears

Figure 2 Bull or short-lived adjustment?

SUMMARY

KEY POINTS

Stock Market Basics (pp. 830–836)

- A stock is a tradable security issued by a firm to certify that its holder owns a share of the firm, is entitled to receive a share of the firm's profit (a dividend), and vote at stockholder meetings.
- The return on a stock consists of a dividend plus a capital gain (or minus a capital loss).
- A firm's accounting profit (called earnings) is used to calculate the price-earnings ratio.
- The S&P Composite, DJIA, NASDAQ, and S&P/TSX indexes provide information about average stock prices.
- The S&P price-earnings ratio between 1871 and 2001 has ranged from 6 to 27 and averaged 13.9. The S&P/TSX price-earnings ratio follows a similar path to that of S&P.

How Are Stock Prices Determined? (pp. 836–839)

- The market fundamental stock price is the discounted present value of the stream of expected future dividend payments, which in turn depend on expected future earnings.
- Some economists believe that stock prices can be understood only as speculative bubbles—periods of rising prices followed by price plunges, both of which occur because people expect them to occur and act on that expectation.

Risk and Return (p. 840)

- Stocks differ in their expected return and risk, and the greater the risk, the higher is the stock's risk premium.
- An investor can lower the risk faced by diversifying across a number of stocks because the returns on different stocks are not perfectly correlated.

The Stock Market and the Economy (pp. 841–845)

- Technological change and the state of the business cycle influence earnings growth and stock prices.

- Earnings growth has come in three main bursts: the 1890s, 1950s and 1960s, and 1990s.
- Each period of rapid earnings growth was also a time of the spread of major new technologies.
- When interest rates rise, stock prices fall, and when interest rates fall, stock prices rise. The change in stock prices precedes anticipated monetary policy actions.
- The capital gains tax and corporate profits tax affect stock prices. A transactions (Tobin) tax would probably not deter speculation.
- As stock prices increased during the 1990s, the saving rate excluding capital gains collapsed but the saving rate including capital gains increased.
- As stock prices increased during the 1990s, the distribution of wealth became more unequal.

KEY FIGURES AND TABLE

KEY TERMS

PROBLEMS

*1. On January 2, 2001, the price of a share of Coca-Cola stock was $60.81. On December 31, 2001, the price was $47.15. During 2001, Coca-Cola paid dividends that totaled 54¢ a share. Coca-Cola's reported accounting profit during 2001 was $1.58 per share.
   a. What was the dividend yield on Coca-Cola stock during 2001?
   b. What was the return on Coca-Cola stock during 2001?
   c. What was the capital gain or loss on Coca-Cola stock during 2001?
   d. What was the rate of return on Coca-Cola stock during 2001?
   e. What were Coca-Cola's earnings during 2001?
   f. What was Coca-Cola's price-earnings ratio on December 31, 2001?

2. On January 2, 2001, the price of a share of General Motors (GM) stock was $52.19. On December 31, 2001, the price was $48.60. During 2001, GM paid a dividend of $2 a share. GM's reported accounting profit during 2001 was $1.40 per share.
   a. What was the dividend yield on GM stock during 2001?
   b. What was the return on GM stock during 2001?
   c. What was the capital gain or loss on GM stock during 2001?
   d. What was the rate of return on GM stock during 2001?
   e. What were GM's earnings during 2001?
   f. What was GM's price-earnings ratio on December 31, 2001?

*3. The financial pages report that the Dow is up by 5 percent, the S&P is up by 8 percent, and the NASDAQ is up by 15 percent. Write a report that interprets these numbers. What can you infer from the data about the changes in stock prices in different sectors of the economy?

4. The financial pages report that the Dow is down by 15 percent, the S&P is down by 10 percent, and the NASDAQ is down by 25 percent. Write a short report that interprets these numbers. What can you infer from the data about the changes in stock prices in different sectors of the economy?

*5. You are trying to figure out whether to buy some stock. You are confident that the stock will pay a dividend of $3 a share next year, and you think that you'll be able to sell the stock at the end of the year for $30 a share. Your discount factor is 0.9. What is the most that you'd be willing to pay for this stock?

6. You are trying to figure out whether to buy some stock. You are confident that the stock will pay a dividend of $5 a share next year, and you think that you'll be able to sell the stock at the end of the year for $30 a share. Your discount factor is 0.8. What is the most that you'd be willing to pay for this stock?

*7. The price of a stock that you're thinking of buying is $20 a share. Your discount factor is 0.75. The firm has announced its dividend for next year of $1 per share. What is the lowest expected price next year that would make it rational for you to go ahead and buy the stock?

8. The price of a stock that you're thinking of buying is $100 a share. Your discount factor is 0.7. The firm has announced that it will pay no dividend next year. What is the lowest expected price next year that would make it rational for you to go ahead and buy the stock?

*9. Suppose there are two pharmaceutical stocks that you might buy: Merck and Pfizer. Merck will provide a return of 50 percent if the firm makes a major breakthrough on its new drug and a 10 percent return otherwise. There is only a 10 percent chance that the firm will make the breakthrough. Pfizer will provide a return of 20 percent if the firm achieves a cost saving and a 15 percent return otherwise. There is a 50 percent chance that the firm will achieve the cost saving.
   a. What is the expected return from investing in Merck?
   b. What is the expected return from investing in Pfizer?
   c. What is the chance of making a return of 50 percent by investing only in Merck?
   d. What is the chance of making a return of 10 percent by investing only in Merck?
   e. What is the chance of making a return of 20 percent by investing only in Pfizer?
   f. What is the chance of making a return of 15 percent by investing only in Pfizer?
   g. If you invest in both Merck and Pfizer in equal amounts, what is your expected return?

h. If you invest in both Merck and Pfizer in equal amounts, what is your chance of making a return of 50 percent?

i. If you invest in both Merck and Pfizer in equal amounts, what is your chance of making a return of 10 percent?

j. Explain why it might be rational to diversify across Merck and Pfizer.

10. Suppose there are two soft drink stocks that you might buy: Coke and Pepsi. Coke will provide a return of 20 percent if the firm's Harry Potter advertising campaign is successful and a 10 percent return otherwise. There is a 60 percent chance that the advertising campaign will be successful. Pepsi will provide a return of 16 percent if the firm achieves a cost saving and a 14 percent return otherwise. There is a 50 percent chance that the firm will achieve the cost saving.

a. What is the expected return from investing in Coke?

b. What is the expected return from investing in Pepsi?

c. What is the chance of making a return of 20 percent by investing only in Coke?

d. What is the chance of making a return of 10 percent by investing only in Coke?

e. What is the chance of making a return of 16 percent by investing only in Pepsi?

f. What is the chance of making a return of 14 percent by investing only in Pepsi?

g. If you invest in both Coke and Pepsi in equal amounts, what is your expected return?

h. If you invest in both Coke and Pepsi in equal amounts, what is your chance of making a return of 20 percent?

i. If you invest in both Coke and Pepsi in equal amounts, what is your chance of making a return of 10 percent?

j. Explain why it might be rational to diversify across Coke and Pepsi.

CRITICAL THINKING

1. Study *Reading Between the Lines* on pp. 846–847 and then answer the following questions:

a. What happened to stock prices during 2002 on the average?

b. Does the performance of stock prices during 2002 look like the result of rational expectations of the fundamentals or of the bursting of a speculative bubble?

c. Assuming that the performance of stock prices during 2002 was the result of rational expectations, what does that performance imply about expectations for profits in 2003 and beyond?

d. What economic development is needed before a new sustained increase in stock prices begins?

WEB EXERCISES

1. Use the link on the Parkin–Bade Web site to visit the New York, London, Frankfurt, Tokyo, and Toronto stock exchanges.

a. Get the latest index numbers from these stock exchanges and get the indexes a year ago.

b. On the basis of the data you have obtained, calculate the percentage changes in the indexes over the past year.

c. Which of the stock markets has delivered the largest percentage gain? Can you think of reasons for the differences in performance of the five stock markets?

2. Use the link on the Parkin–Bade Web site to obtain data on the prices and dividend payments over the past year for five stocks that interest you. Also obtain the value of the S&P/TSX, the DJIA, S&P Composite, and NASDAQ indexes for the same period.

a. For each stock, calculate the rate of return assuming that you bought the stock one year ago.

b. For each index, calculate the percentage change over the past year and compare the performance of each stock with the indexes.

UNDERSTANDING THE GLOBAL ECONOMY

PART 10

It's a Small World

The scale of international trade, borrowing, and lending, both in absolute dollar terms and as a percentage of total world production expands every year. One country, Singapore, imports and exports goods and services in a volume that exceeds its Gross Domestic Product. The world's largest nation, China, returned to the international economic stage during the 1980s and is now a major producer of manufactured goods. ◆ International economic activity is large because today's economic world is small and because communication is so incredibly fast. But today's world is not a new world. From the beginning of recorded history, people have traded over large and steadily increasing distances. The great Western civilizations of Greece and Rome traded not only around the Mediterranean but also into the Gulf of Arabia. The great Eastern civilizations traded around the Indian Ocean. By the Middle Ages, the East and the West were trading routinely overland on routes pioneered by Venetian traders and explorers such as Marco Polo. When, in 1497, Vasco da Gama opened a sea route between the Atlantic and Indian Oceans around Africa, a new trade between East and West began, which brought tumbling prices of Eastern goods in Western markets. ◆ The European discovery of America and the subsequent opening up of Atlantic trade continued the process of steady globalization. So the developments of the 1990s, amazing though many of them are, represent a continuation of an ongoing expansion of human horizons. These three chapters studied the interaction of nations in today's global economy. ◆ Chapter 33 described and explained international trade in goods and services. In this chapter, you came face to face with one of the biggest policy issues of all ages: free trade versus protection and the globalization debate. The chapter explained how all nations can benefit from free international trade. ◆ Chapter 34 explained some of the fundamentals of international borrowing and lending and the exchange rate. It explained the poorly understood fact that the size of a nation's international deficit depends not on how efficient it is, but on how much its citizens save relative to how much they invest. Nations with low saving rates, everything else being the same, have international deficits. ◆ Finally, Chapter 35 studied global stock markets. It described these markets and it explained how stock prices are determined and why they are volatile and impossible to predict. ◆ The global economy is big news these days. And it has always attracted attention. On the next page, you can meet the economist who first understood comparative advantage, David Ricardo. And you can meet one of today's leading international economists, Jagdish Bhagwati of Columbia University.

Gains from International Trade

DAVID RICARDO *(1772–1832) was a highly successful 27-year-old stockbroker when he stumbled on a copy of Adam Smith's* Wealth of Nations *(see p. 54) on a weekend visit to the country. He was immediately hooked and went on to become the most celebrated economist of his age and one of the all-time great economists. One of his many contributions was to develop the principle of comparative advantage, the foundation on which the modern theory of international trade is built. The example he used to illustrate this principle was the trade between England and Portugal in cloth and wine.*

The General Agreement on Tariff and Trade was established as a reaction against the devastation wrought by beggar-my-neighbour tariffs imposed during the 1930s. But it is also a triumph for the logic first worked out by Smith and Ricardo.

Gains from International Trade "Under a system of perfectly free commerce, each country naturally devotes its capital and labour to such employments as are most beneficial to each."

DAVID
RICARDO
The Principles of Political Economy and Taxation,
1817

Until the mid-eighteenth century, it was generally believed that the purpose of international trade was to keep exports greater than imports and pile up gold. If gold was accumulated, it was believed, the nation would prosper; if gold was lost through an international deficit, the nation would be drained of money and impoverished. These beliefs are called *mercantilism*, and the *mercantilists* were pamphleteers who advocated with missionary fervor the pursuit of an international surplus. If exports did not exceed imports, the mercantilists wanted imports restricted.

In the 1740s, David Hume explained that as the quantity of money (gold) changes, so also does the price level, and the nation's *real* wealth is unaffected. In the 1770s, Adam Smith argued that import restrictions would lower the gains from specialization and make a nation poorer. Thirty years later, David Ricardo proved the law of comparative advantage and demonstrated the superiority of free trade. Mercantilism was intellectually bankrupt but remained politically powerful.

Gradually, through the nineteenth century, the mercantilist influence waned and North American and Western Europe prospered in an environment of increasingly free international trade. But despite remarkable advances in economic understanding, mercantilism never quite died. It had a brief and devastating revival in the 1920s and 1930s when tariff hikes brought about the collapse of international trade and accentuated the Great Depression. It subsided again after World War II with the establishment of the General Agreement on Tariffs and Trade (GATT).

But mercantilism lingers on. The often expressed view that the United States should restrict Japanese imports and reduce its deficit with Japan and fears that NAFTA will bring economic ruin to Canada are modern manifestations of mercantilism. It would be interesting to have David Hume, Adam Smith, and David Ricardo commenting on these views. But we know what they would say—the same things that they said to the eighteenth-century mercantilists. And they would still be right today.

THEN

In the eighteenth century, when mercantilists and economists were debating the pros and cons of free international exchange, the transportation technology that was available limited the gains from international trade. Sailing ships with tiny cargo holds took close to a month to cross the Atlantic Ocean. But the potential gains were large, and so was the incentive to cut shipping costs. By the 1850s, the clipper ship had been developed, cutting the journey from Boston to Liverpool to only 12¼ days. Half a century later, 10,000-ton steamships were sailing between North America and England in just 4 days. As sailing times and costs declined, the gains from international trade increased and the volume of trade expanded.

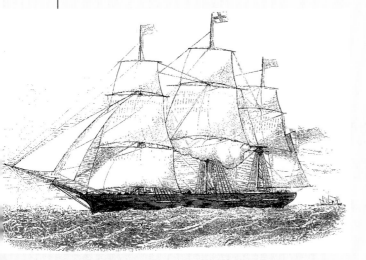

Now

The container ship has revolutionized international trade and contributed to its continued expansion. Today, most goods cross the oceans in containers—metal boxes—packed into and piled on top of ships like this one. Container technology has cut the cost of ocean shipping by economizing on handling and by making cargoes harder to steal, lowering insurance costs. It is unlikely that there would be much international trade in goods such as television sets and VCRs without this technology. High-value and perishable cargoes such as flowers and fresh foods, as well as urgent courier packages, travel by air. Every day, dozens of cargo-laden 747s fly between every major North American city and to destinations across the Atlantic and Pacific oceans.

Jagdish Bhagwati, whom you can meet on the following pages, is one of the most distinguished international economists. He has contributed to our understanding of the effects of international trade and trade policy on economic growth and development and has played a significant role in helping to shape today's global trading arrangements.

TALKING WITH

JAGDISH BHAGWATI *is University Professor at Columbia University. Born in India in 1934, he studied at Cambridge University in England, MIT, and Oxford University before returning to India. He returned to teach at MIT in 1968 and moved to Columbia in 1980. A prolific scholar: Professor Bhagwati also writes in leading newspapers and magazines throughout the world. He has been much honoured for both his scientific work and his impact on public policy. His greatest contributions are in international trade but extend also to developmental problems and the study of political economy.*

Michael Parkin and Robin Bade talked with Jagdish Bhagwati about his work and the progress that economists have made in understanding the benefits of international economic integration since the pioneering work of Ricardo.

Jagdish Bhagwati

Professor Bhagwati, what attracted you to economics?

When you come from India where poverty hits the eye, it is easy to be attracted to economics, which can be used to bring prosperity and create jobs to pull up the poor into gainful employment.

I learned later that there are two broad types of economist: those who treat the subject as an arid mathematical toy, and those who see it as a serious social science.

If Cambridge, where I went as an undergraduate, had been interested in esoteric mathematical economics, I would have opted for something else. But the Cambridge economists from whom I learned—many among the greatest figures in the discipline—saw economics as a social science. I therefore saw the power of economics as a tool to address India's poverty and was immediately hooked.

Who had the greatest impact on you at Cambridge?

Most of all, it was Harry Johnson, a young Canadian of immense energy and profound analytical gifts. Quite unlike the shy and reserved British dons, Johnson was friendly, effusive, and supportive of students who flocked around him. He would later move to Chicago where he became one of the most influential members of the market-oriented Chicago school. Another was Joan Robinson, arguably the world's most impressive female economist.

When I left Cambridge for MIT, going from one Cambridge to the other, I was lucky to transition from one phenomenal set of economists to another. At MIT, I learned much from future Nobel laureates Paul Samuelson and Robert Solow—both would later become great friends and colleagues when I joined the MIT faculty in 1968.

After Cambridge and MIT, you went to Oxford and then back to India. What did you do in India?

I joined the Planning Commission in New Delhi, where my first big job was to find ways of raising the bottom 30 percent of India's population out of poverty to a "minimum income" level.

And what did you prescribe?

My main prescription was to "grow the pie." My research suggested that the share of the bottom 30 percent of the pie did not seem to vary dramatically with differences in economic and political systems. So, growth in the pie seemed to be the principal (but not the only) component of an antipoverty strategy. To supplement growth's good effects on the poor, the Indian planners were also dedicated to education, health, social reforms, and land reforms. Also, the access of the lowest-income and socially disadvantaged groups to the growth process and its benefits was to be improved in many ways, such as extension of credit without collateral.

Today, this strategy has no rivals. Much empirical work shows that where growth has occurred, poverty has lessened. It is nice to know that one's basic take on an issue of such central importance to humanity's well-being has been borne out by experience!

> *My main prescription was to "grow the pie"... Today, this strategy has no rivals. Much empirical work shows that where growth has occurred, poverty has lessened.*

You left India in 1968 to come to America and an academic job at MIT. Why?

While the decision to emigrate often reflects personal factors—and they were present in my case—the offer of a Professorship from MIT certainly helped me make up my mind. At the time, it was easily the world's most celebrated Department: Serendipitously, the highest-ranked Departments at MIT were not in engineering and the sciences but in linguistics (which had Noam Chomsky) and economics (which had Paul Samuelson). Joining the MIT faculty was a dramatic breakthrough: I felt stimulated each year by several fantastic students and by several of the world's most creative economists.

We hear a lot in the popular press about fair trade and level playing fields. What's the distinction between free trade and fair trade? How can the playing field be unlevel?

Free trade simply means allowing no trade barriers such as tariffs, subsidies, and quotas. Trade barriers make domestic prices different from world prices for traded goods. When this happens, resources are not being used efficiently. Basic economics from the time of Ricardo tells us why free trade is good for us and why barriers to trade harm us, though our understanding of this doctrine today is far more nuanced and profound than it was at its creation.

Fair trade, on the other hand, is almost always a sneaky way of objecting to free trade. If your rivals are hard to compete with, you are not likely to get protection simply by saying that you cannot hack it. But if you say that your rival is an "unfair" trader, that is an easier sell! As international competition has grown fiercer, cries of "unfair trade" have therefore multiplied. The lesser rogues among the protectionists ask for "free and fair trade," whereas the worst ones ask for "fair, not free, trade."

> *Fair trade ... is almost always a sneaky way of objecting to free trade.*

At the end of World War II, the General Agreement on Tariffs and Trade (GATT) was established and there followed several rounds of multilateral trade negotiations and reductions in barriers to trade. How do you assess the contribution of GATT and its successor, the World Trade Organization (WTO)?

The GATT has made a huge contribution by overseeing massive trade liberalization in industrial goods among the developed countries. GATT rules, which "bind" tariffs to negotiated ceilings, prevent the raising of tariffs and have prevented tariff wars like those of the 1930s in which mutual and retaliatory tariff barriers were raised to the detriment of everyone.

The GATT was folded into the WTO at the end of the Uruguay Round of trade negotiations and is institutionally stronger. For instance, it has a binding Dispute Settlement Mechanism, whereas the GATT had no such teeth. It is also more ambitious in its scope, extending to new areas such as environment, intellectual property protection, and investment rules.

Running alongside the pursuit of multilateral free trade has been the emergence of bilateral trade agreements such as NAFTA and the EU. How do you view the bilateral free trade areas in today's world?

Unfortunately, there has been an explosion of bilateral free trade areas today. By some estimates, the ones in place and others being plotted approach 400! Each bilateral agreement gives preferential treatment to its trading partner over others. Because there are now so many bilateral agreements, such as between United States and Israel and between United States and Jordan, the result is a chaotic pattern of different tariffs depending on where a product comes from. Also, "rules of origin" must be agreed upon to determine whether a product is, say, Jordanian or Taiwanese if Jordan qualifies for a preferential tariff but Taiwan does not, and Taiwanese inputs enter the Jordanian manufacture of the product.

I have called the resulting criss-crossing of preferences and rules of origin the "spaghetti bowl" problem. The world trading system is choking under these proliferating bilateral deals. Contrast this complexity against the simplicity of a multilateral system with common tariffs for all WTO members.

We now have a world of uncoordinated and inefficient trade policies. The EU makes bilateral free trade agreements with different non-EU countries, so the United States follows with its own bilateral agreements; and with Europe and the United States doing it, the Asian countries, long wedded to multilateralism, have now succumbed to the mania.

Instead, if the United States had provided leadership by rewriting rules to make the signing of such bilateral agreements extremely difficult, this plague on the trading system today might well have been averted.

We now have a world of uncoordinated and inefficient trade policies.

Despite the benefits that economics points to from multilateral free trade, the main organization that pursues this goal, the WTO, is having a very hard time with the anti-globalization movement. What can we say about globalization that puts the WTO and its work in proper perspective?

The anti-globalization movement contains a diverse set of activists. Essentially, they all claim to be stakeholders in the globalization phenomenon. But there are those who want to drive a stake through the system, as in Dracula films, and there are those who want to exercise their stake in the system. The former want to be heard; the latter, to be listened to. For a while, the two disparate sets of critics were milling around together, seeking targets of opportunity at international conferences such as WTO's November 2000 meeting in Seattle where the riots broke out. Now things have settled down; and the groups that want to work systematically and seriously at improving the global economy's functioning are much more in play.

But the WTO is also seen, inaccurately for the most part, as imposing trade sanctions that override concerns such as environmental protection. For example, U.S. legislation bans the importing of shrimp that is harvested without the use of turtle-excluding devices. India and others complained, but the WTO upheld the U.S. legislation. Ignorant of the facts, demonstrators took to the streets dressed as turtles protesting the WTO decision!

What advice do you have for a student who is just starting to study economics? Is economics a good subject in which to major?

I would say: enormously so. In particular, we economists bring three unique insights to good policymaking.

First, economists look for second and subsequent-round effects of actions.

Second, we correctly emphasize that a policy cannot be judged without using a counterfactual. It is a witticism that an economist, when asked how her husband was, said: compared to what?

Third, we uniquely and systematically bring the principle of social cost and benefit to our policy analysis.

CANADIAN
ECONOMY
DATABASE

CANADIAN ECONOMY DATABASE

THE FOLLOWING DATA TABLES PROVIDE A DESCRIPTION of some of the main features of the Canadian economy from 1926 to 2001.

You can make graphs of these data by using *Economics in Action* on the Parkin–Bade Web site. To do so, open the table of contents page for *any* chapter, click on Data Graphing and then click on Canada Historical.

These data are updated annually on the Parkin–Bade Web site.

Sources

CANSIM series: Statistics Canada, Ottawa

HSC series: Statistics Canada, *Historical Statistics of Canada*, Second Edition, F. H. Leacy (ed.), Ottawa, 1983.

HSC(1) series: The MacMillan Company of Canada Limited, *Historical Statistics of Canada*, M.C. Urquhart (ed.), Toronto, 1965.

A break in a series is indicated by *b*.

Variables

1. Real GDP
HSC series F55 and CANSIM series v1992292. The data for 1926–1960 are F55 multiplied by the 1961 ratio of v1992292 to F55.

2. Real consumption expenditure
HSC series F33 and CANSIM series v1992262. The data for 1926–1960 are F33 multiplied by the 1961 ratio of v1992262 to F33.

3. Real investment
HSC is F55 minus the sum of F33, F34, and F51 plus F52; CANSIM series is v1992292 minus the sum of v1992262, v1992268, 1992282 plus v1992286. The data for 1926–1960 are *HSC* multiplied by the 1961 ratio of CANSIM to *HSC*.

4. Real government expenditure
HSC series F34 and CANSIM series v1992268. The data for 1926–1960 are F34 multiplied by the 1961 ratio of v1992268 to F34.

5. Real exports
HSC series F51 and CANSIM series v1992282. The data for 1926–1960 are F51 multiplied by the 1961 ratio of v1992282 to F51.

6. Real imports
HSC series F52 and CANSIM series v1992286. The data for 1926–1960 are F51 multiplied by the 1961 ratio of v1992286 to F52.

7. Real net exports
Real exports *minus* real imports.

8. Potential GDP
Real GDP trends and authors' assumptions and calculations.

9. Fluctuations around potential GDP
Percentage deviation of real GDP from potential GDP.

10. Real GDP growth rate
Annual percentage change in real GDP.

11. GDP deflator
HSC series K172 and CANSIM series v647710 and v3860248. The data for 1961–1980 are v647710 multiplied by the 1981 ratio of v3860248 to v647710. The data for 1926–1960 are K172 multiplied by the 1961 ratio of the above calculation to K172.

12. CPI
Statistics Canada, CANSIM series v737344.

13. Inflation rate
Annual percentage change in the GDP deflator.

14. Inflation rate
Annual percentage change in the CPI.

15. Labour force
CANSIM series v21051 and v2461098.

16. Labour force participation rate
CANSIM series v21051, v21056, and v2461245.

17. Average weekly hours
HSC series E128, E129, E130, E131, E132, E133, E134, E135; Statistics Canada, CANSIM series v2461119 and v2641490, and authors' calculations.

18. Unemployment rate
HSC series D127, D132, and D491 and CANSIM series v2461224.

19. Long-term interest rate
HSC(1) series H605, *HSC* series J475, and Bank of Canada series B14013.

20. Short-term interest rate
HSC series J471 and Bank of Canada series B14060.

21. Federal government revenues
HSC series H18 and CANSIM series v499985.

22. Federal government outlays
HSC series H34 and CANSIM series v500016.

23. Federal government surplus(+)/deficit(-)
HSC series H18 and H34 and CANSIM series v499985 and v500016.

24. Gross federal debt
CANSIM series v151537.

25. M1
Bank of Canada series B2033.

26. M2+
Bank of Canada series B2037.

27. M1 velocity
Series 1 multiplied by series 11 divided by series 25.

28. M2+ velocity
Series 1 multiplied by series 11 divided by series 26.

29. Exchange rate
HSC series J562 and CANSIM series v37426.

30. Current account
HSC series G83 and CANSIM series v114421.

Year		1926	1927	1928	1929	1930	1931	1932	1933	1934	1935
Real GDP (billions of 1997 dollars)	1	61.2	67.0	73.1	73.4	70.3	61.4	55.0	51.3	57.6	62.1
Real consumption expenditure (billions of 1997 dollars)	2	35.6	39.8	43.6	46.3	44.3	42.2	38.9	37.9	39.9	41.6
Real investment (billions of 1997 dollars)	3	12.4	14.5	16.3	14.4	12.7	4.2	1.0	0.0	2.8	4.5
Real government expenditures (billions of 1997 dollars)	4	10.0	10.5	10.6	11.9	13.0	13.8	13.3	11.2	11.9	12.4
Real exports (billions of 1997 dollars)	5	12.1	12.2	13.8	13.0	11.3	10.1	9.4	9.5	10.7	11.8
Real imports (billions of 1997 dollars)	6	8.9	9.9	11.1	12.1	11.0	8.8	7.6	7.2	7.7	8.2
Real net exports (billions of 1997 dollars)	7	3.2	2.3	2.7	0.9	0.3	1.3	1.8	2.2	3.0	3.5
Potential GDP (billions of 1997 dollars)	8	62.0	63.8	65.7	67.7	69.7	71.8	73.9	76.1	78.4	80.8
Fluctuations around potential GDP (percentage)	9	−1.2	5.0	11.3	8.5	0.8	−14.5	−25.6	−32.6	−26.6	−23.2
Real GDP growth rate (percent per year)	10	—	9.5	9.1	0.4	−4.3	−12.7	−10.4	−6.7	12.1	7.8
GDP deflator (1997 = 100)	11	8.7	8.6	8.5	8.6	8.4	7.9	7.1	7.0	7.1	7.1
CPI (1992 = 100)	12	10.9	10.8	10.8	11.0	10.9	9.8	8.9	8.5	8.6	8.7
Inflation rate (GDP deflator percent per year)	13	—	−1.1	−0.6	1.1	−2.5	−6.2	−9.3	−1.7	1.4	0.3
Inflation rate (CPI percent per year)	14	0	−0.9	0	1.9	−0.9	−10.1	−9.2	−4.5	1.2	1.2
Labour force (millions)	15	3.7	3.8	3.9	4.0	4.1	4.2	4.2	4.3	4.3	4.4
Labour force participation rate (percentage)	16	57.8	57.9	58.0	58.1	58.2	58.3	58.2	58.0	57.9	57.8
Average weekly hours (hours per week)	17	—	—	—	—	—	—	—	—	—	—
Unemployment rate (percentage)	18	2.9	1.8	1.7	2.9	9.1	11.6	17.6	19.3	14.5	14.2
Long-term interest rate (percent per year)	19	4.9	4.6	4.5	4.9	4.7	4.6	5.1	4.6	4.0	3.6
Short-term interest rate (percent per year)	20	—	—	—	—	—	—	—	—	2.5	1.5
Federal government revenues (billions of dollars)	21	0.4	0.4	0.5	0.5	0.4	0.3	0.3	0.3	0.4	0.4
Federal government outlays (billions of dollars)	22	0.4	0.4	0.4	0.4	0.4	0.4	0.5	0.5	0.5	0.5
Federal government surplus (+)/deficit(−) (billions of dollars)	23	0	0.1	0.1	0	−0.1	−0.1	−0.2	−0.1	−0.1	−0.2
Gross federal debt (billions of dollars)	24	2.8	2.8	2.7	2.7	2.6	2.7	2.9	3.1	3.2	3.5
M1 (billions of dollars)	25	—	—	—	—	—	—	—	—	—	—
M2+ (billions of dollars)	26	—	—	—	—	—	—	—	—	—	—
M1 velocity (GDP/M1)	27	—	—	—	—	—	—	—	—	—	—
M2+ velocity (GDP/M2+)	28	—	—	—	—	—	—	—	—	—	—
Exchange rate (U.S. dollars per Canadian dollar)	29	1.00	1.00	1.00	1.00	1.00	0.96	0.88	0.92	1.01	0.99
Current account balance (billions of dollars)	30	0.1	0	0	−0.3	−0.3	−0.2	−0.1	0	0.1	0.1

	1936	1937	1938	1939	1940	1941	1942	1943	1944	1945	1946	1947	1948	1949	
	64.8	71.3	71.9	77.2	88.1	100.8	119.5	124.3	129.2	126.3	123.0	128.2	131.4	136.4	1
	43.5	46.2	45.6	46.9	50.3	53.7	55.1	56.7	60.8	66.9	74.4	79.6	77.7	82.1	2
	4.0	8.3	8.8	11.3	6.4	0.5	−20.7	−29.9	−38.0	−19.0	9.5	19.5	23.6	23.4	3
	12.5	12.6	14.1	15.0	26.5	38.3	80.2	87.7	100.7	69.3	32.8	24.7	23.4	25.9	4
	14.2	14.5	13.1	14.4	16.4	21.6	19.3	26.8	25.9	25.2	21.2	21.0	21.7	20.4	5
	9.3	10.3	9.6	10.3	11.5	13.3	14.3	17.0	20.2	16.0	14.8	16.7	15.0	15.4	6
	4.8	4.2	3.4	4.1	4.9	8.3	5.0	9.8	5.7	9.2	6.3	4.4	6.7	5.0	7
	83.2	85.7	88.2	90.9	93.6	97.3	101.1	105.1	109.3	113.7	118.3	123.2	128.2	133.6	8
	−22.1	−16.7	−18.5	−15.0	−5.8	3.6	18.2	18.2	18.2	11.1	3.9	4.1	2.4	2.1	9
	4.4	10.0	0.8	7.4	14.1	14.4	18.6	4.0	4.0	−2.2	−2.7	4.3	2.5	3.8	10
	7.4	7.6	7.6	7.5	7.9	8.5	8.9	9.2	9.4	9.7	10.0	10.8	12.2	12.7	11
	8.8	9.1	9.2	9.2	9.5	10.1	10.5	10.7	10.8	10.9	11.2	12.3	14.0	14.5	12
	3.3	2.6	0	−0.9	4.7	7.9	4.5	3.5	3.1	2.5	2.9	8.8	12.3	4.3	13
	1.1	3.4	1.1	0	3.3	6.3	4.0	1.9	0.9	0.9	2.8	9.8	13.8	3.6	14
	4.5	4.5	4.6	4.6	4.6	4.5	4.6	4.6	4.5	4.5	4.8	4.9	5.0	5.2	15
	57.6	57.5	57.4	57.2	56.6	55.4	56.5	58.0	57.4	56.2	55.0	54.9	54.6	54.4	16
	—	—	—	—	—	—	—	—	—	44.1	42.7	42.5	42.3	42.2	17
	12.8	9.1	11.4	11.4	9.0	4.1	2.7	1.4	1.2	1.4	[b]3.4	2.2	2.3	2.8	18
	[b]3.0	3.2	3.1	3.2	3.3	3.1	3.1	3.0	3.0	2.9	2.6	2.6	2.9	2.8	19
	0.9	0.7	0.6	0.7	0.7	0.6	0.5	0.5	0.4	0.4	0.4	0.4	0.4	0.5	20
	0.5	0.5	0.5	0.6	0.9	1.5	2.3	2.8	2.7	3.0	3.0	2.9	2.8	2.6	21
	0.5	0.5	0.6	0.7	1.3	1.9	4.4	5.3	5.2	5.1	2.6	2.2	2.2	2.4	22
	−0.1	0	−0.1	−0.1	−0.4	−0.4	−2.1	−2.6	−2.6	−2.1	0.4	0.7	0.6	0.1	23
	3.5	3.6	3.6	3.7	4.0	5.0	6.6	8.8	11.8	14.9	17.9	17.7	17.2	16.9	24
	—	—	—	—	—	—	—	—	—	—	—	—	—	—	25
	—	—	—	—	—	—	—	—	—	—	—	—	—	—	26
	—	—	—	—	—	—	—	—	—	—	—	—	—	—	27
	—	—	—	—	—	—	—	—	—	—	—	—	—	—	28
	1.00	1.00	0.99	0.96	0.90	0.90	0.90	0.90	0.90	0.91	1.00	1.00	1.00	0.97	29
	0.2	0.2	0.1	0.1	0.2	0.5	0.1	0.7	0.1	0.7	[b]0.08	0	0.1	0	30

Year		1950	1951	1952	1953	1954	1955	1956	1957	1958	1959
Real GDP (billions of 1997 dollars)	1	146.7	154.1	167.8	176.5	174.3	190.7	206.9	211.7	216.6	224.8
Real consumption expenditure (billions of 1997 dollars)	2	87.5	88.2	94.4	100.9	104.6	113.6	122.1	126.6	131.2	138.5
Real investment (billions of 1997 dollars)	3	27.8	26.2	23.4	26.0	21.8	29.3	37.5	38.0	35.2	38.0
Real government expenditures (billions of 1997 dollars)	4	27.9	36.4	44.8	46.2	44.4	45.4	46.6	45.8	47.2	46.8
Real exports (billions of 1997 dollars)	5	20.3	22.2	24.7	24.5	23.6	25.4	27.3	27.5	27.4	28.5
Real imports (billions of 1997 dollars)	6	16.8	18.9	19.5	21.2	20.2	22.9	26.5	26.2	24.4	26.9
Real net exports (billions of 1997 dollars)	7	3.5	3.3	5.2	3.3	3.4	2.5	0.7	1.3	3.0	1.6
Potential GDP (billions of 1997 dollars)	8	139.1	145.0	151.1	157.6	164.4	171.5	179.0	186.9	195.3	204.1
Fluctuations around potential GDP (percentage)	9	5.5	6.3	11.0	12.0	6.0	11.2	15.5	13.3	10.9	10.2
Real GDP growth rate (percent per year)	10	7.6	5.0	8.9	5.1	−1.2	9.4	8.4	2.4	2.3	3.8
GDP deflator (1997 = 100)	11	13.0	14.5	15.1	15.1	15.3	15.4	16.0	16.3	16.6	16.9
CPI (1992 = 100)	12	14.9	16.4	16.9	16.7	16.8	16.8	17.1	17.6	18.0	18.3
Inflation rate (GDP deflator percent per year)	13	2.4	11.3	4.4	−0.2	1.6	0.6	3.7	2.1	1.5	2.0
Inflation rate (CPI percent per year)	14	2.8	10.1	3.0	−1.2	0.6	0	1.8	2.9	2.3	1.7
Labour force (millions)	15	5.2	5.2	5.3	5.4	5.5	5.6	5.8	6.0	6.1	6.2
Labour force participation rate (percentage)	16	53.7	53.7	53.5	53.1	52.9	52.9	53.5	54.0	53.9	53.8
Average weekly hours (hours per week)	17	42.3	41.7	41.5	41.3	40.7	41.0	41.0	40.4	40.2	40.7
Unemployment rate (percentage)	18	3.6	2.4	2.9	3.0	4.6	4.4	3.4	4.6	7.0	6.0
Long-term interest rate (percent per year)	19	2.8	3.2	3.6	3.7	3.1	3.1	3.6	4.2	4.5	5.0
Short-term interest rate (percent per year)	20	0.6	0.8	1.1	1.7	1.4	1.6	2.9	3.8	2.3	4.8
Federal government revenues (billions of dollars)	21	3.1	4.0	4.6	4.7	4.4	4.7	5.5	5.4	5.1	5.8
Federal government outlays (billions of dollars)	22	2.9	3.8	4.6	4.7	4.7	4.8	5.2	5.5	6.0	6.3
Federal government surplus (+)/deficit(−) (billions of dollars)	23	0.2	0.2	−0.1	0	−0.2	−0.1	0.3	−0.1	−0.8	−0.4
Gross federal debt (billions of dollars)	24	16.7	16.7	16.8	17.4	17.6	17.6	18.7	18.0	18.0	19.7
M1 (billions of dollars)	25	—	—	—	4.2	4.4	4.8	4.8	4.8	5.4	5.2
M2+ (billions of dollars)	26	—	—	—	—	—	—	—	—	—	—
M1 velocity (GDP/M1)	27	—	—	—	6.3	6.1	6.1	6.9	7.2	6.6	7.3
M2+ velocity (GDP/M2+)	28	—	—	—	—	—	—	—	—	—	—
Exchange rate (U.S. dollars per Canadian dollar)	29	[b]0.95	0.95	1.02	1.02	1.03	1.01	1.02	1.04	1.03	1.04
Current account balance (billions of dollars)	30	−0.1	−0.1	0	−0.1	−0.1	−0.2	−0.3	−0.4	−0.3	−0.4

	1960	1961	1962	1963	1964	1965	1966	1967	1968	1969	1970	1971	1972	1973	
	231.3	237.9	254.2	267.1	284.6	303.0	322.9	332.5	350.3	369.0	378.6	399.6	420.9	451.2	1
	143.3	144.9	152.3	158.7	167.1	176.9	185.6	192.5	201.1	210.9	214.5	227.4	243.1	260.0	2
	37.3	33.9	39.4	41.6	46.2	54.5	58.8	52.5	54.3	60.9	52.3	56.8	61.1	70.6	3
	47.9	54.5	57.0	59.0	62.1	64.9	70.7	76.9	81.9	85.4	92.9	96.8	99.8	104.5	4
	29.7	31.9	33.4	36.4	41.4	43.2	49.1	54.3	61.2	66.1	72.3	75.8	82.3	91.1	5
	26.9	27.4	28.0	28.5	32.1	36.5	41.4	43.6	48.1	54.4	53.4	57.3	65.5	75.1	6
	2.8	4.5	5.4	7.9	9.2	6.8	7.7	10.6	13.0	11.7	18.9	18.6	16.9	16.0	7
	212.0	225.8	240.1	254.9	270.2	285.9	302.1	318.7	335.7	353.1	370.8	388.3	406.3	423.7	8
	9.1	5.3	5.8	4.8	5.3	6.0	6.9	4.3	4.3	4.5	2.1	2.9	3.6	6.5	9
	2.9	2.8	6.8	5.1	6.5	6.5	6.6	3.0	5.3	5.3	2.6	5.5	5.4	7.2	10
	17.1	17.2	17.5	17.8	18.3	18.9	19.9	20.8	21.6	22.5	23.6	24.4	25.9	28.3	11
	18.5	18.7	18.9	19.2	19.6	20.0	20.8	21.5	22.4	23.4	24.2	24.9	26.1	28.1	12
	1.3	0.4	1.6	2.1	2.6	3.5	5.3	4.1	4.0	4.3	4.9	3.5	6.0	9.2	13
	1.1	1.1	1.1	1.6	2.1	2.0	4.0	3.4	4.2	4.5	3.4	2.9	4.8	7.7	14
	6.4	6.5	6.6	6.7	6.9	7.1	7.4	7.7	7.9	8.2	8.4	8.6	8.9	9.3	15
	54.2	54.1	53.9	53.8	54.1	54.4	55.1	55.5	55.5	55.8	57.8	58.1	58.6	59.7	16
	40.7	40.5	40.3	40.2	40.2	40.1	39.8	39.1	38.7	38.1	37.5	37.4	37.4	36.8	17
	7.0	7.1	5.9	5.5	4.7	3.9	[b]3.3	3.8	4.5	4.4	5.7	6.2	6.2	5.6	18
	5.1	5.0	5.1	5.1	5.1	5.3	5.7	6.0	6.7	7.6	7.9	7.0	7.2	7.6	19
	3.2	2.8	4.1	3.6	3.8	4.0	5.0	4.6	6.3	7.2	6.0	3.5	3.6	5.5	20
	6.2	6.6	6.7	7.0	8.0	8.8	9.6	10.5	11.7	13.9	14.9	16.5	18.8	21.9	21
	6.6	7.1	7.6	7.7	8.1	8.6	9.8	11.0	12.2	13.2	15.1	17.2	19.6	21.8	22
	−0.3	−0.5	−0.9	−0.7	−0.1	0.2	−0.2	−0.5	−0.5	0.7	−0.2	−0.7	−0.9	0.1	23
	20.4	20.9	22.8	24.5	26.2	26.8	27.7	29.8	32.0	34.4	35.8	39.9	43.8	46.2	24
	5.5	5.9	6.1	6.3	6.7	7.1	7.7	8.4	8.9	9.2	9.8	11.5	13.2	14.6	25
	—	—	—	—	—	—	—	—	34.0	37.1	40.9	46.2	53.3	63.5	26
	7.2	6.9	7.3	7.6	7.8	8.1	8.4	8.2	8.5	9.0	9.1	8.5	8.3	8.7	27
	—	—	—	—	—	—	—	—	2.2	2.2	2.2	2.1	2.0	2.0	28
	1.03	0.99	0.94	0.93	0.93	0.93	0.93	0.93	0.93	0.93	0.96	0.99	1.01	1.00	29
	−0.3	−0.3	−0.3	−0.2	−0.1	−0.4	−0.4	−0.3	−0.3	−0.5	0.1	−0.3	−0.6	−0.5	30

Year		1974	1975	1976	1977	1978	1979	1980	1981	1982	1983
Real GDP (billions of 1997 dollars)	1	469.9	480.3	506.7	524.2	545.6	568.5	576.4	594.1	576.7	592.7
Real consumption expenditure (billions of 1997 dollars)	2	273.5	284.8	300.2	309.2	319.7	328.6	335.2	338.9	330.5	339.9
Real investment (billions of 1997 dollars)	3	79.9	75.5	81.8	78.4	81.4	97.8	97.7	117.0	88.1	95.5
Real government expenditures (billions of 1997 dollars)	4	111.1	118.6	120.9	126.5	128.8	130.1	134.5	136.2	139.0	141.3
Real exports (billions of 1997 dollars)	5	88.7	83.0	91.9	99.0	109.8	113.8	115.9	120.2	118.7	126.3
Real imports (billions of 1997 dollars)	6	83.3	81.6	88.0	88.9	94.0	101.7	106.9	118.2	99.6	110.3
Real net exports (billions of 1997 dollars)	7	5.4	1.4	3.8	10.1	15.8	12.1	9.0	1.9	19.1	15.9
Potential GDP (billions of 1997 dollars)	8	440.4	463.2	484.4	504.0	524.1	547.7	565.7	581.3	598.3	616.7
Fluctuations around potential GDP (percentage)	9	6.7	3.7	4.6	4.0	4.1	3.8	1.9	2.2	−3.6	−3.9
Real GDP growth rate (percent per year)	10	4.1	2.2	5.5	3.5	4.1	4.2	1.4	3.0	−2.9	2.8
GDP deflator (1997 = 100)	11	32.5	35.8	39.1	41.8	44.6	48.8	54.1	60.1	65.1	68.7
CPI (1992 = 100)	12	31.1	34.5	37.1	40.0	43.6	47.6	52.4	58.9	65.3	69.1
Inflation rate (GDP deflator percent per year)	13	14.9	10.2	9.2	6.8	6.6	9.5	10.9	11.0	8.3	5.5
Inflation rate (CPI percent per year)	14	10.7	10.9	7.5	7.8	9.0	9.2	10.1	12.4	10.9	5.8
Labour force (millions)	15	9.6	10.0	10.5	10.8	11.1	11.5	11.9	12.2	12.3	12.5
Labour force participation rate (percentage)	16	60.5	61.1	61.5	61.8	62.6	63.6	64.2	65.0	64.4	64.7
Average weekly hours (hours per week)	17	36.0	35.5	35.4	35.4	35.7	35.8	35.2	34.7	34.5	34.5
Unemployment rate (percentage)	18	5.3	6.9	b7.0	8.0	8.3	7.5	7.5	7.6	11.0	11.9
Long-term interest rate (percent per year)	19	8.9	9.0	9.2	8.7	9.3	10.2	12.5	15.2	14.3	11.8
Short-term interest rate (percent per year)	20	7.8	7.4	8.9	7.3	8.7	11.7	12.7	17.8	13.7	9.3
Federal government revenues (billions of dollars)	21	29.0	30.9	34.5	35.3	36.7	42.0	49.1	63.4	65.1	67.4
Federal government outlays (billions of dollars)	22	28.4	35.4	38.7	43.5	48.2	52.5	60.8	71.7	83.6	91.0
Federal government surplus (+)/deficit(−) (billions of dollars)	23	0.6	−4.5	−4.2	−8.2	−11.4	−10.4	−11.8	−8.3	−18.5	−23.6
Gross federal debt (billions of dollars)	24	49.1	55.1	61.9	69.7	82.4	100.5	110.6	127.7	144.5	173.1
M1 (billions of dollars)	25	15.5	19.0	19.4	21.7	23.6	24.6	27.3	27.4	28.5	30.8
M2+ (billions of dollars)	26	73.7	87.3	102.0	117.8	136.7	160.9	187.5	209.6	226.3	241.6
M1 velocity (GDP/M1)	27	9.9	9.1	10.2	10.1	10.3	11.3	11.4	13.0	13.2	13.2
M2+ velocity (GDP/M2+)	28	2.1	2.0	1.9	1.9	1.8	1.7	1.7	1.7	1.7	1.7
Exchange rate (U.S. dollars per Canadian dollar)	29	1.02	0.98	1.01	0.94	0.88	0.85	0.86	0.83	0.81	0.81
Current account balance (billions of dollars)	30	−1.1	−2.1	−1.9	−1.9	−2.3	−2.5	−1.8	−3.7	0.6	−0.8

1984	1985	1986	1987	1988	1989	1990	1991	1992	1993	1994	1995	1996	1997	
626.4	660.3	677.8	705.7	740.6	759.8	762.4	747.9	754.8	772.5	810.0	832.1	845.2	882.7	1
355.1	373.6	388.5	404.7	422.4	437.4	443.1	437.2	444.8	452.7	467.0	476.9	488.9	510.7	2
108.8	121.3	125.0	137.9	153.9	163.0	149.2	137.5	131.8	133.6	146.6	150.7	151.8	183.0	3
143.0	149.2	151.9	153.9	161.0	165.5	171.6	176.6	178.6	178.7	176.5	175.6	173.5	171.8	4
149.8	158.0	166.3	171.8	188.1	190.5	199.5	204.1	220.2	244.3	276.3	301.3	319.1	348.6	5
130.3	141.8	154.0	162.6	184.9	196.6	201.1	207.6	220.5	236.7	256.4	272.3	288.2	331.3	6
19.4	16.2	12.4	9.2	3.2	−6.1	−1.6	−3.5	−0.3	7.5	19.9	29.0	30.9	17.3	7
634.6	657.7	679.2	699.4	721.8	740.6	751.1	760.0	770.2	784.3	805.2	829.6	857.2	890.8	8
−1.3	0.4	−0.2	0.9	2.6	2.6	1.5	−1.6	−2.0	−1.5	0.6	0.3	−1.4	−0.9	9
5.7	5.4	2.6	4.1	4.9	2.5	0.3	−1.9	0.9	2.3	4.9	2.7	1.6	4.4	10
70.9	73.2	75.4	78.8	82.4	86.1	88.9	91.5	92.7	94.0	95.1	97.2	98.8	100.0	11
72.1	75.0	78.1	81.5	84.8	89.0	93.3	98.5	100.0	101.8	102.0	104.2	105.9	107.6	12
3.2	3.2	3.0	4.5	4.6	4.5	3.3	2.9	1.3	1.4	1.2	2.2	1.6	1.2	13
4.3	4.0	4.1	4.4	4.0	5.0	4.8	5.6	1.5	1.8	0.2	2.2	1.6	1.6	14
12.7	13.0	13.3	13.5	13.8	14.0	14.2	14.3	14.4	14.5	14.6	14.8	14.9	15.2	15
65.0	65.5	66.0	66.4	66.8	67.2	67.1	66.5	65.7	65.4	65.2	64.9	64.7	64.9	16
34.6	34.8	34.8	34.7	35.3	35.7	35.2	34.5	34.0	34.5	34.9	34.6	34.4	34.2	17
11.3	10.7	9.6	8.8	7.8	7.5	8.1	10.3	11.2	11.4	10.4	9.4	9.6	9.1	18
12.8	11.0	9.5	10.0	10.2	9.9	10.9	9.8	8.8	7.8	8.6	8.3	7.5	6.4	19
11.1	9.4	9.0	8.2	9.5	12.1	12.8	8.8	6.6	4.8	5.5	7.1	4.2	3.2	20
73.5	80.2	88.6	97.3	106.6	113.7	120.9	125.8	130.1	128.7	131.9	140.3	148.0	162.6	21
102.2	112.3	114.4	120.6	128.9	138.5	151.5	161.2	164.4	167.2	165.9	172.4	166.1	160.1	22
−28.7	−32.2	−25.8	−23.3	−22.4	−24.8	−30.6	−35.4	−34.4	−38.5	−34.0	−32.1	−18.1	2.5	23
209.3	250.5	284.0	318.3	349.9	380.0	406.6	444.6	476.1	514.4	557.6	595.9	634.9	651.1	24
31.1	34.4	36.7	39.8	42.6	44.1	43.7	46.2	49.2	56.5	61.0	65.5	77.9	86.5	25
262.6	291.2	324.6	351.9	398.8	456.0	499.7	534.8	562.1	582.5	593.1	619.3	643.5	633.7	26
14.3	14.1	13.9	14.0	14.3	14.8	15.5	14.8	14.2	12.8	12.6	12.3	10.7	10.2	27
1.7	1.7	1.6	1.6	1.5	1.4	1.4	1.3	1.2	1.2	1.3	1.3	1.3	1.4	28
0.77	0.73	0.72	0.75	0.81	0.84	0.86	0.87	0.83	0.78	0.73	0.73	0.73	0.72	29
−0.4	−2.0	−3.9	−4.5	−4.6	−6.5	−5.8	−6.4	−6.3	−7.0	−4.4	−1.5	1.2	−2.8	30

Year		1998	1999	2000	2001
Real GDP (billions of 1997 dollars)	1	919.0	967.6	1013.1	1026.9
Real consumption expenditure (billions of 1997 dollars)	2	524.9	545.6	566.3	581.4
Real investment (billions of 1997 dollars)	3	184.9	200.9	219.3	206.4
Real government expenditures (billions of 1997 dollars)	4	177.3	180.7	185.0	191.2
Real exports (billions of 1997 dollars)	5	380.3	416.8	451.7	433.8
Real imports (billions of 1997 dollars)	6	348.4	376.5	409.3	385.9
Real net exports (billions of 1997 dollars)	7	31.9	40.4	42.4	47.8
Potential GDP (billions of 1997 dollars)	8	926.4	962.8	1001.1	1035.1
Fluctuations around potential GDP (percentage)	9	−0.8	0.5	1.2	−0.8
Real GDP growth rate (percent per year)	10	4.1	5.3	4.7	1.4
GDP deflator (1997 = 100)	11	99.6	101.3	105.2	106.3
CPI (1992 = 100)	12	108.6	110.5	113.5	116.4
Inflation rate (GDP deflator percent per year)	13	−0.4	1.7	3.8	1.0
Inflation rate (CPI percent per year)	14	0.9	1.7	2.7	2.6
Labour force (millions)	15	15.4	15.7	16.0	16.2
Labour force participation rate (percentage)	16	65.1	65.6	65.9	66.0
Average weekly hours (hours per week)	17	33.9	34.2	34.5	33.8
Unemployment rate (percentage)	18	8.3	7.6	6.8	7.2
Long-term interest rate (percent per year)	19	5.5	5.7	5.9	5.8
Short-term interest rate (percent per year)	20	4.7	4.7	5.5	3.7
Federal government revenues (billions of dollars)	21	167.5	177.1	193.2	191.4
Federal government outlays (billions of dollars)	22	163.7	172.3	179.5	184.7
Federal government surplus (+)/deficit(−) (billions of dollars)	23	3.8	4.8	13.7	6.7
Gross federal debt (billions of dollars)	24	645.7	648.4	648.2	644.9
M1 (billions of dollars)	25	93.6	101.2	116.1	133.8
M2+ (billions of dollars)	26	641.4	675.0	712.4	771.8
M1 velocity (GDP/M1)	27	9.8	9.7	9.2	8.2
M2+ velocity (GDP/M2+)	28	1.4	1.5	1.5	1.4
Exchange rate (U.S. dollars per Canadian dollar)	29	0.67	0.67	0.67	0.65
Current account balance (billions of dollars)	30	−2.8	0.5	6.9	7.5

GLOSSARY

Above full-employment equilibrium A macroeconomic equilibrium in which real GDP exceeds potential GDP. (p. 510)

Absolute advantage A person has an absolute advantage if that person can produce more goods with a given amount of resources than another person can; a country has an absolute advantage if its output per unit of inputs of all goods is larger than that of another country. (p. 45)

Aggregate demand The relationship between the quantity of real GDP demanded and the price level. (p. 505)

Aggregate hours The total number of hours worked by all the people employed, both full time and part time, during a year. (p. 483)

Aggregate planned expenditure The expenditure that households, firms, governments, and foreigners plan to undertake in given circumstances. It is the sum of planned consumption expenditure, planned investment, planned government expenditures on goods and services, and planned exports minus planned imports. (p. 533)

Aggregate production function The relationship between the quantity of real GDP supplied and the quantities of labour and capital and the state of technology. (pp. 500, 713)

Allocative efficiency A situation in which we cannot produce more of any good without giving up some of another good that we value more highly. (p. 39)

Automatic fiscal policy A change in fiscal policy that is triggered by the state of the economy. (p. 562)

Automatic stabilizers Mechanisms that stabilize real GDP without explicit action by the government. (p. 566)

Autonomous expenditure The sum of those components of aggregate planned expenditure that are not influenced by real GDP. Autonomous expenditure equals the sum of investment, government expenditures, exports, and the autonomous parts of consumption expenditure and imports. (p. 535)

Autonomous tax multiplier The magnification effect of a change in autonomous taxes on equilibrium expenditure and real GDP. (p. 564)

Autonomous taxes Taxes that do not vary with real GDP. (p. 562)

Balance of payments accounts A country's record of international trading, borrowing, and lending. (p. 810)

Balanced budget A government budget in which revenues and outlays are equal. (p. 557)

Bank of Canada The central bank of Canada. (p. 606)

Bank rate The interest rate that the Bank of Canada charges the chartered banks on the reserves it lends them. (p. 609)

Barter The direct exchange of one good or service for other goods and services. (p. 582)

Base period The period in which the CPI is defined to be 100. (p. 490)

Below full-employment equilibrium A macroeconomic equilibrium in which potential GDP exceeds real GDP. (p. 510)

Big tradeoff The conflict between equity and efficiency. (p. 10)

Budget deficit A government's budget balance that is negative—outlays exceed revenues. (p. 557)

Budget surplus A government's budget balance that is positive—revenues exceed outlays. (p. 557)

Business cycle The periodic but irregular up-and-down movement in production and jobs. (p. 8)

Canadian interest rate differential A gap equal to the Canadian interest rate minus the foreign interest rate. (p. 817)

Capital The tools, equipment, buildings, and other constructions that businesses now use to produce goods and services. (p. 4)

Capital account A record of foreign investment in a country minus its investment abroad. (p. 810)

Capital accumulation The growth of capital resources. (p. 40)

Capital consumption The decrease in the capital stock that results from wear and tear and obsolescence. (p. 461)

Capital gain The increase in the price of a stock. (p. 831)

Capital loss The decrease in the price of a stock. (p. 831)

Central bank A public authority that supervises financial institutions and markets and conducts monetary policy. (p. 606)

Ceteris paribus Other things being equal—all other relevant things remaining the same. (p. 13)

Chain-weighted output index An index that uses the prices of two adjacent years to calculate the real GDP growth rate. (p. 466)

Change in demand A change in buyers' plans that occurs when some influence on those plans other than the price of the good changes. It is illustrated by a shift of the demand curve. (p. 63)

Change in supply A change in sellers' plans that occurs when some influence on those plans other than the price of the good changes. It is illustrated by a shift of the supply curve. (p. 67)

Change in the quantity demanded A change in buyers' plans that occurs when the price of a good changes but all other influences on buyers' plans remain unchanged. It is illustrated by a movement along the demand curve. (p. 65)

Change in the quantity supplied A change in sellers' plans that occurs when the price of a good changes but all other influences on sellers' plans remain unchanged. It is illustrated by a movement along the supply curve. (p. 68)

Chartered bank A private firm, chartered under the Bank Act of 1992 to receive deposits and make loans. (p. 585)

Classical growth theory A theory of economic growth based on the view that real GDP growth is temporary and that when real GDP per person increases above subsistence level, a population explosion brings real GDP back to subsistence level. (p. 717)

Comparative advantage A person or country has a comparative advantage in an activity if that person or country can perform the activity at a lower opportunity cost than anyone else or any other country. (p. 42)

Competitive market A market that has many buyers and many sellers, so no single buyer or seller can influence the price. (p. 60)

Complement A good that is used in conjunction with another good. (p. 63)

Consumer Price Index (CPI) An index that measures the average of the prices paid by urban consumers for a fixed "basket" of the consumer goods and services. (p. 490)

Consumption expenditure The total payment for consumer goods and services. (p. 459)

Consumption function The relationship between consumption expenditure and disposable income, other things remaining the same. (p. 528)

Contractionary fiscal policy A decrease in government expenditures or an increase in taxes. (p. 569)

Cost of living The amount of money it takes to buy the goods and services that the average family consumes. (p. 7)

Cost-push inflation An inflation that results from an initial increase in costs. (p. 653)

Credit union A cooperative organization that operates under the Co-operative Credit Association Act of 1992 and that receives deposits and makes loans to its members. (p. 586)

Creditor nation A country that during its entire history has invested more in the rest of the world than

other countries have invested in it. (p. 812)

Cross-section graph A graph that shows the values of an economic variable for different groups in a population at a point in time. (p. 18)

Crowding in The tendency for expansionary fiscal policy to increase investment. (p. 633)

Crowding out The tendency for an expansionary fiscal policy action to decrease investment. (p. 633)

Currency The coins and Bank of Canada notes that we use today. (p. 583)

Currency appreciation The rise in the value of one currency in terms of another currency. (p. 815)

Currency depreciation The fall in the value of one currency in terms of another currency. (p. 815)

Currency drain An increase in currency held outside the banks. (p. 613)

Current account A record of the payments for imports of goods and services, receipts from exports of goods and services, net interest paid abroad, and net transfers. (pp. 449, 810)

Cyclical surplus or deficit The actual surplus or deficit minus the structural surplus or deficit. (p. 567)

Cyclical unemployment The fluctuations in unemployment over the business cycle. (p. 488)

Debtor nation A country that during its entire history has borrowed more from the rest of the world than it has lent to it. (p. 812)

Deflation A falling cost of living—a process in which the price level is falling. (pp. 7, 447)

Demand The relationship between the quantity of a good that consumers plan to buy and the price of the good when all other influences on buyers' plans remain the same. It is described by a demand schedule and illustrated by a demand curve. (p. 62)

Demand curve A curve that shows the relationship between the quantity demanded of a good and its price when all other influences on consumers' planned purchases remain the same. (p. 62)

Demand for labour The relationship between the quantity of labour demanded and the real wage rate when all other influences on firms' hiring plans remain the same. (p. 683)

Demand for money curve The relationship between the quantity of money demanded and the interest rate when all other influences on the amount of money that people wish to hold remain the same. (p. 592)

Demand-pull inflation An inflation that results from an initial increase in aggregate demand. (p. 651)

Deposit multiplier The amount by which an increase in bank reserves is multiplied to calculate the increase in bank deposits. (p. 588)

Depository institution A firm that takes deposits from households and firms and makes loans to other households and firms. (p. 585)

Depreciation The decrease in the capital stock that results from wear and tear and obsolescence. (p. 461)

Desired reserve ratio The ratio of reserves to deposits that banks wish to hold. (p. 587)

Direct relationship A relationship between two variables that move in the same direction. (p. 20)

Discount factor The discounted price is the original price multiplied by the discount factor. (p. 837)

Discouraged workers People who are available and willing to work but have not made specific efforts to find a job within the previous four weeks. (pp. 445, 482)

Discretionary fiscal policy A policy action that is initiated by an act of Parliament. (p. 562)

Discretionary policy A policy that responds to the state of the economy in a possibly unique way that uses all the information available, including perceived lessons from past "mistakes." (p. 763)

Disposable income Aggregate income minus taxes plus transfer payments. (pp. 507, 528)

Dividend The share of a firm's profit paid to stockholders. (p. 830)

Dividend yield The dividend paid on a stock expressed as a percentage of the stock price. (p. 831)

Dumping The sale by a foreign firm of exports at a lower price than the cost of production. (p. 798)

Dynamic comparative advantage A comparative advantage that a person or country possesses as a result of having specialized in a particular activity and then, as a result of learning-by-doing, having become the producer with the lowest opportunity cost. (p. 45)

Earnings A firm's accounting profit. (p. 831)

Economic growth The expansion of production possibilities that results from capital accumulation and technological change. (pp. 40, 439)

Economic growth rate The percentage change in the quantity of goods and services produced from one year to the next. (p. 468)

Economic model A description of some aspect of the economic world that includes only those features of the world that are needed for the purpose at hand. (p. 12)

Economic theory A generalization that summarizes what we think we understand about the economic choices that people make and the performance of industries and entire economies. (p. 12)

Economic welfare A comprehensive measure of the general state of economic well-being. (p. 468)

Economics The social science that studies the choices that we make as we cope with scarcity and the institutions that have evolved to influence and reconcile our choices. (p. 2)

Efficiency wage A real wage rate that is set above the full-employment equilibrium wage rate and that balances the costs and benefits of this higher wage rate to maximize the firm's profit. (p. 694)

Employment-to-population ratio The percentage of people of working age who have jobs. (p. 482)

Entrants People who enter the labour force. (p. 485)

Entrepreneurship The human resource that organizes the other three factors of production: labour, land, and capital. Entrepreneurs come up with new ideas about what and how to produce, make business decisions, and bear the risks that arise from their decisions. (p. 4)

Equation of exchange An equation that states that the quantity of money multiplied by the velocity of circulation equals GDP. (p. 656)

Equilibrium expenditure The level of aggregate expenditure that occurs when aggregate planned expenditure equals real GDP. (p. 536)

Equilibrium price The price at which the quantity demanded equals the quantity supplied. (p. 70)

Equilibrium quantity The quantity bought and sold at the equilibrium price. (p. 70)

Equity capital The value of a firm's stock—also called the firm's equity. (p. 830)

Excess reserves A bank's actual reserves minus its desired reserves. (p. 587)

Exchange rate The price at which the Canadian dollar exchanges for another currency. (p. 596)

Expansion A business cycle phase between a trough and a peak—a phase in which real GDP increases. (p. 440)

Expansionary fiscal policy An increase in government expenditures or a decrease in taxes. (p. 569)

Exports The goods and services that we sell to people in other countries. (pp. 460, 786)

Factors of production The resources that businesses use to produce goods and services. (p. 4)

Federal budget The annual statement of the outlays and revenues of the government of Canada, together with the laws and regulations that approve and support those outlays and revenues. (p. 556)

Feedback-rule policy A rule that specifies how policy actions respond to changes in the state of the economy. (p. 763)

Final good An item that is bought by its final user during a specified time period. (p. 458)

Financial innovation The development of new financial products—new ways of borrowing and lending. (p. 591)

Fiscal policy The government's attempt to achieve macroeconomic objectives such as full employment, sustained economic growth, and price level stability by setting and changing taxes, making transfer payments, and purchasing goods and services. (pp. 451, 507, 556)

Fixed-rule policy A rule that specifies an action to be pursued independently of the state of the economy. (p. 763)

Flow A quantity per unit of time. (p. 461)

Foreign exchange market The market in which the currency of one country is exchanged for the currency of another. (p. 815)

Foreign exchange rate The price at which one currency exchanges for another. (p. 815)

Frictional unemployment The unemployment that arises from normal labour turnover—from people entering and leaving the labour force and from the ongoing creation and destruction of jobs. (p. 487)

Full employment A situation in which the quantity of labour demanded equals the quantity supplied. At full employment, there is no cyclical unemployment—all unemployment is frictional, structural, and seasonal. (p. 488)

GDP deflator One measure of the price level, which is the average of current-year prices as a percentage of base-year prices. (p. 466)

General Agreement on Tariffs and Trade An international agreement signed in 1947 to reduce tariffs on international trade. (p. 793)

Goods and services All the objects that people value and produce to satisfy their wants. (p. 3)

Government budget deficit The deficit that arises when the government spends more than it collects in taxes. (p. 449)

Government budget surplus The surplus that arises when the government collects more in taxes than it spends. (p. 449)

Government debt The total amount of borrowing that the government has undertaken. It equals the sum of past budget deficits minus the sum of past budget surpluses. (p. 559)

Government deposit shifting The transfer of government funds by the Bank of Canada from the government's account at the Bank of Canada to its accounts at the chartered banks or from the government's accounts at the chartered banks to its account at the Bank of Canada. (p. 610)

Government expenditures Goods and services bought by the government. (p. 460)

Government expenditures multiplier The magnification effect of a change in government expenditures on goods and services on equilibrium expenditure and real GDP (p. 562)

Government sector balance An amount equal to net taxes minus government expenditures on goods and services. (p. 813)

Great Depression A decade (1929–1939) of high unemployment and stagnant production throughout the world economy. (p. 438)

Gross domestic product (GDP) The market value of all final goods and services produced within a country during a given time period. (p. 458)

Gross investment The total amount spent on purchases of new capital and on replacing depreciated capital. (p. 461)

Growth accounting A method of calculating how much real GDP growth results from growth of labour and capital and how much is attributable to technological change. (p. 713)

Growth rate cycle downturn A pronounced, pervasive, and persistent decline in the growth rate of aggregate economic activity. (p. 478)

Growth recession A slowdown in the growth rate of real GDP but with the growth rate not becoming negative. (p. 440)

Human capital The knowledge and skill that people obtain from education, on-the-job training, and work experience. (pp. 4, 681)

Imports The goods and services that we buy from people in other countries. (pp. 460, 786)

Incentive An inducement to take a particular action. (p. 11)

Induced expenditure The sum of the components of aggregate planned expenditure that vary with real GDP. Induced expenditure equals consumption expenditure minus imports. (p. 535)

Induced taxes Taxes that vary with real GDP. (p. 565)

Infant-industry argument The argument that it is necessary to protect a new industry to enable it to grow into a mature industry that can compete in world markets. (p. 797)

Inferior good A good for which demand decreases as income increases. (p. 64)

Inflation A rising cost of living—a process in which the price level is rising and money is losing value. (pp. 7, 447, 650)

Inflationary gap The amount by which real GDP exceeds potential GDP. (p. 511)

Inflation rate The percentage change in the price level from one year to the next. (p. 492)

Interest The income that capital earns. (p. 5)

Interest rate The amount received by a lender and paid by a borrower expressed as a percentage of the amount of the loan. (p. 594)

Interest rate parity A situation in which the rates of return on assets in different currencies are equal. (p. 822)

Interest-sensitive expenditure curve The relationship between aggregate expenditure plans and the real interest rate when all other influences on expenditure plans remain the same. (p. 598)

Intermediate good An item that is produced by one firm, bought by another firm, and used as a component of a final good or service. (p. 458)

International crowding out The tendency for an expansionary fiscal policy to decrease net exports. (p. 633)

Inverse relationship A relationship between variables that move in opposite directions. (p. 21)

Investment The purchase of new plant, equipment, and buildings and additions to inventories. (p. 460)

Job leavers People who voluntarily quit their jobs. (p. 485)

Job losers People who are laid off, either permanently or temporarily, from their jobs. (p. 485)

Job rationing The practice of paying a real wage rate above the equilibrium level and then rationing jobs by some method. (p. 694)

Job search The activity of looking for an acceptable vacant job. (p. 693)

Keynesian A macroeconomist who regards the economy as being inherently unstable and requiring active government intervention to achieve stability. (p. 638)

Keynesian activist An economist who believes that fluctuations in aggregate demand combined with sticky wages (and/or sticky prices) are the main source of economic fluctuations. (p. 764)

Keynesian theory of the business cycle A theory that regards volatile expectations as the main source of economic fluctuations. (p. 731)

Labour The work time and work effort that people devote to producing goods and services. (p. 4)

Labour force The sum of the people who are employed and who are unemployed. (pp. 444, 480)

Labour force participation rate The percentage of the working-age population who are members of the labour force. (p. 482)

Labour productivity Real GDP per hour of labour. (pp. 681, 713)

Land All the gifts of nature that we use to produce goods and services. (p. 4)

Law of demand Other things remaining the same, the higher the price of a good, the smaller is the quantity demanded of it. (p. 61)

Law of diminishing returns As a firm uses more of a variable input, with a given quantity of other inputs (fixed inputs), the marginal product of the variable input eventually diminishes. (pp. 683, 714)

Law of supply Other things remaining the same, the higher the price of a good, the greater is the quantity supplied of it. (p. 66)

Learning-by-doing People become more productive in an activity (learn) just by repeatedly producing a particular good or service (doing). (pp. 45, 681)

Linear relationship A relationship between two variables that is illustrated by a straight line. (p. 28)

Liquidity The property of being instantly convertible into a means of payment with little loss in value. (p. 584)

Long-run aggregate supply curve The relationship between the quantity of real GDP supplied and the price level in the long run when real GDP equals potential GDP. (pp. 500, 687)

Long-run macroeconomic equilibrium A situation that occurs when real GDP equals potential GDP—the economy is on its long-run aggregate supply curve. (p. 509)

Long-run neutrality The proposition that in the long run, a change in the quantity of money changes the price level and leaves all real variables unchanged. (p. 641)

Long-run Phillips curve A curve that shows the relationship between inflation and unemployment when the actual inflation rate equals the expected inflation rate. (p. 664)

M1 A measure of money that consists of currency held outside the banks plus demand deposits at chartered banks that are owned by individuals and businesses. (p. 583)

M2+ A measure of money that consists of M1 plus personal savings deposits, and nonpersonal notice deposits at chartered banks plus all types of deposits at trust and mortgage loan companies, credit unions, caisses populaires, and other financial institutions. (p. 583)

Macroeconomic long run A time frame that is sufficiently long for real GDP to return to potential GDP so

that full employment prevails. (p. 500)

Macroeconomic short run A period during which real GDP has fallen below or risen above potential GDP. (p. 501)

Macroeconomics The study of the effects on the national economy and the global economy of the choices that individuals, businesses, and governments make. (p. 2)

Margin When a choice is changed by a small amount or by a little at a time, the choice is made at the margin. (p. 11)

Marginal benefit The benefit that a person receives from consuming one more unit of a good or service. It is measured as the maximum amount that a person is willing to pay for one more unit of the good or service. (pp. 11, 38)

Marginal benefit curve A curve that shows the relationship between the marginal benefit of a good and the quantity of that good consumed. (p. 38)

Marginal cost The opportunity cost of producing one more unit of a good or service. It is the best alternative forgone. It is calculated as the increase in total cost divided by the increase in output. (pp. 11, 37)

Marginal product of labour The additional real GDP produced by an additional hour of labour when all other influences on production remain the same. (p. 683)

Marginal propensity to consume The fraction of a change in disposable income that is consumed. It is calculated as the change in consumption expenditure divided by the change in disposable income. (p. 530)

Marginal propensity to import The fraction of an increase in real GDP that is spent on imports. (p. 533)

Marginal propensity to save The fraction of an increase in disposable income that is saved. It is calculated as the change in saving divided by the change in disposable income. (p. 530)

Market Any arrangement that enables buyers and sellers to get information and to do business with each other. (p. 46)

Means of payment A method of settling a debt. (p. 582)

Microeconomics The study of the choices that individuals and businesses make, the way those choices interact, and the influence governments exert on them. (p. 2)

Minimum wage A regulation that makes the hiring of labour below a specified wage rate illegal. (p. 695)

Monetarist A macroeconomist who believes that fluctuations in the quantity of money are the main source of economic fluctuations. (pp. 638, 764)

Monetarist theory of the business cycle A theory that regards fluctuations in the quantity of money as the main source of economic fluctuations. (p. 732)

Monetary base The sum of the Bank of Canada notes outside the Bank of Canada, chartered banks' deposits at the Bank of Canada, and coins held by households and firms. (p. 607)

Monetary policy The attempt to control inflation and moderate the business cycle by changing the quantity of money and adjusting interest rates and the exchange rate. (pp. 451, 507, 606)

Monetary policy indicators The current features of the economy that the Bank of Canada looks at to determine whether it needs to apply the brake or the accelerator to the economy to influence its future real GDP growth, unemployment, and inflation. (p. 608)

Money Any commodity or token that is generally acceptable as the means of payment. (p. 582)

Money multiplier The amount by which a change in the monetary base is multiplied to determine the resulting change in the quantity of money. (p. 613)

Money wage rate The number of dollars that an hour of labour earns. (p. 683)

Multiplier The amount by which a change in autonomous expenditure is magnified or multiplied to determine the change in equilibrium expenditure and real GDP. (p. 538)

National saving The sum of private saving (saving by households and businesses) and government saving. (p. 461)

Natural rate of unemployment The unemployment rate when the economy is at full employment. There is no cyclical unemployment; all unemployment is frictional, structural, and seasonal. (pp. 488, 500)

Negative relationship A relationship between variables that move in opposite directions. (p. 21)

Neoclassical growth theory A theory of economic growth that proposes that real GDP per person grows because technological change induces a level of saving and investment that makes capital per hour of labour grow. (p. 719)

Net borrower A country that is borrowing more from the rest of the world than it is lending to it. (p. 812)

Net exports The value of exports minus the value of imports. (pp. 460, 786, 813)

Net investment Net increase in the capital stock—gross investment minus depreciation. (p. 461)

Net lender A country that is lending more to the rest of the world than it is borrowing from it. (p. 812)

Net taxes Taxes paid to governments minus transfer payments received from governments. (p. 460)

New classical theory of the business cycle A rational expectations theory of the business cycle that regards unanticipated fluctuations in aggregate demand as the main source of economic fluctuations. (p. 734)

New growth theory A theory of economic growth based on the idea that real GDP per person grows because of the choices that people make in the pursuit of profit and that growth can persist indefinitely. (p. 721)

New Keynesian theory of the business cycle A rational expectations theory of the business cycle that regards unanticipated fluctuations in aggregate demand as the main source of economic fluctuations but leaves room for anticipated demand fluctuations to play a role. (p. 734)

Nominal GDP The value of the final goods and services produced in a given year valued at the prices that

prevailed in that same year. It is a more precise name for GDP. (p. 465)

Nominal interest rate The percentage return on an asset such as a bond expressed in terms of money. (p. 597)

Nontariff barrier Any action other than a tariff that restricts international trade. (p. 793)

Normal good A good for which demand increases as income increases. (p. 64)

North American Free Trade Agreement An agreement, which became effective on January 1, 1994, to eliminate all barriers to international trade between the United States, Canada, and Mexico after a 15-year phasing-in period. (p. 794)

Official Canadian reserves The government's holdings of foreign currency. (p. 810)

Official settlements account A record of the change in a country's official reserves. (p. 810)

One-third rule The rule that, with no change in technology, a 1 percent increase in capital per hour of labour brings, on the average, a one-third of 1 percent increase in real GDP per hour of labour. (p. 714)

Open market operation The purchase or sale of government of Canada securities—Treasury bills and government bonds—by the Bank of Canada from or to a chartered bank or the public. (p. 609)

Opportunity cost The highest-valued alternative that we give up to get something. (p. 11)

Output-inflation tradeoff A tradeoff that arises because a policy action that lowers inflation also lowers output and a policy action that boosts output also increases inflation. (p. 10)

Overnight loans rate The interest rate on large-scale loans that chartered banks make to each other and to dealers in financial markets. (p. 608)

Peak The point at which a business cycle turns from expansion into recession. (p. 440)

Phillips curve A curve that shows a relationship between inflation and unemployment. (p. 662)

Policy conflict A situation in which the government and the Bank of Canada pursue different goals and the actions of one make it harder for the other to achieve its goals. (p. 642)

Policy coordination A situation in which the government and the Bank of Canada work together to achieve a common set of goals. (p. 642)

Positive relationship A relationship between two variables that move in the same direction. (p. 20)

Potential GDP The quantity of real GDP at full employment. (pp. 439, 489)

Preferences A description of a person's likes and dislikes. (p. 38)

Price-earnings ratio The stock price divided by the most recent year's earnings. (p. 831)

Price level The average level of prices as measured by a price index. (pp. 447, 466)

Private sector balance An amount equal to saving minus investment. (p. 813)

Production efficiency A situation in which the economy cannot produce more of one good without producing less of some other good. (p. 35)

Production function The relationship between real GDP and the quantity of labour employed when all other influences on production remain the same. (p. 680)

Production possibilities frontier The boundary between the combinations of goods and services that can be produced and the combinations that cannot. (p. 34)

Productivity curve A relationship that shows how real GDP per hour of labour changes as the amount of capital per hour of labour changes with a given state of technology. (p. 713)

Profit The income earned by entrepreneurship. (p. 5)

Property rights Social arrangements that govern the ownership, use, and disposal of resources or factors of production, goods, and services that are enforceable in the courts. (p. 46)

Provincial budget The annual statement of the outlays and revenues of a provincial government, together with the laws and regulations that approve and support those outlays and revenues. (p. 556)

Purchasing power parity The equal value of different monies. (p. 822)

Quantity demanded The amount of a good or service that consumers plan to buy during a given time period at a particular price. (p. 61)

Quantity of labour demanded The number of labour hours hired by all the firms in the economy. (p. 683)

Quantity of labour supplied The number of labour hours that all households in the economy plan to work. (p. 685)

Quantity supplied The amount of a good or service that producers plan to sell during a given time period at a particular price. (p. 66)

Quantity theory of money The proposition that in the long run, an increase in the quantity of money brings an equal percentage increase in the price level. (p. 656)

Quota A quantitative restriction on the import of a particular good, which specifies the maximum amount that can be imported in a given time period. (p. 796)

Rate of return The return on a stock expressed as a percentage of the stock price. (p. 831)

Rational expectation The most accurate forecast possible, a forecast that uses all the available information, including knowledge of the relevant economic forces that influence the variable being forecasted. (pp. 659, 734, 837)

Real business cycle theory A theory that regards random fluctuations in productivity as the main source of economic fluctuations. (p. 737)

Real GDP (Real gross domestic product) The value of final goods and services produced in a given year when valued at constant prices. (pp. 439, 465)

Real interest rate The percentage return on an asset expressed in terms of what money will buy. It is the nominal interest rate adjusted for inflation and is approximately equal to the nominal interest rate minus the inflation rate. (p. 597)

Real wage rate The quantity of goods and services that an hour's work can buy. It is equal to the money wage rate divided by the price level and multiplied by 100. (pp. 484, 683)

Realized capital gain A capital gain that is obtained when a stock is sold for a higher price than the price paid for it. (p. 843)

Recession A significant decline in activity spread across the economy, lasting for more than a few months, visible in industrial production, employment, real income, and wholesale-retail trade. (p. 440)

Recessionary gap The amount by which potential GDP exceeds real GDP. (p. 510)

Re-entrants People who re-enter the labour force. (p. 485)

Relative price The ratio of the price of one good or service to the price of another good or service. A relative price is an opportunity cost. (p. 60)

Rent The income that land earns. (p. 5)

Rent seeking Lobbying and other political activity that seek to capture the gains from trade. (p. 800)

Reserve ratio The fraction of a bank's total deposits that are held in reserves. (p. 587)

Reserves Cash in a bank's vault plus the bank's deposits at the Bank of Canada. (p. 585)

Return The return on a stock is the sum of the stock's dividend plus its capital gain (or minus its capital loss). (p. 831)

Risk premium The additional return that is earned for bearing an additional risk. (p. 840)

Saving The amount of income that households have left after they have paid their taxes and bought their consumption goods and services. (p. 460)

Saving function The relationship between saving and disposable income, other things remaining the same. (p. 528)

Saving rate Saving as a percentage of disposable income. (p. 843)

Scarcity The state in which the resources available are insufficient to satisfy people's wants. (p. 2)

Scatter diagram A diagram that plots the value of one variable against the value of another. (p. 19)

Seasonal unemployment Unemployment that arises because the number of jobs available has decreased because of the season. (p. 488)

Short-run aggregate supply curve A curve that shows the relationship between the quantity of real GDP supplied and the price level in the short run when the money wage rate, other resource prices, and potential GDP remain constant. (pp. 501, 687)

Short-run macroeconomic equilibrium A situation that occurs when the quantity of real GDP demanded equals the quantity of real GDP supplied—at the point of intersection of the *AD* curve and the *SAS* curve. (p. 508)

Short-run Phillips curve A curve that shows the tradeoff between inflation and unemployment, when the expected inflation rate and the natural rate of unemployment remain the same. (p. 662)

Slope The change in the value of the variable measured on the *y*-axis divided by the change in the value of the variable measured on the *x*-axis. (p. 24)

Speculative bubble A price increase followed by a price plunge, both of which occur because people expect them to occur and act on that expectation. (p. 838)

Standard of living The level of consumption that people enjoy, on the average, and is measured by average income per person. (p. 6)

Stock A quantity that exists at a point in time. (p. 461)

Stock A tradable security that a firm issues to certify that the stockholder owns a share of the firm. (p. 830)

Stock exchange An organized market on which people can buy and sell stock. (p. 830)

Stock price The price at which one

share of a firm's stock trades on a stock exchange. (p. 831)

Structural surplus or deficit The budget balance that would occur if the economy were at full employment and real GDP were equal to potential GDP. (p. 567)

Structural unemployment The unemployment that arises when changes in technology or international competition change the skills needed to perform jobs or change the locations of jobs. (p. 488)

Subsistence real wage rate The minimum real wage rate needed to maintain life. (p. 718)

Substitute A good that can be used in place of another good. (p. 63)

Supply The relationship between the quantity of a good that producers plan to sell and the price of the good when all other influences on producers' plans remain the same. It is described by a supply schedule and illustrated by a supply curve. (p. 66)

Supply curve A curve that shows the relationship between the quantity supplied and the price of a good when all other influences on producers' planned sales remain the same. (p. 66)

Supply of labour The relationship between the quantity of labour supplied and the real wage rate when all other influences on work plans remain the same. (p. 685)

Tariff A tax that is imposed by the importing country when an imported good crosses its international boundary. (p. 793)

Technological change The development of new goods and of better ways of producing goods and services. (p. 40)

Terms of trade The quantity of goods and services that a country exports to pay for its imports of goods and services. (p. 788)

Time-series graph A graph that measures time (for example, months or years) on the x-axis and the variable or variables in which we are interested on the y-axis. (p. 18)

Tradeoff A constraint that involves giving up one thing to get something else. (p. 9)

Trend The general tendency for a variable to move in one direction. (p. 18)

Trough The point at which a business cycle turns from recession into expansion. (p. 440)

Trust and mortgage loan company A privately owned depository institution that operates under the Trust and Loan Companies Act of 1992. (p. 586)

Twin deficits The tendency for the government budget deficit and the current account deficit to move in the same direction. (p. 814)

Unemployment A state in which a person does not have a job but is available for work, willing to work, and has made some effort to find work within the previous four weeks. (p. 444)

Unemployment rate The percentage of the people in the labour force who are unemployed. (pp. 444, 481)

Velocity of circulation The average number of times a dollar of money is used annually to buy the goods and services that make up GDP. (p. 656)

Voluntary export restraint An agreement between two governments in which the government of the exporting country agrees to restrain the volume of its own exports. (p. 796)

Wages The income that labour earns. (p. 5)

Wealth The market value of all the things that people own—the market value of their assets.(pp. 461, 843)

Wealth effect The influence of wealth on consumption expenditure and saving. (p. 843)

Working-age population The total number of people aged 15 years and over. (p. 480)

World Trade Organization An international organization that places greater obligations on its member countries to observe the GATT rules. (p. 793)

INDEX

Key terms and pages on which they are defined appear in **boldface**.

CREDITS

Photo Credits

Part 1: p. 54, Corbis-Bettman; p. 55 (left), Culver Pictures, p. 55 (right), Bruce Ando/Tony Stone Images.

Part 2: p. 148, Stock Montage; p. 149 (left), National Archives; p. 149 (right), PhotoDisc, Inc.

Part 7: p. 522, Stock Montage; p. 523 (left), Corbis-Bettman; p. 523 (right), Mug Shots, First Light.

Part 8: p. 674, Marshall Henrichs/Addison-Wesley; p. 675 (left), UPI/Corbis-Bettman; p. 675 (right), © Carlos Humberto TDC/Contact Press Images.

Part 9: p. 780, Corbis-Bettman; p. 781 (left), North Wind Picture Archives; p. 781 (right), PhotoDisc, Inc.; p. 782, Christopher Irion.

Part 10: p. 852, Corbis-Bettman; p. 853 (left), North Wind Picture Archives; p. 853 (right), © M. Timothy O'Keefe/Weststock.

Figure and Table Credits

The sources below were extracted from the Statistics Canada CANSIM II database <http://cansim2.statcan.ca/cgi-win/CNSMCGI.EXE>.

Figure 1.4: "The Distribution of Income in Canada," adapted from the Statistics Canada Publication "National Income and Expenditure Accounts," Quarterly Estimates, Third Quarter 2002, Catalogue 13-001.

Figure 19.1: "Economic Growth in Canada," adapted from the Statistics Canada CANSIM II database, v1992292.

Figure 19.2: "The Most Recent Canadian Business Cycle," adapted from the Statistics Canada CANSIM II database, v1992292.

Figure 19.3: "Long-Term Growth, Economic Growth in Canada," adapted from the Statistics Canada CANSIM II database, v1992292, and from the Statistics Canada publication *Historical Statistics of Canada*, catalogue 11-516, series F55, 1983.

Figure 19.6: "Unemployment in Canada," adapted from the Statistics Canada CANSIM II database, table 282-0002, and from the Statistics Canada publication *Historical Statistics of Canada*, catalogue 11-516, 1983.

Figure 20.1: "The Circular Flow of Expenditure and Income," adapted from the Statistics Canada CANSIM II database, table 380-0002.

Table 20.1: "The Expenditure Approach," adapted from the Statistics Canada CANSIM II database, table 380-0002.

Table 20.2: "GDP: The Income Approach," adapted from the Statistics Canada CANSIM II database, table 380-0001.

Figure 20.3: "GDP: The Income Approach," adapted from the Statistics Canada CANSIM II database, table 380-0003.

Figure 21.1: Business cycle dates and growth cycle dates: the Economic Cycle Research Institute; Real GDP, Statistics Canada, CANSIM II database, v1992292.

Figure 21.2: "Population Labour Force Categories," adapted from the Statistics Canada CANSIM II database, tables 282-0002 and 051-0001, and from the Statistics Canada publication *Labour Force Historical Review*, catalogue 71F0004, 2001.

Figure 21.3: "Employment, Unemployment and the Labour Force: 1961–2001," adapted from the Statistics Canada CANSIM II database, tables 282-0002, and from the Statistics Canada publication *Labour Force Historical Review*, catalogue 71F0004, 2001.

Figures 21.4, 21.5: "The Changing Face of the Labour Market," data calculated and adapted from the Statistics Canada CANSIM II database, table 282-0002.

Figure 21.6: "Real Wage Rates: 1961–2001," data calculated from the Statistics Canada CANSIM II database, tables 282-0002, 282-0022, and 380-0001.

Figure 21.8: "Unemployment by Reason," adapted from the Statistics Canada publication *Labour Force Historical Review*, catalogue 71F0004, 2001.

Figure 21.9: "Unemployment by Duration," adapted from the Statistics Canada publication *Labour Force Historical Review*, catalogue 71F0004, 2001.

Figure 21.10: "Unemployment by Demographic Group," adapted from the Statistics Canada CANSIM II database, table 282-0002.

Figure 21.11: "Unemployment and the Real GDP," adapted from the Statistics Canada CANSIM II database, tables 282-0002 and 380-0002.

Figure 21.12: "The CPI Basket," adapted from the Statistics Canada publication *Your Guide to the Consumer Price Index*, catalogue 62-557, 1996.

Figure 21.13: "The CPI and the Inflation Rate," adapted from the Statistics Canada CANSIM II database, table 326-0002.

Figure 22.14: "Aggregate Supply and Aggregate Demand 1961–2001," adapted from the Statistics Canada CANSIM II database, tables 326-0002 and 380-0003.

Figure 23.4: "The Canadian Consumption Function," data calculated from the Statistics Canada CANSIM II database, tables 380-0002, 384-0013, and 384-0035.

Figure 24.1: "Revenues, Outlays, and the Budget Balance," adapted from the Statistics Canada CANSIM II database, tables 380-0002 and 380-0007.

Figure 24.2: "Federal Government Revenues," adapted from the Statistics Canada CANSIM II database, tables 380-0002 and 380-0007.

Figure 24.3: "Federal Government Outlays," adapted from the Statistics Canada CANSIM II database, tables 380-0002 and 380-0007.

Figure 24.4: "Federal Government Debt," adapted from the Statistics Canada CANSIM II database, tables 380-0002 and 385-0010.

Figure 24.5: "Provincial Government Budgets," adapted from the Statistics Canada CANSIM II database, tables 384-0002 and 385-0002.

Figure 24.6: "Total Government Budgets," adapted from the Statistics Canada CANSIM II database, tables 380-0002 and 380-0007.

Figure 24.10: "The Business Cycle and the Budget Deficit," adapted from the Statistics Canada CANSIM II database, tables 380-0002 and 380-0007.

Figure 28.7: "Money Growth and Inflation in Canada," data calculated from the Statistics Canada CANSIM database, tables 176-0020 and 380-0056.

Figure 28.14: "Phillips Curves in Canada," data calculated from the Statistics Canada CANSIM II database, tables 380-0002 and 380-0056.

Figure 28.15: "Inflation and the Interest Rate," data calculated in part from the Statistics Canada CANSIM II database, tables 176-0043 and 380-0056.

Figure 30.6: "Growth Accounting and the Productivity Growth Slowdown," data calculated from the Statistics Canada CANSIM II database, tables 282-0002, 378-0004, and 380-0002.

Figure 31.6: "The Real Business Cycle Impulse," data calculated from the Statistics Canada CANSIM II database, tables 282-0002, 378-0004, and 380-0002.

Figure 31.10: "U.S. and Canadian Real GDP Growth: 1989–1995," data calculated in part from the Statistics Canada CANSIM II database, table 380-0002.

Figure 31.12: "Employment and Real Wages," data calculated from the Statistics Canada CANSIM II database, tables 282-0002, 282-0022, and 380-0001.

Figure 32.1: "Macroeconomic Performance: Read GDP and Inflation," data calculated from the Statistics Canada CANSIM II database, table 380-0002.

Figure 32.2: "The Fiscal Policy Record: A Summary," adapted from the Statistics Canada CANSIM II database, tables 380-0002 and 380-0007.

Figure 32.4: "Savings Rate in Canada: 1970–2001," adapted from the Statistics Canada CANSIM II database, table 380-0031.

Figure 33.5: "Canadian Tariffs: 1867–2001," adapted from the Statistics Canada CANSIM II database, tables 380-0002 and 380-0007, and from the Statistics Canada publication *Historical Statistics of Canada*, catalogue 11-516, series G485, 1983.

Table 34.1: "Canadian Balance of Payments Accounts in 2001," adapted from the Statistics Canada CANSIM II database, tables 376-0001 and 376-0002.

Figure 34.1: "The Balance of Payments: 1981–2001," adapted from the Statistics Canada CANSIM II database, tables 376-0001 and 376-0002.

Table 34.2: "Net Exports, the Government Budget, Saving and Investment," adapted from the Statistics Canada CANSIM database, tables 380-0002 and 380-0034.

Figure 34.2: "The Twin Deficits," adapted from the Statistics Canada CANSIM II database, tables 376-0001 and 376-0007.

Figure 35.8: "Two Views of the Personal Saving Rate," adapted from the Statistics Canada CANSIM II database, tables 378-0004 and 380-0031.

KEY TERMS AND CONCEPTS

consumer sovereignty 72
command economy 72
market economy 72
mixed economy 72

labor intensive 73
capital intensive 73
product markets 76
factor (or input) markets 76

simple circular flow model 77
production possibilities curve 78
increasing opportunity cost 82

SECTION QUIZ ANSWERS

3.1 The Three Economic Questions Every Society Faces

1. Why does scarcity force us to decide what to produce?
Because our wants exceed the amount of goods and services that can be produced from our limited resources, it must be decided which wants should have priority over others.

2. How is a command economy different from a market economy?
A command economy makes decisions about what and how much to produce centrally by members of a planning board or organization. A market economy makes those decisions as the result of decentralized decision making by individual producers and consumers, coordinated by their offers to buy and sell on markets.

3. How does consumer sovereignty determine production decisions in a market economy?
Consumer sovereignty determines production decisions in a market economy because producers make what they believe consumers will "vote" for by being willing to pay for them.

4. Do you think that what and how much an economy produces depends on who will get the goods and services produced in that economy? Why or why not?
Who will get the goods produced in an economy affects the incentives of the producers. The less a producer will benefit from increased production, the smaller are

incentives to increase production, and the smaller will be total output in an economy.

5. Why do consumers have to "vote" for a product with their dollars for it to be a success?
In the market sector, products can be profitable only if they attract dollar votes from consumers.

6. Why must we choose among multiple ways of producing the goods and services we want?
We must choose among multiple ways of producing the goods and services we want because goods can generally be produced in several ways, using different combinations of resources.

7. Why might production be labor intensive in one economy but be capital intensive in another?
Production will tend to be labor intensive where labor is relatively plentiful, and therefore relatively less expensive; it will tend to be capital intensive where capital is relatively plentiful, and therefore relatively less expensive. When the manner of production is different in different situations because factors of production have different relative prices, each of those methods will be more efficient where they are used.

8. If a tourist from the United States on an overseas trip notices that other countries don't produce crops "like they do back home," would he be right to conclude that farmers in the other countries produce crops less efficiently than U.S. farmers?
No. The different ways of farming in different areas reflect the different relative scarcities of land, labor,

and capital they face. Factors of production that are relatively scarce in an economy are also relatively costly there as a result. Producers there economize on the use of those more costly resources by using more of relatively less scarce, and less costly, resources instead. For example, where land is scarce, it is intensively cultivated with relatively cheaper (less scarce) labor and capital, but where capital is scarce, relatively cheaper (less scarce) land and labor are substituted for capital.

9. In what way does scarcity determine income?
Relative scarcity determines the market values of the scarce resources people offer to others in exchange for income.

10. What are the most important functions of the market system?
They transmit information through price signals, they provide incentives, and they distribute income.

3.2 The Circular Flow Model

1. Why does the circular flow of money move in the opposite direction from the flow of goods and services?
The circular flow of money moves in the opposite direction from the flow of goods and services because the money flows are the payments made in exchange for the goods and services.

2. What is bought and sold in factor markets?
The factors of production—capital, land, labor, and entrepreneurship—are sold in factor, or input, markets.

3. What is bought and sold in product markets?
Consumer and investment goods and services are sold in product markets.

3.3 The Production Possibilities Curve

1. What does a production possibilities curve illustrate?
The production possibilities curve illustrates the potential output combinations of two goods in an economy operating at full capacity, given the inputs and technology available to the economy.

2. How are opportunity costs shown by the production possibilities curve?
Opportunity cost—the forgone output of one good necessary to increase output of another good—is

illustrated by the slope, or trade-off, between the two goods at a given point on the production possibilities curve.

3. Why do the opportunity costs of added production increase with output?
Opportunity costs of added production increase with output because some resources cannot be easily adapted from their current uses to alternative uses. At first, easily adaptable resources can be switched to producing more of a good. But once those easily adapted resources have been switched, producing further output requires the use of resources less well adapted to expanding that output, raising the opportunity cost of output.

4. How does the production possibilities curve illustrate increasing opportunity costs?
Increasing opportunity costs are illustrated by a bowed (concave from below) production possibilities curve. It shows that initial units of one good can be produced by giving up little of another good, but progressive increases in output will require greater and greater sacrifices of the other good.

5. Why are we concerned with widespread amounts of unemployed or underemployed resources in a society?
We are concerned with widespread amounts of unemployed or underemployed resources in a society because, if we could reduce the extent of unemployed or underemployed resources, people could have more scarce goods and services available for their use.

6. What do we mean by *efficiency*, and how is it related to underemployment of resources?
Efficiency means getting the most we can out of our scarce resources. Underemployment of resources means a society is not getting the most it can out of these resources, either because they are not fully employed or because they are not matched to the uses best suited to them.

7. How are efficiency and inefficiency illustrated by a production possibilities curve?
Efficient combinations of outputs are illustrated by points on the production possibilities curve, along which more of one good can be produced only if less of some other good is also produced. Inefficient combinations of outputs are illustrated by points inside the production possibilities curve because more of both goods could then be produced with the resources available to the economy.

8. Will a country that makes being unemployed illegal be more productive than one that does not? Why or why not?

A more productive economy is one that makes the best use of those who wish to work. Making unemployment illegal (as was true in the old USSR) does not eliminate underemployment, nor does it guarantee that people and other resources are employed where they are most productive (especially because it is more difficult to search for a better job when you are working than when you are not working).

9. If a 68-year-old worker in the United States chooses not to work at all, does that mean that the United States is functioning inside its production possibilities curve? Why or why not?

Individuals who choose retirement rather than work must consider themselves better off not working, when all the relevant considerations are taken into account. They are therefore as fully employed, given their circumstances, as they would like to be, and so the choice does not imply that the United States would be inside its production possibilities curve as a result. However, if such workers became more willing to work, that would shift the U.S. production possibilities curve outward.

3.4 Economic Growth and the Production Possibilities Curve

1. What is the essential question behind issues of economic growth?

The essential question behind issues of economic growth is: How much are we willing to give up today to get more in the future?

2. What is the connection between sacrifices and economic growth?

The more current consumption is sacrificed in an economy, the larger the fraction of its current resources it can devote to producing investment goods, which will increase its rate of economic growth.

3. How is economic growth shown in terms of production possibilities curves?

Economic growth—the expansion of what an economy can produce—is shown as an outward shift in the production possibilities curve, with formerly unattainable output combinations now made possible.

4. Why doesn't economic growth eliminate scarcity?

Economic growth doesn't eliminate scarcity because people's wants still exceed what they are capable of producing, so that trade-offs among scarce goods must still be made.

5. If people reduced their saving (thus reducing the funds available for investment), what would that change do to society's production possibilities curve over time?

The less people save, the slower the capital stock of the economy will grow through new investment (because saving is the source of the funds for investment), and so the slower the production possibilities curve would shift out over time.

PROBLEMS

1. What are the three basic economic questions? How are decisions made differently in a market economy than in planned economies?

2. Recently the American Film Institute selected *Citizen Kane* as the best movie of all time. *Citizen Kane* is a fictional psychological biography of one of the most powerful newspaper publishers in history, William Randolph Hearst. *Avatar* has made the most money of any film in history. Unlike *Avatar*, *Citizen Kane* was not a box office success. Do you think Hollywood will make more movies like *Avatar* or like *Citizen Kane*? Why?

3. As women's wages and employment opportunities have expanded over the past 50 years, Americans have purchased more and more labor-saving home appliances like automatic washers and dryers, dishwashers, and microwave ovens. Do you think these phenomena are related? Could higher wages and better job opportunities lead to a more capital-intensive way of performing household chores? Explain.

4. Identify where the appropriate entries go in the circular flow diagram.

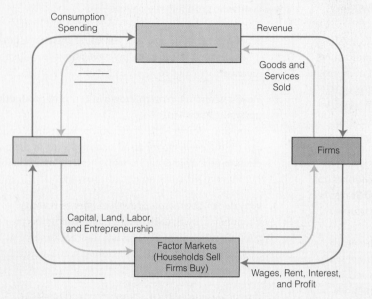

5. Identify whether each of the following transactions takes place in the factor market or the product market.
   a. Billy buys a sofa from Home Time Furniture for his new home.
   b. Home Time Furniture pays its manager her weekly salary.
   c. The manager buys dinner at Billy's Café.
   d. After he pays all of his employees their wages and pays his other bills, the owner of Billy's Café takes his profit.

6. Given the following production possibilities curve:

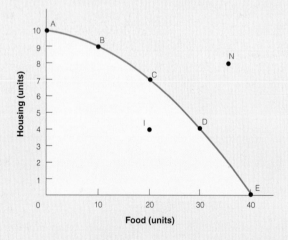

   a. Does this production possibilities curve show increasing opportunity costs? Explain.
   b. What is the opportunity cost of moving from point I to point D? Explain.
   c. What is the opportunity cost of moving from point C to point B?
   d. Which of points A–E is the most efficient? Explain.

7. During wartime, countries shift production from civilian goods, like automobiles and clothing, to military goods, like tanks and military uniforms. When the United States entered World War I in April 1917, for example, the federal government created the War Industries Board and charged it with determining production priorities and converting plants to meet war needs. In the following year, automobile production fell 43 percent as output of military vehicles soared. When the war ended, 19 months later, in November 1918, the government cancelled $2.5 billion in military contracts and the nation resumed normal production. Assuming that in 1917 the United States was at point A on the production possibilities curve shown, show what happened between April 1917 and November 1918. Show what happened once the war ended.

8. How would the following events be shown using a production possibilities curve for housing and food?
    a. The economy is experiencing double-digit unemployment.
    b. Economic growth is increasing at more than 5 percent per year.
    c. Society decides it wants less housing and more food.
    d. Society decides it wants more housing and less food.

9. In *A Bend in the River*, Nobel Prize winner V. S. Naipaul describes a developing country in which the government's constantly changing tax policies and vague laws regarding property ownership cause entrepreneurs to become demoralized and unresponsive to economic opportunities. Could this be a case of idle or unemployed entrepreneurs? How can tax laws and rules governing property affect entrepreneurs' willingness to start new businesses or improve existing enterprises?

10. Using the following table, answer the questions:

			Combinations		
	A	B	C	D	E
Guns	1	2	3	4	5
Butter	20	18	14	8	0

    a. What are the assumptions for a given production possibilities curve?
    b. What is the opportunity cost of one gun when moving from point B to point C? When moving from point D to point E?
    c. Do these combinations demonstrate constant or increasing opportunity costs?

11. Economy A produces more capital goods and fewer consumer goods than Economy B. Which economy will grow more rapidly? Draw two production possibilities curves, one for Economy A and one for Economy B. Demonstrate graphically how one economy can grow more rapidly than the other.

12. Why one nation experiences economic growth and another doesn't is a question that has intrigued economists since Adam Smith wrote *An Inquiry into the Nature and Causes of the Wealth of Nations* in 1776. Explain why each of the following would limit economic growth.
    a. The politically connected elite secure a large share of a country's output and put the proceeds in Swiss banks.
    b. A country has a very low output per person.
    c. The national philosophy is to live for the moment and forget about tomorrow.
    d. The government closes all of the schools so more people will be available for work.
    e. The country fears military invasion and spends half of its income on military goods.

13. How does education add to a nation's capital stock?

14. A politician running for U.S. president promises to build new schools and new space stations during the next four years without sacrificing any other goods and services. Using a production possibilities curve between schools and space stations, explain under what conditions the politician would be able to keep his promise.

PART 2

TECHNOTR/VETTA/GETTY IMAGES

Supply and Demand

Demand, Supply, and Market Equilibrium

Every morning fisherman bring in their daily catch. Along the pier, they negotiate with fish brokers—sellers find buyers and buyers find sellers. Supply and demand is without a doubt the most powerful tool in the economist's toolbox. It can help explain much of what goes on in the world and help predict what will happen tomorrow. In this chapter, we will learn about the law of demand and the law of supply and the factors that can change supply and demand.

We then bring market supply and market demand together to determine equilibrium price and quantity. We also learn how markets with many buyers and sellers adjust to temporary shortages and surpluses.

Markets 4.1

▶ What is a market?   ▶ Why is it so difficult to define a market?

4.1a Defining a Market

The stock market involves many buyers and sellers; and profit statements and stock prices are readily available. New information is quickly understood by buyers and sellers and is incorporated into the price of the stock. When people expect a company to do better in the future, the price of the stock rises; when people expect the company to do poorly in the future, the price of the stock falls.

Although we usually think of a market as a place where some sort of exchange occurs, a market is not really a place at all. A **market** is the process of buyers and sellers exchanging goods and services. Supermarkets, the New York Stock Exchange, drug stores, roadside stands, garage sales, Internet stores, and restaurants are all markets.

Every market is different. That is, the conditions under which the exchange between buyers and sellers takes place can vary. These differences make it difficult to precisely define a market. After all, an incredible variety of exchange arrangements exist in the real world—organized securities markets, wholesale auction markets, foreign exchange markets, real estate markets, labor markets, and so forth. The important point is not what a market looks like, but what it does—it facilitates trade.

market
the process of buyers and sellers exchanging goods and services

Do markets have to be physical places?

ECS

economic content standards

Prices send signals and provide incentives to buyers and sellers. When supply or demand changes, market prices adjust, affecting incentives. Understanding the role of prices as signals and incentives helps people anticipate market opportunities and make better choices as producers and consumers.

4.1b Buyers and Sellers

The roles of buyers and sellers in markets are important. Buyers, as a group, determine the demand side of the market. Buyers include the consumers who purchase the goods and services and the firms that buy inputs—labor, capital, and raw materials. Sellers, as a group, determine the supply side of the market. Sellers include the firms that produce and sell goods and services and the resource owners who sell their inputs to firms—workers who "sell" their labor and resource owners who sell raw materials and capital. The interaction of buyers and sellers determines market prices and outputs—through the forces of supply and demand.

eBay is an Internet auction company that brings together millions of buyers and sellers from all over the world. The gains from these mutually beneficial exchanges are large. Craigslist also uses the power of the Internet to connect many buyers and sellers in local markets.

In the next few chapters, we focus on how supply and demand work in a **competitive market**. A competitive market is one in which a number of buyers and sellers are offering similar products, and no single buyer or seller can influence the market price. That is, buyers and sellers have little market power. Because many markets contain a high degree of competitiveness, the lessons of supply and demand can be applied to many different types of problems.

The supply and demand model is particularly useful in markets like agriculture, finance, labor, construction, services, wholesale, and retail.

In short, a model is only as good as it explains and predicts. The model of supply and demand is very good at predicting changes in prices and quantities in many markets large and small.

competitive market
a market where the many buyers and sellers have little market power—each buyer's or seller's effect on market price is negligible

1. Which of the following is a market?

   a. a garage sale

   b. a restaurant

   c. the New York Stock Exchange

   d. an eBay auction

   e. all of the above

2. In a competitive market,

   a. there are a number of buyers and sellers.

   b. no single buyer or seller can appreciably affect the market price.

   c. sellers offer similar products.

   d. all of the above are true.

3. Buyers determine the _____ side of the market; sellers determine the _____ side of the market.

   a. demand; demand

   b. demand; supply

   c. supply; demand

   d. supply; supply

---

1. Why is it difficult to define a market precisely?

2. Why do you get your produce at a supermarket rather than directly from farmers?

3. Why do the prices people pay for similar items at garage sales vary more than for similar items in a department store?

Answers: 1. e 2. d 3. b

. . . .

4.2 | Demand

▶ What is the law of demand?   ▶ What is a market demand curve?

▶ What is an individual demand curve?

4.2a The Law of Demand

law of demand

the quantity of a good or service demanded varies inversely (negatively) with its price, *ceteris paribus*

Sometimes observed behavior is so pervasive it is called a law—the law of demand, for example. According to the law of demand, the quantity of a good or service demanded varies inversely (negatively) with its price, *ceteris paribus*. More directly, the law of demand says that, other things being equal, when the price (P) of a good or service falls, the quantity demanded (Q_D) increases. Conversely, if the price (P) of a good or service rises, the quantity demanded (Q_D) decreases.

$$P \uparrow \Rightarrow Q_D \downarrow \text{ and } P \downarrow \Rightarrow Q_D \uparrow$$

4.2b Individual Demand

An Individual Demand Schedule

The individual demand schedule shows the relationship between the price of the good and the quantity demanded. For example, suppose Elizabeth enjoys drinking coffee. How many pounds of coffee would Elizabeth be willing and able to buy at various prices during the year? At a price of $3 a pound, Elizabeth buys 15 pounds of coffee over the course of a year. If the price is higher, at $4 per pound, she might buy only 10 pounds; if it is lower, say $1 per pound, she might buy 25 pounds of coffee during the year. Elizabeth's demand for coffee for the year is summarized in the demand schedule in Exhibit 1. Elizabeth might not be consciously aware of the amounts that she would purchase at prices other than the prevailing one, but that does not alter the fact that she has a schedule in the sense that she would have bought various other amounts had other prices prevailed. It must be emphasized that the schedule is a list of alternative possibilities. At any one time, only one of the prices will prevail, and thus a certain quantity will be purchased.

individual demand schedule

a schedule that shows the relationship between price and quantity demanded

ECS

economic content standards

Higher prices for a good or service provide the incentives for buyers to purchase less. Lower prices for goods or services provide incentives to purchase more of the good or service.

Price of Coffee (per pound)	Quantity of Coffee Demanded (pounds per year)
$5	5
4	10
3	15
2	20
1	25

section 4.2 exhibit 1 Elizabeth's Demand Schedule for Coffee

An Individual Demand Curve

By plotting the different prices and corresponding quantities demanded in Elizabeth's demand schedule in Exhibit 1 and then connecting them, we can create the individual demand curve for Elizabeth shown in Exhibit 2. From the curve, we can see that when the price is higher, the quantity demanded is lower, and when the price is lower, the quantity demanded is higher. The demand curve shows how the quantity of the good demanded changes as its price varies.

individual demand curve

a graphical representation that shows the inverse relationship between price and quantity demanded

section 4.2 exhibit 2 Elizabeth's Demand Curve for Coffee

The dots represent various quantities of coffee that Elizabeth would be willing and able to buy at different prices in a given period. The demand curve shows how the quantity demanded varies inversely with the price of the good when we hold everything else constant—*ceteris paribus*. Because of this inverse relationship between price and quantity demanded, the demand curve is downward sloping.

4.2c What Is a Market Demand Curve?

Although we introduced the concept of the demand curve in terms of the individual, economists usually speak of the demand curve in terms of large groups of people—a whole nation, a community, or a trading area. That is, to analyze how the market works, we will need to use market demand. As you know, every individual has his or her demand curve for every product. The horizontal summing of the demand curves of many individuals is called the market demand curve.

Suppose the consumer group is composed of Peter, Lois, and the rest of their small community, Quahog, and that the product is still coffee. The effect of price on the quantity of coffee demanded by Lois, Peter, and the rest of Quahog is

market demand curve

the horizontal summation of individual demand curves

　　Creating a Market Demand Curve

a. Creating a Market Demand Schedule for Coffee

	Quantity of Coffee Demanded (pounds per year)							
Price (per pound)	Peter	+	Lois	+	Rest of Quahog	=	Market Demand
$4	20	+	10	+	2,970	=	3,000
$3	25	+	15	+	4,960	=	5,000

b. Creating a Market Demand Curve for Coffee

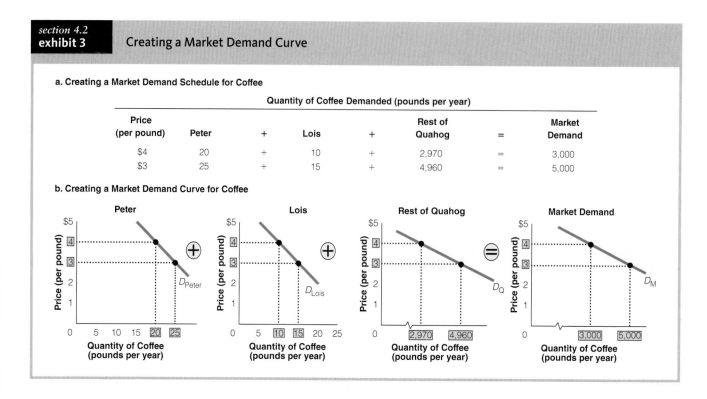

given in the demand schedule and demand curves shown in Exhibit 3. At $4 per pound, Peter would be willing and able to buy 20 pounds of coffee per year, Lois would be willing and able to buy 10 pounds, and the rest of Quahog would be willing and able to buy 2,970 pounds. At $3 per pound, Peter would be willing and able to buy 25 pounds of coffee per year, Lois would be willing and able to buy 15 pounds, and the rest of Quahog would be willing and able to buy 4,960 pounds. The market demand curve is simply the (horizontal) sum of the quantities Peter, Lois, and the rest of Quahog demand at each price. That is, at $4, the quantity demanded in the market would be 3,000 pounds of coffee (20 +10 +2,970 =3,000) , and at $3, the quantity demanded in the market would be 5,000 pounds of coffee (25 +15 +4,960 =5,000).

In Exhibit 4, we offer a more complete set of prices and quantities from the market demand for coffee during the year. Remember, the market demand curve shows the amounts that all the buyers in the market would be willing and able to buy at various prices. For example, when the price of coffee is $2 per pound, consumers in the market collectively would be willing and able to buy 8,000 pounds per year. At $1 per pound, the amount collectively demanded would be 12,000 pounds per year. The market demand curve is the negative (inverse) relationship between price and the quantity demanded, while holding all other factors that affect how much consumers are able and willing to pay constant, *ceteris paribus*. For the most part, we are interested in how the market works, so we will primarily use market demand curves.

4.2d *Ceteris Paribus* and the Law of Demand

When we considered how Elizabeth's demand for coffee is affected by a change in price, we had to hold many other things constant, like her income, her taste, the weather outside, the price of other things that Elizabeth buys, and so on. This *ceteris paribus* assumption allows us to focus on the variable we are interested in, which is the price of coffee.

The *ceteris paribus* assumption also holds when we define a particular good. That is, we are assuming all goods are the same (homogenous). For example, if we are referring

section 4.2
exhibit 4   A Market Demand Curve

a. Market Demand Schedule for Coffee

Price (per pound)	Quantity Demanded (pounds per year)
$5	1,000
4	3,000
3	5,000
2	8,000
1	12,000

b. Market Demand Curve for Coffee

Market Demand Curve

Price (per pound)

Quantity of Coffee
(thousands of pounds per year)

The market demand curve shows the amounts that all the buyers in the market would be willing and able to buy at various prices. We find the market demand curve by adding horizontally the individual demand curves. For example, when the price of coffee is $2 per pound, consumers in the market collectively would be willing and able to buy 8,000 pounds per year. At $1 per pound, the amount collectively demanded would be 12,000 pounds per year.

to the market for frozen yogurt, we would assume that the yogurt is the same size and quality. Not a higher-quality yogurt served in a chocolate-covered waffle cone versus a small scoop in a child-size cup—those would be two different goods. By allowing something other than the price of yogurt to change, you would be violating the *ceteris paribus* assumption.

© ISTOCKPHOTO.COM/HOLGS

Why is gasoline consumption less in Europe than in the United States? The main reason is price. Because of higher taxes, gasoline prices are at least twice as high in Europe. Consequently, Europeans on average consume half as much gasoline—buying smaller cars with better mileage.

SECTION QUIZ

1. If the demand for milk is downward sloping, then an increase in the price of milk will result in a(n)
   a. increase in the demand for milk.
   b. decrease in the demand for milk.
   c. increase in the quantity of milk demanded.
   d. decrease in the quantity of milk demanded.
   e. decrease in the supply of milk.

2. Which of the following is true?
   a. The law of demand states that when the price of a good falls (rises), the quantity demanded rises (falls), *ceteris paribus.*
   b. An individual demand curve is a graphical representation of the relationship between the price and the quantity demanded.
   c. The market demand curve shows the amount of a good that all buyers in the market would be willing and able to buy at various prices.
   d. All of the above are true.

3. Which of the following is true?
   a. The relationship between price and quantity demanded is inverse or negative.
   b. The market demand curve is the vertical summation of individual demand curves.
   c. A change in a good's price causes a movement along its demand curve.
   d. All of the above are true.
   e. Answers (a) and (c) are true.

---

1. What is an inverse relationship?
2. How do lower prices change buyers' incentives?
3. How do higher prices change buyers' incentives?
4. What is an individual demand schedule?
5. What is the difference between an individual demand curve and a market demand curve?
6. Why does the amount of dating on campus tend to decline just before and during final exams?

Answers: 1. d 2. d 3. e

Shifts in the Demand Curve   4.3

▶ What is the difference between a change in demand and a change in quantity demanded?

▶ What are the determinants of demand?

▶ What are substitutes and complements?

▶ What are normal and inferior goods?

▶ How does the number of buyers affect the demand curve?

▶ How do changes in taste affect the demand curve?

▶ How do changing expectations affect the demand curve?

4.3a A Change in Demand versus a Change in Quantity Demanded

Understanding the relationship between price and quantity demanded is so important that economists make a clear distinction between it and the various other factors that can influence consumer behavior. A change in a good's own price is said to lead to a change in quantity demanded. That is, it "moves you along" a given demand curve. The demand curve is the answer to the question: "What happens to the quantity demanded when the price of the good changes?" The demand curve is drawn under the assumption that all other things are held constant, except the price of the good. However, economists know that price is not the only thing that affects the quantity of a good that people buy. The other variables that influence the demand curve are called *determinants of demand,* and a change in these other factors lead to shifts in the demand curve.

change in quantity demanded

a change in a good's own price leads to a change in quantity demanded, a movement along a given demand curve

shifts in the demand curve

A change in one of the variables, other than the price of the good itself, that affects the willingness of consumers to buy

4.3b Shifts in Demand ("PYNTE")

There are two ways the demand curve can shift. We say there is an increase in demand when the curve shifts rightward: at any given price, consumers demand a larger quantity of the good than before. Or when there is a decrease in demand there is a leftward shift in the demand curve: at any given price, consumers demand a smaller quantity of the good than before. These shifts are shown in Exhibit 1.

There are a number of variables that can shift the demand curve but here are some of the most important. It might be helpful to remember the old English spelling of the word pint—PYNTE. This acronym can help you remember the five principle factors that shift the demand curve for a good or service.

Does a movement along the demand curve illustrate a change in demand or a change in quantity demanded?

- Changes in the Prices of Related Goods and Services (P)
- Changes in Income (Y)
- Changes in the Number of Buyers (N)
- Changes in Tastes (T)
- Changes in Expectations (E)

4.3c Changes in the Prices of Related Goods and Services (P)

In deciding how much of a good or service to buy, consumers are influenced by the price of that good or service, a relationship summarized in the law of demand. However, sometimes consumers are also influenced by the prices of *related* goods and services—substitutes and complements.

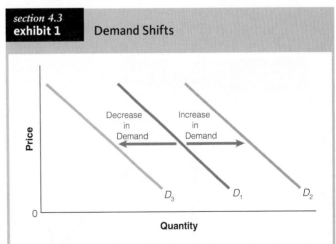

section 4.3 exhibit 1   Demand Shifts

Any change that will cause an increase in the quantity of a good that consumers want to buy at any given price shifts the demand curve to the right. Any change that will cause a decrease in the quantity that consumers want to buy at any given price will shift the demand curve to the left.

• Some cities have tried to reduce traffic congestion by
• lowering the price of substitutes for cars like busses and
• rail services.

© ISTOCKPHOTO.COM/JUANMONINO

Substitutes

Substitutes are generally goods for which one could be used in place of the other. To many, substitutes would include muffins and bagels, Crest and Colgate toothpaste, domestic and foreign cars, movie tickets and video rentals, jackets and sweaters, Exxon and Shell gasoline, and Nikes and Reeboks.

Two goods are substitutes when an increase (decrease) in the price of one good causes an increase (decrease) in the demand for the other good. For example, if an increase in the price of Diet Pepsi (a movement up along the demand curve for Diet Pepsi) causes an increase in demand for Diet Coke (a rightward shift of the demand curve for Diet Coke), we would say that for this buyer, the two goods are substitutes. (See application)

substitutes

two goods are substitutes if an increase (decrease) in the price of one good causes an increase (decrease) in the demand for the other good

Complements

Two goods are complements if they are used together, such as skis and bindings, peanut butter and jelly, hot dogs and buns, digital music players and downloadable music, and printers and ink cartridges. When an increase (decrease) in the price of one good decreases (increases) the demand for another good, the two goods are called complements. For many people, motorcycles and motorcycle helmets are complements, especially in states that have required

USE WHAT YOU'VE LEARNED

Substitute Goods

Q Can you describe the change we would expect to see in the demand curve for Pepsi if the relative price for Coca-Cola increased significantly?

A In Exhibit 2(a), we see that as the price of Coca-Cola increases—a movement up along the demand curve for

Coca-Cola, from point A to point B—causes a reduction in the quantity demanded of Coca-Cola. If the two goods are substitutes, the higher price for Coca-Cola will cause an increase in the demand for Pepsi (a rightward shift), as seen in Exhibit 2(b).

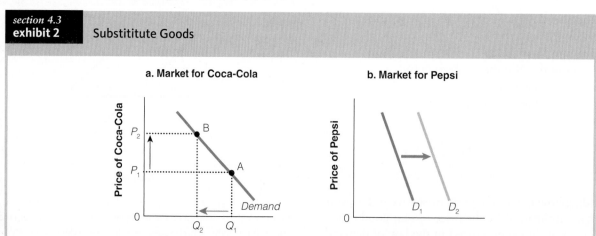

section 4.3
exhibit 2   Substititue Goods

a. Market for Coca-Cola

b. Market for Pepsi

USE WHAT YOU'VE LEARNED

Complementary Goods

Q If the price of computers fell markedly, what do you think would happen to the demand for software?

A If computers and software are complements, the decrease in the price of computers will lead to more computers purchased (a movement down along the demand curve from point A to point B, called an increase in quantity demanded) and an increase in the demand for software (a rightward shift). Of course, the opposite is true, too—an increase in the price of computers will lead to fewer people purchasing computers (a movement up along the demand curve for computers from point B to point A, called a decrease in quantity demanded) and a lower demand for software (a leftward shift).

section 4.3
exhibit 3   **Complementary Goods**

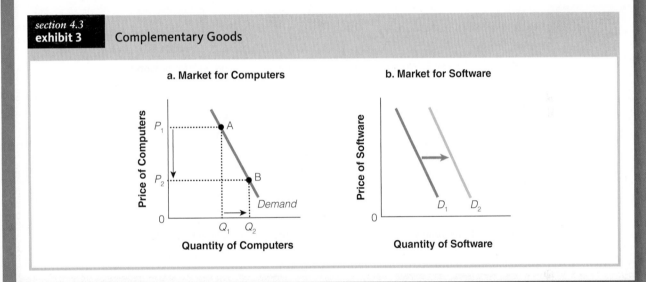

a. Market for Computers

b. Market for Software

helmet laws. So when the price of motorcycles falls, the quantity of motorcycles demanded will rise—a movement down along the demand curve for motorcycles. As more people buy motorcycles, they will demand more motorcycle helmets—the demand curve for motorcycle helmets shifts to the right. However, most pairs of goods are not closely related. For example, ice cream and housing or cars and pizzas are not closely related goods.

complements
two goods are complements if an increase (decrease) in the price of one good leads to a decrease (increase) in the demand for the other good

4.3d Changes in Income (Y)

Why (Y)? The reason is because macroeconomists use the letter (I) for investment, so micro-economists often use the letter (Y) to denote income. Economists have observed that generally the consumption of goods and services is positively related to the income available to consumers. Empirical studies support the notion that as individuals receive more income, they tend to increase their purchases of most goods and services. Other things held equal, rising income usually leads to an increase in the demand for goods (a rightward shift of the demand curve), and decreasing income usually leads to a decrease in the demand for goods (a leftward shift of the demand curve).

Normal and Inferior Goods

If demand for a good increases when incomes rise and decreases when incomes fall, the good is called a **normal good**. Most goods are normal goods. Consumers will typically buy more CDs, clothes, pizzas, and trips to the movies as their incomes rise. However, if demand

normal goods
if income increases, the demand for a good increases; if income decreases, the demand for a good decreases

USE WHAT YOU'VE LEARNED

Normal and Inferior Goods

Q Chester Field owns a high-quality furniture shop. If a boom in the economy occurs (higher average income per person and fewer people unemployed), can Chester expect to sell more high-quality furniture?

A Yes. Furniture is generally considered a normal good, so a rise in income will increase the demand for

high-quality furniture, as shown in (a). However, if Chester sells unfinished, used, or low-quality furniture, the demand for his products might fall, as higher incomes allow customers to buy furniture that is finished, new, or of higher quality. Chester's furniture would then be an inferior good, as shown in Exhibit 4(b).

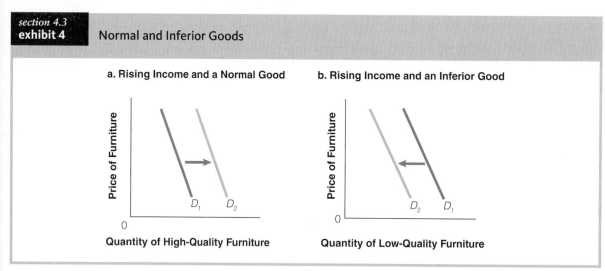

section 4.3
exhibit 4   Normal and Inferior Goods

a. Rising Income and a Normal Good

Price of Furniture

D_1 D_2

0

Quantity of High-Quality Furniture

b. Rising Income and an Inferior Good

Price of Furniture

D_2 D_1

0

Quantity of Low-Quality Furniture

---

inferior goods

if income increases, the demand for a good decreases; if income decreases, the demand for a good increases

for a good decreases when incomes rise or if demand increases when incomes fall, the good is called an inferior good. For example, as your income rises, you may choose to stay in nice hotels rather than youth hostels, or you may purchase fewer fast-food meals. The term *inferior* in this sense does not refer to the quality of the good in question but shows that demand decreases when income increases and demand increases when income decreases.

Or if people's incomes rise and they increase their demand for movie tickets, we say that movie tickets are a normal good. But if people's incomes fall and they increase their demand for bus rides,

In the midst of a recession, is it possible that many people will increase their demand for fast-food restaurants? It is not only possible, it actually happened! If declining income causes demand for a good to rise, is it a normal good or an inferior good?

we say bus rides are an inferior good. Whether goods are normal or inferior, the point here is that income influences demand—usually positively, but sometimes negatively.

4.3e **Changes in the Number of Buyers (N)**

The demand for a good or service will vary with the size of the potential consumer population. The demand for wheat, for example, rises as population increases because the added population wants to consume wheat products, such as bread or cereal. Marketing experts, who closely follow the patterns of consumer behavior regarding a particular good or service, are usually vitally concerned with the *demographics* of the product—the vital statistics of the potential consumer population, including size, race, income, and age characteristics. For example, market researchers for baby food companies keep a close watch on the birth rate.

4.3f **Changes in Tastes (T)**

The demand for a good or service may increase or decrease with changes in people's tastes or preferences. When tastes change in favor a of good, more people want to buy the good at any given price—a rightward shift in the demand curve. When tastes change against a good, fewer people want to buy the good at any given price—a leftward shift in the demand curve.

Changes in taste may be triggered by advertising or promotion, by a news story, by the behavior of some popular public figure, and so on. Changes in taste are particularly noticeable in apparel. Skirt lengths, coat lapels, shoe styles, and tie sizes change frequently.

Changes in preferences naturally lead to changes in demand. A person may grow tired of one type of recreation or food and try another type. People may decide they want more organic food; consequently, we will see more stores and restaurants catering to this change in taste. Changes in occupation, number of dependents, state of health, and age also tend to alter preferences. The birth of a baby might cause a family to spend less on recreation and more on food and clothing. Illness increases the demand for medicine and lessens purchases of other goods. A cold winter increases the demand for heating oil. Changes in customs and traditions also affect preferences, and the development of new products draws consumer preferences away from other goods. Compact discs replaced record albums, just as DVD players replaced VCRs and DVDs are now being replaced by Internet streaming videos like Netflix and Hulu. A change in information can also impact consumers' demand. For example, a breakout of *E. coli* or new information about a defective and/or dangerous product, such as a baby crib, can reduce demand.

© ISTOCKPHOTO.COM/MABE123

Body piercing and tattoos have risen in popularity in recent years. The demand for these services has been pushed to the right. According to the Pew Research Center 36 percent of 18- to 29-year-olds have at least one tattoo.

4.3g **Changes in Expectations (E)**

Sometimes the demand for a good or service in a given period will increase or decrease because consumers expect the good to change in price or availability at some future date. If people expect the future price to be higher, they will purchase more of the good now before the price increase—an increase in the demand today. If people expect the future price to be lower, they will purchase less of the good now and wait for the price decrease—a decrease in the demand today. For example, if you expect the price of computers to fall soon, you may be less willing to buy one today. Or you might buy next year's Halloween decorations on November 1 during a post-Halloween sale. That is, expectations of higher prices in the future could increase your demand now.

A change in consumers' expectations about their future incomes can also shift the demand curve. For example, if you expect to earn additional income next month, you may be more willing to dip into your current savings to buy something this month. If you expect your income to fall in the future, you may choose to save more today and reduce your demand for some goods.

4.3h Changes in Demand versus Changes in Quantity Demanded—Revisited

Economists put particular emphasis on the impact on consumer behavior of a change in the price of a good. We are interested in distinguishing between consumer behavior related to the price of a good itself (movements *along* a demand curve) and behavior related to changes in other factors (shifts of the demand curve).

As indicated earlier, if the price of a good changes, it causes a *change in quantity demanded, ceteris paribus.* If one of the other factors (determinants) influencing consumer behavior changes, it results in a *change in demand.* The effects of some of the determinants that cause changes in demand (shifters) are reviewed in Exhibit 5. For example, there are two different ways to curb teenage smoking: raise the price of cigarettes (a reduction in the quantity of cigarettes demanded) or decrease the demand for cigarettes (a leftward shift in the demand curve for cigarettes). Both would reduce the amount of smoking. Specifically, to increase the price of cigarettes, the government could impose a higher tax on manufacturers. Most of this would be passed on to consumers in the form of higher prices (more on this in Chapter 6). Or to shift the demand curve leftward, the government could adopt policies to discourage smoking, such as advertising bans and increasing consumer awareness of the harmful side effects of smoking—disease and death.

How is a change in demand different than a change in quantity demanded?

section 4.3
exhibit 5   **Possible Demand Shifters**

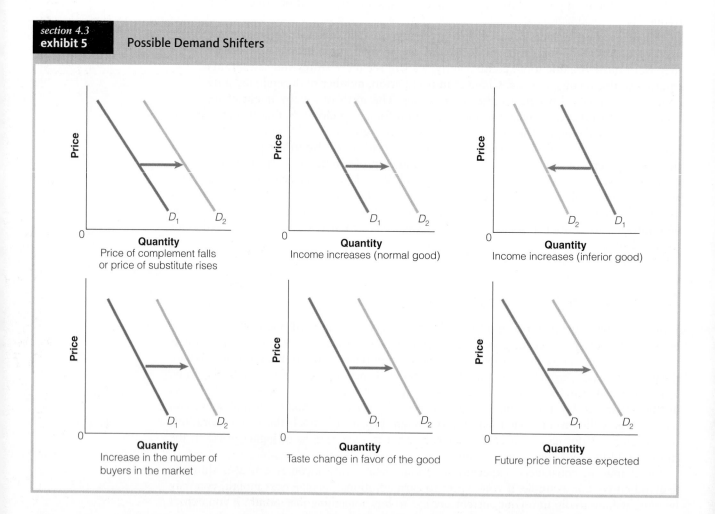

USE WHAT YOU'VE LEARNED

Changes in Demand versus Changes in Quantity Demanded

Q How would you use a graph to demonstrate the two following scenarios? (1) Someone buys more pizzas because the price of pizzas has fallen; and (2) a student buys more pizzas because she just received a 20 percent raise at work, giving her additional income.

A In Exhibit 6, the movement from A to B is called an increase in quantity demanded; the movement from B to A is called a decrease in quantity demanded. Economists use the phrase "increase or decrease in quantity demanded" to describe movements along a given demand curve. However, the change from A to C is called an increase in demand, and the change from C to A is called a decrease in demand. The phrase "increase or decrease in demand" is reserved for a shift in the whole curve. So if an individual buys more pizzas because the price fell, we call it an increase in quantity demanded. However, if she buys more pizzas even at the current price, say $15, we say it is an increase in demand. In this case, the increase in income was responsible for the increase in demand because she chose to spend some of her new income on pizzas.

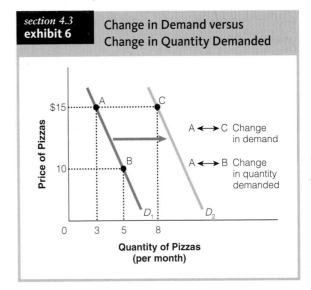

**section 4.3
exhibit 6**   Change in Demand versus Change in Quantity Demanded

Variable	A Change in this Variable Causes
Price of the good itself	a movement along the demand curve
Price of related goods and services	a shift in the demand curve
Income	a shift in the demand curve
Number of buyers	a shift in the demand curve
Tastes	a shift in the demand curve
Expectations	a shift in the demand curve

These are some of the most important variables that affect how much consumers are willing to buy. Remember, changes in the price of the good itself cause a movement along a given demand curve, resulting in a change in quantity demanded. That is what happens to the amount consumers demand when only a good's price changes and all the other variables that influence buyers are held constant. A change in the other variables shifts the curve, causing a change in demand.

SECTION QUIZ

1. Which of the following would be most likely to increase the demand for jelly?

   a. an increase in the price of peanut butter, which is often used with jelly

   b. an increase in income; jelly is a normal good

   c. a decrease in the price of jelly

   d. medical research that finds that daily consumption of jelly makes people live 10 years *less*, on average

(continued)

SECTION QUIZ (cont.)

2. Which of the following would *not* cause a change in the demand for cheese?

    a. an increase in the price of crackers, which are consumed with cheese

    b. an increase in the income of cheese consumers

    c. an increase in the population of cheese lovers

    d. an increase in the price of cheese

3. Whenever the price of Good A decreases, the demand for Good B increases. Goods A and B appear to be

    a. complements.

    b. substitutes.

    c. inferior goods.

    d. normal goods.

    e. inverse goods.

4. Whenever the price of Good A increases, the demand for Good B increases as well. Goods A and B appear to be

    a. complements.

    b. substitutes.

    c. inferior goods.

    d. normal goods.

    e. inverse goods.

5. The difference between a change in quantity demanded and a change in demand is that a change in

    a. quantity demanded is caused by a change in a good's own price, while a change in demand is caused by a change in some other variable, such as income, tastes, or expectations.

    b. demand is caused by a change in a good's own price, while a change in quantity demanded is caused by a change in some other variable, such as income, tastes, or expectations.

    c. quantity demanded is a change in the amount people actually buy, while a change in demand is a change in the amount they want to buy.

    d. This is a trick question. A change in demand and a change in quantity demanded are the same thing.

6. Suppose CNN announces that bad weather in Central America has greatly reduced the number of cocoa bean plants and for this reason the price of chocolate is expected to rise soon. As a result,

    a. the current market demand for chocolate will decrease.

    b. the current market demand for chocolate will increase.

    c. the current quantity demanded for chocolate will decrease.

    d. no change will occur in the current market for chocolate.

7. If incomes are rising, in the market for an inferior good,

    a. demand will rise.

    b. demand will fall.

    c. supply will rise.

    d. supply will fall.

(continued)

Supply   4.4

▶ What is the law of supply?

▶ What is an individual supply curve?

▶ What is a market supply curve?

4.4a The Law of Supply

In a market, the answer to the fundamental question, "What do we produce, and in what quantities?" depends on the interaction of both buyers and sellers. Demand is only half the story. The willingness and ability of sellers to provide goods are equally important factors that must be weighed by decision makers in all societies. As with demand, the price of the good is an important factor. And just as with demand, factors other than the price of the good are also important to sellers, such as the cost of inputs or advances in technology. While behavior will vary among individual sellers, economists expect that, other things being equal, the quantity supplied will vary directly with the price of the good, a relationship called the **law of supply**. According to the law of supply, the higher the price of the good (P), the greater the quantity supplied (Q_s), and the lower the price (P) of the good, the smaller the quantity supplied (Q_s), *ceteris paribus*.

$$P\uparrow \Rightarrow Q_s \uparrow \text{ and } P\downarrow \Rightarrow Q_s \downarrow$$

The relationship described by the law of supply is a direct, or positive, relationship because the variables move in the same direction.

4.4b A Positive Relationship between Price and Quantity Supplied

Firms supplying goods and services want to increase their profits, and the higher the price per unit, the greater the profitability generated by supplying more of that good. For example,

law of supply
the higher (lower) the price of the good, the greater (smaller) the quantity supplied, *ceteris paribus*

economic
content
standards

Higher prices for a good or service provide incentives for producers to make or sell more of it. Lower prices for a good or service provide incentives for producers to make or sell less of it.

**individual supply
curve**

a graphical representation that
shows the positive relationship
between the price and quantity
supplied

market supply curve

a graphical representation of the
amount of goods and services
that sellers are willing and able
to supply at various prices

if you were a coffee grower, wouldn't you much rather be paid $5 a pound than $1 a pound, *ceteris paribus*?

When the price of coffee is low, the coffee business is less profitable and less coffee will be produced. Some sellers may even shut down, reducing their quantity supplied to zero if the price is low enough.

4.4c An Individual Supply Curve

To illustrate the concept of an **individual supply curve**, consider the amount of coffee that an individual seller, Juan Valdés, is willing and able to supply in one year. The law of supply can be illustrated, like the law of demand, by a table or graph. Juan's supply schedule for coffee is shown in Exhibit 1(a). The combinations of price and quantity supplied were then plotted and joined to create the individual supply curve shown in Exhibit 1(b). Note that the individual supply curve is upward sloping as you move from left to right. At higher prices, there will be a greater quantity supplied, other things being equal. That is existing firms or growers will produce more at higher prices than at lower prices.

4.4d The Market Supply Curve

The **market supply curve** may be thought of as the horizontal summation of the supply curves for individual firms. The market supply curve shows how the total quantity supplied varies positively with the price of a good, while holding constant all other factors that affect how much producers are able and willing to supply. The market supply schedule, which reflects the total quantity supplied at each price by all of the coffee producers, is shown in Exhibit 2(a). Exhibit 2(b) illustrates the resulting market supply curve for this group of coffee producers.

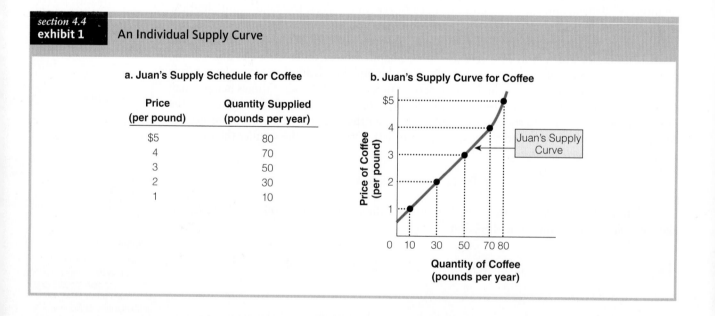

**section 4.4
exhibit 1   An Individual Supply Curve**

a. Juan's Supply Schedule for Coffee

Price (per pound)	Quantity Supplied (pounds per year)
$5	80
4	70
3	50
2	30
1	10

b. Juan's Supply Curve for Coffee

section 4.4
section 4.4
exhibit 2   A Market Supply Curve

a. Market Supply Schedule for Coffee

Price (per pound)	Quantity Supplied (pounds per year)				
	Juan	+	Other Producers	=	Market Supply
$5	80	+	7,920	=	8,000
4	70	+	6,930	=	7,000
3	50	+	4,950	=	5,000
2	30	+	2,970	=	3,000
1	10	+	990	=	1,000

b. Market Supply Curve for Coffee

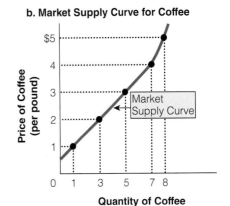

The dots on this graph indicate different quantities of coffee that sellers would be willing and able to supply at various prices. The line connecting those combinations is the market supply curve.

SECTION QUIZ

1. An upward-sloping supply curve shows that
   a. buyers are willing to pay more for particularly scarce products.
   b. sellers expand production as the product price falls.
   c. sellers are willing to increase production of their goods if they receive higher prices for them.
   d. buyers are willing to buy more as the product price falls.

2. Along a supply curve,
   a. supply changes as price changes.
   b. quantity supplied changes as price changes.
   c. supply changes as technology changes.
   d. quantity supplied changes as technology changes.

3. A supply curve illustrates a(n) _____ relationship between _____ and _____.
   a. direct; price; supply
   b. direct; price; quantity demanded
   c. direct; price; quantity supplied
   d. introverted; price; quantity demanded
   e. inverse; price; quantity supplied

4. Which of the following is true?
   a. The law of supply states that the higher (lower) the price of a good, the greater (smaller) the quantity supplied.
   b. The relationship between price and quantity supplied is positive because profit opportunities are greater at higher prices and because the higher production costs of increased output mean that suppliers will require higher prices.
   c. The market supply curve is a graphical representation of the amount of goods and services that suppliers are willing and able to supply at various prices.
   d. All of the above are true.

(continued)

4.5   Shifts in the Supply Curve

▶ What is the difference between a change in supply and a change in quantity supplied?

▶ What are the determinants of supply?

▶ How does the number of suppliers affect the supply curve?

▶ How does technology affect the supply curve?

▶ How do taxes affect the supply curve?

4.5a A Change in Quantity Supplied versus a Change in Supply

Changes in the price of a good lead to changes in the quantity supplied by sellers, just as changes in the price of a good lead to changes in the quantity demanded by buyers. Similarly, a change in supply, whether an increase or a decrease, can occur for reasons other than changes in the price of the product itself, just as changes in demand may be due to factors (determinants) other than the price of the good. In other words, a change in the price of the good in question is shown as a movement along a given supply curve, leading to a change in quantity supplied. A change in any other factor that can affect seller behavior (seller's input prices, the prices of related products, expectations, number of sellers, and technology) results in *a shift in the entire supply curve*. This is called a change in supply.

4.5b Shifts in Supply ("SPENT")

Why is a change in supply different than a change in quantity supplied?

There are two ways the supply curve can shift. We say there is an increase in supply when the curve shifts rightward: at any given price, producers supply a larger quantity of the good than before. Or when there is a decrease in supply there is a leftward shift in the supply curve: at any given price, producers supply a smaller quantity of the good than before. These shifts are shown in Exhibit 1. We now look at some of the possible determinants of supply—factors that determine the position of the supply curve—in greater depth.

There are a number of variables that can shift the supply curve but here are some of the most important. It might be helpful to remember the word "SPENT." This acronym can help you remember the five principle factors that shift the supply curve for a good or service.

- Changes in seller's input prices (S)
- Changes in the prices of related goods and services (P)
- Changes in expectations (E)
- Changes in the number of sellers (N)
- Changes in technology (T)

Changes in Seller's Input Prices (S)

Sellers are strongly influenced by the costs of inputs used in the production process, such as steel used for automobiles or microchips used in computers. Recall that inputs are used to make outputs of goods and services. Inputs, like outputs, also have prices. And if the input prices rise, it increases the cost of producing the output of a good or service. Consequently, the producer is less willing to supply the final good at any given price, causing the supply curve to shift to the left. For example, higher labor, materials, energy, or other input costs increase the costs of producing an automobile, causing the supply curve for automobiles to shift to the left. If input prices fall, producing the final good or service is less costly to the seller; thus, they are more willing to supply the good at any given price, so the supply curve shifts to the right.

Changes in the Prices of Related Goods and Services (P)

The supply of a good increases if the price of one of its substitutes in production falls; and the supply of a good decreases if the price of one of its substitutes in production rises. Suppose you own your own farm, on which you plant cotton and wheat. One year, the price of wheat falls and farmers reduce the quantity of wheat supplied, as shown in Exhibit 2(a). What effect does the lower price of wheat have on your cotton production? It increases the supply of cotton. You want to produce relatively less of the crop that has fallen in price (wheat) and relatively more of the now more attractive other crop (cotton). Cotton and wheat are *substitutes in production* because both goods can be produced using the same resources. Producers tend to substitute the production of more profitable products for that of less profitable products. So the decrease in the price in the wheat market has caused an increase in supply (a rightward shift) in the cotton market, as seen in Exhibit 2(b).

If the price of wheat, a substitute in production, increases, then that crop becomes more profitable. This leads to an increase in the quantity supplied of wheat. Consequently, farmers will shift their resources out of the relatively lower-priced crop (cotton); the result is a decrease in supply of cotton.

Other examples of substitutes in production include automobile producers that have to decide between producing sedans and pick-ups or construction companies that have to choose between building single residential houses or commercial buildings. A producer of soccer balls may produce basketballs if the price of basketballs rises relative to soccer balls. This will increase profitability.

Some goods are *complements in production*. Producing one good does not prevent the production of the other, but actually enables production of the other. For example, leather and beef are complements in production. Suppose the price of beef rises and, as a result, cattle ranchers increase the quantity supplied of beef, moving up the supply curve for beef, as seen in Exhibit 2(c). When cattle ranchers produce more beef, they automatically produce more leather. Thus, when the price of beef increases, the supply of the related good, leather, shifts to the right, as seen in Exhibit 2(d). Suppose the price of beef falls, and as a result, the quantity supplied of beef falls; this leads to a decrease (a leftward shift) in the supply of leather.

Other examples of complements in production where goods are produced simultaneously from the same resource include a lumber mill that produces lumber and sawdust or an oil refinery that can produce gasoline and heating oil from the same resource—crude oil. Another example is that when dairy farmers produce skim milk, they also produce cream. If

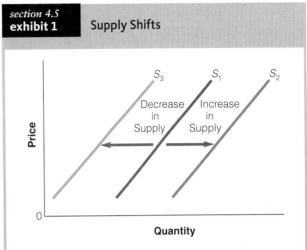

section 4.5
exhibit 1   **Supply Shifts**

Any change that will cause an increase in the quantity that sellers want to produce and sell at any given price shifts the supply curve to the right. Any change that will cause a decrease in the quantity that sellers want to produce and sell at any given price will shift the supply curve to the left.

© ANDRESR/SHUTTERSTOCK.COM

Veterinarians can choose to work on either suburban pets or farm animals. Veterinarians have increasingly chosen to live in metropolitan areas, where they can pursue much more lucrative practices specializing in domestic pets. Since the value of working on pets in the city has risen, the cost of being a farm veterinarian has increased, shifting the supply curve for farm veterinarians to the left.

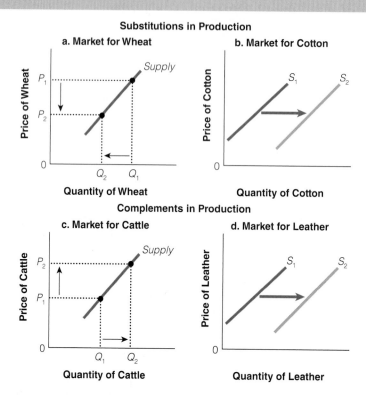

section 4.5
exhibit 2   Substitutes and Complements in Production

If land can be used for either wheat or cotton, a decrease in the price of wheat causes a decease in the quantity supplied, a movement down along the supply curve in Exhibit 2(a). This may cause some farmers to shift out of the production of wheat and into the substitute in production—cotton—shifting the cotton supply curve to the right in Exhibit 2(b). If the price of the complement in production increases (cattle), it becomes more profitable and as a result cattle ranchers increase the quantity supplied of beef, moving up the supply curve for beef, as seen in Exhibit 2(c). When cattle ranchers produce more beef, they also produce more leather. Thus, when the price of beef increases, the supply of the related good, leather, shifts to the right, as seen in Exhibit 2(d).

ERIC GEVAERT/SHUTTERSTOCK.COM

During the global recession of 2007–2009, oil demand dropped substantially. Early in 2009, as oil prices bottomed out, a situation known as contango developed, in which a large gap developed between oil prices trading on the daily spot market and future-dated oil contracts. Traders bought oil on the spot market and parked it in tankers until the prices went back up. Floating storage worldwide peaked in April with nearly 90 million barrels sitting in oil tankers waiting to be sold.

the price of skim milk rises, the dairy farmer produces more skim milk (an increase in the quantity supplied) and the supply of cream increases.

Changes in Expectations (E)

Another factor shifting supply is sellers' expectations. If producers expect a higher price in the future, they will supply less now than they otherwise would have, preferring to wait and sell when their goods will be more valuable. For example, if a cotton producer expected the future price of cotton to be higher next year, he might decide to store some of his current production of cotton for next year when the price will be higher. Similarly, if producers expect now that the price will be lower later, they will supply more now. Oil refiners will often store some of their spring supply of gasoline for summer because gasoline prices typically peak in summer. In addition, some of the heating oil for the fall is stored to supply it in the winter when heating oil prices peak.

Changes in the Number of Sellers (N)

We are normally interested in market demand and supply (because together they determine prices and quantities) rather than in the behavior of individual consumers and firms. As we discussed earlier in the chapter, the supply curves of individual suppliers can be summed horizontally to create a market supply curve. An increase in the number of sellers leads to an increase in supply, denoted by a rightward shift in the supply curve. For example, think of the number of gourmet coffee shops that have sprung up over the last 15 to 20 years, shifting the supply curve of gourmet coffee to the right. An exodus of sellers has the opposite impact, a decrease in supply, which is indicated by a leftward shift in the supply curve.

Changes in Technology (T)

Technological change can lower the firm's costs of production through productivity advances. These changes allow the firm to spend less on inputs and produce the same level of output. Human creativity works to find new ways to produce goods and services using fewer or less costly inputs of labor, natural resources, or capital. That is, changes in production technology, including the way you make, distribute, and sell a good, can change the cost of production. For example, if the technology lowers the cost of production, this will raise sellers' willingness to supply the good or service. Because the firm can now produce the good at a lower cost it will supply more of the good at each and every price—the supply curve shifts to the right.

USE WHAT YOU'VE LEARNED

Change in Supply versus Change in Quantity Supplied

Q How would you graph the following two scenarios: (1) the price of wheat per bushel rises; and (2) good weather causes an unusually abundant wheat harvest?

A In the first scenario, the price of wheat (per bushel) increases, so the quantity supplied changes (i.e., a movement along the supply curve). In the second scenario, the good weather causes the supply curve for wheat to shift to the right, which is called a change in supply (not quantity supplied). A shift in the whole supply curve is caused by one of the other variables, not by a change in the price of the good in question.

As shown in Exhibit 3, the movement from A to B is called an increase in quantity supplied, and the movement from B to A is called a decrease in quantity supplied. However, the change from B to C is called an increase in supply, and the movement from C to B is called a decrease in supply.

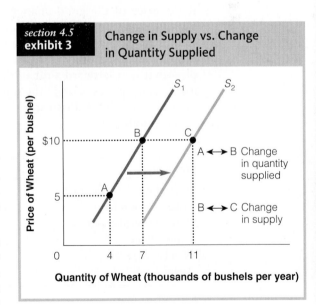

section 4.5 exhibit 3   Change in Supply vs. Change in Quantity Supplied

A ←→ B Change in quantity supplied

B ←→ C Change in supply

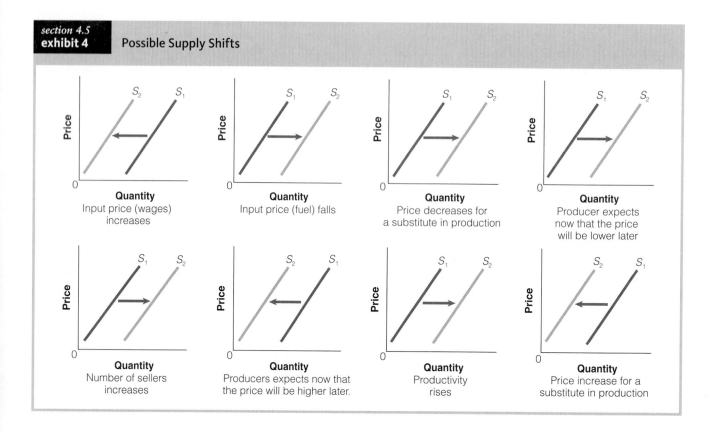

4.5c Change in Supply versus Change in Quantity Supplied—Revisited

If the price of the good changes, it leads to a change in the quantity supplied *ceteris paribus*. If one of the other factors influences sellers' behavior, we say it results in a change in supply. For example, if production costs rise because of a wage increase or higher fuel costs, other things remaining constant, we would expect a decrease in supply—that is, a leftward shift in the supply curve. Alternatively, if some variable, such as lower input prices, causes the costs of production to fall, the supply curve will shift to the right. Exhibit 4 illustrates the effects of some of the determinants that cause shifts in the supply curve.

Variable	A Change in this Variable Causes
Price of the the good itself	a movement along the supply curve
Seller's input prices	a shift in the supply curve
Price of related goods and services	a shift in the supply curve
Expectations	a shift in the supply curve
Number of sellers	a shift in the supply curve
Technology	a shift in the supply curve

These are some of the most important variables that affect how much producers are willing to produce and sell. Remember, changes in the price of the good itself, when all the other variables that influence sellers are held constant, cause movements along a given curve, changing quantity supplied. A change in any of these other variables shifts the curve, causing a change in supply.

SECTION QUIZ

1. All of the following factors will affect the supply of shoes except one. Which will not affect the supply of shoes?

   a. higher wages for shoe factory workers

   b. higher prices for leather

   c. a technological improvement that reduces waste of leather and other raw materials in shoe production

   d. an increase in consumer income

2. The difference between a change in quantity supplied and a change in supply is that a change in

   a. quantity supplied is caused by a change in a good's own price, while a change in supply is caused by a change in some other variable, such as input prices, prices of related goods, expectations, or taxes.

   b. supply is caused by a change in a good's own price, while a change in the quantity supplied is caused by a change in some other variable, such as input prices, prices of related goods, expectations, or taxes.

   c. quantity supplied is a change in the amount people want to sell, while a change in supply is a change in the amount they actually sell.

   d. supply and a change in the quantity supplied are the same thing.

3. Antonio's makes the greatest pizza and delivers it hot to all the dorms around campus. Last week Antonio's supplier of pepperoni informed him of a 25 percent increase in price. Which variable determining the position of the supply curve has changed, and what effect does it have on supply?

   a. future expectations; supply decreases

   b. future expectations; supply increases

   c. input prices; supply decreases

   d. input prices; supply increases

   e. technology; supply increases

4. Which of the following is *not* a determinant of supply?

   a. input prices

   b. technology

   c. tastes

   d. expectations

   e. the prices of related goods

5. A leftward shift in supply could be caused by

   a. an improvement in productive technology.

   b. a decrease in income.

   c. some firms leaving the industry.

   d. a fall in the price of inputs to the industry.

---

1. What is the difference between a change in supply and a change in quantity supplied?

2. If a seller expects the price of a good to rise in the near future, how will that expectation affect the current supply curve?

3. Would a change in the price of wheat change the supply of wheat? Would it change the supply of corn, if wheat and corn can be grown on the same type of land?

4. If a guitar manufacturer increased its wages in order to keep its workers, what would happen to the supply of guitars as a result?

5. What happens to the supply of baby-sitting services in an area when many teenagers get their driver's licenses at about the same time?

Answers: 1. d 2. a 3. c 4. c 5. c

4.6   Market Equilibrium Price and Quantity

▶ What is the equilibrium price?   ▶ What is a shortage?
▶ What is the equilibrium quantity? ▶ What is a surplus?

4.6a The Critical Role of Price

market equilibrium
the point at which the market supply and market demand curves intersect

The glue that brings supply and demand together is the market price. Prices can adapt to make the quantity demanded by consumers equal to the quantity supplied by producers. When that is true, everyone who wants to buy at the current price can do so, and everyone who wants to sell at the current price can also do so. In the next chapter, we will see how non-price determinants can change market outcomes, but for now we focus on the power of price and how it ties supply and demand together.

4.6b Equilibrium Price and Quantity

equilibrium price
the price at the intersection of the market supply and demand curves; at this price, the quantity demanded equals the quantity supplied

The **market equilibrium** is found at the point at which the market supply and market demand curves intersect. The price at the intersection of the market supply curve and the market demand curve is called the **equilibrium price**, and the quantity is called the **equilibrium quantity**. At the equilibrium price, the amount that buyers are willing and able to buy is exactly equal to the amount that sellers are willing and able to produce. The equilibrium market solution is best understood with the help of a simple graph. Let's return to the coffee example we used in our earlier discussions of supply and demand. Exhibit 1 combines the market demand curve for coffee with the market supply curve. At $3 per pound, buyers are willing to buy 5,000 pounds of coffee and sellers are willing to supply 5,000 pounds of coffee. Neither may be "happy" about the price; the buyers would prob-

equilibrium quantity
the quantity at the intersection of the market supply and demand curves; at the equilibrium quantity, the quantity demanded equals the quantity supplied

surplus
a situation where quantity supplied exceeds quantity demanded

ably like a lower price and the sellers would probably like a higher price. But both buyers and sellers are able to carry out their purchase and sales plans at the $3 price. At any other price, either suppliers or demanders would be unable to trade as much as they would like.

4.6c Shortages and Surpluses

| section 4.6 exhibit 1 | Market Equilibrium |

The equilibrium is found at the intersection of the market supply and demand curves. The equilibrium price is $3 per pound, and the equilibrium quantity is 5,000 pounds of coffee. At the equilibrium quantity, the quantity demanded equals the quantity supplied.

What happens when the market price is not equal to the equilibrium price? Suppose the market price is above the equilibrium price, as seen in Exhibit 2(a). At $4 per pound, the quantity of coffee demanded would be 3,000 pounds, but the quantity supplied would be 7,000 pounds. At this price, a **surplus**, or excess quantity supplied, would exist. That is, at this price, growers would be willing to sell more coffee than demanders would be willing to buy. To get rid of the unwanted surplus, frustrated sellers have an incentive to cut their price to attract more buyers and cut back on production. Cutting the price will simultaneously increase the quantity demanded and decrease the quantity supplied. Note that the changes in quantity demanded and quantity supplied are movements along the supply and demand curves, *not* shifts in the curves. This adjustment will continue to reduce the surplus, as long as the price is above the equilibrium price, at $3.

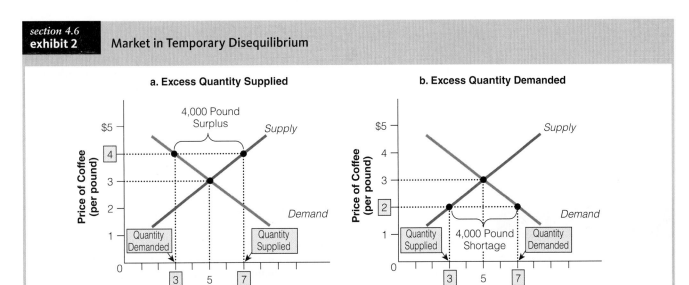

section 4.6
exhibit 2   Market in Temporary Disequilibrium

a. Excess Quantity Supplied

b. Excess Quantity Demanded

In (a), the market price is above the equilibrium price. At $4, the quantity supplied (7,000 pounds) exceeds the quantity demanded (3,000 pounds), resulting in a surplus of 4,000 pounds. To get rid of the unwanted surplus, suppliers cut their prices. As prices fall, consumers buy more, eliminating the surplus and moving the market back to equilibrium. In (b), the market price is below the equilibrium price. At $2, the quantity demanded (7,000 pounds) exceeds the quantity supplied (3,000 pounds), and a shortage of 4,000 pounds is the result. The many frustrated buyers compete for the existing supply, offering to buy more and driving the price up toward the equilibrium level. Therefore, with both shortages and surpluses, market prices tend to pull the market back to the equilibrium level.

What would happen if the market price of coffee were below the equilibrium price? As seen in Exhibit 2(b), at $2 per pound, the yearly quantity demanded of 7,000 pounds would be greater than the 3,000 pounds that producers would be willing to supply at that low price. So at $2 per pound, a **shortage** or excess quantity demanded of 4,000 pounds would exist. Some consumers are lucky enough to find coffee, but others are not able to find any sellers who are willing to sell them coffee at $2 per pound. Some frustrated consumers may offer to pay sellers more than $2. In addition, sellers noticing that there are disappointed consumers will be more than willing to raise their prices. That is, with many buyers chasing few goods, sellers can respond to the shortage by raising prices without the fear of losing sales. These actions by buyers and sellers cause the market price to rise. As the market price rises, the quantity demanded falls and the quantity supplied rises. Notice that these are movements along the supply and demand curves that move the market toward equilibrium. The upward pressure on price continues until equilibrium is reached at $3. Recall our earlier discussion of Adam Smith's invisible hand. Here it is in action. Producers independently decide how much they are going to produce and at what price and consumers will show up at web sites, garage sales, restaurants, and stores to buy those goods and services. Sometimes there might be too much supplied, while at other times there might not be enough. But over time, these mistakes will be corrected by the process of adjustment in supply and demand, which comprises the invisible hand of the market.

So whether the price starts off too high or too low, the activities of the many buyers and sellers will move the market toward equilibrium. Once equilibrium is reached, buyers and sellers are satisfied in their ability to buy and sell at that price, and the there is no longer any pressure on prices. How quickly do markets adjust to equilibrium? It depends on the type of market. But in most competitive markets, shortages and surpluses tend to be temporary.

shortage
a situation where quantity demanded exceeds quantity supplied

economic
content
standards

A market exists when buyers and
sellers interact. This interaction
between supply and demand
curves determines market prices
and thereby allocates scarce
goods and services.

4.6d Don't Confuse Scarcity and Shortages

People often confuse scarcity with shortages. Remember most goods are scarce—desirable
but limited. A shortage occurs when the quantity demanded is greater than the quantity supplied at the current price. We can eliminate shortages by increasing the price but we cannot
eliminate scarcity.

SECTION QUIZ

1. A market will experience a _____ in a situation where quantity supplied exceeds quantity
   demanded and a _____ in a situation where quantity demanded exceeds quantity supplied.

   a. shortage; shortage

   b. surplus; surplus

   c. shortage; surplus

   d. surplus; shortage

2. The price of a good will tend to rise when

   a. a temporary shortage at the current price occurs (assuming no price controls are imposed).

   b. a temporary surplus at the current price occurs (assuming no price controls are imposed).

   c. demand decreases.

   d. supply increases.

3. Which of the following is true?

   a. The intersection of the supply and demand curves shows the equilibrium price and equilibrium quantity in a
      market.

   b. A surplus is a situation where quantity supplied exceeds quantity demanded.

   c. A shortage is a situation where quantity demanded exceeds quantity supplied.

   d. Shortages and surpluses set in motion actions by many buyers and sellers that will move the market toward
      the equilibrium price and quantity unless otherwise prevented.

   e. All of the above are true.

---

1. How does the intersection of supply and demand indicate the equilibrium price and quantity in a market?

2. What can cause a change in the supply and demand equilibrium?

3. What must be true about the price charged for a shortage to occur?

4. What must be true about the price charged for a surplus to occur?

5. Why do market forces tend to eliminate both shortages and surpluses?

6. If tea prices were above their equilibrium level, what force would tend to push tea prices down? If tea prices
   were below their equilibrium level, what force would tend to push tea prices up?

Answers: 1. d 2. a 3. e

Fill in the blanks:

1. A(n) _____ is the process of buyers and sellers _____ goods and services.

2. The important point about a market is what it does—it facilitates _____.

3. _____, as a group, determine the demand side of the market. _____, as a group, determine the supply side of the market.

4. A(n) _____ market consists of many buyers and sellers, no single one of whom can influence the market price.

5. According to the law of demand, other things being equal, when the price of a good or service falls, the _____ increases.

6. An individual _____ curve reveals the different amounts of a particular good a person would be willing and able to buy at various possible prices in a particular time interval, other things being equal.

7. The _____ curve for a product is the horizontal summing of the demand curves of the individuals in the market.

8. A change in _____ leads to a change in quantity demanded, illustrated by a(n) _____ demand curve.

9. A change in demand is caused by changes in any of the other factors (besides the good's own price) that would affect how much of the good is pur-chased: the _____, _____, the _____ of buyers, _____, and _____.

10. An increase in demand is represented by a _____ shift in the demand curve; a decrease in demand is repre-sented by a(n) _____ shift in the demand curve.

11. Two goods are called _____ if an increase in the price of one causes the demand curve for another good to shift to the _____.

12. For normal goods an increase in income leads to a(n) _____ in demand, and a decrease in income leads to a(n) _____ in demand, other things being equal.

13. An increase in the expected future price of a good or an increase in expected future income may _____ current demand.

14. According to the law of supply, the higher the price of the good, the greater the _____, and the lower the price of the good, the smaller the _____.

15. The quantity supplied is positively related to the price because firms supplying goods and services want to increase their _____ and because increasing _____ costs mean that the sellers will require _____ prices to induce them to increase their output.

16. An individual supply curve is a graphical representation that shows the _____ relationship between the price and the quantity supplied.

17. The market supply curve is a graphical representation of the amount of goods and services that sellers are _____ and _____ to supply at various prices.

18. Possible supply determinants (factors that determine the position of the supply curve) are _____ prices; _____; _____ of sellers and _____.

19. A fall in input prices will _____ the costs of production, causing the supply curve to shift to the _____.

20. The supply of a good _____ if the price of one of its substitutes in production falls.

21. The supply of a good _____ if the price of one of its substitutes in production rises.

22. The price at the intersection of the market demand curve and the market supply curve is called the _____ price, and the quantity is called the _____ quantity.

23. A situation where quantity supplied is greater than quantity demanded is called a(n) _____.

24. A situation where quantity demanded is greater than quantity supplied is called a(n) _____.

25. At a price greater than the equilibrium price, a(n) _____, or excess quantity supplied, would exist. Sellers would be willing to sell _____ than demanders would be willing to buy. Frustrated suppliers would _____ their price and _____ on production, and consumers would buy _____, returning the market to equilibrium.

Answers: 1. market; exchanging 2. trade 3. Buyers; Sellers 4. competitive 5. quantity demanded 6. demand 7. market demand 8. a good's price; movement along 9. prices of related goods; income; number; tastes; expectations 10. rightward; leftward 11. substitutes; right 12. increase; decrease 13. increase 14. quantity supplied; quantity supplied 15. profits; production; higher 16. positive 17. willing; able 18. seller's input; technology and the prices of related goods 19. lower; right 20. increases 21. decreases 22. equilibrium; equilibrium 23. surplus 24. shortage 25. surplus; more; lower; cut back; more

KEY TERMS AND CONCEPTS

market 97
competitive market 97
law of demand 98
individual demand schedule 99
individual demand curve 99
market demand curve 99
change in quantity demanded 103

shifts in the demand curve 103
substitutes 104
complements 105
normal goods 105
inferior goods 106
law of supply 111
individual supply curve 112

market supply curve 112
market equilibrium 120
equilibrium price 120
equilibrium quantity 120
surplus 120
shortage 121

SECTION QUIZ ANSWERS

4.1   Markets

1. Why is it difficult to define a market precisely?
Every market is different. An incredible variety of exchange arrangements arise for different types of products, different degrees of organization, different geographical extents, and so on.

2. Why do you get your produce at a supermarket rather than directly from farmers?
Supermarkets act as middlepersons between growers of produce and consumers of produce. You hire them to do this task for you when you buy produce from them, rather than directly from growers, because they conduct those transactions at lower costs than you could. (If you could do it more cheaply than supermarkets, you would buy directly rather than from supermarkets.)

3. Why do the prices people pay for similar items at garage sales vary more than for similar items in a department store?
Items for sale at department stores are more standardized, easier to compare, and more heavily advertised, which makes consumers more aware of the prices at which they could get a particular good elsewhere, reducing the differences in price that can persist among department stores. Garage sale items are nonstandardized, costly to compare, and not advertised, which means people are often quite unaware of how much a given item could be purchased for elsewhere, so that price differences for similar items at different garage sales can be substantial.

4.2   Demand

1. What is an inverse relationship?
An inverse, or negative, relationship is one where one variable changes in the opposite direction from the other—if one increases, the other decreases.

2. How do lower prices change buyers' incentives?
A lower price for a good means that the opportunity cost to buyers of purchasing it is lower than before, and self-interest leads buyers to buy more of it as a result.

3. How do higher prices change buyers' incentives?
A higher price for a good means that the opportunity cost to buyers of purchasing it is higher than before, and self-interest leads buyers to buy less of it as a result.

4. What is an individual demand schedule?
An individual demand schedule reveals the different amounts of a good or service a person would be willing to buy at various possible prices in a particular time interval.

5. What is the difference between an individual demand curve and a market demand curve?
The market demand curve shows the total amounts of a good or service all the buyers as a group are willing to buy at various possible prices in a particular time interval. The market quantity demanded at a given price is just the sum of the quantities demanded by each individual buyer at that price.

6. Why does the amount of dating on campus tend to decline just before and during final exams?
The opportunity cost of dating—in this case, the value to students of the studying time forgone—is higher just before and during final exams than during most of the rest of an academic term. Because the cost is higher, students do less of it.

4.3   Shifts in the Demand Curve

1. What is the difference between a change in demand and a change in quantity demanded?
A change in demand shifts the entire demand curve, while a change in quantity demanded refers to a movement along a given demand curve, caused by a change in the good's price.

2. If the price of zucchini increases, causing the demand for yellow squash to rise, what do we call the relationship between zucchini and yellow squash?

Whenever an increased price of one good increases the demand for another, they are substitutes. The fact that some people consider zucchini an alternative to yellow squash explains in part why zucchini becomes more costly. Therefore, some people substitute into buying relatively cheaper yellow squash now instead.

3. If incomes rise and, as a result, demand for jet skis increases, how do we describe that good?

If income rises and, as a result, demand for jet skis increases, we call jet skis a normal good because for most (or normal) goods, we would rather have more of them than less, so an increase in income would lead to an increase in demand for such goods.

4. How do expectations about the future influence the demand curve?

Expectations about the future influence the demand curve because buying a good in the future is an alternative to buying it now. Therefore, the higher future prices are expected to be compared to the present, the less attractive future purchases become, and the greater the current demand for that good, as people buy more now when it is expected to be cheaper, rather than later, when it is expected to be more costly.

5. Would a change in the price of ice cream cause a change in the demand for ice cream? Why or why not?

No. The demand for ice cream represents the different quantities of ice cream that would be purchased at different prices. In other words, it represents the relationship between the price of ice cream and the quantity of ice cream demanded. Changing the price of ice cream does not change this relationship, so it does not change demand.

6. Would a change in the price of ice cream likely cause a change in the demand for frozen yogurt, a substitute?

Yes. Changing the price of ice cream, a substitute for frozen yogurt, would change the quantity of frozen yogurt demanded at a given price. This change in price means that the whole relationship between the price and quantity of frozen yogurt demanded has changed, which means the demand for frozen yogurt has changed.

7. If plane travel is a normal good and bus travel is an inferior good, what will happen to the demand curves for plane and bus travel if people's incomes increase?

The demand for plane travel and all other normal goods will increase if incomes increase, while the demand for bus travel and all other inferior goods will decrease if incomes increase.

4.4   Supply

1. What are the two reasons why a supply curve is positively sloped?

A supply curve is positively sloped because (1) the benefits to sellers from selling increase as the price they receive increases, and (2) the opportunity costs of supplying additional output rise with output (the law of increasing opportunity costs), so it takes a higher price to make increasing output in the self-interest of sellers.

2. What is the difference between an individual supply curve and a market supply curve?

The market supply curve shows the total amounts of a good all the sellers as a group are willing to sell at various prices in a particular time period. The market quantity supplied at a given price is just the sum of the quantities supplied by each individual seller at that price.

4.5   Shifts in the Supply Curve

1. What is the difference between a change in supply and a change in quantity supplied?

A change in supply shifts the entire supply curve, while a change in quantity supplied refers to a movement along a given supply curve.

2. If a seller expects the price of a good to rise in the near future, how will that expectation affect the current supply curve?

Selling a good in the future is an alternative to selling it now. Therefore, the higher the expected future price relative to the current price, the more attractive future sales become, and the less attractive current sales become. This will lead sellers to reduce (shift left) the current supply of that good, as they want to sell later, when the good is expected to be more valuable, rather than now.

3. Would a change in the price of wheat change the supply of wheat? Would it change the supply of corn, if wheat and corn can be grown on the same type of land?

Would it change the supply of corn, if wheat and corn can be grown on the same type of land? The supply of wheat represents the different quantities of wheat that would be offered for sale at different prices. In other words, it represents the relationship between the price of wheat and the quantity of wheat supplied. Changing the price of wheat does not change this relationship, so it does not change the supply of wheat. However, a change in the price of wheat changes the relative attractiveness of raising wheat instead of corn, which changes the supply of corn.

4. If a guitar manufacturer increased its wages in order to keep its workers, what would happen to the supply of guitars as a result?

An increase in wages, or any other input price, would decrease (shift left) the supply of guitars, making fewer guitars available for sale at any given price, by raising the opportunity cost of producing guitars.

5. What happens to the supply of baby-sitting services in an area when many teenagers get their driver's licenses at about the same time?

When teenagers get their driver's licenses, their increased mobility expands their alternatives to baby-sitting substantially, raising the opportunity cost of baby-sitting. This change decreases (shifts left) the supply of baby-sitting services.

4.6   Market Equilibrium Price and Quantity

1. How does the intersection of supply and demand indicate the equilibrium price and quantity in a market?

The intersection of supply and demand indicates the equilibrium price and quantity in a market because at higher prices, sellers would be frustrated by their inability to sell all they would like, leading sellers to compete by lowering the price they charge; at lower prices, buyers would be frustrated by their inability to buy all they would like, leading buyers to compete by increasing the price they offer to pay.

2. What can cause a change in the supply and demand equilibrium?

Changes in any of the demand curve shifters or the supply curve shifters will change the supply and demand equilibrium.

3. What must be true about the price charged for a shortage to occur?

The price charged must be less than the equilibrium price, with the result that buyers would like to buy more at that price than sellers are willing to sell.

4. What must be true about the price charged for a surplus to occur?

The price charged must be greater than the equilibrium price, with the result that sellers would like to sell more at that price than buyers are willing to buy.

5. Why do market forces tend to eliminate both shortages and surpluses?

Market forces tend to eliminate both shortages and surpluses because of the self-interest of the market participants. A seller is better off successfully selling at a lower equilibrium price than not being able to sell at a higher price (the surplus situation) and a buyer is better off successfully buying at a higher equilibrium price than not being able to buy at a lower price (the shortage situation). Therefore, we expect market forces to eliminate both shortages and surpluses.

6. If tea prices were above their equilibrium level, what force would tend to push tea prices down? If tea prices were below their equilibrium level, what force would tend to push tea prices up?

If tea prices were above their equilibrium level, sellers frustrated by their inability to sell as much tea as they would like at those prices would compete the price of tea down, as they tried to make more attractive offers to tea buyers. If tea prices were below their equilibrium level, buyers frustrated by their inability to buy as much tea as they would like at those prices would compete the price of tea up, as they tried to make more attractive offers to tea sellers.

PROBLEMS

1.   Is the market for laptop computers local, national, or global?

2.   Sid moves from New York City, where he lived in a small condominium, to rural Minnesota, where he buys a big house on five acres of land. Using the law of demand, what do you think is true of land prices in New York City relative to those in rural Minnesota?

3.   The following table shows Hillary's demand schedule for Cherry Blossom Makeup. Graph Hillary's demand curve.

Price (dollars per ounce)	Quantity Demanded (ounces per week)
$15	5 oz.
12	10
9	15
6	20
3	25

4. The following table shows Cherry Blossom Makeup demand schedules for Hillary's friends, Barbara and Nancy. If Hillary, Barbara, and Nancy constitute the whole market for Cherry Blossom Makeup, complete the market demand schedule and graph the market demand curve.

Price (dollars per ounce)	Quantity Demanded (ounces per week)			
	Hillary	Barbara	Nancy	Market
$15	5	0	15	
12	10	5	20	
9	15	10	25	
6	20	15	30	
3	25	20	35	

5. What would be the effects of each of the following on the demand for hamburger in Hilo, Hawaii? In each case, identify the responsible determinant of demand.
    a. The price of chicken falls.
    b. The price of hamburger buns doubles.
    c. Scientists find that eating hamburger prolongs life.
    d. The population of Hilo doubles.

6. What would be the effect of each of the following on the demand for Chevrolets in the United States? In each case, identify the responsible determinant of demand.
    a. The price of Fords plummets.
    b. Consumers believe that the price of Chevrolets will rise next year.
    c. The incomes of Americans rise.
    d. The price of gasoline falls dramatically.

7. The following graph shows three market demand curves for cantaloupe. Starting at point A,
    a. which point represents an increase in quantity demanded?
    b. which point represents an increase in demand?
    c. which point represents a decrease in demand?
    d. which point represents a decrease in quantity demanded?

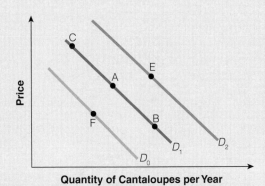

8. Using the demand curve, show the effect of the following events on the market for beef:
    a. Consumer income increases.
    b. The price of beef increases.
    c. An outbreak of "mad cow" disease occurs.
    d. The price of chicken (a substitute) increases.
    e. The price of barbecue grills (a complement) increases.

9. Draw the demand curves for the following goods. If the price of the first good listed rises, what will happen to the demand for the second good, and why?
    a. hamburger and ketchup
    b. Coca-Cola and Pepsi
    c. camera and film
    d. golf clubs and golf balls
    e. skateboard and razor scooter

10. If the price of ice cream increased,
    a. what would be the effect on the demand for ice cream?
    b. what would be the effect on the demand for frozen yogurt?

11. Using the graph below, answer the following questions.
    a. What is the shift from D_1 to D_2 called?
    b. What is the movement from B to A called?
    c. What is the movement from A to B called?
    d. What is the shift from D_2 to D_1 called?

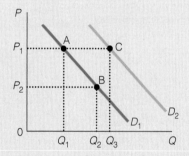

12. Felix is a wheat farmer who has two fields he can use to grow wheat. The first field is right next to his house and the topsoil is rich and thick. The second field is 10 miles away in the mountains and the soil is rocky. At current wheat prices, Felix just produces from the field next to his house because the market price for wheat is just high enough to cover his costs of production including a reasonable profit. What would have to happen to the market price of wheat for Felix to have the incentive to produce from the second field?

13. Show the impact of each of the following events on the oil market.
    a. OPEC becomes more effective in limiting the supply of oil.
    b. OPEC becomes less effective in limiting the supply of oil.
    c. The price for natural gas (a substitute for heating oil) rises.
    d. New oil discoveries occur in Alaska.
    e. Electric and hybrid cars become subsidized and their prices fall.

14. The following table shows the supply schedule for Rolling Rock Oil Co. Plot Rolling Rock's supply curve on a graph.

Price (dollars per barrel)	Quantity Supplied (barrels per month)
$ 5	10,000
10	15,000
15	20,000
20	25,000
25	30,000

15. The following table shows the supply schedules for Rolling Rock and two other petroleum companies. Armadillo Oil and Pecos Petroleum. Assuming these three companies make up the entire supply side of the oil market, complete the market supply schedule and draw the market supply curve on a graph.

	Quantity Supplied (barrels per month)			
Price (dollars per barrel)	Rolling Rock	Armadillo Oil	Pecos Petroleum	Market
$ 5	10,000	8,000	2,000	_____
10	15,000	10,000	5,000	_____
15	20,000	12,000	8,000	_____
20	25,000	14,000	11,000	_____
25	30,000	16,000	14,000	_____

16. If the price of corn rose,
     a. what would be the effect on the supply of corn?
     b. what would be the effect on the supply of wheat?

17. Using the graph below, answer the following questions:
     a. What is the shift from S_1 to S_2 called?
     b. What is the movement from A to B called?
     c. What is the movement from B to A called?
     d. What is the shift from S_2 to S_1 called?

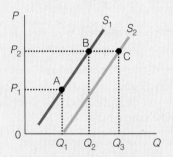

18. What would be the effect of each of the following on the supply of salsa in the United States? In each case, identify the responsible determinant of supply.
     a. Tomato prices skyrocket.
     b. Congress places a 26 percent tax on salsa.
     c. Ed Scissorhands introduces a new, faster vegetable chopper.
     d. J. Lo, Beyonce, and Adam Sandler each introduce a new brand of salsa.

19. What would be the effects of each of the following on the supply of coffee worldwide? In each case, identify the responsible determinant of supply.
     a. Freezing temperatures wipe out half of Brazil's coffee crop.
     b. Wages of coffee workers in Latin America rise as unionization efforts succeed.
     c. Indonesia offers big subsidies to its coffee producers.
     d. Genetic engineering produces a super coffee bean that grows faster and needs less care.
     e. Coffee suppliers expect prices to be higher in the future.

20. The following graph shows three market supply curves for cantaloupe. Compared to point A, which point represents
     a. an increase in quantity supplied?
     b. an increase in supply?
     c. a decrease in quantity supplied?
     d. a decrease in supply?

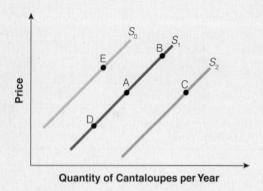

21. The following table shows the hypothetical monthly demand and supply schedules for cans of macadamia nuts in Hawaii.

Price	Quantity Demanded (cans)	Quantity Supplied (cans)
$ 6	700	100
7	600	200
8	500	300
9	400	400
10	300	500

a. What is the equilibrium price of macadamia nuts in Hawaii?
b. At a price of $7 per can, is there equilibrium, a surplus, or a shortage? If it is a surplus or shortage, how large is it?
c. At a price of $10, is there equilibrium, a surplus, or a shortage? If it is a surplus or shortage, how large is it?

22. When asked about the reason for a lifeguard shortage that threatened to keep one-third of the city's beaches closed for the summer, the Deputy Parks Commissioner of New York responded that "Kids seem to want to do work that's more in tune with a career. Maybe they prefer carpal tunnel syndrome to sunburn." What do you think is causing the shortage? What would you advise the Deputy Parks Commissioner to do in order to alleviate the shortage?

23. If a price is above the equilibrium price, explain the forces that bring the market back to the equilibrium price and quantity. If a price is below the equilibrium price, explain the forces that bring the market back to the equilibrium price and quantity.

24. The market for baseball tickets at your college stadium, which seats 2,000, is the following:

Price	Quantity Demanded	Quantity Supplied
$2	4,000	2,000
4	2,000	2,000
6	1,000	2,000
8	500	2,000

a. What is the equilibrium price?
b. What is unusual about the supply curve?
c. At what prices would a shortage occur?
d. At what prices would a surplus occur?
e. Suppose that the addition of new students (all big baseball fans) next year will add 1,000 to the quantity demanded at each price. What will this increase do to next year's demand curve? What is the new equilibrium price?

25. Assume the following information for the demand and supply curves for good Z.

Demand		Supply	
Price	Quantity Demanded	Price	Quantity Supplied
$10	10	$ 1	10
9	20	2	15
8	30	3	20
7	40	4	25
6	50	5	30
5	60	6	35
4	70	7	40
3	80	8	45
2	90	9	50
1	100	10	55

a. Draw the corresponding supply and demand curves.
b. What are the equilibrium price and quantity traded?
c. Would a price of $9 result in a shortage or a surplus? How large?
d. Would a price of $3 result in a shortage or a surplus? How large?
e. If the demand for Z increased by 15 units at every price, what would the new equilibrium price and quantity traded be?
f. Given the original demand for Z, if the supply of Z were increased by 15 units at every price, what would the new equilibrium price and quantity traded be?

Markets in Motion and Price Controls

When four floors of his building caved in, killing three of his neighbors, Uttamchand K. Sojatwala, owner of a successful textile business, refused to leave his two-bedroom, rent-controlled apartment in Mumbai, India. The city then cut off his electricity and water and threatened to arrest his wife, but he still wouldn't leave. In all, fifty-eight tenants refused to leave a rent-controlled apartment building that was considered too dangerous by city officials. Why did these residents take the risks? Cheap rent—$8.50 a month.

There is tremendous tension in "the market" for Mumbai rent-controlled properties between landlords who can't afford to keep up their properties and tenants who will go to extraordinary lengths to keep their units.

SAM HOLLENSHEAD/POLARIS

In this chapter, we study the impact of a change in one or more of the determinants of supply and demand and see how it impacts the market price and quantity exchanged. That is, if you want to know how an event or policy may affect the economy, you must know supply and demand. We then explore the impact of price controls, which are government mandates to set a price above or below the equilibrium price. We also see that policies can have unintended effects—adverse effects that policy makers did not anticipate.

Changes in Market Equilibrium 5.1

▶ What happens to equilibrium price and quantity when the demand curve shifts?

▶ What happens to equilibrium price and quantity when the supply curve shifts?

▶ What happens when both supply and demand shift in the same time period?

▶ What is an indeterminate solution?

When one of the many determinants of demand or supply changes, the demand and/or supply curves will shift, leading to changes in the equilibrium price and equilibrium quantity. There are many events that will have an effect on the supply curve but not much of an impact on the demand curve, such as a flood. Other events shift the demand curve, while having little or no effect on the supply curve. So it is useful to see what happens when just the demand curve or just the supply curve shifts. Supply and demand is a powerful tool that will help us predict what will happen to market equilibrium price and quantity. In the next section, we will see what happens when both supply and demand change. Let us begin with the effects of a change in demand.

What causes the changes in the equilibrium price and equilibrium quantity?

5.1a The Effects of a Change in Demand

A shift in the demand curve—caused by a change in the price of a related good (substitutes or complements), income, the number of buyers, tastes, or expectations—results in a change in both equilibrium price and equilibrium quantity, assuming the supply curve has not changed. But how and why does this relationship happen? The answer can be most clearly explained by means of an example. Suppose a new study claimed that two cups of coffee per day had significant health benefits. We would expect an increase in the demand for coffee. That is, at any given price, buyers want more coffee than before. We are assuming that this new study does not affect how much producers are willing and able to supply—that is, the supply curve does not shift. At the original equilibrium price, P_1, the market is no longer in equilibrium; a shortage occurs because consumers now want to buy Q_3 but sellers only want to sell Q_1, as seen in Exhibit 1(a). This shortage leads to competition among buyers for the limited quantity supplied, putting upward pressure on the price. As the price increases, the quantity demanded decreases (a movement up along the new demand curve, D_2) and the quantity supplied increases (a movement up along the supply curve) until quantity

MATTHEW WILLIAMSON/ALAMY

If demand is greater than the current production schedule, then there will be shortages at the current price. Consequently some dealers were charging prices much higher than the sticker price for the 2014 Corvette Stingray when it first hit the showroom.

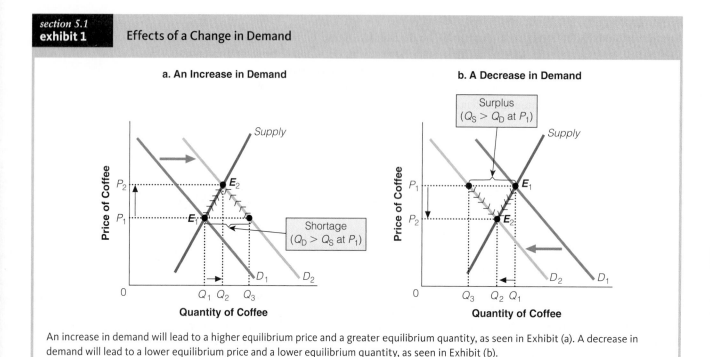

section 5.1
exhibit 1   Effects of a Change in Demand

a. An Increase in Demand

b. A Decrease in Demand

An increase in demand will lead to a higher equilibrium price and a greater equilibrium quantity, as seen in Exhibit (a). A decrease in demand will lead to a lower equilibrium price and a lower equilibrium quantity, as seen in Exhibit (b).

supplied and quantity demanded are equal again at Q_2. This process results in a new equilibrium, E_2, at a higher equilibrium price, P_2, and a greater equilibrium quantity, Q_2.

Now suppose a new study finds that consuming as little as two cups of coffee poses a serious health risk. In Exhibit 1(b), buyers demand less coffee, shifting the demand curve for coffee to the left from D_1 to D_2. Again, we are assuming that this new study does not affect how much producers are willing and able to supply; that is, the supply curve does not shift. At the original price, P_1, a surplus occurs because the quantity supplied is now greater than the quantity demanded. The market is no longer in equilibrium. As sellers compete to sell the surplus, the price falls. As the price falls, coffee growers reduce the quantity supplied (*a movement down along the supply curve*) and buyers increase the quantity demanded (a movement down along the new demand curve, D_2) until quantity supplied and quantity demanded are equal again at Q_2. This process results in a new equilibrium E_2, at a lower equilibrium price, P_2 and a lower equilibrium quantity, Q_2.

In short, given an upward sloping supply curve, an increase in demand will lead to a higher equilibrium price and a greater equilibrium quantity. A decrease in demand will lead to a lower equilibrium price and a lower equilibrium quantity.

5.1b **The Effects of a Change in Supply**

Like a shift in demand, a shift in the supply curve—caused by a change in input prices, prices of related products, expectations, number of suppliers or technology—will also influence both equilibrium price and equilibrium quantity, assuming that demand for the product has not changed. For example, what impact would favorable weather conditions have in coffee-producing countries? Such conditions could cause an increase in the supply of coffee. At any given price, sellers now want to produce and sell more coffee. At the original equilibrium price of P_1, consumers still want to buy Q_1, but sellers are now willing to supply Q_3, as seen in Exhibit 2(a). This creates a surplus at price, P_1. Sellers compete to sell the surplus by reducing the price. As the price falls, the quantity demanded increases (a movement down along the demand curve) and the quantity supplied decreases along the new supply curve, S_2 until quantity supplied and quantity demanded are equal again at the new equilibrium quantity, Q_2. The process results in a new equilibrium, E_2, at a lower equilibrium price, P_2 and a higher equilibrium quantity Q_2.

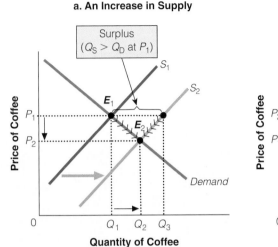

Effects of a Change in Supply

a. An Increase in Supply

Surplus
$(Q_S > Q_D$ at $P_1)$

S_1

S_2

Price of Coffee

E_1

P_1

E_2

P_2

Demand

0   Q_1 Q_2 Q_3

Quantity of Coffee

b. A Decrease in Supply

S_2

S_1

E_2

P_2

E_1

P_1

Shortage
$(Q_D > Q_S$ at $P_1)$

Demand

0   Q_3 Q_2 Q_1

Quantity of Coffee

An increase in supply will lead to a lower equilibrium price and a greater equilibrium quantity, as seen in Exhibit (a). A decrease in supply will lead to a higher equilibrium price and a lower equilibrium quantity, as seen in Exhibit (b).

What impact would unfavorable weather conditions have in coffee-producing countries? Such conditions could cause a reduction in the supply of coffee. At any given price, sellers now want to sell less coffee. At the original equilibrium price of P_1, consumers still want to buy Q_1, but sellers are now only willing to supply Q_3. Thus, a shortage develops as seen in Exhibit 2(b). Competition among competing buyers for the limited quantity supplied forces the price up.

As the price increases, the quantity demanded decreases (a movement along the demand curve) and the quantity supplied increases (a movement up along the new supply curve, S_2) until the quantity demanded and quantity supplied are equal again at the new equilibrium quantity, Q_2. The process results in a new equilibrium, E_2, at a higher equilibrium price, P_2 and a lower equilibrium quantity, Q_2.

In short, given a downward-sloping demand curve, an increase in supply will lead to a lower equilibrium price and a greater equilibrium quantity. A decrease in supply will lead to a higher equilibrium price and a lower equilibrium quantity.

5.1c The Effects of Changes in Both Supply and Demand

We have discussed that, as part of the continual process of adjustment that occurs in the marketplace, supply and demand can each shift in response to many different factors, with the market then adjusting toward the new equilibrium. We have, so far, only considered what happens when just one such change occurs at a time. In these cases, we learned that the results of the adjustments in supply and demand on the equilibrium price and quantity are predictable. However, both supply and demand will often shift in the same time period. Can we predict what will happen to equilibrium prices and equilibrium quantities in these situations?

ECS

economic content standards

Changes in supply or demand cause prices to change; in turn, buyers and sellers adjust their purchases and sales decisions.

ANDREW LICHTENSTEIN/CORBIS

Drought conditions in the United States have led to fewer calves and cows. It is likely that 2014 and 2015 will see beef prices hit record highs as beef production falls further. According to Bloomberg News, herds are at levels we have not seen since 1951. Herd expansion is a slow process, so the higher prices will probably be around for awhile. In addition, there is a slowly growing demand for beef, which will also put upward pressure on prices.

USE WHAT YOU'VE LEARNED

Change in Demand

Q In ski resorts such as Aspen and Sun Valley, hotel prices are higher in February (in-season when more skiers want to ski) than in May (off-season when fewer skiers want to ski). If the May hotel prices were charged in February, what problem would arise? What if we charged February's price in May?

A In the (likely) event that supply is not altered significantly, demand is chiefly responsible for the higher hotel prices in the prime skiing months. In Exhibit 3(a), if prices were maintained at the off-season rates (P_{MAY}) all year long, a shortage would exist—the difference between points A and B in Exhibit 3(a). This excess quantity demanded at the off-peak prices causes prime-season rates to be higher. After all, why would a self-interested resort owner rent you a room for less than its opportunity cost (what someone else would be willing to pay)? For example, at the Hotel Jerome in Aspen, the price per night of a Deluxe King room is almost three times higher in February (in-season) than it is in mid-May (off-season). In Exhibit 3(b), we see that if hotels were to charge the in-season price (P_{FEB}) during the off-season

(May), a surplus would result—the difference between points C and D. Now, it would be this excess quantity supplied during the off-season (at in-season prices) that would cause the price to fall. Who needs all the empty rooms?

What would happen if the Hotel Jerome, pictured above, charged the lower out-of-season rate for resort rentals during peak ski season?

---

section 5.1
exhibit 3   The Market for Aspen Rentals

a. Charging May (Off-Season) Prices in February (In-Season)

b. Charging February (In-Season) Prices in May (Off-Season)

As you will see, when supply and demand move at the same time, we can predict the change in one variable (price or quantity), but we are unable to predict the direction of the effect on the other variable with any certainty. The change in the second variable, then, is said to be *indeterminate* because it cannot be determined without additional information about the size of the relative shifts in supply and demand. This concept will become clearer to you as we work through the following example.

An Increase in Supply and a Decrease in Demand

In Exhibits 4(a) and 4(b), we have an increase in supply and a decrease in demand. These changes will clearly result in a decrease in the equilibrium price because both the increase in supply and the decrease in demand work to push this price down. This drop in equilibrium price (from P_1 to P_2) is shown in the movement from E_1 to E_2 in Exhibits 4(a) and 4(b).

The effect of these changes on equilibrium price is clear, but how does the equilibrium quantity change? The impact on equilibrium quantity is indeterminate because the increase in supply increases the equilibrium quantity and the decrease in demand decreases it. In this scenario, the change in the equilibrium quantity will vary depending on the relative changes in supply and demand. If, as shown in Exhibit 4(a), the decrease in demand is greater than the increase in supply, the equilibrium quantity will decrease. If, however, as shown in Exhibit 4(b), the increase in supply is greater than the decrease in demand, the equilibrium quantity will increase.

What does it mean when it says that one of the variables is indeterminate?

An Increase in Demand and Supply

It is also possible that both supply and demand will increase (or decrease). This situation, for example, has happened with high-definition (HD) televisions (and with laptops, cell phones, tablet computers, digital cameras, and other electronic equipment, too). As a result of

---

**section 5.1
exhibit 4**   **Shifts in Supply and Demand**

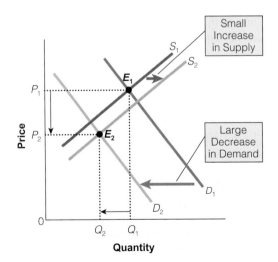

a. A Small Increase in Supply and a Large Decrease in Demand

If the decrease in demand (leftward shift) is greater than the increase in supply (rightward shift), the equilibrium price and equilibrium quantity will fall.

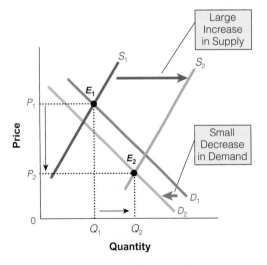

b. A Large Increase in Supply and a Small Decrease in Demand

If the increase in supply (rightward shift) is greater than the decrease in demand (leftward shift), the equilibrium price will fall and the equilibrium quantity will rise.

An Increase in the Demand and Supply of HD Televisions

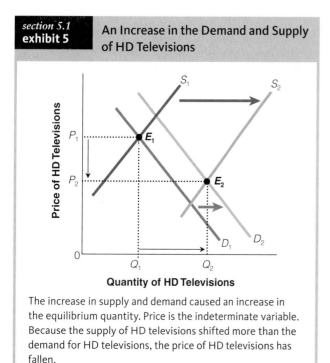

Quantity of HD Televisions

The increase in supply and demand caused an increase in the equilibrium quantity. Price is the indeterminate variable. Because the supply of HD televisions shifted more than the demand for HD televisions, the price of HD televisions has fallen.

technological breakthroughs, the prices of component parts falling, and new factories manufacturing HD televisions, the supply curve for HD televisions shifted to the right. That is, at any given price, more HD televisions were offered than before. But with rising income and an increasing number of buyers in the market, the demand for HD televisions increased as well. As shown in Exhibit 5, both the increased demand and the increased supply caused an increase in the equilibrium quantity—more HD televisions were sold. The equilibrium price could have gone either up (because of increased demand) or down (because of increased supply), depending on the relative sizes of the demand and supply shifts. In this case, price is the indeterminate variable. However, in the case of HD televisions, we know that the supply curve shifted more than the demand curve, so that the effect of increased supply pushing prices down outweighed the effect of increased demand pushing prices up. As a result, the equilibrium price of HD televisions has fallen (from P_1 to P_2) over time.

5.1d The Combinations of Supply and Demand Shifts

The possible changes in demand and/or supply shifts are presented, along with the resulting changes in equilibrium quantity and equilibrium price, in Exhibit 6. Even though you could memorize the impact of the various possible changes in demand and supply, it would be more profitable to draw a graph whenever a situation of changing demand and/or supply arises. Remember that an increase in either demand or supply means a rightward shift in the curve, while a decrease in either means a leftward shift. Also, when both demand and supply change, one of the two equilibrium values, price or quantity, will change in an indeterminate manner (increase or decrease), depending on the relative magnitude of the changes in supply and demand. Specifically, in (a), (c), (g), and (i), both supply and demand change, so one of the variables is indeterminate, which means that the variable, P or Q, may increase, decrease, or remain the same, depending on the size of the change in demand relative to the change in supply.

5.1e Supply, Demand, and the Market Economy

Supply and demand are at the very foundation of the market system. They determine the prices of goods and services and determine how our scarce resources are allocated. What is truly amazing is how producers respond to the complex wants of the population without having tremendous shortages or surpluses, despite the fact that in a "free market," no single individual or agency makes decisions about what to produce. The market system provides a way for millions of producers and consumers to allocate scarce resources. Buyers and sellers indicate their wants through their actions and inactions in the marketplace, and this collective "voice" determines how resources are allocated. But how is this information communicated? Market prices serve as the language of the market system.

We often say the decision is made by "the market" or "market forces," but this is of little help in pinpointing the name and the place of the decision maker. In fact, no single person makes decisions about the quantity and quality of television, cars, beds, or any other goods or services consumed in the economy. Literally millions of people, both producers and consumers, participate in the decision-making process. To paraphrase a statement made popular by the first great modern economist, Adam Smith, it is as if an invisible hand works to coordinate the efforts of millions of diverse participants in the complex process of producing and distributing goods and services.

Market prices communicate important information to both buyers and sellers. They reveal information about the relative availability of products to buyers, and they provide sellers with critical information about the relative value that consumers place on those products. In effect, market prices provide a way for both buyers and sellers to communicate about the relative value of resources. This communication results in a shifting of resources from those uses that are less valued to those that are more valued.

section 5.1
exhibit 6   Summary of Demand Curve and Supply Curve Shifts

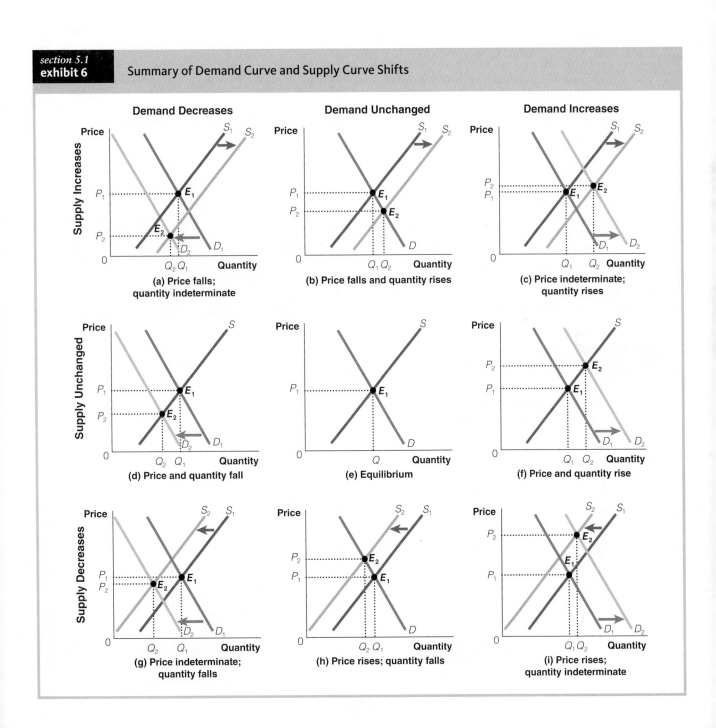

IN THE NEWS

College Enrollment and the Price of Going to College

Q How is it possible that the price of a college education has increased significantly over the past 37 years, yet many more students are attending college? Does this relationship defy the law of demand?

A If we know the price of a college education (adjusted for inflation) and the number of students enrolled in college between 1970 and 2014, we can tell a plausible story using the analysis of supply and demand. In Exhibit 7(a), suppose that we have data for points A and B: the price of a college education and the quantity (the number of college students enrolled in the respective years, 1970 and 2014). In Exhibit 7(b), we connect the two points with supply and demand curves and see a decrease in supply and an increase in demand. Demand increased between 1970 and 2014 for at least two reasons. First, on the demand side, as population grows, a greater number of buyers want a college education. Second, a college education is a normal good; as income increases, buyers increase their demand for a college education. Third, demand has increased because of the availability of student loans. The percentage of U.S. undergraduates who rely on the federal government for financial aid recently soared above 50 percent. On the supply side, several factors caused the supply curve for education to shift to the left: the cost of hiring new staff and faculty (and increases in their salaries), new equipment (computers, lab equipment, and library supplies), and buildings (additional classrooms, labs, cafeteria expansions, and dormitory space).

This situation does not defy the law of demand that states that there is an inverse relationship between price and quantity demanded, *ceteris paribus*. The truth is that supply and demand curves are shifting constantly. In this case, the demand (increasing) and supply (decreasing) caused price and quantity to rise.

section 5.1
exhibit 7   Market for College Education

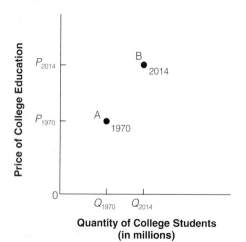

**a. Price of College Education
and Quantity of College Students**

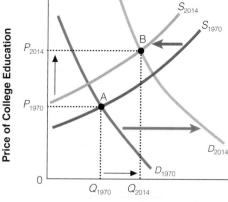

**b. Simultaneous Increase in Demand
and Decrease in Supply**

USE WHAT YOU'VE LEARNED

Supply and Demand Applications

Q During the second half of the 20th century, demand for chicken increased because of rising income and the purported health benefits. However, as the demand for chicken increased, the price fell. Why? (*Hint:* Remember it is supply and demand.)

A Even though the demand for chicken did increase (a small rightward shift), the supply of chicken increased even more. Technological advances in the poultry industry and many new suppliers caused the supply curve to shift rightward. In order for the price to fall, the supply must have shifted further to the right than the demand curve. The result is more chickens consumed at a lower price.

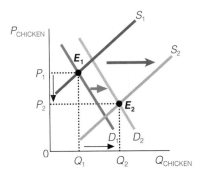

Q Suppose the demand for gasoline increases because of world economic growth and higher incomes. At the same time, supply decreases because of hostilities in the Middle East and refinery problems. What can we predict would happen to the price and quantity of gasoline?

A The increase in demand (rightward shift) and the decrease in supply (leftward shift) would lead to an increase in price. We are not sure about the quantity of gasoline consumed—it depends on the magnitude of the

shifts in the demand and supply curves. That is, quantity is indeterminate.

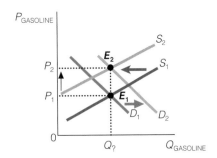

Q Suppose the demand for air travel decreases because of air safety concerns. At the same time, the price of jet fuel increases. What do you think will happen to the price and quantity of air travel?

A Safety concerns would result in a decrease in demand (leftward shift) for air travel and the higher input cost of jet fuel would lead to a decrease in supply (leftward shift). These factors reduce the quantity of air travel. The price change will depend on the magnitude of the shifts in the demand and supply curves. That is, price is indeterminate.

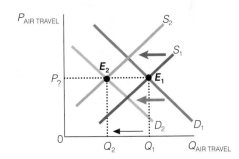

Q Hypothetically, suppose a new study reveals that sugar can have "huge" negative health consequences, causing a large decrease in demand. In addition, a slight reduction in the sugar yield occurs because of bad weather in sugar-producing areas. What do you think will happen to the price and quantity of sugar?

(continued)

Use What You've Learned continued

A

A large decrease in demand (leftward shift) for sugar and a small decrease in supply (leftward shift) because of bad weather lead to a reduction in price and a large reduction in quantity.

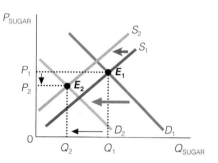

Q

As the price of oil rises, many may switch to burning natural gas to save money. Can buyers of natural gas expect any surprises?

A

If oil and natural gas are substitutes, then the higher price for oil will cause an increase in demand for natural gas (rightward shift). As a result, the price and quantity of natural gas will rise.

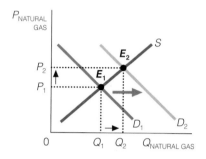

Stub Hub tickets can make supply and demand come alive as prices respond to changes in supply and demand. A ticket with little appeal—low demand—can sell for below face value and tickets in huge demand can sell for well above face value.

© ISTOCKPHOTO.COM/WDSTOCK

SECTION QUIZ

1. Other things equal, a decrease in consumer income would

   a. increase the price and increase the quantity of autos exchanged.

   b. increase the price and decrease the quantity of autos exchanged.

   c. decrease the price and increase the quantity of autos exchanged.

   d. decrease the price and decrease the quantity of autos exchanged.

(continued)

SECTION QUIZ (cont.)

2. An increase in the expected future price of a good by consumers would, other things being equal,

   a. increase the current price and increase the current quantity exchanged.

   b. increase the current price and decrease the current quantity exchanged.

   c. decrease the current price and increase the current quantity exchanged.

   d. decrease the current price and decrease the current quantity exchanged.

3. Assume that airline travel is a normal good. Higher incomes would

   a. increase both the price and the quantity of airline travel.

   b. decrease both the price and quantity of airline travel.

   c. increase the price and decrease the quantity of airline travel.

   d. decrease the price and increase the quantity of airline travel.

4. If you observed the price of a good increasing and the quantity exchanged decreasing, it would be most likely caused by a(n)

   a. increase in demand.

   b. decrease in demand.

   c. increase in supply.

   d. decrease in supply.

5. If you observed the price of a good decreasing and the quantity exchanged decreasing, it would be most likely caused by a(n)

   a. increase in demand.

   b. decrease in demand.

   c. increase in supply.

   d. decrease in supply.

6. If both supply and demand decreased, but supply decreased more than demand, the result would be

   a. a higher price and a lower equilibrium quantity.

   b. a lower price and a lower equilibrium quantity.

   c. no change in the price and a lower equilibrium quantity.

   d. a higher price and a greater equilibrium quantity.

   e. a lower price and a greater equilibrium quantity.

7. Which of the following are true statements?

   a. Changes in demand will cause a change in the equilibrium price and/or quantity, *ceteris paribus*.

   b. Changes in supply will cause a change in the equilibrium price and/or quantity, *ceteris paribus*.

   c. Supply and demand curves can shift simultaneously in response to changes in both supply and demand determinants.

   d. When simultaneous shifts occur in both supply and demand curves, we will be able to determine one, but not both, of the variables.

   e. All of the above are true.

---

1. Does an increase in demand create a shortage or surplus at the original price?

2. What happens to the equilibrium price and quantity as a result of a demand increase?

3. Does an increase in supply create a shortage or surplus at the original price?

(continued)

SECTION QUIZ (cont.)

4. Assuming the market is already at equilibrium, what happens to the equilibrium price and quantity as a result of a supply increase?

5. Why are evening and weekend long-distance calls cheaper than weekday long-distance calls?

6. What would have to be true for both supply and demand to shift in the same time period?

7. When both supply and demand shift, what added information do we need to know in order to determine in which direction the indeterminate variable changes?

8. If both buyers and sellers of grapes expect grape prices to rise in the near future, what will happen to grape prices and sales today?

9. If demand for peanut butter increases and supply decreases, what will happen to equilibrium price and quantity?

Answers: 1. d 2. a 3. a 4. d 5. b 6. a 7. e

5.2   Price Controls

▶ What are price controls?

▶ What are price ceilings?

▶ What are price floors?

▶ What is the law of unintended consequences?

5.2a Price Controls

price ceiling
a legally established maximum price

price floor
a legally established minimum price

economic content standards

Government-enforced price ceilings set below the market clearing price and government-enforced price floors set above the market clearing price distort price signals and incentives to producers and consumers. The price ceilings cause persistent shortages, while price floors cause persistent surpluses.

Although non-equilibrium prices can occur naturally in the private sector, reflecting uncertainty, they seldom last for long. Governments, however, may impose non-equilibrium prices for significant periods. Price controls involve the use of the power of the state to establish prices different from the equilibrium prices that would otherwise prevail. The motivations for price controls vary with the market under consideration. For example, a price ceiling, a legal maximum price, is often set for goods deemed important to low-income households, such as housing. Or a price floor, a legal minimum price, may be set on wages because wages are the primary source of income for most people.

Price controls are not always implemented by the federal government. Local governments (and more rarely, private companies) can and do impose local price controls. One fairly well-known example is rent control. The inflation of the late 1970s meant rapidly rising rents; some communities, such as Santa Monica, California, decided to do something about it. In response, they limited how much landlords could charge for rental housing.

5.2b Price Ceilings: Rent Controls

Rent control experiences can be found in many cities across the country. San Francisco, Berkeley, and New York City all have had some form of rent control. Although the rules may vary from city to city and over time, generally the price (or rent) of an apartment remains fixed over the tenure of an occupant, except for allowable annual increases tied to the cost of living or some other price index. When an occupant moves out, the owners can usually, but not always, raise the rent to a near-market level for the next occupant. The controlled rents for existing occupants, however, are generally well below market rental rates.

Results of Rent Controls

Most people living in rent-controlled apartments are getting a good deal, one that they would lose by moving as their family circumstances or income changes. Tenants thus are reluctant to give up their governmentally granted right to a below-market-rent apartment. In addition, because the rents received by landlords are constrained and below market levels, the rate of return (roughly, the profit) on housing investments falls compared with that on other forms of real estate not subject to rent controls, such as office rents or mortgage payments on condominiums. Hence, the incentive to construct new housing is reduced.

Furthermore, when landlords are limited in the rents they can charge, they have little incentive to improve or upgrade apartments—by putting in new kitchen appliances or new carpeting, for instance. In fact, rent controls give landlords some incentive to avoid routine maintenance, thereby lowering the cost of apartment ownership to a figure approximating the controlled rental price, although the quality of the housing stock will deteriorate over time.

Another impact of rent controls is that they promote housing discrimination. Where rent controls do not exist, prejudiced landlords might willingly rent to people they believe are undesirable simply because the undesirables are the only ones willing to pay the requested rents (and the landlords are not willing to lower their rents substantially to get desirable renters because of the possible loss of thousands of dollars in income). With rent controls, each rent-controlled apartment is likely to attract many possible renters, some desirable and some undesirable as judged by the landlord, simply because the rent is at a below-equilibrium price. Landlords can indulge in their "taste" for discrimination without any additional financial loss beyond that required by the controls. Consequently, they will be more likely to choose to rent to desirable people, perhaps a family without children or pets, rather than to undesirable ones, perhaps a family with lower income and so a greater risk of nonpayment.

Exhibit 1 shows the impact of rent controls. If the price ceiling (P_{RC}) is set below the equilibrium price (P_E), consumers are willing to buy Q_D, but producers are only willing to supply Q_S. The rent control policy will therefore create a persistent shortage, the difference between Q_D and Q_S.

Many have blamed the late President Hugo Chavez and his successor Nicolas Maduro for the severe shortages in Venezuela. Chavez accused companies of holding products off the market to drive the price up. In an effort to control price increases, Chavez imposed price controls on a number of goods. The outcome was predictable: widespread shortages of many basic goods, including milk, toilet paper, and meats. In January, 2012, the Bank of Venezuela compiled a scarcity index and found that the difficulty of finding basic goods on store shelves was at its worst level since 2008. And those shortages affected both the poor and the well-to-do.

JORGE SILVA/REUTERS/CORBIS

Can rent controls promote housing discrimination?

5.2c Price Floors: The Minimum Wage

The argument for a minimum wage is simple: Existing wages for workers in some types of labor markets do not allow for a very high standard of living, and a minimum wage allows those workers to live better than before. Ever since 1938, when the first minimum wage was established (at 25 cents per hour), the federal government has, by legislation, made it illegal to pay most workers an amount below the current legislated minimum wage. In 2014, the federal minimum wage was set at $7.25. A number of states also have minimum-wage laws. In cases where an employee is subject to both state and federal minimum-wage laws, the employee is entitled to the higher minimum wage.

Let's examine graphically the impact of a minimum wage on low-skilled workers. In Exhibit 2, suppose the government sets the minimum wage, W_{MIN}, above the market equilibrium wage, W_E. In Exhibit 2, we see that the price floor is binding. That is, there is a surplus of low-skilled workers at W_{MIN} because the quantity of labor supplied is greater than the quantity

What does a binding price ceiling or binding price floor mean?

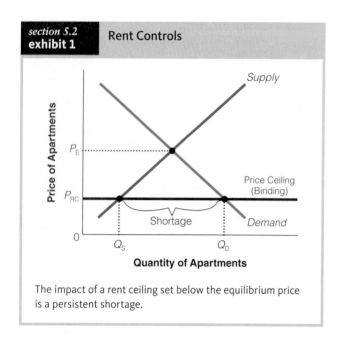

section 5.2
exhibit 1   Rent Controls

The impact of a rent ceiling set below the equilibrium price is a persistent shortage.

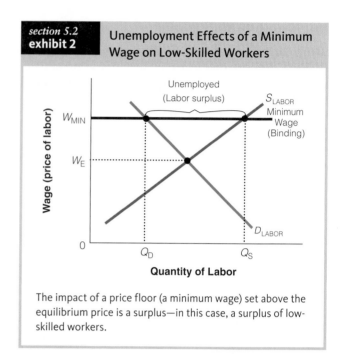

section 5.2
exhibit 2   Unemployment Effects of a Minimum Wage on Low-Skilled Workers

The impact of a price floor (a minimum wage) set above the equilibrium price is a surplus—in this case, a surplus of low-skilled workers.

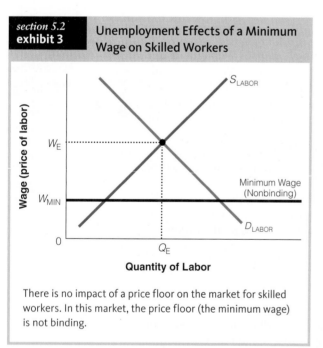

section 5.2
exhibit 3   Unemployment Effects of a Minimum Wage on Skilled Workers

There is no impact of a price floor on the market for skilled workers. In this market, the price floor (the minimum wage) is not binding.

Who loses and who wins with higher minimum wages?

Are consumers hurt by a higher minimum wage?

of labor demanded. The reason for the surplus of low-skilled workers (unemployment) at W_{MIN} is that more people are willing to work than employers are willing and able to hire.

Notice that not everyone loses from a minimum wage. Workers who continue to hold jobs have higher incomes—those between 0 and Q_D in Exhibit 2. However, many low-skilled workers suffer from a minimum wage—those between Q_D and Q_S in Exhibit 2—because they either lose their jobs or are unable to get them in the first place. Although studies disagree somewhat on the precise magnitudes, they largely agree that minimum-wage laws do create some unemployment and that the unemployment is concentrated among teenagers—the least-experienced and least-skilled members of the labor force. Many teenagers are willing to accept the lower wage in exchange for on-the-job training. In fact, some college students accept non-paying intern jobs for the experience. Minimum-wage laws do not apply to internships, and if they did, many of those jobs might not exist.

Most U.S. workers are not directly affected by the minimum wage because in the market for their skills, they earn wages that exceed the minimum wage. For example, a minimum wage will not affect the unemployment rate for physicians. In Exhibit 3, we see the labor market for skilled and experienced workers. In this market, the minimum wage (the price floor) is not binding because these workers are earning wages that far exceed the minimum wage—W_E is much higher than W_{MIN}.

This analysis does not "prove" that minimum-wage laws are "bad" and should be abolished. In fact, a recent poll of Ph.D. economists showed that 47 percent favored eliminating the minimum wage, while 38 percent would increase it and 15 percent would keep it at its current level. Let's take a more careful look. First, consider the empirical question of how much unemployment is caused by minimum wages. Economists David Card and Alan Kreuger published a controversial study on the increase in minimum wage in the fast-food industry in New Jersey and Pennsylvania. They found the effect on employment to be quite small. However, other researchers using similar data have come to the opposite conclusion. In fact, most empirical studies indicate that a 10 percent increase in the minimum wage would reduce employment of teenagers between 1 and 3 percent. Second, some might believe that the cost of unemployment resulting from a minimum wage is a reasonable price to pay for ensuring that those with jobs get a "decent" wage. However, opponents of minimum wage argue that it might induce teenagers to drop out of school and prevent some young, low-skilled workers from getting on-the-job training that would increase their productivity and earning prospects. Less than one-third of minimum-wage earners are from families with incomes below the poverty line. In fact, many recipients of the minimum wage are part-time teenage workers from middle-income families. More efficient methods transfer income to low-wage workers, such as a wage subsidy like the earned income tax credit. This is a government program that supplements low-wage workers. Of course, there are no free lunches so subsidies in the form of wages, income, or rent ultimately cost taxpayers. We revisit this topic in upcoming chapters.

However, the analysis does point out there is a cost to having a minimum wage: The burden of the minimum wage falls also on consumers of products made more costly by the minimum wage. In addition, a higher minimum wage might tempt some businesses to substitute robots or other forms of automation for low-skilled labor.

What do you think would happen to the number of teenagers getting jobs if we raised the minimum wage to $50 an hour? The first jobs many young people could find would reflect their low productivity. That productivity may not yet be great enough to be worth even the current minimum wage to employers. And a higher minimum wage reduces the incentive for an employer to take a chance on a "marginal" low-skilled applicant.

5.2d Price Ceilings: Price Controls on Gasoline

Another example of price ceilings leading to shortages is the price controls imposed on gasoline in 1974. In 1973, the Organization of Petroleum Exporting Countries (OPEC) reduced the supply of oil. Because crude oil is the most important input in the production of gasoline, this reduction in the supply of oil caused a shift in the supply curve for gasoline leftward from S_1 to S_2 in Exhibit 4. In an effort to prevent sharply rising prices, the government imposed price controls on gasoline in 1974. The government told gasoline stations they could not charge more than P_C for gasoline. But people wanted to buy more gasoline than was available at the controlled price, P_C. That is, a shortage developed at P_C, as you can see in Exhibit 4. Some customers were lucky enough to get their gasoline at P_C (0 to Q_S), but others were left wanting

In 1974, the government imposed price ceilings on gasoline. The result was shortages. In some cities, such as Chicago, Portland, and New York, drivers waited over an hour to fill up their tanks. As you know, the value of your time has an opportunity cost.

(Q_S to Q_D). The price ceiling was binding. Consequently, people wasted hours waiting in line for gasoline. Some gas stations sold their gas on a first-come, first-served basis. Some states implemented an even/odd license plate system. If your license plate ended in an odd number, you could buy gas on only odd-numbered days. In addition, quantity restrictions meant that some stations would only allow you to buy a few gallons a day; when they ran out of gas, they closed for the day. Many gas stations were closed in the evenings and on weekends.

A number of government officials wanted to put the blame on OPEC, but if prices were allowed to rise to their equilibrium at E_2, shortages would have been avoided. Instead, it would have meant higher prices at P_2 and a greater quantity sold, Q_2 rather than Q_S. Of course, not everybody was unhappy with the price ceiling. Recall our discussion of opportunity cost in Chapter 2. People place different values on their time. People with a low opportunity cost

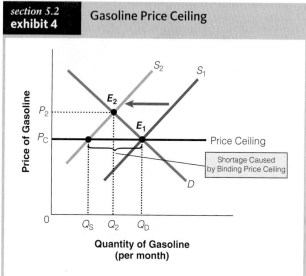

section 5.2 exhibit 4   Gasoline Price Ceiling

The higher price of crude oil (a major input for gasoline) caused the supply curve to shift leftward from S_1 to S_2. Without price controls, the price would have risen to P_2. However, with the binding price ceiling consumers were able and willing to buy Q_D but producers were able and willing to sell Q_S. Therefore, a shortage of $Q_D - Q_S$ occurred at P_C.

unintended consequences

the secondary effects of an action that may occur as well as the initial effects

of time but who cannot as easily afford the higher price per gallon (e.g., poor retired senior citizens) would be more likely to favor the controls. Surgeons, lawyers, and others who have high hourly wages and salaries would view the controls less favorably because the time spent waiting in line may be worth more to them than paying the higher price for gasoline.

5.2e Unintended Consequences

When markets are altered for policy reasons, it is wise to remember that actions do not always have the results that were initially intended—in other words, actions can have **unintended consequences**. As economists, we must always look for the secondary effects of an action, which may occur along with the initial effects. For example, the government is often well intentioned when it adopts price controls to help low-skilled workers or tenants in search of affordable housing; however, such policies may also cause unintended consequences that could completely undermine the intended effects. For example, rent controls may have the immediate effect of lowering rents, but secondary effects may well include low vacancy rates, discrimination against low-income and large families, deterioration of the quality of rental units, and black markets. Similarly, a sizable increase in the minimum wage may help many low-skilled workers or apprentices but may also result in higher unemployment and/or a reduction in fringe benefits, such as vacations and discounts to employees. Society has to make tough decisions, and if the government subsidizes some programs or groups of people in one area, then something must always be given up somewhere else. The "law of scarcity" cannot be repealed!

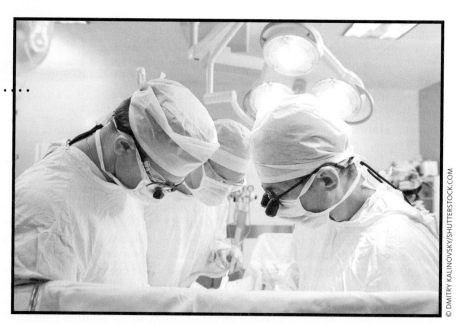

When the sale of organs is illegal, it is like setting a price ceiling at zero. The only available supply comes from altruistic donors at a zero price. Since the quantity demanded of kidneys is much greater than the quantity supplied, there is a shortage. A number of economists believe that society would benefit from allowing a free market in organs, especially kidneys. Everybody is born with two kidneys. So if those needing a kidney bought one from those who were willing to sell one of their two, the price would rise and the shortage would disappear.

Critics argue a free market for kidneys may be efficient, but it is not fair. That is, kidneys would be allocated on the basis of who was willing and able to pay the most. But under the current system, people are walking around with two kidneys while some are dying to get one. Is that fair?

Use What You've Learned

Binding Price Controls

Q If binding price controls are imposed by the government at levels that are either above or below the equilibrium price, is the quantity of goods bought (and sold) less than the equilibrium quantity?

A If a price ceiling (a legally established maximum price) is set below the equilibrium price, quantity demanded will be greater than quantity supplied, resulting in a shortage at that price. Because producers will only increase the quantity supplied at higher prices, *ceteris paribus*, only Q_1 will be bought and sold. Alternatively, if a price floor (a legally established minimum price) is set above the equilibrium price, quantity supplied will be greater than quantity demanded, causing a surplus at that price. Because consumers will only increase

their quantity demanded, *ceteris paribus*, at lower prices, only Q_1 will be bought and sold.

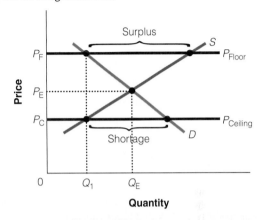

SECTION QUIZ

1. If the equilibrium price of wheat is $3 per bushel and then a price floor of $2.50 per bushel is imposed by the government,

   a. there will be no effect on the wheat market.

   b. there will be a shortage of wheat.

   c. there will be a surplus of wheat.

   d. the price of wheat will decrease.

2. Which of the following is true?

   a. A price ceiling reduces the quantity exchanged in the market, but a price floor increases the quantity exchanged in the market.

   b. A price ceiling increases the quantity exchanged in the market, but a price floor decreases the quantity exchanged in the market.

   c. Both price floors and price ceilings reduce the quantity exchanged in the market.

   d. Both price floors and price ceilings increase the quantity exchanged in the market.

3. If a price floor was set at the current equilibrium price, which of the following would cause a surplus as a result?

   a. an increase in demand

   b. a decrease in demand

   c. an increase in supply

   d. a decrease in supply

   e. either (b) or (c)

(continued)

SECTION QUIZ (cont.)

4. A current shortage is due to a price ceiling. If the price ceiling is removed,

   a. price would increase, quantity supplied would increase, and quantity demanded would decrease.

   b. price would increase, quantity supplied would decrease, and quantity demanded would increase.

   c. price would decrease, quantity supplied would increase, and quantity demanded would decrease.

   d. price would decrease, quantity supplied would decrease, and quantity demanded would increase.

5. A current surplus is due to a price floor. If the price floor is removed,

   a. price would increase, quantity demanded would increase, and quantity supplied would increase.

   b. price would increase, quantity demanded would decrease, and quantity supplied would decrease.

   c. price would decrease, quantity demanded would increase, and quantity supplied would decrease.

   d. price would decrease, quantity demanded would decrease, and quantity supplied would increase.

6. Which of the following will most likely occur with a 20 percent increase in the minimum wage?

   a. higher unemployment rates among experienced and skilled workers

   b. higher unemployment rates among young and low-skilled workers

   c. lower unemployment rates for young and low-skilled workers

   d. the price floor (minimum wage) will be binding in the young and low-skilled labor market but not in the experienced and skilled labor market

   e. both (b) and (d)

---

1. How is rent control an example of a price ceiling?

2. What predictable effects result from price ceilings such as rent control?

3. How is the minimum-wage law an example of a price floor?

4. What predictable effects result from price floors such as the minimum wage?

5. What may happen to the amount of discrimination against groups such as families with children, pet owners, smokers, or students when rent control is imposed?

6. Why does rent control often lead to condominium conversions?

7. What is the law of unintended consequences?

8. Why is the law of unintended consequences so important in making public policy?

Answers: 1. a 2. c 3. e 4. a 5. c 6. e

Fill in the blanks:

1. An increase in demand results in a(n) _____ equilibrium price and a(n) _____ equilibrium quantity.

2. A decrease in supply results in a(n) _____ equilibrium price and a(n) _____ equilibrium quantity.

3. If demand decreases and supply increases, but the decrease in demand is greater than the increase in supply, the equilibrium quantity will _____.

4. If supply decreases and demand increases, the equilibrium price will _____ and the equilibrium quantity will be _____.

5. A price _____ is a legally established maximum price; a price _____ is a legally established minimum price.

6. Rent controls distort market signals and lead to _____ of rent-controlled apartments.

7. The quality of rent-controlled apartments would tend to _____ over time.

8. An increase in the minimum wage would tend to create _____ unemployment for low-skilled workers.

9. The secondary effects of an action that may occur after the initial effects are called _____.

Answers: 1. greater; greater 2. higher; lower 3. decrease 4. increase; indeterminate 5. ceiling; floor 6. shortages 7. decline 8. additional 9. unintended consequences

price ceiling 144

price floor 144

unintended consequences 148

5.1 Changes in Market Equilibrium

1. **Does an increase in demand create a shortage or surplus at the original price?**

   An increase in demand increases the quantity demanded at the original equilibrium price, but it does not change the quantity supplied at that price, meaning that it would create a shortage at the original equilibrium price.

2. **What happens to the equilibrium price and quantity as a result of a demand increase?**

   Frustrated buyers unable to buy all they would like at the original equilibrium price will compete the market price higher, and that higher price will induce suppliers to increase their quantity supplied. The result is a higher market price and a larger market output.

3. **Does an increase in supply create a shortage or surplus at the original price?**

   An increase in supply increases the quantity supplied at the original equilibrium price, but it does not change the quantity demanded at that price, meaning that it would create a surplus at the original equilibrium price.

4. **Assuming the market is already at equilibrium, what happens to the equilibrium price and quantity as a result of a supply increase?**

   Frustrated sellers unable to sell all they would like at the original equilibrium price will compete the market price lower, and that lower price will induce demanders to increase their quantity demanded. The result is a lower market price and a larger market output.

5. **Why do heating oil prices tend to be higher in the winter?**

   The demand for heating oil is higher in the cold winter months. The result of this higher winter heating oil demand, for a given supply curve, is higher prices for heating oil in the winter.

6. **What would have to be true for both supply and demand to shift in the same time period?**

   For both supply and demand to shift in the same time period, one or more of both the supply curve shifters and the demand curve shifters would have to change in that same time period.

7. **When both supply and demand shift, what added information do we need to know in order to determine in which direction the indeterminate variable changes?**

When both supply and demand shift, we need to know which of the shifts is of greater magnitude, so we can know which of the opposing effects in the indeterminate variable is larger; whichever effect is larger will determine the direction of the net effect on the indeterminate variable.

8. **If both buyers and sellers of grapes expect grape prices to rise in the near future, what will happen to grape prices and sales today?**

If grape buyers expect grape prices to rise in the near future, it will increase their current demand to buy grapes, which would tend to increase current prices and increase the current quantity of grapes sold. If grape sellers expect grape prices to rise in the near future, it will decrease their current supply of grapes for sale, which would tend to increase current prices and decrease the current quantity of grapes sold. Because both these effects tend to increase the current price of grapes, grape prices will rise. However, the supply and demand curve shifts tend to change current sales in opposing directions, so without knowing which of these shifts was of a greater magnitude, we do not know what will happen to current grape sales. They could go up, go down, or even stay the same.

9. **If demand for peanut butter increases and supply decreases, what will happen to equilibrium price and quantity?**

An increase in the demand for peanut butter increases the equilibrium price and quantity of peanut butter sold. A decrease in the supply of peanut butter increases the equilibrium price and decreases the quantity of peanut butter sold. The result is an increase in peanut butter prices and an indeterminate effect on the quantity of peanut butter sold.

5.2 Price Controls

1. **How is rent control an example of a price ceiling?**

A price ceiling is a maximum price set below the equilibrium price by the government. Rent control is an example because the controlled rents are held below the market equilibrium rent level.

2. **What predictable effects result from price ceilings such as rent control?**

The predictable effects resulting from price ceilings include shortages, reduced amounts of the controlled good being made available by suppliers, reductions in the quality of the controlled good, and increased discrimination among potential buyers of the good.

3. **How is the minimum-wage law an example of a price floor?**

A price floor is a minimum price set above the equilibrium price by the government. The minimum-wage law is an example because the minimum is set above the market equilibrium wage level for some low-skill workers.

4. **What predictable effects result from price floors such as the minimum wage?**

The predictable effects resulting from price floors include surpluses, reduced amounts of the controlled good being purchased by demanders, increases in the quality of the controlled good, and increased discrimination among potential sellers of the good.

5. **What may happen to the amount of discrimination against groups such as families with children, pet owners, smokers, or students when rent control is imposed?**

Rent control laws prevent prospective renters from compensating landlords through higher rents for any characteristic landlords find less attractive, whether it is bothersome noise from children or pets, odors from smokers, increased numbers of renters per unit, risks of nonpayment by lower-income tenants such as students, and so on. As a result, it lowers the cost of discriminating against anyone with what landlords consider unattractive characteristics because other prospective renters without those characteristics are willing to pay the same controlled rent.

6. **Why does rent control often lead to condominium conversions?**

Rent control applies to rental apartments, but not to apartments owned by their occupants. Therefore, one way to get around rent control restrictions on apartment owners' ability to receive the market value of their apartments is to convert those apartments to condominiums by selling them to tenants instead (what was once a controlled rent becomes part of an uncontrolled mortgage payment).

7. **What is the law of unintended consequences?**

The law of unintended consequences is the term used to indicate that the results of actions are not always as clear as they appear. The secondary effects of an action may cause its results to include many consequences that were not part of what was intended.

8. **Why is the law of unintended consequences so important in making public policy?**

It is impossible to change just one incentive to achieve a particular result through a government policy. A policy will change the incentives facing multiple individuals making multiple decisions, and changes in all those affected choices will result. Sometimes, the unintended consequences can be so substantial that they completely undermine the intended effects of a policy.

1. Using supply and demand curves, show the effect of each of the following events on the market for wheat.
    a. The Midwestern United States (a major wheat-producing area) suffers a flood.
    b. The price of corn decreases (assume that many farmers can grow either corn or wheat).
    c. The Midwest has great weather.
    d. The price of fertilizer declines.
    e. More individuals start growing wheat.

2. Beginning from an initial equilibrium, draw the effects of the changes in the following list in terms of the relevant supply and demand curves.
    a. An increase in the price of hot dogs on the hamburger market
    b. A decrease in the number of taxicab companies in New York City on cab trips
    c. Effect of El Niño rain storms destroying the broccoli crop in two California counties

3. Use supply and demand curves to show
    a. simultaneous increases in supply and demand, with a large increase in supply and a small increase in demand.
    b. simultaneous increases in supply and demand, with a small increase in supply and a large increase in demand.
    c. simultaneous decreases in supply and demand, with a large decrease in supply and a small decrease in demand.
    d. simultaneous decrease in supply and demand, with a small decrease in supply and a large decrease in demand.

4. What would be the impact of a rental price ceiling set above the equilibrium rental price for apartments? below the equilibrium rental price?

5. What would be the impact of a price floor set above the equilibrium price for dairy products? below the equilibrium price?

6. Giving in to pressure from voters who charge that local theater owners are gouging their customers with ticket prices as high as $10 per movie, the city council of a Midwestern city imposes a price ceiling of $2 on all movies. What effect is this likely to have on the market for movies in this particular city? What will happen to the quantity of tickets demanded? What will happen to the quantity supplied? Who gains? Who loses?

7. Why do price floors and price ceilings both reduce the quantity of goods traded in those markets?

8. Why do 10:00 A.M. classes fill up before 8:00 A.M. classes during class registration? Use supply and demand curves to help explain your answer.

9. What would happen to the equilibrium price and quantity exchanged in the following cases?
    a. An increase in income and a decreasing price of a complement, for a normal good
    b. A technological advance and lower input prices
    c. An increase in the price of a substitute and an increase in income, for an inferior good
    d. Producers' expectations that prices will soon fall, and increasingly costly government regulations

10. Refer to the following supply and demand curve diagram.

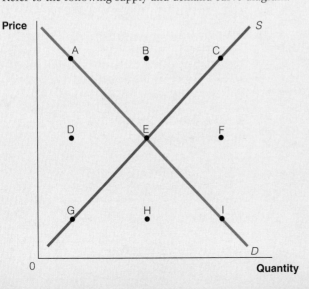

a. Starting from an initial equilibrium at E, what shift or shifts in supply and/or demand could move the equilibrium price and quantity to each of points A through I?

b. Starting from an initial equilibrium at E, what would happen if both a decrease in the price of a substitute in production and an increase in income occurred, if it is a normal good?

c. Starting from an initial equilibrium at E, what would happen if both an increase in the price of an input and an advance in technology occurred?

d. If a price floor is imposed above the equilibrium price, which of A through I would tend to be the quantity supplied, and which would tend to be the quantity demanded? Which would be the new quantity exchanged?

e. If a price ceiling is imposed below the equilibrium price, which of A through I would tend to be the quantity supplied, and which would tend to be the quantity demanded? Which would be the new quantity exchanged?

Elasticities

If a rock band increases the price it charges for concert tickets, what impact will that have on ticket sales? More precisely, will ticket sales fall a little or a lot? Will the band make more money by lowering the price or by raising the price? This chapter allows you to answer these types of questions and more.

Some of the results in this chapter may surprise you. A huge flood in the Midwest that destroyed much of this year's wheat crop would leave some wheat farmers better off. Ideal weather that led to a bountiful crop of wheat everywhere would leave wheat farmers worse off. As you will soon find out, these issues hinge importantly on the tools of elasticity.

In this chapter, we also see the importance of elasticity in determining how the burden of a tax is allocated between buyers and sellers. If a tax is levied on the seller, will the seller pay all of the taxes? If the tax were levied on the buyer—who pays the larger share of taxes? We will see that elasticity is critical in the determination of tax burden. Elasticities will also help us to more fully understand many policy issues—from illegal drugs to luxury taxes. For example, if Congress were to impose a large tax on yachts, what do you think would happen to yacht sales? What would happen to employment in the boat industry?

IMAGINECHINA/CORBIS

6.1   **Price Elasticity of Demand**

▶ What is price elasticity of demand?

▶ How do we measure consumers' responses to price changes?

▶ What determines the price elasticity of demand?

In learning and applying the law of demand, we have established the basic fact that quantity demanded changes inversely with change in price, *ceteris paribus*. But how much does quantity demanded change? The extent to which a change in price affects quantity demanded may vary considerably from product to product and over the various price ranges for the same product. The price elasticity of demand measures the responsiveness of quantity demanded to a change in price. Specifically, price elasticity is defined as the percentage change in quantity demanded divided by the percentage change in price, or

price elasticity of demand
the measure of the responsiveness of quantity demanded to a change in price

$$\text{Price elasticity of demand } (E_D) = \frac{\text{Percentage change in quantity demanded}}{\text{Percentage change in price}}$$

Note that, following the law of demand, price and quantity demanded show an inverse relationship. For this reason, the price elasticity of demand is, in theory, always negative. But in practice and for simplicity, this quantity is always expressed in absolute value terms—that is, as a positive number.

6.1a **Is the Demand Curve Elastic or Inelastic?**

It is important to understand the basic intuition behind elasticities, which requires a focus on the percentage changes in quantity demanded and price.

Think of elasticity as an elastic rubber band. If the quantity demanded is responsive to even a small change in price, we call it elastic. On the other hand, if even a huge change in price results in only a small change in quantity demanded, then the demand is said to be inelastic. For example, if a 10 percent increase in the price leads to a 50 percent reduction in the quantity demanded, we say that demand is elastic because the quantity demanded is sensitive to the price change.

$$E_D = \frac{\%\Delta Q_D}{\%\Delta P} = \frac{50\%}{10\%} = 5$$

Demand is elastic in this case because a 10 percent change in price led to a larger (50 percent) change in quantity demanded.

Alternatively, if a 10 percent increase in the price leads to a 1 percent reduction in quantity demanded, we say that demand is *inelastic* because the quantity demanded did not respond much to the price reduction.

$$E_D = \frac{\%\Delta Q_D}{\%\Delta P} = \frac{1\%}{10\%} = 0.10$$

Demand is inelastic in this case because a 10 percent change in price led to a smaller (1 percent) change in quantity demanded.

Think of price elasticity like an elastic rubber band. When small price changes greatly affect, or "stretch," quantity demanded, the demand is elastic, much like a very stretchy rubber band. When large price changes can't "stretch" demand, however, then demand is inelastic, more like a very stiff rubber band.

BLUE JEAN IMAGES/ALAMY

6.1b **Types of Demand Curves**

Economists refer to a variety of demand curves based on the magnitude of their elasticity. A demand curve, or a portion of a demand curve, can be elastic, inelastic, or unit elastic.

Demand is **elastic** when the elasticity is greater than 1 ($E_D > 1$)—the quantity demanded changes proportionally more than the price changes. In this case, a given percentage increase in price, say 10 percent, leads to a larger percentage change in quantity demanded, say 20 percent, as seen in Exhibit 1(a). If the curve is *perfectly elastic,* the demand curve becomes horizontal. When the demand is perfectly elastic, the quantity demanded is extremely responsive to changes in prices. For example, buyers might be willing to buy all of a seller's wheat at $5 a bushel but none at $5.10. That is, a small percentage change in price causes an enormous change in quantity demanded (from buying all to buying nothing). In Exhibit 1(b), a *perfectly elastic* demand curve (horizontal) is illustrated.

Demand is **inelastic** when the elasticity is less than 1; the quantity demanded changes proportionally less than the price changes. In this case, a given percentage (for example, 10 percent) change in price is accompanied by a smaller (for example, 5 percent) reduction in quantity demanded, as seen in Exhibit 2(a). If the demand curve is *perfectly inelastic*, the quantity demanded is the same regardless of the price. Examples of goods that are extremely price inelastic are insulin and heroin. Insulin to a person who has an acute case of diabetes is so important that a rise or fall in price will not have an impact on the quantity the person buys. Similarly, the same may be true for a heroine addict. The elasticity coefficient is zero because the quantity demanded does not respond to a change in price. This relationship is illustrated in Exhibit 2(b).

Goods for which E_D equals one ($E_D = 1$) are said to have **unit elastic demand**. In this case, the quantity demanded changes proportionately to price changes. For example, a 10 percent increase in price will lead to a 10 percent reduction in quantity demanded. This relationship is illustrated in Exhibit 3.

The price elasticity of demand is closely related to the slope of the demand curve. The flatter the demand curve passing through a given point, the more elastic the demand. The steeper the demand curve passing through a given point, the less elastic the demand. But elasticity is different than slope. The slope depends on the units of measurement we choose—like dollars

elastic
when the percentage change in quantity demanded is greater than the percentage change in price ($E_D > 1$)

inelastic
when the percentage change in quantity demanded is less than the percentage change in price ($E_D < 1$)

unit elastic demand
demand with a price elasticity of 1; the percentage change in quantity demanded is equal to the percentage change in price

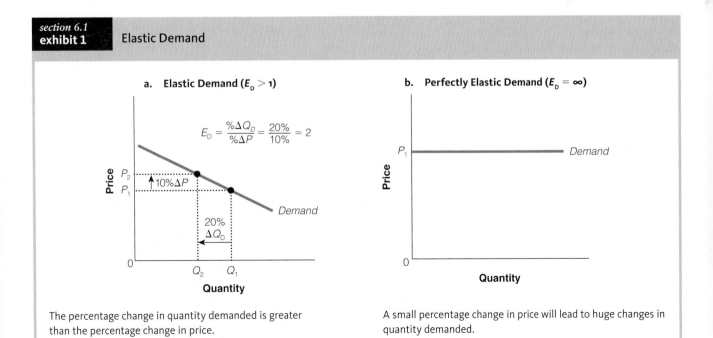

section 6.1
exhibit 1   **Elastic Demand**

a.   Elastic Demand ($E_D > 1$)

$$E_D = \frac{\%\Delta Q_D}{\%\Delta P} = \frac{20\%}{10\%} = 2$$

b.   Perfectly Elastic Demand ($E_D = \infty$)

The percentage change in quantity demanded is greater than the percentage change in price.

A small percentage change in price will lead to huge changes in quantity demanded.

Inelastic Demand

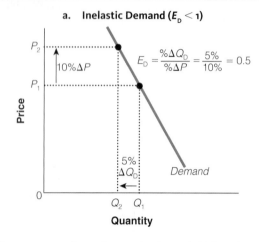

a.   Inelastic Demand ($E_D < 1$)

$$E_D = \frac{\%\Delta Q_D}{\%\Delta P} = \frac{5\%}{10\%} = 0.5$$

The percentage change in quantity demanded is less than the percentage change in price.

b.   Perfectly Inelastic Demand ($E_D = 0$)

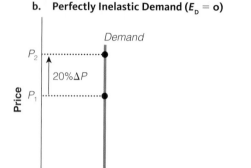

The quantity demanded does not change regardless of the percentage change in price.

Unit Elastic Demand

$$E_D = \frac{\%\Delta Q_D}{\%\Delta P} = \frac{10\%}{10\%} = 1$$

The percentage change in quantity demanded is the same as the percentage change in price ($E_D = 1$).

Does it matter whether we move up or down the demand curve when we calculate the price elasticity of demand?

or cents, or ounces or pounds. Using elasticities and measuring the relative percentage changes eliminates the unit problem. For example, a 5% change is a 5% change whether we are talking about pounds or ounces.

6.1c Calculating the Price Elasticity of Demand: The Midpoint Method

To get a clear picture of exactly how the price elasticity of demand is calculated, consider the case for a hypothetical pizza market. Say the price of pizza increases from $19 to $21. If we take an average between the old price, $19, and the new price, $21, we can calculate an average price of $20. Exhibit 4 shows that as a result of the increase in the price of pizza, the quantity demanded has fallen from 82 million pizzas to 78 million pizzas per year. If we take an average between the old quantity demand, 82 million, and the new quantity demanded, 78 million, we have an average quantity demanded of 80 million pizzas per year. That is, the $2 increase in the price of pizza has led to a 4-million pizza reduction in quantity demanded. How can we figure out the price elasticity of demand?

You might ask why we are using the average price and average quantity. The answer is that if we did not use the average amounts, we would come up with different values for the elasticity of demand depending on whether we moved up or down the demand curve. When the change in price and quantity are of significant magnitude, the exact meaning of the term *percentage change* requires clarification, and the terms *price* and *quantity* must be defined more precisely. The issue thus is, should the percentage change be figured on the basis of price and quantity before or after the change has occurred? For example, a price rise from $10 to $15 constitutes a 50 percent change if the original price ($10) is used in figuring the percentage ($5/$10), or a 33 percent change if the price after the change ($15) is used ($5/$15).

For small changes, the distinction is not important, but for large changes, it is. To avoid this confusion, economists often use this average technique. Specifically, we are actually calculating the elasticity at a midpoint between the old and new prices and quantities.

Now to figure out the price elasticity of demand, we must first calculate the percentage change in price. To find the percentage change in price, we take the change in price (ΔP) and divide it by the average price (P_{avg}). (Note: The Greek letter delta, Δ, means "change in.")

$$\text{Percentage change in price} = \Delta P / P_{avg}$$

In our pizza example, the original price was $19, and the new price is $21. The change in price (ΔP) is $2, and the average price (P_{avg}) is $20. The percentage change in price can then be calculated as

$$\text{Percentage change in price} = \$2/\$20$$
$$= 1/10 = 0.10 = 10\%$$

Next, we must calculate the percentage change in quantity demanded. To find the percentage change in quantity demanded, we take the change in quantity demanded (ΔQ_D) and divide it by the average quantity demanded (Q_{avg}).

$$\text{Percentage change in quantity demanded} = \Delta Q_D / Q_{avg}$$

In our pizza example, the original quantity demanded was 82 million, and the new quantity demanded is 78 million. The change in quantity demanded (ΔQ_D) is 4 million, and the average quantity demanded (Q_{avg}) is 80 million. The percentage change in quantity demanded can then be calculated as

$$\text{Percentage change in quantity demanded} = 4 \text{ million}/80 \text{ million} = 1/20 = 0.05 = 5\%$$

Because the price elasticity of demand is equal to the percentage change in quantity demanded divided by the percentage change in price, the price elasticity of demand for pizzas between point A and point B can be shown as

$$E_D = \frac{\text{Percentage change in quantity demanded}}{\text{Percentage change in price}}$$

$$= \frac{\Delta Q_D / Q_{avg}}{\Delta P / P_{avg}} = \frac{4 \text{ million}/80 \text{ million}}{\$2/\$20}$$

$$= \frac{1/20}{1/10} = \frac{5\%}{10\%} = 0.5$$

However, in this text, we rarely perform this type of calculation. For the most part, it is about—the responsiveness of quantity demanded to a change in price—and what it implies.

6.1d The Determinants of the Price Elasticity of Demand

As you have learned, the elasticity of demand for a specific good refers to movements along its demand curve as its price changes. A lower price will increase quantity demanded, and a higher price will reduce quantity demanded. But what factors will influence the magnitude of

section 6.1 exhibit 4 — Calculating the Price Elasticity of Demand

Price per Pizza

- $21 ··· B
- P_{avg} $20 — $\Delta P = \$2$ — $E_D = 0.5$ at midpoint between A and B
- $19 ··· A
- $\Delta Q_D = 4$ million
- D
- 0
- 78   80   82
- Q_{avg}

Quantity of Pizzas (millions per month)

The price elasticity of demand is found with the formula

$$\frac{\Delta Q_D / Q_{avg}}{\Delta P / P_{avg}}$$

Why are demand curves for goods with close substitutes more elastic?

If bus fares increase, will ridership fall a little or a lot? It all depends on the price elasticity of demand. If the price elasticity of demand is elastic, a 50-cent price increase will lead to a relatively large reduction in bus travel as riders find viable substitutes. If the price elasticity of demand is inelastic, a 50-cent price increase will lead to a relatively small reduction in bus ridership as riders are not able to find good alternatives to bus transportation.

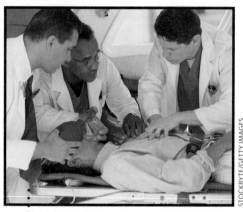

Unlike most tangible items (such as specific types of food or cars), there are few substitutes for a physician and medical care when you have an emergency. Because the number of available substitutes is limited, the demand for emergency medical care is relatively inelastic.

the change in quantity demanded in response to a price change? That is, what will make the demand curve relatively more elastic (where Q_D is responsive to price changes), and what will make the demand curve relatively less elastic (where Q_D is less responsive to price changes)?

For the most part, the price elasticity of demand depends on three factors: (1) the availability of close substitutes, (2) the proportion of income spent on the good, and (3) the amount of time that has elapsed since the price change.

Availability of Close Substitutes

Goods *with* close substitutes tend to have more elastic demands. Why? Because if the price of such a good increases, consumers can easily switch to other now relatively lower-priced substitutes. In many examples, such as one brand of root beer as opposed to another, or different brands of gasoline, the ease of substitution will make demand quite elastic for most individuals. Goods *without* close substitutes, such as insulin for diabetics, cigarettes for chain smokers, heroin for addicts, or emergency medical care for those with appendicitis, a broken leg or a rattlesnake bite, tend to have inelastic demands.

The degree of substitutability can also depend on whether the good is a necessity or a luxury. Goods that are necessities, such as food, have no ready substitutes and thus tend to have lower elasticities than do luxury items, such as jewelry.

When the good is broadly defined, it tends to be less elastic than when it is narrowly defined. For example, the elasticity of demand for food, a broad category, tends to be inelastic over a large price range because few substitutes are available for food. But for a certain type of food, such as pizza, a narrowly defined good, it is much easier to find a substitute—perhaps tacos, burgers, salads, burritos, or chili fries. That is, the demand for a particular type of food is more elastic because more and better substitutes are available than for food as an entire category.

Proportion of Income Spent on the Good

The smaller the proportion of income spent on a good, the lower its elasticity of demand. If the amount spent on a good relative to income is small, then the impact of a change in its price on one's budget will also be small. As a result, consumers will respond less to price changes for small-ticket items than for similar percentage changes in large-ticket items, where a price change could potentially have a large impact on the consumer's budget. For example, a 50 percent increase in the price of salt will have a much smaller impact on consumers' behavior than a similar percentage increase in the price of a new automobile.

What impact does time have on elasticity?

Time

For many goods, the more time that people have to adapt to a new price change, the greater the elasticity of demand. Immediately after a price change, consumers may be unable to locate good alternatives or easily change their consumption patterns. But as time passes, consumers have more time to find or develop suitable substitutes and to plan and implement changes in their patterns of consumption. For example, drivers may not respond immediately to an increase in gas prices, perhaps believing it to be temporary. However, if the price persists over a longer period, we would expect people to drive less, buy more fuel-efficient cars, move closer to work, carpool, take the bus, or even bike to work. So for many goods, especially nondurable goods (goods that do not last a long time), the short-run demand curve is generally less elastic than the long-run demand curve, as illustrated in Exhibit 5.

Estimated Price Elasticities of Demand

Because of shifts in supply and demand curves, researchers have a difficult task when trying to estimate empirically the price elasticity of demand for a particular good or service. Despite this difficulty, Exhibit 6 presents some estimates for the price elasticity of demand for certain goods. As you would expect, certain goods like medical care, air travel, and gasoline are all relatively price inelastic in the short run because buyers have fewer substitutes. On the other hand, air travel in the long run is much more sensitive to price (elastic) because the available substitutes are much more plentiful. Exhibit 6 shows that the price elasticity of demand for air travel is 2.4, which means that a 1 percent increase in price will lead to a 2.4 percent reduction in quantity demanded. Notice, in each case where the data are available, the estimates of the long-run price elasticities of demand are greater than the short-run price elasticities of demand. In short, the price elasticity of demand is greater when the price change persists over a longer time periods.

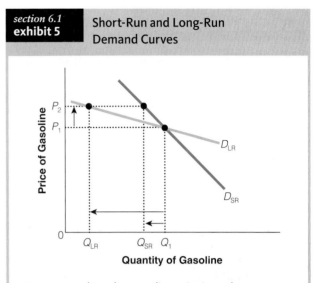

section 6.1 exhibit 5   Short-Run and Long-Run Demand Curves

For many goods, such as gasoline, price is much more elastic in the long run than in the short run because buyers have more time to find suitable substitutes or change their consumption patterns. In the short run, the increase in price from P_1 to P_2 has only a small effect on the quantity demanded for gasoline. In the long run, the effect of the price increase will be much larger.

section 6.1 exhibit 6	Price Elasticities of Demand for Selected Goods	
Good	**Short Run**	**Long Run**
Salt	—	0.1
Air travel	0.1	2.4
Gasoline	0.2	0.7
Medical care and hospitalization	0.3	0.9
Jewelry and watches	0.4	0.7
Physician services	0.6	—
Alcohol	0.9	3.6
Movies	0.9	3.7
China, glassware	1.5	2.6
Automobiles	1.9	2.2
Chevrolets	—	4.0

SOURCES: Adapted from Robert Archibald and Robert Gillingham, "An Analysis of the Short-Run Consumer Demand for Gasoline Using Household Survey Data," *Review of Economics and Statistics* 62 (November 1980): 622–628; Hendrik S. Houthakker and Lester D. Taylor, *Consumer Demand in the United States: Analyses and Projections* (Cambridge, Mass.: Harvard University Press, 1970), pp. 56–149; Richard Voith, "The Long-Run Elasticity of Demand for Commuter Rail Transportation," *Journal of Urban Economics* 30 (November 1991): 360–372.

SECTION QUIZ

1. Price elasticity of demand is defined as the _____ change in quantity demanded divided by the _____ change in price.

   a. total; percentage

   b. percentage; marginal

   c. marginal; percentage

   d. percentage; percentage

   e. total; total

2. Demand is said to be _____ when the quantity demanded is not very responsive to changes in price.

   a. independent

   b. inelastic

   c. unit elastic

   d. elastic

3. When demand is inelastic,

   a. price elasticity of demand is less than 1.

   b. consumers are not very responsive to changes in price.

   c. the percentage change in quantity demanded resulting from a price change is less than the percentage change in price.

   d. all of the above are correct.

4. Which of the following will not tend to increase the elasticity of demand for a good?

   a. An increase in the availability of close substitutes

   b. An increase in the amount of time people have to adjust to a change in the price

   c. An increase in the proportion of income spent on the good

   d. All of the above will increase the elasticity of demand for a good

5. Which of the following would tend to have the most elastic demand curve?

   a. Automobiles

   b. Chevrolet automobiles

   c. (a) and (b) would be the same

   d. None of the above

6. Price elasticity of demand is said to be greater

   a. the shorter the period of time consumers have to adjust to price changes.

   b. the longer the period of time consumers have to adjust to price changes.

   c. when there are fewer available substitutes.

   d. when the elasticity of supply is greater.

7. The long-run demand curve for gasoline is likely to be

   a. more elastic than the short-run demand curve for gasoline.

   b. more inelastic than the short-run demand curve for gasoline.

   c. the same as the short-run demand curve for gasoline.

   d. more inelastic than the short-run supply of gasoline.

(continued)

SECTION QUIZ (cont.)

8. Demand curves for goods tend to become more inelastic

    a. when more good substitutes for the good are available.

    b. when the good makes up a larger portion of a person's income.

    c. when people have less time to adapt to a given price change.

    d. when any of the above is true.

    e. in none of the above situations.

---

1. What question is the price elasticity of demand designed to answer?

2. How is the price elasticity of demand calculated?

3. What is the difference between a relatively price elastic demand curve and a relatively price inelastic demand curve?

4. What is the relationship between the price elasticity of demand and the slope at a given point on a demand curve?

5. What factors tend to make demand curves more price elastic?

6. Why would a tax on a particular brand of cigarettes be less effective at reducing smoking than a tax on all brands of cigarettes?

7. Why is the price elasticity of demand for products at a 24-hour convenience store likely to be lower at 2:00 A.M. than at 2:00 P.M.?

8. Why is the price elasticity of demand for turkeys likely to be lower, but the price elasticity of demand for turkeys at a particular store at Thanksgiving likely to be greater than at other times of the year?

Answers: 1. d 2. b 3. d 4. d 5. b 6. b 7. a 8. c

. . . .

Total Revenue and the Price Elasticity of Demand   6.2

▶ What is total revenue?

▶ What is the relationship between total revenue and the price elasticity of demand?

▶ Does the price elasticity of demand vary along a linear demand curve?

6.2a How Does the Price Elasticity of Demand Impact Total Revenue?

The price elasticity of demand for a good also has implications for total revenue. Total revenue (TR) is the amount sellers receive for a good or service. Total revenue is simply the price of the good (P) times the quantity of the good sold (Q): $TR = P \times Q$. The elasticity of demand will help to predict how changes in the price will impact total revenue earned by the producer for selling the good. Let's see how this works.

In Exhibit 1, we see that when the demand is price elastic ($E_D > 1$), total revenues will rise as the price declines, because the percentage increase in the quantity demanded is greater than the percentage reduction in price. For example, if the price of a good is cut in half (say from \$10 to \$5) and the quantity demanded more than doubles (say from 40 to 100), total

total revenue (TR)

the amount sellers receive for a good or service, calculated as the product price times the quantity sold

Elastic Demand and Total Revenue

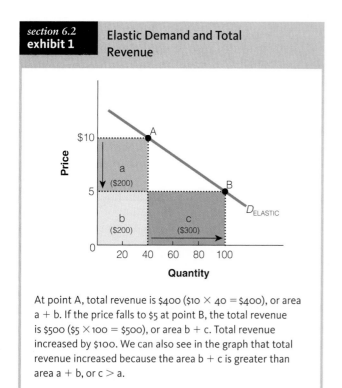

At point A, total revenue is $400 ($10 × 40 = $400), or area a + b. If the price falls to $5 at point B, the total revenue is $500 ($5 × 100 = $500), or area b + c. Total revenue increased by $100. We can also see in the graph that total revenue increased because the area b + c is greater than area a + b, or c > a.

Inelastic Demand and Total Revenue

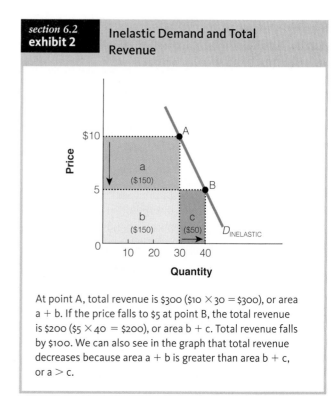

At point A, total revenue is $300 ($10 × 30 = $300), or area a + b. If the price falls to $5 at point B, the total revenue is $200 ($5 × 40 = $200), or area b + c. Total revenue falls by $100. We can also see in the graph that total revenue decreases because area a + b is greater than area b + c, or a > c.

Can the relationship between price and total revenue tell you whether a good is elastic or inelastic?

revenue will rise from $400 ($10 × 40 = $400) to $500 ($5 × 100 = $500). Equivalently, if the price rises from $5 to $10 and the quantity demanded falls from 100 to 40 units, then total revenue will fall from $500 to $400. As this example illustrates, if the demand curve is relatively elastic, total revenue will vary inversely with a price change.

You can see from the following what happens to total revenue when demand is price elastic. (*Note:* The size of the price and quantity arrows represents the size of the percentage changes.)

When Demand Is Price Elastic

$$\downarrow TR = \uparrow P \times \downarrow Q$$

or

$$\uparrow TR = \downarrow P \times \uparrow Q$$

On the other hand, if demand for a good is relatively inelastic ($E_D < 1$), the total revenue will be lower at lower prices than at higher prices because a given price reduction will be accompanied by a proportionately smaller increase in quantity demanded. For example, as shown in Exhibit 2, if the price of a good is cut (say from $10 to $5) and the quantity demanded less than doubles (say it increases from 30 to 40), then total revenue will fall from $300 ($10 × 30 = $300) to $200 ($5 × 40 = $200). Equivalently, if the price increases from $5 to $10 and the quantity demanded falls from 40 to 30, total revenue will increase from $200 to $300. That is, if the demand curve is inelastic, total revenue will vary directly with a price change.

When Demand Is Price Inelastic

$$\uparrow TR = \uparrow P \times \downarrow Q$$

or

$$\downarrow TR = \downarrow P \times \uparrow Q$$

In this case, the "net" effect on total revenue is reversed but easy to see. (Again, the size of the price and quantity arrows represents the size of the percentage changes.)

6.2b Price Elasticity Changes along a Linear Demand Curve

As already shown (Section 6.1, Exhibit 1), the slopes of demand curves can be used to estimate their *relative* elasticities of demand: The steeper one demand curve is relative to another, the more inelastic it is relative to the other. However, except for the extreme cases of perfectly elastic and perfectly inelastic curves, great care must be taken when trying to estimate the degree of elasticity of one demand curve from its slope. In fact, as we will soon see, a straight-line demand curve with a constant slope will change elasticity continuously as you move up or down it. It is because the slope is the ratio of changes in the two variables (price and quantity) while the elasticity is the ratio of percentage changes in the two variables.

   We can easily demonstrate that the elasticity of demand varies along a linear demand curve by using what we already know about the interrelationship between price and total revenue.

How is it possible that elasticity changes along a straight-line demand curve when the slope is constant?

USE WHAT YOU'VE LEARNED

Elasticities and Total Revenue

Q Is a poor wheat harvest bad for all farmers and is a great wheat harvest good for all farmers? (Hint: Assume that demand for wheat is inelastic. The demand for basic foodstuffs, such as wheat, is usually inelastic because it is relatively inexpensive and has few good substitutes.

A Without a simultaneous reduction in demand, a reduction in supply from a poor harvest results in higher prices. With that, if demand for the wheat is inelastic over the pertinent portion of the demand curve, the price increase will cause farmers' total revenues to rise. As shown in Exhibit 3(a), if demand for the crop is inelastic, an increase in price will cause farmers to lose the revenue indicated by area c. They will, however, experience an increase in revenue equal to area a, resulting in an overall increase in total revenue equal to area a − c. Clearly, if some farmers lose their entire crop because of, say, bad weather, they will be worse off; but collectively, farmers can profit from events that reduce crop size—and they do because the demand for most agricultural products is inelastic. Interestingly, if all farmers were hurt equally, say losing one-third of their crop, each farmer would be better off. Of course, consumers would be worse off because the price of agricultural products would be higher. Alternatively, what if phenomenal weather led to record wheat harvests or a technological advance led to more productive wheat farmers? Either event would increase the supply from S_1 to S_2 in Exhibit 3(b). The increase in supply leads to a decrease in price, from P_1 to P_2. Because the demand for wheat is inelastic, the quantity sold of wheat

ROBERT L. SEXTON

rises less than proportionately to the fall in the price. That is, in percentage terms, the price falls more than the quantity demanded rises. Each farmer is selling a few more bushels of wheat, but the price of each bushel has fallen even more, so collectively wheat farmers will experience a decline in total revenue despite the good news.

   The same is also true for the many government programs that attempt to help farmers by reducing production—crop restriction programs. These programs, like droughts or floods, tend to help farmers because the demand for food

(continued)

Use What You've Learned continued

is relatively inelastic. But it hurts consumers, who now have to pay a higher price for less food. Farm technology may be good for consumers because it shifts the supply curve to the right and lowers prices. However, it may be bad for some small farmers because it could put them out of business. See Exhibit 3(b).

section 6.2
exhibit 3   Elasticities and Total Revenue

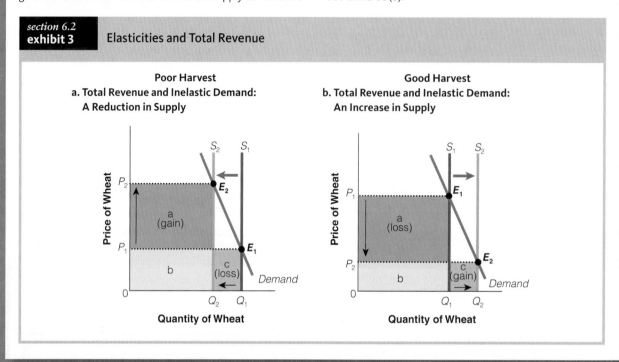

Exhibit 4 shows a linear (constant slope) demand curve. In Exhibit 4(a), we see that when the price falls on the upper half of the demand curve from P_1 to P_2, and quantity demanded increases from Q_1 to Q_2, total revenue increases. That is, the new area of total revenue (area b + c) is larger than the old area of total revenue (area a + b). It is also true that if price increased in this region (from P_2 to P_1), total revenue would fall because b + c is greater than a + b.

section 6.2
exhibit 4   Price Elasticity along a Linear Demand Curve

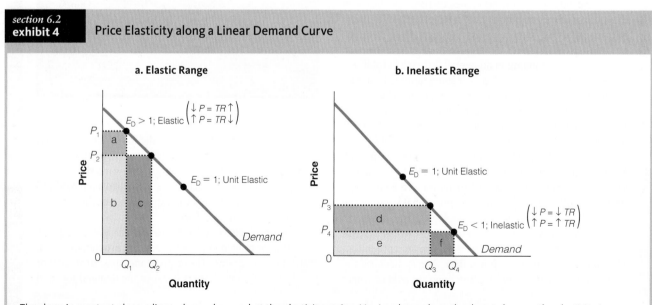

The slope is constant along a linear demand curve, but the elasticity varies. Moving down along the demand curve, the elasticity is elastic at higher prices and inelastic at lower prices. It is unit elastic between the inelastic and elastic ranges.

USE WHAT YOU'VE LEARNED

Elasticity Varies along a Linear Demand Curve

Q Why do economists emphasize elasticity at the current price?

A Because for most demand (and supply) curves, the price elasticity varies along the curve. Thus, for most goods we usually refer to a particular point or a section of the demand (or supply) curves. In Exhibit 5, we see that the upper half of the straight-line demand curve is elastic and the lower half is inelastic. Notice on the lower half of the demand curve, a higher (lower) price increases (decreases) total revenue—that is, in this lower region, demand is inelastic. However, on the top half of the demand curve, a lower (higher) price increases (decreases) total revenue—that is, in this region demand is elastic.

For example, when the price increases from $2 to $3, the total revenue increases from $32 to $42—an increase in price increases total revenue, so demand is inelastic in this portion of the demand curve. But when the price increases from $8 to $9, the total revenue falls from $32 to $18—an increase in price lowers total revenue, so demand is elastic in this portion of the demand curve.

Specifically, when the price is high and the quantity demanded is low, this portion of the demand curve is elastic. Why? It is because a $1 reduction in price is a smaller percentage change when the price is high than when it is low. Similarly, an increase in 2 units of output is a larger percentage change when quantity demanded is lower. So we have a relatively small change in price leading to a proportionately greater change in quantity demanded—that is, demand is elastic on this portion of the demand curve. Of course, the opposite is true when the price is low and the quantity demanded is high. Why? It is because a $1 change in price is a larger percentage change when the price is low and an increase in 2 units of output is a smaller percentage change when the quantity demanded is larger. That is, a relatively larger percentage change in price will lead to a relatively smaller change in quantity demanded—demand is relatively inelastic on this portion of the demand curve.

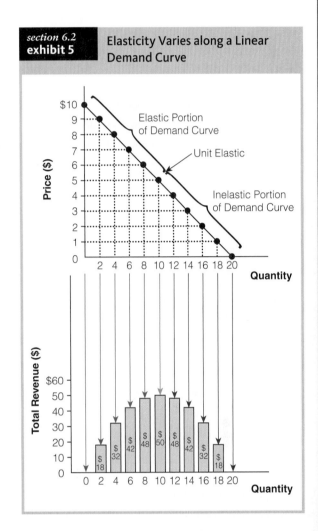

section 6.2 **exhibit 5** — Elasticity Varies along a Linear Demand Curve

In this region of the demand curve, then, there is a negative relationship between price and total revenue. As we discussed earlier, this is characteristic of an elastic demand curve ($E_D > 1$).

Exhibit 4(b) illustrates what happens to total revenue on the lower half of the same demand curve. When the price falls from P_3 to P_4 and the quantity demanded increases from Q_3 to Q_4, total revenue actually decreases because the new area of total revenue (area e + f) is less than the old area of total revenue (area d + e). Likewise, it is clear that an increase in price from P_4 to P_3 would increase total revenue. In this case, there is a positive relationship between price and total revenue, which, as we discussed, is characteristic of an inelastic demand curve ($E_D < 1$). Together, parts (a) and (b) of Exhibit 4 illustrate that, although the slope remains constant, the elasticity of a linear demand curve changes along the length of the curve—from relatively elastic at higher price ranges to relatively inelastic at lower price ranges.

Is a good wheat harvest always good for all wheat farmers?

SECTION QUIZ

1. When the local symphony recently raised the ticket price for its summer concerts in the park, the symphony was surprised to see that its total revenue had actually decreased. The reason was that the elasticity of demand for tickets was

   a. unit elastic.

   b. unit inelastic.

   c. inelastic.

   d. elastic.

2. A straight-line demand curve would

   a. have the same elasticity along its entire length.

   b. have a higher elasticity of demand near its top than near its bottom.

   c. have a higher elasticity of demand near its bottom than near its top.

   d. be relatively inelastic at high prices, but relatively elastic at low prices.

3. Which of the following is a true statement?

   a. Total revenue is the price of the good times the quantity sold.

   b. If demand is price elastic, total revenue will vary inversely with a change in price.

   c. If demand is price inelastic, total revenue will vary in the same direction as a change in price.

   d. A linear demand curve is more price elastic at higher price ranges and more price inelastic at lower price ranges, and it is unit elastic at the midpoint.

   e. All of the above are true statements.

4. If demand was relatively inelastic in the short run, but elastic in the long run, a price increase would _____ total revenue in the short run and _____ total revenue in the long run.

   a. increase; increase

   b. increase; decrease

   c. decrease; increase

   d. decrease; decrease

---

1. Why does total revenue vary inversely with price if demand is relatively price elastic?

2. Why does total revenue vary directly with price if demand is relatively price inelastic?

3. Why is a linear demand curve more price elastic at higher price ranges and more price inelastic at lower price ranges?

4. If demand for some good was perfectly price inelastic, how would total revenue from its sales change as its price changed?

5. Assume that both you and Art, your partner in a picture-framing business, want to increase your firm's total revenue. You argue that in order to achieve this goal, you should lower your prices; Art, on the other hand, thinks that you should raise your prices. What assumptions are each of you making about your firm's price elasticity of demand?

Answers: 1. d   2. b   3. e   4. b

Other Types of Demand Elasticities   6.3

▶ What is the cross-price elasticity of demand?   ▶ What is the income elasticity of demand?

6.3a The Cross-Price Elasticity of Demand

The price of a good is not the only factor that affects the quantity consumers will purchase. Sometimes the quantity of one good demanded is affected by the price of a related good. For example, if the price of potato chips falls, what is the impact, if any, on the demand for soda (a complement)? Or if the price of soda increases, to what degree will the demand for iced tea (a substitute) be affected? The cross-price elasticity of demand measures both the direction and magnitude of the impact that a price change for one good will have on the demand for another good. Specifically, the **cross-price elasticity of demand** is defined as the percentage change in the demand of one good (good A) divided by the percentage change in price of another good (good B), or

$$\text{Cross-price elasticity demand} = \frac{\% \,\Delta \text{ in the demand for Good A}}{\% \,\Delta \text{ in the price for Good B}}$$

cross-price elasticity of demand

the measure of the impact that a price change of one good will have on the demand of another good

The cross-price elasticity of demand indicates not only the degree of the connection between the two variables but also whether the goods in question are substitutes or complements for one another.

Calculating the Cross-Price Elasticity of Demand

Let's calculate the cross-price elasticity of demand between soda and iced tea, where a 10 percent increase in the price of soda results in a 20 percent increase in the demand for iced tea. In this case, the cross-price elasticity of demand would be +2 (+20% ÷ +10% = +2).

Consumers responded to the soda price increase by buying less soda (moving along the demand curve for soda) and increasing the demand for iced tea (shifting the demand curve for iced tea). In general, if the cross-price elasticity is positive, we can conclude that the two goods are substitutes because the price of one good and the demand for the other move in the same direction.

As another example, let's calculate the cross-price elasticity of demand between potato chips and soda, where a 10 percent decrease in the price of potato chips results in a 30 percent increase in the demand for soda. In this case, the cross-price elasticity of demand is −3 (+30% ÷ −10% = −3). The demand for chips increases as a result of the price decrease, as consumers then purchase additional soda to wash down those extra bags of salty chips. Potato chips and soda, then, are complements. In general, if the cross-price elasticity is negative, we can conclude that the two goods are complements because the price of one good and the demand for the other move in opposite directions.

© ISTOCKPHOTO.COM/JO UNRUH

A 10 percent increase in the price of a six-pack of Diet Coke will lead to a 11.5 percent increase in the sales of six-packs of Coca-Cola. That is a cross-price elasticity of 1.15.

6.3b Cross-Price Elasticity and Sodas

According to economist Jean-Pierre Dube, Coca-Cola is a good substitute for Pepsi—the cross-price elasticity is a 0.34. In other words, a 10 percent increase in the price of a Pepsi 12-pack will lead to an increase in the sales of Coca-Cola 12-packs by 3.4 percent. But six-packs of Coca-Cola and Diet Coke are an even better substitute—with a cross-price elasticity of 1.15; a 10 percent increase in the price of a six-pack of Diet Coke will lead to an 11.5 percent increase in the sales of six-packs of Coca-Cola. And a 10 percent increase in the price of a 12-pack of Mountain Dew will lead to a 7.7 percent increase in the sales of 12-packs of Pepsi.

6.3c **The Income Elasticity of Demand**

income elasticity of demand

the percentage change in demand divided by the percentage change in consumers' income

Sometimes it is useful to measure how responsive demand is to a change in income. The income elasticity of demand is a measure of the relationship between a relative change in income and the consequent relative change in demand, *ceteris paribus*. The income elasticity of demand coefficient not only expresses the degree of the connection between the two variables, but it also indicates whether the good in question is normal or inferior. Specifically, the income elasticity of demand is defined as the percentage change in the demand divided by the percentage change in income, or

$$\text{Income elasticity of demand} = \frac{\%\Delta \text{ in demand}}{\%\Delta \text{ in income}}$$

Calculating the Income Elasticity of Demand

Let's calculate the income elasticity of demand for lobster, where a 10 percent increase in income results in a 15 percent increase in the demand for lobster. In this case, the income elasticity of demand is $+1.5$ ($+15\% \div +10\% = +1.5$). Lobster, then, is a normal good because an increase in income results in an increase in demand. In general, if the income elasticity is positive, then the good in question is a normal good because income and demand move in the same direction.

In comparison, let's calculate the income elasticity of demand for beans, where a 10 percent increase in income results in a 15 percent decrease in the demand for beans. In this case, the income elasticity of demand is -1.5 ($-15\% \div +10\% = -1.5$). In this example, then, beans are an inferior good because an increase in income results in a decrease in the demand for beans. If the income elasticity is negative, then the good in question is an inferior good because the change in income and the change in demand move in opposite directions.

SECTION QUIZ

1. If the cross-price elasticity of demand between two goods is negative, we know that
    a. they are substitutes.
    b. they are complements.
    c. they are both inferior goods.
    d. they are both normal goods.

2. If the income elasticity of demand for good A is 0.5 and the income elasticity of demand for good B is 1.5, then
    a. both A and B are normal goods.
    b. both A and B are inferior goods.
    c. A is a normal good, but B is an inferior good.
    d. A is an inferior good, but B is a normal good.

3. If good X has a negative cross-price elasticity of demand with good Y and good X also has a negative income elasticity of demand, then
    a. X is a substitute for Y, and X is a normal good.
    b. X is a substitute for Y, and X is an inferior good.
    c. X is a complement for Y, and X is a normal good.
    d. X is a complement for Y, and X is an inferior good.

(continued)

4. Which of the following statements is true?

    a. The cross-price elasticity of demand is the percentage change in the demand of one good divided by the percentage change in the price of another good.

    b. If the sign on the cross-price elasticity is positive, the two goods are substitutes; if it is negative, the two goods are complements.

    c. The income elasticity of demand is the percentage change in demand divided by the percentage change in consumers' income.

    d. If the income elasticity is positive, then the good is a normal good; if it is negative, the good is an inferior good.

    e. All of the above are true statements.

---

1. How does the cross-price elasticity of demand tell you whether two goods are substitutes? Complements?

2. How does the income elasticity of demand tell you whether a good is normal? Inferior?

3. If the cross-price elasticity of demand between potato chips and popcorn was positive and large, would popcorn makers benefit from a tax imposed on potato chips?

4. As people's incomes rise, why will they spend an increasing portion of their incomes on goods with income elasticities greater than 1 (DVDs) and a decreasing portion of their incomes on goods with income elasticities less than 1 (food)?

5. If people spent three times as much on restaurant meals and four times as much on DVDs as their incomes doubled, would restaurant meals or DVDs have a greater income elasticity of demand?

Answers: 1. b   2. a   3. d   4. e

· ·

Price Elasticity of Supply   6.4

▶ What is the price elasticity of supply?

▶ How does time affect the supply elasticity?

▶ How does the relative elasticity of supply and demand determine the tax burden?

6.4a What is the Price Elasticity of Supply?

According to the law of supply, there is a positive relationship between price and quantity supplied, *ceteris paribus*. But by how much does quantity supplied change as price changes? It is often helpful to know the degree to which a change in price changes the quantity supplied. The **price elasticity of supply** measures how responsive the quantity sellers are willing and able to sell is to changes in price. In other words, it measures the relative change in the quantity supplied that results from a change in price. Specifically, the price elasticity of supply (E_s) is defined as the percentage change in the quantity supplied divided by the percentage change in price, or

price elasticity of supply
the measure of the sensitivity of the quantity supplied to changes in price of a good

$$E_s = \frac{\%\Delta \text{ in the quantity supplied}}{\%\Delta \text{ in price}}$$

Calculating the Price Elasticity of Supply

The price elasticity of supply is calculated in much the same manner as the price elasticity of demand. Consider, for example, the case in which it is determined that a 10 percent increase in the price of artichokes results in a 25 percent increase in the quantity of artichokes supplied after, say, a few harvest seasons. In this case, the price elasticity is +2.5 (+25% ÷ +10% = +2.5). This coefficient indicates that each 1 percent increase in the price of artichokes induces a 2.5 percent increase in the quantity of artichokes supplied.

Types of Supply Curves

As with the elasticity of demand, the ranges of the price elasticity of supply center on whether the elasticity coefficient is greater than or less than 1. Goods with a supply elasticity that is greater than 1 ($E_s > 1$) are said to be relatively elastic in supply. With that, a 1 percent change in price will result in a greater than 1 percent change in quantity supplied. In our example, artichokes were elastic in supply because a 1 percent price increase resulted in a 2.5 percent increase in quantity supplied. An example of an *elastic supply curve* is shown in Exhibit 1(a).

section 6.4 exhibit 1	The Price Elasticity of Supply

a. Elastic Supply ($E_s > 1$)

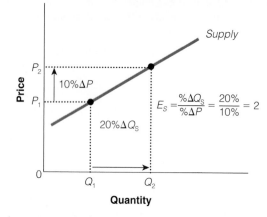

$$E_S = \frac{\%\Delta Q_S}{\%\Delta P} = \frac{20\%}{10\%} = 2$$

A change in price leads to a larger percentage change in quantity supplied.

b. Inelastic Supply ($E_s < 1$)

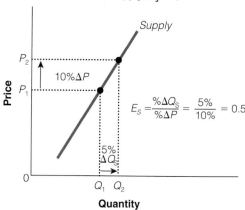

$$E_S = \frac{\%\Delta Q_S}{\%\Delta P} = \frac{5\%}{10\%} = 0.5$$

A change in price leads to a smaller percentage change in quantity supplied.

c. Perfectly Inelastic Supply ($E_s = 0$)

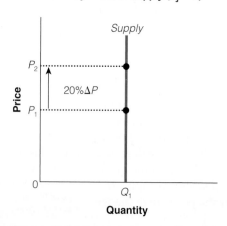

The quantity supplied does not change regardless of the change in price.

d. Perfectly Elastic Supply ($E_s = \infty$)

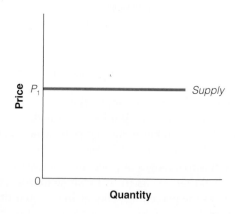

Even a small percentage change in price will change quantity supplied by an infinite amount.

Goods with a supply elasticity that is less than 1 ($E_S < 1$) are said to be inelastic in supply. In other words, a 1 percent change in the price of these goods will induce a proportionately smaller change in the quantity supplied. An example of an *inelastic supply curve* is shown in Exhibit 1(b).

Finally, two extreme cases of price elasticity of supply are perfectly inelastic supply and perfectly elastic supply. In a condition of *perfectly inelastic supply*, an increase in price will not change the quantity supplied. In this case the elasticity of supply is zero. For example, in a sports arena in the short run (that is, in a period too brief to adjust the structure), the number of seats available will be almost fixed, say at 20,000 seats. Additional portable seats might be available, but for the most part, even if a higher price is charged, only 20,000 seats will be available. We say that the elasticity of supply is zero, which describes a perfectly inelastic supply curve. Famous paintings, such as Van Gogh's *Starry Night*, provide another example: Only one original exists; therefore, only one can be supplied, regardless of price. An example of this condition is shown in Exhibit 1(c).

At the other extreme is a perfectly elastic supply curve, where the elasticity equals infinity, as shown in Exhibit 1(d). In a condition of *perfectly elastic supply*, the price does not change at all. It is the same regardless of the quantity supplied, and the elasticity of supply is infinite. Firms would supply as much as the market wants at the market price (P_1) or above. However, firms would supply nothing below the market price because they would not be able to cover their costs of production. Most cases fall somewhere between the two extremes of perfectly elastic and perfectly inelastic.

Immediately after harvest season is over, the supply of pumpkins is inelastic. That is, even if the price for pumpkins rises, say 10 percent, the amount of pumpkins produced will change hardly at all until the next harvest season. Some pumpkins may be grown in greenhouses (at a much higher price to consumers), but most farmers will wait until the next growing season.

What does it mean if the supply of elasticity is less than 1? greater than 1?

How Does Time Affect Supply Elasticities?

Time is usually critical in supply elasticities (as well as in demand elasticities) because it is more costly for sellers to bring forth and release products in a shorter period. For example, higher wheat prices may cause farmers to grow more wheat, but big changes cannot occur until the next growing season. That is, immediately after harvest season, the supply of wheat is relatively inelastic, but over a longer time extending over the next growing period, the supply curve becomes much more elastic. Thus, supply tends to be more elastic in the long run than in the short run, as shown in Exhibit 2.

In the short run, firms can increase output by using their existing facilities to a greater capacity, paying workers to work overtime, and hiring additional workers. However, firms will be able to change output much more in the long run when firms can build new factories or close existing ones. In addition, some firms can enter as others exit. In other words, the quantity supplied will be much more elastic in the long run than in the short run.

Elasticities and Taxes: Combining Supply and Demand Elasticities

Who pays the tax? Someone may be legally required to send the check to the government but that is not necessarily the party that bears the burden of the tax.

The relative elasticity of supply and demand determines the distribution of the tax burden for a good. As we will see, if demand is relatively less elastic than supply in the relevant tax region, the largest portion of the tax is paid by

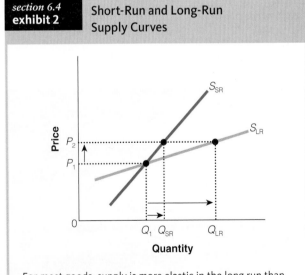

section 6.4 exhibit 2   Short-Run and Long-Run Supply Curves

For most goods, supply is more elastic in the long run than in the short run. For example, if the price of a certain good increases, firms have an incentive to produce more but are constrained by the size of their plants. In the long run, they can increase their capacity and produce more.

Consider an increase in demand for housing in two cities: New York and Houston. In New York, land is extremely scarce, resulting in dense development. Further development is also regulated, making the supply curve of housing in NYC very steep, or inelastic. However, in Houston, there is a lot more space, resulting in much lower density. Furthermore, new development is much less regulated, making the supply curve of housing in Houston much more elastic. So what could we predict about the results if there was an increase in demand of roughly the same magnitude in both cities? We would expect a large increase in price and a small increase in equilibrium quantity of housing in NYC. In Houston, we would predict a relatively small increase in price and a relatively large increase in quantity for a similarly sized demand shift. Draw the graphs to see for yourself.

the consumer. However, if demand is relatively more elastic than supply in the relevant tax region, the largest portion of the tax is paid by the producer.

In Exhibit 3(a), the pretax equilibrium price is $1.00 and the pretax equilibrium quantity is Q_{BT}—the quantity before tax. If the government imposes a $0.50 tax on the seller, the supply curve shifts vertically by the amount of the tax (just as if an input price rose $0.50).

When demand is relatively less elastic than supply in the relevant region, the consumer bears more of the burden of the tax. For example, in Exhibit 3(a), the demand curve is relatively less elastic than the supply curve. In response to the tax, the consumer pays $1.40 per unit, $0.40 more than the consumer paid before the tax increase. The producer, however, receives $0.90 per unit, which is $0.10 less than the producer received before the tax.

In Exhibit 3(b), demand is relatively more elastic than the supply in the relevant region. Here we see that the greater burden of the same $0.50 tax falls on the producer. That is, the producer is now responsible for $0.40 of the tax, while the consumer only pays $0.10. In general, then, the tax burden falls on the side of the market that is relatively less elastic.

Why does supply tend to be more elastic in the long run than in the short run?

Yachts, Taxes, and Elasticities

In 1991, Congress levied a 10 percent luxury tax. The tax applied to the "first retail sale" of luxury goods with sales prices above the following thresholds: automobiles, $30,000; boats, $100,000; private planes, $250,000; and furs and jewelry, $10,000. The Congressional Budget Office forecasted that the luxury tax would raise about $1.5 billion over five years. However, in 1991, the luxury tax raised less than $30 million in tax revenues. Why? People stopped buying items subject to the luxury tax.

Let's focus our attention on the luxury tax on yachts. Congress passed this tax thinking that the demand for yachts was relatively inelastic and that the tax would have only a small impact on the sale of new yachts. However, the people in the market for new boats had plenty of substitutes—used boats, boats from other countries, new houses, vacations, and so on. In short, the demand for new yachts was more elastic than Congress thought. Remember, when demand is relatively more elastic than supply, most of the tax is

If the demand for yachts is elastic, will most of a luxury tax on yachts get passed on to producers of yachts? And if so, how will that impact employment in the boat-building industry?

section 6.4
exhibit 3   Elasticity and the Burden of Taxation

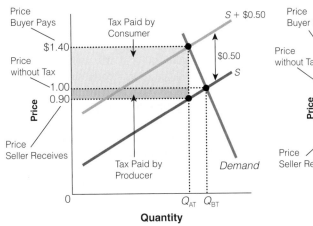

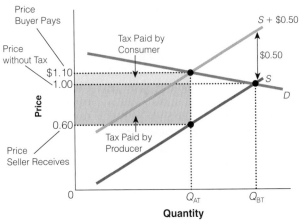

a. Demand is Relatively Less Elastic than Supply

b. Demand is Relatively More Elastic than Supply

When demand is less elastic (or more inelastic) than supply, the tax burden falls primarily on consumers, as shown in (a). When demand is more elastic than supply, as shown in (b), the tax burden falls primarily on producers.

passed on to the seller—in this case, the boat industry (workers and retailers). And supply was relatively inelastic because boat factories are not easy to change in the short run. So sellers received a lower price for their boats, and sales fell. In the first year after the tax, yacht retailers reported a 77 percent drop in sales, and approximately 25,000 workers were laid off. The point is that incorrectly predicting elasticities can lead to huge social, political, and economic problems. After intense lobbying by industry groups, Congress repealed the luxury tax on boats in 1993, and on January 1, 2003, the tax on cars finally expired.

USE WHAT YOU'VE LEARNED

Farm Prices Fall over the Last Half-Century

Q In the last half-century, farm prices experienced a steady decline—roughly 2 percent per year. Why?

A The demand for farm products grew more slowly than supply. Productivity advances in agriculture caused large increases in supply. And because of the inelastic demand for farm products, farmers' incomes fell considerably. That is, the total revenues ($P \times Q$) that farmers collected at the higher price, P_1, was much greater, area $oP_1E_1Q_1$, than the total revenue collected by farmers now when prices are lower, P_2, at area $oP_2E_2Q_2$. In addition, with the low prices for farm products, only the most efficiently run farms have been able to remain profitable. Many of the smaller, family-run farms have found it difficult to survive. Hence, many of these small farms have disappeared.

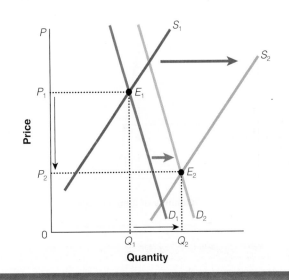

IN THE NEWS

Drugs across the Border

The United States spends billions of dollars a year to halt the importation of illegal drugs across the border. Although these efforts are clearly targeted at suppliers, who really pays the higher enforcement and evasion costs? The government crackdown has increased the probability of apprehension and conviction for drug smugglers. That increase in risk for suppliers increases their cost of doing business, raising the cost of importing and distributing illegal drugs. This would shift the supply curve for illegal drugs to the left, from S_1 to S_2, as seen in Exhibit 4. For most drug users—addicts, in particular—the price of drugs such as cocaine and heroin lies in the highly inelastic region of the demand curve. Because the demand for drugs is relatively inelastic in this region, the seller would be able to shift most of this cost onto the consumer (think of it as similar to the tax shift just discussed). The buyer now has to pay a much higher price, P_B, and the seller receives a slightly lower price, P_S. That is, enforcement efforts increase the price of illegal drugs, but only a small reduction in quantity demanded results from this price increase. Increased enforcement efforts may have unintended consequences due to the fact that buyers bear the majority of the burden of this price increase. Tighter smuggling controls may, in fact, result in higher levels of burglary, muggings, and white-collar crime, as more cash-strapped buyers search for alternative ways of funding their increasingly expensive habit. In addition, with the huge financial rewards in the drug trade, tougher enforcement and higher illegal drug prices could lead to even greater corruption in law enforcement and the judicial system.

These possible reactions do not mean we should abandon our efforts against illegal drugs. Illegal drugs can impose huge personal and social costs—billions of dollars of lost productivity and immeasurable personal tragedy. However, solely targeting the supply side can have unintended consequences. Policy makers may get their best results by focusing on a reduction in demand—changing user preferences. For example, if drug education leads to a reduction in the demand for drugs, the demand curve will shift to the left—reducing the price and the quantity of illegal drugs exchanged, as shown in Exhibit 5. The remaining drug users, at Q_2, will now pay a lower price, P_2. This lower price for drugs will lead to fewer drug-related crimes, *ceteris paribus*.

It is also possible that the elasticity of demand for illegal drugs may be more elastic in the long run than the short run. In the short run, as the price rises, the quantity demanded falls less than proportionately because of the addictive nature of illegal drugs (this relationship is also true for goods such as tobacco and alcohol). However, in the long run, the demand for illegal drugs may be more elastic; that is, the higher price may deter many younger, and poorer, people from experimenting with illegal drugs.

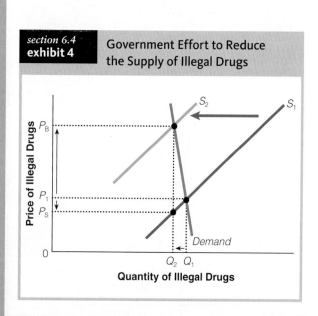

section 6.4 exhibit 4 Government Effort to Reduce the Supply of Illegal Drugs

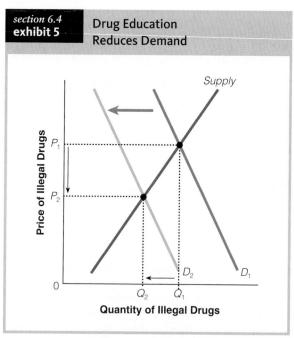

section 6.4 exhibit 5 Drug Education Reduces Demand

Use What You've Learned

Oil Prices

One reason that small changes in supply (or demand) lead to large changes in oil prices and small changes in quantity is because of the inelasticity of demand (and supply) in the short run. Because bringing the production of oil to market takes a long time, the elasticity of supply is relatively low—supply is inelastic. Few substitutes for oil products (e.g., gasoline) are available in the short run, as seen in Exhibit 6(a).

However, in the long run, demand and supply are more elastic. At higher prices, consumers will replace gas guzzlers with more fuel-efficient cars, and non-OPEC oil producers will expand exploration and production. Thus, in the long run, when supply and demand are much more elastic, the same size reduction in supply will have a smaller impact on price, as seen in Exhibit 6(b).

section 6.4
exhibit 6

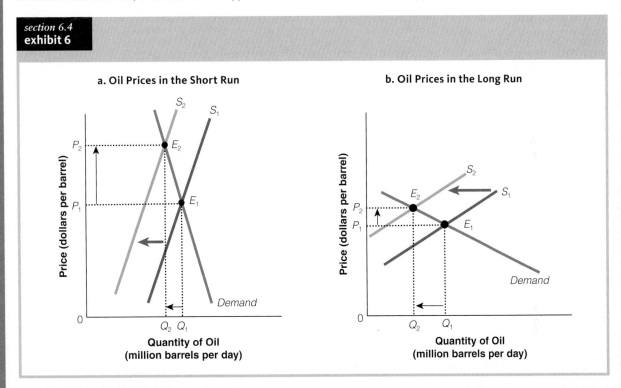

a. Oil Prices in the Short Run

b. Oil Prices in the Long Run

SECTION QUIZ

1. For a given increase in price, the greater the elasticity of supply, the greater the resulting

   a. decrease in quantity supplied.

   b. decrease in supply.

   c. increase in quantity supplied.

   d. increase in supply.

2. If the demand for gasoline is highly inelastic and the supply is highly elastic, and then a tax is imposed on gasoline, it will be paid

   a. largely by the sellers of gasoline.

   b. largely by the buyers of gasoline.

   c. equally by the sellers and buyers of gasoline.

   d. by the government.

(continued)

SECTION QUIZ (cont.)

3. Which of the following statements is true?

   a. The price elasticity of supply measures the relative change in the quantity supplied that results from a change in price.

   b. If the supply price elasticity is greater than 1, it is elastic; if it is less than 1, it is inelastic.

   c. Supply tends to be more elastic in the long run than in the short run.

   d. The relative elasticity of supply and demand determines the distribution of the tax burden for a good.

   e. All of the statements above are true.

4. Which of the following statements is true?

   a. The price elasticity of supply measures the relative change in the quantity supplied that results from a change in price.

   b. When supply is relatively elastic, a 10 percent change in price will result in a greater than 10 percent change in quantity supplied.

   c. Goods with a supply elasticity that is less than 1 are called relatively inelastic in supply.

   d. Who bears the burden of a tax has nothing to do with who actually pays the tax at the time of the purchase.

   e. All of the statements above are true.

---

1. What does it mean to say the elasticity of supply for one good is greater than that for another?

2. Why does supply tend to be more elastic in the long run than in the short run?

3. How do the relative elasticities of supply and demand determine who bears the greater burden of a tax?

Answers: 1. c 2. b 3. e 4. e

INTERACTIVE SUMMARY

Fill in the blanks:

1. The price elasticity of demand measures the responsiveness of quantity _____ to a change in price.

2. The price elasticity of demand is defined as the percentage change in _____ divided by the percentage change in _____.

3. If the price elasticity of demand is elastic, it means the quantity demanded changes by a relatively _____ amount than the price change.

4. If the price elasticity of demand is inelastic, it means the quantity demanded changes by a relatively _____ amount than the price change.

5. A demand curve or a portion of a demand curve can be relatively _____, _____, or relatively _____.

6. For the most part, the price elasticity of demand depends on the availability of _____, the _____ spent on the good, and the amount of _____ people have to adapt to a price change.

7. The elasticity of demand for a Ford automobile would likely be _____ elastic than the demand for automobiles because there are more and better substitutes for a certain type of car than for a car itself.

8. The smaller the proportion of income spent on a good, the _____ its elasticity of demand.

9. The more time that people have to adapt to a new price change, the _____ the elasticity of demand. The more time that passes, the more time consumers have to find or develop suitable _____ and to plan and implement changes in their patterns of consumption.

10. When demand is price elastic, total revenues will _____ as the price declines because the percentage increase in the _____ is greater than the percentage reduction in price.

11. When demand is price inelastic, total revenues will _____ as the price declines because the percentage increase in the _____ is less than the percentage reduction in price.

12. When the price falls on the _____ half of a straight-line demand curve, demand is relatively _____. When the price falls on the lower half of a straight-line demand curve, demand is relatively _____.

13. The cross-price elasticity of demand is defined as the percentage change in the _____ of good A divided by the percentage change in _____ of good B.

14. The income elasticity of demand is defined as the percentage change in the _____ by the percentage change in _____.

15. The price elasticity of supply measures the sensitivity of the quantity _____ to changes in the price of the good.

16. The price elasticity of supply is defined as the percentage change in the _____ divided by the percentage change in _____.

17. Goods with a supply elasticity that is greater than 1 are called relatively _____ in supply.

18. When supply is inelastic, a 1 percent change in the price of a good will induce a _____ 1 percent change in the quantity supplied.

19. Time is usually critical in supply elasticities because it is _____ costly for sellers to bring forth and release products in a shorter period of time.

20. The relative _____ determines the distribution of the tax burden for a good.

21. If demand is relatively _____ elastic than supply in the relevant region, the largest portion of a tax is paid by the producer.

Answers: 1. demanded 2. quantity demanded; price 3. larger 4. smaller 5. elastic; unit elastic; inelastic 6. close substitutes; proportion of income; time 7. more 8. lower 9. greater; substitutes 10. rise; quantity demanded 11. fall; quantity demanded 12. upper; elastic; inelastic 13. demand; price 14. demand; income 15. supplied 16. quantity supplied; price 17. elastic 18. less than 19. more 20. elasticity of supply and demand 21. more.

KEY TERMS AND CONCEPTS

price elasticity of demand 156
elastic 157
inelastic 157

unit elastic demand 157
total revenue (TR) 163
cross-price elasticity of demand 169

income elasticity of demand 170
price elasticity of supply 171

SECTION QUIZ ANSWERS

6.1 Price Elasticity of Demand

1. **What question is the price elasticity of demand designed to answer?**
   The price elasticity of demand is designed to answer the question, How responsive is quantity demanded to changes in the price of a good?

2. **How is the price elasticity of demand calculated?**
   The price elasticity of demand is calculated as the percentage change in quantity demanded, divided by the percentage change in the price that caused the change in quantity demanded.

3. **What is the difference between a relatively price elastic demand curve and a relatively price inelastic demand curve?**
   Quantity demanded changes relatively more than price along a relatively price elastic segment of a demand curve, while quantity demanded changes relatively less than price along a relatively price inelastic segment of a demand curve.

4. **What is the relationship between the price elasticity of demand and the slope at a given point on a demand curve?**
   At a given point on a demand curve, the flatter the demand curve, the more quantity demanded changes for a given change in price, so the greater is the elasticity of demand.

5. **What factors tend to make demand curves more price elastic?**

   Demand curves tend to become more elastic, the larger the number of close substitutes available for the good, the larger proportion of income spent on the good, and the greater the amount of time that buyers have to respond to a change in the good's price.

6. **Why would a tax on a particular brand of cigarettes be less effective at reducing smoking than a tax on all brands of cigarettes?**

   A tax on one brand of cigarettes would allow smokers to avoid the tax by switching brands rather than by smoking less, but a tax on all brands would raise the cost of smoking any cigarettes. A tax on all brands of cigarettes would therefore be more effective in reducing smoking.

7. **Why is the price elasticity of demand for products at a 24-hour convenience store likely to be lower at 2:00 A.M. than at 2:00 P.M.?**

   Fewer alternative stores are open at 2:00 A.M. than at 2:00 P.M., and with fewer good substitutes, the price elasticity of demand for products at 24-hour convenience stores is greater at 2:00 P.M.

8. **Why is the price elasticity of demand for turkeys likely to be lower, but the price elasticity of demand for turkeys at a particular store at Thanksgiving likely to be greater than at other times of the year?**

   For many people, far fewer good substitutes are acceptable for turkey at Thanksgiving than at other times, so that the demand for turkeys is more inelastic at Thanksgiving. But grocery stores looking to attract customers for their entire large Thanksgiving shopping trip also often offer and heavily advertise turkeys at far better prices than normally. This means shoppers have available more good substitutes and a more price elastic demand curve for buying a turkey at a particular store than usual.

6.2 Total Revenue and the Price Elasticity of Demand

1. **Why does total revenue vary inversely with price if demand is relatively price elastic?**

   Total revenue varies inversely with price if demand is relatively price elastic because the quantity demanded (which equals the quantity sold) changes relatively more than price along a relatively elastic demand curve. Therefore, total revenue, which equals price times quantity demanded (sold) at that price, will change in the same direction as quantity demanded and in the opposite direction from the change in price.

2. **Why does total revenue vary directly with price, if demand is relatively price inelastic?**

   Total revenue varies in the same direction as price if demand is relatively price inelastic because the quantity demanded (which equals the quantity sold) changes relatively less than price along a relatively inelastic demand curve. Therefore, total revenue, which equals price times quantity demanded (and sold) at that price, will change in the same direction as price and in the opposite direction from the change in quantity demanded.

3. **Why is a linear demand curve more price elastic at higher price ranges and more price inelastic at lower price ranges?**

   Along the upper half of a linear (constant slope) demand curve, total revenue increases as the price falls, indicating that demand is relatively price elastic. Along the lower half of a linear (constant slope) demand curve, total revenue decreases as the price falls, indicating that demand is relatively price inelastic.

4. **If demand for some good was perfectly price inelastic, how would total revenue from its sales change as its price changed?**

   A perfectly price inelastic demand curve would be one where the quantity sold did not vary with the price. In such an (imaginary) case, total revenue would increase proportionally with price—a 10 percent increase in price with the same quantity sold would result in a 10 percent increase in total revenue.

5. **Assume that both you and Art, your partner in a picture-framing business, want to increase your firm's total revenue. You argue that in order to achieve this goal, you should lower your prices; Art, on the other hand, thinks that you should raise your prices. What assumptions are each of you making about your firm's price elasticity of demand?**

   You are assuming that a lower price will increase total revenue, which implies you think the demand for your picture frames is relatively price elastic. Art is assuming that an increase in your price will increase your total revenue, which implies he thinks the demand for your picture frames is relatively price inelastic.

6.3 Other Types of Demand Elasticities

1. **How does the cross-price elasticity of demand tell you whether two goods are substitutes? Complements?**

   Two goods are substitutes when an increase (decrease) in the price of one good causes an increase (decrease) in the demand for another good. Substitutes have a positive cross-price elasticity. Two goods are complements when an increase (decrease) in the price of one good decreases (increases) the demand for another good. Complements have a negative cross-price elasticity.

2. **How does the income elasticity of demand tell you whether a good is normal? Inferior?**

If demand for a good increases (decreases) when income rises (falls), it is a normal good and has a positive income elasticity. If demand for a good decreases (increases) when income rises (falls), it is an inferior good and has a negative income elasticity.

3. **If the cross-price elasticity of demand between potato chips and popcorn was positive and large, would popcorn makers benefit from a tax imposed on potato chips?**

A large positive cross-price elasticity of demand between potato chips and popcorn indicates that they are close substitutes. A tax on potato chips, which would raise the price of potato chips as a result, would also substantially increase the demand for popcorn, increasing the price of popcorn and the quantity of popcorn sold, increasing the profits of popcorn makers.

4. **As people's incomes rise, why will they spend an increasing portion of their incomes on goods with income elasticities greater than 1 (DVDs) and a decreasing portion of their incomes on goods with income elasticities less than 1 (food)?**

An income elasticity of 1 would mean people spent the same fraction or share of their income on a particular good as their incomes increase. An income elasticity greater than 1 would mean people spent an increasing fraction or share of their income on a particular good as their incomes increase, and an income elasticity less than 1 would mean people spent a decreasing fraction or share of their income on a particular good as their incomes increase.

5. **If people spent three times as much on restaurant meals and four times as much on DVDs as their incomes doubled, would restaurant meals or DVDs have a greater income elasticity of demand?**

DVDs would have a higher income elasticity of demand (4) in this case than restaurant meals (3).

6.4 Price Elasticity of Supply

1. **What does it mean to say the elasticity of supply for one good is greater than that for another?**

For the elasticity of supply for one good to be greater than for another, the percentage increase in quantity supplied that results from a given percentage change in price will be greater for the first good than for the second.

2. **Why does supply tend to be more elastic in the long run than in the short run?**

Just as the cost of buyers changing their behavior is lower the longer they have to adapt, which leads to long-run demand curves being more elastic than short-run demand curves, the same is true of suppliers. The cost of producers changing their behavior is lower the longer they have to adapt, which leads to long-run supply curves being more elastic than short-run supply curves.

3. **How do the relative elasticities of supply and demand determine who bears the greater burden of a tax?**

When demand is more elastic than supply, the tax burden falls mainly on producers; when supply is more elastic than demand, the tax burden falls mainly on consumers.

PROBLEMS

1. In each of the following cases, indicate which good you think has a relatively *more* price elastic demand and identify the most likely reason, in terms of the determinants of the elasticity of demand (more substitutes, greater share of budget, or more time to adjust).
   a. Cars or Chevrolets
   b. Salt or housing
   c. Going to a New York Mets game or a Cleveland Indians game
   d. Natural gas this month or over the course of a year

2. How might your elasticity of demand for copying and binding services vary if your work presentation is next week versus in 2 hours?

3. The San Francisco Giants want to boost revenues from ticket sales next season. You are hired as an economic consultant and asked to advise the Giants whether to raise or lower ticket prices next year. If the elasticity of demand for Giants game tickets is estimated to be −1.6, what would you advise? If the elasticity of demand equals −0.4?

4. For each of the following pairs, identify which one is likely to exhibit more elastic demand.
    a. Shampoo; Paul Mitchell Shampoo
    b. Air travel prompted by an illness in the family; vacation air travel
    c. Paper clips; an apartment rental
    d. Prescription heart medication; generic aspirin

5. Using the midpoint formula for calculating the elasticity of demand, if the price of a good fell from $42 to $38, what would be the elasticity of demand if the quantity demanded changed from:
    a. 19 to 21?
    b. 27 to 33?
    c. 195 to 205?

6. Explain why using the midpoint formula for calculating the elasticity of demand gives the same result whether price increases or decreases, but using the initial price and quantity instead of the average does not.

7. Why is a more narrowly defined good (pizza) likely to have a greater elasticity of demand than a more broadly defined good (food)?

8. If the elasticity of demand for hamburgers equals −1.5 and the quantity demanded equals 40,000, predict what will happen to the quantity demanded of hamburgers when the price increases by 10 percent. If the price falls by 5 percent, what will happen?

9. Evaluate the following statement: "Along a downward-sloping linear demand curve, the slope and therefore the elasticity of demand are both 'constant.'"

10. If the midpoint on a straight-line demand curve is at a price of $7, what can we say about the elasticity of demand for a price change from $12 to $10? What about from $6 to $4?

11. Assume the following weekly demand schedule for Sunshine Yogurt in Cloverdale.

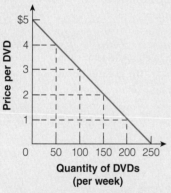

    a. When Sunshine Yogurt lowers its price from $4 to $3, what happens to its total revenue?
    b. Between a price of $4 and a price of $3, is the demand for Sunshine Yogurt in Cloverdale elastic or inelastic?
    c. Between a price of $2 and a price of $1, is the demand for Sunshine Yogurt in Cloverdale elastic or inelastic?

12. The Cowtown Hotel is the only first-class hotel in Fort Worth, Texas. The hotel owners hired economics advisors for advice about improving the hotel's profitability. They suggested the hotel could increase this year's revenue by raising prices. The owners asked, "Won't raising prices reduce the quantity of hotel rooms demanded and increase vacancies?" What do you think the advisors replied? Why would they suggest increasing prices?

13. A movie production company faces a linear demand curve for its film, and it seeks to maximize total revenue from the film's distribution. At what level should the price be set? Where is demand elastic, inelastic, or unit elastic? Explain.

14. Isabella always spends $50 on red roses each month and simply adjusts the quantity she purchases as the price changes. What can you say about Isabella's elasticity of demand for roses?

15. If taxi fares in a city rise, what will happen to the total revenue received by taxi operators? If the fares charged for subway rides, a substitute for taxi rides, do not change, what will happen to the total revenue earned by the subway as a result?

16. Mayor George Henry has a problem. He doesn't want to anger voters by taxing them because he wants to be reelected, but the town of Gapville needs more revenue for its schools. He has a choice between taxing tickets to professional basketball games or taxing food. If the demand for food is relatively inelastic while the supply is relatively elastic, and if the demand for professional basketball games is relatively elastic while the supply is relatively inelastic, in which case would the tax burden fall primarily on consumers? In which case would the tax burden fall primarily on producers?

17. Indicate whether a pair of products are substitutes, complements, or neither based on the following estimates for the cross-price elasticity of demand:
    a. 0.5.
    b. −0.5.

18. Using the midpoint formula for calculating the elasticity of supply, if the price of a good rose from $95 to $105, what would be the elasticity of supply if the quantity supplied changed from:
    a. 38 to 42?
    b. 78 to 82?
    c. 54 to 66?

19. Why is an increase in price more likely to decrease the total revenue of a seller in the long run than in the short run?

20. If both supply curves and demand curves are more elastic in the long run than in the short run, how does the incidence of a tax change from the short run to the long run as a result? What happens to the revenue raised from a given tax over time, *ceteris paribus*?

PART 3

TECHNOTR/VETTA/GETTY IMAGES

Market Efficiency, Market Failure, and the Public System

Market Efficiency and Welfare

We can use the tools of consumer and producer surplus to study the welfare effects of government policy—rent controls, taxes, and agricultural support prices. To economists, welfare does not mean a government payment to the poor; rather, it is a way that we measure the impact of a policy on a particular group, such as consumers or producers. By calculating the changes in producer and consumer surplus that result from government intervention, we can measure the impact of such policies on buyers and sellers. For example, economists and policy makers may want to know how much a consumer or producer might benefit or be harmed by a tax or subsidy that alters the equilibrium price and quantity of a good or service. Take the price support programs for farmers. For years, the government has tried to phase out the price floors and the government purchases of surpluses and return to free agriculture. To allow

farmers time to adjust they have implemented subsidies but the subsidies continue and in 2013 the Congressional Budget office (CBO) estimated that the new farm bill would cost roughly $960 billion over the next ten years. Who gains and who loses with these policies?

By using the concepts of consumer surplus, producer surplus, and deadweight loss we can understand more clearly the economic inefficiencies that result from price floors and price ceilings. We will see how moving away from a competitive equilibrium will reduce economic efficiency.

Maximizing total surplus (the sum of consumer and producer surplus) leads to an efficient allocation of resources. Efficiency makes the size of the economic pie as large as possible. How we distribute that economic pie (equity) is the subject of future chapters. Efficiency can be measured on objective, positive grounds while equity involves normative analysis.

Let's begin by presenting the most widely used tool for measuring consumer and producer welfare.

Consumer Surplus and Producer Surplus   7.1

▶ What is consumer surplus?

▶ What is producer surplus?

▶ How do we measure the total gains from trade?

7.1a Consumer Surplus

In a competitive market, consumers and producers buy and sell at the market equilibrium price. However, some consumers will be willing and able to pay more for the good than they have to. But they would never knowingly buy something that is worth less to them. That is, what a consumer actually pays for a unit of a good is usually less than the amount she is *willing* to pay. For example, would you be willing to pay more than the market price for a rope ladder to get out of a burning building? Would you be willing to pay more than the market price for a tank of gasoline if you had run out of gas on a desolate highway in the desert? Would you be willing to pay more than the market price for an anti-venom shot if you had been bitten by a rattlesnake? Consumer surplus is the monetary difference between the amount a consumer is willing and able to pay for an additional unit of a good and what the consumer actually pays—the market price. Consumer surplus for the whole market is the sum of all the individual consumer surpluses for those consumers who have purchased the good.

ROBERT L. SEXTON

Imagine it is 115 degrees in the shade. Do you think you would get more consumer surplus from your first glass of iced tea than you would from a fifth glass?

7.1b Marginal Willingness to Pay Falls as More Is Consumed

Suppose it is a hot day and iced tea is going for $1 per glass, but Emily is willing to pay $4 for the first glass (point a), $2 for the second glass (point b), and $0.50 for the third glass (point c), reflecting the law of demand. How much consumer surplus will Emily receive? First,

consumer surplus
the difference between the price a consumer is willing and able to pay for an additional unit of a good and the price the consumer actually pays; for the whole market, it is the sum of all the individual consumer surpluses

it is important to note the general fact that if the consumer is a buyer of several units of a good, the earlier units will have greater marginal value and therefore create more consumer surplus because *marginal willingness to pay* falls as greater quantities are consumed in any period. In fact, you can think of the demand curve as a marginal benefit curve—the additional benefit derived from consuming one more unit. Notice in Exhibit 1 that Emily's demand curve for iced tea has a step-like shape. This is demonstrated by Emily's willingness to pay $4 and $2 successively for the first two glasses of iced tea. Thus, Emily will receive $3 of consumer surplus for the first glass ($4 – $1) and $1 of consumer surplus for the second glass ($2 – $1), for a total consumer surplus of $4, as seen in Exhibit 1. Emily will not be willing to purchase the third glass because her willingness to pay is less than its price ($0.50 versus $1.00).

In Exhibit 2, we can easily measure the consumer surplus in the market by using a market demand curve rather than an individual demand curve. In short, the market consumer surplus is the area under the market demand curve and above the market price (the shaded area in Exhibit 2). The market for chocolate contains millions of potential buyers, so we will get a smooth demand curve. That is, each of the millions of potential buyers has their own willingness to pay. Because the demand curve represents the *marginal benefits* consumers receive from consuming an additional unit, we can conclude that all buyers of chocolate receive at least some consumer surplus in the market because the marginal benefit is greater than the market price—the shaded area in Exhibit 2.

7.1c Price Changes and Changes in Consumer Surplus

We may want to know how much consumers are hurt or helped when prices change. So let's see what happens to consumer surplus when the price of a good rises or falls, when demand remains constant. Suppose that the price of your favorite beverage fell because of an increase in supply. Wouldn't you feel better off? An increase in supply and a lower price will increase your consumer surplus for each unit you were already consuming and will also increase your consumer surplus from additional purchases at the lower price. Conversely, a decrease in supply and increase in price will lower your consumer surplus.

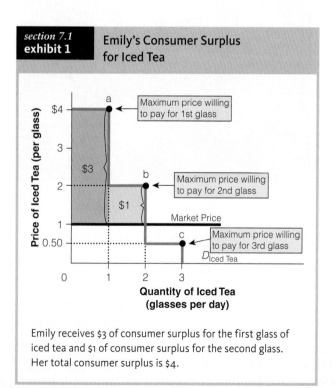

section 7.1
exhibit 1   Emily's Consumer Surplus for Iced Tea

Emily receives $3 of consumer surplus for the first glass of iced tea and $1 of consumer surplus for the second glass. Her total consumer surplus is $4.

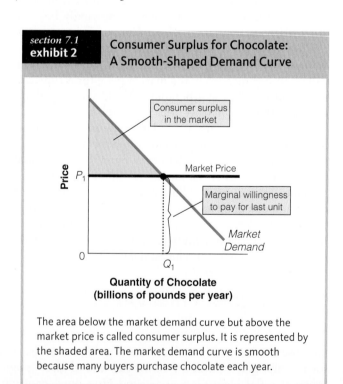

section 7.1
exhibit 2   Consumer Surplus for Chocolate: A Smooth-Shaped Demand Curve

The area below the market demand curve but above the market price is called consumer surplus. It is represented by the shaded area. The market demand curve is smooth because many buyers purchase chocolate each year.

Exhibit 3 shows the gain in consumer surplus associated with a fall in the market price of pizza from P_1 to P_2. The fall in the market price leads to an increase in quantity demanded and an increase in consumer surplus. More specifically, consumer surplus increases from area P_1AB to area P_2AC, for a gain in consumer surplus of P_1BCP_2. The increase in consumer surplus has two parts. First, there is an increase in consumer surplus, because Q_1 can now be purchased at a lower price; this amount of additional consumer surplus is illustrated by area P_1BDP_2 in Exhibit 3. That is, these consumers would have purchased those pizzas at the original price of P_1, but now can purchase them at the new lower price of P_2. Second, the lower price makes it advantageous for buyers to expand their purchases from Q_1 to Q_2. The net benefit to buyers from expanding their consumption from Q_1 to Q_2 is illustrated by area BCD. That is, buyers would purchase those additional pizzas because the price was reduced. Similarly, if the market price of pizzas rose, the quantity demanded would fall. As a result, the two effects triggered by a decrease in price would increase consumer surplus, while an increase in price would decrease consumer surplus by P_1BCP_2.

In sum, consumer surplus measures the net gains buyers *perceive* that they receive, over and above the market price they must pay. So in this sense, it is a good measure of changes in economic well-being, if we assume that individuals make rational choices—self-betterment choices—and that individuals are the best judges of how much benefit they derive from goods and services.

section 7.1 exhibit 3   A Fall in Price Increases Consumer Surplus

A fall in the price from P_1 to P_2 leads to an increase in quantity demanded from Q_1 to Q_2 and an increase in consumer surplus. The increase in consumer surplus has two parts: the gain to those who would have bought pizza at the higher original price, P_1 (area P_1BDP_2), and the gain to those who would not have bought the good at P_1 but are willing to do so at P_2 (area BCD). The gain in the consumer surplus is both those areas, or P_1BCP_2. Similarly, if the market price of pizzas rises, the quantity demanded would fall and it would lead to a decrease in consumer surplus of P_1BCP_2.

7.1d Producer Surplus

As we have just seen, the difference between what a consumer would be willing and able to pay for a given quantity of a good and what a consumer actually has to pay is called consumer surplus. The parallel concept for producers is called producer surplus. Producer surplus is the difference between what a producer is paid for a good and the cost of producing one unit of that good. Producers would never knowingly sell a good that is worth more to them than the asking price. Imagine selling coffee for half of what it cost to produce—you won't be in business very long with that pricing strategy. The supply curve shows the minimum amount that sellers must receive to be willing to supply any given quantity; that is, the supply curve reflects the marginal cost to sellers. The **marginal cost** is the cost of producing one more unit of a good. In other words, the supply curve is the marginal cost curve, just like the demand curve is the marginal benefit curve. Because some units can be produced at a cost that is lower than the market price, the seller receives a surplus, or a net benefit, from producing those units. For each unit produced, the producer surplus is the difference between the market price and the marginal cost of producing that unit. For example, in Exhibit 4, the market price is $4.50. Say the firm's marginal cost is $2 for the first unit, $3 for the second unit, $4 for the third unit, and $5 for the fourth unit. Because producer surplus for a particular unit is the difference between the market price and the seller's cost of producing that unit, producer surplus would be as follows: The first unit would yield $2.50, the second unit would yield $1.50, the third unit would yield $.50, and the fourth unit would add nothing to producer surplus because the market price is less than the seller's cost.

When there are a lot of producers, the supply curve is more or less smooth, like in Exhibit 5. Total producer surplus for the market is obtained by summing all the producer surpluses of all the sellers—the area above the market supply curve and below the market

producer surplus
the difference between what a producer is paid for a good and the cost of producing that unit of the good; for the market, it is the sum of all the individual sellers' producer surpluses—the area above the market supply curve and below the market price

marginal cost
the cost of producing one more unit of a good

section 7.1
exhibit 4   A Firm's Producer Surplus

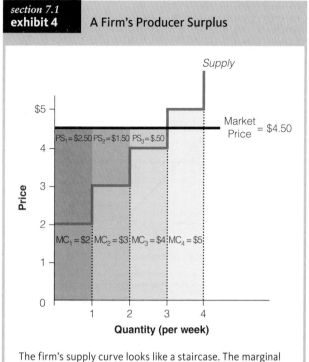

The firm's supply curve looks like a staircase. The marginal cost is under the stairs and the producer surplus is above the red stair and below the market price for each unit.

section 7.1
exhibit 6   A Rise in Price Increases Producer Surplus

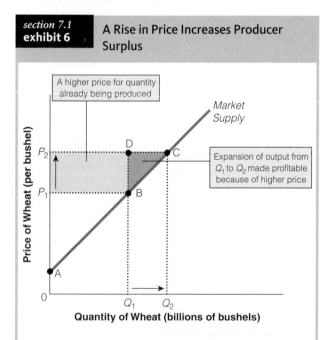

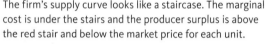

A rise in the price of wheat from P_1 to P_2 leads to an increase in quantity supplied and an increase in producer surplus. The increase in producer surplus has two parts: part of the added surplus (area P_2DBP_1) is due to a higher price and part (area DCB) is due to the expansion of output made profitable by the higher price. Similarly, a fall in the price of wheat from P_2 to P_1 would lead to a reduction in producer surplus of area P_2CBP_1.

section 7.1
exhibit 5   Market Producer Surplus

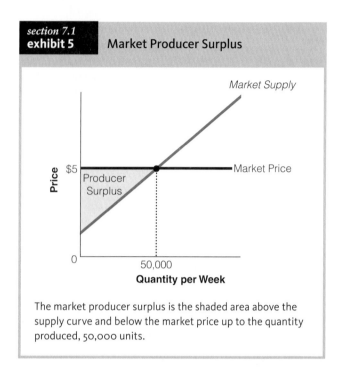

The market producer surplus is the shaded area above the supply curve and below the market price up to the quantity produced, 50,000 units.

price up to the quantity actually produced—the shaded area in Exhibit 5. Producer surplus is a measurement of how much sellers gain from trading in the market. Producer surplus represents the benefits that lower costs producers receive by selling at the market price.

Suppose the market price of wheat rises, from P_1 to P_2; wheat farmers now receive a higher price per unit, so additional producer surplus is generated, area P_2CBP_1. In Exhibit 6, we see the additions to producer surplus. Part of the added surplus (area P_2DBP_1) is due to a higher price for the quantity already being produced (up to Q_1) and part (area DCB) is due to the expansion of output made profitable by the higher price (from Q_1 to Q_2). That is, there are gains to farmers who would have supplied the wheat at the original price, P_1, and gains to the producers of added output who are drawn into the market at the higher market price, P_2. Similarly, a fall in the price of wheat from P_2 to P_1 would lead to a reduction in producer surplus of area P_2CBP_1.

Just as consumer surplus measures the net gains in economic well-being received by buyers, producer surplus measures the net gains in economic well-being received by sellers. In the next section we see that maximizing total surplus (both consumer and producer surplus) will lead to an efficient allocation of resources.

7.1e Market Efficiency and Producer and Consumer Surplus

With the tools of consumer and producer surplus, we can better analyze the total gains from exchange. The demand curve represents a collection of maximum prices that consumers are willing and able to pay for additional quantities of a good or service. It also shows the marginal benefits derived by consumers. That is, the demand curve represents the benefits that buyers receive from each marginal unit of the good consumed. The supply curve represents a collection of minimum prices that suppliers require to be willing and able to supply each additional unit of a good or service. It also shows the marginal cost of production. It represents the costs that sellers must bear to produce each marginal unit for the market. Both are shown in Exhibit 7. For example, for the first unit of output, the buyer is willing to pay up to $7, while the seller would have to receive at least $1 to produce that unit. However, the equilibrium price is $4, as indicated by the intersection of the supply and demand curves. It is clear that the two would gain from getting together and trading that unit because the consumer would receive $3 of consumer surplus ($7 – $4), and the producer would receive $3 of producer surplus ($4 – $1). Both would also benefit from trading the second and third units of output—in fact, both would benefit from trading every unit up to the market equilibrium output. That is, the buyer purchases the good, except for the very last unit, for less than the maximum amount she would have been willing to pay; the seller receives for the good, except for the last unit, more than the minimum amount for which he would have been willing to supply the good. Once the equilibrium output is reached at the equilibrium price, all the mutually beneficial trade opportunities between the demander and supplier will have taken place, and the sum of consumer surplus and producer surplus is maximized. This is where the marginal benefit to buyers is equal to the marginal cost to producers. Both buyer and seller are better off from each of the units traded than they would have been if they had not exchanged them.

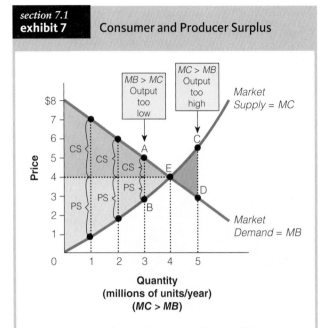

section 7.1
exhibit 7   **Consumer and Producer Surplus**

Increasing output beyond the competitive equilibrium output, 4 million units, decreases welfare because the cost of producing this extra output exceeds the value the buyer places on it (MC > MB)—producing 5 million units rather than 4 million units leads to a deadweight loss of area ECD. Reducing output below the competitive equilibrium output level, 4 million units, reduces total welfare because the buyer values the extra output by more than it costs to produce that output—producing 3 million units rather than 4 million units leads to a deadweight loss of area EAB, MB > MC, only at equillibrium, E, is MB = MC.

It is important to recognize that, in this case, the **total welfare gains** to the economy from trade in this good is the sum of the consumer and producer surpluses created. That is, consumers benefit from additional amounts of consumer surplus, and producers benefit from additional amounts of producer surplus. Improvements in welfare come from additions to both consumer and producer surpluses. In competitive markets with large numbers of buyers and sellers, at the market equilibrium price and quantity, the net gains to society are as large as possible.

Why would it be inefficient to produce only 3 million units? The demand curve in Exhibit 7 indicates that the buyer is willing to pay $5 for the 3 millionth unit. The supply curve shows that it only costs the seller $3 to produce that unit. That is, as long as the buyer values the extra output by more than it costs to produce that unit, total welfare would increase by expanding output. In fact, if output is expanded from 3 million units to 4 million units, total welfare (the sum of consumer and producer surpluses) will increase by area AEB in Exhibit 7.

What if 5 million units are produced? The demand curve shows that the buyer is only willing to pay $3 for the 5 millionth unit. However, the supply curve shows that it would cost about $5.50 to produce that 5 millionth unit. Thus, increasing output beyond equilibrium decreases total welfare because the cost of producing this extra output is greater than the value the buyer places on it. If output is reduced from 5 million units to 4 million units, total welfare will increase by area ECD in Exhibit 7.

Not producing the efficient level of output, in this case 4 million units, leads to what economists call a **deadweight loss**. A deadweight loss is the reduction in both consumer and

total welfare gains
the sum of consumer and producer surpluses

Why is total welfare maximized at the competitive equilibrium output?

How do we know when we have achieved market efficiency?

deadweight loss
net loss of total surplus that results from an action that alters a market equilibrium

SILICONVALLEYSTOCK/ALAMY

In an attempt to gain greater efficiency from limited parking space, the city of San Francisco has chosen to use variable parking meter pricing. That is, using the price system to get a more efficient use of a scarce resource—parking. Parking meter prices vary on the basis of location and time of day. The goal is to have at least one space available on every targeted block at any given time. To see how often a parking space is being used, the system employs sensors that track occupancy. The prices are then adjusted. Recently, blocks with less than 60 percent occupancy had meter price reductions and those with over 80 percent occupancy had meter price increases. Rates are adjusted no more than once a month and can vary between $1.25 and $4 per hour. In special short-term cases, such as major public events, meters can cost as much as $18 per hour.

producer surpluses—it is the net loss of total surplus that results from the misallocation of resources. In short, a deadweight loss measures the consumer and producer surplus that is destroyed. The deadweight loss gets larger and larger as we move further and further away from the efficient equilibrium output.

In a competitive equilibrium, supply equals demand at the equilibrium. This means that the buyers value the last unit of output consumed by exactly the same amount that it cost to produce. If consumers valued the last unit by more than it cost to produce, welfare could be increased by expanding output. If consumers valued the last unit by less than it cost to produce, then welfare could be increased by producing less output.

In sum, *market efficiency* occurs when we have maximized the sum of consumer and producer surplus, when the marginal benefits of the last unit produced is equal to the marginal cost of producing it, $MB = MC$.

7.1f Market Efficiency and Market Failure: A Caveat

It is worth repeating what we discussed in Chapter 2, that markets can fail to allocate resources efficiently when there is a lack of competition and/or externalities are present. Recall that we assume in our supply and demand analysis that markets are perfectly competitive. But markets are often not *perfectly* competitive and some firms may have considerable market power. These firms may keep market prices and quantities far from the equilibrium levels that would occur under competitive conditions, that is, the levels determined by market supply and demand.

In addition, we assumed that equilibrium prices and output only impact the buyers and sellers, but that is not always the case. Sometimes innocent bystanders are impacted by the decisions of buyers and sellers. For example, the farmer that uses dangerous pesticides may impact those that live in surrounding areas who drink the water and breathe the air. If buyers and sellers ignore these externalities, the market will not produce the efficient equilibrium output from society's standpoint—a topic we return to in Chapter 8. Fortunately, policy makers can help regulate markets when market power is present and try to correct for externalities with taxes and subsidies. However, despite these shortcomings, the concepts of economic efficiency and economic welfare presented in this chapter work remarkably well and can help guide policy makers into making better decisions.

GREAT ECONOMIC THINKERS

Alfred Marshall (1842–1924)

Alfred Marshall was born outside of London in 1842. His father, a domineering man who was a cashier for the Bank of England, wanted nothing more than for Alfred to become a minister. But the young Marshall enjoyed math and chess, both of which were forbidden by his authoritarian father. When he was older, Marshall turned down a theological scholarship to Oxford to study at Cambridge, with the financial

support of a wealthy uncle. Here he earned academic honors in mathematics. Upon graduating, Marshall set upon a period of self-discovery. He traveled to Germany to study metaphysics, later adopting the philosophy of agnosticism, and moved on to studying ethics. He found within himself a deep sorrow and disgust over the condition of society. He resolved to use his skills to lessen poverty and human suffering, and in

(continued)

Great Economic Thinkers continued

wanting to use his mathematics in this broader capacity, Marshall soon developed a fascination with economics.

Marshall became a fellow and lecturer in political economy at Cambridge. He had been teaching for nine years when, in 1877, he married a former student, Mary Paley. Because of the university's celibacy rules, Marshall had to give up his position at Cambridge. He moved on to teach at University College at Bristol and at Oxford. But in 1885, the rules were relaxed and Marshall returned to Cambridge as the Chair in Political Economy, a position that he held until 1908, when he resigned to devote more time to writing.

Before this point in time, economics was grouped with philosophy and the "moral sciences." Marshall fought all of his life for economics to be set apart as a field all its own. In 1903, Marshall finally succeeded in persuading Cambridge to establish a separate economics course, paving the way for the discipline as it exists today. As this event clearly demonstrates, Marshall exerted a great deal of influence on the development of economic thought in his time. Marshall popularized the heavy use of illustration, real-world examples, and current events in teaching, as well as the modern diagrammatic approach to economics.

Relatively early in his career, it was being said that Marshall's former students occupied half of the economic chairs in the United Kingdom. His most famous student was John Maynard Keynes.

Marshall is most famous for refining the marginal approach. He was intrigued by the self-adjusting and self-correcting nature of economic markets, and he was also interested in time—how long did it take for markets to adjust? Marshall coined the analogy that compares the tools of supply and demand to the blades on a pair of scissors—that is, it is fruitless to talk about whether it was supply or demand that determined the market price; rather, one should consider both in unison. After all, the upper blade is not of more importance than the lower when using a pair of scissors to cut a piece of paper. Marshall was also responsible for refining some of the most important tools in economics—elasticity and consumer and producer surplus. Marshall's book *Principles of Economics* was published in 1890; immensely popular, the book went into eight editions. Much of the content in *Principles* is still at the core of microeconomics texts today.

SECTION QUIZ

1. In a supply and demand graph, the triangular area under the demand curve but above the market price is
   a. the consumer surplus.
   b. the producer surplus.
   c. the marginal cost.
   d. the deadweight loss.
   e. the net gain to society from trading that good.

2. Which of the following is not true about consumer surplus?
   a. Consumer surplus is the difference between what consumers are willing to pay and what they actually pay.
   b. Consumer surplus is shown graphically as the area under the demand curve but above the market price.
   c. An increase in the market price due to a decrease in supply will increase consumer surplus.
   d. A decrease in market price due to an increase in supply will increase consumer surplus.

3. Which of the following is not true about producer surplus?
   a. Producer surplus is the difference between what sellers are paid and their cost of producing those units.
   b. Producer surplus is shown graphically as the area under the market price but above the supply curve.
   c. An increase in the market price due to an increase in demand will increase producer surplus.
   d. All of the above are true about producer surplus.

(continued)

SECTION QUIZ (cont.)

4. At the market equilibrium price and quantity, the total welfare gains from trade are measured by

   a. the total consumer surplus captured by consumers.

   b. the total producer surplus captured by producers.

   c. the sum of consumer surplus and producer surplus.

   d. the consumer surplus minus the producer surplus.

5. In a supply and demand graph, the triangular area under the demand curve but above the supply curve is

   a. the consumer surplus.

   b. the producer surplus.

   c. the marginal cost.

   d. the deadweight loss.

   e. the net gain to society from trading that good.

6. Which of the following are true statements?

   a. The difference between how much a consumer is willing and able to pay and how much a consumer has to pay for a unit of a good is called consumer surplus.

   b. An increase in supply will lead to a lower price and an increase in consumer surplus; a decrease in supply will lead to a higher price and a decrease in consumer surplus.

   c. Both (a) and (b) are true.

   d. None of the above is true.

7. Which of the following are true statements?

   a. Producer surplus is the difference between what a producer is paid for a good and the cost of producing that good.

   b. An increase in demand will lead to a higher market price and an increase in producer surplus; a decrease in demand will lead to a lower market price and a decrease in producer surplus.

   c. We can think of the demand curve as a marginal benefit curve and the supply curve as a marginal cost curve.

   d. Total welfare gains from trade to the economy can be measured by the sum of consumer and producer surpluses.

   e. All of the above are true statements.

---

1. What is consumer surplus?

2. Why do the earlier units consumed at a given price add more consumer surplus than the later units consumed?

3. Why does a decrease in a good's price increase the consumer surplus from consumption of that good?

4. Why might the consumer surplus from purchases of diamond rings be less than the consumer surplus from purchases of far less expensive stones?

5. What is producer surplus?

6. Why do the earlier units produced at a given price add more producer surplus than the later units produced?

7. Why does an increase in a good's price increase the producer surplus from production of that good?

8. Why might the producer surplus from sales of diamond rings, which are expensive, be less than the producer surplus from sales of far less expensive stones?

9. Why is the efficient level of output in an industry defined as the output where the sum of consumer and producer surplus is maximized?

10. Why does a reduction in output below the efficient level create a deadweight loss?

11. Why does an expansion in output beyond the efficient level create a deadweight loss?

Answers: 1. a   2. c   3. d   4. c   5. e   6. c   7. e

The Welfare Effects of Taxes, Subsidies, and Price Controls

▶ What are the welfare effects of a tax?

▶ What is the relationship between a deadweight loss and price elasticities?

▶ What are the welfare effects of subsidies?

▶ What are the welfare effects of price controls?

In the previous section we used the tools of consumer and producer surplus to measure the efficiency of a competitive market—that is, how the equilibrium price and quantity in a competitive market lead to the maximization of aggregate welfare (for both buyers and sellers). Now we can use the same tools, consumer and producer surplus, to measure the welfare effects of various government programs—taxes and price controls. When economists refer to the **welfare effects** of a government policy, they are referring to the gains and losses associated with government intervention. This use of the term should not be confused with the more common reference to a welfare recipient who is getting aid from the government.

welfare effects

the gains and losses associated with government intervention in markets

7.2a Using Consumer and Producer Surplus to Find the Welfare Effects of a Tax

To simplify the explanation of elasticity and the tax incidence, we will not complicate the illustration by shifting the supply curve (tax levied on sellers) or demand curve (tax levied on buyers) as we did in Section 6.4. We will simply show the result a tax must cause. The tax is illustrated by the vertical distance between the supply and demand curves at the new after-tax output—shown as the bold vertical line in Exhibit 1. After the tax, the buyers pay a higher price, P_B, and the sellers receive a lower price, P_S; and the equilibrium quantity of the good (both bought and sold) falls from Q_1 to Q_2. The tax revenue collected is measured by multiplying the amount of the tax times the quantity of the good sold after the tax is imposed ($T \times Q_2$).

In Exhibit 2, we can now use consumer and producer surpluses to measure the amount of welfare loss associated with a tax. First, consider the amounts of consumer and producer surplus before the tax. Before the tax is imposed, the price is P_1 and the quantity is Q_1; at that price and output, the amount of consumer surplus is area a + b + c, and the amount of producer surplus is area d + e + f. To get the total surplus, or total welfare, we add consumer and producer surpluses, area a + b + c + d + e + f. Without a tax, tax revenues are zero.

After the tax, the price the buyer pays is P_B, the price the seller receives is P_S, and the output falls to Q_2. As a result of the higher price and lower output from the tax, consumer surplus is smaller—area a. After the tax, sellers receive a lower price, so producer surplus is smaller—area f. However, some of the loss in consumer and producer surpluses is transferred in the form of tax revenues to the government, which can be used to reduce other taxes, fund public projects, or be redistributed to others in society. This transfer of

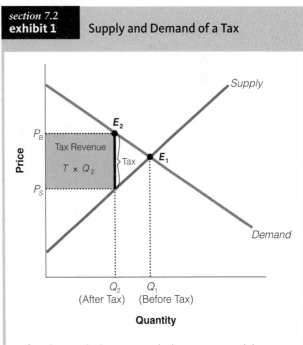

section 7.2
exhibit 1   **Supply and Demand of a Tax**

After the tax, the buyers pay a higher price, P_B, and the sellers receive a lower price, P_S; and the equilibrium quantity of the good (both bought and sold) falls from Q_1 to Q_2. The tax revenue collected is measured by multiplying the amount of the tax times that quantity of the good sold after the tax is imposed ($T \times Q_2$).

USE WHAT YOU'VE LEARNED

Should We Use Taxes to Reduce Dependency on Foreign Oil?

Q What if we placed a $0.50 tax on gasoline to reduce dependence on foreign oil and to raise the tax revenue?

A If the demand and supply curves are both equally elastic, as in Exhibit 2, both consumers and producers will share the burden equally. the tax collected would be b + d, but total loss in consumer surplus (b + c) and producer surplus (d + e) would be greater than the gains in tax revenue. Not surprisingly, both consumers and producers fight such a tax every time it is proposed.

How do taxes distort market incentives?

society's resources is not a loss from society's perspective. The net loss to society can be found by measuring the difference between the loss in consumer surplus (area b + c) plus the loss in producer surplus (area d + e) and the gain in tax revenue (area b + d). The reduction in total surplus is area c + e, or the shaded area in Exhibit 2. This deadweight loss from the tax is the reduction in producer and consumer surpluses minus the tax revenue transferred to the government.

section 7.2
exhibit 2   Welfare Effects of a Tax

The net loss to society due to a tax can be found by measuring the difference between the loss in consumer surplus (area b + c) plus the loss in producer surplus (area d + e) and the gain in tax revenue (area b + d). The deadweight loss from the tax is the reduction in the consumer and producer surpluses minus the tax revenue transferred to the government, area c + e.

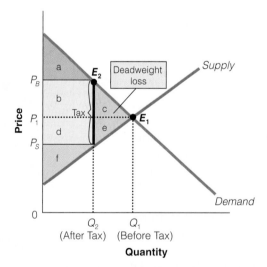

	Before Tax	After Tax	Change
Consumer Surplus	a + b + c	a	−b − c
Producer Surplus	d + e + f	f	−d − e
Tax Revenue ($T \times Q_2$)	zero	b + d	b + d
Total Welfare	a + b + c + d + e + f	a + b + d + f	−c − e

Deadweight loss occurs because the tax reduces the quantity exchanged below the original output level, Q_1, reducing the size of the total surplus realized from trade. The problem is that the tax distorts market incentives: The price to buyers is higher than before the tax, so they consume less; and the price to sellers is lower than before the tax, so they produce less. These effects lead to deadweight loss, or market inefficiencies—the waste associated with not producing the efficient level of output. That is, the tax causes a deadweight loss because it prevents some mutual beneficial trade between buyers and sellers. And when the tax gets larger, the deadweight loss get *much* larger. So a big tax is much worse than a small tax.

All taxes lead to deadweight loss. The deadweight loss is important because if the people are to benefit from the tax, then more than $1 of benefit must be produced from $1 of government expenditure. For example, if a gasoline tax leads to $100 million in tax revenues and $20 million in deadweight loss, then the government needs to provide a benefit to the public of more than $120 million with the $100 million revenues.

7.2b Elasticity and the Size of the Deadweight Loss

The size of the deadweight loss from a tax, as well as how the burdens are shared between buyers and sellers, depends on the price elasticities of supply and demand. In Exhibit 3(a) we can see that, other things being equal, the less elastic the demand curve, the smaller the deadweight loss. Similarly, the less elastic the supply curve, other things being equal, the smaller the deadweight loss, as shown in Exhibit 3(b). However, when the supply and/or demand curves become more elastic, the deadweight loss becomes larger because a given tax reduces the quantity exchanged by a greater amount, as seen in Exhibit 3(c). Recall that elasticities measure how responsive buyers and sellers are to price changes. That is, the more elastic the curves are, the greater the change in output and the larger the deadweight loss.

Does the elasticity affect the size of the deadweight loss?

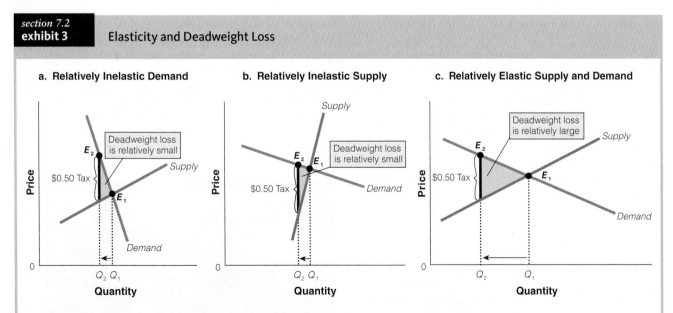

section 7.2
exhibit 3   **Elasticity and Deadweight Loss**

a. Relatively Inelastic Demand

b. Relatively Inelastic Supply

c. Relatively Elastic Supply and Demand

In (a) and (b), we see that when one of the two curves is relatively price inelastic, the deadweight loss from the tax is relatively small. However, when the supply and/or demand curves become more elastic, the deadweight loss becomes larger because a given tax reduces the quantity exchanged by a greater amount, as seen in (c). The more elastic the curves are, the greater the change in output and the larger the deadweight loss.

Elasticity differences can help us understand tax policy. Goods that are heavily taxed, such as alcohol, cigarettes, and gasoline, often have a relatively inelastic demand curve in the short run, so the tax burden falls primarily on the buyer. It also means that the deadweight loss to society is smaller for the tax revenue raised than if the demand curve were more elastic. In other words, because consumers cannot find many close substitutes in the short run, they reduce their consumption only slightly at the higher after-tax price. Even though the deadweight loss is smaller, it is still positive because the reduced after-tax price received by sellers and the increased after-tax price paid by buyers reduces the quantity exchanged below the previous market equilibrium level.

7.2c **The Welfare Effects of Subsidies**

If taxes cause deadweight loss, why don't subsidies cause welfare gains?

If taxes cause deadweight or welfare losses, do subsidies create welfare gains? For example, what if a government subsidy (paid by taxpayers) was provided in a particular market? Think of a subsidy as a negative tax. Before the subsidy, say the equilibrium price was P_1 and the equilibrium quantity was Q_1, as shown in Exhibit 4. The consumer surplus is area a + b, and the producer surplus is area c + d. The sum of producer and consumer surpluses is maximized (a + b + c + d), with no deadweight loss.

In Exhibit 4, we see that the subsidy lowers the price to the buyer to P_B and increases the quantity exchanged to Q_2. The subsidy results in an increase in consumer surplus from area a + b to area a + b + c + g, a gain of c + g. And producer surplus increases from area c + d to area c + d + b + e, a gain of b + e. With gains in both consumer and producer

In The News

Gift Giving and Deadweight Loss

Only about 15 percent of gifts during the holidays are money. Money fits the description as an efficient gift. An efficient gift is one that the recipient values at least as much as it costs the giver.

There are a lot of unwanted gifts that recipients receive during the holidays. What do people do with their unwanted gifts? Many people exchange or repackage unwanted gifts. Gift cards are becoming more popular. While they provide less flexibility to recipients than cash, gift cards might be seen as less "tacky" than cash. So why don't more people give cash and gift cards?

Over the past 20 years, University of Minnesota Professor Joel Waldfogel has done numerous surveys asking gift recipients about the items they've received: Who bought it? What did the buyer pay? What's the most you would have been willing to pay for it? Based on these surveys, he's concluded that we value items we receive as gifts 20 percent less, per dollar spent, than items we buy for ourselves. Given the $65 billion in U.S. holiday spending per year, that means we get $13 billion less in satisfaction than we would receive if we spent that money the usual way on ourselves. That is, deadweight loss is about $13 billion a year, the difference between the price of the gifts and the value to their recipients. This is like the deadweight loss associated with subsidies; the recipient values the gift less than the cost to the giver who buys it.

That is, the marginal costs are greater than the marginal benefits.

Of course, people may derive satisfaction from trying to pick "the perfect gift." if that is the case, then the deadweight loss would be smaller. In addition, gift giving can provide a signal. If you really love a person, you will try to get enough information and spend enough time to get the right gift. This sends a strong signal that a gift card or money does not provide. If the recipients are adult children, they may already know of your affection for them so sending a gift card or cash might be less offensive.

Welfare Effects of a Subsidy

With a subsidy, the price producers receive (P_S) is the price consumers pay (P_B) plus the subsidy ($\$S$). Because the subsidy leads to the production of more than the efficient level of output Q_1, a deadweight loss results. For each unit produced between Q_1 and Q_2, the supply curve lies above the demand curve, indicating that the marginal benefits to consumers are less than society's cost of producing those units.

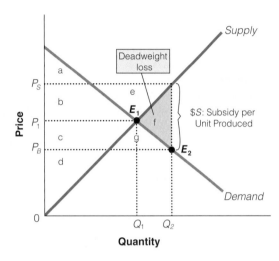

	Before Subsidy	After Subsidy	Change
Consumer Surplus (CS)	a + b	a + b + c + g	c + g
Producer Surplus (PS)	c + d	c + d + b + e	b + e
Government (Taxpayers, G)	zero	−b − e − f − c − g	−b − e − f − c − g
Total Welfare (CS + PS − G)	a + b + c + d	a + b + c + d − f	−f

surpluses, it looks like a gain in welfare, right? Not quite. Remember that the government is paying for this subsidy, and the cost to government (taxpayers) of the subsidy is area b + e + f + c + g (the subsidy per unit times the number of units subsidized). That is, the cost to government (taxpayers), area b + e + f + c + g, is greater than the gains to consumers, c + g, and the gains to producers, b + e, by area f. Area f is the deadweight or welfare loss to society from the subsidy because it results in the production of more than the competitive market equilibrium, and the market value of that expansion to buyers is less than the marginal cost of producing that expansion to sellers. In short, the market overproduces relative to the efficient level of output, Q_1.

7.2d **Price Controls and Welfare Effects**

As we saw in Chapter 5, price controls involve the use of the power of the government to establish prices different from the equilibrium market price that would otherwise prevail. The motivations for price controls vary with the markets under consideration. A maximum, or ceiling, is often set for goods deemed important, such as housing. A minimum price, or floor, may be set on wages because wages are the primary source of income for most people, or on agricultural products, in order to guarantee that producers will get a certain minimum price for their products. Consequently, most of the support for government price ceilings comes from buyers who wish to pay less, and most of the support for government price floors comes from sellers who wish to receive more.

Do consumers and producers both gain with a subsidy if it lowers the price to consumers and raises the price to producers? How about taxpayers?

7.2e **Price Ceilings**

Historically, price ceilings have been set on a whole array of goods: apartments, auto insurance, electricity, cable television, food, gasoline, and many other products. What's the impact of a price ceiling on buyers and sellers?

If a price ceiling (that is, a legally established maximum price) is binding and set below the equilibrium price at P_{MAX}, the quantity demanded will be greater than the quantity supplied at that price, and a shortage will occur. At this price, buyers will compete for the limited supply, Q_2.

We can see the welfare effects of a price ceiling by observing the change in consumer and producer surpluses from the implementation of the price ceiling in Exhibit 5. Before the price ceiling, the buyer receives area a + b + c of consumer surplus at price P_1 and quantity Q_1. However, after the price ceiling is implemented at P_{MAX}, consumers can buy the good at a lower price but cannot buy as much as before (they can only buy Q_2 instead of Q_1). Because consumers can now buy Q_2 at a lower price, they gain area d of consumer surplus after the price ceiling. However, they lose area c of consumer surplus because they can only purchase Q_2 rather than Q_1 of output. Thus, the change in consumer surplus is d − c. In this case, area d is larger than area e and area c and the consumer gains from the price ceiling.

The price the seller receives for Q_2 is P_{MAX} (the ceiling price), so producer surplus falls from area d + e + f before the price ceiling to area f after the price ceiling, for a loss of area d + e. That is, any possible gain to consumers will be more than offset by the losses to

section 7.2 exhibit 5	Welfare Effects of a Price Ceiling

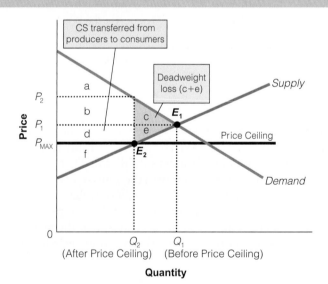

	Before Price Ceiling	After Price Ceiling	Change
Consumer Surplus (CS)	a + b + c	a + b + d	d − c
Producer Surplus (PS)	d + e + f	f	−d − e
Total Welfare (CS + PS)	a + b + c + d + e + f	a + b + d + f	−c − e

If area d is larger than area c, consumers in the aggregate would be better off from the price ceiling. However, any possible gain to consumers will be more than offset by the losses to producers, area d + e. Price ceiling causes a deadweight loss of c + e.

producers. The price ceiling has caused a deadweight loss of area c + e. Notice, too, that area d, after the price ceiling, is a transfer of producer surplus to consumer surplus. That is, a transfer of surplus from sellers to buyers.

There is a deadweight loss because less is sold at Q_2 than at Q_1; and consumers value those units between Q_2 and Q_1 by more than it cost to produce them. For example, at Q_2, consumers will value the unit at P_2, which is much higher than it cost to produce it—the point on the supply curve at Q_2.

Who gains and who loses with rent controls? If the shortage of apartments leads tenants to pay rents that are higher than the law allows, what will happen to consumer and producer surplus?

7.2f Rent Controls

As we have seen, price controls create winners and losers. Let's now look at the winners and losers from rent control. If consumers use no additional resources, search costs, or side payments for a rent-controlled unit, the consumer gains area b − e of consumer surplus from rent control. The producer loses area d + e of producer surplus from rent control. However, landlords may be able to collect higher "rent" using a variety of methods. They might have the tenant slip them a couple hundred dollars or more each month; they might charge a high rate for parking in the garage; they might rent used furniture at a high rate; or they might charge an exorbitant key price—the price for changing the locks for a new tenant. These types of arrangements take place in so-called black markets—markets where goods are transacted outside the boundaries of the law. One problem is that law-abiding citizens will be among those least likely to find a rental unit. Other problems include black-market prices that are likely to be higher than the price would be if restrictions were lifted and the inability to use legal means to enforce contracts and resolve disputes.

If the landlord is able to charge P_2, then the area b + d of consumer surplus will be lost by consumers and gained by the landlord. This redistribution from the buyer to the seller does not change the size of the deadweight loss; it remains area c + e.

The measure of the deadweight loss in the price ceiling case may underestimate the true cost to consumers. At least two inefficiencies are not measured. One, consumers may spend a lot of time looking for rental units because vacancy rates will be very low—only Q_2 is available and consumers are willing to pay as much as P_2 for Q_2 units. Two, someone may have been lucky to find a rental unit at the ceiling price, P_{MAX}, but someone who values it more, say at P_2, may not be able to find a rental unit.

It is important to distinguish between deadweight loss, which measures the overall efficiency loss, and the distribution of the gains and losses from a particular policy. For example, as a rent-control tenant, you may be pleased with the outcome—a lower price than you would ordinarily pay (a transfer from landlord to tenant) providing that you can find a vacant rent-controlled unit. In short, there are winners and losers from rent control. The winners are those tenants that are paying less than they would if there was no rent control. Landlords could also win if they broke the law and charged higher rents than the competitive equilibrium price. The losers are the landlords that abide by the laws and the renters who cannot find apartments to rent at the controlled price. The deadweight loss exists because there are fewer apartments rented than would occur in a competitive market.

7.2g Rent Controls—Short Run versus Long Run

In the absence of rent control (a price ceiling), the equilibrium price is P_1 and the equilibrium quantity is Q_1, with no deadweight loss. However, a price ceiling leads to a deadweight loss, but the size of the deadweight loss depends on elasticity: The deadweight loss is smaller in the short run (less elastic supply) than in the long run (more elastic supply). Why? A city that enacts a rent-control program will not lose many rental units in the next week. That is, even at lowered legal prices, roughly the same number of units will be available this week as last week; thus, in the short run the supply of rental units is virtually fixed—relatively inelastic,

Is it possible that removing rent controls in New York City is good economics but bad politics?

as seen in Exhibit 6(a). In the long run, however, the supply of rental units is much more elastic; landlords respond to the lower rental prices by allowing rental units to deteriorate and by building fewer new rental units. In the long run, then, the supply curve is much more elastic, as seen in Exhibit 6(b). It is also true that demand becomes more elastic over time as buyers respond to the lower prices by looking for their own apartment (rather than sharing one) or moving to the city to try to rent an apartment below the equilibrium rental price. What economic implications do these varying elasticities have on rent control policies?

In Exhibit 6(a), only a small reduction in rental unit availability occurs in the short term as a result of the newly imposed rent-control price—a move from Q_1 to Q_{SR}. The corresponding deadweight loss is small, indicated by the shaded area in Exhibit 6(a). However, the long-run response to the rent ceiling price is much larger: The quantity of rental units falls from Q_1 to Q_{LR}, and the size of the deadweight loss and the shortage are both larger, as seen in Exhibit 6(b). Hence, rent controls are much more harmful in the long run than the short run, from an efficiency standpoint.

ECS

economic content standards

Price controls are often advocated by special interest groups. Price controls reduce the quantity of goods and services produced, thus depriving consumers of some goods and services whose value would exceed their cost.

7.2h **Price Floors**

Since the Great Depression, several agricultural programs have been promoted as assisting small-scale farmers. Such a price-support system guarantees a minimum price—promising a dairy farmer a price of $4 per pound for cheese, for example. The reasoning is that the equilibrium price of $3 is too low and would not provide enough revenue for small-volume farmers to maintain a "decent" standard of living. A price floor sets a minimum price that is the lowest price a consumer can legally pay for a good.

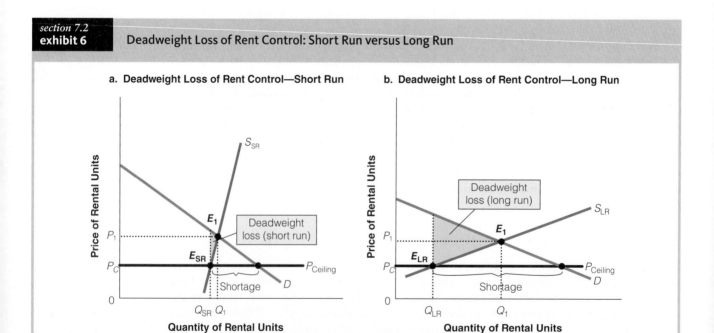

section 7.2
exhibit 6   Deadweight Loss of Rent Control: Short Run versus Long Run

a. Deadweight Loss of Rent Control—Short Run

b. Deadweight Loss of Rent Control—Long Run

The reduction in rental units in response to the rent ceiling price P_C is much smaller in the short run (Q_1 to Q_{SR}) than in the long run (Q_1 to Q_{LR}). The deadweight loss is also much greater in the long run than in the short run, as indicated by the shaded areas in the two graphs. In addition, the size of the shortage is much greater in the long run than in the short run.

7.2i The Welfare Effects of a Price Floor When the Government Buys the Surplus

In the United States, price floors have been used to increase the price of dairy products, tobacco, corn, peanuts, soybeans, and many other goods since the Great Depression. The government sets a price floor that guarantees producers will get a certain price. The intent of the law was to protect farmers from fluctuating prices. To ensure the support price, the government buys as much output as necessary to maintain the price at that level.

Who gains and who loses under price-support programs? In Exhibit 7, the equilibrium price and quantity without the price floor are at P_1 and Q_1, respectively. Without the price floor, consumer surplus is area a + b + c, and producer surplus is area e + f, for a total surplus of area a + b + c + e + f.

To maintain the price support, the government must buy up the excess supply at P_S; that is, the quantity $Q_S - Q_2$. As shown in Exhibit 7, the government

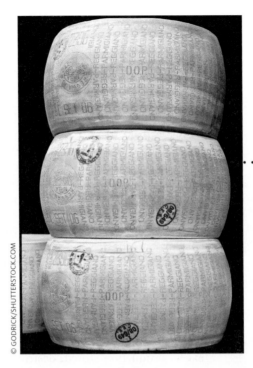

© GODRICK/SHUTTERSTOCK.COM

In an effort to help producers of the cheese commonly grated over spaghetti, fettuccine, and other pastas, the Italian government is buying 100,000 wheels of Parmigiano Reggiano and donating them to charity. This is similar to the price floors where the government buys up the surplus.

---

section 7.2
exhibit 7   Welfare Effects of a Price Floor When Government Buys the Surplus

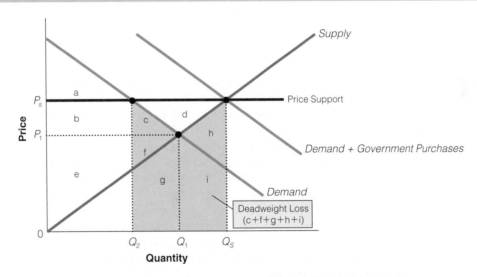

	Before Price Support	After Price Support	Change
Consumer Surplus (CS)	a + b + c	a	−b − c
Producer Surplus (PS)	e + f	b + c + d + e + f	b + c + d
Government (Taxpayers, G)	zero	−c − d − f − g − h − i	b + d
Total Welfare	a + b + c + e + f	a + b + e − g − h − i	−c − f − g − h − i

After the price support is implemented, the price rises to P_S and output falls to Q_2; the result is a loss in consumer surplus of area b + c but a gain in producer surplus of area b + c + d. However, these changes are not the end of the story because the cost to the government (taxpayers), area c + d + f + g + h + i, is greater than the gain to producers, area d, so the deadweight loss is area c + f + g + h + i.

purchases are added to the market demand curve (D + government purchases). This additional demand allows the price to stay at the support level. After the price floor is in effect, price rises to P_S; output falls to Q_2; and consumer surplus falls from area a + b + c to area a, a loss of b + c. Some of the loss of consumer surplus occurs because at the higher price, P_S, some consumers will buy less of the good or not buy the good at all. Consumers also lose area b because they now have to pay a higher price, P_S, for Q_2 output. However, the policy was not intended to help the consumer, but to help the producer. And it does. Producer surplus increases from area e + f to area b + c + d + e + f, a gain of area b + c + d. If those changes were the end of the story, we would say that producers gained (area b + c + d) more than consumers lost (area b + c), and, on net, society would benefit by area d from the implementation of the price support. However, those changes are *not* the end of the story. The government (taxpayers) must pay for the surplus it buys, area c + d + f + g + h + i. That is, the cost to government is area c + d + f + g + h + i. The total welfare cost of the program is found by adding the change in consumer surplus (lost area b + c) and the change in producer surplus (gained area b + c + d) and then subtract the government costs. After adding the change in consumer surplus to the change in producer surplus we end up with a + d than we subtract the government costs c + d + f + g + h + i. Assuming no alternative use of the surplus the government purchases, the result is a deadweight loss from the price floor of area c + f + g + h + i. Why? Consumers are consuming less than the previous market equilibrium output, eliminating mutually beneficial exchanges (that is, exchanges for which the MB is greater than the MC), while sellers are producing more than is being consumed, with the excess production stored, destroyed, or exported. Note that the government can't sell the surplus domestically because it would drive the domestic price down. Since the objective of the policy is to support the higher price, it must either store it or ship it abroad. If the objective is to help the farmers, wouldn't it be less costly to just give them the money directly rather than through price supports? Then the program would only cost b + c + d. However, price supports may be more palatable from a political standpoint than an outright handout.

Wouldn't it cost less to give farmers money directly rather than through price supports?

7.2j **Deficiency Payment Program**

Another possibility is the deficiency payment program. In Exhibit 8, if the government sets the support price at P_S, producers will supply Q_2 and sell all they can at the market price, P_M. The government then pays the producers a deficiency payment (DP)—the vertical distance between the price the producers receive, P_M, and the price they were guaranteed, P_S. Producer surplus increases from area c + d to area c + d + b + e, which is a gain of area b + e because producers can sell a greater quantity at a higher price. Consumer surplus increases from area a + b to area a + b + c + g, which is a gain of area c + g because consumers can buy a greater quantity at a lower price. The cost to government ($Q_2 \times$ DP), area b + e + f + c + g, is greater than the gains in producer and consumer surpluses (area b + e + c + g), and the deadweight loss is area f. The deadweight loss occurs because the program increases the output beyond the efficient level of output, Q_1. From Q_1 to Q_2, the marginal cost to sellers for producing the good (the height of the supply curve) is greater than the marginal benefit to consumers (the height of the demand curve).

Compare area f in Exhibit 8 with the much larger deadweight loss for price supports in Exhibit 7. The deficiency payment program does not lead to the production of crops that will not be consumed, or to the storage problem we saw with the previous price-support program in Exhibit 7.

The purpose of these farm programs is to help poor farmers. However, large commercial farms (roughly 10 percent of all farms) receive the bulk of the government subsidies. Small farms (roughly 60 percent of all farms) receive less than 20 percent of the farm subsidies. Many other countries around the world also provide subsidies to their farmers.

Welfare Effects of a Deficiency Payment Plan

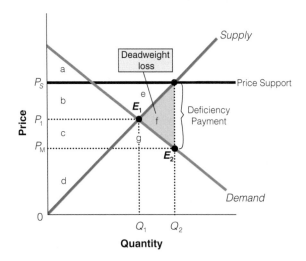

	Before Plan	**After Plan**	**Change**
Consumer Surplus (CS)	a + b	a + b + c + g	c + g
Producer Surplus (PS)	c + d	c + d + b + e	b + e
Government (Taxpayers, G)	zero	−b − e − f − c − g	−b − e − f − c − g
Total Welfare (CS + PS − G)	a + b + c + d	a + b + c + d − f	−f

The cost to government (taxpayers), area b + e + f + c + g, is greater than the gains to producer and consumer surplus, area b + e + c + g. the deficiency payment program increases the output level beyond the efficient output level of Q_1. From Q_1 to Q_2, the marginal cost of producing the good (the height of the supply curve) is greater than the marginal benefit to the consumer (the height of the demand curve)—area f.

SECTION QUIZ

1. In a supply and demand graph, the triangular area between the demand curve and the supply curve lost because of the imposition of a tax, price ceiling, or price floor is

   a. the consumer surplus.

   b. the producer surplus.

   c. the marginal cost.

   d. the deadweight loss.

   e. the net gain to society from trading that good.

(continued)

SECTION QUIZ (cont.)

2. After the imposition of a tax,

   a. consumers pay a higher price, including the tax.

   b. consumers lose consumer surplus.

   c. producers receive a lower price after taxes.

   d. producers lose producer surplus.

   e. all of the above occur.

3. With a subsidy,

   a. the price producers receive is the price consumers pay plus the subsidy.

   b. the subsidy leads to the production of more than the efficient level of output.

   c. there is a deadweight loss.

   d. all of the above are true.

4. In the case of a price floor, if the government buys up the surplus,

   a. consumer surplus decreases.

   b. producer surplus increases.

   c. a greater deadweight loss occurs than with a deficiency payment system.

   d. all of the above are true.

5. The longer a price ceiling is left below the equilibrium price in a market, the _____ is the reduction in the quantity exchanged and the _____ is the resulting deadweight loss.

   a. greater; greater

   b. greater; smaller

   c. smaller; greater

   d. smaller; smaller

6. With a deficiency payment program,

   a. the government sets the target price at the equilibrium price.

   b. producer and consumer surplus falls.

   c. there is a deadweight loss because the program increases the output beyond the efficient level of output.

   d. all of the above are true.

---

1. Could a tax be imposed without a welfare cost?

2. How does the elasticity of demand represent the ability of buyers to "dodge" a tax?

3. If both supply and demand were highly elastic, how large would the effect be on the quantity exchanged, the tax revenue, and the welfare costs of a tax?

4. What impact would a larger tax have on trade in the market? What will happen to the size of the deadweight loss?

5. What would be the effect of a price ceiling?

6. What would be the effect of a price floor if the government does not buy up the surplus?

7. What causes the welfare cost of subsidies?

8. Why does a deficiency payment program have the same welfare cost analysis as a subsidy?

Answers: 1. d 2. e 3. d 4. d 5. a 6. c

Fill in the blanks:

1. The monetary difference between the price a consumer is willing and able to pay for an additional unit of a good and the price the consumer actually pays is called _____.

2. We can think of the demand curve as a _____ curve.

3. Consumer surplus for the whole market is shown graphically as the area under the market _____ (willingness to pay for the units consumed) and above the _____ (what must be paid for those units).

4. A lower market price due to an increase in supply will _____ consumer surplus.

5. A(n) _____ is the difference between what a producer is paid for a good and the cost of producing that unit of the good.

6. We can think of the supply curve as a(n) _____ curve.

7. Part of the added producer surplus when the price rises as a result of an increase in demand is due to a higher price for the quantity _____ being produced, and part is due to the expansion of _____ made profitable by the higher price.

8. The demand curve represents a collection of _____ prices that consumers are willing and able to pay for additional quantities of a good or service, while the supply curve represents a collection of _____ prices that suppliers require to be willing to supply additional quantities of that good or service.

9. The total welfare gain to the economy from trade in a good is the sum of the _____ and _____ created.

10. In competitive markets, with large numbers of buyers and sellers at the market equilibrium price and quantity, the net gains to society are _____ as possible.

11. After a tax is imposed, consumers pay a(n) _____ price and lose the corresponding amount of consumer surplus as a result. Producers receive a(n) _____ price after tax and lose the corresponding amount of producer surplus as a result. The government _____ the amount of the tax revenue generated, which is transferred to others in society.

12. The size of the deadweight loss from a tax, as well as how the burdens are shared between buyers and sellers, depends on the relative _____.

13. When there is a subsidy, the market _____ relative to the efficient level of output.

14. Because the _____ leads to the production of more than the efficient level of output, a(n) _____ results.

15. With a(n) _____, any possible gain to consumers will be more than offset by the losses to producers.

16. With a price floor where the government buys up the surplus, the cost to the government is _____ than the gain to _____.

17. With no alternative use of the government purchases from a price floor, a(n) _____ will result because consumers are consuming _____ than the previous market equilibrium output and sellers are producing _____ than is being consumed.

18. With a deficiency payment program, the deadweight loss is _____ than with an agricultural price support program when the government buys the surplus.

consumer surplus 187
producer surplus 189

marginal cost 189
total welfare gains 191

deadweight loss 191
welfare effects 195

SECTION QUIZ ANSWERS

7.1 Consumer Surplus and Producer Surplus

1. What is consumer surplus?

Consumer surplus is defined as the monetary difference between what a consumer is willing to pay for a good and what the consumer is required to pay for it.

2. Why do the earlier units consumed at a given price add more consumer surplus than the later units consumed?

Because what a consumer is willing to pay for a good declines as more of that good is consumed; the difference between what he is willing to pay and the price he must pay also declines for later units.

3. Why does a decrease in a good's price increase the consumer surplus from consumption of that good?

A decrease in a good's price increases the consumer surplus from consumption of that good by lowering the price for those goods that were bought at the higher price and by increasing consumer surplus from increased purchases at the lower price.

4. Why might the consumer surplus from purchases of diamond rings be less than the consumer surplus from purchases of far less expensive stones?

Consumer surplus is the difference between what people would have been willing to pay for the amount of the good consumed and what they must pay. Even though the marginal value of less expensive stones is lower than the marginal value of a diamond ring to buyers, the difference between the total value of the far larger number of less expensive stones purchased and what consumers had to pay may well be larger than that difference for diamond rings.

5. What is producer surplus?

Producer surplus is defined as the monetary difference between what a producer is paid for a good and the producer's cost.

6. Why do the earlier units produced at a given price add more producer surplus than the later units produced?

Because the earlier (lowest cost) units can be produced at a cost that is lower than the market price, but the cost of producing additional units rises, the earlier units produced at a given price add more producer surplus than the later units produced.

7. Why does an increase in a good's price increase the producer surplus from production of that good?

An increase in a good's price increases the producer surplus from production of that good because it results in a higher price for the quantity already being produced and because the expansion in output in response to the higher price also increases profits.

8. Why might the producer surplus from sales of diamond rings, which are expensive, be less than the producer surplus from sales of far less expensive stones?

Producer surplus is the difference between what a producer is paid for a good and the producer's cost. Even though the price, or marginal value, of a less expensive stone is lower than the price, or marginal value of a diamond ring to buyers, the difference between the total that sellers receive for those stones in revenue and the producer's cost of the far larger number of less expensive stones produced may well be larger than that difference for diamond rings.

9. Why is the efficient level of output in an industry defined as the output where the sum of consumer and producer surplus is maximized?

The sum of consumer surplus plus producer surplus measures the total welfare gains from trade in an industry, and the most efficient level of output is the one that maximizes the total welfare gains.

10. Why does a reduction in output below the efficient level create a deadweight loss?

A reduction in output below the efficient level eliminates trades whose benefits would have exceeded their costs; the resulting loss in consumer surplus and producer surplus is a deadweight loss.

11. Why does an expansion in output beyond the efficient level create a deadweight loss?

An expansion in output beyond the efficient level involves trades whose benefits are less than their costs; the resulting loss in consumer surplus and producer surplus is a deadweight loss.

7.2 The Welfare Effects of Taxes, Subsidies, and Price Controls

1. Could a tax be imposed without a welfare cost?

A tax would not impose a welfare cost only if the quantity exchanged did not change as a result—only when supply was perfectly inelastic or in the nonexistent case where the demand curve was perfectly inelastic. In all other cases, a tax would create a welfare cost by eliminating some mutually beneficial trades (and the wealth they would have created) that would otherwise have taken place.

2. How does the elasticity of demand represent the ability of buyers to "dodge" a tax?

The elasticity of demand represents the ability of buyers to "dodge" a tax because it represents how easily buyers could shift their purchases into other goods. If it is relatively low cost to consumers to shift out of buying a particular good when a tax is imposed on it—that is, demand is relatively elastic— they can dodge much of the burden of the tax by shifting their purchases to other goods. If it is relatively high cost to consumers to shift out of buying a particular good when a tax is imposed on it—that is, demand is relatively inelastic— they cannot dodge much of the burden of the tax by shifting their purchases to other goods.

3. If both supply and demand were highly elastic, how large would the effect be on the quantity exchanged, the tax revenue, and the welfare costs of a tax?

The more elastic are supply and/or demand, the larger the change in the quantity exchanged that would result from a given tax. Given that tax revenue equals the tax per unit times the number of units traded after the imposition of a tax, the smaller after-tax quantity traded would reduce the tax revenue raised, other things being equal. Because the greater change in the quantity traded wipes out more mutually beneficial trades than if demand and/or supply was more inelastic, the welfare cost in such a case would also be greater, other things being equal.

4. What impact would a larger tax have on trade in the market? What will happen to the size of the deadweight loss?

A larger tax creates a larger wedge between the price including tax paid by consumers and the price net of tax received by producers, resulting in a greater increase in prices paid by consumers and a greater decrease in price received by producers, and the laws of supply and demand imply that the quantity exchanged falls more as a result. The number of mutually beneficial trades eliminated will be greater and the consequent welfare cost will be greater as a result.

5. What would be the effect of a price ceiling?

A price ceiling reduces the quantity exchanged because the lower regulated price reduces the quantity sellers are willing to sell. This lower quantity causes a welfare cost equal to the net gains from those exchanges that no longer take place. However, that price ceiling would also redistribute income, harming sellers, increasing the well-being of those who remain able to buy successfully at the lower price, and decreasing the well-being of those who can no longer buy successfully at the lower price.

6. What would be the effect of a price floor if the government does not buy up the surplus?

Just as in the case of a tax, a price floor where the government does not buy up the surplus reduces the quantity exchanged, thus causing a welfare cost equal to the net gains from the exchanges that no longer take place. However, that price floor would also redistribute income, harming buyers, increasing the incomes of those who remain able to sell successfully at the higher price, and decreasing the incomes of those who can no longer sell successfully at the higher price.

7. What causes the welfare cost of subsidies?

Subsidies cause people to produce units of output whose benefits (without the subsidy) are less than the costs, reducing the total gains from trade.

8. Why does a deficiency payment program have the same welfare cost analysis as a subsidy?

Both tend to increase output beyond the efficient level, so that units whose benefits (without the subsidy) are less than the costs, reducing the total gains from trade in the same way; furthermore, the dollar cost of the deficiency payments are equal to the dollar amount of taxes necessary to finance the subsidy, in the case where each increases production the same amount.

PROBLEMS

1. Refer to the following exhibit.

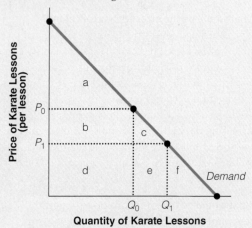

Quantity of Karate Lessons

a. If the price of each karate lesson is P_0, the consumer surplus is equal to what area?
b. If the price falls from P_0 to P_1, the change in consumer surplus is equal to what area?

2. Steve loves potato chips. His weekly demand curve is shown in the following exhibit.

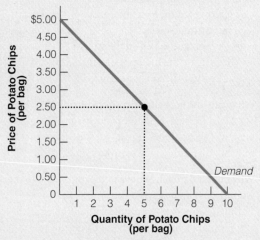

Quantity of Potato Chips (per bag)

a. How much is Steve willing to pay for one bag of potato chips?
b. How much is Steve willing to pay for a second bag of potato chips?
c. If the actual market price of potato chips is $2.50, and Steve buys five bags as shown, what is the value of his consumer surplus?
d. What is Steve's total willingness to pay for five bags?

3. If a freeze ruined this year's lettuce crop, show what would happen to consumer surplus.

4. If demand for apples increased as a result of a news story that highlighted the health benefits of two apples a day, what would happen to producer surplus?

5. How is total surplus (the sum of consumer and producer surpluses) related to the efficient level of output? Using a supply and demand curve, demonstrate that producing less than the equilibrium output will lead to an inefficient allocation of resources—a deadweight loss.

6. If the government's goal is to raise tax revenue, which of the following are good markets to tax?
    a. luxury yachts
    b. alcohol
    c. movies
    d. gasoline
    e. grapefruit juice

7. Which of the following do you think are good markets for the government to tax if the goal is to boost tax revenue? Which will lead to the least amount of deadweight loss? Why?
    a. luxury yachts
    b. alcohol
    c. motor homes
    d. cigarettes
    e. gasoline
    f. pizza

8. Elasticity of demand in the market for one-bedroom apartments is 2.0, elasticity of supply is 0.5, the current market price is $1,000, and the equilibrium number of one-bedroom apartments is 10,000. If the government imposes a price ceiling of $800 on this market, predict the size of the resulting apartment shortage.

9. Use the diagram to answer the following questions (a–d).

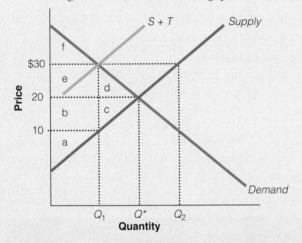

    a. At the equilibrium price before the tax is imposed, what area represents consumer surplus? What area represents producer surplus?
    b. Say that a tax of T per unit is imposed in the industry. What area now represents consumer surplus? What area represents producer surplus?
    c. What area represents the deadweight cost of the tax?
    d. What area represents how much tax revenue is raised by the tax?

10. Use consumer and producer surplus to show the deadweight loss from a subsidy (producing more than the equilibrium output). (*Hint:* Remember that taxpayers will have to pay for the subsidy.)

11. Use the diagram to answer the following questions (a)–(c).

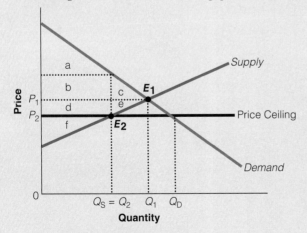

    a. At the initial equilibrium price, what area represents consumer surplus? What area represents producer surplus?
    b. After the price ceiling is imposed, what area represents consumer surplus? What area represents producer surplus?
    c. What area represents the deadweight loss cost of the price ceiling?

Market Failure

Drivers on congested "freeways" compete for limited space.
One way to internalize the externality is with a higher gasoline tax that would encourage people to drive less, carpool more, buy more fuel-efficient vehicles, and take public transportation. Some economists have estimated that in the United States, the optimal corrective tax is at least five times higher than the current level.

In the last several chapters, we concluded that markets are efficient. But we made some assumptions about how markets work. If these assumptions do not hold, our conclusion about efficiency may be flawed. What are the assumptions?

First, in our model of supply and demand, we assumed that markets are perfectly competitive—many buyers and sellers exchanging similar goods in an environment where buyers and sellers can easily enter and exit the market. This is not always true. In some markets, few firms may have control over the market price. When firms can control the market price, we say that they have market power. This market power can cause inefficiency because it will lead to higher prices and lower quantities than the competitive solution.

Sometimes the market system fails to produce efficient outcomes because of side effects economists call *externalities*. An externality occurs when a person engages in an activity that influences a bystander and is neither paid or compensated for the action. If the bystander is impacted adversely it is called a negative externality; if the bystander is impacted beneficially it is called a positive externality. Another possible source of market failure is that competitive markets provide less than the efficient quantity of public goods. A public good is a good or service that someone can consume simultaneously with everyone else, even if he or she doesn't pay for it. For example, everyone enjoys the benefits of national defense and yet it would be difficult to exclude anyone from receiving these benefits. The problem is that if consumers know it is too difficult to exclude them, then they could avoid paying their share of the public good (take a free ride), and producers would find it unprofitable to provide the good. Therefore, the government provides important public goods such as national defense.

Many economists believe that asymmetric information can cause market failures. *Asymmetric information* is a situation where some people know what other people don't know. This can lead to adverse selection where an informed party benefits in an exchange by taking advantage of knowing more than the other party.

Externalities 8.1

▶ What is a negative externality?

▶ How are negative externalities internalized?

▶ What is a positive externality?

▶ How are positive externalities internalized?

Even if the economy is competitive, it is still possible that the market system fails to produce the efficient level of output because of side effects economists call **externalities**. With **positive externalities**, the private market supplies too little of the good in question (such as education). In the case of **negative externalities** (such as pollution), the market supplies too much. Both types of externalities are caused by economic agents—producers and consumers—receiving the wrong signals. That is, the free market works well in providing most goods but does less well without regulations, taxes, and subsidies in providing others.

8.1a Negative Externalities in Production

The classic example of a negative externality in production is air pollution from a factory, such as a steel mill. If the firm uses clean air in production and returns dirty air to the atmosphere, it creates a negative externality. The polluted air "spills over" to outside parties. Now people in the neighboring communities may experience higher incidences of disease, dirtier houses, and other property damage. Such damages are real costs; but because no one owns the air, the firm does not have to pay for its use, unlike the other resources the firm uses in production. A steel mill pays for labor, capital, energy, and raw materials because it must compensate the owners of those inputs for their use. If a firm can avoid paying the costs it imposes on others—the external costs—it has lowered its own costs of production, but not the true costs to society.

Examples of negative externalities are numerous: the roommate who plays his stereo too loud at 2:00 A.M., the neighbor's dog that barks all night long or leaves "messages" on your front lawn, or the gardener who runs the leaf blower on full power at 7:00 A.M. on the weekend. Driving our cars may be another area in which people don't bear the full costs of their choices. We pay the price to purchase cars, as well as to maintain, insure, and fuel them—those are the private costs. But do we pay for all of our external costs such as emissions, congestion, wear and tear on our highways, and the possible harm to those driving in cars smaller than ours?

externality

a benefit or cost from consumption or production that spills over onto those who are not consuming or producing the good

positive externality

when benefits spill over to an outside party who is not involved in producing or consuming the good

negative externality

when costs spill over to an outside party who is not involved in producing or consuming the good

What are externalities? Are they always bad?

*economic
content
standards*

Externalities exist when some of the costs or benefits associated with production and/or consumption of a good or service falls on someone other than the producers or consumers of the product or service.

When a price fails to reflect all the costs of a product, too much of it is produced and/or consumed.

**internalizing
externalities**

changing incentives so people will take into account the effects of the external costs or benefits imposed on, or enjoyed by, others.

Graphing Negative External Costs in Production

Let's take a look at the steel industry. In Exhibit 1, we see the market for steel. Notice that at each level of output, the first supply curve, $S_{Private}$, is lower than the second, S_{Social}. The reason is simple: $S_{Private}$ only includes the private costs to the firm—the capital, entrepreneurship, land, and labor for which it must pay. However, S_{Social} includes all of these costs, plus the external costs that production imposes on others. If the firm could somehow be required to compensate society for the damage it causes, the cost of production for the firm would increase and would shift the supply curve to the left. That is, the true social cost of producing steel is represented by S_{Social} in Exhibit 1. The equilibrium at P_2 and Q_2 is efficient. The market equilibrium is not efficient because the true supply curve is above the demand curve at Q_1. At Q_1 the marginal benefits (point a) are less than the marginal cost (point b) and society would be better off if the firm produced less steel. The deadweight loss from overproduction is measured by the shaded area in Exhibit 1. From society's standpoint, Q_2 is the efficient level of output because it represents all the costs (private plus external costs) associated with the production of this good. If the suppliers of steel are not aware of or not responsible for the external costs, they will tend to produce too much Q_1 from society's standpoint and efficiency would be improved if less were produced and consumed.

8.1b What Can the Government Do to Correct for Negative Externalities?

The government can intervene in market decisions in an attempt to take account of these negative externalities. It may do this by estimating the amount of those external costs and then taxing the manufacturer by that amount, forcing the manufacturer to internalize (bear) the costs.

Pollution Taxes

Pollution taxes are designed to internalize negative externalities. If the government could impose a pollution tax equal to the exact size of the external cost, then the firm would produce the efficient level of output, Q_2. That is, by imposing a tax on the production of steel equal to the external cost of pollution, the government could cause steel producers to internalize the negative externality. Now the cost of pollution caused by the steel plant will be a private cost borne by the steel plant and the supply curve for steel will shift leftward to S_{Social}. This provides an incentive for the firm to produce at the efficient level of output. Additionally, tax revenues would be generated that could be used to compensate those who had suffered damage from the pollution or in some other productive way.

Regulation

Alternatively, the government could use regulation. The government might simply prohibit certain types of activities that cause pollution or force firms to adopt a specific technology to reduce their emissions. However, regulators would have to know the best available technology for each and every industry. The purchase and use of new pollution control devices will increase the cost of production and shift the supply curve to the left, from $S_{Private}$ to S_{Social}.

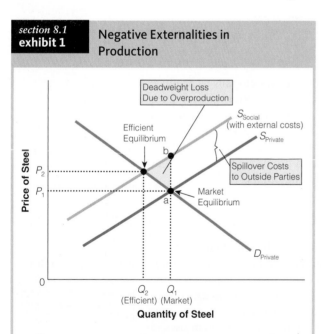

section 8.1
exhibit 1   Negative Externalities in Production

When a negative externality in production is present, firms do not bear the full cost of their actions, and they will produce more than the efficient level of output: Q_1 rather than Q_2. $S_{Private}$ reflects the private cost of the firm. S_{Social} reflects the private costs plus the external (or spillover) costs that the steel production imposes on others. If the supply curve is $S_{Private}$, the market equilibrium is at P_1 and Q_1. This level is not efficient and leads to a deadweight loss—the shaded area. However, when the supply curve is S_{Social}, then the equilibrium occurs at P_2 and Q_2, which is the efficient equilibrium.

Which Is Better—Pollution Tax or Regulation?

Most economists agree that a pollution tax, or a corrective tax, is more efficient than regulation. The pollution tax is good because it gets rid of the externality and moves society closer to an efficient level of output. The tax also gives firms an incentive to find and apply new technology to further reduce pollution levels in their plants and consequently lower the tax they would have to pay. Under regulation, a firm has little incentive to further reduce emissions once it reaches the predetermined level set by the regulated standard.

For example, a gas tax is a form of pollution tax: It helps reduce the externalities of pollution and congestion. The higher the tax, then fewer vehicles are on the road, fewer miles are driven, and more fuel-efficient vehicles are purchased, each of which leads to less congestion and pollution. Therefore, the pollution tax, unlike other taxes, can enhance economic efficiency while generating revenue for the government.

Many economists like the gas tax because it is easy to collect, difficult for users to avoid, and encourages fuel economy. It puts the tax on highway users but completely internalizing the externality may cost much more than U.S. drivers are currently charged. In Europe, the gas tax is over $4 per gallon. Proposals for similar types of taxes to reduce negative externalities imposed on others by secondhand smoke, alcohol consumption, and sugary sodas have also been proposed.

© BURLINGHAM/SHUTTERSTOCK.COM

According to a University of Utah study, using a cell phone while driving, whether it's handheld or hands-free, delays a driver's reactions as much as having a blood alcohol concentration at the legal limit of .08 percent. That is, driving while texting can create a serious negative externality.

8.1c Positive Externalities in Consumption

Unlike negative externalities, positive externalities benefit others. For some goods, the individual consumer receives all the benefits. If you buy a hamburger, for example, you get all its benefits. On the other hand, consider education. This is a positive externality in consumption whose benefits extend beyond the individual consumer of education. Certainly, when you "buy" an education, you receive many of its benefits: greater future income, more choice of future occupations, and the consumption value of knowing more about life as a result of learning. However, these benefits, great as they may be, are not all the benefits associated with your education. You may be less likely to be unemployed or commit crimes; you may end up curing cancer or solving some other social problem or create some technological innovation that raises productivity and wages for many workers. These nontrivial benefits are the positive external benefits of education.

The government frequently subsidizes education. Why? Presumably because the private market does not provide enough. It is argued that the education of a person benefits not only that person but all society because a more informed citizenry can make more intelligent collective decisions, which benefits everyone.

Public health departments sometimes offer "free" inoculations against certain communicable diseases, such as influenza, because by protecting one group of citizens, everyone gets some protection; if one citizen is prevented from getting the disease, that person cannot pass it on to others. Many governmental efforts in the field of health and education are justified on the basis of positive externalities. Of course, because positive externalities are often difficult to measure, it is hard to demonstrate empirically whether many governmental education and health programs achieve their intended purposes.

In short, the presence of positive externalities interferes with reaching economic efficiency because of the tendency for the market to underallocate (produce too little) of this good.

economic content standards

Government can use taxes or regulation to correct for excessive output of a good whose production generates external costs.

When a price fails to reflect all the benefits of a product, too little of the product is produced and consumed.

The government can use subsidies to help correct for insufficient output of a good that generates external benefits, or it can regulate output directly to correct for underproduction or underconsumption of a good.

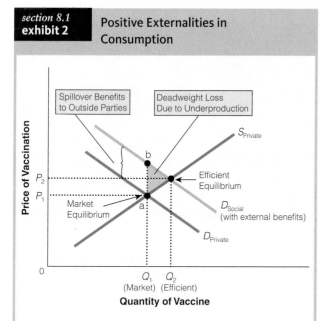

section 8.1
exhibit 2   Positive Externalities in Consumption

The private demand curve plus external benefits is presented as the demand curve D_{Social}. This demand curve is to the right of the private demand curve, $D_{Private}$. At Q_1 the marginal benefits (point b) are greater than the marginal cost (point a) leading to a deadweight loss—the shaded area. The market equilibrium output, Q_1, falls short of the efficient level of output, Q_2. The market produces too little of the good or service.

These types of systems use a radio transmitter to help owners track and find their cars if they are stolen. If the devices also help law enforcement break up rings of car thieves, they will have spillover benefits (positive externalities) for car owners that do not own the device because they will reduce the probability of their car being stolen. Thus, the social value of LoJack devices is likely to be greater than their private value to customers. In short, society may be better off if more people had LoJack units.

EDDIE MOORE/ZUMA PRESS/NEWSCOM

Graphing Positive External Benefits of Consumption

Let's take the case of a new vaccine against the common cold. The market for the vaccine is shown in Exhibit 2. The demand curve, $D_{Private}$, represents the prices and quantities that buyers would be willing to pay in the private market to reduce their probability of catching the common cold. The supply curve shows the amounts that suppliers would offer for sale at different prices. However, at the equilibrium market output, Q_1, the output of vaccinations falls far short of the efficient level, Q_2. Why? Many people benefit from the vaccines, including those who do not have to pay for them; they are now less likely to be infected because others took the vaccine. If we could add the benefits derived by nonpaying consumers, the demand curve would shift to the right, from $D_{Private}$ to D_{Social}. The greater level of output, Q_2, that would result if D_{Social} were the observed demand reflects the efficient output level.

The market equilibrium at P_1 and Q_1 is not efficient because D_{Social} is above $D_{Private}$ for all levels of output between Q_1 and Q_2. That is, at Q_1 the marginal benefits (D_{Social}) at point b are greater than the marginal cost (S_{Social}) at point a. Consequently, a deadweight loss is associated with underproduction. In short, too little of the good is produced. Because producers are unable to collect payments from all those who benefit from the good or service, the market has a tendency to underproduce. In this case, the market is not producing enough vaccinations from society's standpoint and an *underallocation* of resources occurs.

Technology Spillover

Another potentially important positive externality is called a technology spillover. One firm's research and production can spill over to increase another firm's access to technological advances. For example, in technology industries like semiconductors, bioengineering and software design, one firm's innovations are often imitated and improved on by other firms. The firm benefits from the new knowledge, but that knowledge also generates positive externalities that spill over to other firms. That is one reason why many technology firms are clustered together in California's Silicon Valley. That clustering allows workers to more easily share knowledge and collaborate in a rapidly changing industry. However, if other firms can easily imitate the developing firm's design, it can capture some of the developing firm's profits away from it. This will cause firms to engage in less research and development, and therefore R & D will be underfunded in the market. Should the government encourage firms with large spillovers by providing subsidies? The problem is that technology spillovers are difficult to measure. Patent protection is one way to deal with technology spillovers.

Under the patent system, the firm that makes a technological breakthrough can capture most of the profits. The patent internalizes the externality and gives firms a greater incentive to invest in research and development.

8.1d What Can the Government Do to Correct for Positive Externalities?

How could society correct for this market failure? Two particular methods of achieving the higher preferred output are subsidies and regulation.

Subsidies

Government could provide a subsidy—either give refunds to individuals who receive an inoculation or provide an incentive for businesses to give their employees "free" inoculations at the office. If the subsidy was exactly equal to the external benefit of inoculation, the demand curve would shift from $D_{Private}$ to D_{Social}, resulting in an efficient level of output, Q_2. That is, the government could internalize a positive externality of consumption by providing a subsidy equal to the value of the positive externality.

Regulation

The government could also pass a regulation requiring each person to get an inoculation. This approach would also shift the demand curve rightward toward the efficient level of output.

In summary, with positive externalities, the private market supplies too little of the good in question (such as education or inoculations for communicable diseases). In the case of negative externalities, the market supplies too much. In either case, buyers and sellers are receiving the wrong signals. The producers and consumers are not doing what they do because they are evil; rather, whether well-intentioned or ill-intentioned, they are behaving according to the incentives they face. The free market, then, works fine in providing most goods, but it functions less well without regulations, taxes, and subsidies in providing others.

8.1e Nongovernmental Solutions to Externalities

Sometimes externality problems can be handled by individuals without the intervention of government, where people may decide to take steps on their own to minimize negative externalities. Moral and social codes may prevent some people from littering, driving gas-guzzling cars, or using gas-powered mowers and log-burning fireplaces. The same self-regulation also applies to positive externalities. Philanthropists, for example, frequently donate money to public and private schools. In part, this must be because they view the positive externalities from education as a good buy for their charitable dollars.

SECTION QUIZ

1. The presence of negative externalities leads to a misallocation of societal resources because
   a. whenever external costs are imposed on outside parties, the good should not be produced at all.
   b. less of the good than is ideal for society is produced.
   c. some costs are associated with production that the producer fails to take into consideration.
   d. the government always intervenes in markets when negative externalities are present, and the government is inherently inefficient.

(continued)

SECTION QUIZ (cont.)

2. A tax equal to the external cost on firms that emit pollutants would

    a. provide firms with the incentive to increase the level of activity creating the pollution.

    b. provide firms with the incentive to decrease the level of activity creating the pollution.

    c. provide firms with little incentive to search for less environmentally damaging production methods.

    d. not reduce pollution levels at all.

3. In the case of a good whose production generates negative externalities,

    a. those not directly involved in the market transactions are harmed.

    b. internalizing the externality would tend to result in a greater output of the good.

    c. too little of the good tends to be produced.

    d. a subsidy would be the appropriate government corrective action.

    e. all of the above are true.

4. If firms were required to pay the full social costs of the production of goods, including both private and external costs, other things being equal, there would probably be a(n)

    a. increase in production.

    b. decrease in production.

    c. greater misallocation of resources.

    d. decrease in the market price of the product.

5. Which of the following will most likely generate positive externalities of consumption?

    a. A hot dog vendor

    b. Public education

    c. An automobile

    d. A city bus

    e. A polluting factory

6. Assume that production of a good imposes external costs on others. The market equilibrium price will be _____ and the equilibrium quantity _____ for efficient resource allocation.

    a. too high; too high

    b. too high; too low

    c. too low; too high

    d. too low; too low

7. Assume that production of a good generates external benefits of consumption. The market equilibrium price of the good will be _____ and the equilibrium quantity _____ for efficient resource allocation.

    a. too high; too high

    b. too high; too low

    c. too low; too high

    d. too low; too low

8. In the case of externalities, appropriate government corrective policy would be

    a. taxes in the case of external benefits and subsidies in the case of external costs.

    b. subsidies in the case of external benefits and taxes in the case of external costs.

    c. taxes in both the case of external benefits and the case of external costs.

    d. subsidies in both the case of external benefits and the case of external costs.

    e. none of the above; the appropriate thing to do would be to do nothing.

(continued)

SECTION QUIZ (cont.)

1. Why are externalities also called spillover effects?
2. How do external costs affect the price and output of a polluting activity?
3. How can the government intervene to force producers to internalize external costs?
4. How do external benefits affect the output of an activity that causes them?
5. How can the government intervene to force external benefits to be internalized?
6. Why do most cities have more stringent noise laws for the early morning and late evening hours than for during the day?

Answers: 1. c 2. b 3. a 4. b 5. b 6. c 7. d 8. b

Public Policy and the Environment   8.2

▷ What is the "best" level of pollution?
▷ What are command and control regulations?

▷ What is a pollution tax?
▷ What are transferable pollution rights?

8.2a Why Is a Clean Environment Not Free?

In many respects, a clean environment is no different from any other desirable good. In a world of scarcity, we can increase our consumption of a clean environment only by giving up something else. The problem that we face is choosing the combination of goods that does the most to enhance human well-being. Few people would enjoy a perfectly clean environment if they were cold, hungry, and generally destitute. On the other hand, an individual choking to death in smog is hardly to be envied, no matter how great his or her material wealth.

Only by considering the additional cost as well as the additional benefit of increased consumption of all goods, including clean air and water, can decisions on the desirable combination of goods to consume be made properly.

8.2b The Costs and Benefits of Pollution Control

It is possible, even probable, that pollution elimination, like nearly everything else, is subject to diminishing returns. Initially, a large amount of pollution can be eliminated fairly inexpensively, but getting rid of still more pollution may prove more costly. Likewise, it is also possible that the marginal benefits from eliminating "crud" from the air might decline as more and more pollution is eliminated. For example, perhaps some pollution elimination initially would have a profound impact on health care costs, home repair expenses, and so on, but as pollution levels fall, further elimination of pollutants brings fewer marginal benefits.

The cost–benefit trade-off just discussed is illustrated in Exhibit 1, which examines the marginal social benefits and marginal social costs associated with the elimination of air pollution. In the early 1960s, as a nation we had few regulations on pollution control and, as a result, private firms had little incentive to eliminate the problem. In the context of Exhibit 1, we may have spent Q_1 on controls, meaning that the marginal social benefits of greater pollution control expenditures exceeded the marginal costs associated with having the controls. Investing more capital and labor to reduce pollution is efficient in such a situation.

Optimum pollution control occurs when Q^* of pollution is eliminated. Up to that point, the benefits from the elimination of pollution exceed the marginal costs, both pecuniary and

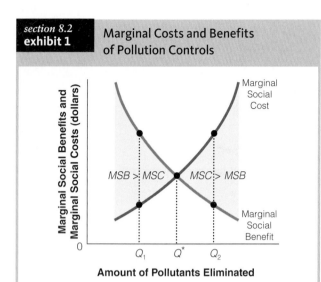

section 8.2 exhibit 1   Marginal Costs and Benefits of Pollution Controls

Pollution has costs and benefits. At output Q_1, pollution control is inadequate; on the other hand, elimination of Q_2 pollution will entail marginal costs that exceed the marginal benefits. Only at Q^* is pollution control expenditure at an optimum level. Of course, in practice, it is difficult to know exactly the position and slope of these curves.

Can skyscrapers be good for the environment? People who live in the city drive less, use more public transportation, and also use less electricity and home heating because they tend to live in smaller living spaces compared to suburbanites. As a result, central city residents may emit less carbon into the atmosphere than suburbanites.

ROBERT L. SEXTON

nonpecuniary, of the pollution control. Overly stringent compliance levels force companies to control pollution to the level indicated by Q_2 in Exhibit 1, where the additional costs from the controls far outweigh the environmental benefits. It should be stated, however, that increased concerns about pollution have probably caused the marginal social benefit curve to shift to the right over time, increasing the optimal amount of pollution control. Because of measurement problems, however, it is difficult to state whether we are generally below, at, or above the optimal pollution level.

Measuring Externalities

How much damage, at the margin, does a steel mill's air pollution do to nonconsumers of the steel? No one really knows because no market fully measures those costs. Indeed, the costs are partly nonpecuniary, meaning that no outlay of money occurs. Even though we pay dollars to see the doctor for respiratory ailments and pay dollars to repaint pollution-caused peeling on buildings, we do not make explicit money payments for the visual pollution and undesirable odors that the mill might produce as a by-product of making steel. Nonpecuniary costs are real costs and potentially have a monetary value that can be associated with them, but assessing that value in practical terms is immensely difficult. You might be able to decide how much you would be willing to pay to live in a pollution-free world, but no current mechanism allows anyone to express the perceived monetary value of having clear air to breathe and smell. Even some pecuniary, or monetary, costs are difficult to truly measure: How much respiratory disease is caused by pollution and how much by other factors? Environmental economists continue to make progress in valuing these difficult-to-measure damages.

Even though measuring externalities, both negative and positive, is often nearly impossible, it does not necessarily mean that it is better to ignore the externality and allow the market solution to operate. As already explained, the market solution will almost certainly result in excessive output by polluters unless some intervention occurs. What form should the intervention take?

8.2c Command and Control Policies: Regulation

One approach to dealing with externalities is to require private enterprise to produce their outputs in a manner that would reduce negative externalities below the amounts that would persist in the absence of regulation. For example, the Environmental Protection Agency (EPA) was established by the Clean Air Act of 1970 to serve as a watchdog over the production of goods and services in areas where externalities, especially negative externalities, exist. The EPA's main duty is to enforce environmental standards.

However, the EPA might also require a firm to use a certain technology to reduce emissions. In order to design good policies, the government regulators need information on specific industries and the technologies they could employ. This is not easy information for the government to obtain.

At the turn of the 20th century, horses and carriages were the predominant form of transportation in New York City. During inclement weather, the city was knee high in mud and manure. Horses that died on the job had to be dealt with as well. Ironically, the solution to the pollution problem was the horseless carriage—the automobile.

MUSEUM OF THE CITY OF NEW YORK/THE ART ARCHIVE AT ART RESOURCE, NY

For example, the EPA may identify and then enforce a standard equal to the maximum amount of pollution that firms can produce per unit of output per year. To be effective in pollution reduction, of course, these standards must result in less pollution than would exist in the absence of regulation. The regulations, then, force companies to find less pollution-intensive ways of producing goods and services. Or in the case of consumer products that pollute—such as automobiles, for example—manufacturers have been forced to reduce the emissions from the products themselves. In 1984, the federal government required that auto producers install catalytic converters in new cars to reduce auto emissions.

How can we determine the optimum level of pollution control?

transferable pollution rights
a right given to a firm to discharge a specified amount of pollution; its transferable nature creates incentive to lower pollution levels

8.2d Pollution Taxes: A Market-Based Policy

Using taxes to internalize external costs is appealing because it allows the relatively efficient private sector to operate according to market forces in a manner that takes socially important spillover costs into account. A major objection to the use of such taxes and subsidies is that, in most cases, it is difficult to measure externalities with any precision. Choosing a tax rate involves some guesswork, and poor guessing might lead to a solution that is far from optimal. But it is likely to be better than ignoring the problem. In spite of the severe difficulties in measurement, however, many economists would like to see greater effort made to force internalization of externalities through taxes rather than using alternative approaches. Why? We know that firms will seek out the least-expensive (in terms of using society's scarce resources) approaches to cleanup because they want more profits.

What is the advantage to the pollution rights approach?

8.2e Transferable Pollution Rights

Economists see an opportunity to control pollution through a government-enforced system of property rights. In this system, the government issues transferable pollution rights that give the holder the right to discharge a specified amount (smaller than the uncontrolled amount) of pollution into the air. In this plan, firms have an incentive to lower their levels of pollution because they can sell their permits if they go unused. Specifically, firms that can lower their emissions at the lowest costs will do so and trade their pollution rights to firms that cannot reduce their pollution levels as easily. That is, each polluter— required either to reduce pollution to the level allowed by the number of rights it holds or buy more rights—will be motivated to eliminate all pollution that is cheaper than the price of pollution rights. The crucial advantage to the pollution rights approach comes from the fact that the rights are private property and can be sold.

It is worth emphasizing that this least-cost pattern of abatement does not require any information about the techniques of pollution abatement on the part of the government—more specifically, the EPA. The EPA does not need to know the cheapest abatement strategy for each and every polluter. Faced

ROMANA CHAPMAN/GETTY IMAGES

Do countries with greater gross domestic product per capita have cleaner environments? According to researchers at Yale University, wealth matters. For the most part, richer countries can and do spend more money on producing a healthy environment than poorer countries.

with a positive price for pollution rights, each polluter has every motivation to discover and use the cheapest way to reduce pollution. Nor does the EPA need to know anything about the differences in abatement costs among polluters. Each polluter is motivated to reduce pollution as long as the cost of reducing one more unit is less than the price of pollution rights. The information and incentives generated by private ownership and market exchange of these pollution rights automatically leads to the desirable pattern of pollution.

The pollution rights approach also creates an incentive for polluters to develop improved pollution abatement technologies.

The prospect of buying and selling pollution permits would allow firms to move into an area that is already as polluted as allowed by EPA standards. Under the tradeable permits policy, the firm can set up operation by purchasing pollution permits from an existing polluter in the area. This type of exchange allows the greatest value to be generated with a given amount of pollution. It also encourages polluters to come up with cheaper ways of reducing pollution because the firm that reduces pollution is able to sell its pollution credits to others, making pollution reduction profitable.

SECTION QUIZ

1. Taxes on the emissions of polluting firms are primarily intended to
   a. encourage firms to reduce product prices.
   b. encourage firms to increase production of output.
   c. raise revenue for general spending needs.
   d. encourage firms to pollute less.

2. An ideal pollution tax
   a. does not affect the quantity of the good produced.
   b. forces a firm to internalize the externality.
   c. causes a polluting firm to increase production to the socially efficient level of output.
   d. leads to a reduction in price to the consumer of the polluting firm's output.

3. If compliance standards are too stringent,
   a. the marginal social benefit of pollution reduction may outweigh the marginal social cost of pollution reduction.
   b. the marginal social cost of pollution reduction may outweigh the marginal social benefit of pollution reduction.
   c. the marginal social cost of pollution reduction will just equal the marginal social benefit from pollution reduction.
   d. none of the above is correct.

4. An advantage that emission taxes and tradable emissions permits have over compliance standards is that the former
   a. work well even if pollution output cannot be accurately measured.
   b. result in equal levels of pollution abatement across all firms.
   c. make it in the interests of firms to reduce pollution in the most efficient manner possible.
   d. reduce pollution to zero.

5. Which of the following is *not* an advantage of transferable pollution rights?
   a. They create incentives for polluters to develop cheaper ways to reduce pollution.
   b. They allow the greatest value of output to be produced with a given amount of pollution.
   c. They require polluters to reduce emissions, regardless of the cost.
   d. The rights are private property and may be bought or sold freely.

(continued)

Property Rights and the Environment   8.3

▶ What is the relationship between externalities and property rights?

▶ What is the Coase theorem?

The existence of externalities and the efforts to deal with them in a manner that will enhance the social good can be considered a question of the nature of property rights. If the EPA limits the soot that a steel company emits from its smokestack, then the property rights of the steel company with respect to its smokestack have been altered or restricted. Similarly, zoning laws restrict how property owners can use their property. Sometimes, to deal with externalities, governments radically alter arrangements of property rights.

Indeed, the entire matter of dealing with externalities ultimately evolves into a question of how property rights should be altered. If no externalities existed in the world, reasons for prohibiting property owners from using their property in any manner they voluntarily chose would be few. Ultimately, then, externalities involve an evaluation of the legal arrangements under which we operate our economy and thus illustrate one area where law and economics merge.

What is the Coase theorem?

8.3a The Coase Theorem

In a classic paper, Nobel laureate Ronald Coase observed that when the benefits are greater than the costs for some course of action (say, environmental cleanup), potential transactions can make some people better off without making anyone worse off. This idea is known as the **Coase theorem**. To appreciate this important insight, consider the following problem: A cattle rancher lives downstream from a paper mill. The paper mill dumps waste into the stream, which injures the rancher's cattle. If the rancher is not compensated, an externality exists.

Suppose the courts have established (perhaps because the paper mill was there first) that the property rights to use (or abuse) the stream reside with the mill. If the benefits of cleanup are greater than the costs, the rancher should be willing to pay the mill owner to stop polluting. Let's assume that the rancher's benefits (say $10,000) from the cleanup undertaken by the mill are greater than the cost (say $5,000). If the rancher were to offer $7,500 to the mill owner to clean up the stream, both the rancher and the mill owner would be better off than with continued pollution. If, on the other hand, the rancher had the property rights to the stream, and the mill owner received a sufficiently high benefit from polluting the river, then it would be rational for the mill owner to pay the rancher up to the point where the marginal benefit to the mill owner of polluting equaled the marginal damage to the rancher from pollution.

Coase theorem
where property rights are defined in a clear-cut fashion, and externalities are internalized if transaction costs are low

8.3b **Transaction Costs and the Coase Theorem**

The mill owner and rancher example hinges critically on low transaction costs. Transaction costs are the costs of negotiating and executing an exchange, excluding the cost of the good or service bought. For example, when buying a car, it is usually rational for the buyer to spend some time searching for the "right" car and negotiating a mutually agreeable price.

Suppose instead that the situation involved 1,000 ranchers and 10 mill owners. Trying to coordinate the activity between the ranch owners and mill owners would be almost impossible. Now imagine the complexities of more realistic cases: millions of people live within 60 miles of downtown Los Angeles. Each of them is damaged a little by a large number of firms and other individuals (for example, automobile drivers) in Los Angeles.

It thus becomes apparent why the inefficiencies resulting from pollution control are not eliminated by private negotiations. First is the issue of ambiguity regarding property rights in air, water, and other environmental media. Firms that have historically polluted resent controls, giving up their rights to pollute only if bribed, yet consumers feel they have the right to breathe clean air and use clean bodies of water. These conflicting positions must be resolved in court, with the winner being, of course, made wealthier. Second, transaction costs increase greatly with the number of transactors, making it next to impossible for individual firms and citizens to negotiate private agreements. Finally, the properties of air or water quality (and similar public goods) are such that additional people can enjoy the benefits at no additional cost and cannot be excluded from doing so. Hence, in practice, private agreements are unlikely to solve many problems of market failure.

It is, however, too easy to jump to the conclusion that governments should solve any problems that cannot be solved by private actions. No solution may be possible, or all solutions may involve costs that exceed benefits. In any event, the ideas developed in this chapter should enable you to think critically about such problems and the difficulties in formulating appropriate policies.

SECTION QUIZ

1. According to the Coase theorem, one way to deal with an externality problem when transaction costs are low is
   a. for the government to impose pollution taxes.
   b. for the government to make certain that property rights are well defined.
   c. for the government to issue transferable pollution permits.
   d. for the government to impose compliance standards.

2. The Coase theorem suggests that private solutions to externality problems
   a. can lead to an optimal allocation of resources if private parties can bargain at relatively low cost.
   b. result in the efficient outcome under all conditions.
   c. will result in the same distribution of wealth no matter how property rights are assigned.
   d. will result in different efficiency levels of production, depending crucially on how property rights are assigned.

3. In the case of a private solution to the externality problem, the distribution of rights
   a. restricts the ability of private parties to properly price the externalities.
   b. enhances the market incentive to reach an efficient solution.
   c. determines who bears the cost of the solution but does not affect the efficient result.
   d. affects the efficiency of the outcome, but does not determine who bears the cost.

(continued)

4. Pollution reduction will be achieved for the least cost when

   a. large polluters are required to reduce pollution by a greater extent than small polluters.

   b. small polluters are required to reduce pollution by a greater extent than large polluters.

   c. all firms are required to reduce pollution by a proportionate amount.

   d. all firms are required to reduce pollution by an equal absolute amount.

   e. the cost of reducing pollution by an additional unit is the same for all polluting firms.

___

1. Why can externalities be considered a property rights problem?

2. Why, according to the Coase theorem, will externalities tend to be internalized when property rights are clearly defined and information and transaction costs are low?

3. How do transaction costs limit the market's ability to efficiently solve externality problems?

Answers: 1. b   2. a   3. c   4. e

Public Goods   8.4

▶ What is a public good?

▶ What is the free-rider problem?

▶ Why does the government provide public goods?

▶ What is a common resource good?

▶ What is the tragedy of the commons?

What is a public good? Is it any good that is purchased by the government?

8.4a Private Goods versus Public Goods

Externalities are not the only culprit behind resource misallocation. A **public good** is another source of market failure. As used by economists, this term refers not to how these particular goods are purchased—by a government agency rather than some private economic agent—but to the properties that characterize them. In this section, we learn the difference between private goods, public goods, and common resources.

public good
a good that is nonrivalrous in consumption and nonexcludable

Private Goods

A **private good** such as a cheeseburger has two critical properties in this context: it is rival and excludable. First, a cheeseburger is rival in consumption because if one person eats a particular cheeseburger, nobody else can eat the same cheeseburger. Second, a cheeseburger is excludable. It is easy to keep someone from eating your cheeseburger by not giving it to him. Most goods in the economy, like food, clothing, cars, and houses, are private goods that are rival and excludable.

private good
a good with rivalrous consumption and excludability

economic content standards

Public goods provide benefits to more than one person at a time, and their use cannot be restricted to only those people who have paid to use them.

Public Goods

The consumption of public goods, unlike private goods, is neither rival nor excludable. A public good is not rival because everyone can consume the good simultaneously; that is, one person's use of it does not diminish another's ability to use it. A public good is likewise *not excludable* because once the good is produced, it is prohibitively costly to exclude anyone

Voters may disagree on whether we have too much or too little, but most agree that we must have national defense. If national defense were provided privately and people were asked to pay for the use of national defense, many would be free riders, knowing they could derive the benefits of the good without paying for it. For this reason, the government provides important public goods, such as national defense.

from consuming the good. Consider national defense. Everyone enjoys the benefits of national defense (not rival) and it would be too costly to exclude anyone from those benefits (not excludable). That is, once the military has its defense in place, everyone is protected simultaneously (not rival) and it would be prohibitively costly to exclude anyone from consuming national defense (not excludable).

Another example of a public good is a flood control project. A flood control project would allow all the people who live in the flood plain area to enjoy the protection of the new program simultaneously (not rival). It would also be very difficult to exclude someone who lived in the middle of the project who said she did not want to pay (not excludable).

8.4b Public Goods and the Free-Rider Problem

The fact that a public good is not rival and not excludable makes the good difficult to produce privately. Some would know they could derive the benefits from the good without paying for it because once it is produced, it is too difficult to exclude them. Some would try to take a *free ride*—derive benefits from something they did not pay for. Let's return to the example of national defense. Suppose the private protection of national defense is actually worth $100 to you. Assume that 100 million households in the United States are willing to make a $100 contribution for national defense. These contributions would add up to $10 billion. You might write a check for $100, or you might reason as follows: "If I don't give $100 and everybody else does, I will be equally well protected plus derive the benefits of $100 in my pocket." Taking the latter course represents a rational attempt to be a free rider. The rub is that if everyone attempts to take a free ride, the ride will not exist.

free rider

deriving benefits from something not paid for

The free-rider problem prevents the private market from supplying the efficient amounts of public goods. That is, no private firm would be willing to supply national defense because people can consume it without paying for it—the free-rider problem. Therefore, the government provides important public goods such as national defense.

8.4c The Government and Benefit–Cost Analysis

Everything the government provides has an opportunity cost. What is the best level of national defense? More national defense means less of something else that society may value more, like health care or Social Security. To be efficient, additional goods from the public sector must also follow the rule of rational choice—pursue additional government activities if and only if the expected marginal benefits exceed the expected marginal costs. It all comes back to the adage "there are no free lunches."

In addition, there is also the problem of assessing the value of these goods. Consider the case of a new highway. Before it builds the highway, the appropriate government agency will undertake a benefit–cost analysis of the situation. In this case, it must evaluate consumers' willingness to pay for the highway against the costs that will be incurred for construction and maintenance. However, those individuals who want the

Is busking, or street entertaining, a public good? The nonpaying public can benefit so you have a free-rider problem. It is difficult to exclude someone from the pitch (where buskers play). However, if the street entertainers are really good, it is possible that local vendors will pay them because they may attract customers. Did you know busking has been around since the Roman Empire?

highway have an incentive to exaggerate their desire for it. At the same time, individuals who will be displaced or otherwise harmed by the highway have an incentive to exaggerate the harm that will be done to them. Together, these elements make it difficult for the government to accurately assess benefits and costs. Ultimately, their evaluations are reduced to educated guesses about the net impact, weighing both positive and negative effects, of the highway on all parties concerned.

8.4d Common Resources and the Tragedy of the Commons

In many cases we do not have exclusive private property rights to things such as the air around us or the fish in the sea. They are common resources—goods that are owned by everyone and therefore not owned by anyone. When a good is not owned by anyone, individuals feel little incentive to conserve or use the resource efficiently.

A **common resource** is a rival good that is nonexcludable; that is, nonpayers cannot be easily excluded from consuming the good, and when one unit is consumed by one person, it means that it cannot be consumed by another. Fish in the vast ocean waters are a good example of a common resource. They are rival because fish are limited—a fish taken by one person is not available for others. They are nonexcludable because it is prohibitively costly to keep anyone from catching them—almost anyone with a boat and a fishing rod could catch one. Common resources can lead to the tragedy of the commons. This is the case of private incentives failing to provide adequate maintenance of public resources.

In early America, New Englanders had privately owned gardens to grow their own food, but they also had established commons for grazing livestock. Settlers had an incentive to protect their own private lands but not the publicly owned commons. As a result, the commons were soon overgrazed and no longer able to support the villagers' cattle, creating the so-called Tragedy of the Commons.

Other examples of common resources where individuals have relatively free access and the resources can be easily exploited are congested roads and the Internet. "Free" way is a misnomer. No one owns the space on the freeway. Because there are no property rights to the freeway, you cannot exclude others from driving on and sharing the freeway. When you occupy a part of the freeway, you are keeping others from using that portion. So, all drivers compete for limited space, causing a negative externality in the form of congestion.

The Internet poses a similar problem. If everyone attempts to access the same website at the same time, overcrowding occurs and congestion can cause the site to slow down.

There are two possible solutions to the common property rights problem. First, the government, through taxes and fees, can attempt to internalize the externality. To prevent road congestion, the government could charge drivers a toll—a corrective tax on congestion—or it could charge higher tolls on bridges during rush hour. A gasoline tax would be an inferior policy solution because while it would reduce driving, it would not necessarily reduce driving during peak periods.

If a tornado siren in a small town is not rival, and not excludable, is it a public good?

ECS

economic content standards

Governments provide an alternative method to markets for supplying goods and services when it appears that the benefits to society of doing so outweigh the costs to society. Not all individuals will bear the same costs or share the same benefits of those policies.

A government policy to correct a market imperfection is not justified economically if the cost of implementing it exceeds its expected benefits.

common resource
a good that is rival in consumption and nonexcludable

Poachers in Africa hunt elephants for their tusks. Where no one owns them, allowing owners to capture both the benefits and the costs from them, elephants roam free and they are treated as a common resource. Poachers are numerous in those places and each poacher has an incentive to kill as many elephants as possible to get their tusks before someone else does. However, in Botswana and Zimbabwe. elephants are a private good. In these countries safari hunting is legal on private property, allowing effective ownership of the elephants on that property and providing the ability to protect its herds against poachers and the incentive to efficiently manage its herds. Consequently, the elephant population in those countries has started to rise because of private ownership and profit motives.

Similarly, the government can charge fees to reduce congestion in national parks during peak periods. They can have restrictions through licensing on hunting and fishing to control animal populations.

Second, the government could assign private property rights to common resources. For example, private fish farms have become more profitable as overfishing depletes the stock of fish in open waters.

SECTION QUIZ

1. The market system fails to provide the efficient output of public goods because
   a. people place no value on public goods.
   b. private firms cannot restrict the benefits from those goods to consumers who are willing to pay for them.
   c. public enterprises can produce those goods at lower cost than private firms.
   d. public goods create widespread spillover costs.

2. Public goods, like national defense, are usually funded through government because
   a. no one cares about them because they are public.
   b. it is prohibitively difficult to withhold national defense from someone unwilling to pay for it.
   c. they cost too much for private firms to produce them.
   d. they provide benefits only to individuals and not firms.

3. A public good is both _____ in consumption and _____.
   a. nonrivalrous; exclusive
   b. nonrivalrous; nonexclusive
   c. rivalrous; exclusive
   d. rivalrous; nonexclusive

4. Public goods
   a. do not need to be produced by government.
   b. are subject to free-rider problems.
   c. tend to be underproduced in the marketplace.
   d. All of the above are true.

5. A common resource
   a. is rivalrous in consumption.
   b. is nonexcludable.
   c. can lead to the tragedy of the commons.
   d. All of the above are true.

---

1. How are public goods different from private goods?
2. Why does the free-rider problem arise in the case of public goods?
3. In what way can government provision of public goods solve the free-rider problem?
4. What is a common resource?
5. What is the tragedy of the commons?

Answers: 1. b 2. b 3. b 4. d 5. d

Asymmetric Information 8.5

▶ What is asymmetric information?

▶ What is moral hazard?

▶ What is adverse selection?

8.5a What Is Asymmetric Information?

When the available information is initially distributed in favor of one party relative to another, **asymmetric information** is said to exist. Suppose you just bought a used car that had 3,000 miles on the odometer. The car was in pristine shape—no dents, no scratches, good tires, and so on. Would you be willing to pay close to the same price for this car as you would for a new car (same model, same accessories) from the dealer? Probably not, because you are going to suspect that something is wrong with the car.

Sellers are at an information advantage over potential buyers when selling a used car because they have more information about the car than does the potential buyer. However, potential buyers know that sellers are more likely to sell a lemon. As a result, potential buyers will offer a lower price than they would if they could be certain of the quality. This is known as the lemon problem. Without incurring significant quality detection costs, such as having it inspected by a mechanic, the potential buyer is at an informational disadvantage relative to the seller. It is rational for the seller to claim that the car is in good shape and has no known defects, but the potential buyer cannot detect whether the car is a lemon or not without incurring costs. If the quality detection costs are sufficiently high, a solution is to price all used cars as if they are average quality. That is, used cars of the same year, make, and model generally will be offered at the same price, regardless of their known conditions. The seller of a lemon will then receive a payment that is more than the car is worth, and the seller of a relatively high-quality car will receive less than the car is worth. However, if a seller of a high-quality car does *not* receive what the car would sell for if the potential buyer knew its quality, the seller will rationally withdraw the offer to sell the car. Given the logical response of sellers of higher-than-average quality cars, the average quality of used cars on the market will fall, and consequently, many people will avoid buying in the used-car market. In other words, the bad cars will drive the good cars out of the market. Thus, fewer used cars are bought and sold because fewer good cars are offered for sale. That is, information problems reduce economic efficiency. A situation where an informed party benefits in an exchange by taking advantage of knowing more than the other party is called **adverse selection**.

This distortion in the used-car market resulting from adverse selection can be reduced by the buyer acquiring more information so that the buyer and seller have equal information. In the used-car example, it might mean that an individual buyer would demand that an independent mechanic do a detailed inspection of the used car or that the dealership provide an extended warranty. A warranty provides a credible signal that this dealer is not selling lemons. In addition, new services such as carfax.com allow you to pay to find the history of a used car before you buy it. These services help eliminate the adverse selection problem because buyers have more information about the product they are buying.

The least-cost solution would have sellers reveal their superior information to potential buyers. The problem is that it is not individually rational for the seller to provide a truthful and complete disclosure, a point that is known by a potential buyer. Only if the

asymmetric information
when the available information is initially distributed in favor of one party relative to another in an exchange

adverse selection
a situation where an informed party benefits in an exchange by taking advantage of knowing more than the other party

Because the seller of a car has more information than the buyer has, the potential buyer does not know whether the car is a cherry or a lemon. So the buyer guesses the car is average quality and consequently he offers an average price. The owner of a carefully maintained, good used car will be unable to get a high enough price to make selling that car worthwhile. Consequently, owners of good cars will not place their cars on the used-car market. But those with cars of less than average quality will dump their cars on the market. Hence, the lemon problem.

When players get traded from one team to another, a potential asymmetric information and adverse selection problem occurs—especially with pitchers. The team that is trading the pitcher knows more about his medical past, his pitching mechanics, his demeanor on and off the field, and so on, than the team that is trading for him. Even though trades are not finalized until the player passes a physical, many ailments or potential problems may go undetected.

seller is punished for not truthfully revealing exchange-relevant information will a potential buyer perceive the seller's disclosure as truthful.

Adverse selection also occurs in the insurance market. Imagine an auto insurance company that has a one-size-fits-all policy for its insurance premiums. Careful drivers would be charged the same premium as careless drivers. The company would assess the average risk of accidents for all drivers and then set the premium. Of course, this would be very appealing to careless drivers, who are more likely to get in an accident, but not very appealing to careful drivers, who have a much lower probability of getting in an accident. Under this pricing scheme, the bad drivers would drive the good drivers out of the market. Good drivers would be less likely to buy a policy, thinking that they are paying too much, since they are less likely to get in an accident than a careless driver. Many good drivers would exit the market, leaving a disproportionate share of bad drivers—exactly what the insurance companies do not want—people with a higher risk of getting in accidents. So what do they do?

Insurance companies set premiums according to the risk associated with particular groups of drivers, so good drivers do not exit the market. One strategy they use for dealing with adverse selection is called *screening*, where they use observable information about people to reveal private information. For example, a 17-year-old male driving a sports car will be charged a much higher premium than a 40-year-old female driving a minivan, even if he is a careful driver. Or someone with a good driving record or good grades gets a discount on his insurance. Insurance companies have data on different types of drivers and the probability of those drivers being in accidents, and they use these data to set insurance premiums. They may be wrong on an individual case (the teenager may be accident-free for years), but they are likely to be correct on average.

Reputation and Standardization

Asymmetric information is also present in other markets like rare stamps, coins, paintings, and sports memorabilia where the dealer (seller) knows more about the product than does the potential buyer. Potential buyers want to be assured that these items are authentic, not counterfeits. Unless the seller can successfully provide evidence of the quality of the product, bad products will tend to drive good products out of the market, resulting in a market failure.

One method that sellers can use to convince potential buyers that their products are high quality is *reputation*. For example, if a supermarket has a reputation of selling fresh produce, you are more likely to shop there. The same is true when you choose an electrician, plumber, or physician. In the used-car market, the dealer might advertise how long he has been in business. This provides a signal that he has many satisfied customers. Therefore, he is likely to sell more used cars. In short, if there is a reputation of high quality, it will minimize the market failure problem.

However, there may be cases where it is difficult to develop a reputation. For example, take a restaurant or a motel on a desolate highway. These establishments may not receive repeat customers. Customers have little idea of the quality of food, the probability of bedbugs, and so on. In this case, *standardization* is important.

When confronted with the choice between a little-known motel and a reputable hotel chain, like Holiday Inn or Hilton, you may pick the national chain because of its reputation.

Asymmetric Information and Job Market Signaling

Why does non-job-related schooling raise your income? Why would salaried workers work longer hours—putting in 60 to 70 hours a week? The reason is this behavior provides a useful signal to the employer about the person's intelligence and work ethic.

Signaling is important because it reduces information costs associated with asymmetric information; the seller of labor (potential employee) has more information about her work ethic and reliability than the buyer of labor (potential employer). Imagine how costly it would be to try out 150 potential employees for a job. In short, signals provide a measure that can help reduce asymmetric information and lower hiring costs.

There are strong signals and weak signals. Wearing a nice suit to work would be a weak signal because it does not necessarily distinguish a highly productive worker from a less productive worker—a less productive worker can dress well too. To provide a strong signal, it must be harder for a low-productivity worker to give the signal than a high-productivity worker. Education is a strong signal in labor markets because it requires achievements that many low productivity workers may find too difficult to obtain. The education signal is also relatively easy to measure—years of education, grade point average, highest degree attained, reputation of the university or college, rigor of courses attempted, and so on. Education can clearly improve a person's productivity; even if it did not, however, it would be a useful signal because more productive people find it easier to obtain education than lazy people. Furthermore, productive people are more likely to attain more education in order to signal to their employer that they are productive. So it may not just be the knowledge obtained from a college education, it may be the effort that you are signaling—something you presumably already had before you entered college. So according to the signaling model, workers go to college not for the knowledge gained, but to send the important signal that they are highly productive.

In all likelihood, education provides knowledge and enhances productivity. However, it also sends an important signal. For example, many firms will not hire managers without an MBA because of the knowledge potential employees gained in courses like finance and economics, but also because an MBA sends a powerful signal that the worker is disciplined and hard working.

Durable Goods, Signals, and Warranties

Why are people reluctant to buy durable goods like televisions, refrigerators, and cameras without a warranty? Warranties are a signal. Honest and reliable firms find it less expensive to provide a warranty than dishonest firms do. The dilemma for consumers is that they are trying to distinguish the good brands from the bad brands. One way to do this is to see what kind of warranty the producer offers. Low-quality items would require more frequent and expensive servicing than high-quality items. Thus, producers of low-quality items will tend to not offer extensive warranties. In short, extensive warranties signal high quality, while low-quality items without extensive warranties signal poor quality. With this knowledge, consumers will pay more for high-quality products with good warranties.

8.5b What Is Moral Hazard?

Another information problem is associated with the insurance market and is called moral hazard. If an individual is fully insured for fire, theft, auto, life, and so on, what incentives will this individual have to take additional precautions from risk? For example, a person with auto insurance may drive less cautiously than would a person without auto insurance.

Insurance companies do, however, try to remedy the adverse selection problem by requiring regular checkups, discounts for nonsmokers, charging different deductibles and different rates for different age and occupational groups, and so on.

Gift-giving can illustrate asymmetric information issues because each person knows more about their preferences than others do. For example, if the question being addressed is "Does he really love me?", perhaps choosing the "right" gift is a way to send a signal of love. But giving the "right" gift rather than money is costly because it takes more time and information to choose. However, if he truly loves her, this might be an easier task because he will know more, and care more, about her tastes. Giving cash can send a signal that you really don't care very much.

Additionally, those with health insurance may devote less effort and resources to staying healthy than those who are not covered. The problem, of course, is that if the insured are behaving more recklessly than they would if they were not insured, the result might be much higher insurance rates. The moral hazard arises from the fact that it is costly for the insurer to monitor the behaviors of the insured party. Suppose an individual knew that his car was protected with a "bumper-to-bumper" warranty. He might have less incentive to take care of the car, despite the manufacturer's contract specifying that the warranty was only valid under "normal wear and tear." It would be too costly for the manufacturer to detect if a product failure was the consequence of a manufacturing defect or the abuse of the owner-user.

moral hazard

taking additional risks because you are insured, thus lowering the cost to you of taking those risks

Adverse Selection versus Moral Hazard

Don't confuse adverse selection and moral hazard. Adverse selection is the phenomenon that occurs when one party in the exchange takes advantage of knowing more than the other party. Moral hazard involves the action taken *after* the exchange, such as if you were a nonsmoker who had just bought a life insurance policy and then started smoking heavily.

SECTION QUIZ

1. Adverse selection refers to

   a. the phenomenon that occurs when one party in an exchange takes advantage of knowing more than another party.

   b. the tendency for individuals to alter their behavior once they are insured against loss.

   c. the tendency for individuals to engage in insurance fraud.

   d. both (b) and (c).

2. If, after you buy a car with air bags, you start to drive recklessly, it would be an illustration of

   a. the moral hazard problem.

   b. the free-rider problem.

   c. the adverse selection problem.

   d. the "lemon" problem.

3. In the market for insurance, the moral hazard problem leads

   a. those most likely to collect on insurance to buy it.

   b. those who buy insurance to take fewer precautions to avoid the insured risk.

   c. those with more prior insurance claims to be charged a higher premium.

   d. to none of the above.

---

1. How do substantial warranties offered by sellers of used cars act to help protect buyers from the problem of asymmetric information and adverse selection? Why might too extensive a warranty lead to a moral hazard problem?

2. If where you got your college degree acted as a signaling device to potential employers, why would you want the school from which you graduated to raise its academic standards after you leave?

3. Why might withdrawals in several classes send a poor signal to potential employers?

Answers: 1. a 2. a 3. b

Fill in the blanks:

1. Sometimes the market system fails to produce efficient outcomes because of side effects economists call _____.

2. Whenever an activity has physical impacts on individuals not directly involved in the activity, if the impact on the outside party is negative, it is called a _____; if the impact is positive, it is called a _____.

3. If a firm can avoid paying the external costs it imposes on others, it _____ its own costs of production but not the _____ cost to society.

4. If the government taxed a manufacturer by the amount of those external costs it imposes on others, it would force the manufacturer to _____ the costs.

5. The benefits of a product or service that spill over to an outside party not involved in producing or consuming the good are called _____.

6. If suppliers are unaware of or not responsible for the external costs created by their production, the result is a(n) _____ of scarce resources to the production of the good.

7. Because producers are unable to collect payments from all who are benefiting from the good or service, the market has a tendency to _____ goods with external benefits.

8. In the case of either external benefits or external costs, buyers and sellers are receiving the wrong signals: The apparent benefits or costs of some actions differ from the _____ benefits or costs.

9. Unlike the consumption of private goods, the consumption of public goods is both _____ and _____.

10. Pollution reduction, like other forms of production, is subject to _____ returns.

11. The marginal cost of pollution abatement _____ with increasing levels of abatement.

12. The optimal quantity of pollution is where the _____ of pollution abatement equals the _____ from pollution abatement.

13. Compliance standards should be stricter where the marginal benefit from pollution reduction is _____.

14. Eliminating nearly all pollution would be economically _____ because the marginal _____ would exceed the marginal _____.

15. The economically ideal tax to impose on a polluter would be _____ the marginal external costs imposed on others by its production.

16. Compared to compliance standards, pollution taxes lead to abatement by firms who can do so at the _____ cost.

17. The imposition of per-unit pollution taxes would likely be _____ costly than compliance standards for the same degree of pollution abatement.

18. Firms buy and sell rights to pollute under a system of _____ rights.

19. Transferable pollution rights _____ work when the EPA does not know the cheapest way for polluters to reduce their emissions because they make it in polluters' interests to reduce pollution the cheapest way.

20. Under a system of transferable pollution rights, firms with high costs of abatement would likely be _____, and firms with low costs of abatement would be _____.

21. Problems of external costs are largely a question of how _____ should be assigned.

22. _____, the costs of negotiating and executing exchanges, must be low for well-defined property rights to allow externalities to be internalized.

23. According to the Coase theorem, markets can internalize externalities as long as _____ are well-defined and _____ costs are low.

24. When large numbers of individuals are affected by an external cost, the transaction costs of using voluntary negotiation to internalize it is likely to be _____.

25. If once a good is produced it is prohibitively costly to exclude anyone from consuming the good, consumption of that good is called _____.

26. If everyone can consume a good simultaneously, it is _____.

27. When individuals derive the benefits of a good without paying for it, it is called a(n) _____.

28. The government may be able to overcome the freerider problem by _____ the public good and imposing taxes to pay for it.

29. Goods that are owned by everyone and therefore not owned by anyone are called _____ resources.

30. A common resource is a(n) _____ good that is _____.

31. Fish in the vast ocean are a good example of a(n) _____ resource.

32. The failure of private incentives to provide adequate maintenance of public resources is known to economists as the _____.

33. When the available information is initially distributed in favor of one party relative to another, _____ is said to exist.

34. The existence of _____ may give rise to signaling behavior.

35. When one party enters into an exchange with another party that has more information, we call it _____ selection.

36. A college education can provide a(n) _____ about a person's intelligence and perseverance.

37. Good warranties are an example of _____ behavior that takes place because the _____ may know the actual quality of durable goods better than the _____.

38. _____ arises from the cost involved for the insurer to monitor the behaviors of the insured party.

Answers: 1. externalities 2. negative externality; positive externality 3. lowers; true 4. internalize (bear) 5. positive externalities 6. overallocation 7. underproduce 8. true social 9. nonexcludable; nonrivalous 10. diminishing 11. rises 12. marginal benefit; marginal cost 13. greater 14. inefficient; costs; benefits 15. equal to 16. lowest 17. less 18. transferable pollution 19. can 20. buyers; sellers 21. property rights 22. Transaction costs 23. property rights; transaction 24. large 25. nonexcludable 26. nonrivalous 27. free ride 28. providing 29. common 30. rival; nonexcludable 31. common 32. tragedy of the commons 33. asymmetric information 34. asymmetric information 35. adverse 36. signal 37. signaling; sellers; buyers 38. Moral hazard

KEY TERMS AND CONCEPTS

externality 213
positive externality 213
negative externality 213
internalizing externalities 214
transferable pollution rights 221

Coase theorem 223
public good 225
private good 225
free rider 226

common resource 227
asymmetric information 229
adverse selection 229
moral hazard 232

SECTION QUIZ ANSWERS

8.1 Externalities

1. Why are externalities also called spillover effects?
An externality exists whenever the benefits or costs of an activity impact individuals outside the market mechanism. That is, some of the effects spill over to those who have not voluntarily agreed to bear them or compensate others for them, unlike the voluntary exchange of the market.

2. How do external costs affect the price and output of a polluting activity?
If the owner of a firm that pollutes does not have to bear the external costs of pollution, she can ignore those real costs of pollution to society. The result is that the private costs she must pay are less than the true social costs of production, so that the market output of the polluting activity is greater, and the resulting market price less, than it would be if producers did have to bear the external costs of production.

3. How can the government intervene to force producers to internalize external costs?
If the government could impose a tax or fee on producers equal to the external costs imposed on people without their consent, producers would have to take those costs into account. The result would be that those costs would no longer be external costs, but internalized by producers.

4. How do external benefits affect the output of an activity that causes them?
External benefits are benefits that spill over to others because the party responsible need not be paid for those benefits. Therefore, some of the benefits of an activity to society will be ignored by the relevant

decision makers in this case, and the result will be a smaller output and a higher price for goods that generate external benefits to others.

5. How can the government intervene to force external benefits to be internalized?

Just as taxes can be used to internalize external costs imposed on others, subsidies can be used to internalize external benefits generated for others.

6. Why do most cities have more stringent noise laws for the early morning and late evening hours than for during the day?

The external costs to others from loud noises in residential areas early in the morning and late in the evening are higher because most residents are home and trying to sleep, than when many people are gone at work or are already awake in the daytime. Given those higher potential external costs, most cities impose more restrictive noise laws for nighttime hours to reduce them.

8.2 Public Policy and the Environment

1. How does pollution control lead to both rising marginal costs and falling marginal benefits?

The marginal costs of pollution control rise for the same reason it is true of other goods. Pollution will be reduced in the lowest cost manner first. Once lower cost pollution control methods are exhausted, if we wish to reduce pollution further, we will have to turn to progressively more costly methods. The marginal benefits from pollution controls will fall because the value of reducing crud in the atmosphere is higher the more crud there is. As controls reduce the level of crud in the air, the marginal benefit of further crud reductions will fall.

2. How is the optimal amount of pollution control determined, in principle?

In principle, the optimal amount of pollution control is the amount at which the marginal social benefit of pollution reduction equals the marginal cost of pollution reduction. But there is no clear agreement about what those marginal benefits or costs are, leading to disagreements about the optimal amount of pollution.

3. How do command and control policies act to internalize external costs?

By forcing companies to find less pollution-intensive ways of production rather than imposing the costs of additional pollution on others, they are forced to internalize those costs formerly imposed on others.

4. How could transferable pollution rights lead to pollution being reduced at the lowest possible opportunity cost?

Transferable pollution rights would create a market for pollution reduction. Every polluter would then find it

profitable to reduce pollution as long as they could do it more cheaply than the price of a pollution right. Therefore, producers would employ the lowest-cost pollution control methods for a given amount of pollution reduction.

5. What are the objectives of an ideal pollution control policy from the perspective of economists interested in resource allocation?

An ideal pollution control strategy from the perspective of economists interested in resource allocation would reduce pollution to the efficient level, it would do so at the lowest possible opportunity cost, and it would create incentives to motivate advances in pollution abatement technology.

8.3 Property Rights and the Environment

1. Why can externalities be considered a property rights problem?

If the rights to clean air, water, and so on, were clearly owned, those that infringe on those rights would be forced to compensate the owners. Such costs would be internalized, rather than external, to the relevant decision makers. Therefore, externalities are the result of the absence of clear and enforceable property rights in certain goods.

2. Why, according to the Coase theorem, will externalities tend to be internalized when property rights are clearly defined and information and transaction costs are low?

When property rights are clearly defined and information and transaction costs are low, whoever wants to exercise their right faces an opportunity cost of what others would pay for that right. That opportunity cost, represented by the potential payment from others to sell the right, is what forces decision makers to internalize what would otherwise be an externality.

3. How do transaction costs limit the market's ability to efficiently solve externality problems?

Transaction costs limit the ability of the market mechanism to internalize externalities because trading becomes more difficult. The free-rider problem—where those who benefit from some action cannot be forced to pay for it—also hinders the ability for voluntary trade across markets to generate efficient levels of goods such as cleaner air.

8.4 Public Goods

1. How are public goods different from private goods?

Private goods are rival in consumption (we can't both consume the same unit of a good) and exclusive (nonpayers can be prevented from consuming the good unless they pay for it). Public goods are nonrival in consumption (more than one person can consume the same good) and nonexclusive (nonpayers can't be effectively kept from consuming the good, even if they don't voluntarily pay for it).

2. Why does the free-rider problem arise in the case of public goods?

The free-rider problem arises in the case of public goods because people cannot be prevented from enjoying the benefits of public goods once they are provided. Therefore, people have an incentive not to voluntarily pay for those benefits, making it difficult or even impossible to finance the efficient quantity of public goods through voluntary market arrangements.

3. In what way can government provision of public goods solve the free-rider problem?

The government can overcome the free-rider problem by forcing people to pay for the provision of a public good through taxes.

4. What is a common resource?

A common resource good is rival in consumption but nonexcludable.

5. What is the tragedy of the commons?

Common resource goods often lead to overuse because if no one owns the resource, they are not likely to consider the cost of their use of the resource on others. This is the so-called tragedy of the commons. This problem has led to overfishing. Of course, you could remove the common and make the resource private property, but assigning private property rights to a vast ocean area would be virtually impossible.

8.5 Asymmetric Information

1. How do substantial warranties offered by sellers of used cars act to help protect buyers from the problem of asymmetric information and adverse selection? Why might too extensive a warranty lead to a moral hazard problem?

In the used-car market, the seller has superior information about the car's condition, placing the buyer at an information disadvantage. It also increases the chance that the car being sold is a "lemon." A substantial warranty can provide the buyer with valuable additional information about the condition of the car, reducing both asymmetric information and adverse selection problems.

Too extensive a warranty (e.g., an unlimited "bumper-to-bumper" warranty) will give the buyer less incentive to take care of the car because the buyer is effectively insured against the damage that lack of care would cause.

2. If where you got your college degree acted as a signaling device to potential employers, why would you want the school from which you graduated to raise its academic standards after you leave?

If an employer used your college's academic reputation as a signal of your likely "quality" as a potential employee, you want the school to raise its standards after you graduate because it would improve the average quality of its graduates, improving the quality it signals about you to an employer.

3. Why might withdrawals in several classes send a poor signal to potential employers?

It would indicate a failure to stick to difficult tasks relative to other students.

PROBLEMS

1. Indicate which of the following activities create a positive externality, a negative externality, or no externality at all.
   a. During a live theater performance, an audience member's cell phone rings loudly.
   b. You are given a flu shot.
   c. You purchase and drink a soda during a break from class.
   d. A college fraternity and sorority clean up trash along a 2 mile stretch on the highway.
   e. A firm dumps chemical waste into a local water reservoir.
   f. The person down the hall in your dorm plays loud music while you are trying to sleep.

2. Draw a standard supply-and-demand diagram for televisions, and indicate the equilibrium price and output.
   a. Assuming that the production of televisions generates external costs, illustrate the effect of the producers being forced to pay a tax equal to the external costs generated, and indicate the equilibrium output.
   b. If instead of generating external costs, television production generates external benefits, illustrate the effect of the producers being given a subsidy equal to the external benefits generated, and indicate the equilibrium output.

3. For each of the following goods, indicate whether they are nonrival and/or nonexclusive. Indicate whether they are private or public goods.
   a. Hot dogs
   b. Cable TV
   c. Broadcast TV
   d. Automobiles
   e. National defense
   f. Pollution control
   g. Parking in a parking structure
   h. A sunset
   i. Admission to a theme park

4. Is a lighthouse a public good if it benefits many ship owners? What if it primarily benefits ships going to a port nearby?

5. Why do you think buffaloes became almost completely extinct on the Great Plains but cattle did not? Why is it possible that you can buy a buffalo burger in a store or diner today?

6. What kind of problems does the government face when trying to perform a cost–benefit analysis of whether or how much of a public project to produce?

7. How does a TV broadcast have characteristics of a public good? What about cable services such as HBO?

8. In order to get a license to practice in the United States, foreign-trained veterinarians must take an exam given by the American Veterinary Association. Only 48 people per year are allowed to take the exam, which is administered at only two universities. The fee for the exam, which must be booked at least 18 months in advance, was recently raised from $2,500 to $6,000. What effects does this clinical competency exam have on the number of veterinarians practicing in the United States? Do you think it improves the quality of veterinary services?

9. How would the adverse selection problem arise in the insurance market? How is it like the "lemon" used-car problem?

10. In terms of signaling behavior:
    a. Why is wearing a suit a weaker signal of ability than higher educational achievement?
    b. Why do some majors in college provide more powerful signals to future employers than others?
    c. Why could double-majoring provide a more powerful labor market signal than having a single major?
    d. How would you explain why students might be said to "overinvest" in grades as opposed to learning course material?

11. In terms of moral hazard:
    a. Why does someone's willingness to pay a large deductible on an insurance policy tell an insurer something valuable about the seriousness of the moral hazard problem they might expect from the policyholder?
    b. Why does car insurance that explicitly excludes insuring the car for commercial use act to reduce moral hazard?
    c. Why does vehicle insurance based in part on miles driven reduce moral hazard problems?
    d. Why would a GPS monitor that can record the location and the speed a rental car is driven help reduce the moral hazard problem that rental companies are exposed to?

Public Finance and Public Choice

Ben Franklin is famous for saying that "nothing is certain but death and taxes." When Franklin made this statement, Americans were paying on average less than 5 percent of their income. Today, that figure is roughly 25 percent when you add up personal income taxes, sales taxes, corporate income taxes, payroll taxes, property taxes, and other taxes.

In the last chapter, we discussed the role of government in the case of externalities and public goods. We argued that the government can sometimes improve economic well-being by remedying externalities through pollution taxes, regulation and subsidies, and providing public goods.

In this chapter, we see how the government obtains revenues through taxation to provide these goods and services. We also examine the different types of taxation. The last section of the chapter is on public choice economics, the application of economic principles to politics.

Public Finance: Government Spending and Taxation   9.1

▶ How does government finance its spending?

▶ On what does the public sector spend its money?

▶ What are progressive and regressive taxes?

▶ What is a flat tax?

▶ What is the ability-to-pay principle?

▶ What is vertical equity?

▶ What is the benefits-received principle?

▶ What is a value-added tax?

9.1a Growth in Government

Government plays a large role in the economy, and its role increased markedly during World War II. From 1950 to 1975, government expenditures grew slowly from about 25 percent of GDP to 33 percent GDP. However, government expenditures increased sharply with the recession that began in 2008. By 2009, government expenditures reached a peacetime record of 39 percent of GDP, as seen in Exhibit 1.

National defense spending fluctuates with international tension. The aftermath of the terrorist attacks of September 11, 2001, and the wars in Iraq and Afghanistan, led to increases in defense spending. Consequently, defense spending, as a percentage of total federal spending, rose from 17 percent in 2001 to 20 percent in 2010. Terrorism is probably not going away anytime soon, so defense expenditures will most likely remain high; however, it was much higher in 1970, when it was 40 percent of federal expenditures (see Exhibit 2). The global

ECS

economic content standards

Most federal government tax revenue comes from individual income and payroll taxes. Payments to Social Security recipients, the costs of national defense, medical expenditures, and interest payments on the national debt constitute the bulk of federal government spending.

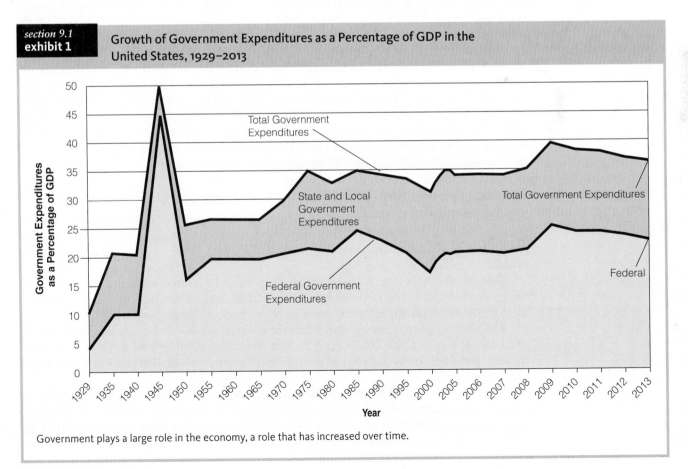

section 9.1 **exhibit 1**   Growth of Government Expenditures as a Percentage of GDP in the United States, 1929–2013

Government plays a large role in the economy, a role that has increased over time.

SOURCE: *Economic Report of the President,* 2014.

Federal Government Expenditures

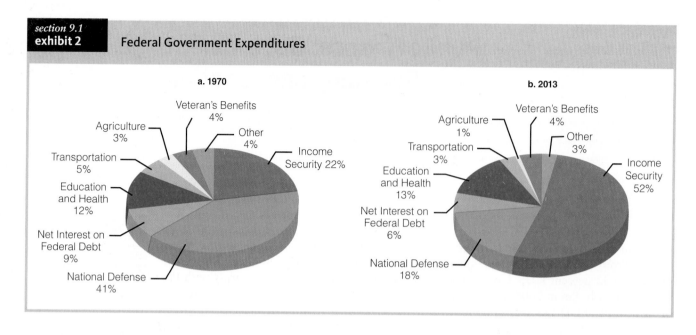

recession of 2008–2009 also expanded the size of government further. In addition, the Obama administration has created a greater role for government in the health care and energy sectors. Finally, as baby boomers age, there will be an even greater demand on public pensions and health care. Government spending will probably not be shrinking any time soon. Areas of government growth can be identified at least in part by looking at statistics on the types of government spending. In Exhibit 2, we compare federal expenditures in 1970 and 2013. In 2013, the largest category by far, was income security. This category includes Social Security, Medicare and income maintenance programs for the aged, persons with handicaps and disabilities, the unemployed, retired and families without breadwinners. In 2013, roughly 70 percent of income security expenditures was spent on Social Security and Medicare. Income security was only 22 percent of federal expenditures in 1970 and grew to over 52 percent by 2013.

The second largest federal expenditure category in 2013 was national defense; 18 percent of federal expenditures. But notice in Exhibit 2, national defense was much larger in 1970, when it was 41 percent of federal expenditures. Combined, income security and national defense, account for slightly over 70 percent of the federal outlays.

Mandatory Spending, Discretionary Spending, and Net Interest

Mandatory spending is government spending that is committed for the long run, such as Social Security and Medicare. Other mandatory programs include Medicaid (health care for the poor), retirement and disability programs. Current laws passed by Congress make it mandatory to fund these programs.

Discretionary spending includes programs that can be altered on an annual basis, when the government proposes a new budget. They include defense spending, payment to government workers, money for infrastructure like ports, bridges and highways, etc.

The final category is net interest. When the government borrows from the public it must pay interest, just as when you borrow from a bank. The payments made to owners of US treasury bond holders is included in net interest. They cannot be changed just by passing a new budget, either.

In recent years, much of the growth in federal expenditures has occurred in mandatory spending—particularly Social Security and Medicare. Today, Social Security and Medicare alone make up 8.5 percent of GDP. In 1962, that figure was less than 1 percent. Part of the explanation is demographics—an aging population—and part is due to expanded benefits. In short, the number of workers continues to decline relative to those receiving benefits, and benefits per recipient are also rising.

The fiscal challenge of a growing budget deficit can be answered by cutting costs, reducing benefits, raising taxes, or some combination of the three. That topic will be dealt with in the macroeconomic chapters of the text.

9.1b State and Local Spending

State and local spending differs greatly from federal spending. Education and health care account for roughly 55 percent of state and local expenditures. Other significant areas of state and local spending include highways, utilities, and police and fire protection.

9.1c Generating Government Revenue

economic content standards

Governments have to pay their bills like any person or institution that spends money. But how do they obtain revenue? In most years, a large majority of government activity is financed by taxation. What kinds of taxes are levied on the American population?

At the federal level, most taxes or levies are on income. Exhibit 3 shows that 81 percent of tax revenues come in the form of income taxes on individuals and Social insurance taxes (payroll taxes), which are levied on work-related income, that is, payrolls. These taxes are used to pay for Social Security and compulsory insurance plans such as Medicare. Payroll taxes are split between employees and employers. The Social Security share of federal taxes has steadily risen as the proportion of the population over age 65 has grown and as Social Security benefits have been increased.

At the state and local level, most of the revenue comes from sales taxes and property taxes. State and local governments also receive substantial funds from the federal government. States and local government also levy individual and corporate income taxes (see Exhibit 3). Consequently, payroll taxes have risen significantly in recent years. Other taxes, on such items as gasoline, liquor, and tobacco products, provide for a small proportion of government revenues, as do customs duties, estate and gift taxes, and some minor miscellaneous taxes and user charges.

The U.S. federal government relies more heavily on income-based taxes than nearly any other government in the world. Most other governments rely more heavily on sales taxes, excise taxes, and customs duties.

Most federal government tax revenue comes from personal income and payroll taxes. Payments to Social Security recipients, the costs of national defense, Medicare/Medicaid expenditures, and interest payments on the national debt constitute the bulk of federal government spending.

Most state and local government revenues come from sales taxes, grants from the federal government, personal income taxes, and property taxes. The bulk of state and local government revenue is spent for education, public welfare, road construction and repair, and public safety.

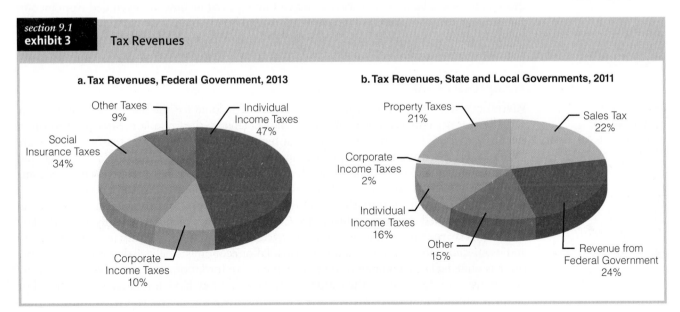

section 9.1
exhibit 3   Tax Revenues

a. Tax Revenues, Federal Government, 2013

Other Taxes 9%
Individual Income Taxes 47%
Social Insurance Taxes 34%
Corporate Income Taxes 10%

b. Tax Revenues, State and Local Governments, 2011

Property Taxes 21%
Sales Tax 22%
Corporate Income Taxes 2%
Individual Income Taxes 16%
Other 15%
Revenue from Federal Government 24%

SOURCE: *Economic Report of the President and Bureau of Economic Analysis,* 2014.

POLICY WATCH

Social Security: How Can We Save It?

What are the options for saving Social Security?

1. Increase the payroll taxes to a rate closer to 15 percent. It is currently 12.4 percent.

2. Increase the age of full-time benefits to age 70. The problem is that seniors already have a difficult time finding employment and may not be able to do the physical work expected of them.

3. Implement "means testing." Means testing would reduce the benefits to retirees who have "sufficient means" for retirement.

4. Increase the return to Social Security funds. The government might be interested in investing part of Social Security in the stock market. The historical returns are much greater in the stock market. The real rate of return (indexed for inflation) has been roughly 7 percent in the stock market compared with only 2 percent for government bonds. However, one of the drawbacks of government investment in the stock market is the potential for political abuse. With such a large amount of funds, the temptation emerges for the government to favor some firms and punish others.

5. Put some of the payroll tax in an individual retirement plan and let individuals manage their own funds—perhaps choosing from a list of mutual funds.

6. Let individuals choose to continue with the current Social Security system or contribute a minimum of, say, 10 percent or 20 percent of their wages to a private investment fund. This option has been tried in a number of Central and South American countries. In Chile, almost 90 percent of workers choose to leave the government Social Security program to invest privately.

Critics of the private plan argue that it is risky, individuals might make poor investment decisions, and the government might ultimately have to pay for their mistakes. That is, the stock market may have a good long-term track record, but it is still inherently uncertain and risky because of economic fluctuations. This may not be consistent with a guaranteed stream of retirement income.

A Progressive Tax

Progressive tax

a tax designed so that a larger percentage of taxable income is taken as taxable income increases.

One effect of substantial taxes on income is that the "take home" income of Americans is significantly altered by the tax system. Progressive taxes, of which the federal income tax is one example, are designed so that those with higher incomes pay a greater proportion of their income in taxes. A progressive tax is one tool that the government can use to redistribute income. It should be noted, however, that certain types of income are excluded from income for taxation purposes, such as interest on municipal bonds and income in kind—food stamps or Medicare, for example. The federal income tax is an example of a progressive income tax. Exhibit 4 shows the federal income tax brackets for a single taxpayer.

A Regressive Tax

regressive tax

a tax designed so that a smaller percentage of taxable income is taken as taxable income increases.

What is a progressive income tax?

Payroll taxes, the second most important source of income for the federal government, are actually regressive taxes, when considered alone. That is, they take a greater proportion of the income of lower-income groups than of higher-income groups. The reasons for this are simple. Social Security, for example, is imposed as a fixed proportion (6.2%) of wage and salary income up to $117,000 as of 2014. Also, wealthy persons have relatively more income from sources such as dividends and interest that are not subject to payroll taxes.

At first glance, it appears that employers and employees split the burden of the Social Security tax (called the Federal Insurance Contribution Act, or FICA) equally, since the law takes equal shares from employers and employees. However, recall our discussion of elasticity and its effects on the burden of taxation. Most labor economists believe that the labor supply curve is quite inelastic compared to the demand curve for labor. Since workers are relatively unresponsive to decreases in their after-tax wage rate (they have a relatively inelastic labor

section 9.1
exhibit 4

section 9.1 **exhibit 4** Federal Income Tax Brackets for Single Taxpayer, 2013	
Income	**Tax Rate**
$0–$8,925	10%
$8,926–$36,250	15
$36,251–$87,850	25
$87,851–$183,250	28
$183,251–$398,350	33
$398,351–$400,000	35
Over $400,000	39.6

SOURCE: Internal Revenue Service

section 9.1
exhibit 5   Payroll Tax

A payroll (FICA) tax puts "a wedge" between the wage firms pay and the wage workers receive. The wedge does not depend on whether the tax was imposed on the buyers or sellers. But the effects depend on elasticity of supply and demand. If, as most labor economists believe the supply of labor is less elastic than the demand for labor. The worker (not the firm) bears most of the burden of the payroll tax.

supply curve), employers can pass most of the tax on to employees in the form of lower wages, as seen in Exhibit 5.

Congress may have intended an even split on the payroll tax between workers and firms. That is, half is paid by employers and half is deducted from the paychecks of employees. However, the burden of the tax does not depend on whether it is levied on the buyer or the seller, but rather on the price elasticities of supply and demand.

An Excise Tax

Some consider an excise tax—a sales tax on individual products such as alcohol, tobacco, and gasoline—to be the most unfair type of tax because it is generally the most regressive. Excise taxes on specific items impose a far greater burden, as a percentage of income, on the poor and middle classes than on the wealthy because low-income families generally spend a greater proportion of their income on these items than do high-income families.

excise tax
a sales tax on individual products such as alcohol, tobacco, and gasoline

USE WHAT YOU'VE LEARNED

Marginal Versus Average Tax Rates

Suppose you make $100,000 this year. If you were a single taxpayer (ignoring exemptions and deductions), how much will you owe to the federal government on April 15 using the current marginal tax brackets? What is the difference between the marginal and average tax rates?

On the first $8,925 you will owe $892.50 (10% of $8,925). On the next $27,325 you will owe $4,098.75 (15% of $27,325). On the next $51,600 you will owe $12,900 (25%

of $51,600). And on the last $12,150 you will owe $3,402 (28% of $12,150). If we add this all together, you will need to write a check for $21,293.25 to the federal government. And your average tax rate would be roughly 21.29%. This is different than the marginal tax rate, the rate paid on your last dollar of income: 28 percent. Of course, many people will have exemptions and deductions to reduce the amount of income subject to taxes.

If a person who earns $20,000 a year spends $2,000 of it on lottery tickets, he will spend 10 percent of his income. However, if a person who earns $200,000 a year spends $2,000 of it on lottery tickets, she will only pay 1 percent. They both have the same chance of winning. But if people in different income brackets spend the same amount on the lottery, then the lottery acts as a regressive tax because it places a heavier burden on the poor than the rich. Studies show that lottery sales tend to be higher in zip codes where per capita income is lower. Thus, non-winning lottery tickets may act like a regressive tax for the state.

flat tax

a tax that charges all income earners the same percentage of their income

Excise taxes are sales taxes on goods like cigarettes and alcohol. This type of tax can impose a greater burden on the middle and lower class if they spend a greater proportion of their income on these items compared to higher income families.

In addition, excise taxes may lead to economic inefficiencies. By isolating a few products and subjecting them to discriminatory taxation, excise taxes subject economic choices to political manipulation, and leads to inefficiency.

9.1d Financing State and Local Government Activities

Historically, the primary source of state and local revenue has been property taxes. In recent decades, state and local governments have relied increasingly on sales and income taxes for revenues (see Exhibit 3). Today, sales taxes account for roughly 22 percent of revenues, property taxes account for 21 percent, and personal and corporate income taxes account for another 18 percent. Approximately 20 percent of state and local revenues come from the federal government as grants. The remaining share of revenues comes from license fees and user charges (e.g., payment for utilities, occupational license fees, tuition fees) and other taxes.

9.1e Should We Have a Flat Tax?

Some politicians and individuals believe that we should scrap the current progressive income tax and replace it with a **flat tax**. A flat tax, also called a proportional tax, is designed so that everybody would be charged the same percentage of their income. How would a flat tax work? What do you think would be the advantages and disadvantages of a flat tax?

With a flat tax, a household could simply report its income, multiply it by the tax rate, and send in the money. Because no deductions are involved, the form could be a simple page! But most flat tax proposals call for exempting income to a certain level—say, the poverty line.

Actually, if the flat tax plan allowed individuals to deduct a standard allowance of, say, $20,000 from their wages, the tax would still be progressive. Here's how it would work: If you were earning less than $20,000 a year, you would not have to pay any income taxes. However, if you earned $50,000 a year, and the flat tax rate was 15 percent, after subtracting your $20,000 allowance you would be paying taxes on $30,000. In this system, you would have to pay $4,500 in taxes ($0.15 \times \$30,000$) and your average tax rate would be 9 percent ($\$4,500/\$50,000 = 0.09$). Now, say you made $100,000 a year. After taking your $20,000 allowance, you would have to pay a 15 percent tax on $80,000, and you would owe the government $12,000. Notice, however, that your average tax rate would be higher: 12 percent ($\$12,000/\$100,000 = 0.12$) as opposed to 9 percent. So if the flat tax system allows individual taxpayers to take a standard allowance, like most flat tax proposals, then the tax is actually progressive. That is, lower- and middle-income families will pay, on average, a smaller average tax rate, even though everyone has the same marginal tax rate over the stipulated allowance.

The advantages of the flat tax are that all of the traditional exemptions, like entertainment deductions, mortgage interest deductions, business travel expenses, and charitable contribution deductions, would be out the door, along with the possibilities of abuses and misrepresentations that go with tax deductions. Taxpayers could fill out tax returns in the way they did in the old days, in a space about the size of a postcard. Advocates argue that the government could collect the same amount of tax revenues, but the tax would be much more efficient, as many productive resources would be released from looking for tax loopholes to doing something productive from society's standpoint.

Of course, some versions of the flat tax will hurt certain groups. Not surprisingly, realtors and home owners, who like the mortgage interest deductions, and tax accountants, who make billions every year preparing tax returns, will not be supportive of a flat tax with no deductions. And, of course, many legitimate questions would inevitably arise, such as: What would happen to the size of charitable contributions if the charitable contribution deduction was eliminated? And how much will the housing sector be hurt if the mortgage interest deduction was eliminated or phased out? After all, the government's intent of the tax break was to increase home ownership. And the deductions for hybrid cars are intended to get drivers into cleaner, more fuel-efficient cars. These deductions could be gone in most flat tax proposals. In addition, the critics of the flat tax believe that the tax is not progressive enough to eliminate the inequities in income and are skeptical of the tax-revenue-raising capabilities of a flat tax.

Some flat-tax proposals exclude taxing income from savings and investments like interest, dividends, and capital gains. This exemption is intended to encourage investment, saving, and economic growth. However, it raises some equity issues. Under this proposal, a family earning $70,000 a year would have to pay taxes while a wealthy retiree, living on his or her interest and dividends, might pay zero taxes. Is that fair?

In short, many people like the appeal of a flat tax but may not like the particulars. For example, think of middle-income households that would lose their mortgage interest deduction. Eliminating this exemption could lead to falling home values. Reworking the tax code might provide a better alternative.

9.1f Taxes: Efficiency and Equity

In the last few chapters, we talked about efficiency—getting the most out of our scarce resources. However, taxes for the most part are *not* efficient (except for internalizing externalities and providing public goods) because they change incentives and distort the values that buyers and sellers place on goods and services. That is, decisions made by buyers and sellers are different from what they would be without the tax. Taxes can be inefficient because they may lead to less work, less saving, less investment, and lower output.

Why are most taxes inefficient?

Economists spend a lot of time on issues of efficiency, but policy makers (and economists) are also concerned about other goals, such as fairness. Income redistribution through taxation may also lead to greater productivity for low-income workers through improvements in health and education. Even though what is fair to one person may not be fair to another, most people would agree that we should have a fair tax system based on either ability to pay or benefits received. While economists cannot determine the best balance between efficiency and equity, they can at least provide input on the trade-offs between efficiency and equity when they evaluate and design tax policies.

Ability-to-Pay Principle and Vertical Equity

The **ability-to-pay principle** is simply that those with the greatest ability to pay taxes (richer people) should pay more than those with the least ability to pay taxes (poorer people). This concept is known as **vertical equity**—people with different levels of income should be treated differently. The federal income tax is a good example of the ability-to-pay principle because the rich pay a larger percentage of their income in taxes. That is, high-income individuals will pay a higher percentage of their income in taxes than low-income individuals. Sales taxes are not a good example of the ability-to-pay principle because low-income individuals pay a larger percentage of their income in such taxes.

In Exhibit 6, we see three different tax systems. Under each tax system the rich pay more than the poor. Under the progressive system, the high-income taxpayers pay the largest fraction of their income. If it was a proportional tax system, each taxpayer would pay the same fraction of their income. And under a regressive tax system, the high-income taxpayers would pay a smaller fraction of their income but they still pay a larger absolute amount. All three of these systems deal with vertical equity, but no one system will be considered fair to everyone.

ability-to-pay principle
the belief that those with the greatest ability to pay taxes should pay more than those with less ability to pay

vertical equity
the concept that people with different levels of income should be treated differently

section 9.1 exhibit 6	Three Tax Systems					
	Progressive Tax		**Proportional Tax**		**Regressive Tax**	
Income	**Amount of Tax**	**Percentage of Income**	**Amount of Tax**	**Percentage of Income**	**Amount of Tax**	**Percentage of Income**
$50,000	$10,000	20%	$10,000	20%	$10,000	20%
100,000	25,000	25	20,000	20	15,000	15
200,000	60,000	30	40,000	20	20,000	10

In Exhibit 7, we see data for different income groups share in the federal tax burden. We break the groups into quintiles from lowest to highest and also look at the richest 1 percent of income earners. In column 2, we have average income. This includes income from work and savings and also transfer payments (such as Social Security and welfare). The poorest households had average income of $24,100 and the richest quintile had an average of $239,100 and the top 1 percent had average income of $1,434,900. The third column shows the progressive nature of the income tax. Notice that the lowest quintile only pays 1.5 of their income in federal taxes while the richest quintile pays 24 percent of their income and the top 1 percent pays 29.4 of their incomes. The last two columns show the distribution of income and the distribution of taxes. That is, the poorest quintile makes 5.1 of all the income and pays .04 percent of all the federal taxes. Compare this with the richest quintile, which earned 51.9 percent of the income and paid 68.8 percent of the taxes. The richest 1 percent earned almost 15 percent of the income and paid over 24 percent of the federal taxes. That is, 1/20th of the breadwinners paid almost one-quarter of the federal taxes.

However, this is just part of the story—the system is even more progressive because people in the bottom quintile receive more in transfers than they pay in taxes. That is, the average tax rate for the bottom quintile would be very negative.

There is no way to evaluate the current tax law objectively, but at least we can objectively see how much different families with different incomes pay.

Benefits-Received Principle

The *benefits-received principle* means that the individuals receiving the benefits are those who pay for them. Take the gasoline tax: the more miles one drives on the highway, the more gasoline used and the more taxes collected. The tax revenues are then used to maintain the highways. Or those who benefit from a new airport or an opera house should be the ones who pay for such public spending. Although this principle may work for some private goods, it does not work well for public goods such as national defense and the judicial system.

section 9.1 exhibit 7	Federal Tax Burden			
Quintile	**Average Income**	**Taxes as a Percentage of Income**	**Percentage of All Income**	**Percentage of All Taxes**
Lowest	$24,000	1.5%	5.1%	0.04%
Second	44,200	7.2	9.6	3.8
Middle	65,400	11.5	14.2	9.1
Fourth	95,500	15.6	20.4	17.6
Highest	239,100	24.0	51.9	68.8
Top 1%	1,434,900	29.4	14.9	24.2

SOURCE: *Congressional Budget Office (CBO)*, December 4, 2013.

USE WHAT YOU'VE LEARNED

The Burden of the Corporate Income Tax

Corporate income taxes are generally popular among voters because they think the tax comes from the corporation. Of course, it does write the check to the IRS, but that does not mean that the corporation (and its stockholders) bears the burden of the tax. Some of the tax burden (perhaps a great deal) is passed on to consumers in the form of higher prices. It will also impact investors' rates of return. Less investment leads to less capital for workers, which lowers workers' productivity and wages. So the tax appears to be paid by rich corporations but it is in the end borne by workers, customers, and those that own stocks in their retirement plans. The corporations are more tax collectors rather than taxpayers. If voters only knew, these taxes would be a lot less popular. The key here is to be careful to distinguish between who pays the tax and who incurs the burden of the tax.

Because we collectively consume national defense, it is not possible to find out who benefits and by exactly how much.

Administration Burden of Taxation

The administration burden of the income tax also leads to another deadweight loss. Imagine if everyone filled out a one-page tax form that took no more than 5 minutes. Instead the opportunity cost of the hours of time and services used in tax preparation is in the billions of dollars. The government also spends a great deal to enforce these taxes. A simplified tax system would reduce the deadweight loss.

Social Policy of Taxes

Taxes and subsidies can be efficiency enhancing when used to correct for externalities. For example, the government may view it as good social policy to subsidize cleaner, more efficient hybrid vehicles. Or they may want to put a high tax on cigarettes in an attempt to reduce teen smoking. In other words, taxes on alcohol and cigarettes may be used to discourage these activities—sometimes we call these "sin taxes."

POLICY WATCH

Should We Have a Consumption Tax?

In Chapter 8, we discussed the deadweight loss associated with taxes. A higher marginal tax rate on income may discourage people from working as hard as they otherwise would. In addition, the individual income tax might discourage people from saving.

Consequently, many economists favor the idea of replacing the individual income tax with a consumption tax. A consumption tax would tax the amount that is spent rather than what is earned. In that sense, people are taxed based on what they take out of the economy, not on what they earn (in exchange for the benefits provided to others).

Under a consumption tax, saved income is not taxed. As a result, people would save more. That would provide increased funds for investment, which would expand the capital stock over time, increasing worker productivity, economic output, and real wages.

Unfortunately, there are issues with transitioning from an income tax to a consumption tax. Some argue that low-income individuals spend a large fraction of their income, and therefore save little, so they would benefit little from a consumption tax. The transition from an income tax to a consumption tax would also shift tax burdens to older generations that would have to pay a consumption tax on spending, in addition to the income taxes they already had to pay when that income was earned. And equity issues might require a phase-in period, which would increase tax complexity during that period. Furthermore, people can already invest in individual retirement accounts (IRAs), which allow them to defer paying taxes until after retirement, much like with a consumption tax.

SECTION QUIZ

1. Which of the following are important roles of the government?

   a. Protecting property rights

   b. Providing a legal system

   c. Intervening when insufficient competition occurs in the marketplace

   d. Promoting stability and economic growth

   e. All of the above

2. Social Security and Medicare are financed by

   a. personal income taxes.

   b. payroll taxes.

   c. excise taxes.

   d. corporation income taxes.

   e. none of the above taxes.

3. Who must legally pay social security and medicare taxes?

   a. Employers

   b. Employees

   c. Both employers and employees

   d. Neither employers nor employees

4. Expenditures on _____ comprise the largest component of state and local government budgets.

   a. education

   b. public safety

   c. public infrastructure (such as roads and water works)

   d. public welfare (such as food stamps and income supplemental programs)

5. _____ taxes are designed to take a larger percentage of high incomes as compared to lower incomes.

   a. Progressive

   b. Regressive

   c. Proportional

   d. Negative

6. An example of a proportional tax would be

   a. a state sales tax.

   b. a local property tax.

   c. a flat rate income tax.

   d. the current U.S. income tax.

7. The largest single source of revenue for the federal government is the

   a. corporate income tax.

   b. federal excise tax.

   c. personal income tax.

   d. social security tax.

8. The U.S. federal income tax is an example of a

   a. progressive tax.

   b. proportional tax.

   c. regressive tax.

   d. value-added tax.

(continued)

SECTION QUIZ (cont.)

9. The ability-to-pay principle states:

   a. Those with the greatest ability to pay taxes should pay more.

   b. Those with the least ability to pay taxes should pay more.

   c. Individuals receiving the benefits should pay for them.

   d. All of the above are true.

---

1. Has federal government spending as a fraction of GdP changed much since the 1960s?

2. What finances the majority of federal government spending?

3. What happens to the proportion of income paid as taxes when income rises, for a progressive tax? What is an example of such a progressive tax?

4. Why are excise taxes on items such as alcohol, tobacco, and gasoline considered regressive taxes?

5. How could a flat tax also be a progressive tax?

6. Why is the federal income tax an example of the ability-to-pay principle?

7. How is a gas tax an example of the benefits-received principle?

Answers: 1. e 2. b 3. c 4. a 5. a 6. c 7. c 8. a 9. a

. . . .

Public Choice 9.2

▶ What is public choice theory?
▶ What is the median voter model?

▶ What is rational ignorance?
▶ Why do special interest groups arise?

When the market fails, as in the case of an externality or public good, it may be necessary for the government to intervene and make public choices. However, it is possible for government actions in response to externalities to make matters worse. Our discussion of public goods considered what goods the government should provide, like national defense or flood control programs, but it did not specify how much of the public good the government would provide. How many new jet fighters, missiles, or aircraft carriers? The same is true with law enforcement and environmental protection: how much should the government provide? In addition, as we discussed in the section on public goods, we do not know the true demand for public services. A vote does not signal how much an individual values that good or service. What if 51 percent of the voters are going to vote for a new highway but do not have very strong preferences while 49 percent felt very strongly that the highway should not get built? The highway is built. The political system uses majority rules. The market system uses a proportional rule; so if 20 percent of the dollar votes want hybrid vehicles, 20 percent of the money would go to purchase hybrids. That is, just because markets have failed to generate efficient results does not necessarily mean that government can do a better job. One explanation for this outcome is presented by public choice theory.

ECS
economic content standards

Costs of government policies sometimes exceed benefits. This may occur because voters, government officials, and government employees have opposing incentives; actions by special interest groups can impose costs on the general public; or social goals other than economic efficiency are being pursued.

9.2a What Is Public Choice Theory?

Public choice theory is the application of economic principles to politics. Public choice economists believe that government actions are an outgrowth of individual behavior. Specifically, they assume that the behavior of individuals in politics, as in the marketplace, will be influenced by self-interest. Bureaucrats, politicians, and voters make choices that they believe will yield them expected marginal benefits that will be greater than their expected marginal costs. Of course, the private sector and the public sector differ when it comes to the "rules of the game" that they must follow. The self-interest assumption is, however, central to the analysis of behavior in both arenas.

9.2b Scarcity and the Public Sector

The self-interest assumption is not the only similarity between the market and public sectors. For example, scarcity is present in the public sector as well as in the private sector. Public schools and public libraries come at the expense of something else. While the cost to the consumer of a new park may seem free—zero price—like everything else, it has an opportunity cost. What else could that land be used for? Competition is also present in the public sector, as different government agencies compete for government funds and lobbyists compete with each other to get favored legislation through Congress.

9.2c The Individual Consumption–Payment Link

In private markets, when a shopper goes to the supermarket to purchase groceries, the shopping cart is filled with many different goods that the consumer presumably wants and is willing to pay for; the shopping cart reflects the individual consumption–payment link. The link breaks down when an assortment of political goods is decided on by majority rule. These political goods might include such items as additional national defense, additional money for the space program, new museums, new public schools, increased foreign aid, and so on. Even though an individual may be willing to pay for some of these goods, it is unlikely that she will want to consume or pay for everything placed in the political shopping cart. However, if the majority decides that these political goods are important, the individual will have to purchase the goods through higher taxes, whether she values the goods or not.

9.2d Majority Rule and the Median Voters

In a two-party system, the candidate with the most votes wins the election. Because voters are likely to vote for the candidate who holds views similar to theirs, candidates must pay close attention to the preferences of the majority of voters.

For example, in Exhibit 1, we assume a normal distribution, with a continuum of voter preferences from the liberal left to the conservative right. We can see from the figure that only a few are extremely liberal or extremely conservative. A successful campaign would have to address the concerns of the median voters (those in the middle of the distribution in Exhibit 1), resulting in moderate policies. For example, if one candidate ran a fairly conservative campaign, attracting voters at and to the right of V_1, an opponent could win by a landslide by taking a fairly conservative position just to the left of this candidate. Alternatively, if the candidate takes a liberal position, say V_2, then the opponent can win by campaigning just to the right of that position. In this case, it is easy to see that the candidate who takes the median position, V_M, is least likely to be defeated. Of course, the distribution does not

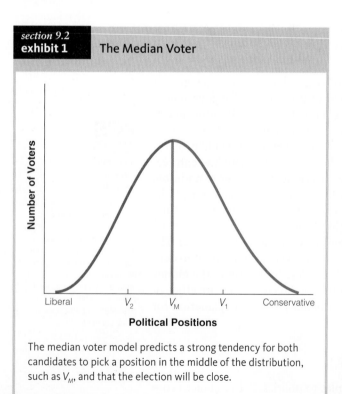

section 9.2 exhibit 1   **The Median Voter**

Political Positions

(x-axis labels: Liberal, V_2, V_M, V_1, Conservative; y-axis label: Number of Voters)

The median voter model predicts a strong tendency for both candidates to pick a position in the middle of the distribution, such as V_M, and that the election will be close.

have to be normal or symmetrical; it could be skewed to the right or left. Regardless of the distribution, however, the successful candidate will still seek out the median voters. In fact, the median voter model predicts a strong tendency for both candidates to choose a position in the middle of distribution, and therefore the election will be close. If the model predicts correctly, then the median voter will determine the outcome of the election because those voters whose preferences are in the tails—the two extremes—will prefer the middle position rather than the other extreme position.

median voter model
a model that predicts candidates will choose a position in the middle of the distribution

Of course, this model does not mean that all politicians will find or even attempt to find the median. Politicians, for example, may take different positions because they have arrived at different predictions of voter preferences or have merely misread public sentiment; or they may think they have the charisma to change voter preferences.

9.2e **Voters and Rational Ignorance**

Representative democracy provides a successful mechanism for making social choices in many countries. But some important differences are evident in the way democracy is ideally supposed to work and how it actually works.

One of the keys to an efficiently working democracy is a concerned and informed electorate. Everyone is supposed to take time to study the issues and candidates and then carefully weigh the relevant information before deciding how to vote. Although an informed citizenry is desirable from a social point of view, it is not clear that individuals will find it personally desirable to become politically informed.

Obtaining detailed information about issues and candidates is costly. Many issues are complicated, and a great deal of technical knowledge and information is necessary to make an informed judgment on them. To find out what candidates are really going to do requires a lot more than listening to their campaign slogans. It requires studying their past voting records, reading a great deal that has been written either by or about them, and asking them questions at public meetings. Taking the time and trouble to do these things—and more—is the cost that each eligible voter has to pay personally for the benefits of being politically informed. These costs may help to explain why the majority of Americans cannot identify their congressional representatives and are unlikely to be acquainted with their representatives' views on Social Security, health care, tariffs, and agricultural policies.

Are political goals and economic goals always the same?

For many people, the costs of becoming politically informed are high, whereas the benefits are low. As a result, they limit their quest for political information to listening to the radio on the way to work, talking with friends, casual reading, and other things they would normally do anyway. Even though most people in society might be better off if everyone became more informed, it isn't worth the cost for most individuals to make the requisite effort to become informed themselves. Public choice economists refer to this lack of incentive to become informed as rational ignorance. People will generally make much more informed decisions as buyers than as voters. For example, you are likely to gather more information when making a decision on a car purchase than when you are deciding between candidates in an upcoming election. An uninformed decision on a car purchase will most likely affect your life much more than an uninformed decision on a candidate, especially when your vote will most likely not alter the outcome of the election. Because you cannot disbundle, you are voting for a candidate who takes a stand on many issues—that is, you are voting on a bundle of issues that are difficult to assess.

rational ignorance
lack of incentive to be informed

Can we predict what would happen to voter turnout on a day like this? Some potential voters might rationally decide to stay home if they perceive the cost of going to the polls outweighs the benefit.

The fact that one vote, especially in a state or national election, is highly unlikely to affect the outcome of the election may explain why some citizens choose not to vote.

Many factors may determine the net benefits for voting, including candidates and issues on the ballot, weather, and distance to the polling booths. For example, we would certainly expect fewer voters to turn out at the polls on the day of a blizzard; the blizzard would change the net benefits. We would also expect more voters at the polls if the election were predicted to be a close one, with emotions running higher and voters perceiving their individual votes as more significant.

If the cost of being an informed voter is high and the benefits low, why do people vote? Many people vote for reasons other than to affect the outcome of the election. They vote because they believe in the democratic process and because of civic pride. In other words, they perceive that the benefits they derive from being involved in the political process outweigh the costs.

Furthermore, rational ignorance does not imply that people should not vote; it is merely one explanation for why some people do not vote. The point that public choice economists are making is that some people will vote only if they think that their vote will make a difference; otherwise, they will not vote.

9.2f Special Interest Groups

Even though many voters may be uninformed about specific issues, others may feel a strong need to be politically informed. Such individuals may be motivated to organize a **special interest group**. These groups may have intense feelings about and a degree of interest in particular issues that is at variance with the general public. However, as a group these individuals are more likely to influence decision makers and have a far greater impact on the outcome of a political decision than they would with their individual votes.

If a special interest group is successful in getting everyone else to pay for a project that benefits them, the cost will be spread over so large a number of taxpayers that the amount any one person will have to pay is negligible. Hence, the motivation for an individual citizen to spend the necessary time and effort to resist an interest group is minimal, even if she had a guarantee that this resistance would be effective.

Public choice economists believe that if government becomes a vehicle for promoting special interests, it fails in its primary responsibility of expanding opportunities for all. That is, instead of creating opportunities to benefit through productive cooperation with each other, government will have created the illusion that people can benefit at the expense of each other. Public choice economists are not callously indifferent to the social benefits that government can provide. In fact, the difference between public choice economists and those who see every social ill as justification for expanding government is not a difference in moral vision. Instead, it is a difference in their interpretation of how government works. Public choice economists lean toward less government not because they want less from government, but because they, like many others, want less waste from government.

Politicians and Logrolling

Sometimes members of Congress engage in **logrolling**. Logrolling involves politicians trading votes for their legislation. For example, Representative A may tell Representative B that he will vote for her water bill if she votes for his new highway bill. Of course, if Representative B does not go along with Representative A's legislation, she runs the risk of not getting support for her legislation at a later date. Local projects such as federally funded dams, bridges, highways, housing projects, VA hospitals, job-training centers, and military bases are often pushed through Congress and state legislatures by logrolling.

The trading of votes could lead to an outcome where the majority of Congress now supports the economic interests of a few at the economic expense of many. This is especially true if the cost to the many is so low that they are rationally ignorant to the effects of rent-seeking behavior. Rent seeking occurs when individuals and firms use resources, like money and lobbyists, to influence government to grant them special privileges.

SECTION QUIZ

1. The amount of information that is necessary to make an efficient choice is generally _____ in the public sector than in the private sector.

   a. less

   b. more

   c. the same

   d. None of the above is true.

2. Voters will tend to be _____ informed about their political choices than their private market choices, other things being equal.

   a. more

   b. equally

   c. less

   d. Any of the above are equally likely to be true.

3. The median voter result implies that

   a. elections will often be very close.

   b. elections will usually be landslides for the same party year after year.

   c. elections will usually be landslides, with victories alternating between parties each year.

   d. when the preferences of most voters change substantially, winning political positions will also tend to change.

   e. both (a) and (d) are true.

4. For a voter to become more informed on a political issue is likely to have _____ benefits and _____ costs than for similar market decisions, other things being equal.

   a. smaller; larger

   b. smaller; smaller

   c. larger; larger

   d. larger; smaller

5. Which of the following would tend to raise voter turnout?

   a. a blizzard or heavy rainstorm on election day

   b. an election that is expected to be a landslide

   c. the longer the wait is expected to be at the voting locations

   d. a feeling that the candidates are basically running on the same platforms

   e. none of the above would tend to raise voter turnout.

6. if there are far fewer sugar growers than sugar consumers,

   a. the growers are likely to be more informed and influential on policy than voters.

   b. the consumers are likely to be more informed and influential on policy than voters.

   c. individual sugar growers are likely to have more at stake than individual sugar consumers.

   d. individual sugar consumers are likely to have more at stake than individual sugar growers.

   e. Because (c) is likely to be true, (a) is also likely to be true.

(continued)

SECTION QUIZ (cont.)

1. What principles does the public choice analysis of government behavior share with the economic analysis of market behavior?

2. Why is the tendency strong for candidates to choose positions in the middle of the distribution of voter preferences?

3. Why is it rational to be relatively less informed about most political choices than about your own market choices?

4. Why can't the majority of citizens effectively counter the political power of special interest groups?

Answers: 1. b 2. c 3. e 4. a 5. d 6. e

INTERACTIVE SUMMARY

Fill in the blanks:

1. Governments obtain revenue through two major avenues: _____ and _____.

2. The government share of GDP changed _____ between 1975 and 2013, but its composition has changed _____.

3. From 1970 to 2013, national defense spending as a fraction of GDP _____.

4. By the mid-1970s, for the first time in history, roughly half of government spending in the United States was for _____.

5. Income transfer payments _____ in the 1980s and 1990s.

6. _____ and _____ account for roughly half of state and local government expenditures.

7. At the federal level, _____ half of taxes are from personal income taxes and corporate income taxes.

8. The United States relies _____ heavily on income-based taxes than most other developed countries in the world.

9. If a higher-income person paid the same taxes as a lower-income person, that tax would be considered _____.

10. Excise taxes are considered regressive because lower-income people spend a(n) _____ fraction of their incomes on such taxes than do higher-income people.

11. Sales taxes account for _____ state and local tax revenue than property taxes.

12. Most people agree that the tax system should be based on either _____ or _____.

13. When people with different levels of income are treated differently, it is called _____ equity.

14. Federal income tax is a good example of the _____ principle.

15. The _____ principle means that the individuals receiving the benefits are those who pay for them.

16. The _____ burden of a tax leads to a deadweight loss.

17. With a(n) _____ tax, individuals are taxed on what they take out of the economy, not on what they put in.

18. Public choice theory is the application of _____ principles to politics.

19. Public choice economists believe that the behavior of individuals in politics, as in the marketplace, will be influenced by _____.

20. The amount of information that is necessary to make an efficient decision is much _____ in political markets than in private markets.

21. In private markets, an individual _____ link indicates that the goods consumers get reflect what they are willing to pay for.

22. Even though actors in both the private and public sectors are _____, the _____ are different.

23. A successful political campaign would have to address the concerns of the _____ voters.

24. _____ implies that most private-sector buyers will tend to be more informed than voters on a given issue.

25. If voters were _____ informed, special-interest groups would have less influence on political results, other things being equal.

26. Compared to private-sector decisions, acquiring information to make public-sector decisions will tend to have _____ benefits and _____ costs.

27. _____ positions tend to win in elections decided by majority votes.

Answers: 1. taxation; borrowing 2. little; considerably 3. fell 4. social concerns 5. increased 6. Education; public welfare 7. more than 8. more 9. regressive 10. larger 11. more 12. ability-to-pay 13. vertical 14. ability-to-pay 15. benefits-received 16. administrative 17. consumption 18. economic 19. self-interest 20. greater 21. consumption-payment 22. self-interested; "rules of the game" 23. median 24. Rational ignorance 25. more 26. smaller; larger 27. Middle-of-the-road

progressive tax 242
regressive tax 242
excise tax 243
flat tax 244

ability-to-pay principle 245
vertical equity 245
median voter model 251
rational ignorance 251

special interest groups 252
logrolling 252

9.1 Public Finance: Government spending and Taxation

1. **Has federal government spending as a fraction of GDP changed much since the 1960s?**
Overall federall government spending as a fraction of GDP has not changed much since the 1960s. However, the composition of federal government spending has changed, with substantial decreases in national defense spending and substantial increases in income security spending, such as for Social Security and Medicare.

2. **What finances the majority of federal government spending?**
The majority of federal government spending is financed by taxes on personal and corporate incomes, although payroll taxes have risen substantially in recent years.

3. **What happens to the proportion of income paid as taxes when income rises, for a progressive tax? What is an example of such a progressive tax?**
A progressive tax is one that takes an increasing proportion of income as income rises. The personal income tax is an example because higher-income

earners pay a larger proportion of their incomes than lower-income earners.

4. **Why are excise taxes on items such as alcohol, tobacco, and gasoline considered regressive taxes?**
Lower-income people pay a larger fraction of their incomes for such items, so that they pay a larger fraction of their incomes for taxes on those items, even though all users pay the same tax rate on them.

5. **How could a flat tax also be a progressive tax?**
With a standard allowance or deduction amount, a proportional tax on taxable income would represent a larger fraction of total income for a high-income earner than for a low-income earner.

6. **Why is the federal income tax an example of the ability-to-pay principle?**
Higher-income people, with a greater ability to pay, pay a larger fraction of their income in taxes.

7. **How is a gas tax an example of the benefits received principle?**
Those who drive more benefit more from the highway system, but they also pay more in total gasoline taxes.

9.2 Public Choice

1. What principles does the public choice analysis of government behavior share with the economic analysis of market behavior?

Public choice analysis of government behavior is based on the principle that the behavior of individuals in politics, just like that in the marketplace, is influenced by self-interest. That is, it applies basic economic theory to politics, looking for differences in incentives to explain people's behavior.

2. Why is the tendency strong for candidates to choose positions in the middle of the distribution of voter preferences?

This is what we would predict from the median voter model because the candidate closer to the median is likely to attract a majority of the votes.

3. Why is it rational to be relatively less informed about most political choices than about your own market choices?

It is rational to be relatively less informed about most political choices because the costs of becoming more informed about political issues tend to be higher and the benefits of becoming more informed about political choices tend to be lower than for your own market choices.

4. Why can't the majority of citizens effectively counter the political power of special interest groups?

The majority of citizens can't effectively counter the political power of special interest groups because even if a special interest group is successful in getting everyone else to pay for a project that benefits that group, the cost to each citizen will be small. In fact, this cost is very likely to be far smaller than the cost to a member of the majority of becoming sufficiently informed and active to successfully oppose it.

PROBLEMS

1. Why would means-tested transfer payments (such as food stamps, in which benefits are reduced as income rises) act like an income tax facing recipents?

2. Why are income taxes more progressive than excise taxes such as those on alcohol, tobacco, and gasoline?

3. Why is the Social Security payroll tax considered regressive?

4. Could the burdens of a regulation be either progressive or regressive, like the effects of a tax?

5. Is a gas tax better described as reflecting the ability-to-pay principle or the benefits-received principle? What about the federal income tax?

6. Why would the benefits-received principle be difficult to apply to national defense and the provision of the justice system?

7. Illustrate the median voter model graphically and explain it.

8. Why would a candidate offering "a choice, not an echo," run a risk of losing in a landslide?

9. Why might the party favorites at a political convention sometimes be harder to elect than more moderate candidates?

10. How can you be forced to pay for something you do not want to "buy" in the political sector? Is this sometimes good?

11. Why does the creation of a government program create a special interest group, which makes it difficult to reduce or eliminate it in the future?

12. Why are college students better informed about their own teachers' and schools' policies than about national education issues?

13. Why do you think news reporters are more informed than average citizens about public policy issues?

TECHNOTR/VETTA/GETTY IMAGES

PART 4

Households and Market Structure

Consumer Choice Theory

Why do most individuals take only one newspaper from covered, coin-operated newspaper racks when it would be so easy to take more? Do you think potato chips, candy, or sodas could be sold profitably in the same kind of dispenser? Although ethical considerations keep some people from taking additional papers, the law of diminishing marginal utility is also at work here. The second newspaper adds practically zero utility to most individuals on most days, so they typically feel no incentive to take more than one.

On the other hand, if putting money in a vending machine gave access to many bags of potato chips, candy bars, or sodas, the temptation to take more than one might be too great for some people. After all, the potato chip bags would still be good tomorrow. Therefore, vending machines with foods and drinks only dispense one item at a time because it is likely that, for most people, the marginal utility gained from another unit of food or drink is higher than for a second newspaper.

In this chapter, we discuss how individuals allocate their income between different bundles of goods. This decision involves trade-offs—if you buy more of one good, you cannot afford as much of other goods. How do we as consumers choose certain bundles of goods with our available budget to fit our desires? We address these questions in this chapter to strengthen our understanding of the law of demand.

Consumer Behavior | 10.1

▶ What is utility?

▶ Can we make interpersonal utility comparisons?

▶ What is diminishing marginal utility?

As you may recall from Chapter 4, the law of demand is intuitive. Put simply, at a higher price, consumers will buy less (a decrease in the quantity demanded); at a lower price, consumers will buy more (an increase in quantity demanded), *ceteris paribus*. However, the downward-sloping demand curve has three other explanations: (1) the income and substitution effects of a price change, (2) the law of diminishing marginal utility, and (3) an interpretation using indifference curves and budget lines (in the appendix).

Let's start with out first explanation of a downward-sloping demand curve—the substitution and income effects of a price change. For example, if the price of pizza increases, the quantity of pizza demanded will fall because some consumers might switch out of pizza into hamburgers, tacos, burritos, submarine sandwiches, or some other foods that substitute for pizza. This behavior is called the **substitution effect** of a price change. In addition, a price increase for pizza will reduce the quantity of pizza demanded because it reduces a buyer's purchasing power. The buyer cannot buy as many pieces of pizza at higher prices as she could at lower prices, which is called the **income effect** of a price change.

The second explanation for the negative relationship between price and quantity demanded is what economists call **diminishing marginal utility**. In a given time period, a buyer will receive less satisfaction from each successive unit consumed. For example, a second ice cream cone will yield less satisfaction than the first, a third less satisfaction than the second, and so on. It follows from diminishing marginal utility that if people are deriving less satisfaction from successive units, consumers would buy added units only if the price were reduced. Let's now take a closer look at utility theory.

Economists conducted an experiment with rats to see how they would respond to changing prices of different drinks (changing the number of times a rat had to press a bar). Rats responded by choosing more of the beverage with a lower price, showing they were willing to substitute when the price changed. That is, even rats seem to behave rationally—responding to incentives and opportunities to make themselves better off.

substitution effect
a consumer's switch to another similar good when the price of the preferred good increases

income effect
reduction in quantity demanded of a good when its price increases because of a consumer's decreased purchasing power

diminishing marginal utility
a good's ability to provide less satisfaction with each successive unit consumed

utility
a measure of the relative levels of satisfaction consumers get from consumption of goods and services

util
one unit of satisfaction

Can we accurately compare utility between two people?

10.1a Utility

To more clearly define the relationship between consumer choice and resource allocation, economists developed the concept of **utility**—a measure of the relative levels of satisfaction that consumers get from the consumption of goods and services. Defining one **util** as equivalent to one unit of satisfaction, economists can indicate relative levels of consumer satisfaction that result from alternative choices. For example, for a coffee lover who wouldn't dream of starting the day without a strong dose of caffeine, a cup of coffee might generate 150 utils of satisfaction while a cup of herbal tea might only generate 10 utils.

Inherently, utility varies from individual to individual depending on specific preferences. For example, Jason might get 50 utils of satisfaction from eating his first piece of apple pie, while Brittany might only derive 4 utils of satisfaction from her first piece of apple pie.

In fact, a whole school of thought called utilitarianism, based on utility theory, was developed by Jeremy Bentham. Bentham believed that society should seek the greatest happiness for the greater number. (See Bentham's biography.)

10.1b Utility Is a Personal Matter

Economists recognize that it is not really possible to make interpersonal utility comparisons. That is, they know that it is impossible to compare the relative satisfactions of different persons. The relative satisfactions gained by two people drinking cups of coffee, for example, simply cannot be measured in comparable terms. Likewise, although we might be tempted to believe that a poorer person would derive greater utility from finding a $100 bill than would a richer person,

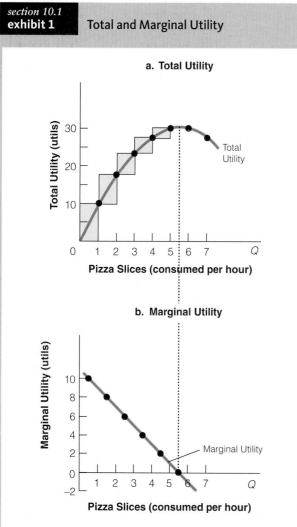

section 10.1
exhibit 1   Total and Marginal Utility

a. Total Utility

As you can see in (a), the total utility from pizza increases as consumption increases. In (b) marginal utility decreases as consumption increases. That is, as you eat more pizza, your satisfaction from each additional slice diminishes.

Slices of Pizza (per day)	Total Utility (utils)	Marginal Utility (utils)
0	0	
		10
1	10	
		8
2	18	
		6
3	24	
		4
4	28	
		2
5	30	
		0
6	30	
		−2
7	28	

How many utils is this woman deriving from this cup of coffee? Can we accurately compare her satisfaction from a cup of coffee with another person's?

ROBERT L. SEXTON

we should resist the temptation. We simply cannot prove it. The poorer person may be "monetarily" poor because money and material things are not important to her, and the rich person may have become richer because of his lust for the things money can buy.

10.1c **Total Utility and Marginal Utility**

Economists recognize two different dimensions of utility: total utility and marginal utility. **Total utility** is the total amount of satisfaction derived from the consumption of a certain number of units of a good or service. In comparison, **marginal utility** is the extra satisfaction generated by an additional unit of a good that is consumed in a particular time period. For example, eating four slices of pizza in an hour might generate a total of 28 utils of satisfaction. The first three slices of pizza might generate a total of 24 utils, while the last slice generates only 4 utils. In this case, the total utility of eating four slices of pizza is 28 utils, and the marginal utility of the fourth slice is 4 utils. Notice in Exhibit 1(a) how total utility increases as consumption increases (we see more total utility after the fourth slice of pizza than after the third). But notice, too, that the increase in total utility from each additional unit (slice) is less than the unit before, which indicates the marginal utility. In Exhibit 1(b) we see how the marginal utility falls as consumption increases.

total utility
total amount of satisfaction derived from the consumption of a certain number of goods or services

marginal utility
extra satisfaction generated by consumption of an additional good or service during a specific time period

USE WHAT YOU'VE LEARNED

The Diamond-Water Paradox: Marginal and Total Utility

"Nothing is more useful than water: but it will not purchase scarce anything. . . . Diamond, on the contrary, has scarce any value in use; but a very great quantity of other goods may frequently be had in exchange for it."

—Adam Smith, *Wealth of Nations*, 1776

C SQUARED STUDIOS/PHOTODISC/GETTY IMAGES

Q Why are those things that are necessary for life, like water, are inexpensive, and those items that are not necessary for life, like diamonds, are expensive?

A The classic diamond–water paradox puzzled philosophers for centuries. The answer lies in making the distinction between total utility and marginal utility. The amount of total utility is indeed higher for water than for diamonds because of its importance for survival. But price is not determined by total utility; it is determined by marginal utility. Total utility measures the total amount of satisfaction someone derives from a good, whereas marginal utility determines the price. Market value—the value of the last, or marginal, unit traded—depends on both supply and demand. Thus, the limited supply of diamonds relative to the demand generates a high price, but an abundant supply of water relative to the demand results in a low price. The total utility (usefulness) for water is very large compared to the marginal utility. Because the price of water is so low, we use so much water

that the marginal utility we receive from the last glass of water is small. Diamonds have a much smaller total utility (usefulness) relative to water, but because the price of diamonds is so high, we buy so few diamonds that they have a high marginal utility. Could water ever have a higher marginal utility than diamonds? Yes, if you had no water and no diamonds, your first cup of water would give you a much higher marginal value than your first cup of diamonds. Furthermore, if diamonds were very plentiful and water was very scarce, which would have the higher marginal utility? In this case, water would be expensive and diamonds would be inexpensive.

10.1d **Diminishing Marginal Utility**

diminishing marginal utility

the concept that states that as an individual consumes more and more of a good, each successive unit generates less and less utility (or satisfaction)

Although economists believe that total utility increases with additional consumption, they also argue that the incremental satisfaction—the marginal utility—that results from the consumption of additional units tends to decline as consumption increases. In other words, each successive unit of a good that is consumed generates less satisfaction than did the previous unit. This concept is traditionally referred to as the diminishing marginal utility. Exhibit 1(b) demonstrates this graphically, where the marginal utility curve has a negative slope.

GREAT ECONOMIC THINKERS

Jeremy Bentham (1748–1832)

Jeremy Bentham was born in London in 1748. He was a gifted child, reading history and other "serious" books at age 3, playing the violin at age 5, and studying Latin and French when he was only 6. At 12, he entered Queens College, in Oxford, where he studied law. In his late teens, Bentham decided to concentrate on his writings. With funding provided by his father, he wrote a series of books on philosophy, economics, and politics. He would often write for 8 to 12 hours a day, a practice that continued through his life, leaving scholars material to compile for years to come. Most of his writings were not published until well over a century after his death.

Jeremy Bentham was a social philosopher. His most famous contribution to economics was the idea of utility and how it was a driving force in economic and social behavior. According to Bentham, "pain and pleasure are the sovereign masters governing man's conduct": People will tend to pursue things that are pleasurable and avoid things that are painful. To this day, the rule of rational choice—weighing marginal benefits against marginal costs—has its roots in the earlier works of Jeremy Bentham. That is, economists predict human behavior on the basis of people's responses to changing incentives; people make choices on the basis of their expected marginal benefits and their expected marginal costs.

Although Bentham was most well known for utilitarianism, a philosophy stemming from his rational-choice ideas, he also had much to say on the subjects of prison reform, religion, relief to the poor, international law, and animal welfare. He was an ardent advocate of equality. Good humored, meditative, and kind, he was thought to be a visionary and ahead of his time.

Bentham died in London in 1832. He left behind a strange legacy. At his request, his body was dissected, his

ROBERT L. SEXTON

skeleton padded and fully clothed, and his head preserved in the manner of South American headhunters. He asked that this "autoicon," as it is now called, be seated in a glass case at the University College in London, and that his remains should be present at all meetings for the board. The autoicon is still there today, although the mummified head, which did not preserve well, has been replaced by a wax head. The real head became an easy target for students and one story has the head being used at soccer practice! No one is quite sure why Bentham desired such an odd afterlife for his body; explanations range from it being a testament to an inflated sense of self-worth to a statement about religion or a practical joke.

It follows from the law of diminishing marginal utility that as a person uses more and more units of a good to satisfy a given want, the intensity of the want, and the utility derived from further satisfying that want, diminishes. Think about it: If you are starving, your desire for that first piece of pizza will be great, but as you eat, you gradually become more and more full, reducing your desire for yet another piece.

SECTION QUIZ

1. The increase in total utility that one receives from eating an additional piece of sushi is called
   a. marginal utility.
   b. interpersonal utility.
   c. marginal cost.
   d. average utility.
   e. average cost.

2. Marginal utility is
   a. the total satisfaction derived from consuming all goods.
   b. always the total satisfaction derived from consuming the first unit of a good.
   c. always positive.
   d. always negative.
   e. the change in total satisfaction derived from consuming one more unit of a particular good.

3. As one eats more and more oranges,
   a. total utility falls, but the marginal utility of each orange rises.
   b. marginal utility rises as long as the total utility derived from the oranges remains positive.
   c. total utility rises, as does the marginal utility of each orange.
   d. total utility rises as long as the marginal utility of the oranges is positive, but the marginal utility of each additional orange likely falls.

4. The marginal utility from a hot fudge sundae
   a. is always increasing.
   b. is always greater than the average utility derived from all hot fudge sundaes consumed.
   c. generally depends on how many hot fudge sundaes the consumer has already consumed.
   d. is always equal to the price paid for the hot fudge sundae.

5. Total utility will decline when
   a. marginal utility is falling.
   b. marginal utility is rising.
   c. marginal utility equals zero.
   d. marginal utility is constant.
   e. marginal utility is negative.

6. When total utility is at its maximum,
   a. marginal utility is negative.
   b. marginal utility is positive.
   c. marginal utility is at its maximum.
   d. marginal utility equals zero.
   e. marginal utility stops decreasing and starts increasing.

(continued)

7. The law of diminishing marginal utility implies that the more of a commodity you consume,

   a. the more you value additional units of output.

   b. the less you value additional units of output.

   c. the happier you are.

   d. the higher the price that is paid for the commodity.

8. The fact that a gallon of gasoline commands a higher market price than a gallon of water indicates that

   a. gasoline is a scarce good but water is not.

   b. the total utility of gasoline exceeds the total utility of water.

   c. the marginal utility of a gallon of gasoline is greater than the marginal utility of a gallon of water.

   d. the average utility of a gallon of gasoline is greater than the average utility of a gallon of water.

1. How do economists define utility?

2. Why can't interpersonal utility comparisons be made?

3. What is the relationship between total utility and marginal utility?

4. Why could you say that a millionaire gets less marginal utility from a second piece of pizza than from the first piece, but you couldn't say that the millionaire derives more or less marginal utility from a second piece of pizza than someone else who has a much lower level of income?

5. Are you likely to get as much marginal utility from your last piece of chicken at an all-you-can-eat restaurant as at a restaurant where you pay $2 per piece of chicken?

Answers: 1. a 2. e 3. d 4. c 5. e 6. d 7. b 8. c

10.2   The Consumer's Choice

▶ How do consumers maximize satisfaction?

▶ What is the connection between the law of demand and the law of diminishing marginal utility?

10.2a What Is the "Best" Decision for Consumers?

We established the fact that marginal utility diminishes as additional units of a good are acquired. But what significance does this idea have for consumers? Remember, consumers try to add to their own total utility, so when the marginal utility generated by the purchase of additional units of one good drops too low, it can become rational for the consumer to purchase other goods rather than purchase more of the first good. In other words, a rational consumer will avoid making purchases of any one good beyond the point at which other goods will yield greater satisfaction for the amount spent—the "bang for the buck."

Marginal utility, then, is an important concept in understanding and predicting consumer behavior, especially when combined with information about prices. By comparing the marginal utilities generated by units of the goods that they desire as well as the prices, rational consumers seek the combination of goods that maximizes their satisfaction for a given amount spent. In the next section, we see how this concept works.

When the marginal utility generated by the purchase of one good falls too low, is it rational for consumers to purchase other goods?

10.2b Consumer Equilibrium

To reach consumer equilibrium, consumers must allocate their incomes in such a way that the marginal utility per dollar's worth of any good is the same for every good. That is, the "bang for the buck" must be equal for all goods at consumer equilibrium. When this goal is realized, one dollar's worth of additional gasoline will yield the same marginal utility as one dollar's worth of additional bread or apples or movie tickets or soap. This concept will become clearer to you as we work through an example illustrating the forces present when consumers are not at equilibrium.

Given a fixed budget, if the marginal utilities per dollar spent on additional units of two goods are not the same, you can increase total satisfaction by buying more of one good and less of the other. For example, assume that the price of a loaf of bread is $1, the price of a bag of apples is $1, the marginal utility of a dollar's worth of apples is 1 util, and the marginal utility of a dollar's worth of bread is 5 utils. In this situation, your total satisfaction can be increased by buying more bread and fewer apples because bread is currently giving you greater satisfaction per dollar than apples—5 utils versus 1 util, for a net gain of 4 utils to your total satisfaction. By buying more bread, though, you alter the marginal utility of both bread and apples. Consider what would happen if, next week, you buy one more loaf of bread and one less bag of apples. Because you are consuming more of it now, the marginal utility for bread will fall, say to 4 utils. On the other hand, the marginal utility for apples will rise, perhaps to 2 utils, because you now have fewer apples.

A comparison of the marginal utilities for these goods in week 2 versus week 1 would look something like this:

Week 1

$MU_{bread}/\$1 > MU_{apples}/\$1$

5 utils/$1 > 1 util/$1

Week 2

$MU_{bread}/\$1 > MU_{apples}/\$1$

4 utils/$1 > 2 utils/$1

Notice that although the marginal utilities of bread and apples are now closer, they are still not equal. Because of this difference, it is still in the consumer's interest to purchase an additional loaf of bread rather than the last bag of apples; in this case, the net gain would be 2 utils (3 utils for the unit of bread added at a cost of 1 util for the apples given up). By buying yet another loaf of bread, you once again push further down your marginal utility curve for bread, and as a result, the marginal utility for bread falls. With that change, the relative value of apples to you increases again, changing the ratio of marginal utility to dollar spent for both goods in the following way:

Week 3

$MU_{bread}/\$1 = MU_{apples}/\$1$

3 utils/$1 = 3 utils/$1

What this example shows is that, to achieve maximum satisfaction—**consumer equilibrium**—consumers have to allocate income in such a way that the ratio of the marginal utility to the price of the goods is equal for all goods purchased. In other words, in a state of consumer equilibrium,

$$MU_1/P_1 = MU_2/P_2 = MU_3/P_3 = \ldots MU_N/P_N$$

In this situation, each good provides the consumer with the same level of marginal utility per dollar spent.

consumer equilibrium
allocation of consumer income that balances the ratio of marginal utility to the price of goods purchased

10.2c The Law of Demand and the Law of Diminishing Marginal Utility

Are the law of demand and the law of diminishing marginal utility related?

The law of demand states that when the price of a good is reduced, the quantity of that good demanded will increase. But why is this the case? By examining the law of diminishing marginal utility in action, we can determine the basis for this relationship between price and quantity demanded.

For example, let's say that you are in consumer equilibrium when the price of a personal-sized pizza is $4 and the price of a hamburger is $1. Furthermore, in equilibrium, the marginal utility on the last pizza consumed is 40 utils, and the marginal utility on the last hamburger is 10 utils. So in consumer equilibrium, the MU/P ratio for both the pizza and the hamburger is 10 utils per dollar:

$$MU_{pizza} \ (40 \text{ utils})/\$4 = MU_{hamburger} \ (10 \text{ utils})/\$1$$

Now suppose the price of the personal-sized pizza falls to $2, *ceteris paribus*. Instead of the MU/P ratio of the pizza being 10 utils per dollar, it is now 20 utils per dollar (40 utils/$2). This calculation implies, *ceteris paribus*, that you will now buy more pizza at the lower price because you are getting relatively more satisfaction for each dollar you spend on pizza.

$$MU_{pizza} \ (40 \text{ utils})/\$2 > MU_{hamburger} \ (10 \text{ utils})/\$1$$

In other words, because the price of the personal-sized pizza fell, you are now willing to purchase more pizzas and fewer hamburgers.

USE WHAT YOU'VE LEARNED

Marginal Utility

A consumer is faced with choosing between hamburgers and milkshakes that are priced at $2 and $1, respectively. He has $11 to spend for the week. The marginal utility derived from each of the two goods is as follows.

If you did not have a budget constraint, you would choose five hamburgers and five milkshakes because you would maximize your total utility (68 + 34 = 102); that is, adding up all the marginal utilities for all hamburgers (68 utils) and all milkshakes (34 utils). And that would cost you $15: $10 for the five hamburgers and $5 for the five milkshakes. However, you can only spend $11; so what is the best way to spend it? Remember economic decisions are made at the margin. This idea is the best "bang for the buck" principle; we must equalize the marginal utility per dollar spent. Looking at the table, we accomplish this at four hamburgers and three milkshakes per week.

Or

$$MU_H/P_H = MU_M/P_M$$
$$10/\$2 = 5/\$1$$
$$(Q_H \times P_H) + (Q_M \times P_M) = \$11$$
$$(4 \times \$2) + (3 \times \$1) = \$11$$

Marginal Utility from Last Hamburger	Quantity of Hamburgers Consumed Each Week	(MU_H/P_H)
20	1	10
16	2	8
14	3	7
10	4	5
8	5	4

Marginal Utility from Last Milkshake	Quantity of Milkshakes Consumed Each Week	(MU_M/P_M)
12	1	12
10	2	10
5	3	5
4	4	4
3	5	3

SECTION QUIZ

1. When a consumer spends her income on goods and services in such a way that her utility is maximized, she reaches

    a. monetary equilibrium.

    b. market equilibrium.

    c. consumer equilibrium.

    d. marginal equilibrium.

2. The total utility derived from consuming scoops of ice cream can be found by

    a. multiplying the marginal utility of the last scoop consumed by the number of scoops consumed.

    b. multiplying the marginal utility of the last scoop consumed by the price of a scoop of ice cream.

    c. dividing the marginal utility of the last scoop consumed by its price.

    d. summing the marginal utilities of each scoop consumed.

    e. multiplying together the marginal utilities of each scoop of ice cream consumed.

3. In consumer equilibrium,

    a. the marginal utility from consumption is the same across all goods.

    b. individuals consume so as to maximize their total satisfaction, given limited income.

    c. the ratio of the marginal utility of each good divided by its price is equal across all goods consumed.

    d. all of the above are true.

    e. all of the above are generally true except (a).

4. Hamburgers cost $2 and hot dogs cost $1, and Juan is in consumer equilibrium. What must be true about the marginal utility of the last hamburger Juan consumes?

    a. The marginal utility of the last hamburger consumed must be less than that of the last hot dog.

    b. The marginal utility of the last hamburger consumed must be equal to that of the last hot dog.

    c. The marginal utility of the last hamburger consumed must be greater than that of the last hot dog.

    d. The marginal utility of the last hamburger consumed must be equal to zero.

5. Melissa spent the week at an amusement park and used all of her money on rides and popcorn. Both rides and bags of popcorn are priced at $1 each. Melissa realizes that the last bag of popcorn she consumed increased her utility by 40 utils, while the marginal utility of her last ride was only 20 utils. What should Melissa have done differently to increase her satisfaction?

    a. Reduced the number of bags of popcorn she consumed and increased the number of rides

    b. Increased the number of bags of popcorn she consumed and reduced the number of rides

    c. Decreased both the number of bags of popcorn and rides consumed

    d. Increased both the number of bags of popcorn and rides consumed

    e. Nothing, her utility was maximized.

---

1. What do economists mean by consumer equilibrium?

2. How could a consumer raise his total utility if the ratio of his marginal utility to the price for good A was greater than that for good B?

3. What must be true about the ratio of marginal utility to the price for each good consumed in consumer equilibrium?

4. How does the law of demand reflect the law of diminishing marginal utility?

5. Why doesn't consumer equilibrium imply that the ratio of total utility per dollar is the same for different goods?

6. Why does the principle of consumer equilibrium imply that people would tend to buy more apples when the price of apples is reduced?

7. Suppose the price of walnuts is $6 per pound and the price of peanuts is $2 per pound. If a person gets 20 units of added utility from eating the last pound of peanuts she consumes, how many utils of added utility would she have to get from eating the last pound of walnuts in order to be in consumer equilibrium?

Answers: 1. c 2. d 3. e 4. c 5. b

10.3 Behavioral Economics

▶ What is behavioral economics?

▶ What are rules of thumb?

▶ What is gambler's fallacy?

▶ What is compartmentalizing?

▶ What is framing?

▶ If we own something, do we value it more?

▶ What is the ultimatum game?

The model of consumer theory and the appendix in this chapter on indifference curves make some strong simplifying assumptions about rationality and decision making. More precisely, we saw that consumers have clear preferences for some goods over other goods, consumers face budget constraints, and consumers choose to maximize their utility subject to their budget constraints and the price of different goods. This basic model of consumer behavior has done extremely well in predicting actual behavior such as how consumers respond to changes in prices, income, and other factors.

However, economists have recently been developing models that incorporate more real-istic assumptions about rationality and decision making in a relatively new field called **behavioral economics**. Calling themselves behavioral economists, they are attempting to go beyond the basic assumptions of the traditional economic model and augment it with findings from psychology to gain a greater understanding of complex consumer behavior.

For example, do consumers really purchase combinations of goods and services to maxi-mize their utility? Are consumers really as rational and informed as economists typically presume? And are preferences always clear? These are just a few of the questions with which behavioral economists are wrestling.

behavioral economics

a field of economics that incorporates insights from human psychology into the models of economic behavior

10.3a Bounded Rationality and Rule of Thumb

The late Nobel laureate Herbert Simon was an early critic of the assumption, often implicit, that people have unlimited information-processing capabilities. He suggested the term "bounded rationality" to describe a more realistic conception of human problem-solving ability. People might *satisfice* in some circumstances rather than trying to accurately calculate the best decision. If the likely improvement for a range of decisions is judged to be less than the increased cost of calculating necessity, people may adopt rules of thumb—relying on deci-sions that are felt to have worked well enough in the past.

You may be trying to decide between two movies that you would like to see tonight, but cannot decide which movie would give you the greatest utility. So you rely on reviews on

Fandango and word of mouth. Or on a trip across the country, you may visit a restaurant to which you will never return, but you leave a 15 percent tip anyway because it is a rule of thumb and you do not have to carefully assess the value of the service. This cannot easily be explained by standard utility maximizing theory. Behavioral economists think of such rules of thumb as mental shortcuts to making decisions that may turn out to be non-optimal in some cases.

Behavioral economists understand that individuals make decisions in a world of uncertainty; part of the uncertainty comes from a lack of understanding of the probabilities of outcomes. For example, many people fall victim to the gambler's fallacy—the false belief that past outcomes affect future events. For example, if you flip a coin six times, and it comes up heads each time, some believe that when you flip for the seventh time the odds are better that it will come up tails. This is incorrect. Since these are independent events, the chances are the same each time a coin is flipped; the past does not impact the present in coin flipping. This can become problematic. For example, when people think that housing prices will continue to rise because they have continually risen over, say, the last 7–10 years, it can fuel a housing bubble.

People tend to be *overconfident* in certain circumstances. Experiments with football bettors found that those that bet "parlays" miscalculated the odds of winning. A parlay is a type of bet that requires you to pick multiple games to beat the point spread. If any of the games picked fail to cover the spread, you lose the whole parlay. Researchers found that parlay bettors estimated their chances of winning at 45 percent, when the actual probability was closer to 20 percent. People often miscalculate probabilities.

Overconfident people might think they are going to stick to their New Year's resolution and exercise five times a week. The gym knows that most people will work out a lot in the beginning and will taper off during the year. So their pricing strategy is not to charge per visit but rather charge a yearly rate and take advantage of their overconfidence. In short, most consumers would have been better off paying higher per-visit rates rather than a yearly membership because of the number of visits.

People also tend to give too much weight to a small sample. For example, a friend might tell you about a particular car that you are thinking of buying and you might take her opinion more seriously than a J.D. Power survey that polled thousands of owners of that vehicle.

10.3b Self-Control

Standard economics assumes complete self-control. However, people, even when they know what is best, sometimes lack self-control. Most of us, at some point, have eaten, drunk, or spent too much, and exercised, saved, studied, or worked too little. Though people have these self-control problems, they are at least somewhat aware of them: they sometimes join diet plans and buy food in small packs, rather than in bulk, to control their weight problem.

Some of this can be explained by people being unrealistic about the future. Roughly 70 percent of Americans are overweight. Perhaps they get more utility out of eating too much than being thin. While some people may be heavy because of medical conditions, others may eat a lot today because they think they are going to be more controlled in the future and eat less. But if that doesn't happen, they gain weight. A similar scenario can apply to smoking. People may realize it is not a healthy habit but plan on giving it up in the near future—but those healthier days in the future may never come. In other words, they may be overvaluing the current choice of smoking or eating too many desserts and undervaluing the value they would get in the future from having healthier lungs and a thinner body.

10.3c Compartmentalizing

Is $1 always a dollar? Traditional economics says it is. But behavioral economists say that people may treat $1 they received as a gift differently than $1 they earned through their hard work. They call this compartmentalizing—they are storing the gift and the money earned from hard work in different parts of the brain. Or, if you win money at a casino, you may be more likely to spend that money than you would to spend your hard-earned cash. Yet money is money.

10.3d Framing

People sometimes alter their preferences when a problem is posed or presented in different language. In a famous experiment, psychologists Amos Tversky and Daniel Kahneman found that different phrasing affected participants' responses to a question about a disease prevention strategy. Participants were offered two alternative solutions to combat a hypothetical disease that could kill 600 people:

- If Program A is adopted, 200 people will be saved.
- If Program B is adopted, there is a 33 percent chance of saving all 600 people and a 66 percent possibility of saving no one.

These decisions have the same expected outcome of 200 lives saved, but Program B is risky. Seventy-two percent of participants chose Program A, while only 28 percent of participants chose Program B.

The second problem, given to another group of participants, offered the same scenario with identical statistics, but different wording was used:

- If Program C is adopted, then 400 people will die.
- If Program D is adopted, there is a 33 percent chance that no people will die and a 66 percent probability that all 600 will die.

In this group, 78 percent of participants chose Program D (equivalent to Program B), while only 22 percent of participants chose Program C (equivalent to Program A).

In the first problem, a positive frame emphasized lives gained; in the second, a negative frame emphasized lives lost. The two groups chose quite differently when equivalent policies were expressed employing such different framing.

10.3e Anchoring

Another framing bias is called anchoring. People will often tend to make their decisions based on pieces of information they are already given. People's common tendency is to rely heavily on the first piece of information offered (the "anchor") when making a purchase. Once the anchor is established, decisions are then made by adjusting around the initial anchor price, regardless of the legitimacy of the actual anchor price. That is, the presentation of the product and prices influence a consumer's choice. In conventional consumer theory, taste influences a person's willingness to pay.

Let's use anchoring in an example. Suppose you are shopping for a used car; the initial price offered for the used car is the anchor; it sets the standard for the rest of the negotiation, regardless of the legitimacy of the initial price. This way any price lower than the initial anchor price seems more reasonable, even if the price is higher than what the car is really worth. If the salesperson can get the customer anchored on the higher price, the consumer will estimate that the lower price is a good deal.

10.3f The Endowment Effect

When we own something, we typically value it more than other people do. This is true of cars, homes, and many other things we possess. In standard consumer theory, the price you would be willing to accept to give up something you own should be the same as the price you would pay for an identical one. In one experiment, students were given coffee mugs. Researchers found that the price students were willing to pay for an identical coffee mug was less than the price they would be willing to accept to give up the coffee mug that they already owned.

People may be reluctant to sell a stock at a loss even if they could put their money in another stock they believe might yield higher returns. Why? It may be that the stock owner incorrectly views the original price of the stock, which was apparently too high, as the reference point of how much the stock is worth. That is, individuals tend to place a higher value on something they own.

People will also be averse to selling their house for less than they paid for it. However, the price they paid for the house is irrelevant to how much the house is now worth. That is determined by current market conditions. The market doesn't care what you paid for your house 8 years ago!

10.3g **Fairness Matters**

Suppose there is a hurricane warning and the stores are filled with people wanting to stock up on batteries. When you arrive at the store, you notice the price of batteries has doubled. You think this is unfair, so out of spite, you don't buy the batteries. This is inconsistent with standard consumer choice theory, but may be how some consumers behave. People care about fairness.

People's concerns about fairness are illustrated in an experiment called the *ultimatum game*. The experiment begins with two players and a coin toss to determine their roles: the proposer and the responder. Suppose they are told they can win a total of $100. The proposer then makes an offer of any amount between $100 and $1, to the other player; the responder must decide whether to accept or reject the offer. Suppose the proposer offers $1 to the responder, and he or she accepts the offer. The proposer would get $99, and the responder would get $1. Standard economic theory predicts that wealth maximizers would accept this offer. After all, once the proposal is made, it is better for the responder to receive $1 than nothing. And if the proposer knows the responder will take $1, why offer more? However, when this experiment was conducted, responders usually rejected offers of 20 percent or less. Realizing this, the proposer usually offered something along a 70/30 split—which may be unfair compared to a 50/50 split, but not so unfair that the responder would reject the offer. That is, people may be motivated by some innate sense of fairness in addition to other motivations.

Does Behavioral Economics Make the Traditional Consumer Behavior Models Worthless?

Arguments on whether rational consumers maximize utility will undoubtedly continue. Does the bounded rationality model yield better results than the traditional utility-based consumer choice theory? Are the traditional explanations, while not completely accurate, true enough to yield fruitful results? Are these deviations from rationality critical to our understanding of consumer behavior? Will the two interpretations of human behavior end up as competing or complementary frameworks? Many economists like to consider such apparent anomalies to see if they are not anomalies at all. Only time will tell where these new studies may take us. In the meantime, the traditional consumer choice model, with its simplifying assumptions of rationality, predicts and explains most consumer behavior quite well most of the time. In addition, by tweaking the basic economic model, a suitable alternative explanation to the observed behavior may be crafted.

SECTION QUIZ

1. Economists that use models that incorporate more realistic assumptions about rationality and decision making are called

    a. utility maximizers.

    b. behavioral economists.

    c. profit maximizers.

    d. none of the above.

2. Because of bounded rationality, people

    a. have limited information processing capabilities.

    b. may "satisfice" rather than trying to accurately calculate the best decision.

    c. may use rules of thumb as mental shortcuts to making decisions that may be nonoptimal.

    d. all of the above.

3. The gambler's fallacy is

    a. when people give too much weight to a small sample.

    b. the false belief that past outcomes affect future events.

    c. assumes that people have self-control when it comes to gambling.

    d. none of the above

4. When you treat a dollar that you received as a gift differently than a dollar you received from hard work, it is called

    a. bounded rationality.

    b. framing.

    c. the endowment effect.

    d. compartmentalizing.

---

1. Instead of asking you for a donation of any amount, a charity might ask you to choose $25, $50, $100, $250, or $500. Why would the charity organization use this strategy and what concept of behavioral economics is being used here?

2. There is a phone app called StickK that was founded by Economics Professor Dean Karlan at Yale University. He wanted to open an online 'Commitment Store'. He envisioned that people would come to the Commitment Store to sign contracts obliging them to achieve their personal goals such as losing weight or quitting smoking. Standard economic theory assumes that people have self-control. So why is this app important to people and what do behavioral economists believe are the flaws of conventional economic theory when it comes to self-control? Would a penalty help people keep their commitment?

3. Katherine was shopping at the mall and saw a dress she really liked. The problem was that the price was $100, which was more than she was willing to pay for the dress. The next week, the dress went on sale for $50, and she bought it. The following week, a friend, who wears the same size dress, offers to pay her $100 for the dress, but she refuses to sell. How might a behavioral economist explain this behavior?

Answers: 1. b 2. d 3. b 4. d

Fill in the blanks:

1. _____ utility implies that people will derive less satisfaction from successive units.

2. You would expect a third ice cream cone to provide _____ additional utility, or satisfaction, on a given day, than the second ice cream cone the same day.

3. _____ is the satisfaction or enjoyment derived from consumption.

4. The relative satisfaction gained by two people drinking cups of coffee _____ be measured in comparable terms.

5. _____ is the total amount of satisfaction derived from the consumption of a certain number of units of a good.

6. _____ utility is the extra satisfaction generated by an additional unit of a good that is consumed in a given time period.

7. If the first of three slices of pizza generates 24 utils and four slices of pizza generates 28 utils, then the marginal utility of the fourth slice of pizza is _____ utils.

8. Marginal utility _____ as consumption increases, which is called the law of _____.

9. Market prices of goods and services are determined by _____ utility.

10. If total utility fell for consuming one more unit of a good, the marginal utility for that good would be _____.

11. To reach _____, consumers must allocate their incomes in such a way that the marginal utility per dollar's worth of any good is the same for every good.

12. If the last dollar spent on good A provides more marginal utility per dollar than the last dollar spent on good B, total satisfaction would increase if _____ was spent on good A and _____ was spent on good B.

13. As an individual approaches consumer equilibrium, the ratio of marginal utility per dollar spent on different goods gets _____ apart across goods.

14. In consumer equilibrium, if the price of good A is three times that of the price of good B, then the marginal utility from the last unit of good A will be _____ times the marginal utility from the last unit of good B.

15. Starting in consumer equilibrium, when the price of good A falls, it makes the marginal utility per dollar spent on good A _____ relative to that of other goods, leading to a _____ quantity of good A purchased.

16. _____ are attempting to go beyond the basic assumptions of the traditional economic model and augment it with findings from psychology to gain a greater understanding of complex consumer behavior.

17. If the likely improvement for a range of decisions is judged to be less than the increased cost of calculating necessity, people may adopt _____, relying on decisions that are felt to have worked well enough in the past.

18. _____ is the false belief that past outcomes affect future events.

19. Behavioral economists say that people may treat $1 they received as a gift differently than $1 they earned through their hard work. They call this _____.

20. People's concerns about fairness are illustrated in an experiment called the _____ game.

Answers: 1. Diminishing marginal 2. less 3. Utility 4. cannot 5. Total utility 6. Marginal 7. 4 8. declines; diminishing marginal utility 9. marginal 10. negative 11. consumer equilibrium 12. more; less 13. less far 14. three 15. rise; larger 16. behavioral economists 17. rules of thumb 18. The gambler's fallacy 19. compartmentalizing 20. ultimatum

substitution effect 259
income effect 259
diminishing marginal utility 259

utility 259
util 259
total utility 261

marginal utility 261
consumer equilibrium 265
behavioral economists 268

SECTION QUIZ ANSWERS

10.1 Consumer Behavior

1. How do economists define utility?

Economists define utility as the level of satisfaction or well-being an individual receives from consumption of a good or service.

2. Why can't interpersonal utility comparisons be made?

We can't make interpersonal utility comparisons because it is impossible to measure the relative satisfaction of different people in comparable terms.

3. What is the relationship between total utility and marginal utility?

Marginal utility is the increase in total utility from increasing consumption of a good or service by one unit.

4. Why could you say that a millionaire gets less marginal utility from a second piece of pizza than from the first piece, but you couldn't say that the millionaire derives more or less marginal utility from a second piece of pizza than someone else who has a much lower level of income?

Both get less marginal utility from a second piece of pizza than from the first piece because of the law of diminishing marginal utility. However, it is impossible to measure the relative satisfaction of different people in comparable terms, even when we are comparing rich and poor people, so we cannot say who got more marginal utility from a second slice of pizza.

5. Are you likely to get as much marginal utility from your last piece of chicken at an all-you-can-eat restaurant as at a restaurant where you pay $2 per piece of chicken?

No. If you pay $2 per piece, you only eat another piece as long as it gives you more marginal utility than spending the $2 on something else. But at an all-you-can-eat restaurant, the dollar price of one more piece of chicken is zero, so you consume more chicken and get less marginal utility out of the last piece of chicken you eat.

10.2 The Consumer's Choice

1. What do economists mean by consumer equilibrium?

Consumer equilibrium means that a consumer is consuming the optimum, or utility-maximizing, combination of goods and services, for a given level of income.

2. How could a consumer raise his total utility if the ratio of his marginal utility to the price for good A was greater than that for good B?

Such a consumer would raise his total utility by spending less on good B and more on good A because a dollar less spent on B would lower his utility less than a dollar more spent on A would increase it.

3. What must be true about the ratio of marginal utility to the price for each good consumed in consumer equilibrium?

In consumer equilibrium, the ratio of marginal utility to price for each good consumed must be the same; otherwise, the consumer could raise his total utility by changing his consumption pattern to increase consumption of those goods with higher marginal utility per dollar and decrease consumption of those goods with lower marginal utility per dollar.

4. How does the law of demand reflect the law of diminishing marginal utility?

In consumer equilibrium, the marginal utility per dollar spent is the same for all goods and services consumed. Starting from that point, reducing the price of one good increases its marginal utility per dollar, resulting in increased consumption of that good. But that is what the law of demand states—that the quantity of a good demanded will increase, the lower its price, *ceteris paribus*.

5. Why doesn't consumer equilibrium imply that the ratio of total utility per dollar is the same for different goods?

It is the additional, or marginal, utility per dollar spent for different goods, not the total utility you get per dollar spent, that matters in determining whether consuming more of some goods and less of others will increase total utility.

6. Why does the principle of consumer equilibrium imply that people would tend to buy more apples when the price of apples is reduced?

A fall in the price of apples will increase the marginal utility per dollar spent on the last apple a person was willing to buy before their price fell. This means a person could increase his or her total utility for a given income by buying more apples and less of some other goods.

7. Suppose the price of walnuts is $6 per pound and the price of peanuts is $2 per pound. If a person gets 20 units of added utility from eating the last pound of peanuts she consumes, how many utils of added utility

would she have to get from eating the last pound of walnuts in order to be in consumer equilibrium?

Since consumer equilibrium requires that the marginal utility per dollar spent must be the same across goods that are consumed, the last pound of walnuts would have to provide 60 units of added or marginal utility in this case ($60/6 = 20/2$).

10.3 Behavioral Economics

1. **Instead of asking you for a donation of any amount, a charity might ask you to choose $25, $50, $100, $250, or $500. Why would the charity organization use this strategy and what concept of behavioral economics is being used here?**

    Anchoring. The charity might feel that somebody thinking about donating $40 might now donate $50 or someone might think about $10, but see that is not an option and donate $25. That is, by anchoring, relying on a suggested piece of information, it may cause donors to give more than they had originally intended.

2. **There is a phone app called StickK that was founded by economics professor Dean Karlan at Yale University. He wanted to open an online "Commitment Store." He envisioned that people would come to the Commitment Store to sign contracts obliging them to achieve their personal goals such as losing weight or quitting smoking. Standard economic theory assumes that people have self-control. So why is this app important to people and what do behavioral economists believe are the flaws of conventional economic theory when**

it comes to self-control? Would a penalty help people keep their commitment?

The problem is that people may overvalue current choices and undervalue future choices, so commitment to a program like StickK might help, especially if there is a penalty for not keeping your commitment. According to their website, "We all start off wanting to achieve our goal, but most of the time there's simply nothing out there to make us "stickK" to our word. By entering into a Commitment Contract, backing out on that promise just got a whole lot harder. If drinking a can of soda meant you'd have to fork over $10 to your friend, just about anyone would look for something else to drink."

The Commitment Contract concept is based on two well-known principles of behavioral economics: (1) people don't always do what they claim they want to do, and (2) incentives get people to do things.

3. **Katherine was shopping at the mall and saw a dress she really liked. The problem was that the price was $100, which was more than she was willing to pay for the dress. The next week the dress went on sale for $50, and she bought it. The following week, a friend, who wears the same-size dress, offered to pay her $100 for the dress, but she refused to sell. How would behavioral economists explain this behavior?**

    This is called the endowment effect. This is when someone places a higher value on something they own than when they do not—that is, possessing a good makes it more valuable. The possessor must be paid more to give up the good than she would have paid for it in the first place.

PROBLEMS

1. Why can we *not* say that two people who chose to buy the same quantity of a good at the same price have the same marginal utility?

2. If someone said, "You would have to pay me to eat one more bite," what do we know about his marginal utility? What do we know about his total utility?

3. Why would you not continue to consume a good in the range where there was diminishing total utility?

4. The following table shows Rene's total utility from eating escargot. Fill in the blanks that show the marginal utility that Rene derives from eating escargot.

Escargot per Day	Total Utility	Marginal Utility
1	10	_____
2	18	_____
3	24	_____
4	28	_____
5	30	_____
6	30	_____

5. Plot both Rene's total and marginal utility curves on graphs.

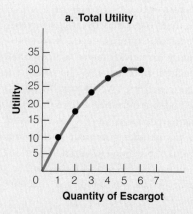

a. Total Utility

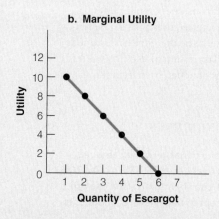

b. Marginal Utility

6. Suppose it is all-you-can-eat night at your favorite restaurant. Once you've paid $9.95 for your meal, how do you determine how many helpings to consume? Should you continue eating until your food consumption has yielded $9.95 worth of satisfaction? What happens to the marginal utility from successive helpings as consumption increases?

7. Suppose you currently spend your weekly income on movies and video games such that the marginal utility per dollar spent on each activity is equal. If the price of a movie ticket rises, how will you reallocate your fixed income between the two activities? Why?

8. Brandy spends her entire weekly budget of $20 on soda and pizza. A can of soda and a slice of pizza are priced at $1 and $2, respectively. Brandy's marginal utility from soda and pizza consumption is 6 utils and 4 utils, respectively. What advice could you give Brandy to help her increase her overall satisfaction from the consumption of soda and pizza? What will happen to the marginal utility per dollar from soda consumption if Brandy follows your advice? What will happen to the marginal utility per dollar from pizza consumption?

9. Suppose you were studying late one night and you were craving a Papa John's pizza. How much marginal utility would you receive? How much marginal utility would you receive from a pizza that was delivered immediately after you finished a five-course Thanksgiving dinner? Where would you be more likely to eat more pizza in a single setting, at home or at a crowded party (particularly if you are not sure how many pizzas have been ordered)? Use marginal utility analysis to answer the last question.

10. The Consumer Price Index (CPI) measures changes in the cost of living by comparing the cost of buying a certain bundle of goods and services over time. The quantities of each commodity remain the same from year to year but their prices change, so changes in the index reflect the weighted average of changes in the prices of goods and services. Explain how the behavior assumed in the CPI conflicts with the way consumers actually respond to price changes. Do you think the CPI overestimates or underestimates the effect of price changes on consumers?

11. A restaurant offers a free dinner with a six-pound steak, potatoes, and all the trimmings, but only if the patron can eat it all. Otherwise, he must pay $80 for the steak dinner. What does this say about the likely marginal utility most people expect to get from the sixth pound of steak during that dinner?

12. How does the water–diamond paradox explain why there is such a poor correlation between the price of a good and the total utility a person receives from it?

13. Explain the income and substitution effects of a price reduction of a good.

14. Explain the book's distinction between newspaper racks, where the price allows you access to multiple papers, and food vending machines, where you can only get one of the items purchased. Would you expect the policy used by newspaper racks to change if each newspaper routinely included hundreds of dollars of valuable coupons?

15. Some programs have an opt-out system where people are automatically put in the program unless they opt out. Other programs are opt-in programs; people must choose to participate. Opt-out programs are far more popular than opt-in programs for 401(k) programs. How do you think a behavioral economist would explain this?

A More Advanced Theory of Consumer Choice

In this appendix, we develop a slightly more advanced set of tools using indifference curves and budget lines to aid in our understanding of the theory of consumer choice. These approaches allow us to express our total utility as a function of two goods. The tools developed here allow us to see how the optimal combination changes in response to changing prices and income. Let's begin with indifference curves.

The notion of utility in some cardinally measurable sense where we can quantify the precise measurement of each util is not necessary to our analytical framework when we use indifference curves. All that matters is that we are able to rank commodity bundles in order of increasing satisfaction, not that we should be able to say by exactly how much satisfaction increases as we move from one market bundle to another. This is called an ordinal measure. For example, a person can compare the satisfaction gained from a second car with that obtained from the first car, and with the satisfaction from a trip to Europe. Again, ordering these preferences does not depend on how much one good is preferred to another but rather that one is merely preferred to the other.

Indifference Curves

On the basis of their tastes and preferences, consumers must subjectively choose the bundle of goods and services that yield the highest level of satisfaction given their money income and prices.

What Is an Indifference Curve?

A consumer's indifference curve, shown in Exhibit 1, contains various combinations of two commodities, and each combination of goods (like points A, B, and C) on the indifference curve will yield the same level of total utility to this consumer. The consumer is said to be indifferent between any combination of the two goods along an individual indifference curve because she receives the same level of satisfaction from each bundle.

The Properties of the Indifference Curve

Indifference curves have the following three properties: (1) Higher indifference curves represent greater satisfaction, (2) they are negatively sloped, and (3) they are convex from the origin.

Higher Indifference Curves Represent Greater Satisfaction

Although consumers are equally happy with any bundle of goods along the indifference curve, they prefer to be on the highest indifference curve possible. This preference follows from the assumption that more of a good is preferred to less of a good. For example, in Exhibit 2, the consumer would prefer I_2 to I_1. The higher indifference curve represents more satisfaction. As you can

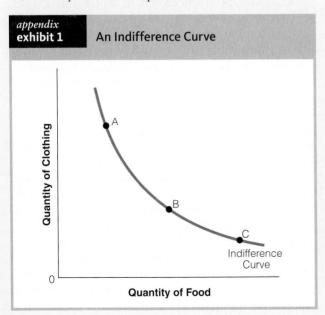

appendix
exhibit 1   An Indifference Curve

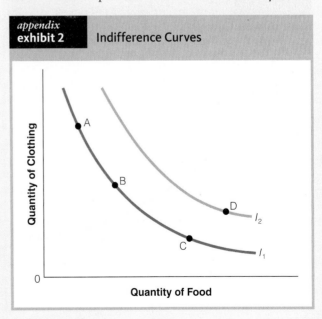

appendix
exhibit 2   Indifference Curves

see in Exhibit 2, bundle D gives the consumer more of both goods than does bundle C, which is on a lower indifference curve. Bundle D is also preferred to bundle A because there is more than enough extra food to compensate the consumer for the loss of clothing; total utility has risen because the consumer is now on a higher indifference curve.

Indifference Curves Are Negatively Sloped

Indifference curves must slope downward from left to right if the consumer views both goods as desirable. If the quantity of one good is reduced, the quantity of the other good must be increased to maintain the same level of total satisfaction.

Indifference Curves Are Convex from the Origin

The slope of an indifference curve at a particular point measures the marginal rate of substitution (MRS), the rate at which the consumer is willing to trade one good to gain one more unit of another good. If the indifference curve is steep, the marginal rate of substitution is high. The consumer would be willing to give up a large amount of clothing for a small amount of food as she moves from point A to point B in Exhibit 3. The MRS between points A and B is 5—the consumer is willing to give up 5 units of clothing for one unit of food. If the indifference curve is flatter, the marginal rate of substitution is low. For example, the MRS between point C and

D is -1. The consumer is only willing to give up a small amount of clothing in exchange for an additional unit of food to remain indifferent. A consumer's willingness to substitute one good for another depends on the relative quantities he consumes. If he has lots of something, say food relative to clothing, he will not value the prospect of getting even more food very highly, which is just the law of demand, which is based on the law of diminishing marginal utility.

Complements and Substitutes

As we learned in Chapter 4, many goods are complements to each other; that is, the use of more units of one encourages the acquisition of additional units of the other. Gasoline and automobiles, baseballs and baseball bats, snow skis and bindings, bread and butter, and coffee and cream are examples of complementary goods. When goods are complements, units of one good cannot be acquired without affecting the want-satisfying power of other goods. Some goods are substitutes for one another; that is, the more you have of one, the less you desire the other. (The relationship between substitutes is thus the opposite of the relationship between complements.) Examples of substitutes include coffee and tea, sweaters and jackets, and home-cooked and restaurant meals.

The degree of convexity of an indifference curve—that is, the extent to which the curve deviates from a straight line—depends on how easily the two goods can be substituted for each other. If two commodities are perfect substitutes—one $10 bill and two $5 bills, for example—the indifference curve is a straight line (in this case, the line's slope is -1). As depicted in Exhibit 4(a), the marginal rate of substitution is the same regardless of the extent to which one good is replaced by the other.

At the other extreme are two commodities that are not substitutes but are perfect complements, such as left and right shoes. For most people, these goods are never used separately but are consumed only together. Because it is impossible to replace units of one with units of the other and maintain satisfaction, the marginal rate of substitution is undefined; thus, the indifference curve is a right angle, as shown in Exhibit 4(b). Because most people only care about pairs of shoes, 4 left shoes and 2 right shoes (bundle B) would yield the same level of satisfaction as 2 left shoes and 2 right shoes (bundle A). Two pairs of shoes (bundle A) are also as good as 4 right shoes and 2 left shoes (bundle C). That is, bundles A, B, and C all lie on the same indifference curve and yield the same level of satisfaction. But the combination of three right shoes and three left shoes (bundle D) is preferred to any combination of bundles on indifference curve I_1.

appendix exhibit 3 Indifference Curves Are Convex from the Origin

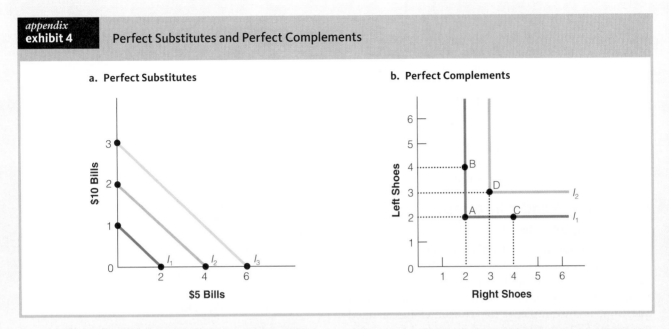

appendix
exhibit 4   Perfect Substitutes and Perfect Complements

a. Perfect Substitutes

b. Perfect Complements

If two commodities can easily be substituted for one another, the nearer the indifference curves will approach a straight line; in other words, it will maintain more closely the same slope along its length throughout. The greater the complementarity between the two goods, the nearer the indifference curves will approach a right angle.

The Budget Line

A consumer's purchase opportunities can be illustrated by a budget line. More precisely, a budget line represents the various combinations of two goods that a consumer can buy with a given income, holding the prices of the two goods constant. For simplicity, we only examine the consumer's choices between two goods. We recognize

that this example is not completely realistic, as a quick visit to the store shows consumers buying a variety of different goods and services. However, the two-good model allows us to focus on the essentials, with a minimum of complication.

First, let's look at a consumer who has $50 of income a week to spend on two goods—food and clothing. The price of food is $10 per unit, and the price of clothing is $5 per unit. If the consumer spends all her income on food, she can buy 5 units of food per week ($50/$10 = 5). If she spends all her income on clothing, she can buy 10 units of clothing per week ($50/$5 = 10). However, it is likely that she will spend some of her income on each. Six of the affordable combinations are presented in the table in Exhibit 5.

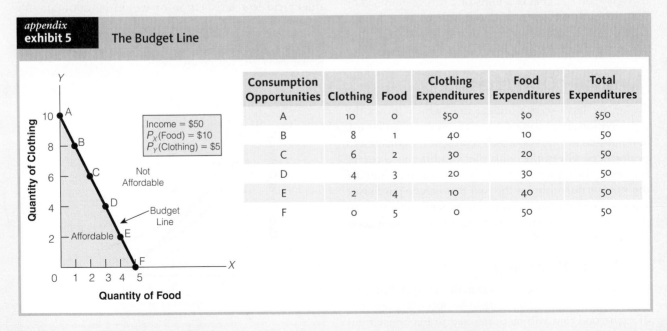

appendix
exhibit 5   The Budget Line

Consumption Opportunities	Clothing	Food	Clothing Expenditures	Food Expenditures	Total Expenditures
A	10	0	$50	$0	$50
B	8	1	40	10	50
C	6	2	30	20	50
D	4	3	20	30	50
E	2	4	10	40	50
F	0	5	0	50	50

Income = $50
P_X(Food) = $10
P_Y(Clothing) = $5

In the graph in Exhibit 5, the horizontal axis measures the quantity of food and the vertical axis measures the quantity of clothing. Moving along the budget line we can see the various combinations of food and clothing the consumer can purchase with her income. For example, at point A, she could buy 10 units of clothing and 0 units of food; at point B, 8 units of clothing and 1 unit of food; and so on.

Of course, any other combination along the budget line is also affordable. However, any combination of goods beyond the budget line is not feasible.

Finding the *X*- and *Y*-Intercepts of the Budget Line

The intercept on the vertical *Y*-axis (the clothing axis) and the intercept on the horizontal *X*-axis (the food axis) can easily be found by dividing the total income available for expenditures by the price of the good in question. For example, if the consumer has a fixed income of $50 a week and clothing costs $5 per unit, we know that if he spends all his income on clothing, he can afford 10 (Income/P_Y = $50/$5 = 10); so 10 is the intercept on the *Y*-axis. Now if he spends all his $50 on food and food costs $10 per unit, he can afford to buy 5 (Income/P_X = $50/$10 = 5); so 5 is the intercept on the *X*-axis, as shown in Exhibit 6.

Finding the Slope of the Budget Line

The slope of the budget line is equal to $-P_X/P_Y$. The negative coefficient of the slope indicates that the budget line is negatively sloped (downward sloping), reflecting the fact that you must give up some of one good to get more of the other. For example, if the price of *X* (food) is $10 and the price of *Y* (clothing) is $5, then the slope is equal to $-10/5$, or -2. That is, 2 units of *Y* can be obtained by forgoing the purchase of 1 unit of *X*; hence, the slope of the budget line is said to be -2 (or 2, in absolute value terms) as seen in Exhibit 6.

Consumer Optimization

So far, we have seen a budget line, which shows the combinations of two goods that a consumer can afford, and indifference curves, which represent the consumer's preferences. Given the consumer's indifference curves for two goods, together with the budget line showing the various quantities of the two that can be purchased with a given money income for expenditure, we can determine the optimal (or best) quantities of each good the consumer can purchase.

The Point of Tangency

The point of tangency between the budget line and an indifference curve indicates the optimal quantities of each good that will be purchased to maximize total

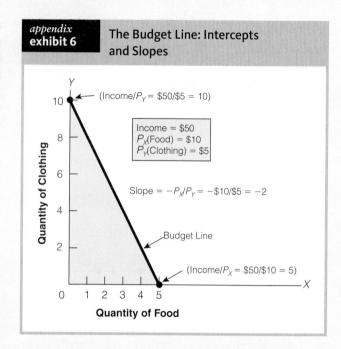

appendix
exhibit 6   The Budget Line: Intercepts and Slopes

satisfaction. At that point of tangency, $-MRS$ (the slope of the indifference curve) will be equal to $-P_X/P_Y$ (the slope of the budget line). Exhibit 7 shows the consumer's optimal combination of clothing and food. The optimum occurs where the budget line is tangent to indifference curve I_2, at point A: The consumer will acquire 2 units of food and 6 units of clothing.

To maximize satisfaction, the consumer must acquire the most preferred attainable bundle—that is, reach the highest indifference curve that can be reached with a given level of income. The highest curve that can be reached is the one to which the budget line is tangent, at point A. Any other possible combination of the two goods either would be on a lower indifference curve and thus yield less satisfaction or would be unobtainable

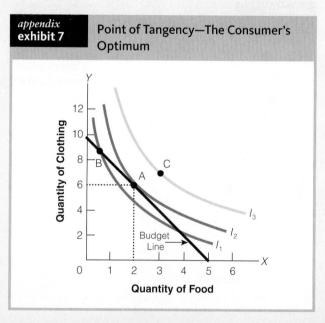

appendix
exhibit 7   Point of Tangency—The Consumer's Optimum

with the given income. For example, point B is afford-able but would place the consumer on a lower indif-ference curve. In other words, if the consumer were at point B, she could be made better off moving to point A by consuming less clothing and more food. How about point C? That move would be nice because it is on a higher indifference curve and would yield greater total utility, but unfortunately it is unattainable with the current budget line.

Changes in the Budget Line

So far, we have seen how the prices of goods along with a consumer's income determine a budget line. Now let us examine how the budget line can change as a result of a change in the income level or the price of either good.

The Position of the Budget Line If Income Rises

An increase in income, holding relative prices constant, will cause the curve to shift outward, parallel to the old curve. As seen in Exhibit 8, a richer person can afford more of both goods than a poorer person because of the higher budget line. Suppose you just received an inheritance from a relative; this money will allow you to now buy more of the things that you want. The change in income, holding relative prices constant, is called the income effect and it causes this parallel shift in the budget line.

With a given pattern of indifference curves, larger amounts available for spending will result in an income-consumption curve (*ICC*) connecting the best consumption points (tangencies) at each income level.

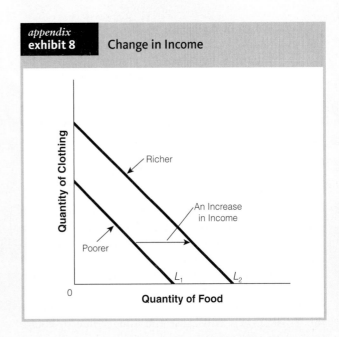

appendix
exhibit 8   Change in Income

Consider what happens to consumer purchases with a rise in income. In Exhibit 9(a), the rise in income shifts the budget line outward. If both goods, clothing and food, are normal goods in this range, then the consumer will buy more of both goods, as seen in Exhibit 9(a). If income rises and the consumer buys less of one good, we say that good is an inferior good. In Exhibit 9(b), we see that the consumer buys more clothing (normal good) but less liver (inferior good). In this example, as income rises, the consumer may choose to consume fewer units of liver—the lower-quality meat. Other examples of inferior goods include second-hand clothing or do-it-yourself

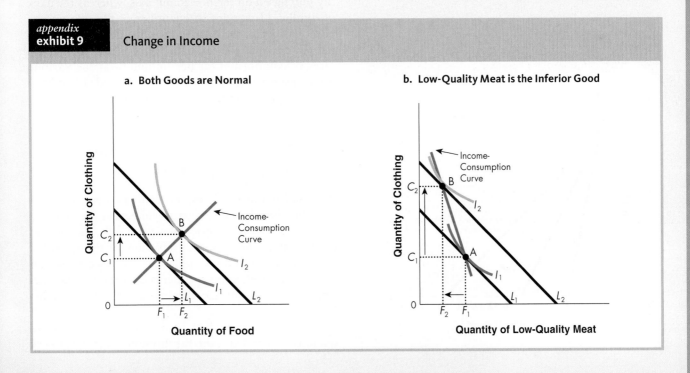

appendix
exhibit 9   Change in Income

haircuts, which consumers generally buy only because they cannot afford more expensive substitutes.

In Exhibit 9(a), both goods are normal goods, so the consumer responds to the increase in income by buying more of both clothing and food. In Exhibit 9(b), clothing is normal and hamburger is an inferior good, so the consumer responds to the increase in income by buying more clothing and less hamburger.

The Budget Line Reflects Price Changes

Purchases of goods and services depend on relative prices as well as a consumer's level of income. However, when the price of one good changes, holding income and the price of the other good constant, it causes a relative price effect. Relative prices affect the way consumers allocate their income among different goods. For example, a change in the price of the good on either the Y- or X-axis will cause the budget line to rotate inward or outward from the budget line's intercept on the other axis.

Let's return to our two-good example—clothing and food. Say the price of food falls from $10 to $5. This decrease in price comes as good news to consumers because it expands their buying opportunities—rotating the budget line outward, as seen in Exhibit 10. Thus, a consumer who spends all his income on food can now buy 10 units of food, as Income/P_X = $50/$5 = 10. If the price per unit of food rose from $10 to $25, it would contract the consumer's buying opportunities and rotate the budget line inward; so the consumer who spends all his income on food would be able to buy only 2 units of food, as Income/P_X = $50/$25 = 2.

The tangency relationship between the budget line and the indifference curve indicates the optimal amounts of each of the two goods the consumer will purchase, given the prices of both goods and the consumer's total available income for expenditures. At different possible prices for one of the goods, given the price of the other and given total income, a consumer would optimally purchase different quantities of the two goods.

A change in the price of one of the goods will alter the slope of the budget line because a different amount of the good can be purchased with a given level of income. If, for example, the price of food falls, the budget line becomes flatter because the consumer can purchase more food with a given income than she previously could. As shown in Exhibit 11, the new budget line rotates outward, from L_1 to L_2, as a result of the price reduction. Thus, the new point of tangency with an indifference curve will be on a higher indifference curve. In Exhibit 11(a), the point of tangency moves from point A to point B as a result of the decline in price of food from $10 to $5; the equilibrium quantity of food purchased increases from 2 to 5 units.

A relation known as the price–consumption curve (*PCC*) may be drawn through these points of tangency, indicating the optimum quantities of food (and clothing) at various possible prices of food (given the price of clothing). From this price–consumption curve, we can derive the usual demand curve for the good. Thus, Exhibit 11(a) shows that if the price of food is $10, the consumer will purchase 5 units. These data may be plotted, as in Exhibit 11(b), to derive a demand curve of the usual form. Notice that in Exhibit 11(b) the price of food is measured on the vertical axis and the quantity purchased on the horizontal axis, whereas the axes of Exhibit 11(a) refer to quantities of the two goods. Notice also that the quantities demanded, as shown in Exhibit 11(b), are those with the consumer's expenditures in equilibrium (at her optimum) at the various prices. Essentially, the demand curve is made up of various price and quantity optimum points.

The Income and Substitution Effects of a Price Change

With indifference curves, we can easily see the two ways in which a price reduction influences the quantity demanded. When the price of a good falls, the income effect enables the person to buy more of this good (or other goods) with a given income; the price reduction has the same effect as an increase in money income. That is, the consumer can now move onto a higher indifference curve.

The second influence of the price decline on the quantity demanded is the substitution effect. The lower

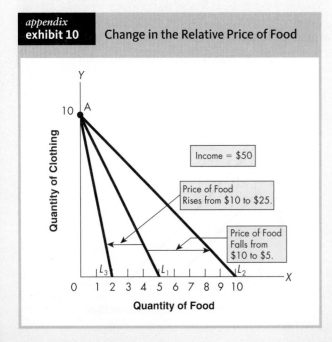

appendix
exhibit 10   **Change in the Relative Price of Food**

Income = $50

Price of Food Rises from $10 to $25.

Price of Food Falls from $10 to $5.

Quantity of Clothing

Quantity of Food

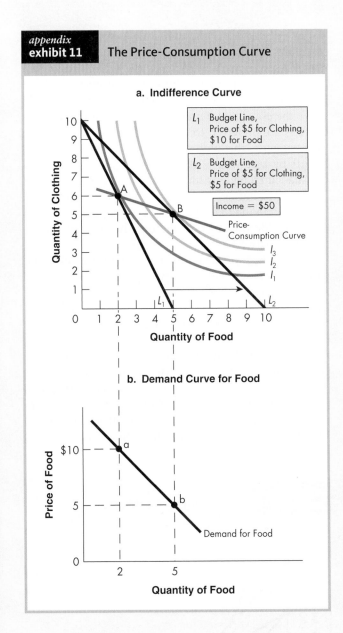

appendix
exhibit 11   The Price-Consumption Curve

a. Indifference Curve

L_1 Budget Line, Price of $5 for Clothing, $10 for Food

L_2 Budget Line, Price of $5 for Clothing, $5 for Food

Income = $50

Price-Consumption Curve

I_3 I_2 I_1

b. Demand Curve for Food

Demand for Food

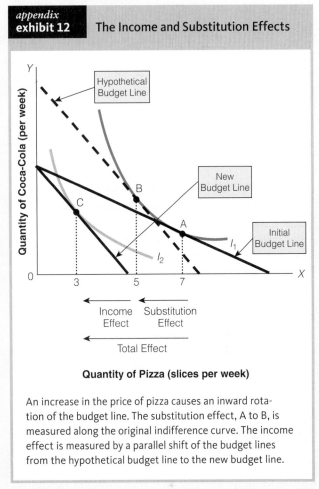

appendix
exhibit 12   The Income and Substitution Effects

Hypothetical Budget Line

New Budget Line

Initial Budget Line

Income Effect   Substitution Effect

Total Effect

An increase in the price of pizza causes an inward rotation of the budget line. The substitution effect, A to B, is measured along the original indifference curve. The income effect is measured by a parallel shift of the budget lines from the hypothetical budget line to the new budget line.

price encourages the consumer to buy larger quantities of this good. *The substitution effect is always negative.* That is, price and quantity demanded are negatively correlated; lower prices mean higher quantities demanded, and vice versa.

Exhibit 12 shows the income and substitution effects for an *increase* in the price of pizza. Because the relative price of pizza increases, the budget line rotates inward. (Note that the Y-intercept did not change because neither income nor the price of pizza changed. Hence if all income is spent on Coca-Cola before and after the price increase of pizza, the same amount of Coca-Cola can be purchased.) The total effect of the increase in the price of pizza is indicated by point C; that is, a reduction in the quantity of pizza from seven slices of pizza to three slices of pizza.

Within the total effect are the substitution effect and the income effect. First consider how much of the total effect is substituting away from the now higher-priced good, pizza. This comparison can easily be made by taking the new budget line and drawing a new hypothetical budget line parallel to the new budget line but tangent to the old indifference curve I_1. Why? It shows the effect of the new relative price on the old indifference curve—in effect, the consumer is compensated for the loss of welfare associated with the price rise by enough income to return to the original indifference curve, I_1. Remember that as long as the new budget line and the hypothetical budget line are parallel, the relative prices are the same; the only difference is the level of income. Thus, we are able to isolate the one effect—the amount of substitution that would prevail without the real income effect—which is the movement from A to B, or the substitution effect.

The movement from B to C is a change in the real income when the relative prices are constant because this move requires a parallel shift in the budget line. Thus, the movement from B to C results from the decrease in real income because of the higher price of pizza while all other prices remain constant—the income effect. Remember that the slope of the budget line indicates relative prices; thus, by shifting the new budget line next to the old indifference curve, we can see the change that took place holding real income (measured by utility) constant. Then when we make the parallel shift, we see the change in income because the size of the parallel shift measures only the amount of real income change, with relative prices remaining constant.

Subsidies and Indifference Curves

The indifference curve is a convenient tool to aid in our understanding of subsidies. In this final section, we consider two examples demonstrating the effects of subsidies in income as compared to subsidies in price. The first question is whether the poor would be better off with cash or food stamps. The second example has to do with the more general question of subsidizing the price of a good like buses or trains.

Using the indifference curve approach, we can show that the poor would be at least equally as well off receiving cash rather than a subsidy like food stamps.

In Exhibit 13, if the individual's initial position is at bundle A (consuming F_1 amount of food, an amount deemed insufficient by society), the introduction of a food stamp program that allowed the recipient to spend an additional $100 per month exclusively on food would make the consumer better off (bundles of indifference curve I_2 are preferred to those on I_1). However, for the same expense, this individual might be made even better off by receiving $100 in cash. The reason is that the shaded triangle is unobtainable to the recipient of food stamps but not to those receiving a cash payment. Unless the individual intended to spend *all* of the next $100 of additional income on food, he or she would be better off with a choice.

Similarly, subsidizing the price of a good (like education, postal services, mass transportation, or medical services) is usually *not* the best method to ensure that society's scarce resources are properly allocated. If the price of a good is subsidized, it distorts market signals and results in output levels of the subsidized good that are inefficiently large. In other words, the opportunity cost of forgone other goods that could have been produced with those resources is greater than the (marginal) value of the subsidized good. (Recall the ordinary supply and demand diagram for a subsidy from Chapter 7.) Exhibit 14 shows that if the whole budget constraint is

appendix exhibit 13 — Cash Grants versus Food Stamp Income Subsidy

With no government assistance, the consumer chooses bundle A. The availability of food stamps increases the budget and allows the buyer to purchase bundle B, consuming more food and more other goods and attaining a higher level of utility. A cash grant, however, expands the budget set further. The recipient would purchase bundle C, which contains more nonfood items and less food than bundle B. The consumer reaches a higher level of utility with a cash grant than with food stamps.

appendix exhibit 14 — Cash Grants versus Price Subsidies

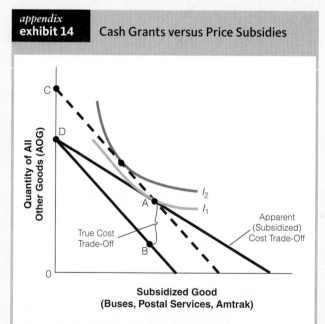

A subsidy lowers the price paid for the good, pivoting the budget line to the right, whereas a cash grant causes a parallel shift of the budget line to the right. The consumer chooses bundle A with the subsidy but attains more satisfaction under a cash grant program. More units of the subsidized good and fewer units of other goods are consumed with a subsidy than with a cash grant of equivalent value.

shifted parallel by an amount equivalent to the price subsidy, AB (AB = CD), then a higher indifference curve can be reached, I_2 rather than I_1. Because reaching the highest indifference curve subject to the budget constraint maximizes consumer satisfaction, this simple diagram shows that it is better to subsidize income (parallel shift) than to subsidize price (altering the slope), if one is interested in making some group better off.

Of course, if you want certain groups (say, the poor) to consume more of *particular goods* (housing or food), rather than just raising their utility, you may not wish to give unconstrained income subsidies. Recall that economists can never, in their role as economists, recommend one approach over the other but they can point out the implications of alternative choices.

PROBLEMS

1. If you had a budget of $200, and P_Y is $5 and P_X is $10, draw the budget line. Draw the budget lines when P_X falls to $8. Show the budget line when the money available for expenditures increases to $400. What is the slope of the budget line when P_Y is $5 and P_X is $10? How about when P_X falls to $8?

   Answer:

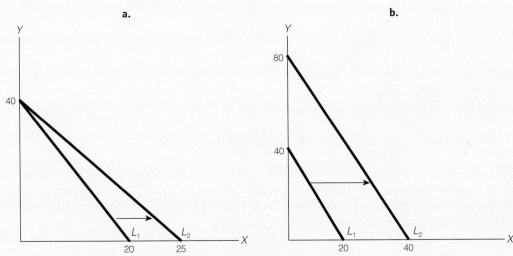

2. Joe buys more clothes than Jim.

   a. Using indifference curves, show how Jim's consumption of clothing and food may differ from Joe's because they have different tastes, *ceteris paribus*.

   b. Suppose that Jim and Joe have the same tastes and income. Joe's father manages a clothing store, and Joe is able to buy all his clothes at wholesale prices. Show why Jim's choices of food and clothing differ from Joe's in this situation.

   c. Now suppose that Jim and Joe have the same tastes and face the same prices, but that Joe has more money to spend than Jim. Demonstrate how this difference affects Joe's consumption pattern compared with Jim's.

Answer:

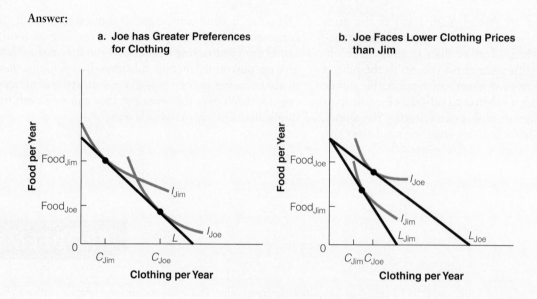

a. Joe has Greater Preferences
   for Clothing

b. Joe Faces Lower Clothing Prices
   than Jim

c. Joe has More Money Available
   for Expenditures

3.   Cigarette taxes are imposed to discourage consumption of so-called "undesirable goods." Using indifference curves, show the effect of an increase in taxes on cigarettes. What is the total effect? How much of the change is due to the income effect? How much is due to the substitution effect?

Answer:

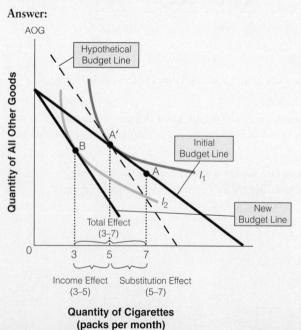

The Firm: Production and Costs

What questions do you think Toyota had to ask when it decided to build this auto plant? How long would it take to get it up and running? What about the other possible uses of the building funds? Perhaps those could have been diverted to researching new engine technology. What if the economy slows down and Toyota finds it doesn't need the extra capacity anymore? Should it shut the plant down? What about all the money it already invested in the plant?

Costs exist because resources are scarce and have competing uses—to produce more of one good means forgoing the production of another good. The cost of producing a good is measured by the worth of the most valuable alternative that was given up to obtain the resource, which is called the *opportunity cost*. In Chapter 3, the production possibilities curve highlighted this trade-off. Recall that the opportunity cost of producing additional houses was the food that had to be sacrificed.

Other examples of opportunity costs abound: Paper used in this book could have been used in newspapers or magazines; the steel used in the construction of a new building could have been used in the production of an automobile or a washing machine.

In this chapter, we turn our attention away from the behavior of consumers and toward the behavior of producers; that is, we examine the firm's costs in more detail—what really lies behind the firm's supply curve? A firm's costs are a key determinant in pricing and production decisions and a very important building block for the theory of the firm. However, costs by themselves do not tell us what decisions firms will make. We will have to wait until the next chapter to find the complete answer to that question, but costs are a major component.

But what exactly makes up a firm's cost of production? Let's begin by looking at explicit and implicit costs.

11.1 Firms and Profits: Total Revenues Minus Total Costs

▶ What are explicit and implicit costs?

▶ What are accounting profits?

▶ What are economic profits?

▶ What are sunk costs?

explicit costs
the opportunity costs of production that require a monetary payment

implicit costs
the opportunity costs of production that do not require a monetary payment

11.1a Explicit Costs

Explicit costs are the input costs that require a monetary payment—the out-of-pocket expenses that pay for labor services, raw materials, fuel, transportation, utilities, advertising, and so on. It is important to note that the explicit costs are opportunity costs to the firm. For example, money spent on electricity cannot be used for advertising. Remember that in a world of scarcity we are always giving up something to get something else. Trade-offs are pervasive. The costs discussed so far are relatively easy to measure, and an economist and an accountant would most likely arrive at the same figures. However, that will not always be the case.

11.1b Implicit Costs

Some of the firm's (opportunity) costs of production are implicit. Implicit costs do not require an outlay of money. Here is where the economist's and accountant's measures of costs diverge because accountants do *not* include implicit costs. For example, what if you start your own yogurt shop? You give up the opportunity to make a salary working for someone else. And the money invested in your new business could have been invested elsewhere and earned interest. And what do you give up if you own the building where you have your new yogurt shop? The opportunity to rent it to someone else. These opportunity costs are less visible than explicit costs but are still part of the costs of doing business.

What explicit and implicit costs might the owner of this salon incur? His explicit costs include chairs, rent for the shop, scissors, the rinse sinks, electricity, blow dryers, and so on. The implicit costs include the salary he could make at another job or the leisure he could enjoy if he retired.

USE WHAT YOU'VE LEARNED

Explicit and Implicit Costs

If a company owns its own building in a growing urban area, can it protect itself from rising rents?

 The company cannot avoid implicit costs. If the company owned the building and rents increased, so would the opportunity cost of owning the building. That is, by occupying the building, the company is giving up the new, higher rents it could receive from renters if it leased out the space. Even though the firm pays zero rent by owning the building, the rent it could receive by leasing it to another company is a real economic cost (but not an accounting cost) to the firm.

11.1c Profits

Economists generally assume that the ultimate goal of every firm is to maximize its **profits**. In other words, firms try to maximize the difference between what they give up for their inputs—their total costs (explicit and implicit)—and the amount they receive for their goods and services—their total revenues. Like revenues and costs, profits refer to flows over time. When we say that a firm earned $5 million in profit, we must specify the period in which the profit was earned—a week, month, year, and so on.

11.1d Are Accounting Profits the Same as Economic Profits?

A firm can make profits in the sense that the total revenues it receives exceed the explicit costs it incurs in the process of doing business. We call these profits **accounting profits**. Profits as accountants record them are based on total revenues and explicit costs and do not include implicit costs. An accountant's job is to keep track of money flows, money flowing into and out of businesses, which is why they measure explicit costs and usually ignore implicit costs.

 Economists prefer an alternative way of measuring profits; they are interested in total revenues minus total costs (both explicit and implicit). Economists include the implicit costs—as well as the explicit costs—when calculating the total costs of the firm.

 Measured in terms of accounting profits such as those reported in real-world financial statements, a firm has a profit if its total revenues exceed its explicit costs. In terms of **economic profits**, a firm has profits if its total revenues exceed its total opportunity costs—both its explicit costs and implicit costs. Exhibit 1 illustrates the difference between accounting profits and economic profits.

How do accounting profits differ from economic profits?

profits
the difference between total revenues and total costs

accounting profits
total revenues minus total explicit costs

economic profits
total revenues minus explicit and implicit costs

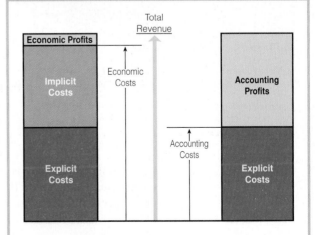

**section 11.1
exhibit 1**   **Accounting Profits versus Economic Profits**

Economic profits equal total revenues minus economic costs (explicit plus implicit costs). Accounting profits equal total revenues minus accounting costs (explicit costs).

USE WHAT YOU'VE LEARNED

Accounting Profits and Economic Profits

Q Emily, an energetic 10-year-old, set up a lemonade stand in front of her house. One Saturday, she sold 50 cups of lemonade at 50 cents apiece to her friends, who were hot and thirsty from playing. These sales generated $25 in total revenues for Emily. Emily was pleased because she knew her total costs—for lemonade, mix, cups, and so on—was only $5. As she was closing up shop for the day, her neighbor, an accountant, stopped by to say hello. Emily told him about her successful day. He said, "What a great job! You made a $20 profit!" Excited, Emily rushed into the house to tell her mother, an economist, the great news. Will Emily's mother agree with the accountant's calculation of Emily's profits? If not, why?

A No, Emily's mother will not agree with the accountant because he forgot to include the implicit costs when calculating Emily's profits. That is, he neglected to take into account what Emily could have been doing with her time if she had not been selling lemonade. For example, she could have been playing with her friends, cleaning her room, or perhaps helping her friends make money at their garage sale. These lost opportunities are implicit costs that should be included in the calculation of Emily's economic profits.

UPI/BRIAN KERSEY/LANDOV

At the beginning of the week, suppose you bought two tickets for $2,000 online at eBay for a sold-out Monday night game between the Bears and the Patriots at Soldier Field. The weather was forecasted for the high 50s at game time. However, an unexpected blizzard hits, taking the wind chill down to −30 on game day. Do you go to the game because you paid so much for the tickets? What if someone offers you $1,000 for the two tickets; would that necessarily be a bad decision if you lose $1,000? If you now valued the $1,000 more than the tickets, what are your sunk costs?

11.1e A Zero Economic Profit Is a Normal Profit

As we just discussed, an economic profit is less than an accounting profit because an economic profit includes implicit as well as explicit costs. In fact, an economist considers a zero economic profit a normal profit. A zero economic profit means that the firm is covering both explicit and implicit costs—the total opportunity costs of its resources. In other words, the firm's total revenues are sufficient to compensate for the time and money that owners put in the business. This is not as bad as it sounds. For example, suppose you become a farmer and make $80,000 a year. Initially you had to invest $1 million for the property, seed, and equipment. However, if you had put that money in the bank at, say, 3 percent interest, you would make $30,000 a year; so you have an implicit cost of $30,000 per year in lost interest. In addition, you have an implicit cost of $50,000 a year because you did not take the job you were offered at the tractor dealership. So an accountant would have you making an economic profit of $80,000 but an economist would say you made zero economic profit because your total revenue minus total costs (explicit + implicit costs) are zero. But even though your profits are driven to zero, your revenue from farming compensates you for your total costs, so you stay in business. This view is clearly different from making a zero accounting profit, when revenues would only cover the explicit costs. That is, at a zero economic profit, economic profits are zero but accounting profits are positive.

11.1f Sunk Costs

sunk costs
costs that have been incurred and cannot be recovered

We just saw how opportunity costs are often hidden, as in the case of implicit costs, and that economists believe they should be taken into account when making economic decisions. Another type of cost should also be discussed: sunk costs. Sunk costs have already been incurred and cannot be recovered. These costs are visible but should be ignored when making economic decisions. Suppose you attend a concert at the advice of a friend. The tickets were very expensive. But the concert is half over and you are bored out of your mind. Should you stay because the ticket was so expensive? No, now that you are half way through the concert, and the ticket can probably not be resold, the ticket price is sunk. The ticket cost cannot be recovered whether you stay or leave. The only question now is will you have more fun doing something else.

Or suppose a donut shop has a one-year lease, but after 3 months the owner decides that the shop would do much better by relocating to a new mall that just opened. Should the donut shop just stay put until the end of the year because it is legally obligated to pay the 12-month lease? No, the non-refundable lease payment is sunk and irrelevant to the decision to relocate. If moving means greater economic profits, it makes sense to move.

In short, sunk costs are irrelevant for any future action because they have already been incurred and cannot be recovered. Once sunk costs are paid, they should not impact current or future production decisions. They are lost, no matter what decision is made now or in the future.

Gym memberships are generally sunk costs that cannot be recovered. Once you have paid for the membership it is sunk. Your decision to go to the gym now depends on opportunity cost, not sunk cost. Would I rather do something else than go to the gym?

Why would you stay in business if you were making zero economic profits?

SECTION QUIZ

1. An explicit cost
   a. is an opportunity cost.
   b. is an out-of-pocket expense.
   c. does not require an outlay of money.
   d. is characterized by both (a) and (b).
   e. is characterized by both (a) and (c).

2. Which of the following is false?
   a. Explicit costs are input costs that require a monetary payment.
   b. Implicit costs do not represent an explicit outlay of money.
   c. Both implicit and explicit costs are opportunity costs.
   d. Sunk costs are irrelevant for any future action.
   e. All of the above are *true*.

3. Which of the following is false?
   a. Profits are a firm's total revenue minus its total costs.
   b. Accounting profits are actual revenues minus actual expenditures of money.
   c. Economic profits are actual revenues minus all explicit and implicit costs.
   d. If a firm has any implicit costs, its economic profits exceed its accounting profits.

4. The crucial difference between how economists and accountants analyze the profitability of a business has to do with whether or not _____ are included when calculating total production costs.
   a. implicit costs
   b. cash payments
   c. sunk costs
   d. explicit costs

(continued)

5. Which of the following is true?

   a. If a firm's implicit costs are zero, accounting profits equal economic profits.

   b. If a firm's implicit costs are positive, accounting profits exceed economic profits.

   c. If a firm's implicit costs are positive, economic profits exceed accounting profits.

   d. Both (a) and (b) are true.

   e. Both (a) and (c) are true.

6. Sunk costs

   a. should be included when weighing the marginal costs of production against the marginal benefits received.

   b. have already been incurred and cannot be recovered.

   c. plus variable costs equal the total costs of production.

   d. are relevant to future decisions and should be carefully considered.

1. What is the difference between explicit costs and implicit costs?

2. Why are both explicit costs and implicit costs relevant in making economic decisions?

3. How do we measure profits?

4. Why is it important to look at all the opportunity costs of production?

5. If you turn down a job offer of $45,000 per year to work for yourself, what is the opportunity cost of working for yourself?

Answers: 1. d 2. e 3. d 4. a 5. d 6. b

11.2   Production in the Short Run

▶ What is the difference between the short run and the long run?

▶ What is a production function?

▶ What is diminishing marginal product?

11.2a The Short Run versus the Long Run

short run

a period too brief for some production inputs to be varied

What is the difference between the short run and the long run?

long run

a period over which all production inputs are variable

Of fundamental importance for cost and production behavior is the extent to which a firm is able to adjust inputs as it varies output. Because it takes more time to vary some inputs than others, we must distinguish between the short run and the long run. The short run is defined as a period too brief for some inputs to be varied. For example, a firm cannot alter the current size of its plant in a day, and it cannot obtain new equipment overnight. If demand increases for the firm's product and the firm chooses to produce more output in the short run, it must do so with its existing equipment and factory. Inputs such as buildings and equipment that do not change with output are called *fixed* inputs.

The long run is a period in which a firm can adjust all inputs. That is, in the long run, all inputs to the firm are *variable*, changing as output changes. The length of the long run can vary considerably from industry to industry. For a chain of coffeehouses that wants to add a few more stores, the long run may only be a few months. In other industries, such as automobiles or steel, the long run might be a couple of years, as a new plant or factory in this type of industry takes much longer to build.

11.2b Production in the Short Run

Exhibit 1 shows how the quantity of bagels produced by Moe's Bagel Shop per hour varies with the number of workers. This relationship between the quantity of inputs (workers) and the quantity of outputs (bagels) is called the **production function.** Suppose that Moe's has just one input that is variable (labor) and the size of the bagel shop is fixed in the short run. What will happen to **total product (TP),** the total amount of output (bagels) generated by Moe's, as the level of the variable input, labor, rises? Common sense suggests that total product will start at a low level and increase—perhaps rapidly at first and then more slowly—as the amount of the variable input increases. It will continue to increase until the quantity of the variable input (labor) becomes so large in relation to the quantity of other inputs— the size of the bagel shop, for example—that further increases in output become more and more difficult or even impossible. In the second column of Exhibit 1, we see that as Moe increases the number of workers in his bagel shop, the number of bagels Moe is able to produce increases. The addition of the first worker results in a total output of 10 bagels per hour. When Moe adds a second worker, bagel output climbs to 24, an increase of 14 bagels per hour. Total product continues to increase even with the sixth worker hired; but you can see that it has slowed considerably, with the sixth worker only increasing total product by one bagel per hour. Beyond this point, additional workers may even result in a decline in total bagel output as workers bump into each other in the small bagel shop. This outcome is evident both in Exhibit 1 and in the total product curve shown in Exhibit 2(a).

section 11.2 exhibit 1	Moe's Production Function with One Variable, Labor	
Variable Input Labor (Workers)	**Total Output (Bagels per hour) Q**	**Marginal Product of Labor (Bagels per hour) $\Delta Q/\Delta V$**
0	0	
		10
1	10	
		14
2	24	
		12
3	36	
		10
4	46	
		4
5	50	
		1
6	51	

production function
the relationship between the quantity of inputs and the quantity of outputs produced

total product (TP)
the total output of a good produced by the firm

11.2c Diminishing Marginal Product

The **marginal product (MP)** of any single input is defined as the change in total product resulting from a one-unit change in the amount of input used. This concept is shown in the final column in Exhibit 1 and is illustrated by the *MP* curve in Exhibit 2(b). As you can see in Exhibit 2(b), the *MP* curve first rises and then falls.

marginal product (MP)
the change in total output of a good that results from a one-unit change in input

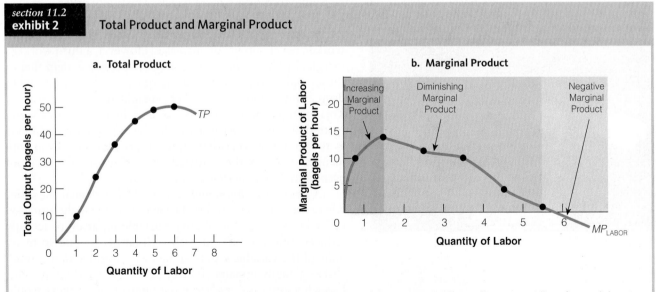

section 11.2 exhibit 2   Total Product and Marginal Product

a. Total Product

b. Marginal Product

In (a), we see that total output increases as the amount of the variable input, labor, is increased—usually more rapidly at first and then more slowly. In (b), we see that the marginal product first rises (increasing marginal product) as workers are added to the fixed input (a machine, for example), which is thus used more efficiently. Then the marginal product falls; the crowding of the fixed input with more and more workers causes marginal product to fall. Finally, negative marginal product occurs as additional inputs cause output to fall.

How many workers could be added to this jackhammer and still be productive (not to mention safe)? If more workers were added, how much output would be derived from each additional worker? Slightly more total output might be realized from the second worker because the second worker would be using the jackhammer while the first worker was taking a break from "the shakes." However, the fifth or sixth worker would clearly not create any additional output, as workers would just be standing around for their turn. That is, the marginal product (additional output) would eventually fall because of diminishing marginal product.

BRUCE BURKHARDT/FLIRT/CORBIS

The Rise in Marginal Product

The initial rise in the marginal product is the result of more effective use of fixed inputs as the number of workers increases. For example, certain types of capital equipment may require a minimum number of workers for efficient operation, or perhaps any operation at all. With a small number of workers (the variable input), some machines cannot operate at all, or only at a low level of efficiency. As additional workers are added, machines are brought into efficient operation and thus the marginal product of the workers rises. Similarly, if one person tried to operate a large department store alone—doing all the types of work necessary in the store—her energies would be spread so thin in so many directions that total output (sales) might be less than if she were operating a smaller store (working with less capital). As successive workers are added, up to a certain number, each worker adds more to total product than the previous one, and the marginal product rises. This relationship is seen in the shaded area of Exhibit 2(b) labeled "Increasing Marginal Product."

Would a firm ever knowingly operate at a point where its marginal product is negative?

diminishing marginal product

as a variable input increases, with other inputs fixed, a point will be reached where the additions to output will eventually decline

The Fall in Marginal Product

Too many workers in a store make it more difficult for customers to shop; too many workers in a factory get in each other's way. Adding more and more of a variable input to a fixed input will eventually lead to diminishing marginal product. Specifically, as the amount of a variable input is increased, with the amount of other (fixed) inputs held constant, a point will ultimately be reached beyond which marginal product will decline. Beyond this point, output increases but at a decreasing rate. It is the crowding of the fixed input with more and more workers that causes the decline in the marginal product.

The point of this discussion is that production functions conform to the same general pattern as that shown by Moe's Bagel Shop in the third column of Exhibit 1 and illustrated in Exhibit 2(b). In the third column of Exhibit 1, we see that as the number of workers in Moe's Bagel Shop increases, Moe is able to produce more bagels. The first worker is able to produce 10 bagels per hour. When Moe adds a second worker, total bagel output climbs to 24, an increase of 14 bagels per hour. When Moe hires a third worker, bagel output still increases. However, a third worker's marginal production (12 bagels per hour) is less than that of the second worker. In fact, the marginal product continues to drop as more and more workers are added to the bagel shop. This example shows diminishing marginal product at work. Note that it is *not* because the third worker is not as "good" as the second worker that marginal product falls. Even with identical workers, the increased "crowding" of the fixed input eventually causes marginal output to fall.

A firm never *knowingly* allows itself to reach the point where the marginal product becomes negative—the situation in which the use of additional variable input units actually reduces total product. In such a situation, having so many units of the variable input—inputs with positive opportunity costs—actually impairs efficient use of the fixed input units. In such a situation, *reducing* the number of workers would actually *increase* total product.

© ISTOCKPHOTO.COM/MEDIAPHOTOS

Suppose the second hour of studying leads to less learning than the first, but the fifth straight hour makes you forget what you learned in the first hour. What can we say about the diminishing marginal product of your study time? It is declining and eventually becomes negative.

SECTION QUIZ

1. The short run
   a. is a period too brief for any inputs to be varied.
   b. is a period that involves no fixed costs.
   c. is normally a period of one year.
   d. is none of the above.

2. The long run
   a. is a period in which a firm can adjust all its inputs.
   b. can vary in length from industry to industry.
   c. is a period in which all costs are variable costs.
   d. is characterized by all of the above.

3. Which of the following most accurately describes the long-run period?
   a. The long run is a period of time in which a firm is unable to vary some of its factors of production.
   b. In the long run, a firm is able to expand output by utilizing additional workers and raw materials, but not physical capital.
   c. The long run is of sufficient length to allow a firm to alter its plant capacity and all other factors of production.
   d. The long run is of sufficient length to allow a firm to transform economic losses into economic profits.
   e. Both (a) and (b) most accurately describe the long-run period.

4. Production in the short run
   a. is subject to the law of diminishing marginal product.
   b. involves some fixed factors.
   c. can be increased by employing another unit of a variable input, as long as the marginal product of that input is positive.
   d. is characterized by all of the above.
   e. is characterized by none of the above.

5. A production function shows the relationship between
   a. variable inputs and fixed inputs.
   b. variable inputs and output.
   c. costs and output.
   d. inputs and costs.
   e. production and sales revenue.

6. Diminishing marginal productivity in a frozen-pizza company means that
   a. hiring additional workers causes the total output of pizza to fall.
   b. hiring additional workers does not change the total output of pizza produced.
   c. hiring additional workers adds fewer and fewer pizzas to total output.
   d. the average total cost of production must be decreasing.

---

1. What is the difference between fixed and variable inputs?
2. Why are all inputs variable in the long run?
3. What relationship does a production function represent?
4. What is diminishing marginal product? What causes it?

Answers: 1. d   2. d   3. c   4. d   5. b   6. c

Costs in the Short Run

▷ What are fixed costs?

▷ What are variable costs?

▷ What are marginal costs?

▷ What are average fixed, average variable, and average total costs?

In the last section, we discussed the relationship between a firm's inputs and its level of output. But that relationship is only one part of the discussion; we must also consider how much it will cost the firm to use each of these inputs in production. In this section, we examine the short-run costs of the firm—what they are and how they vary with the output levels that are produced. The short-run total costs of a business fall into two distinct categories: fixed costs and variable costs.

11.3a Fixed Costs, Variable Costs, and Total Costs

fixed costs
costs that do not vary with the level of output

total fixed cost (TFC)
the sum of the firm's fixed costs

variable costs
costs that vary with the level of output

total variable cost (TVC)
the sum of the firm's variable costs

total cost (TC)
the sum of the firm's total fixed costs and total variable costs

Fixed costs are those costs that do not vary with the level of output. For example, the rent on buildings or equipment is usually fixed, at least for some period; whether the firm produces lots of output or little output, the rent stays the same. Insurance premiums, property taxes, and interest payments on debt used to finance capital equipment are other examples of fixed costs; they have to be paid even if no output is produced. In the short run, fixed costs cannot be avoided. The sum of the firm's fixed costs is called the total fixed cost (TFC).

Variable costs vary with the level of output. As more variable inputs such as labor and raw materials are added, output increases. The variable cost (expenditures for wages and raw materials) increases as output increases. The sum of the firm's variable costs is called the total variable cost (TVC). The sum of the total fixed costs and total variable costs is called the firm's total cost (TC).

11.3b Average Total Costs

average total cost (ATC)
a per-unit cost of operation; total cost divided by output

average fixed cost (AFC)
a per-unit measure of fixed costs; fixed costs divided by output

average variable cost (AVC)
a per-unit measure of variable costs; variable costs divided by output

Although we are often interested in the total amount of costs incurred by the firm, sometimes we find it convenient to discuss these costs on a per-unit-of-output, or an average, basis. For example, if Pizza Shack Company has a total fixed cost of $1,600 and a total variable cost of $2,400, its total cost is $4,000. If it produces 800 pizzas in the period in question, its total cost per unit of output equals $5 ($4,000 total cost ÷ 800 units of output = $5). We call this per-unit cost the average total cost (ATC). Likewise, we might talk about the fixed cost per unit of output, or average fixed cost (AFC). In the case of Pizza Shack, the average fixed cost, or AFC, would equal $2 ($1,600 fixed cost ÷ 800 units of output = $2). Similarly, we can speak of the per-unit variable cost, or average variable cost (AVC). In this example, the average variable cost would equal $3 ($2,400 variable cost ÷ 800 units of output = $3).

11.3c Marginal Costs

marginal cost (MC)
the change in total costs resulting from a one-unit change in output

Up to this point, six different short-run cost concepts have been introduced: total cost, total fixed cost, total variable cost, average total cost, average fixed cost, and average variable cost. All these concepts are relevant to a discussion of firm behavior and profitability. However, the most important single cost concept has yet to be mentioned: marginal (or additional) cost. You may recall this concept from Chapter 2, where we highlighted the importance of using marginal analysis—that is, analysis that focuses on *additional* or marginal choices. Specifically, marginal cost (MC) shows the change in total cost (TC) associated with a change in output (Q) by one unit ($\Delta TC/\Delta Q$). Put a bit differently, marginal cost is the cost of producing one more unit of output. As such, looking at marginal cost is a useful way to view variable cost—cost that varies as output varies. Marginal cost represents the added labor, raw materials, and miscellaneous expenses incurred in making an additional unit of output. Marginal cost is the additional, or incremental, cost associated with the "last" unit of output produced.

11.3d How Are These Costs Related?

Exhibit 1 summarizes the definitions of the seven different short-run cost concepts introduced in this chapter. To further clarify these concepts and to illustrate the relationships between them, let's return to our discussion of the costs faced by Pizza Shack.

Exhibit 2 presents the costs incurred by Pizza Shack at various levels of output. Notice that the total fixed cost is the same at all output levels and that at low output levels (four or fewer units in the example), total fixed cost is the dominant portion of total costs. At high output levels (eight or more units in the example), total fixed cost becomes quite small relative to total variable cost. As the firm increases its output, it spreads its total fixed cost across more units; as a result, the average fixed cost declines continuously.

It is often easier to understand these cost concepts by examining graphs that show the levels of the various costs at different output levels. The graph in Exhibit 3 shows the first

---

section 11.3
exhibit 1   A Summary of the Short-Run Cost Concept

Concept	Abbreviation	Definition
Total fixed cost	TFC	Costs that are the same at all output levels (e.g., insurance, rent)
Total variable cost	TVC	Costs that vary with the level of output (e.g., hourly labor, raw materials)
Total cost	TC	Sum of the firm's total fixed costs and total variable costs at a level of output ($TC = TFC + TVC$)
Marginal cost	MC	Added cost of producing one more unit of output; change in TC associated with one more unit of output ($\Delta TC/\Delta Q$)
Average total cost	ATC	TC per unit of output; TC divided by output (TC/Q)
Average fixed cost	AFC	TFC per unit of output; TFC divided by output (TFC/Q)
Average variable cost	AVC	TVC per unit of output; TVC divided by output (TVC/Q)

---

section 11.3
exhibit 2   Cost Calculations for Pizza Shack Company

(1) Hourly Output (Q)	(2) Total Fixed Cost (TFC)	(3) Total Variable Cost (TVC)	(4) Total Cost (TC = TVC + TFC)	(5) Average Fixed Cost (AFC = TFC/Q)	(6) Average Variable Cost (AVC = TVC/Q)	(7) Average Total Cost (ATC = TC/Q or AFC + AVC)	(8) Marginal Cost (MC = ΔTC/ΔQ)
0	$40	$0	$40	—	—	—	
1	40	10	50	$40.00	$10.00	$50.00	$10
2	40	18	58	20.00	9.00	29.00	8
3	40	25	65	13.33	8.33	21.66	7
4	40	33	73	10.00	8.25	18.25	8
5	40	43	83	8.00	8.60	16.60	10
6	40	56	96	6.67	9.33	16.00	13
7	40	73	113	5.71	10.43	16.14	17
8	40	94	134	5.00	11.75	16.75	21
9	40	120	160	4.44	13.33	17.77	26
10	40	152	192	4.00	15.20	19.20	32

section 11.3
exhibit 3

Total and Fixed Costs

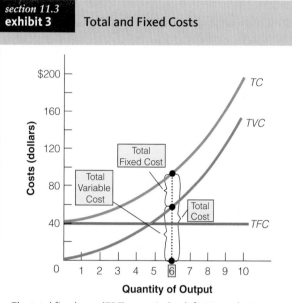

The total fixed cost (*TFC*) curve is, by definition, a horizontal line. The total cost (*TC*) curve is the vertical summation of the total variable cost (*TVC*) and total fixed cost (*TFC*) curves. Notice that *TVC* = 0 when *Q* = 0 and that *TFC* = $40 even when no output is being produced.

three cost concepts: fixed, variable, and total costs. The total fixed cost (*TFC*) curve is always a horizontal line because, by definition, fixed costs are the same at all output levels—even at zero level of output. In Exhibit 3, notice that *TVC* = 0 when *Q* = 0; if no output is being produced, no variable costs are incurred.

The total cost (*TC*) curve is the summation of the total variable cost (*TVC*) and total fixed cost (*TFC*) curves. Because the total fixed cost curve is horizontal, the total cost curve lies above the total variable cost curve by a fixed (vertical) amount.

Exhibit 4 shows the average fixed cost curve, the average variable cost curve, the average total cost curve, and the associated marginal cost curve. In this exhibit, notice how the average fixed cost (*AFC*) curve constantly declines, approaching but never reaching zero. Remember, *AFC* is simply *TFC/Q*, so as output expands, *AFC* declines, because the total fixed cost is being spread over successively larger volumes of output. Also observe how the marginal cost (*MC*) curve crosses the average variable cost (*AVC*) and average total cost (*ATC*) curves at their lowest points. At higher output levels, high marginal costs pull up the average variable cost and average total cost curves, while at low output levels, low marginal costs pull the curves down. In the next section, we explain why the marginal cost curve intersects the average variable cost curve and the average total cost curve at their minimum points.

Why does average fixed cost decrease with added output?

section 11.3
exhibit 4

Average and Marginal Costs

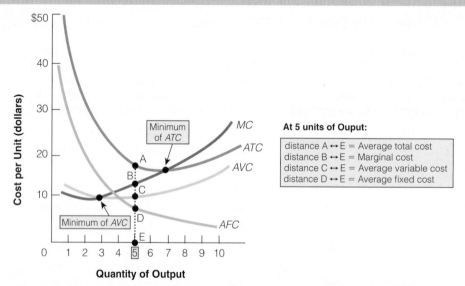

At 5 units of Ouput:

distance A ↔ E = Average total cost
distance B ↔ E = Marginal cost
distance C ↔ E = Average variable cost
distance D ↔ E = Average fixed cost

The marginal cost (*MC*) curve always intersects the average total cost (*ATC*) and average variable cost (*AVC*) curves at those curves' minimum points. Average fixed cost (*AFC*) curves always decline and approach—but never reach—zero. The *ATC* curve is the vertical summation of the *AFC* and *AVC* curves; it reaches its minimum (lowest unit cost) point at a higher output than the minimum point of the *AVC* curve.

SECTION QUIZ

1. Total fixed costs
   a. do not vary with the level of output.
   b. cannot be avoided in the short run without going out of business.
   c. do not exist in the long run.
   d. are characterized by all of the above.

2. Which of the following is most likely a variable cost for a business?
   a. The loan payment on funds borrowed when a new building is constructed
   b. Payments for electricity
   c. The lease payment on a warehouse used by a business
   d. Contracted shipments of materials

3. The change in total cost that results from the production of one additional unit of output is called
   a. marginal revenue.
   b. average variable cost.
   c. marginal cost.
   d. average total cost.
   e. average fixed cost.

4. Which short-run curve typically declines continuously as output expands?
   a. Average variable cost
   b. Average total cost
   c. Average fixed cost
   d. Marginal cost
   e. None of the above

---

1. What is the difference between fixed costs and variable costs?
2. How are the average fixed cost, average variable cost, and average total cost calculated?
3. Why is marginal cost the relevant cost to consider when a producer is deciding whether to produce more or less of a product?
4. If the average variable cost curve were constant over some range of output, why would the average total cost be falling over that range of output?
5. If your season batting average going into a game was .300 (three hits per 10 at bats) and you got two hits in five at bats during the game, would your season batting average rise or fall as a result?

Answers: 1. d 2. b 3. c 4. c

11.4 The Shape of the Short-Run Cost Curves

▶ What is the relationship between marginal costs and marginal product?

▶ Why is the average total cost curve U-shaped?

▶ When marginal cost is greater than average cost, what happens to the average?

11.4a The Relationship between Marginal Costs and Marginal Product

What is the relationship between marginal cost and marginal product?

The behavior of marginal costs bears a definite relationship to marginal product (*MP*). Say, for example, that the variable input is labor. Initially, as the firm adds more workers, the marginal product of labor tends to rise. When the marginal product of labor is rising, marginal costs are falling because each additional worker adds more to the total product than the previous worker. Thus, the increase in total cost resulting from the production of another unit of output—marginal cost—falls. However, when marginal product of labor is declining, marginal costs are rising because additional workers are adding less to total output. In sum, if an additional worker's marginal product is lower (higher) than that of previous workers, marginal costs increase (decrease), as seen in Exhibit 1. In area a of the two graphs in Exhibit 1, we see that as marginal product rises, marginal costs fall; in area b, we see that as marginal product falls, marginal costs rise. For example, if we are only producing a few bagels in our bagel shop, we have some idle resources like the equipment (ovens, cash registers and so on). At this point, the marginal product of an extra worker is large and the marginal cost of producing one more bagel is small. However, when the bagel shop is crowded, producing many bagels with many workers and the equipment is being used to capacity, the marginal product of hiring another worker is low. Why? Because the new worker has to work in crowded conditions where she may be bumping into other workers as she waits to use the toasters and cash register. The flip side of the coin is that when the bagel shop is crowded with workers, producing an additional bagel requires a lot of additional workers—higher marginal costs. In short, when the number of bagels produced is high, the marginal product of another worker is low and the marginal cost of an additional bagel is large. Recall that for many firms, over some range of output, marginal product actually rises when additional workers are added. That is, initially there is increasing marginal product. Depending on the production process, the second and third workers might be more productive than the first. As more workers are added, and additional output is produced, the firm may have its workers specialize in certain tasks. But once enough workers are hired to capture all the benefits from further specialization, diminishing returns of labor set in and the marginal costs turn upward.

section 11.4 exhibit 1   Marginal Product and Marginal Costs

Area a

Area b

Area a: MP↑ and MC↓

Area b: MP↓ and MC↑

Marginal Product (units per hour)

MP

Number of Workers

Area a

Area b

MC

Marginal Cost (dollars)

Quantity of Output

An inverse relationship exists between marginal product (*MP*) and marginal costs (*MC*). When marginal product is rising, marginal costs must fall, and when marginal product falls, marginal costs must rise.

11.4b The Relationship between Marginal and Average Amounts

The relationship between the marginal and the average is simply a matter of arithmetic; when a number (the marginal cost) being added into a series is smaller than the previous average of the series, the new average will be lower than the previous one. Likewise, when the marginal number is larger than the average, the average will rise. For example, if you have taken two economics exams and received a 90 percent on your first exam and an 80 percent on your second exam, you have an 85 percent average. If, after some serious studying, you get a 100 percent on the third exam (the marginal exam), what happens to your average? It rises to 90 percent. Because the marginal is greater than the average, it "pulls" the average up. However, if the score on your third (marginal) exam is lower—a 70 percent—your average will fall to 80 percent because the marginal is below the average. A baseball or softball player will improve on their batting average if the next trip to the plate is a hit; their average will fall if they strike out.

11.4c The Average Total Cost Curve Is Usually U-Shaped

Why is the average total cost curve usually U-shaped, as seen in Exhibit 2? At very small levels of output and very large levels of output, average total cost is very high. The reason for the high average total cost when the firm is producing a very small amount of output is the high average fixed cost—when the output rate of the plant is small relative to its capacity, the plant is being underutilized. But as the firm expands output beyond this point, the average total cost falls. Why? Remember that $ATC = AFC + AVC$, and average fixed cost always falls when output expands because the fixed costs are being spread over more units of output. Thus, it is the declining AFC that is primarily responsible for the falling ATC.

Is ATC high at both low and high levels of output for the same reason?

The average total cost rises at high levels of output because of diminishing marginal product. For example, as more and more workers are put to work using a fixed quantity of machines, the result may be crowded working conditions and/or increasing maintenance costs as equipment is used more intensively or as older, less-efficient machinery is called on to handle the greater output. In fact, diminishing marginal product sets in at the bottom of the marginal cost curve, as seen in Exhibit 2. That is, it is diminishing marginal product that causes marginal costs to increase, eventually causing the average variable cost and average total cost curves to rise. At large levels of output, relative to plant capacity, the fixed plant is overutilized, leading to high marginal costs that cause a high average total cost.

11.4d The Relationship between Marginal Costs and Average Variable and Average Total Costs

Certain relationships exist between marginal costs and average variable and average total costs. For example, when the average variable cost is falling, marginal costs must be less than the average variable cost; and when the average

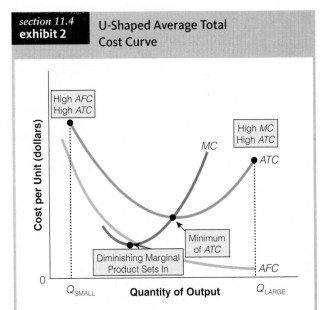

section 11.4 exhibit 2   U-Shaped Average Total Cost Curve

At low levels of output, *ATC* is high because *AFC* is high—the fixed plant is underutilized. At high levels of output (close to capacity), the fixed plant is overutilized, leading to high *MC* and, consequently, high *ATC*. It is diminishing marginal product that causes the *MC*, and eventually the *AVC* and *ATC*, to rise.

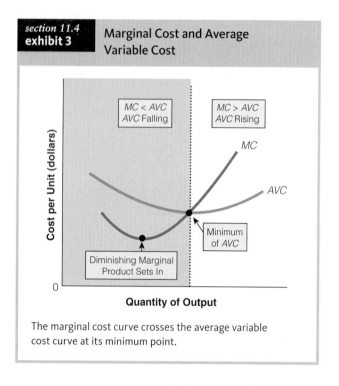

Marginal Cost and Average Variable Cost

The marginal cost curve crosses the average variable cost curve at its minimum point.

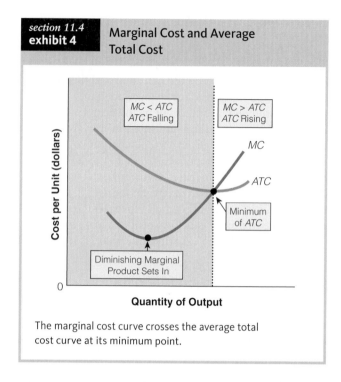

Marginal Cost and Average Total Cost

The marginal cost curve crosses the average total cost curve at its minimum point.

How are the marginal cost curve and the average total cost curve related?

variable cost is rising, marginal costs are greater than the average variable cost. Marginal costs are equal to the average variable cost at the lowest point of the average variable cost curve, as seen in Exhibit 3. In the left-hand (shaded) portion of Exhibit 3, marginal costs are less than the average variable cost, and the average is falling. On the right side, marginal costs are greater than the average variable cost, and the average is rising. The same relationship holds for the marginal cost curve and the average total cost curve. In the left-hand (shaded) portion of Exhibit 4, marginal costs are less than the average total cost, and the average is falling. On the right side, marginal costs are greater than the average total cost, and the average is rising. So it is the marginal cost curve that determines the U-shape of the *AVC* and *ATC* curves.

USE WHAT YOU'VE LEARNED

Marginal versus Average Amounts

Q If a small horse-racing jockey decided to join your economics class of 10 students, what would happen to the *average* height of the class?

A The marginal addition, the jockey, would presumably be smaller than the average person in the class, so the average height of the class would fall. Now, if the star seven-foot center on the basketball team joined your class, the average height would rise, because the newer marginal member would presumably be taller than the average person. In sum, if the margin is greater (less) than the average, the average will rise (fall).

SECTION QUIZ

1. Which of the following is true?

   a. The short-run *ATC* exceeds the short-run *AVC* at any given level of output.

   b. If the short-run *ATC* curve is rising, the short-run *AVC* curve is also rising.

   c. The short-run *AFC* is always falling with increased output, whether the short-run *MC* curve is greater or less than short-run *AFC*.

   d. If short-run *MC* is less than short-run *AVC*, short-run *AVC* is falling.

   e. All of the above are true.

2. Which of the following is true in the short run?

   a. MC equals *ATC* at the lowest point of *ATC*.

   b. MC equals *AVC* at the lowest point of *AVC*.

   c. When *AVC* is at its minimum point, *ATC* is falling.

   d. When *ATC* is at its minimum point, *AVC* is rising.

   e. All of the above are true.

3. Which of the following is always true?

   a. When marginal cost is less than average total cost, average total cost is increasing.

   b. When average fixed cost is falling, marginal cost must be less than average fixed cost.

   c. When average variable cost is falling, marginal cost must be greater than average variable cost.

   d. When marginal cost is greater than average total cost, average total cost is increasing.

4. When marginal product is increasing,

   a. marginal cost is increasing.

   b. marginal cost is decreasing.

   c. average variable cost is increasing.

   d. average total cost is increasing.

   e. total cost is decreasing.

5. If a taxi service is operating in the region of diminishing marginal product and more taxi service is added in the short run, what will happen to the marginal cost of providing the additional service?

   a. It is impossible to say anything about marginal cost with the information provided.

   b. Marginal cost will decrease.

   c. Marginal cost will increase.

   d. Marginal cost will stay the same.

---

1. What is the primary reason that the average total cost falls as output expands over low output ranges?

2. Why does the average total cost rise at some point as output expands further?

3. If marginal costs are less than the average total cost, why does *ATC* fall? If *MC* is greater than *ATC*, why does *ATC* rise?

Answers: 1. e   2. e   3. d   4. b   5. c

11.5   Cost Curves: Short Run versus Long Run

▶ Why are long-run costs different than short-run costs?
▶ What are economies of scale?

▶ What are diseconomies of scale?
▶ What are constant returns to scale?

Larger plants may be built in the long run.

BRAND X PICTURES/GETTY IMAGES

11.5a Long-Run Cost Curves

Over long enough periods, firms can vary all of their productive inputs. That is, time provides an opportunity to substitute lower-cost capital, like larger plants or newer, more sophisticated equipment, for more expensive labor inputs. However, in the short run a firm cannot alter its plant size and equipment. These inputs are fixed in the short run, so the firm can only expand output by employing more variable inputs (e.g., workers and raw materials) in order to get extra output from the existing factory. If a company has to pay many workers overtime wages to expand output in the short run, over the long run firms may opt to invest in new equipment to conserve on expensive labor. That is, in the long run, the firm can expand its factories, build new ones, or shut down unproductive ones. Of course, the time it takes for a firm to get to the long run varies from firm to firm. For example, it may take only a couple of months to build a new coffee shop, while it may take a few years to build a new automobile plant.

Why are long-run cost curves different from short-run cost curves?

In Exhibit 1, we see that the long-run average total cost ($LRATC$) curve lies equal to or below the short-run average total cost ($SRATC$) curves. The reason for the difference between the firm's long-run total cost curve and the short-run total cost curve is that in the long run, costs are lower because firms have greater flexibility in changing inputs that are fixed in the short run. In Exhibit 1, we present three possible plant sizes: $SRATC_1$ (small), $SRATC_2$ (medium) and $SRATC_3$ (large).

It also shows the long-run average total cost curve. In the *short run*, the firm is restricted to the current plant size, but in the long run it can choose the short-run cost curve for the level of production it is planning on producing. As the firm moves along the long-run average total cost curve, it is adjusting the size of the factory to the quantity of production.

11.5b Creating the Long-Run Average Total Cost Curve

Certain relationships among the successive curves should be emphasized. For very small output levels, q_1, costs are lowest with the smallest plant size, $SRATC_1$, point A. Costs with plant size $SRATC_2$ (the medium-sized plant) are relatively high for these low levels of output because the plant's fixed costs are far too high for low levels of output—machinery, buildings, and so on would be poorly utilized. In Exhibit 1, we can see that if q_1 output is produced with plant size $SRATC_2$, the plant would be operating at below capacity, at point B, and the cost would be higher at $10 per unit rather than $7 per unit, at point A. However, if the firm planned to produce output level q_2, costs with plant size $SRATC_2$ are lower that those with $SRATC_1$. If output levels in this range were produced with the smaller plant, $SRATC_1$, the plant would be operating beyond designed capacity, at point D, and cost would be higher at $7 per unit rather than at $5 per unit, at point C. That

section 11.5
exhibit 1   The Short-Run and Long-Run Average Total Cost Curves

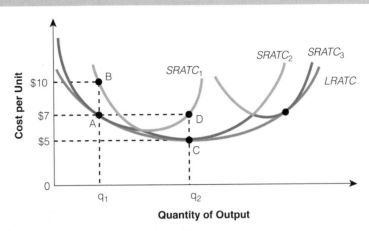

The long run average total is made up of segments of the short run average total cost curves ($SRATC_1$, $SRATC_2$, and $SRATC_3$) of the various size plants the firm can choose. Each point along the red scalloped portion of the the three cost curves represents the $LRATC$ when there are only three plants. The blue smooth U-shaped long-run average is the long-run average total cost curve if there were many possible short-run average total cost curves. The long-run average total cost curve represents the lowest unit cost cost attainable for any output when the firm has time to make all the desired changes in its plant size.

is, plant $SRATC_2$, designed for a larger volume of output than the small plant, would minimize costs for producing quantity q_2.

If a straight line were extended upward from the horizontal output axis on a graph containing the various $SRATC$ curves for different-sized plants, the point at which it first struck an $SRATC$ curve would indicate the relevant value of $LRATC$ for that output level. Thus, in Exhibit 1, for low levels of output, q_1, the lowest average cost point is on curve $SRATC_1$; at output q_2, it is on $SRATC_2$, and so on. If there are only three possible plant sizes ($SRATC_1$, $SRATC_2$, and $SRATC_3$) the long-run average cost curve is the red scalloped portion of the three short-run cost curves. When there are many possible plant sizes, the successive $SRATC$ curves will be close to one another, and the $LRATC$ curve will be smooth and U-shaped, like the dark solid blue line in Exhibit 1.

The $LRATC$ curve is often called a *planning curve*, since it represents the cost data relevant to the firm when it is planning policy relating to scale of operations, output, and price over a long period of time. At a particular time, a firm already in operation has a certain plant and must base its current price and output decisions on the costs with the existing plant. However, when the firm considers the possibility of adjusting its scale of operations, long-run cost estimates are relevant.

11.5c **The Shape of the Long Run ATC Curve**

By examining the long-run average total cost in Exhibit 2, we can see three possible production patterns. In Exhibit 2(a), when ATC falls as output expands, we say that there are economies of scale present. In Exhibit 2(c), when ATC rises as output expands, we say that the firm is facing diseconomies of scale. And in Exhibit 2(b) when the ATC does not vary with output, the firm is facing constant returns to scale.

economies of scale
occur in an output range where
$LRATC$ falls as output increases

diseconomies of scale
occur in an output range where
$LRATC$ rises as output expands

constant returns to scale
occur in an output range where
$LRATC$ does not change as
output varies

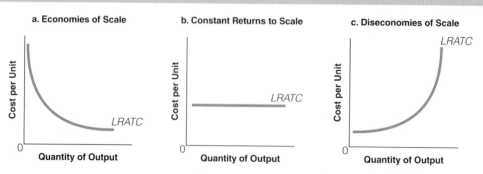

a. Economies of Scale   b. Constant Returns to Scale   c. Diseconomies of Scale

At very low output levels, some reduction of average costs per unit are obtainable by expanding output; in those output ranges, economies of scale exist, as seen in Exhibit 2(a). At higher output ranges, average costs per unit will start rising if the firm enters an output range characterized by diseconomies of scale, as seen in Exhibit 2(c). If the *LRATC* is flat, the average per unit costs will be constant over this range of output, the firm is experiencing constant returns to scale, as seen in Exhibit 2(b). The typical firm in an industry may well experience economies of scale at low levels of output, constant returns to scale at higher levels of output, and diseconomies of scale at still higher levels of output, as seen in Exhibit 3. The minimum efficient scale plant is one in which the economies of scale are exhausted and the long-run average total costs are minimized. This is shown in Exhibit 3. In this constant returns to scale range (the flat portion of the *LRATC*), firms of differing size can compete on a roughly equal basis as far as costs are concerned—that is, they have no cost advantage over firms that are operating at the minimum efficient scale.

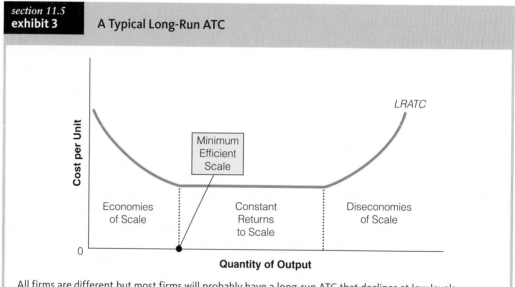

All firms are different but most firms will probably have a long-run ATC that declines at low levels of output and then remains constant and then eventually will rise at the higher levels of output. The **minimum efficient scale** is the lowest level of output at which average total costs are minimized.

minimum efficient scale

the output level where economies of scale are exhausted and constant returns to scale begin

11.5d Why Do Economies and Diseconomies of Scale Occur?

As we have just seen, economies of scale exist when there is a reduction in the firm's long-run average costs as output expands. Firms may experience economies of scale for several reasons. First, if a firm operates on a larger scale, both workers and managers can become more specialized, allowing workers and managers to be more productive as output expands. Second, large initial setup costs in some industries, such as in some manufacturing sectors and in oil

FUSE/GETTY IMAGES

By having several screens in one complex, the cinema company can cut down on advertising and employee costs as well as rent. Because of economies of scale, it may be less expensive to have eight screens in one building with one concession area than eight separate theaters, each with one screen and a concession area. However, at some level diseconomies may set in—perhaps at 10 or 20 screens. Too many screens may lead to traffic congestion, the supply of popular movies may be limited, and there may be a problem coordinating the starts and finishes of 10–20 films so you do not have lobby congestion during prime time.

© TONYV3112/SHUTTERSTOCK.COM

As a result of economies of scale derived from these large container ships it is easy to see how a t-shirt in China can be shipped to Europe for just a few cents, ultimately driving down prices for consumers.

refining, means that high fixed costs are necessary to produce any output. That is, large firms can take advantage of highly efficient mass production techniques and equipment, which are only economical if spread over a large output. Third, larger firms such as Walmart may be able to purchase inputs at lower costs than smaller firms.

Recall that diseconomies of scale exist when there is an increase in the firm's long-run average costs as output expands. This may occur as the firm finds it increasingly difficult to handle the complexities of large-scale management. For example, information and coordination problems tend to increase when a firm becomes very large. For example, some companies with numerous production facilities all over the world may witness management and communication coordination problems that could ultimately lead to higher costs as output expands. This is why the *LRATC* is usually U-shaped. At low levels of output, firms generally benefit from increased size because they can take advantage of specialization. However, at high levels of output, the gains from specialization have already occurred but coordination and bureaucratic problems increase.

SECTION QUIZ

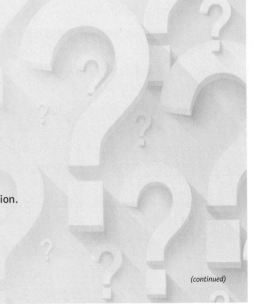

1. If a firm's *ATC* is falling in the long run, then
   a. it is subject to economies of scale over that range of output.
   b. it is subject to diseconomies of scale over that range of output.
   c. it is subject to constant return to scale over that range of output.
   d. it has reached the minimum efficient scale of production.
   e. both (c) and (d) are true.

2. In the long run,
   a. the average fixed cost curve is U-shaped.
   b. the average fixed cost exceeds the average variable cost of production.
   c. all costs are variable.
   d. all costs are fixed.
   e. none of the above is correct.

(continued)

SECTION QUIZ (cont.)

3. When a firm experiences economies of scale in production,

   a. long-run average total cost declines as output expands.

   b. long-run average total cost increases as output expands.

   c. marginal cost increases as output expands.

   d. the marginal product of an input diminishes with increased utilization.

4. The lowest level of output at which a firm's goods are produced at minimum long-run average total cost is called

   a. the point of zero marginal cost.

   b. the point of diminishing returns.

   c. the minimum total product.

   d. the minimum efficient scale.

   e. plant capacity.

1. What are economies of scale, diseconomies of scale, and constant returns to scale?

2. How might cooking for a family dinner be subject to falling average total cost in the long run as the size of the family grows?

3. What may cause economies or diseconomies of scale?

Answers: 1. a 2. c 3. a 4. d

INTERACTIVE SUMMARY

1. Profits are defined as _____ minus _____.

2. The cost of producing a good is measured by the worth of the _____ alternative that was given up to obtain the resource.

3. Explicit costs are input costs that require a(n) _____ payment.

4. Whenever we talk about cost—explicit or implicit—we are talking about _____ cost.

5. Economists generally assume that the ultimate goal of a firm is to _____ profits.

6. Accounting profits equal actual revenues minus actual expenditures of cash (explicit costs), so they do not include _____ costs.

7. Economists consider a zero economic profit a normal profit because it means that the firm is covering both _____ and _____ costs—the total opportunity cost of its resources.

8. _____ costs are costs that have already been incurred and cannot be recovered.

9. Because it takes more time to vary some inputs than others, we must distinguish between the _____ run and the _____ run.

10. The long run is a period of time in which the firm can adjust _____ inputs.

11. In the long run, all costs are _____ costs and will change as output changes.

12. The total product schedule shows the total amount of _____ generated as the level of the variable input increases.

13. The marginal product of any single input is the change in total product resulting from a(n) _____ change in the amount of that input used.

14. As the amount of a variable input is increased, the amount of other fixed inputs being held constant, a point will ultimately be reached beyond which marginal product will decline. This point is called _____.

15. The short-run total costs of a business fall into two distinct categories: _____ costs and _____ costs.

16. Fixed costs are costs that _____ with the level of output.

17. In the short run, fixed costs cannot be avoided without _____.

18. The sum of a firm's fixed costs is called its _____.

19. Costs that are not fixed are called _____ costs.

20. The sum of a firm's variable costs is called its _____.

21. The sum of a firm's total _____ costs and total _____ costs is called its total cost.

22. Average total cost equals _____ divided by the _____ produced.

23. Average fixed cost equals _____ divided by the _____ produced.

24. _____ equals total variable cost divided by the level of output produced.

25. Marginal costs are the _____ costs associated with the "last" unit of output produced.

26. A fixed cost curve is always a(n) _____ line because, by definition, fixed costs are the same at all output levels.

27. The reason for high average total costs when a firm is producing a very small amount of output is the high _____ costs.

28. The average total cost curve rises at high levels of output because of _____ product.

29. When *AVC* is falling, *MC* must be _____ than *AVC*; and when *AVC* is rising, *MC* must be _____ than *AVC*.

30. In the _____ run, a company cannot vary its plant size and equipment, so the firm can only expand output by employing more _____ inputs.

31. The *LRATC* curve is often called a(n) _____ curve because it represents the cost data relevant to a firm when it is planning policy relating to scale of operations, output, and price over a long period of time.

32. When *LRATC* falls as output expands, _____ of scale occur. When the *LRATC* does not vary with output, the firm faces _____ to scale. When the *LRATC* rises as output expands, _____ of scale occur.

33. At the _____ scale, a plant has exhausted its economies of scale and the long-run average total costs are minimized.

34. Any particular cost curve is based on the assumption that _____ prices and _____ are constant.

35. _____ may occur as a firm finds it increasingly difficult to handle the complexities of large-scale management.

Answers: 1. total revenues; total costs 2. most valuable 3. monetary 4. opportunity 5. maximize 6. implicit 7. implicit; explicit 8. Sunk 9. short; long 10. all 11. variable 12. output 13. small 14. diminishing marginal product 15. fixed; variable 16. do not vary 17. going out of business 18. total fixed cost 19. variable 20. total variable cost 21. fixed; variable 22. total cost; level of output 23. total fixed cost; level of output 24. Average variable cost 25. additional 26. horizontal 27. average fixed 28. diminishing marginal 29. less; more 30. short; variable 31. planning 32. economies; constant returns; diseconomies 33. minimum efficient 34. input. technology 35. Diseconomies of scale

SECTION QUIZ ANSWERS

11.1 Firms and Profits: Total Revenues Minus Total Costs

1. What is the difference between explicit costs and implicit costs?

Explicit costs are those costs readily measured by the money spent on the resources used, such as wages. Implicit costs are those that do not represent an explicit outlay of money, but do represent opportunity costs, such as the opportunity cost of your time when you work for yourself.

2. Why are both explicit costs and implicit costs relevant in making economic decisions?

In making economic decisions, where expected marginal benefits must be weighed against expected marginal costs, all relevant costs must be included, whether they are explicit or implicit.

3. How do we measure profits?

Profit is measured as total revenue minus total cost.

4. Why is it important to look at all the opportunity costs of production?

Economic profit equals total revenue minus both explicit and implicit costs, including the opportunity cost (forgone earnings) of financial resources invested in the firm. All of your owned inputs—including your own time, equipment, structures, land, and so on—have opportunity costs that aren't revealed in explicit dollar payments. Correctly assigning implicit costs to all these owned inputs is necessary so that a correct measure of economic profits can be made. To be earning economic profits means that a firm is earning an above-normal rate of return.

5. If you turn down a job offer of $45,000 per year to work for yourself, what is the opportunity cost of working for yourself?

Other things being equal, you incur a $45,000 per year implicit cost of working for yourself in this case because it is what you give up when you choose to turn down the alternative job offer. If you turned down even better offers, your opportunity cost of working for yourself would be even higher.

11.2 Production in the Short Run

1. What is the difference between fixed and variable inputs?

Fixed inputs are those, such as plants and equipment, that cannot be changed in the short run, while variable inputs are those, such as hourly labor, that can be changed in the short run.

2. Why are all inputs variable in the long run?

All inputs are variable in the long run by definition because the long run is defined as that time period necessary to allow all inputs to be varied.

3. What relationship does a production function represent?

A production function represents the relationship between different combinations of inputs and the maximum output of a product that can be produced with those inputs, with given technology.

4. What is diminishing marginal product? What causes it?

Diminishing marginal product means that as the amount of a variable input is increased—the amount of other inputs being held constant—a point will ultimately be reached beyond which marginal product will decline. It is caused by reductions in the amount of fixed inputs that can be combined with each unit of a variable input, as the amount of that variable input used increases.

11.3 Costs in the Short Run

1. What is the difference between fixed costs and variable costs?

Fixed costs are the expenses associated with fixed inputs (that therefore only exist in the short run), which are constant regardless of output. Variable costs are the expenses associated with variable inputs, which change as the level of output changes.

2. How are the average fixed cost, average variable cost, and average total cost calculated?

For a given level of output, any average cost is calculated as the relevant total cost divided by the level of output. Average fixed cost is therefore total fixed cost divided by output; average variable cost is total variable cost divided by output; and average total cost is total cost (fixed cost plus variable cost) divided by output.

3. Why is marginal cost the relevant cost to consider when a producer is deciding whether to produce more or less of a product?

Marginal cost is the additional cost of increasing output by one unit. That is, it is the cost relevant to the choice of whether to produce and sell one more unit of a good. For producing and selling one more unit of a product to increase profits, the addition to revenue from selling that output (marginal revenue) must exceed the addition to cost from producing it (marginal cost).

4. If the average variable cost curve were constant over some range of output, why would the average total cost be falling over that range of output?

Average total cost is the sum of average variable cost and average fixed cost. Average fixed costs fall over the entire possible range of output. Therefore, if the average variable cost curve were constant over a range of output, the average total cost curve must be falling over that range of output.

5. **If your season batting average going into a game was .300 (three hits per 10 at bats) and you got two hits in five at bats during the game, would your season batting average rise or fall as a result?**
Your "marginal" batting average in the game was .400 (two hits per five at bats), which was higher than your previous batting average. As a consequence, because that game's marginal results were above your previous average, it raises your season batting average as a result.

11.4 The Shape of the Short-Run Cost Curves

1. **What is the primary reason that the average total cost falls as output expands over low output ranges?**
The primary reason average total cost falls as output expands over low output ranges is that average fixed cost declines sharply with output at low levels of output.

2. **Why does the average total cost rise at some point as output expands further?**
Average total cost begins to rise at some point as output expands further because of the law of diminishing marginal product, also called the law of increasing costs. Over this range of output, adding more variable inputs does not increase output by the same proportion, so the average cost of production increases over this range of output.

3. **If marginal costs are less than the average total cost, why does *ATC* fall? If *MC* is greater than *ATC*, why does *ATC* rise?**
When the marginal cost of a unit of output is less than its average total cost, including the lowercost unit will

lower the average (just as getting lower marginal grades this term will decrease your GPA). When the marginal cost of a unit of output exceeds its average total cost, including the higher-cost unit will raise the average (just as getting higher marginal grades this term will increase your GPA).

11.5 Cost Curves: Short Run versus Long Run

1. **What are economies of scale, diseconomies of scale, and constant returns to scale?**
Each of these terms refers to average or per-unit costs as output expands. Economies of scale means that long-run average cost falls as output expands; diseconomies of scale means that long-run average cost rises as output expands; and constant returns to scale means that long-run average cost is constant as output expands.

2. **How might cooking a family dinner be subject to falling average total cost in the long run as the size of the family grows?**
Once the appropriate larger-scale cooking technology has been adopted (i.e., in the long run, when all inputs can be varied), such as larger cooking pots, pans, and baking sheets, larger ovens, dishwashers, and so on, and more family members can be involved, each specializing in fewer tasks, this larger scale can reduce the average cost per meal served.

3. **What may cause economies or diseconomies of scale?**
Economies of scale can result when expanding output allows the use of mass production techniques such as assembly lines or allows gains from further labor specialization that may not be possible at lower levels of output. Diseconomies of scale can result when a firm finds it increasingly difficult to handle the complexity as well as the information and coordination problems of large-scale management.

PROBLEMS

1. What happens to the cost of growing strawberries on your own land if a housing developer offers you three times what you thought your land was worth?

2. As a farmer, you work for yourself using your own tractor, equipment, and farm structures, and you cultivate your own land. Why might it be difficult to calculate your profits from farming?

3. The salmon fishery in Alaska's Bristol Bay has historically been one of the world's richest. Over the past few years, poor returns of salmon to the bay and competition from farm-raised salmon have reduced the economic returns to the fishermen. One response to lower revenues has been for fishermen to use family members instead of hiring crew "in order to reduce their costs." Evaluate this business strategy. Will employing relatives really keep profits from falling? Under what conditions is this a good strategy?

4. Use the table below for a–c.

Willie's Water Park Short-Run Production Function

Labor (workers)	Total Product (visitors per hour)	Marginal Product
0	_____	0
1	_____	10
2	_____	12
3	_____	9
4	_____	8
5	_____	4
6	_____	−2

a. Fill in the Total Product column.
b. Willie's Water Park experiences diminishing marginal product beginning with which worker?
c. Willie's Water Park experiences diminishing total product beginning with which worker?

5. Harry's Hat Company makes hats using the technology described in the following data:

	With Three Machines			With Four Machines	
Labor	Total Product (hats)	Marginal Product (hats)	Labor	Total Product (hats)	Marginal Product (hats)
1 day	8	_____	1 day	9	_____
2 days	18	_____	2 days	20	_____
3 days	30	_____	3 days	35	_____
4 days	45	_____	4 days	55	_____
5 days	57	_____	5 days	76	_____
6 days	67	_____	6 days	88	_____
7 days	72	_____	7 days	95	_____

a. Fill in the Marginal Product columns of these tables.
b. At what point does diminishing marginal product set in with three machines? With four?
c. Why is the point of diminishing marginal product different in each case?

6. Fill in the rest of the production function for Candy's Candies from the information provided.

With Four Machines

Labor (workers)	Total Product (pounds)	Marginal Product (pounds)
0	_____	_____
1	20	_____
2	44	_____
3	62	_____
4	_____	12
5	_____	6
6	78	_____

a. Candy's Candies begins to experience diminishing marginal product with which worker?
b. Does Candy's Candies ever experience negative marginal product? If so, with the addition of which worker?

7. Draw a typically shaped total product curve and the marginal product curve derived from it, and indicate the ranges of increasing, diminishing, and negative marginal product.

8. Say that your firm's total product curve includes the following data: one worker can produce 8 units of output; two workers, 20 units; three workers, 34 units; four workers, 50 units; five workers, 60 units; six workers, 70 units; seven workers, 76 units; eight workers, 78 units; and nine workers, 77 units.
   a. What is the marginal product of the seventh worker?
   b. When does the law of diminishing product set in?
   c. Under these conditions, would you ever choose to employ nine workers?

9. Why does the law of diminishing marginal product imply the law of increasing costs?

10. Complete the following table describing the short-run daily costs of the Attractive Magnet Co. for 2012.

Total Product (magnets)	Total Fixed Costs	Total Variable Costs	Total Costs	Average Fixed Costs	Average Variable Costs	Average Total Costs	Marginal Costs
1	$100	$ 30	$130	$100	$30	$130	$30
2	___	___	___	___	25	___	___
3	___	___	___	___	20	___	___
4	___	___	___	___	16	___	___
5	___	___	___	___	18	___	___
6	___	___	___	___	21	___	___
7	___	___	___	___	24	___	___
8	___	218	318	___	___	___	___

11. A one-day ticket to visit the Screaming Coasters theme park costs $36, but you can also get a two-consecutive-day ticket for $40. What is the average cost per day for the two-day ticket? What is the marginal cost of the second consecutive day?

12. As a movie exhibitor, you can choose between paying a flat fee of $5,000 to show a movie for a week or paying a fee of $2 per customer. Will your choice affect your fixed and variable costs? How?

13. What is likely to happen to your marginal costs when adding output requires working beyond an eight-hour day, if workers must be paid time-and-a-half wages beyond an eight-hour day?

14. If your university pays lecture note takers $20 per hour to take notes in your economics class and then sells subscriptions for $15 per student, is the cost of the lecture note taker a fixed or variable cost of selling an additional subscription?

15. The Lighthouse Safety Vest Co. makes flotation vests for recreational boaters. They currently employ 50 people and produce 12,000 vests per month. Lighthouse managers know that when they hire one more person, monthly vest production will increase by 200 vests. They pay workers $1,600 per month.
    a. What is the marginal product of the 51st worker?
    b. What is the marginal cost to produce one more vest? (*Hint:* Think of the marginal cost as the additional worker's pay divided by the changes in output.)
    c. If labor is the only variable factor of production, will the average variable cost of production rise or fall as a result of hiring a 51st worker? Why?
    d. What happens to the marginal cost of a vest when the 52nd worker is added and the marginal product drops to 160 vests per month?

16. Illustrate how the shape of the marginal product curve relates to the shape of the marginal cost curve.

17. Use the graph to answer the following questions.
    a. Curve A represents which cost curve?
    b. Curve B represents which cost curve?
    c. Curve C represents which cost curve?
    d. Curve D represents which cost curve?

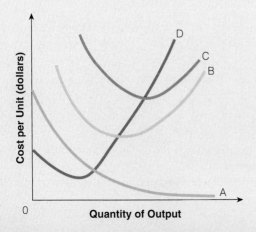

e. Why must curve D pass through the minimum points of both curve B and curve C?

f. What significance does the point where curve A intersects curve D have?

18. Fill in the rest of the cost function for Bob's Bowling Balls.

Output	Total Fixed Costs	Total Variable Costs	Total Costs	Average Fixed Costs	Average Variable Costs	Average Total Cost	Marginal Costs
1	$200	$ 60	$_____	$_____	$_____	$_____	$_____
2	_____	100	_____	_____	_____	_____	_____
3	_____	120	_____	_____	_____	_____	_____
4	_____	128	_____	_____	_____	_____	_____
5	_____	180	_____	_____	_____	_____	_____
6	_____	252	_____	_____	_____	_____	_____
7	_____	316	_____	_____	_____	_____	_____
8	_____	436	_____	_____	_____	_____	_____

19. Buffalo Bill has a potato chip company, Buffalo's Chips. He is currently losing money on every bag of chips he sells. Mrs. Bill, who has just completed an economics class, tells Buffalo Bill he could make a profit if he adds more machines and produces more chips. How could this be possible? What is Mrs. Bill assuming about the output range in which Buffalo Bill is currently producing?

20. You have the following information about long-run total cost for the following firms:

Quantity	Arnold's Apples LRTC	Belle's Bananas LRTC	Cam's Cantaloupes LRTC
1	120	33	42
2	140	72	68
3	160	117	98
4	180	168	132
5	200	225	170
6	220	288	212
7	240	357	258

a. Do any of these firms experience constant returns to scale? How do you know?

b. Do any of these firms experience diseconomics of scale? How do you know?

c. Do any of these firms experience economics of scale? How do you know?

21. Refer to the cost curve in the following exhibit:

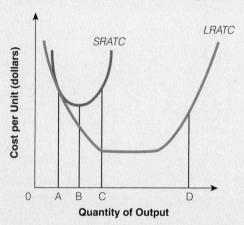

a. What is the lowest level of output at which the efficient scale of production is reached in the long run?

b. In the short run described by SRATC, what is the efficient output level?

c. When the firm is producing at the level of output described by D, will it be experiencing constant returns to scale, economies of scale, or diseconomies of scale?

Using Isoquants and Isocosts

Optimal Factor Combinations: Two Variable Inputs

If the production manager had to deal with just one variable input, decision problems would be relatively easy. Given the output target, the production manager would purchase the minimum quantity of input needed to produce the assigned output and would inform the output manager of the costs incurred. However, the production manager's job becomes much more complicated when the output can be produced with several alternative combinations of inputs. For the sake of simplicity, we shall confine ourselves to two variable inputs: capital and labor.

The Isoquant

The various combinations of two factors that allow the firm to produce a given quantity of output can be illustrated graphically. The curve showing the various factor combinations that can produce a given level of output is known as an isoquant. Exhibit 1 shows that units of capital are measured on the vertical axis, and units of labor on the horizontal axis; isoquant q shows the various combinations of capital and labor that allow the firm to produce a given level (20 units) of output.

isoquant

curve showing the various factor combinations that can produce a given level of output

---

appendix exhibit 1 — Isoquant Showing Various Combinations of Labor and Capital That Can Be Used to Produce 20 Units of Output per Day

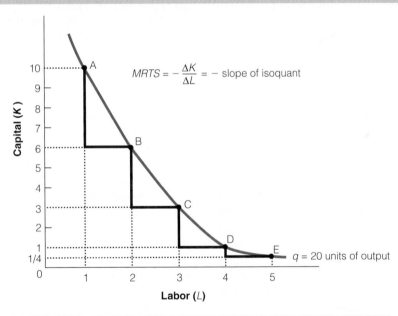

$$MRTS = -\frac{\Delta K}{\Delta L} = -\text{ slope of isoquant}$$

$q = 20$ units of output

Combination	Labor (L)	Capital (K)	Marginal Rate of Technical Substitution
A	1	10	
			4
B	2	6	
			3
C	3	3	
			2
D	4	1	
			3/4
E	5	1/4	

The isoquant q indicates that 20 units of output can be produced with 10 units of capital and 1 unit of labor (combination A), or 3 units of capital and 3 units of labor (combination C). All other combinations of capital and labor capable of producing 20 units of output are also charted along isoquant q.

Isoquants, like indifference curves, have several important properties. Isoquants are negatively sloped, nonintersecting, convex, and they increase in value as we move in a northeast direction from the origin. However, unlike indifference curves, isoquants are measured cardinally. That is, an output of 40 is twice as large as an output of 20.

The Marginal Rate of Technical Substitution

Explanation of the optimal factor combination can be facilitated by discussing the concept of the marginal rate of technical substitution (MRTS) of labor for capital (to distinguish it from the marginal rate of substitution along an indifference curve). The slope of the isoquant is

marginal rate of technical substitution (MRTS) of labor for capital
the quantity of capital that can be given up by using one additional unit of labor while producing the same level of output

the number of units of one factor necessary to replace a unit of another factor, in order to maintain the same level of output, $-\Delta K/\Delta L$. If we remove the negative sign on the slope we have the *MRTS*.

Suppose that various combinations of labor and capital (together with given quantities of other factors) are used to produce a given level of output, as illustrated in Exhibit 1. Various combinations will produce 20 units of output per day; for example, if two units of labor are used, six units of capital will be needed (Combination B); and if three units of labor are used, then three units of capital will be required (Combination C). Note that the various combinations are alternative possibilities for the production of a given quantity of the product, 20 units of output per day in this example.

The *MRTS* measures the quantity of capital that can be given up by using one additional unit of labor, while still producing the same level of output. For example, if two units of labor (and six units of capital) are now being used, three units of capital can be given up by using one additional unit of labor.

As the data in Exhibit 1 illustrate, the isoquants are convex. That is, the *MRTS* diminishes as we move down along the isoquant. We also see that labor becomes more abundant and capital more scarce. Hence, it becomes increasingly difficult to substitute even more labor for capital.

As the quantity of one factor, say labor, is increased relative to the quantity of the other, say capital, output being constant, the number of units of capital that can be replaced by one unit of labor falls. In other words, the marginal product of labor falls as we use more of it, and the marginal product of capital rises as we use less of it.

Under ordinary circumstances, the isoquant will be convex to the point of origin because of the principle of diminishing marginal rate of technical substitution. The greater the quantity of labor used, the smaller is the quantity of the capital needed to replace a unit of labor and maintain output. Thus, the right-hand portion of the isoquant is almost parallel to the horizontal axis, while the left-hand portion is almost parallel to the vertical axis.

The marginal rate of technical substitution is equal to $-\Delta K/\Delta L$, which is the slope of the isoquant. Recall that all combinations on a given isoquant yield the same level of output. Thus, if labor is substituted for capital, with output remaining constant, we know that:

$$(\Delta K)(MP_K) + (\Delta L)(MP_L) = 0$$

Rearranging the terms in this equation we have:

$$MRTS = -(\Delta K)/(\Delta L) = MP_L/MP_K$$

That is, the slope of the isoquant at any point is equal to the ratio of the marginal product of labor to the marginal product of capital.

The *MRTS* is a measure of the extent to which the two factors are substitutes for each other. If they are perfect substitutes—that is, if either factor can be used equally well to produce the product—the marginal rate of technical substitution will be a constant. If capital and labor can be used equally well, the *MRTS* will remain unchanged, regardless of the extent to which substitution is carried in either direction, as seen in Exhibit 2. For example, a woven rug or a sweater could either be done almost exclusively by machine or with a few tools and hand labor.

At the other extreme, two factors may not be substitutes for a particular purpose (such as carpenters and hammers or taxicab drivers and taxicabs). Here, the *MRTS* is undefinable because output cannot be maintained if one factor is replaced by the other. If this relationship exists between all factors the firm uses, the factor combination the firm employs is dictated entirely by technological conditions, and no substitution is possible. The curve in Exhibit 3 is a right angle indicating that the same output would be forthcoming if more of either (but not more of both!) of the inputs were used. That is, you are equally well off producing q_1 output using factor combination A as you would be using factor combination B. However, you can clearly produce more output, q_2, if you increase both labor and capital, a move from A to C. This type of production relationship is called fixed-proportions production function.

fixed-proportions production function
when it is impossible to substitute one input for another so inputs must be used in fixed proportions

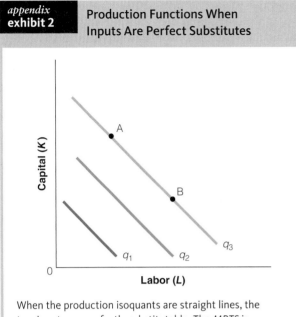

appendix
exhibit 2
Production Functions When Inputs Are Perfect Substitutes

When the production isoquants are straight lines, the two inputs are perfectly substitutable. The *MRTS* is constant along a given isoquant; that is, either combination A or combination B could be used equally well to produce q_3.

appendix
exhibit 3
Production Functions with Fixed Proportions

If the production function is L-shaped, it is a fixed proportions production function. The addition of more labor (A to B) does not produce more output. You can, however, produce more output (q_2) if you increase both labor and capital (A to C).

Cost Schedules with Long-Run Adjustments Completed

The long-run period has been defined as a period sufficiently long for a firm to adjust all factors of production. The long run, as emphasized earlier, is always a *planning period* because at any moment, firms are inevitably in some short-run situation. In the long run, however, a firm can choose any short-run plant configuration. The actual time interval depends on the nature of the production processes and particularly on the extent to which specialized capital equipment, requiring a substantial period to construct and having a certain lifespan, are used. The time a firm needs to adjust all factors is much greater for a steel mill or a railroad than for a service station or a grocery store. Over a long-run period, because all factors are adjustable, all costs are variable.

In the long run, the firm can alter all its inputs. Thus, the manager must choose among alternative inputs that minimize the cost of producing a given output. In addition, we need to obtain information on long-run costs and output levels.

Isocost Lines and the Optimum Factor Combination

The optimal factor combination can be shown graphically by combining isoquants with **isocost (equal cost) lines**, each of which shows the various possible quantities

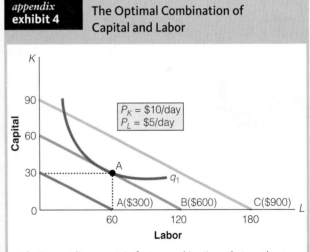

appendix
exhibit 4
The Optimal Combination of Capital and Labor

$P_K = \$10/\text{day}$
$P_L = \$5/\text{day}$

The isocost lines contain factor combinations that can be hired at the same expense. Minimizing the cost of producing q_1 output involves choosing a factor combination that coincides with q_1 output. The optimum input combination occurs at point A, where 60 units of labor and 30 units of capital are utilized to produce q_1 output.

of the two factors that can be purchased with a given outlay of money. Exhibit 4 shows isoquants when isocost lines are added. Specifically, Exhibit 4 shows

isocost (equal cost) lines
graphical display of the various possible quantities of the two factors that can be purchased with a given outlay of money

the various quantities of capital and labor that can be purchased with a given outlay of money, assuming that the prices of labor and capital are $5 and $10 per hour, respectively. If the given outlay is $600, for example, the isocost line is represented in Exhibit 4 by line B, which indicates that 60 units of capital can be purchased if only capital is purchased, 120 units of labor if only labor is purchased, and 60 units of labor if 30 units of capital are used. The isocost relation is a straight line as a matter of mathematical necessity as long as prices paid for factor units are the same regardless of the quantities purchased. The various possible isocost lines, one for each potential level of outlay on factors, are parallel to each other (see lines A, B, and C in Exhibit 4). The farther to the right an isocost line is located, the higher is the level of outlay that it represents.

Minimum cost is achieved when the firm chooses the least expensive combination of factor inputs for a given level of output. This combination is represented graphically by the lowest isocost line (the farthest one to the left) that touches the isoquant representing the quantity to be produced. Thus, the optimum factor combination is represented by a point of tangency between the given isoquant and the lowest possible isocost line, point A in Exhibit 4.

The isocost line that is just tangent to the isoquant allows a firm to acquire the necessary factor units with the lowest possible outlay.* Any lower line would not allow the firm to purchase enough factors to produce the desired output, while any higher isocost line would entail unnecessarily high factor costs. At any point on the isoquant other than the point of tangency, the outlay on the factors to produce the given output would be higher than that at the tangency point. At the tangency, the slope of the isoquant (which represents the marginal rate of technical substitution between the two factors) is equal to the slope of the isocost line (which represents the ratio of the prices of the two factors), and thus the marginal rate of technical substitution is equal to the ratio of the factor prices.

Therefore at the tangency points, the isoquant and the isocost line will have identical slopes. The slope of the MRTS is equal to the ratio of the factor prices:

$$MRTS_{LK} = w/r.$$

where

w = wages (the price of labor)
r = rental rate of capital

For example, in Exhibit 5(a), to minimize the cost of producing 100 units of output, the firm should produce at point A, where the isoquant is tangent to the isocost line. Point B is an input combination that can produce 100 units of output. However, B costs more than A. Point C represents a cheaper factor combination, but it is impossible to produce 100 units of output with so few inputs. Exhibit 5(b) illustrates the alternative optimization process, maximizing output for a given

optimum factor combination

a point of tangency between the given isoquant and the lowest possible isocost line

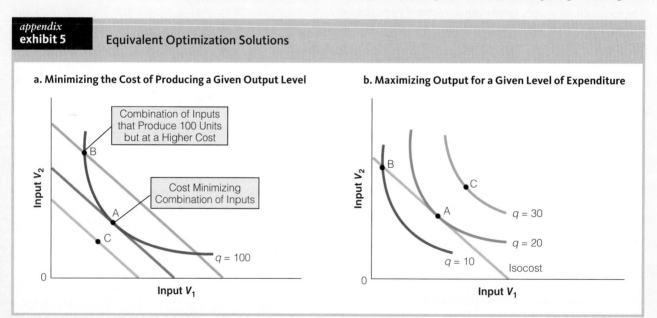

appendix
exhibit 5   **Equivalent Optimization Solutions**

a. Minimizing the Cost of Producing a Given Output Level

Combination of Inputs that Produce 100 Units but at a Higher Cost

Cost Minimizing Combination of Inputs

$q = 100$

Input V_2

Input V_1

b. Maximizing Output for a Given Level of Expenditure

$q = 30$
$q = 20$
$q = 10$
Isocost

Input V_2

Input V_1

---

*Remember that an isoquant shows the various quantities of the two factors necessary to produce a given output, while each isocost line shows the various quantities of two factors that can be acquired with the expenditure of a given sum of money.

The Expansion Path

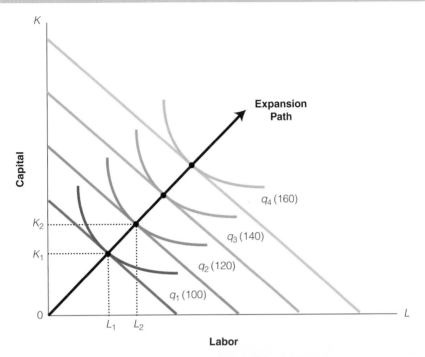

An expansion path connects the firm's least-cost input combinations of producing each level of output in the long run, when all inputs can be varied. The least-cost input combination for producing 120 units of output is K_2 units of capital and L_2 units of labor.

level of costs. The producer attempts to reach the highest isoquant for a given isocost line. Again point A, the tangency point between the isoquant and the isocost line, gives the optimum factor combination. Point B is feasible, but produces a lower level of output. Greater output is attained at point C, but costs are too high. Hence, both strategies result in the same optimization conditons: the isoquant and the isocost line are tangent, and the *MRTS* equals the ratio of input prices.

Recall that *MRTS* is a measure of the extent to which the two factors are substitutes for each other. Also recall that the *MRTS* is equal to the ratio of the marginal product of labor to capital. So we can rewrite our previous equation as:

$$\text{(slope of the isoquant)} - MP_L/MP_K =$$
$$-w/r \text{ (slope of the isocost line)}$$

or

$$MP_L/MP_K = w/r$$

Rearranging our terms, we find that

$$MP_{L/W} = MP_{K/r}$$

In other words, at the tangency solution, the ratio of the marginal product to input price must be the same for all inputs used in production.

The Expansion Path

In Exhibit 6, the optimal factor bundles are presented for different levels of output. For example, the leastcost method for producing 100 units of output is using L_1 units of labor and K_1 units of capital, while the least-cost method of producing 120 units of output would be combining L_2 units of labor and K_2 units of capital. The expansion path is the line that connects these least-cost input combinations, holding input prices constant.

The expansion path provides us information regarding the longrun total cost curve. Specifically, it shows the least-cost input solutions for providing a given output, or equivalently, the lowest long-run total cost for producing each level of output. The connection between long-run total cost and the expansion path is seen in Exhibit 7. Points A, B, and C are the cost-minimizing input combinations along the expansion path in part (a). The corresponding points on the long-run total cost curve are A, B, and C in part (b). Long-run total cost is simply the optimum amount of labor times the wage plus the optimum amount of capital times the price of capital.

> **expansion path**
> shows the least-cost input solutions for providing a given output

appendix
exhibit 7   Deriving *LRTC* from an Isoquant-Isocost Map

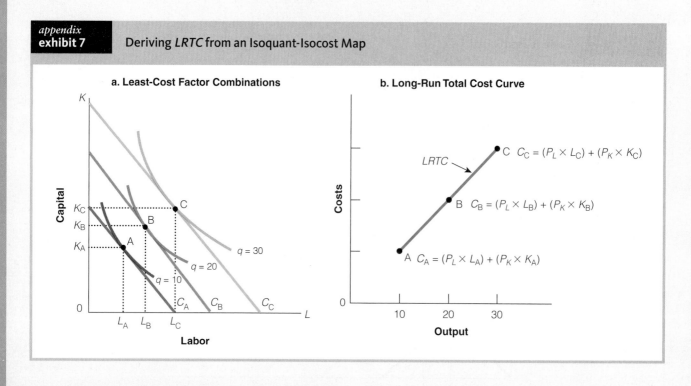

a. Least-Cost Factor Combinations

b. Long-Run Total Cost Curve

KEY TERMS AND CONCEPTS

isoquant 315
marginal rate of technical substitution
   (MRTS) of labor for capital 316

fixed-proportions production
   function 316
isocost (equal cost) lines 317

optimum factor combination 318
expansion path 319

PROBLEMS

1. Would a firm ever choose a factor combination on a positively sloped portion of an isoquant? Explain.

Answer
The following figure reveals two isoquants with positively sloped sections. If the amount of input V_2 is fixed at V_2, one unit of output can be produced at either V_1 or V''_1. The input combination at point C would clearly be less efficient than at point A because C uses more of input V_1 and would be more costly. Note that the positively sloped segment of an isoquant corresponds to stage three of production because an increase in V'_1 from V''_1 to V_1 when V_2 is fixed at V_2 results in a lower quantity of output (q falls from 2 to 1).

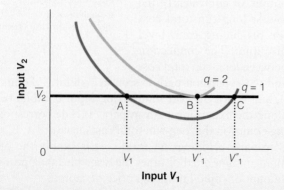

2. If two factors are partial substitutes for one another, will the marginal rate of substitution vary as factor proportions are altered, ranging from infinity to values of, or equal to, zero? Explain.

    Answer

    Suppose, for example, that in the production of DVDs, either metal or plastic can be used for most purposes, but metal is essential for some purposes because plastic lacks sufficient strength for performing the task. In this case, once the quantity of metal has been reduced to the minimum amount required, the *MRTS* will become infinite because output cannot be maintained if substitution is carried further.

3. A firm is producing 50 units of output. The marginal rate of technical substitution at the current usage rates of V_1 and V_2 is 1. The price of $V_1 = \$8$ per unit, and the price of $V_2 = \$9$ per unit. Should the firm change its purchases of V_1 and V_2?

    Answer

    The firm can substitute one unit of V_1 for one unit of V_2 and still produce the same output level, but the price of V_1 is less than the price of V_2. Thus, the firm should decrease the amount of V_2 and increase the amount of V_1. The situation is depicted in the following graph. The input price ratio, 8/9, is less than the *MRTS*, 1, which is demonstrated by the flatter slope of the isocost than the isoquant at point A, the current factor combination. The firm can, however, lower its expenditure by moving to point B and hiring more V_1 and less V_2.

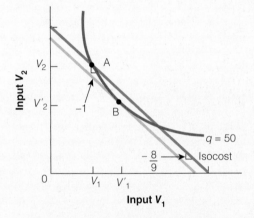

4. Suppose a union raises earnings for workers, and management decides to continue to produce the same output level. How will the firm's optimum combination of labor and capital change, assuming only two inputs? Illustrate graphically. Under what conditions will the effect be large?

    Answer

    The original factor combination is L and K at point A in the figure. A pay raise increases the slope of the isocost line, the price of labor divided by the price of capital. If the firm continues to produce along the same isoquant, the new quantities of labor and capital are L' and K''. If labor and capital are roughly equally good substitutes over a wide range of input combinations, the isoquant will have little curvature, and the substitution of capital for labor will be great.

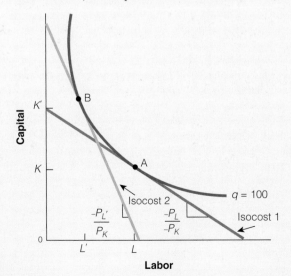

5. Use isoquants to demonstrate how a technological advance allows a firm to produce the same level of output with fewer inputs.

    Answer

    In the following figure, a technological advance is illustrated by the inward shift of the isoquant from $q' = 100$ to $q = 100$. Both isoquants represent the same level of output, but q'' demonstrates that the new technology requires fewer inputs to do so. Thus, the same level of output can be produced at lower costs.

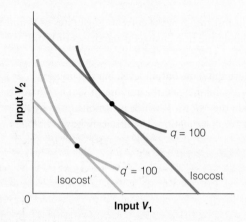

CHAPTER 12

Firms in Perfectly Competitive Markets

At the Chicago Board of Trade (CBOT), prices are set by thousands of buyers interacting with thousands of sellers. The goods in question are standardized (e.g., grade A winter wheat) and information is readily available. Every buyer and seller in the market knows the price, the quantity, and the quality of the wheat available. Transaction costs are negligible. For example, if a news story breaks on an infestation in the cotton crop, the price of cotton will rise immediately. CBOT price information is used to determine the value of some commodities throughout the world.

A firm must answer two critical questions: What price should we charge for the goods and services we sell, and how much should we produce? The answers to these two questions will depend on the market structure. The behavior of firms will depend on the number of firms in the market, the ease with which firms can

CHICAGO BOARD OF TRADE

enter and exit the market, and the ability of firms to differentiate their products from those of other firms. There is no typical industry. An industry might include one firm that dominates the market, or it might consist of thousands of smaller firms that each produce a small fraction of the market supply. Between these two end points are many other industries. However, because we cannot examine each industry individually, we break them into four main categories: perfect competition, monopoly, monopolistic competition, and oligopoly.

In a perfectly competitive market, the market price is the critical piece of information that a firm needs to know. A firm in a perfectly competitive market can sell all it wants at the market price. A firm in a perfectly competitive market is said to be a price taker, because it cannot appreciably affect the market price for its output or the market price for its inputs. For example, suppose a Washington apple grower decides that he wants to get out of the family business and go to work for Microsoft. Because he may be one of 50,000 apple growers in the United States, his decision will not appreciably change the price of the apples, the production of apples, or the price of inputs. In this chapter we see that a market supply curve is closely related to a firm's costs of production. Which of a firm's many costs (fixed, variable, average, and marginal) are most relevant to the firm for its supply decisions?

12.1 A Perfectly Competitive Market

▶ What are the characteristics of a firm in   ▶ What is a price taker?
   a perfectly competitive market?

12.1a A Perfectly Competitive Market

This chapter examines perfect competition, a market structure characterized by (1) many buyers and sellers, (2) identical (homogeneous) products, and (3) easy market entry and exit. Let's examine these characteristics in greater detail.

Many Buyers and Sellers

Why do they call firms in a perfectly competitive market price takers?

In a perfectly competitive market, there are *many buyers and sellers*, perhaps thousands or conceivably millions. Because each firm is so small in relation to the industry, its production decisions have no impact on the market—each regards price as something over which it has no control. For this reason, perfectly competitive firms are called price takers: They must take the price given by the market because their influence on price is insignificant. If the price of wheat in the wheat market is $5 a bushel, then individual wheat farmers will receive $5 a bushel for their wheat. Similarly, no single buyer of wheat can influence the price of wheat, because each buyer purchases only a small amount of wheat. We see how this relationship works in more detail in Section 12.2.

Identical (Homogeneous) Products

Consumers believe that all firms in perfectly competitive markets *sell identical (or homogeneous) products*. For example, in the wheat market, we are assuming it is not possible to determine any significant and consistent qualitative differences in the wheat produced by different farmers. Wheat produced by Farmer Jones looks, feels, smells, and tastes like that produced by Farmer Smith. In short, a bushel of wheat is a bushel of wheat. The products of all the firms are considered to be perfect substitutes.

Easy Entry and Exit

Product markets characterized by perfect competition *have no significant barriers to entry or exit.* Therefore it is fairly easy for entrepreneurs to become suppliers of the product or, if they are already producers, to stop supplying the product. "Fairly easy" does not mean that any person on the street can instantly enter the business but rather that the financial, legal, educational, and other barriers to entering the business are modest, enabling large numbers of people to overcome the barriers and enter the business, if they so desire, in any given period. If buyers can easily switch from one seller to another and sellers can easily enter or exit the industry, then they have met the perfectly competitive condition of easy entry and exit. Because of this easy market entry, perfectly competitive markets generally consist of a large number of small suppliers.

Can the owner of this orchard charge a noticeably higher price for apples of similar quality to those sold at the orchard down the road? What if she charges a lower price for apples of similar quality? How many apples can she sell at the market price?

A perfectly competitive market is approximated most closely in highly organized markets for securities and agricultural commodities, such as the New York Stock Exchange or the Chicago Board of Trade. Wheat, corn, soybeans, cotton, and many other agricultural products are sold in perfectly competitive markets. Although all the criteria for a perfectly competitive market are rarely met, a number of markets come close to satisfying them. Even when all the assumptions don't hold, it is important to note that studying the model of perfect competition is useful because many markets resemble perfect competition—that is, markets in which firms face highly elastic (flat) demand curves and relatively easy entry and exit. The model also gives us a standard of comparison—a benchmark to evaluate the efficiency of other types of markets.

What are the three characteristics of a perfectly competitive market?

SECTION QUIZ

1. Perfectly competitive markets tend to have a _____ number of sellers and a(n) _____ entry.

   a. large; easy

   b. large; difficult

   c. small; easy

   d. small; difficult

2. In perfectly competitive markets, products are _____ and sellers are _____.

   a. homogeneous; price takers

   b. homogeneous; price searchers

   c. substantially different; price takers

   d. substantially different; price searchers

3. Perfectly competitive markets have _____ sellers, each of which produces a _____ share of industry output.

   a. few; substantial

   b. few; small

   c. many; substantial

   d. many; small

(continued)

SECTION QUIZ (cont.)

4. Which of the following is false about perfect competition?

   a. Perfectly competitive firms sell homogeneous products.

   b. A perfectly competitive industry allows easy entry and exit.

   c. A perfectly competitive firm must take the market price as given.

   d. A perfectly competitive firm produces a substantial fraction of the industry output.

   e. All of the above are true.

5. An individual, perfectly competitive firm

   a. may increase its price without losing sales.

   b. is a price maker.

   c. has no perceptible influence on the market price.

   d. sells a product that is differentiated from those of its competitors.

1. Why do firms in perfectly competitive markets involve homogeneous goods?

2. Why does the absence of significant barriers to entry tend to result in a large number of suppliers?

3. Why does the fact that perfectly competitive firms are small relative to the market make them price takers?

Answers: 1. a 2. a 3. d 4. d 5. c

12.2 An Individual Price Taker's Demand Curve

▶ Why won't individual price takers raise or lower their prices?

▶ Can individual price takers sell all they want at the market price?

▶ Will the position of individual price takers' demand curves change when market price changes?

12.2a An Individual Firm's Demand Curve

In perfectly competitive markets, buyers and sellers must accept the price that the market determines, so they are said to be *price takers*. The market price and output are determined by the intersection of the market supply and demand curves, as seen in Exhibit 1(b). As we stated earlier, perfectly competitive markets have many buyers and sellers and the goods offered for sale are essentially identical. Consequently, no buyer or seller can influence the market price. They take the market price as given.

For example, no single consumer of wheat can influence the market price of wheat because each buyer purchases such a small percentage of the total amount sold in the wheat market. Likewise, each wheat farmer sells relatively small amounts of almost identical wheat, so the farmer has little control over wheat prices.

Individual wheat farmers know that they cannot dispose of their wheat at any figure higher than the current market price; if they attempt to charge a higher price, potential buyers will simply make their purchases from other wheat farmers. Further, the farmers certainly would not knowingly charge a lower price, because they could sell all they want at the market price.

Likewise, in a perfectly competitive market, individual sellers can change their outputs, and it will not alter the market price. The large number of sellers who are selling identical

Can an individual wheat farmer influence the market price of wheat? Can an individual consumer of wheat influence the market price of wheat?

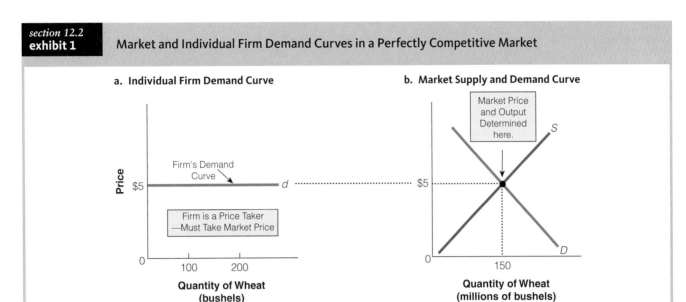

Market and Individual Firm Demand Curves in a Perfectly Competitive Market

a. Individual Firm Demand Curve

b. Market Supply and Demand Curve

Price

Firm's Demand Curve

$5 .... d $5

Firm is a Price Taker —Must Take Market Price

Market Price and Output Determined here.

S

D

0

100   200

0   150

Quantity of Wheat (bushels)

Quantity of Wheat (millions of bushels)

At the market price for wheat, $5, the individual farmer can sell all the wheat he wishes. Because each producer provides only a small fraction of industry output, any additional output will have an insignificant impact on market price. The firm's demand curve is perfectly elastic at the market price.

products make this situation possible. Each producer provides such a small fraction of the total supply that a change in the amount he offers does *not* have a noticeable effect on market equilibrium price. In a perfectly competitive market, then, an individual firm can sell as much as it wishes to place on the market at the prevailing price; the demand, as seen by the seller, is perfectly elastic.

It is easy to construct the demand curve for an individual seller in a perfectly competitive market. Remember, she won't charge more than the market price because no one will buy it, and she won't charge less because she can sell all she wants at the market price. Thus, the farmer's demand curve is horizontal over the entire range of output that she could possibly produce. If the prevailing market price of the product is $5, the farmer's demand curve will be represented graphically by a horizontal line at the market price of $5, as shown in Exhibit 1(a).

In short, both consumers and producers are price takers in the perfectly competitive market. Consumers, for the most part, are price takers. Consumers cannot generally affect the prices they pay. However, in a number of market situations the producer can affect the market price and we study those in the following chapters.

Why is the perfectly competitive firm's demand curve perfectly elastic?

12.2b A Change in Market Price and the Firm's Demand Curve

To say that under perfect competition producers regard price as a given is not to say that price is constant. The *position* of the firm's demand curve varies with every change in the market price. In Exhibit 2, we see that when the market price for wheat increases, say as a result of an increase in market demand, the price-taking firm will receive a higher price for all its output. Or when the market price decreases, say as a result of a decrease in market demand, the price-taking firm will receive a lower price for all its output.

In effect, sellers are provided with current information about market demand and supply conditions as a result of price changes. It is an essential aspect of the perfectly competitive model that sellers respond to the signals provided by such price movements, so they must alter their behavior over time in light of actual experience, revising their production decisions to reflect changes in market price. In this respect, the perfectly competitive model is straightforward; it does not assume any knowledge on the part of individual buyers and sellers about market demand and supply—they only have to know the price of the good they sell.

What happens to the perfectly competitive firm's demand curve if there is an increase in the market price?

section 12.2
exhibit 2 — Market Prices and the Position of a Firm's Demand Curve

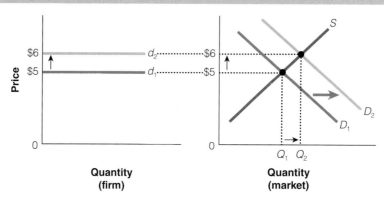

The position of the firm's demand curve will vary with every change in the market price.

SECTION QUIZ

1. Which of the following is false?

   a. A perfectly competitive firm cannot sell at any price higher than the current market price and would not knowingly charge a lower price because it could sell all it wants at the market price.

   b. In a perfectly competitive market, individual sellers can change their output without altering the market price.

   c. In a perfectly competitive industry, the firm's demand curve is downward sloping.

   d. The perfectly competitive model does not assume any knowledge on the part of individual buyers and sellers about market demand and supply—they only have to know the price of the good they sell.

2. When market demand shifts _____, a perfectly competitive firm's demand curve shifts _____.

   a. rightward; upward

   b. rightward; downward

   c. leftward; upward

   d. leftward; downward

   e. Both (a) and (d) are correct.

3. When will a perfectly competitive firm's demand curve shift?

   a. never

   b. when the market demand curve shifts

   c. when new producers enter the industry in large numbers

   d. when either (b) or (c) occurs

4. In a market with perfectly competitive firms, the market demand curve is _____ and the demand curve facing each individual firm is _____.

   a. upward sloping; horizontal

   b. downward sloping; horizontal

   c. horizontal; downward sloping

   d. horizontal; upward sloping

   e. horizontal; horizontal

(continued)

Profit Maximization 12.3

▶ What is total revenue?

▶ What is average revenue?

▶ What is marginal revenue?

▶ Why does the firm maximize profits where marginal revenue equals marginal cost?

12.3a Revenues in a Perfectly Competitive Market

The objective of the firm is to maximize profits. To maximize profits, the firm wants to produce the amount that maximizes the difference between its total revenues and total costs. In this section, we examine the different ways to look at revenue in a perfectly competitive market: total revenue, average revenue, and marginal revenue.

12.3b Total Revenue

Total revenue (TR) is the revenue that the firm receives from the sale of its products. Total revenue from a product equals the price of the good (P) times the quantity (q) of units sold ($TR = P \times q$). For example, if a farmer sells 10 bushels of wheat a day for $5 a bushel, his total revenue is $50 ($5 × 10 bushels). (*Note:* We will use the lowercase letter q to denote the single firm's output and reserve the uppercase letter Q for the output of the entire market. For example, q would be used to represent the output of one lettuce grower, while Q would be used to represent the output of all lettuce growers in the lettuce market.)

total revenue (TR)
the product price times the quantity sold

12.3c Average Revenue and Marginal Revenue

Average revenue (AR) equals total revenue divided by the number of units of the product sold ($TR \div q$, or $[P \times q] \div q$). For example, if the farmer sells 10 bushels at $5 a bushel, total revenue is $50 and average revenue is $5 per bushel ($50 ÷ 10 bushels). Thus, in perfect competition, average revenue is equal to the price of the good.

average revenue (AR)
total revenue divided by the number of units sold

Marginal revenue (MR) is the additional revenue derived from the production of one more unit of the good. In other words, marginal revenue represents the increase in total revenue that results from the sale of one more unit ($MR = \Delta TR \div \Delta q$). In a perfectly competitive market, because additional units of output can be sold without reducing the price of the product, marginal revenue is constant at all outputs and equal to average revenue. For example, if the price of wheat per bushel is $5, the marginal revenue is $5. Because total revenue is equal

marginal revenue (MR)
the increase in total revenue resulting from a one-unit increase in sales

Revenues for a Perfectly Competitive Firm

Quantity (q)	Price (P)	Total Revenue (TR = P × q)	Average Revenue (AR = TR/q)	Marginal Revenue (MR = ΔTR/Δq)
1	$5	$5	$5	
2	5	10	5	$5
3	5	15	5	5
4	5	20	5	5
5	5	25	5	5

How does a perfectly competitive firm decide how much to produce and at what price?

profit-maximizing level of output

a firm should always produce at the output where MR = MC

to price multiplied by quantity $(TR = P \times q)$, as we add one additional unit of output, total revenue will always increase by the amount of the product price, $5. Marginal revenue facing a perfectly competitive firm is equal to the price of the good.

In perfect competition, then, we know that marginal revenue, average revenue, and price are all equal: $P = MR = AR$. These relationships are clearly illustrated in the calculations presented in Exhibit 1.

12.3d How Do Firms Maximize Profits?

Now that we have discussed the firm's cost curves (in Chapter 11) and its revenues, we are ready to see how a firm maximizes its profits. A firm's profits equal its total revenues minus its total costs. However, at what output level must a firm produce and sell to maximize profits? In all types of market environments, the firm will maximize its profits at the output that maximizes the difference between total revenue and total cost, which is at the same output level at which marginal revenue equals marginal cost.

Finding the Profit-Maximizing Level of Output

A Firm Maximizes Profits by Producing the Quantity where MR = MC at q*.

Lost Profit $q_1 < q^*$

Lost Profit $q_2 > q^*$

MC

$5   ································ P = MR

Price

0   q_1 q^* q_2

Quantity of Wheat (bushels per year)

At any output below q*—at q_1, for example—the marginal revenue (MR) from expanding output exceeds the added costs (MC) of that output, so additional profits can be made by expanding output. Beyond q*—at q_2, for example—marginal costs exceed marginal revenue, so output expansion is unprofitable and output should be reduced. The profit-maximizing level of output is at q*, where the profit-maximizing output rule is followed—the firm should produce the level of output where MR = MC.

12.3e Equating Marginal Revenue and Marginal Cost

The importance of equating marginal revenue and marginal cost is seen in Exhibit 2. As output expands beyond zero up to q^*, the marginal revenue derived from each unit of the expanded output exceeds the marginal cost of that unit of output, so the expansion of output creates additional profits. This addition to profit is shown as the leftmost shaded section in Exhibit 2. As long as marginal revenue exceeds marginal cost, profits continue to grow. For example, if the firm decides to produce q_1, the firm sacrifices potential profits because the marginal revenue from producing more output is greater than the marginal cost. Only at q^*, where $MR = MC$, is the output level just right—not too large, not too small. Further expansion of output beyond q^* will lead to losses on the additional output (i.e., decrease the firm's overall profits) because $MC > MR$. For example, if the firm produces q_2, the firm incurs losses on the output produced beyond q^*; the firm should reduce its output. Only at output q^*, where $MR = MC$, can we find the **profit-maximizing level of output**.

section 12.3 exhibit 3	Cost and Revenue Calculations for a Perfectly Competitive Firm						
Quantity (1)	Total Revenue (2)	Total Cost (3)	Profit (TR − TC) (4)	Marginal Revenue $\Delta TR/\Delta q$ (5)	Marginal Cost $\Delta TC/\Delta q$ (6)	Change in Profit (MR − MC) (7)
0	$0	$2	$−2			
				$5	$2	$3
1	5	4	1			
				5	3	2
2	10	7	3			
				5	4	1
3	15	11	4			
				5	5	0
4	20	16	4			
				5	6	−1
5	25	22	3			

Be careful not to make the mistake of focusing on profit per unit rather than total profit. That is, you might think that at q_1, if MR is much greater than MC, the firm should not produce more because the profit per unit is high at this point. However, that would be a mistake because a firm can add to its total profits as long as MR > MC—that is, all the way to q^*.

Should we focus on profit per unit or total profit?

The Marginal Approach

We can use the data from the table in Exhibit 3 to find Farmer Jones's profit-maximizing position. Columns 5 and 6 show the marginal revenue and marginal cost, respectively. The first bushel of wheat that Farmer Jones produces has a marginal revenue of $5 and a marginal cost of $2; so producing that bushel of wheat increases profits by $3 ($5 − $2). The second bushel of wheat produced has a marginal revenue of $5 and a marginal cost of $3; so producing that bushel of wheat increases profits by $2 ($5 − $3). Farmer Jones wants to produce those units and more. That is, as long as marginal revenue exceeds marginal cost, producing and selling those units add more to revenues than to costs; in other words, they add to profits. However, once he expands production beyond four units of output, Farmer Jones's costs are less than his marginal revenues, and his profits begin to fall. Clearly, Farmer Jones should not produce beyond four bushels of wheat.

Let's take another look at profit maximization, using the table in Exhibit 3. Comparing columns 2 and 3—the calculations of total revenue and total cost, respectively—we see that Farmer Jones maximizes his profits at output levels of three or four bushels, where he will make profits of $4. In column 4—profit—you can see that there is no higher level of profit at any of the other output levels. Producing five bushels would reduce profits by $1 because marginal revenue, $5, is less than the marginal cost, $6. Consequently, Farmer Jones would not produce this level of output. If MR > MC, Farmer Jones should increase production; if MR < MC, Farmer Jones should decrease production.

In the next section we use the profit-maximizing output rule to see what happens when changes in the market cause the price to fall below average total cost and even below average variable costs. We introduce the three-step method to determine whether the firm is making an economic profit, minimizing its losses, or should be temporarily shut down.

SECTION QUIZ

1. The marginal revenue of a perfectly competitive firm
   a. decreases as output increases.
   b. increases as output increases.
   c. is constant as output increases and is equal to price.
   d. increases as output increases and is equal to price.

(continued)

2. A perfectly competitive firm seeking to maximize its profits would want to maximize the difference between

   a. its marginal revenue and its marginal cost.

   b. its average revenue and its average cost.

   c. its total revenue and its total cost.

   d. its price and its marginal cost.

   e. either (a) or (d).

3. If a perfectly competitive firm's marginal revenue exceeded its marginal cost,

   a. it would cut its price in order to sell more output and increase its profits.

   b. it would expand its output but not cut its price in order to increase its profits.

   c. it would raise its price and expand its output to increase its profits.

   d. none of the above would be true.

4. Which of the following is true?

   a. Total revenue is price times the quantity sold.

   b. Average revenue is total revenue divided by the quantity sold.

   c. Marginal revenue is the change in total revenue from the sale of an additional unit of output.

   d. In a competitive industry, the price of the good equals both the average revenue and the marginal revenue.

   e. All of the above are true.

1. How is total revenue calculated?

2. How is average revenue derived from total revenue?

3. How is marginal revenue derived from total revenue?

4. Why is marginal revenue equal to price for a perfectly competitive firm?

Answers: 1. c 2. c 3. b 4. e

12.4 Short-Run Profits and Losses

▶ How do we determine whether a firm is generating an economic profit?

▶ How do we determine whether a firm is experiencing an economic loss?

▶ How do we determine whether a firm is making zero economic profits?

▶ Why doesn't a firm produce when price is below average variable cost?

In the previous section, we discussed how to determine the profit-maximizing output level for a perfectly competitive firm. How do we know whether a firm is actually making economic profits or losses?

12.4a The Three-Step Method

What Is the Three-Step Method?

Determining whether a firm is generating economic profits, economic losses, or zero economic profits at the profit-maximizing level of output, q^*, can be done in three easy steps. First, we walk through these steps, and then we apply the method to three situations for a hypothetical firm in the short run in Exhibit 1.

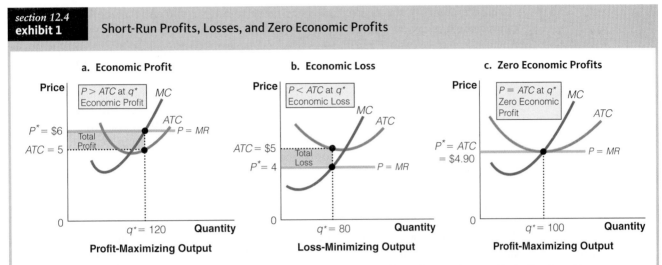

section 12.4 exhibit 1   **Short-Run Profits, Losses, and Zero Economic Profits**

a. Economic Profit

b. Economic Loss

c. Zero Economic Profits

In (a), the firm is earning short-run economic profits of $120. In (b), the firm is suffering losses of $80. In (c), the firm is making zero economic profits, with the price just equal to the average total cost in the short run.

1. Find where marginal revenue equals marginal cost and proceed straight down to the horizontal quantity axis to find q^*, the profit-maximizing output level.
2. At q^*, go straight up to the demand curve and then to the left to find the market price, P^*. Once you have identified P^* and q^*, you can find total revenue at the profit-maximizing output level because $TR = P \times q$.
3. The last step is to find the total cost. Again, go straight up from q^* to the average total cost (ATC) curve and then left to the vertical axis to compute the average total cost *per unit*. If we multiply average total cost by the output level, we can find the total cost ($TC = ATC \times q$).

If total revenue is greater than total cost at q^*, the firm is generating economic profits. If total revenue is less than total cost at q^*, the firm is generating economic losses. If total revenue is equal to total cost at q^*, there are zero economic profits (or a normal rate of return).

Alternatively, to find total economic profits, we can take the product price at P^* and subtract the average total cost at q^*. This will give us per-unit profit. If we multiply this by output, we will arrive at total economic profit; $(P^* - ATC) \times q^* = $ Total economic profit.

Remember, the cost curves include implicit and explicit costs—that is, we are covering the opportunity costs of our resources. Therefore, even with zero economic profits, no tears should be shed because the firm is covering both its implicit and explicit costs. Because firms are also covering their implicit costs, or what they could be producing with these resources in another endeavor, economists sometimes call this zero economic profit *a normal rate of return*. That is, the owners are doing as well as they could elsewhere, in that they are getting the normal rate of return on the resources they invested in the firm.

The Three-Step Method in Action

Exhibit 1 shows three different short-run equilibrium positions; in each case, the firm is producing at a level where marginal revenue equals marginal cost. Each of these alternatives shows that the firm is maximizing profits or minimizing losses in the short run.

Assume that three alternative prices—$6, $5, and $4—are available for a firm with given costs. In Exhibit 1(a), the firm receives $6 per unit at an equilibrium level of output ($MR = MC$) of 120 units. Total revenue ($P \times q^*$) is $6 × 120, or $720. The average total cost at 120 units of output is $5, and the total cost ($ATC \times q^*$) is $600. Following the three-step method, we can calculate that this firm is earning a total economic profit of $120. Or we can calculate total economic profit by using the following equation: $(P^* - ATC) \times q^* = ($6 - $5) \times 120 = 120.

Why do economists sometimes call a zero economic profit a normal rate of return?

In Exhibit 1(b), the market price has fallen to $4 per unit. At the equilibrium level of output, the firm is now producing 80 units of output at an average total cost of $5 per unit. The total revenue is now $320 ($4 × 80), and the total cost is $400 ($5 × 80). We can see that the firm is now incurring a total economic loss of $80. Or we can calculate total economic profit by using the following equation: $(P^* - ATC) \times q^* = (\$4 - \$5) \times 80 = -\$80$.

In Exhibit 1(c), the firm is earning zero economic profits, or a normal rate of return. The market price is $4.90, and the average total cost is $4.90 per unit for 100 units of output. In this case, economic profits are zero because total revenue, $490, minus total cost, $490, is equal to zero. This firm is just covering all its costs, both implicit and explicit. Or we can calculate total economic profit by using the following equation: $(P^* - ATC) \times q^* = \$4.90 - \$4.90 \times 100 = \$0$.

12.4b Evaluating Economic Losses in the Short Run

A firm generating an economic loss faces a tough choice: Should it continue to produce or should it shut down its operation? To make this decision, we need to add another variable to our discussion of economic profits and losses: average variable cost. Variable costs are costs that vary with output—for example, wages, raw material, transportation, and electricity. If a firm cannot generate enough revenues to cover its variable costs, it will have larger losses if it operates than if it shuts down (when losses are equal to fixed costs). That is, the firm will shut down if its total revenue ($p \times q$) is less than its variable costs (VC). If we divide $p \times q$ by q, we get p, and if we divide VC by q, we get AVC, so if $p < AVC$, a profit-maximizing firm will shut down. Thus, a firm will not produce at all unless the price is greater than its average variable cost.

Operating at a Loss

At price levels greater than or equal to the average variable cost, a firm may continue to operate in the short run even if its average total cost—variable and fixed costs—is not completely covered. That is, the firm may continue to operate even though it is experiencing an economic loss. Why? Because fixed costs continue whether the firm produces or not; it is better to earn enough to cover a portion of fixed costs than to earn nothing at all.

Why doesn't a firm just shut down whenever it is making economic losses?

For example, a restaurant may decide to stay open for lunch even with few customers if its revenues can cover variable costs. Many of a restaurant's costs are fixed—rent, insurance, kitchen appliances, pots, pans, tableware, and so on. These are sunk costs in the short run, so shutting down for lunch would not reduce these costs; the restaurant can ignore them when making its business strategy decisions.

The restaurant's lunch decision hinges on whether or not the revenue from the few lunchtime customers can cover the variable costs like staff and extra food. If the restaurant owner cannot cover the variable costs at lunchtime, she shuts it down for lunch.

Similarly, a grocery store may stay open all night even if it anticipates only a few customers. To the person on the street, this may look unprofitable. However, the relevant question to the store owner is not whether all the costs can be covered, but whether the additional sales from staying open all night cover the variable costs of electricity, staff, and extra food. Many businesses that are "failing" may continue to operate because they can cover their variable costs and at least part of their fixed costs, like rent.

In Exhibit 2, price is less than average total cost but more than average variable cost. In this case, the firm produces in the short run, but at a loss. To shut down would make this firm worse off because it can cover at least *some* of its fixed costs with the excess of revenue over its variable costs.

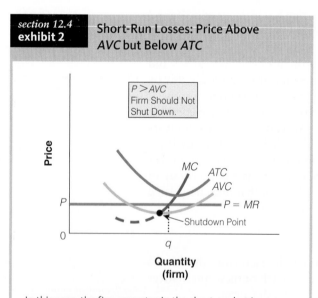

section 12.4 exhibit 2   Short-Run Losses: Price Above AVC but Below ATC

In this case, the firm operates in the short run but incurs a loss because $P < ATC$. Nevertheless, $P > AVC$, and revenues cover variable costs and partially defray fixed costs. This firm will leave the industry in the long run unless prices are expected to rise in the near future; but in the short run, it continues to operate at a loss as long as $P > AVC$, the shutdown point.

© ISTOCKPHOTO.COM/SLOBO

Why might a restaurant stay open at lunch even though there are only a few customers?

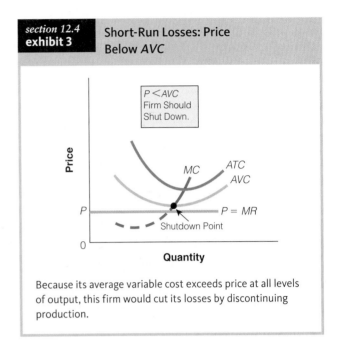

section 12.4
exhibit 3   **Short-Run Losses: Price Below *AVC***

$P < AVC$
Firm Should
Shut Down.

Because its average variable cost exceeds price at all levels of output, this firm would cut its losses by discontinuing production.

The Decision to Shut Down

Exhibit 3 illustrates a situation in which the price a firm is able to obtain for its product is below its average variable cost at all ranges of output. In this case, the firm is unable to cover even its variable costs in the short run. Because the firm is losing even more than the fixed costs it would lose if it shut down, it is more logical for the firm to cease operations. Hence, if $P < AVC$, the firm can cut its losses by shutting down.

For example, the owner of a miniature golf course in a summer resort may shut down for the winter months because of insufficient demand. But the fixed costs are irrelevant. The miniature golf course will shut down if $TR < VC$, or $(P \times q) < VC$. If we divide both sides by q, the firm will shut down if $P < AVC$, or $(P \times q)/q < VC/q$. So the course will shut down when its total revenues do not cover its variable costs.

Is the shutdown rule ($P < AVC$) related to a perfectly competitive firm's supply curve?

We must be careful to distinguish between a firm's decision to temporarily shut down and a permanent exit from the market. We reserve the language "shut down" to describe a firm that has made a short run decision not to produce any out put in the specific time period because of current market conditions. Exit, on the other hand, is a long run decision to leave the market permanently. Remember, the firm cannot avoid fixed costs in the short run, but it can in the long run. That is, in the short run, a firm may shut down, but it still has to pay its fixed costs. In the long run, a firm that exits does not have to pay fixed or variable costs.

The Short-Run Supply Curve

As we have just seen, at all prices above the minimum *AVC*, a firm produces in the short run even if average total cost (*ATC*) is not completely covered; at all prices below the minimum AVC, the firm shuts down. The firm produces above the minimum AVC even if it is incurring economic losses because it can still earn enough in total revenues to cover all its average variable cost and a portion of its fixed costs, which is better than not producing and earning nothing at all.

ROBERT L. SEXTON

Because the demand for summer camps will be lower during the off-season, it is likely that revenues may be too low for the camp to cover its variable costs, and the owner will choose to shut down. Remember, the owner will still have to pay the fixed costs: property tax, insurance, the costs associated with the building and land. However, if the camp is not in operation during the off-season, the owner will at least not have to pay the variable costs: salaries for the camp staff, food, and electricity.

section 12.4
exhibit 4   The Firm's Short-Run Supply Curve

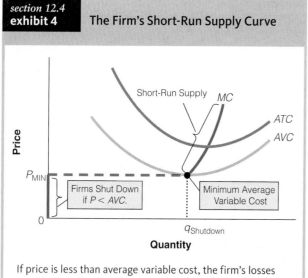

If price is less than average variable cost, the firm's losses would be smaller if it shut down and stopped producing. That is, if $P < AVC$, the firm is better off producing zero output. Hence, the firm's short-run supply curve is the marginal cost curve above average variable cost.

In graphical terms, the **short-run supply curve** of an individual competitive seller is identical to the portion of the *MC* curve that lies above the minimum of the *AVC* curve. As a cost relation, this curve shows the marginal cost of producing any *given output;* as a supply curve, it shows the *equilibrium output* that the firm will supply at various prices in the short run. The thick line above the dot in Exhibit 4 is the firm's supply curve—the portion of MC above its intersection with AVC. The declining portion of the MC curve has no significance for supply, because if the price falls below the average variable cost, the firm is better off shutting down— producing no output. The shutdown point is at the minimum point on the average variable cost curve where the output level is $q_{\text{Shut Down}}$. Beyond the point of lowest *AVC*, the marginal costs of successively larger amounts of output are progressively greater, so the firm will supply larger and larger amounts only at higher prices.

12.4c Deriving the Short-Run Market Supply Curve

The **short-run market supply curve** is the summation of all the individual firms' supply curves (that is, the portion of the firms' *MC* above *AVC*) in the market. Because the short run is too brief for new firms to enter the market, the market supply curve is the summation of *existing* firms. For example, in Exhibit 5, at P_1, each of the 1,000 identical firms in the industry produces 500 bushels of wheat per day at point a, in Exhibit 5(a); and the quantity supplied in the market is 500,000 bushels of wheat, point A, in Exhibit 5(b). We can again sum horizontally at P_2; the quantity supplied for each of the 1,000 identical firms is 800 bushels of wheat per day at point b in Exhibit 5(a), so the quantity supplied for the industry is 800,000 bushels of wheat per day, point B in Exhibit 5(b). Continuing this process gives us the market supply curve for the wheat market. In a market of 1,000 identical wheat farmers, the market supply curve is 1,000 times the quantity supplied by each firm, as long as the price is above *AVC*.

short-run supply curve

the portion of the *MC* curve above the *AVC* curve

short-run market supply curve

the horizontal summation of the individual firms' supply curves in the market

section 12.4
exhibit 5   Deriving the Short-Run Market Supply Curve

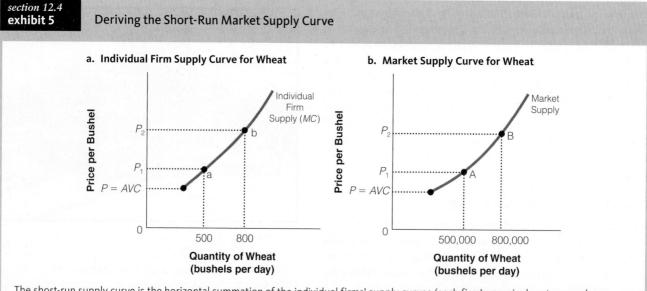

The short-run supply curve is the horizontal summation of the individual firms' supply curves (each firm's marginal cost curve above *AVC*), shown in (a). In a market of 1,000 identical wheat farmers, the market supply curve is 1,000 times the quantity supplied by each firm, shown in (b).

USE WHAT YOU'VE LEARNED

Reviewing the Short-Run Output Decision

Exhibit 6 shows the firm's short-run output at these various market prices: P_1, P_2, P_3, and P_4.

At the market price of P_1, the firm would not cover its average variable cost—the firm would produce zero output because the firm's losses would be smaller if it shut down and stopped producing. At the market price of P_2, the firm would produce at the loss-minimizing output of q_2 units. It would operate rather than shut down because it could cover all its average variable costs and some of its fixed costs. At the market price of P_3, the firm would produce q_3 units of output and make zero economic profit (a normal rate of return). At the market price of P_4, the firm would produce q_4 units of output and be making short-run economic profits.

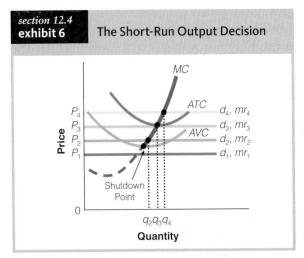

section 12.4
exhibit 6   The Short-Run Output Decision

USE WHAT YOU'VE LEARNED

Evaluating Short-Run Economic Losses

Q Lei-ann is one of many florists in a medium-size urban area. That is, we assume that she works in a market similar to a perfectly competitive market and operates, of course, in the short run. Lei-ann's cost and revenue information is shown in Exhibit 7. Based on this information, what should Lei-ann do in the short run, and why?

A Fixed costs are unavoidable unless the firm goes out of business. Lei-ann really has two decisions in the short run—either to operate or to shut down temporarily. In Exhibit 7, we see that Lei-ann makes $2,000 a day in total revenue, but her daily costs (fixed and variable) are $2,500. She has to pay her workers, pay for fresh flowers, and pay for the fuel used by her drivers in picking up and delivering flowers. She must also pay the electricity bill to heat her shop and keep her refrigerators going to protect her flowers. That is, every day, poor Lei-ann is losing $500; but she still might want to operate the shop despite the loss. Why? Lei-ann's average variable cost (comprising flowers, transportation, fuel, daily wage earners, and so on) amounts to $1,500 a day; her fixed costs (insurance, property taxes, rent for the building, and refrigerator payments) are $1,000 a day. Now, if Lei-ann does not operate, she will save on her variable cost—$1,500

If Lei-ann cannot cover her fixed costs, will she continue to operate?

a day—but she will be out the $2,000 a day she makes in revenue from selling her flowers. Thus, every day she operates, she is better off than if she had not operated at all. That is, if the firm can cover the average variable cost, it is better off operating than not operating. But suppose Lei-ann's *VC* were $2,100 a day. Then Lei-ann should not operate because

(continued)

Use What You've Learned continued

every day she does, she is $100 worse off than if she shut down altogether. In short, a firm will shut down if $TR < VC$ or $(P \times q) < VC$. If we divide both sides by q, the firm will shut down if $P < AVC$ or $(P \times q)/q < VC/q$.

Why does Lei-ann even bother operating if she is making a loss? Perhaps the economy is in a recession and the demand for flowers is temporarily down, but Lei-ann thinks things will pick up again in the next few months. If Lei-ann is right and demand picks up, her prices and marginal revenue will rise, and she may have a chance to make short-run economic profits.

section 12.4
exhibit 7
Lei-ann's Daily Revenue and Cost Schedule

Total Revenue	$2,000
Total Costs	**2,500**
Variable Costs	1,500
Fixed Costs	1,000

SECTION QUIZ

1. If a perfectly competitive firm's marginal revenue exceeded its marginal cost,
   a. it would cut its price in order to sell more output and increase its profits.
   b. it would expand its output but not cut its price in order to increase its profits.
   c. it is currently earning economic profits.
   d. both (a) and (c) are true.
   e. both (b) and (c) are true.

2. A perfectly competitive firm maximizes its profit at an output in which
   a. total revenue exceeds total cost by the greatest dollar amount.
   b. marginal cost equals the price.
   c. marginal cost equals marginal revenue.
   d. all of the above are true.

3. In perfect competition, at a firm's short-run profit-maximizing (or loss minimizing) output,
   a. its marginal revenue equals zero.
   b. its price could be greater or less than average cost.
   c. its marginal revenue will be falling.
   d. both (b) and (c) will be true.

4. The minimum price at which a firm would produce in the short run is the point at which
   a. price equals the minimum point on its marginal cost curve.
   b. price equals the minimum point on its average variable cost curve.
   c. price equals the minimum point on its average total cost curve.
   d. price equals the minimum point on its average fixed cost curve.

5. A profit-maximizing perfectly competitive firm would never knowingly operate at an output level at which
   a. it would lose more than its total fixed costs.
   b. it was not earning a positive economic profit.
   c. it was not earning a zero economic profit.
   d. it was not earning an accounting profit.

(continued)

SECTION QUIZ (cont.)

6. If a perfectly competitive firm finds that price is greater than *AVC* but less than *ATC* at the quantity where its marginal cost equals the market price,

   a. the firm will produce in the short run but may eventually go out of business.

   b. the firm will produce in the short run, and new entrants will tend to enter the industry over time.

   c. the firm will immediately shut down.

   d. the firm will be earning economic profits.

   e. both b and d are true.

7. The short-run supply curve of a perfectly competitive firm is

   a. its *MC* curve.

   b. its *MC* curve above the minimum point of *AVC*.

   c. its *MC* curve above the minimum point of *ATC*.

   d. none of the above.

---

1. How is the profit-maximizing output quantity determined?

2. How do we determine total revenue and total cost for the profit-maximizing output quantity?

3. If a profit-maximizing, perfectly competitive firm is earning a profit because total revenue exceeds total cost, why must the market price exceed average total cost?

4. If a profit-maximizing, perfectly competitive firm is earning a loss because total revenue is less than total cost, why must the market price be less than average total cost?

5. If a profit-maximizing, perfectly competitive firm is earning zero economic profits because total revenue equals total cost, why must the market price be equal to the average total cost for that level of output?

6. Why would a profit-maximizing, perfectly competitive firm shut down rather than operate if price was less than its average variable cost?

7. Why would a profit-maximizing, perfectly competitive firm continue to operate for a period of time if price was greater than average variable cost but less than average total cost?

Answers: 1. b 2. d 3. b 4. b 5. a 6. a 7. b

Long-Run Equilibrium   12.5

▶ When an industry is earning profits, will it encourage the entry of new firms?

▶ Why do perfectly competitive firms make zero economic profits in the long run?

12.5a Economic Profits and Losses Disappear in the Long Run

If farmers are able to make economic profits producing wheat, what will their response be in the long run? Farmers will increase the resources that they devote to the lucrative business of producing wheat. Suppose Farmer Jones is making an economic profit (he is earning an above-normal rate of return) producing wheat. To make even more profits, he may take land out of producing other crops and plant more wheat. Other farmers or people who are holding land for speculative purposes may also decide to plant wheat on their land.

Do economic profits and losses provide incentives for perfectly competitive firms to enter or exit?

a. Individual Firm

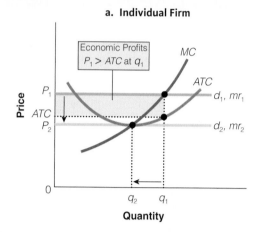

b. Market

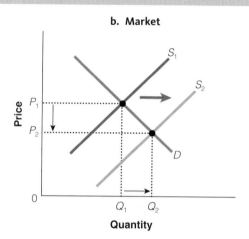

As the industry-determined price of wheat falls in (b), Farmer Jones's marginal revenue curve shifts downward from mr_1 to mr_2 in (a). A new profit-maximizing ($MC = MR$) point is reached at q_2. When the price is P_1, Farmer Jones is making a profit because $P_1 > ATC$. When the market supply increases, causing the market price to fall to P_2, Farmer Jones's profits disappear because $P_2 = ATC$.

As word gets out that wheat production is proving profitable, it will cause a supply response—the market supply curve will shift to the right as more firms enter the industry and existing firms expand, as shown in Exhibit 1(b). With this shift, the quantity of wheat supplied at any given price is greater than before. It may take a year or even longer, of course, for the complete supply response to take place, simply because it takes some time for information on profit opportunities to spread and still more time to plant, grow, and harvest the wheat. Note that the effect of increasing supply, other things being equal, is a reduction in the equilibrium price of wheat.

JIM WEST/ALAMY

In the late 1990s, when the organic food industry was in its infancy, an organic apple grower could sell its apples at a much higher price than regular apples. A price that covered more than its cost of production—an economic profit. Today, there are many more organic farmers, increasing market supply and decreasing the market price and moving firms toward zero economic profits—normal rate of return.

Suppose that, as a result of the supply response, the price of wheat falls from P_1 to P_2. The impact of the change in the market price of wheat, over which Farmer Jones has absolutely no control, is simple. If his costs don't change, he moves from making a profit ($P_1 > ATC$) to zero economic profits ($P_2 = ATC$), as shown in Exhibit 1(a). In long-run equilibrium, perfectly competitive firms make zero economic profits. Remember, a zero economic profit means that the firm actually earns a normal return on the use of its capital. Zero economic profit is an equilibrium or stable situation because any positive economic (above-normal) profit signals resources into the industry, beating down prices and therefore revenues to the firm.

Any economic losses signal resources to leave the industry, causing supply reductions that lead to increased prices and higher firm revenues for the remaining firms. For example, in Exhibit 2 we see a firm that continues to operate despite its losses—ATC is greater than P_1 at q_1. With losses, however, some firms will exit the industry, causing the market supply curve to shift from S_1 to S_2 and driving up the market price to P_2. This price increase reduces the losses for the firms remaining in the industry, until the losses are completely eliminated at P_2. The remaining firms will maximize profits by producing at q_2 units of output, where profits and losses are zero. Only at zero economic profits is there no tendency for firms to either enter or leave the industry.

section 12.5 exhibit 2   Losses Disappear with Exit

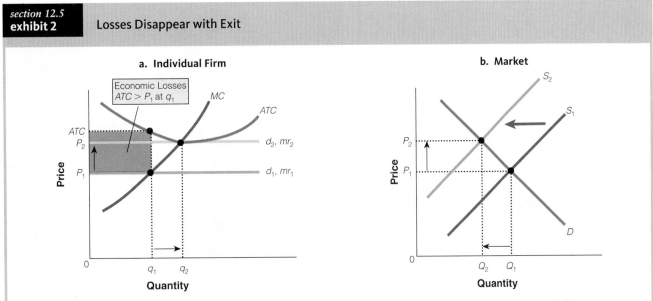

a. Individual Firm

b. Market

When firms in the industry suffer losses, some firms will exit in the long run, shifting the market supply curve to the left from S_1 to S_2. This shift causes market price to rise from P_1 to P_2 and market output to fall from Q_1 to Q_2. When the price is P_1, the firm is incurring a loss because ATC is greater than P_1 at q_1. When the market supply decreases from S_1 to S_2, it causes the market price to rise and the firm's losses disappear because $P_2 = ATC$.

12.5b The Long-Run Equilibrium for the Competitive Firm

The long-run competitive equilibrium for a perfectly competitive firm is illustrated graphically in Exhibit 3. At the equilibrium point, e (where $MC = MR$), short-run and long-run average total costs are also equal. The average total cost curves touch the marginal cost and marginal revenue (demand) curves at the equilibrium output point. Because the marginal revenue curve is also the average revenue curve, average revenue and average total cost are equal at the equilibrium point. The long-run equilibrium in perfect competition depicted in Exhibit 3 has an interesting feature. Note that the equilibrium output occurs at the lowest point on the average total cost curve. As you may recall, this occurs because the marginal cost curve must intersect the average total cost curve at the latter curve's lowest point. Hence, the equilibrium condition in the long run in perfect competition is for each firm to produce at the output that minimizes average total cost. At this longrun equilibrium, all firms in the industry earn zero economic profit; consequently, new firms have no incentive to enter the market, and existing firms have no incentive to exit the market.

section 12.5 exhibit 3   The Long-Run Competitive Equilibrium

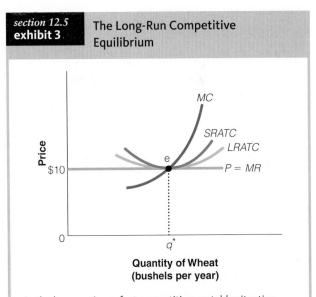

In the long run in perfect competition, a stable situation or equilibrium is achieved when economic profits are zero. In this case, at the profit-maximizing point where $MC = MR$, short-run and long-run average total costs are equal. Industry-wide supply shifts would change prices and average revenue, wiping out any losses or profits that develop in the short run and leading to the situation depicted here.

Real estate in Malibu is very pricey—the median price of a home is about $1.2 million. An agent might be able to make a nice commission. But that might be her only sale for two years. In contrast, a real estate agent in Fargo, North Dakota might be selling homes for $200,000. How could they make the same annual salary? The answer is free entry. It is relatively easy to pick up a real estate license and be in business in a couple of months. If profits from being a real estate agent are much higher in Malibu, then there will be more agents competing to sell houses. So a typical agent will make higher commissions per house sold but will sell fewer houses. In North Dakota, an agent might sell far more houses, even though his commission is less. This is exactly what Economists Hseih and Moretti found in a 2003 study. This happens over the housing cycle, as well. When housing prices rise—more agents enter the market; when housing prices fall, there are less agents in the market. Relatively free entry explains why average salaries tend to be similar across space and time.

SECTION QUIZ

1. The entry of new firms into an industry will likely

   a. shift the industry supply curve to the right.

   b. cause the market price to fall.

   c. reduce the profits of existing firms in the industry.

   d. do all of the above.

2. In long-run equilibrium under perfect competition, price does not equal which of the following?

   a. Long-run marginal cost

   b. Minimum average total cost

   c. Average fixed cost

   d. Marginal revenue

   e. Average revenue

3. Which of the following is true?

   a. Economic profits encourage the entry of new firms, which shift the market supply curve to the right.

   b. Any positive economic profits signal resources into the industry, driving down prices and revenues to the firm.

   c. Any economic losses signal resources to leave the industry, leading to supply reduction, higher prices, and increased revenues.

   d. Only at zero economic profits is there no tendency for firms to either enter or exit the industry.

   e. All of the above are true.

(continued)

SECTION QUIZ (cont.)

4. The exit of firms from an unprofitable industry
   a. will shift the market supply curve left.
   b. will cause the market price to rise.
   c. will increase the economic profits of the firms that remain.
   d. will do all of the above.

5. In long-run equilibrium, firms make zero _____ profits, earning a _____ rate of return.
   a. economic; normal
   b. economic; zero
   c. accounting; normal
   d. accounting; zero

1. Why do firms enter profitable industries?
2. Why does entry eliminate positive economic profits in a perfectly competitive industry?
3. Why do firms exit unprofitable industries?
4. Why does exit eliminate economic losses in a perfectly competitive industry?
5. Why is a situation of zero economic profits a stable long-run equilibrium situation for a perfectly competitive industry?

Answers: 1. d 2. c 3. e 4. d 5. a

Long-Run Supply   12.6

► What are constant-cost industries?
► What are increasing-cost industries?
► What are decreasing-cost industries?

► What is productive efficiency?
► What is allocative efficiency?

The preceding sections considered the costs for an individual, perfectly competitive firm as it varies output, on the assumption that the prices it pays for inputs (costs) are given. However, when the output of an entire industry changes, the likelihood is greater that changes in costs will occur. How will the changes in the number of firms in an industry affect the input costs of individual firms? In this section, we develop the long-run supply (*LRS*) curve. As we will see, the shape of the long-run supply curve depends on the extent to which input costs change with the entry or exit of firms in the industry. We look at three possible types of industries, when considering long-run supply: constant-cost industries, increasing-cost industries, and decreasing-cost industries.

12.6a A Constant-Cost Industry

In a **constant-cost industry**, the prices of inputs do not change as output is expanded. The industry may not use inputs in sufficient quantities to affect input prices. For example, say the firms in the industry use a lot of unskilled labor, but the industry is small. Therefore, as output expands, the increase in demand for unskilled labor will not cause the market wage

constant-cost industry
an industry where input prices (and cost curves) do not change as industry output changes

for unskilled labor to rise. Similarly, suppose a paper clip maker decides to double its output. It is highly unlikely that its demand for steel will have an impact on steel prices because its demand for the input is so small.

Once long-run adjustments are complete, by necessity each firm operates at the point of lowest long-run average total cost because supply shifts with entry and exit, eliminating profits. Therefore, each firm supplies the market with the quantity of output that it can produce at the lowest possible long-run average total cost.

In Exhibit 1, we can see the impact of an unexpected increase in market demand. Suppose that recent reports show that blueberries can lower cholesterol, lower blood pressure, and significantly reduce the risk of all cancers. The increase in market demand for blueberries leads to a price increase from P_1 to P_2 as the firm increases output from q_1 to q_2, and blueberry industry output increases from Q_1 to Q_2, as seen in Exhibit 1(b). The increase in market demand generates a higher price and positive profits for existing firms in the short run. The existence of economic profits will attract new firms into the industry, causing the short-run supply curve to shift from S_1 to S_2 and lowering price until excess profits are zero. This shift results in a new equilibrium, point C in Exhibit 1(c). Because the industry is one with constant costs, industry expansion does not alter firms' cost curves, and the industry long-run supply curve is horizontal. That is, the long-run equilibrium price is at the same level that prevailed before demand increased; the only long-run effect of the increase in demand is an increase in industry output, as more firms enter that are just like existing firms [shown in Exhibit 1(c)]. The long-run supply curve is horizontal when the market has free entry and exit; there are a large number of firms with identical costs and input prices are constant. Because these strong assumptions do not generally hold, we now discuss when the long-run supply curve has a positive or negative slope. Studies have shown that retail trade may fall into the category of a constant-cost industry because output can be expanded or contracted without a noticeable impact on input prices. The same may be true of the banking industry.

12.6b An Increasing-Cost Industry

increasing-cost industry

an industry where input prices rise (and cost curves rise) as industry output rises

In an increasing-cost industry, a more common scenario, the cost curves of individual firms rise as the total output of the industry increases. Increases in input prices (upward shifts in cost curves) occur as larger quantities of factors are employed in the industry. When an industry utilizes a large portion of an input, input prices will rise when the industry uses more of the input.

Increasing cost conditions are typical of "extractive" industries such as agriculture, fishing, mining, and lumbering, which utilize large portions of the total supply of specialized natural resources such as land or mineral deposits. As the output of such an industry expands, the increased demand for the resources raises the prices that must be paid for their use. Because additional resources of given quality cannot be produced, greater supplies can be obtained (if at all) only by luring them away from other industries, or by using lower-quality (and less-productive, thus higher-cost) resources.

Wheat production is a typical example of an increasing-cost industry. As the output of wheat increases, the demand for land suitable for the production of wheat rises, and thus the price paid for the use of land of any given quality increases.

If there were a construction boom in a fully employed economy, would it be more costly to get additional resources like skilled workers and raw materials? Yes, if this is an increasingcost industry, the industry can only produce more output if it gets a higher price because the firm's costs of production rise as output expands. As new firms enter and output expands, the increase in demand for inputs causes the price of inputs to rise—the cost curves of all construction firms shift upward as the industry expands. Or consider a downtown building boom where the supply of workers who are willing to work on tall skyscrapers is very inelastic, a very steep supply of labor curve. The high demand for these few workers causes their wages to rise sharply and the cost of skyscrapers to rise. The industry can produce more output but only at a higher price, enough to compensate the firm for the higher input costs. In an increasing-cost industry, the long-run supply curve is upward sloping.

section 12.6
exhibit 1   Demand Increase in a Constant-Cost Industry

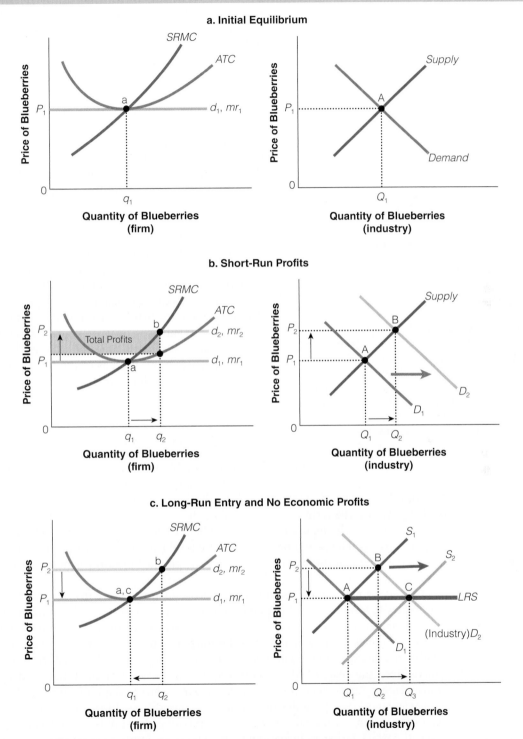

An unexpected increase in market demand for blueberries leads to an increase in the market price in (b). The new market price leads to positive profits for existing firms, which attracts new firms into the industry, shifting market supply from S_1 to S_2 in (c). This increased short-run industry supply curve intersects D_2 at point C. Each firm (of a new, larger number of firms) is again producing at q_1 and earning zero economic profits.

Increasing-Cost Industry

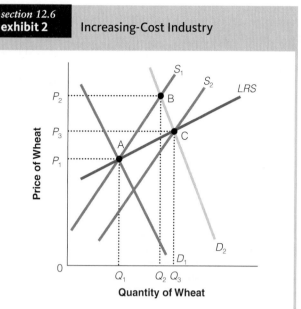

The unexpected increase in demand for wheat shifts the demand curve from D_1 to D_2. The increase in demand leads to higher prices from P_1 to P_2. The short-run economic profits induce other firms to enter the industry. This causes the short-run supply curve to shift right, from S_1 to S_2. As new firms enter and output expands, the increase in demand for inputs causes the price of inputs to rise, leading to higher cost curves for the firm. This means the supply curve does not shift rightward as much as in the constant-cost industry. The new long-run equilibrium is at P_3 and Q_3. The LRS is positively sloped. This means the industry must receive a higher market price to produce more output, Q_3, because the increased output causes input prices to rise.

For example, in Exhibit 2, we see that an unexpected increase in the market demand for wheat will shift the market demand curve from D_1 to D_2. Consequently, price will increase from P_1 to P_2 in the short run and the industry output increases from Q_1 to Q_2. The typical firm (farm) will have positive short-run profits and expand output. With the presence of short-run economic profits, new firms will enter the industry, shifting the short-run market supply curve to the right from S_1 to S_2. The prices of inputs, like farm land, fertilizer, seed, farm machinery, and so on, will be bid up by competing farmers, causing the firm's marginal and long-run average cost curves to rise. The cost increases mean that the market supply curve shifts right less than it would in a constant-cost industry. This leads to an upward-sloping long-run industry supply curve, as seen in Exhibit 2.

Another example is provided by the airlines. Growth in the airline industry results in more congestion of airports and airspace. That is, as the output of the airline industry increases, the firm's cost increases, *ceteris paribus*. This situation of an upward-sloping long-run industry supply curve is what economists call *external diseconomies of scale*—factors that are beyond the firm's control (that is, external) raise the firm's costs as industry output expands. In contrast, recall the discussion of diseconomies of scale in the last chapter where the costs were internal to the firm—increased costs due to managing a larger firm.

12.6c A Decreasing-Cost Industry

It is also possible that an expansion in the output of an industry can lead to a reduction in input costs and shift the MC and ATC curves downward, and the market price falls because of *external economies of scale*. We use the term *external* because the cost decreases are external to the firm; no one firm can gain by its own expansion. That is, the gain occurs when the total industry's output expands. The new long-run market equilibrium has more output at a lower price—that is, the long-run supply curve for a **decreasing-cost industry** is downward sloping (not shown).

Consider a new mining region, developed in an area remote from railroad facilities back in the days before motor vehicles. So long as the total output of the mines were small, the ore was hauled by wagon, an extremely expensive form of transportation. But when the number of mines increased, and the total output of the region rose substantially, it became feasible to construct a railroad to serve the area. The railroad lowered transportation costs and reduced the costs of all firms in the industry. As a practical matter, decreasing-cost industries are rarely encountered, at least over a large range of output. However, some industries may operate under decreasing-cost conditions in the short intervals of output expansion when continued growth makes possible the supply of materials or services at reduced cost. A larger industry might benefit from improved transportation or financial services, for example.

This situation might occur in the computer industry. The firms in the industry may be able to acquire computer chips at a lower price as the industry's demand for computer chips rises. Why? Perhaps it is because the computer chip industry can employ cost-saving techniques that become more economical at higher levels of output. That is, the marginal and average costs of the firm fall as input prices fall because of expanded output in the industry.

decreasing-cost industry

an industry where input prices fall (and cost curves fall) as industry output rises

12.6d **Perfect Competition and Economic Efficiency**

In this chapter, we have seen that a firm in a perfectly competitive market produces at the minimum point of the *ATC* curve in the long run and charges a price equal to that cost. Because competitive firms are producing using the least-cost method, the minimum value of resources is being used to produce a given level of output. This leads to lower product prices for consumers. In short, **productive efficiency** requires that firms produce goods and services in the least costly way, where *P* = Minimum *ATC*, as seen in Exhibit 3 in section 12.5 on page 341. However, productive efficiency alone does not guarantee that markets are operating efficiently—society must also produce the goods and services that society wants most. This leads us to what economists call allocative efficiency.

productive efficiency
where a good or service is produced at the lowest possible cost

We say that the output that results from equilibrium conditions of market demand and market supply in perfectly competitive markets achieve an efficient allocation of resources.

At the intersection of market supply and market demand, we find the competitive equilibrium price, *P**, and the competitive equilibrium output, *Q**. In competitive markets, market supply equals market demand, and *P* = *MC*. When *P* = *MC*, buyers value the last unit of output by the same amount that it cost sellers to produce it. If buyers value the last unit by more than the marginal cost of production, resources are not being allocated efficiently, as at Q_1 in Exhibit 3(a). Think of the demand curve as the marginal benefit curve (*D* = *MB*) and the supply curve as the marginal cost curve (*S* = *MC*). According to the rule of rational choice, we should pursue an activity as long as the expected marginal benefits are greater than the expected marginal costs. For example, in Exhibit 3(a), if Q_1 is produced, then the marginal benefits from producing additional units are greater than the marginal costs. The shaded area is deadweight loss. That is, at Q_1, resources are not being allocated efficiently, and output should be expanded.

We can also produce too much output. For example, if output is expanded beyond *Q** in Exhibit 3(b), the cost to sellers for producing the good is greater than the marginal benefit to consumers. The shaded area is deadweight loss. Society would gain from a reduction in output back to *Q**. Once the competitive equilibrium is reached, the buyers' marginal benefit equals the sellers' marginal cost. That is, in a competitive market, producers efficiently use their scarce resources (labor, machinery, and other inputs) to produce what consumers want. In this sense, perfect competition achieves **allocative efficiency**.

What is the difference between productive efficiency and allocative efficiency?

allocative efficiency
where *P* = *MC* and production will be allocated to reflect consumer preferences

---

section 12.6
exhibit 3   **Allocative Efficiency and Perfect Competition**

a. Producing Less Than the Competitive Level of Output Lowers Welfare

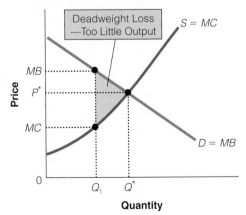

b. Producing More Than the Competitive Level of Output Lowers Welfare

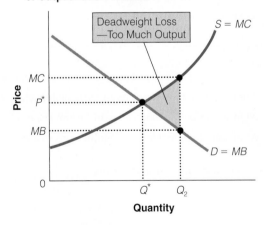

The demand curve measures the marginal benefits to the consumer and the supply curve measures the marginal cost to the sellers. At *P** and *Q**, resources are being allocated efficiently—the marginal benefits of these resources are equal to the marginal cost of these resources. If Q_1 is produced, then the marginal benefits from producing additional units are greater than the marginal costs. Society gains from expanding output up to the point where *MB* = *MC* at *Q**. If output is expanded beyond *Q** (*MC* > *MB*) society, gains from a reduction in output back to *Q**.

SECTION QUIZ

1. If the domino-making industry is a constant-cost industry, one would expect the long-run result of an increase in demand for dominos to include

   a. a greater number of firms and a higher price.

   b. a greater number of firms and the same price.

   c. the same number of firms and a higher price.

   d. the same number of firms and the same price.

2. In an increasing-cost industry, an unexpected increase in demand would lead to what result in the long run?

   a. Higher costs and a higher price

   b. Higher costs and a lower price

   c. No change in costs or prices

   d. Impossible to determine from the information given

3. Which of the following is true?

   a. In constant-cost industries, the cost curves of the firm are not affected by changes in the output of the entire industry.

   b. In an increasing-cost industry, the cost curves of the individual firms rise as total output increases.

   c. A decreasing-cost industry has a downward-sloping long-run supply curve; firms experience lower cost as industry expands.

   d. All of the above are true.

4. Which of the following is true?

   a. Productive efficiency occurs in perfect competition because the firm produces at the minimum of the *ATC* curve.

   b. Allocative efficiency occurs when $P = MC$; production is allocated to reflect consumers' want.

   c. Both (a) and (b) are true.

   d. None of the above is true.

5. In an increasing-cost industry, an increase in industry demand would lead to _____ in the number of firms and _____ in firms' average cost curves in the long run.

   a. no change; no change

   b. no change; an upward shift

   c. an increase; no change

   d. an increase; an upward shift

---

1. What must be true about input costs as industry output expands for a constant-cost industry?

2. What must be true about input costs as industry output expands for an increasing-cost industry?

3. What would be the long-run equilibrium result of an increase in demand in a constant-cost industry?

4. What would be the long-run equilibrium result of an increase in demand in an increasing-cost industry?

Answers: 1. b 2. a 3. d 4. c 5. d

Fill in the blanks:

1. Perfect competition is a market structure involving a(n) _____ number of buyers and sellers, a(n) _____ product, and _____ market entry and exit.

2. Perfectly competitive firms are _____, who must accept the market price as determined by the forces of demand and supply.

3. Because perfectly competitive markets have _____ buyers and sellers, each firm is so _____ in relation to the industry that its production decisions have no impact on the market.

4. Because consumers believe that all firms in a perfectly competitive market sell _____ products, the products of all the firms are perfect substitutes.

5. Because of _____ market entry and exit, perfectly competitive markets generally consist of a(n) _____ number of small suppliers.

6. In a perfectly competitive industry, each producer provides such a(n) _____ fraction of the total supply that a change in the amount he or she offers does not have a noticeable effect on the market price.

7. Because perfectly competitive sellers can sell all they want at the market price, their demand curve is _____ at the market price over the _____ range of output that they could possibly produce.

8. The objective of a firm is to maximize profits by producing the amount that maximizes the difference between its _____ and _____.

9. Total revenue for a perfectly competitive firm equals the _____ times the _____.

10. _____ equals total revenue divided by the number of units of the product sold.

11. _____ is the additional revenue derived from the sale of one more unit of the good.

12. In perfect competition, we know that _____ and price are equal.

13. In all types of market environments, firms will maximize profits at that output that maximizes the difference between _____ and _____, which is the same output level where _____ equals _____.

14. At the level of output chosen by a competitive firm, total cost equals _____ times quantity,

while total revenue equals _____ times quantity.

15. If total revenue is greater than total costs at its profit-maximizing output level, a firm is generating _____. If total revenue is less than total costs, the firm is generating _____. If total revenue equals total costs, the firm is earning _____.

16. If a firm cannot generate enough revenues to cover its _____ costs, then it will have larger losses if it operates than if it shuts down in the short run.

17. The loss a firm would bear if it shuts down would be equal to _____.

18. When price is less than _____ but more than _____, a firm produces in the short run, but at a loss.

19. The short-run supply curve of an individual competitive seller is identical with that portion of the _____ curve that lies above the minimum of the _____ curve.

20. The short-run market supply curve is the horizontal summation of the individual firms' supply curves, providing that _____ are not affected by increased production by existing firms.

21. If perfectly competitive producers are currently making economic profits, the market supply curve will shift to the right over time as more firms _____ and existing firms _____.

22. As entry into a profitable industry pushes down the market price, producers will move from a situation where price _____ average total cost to one where price _____ average total cost.

23. Only at _____ is the tendency for firms either to enter or leave the business eliminated.

24. The long-run equilibrium output in perfect competition occurs at the lowest point on the average total cost curve, so the equilibrium condition in the long run in perfect competition is for firms to produce at that output that minimizes the _____.

25. The shape of the long-run supply curve depends on the extent to which _____ change with the entry or exit of firms in the industry.

26. In a constant-cost industry, the prices of inputs _____ as output is expanded.

27. In an increasing-cost industry, the cost curves of the individual firms _____ as the total output of the industry increases.

28. There is a(n) _____ efficiency in perfect competition because the firm produces at the minimum of the *ATC* curve.

29. There is _____ efficiency in perfect competition because $P = MC$ and production is allocated to reflect consumers' wants.

30. Once the competitive equilibrium is reached, the buyers' _____ equals the sellers' _____.

Answers: 1. large; homogeneous (standardized); easy 2. price takers 3. many; small 4. identical (homogeneous) 5. easy; large 6. small 7. horizontal; entire 8. total revenues; total costs 9. market price; quantity of units sold 10. Average revenue 11. Marginal revenue 12. marginal revenue 13. total revenue; total costs; marginal costs 14. average total cost; the market price 15. economic profits; economic losses; zero economic profits 16. variable 17. fixed costs 18. average total costs; average variable costs 19. marginal cost; average variable cost 20. input prices 21. enter the industry; expand 22. exceeds; equals 23. zero economic profits 24. average total cost curve 25. input costs 26. do not change 27. rise 28. productive 29. allocative 30. marginal benefit; marginal cost

KEY TERMS AND CONCEPTS

total revenue (TR) 329
average revenue (AR) 329
marginal revenue (MR) 329
profit-maximizing level of output 330

short-run supply curve 336
short-run market supply curve 336
constant-cost industry 343
increasing-cost industry 344

decreasing-cost industry 346
productive efficiency 347
allocative efficiency 347

SECTION QUIZ ANSWERS

12.1 A Perfectly Competitive Market

1. **Why do firms in perfectly competitive markets involve homogeneous goods?**
For there to be a large number of sellers of a particular good, so that no seller can appreciably affect the market price (i.e., sellers are price takers), the goods in question must be the same, or homogeneous.

2. **Why does the absence of significant barriers to entry tend to result in a large number of suppliers?**
With no significant barriers to entry, it is fairly easy for entrepreneurs to become suppliers of a product. With such easy entry, as long as an industry is profitable it will attract new suppliers, typically resulting in large numbers of sellers.

3. **Why does the fact that perfectly competitive firms are small relative to the market make them price takers?**
If a perfectly competitive firm sells only a small amount relative to the total market supply, even sharply reducing its output will make virtually no difference in the market quantity supplied; therefore, it will make virtually no difference in the market price. In this case, a firm is able to sell all it wants at the market equilibrium price but is unable to appreciably affect that price; therefore, it takes the market equilibrium price as given—that is, it is a price taker.

12.2 An Individual Price Taker's Demand Curve

1. **Why would a perfectly competitive firm not try to raise or lower its price?**
A perfectly competitive firm is able to sell all it wants at the market equilibrium price. Therefore, it has no incentive to lower prices (sacrificing revenues and therefore profits) in an attempt to increase sales. Because other firms are willing to sell perfect substitutes for each other's product (because goods are homogeneous) at the market equilibrium price, trying to raise the price would lead to the firm losing all its sales. Therefore, it has no incentive to try to raise its price, either.

2. **Why can we represent the demand curve of a perfectly competitive firm as perfectly elastic (horizontal) at the market price?**
If a perfectly competitive firm can sell all it would like at the market equilibrium price, the demand curve it faces for its output is perfectly elastic (horizontal) at that market equilibrium price.

3. **How does an individual perfectly competitive firm's demand curve change when the market price changes?**
If a perfectly competitive firm can sell all it would like at the market equilibrium price, it faces a perfectly

elastic demand curve at the market equilibrium price. Therefore, anything that changes the market equilibrium price (any of the market demand curve shifters or the market supply curve shifters) will change the price at which each perfectly competitive firm's demand curve is perfectly elastic (horizontal).

4. If the marginal cost facing every producer of a product shifted upward, would the position of a perfectly competitive firm's demand curve be likely to change as a result? Why or why not?

Yes. If the marginal cost curves facing each producer shifted upward, a decrease (leftward shift) would occur in the industry supply curve. This shift would result in a higher market price that each producer takes as given, which would shift each producer's horizontal demand curve upward to that new market price.

12.3 Profit Maximization

1. How is total revenue calculated?

Total revenue is equal to the price times the quantity sold. However, because the quantity sold at that price must equal the quantity demanded at that price (to sell a product you need a willing buyer), it can also be described as price times quantity demanded at that price.

2. How is average revenue derived from total revenue?

Average or per-unit revenue for a given quantity of output is just the total revenue from that quantity of sales divided by the quantity sold.

3. How is marginal revenue derived from total revenue?

Marginal revenue is the change in total revenue from the sale of one more unit of output. It can be either positive (total revenue increases with output) or negative (total revenue decreases with output).

4. Why is marginal revenue equal to price for a perfectly competitive firm?

If a perfectly competitive seller can sell all it would like at the market equilibrium price, it can sell one more unit at that price without having to lower its price on the other units it sells (which would require sacrificing revenues from those sales). Therefore, its marginal revenue from selling one more unit equals the market equilibrium price, and its horizontal demand curve therefore is the same as its horizontal marginal revenue curve.

12.4 Short-Run Profits and Losses

1. How is the profit-maximizing output quantity determined?

The profit-maximizing output is the output where marginal revenue equals marginal cost (because profits increase for every unit of output for which marginal revenue exceeds marginal cost).

2. How do we determine total revenue and total cost for the profit-maximizing output quantity?

At the profit-maximizing quantity, total revenue is equal to average revenue (price) times quantity (because average revenue is total revenue divided by quantity), and total cost is equal to average cost times quantity (because average cost equals total cost divided by quantity).

3. If a profit-maximizing, perfectly competitive firm is earning a profit because total revenue exceeds total cost, why must the market price exceed average total cost?

If total revenue exceeds total cost, total revenue divided by the quantity of output, which is average revenue or price, must also exceed total cost divided by the same quantity of output, which is average total cost, for that level of output.

4. If a profit-maximizing, perfectly competitive firm is earning a loss because total revenue is less than total cost, why must the market price be less than average total cost?

If total revenue is less than total cost, total revenue divided by the quantity of output, which is average revenue or price, must also be less than total cost divided by the same quantity of output, which is average total cost, for that level of output.

5. If a profit-maximizing, perfectly competitive firm is earning zero economic profits because total revenue equals total cost, why must the market price be equal to the average total cost for that level of output?

If total revenue equals total cost, total revenue divided by the quantity of output, which is average revenue or price, must also be equal to total cost divided by the same quantity of output, which is average total cost, for that level of output.

6. Why would a profit-maximizing, perfectly competitive firm shut down rather than operate if price was less than its average variable cost?

If a firm shuts down, its losses will equal its fixed costs (because it has no revenue or variable costs). If a firm operates, and revenues exactly cover variable costs, it will also suffer losses equal to fixed costs. But if a firm cannot cover even all its variable costs with its revenues, it will lose its fixed costs plus part of its variable costs. But because these losses are greater than the losses from shutting down, a firm would choose to shut down rather than continue to operate in this situation.

7. Why would a profit-maximizing, perfectly competitive firm continue to operate for a period of time if price was greater than average variable cost but less than average total cost?

If price was greater than average variable cost but less than average total cost, a firm would be earning losses and would eventually go out of business if that situation continued. However, in the short run, as long as revenues more than covered variable costs, losses from operating would be less than the losses from shutting down (these losses equal total fixed cost), as at least part of fixed costs would be covered by revenues; so a firm would continue to operate in the short run in this situation.

12.5 Long-Run Equilibrium

1. **Why do firms enter profitable industries?**
Profitable industries generate a higher rate of return to productive assets than other industries. Therefore, firms will enter such industries in their search for more profitable uses for their assets.

2. **Why does entry eliminate positive economic profits in a perfectly competitive industry?**
Entry eliminates positive economic profits (above-normal rates of return) in a perfectly competitive industry because entry will continue as long as economic profits remain positive (rates of return are higher than in other industries), that is, until no more positive economic profits can be earned.

3. **Why do firms exit unprofitable industries?**
Unprofitable industries generate lower rates of return to productive assets than other industries. Therefore, firms will exit such industries in their search for more profitable uses for their assets elsewhere.

4. **Why does exit eliminate economic losses in a perfectly competitive industry?**
Exit eliminates negative economic profits (below-normal rates of return) in a perfectly competitive industry because exit will continue as long as economic profits remain negative (rates of return are lower than in other industries); that is, until no firms are experiencing economic losses.

5. **Why is a situation of zero economic profits a stable long-run equilibrium situation for a perfectly competitive industry?**
A situation of zero economic profits is a stable long-run equilibrium situation for a perfectly competitive industry because that situation offers no profit incentives for firms to either enter or leave the industry.

12.6 Long-Run Supply

1. **What must be true about input costs as industry output expands for a constant-cost industry?**
Input costs remain constant as industry output expands for a constant-cost industry (which is why it is a constant-cost industry).

2. **What must be true about input costs as industry output expands for an increasing-cost industry?**
Input costs increase as industry output expands for an increasing-cost industry (which is why it is an increasing-cost industry).

3. **What would be the long-run equilibrium result of an increase in demand in a constant-cost industry?**
The long-run equilibrium result of an increase in demand in a constant-cost industry is an increase in industry output with no change in price because output will expand as long as price exceeds the constant level of long-run average cost.

4. **What would be the long-run equilibrium result of an increase in demand in an increasing-cost industry?**
The long-run equilibrium result of an increase in demand in an increasing-cost industry is an increase in industry output (but a smaller increase than in the constant-cost case) and a higher price. Output will expand as long as price exceeds long-run average cost; but that expansion of output increases costs by raising input prices, so in the long run prices just cover the resulting higher costs of production.

PROBLEMS

1. Which of the following are most likely to be perfectly competitive?
   a. Chicago Board of Trade
   b. fast-food industry
   c. computer software industry
   d. New York Stock Exchange
   e. clothing industry

2. Using the following information, which of the industries described are perfectly competitive? Check the perfectly competitive market characteristics each industry possesses and determine whether it is a perfectly competitive industry.

Industry	Many Firms and Buyers	Identical Products	Ease of Entry and Exit	Perfectly Competitive Market?
New York taxi business: City issues a limited number of permits.	☐	☐	☐	_____
Commercial aircraft industry: The costs of starting such a business are significant.	☐	☐	☐	_____
Window-washing business: Low cost of entry and limited specialized training.	☐	☐	☐	_____
Fast-food business: Restaurant chains produce meals that are distinct.	☐	☐	☐	_____
Broccoli farming: There are many producers of broccoli, which requires no special growing conditions.	☐	☐	☐	_____

3.

Output	Total Cost	Total Revenue
0	$ 30	$ 0
1	45	25
2	65	50
3	90	75
4	120	100
5	155	125

Given these data, determine *AR, MR, P,* and the short-run profit-maximizing (loss-minimizing) level of output.

4. Illustrate the *SRATC, AVC, MC,* and *MR* curves for a perfectly competitive firm that is operating at a loss. What is the output level that minimizes losses? Why is it more profitable to continue producing in the short run rather than shut down?

5. Industry councils promote the consumption of particular types of farm products. These groups urge us to "Drink Milk" or "Eat Apples." Very little advertising is done by individual farmers. Using your understanding of the perfectly competitive market, explain this advertising strategy.

6. Complete the following table and identify the profit-maximizing output.
   a.

Quantity	Price	Total Revenue	Marginal Revenue	Marginal Cost	Total Profit
10	$12	$120	$12	$8	$25
11	12	_____	_____	9	_____
12	12	_____	_____	11	_____
13	12	_____	_____	12	_____
14	12	_____	_____	14	_____

   b. What is true about marginal revenue and marginal costs when profit is maximized?
   c. What would be the profit-maximizing level of output if price fell to $9?

7. Explain why the following conditions are typical under perfect competition in the long run.
   a. *P = MC*
   b. *P* = minimum *ATC*

8. Discuss the following questions.
   a. Why must price cover *AVC* if firms are to continue to operate?
   b. If the firm is covering its *AVC* but not all its fixed costs, will it continue to operate in the short run? Why or why not?
   c. Why is it possible for price to remain above the average total cost in the short run but not in the long run?

9. At a price of $5, the profit-maximizing output for a perfectly competitive firm is 1,000 units per year. If the average total cost is $3 per unit, what will be the firm's profit? If the average total cost is $6 per unit, what will be the firm's profit? What is the relationship between profit, price, and average total cost?

10. Use the following diagram to answer (a), (b), and (c).

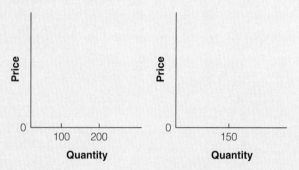

   a. Illustrate the relationship between a perfectly competitive firm's demand curve and the market supply and demand curve.
   b. Illustrate the effects of an increase in market demand on a perfectly competitive firm's demand curve.
   c. Illustrate the effects of a decrease in market demand on a perfectly competitive firm's demand curve.

11. Complete the following table for a perfectly competitive firm, and indicate its profit-maximizing output.

Quantity	Price	Total Revenue	Marginal Revenue	Total Cost	Marginal Cost	Total Profit
6	$10	$ _____	$ _____	$30	$3	$30
7	_____	_____	_____	35	_____	_____
8	_____	_____	_____	42	_____	_____
9	_____	_____	_____	51	_____	_____
10	_____	_____	_____	62	_____	_____
11	_____	_____	_____	75	_____	_____
12	_____	_____	_____	90	_____	_____

12. Use the following diagram to answer (a)–(d).

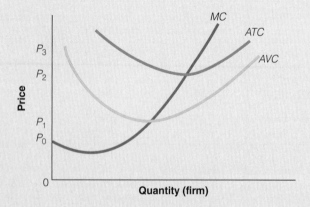

   a. How much would a perfectly competitive firm produce at each of the indicated prices?
   b. At which prices is the firm earning economic profits? Zero economic profits? Negative economic profits?
   c. At which prices would the firm shut down?
   d. Indicate what this firm's supply curve would be.

13. Use the following diagram to answer (a)–(d).

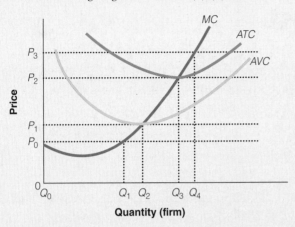

a. How much would a perfectly competitive firm produce at each of the indicated prices?
b. At which prices is the firm earning economic profits? Zero economic profits? Negative economic profits?
c. At which prices would the firm shut down?
d. Indicate what this firm's supply curve would be.

14. Use the following diagrams to answer (a) and (b).

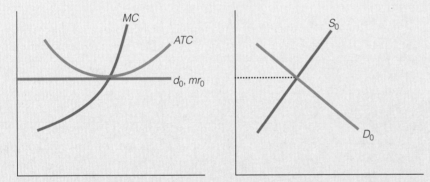

a. Show the effect of an increase in demand on the perfectly competitive firm's price, marginal revenue, output, and profits in the short run.
b. Show the long-run effects of an increase in demand for the industry and the effects on a perfectly competitive firm's price, marginal revenue, output, and profits for a constant-cost industry.

15. In *The Wealth of Nations*, Adam Smith wrote, "Every individual endeavors to employ his capital so that its produce may be of greatest value. He generally neither intends to promote the public interest, nor knows how much he is promoting it. He intends only his own security, only his own gain. And he is led by an invisible hand to promote an end which was no part of his intention. By pursuing his own interest he frequently promotes that of society more effectively than when he really intends to promote it." How does the story of long-run equilibrium in a perfectly competitive industry illustrate Adam Smith's invisible hand?

16. Graph and explain the adjustments to long-run equilibrium when market demand decreases in a constant-cost industry.

17. Evaluate the following statements. Determine whether each is true or false and explain your answer.
a. If economic profits are zero, firms will exit the industry in the long run.
b. A firm cannot maximize profits without minimizing costs.
c. If a firm is minimizing costs, it must be maximizing profits.

18. Describe what would happen to the industry supply curve and the economic profits of the firms in a competitive industry if those firms were currently earning economic profits. What if they were currently earning economic losses?

19. Given the industry description, identify each of the following as an increasing- or constant-cost industry.
a. Major League Baseball: Uses the majority of pitchers. As the number of pitchers used increased, the quality declines.
b. Fast-food restaurants: Uses a relatively small share of land and unskilled labor in most cities.
c. Trucking industry: Uses a large portion of trained and experienced drivers, especially long-distance drivers.

Monopoly and Antitrust

Richard Branson, the owner of Virgin Atlantic Airlines, currently has a monopoly on commercial space travel. Here is an ad for space travel.

> Book your place in space now and join around 600 Virgin Galactic astronauts who will venture into space. Tickets cost $250,000. If you are interested in discussing your reservation with us directly, please fill in the form below and we will be in touch as soon as possible to answer any questions you may have. Or you can contact one of our "local" Accredited Space Agents around the world. They have been specially selected and trained by us to handle all aspects of your spaceflight reservation.
>
> Virgin Galactic Mission Control

Monopoly is at the other end of the spectrum from perfect competition. Pure monopoly is a market with a single seller. Because it is the sole supplier, a monopoly faces the market demand curve for its product. Consequently, the monopolist has control over the market price—it is a price maker. The monopolist can choose any combination of price and quantity along its market demand curve. But do not confuse ability with incentive. The monopolist, just like the perfectly competitive firm, will maximize profits (or minimize losses) by producing at the output level where $MR = MC$.

A pure monopoly, with literally one seller, is rare in the real world. But situations in which a few firms compete with each other are quite common. For example, Microsoft's Windows system, certain patented prescription drugs, the DeBeers diamond company, and your cable company are all examples of near monopolies. All of these firms have some monopoly power—control over prices and output.

In this chapter, we see how a monopolist determines the profit-maximizing price and output. We also compare monopoly and perfect competition to see which is more efficient. Does the monopoly equilibrium solution lead to higher prices and lower output levels than the perfectly competitive equilibrium solution? If so, what can the government do about it?

Monopoly: The Price Maker | 13.1

▸ What is a monopoly?

▸ Why is pure monopoly rare?

▸ What are the sources of monopoly power?

▸ What is a natural monopoly?

13.1a What Is a Monopoly?

A true or pure **monopoly** exists when a market consists of only one seller of a product with no close substitute and natural or legal barriers to prevent competition from new entrants. The reason a monopoly is the only firm in the market is because other firms cannot enter—there are barriers to entry. In monopoly, the firm and "the industry" are one and the same. Consequently, the firm sets the price of the good because the firm faces the industry demand curve and can pick the most profitable point on that demand curve. Monopolists are price makers (rather than price takers) that try to pick the price that will maximize their profits.

monopoly
the single supplier of a product that has no close substitute

13.1b Pure Monopoly Is a Rarity

Few goods and services truly have only one producer. One might think of a small community with a single bank, a single newspaper, or even a single grocery store. Even in these situations, however, most people can bank out of town, use a substitute financial institution, buy out-of-town newspapers or read them on the Web, go to a nearby town to buy groceries, and so on. Near-monopoly conditions exist, but absolutely pure monopoly is unusual.

One market in which there is typically only one producer of goods and services within an area is public utilities. In any given market, usually only one company provides natural gas or supplies water. Moreover, governments themselves provide many services for which they are often the sole provider—sewer services, fire and police protection, and military protection. Most of these situations resemble a pure monopoly. However, for most of these goods and services, substitute goods and services are available. People heating their homes with natural gas can switch to electric heat (or vice versa). In some areas, residents can even substitute home-collected rainwater or well water for what the local water company provides.

Even though the purist may correctly deny the existence of monopoly, the number of situations where monopoly conditions are closely approximated is numerous enough to make the study of monopoly more than a theoretical abstraction; moreover, the study of monopoly is useful in clarifying certain desirable aspects of perfect competition. In short, monopoly is a matter of degree. Many firms have some monopoly power but it is usually limited.

13.1c Barriers to Entry

A monopolist can use several ways to make it very difficult for other firms to overcome barriers to entry. For example, a monopolist might prevent potential rivals from entering the market by establishing legal barriers, taking advantage of economies of scale, or controlling important inputs.

If pure monopoly is a rarity, why do we study monopoly?

Legal Barriers

In the case of legal barriers, the government might franchise only one firm to operate an industry, as is the case for postal services in most countries. The government can also provide licensing designed to ensure a certain level of quality and competence. Workers in many trade

Economies of Scale

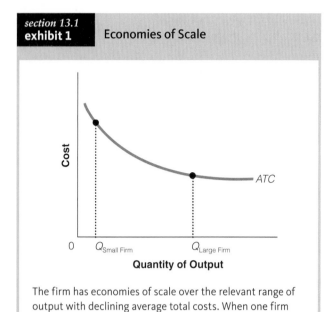

The firm has economies of scale over the relevant range of output with declining average total costs. When one firm can produce the total output at a lower cost than several small firms, it is called a natural monopoly.

natural monopoly
a firm that can produce at a lower cost than a number of smaller firms can

industries must obtain government licensing—hairstylists, bartenders, contractors, electricians, and plumbers, for instance.

Also, the government could award patents that encourage inventive activity. It can cost millions of dollars to develop a new drug or computer chip, for example, and without a patent to recoup some of the costs, a company would certainly be less motivated to pursue inventive activity. As long as the patent is in effect, the company has the potential to enjoy monopoly profits for many years. After all, why would a firm engage in costly research if any company could take a free ride on their discovery and produce and sell the new drug or computer chip?

Economies of Scale

The situation in which one large firm can provide the output of the market at a lower cost than two or more smaller firms is called a **natural monopoly**. With a natural monopoly, it is more efficient to have one firm produce the good. The reason for the cost advantage is economies of scale; that is, *ATC* falls as output expands throughout the relevant output range, as seen in Exhibit 1. Public utilities, such as water, gas, and electricity, are examples of natural monopoly. It is less costly for one firm to lay down pipes and distribute water than for competing firms to lay down a maze of competing pipes. That is, a single water company can supply the town water more efficiently than a large number of competing firms. Recall a few years ago when Sirius and XM Radio merged because both their fixed costs were huge and neither was going to make it on their own. Average costs were much lower with one company than two. So in 2008, they merged and average costs fell.

IN THE NEWS

Is a Diamond Monopoly Forever?

At one time, the De Beers diamond company had control of roughly 80 percent of the world's output of diamonds. However, today De Beers accounts for less than 40 percent of diamond production. Increased competition and the discovery of new diamond deposits has finally broken the monopoly in the diamond industry. A number of producers from countries such as Russia, Canada, and Australia chose to start distributing diamonds outside of the De Beers channel, thus effectively ending the monopoly. De Beers realized it was no longer profitable to buy diamonds to keep them off the market. Also, the demand for diamond jewelry had fallen. To keep its share of the market from falling further, De Beers has differentiated its diamonds by branding with a mark visible only with a microscope. Other diamond firms have followed suit to assure customers that these diamonds are mined under ethical and environmentally friendly conditions. By branding diamonds, sellers are assuring their customers that they are not buying "blood" diamonds that have been exported from war-ravaged

areas of Africa where the revenues are used to bolster military efforts. De Beers's new strategy has been effective; it is now more profitable today with a 40 percent market share than when it maintained an 80 percent market share.

Control over an Important Input

Another barrier to entry could exist if a firm had control over an important input. For example, from the late nineteenth century to the early 1940s, the Aluminum Company of America (Alcoa) had a monopoly in the production of aluminum. Its monopoly power was guaranteed because of its control over an important ingredient in the production of aluminum—bauxite.

However, the ownership of key resources is rarely the source of monopoly power. Many goods are traded internationally, and resources are owned by many different people around the world. It is uncommon that a firm would control the worldwide supply of a resource that did not have a close substitute.

SECTION QUIZ

1. Pure monopoly is defined as
   a. an industry consisting of a single seller.
   b. a market structure that involves many substitute products.
   c. a market in which many rival firms compete for sales.
   d. a market structure consisting of a single buyer.

2. For a true, or pure, monopoly,
   a. there is only one seller of the product.
   b. no close substitutes are available.
   c. the firm and the industry are the same.
   d. it must be virtually impossible for other firms to overcome barriers to entry.
   e. all of the above are true.

3. Which of the following is inconsistent with monopoly?
   a. a single seller
   b. economies of scale
   c. $MR < P$
   d. free entry and exit
   e. selling in the elastic portion of the demand curve in order to maximize profits

4. Which of the following is potentially a barrier to entry into a product market?
   a. patent protection on the design of the product
   b. economies of scale in the product market
   c. government licensing of the product's producers
   d. the control of a crucial input necessary to produce the product
   e. all of the above

---

1. Why does monopoly depend on the existence of barriers to entry?
2. Why is a pure monopoly a rarity?
3. Why does the government grant some companies, such as public utilities, monopoly power?

Answers: 1. a 2. e 3. d 4. e

13.2   Demand and Marginal Revenue in Monopoly

▶ How does the demand curve for a monopolist differ from that for a perfectly competitive firm?

▶ Why is marginal revenue less than price in monopoly?

Why can't a monopolist set both its price and the quantity it sells?

ECS

economic content standards

Monopolists, and all other firms that are price makers, face a downward-sloping demand curve. If the monopolist raises its price, it will lose some—but not all—of its customers.

In monopoly, the market demand curve may be regarded as the demand curve for the firm's product because the monopoly firm is the market for that particular product. The demand curve indicates the quantities that the firm can sell at various possible prices. In monopoly, the demand curve for the firm's product declines as additional units are placed on the market—the demand curve is downward sloping. In monopoly, the firm cannot set both its price and the quantity it sells. That is, a monopolist would love to sell a larger quantity at a high price, but it can't. If the monopolist raises the price, the amount sold will fall; if the monopolist lowers the price, the amount sold will rise.

Recall that in perfect competition, many buyers and sellers of homogeneous goods (resulting in a perfectly elastic demand curve) mean that competitive firms can sell all they want at the market price. They face a horizontal demand curve. The firm takes the price of its output as determined by the market forces of supply and demand. Monopolists, and all other firms that are price makers, face a downward-sloping demand curve. If the monopolist raises its price, it will lose some—but not all—of its customers. The two demand curves are displayed side by side in Exhibit 1.

In Exhibit 2, we see the price of the good, the quantity of the good, the *total revenue*, which is the quantity sold times the price ($TR = P \times Q$), and the *average revenue*, that is, the amount of revenue the firm receives per unit sold ($AR = TR \div Q$). The average revenue is simply the price per unit sold, which is exactly equal to the market demand curve, and the *marginal revenue* (MR)—the amount of revenue the firm receives from selling an additional unit—is equal to $\Delta TR \div \Delta Q$.

Taking the information from Exhibit 2, we can create the demand and marginal revenue curves as seen in Exhibit 3. We see that the marginal revenue is always less than the price of the good. To understand why, suppose the firm cuts its price from $4 to $3.

---

section 13.2 exhibit 1   **Comparing Demand Curves: Perfect Competition versus Monopoly**

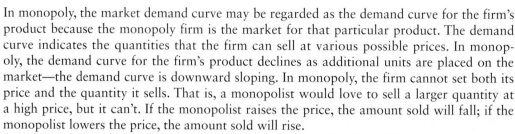

a. Perfectly Competitive Firm's Demand Curve

b. Monopolist's Demand Curve

The demand curve for a perfectly competitive firm is perfectly elastic; competitive firms can sell all they want at the market price. The firm is a price taker. The demand curve for a monopolist is downward sloping; if the monopolist raises its price, it will lose some but not all of its customers. The monopolist is a *price maker*. Because a monopoly has no close competitors, it can change the product price by adjusting its output.

section 13.2
exhibit 2   Total, Marginal, and Average Revenue

Price	Quantity	Total Revenue $(TR = P \times Q)$	Average Revenue $(AR = TR/Q)$	Marginal Revenue $(MR = \Delta TR/\Delta Q)$
$6	0	—	—	
5	1	$5	$5	$5
4	2	8	4	3
3	3	9	3	1
2	4	8	2	−1
1	5	5	1	−3

To induce a third daily customer to purchase the good, the firm must cut its price to $3. In doing so, it gains $3 in revenue from the newest customer—the output effect. However, it loses $2 in revenue because each of the first two customers are now paying $1 less than previously—the price effect. The marginal revenue is $1 ($3 − $2), which is less than the price of the good ($3).

Why is the monopolist's marginal revenue always less than the price?

Exhibit 3 graphs the relationship between the demand curve and the marginal revenue curve for a monopolist. Because a *monopolist's marginal revenue is always less than the price*, the marginal revenue curve will always lie below the demand curve, as shown in Exhibit 3. Recall that in perfect competition, the firm could sell all it wanted at the market price, and the price was equal to marginal revenue. However, in monopoly, if the seller wants to expand output, it will have to lower the price on *all* units; the monopolist receives additional revenue from the new unit sold—the output effect, but will receive less revenue on all the units it was previously selling—the price effect. Thus, when the monopolist cuts the price to attract new customers, the old customers benefit.

In Exhibit 4, we can compare marginal revenue for the competitive firm with marginal revenue for the monopolist. The firm in perfect competition can sell another unit of output without lowering its price; hence, the marginal revenue from selling its last unit of output is the market price. That is, when the perfectly competitive firm increases output by one unit, it receives the market price for that unit and it does not receive any less for the units that it was already selling. However, the monopolist has a downward-sloping demand curve. To sell an extra unit of output, the price falls from P_1 to P_2, and the monopolist loses area c in Exhibit 4(b). Because the monopolist must lower the price on every unit it sells, it will cut into revenue it was originally selling. Consequently, a monopolist's marginal revenue is less than the price.

It is important to note that even though a monopolist can set its price anywhere it wants, it will not set its price as high as possible—be careful not to confuse ability with incentive. As we will see in the next section, some prices along the demand curve will not be profitable for a firm. In other words, the monopolist can enhance profits by either lowering the price or raising it, depending on the circumstances.

section 13.2
exhibit 3   **Demand and Marginal Revenue for the Monopolist**

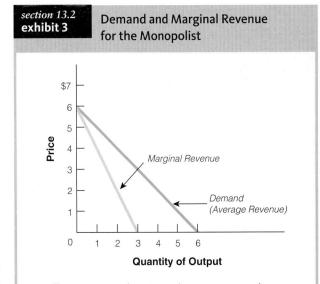

To sell more output, the monopolist must accept a lower price on all units sold—the price effect; the monopolist receives additional revenue from the new unit sold—the output effect, but less revenue on all the units it was previously selling. Thus, the marginal revenue curve for the monopolist always lies below the demand curve.

| section 13.2 |
| **exhibit 4** | Marginal Revenue—Competitive Firm versus Monopolist |

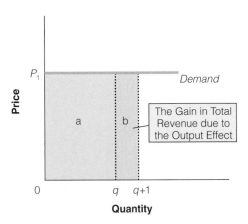

a. **Perfect Competitive Firm's Demand Curve**

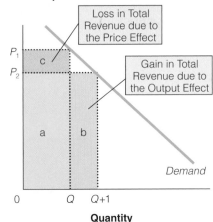

b. **Monopolist's Demand Curve**

Area b in (a) represents the marginal revenue from an extra unit of output ($q + 1$) for the firm in perfect competition. The competitive firm's marginal revenue (area b) is equal to the market price, P_1 ($P_1 \times 1$). Area b is the gain in total revenue from the output effect and area c is the loss in total revenue from the price effect. Notice there is no price effect for the perfectly competitive firm. The marginal revenue for the monopolist is the change in total revenue (b − c) for one more unit of output ($Q + 1$); this is less than the price, P_2.

USE WHAT YOU'VE LEARNED

Demand and Marginal Revenue

Q Using the concepts of total revenue and marginal revenue, show why marginal revenue is less than price in a monopoly situation. Suppose a monopolist wants to expand output from one unit to two units. To sell two units rather than one, the monopolist must lower its price from $10 to $8, as shown in Exhibit 5. Will the marginal revenue be less than the price?

A In Exhibit 5, we see that to sell two units, the monopolist will have to lower the price on both units to $8. That is, the seller doesn't receive $10 for unit one and $8 for unit two but receives $8 for both units. Therefore, what happens to marginal revenue? This answer involves two parts: First, a loss in revenue, $2, occurs from selling the first unit at $8 instead of $10. Second, the gain in revenue from the additional output—the second unit—is $8. Thus, the marginal revenue is $6 ($8 − $2), which is less than the price of the good, $8. The monopolist's marginal revenue will always be less than the price of the downward-sloping demand curve.

| section 13.2 | | | |
| **exhibit 5** | The Demand and Marginal Revenue Curve | | |

Price	Quantity	Total Revenue	Marginal Revenue
$10	1	$10	
			$6
8	2	16	
			2
6	3	18	

13.2a The Monopolist's Price in the Elastic Portion of the Demand Curve

The relationships between the elasticity of demand and the marginal and total revenue are shown in Exhibit 6. In Exhibit 6(a), elasticity varies along a linear demand curve. Recall from Chapter 6 that above the midpoint, the demand curve is elastic ($E_D > 1$); below the midpoint, it is inelastic ($E_D < 1$); and at the midpoint, it is unit elastic ($E_D = 1$). How does elasticity relate to total and marginal revenue? In the elastic portion of the curve shown in Exhibit 6(b), when the price falls, total revenue rises and marginal revenue is positive. In the inelastic region of the demand curve, when the price falls, total revenue falls, and marginal revenue is negative. At the midpoint of the linear demand curve in Exhibit 6(b), the total revenue curve reaches its highest point and $MR = 0$.

For example, suppose the price falls on the top half of the demand curve in Exhibit 6(a) from $90 to $80; total revenue increases from $90 ($90 × 1) to $160 ($80 × 2), and marginal revenue is positive at $70. Because a reduction in price leads to an increase in total revenue, the demand curve is elastic in this region. Now suppose the price falls from $20 to $10 on the lower portion of the demand curve, total revenue falls from $160 ($20 × 8) to $90 ($10 × 9), and marginal revenue is negative at −$70. Because a reduction in price leads to a decrease in total revenue, the demand curve is inelastic in this region.

A monopolist will never knowingly operate on the inelastic portion of its demand curve, because increased output will lead to lower total revenue in this region. Not only are total revenues falling, but total costs will rise as the monopolist produces more output. Similarly, if the monopolist were to lower its output, it could increase its total revenue and lower its total costs (because it costs less to produce fewer units), leading to greater economic profits.

section 13.2 exhibit 6 — The Relationship between the Elasticity of Demand and Total and Marginal Revenue

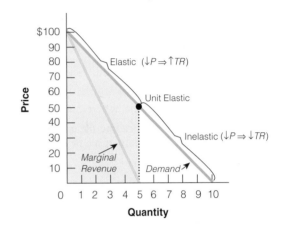

a. Demand and Marginal Revenue

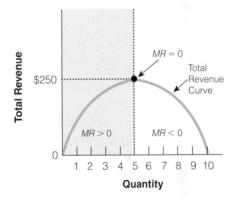

b. Total Revenue

In (a), we see that along a linear demand curve, the elastic segment lies above the midpoint, the inelastic segment lies below the midpoint, and at the midpoint the demand is unit elastic. When demand is elastic, a decline in price will increase total revenue; when demand is inelastic, a decline in price will lead to a decrease in total revenue. In (b), we see that over the range from zero to five units, total revenue is rising, so marginal revenue is positive. Over the range from five units to ten units, total revenue is falling, so marginal revenue is negative. At five units of output, total revenue is maximized at $250 ($50 × 5), so marginal revenue is zero.

Why would a monopolist not operate on the bottom half of the demand curve?

SECTION QUIZ

1. The monopolist's demand curve is

   a. upward sloping.

   b. downward sloping.

   c. horizontal, like the perfectly competitive firm's demand curve.

   d. The monopolist does not have a demand curve.

2. In monopoly, the firm

   a. is a price taker.

   b. will only operate on the bottom half of its demand curve.

   c. cannot set both its price and the quantity sold; if the monopolist reduces output, the price will rise, and if the monopolist expands output, the price will fall.

   d. All of the above are true.

3. In monopoly,

   a. the firm's demand curve is the market demand curve for the product.

   b. the marginal revenue is less than the price.

   c. the firm can set its price anywhere but will enhance its profits by raising or lowering the price, depending on the circumstances.

   d. all of the above are true.

4. Which of the following is true?

   a. The monopolist's marginal revenue will always be less than the price because of its downward-sloping demand curve.

   b. In order to sell more output, the monopolist must accept a lower price on all units sold.

   c. The monopolist will receive additional revenue from the sale of an additional new unit but will receive less revenue on all of the units it was previously selling as well.

   d. All of the above statements are true.

---

1. Why are the market and firm demand curves the same for a monopoly?

2. Why is a monopoly a price maker, but a perfectly competitive firm a price taker?

3. Why is marginal revenue less than price for a profit-maximizing monopolist?

4. Why would a monopolist never knowingly operate in the inelastic portion of its demand curve?

Answers: 1. b. 2. c. 3. d 4. d

The Monopolist's Equilibrium 13.3

▶ How does the monopolist decide what output to produce?

▶ How does the monopolist decide what price to charge?

▶ How do we know whether the monopolist is making a profit?

▶ How do we know whether the monopolist is incurring a loss?

▶ Can the monopolist's economic profits last into the long run?

13.3a How Does the Monopolist Determine the Profit-Maximizing Output?

In the preceding section, we saw how a monopolist could choose any point along a demand curve. However, the monopolist's decision as to what level of output to produce depends on more than the marginal revenue derived at various outputs. The firm faces production costs; and the monopolist, like the perfect competitor, will maximize profits at that output where $MR = MC$. This point is demonstrated graphically in Exhibit 1.

As you can see in Exhibit 1, at output level Q_1, the marginal revenue exceeds the marginal cost of production, so it is profitable for the monopolist to expand output. Profits continue to grow until output Q_M is reached. Beyond that output, say at Q_2, the marginal cost of production exceeds the marginal revenue from production, so profits decline. The monopolist should cut production back to Q_M. Therefore, the equilibrium output is Q_M. At this output, marginal cost and marginal revenue are equal.

What are the three steps to determine whether a monopolist is making an economic profit, an economic loss, or just breaking even (zero economic profit)?

13.3b Three-Step Method for the Monopolist

Let's return to the three-step method we used in Chapter 12. Determining whether a firm is generating positive economic profits, economic losses, or zero economic profits at the profit-maximizing level of output, Q_M, can be done in three easy steps.

1. Find where marginal revenue equals marginal cost and proceed straight down to the horizontal (quantity) axis to find Q_M, the profit-maximizing output level for the monopolist.
2. At Q_M, go straight up to the demand curve and then to the left to find the market price, P_M. Once you have identified P_M and Q_M, you can find total revenue at the profit-maximizing output level because $TR = P \times Q$.
3. The last step is to find total cost. Again, go straight up from Q_M to the average total cost (ATC) curve and then left to the vertical axis to compute the average total cost at Q_M. If we multiply average total cost by the output level, we can find the total cost ($TC = ATC \times Q$).

13.3c Profits for a Monopolist

Exhibit 1 does not show what profits, if any, the monopolist is actually making. This missing information is found in Exhibit 2, which shows the equilibrium position for a

section 13.3 exhibit 1 **Equilibrium Output and Price for a Monopolist**

Lost total profits from producing too little output: $MR > MC$

Marginal Cost

The demand curve shows the price, P_M, consistent with the profit-maximizing output, Q_M

$MR = MC$ determines the profit-maximizing output, Q_M

Lost total profits from producing too much output: $MC > MR$

Marginal Revenue

D

Price — P_M

0   Q_1 Q_M Q_2

Quantity

The monopolist maximizes profits at that quantity where $MR = MC$, that is, at Q_M. At Q_M the monopolist finds P^* by extending a vertical line up to the demand curve and over to the vertical axis to find the price. Rather than charging a price equal to marginal cost or marginal revenue at their intersection, however, the monopolist charges the price that customers are willing to pay for that quantity as indicated on the demand curve at P_M. At Q_1, $MR > MC$, and the firm should expand output. At Q_2, $MC > MR$, the firm should cut back production.

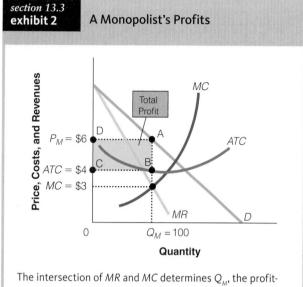

The intersection of *MR* and *MC* determines Q_M, the profit-maximizing level of output. The demand curve shows the price that can be charged for Q_M. Total profits equal the area DABC—the difference between total revenues (DAQ_M0) and total costs (CBQ_M0).

monopolist, this time adding an average total cost (*ATC*) curve. As we just discussed, the firm produces where *MC* = *MR*, at output Q_M. At output Q_M (100) and price P_M ($6) the firm's total revenue is equal to DAQ_M0, which is $P_M \times Q_M$ ($600). At output Q_M, the firm's total cost is CBQ_M0, which is $ATC \times Q_M$ ($400). In Exhibit 2, we see that total revenue is greater than total cost, so the firm has a total profit of area DABC. Or, $P_M - ATC$ (price minus average total cost) is the per-unit profit, $2. The width of the box (segment CB) is the quantity sold (0 to Q_M), 100 units. Hence, the area of the box is the monopoly firm's total profit, $200 (per-unit profit $\times$ quantity sold).

In perfect competition, profits in an economic sense will persist only in the short run. In the long run, new firms will enter the industry and increase industry supply, thereby driving down the price of the good and eliminating profits. In monopoly, however, profits are not eliminated because one of the conditions for monopoly is that barriers to entry exist. Other firms cannot enter, so economic profits can persist in the long run.

13.3d **Losses for the Monopolist**

It is easy to imagine a monopolist ripping off consumers by charging prices that result in long-run economic profits. However, many companies with monopoly power have gone out of business. Imagine that you received a patent on a bad idea such as a roof ejection seat for a helicopter, or that you had the sole rights to turn an economics textbook into a screenplay for a motion picture. Although you may be the sole supplier of a product, you are not guaranteed that consumers will demand your product. Even without a close substitute for your product, you will always face competition for the consumer dollar, and other goods may provide greater satisfaction.

Exhibit 3 illustrates loss in a monopoly situation. In this graph, notice that the demand curve is below the average total cost curve. In this case, the monopolist will incur a loss

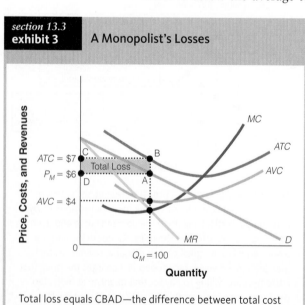

Total loss equals CBAD—the difference between total cost (CBQ_M0) and total revenue (DAQ_M0).

because of insufficient demand to cover the average total cost at any price and output combination along the demand curve. At Q_M, total cost, CBQ_M0, is greater than total revenue, DAQ_M0, so the firm incurs a total loss of CBAD. Or total revenue is $600 ($P_M \times Q_M = \$6 \times 100$) and total cost is $700 ($ATC \times Q_M = \$7 \times 100$), for an economic loss of $100. Notice that the total revenue is great enough to cover the variable costs of $400 ($TVC = \$4 \times 100$). That is, the firm can reduce its losses by operating rather than shutting down in the short run. However, in monopoly as in perfect competition, a firm will go out of business in the long run if it cannot generate enough revenue to cover its total costs.

If total revenue is greater than total cost at Q_M, the firm generates a total economic profit; and if total revenue is less than total cost at Q_M, the firm generates a total economic loss. If total revenue is equal to total cost at Q_M, the firm earns zero economic profit. Remember, the cost curves include implicit and explicit costs, so in this case, the monopolist is covering the total opportunity costs of its resources and earning a normal profit or rate of return.

13.3e **Patents**

Governments confer one form of monopoly power through patents and copyrights. A patent puts the government's police power behind the patent-holder's exclusive right to make a product for a specified period (up to 20 years) without anyone else being able to make an identical product. As Exhibit 4 suggests, the patent gives the supplier at least temporary monopoly power over that good or service. The firm with the patent can then price its product well above marginal costs, at P_M. In Exhibit 4, the marginal cost of producing the drug is constant, which is true for many prescription drugs. When the patent expires, the price of the patented good or service usually falls substantially with the entry of competing firms into the market. The price will fall toward the perfectly competitive price P_{PC}, and the output will increase toward Q_{PC}.

Why will entry eliminate economic profits for perfectly competitive firms, but not for monopolies?

Why does the government give inventors this limited monopoly power, raising the prices of pharmaceutical drugs and other "vital" goods? The rationale is simple. Without patents, inventors would have little incentive to incur millions of dollars in research and development expenses to create new products (e.g., lifesaving drugs) because others could immediately copy the idea and manufacture the products without incurring the research expenses. Similarly, copyrights stimulate creative activity of other kinds, giving writers the incentive to write books that earn royalties and are not merely copied for free. The enormous number of computer programs written for home computers reflects the fact that program writers receive royalties from the sale of each copy sold; that is why they and the firms they work for vehemently oppose unauthorized copying of their work.

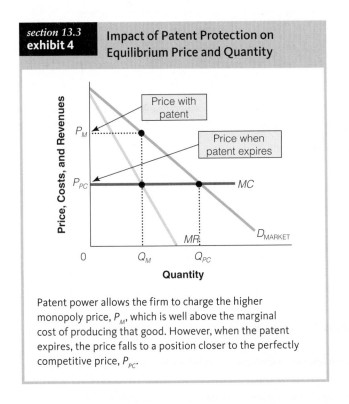

section 13.3 exhibit 4 — **Impact of Patent Protection on Equilibrium Price and Quantity**

Patent power allows the firm to charge the higher monopoly price, P_M, which is well above the marginal cost of producing that good. However, when the patent expires, the price falls to a position closer to the perfectly competitive price, P_{PC}.

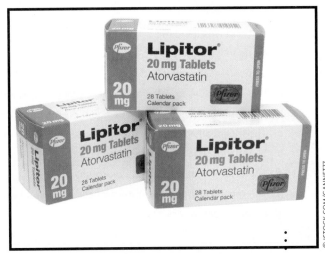

Without patents, would some lifesaving drugs have been invented? Some drugs cost millions of dollars in research. Without the protection of a patent, the firm might not have been able to make profits from its inventive activity for very long, which is why the government issues patents that last up to 20 years. However, after the patent expires, many popular drugs soon lose their protection. Lipitor lost its patent in November 2011. In most cases, less costly generic drugs hit the market soon after patent expiration. Prices then move closer to the competitive price, although perhaps not all the way to the competitive level, as some companies are able to keep customers through brand loyalty.

Some studies have shown prices falling over 30 percent after generics are introduced into the market. The generic market makes up almost 65 percent of the U.S. prescription drug market as many insurance plans encourage or require their subscribers to use generics.

SECTION QUIZ

1. A profit-maximizing monopolist sets

   a. the product price where marginal cost equals marginal revenue.

   b. output where marginal cost equals marginal revenue.

   c. output where marginal cost equals average revenue.

   d. output where demand equals average total cost.

   e. price equal to the highest dollar amount that any customer is willing to pay.

2. For a monopolist,

   a. its demand curve is downward sloping.

   b. its marginal revenue is less than price.

   c. existing economic profits can be sustained over time.

   d. all of the above are true.

3. If a profit-maximizing monopolist is currently charging a price on the inelastic portion of its demand curve, it should

   a. raise price and decrease output.

   b. lower price and increase output.

   c. reduce both output and price.

   d. hold output constant and raise price.

   e. do none of the above.

4. If a monopolist had a zero marginal cost of production, it would maximize profits by choosing to produce a quantity where

   a. demand was inelastic.

   b. demand was unit elastic.

   c. demand was elastic.

   d. It is impossible to determine where along a demand curve such a monopolist would choose to produce.

5. Which of the following is *not* true about a profit-maximizing monopolist?

   a. The monopolist faces the downward-sloping market demand curve.

   b. The monopolist always earns an economic profit.

   c. The price of output exceeds marginal revenue.

   d. The monopolist chooses output where marginal revenue equals marginal cost.

   e. All of the above are true.

---

1. What is a monopolist's principle for choosing the profit-maximizing output?

2. How do you find the profit-maximizing price for a monopolist?

3. For a monopolist making positive economic profits, what must be true about the relationship between price and average total cost?

4. For a monopolist making negative economic profits, what must be true about the relationship between price and average total cost?

5. Why, unlike perfectly competitive firms, can a monopolist continue to earn positive economic profits in the long run?

Answers: 1. b 2. d 3. a 4. b 5. b

Monopoly and Welfare Loss   13.4

▶ How does monopoly lead to inefficiencies?

▶ What is the welfare loss in monopoly?

▶ Does monopoly retard innovation?

13.4a Does Monopoly Promote Inefficiency?

Monopoly is often considered to be bad. Two main objections form the basis for concerns about the establishment of monopoly power. First, on equity grounds, many people feel that it is not "fair" for monopoly owners to have persistent economic profits when they work no harder than other firms. However, to most economists, the more serious objection is that monopolies result in market inefficiencies. That is, monopoly leads to a lower output and higher prices than would exist under perfect competition. Exhibit 1 demonstrates why. In monopoly, the firm produces output Q_M and charges price P_M. Suppose, however, that perfect competition exists and the industry is characterized by many small firms that could produce output with the same efficiency (at the same cost) as one large firm. Then the marginal cost curve shown in Exhibit 1 is the sum of all the individual marginal cost curves of the individual firms, which is the industry supply curve.

In the perfectly competitive market, the equilibrium price and quantity would be determined where the marginal cost (or supply) curve intersects with the demand curve, at output Q_{PC} and price P_{PC}. Thus, the competitive equilibrium solution provides for more output and lower prices than the solution prevailing in monopoly, which leads to the major efficiency objection to monopoly: Monopolists charge higher prices and produce less output. This situation may also be viewed as "unfair," in that consumers are burdened more than under the alternative competitive arrangement. In short, a monopolist is unchecked by competition, so the market outcome is not usually in the best interest of society.

Welfare Loss in Monopoly

In addition to the monopolist producing lower levels of output at higher prices, notice that the monopolist produces at an output where the price (P_M) is greater than the marginal cost (MC_M). Because $P > MC$, the value to society from the last unit produced is greater than its

Why is monopoly less efficient than perfect competition?

---

section 13.4
exhibit 1   **Perfect Competition versus Monopoly**

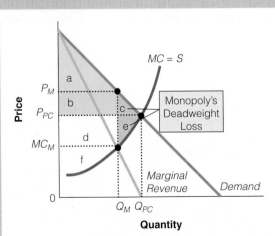

Compared with perfect competition, the monopolist's equilibrium price is higher, P_M, and its equilibrium output is lower, Q_M. Also notice that P_M is greater than MC_M, which means that the value of the last unit produced by the monopolist (P_M) is greater than the cost (MC_M), so from society's point of view the monopolist is producing too little output. Under monopoly, consumer surplus is area a, producer surplus is area b + d + f, and the deadweight loss of monopoly is c + e.

	Perfect Competition	**Monopoly**	**Change**
Consumer Surplus	a + b + c	a	−b − c
Producer Surplus	d + e + f	b + d + f	b − e
Welfare	a + b + c + d + e + f	a + b + d + f	−c − e

costs (MC_M). That is, the monopoly is *not* producing enough of the good from society's perspective. We call the area c + e in Exhibit 1 the welfare or deadweight loss due to monopoly. In perfect competition, the equilibrium is P_{PC} and the equilibrium quantity is Q_{PC}. Consumer surplus is area a + b + c, and the product surplus is area d + e + f. In monopoly, the equilibrium price is higher at P_M and the equilibrium quantity is lower at Q_M. Under monopoly, consumer surplus is area a, producer surplus is area b + d + f, and lost welfare or the deadweight loss of monopoly is c + e.

There are relatively few true monopolies, so the size of the deadweight loss is probably very small. Most economists believe that it is less than 1 percent of the total production of the United States. That is, if every industry were perfectly competitive ($P = MC$) the gain in total output would be less than 1 percent.

As we stated, firms with substantial monopoly power are rare. Some firms have monopoly power, but it is limited. Most goods have relatively good substitutes—for example, foreign-produced automobiles are a substitute for domestically-produced automobiles. So monopoly is a matter of degree. Thus, in most instances, we are safe in assuming that firms operate in a relatively competitive market.

13.4b Does Monopoly Retard Innovation?

Another argument against monopoly is that a lack of competition tends to retard technological advancement. Monopolists become comfortable, reaping their monopolistic profits, so they do not work hard at product improvement, technical advances designed to promote efficiency, and so forth. The American railroad is sometimes cited as an example of this situation. Early in the last century, railroads had strong monopoly power, but they did not spend much on research or development; they did not aggressively try to improve rail transport. Consequently, technical advances in substitute modes of transportation—like cars, trucks, and airplanes—led to a loss of monopoly power for the railroads.

Can monopoly change the level of innovation?

However, the notion that monopoly retards all innovation can be disputed. Many near monopolists are, in fact, important innovators. Companies such as Microsoft, IBM, Polaroid, and Xerox have all, at one time or another, had strong market positions, in some instances approaching monopoly secured by patent protection, but they were also important innovators. Indeed, innovation helps firms initially obtain a degree of monopoly status because patents can give a monopoly to new products and/or cost-saving technology. Even the monopolist wants more profits, and any innovation that lowers costs or expands revenues creates profits for the monopolist. In addition, because patents expire, a monopolist may be expected to innovate in order to obtain additional patents and preserve its monopoly power. Therefore, the incentive to innovate might well exist in monopolistic market structures.

SECTION QUIZ

1. Monopolists are like perfectly competitive firms in that
   a. both maximize profits at the output level where marginal revenue equals marginal cost.
   b. both could be earning either profits or losses in the short run.
   c. both are in industries with downward-sloping demand curves.
   d. all of the above are true of both of them.
   e. (a) and (b) are true of both of them, but not (c).

(continued)

SECTION QUIZ (cont.)

2. Monopoly is unlike perfect competition in that

   a. a monopolist's price is greater than marginal cost.

   b. there are no barriers to entry into a monopoly industry.

   c. a monopolist earns an economic profit only if its price is greater than *ATC*.

   d. all of the preceding are ways in which monopoly is unlike perfect competition.

   e. (a) and (b), but not (c), are ways in which monopoly is unlike perfect competition.

3. A price-taking firm and a monopolist are alike in that

   a. price equals marginal revenue for both.

   b. both maximize profits by choosing an output where marginal revenue equals marginal cost, provided that price exceeds average variable cost.

   c. price exceeds marginal cost at the profit-maximizing level of output for both.

   d. in the long run, both earn zero economic profits.

4. Which of the following is true of perfect competition but not true of monopoly?

   a. The firm's average total cost curve is U-shaped.

   b. Marginal revenue is equal to price.

   c. A profit-maximizing firm chooses output where marginal revenue equals marginal cost.

   d. Profits may exist in the short run.

5. Objections to monopolies do *not* include which of the following?

   a. They reduce output below the efficient level of output that would be produced in perfect competition.

   b. They reduce the price below what would be charged in perfect competition.

   c. They charge a price that is greater than marginal cost.

   d. They create a welfare cost.

   e. All of the preceding are objections to monopolies.

6. Which of the following statements is true?

   a. Monopoly results in smaller output and a higher price than would be the case under perfect competition.

   b. The monopolist produces at an output where $P > MC$ and the marginal value to society of the last unit produced is greater than its marginal cost.

   c. The monopoly is not producing enough output from society's standpoint.

   d. Monopoly may lead to greater concentration of economic power and could retard innovation.

   e. All of the above statements are true.

---

1. Why does the reduced output under monopoly cause inefficiency?

2. Does monopoly power retard innovation? Why or why not?

3. What does the welfare cost of monopoly represent? How is it measured?

4. How can economies of scale lead to monopoly? How could it result in monopoly increasing rather than decreasing market output, relative to the competitive market structure?

5. Can monopoly be the result of a new innovation that leaves consumers better off than before? Why or why not?

Answers: 1. e 2. a 3. b 4. b 5. b 6. e

13.5   Monopoly Policy

▶ What is the objective of antitrust policy?

▶ What is regulation?

▶ What is average cost pricing?

Because monopolies pose certain problems with respect to efficiency, equity, and power, the public, through its governments, must decide how to deal with the phenomenon. Two major approaches to dealing with such problems are commonly employed: antitrust policies and regulation. It should be pointed out that in these discussions, the word *monopoly* is sometimes used in a loose, general sense to refer to imperfectly competitive markets, not just to "pure" monopoly.

13.5a   Antitrust Policies

Perhaps the most obvious way to deal with monopoly is to make it illegal. The government can bring civil lawsuits or even criminal actions against businesspeople or corporations engaged in monopolistic practices. By imposing costs on monopolists that can be either monetary or nonmonetary (such as the fear of lawsuits or even jail sentences), antitrust policies reduce the profitability of monopoly.

13.5b   Antitrust Laws

The first important law regulating monopoly was the Sherman Antitrust Act. The Sherman Act prohibited "restraint of trade"—price fixing and collusion—but narrow court interpretation of the legislation led to a number of large mergers, such as U.S. Steel. Some important near-monopolies were broken up, however. For example, in 1911, the Standard Oil Trust, which controlled most of the country's oil refining, and the American Tobacco Co., which had similar dominance in tobacco, were both forcibly divided up into smaller companies.

Antitrust Acts Strengthened

Antitrust efforts were strengthened by subsequent legislation, the most important of which was the Clayton Act in 1914. Additional legislation in the same year created the Federal Trade Commission (FTC), which became the second government agency concerned with antitrust actions. The Clayton Act made it illegal to engage in predatory pricing—setting prices to drive out competitors or deter potential entrants in order to ensure higher prices in the future. The Clayton Act also prohibited mergers if it led to weakened competition. Not all of the later legislation actually served to enhance competition. A case in point is the Robinson-Patman Act of 1936 (forbidding most forms of price discrimination) and the Cellar-Kefauver Act in 1950, legislation that toughened restrictions on mergers that reduced competition.

However, antitrust laws may have costs as well as benefits because mergers may lead to lower costs and greater efficiency. A number of banks recently merged, lowering costs. So good antitrust policy must be able to recognize which mergers are desirable and which are not.

What do antitrust laws do?

13.5c   Have Antitrust Policies Been Successful?

The success of antitrust policies can be debated. It is true that few giant monopolies were disbanded as a consequence of antitrust policies. Studies showed little change in the degree of monopoly/oligopoly power in the first 100 years or so of U.S. antitrust legislation. Manufacturing, as a whole, actually became more concentrated; that is, fewer firms are now in the industry. However, it is likely that at least some anticompetitive practices were prevented simply by the existence of laws prohibiting monopoly-like practices. Although the laws were probably enforced in an imperfect fashion, on balance they impeded monopoly influences to at least some degree.

The Microsoft Case

The most important and controversial antitrust case in recent years was a U.S. government suit against Microsoft that began in 1998. Government prosecutors argued that Microsoft engaged in a pattern of using its monopoly power to crush its rivals and prevent real competition. More specifically, the government claimed that Microsoft was bundling its Internet browser into its Windows operating system. This, the government argued, would deter other software companies from competing.

Microsoft countered that they were merely adding new features to existing products, a natural technological progress. They argued that this was better for consumers because they could now be assured that the different pieces of software would work well together. The government also argued that Microsoft had substantial monopoly power. At the time, 80 percent of personal computers were using the Microsoft operating system. Microsoft maintained that they were competing in a changing and competitive environment. They argued that the low price they were charging for Windows was evidence that their market power was limited.

After a 2-year investigation of Google, the Federal Trade Commission (FTC) closed their antitrust investigation after Google agreed to change some of their business practices. Google had to give online advertisers more flexibility to use rival ad platforms. Google's competitors had complained that about 65 percent of all web searches went through Google, which was stifling competition. Google claimed they were defining the market incorrectly. That is, it should not be considered to be solely in the search engine business, but rather that it competes with all advertisers (newspaper, radio, television, highway billboards, etc.). In addition, consumers could search with Yahoo or Bing. Does the Google search engine hurt consumers? The FTC said no. Google will only lead in the search market as long as consumers believe it is the best search engine.

In June 2001, a federal appeals court unanimously threw out a lower court order to split Microsoft into two companies. However, the appeals court did find that the company repeatedly abused its monopoly power in the software business. A settlement was finally reached in November 2002 that led to some restrictions on Microsoft's business practices. In the end, Microsoft had to agree to some business restrictions but was allowed to keep its browser as part of its operating system. In 2005, the European Union cracked down on Microsoft because it bundled its media player with its Windows operating system. Microsoft was fined and required to offer both bundled and unbundled versions of its operating system.

13.5d **Government Regulation**

Government regulation is an alternative approach to dealing with monopolies. Under regulation, a company would not be allowed to charge any price it wants. This is a common practice when the government does not want to break up a natural monopoly in the water or power industry. Remember that natural monopolies occur when one large firm can produce as much output as many smaller firms but at a lower average cost per unit. The government may decide to regulate the monopoly price, but what price does it let the firm charge? The goal is to achieve the efficiency of large-scale production without permitting the high monopoly prices and low output that can promote allocative *inefficiency*.

The basic policy dilemma that regulators often face in attempting to fix maximum prices can be illustrated rather easily. Consider Exhibit 1. Without regulation, say the profit-maximizing monopolist operates at point A—at output Q_M and price P_M. At this output, the

Why don't we want to break up a natural monopoly?

Marginal Cost Pricing versus Average Cost Pricing

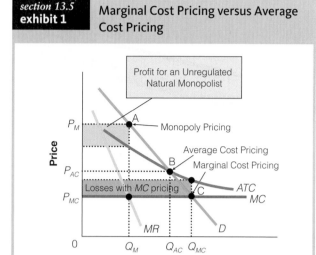

The marginal cost (MC) curve is less than the average total cost (ATC) curve for the natural monopolist as the average cost falls. If the monopolist is unregulated, it could produce a relatively small level of output, Q_M, at a relatively high price, P_M, and make an economic profit. If regulators require the natural monopolist to use marginal cost pricing, the monopoly will lose money because P_{MC} is less than ATC. Average cost pricing (at point B) would permit firms to make a normal rate of return, where $P_{AC} = ATC$. The monopolist's unregulated output at point A is not optimal from society's standpoint, and the optimal output at point C is not feasible without subsidy.

price exceeds the average total cost, so economic profits exist, as seen in Exhibit 1. However, the monopolist is producing relatively little output and is charging a relatively high price, and it is producing at a point where price is above marginal cost. This point is not the best from society's perspective.

Allocative Efficiency

From society's point of view, what would be the best price and output position? As we discussed in Chapter 12, the best position is at the competitive equilibrium output, where $P = MC$, because the equilibrium price represents the marginal value of output. The marginal cost represents society's opportunity costs of making the good as opposed to something else. Where price equals marginal cost, society matches marginal value and marginal cost—that is, it achieves allocative efficiency, as seen at point C in Exhibit 1.

Can the Regulated Monopolist Operate at $P = MC$?

Unfortunately, the natural monopoly cannot operate profitably at the allocative efficient point, where $P = MC$, indicated as point C in Exhibit 1. At point C, the intersection of the demand and marginal cost curves, average total cost is greater than price. The optimal output, then, is an output that results in losses for the producer. Any regulated business that produced for long at this "optimal" output would go bankrupt; it would be impossible to attract new capital to the industry.

Therefore, the "optimal" output from a welfare perspective is not really viable because firms incur losses. The regulators cannot force firms to price their products at P_{MC} and to sell Q_{MC} output because they would go out of business. Indeed, in the long run, the industry's capital would deteriorate as investors failed to replace old capital as it became worn out or obsolete. If the monopolist's unregulated output at point A is not optimal from society's standpoint, and the short-run optimal output at point C is not feasible from the monopolist's standpoint, where should the regulated monopolist be allowed to operate?

One possible solution to the problem is for the government to subsidize the losses associated with marginal cost pricing. However, the burden of this solution would ultimately fall on the taxpayers, as the government would have to raise the money to pay for the losses. And remember, taxation has its own deadweight loss.

The Compromise: Average Cost Pricing

A compromise between monopoly pricing and marginal cost pricing is found at point B in Exhibit 1, at output Q_{AC}, which is somewhere between the excessively low output and high prices of an unregulated monopoly and the excessively high output and low prices achieved when prices are equated with marginal cost pricing. At point B, price equals average total cost. The monopolist is permitted to price the product where economic profit is zero, earning a normal economic profit or rate of return, such as firms experience in perfect competition in the long run. This compromise is called average cost pricing. However, average cost pricing is not a perfect solution as it leads to a deadweight loss because price is not equal to marginal cost.

In the real world, regulators often permit utilities to receive a "fair and reasonable" return that is a rough approximation to that suggested by average cost pricing, at point B. Point B

average cost pricing

setting price equal to average total cost

would seem "fair" in that the monopolist is receiving rewards equal to those that a perfect competitor would ordinarily receive—no more, no less. Point B permits more output at a significantly lower price than is possible at point A, where the monopolist is unregulated, even though output is still somewhat less and price somewhat more than that suggested by point C, the socially optimum or best position.

Inaccurate Calculations of Costs

The actual implementation of a rate (price) that permits a "fair and reasonable" return is more difficult than the analysis suggests. The calculations of costs and values are difficult. In reality, the firm may not know exactly what its demand and cost curves look like, which forces regulatory agencies to use profits, another somewhat ambiguous target, as a guide. If profits are "too high," lower the price; if profits are "too low," raise the price. In addition, what if the regulated firm has more information than the regulators do about its firm, workers, and technology—asymmetric information? If the firm can persuade regulators that its average cost is higher than it actually is, then the regulated price could be set higher, closer to the monopoly price.

No Incentives to Keep Costs Down

Another problem is that average cost pricing offers the monopolist no incentive to reduce costs. Recall that firms in competitive markets try to lower costs to increase profits. But with a regulated natural monopolist, if the firm's costs rise from ATC_1 to ATC_2 in Exhibit 2, the price will rise from P_1 to P_2. If costs fall, the firm's price will fall. In either scenario, the firm will still be earning a normal rate of return. In other words, if the regulatory agency sets the price at any point where the ATC curve intersects the demand curve, the firm will earn a normal rate of return. Thus, if the agency is going to set the price wherever ATC intersects the demand curve, the firm might just think, Why not let average costs rise? Why not let employees fly first class and dine in the finest restaurants? Why not buy concert tickets and season tickets to sporting events? And if the regulated monopolist knows that the regulators will reduce prices if costs fall, the regulated monopolist does not benefit from lower costs. Regulators have tackled this problem by allowing the regulated firm to keep some of the profits that come from lower costs; that is, they do not adhere strictly to average cost pricing.

Special Interest Groups

In the real world, consumer groups are constantly battling for lower utility rates, while the utilities themselves are lobbying for higher rates so they can approach the monopoly profits indicated by point A in Exhibit 1. Decisions are not always made in a calm, objective, dispassionate atmosphere free from outside involvement. It is precisely the political economy of rate setting that disturbs some critics of this approach to dealing with the monopoly problem. For example, a rate-making commissioner could become friendly with a utility company, believing that he could obtain a nice job after his tenure as a regulator expires. The temptation would be great for the commissioner to be generous to the utilities. On the other hand, the tendency might be for regulators to bow to pressure from consumer groups. A politician who wants to win votes can almost always succeed by attacking utility rates and promising rate "reform" (lower rates). If zealous rate regulators listen too closely

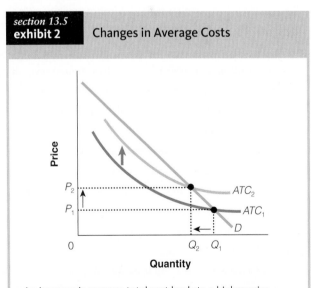

section 13.5
exhibit 2   **Changes in Average Costs**

An increase in average total cost leads to a higher price and lower output (P_2Q_2); lower average total cost leads to a lower price and greater output (P_1Q_1). However, both situations lead to a normal rate of return. Because the regulated firm has little incentive to minimize costs, average total cost would have a tendency to rise.

What makes average cost pricing so difficult?

to consumer groups and push rates down to a level indicated by point C in Exhibit 1, the industry might be too unstable to attract capital for expansion.

13.5e **Public Ownership**

If antitrust or regulation does not work with the problems created by monopoly the government could run the monopoly. This is common in many European countries where the government operates water, electric and telephone companies. In the United States, the government runs the postal service—some argue that first class mail is a natural monopoly. However, many economists prefer private to public ownership of monopolies because of the incentive structure. Private owners want to minimize costs to increase their profits. If the private firm is doing a poor job on minimizing costs there will be firings. When a government fails to minimize costs, it is often the customers and the taxpayers who foot the bill.

SECTION QUIZ

1. A natural monopoly is defined as an industry in which

   a. one firm can produce the entire industry output at a lower average cost than can two or more firms.

   b. a single firm controls crucial inputs to the production process.

   c. one firm is especially large relative to other firms that could enter the industry.

   d. a single seller exists as a result of patent protection.

2. If regulators set a price according to marginal cost pricing, the firm will

   a. earn positive economic profits.

   b. make zero economic profits.

   c. suffer an economic loss.

   d. earn the same level of profits as it would absent regulation.

3. Average cost pricing for a natural monopoly will

   a. result in the socially efficient level of output.

   b. result in a less than socially efficient level of output.

   c. result in a greater than socially efficient level of output.

   d. result in the firm suffering economic losses.

   e. result in the firm earning economic profit.

4. Under average cost pricing by a natural monopoly,

   a. price is greater than marginal cost.

   b. a welfare cost will be incurred.

   c. the producer will earn a normal rate of return.

   d. a producer experiences little or no incentive to hold down costs.

   e. all of the preceding are true.

5. Which of the following is not a limitation that regulators face when they implement average cost pricing?

   a. Average cost pricing provides little or no incentive for firms to keep costs down.

   b. The accurate calculation of a firm's costs is difficult.

   c. Decisions are political and often influenced by special interests.

   d. All of the preceding are limitations faced by regulators implementing average cost pricing.

(continued)

6. Which of the following statements is true?

   a. Antitrust policies are government policies designed to reduce the profitability of a monopoly and push production closer to the social optimum.

   b. Antitrust laws can promote greater competition.

   c. Average cost pricing sets price equal to marginal cost, where the demand curve intersects the marginal cost curve.

   d. Both (a) and (b) are true.

---

1. What alternative ways of dealing with the monopoly problem are commonly used?

2. How do antitrust laws promote greater price competition?

3. What price and output are ideal for allocative efficiency for a regulated natural monopolist? Why is an unregulated natural monopolist unlikely to pick this solution?

4. What is average cost pricing? How is it different from marginal cost pricing?

5. What are some difficulties encountered when regulators try to implement average cost pricing for natural monopolies?

6. Why might a job with a regulated natural monopolist that is allowed to earn a "fair and reasonable" return have more perks (noncash forms of compensation) than a comparable job in a nonregulated firm?

Answers: 1. a 2. c 3. b 4. e 5. d 6. d

Price Discrimination and Peak Load Pricing   13.6

▸ What is price discrimination?

▸ Why does price discrimination exist?

▸ Does price discrimination work when reselling is easy?

▸ What is peak load pricing?

13.6a Price Discrimination

Sometimes sellers will charge different customers different prices for the same good or service when the cost of providing that good or service does not differ among customers. This practice is called price discrimination. Under certain conditions, the monopolist finds it profitable to discriminate among various buyers, charging higher prices to those who are more willing to pay and lower prices to those who are less willing to pay.

price discrimination
the practice of charging different consumers different prices for the same good or service

13.6b Conditions for Price Discrimination

The ability to practice price discrimination is not available to all sellers. To practice price discrimination, the following three conditions must hold.

Why is it unlikely that competitive firms will price-discriminate?

Market Power

Price discrimination is possible only with market power. A monopoly, an oligopoly, a monopolistically competitive firm, or a cartel may be able to price-discriminate. In cases with a large number of competing firms, discrimination is less likely because competitors tend to undercut the high prices charged by the firms that are engaging in price discrimination.

Market Segregation

Price discrimination can only occur if the demand curves for markets, groups, or individuals are different. If the demand curves are not different, a profit-maximizing monopolist would charge the same price in both markets. Price discrimination requires the ability to separate customers according to their willingness to pay. That is, consumers must differ in their sensitivity to price (elasticity of demand) and firms must be able to identify how consumers differ in their sensitivities to price.

Difficulty in Reselling

For price discrimination to work, the person buying the product at a discount must have difficulty in reselling the product to customers being charged more. Otherwise, those getting the items cheaply would want to buy extra amounts of the product at the discounted price and sell it at a profit to others. Price differentials between groups erode if reselling is easy.

13.6c Price Discrimination and the Profit-Maximization Motive

Price discrimination results from the profit-maximization motive. Our graphical analysis of monopoly described the demand curve for the product and the corresponding marginal revenue curve. Sometimes, however, different groups of people have different demand curves and therefore react differently to price changes. A producer can make more money by charging these different buyers different prices.

A different demand curve applies for those that want to go to a matinee (afternoon) movie and those that want to go to movies in the evening. Movie theater owners know that more people are willing to see a movie in the evening than the afternoon. Because the time and price is provided on the ticket and can be easily detected, the two markets, matinee and evening, can be separated. Specifically, the elasticity of demand with respect to price is greater for afternoon movie-goers than for evening movie-goers. Assume, for simplicity, that the marginal cost is constant. The profit-maximizing movie theater owner will price where the constant marginal costs equal marginal revenue for each group. As you can see in Exhibit 1(a), the demand curve for afternoon tickets is relatively elastic—firms will charge these customers a lower price. If the owners charged the evening price, $11, they would sell too few tickets in the afternoon, and MR would exceed MC. The demand curve for evening shows, shown in Exhibit 1(b), is less elastic; firms will charge evening movie-goers a higher price—$11. If the firm charged $9 (the matinee price), it would lead to too many tickets sold, and MR would be less than MC. To maximize profit, the firm charges the group with the less elastic demand curve (evening movie-goers) a higher price and the group with the more elastic demand curve (afternoon movie-goers) a lower price.

© ISTOCK.COM/EDSTOCK

Disneyland practices price discrimination. During the off-season, locals are charged less than out-of-town visitors. If nonlocals have a greater willingness to pay (a less elastic demand curve) for the park hopper ticket (which is good for both Disneyland and its next-door neighbor, California Adventure) than locals do, Disneyland can increase its profits with this pricing strategy as long as it can prevent reselling. Charging both groups the same price is not in the best interest of Disneyland.

13.6d Examples of Price Discrimination

Examples of price discrimination in the United States are plentiful. Here are just a few.

Airline Tickets

Seats on airplanes usually go for different prices. They sell high-priced, no-strings-attached fares, and they sell restricted fares—tickets that require Saturday night layovers or must be

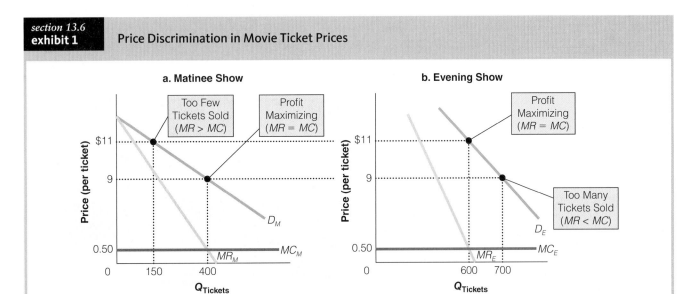

section 13.6
exhibit 1   **Price Discrimination in Movie Ticket Prices**

a. Matinee Show

Too Few Tickets Sold ($MR > MC$)

Profit Maximizing ($MR = MC$)

Price (per ticket)

$11

9

0.50

D_M

MR_M

MC_M

0   150   400

$Q_{Tickets}$

b. Evening Show

Profit Maximizing ($MR = MC$)

Too Many Tickets Sold ($MR < MC$)

Price (per ticket)

$11

9

0.50

D_E

MR_E

MC_E

0   600   700

$Q_{Tickets}$

If the movie theaters in the area have some monopoly power and if matinee (afternoon) movie attendees have a lower willingness to pay than evening movie attendees, then movie theaters can increase profits by price discriminating. Because the demand curve for matinee movie tickets is relatively more elastic than the demand curve for evening movie tickets, the firm finds it profitable to charge the two different groups a different price. To maximize profit, the firm charges the group with the less elastic demand curve (evening) a higher price and the group with the more elastic demand curve (matinee) a lower price.

purchased weeks in advance. This airline pricing strategy allows the airlines to discriminate against business travelers, who usually have little advance warning, travel on the weekdays, and are not as willing to spend their weekends away from home and family. Because business travelers have a high willingness to pay (a relatively inelastic demand curve), the airlines can charge them higher prices. If the airlines were to cut prices for these clients, their revenues would fall. On the other hand, the personal traveler (perhaps a vacationer) can choose among many substitutes, such as other modes of transportation and different times. In short, the personal traveler has a lower willingness to pay (a relatively elastic demand curve). Thus, the airlines can clearly make more money by charging a higher price to those who have a higher willingness to pay (less elastic demand) and a lower price to those who have a lower willingness to pay (more elastic demand)—those who are willing to book in advance and stay over on Saturday nights. If the airlines charged a higher single price to everyone, those with a lower willingness to pay would not travel; if they charged a lower single price to everyone, they would lose profits by receiving less revenue from those who were willing to pay more.

How does price discrimination increase a firm's profits?

Coupons

The key to price discrimination is observing the difference in demand curves for different customers. The coupon cutter, who spends an hour looking through the Sunday paper for coupons, will probably have a relatively more elastic demand curve than, say, a busy and wealthy physician or executive. Consequently, firms charge a lower price to customers with a lower willingness to pay (more elastic demand)—the coupon cutter—and a higher price to those who don't use coupons (less elastic demand). Digital coupons have made it easier for firms to target particular customers. It also has lowered the cost to consumers of using coupons. So we would expect even more people to use coupons.

College and University Tuition

Another example of price discrimination is the financial aid packages given by many colleges and universities. That is, even though colleges do not charge different tuitions to different students, they do offer different financial aid packages. Furthermore, to receive financial aid,

Use What You've Learned

Price Discrimination Over Time

Q Why do people pay a lot more for a hardcover book than a paperback book?

A Sometimes firms engage in price discrimination over time to increase their profits. Although a hardcover book is only slightly more expensive to publish, the real reason for the price differential between hardcover and paper- back books is the price elasticity of demand. Some people are willing to pay a higher price to be among the first to read a book; the demand curve is relatively inelastic for these devoted fans. Other individuals have a more elastic demand curve for these goods and are willing to wait for the book to come out in paperback. Other customers, such as libraries, find that paperbacks are not durable enough to be good substitutes for hardbacks. Sellers are able to profit from this difference in elasticities of demand by charging more to those who are more willing to pay and charging a

Why do hardcover texts come out before the paperback version?

lower price to those who are less willing to pay. Thus, book publishers are able to profit.

Policy Watch

Misconceptions 101: Why College Costs Aren't Soaring

Evan Soltas, bloomberg.com, November 27, 2012

Conventional wisdom suggests that U.S. colleges and univer- sities have become sharply more expensive in recent years. "When kids do graduate, the most daunting challenge can be the cost of college," President Barack Obama said in his 2012 State of the Union address. "We can't just keep subsidizing skyrocketing tuition; we'll run out of money."

At first, the view that the cost of college is rising appears to have data on its side. Published tuition prices and fees at colleges have risen three times faster than the rate of Consumer Price Index inflation since 1978, according to the Bureau of Labor Statistics.

Real tuition and fees have increased, to be sure, but hardly as significantly as the media often report or the data suggest at face value. The inflation-adjusted net price of college has risen only modestly over the last two decades, according to data from the College Board's Annual Survey of Colleges.

What has happened is a shift toward price discrimination— offering multiple prices for the same product. Universities have offset the increase in sticker price for most families

through an expansion of grant-based financial aid and schol- arships. That has caused the BLS measure to rise without increasing the net cost.

Wealthier families now pay more than ever to send their children to college. But for much of the middle class, the real net cost of college has not changed significantly; for much of the poor, the expansion of aid has increased the accessibility and affordability of a college education.

Data from the College Board show effectively no change in real net tuition and fees for dependent students at 4-year public or private universities whose families are in the lower- income quartiles. There have been some increases in the real cost of room and board, but for families with below-average incomes, the rise has been on the order of 20 percent over 20 years.

In other words, the cost burden of college has become significantly more progressive since the 1990s. Students from wealthier families not only now pay more for their own educations but also have come to heavily subsidize the costs of the less fortunate.

parents must disclose their family income and wealth. In short, students who are well off financially tend to pay more for their education than do students who are less well off.

Quantity Discounts

Another form of price discrimination occurs when customers buy in large quantities, as with public utilities and wholesalers. But even stores will sell a six-pack of soda for less than six single cans. For example, the local bagel shop might sell you a bagel for $1 each, but a dozen bagels for $10. This is price discrimination, because the buyer is paying less for the twelfth bagel than the first bagel. This form of price discrimination is effective because a buyer's willingness to pay declines as additional units are purchased.

Why is the price a lot higher to launder a woman's blouse than a man's shirt? Why are women charged more for haircuts than are men? Are these differences based on costs—perhaps it is more costly to launder a delicate blouse or cut longer hair? Or is it a form of price discrimination where one group may have a greater willingness to pay than the other group?

13.6e The Welfare Effects of Price Discrimination

In Exhibit 2, we analyze the welfare effects of perfect price discrimination using consumer and producer surplus and then compare this with perfect competition and single-price monopoly. When the firm is able to perfectly price-discriminate, each unit is sold at its **reservation price**; that is, the firm sells each unit at the maximum amount that the customer would be willing to pay. Because each customer pays exactly the amount he is willing to pay, the marginal revenue is the same as the demand curve.

reservation price

the maximum amount a customer would be willing to pay for a unit of output

In Exhibit 2, we see that the firm sells its first unit at P_1 to the customer who is willing to pay the most. The marginal cost for producing that good is MC, so the firm makes $P_1 - MC$ on that unit. For each successive unit, the firm receives a lower price (moving down the demand curve) and has a higher marginal cost (moving up the marginal cost curve). The firm will continue to sell units as long as price exceeds marginal cost. Perfect price discrimination leads to an economically efficient level of output because price equals marginal cost on the last unit sold. However, what is efficient may not always be viewed as fair. In particular, consumers may not be happy with the outcome because the entire surplus (a + b + c + d + f) goes to the monopolist in the form of producer surplus. Consumer surplus is zero because each consumer pays exactly the amount she is willing to pay—her reservation price.

In Exhibit 2, we see that in the competitive market, the equilibrium is established at the intersection of the demand curve and the marginal cost curve, where the equilibrium price is P_{PC} and the equilibrium quantity is Q_{PC}. The perfectly competitive market is efficient because price equals marginal cost. Consumer surplus is a + b + c, producer surplus is d + f, and total welfare is maximized (a + b + c + d + f). The deadweight loss is zero.

We can also see in Exhibit 2 that if the monopolist charges a single price (the monopoly price), deadweight loss is area c + f; that is, some potential buyers value the good at more than the marginal cost but are not able to buy the good at the monopoly price. The market is not efficient because $P < MC$ at Q_M. In this market, the consumer surplus is area a and the producer surplus is area b + d. While consumers receive the most consumer surplus from perfect competition, they are better off with the single-price monopoly than with perfect price discrimination, where consumer surplus is totally eliminated.

You can go to the TKTS booth on the day of a Broadway play and often get a substantial discount on theater tickets. This is a form of price discrimination where once producers know how many empty seats they have, they offer discounts to fill the rest. Once the show starts, an empty seat brings in no revenue. By offering tickets at a heavy discount to those who are willing to wait in line, the theater is able to increase attendance and raise revenue.

section 13.6 exhibit 2   The Welfare Effects of Perfect Price Discrimination

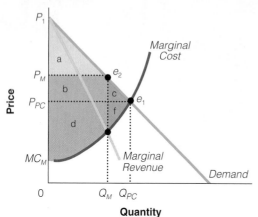

In perfect competition, the market equilibrium price is P_{PC} and the market equilibrium quantity is Q_{PC}. Consumer surplus is area a + b + c, producer surplus is area d + f, and there is no deadweight loss. In a single-price monopoly, the monopoly equilibrium price is P_M and the equilibrium quantity is Q_M. Compared with perfect competition, consumer surplus falls to area a, producer surplus is area b + d, and the deadweight loss is area c + f.

In perfect price discrimination, the monopolist sells each unit at the buyer's reservation price—the consumer surplus falls to zero, producer surplus increases to area a + b + c + d + f, and there is no deadweight loss.

	Perfect Competition	Single Price Monopoly	Perfect Price Discrimination
Customer Surplus	a + b + c	a	o
Producer Surplus	d + f	b + d	a + b + c + d + f
Total Welfare	a + b + c + d + f	a + b + d	a + b + c + d + f
Deadweight Loss	o	c + f	o

Market conditions obviously do not permit perfect price discrimination to be carried out to any significant extent. It is much too difficult to know each consumer's demand curve. However, rough approximations of perfect price discrimination are possible. Lawyers, accountants, and doctors might try to figure out whether their customers are rich or poor and charge accordingly. Car dealers might try to figure out how much a prospective buyer is willing to pay. We do know that price discrimination increases the monopolist's profits; otherwise, it would simply charge a single uniform price to all its customers.

peak load pricing

when producers charge different prices during different periods because the demand and the cost of producing a product vary over time

NETPHOTOS/ALAMY

Google is attempting to price-discriminate when they place ads on your computer or phone, based on your search results. By giving firms data on your search preferences, firms can find difficult-to-reach customers and blast them with targeted ads. This is a lot less costly than less-well-targeted mailers and print and broadcast ads. Now if advertisers can alter the price to find the buyers' willingness to pay, they can more closely approach perfect price discrimination.

13.6f Peak Load Pricing

In our earlier discussion of price discrimination, we assumed that the marginal costs associated with selling output over time were constant, but this assumption is not always true. Sometimes producers will charge different prices during different periods because the demand and the cost of producing the product vary over time. For a number of goods and services, demand peaks at particular times—bridges, roads, and tunnels during rush-hour traffic; telephone services during business hours; electricity during late summer afternoons; movie theaters on weekend evenings; and amusement parks and ski resorts during holidays.

In price discrimination, we saw that prices reflected different demands from buyers. With peak load pricing, demand levels and costs are different. Peak load pricing leads to greater efficiency because consumer prices reflect the higher marginal costs of production during peak periods. That is, buyers pay higher prices for goods and services during peak periods and lower prices during nonpeak periods.

Suppose a regulatory agency for an electric utility company is deciding whether to change its pricing strategy from constant pricing to peak load pricing. In Exhibit 3, the utility company is presently charging 4 cents per kilowatt-hour 24 hours a day. This constant price is based on the average cost to the electricity company in the combined peak and nonpeak periods. Notice, however, that a separate demand curve applies for each of two different times of day. Let's look at the nonpeak demand curve first. During nonpeak hours, at a price of 4 cents, customers will purchase 200,000 kilowatts. If we look at the marginal cost of producing 200,000 kilowatts (by looking at the supply curve), we see that it costs less than 3 cents per kilowatt-hour. This solution is clearly not efficient because society would be better off if the marginal benefit (demand curve) was equal to the marginal cost (supply curve), which is where supply intersects demand—at a price of 3 cents and a quantity of 300,000 kilowatt-hours (point C).

Now let's look at the demand curve during peak hours. Notice that if the company stuck with its price of 4 cents per kilowatt-hour, it would sell 600,000 kilowatts. However, how much does it cost to produce 600,000 kilowatts? Looking at the supply curve, we see that the marginal cost is more than 6 cents per kilowatt-hour. This solution is not efficient because, once again, society would be better off if the marginal benefit (demand curve) equaled the marginal cost (supply curve), which is where supply intersects demand—at a price of 5 cents and a quantity of 500,000 kilowatt-hours (point D).

In sum, the most economically efficient solution is to charge the lower price during the nonpeak period and the higher price during the peak period. The gain from peak load pricing, compared with constant pricing, can be seen graphically as the sum of the two shaded triangles in Exhibit 3. With this pricing strategy, consumers have an incentive to give their appliances a rest during the peak period when the cost of providing electricity is the highest.

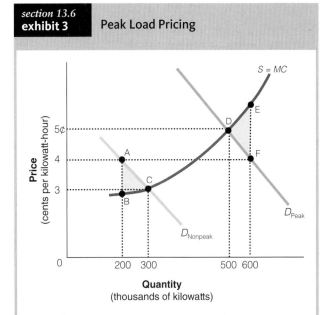

section 13.6
exhibit 3   Peak Load Pricing

Demand for some goods and services fluctuates considerably and predictably between peak and nonpeak periods. It is more efficient to charge a higher price, 5 cents, during peak periods (when marginal costs are higher) and a lower price, 3 cents, during nonpeak periods (when marginal costs are lower) compared with charging a single price, 4 cents, at all times.

Why is peak load pricing more efficient than charging a constant price?

(continued)

SECTION QUIZ (cont.)

3. Which of the following is not true of successful price discriminators?

   a. They could make greater profits by charging everyone a higher, uniform price.

   b. Their customers must differ in their willingness to pay.

   c. Their customers must have difficulty reselling the good to other customers.

   d. They must have monopoly power.

4. Price discrimination may be a rational strategy for a profit-maximizing monopolist when

   a. it can separate willingness to pay across customers.

   b. it has a substantial opportunity for reselling across market segments.

   c. consumers are unable to be segmented into identifiable markets.

   d. the willingness to pay is the same across all customers.

_____

1. How do we define price discrimination?

2. Why does price discrimination arise from the profit-maximization motive?

3. Why is preventing resale the key to successful price discrimination?

4. Why is it generally easier to price-discriminate for services than for goods?

5. What principle will a profit-maximizing monopolist use in trying to price-discriminate among different groups of customers?

6. How can offering quantity discounts increase a producer's profits?

7. Why does perfect price discrimination lead to the economically efficient level of output while reducing consumer surplus to zero?

8. What does perfect price discrimination do to the deadweight cost of monopoly?

9. Why is peak load pricing more efficient than constant pricing for a good with sharp swings in demand over time?

Answers: 1. d 2. a 3. a 4. a

INTERACTIVE SUMMARY

Fill in the blanks:

1. A true or pure monopoly exists in cases of only _____ seller of a product for which no close substitute is available.

2. Monopolists are _____ rather than price takers.

3. A monopolist's barriers to entry can include _____, _____, and _____.

4. _____ include franchising, licensing, and patents.

5. The situation in which one large firm can provide the output of the market at a lower cost than two or more smaller firms is called a(n) _____.

6. A barrier to entry is control over an important _____, such as Alcoa's control over bauxite in the 1940s and De Beers's control over much of the world's output of diamonds.

7. In monopoly, the market demand curve may be regarded as the demand curve for the _____ because it is the market for that particular product.

8. If a monopolist reduces output, the price will _____; if the monopolist expands output, the price will _____.

9. In monopoly, if the seller wants to expand output, it will have to lower its price on _____ units.

10. The monopolist, like the perfect competitor, will maximize profits at that output where _____ = *MC*.

11. The monopolist, unlike the perfect competitor, will not maximize profits at that output where _____ = *MC*.

12. If at a monopolist's profit-maximizing price and output, the price is less than _____, the monopolist is generating economic losses.

13. In monopoly, economic profits are not eliminated by entry, because one of the conditions for monopoly is that _____ exist.

14. Patents and copyrights are examples of _____ power designed to provide an incentive to develop new products.

15. The major efficiency objection to monopoly is that a monopolist charges _____ prices and produces _____ output than would exist under perfect competition.

16. A monopolist produces at an output where the price is _____ than its marginal cost, so the value to society from the last unit produced is _____ than its marginal cost.

17. An argument against monopoly is that a lack of competition tends to retard _____ advance; but, in fact, many near monopolists are important innovators.

18. Three major approaches to dealing with the monopoly problem are commonly used: _____ policies, _____, and _____ ownership.

19. It is likely that at least some anticompetitive practices have been prevented by _____ policies simply by their prohibition of monopoly-like practices.

20. The goal of government regulation as an alternative approach to dealing with monopolies is to achieve the efficiency of large-scale production without permitting the _____ monopoly prices and _____ output that can cause allocative inefficiency.

21. From society's point of view, allocative efficiency occurs where the price of the good is equal to _____. But with natural monopoly, at the "optimal" level of output for allocative efficiency, _____ are incurred.

22. A compromise between unregulated monopoly and marginal cost pricing is _____ pricing, where the monopolist is permitted to price the product where price equals _____.

23. Average cost pricing _____ the incentives for a monopolist to find ways to reduce its costs.

24. _____ occurs when sellers charge different customers different prices for the same good or service when the cost does not differ.

25. In the case of a number of competing firms, price discrimination is _____ likely because competitors tend to undercut the _____ prices charged.

26. A profit-maximizing seller will charge a(n) _____ price for more inelastic demanders and a(n) _____ price for more elastic demanders.

27. The profit-maximizing rule for a price-discriminating monopolist is to price where _____ equals _____ for each different group of demanders.

28. For price discrimination to work, the person buying the product at a discount must have difficulty in _____ the product to customers being charged more.

29. _____, which allow sellers to charge a higher price for the first unit than for later units, are another form of price discrimination.

Answers: 1. monopoly 2. price makers 3. legal barriers; economies of scale; control of important inputs 4. Legal barriers to entry 5. natural monopoly 6. input 7. firm 8. rise; fall 9. all 10. *MR* 11. *P* 12. average total cost 13. barriers to entry 14. barriers to entry 15. higher; less 16. greater; greater 17. technological 18. antitrust; regulation; public 19. antitrust 20. high; low 21. marginal cost; losses 22. average cost; average total cost 23. reduces 24. Price discrimination 25. less; high 26. higher; lower 27. marginal revenue; marginal cost 28. reselling 29. Quantity discounts

SECTION QUIZ ANSWERS

13.1 Monopoly: The Price Maker

1. **Why does monopoly depend on the existence of barriers to entry?**

   If a monopoly were unusually profitable (earning a higher than normal rate of return), entry by other firms would occur, driving its economic profits down and increasing the number of sellers, unless some barrier to entry prevented it.

2. **Why is a pure monopoly a rarity?**

   Pure monopolies are a rarity because there are very few goods or services for which there are no close substitutes and for which there is only one producer.

3. **Why does the government grant some companies, such as public utilities, monopoly power?**

   In some industries, it is inherently inefficient to have more than one firm producing the good or service (i.e., the good or service is a natural monopoly).

13.2 Demand and Marginal Revenue in Monopoly

1. **Why are the market and firm demand curves the same for a monopoly?**

   The market and firm demand curves are the same for a monopoly because a monopoly is the only seller of the product under consideration. Since a monopolist is the only seller in the industry, its demand curve is the industry or market demand curve.

2. **Why is a monopoly a price maker, but a perfectly competitive firm a price taker?**

   A perfectly competitive firm is a price taker because it cannot appreciably change the quantity offered for sale on a market, and therefore it cannot change the equilibrium market price appreciably. However, since a monopoly controls the quantity offered for sale, it can alter the price by changing its output—it "makes" the price through its decision of how much to produce.

3. **Why is marginal revenue less than price for a profit-maximizing monopolist?**

   For a monopolist, selling an additional unit requires it to reduce its price, and reducing its price reduces its revenues from units it was selling before at its previous higher price. Therefore, the monopolist's marginal revenue equals price minus this lost revenue from the reduced price on other units, and is less than price as a result.

4. **Why would a monopolist never knowingly operate in the inelastic portion of its demand curve?**

   To maximize its profits, a monopolist will produce the output where marginal revenue equals marginal cost. But since marginal cost will be positive, this requires that marginal revenue is also positive at the profit-maximizing level. Since a positive marginal revenue means that total revenue increases as quantity sold increases along a demand curve, and this only occurs if demand is relatively elastic (the elasticity of demand is greater than one), this means that a monopolist will always choose to operate on the elastic portion of its demand curve.

13.3 The Monopolist's Equilibrium

1. **What is a monopolist's principle for choosing the profit-maximizing output?**

   A monopolist's principle for choosing the profit-maximizing output is the same as for a perfectly competitive firm: Produce all those units for which marginal revenue exceeds marginal cost, resulting in a profit-maximizing equilibrium quantity where marginal revenue equals marginal cost. The differences between a monopoly and a perfectly competitive firm arise because marginal revenue also equals price for a perfectly competitive firm, but marginal revenue is less than price for a monopolist.

2. **How do you find the profit-maximizing price for a monopolist?**

   A monopolist produces the quantity where marginal revenue equals marginal cost. The height of its demand curve at that quantity indicates the price at which that profit-maximizing quantity can be sold.

3. **For a monopolist making positive economic profits, what must be true about the relationship between price and average total cost?**

   Just as with a perfectly competitive firm, for a monopoly to be earning economic profits, its total revenue must exceed total cost at the profit-maximizing output. But this means that price (average revenue) must also exceed average cost at the profit-maximizing output level for positive economic profits to be earned.

4. **For a monopolist making negative economic profits, what must be true about the relationship between price and average total cost?**

   Just as with a perfectly competitive firm, for a monopoly to be earning negative economic profits, its total revenue must be less than its total cost at the profit-maximizing output. But this means that price (average revenue) must also be less than average cost at the profit-maximizing output level for negative economic profits to be earned.

5. **Why, unlike perfectly competitive firms, can a monopolist continue to earn positive economic profits in the long run?**

Unlike perfectly competitive firms, a monopolist can continue to earn positive economic profits in the long run because barriers to entry keep entrants, whose entry would erode those economic profits, from entering the industry.

13.4   Monopoly and Welfare Loss

1. **Why does the reduced output under monopoly cause inefficiency?**

The reduced output and higher prices under monopoly cause inefficiency because some units for which the marginal value (indicated by willingness to pay along the demand curve) exceeds the marginal cost are no longer exchanged (unlike in perfect competition), eliminating the net gains that such trades would have generated.

2. **Does monopoly power retard innovation? Why or why not?**

Monopoly has been claimed to retard innovation, but many near-monopolists are important innovators. Therefore the incentive to innovate exists in monopolistic as well as competitive market structures.

3. **What does the welfare cost of monopoly represent? How is it measured?**

The welfare cost of monopoly represents the net gains from trade (the difference between the marginal values of those goods indicated by the demand curve and the marginal costs of producing them) from those units of a good that would have been traded, but are no longer traded because of the output restriction of monopoly. It is measured by the area between the demand curve and the marginal cost curve for those units that are no longer traded because of the monopoly output restriction.

4. **How can economies of scale lead to monopoly? How could it result in monopoly increasing rather than decreasing market output, relative to the competitive market structure?**

Economies of scale can lead to monopoly because output can be produced at lower costs on a larger scale than on a smaller scale, and this efficiency (cost) advantage can result in a larger firm outcompeting smaller firms. Industries with economies of scale over the entire range of industry output therefore tend toward

monopoly. But if the production cost savings are greater than the price-increasing effect of monopoly output restriction, the result of such a monopoly would be a lower price and a higher quantity than would be the case with a larger number of firms (i.e., a more competitive market structure).

5. **Can monopoly be the result of a new innovation that leaves consumers better off than before? Why or why not?**

A new innovation may result in its innovator having a monopoly on it, which would give its creator incentives to raise prices and reduce outputs like any other monopoly. But for that monopoly innovator to attract customers away from the products customers currently purchase, those customers must expect to be made better off buying the product at the price charged. This means that such a monopoly has no ability to harm consumers compared to their earlier situation, but can make them better off.

13.5   Monopoly Policy

1. **What alternative ways of dealing with the monopoly problem are commonly used?**

The monopoly problem (with respect to efficiency, equity, and power) is commonly dealt with through antitrust policies, regulation, and public ownership.

2. **How do antitrust laws promote greater price competition?**

Antitrust laws promote more price competition by making monopolistic practices and restrictions on price competition illegal.

3. **What price and output are ideal for allocative efficiency for a regulated natural monopolist? Why is an unregulated natural monopolist unlikely to pick this solution?**

The efficient price and output are where demand (marginal value) equals marginal cost, since this guarantees that every mutually beneficial trade takes place. However, with economies of scale (falling average cost curves), marginal cost is less than average cost for a natural monopolist, so that marginal cost prices would result in economic losses. An unregulated natural monopolist would not choose such a solution.

4. **What is average cost pricing? How is it different from marginal cost pricing?**

Average cost pricing is a regulatory approach to natural monopoly that permits the regulated natural monopolist to earn a normal rate of return on capital investment (zero economic profits). Zero economic profits requires that total revenues equal total (opportunity) costs, which requires that average revenue, or price, equals average cost. Forcing such a natural monopolist to charge prices equal to marginal cost would require a price below average cost because marginal cost is less than average cost for a natural monopolist, implying losses to the producer, which is not sustainable over the long run.

5. What are some difficulties encountered when regulators try to implement average cost pricing for natural monopolies?

Difficulties encountered when regulators try to implement average cost pricing include difficulties in calculating costs, eroded incentives for regulated firms to keep costs down, and the risk that the regulatory agency will make decisions on a political rather than on an economic basis.

6. Why might a job with a regulated natural monopolist that is allowed to earn a "fair and reasonable" return have more perks (noncash forms of compensation) than a comparable job in a nonregulated firm?

A regulated natural monopolist that is allowed to earn a "fair and reasonable" rate of return has little or no incentive to keep costs down, since reducing costs won't allow them to earn higher profits as a result. Those potential profits the monopolist is not allowed to keep are converted instead into business expenses that benefit the management, such as lavish perks (first-class air travel, hotels, meals, etc.).

13.6 Price Discrimination and Peak Load Pricing

1. How do we define price discrimination?

Price discrimination is defined as charging different customers different prices for the same good or service.

2. Why does price discrimination arise from the profit-maximization motive?

Price discrimination arises from the profit-maximization motive because different customers react differently to price changes (i.e., they have different elasticities of demand). Therefore, profit-maximization implies treating these different customers differently.

3. Why is preventing resale the key to successful price discrimination?

If customers who are being charged different prices for the same goods can resell the goods among themselves, the lower price group will resell to the higher price group, undermining the seller's ability to charge a higher price to the groups with more inelastic demand curves.

4. Why is it generally easier to price-discriminate for services than for goods?

Preventing resale is a key to successful price discrimination, and it is typically easier to prevent resale of services provided directly to customers than for goods sold to them (e.g., it is harder to resell a gall bladder surgery or plumbing repairs than to resell a computer).

5. What principle will a profit-maximizing monopolist use in trying to price-discriminate among different groups of customers?

A profit-maximizing monopolist will attempt to charge higher prices to those who are more willing to pay (more inelastic demanders) and lower prices to those who are less willing to pay (more elastic demanders).

6. How can offering quantity discounts increase a producer's profits?

Quantity discounts can allow a producer to charge a lower price for additional units, without having to reduce the price on the earlier units; it is effective because a buyer's willingness to pay declines as additional units are purchased.

7. Why does perfect price discrimination lead to the economically efficient level of output while reducing consumer surplus to zero?

Perfect price discrimination allows a seller to sell each unit for a price equal to the buyer's reservation price, which eliminates any consumer surplus. But since a perfect price-discriminating monopolist need not lower its price on previous units when it sells more, its marginal revenue is the same as its price, so when it produces to the output level where marginal revenue equals marginal cost, it also produces to the output level where price equals marginal cost, which is the efficient level of output.

8. What does perfect price discrimination do to the deadweight cost of monopoly?

Since perfect price discrimination makes marginal revenue equal to price for each unit sold, such a monopolist has no reason to restrict output to increase profits; with no incentive to reduce output below the efficient level, there would be no deadweight cost.

9. Why is peak load pricing more efficient than constant pricing for a good with sharp swings in demand over time?

A constant price would result in price being too low in the peak demand period, and too high in the low demand period; both of these pricing "errors" would cause a deadweight cost that could be avoided by peak load pricing.

1. Which of the following could be considered a monopoly?
   a. Kate Hudson (an actress)
   b. De Beers diamond company
   c. the only doctor in a small town
   d. Ford Motor Company

2. Barriers to entry are important in the creation of monopolies because they keep competitors out of the industry. Although many types of barriers exist, historically, ownership of an essential resource, government patents and licenses, and large entry costs have served as the primary barriers to entry. For each of the following cases, indicate which type of barrier created the monopoly.
   a. In the 1940s, Aluminum Company of America owned all of the world's known bauxite deposits.
   b. The local cable TV company has the only government-issued license to supply services in the area.
   c. The pharmaceutical company MAXCO invents and patents a new drug curing baldness.
   d. In the 1950s, AT&T provided long-distance telephone service by stringing millions of miles of copper wiring across the United States.

3. Is it optimal for the monopolist to operate on the inelastic portion of the demand curve? Why or why not?

4. Fill in the missing data in the following table for a monopolist.

Quantity	Price	Total Revenue	Marginal Revenue	Demand Elastic or Inelastic?
1	$11	_____	_____	_____
2	10	_____	_____	_____
3	9	_____	_____	_____
4	8	_____	_____	_____
5	7	_____	_____	_____
6	6	_____	_____	_____
7	5	_____	_____	_____
8	4	_____	_____	_____
9	3	_____	_____	_____
10	2	_____	_____	_____
11	1	_____	_____	_____

5. Assume that the monopolist in problem 4 had fixed costs of $10 and a constant marginal cost of $4 per unit. Add columns to the above table for Total Cost, Marginal Cost, and Profit.

6. The Mobile Phone Company has served Mobile, Alabama, since the 1930s as a government-authorized natural monopoly. The following table describes a portion of the demand curve for long-distance service facing Mobile Phone Company.
   a. Complete the table.

MOBILE PHONE COMPANY DEMAND FOR PHONE HOURS

Quantity	Price	Total Revenue	Marginal Revenue	Elastic or Inelastic?
30	$3.65	_____	_____	_____
31	3.58	_____	_____	_____
32	3.50	_____	_____	_____
33	3.43	_____	_____	_____
34	3.35	_____	_____	_____
35	3.27	_____	_____	_____
36	3.20	_____	_____	_____
37	3.12	_____	_____	_____
38	3.05	_____	_____	_____

Quantity	Price	Total Revenue	Marginal Revenue	Elastic or Inelastic?
39	2.97	_____	_____	_____
40	2.89	_____	_____	_____
41	2.82	_____	_____	_____
42	2.74	_____	_____	_____
43	2.67	_____	_____	_____
44	2.59	_____	_____	_____
45	2.51	_____	_____	_____
46	2.44	_____	_____	_____
47	2.36	_____	_____	_____
48	2.29	_____	_____	_____
49	2.21	_____	_____	_____
50	2.13	_____	_____	_____

b. How does the company's marginal revenue change as the price changes? What is the relationship between marginal revenue and price?

c. At what price does demand become inelastic?

d. What will happen to the elasticity of demand when a new company, Mobile Phones of Mobile, starts a competing wireless phone company?

7. The following table shows the demand for water and cost conditions for the New South Springdale Water Utility, a pure monopoly.

a. Complete the table.

Quanity (gallons)	Price (per gallon)	Total Revenue	Marginal Revenue	Marginal Costs	Average Total Costs	Profit
100	$1.28	_____	_____	$0.15	$1.252	_____
101	1.27	_____	_____	0.18	1.241	_____
102	1.26	_____	_____	0.21	1.231	_____
103	1.25	_____	_____	0.23	1.221	_____
104	1.24	_____	_____	0.26	1.212	_____

b. What is true about the relationship between marginal revenue and marginal costs when profit is the greatest?

c. Suppose the government imposed a tax on the firm of $103, which the firm had to pay even if it went out of business. What would be the profit-maximizing level of output? What would happen to profits? Would the firm stay in business?

8. A patent gives a firm a monopoly in production of the patented good. While the monopoly profits provide an incentive for firms to innovate, the monopoly power imposes a cost on consumers. Why do consumers suffer a cost? Is it greater than the profits earned by the monopolist?

9. Use the accompanying diagram to answer a–c.

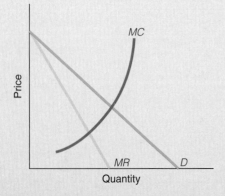

a. Assuming the monopolist indicated in the diagram produced at all, indicate its profit-maximizing quantity and price.

b. Add an *ATC* curve that would show this monopolist earning an economic profit.

c. Add an *ATC* curve that would show this monopolist experiencing an economic loss.

10. If economic profits were zero, would a monopolist stay in business? Why might it be possible for a monopolist to earn positive economic profits in the long run?

11. What is meant by the "welfare loss" of monopoly? Why does no welfare loss occur if a monopolist successfully practices perfect price discrimination?

12. Consider the data in the following table:

Price	Quantity	Fixed Cost	Variable Cost
$100	0	$60	$ 0
90	1	60	25
80	2	60	40
70	3	60	50
60	4	60	70
50	5	60	100
40	6	60	140
30	7	60	190
20	8	60	250

A simple monopolist with these fixed and variable cost schedules maximizes profits at what level of output?

13. Explain how each of the following is a form of price discrimination.

a. A student discount at the movie theater

b. Long-distance phone service that costs 15 cents per minute for the first 10 minutes and 5 cents per minute after 10 minutes

c. A psychic who charges each customer his or her maximum reservation price for palm readings

d. A senior citizen breakfast discount at a local restaurant

e. Coupon discounts on laundry detergent

14. In October 1999, Coca-Cola announced that it was considering testing a new vending machine that was temperature sensitive. The price of the soft drinks in the machines would be higher on hot days. The *Miami Herald* story read "Soda jerks." How is this practice a form of price discrimination? How can the placement of the vending machines create a monopoly? What if other vending machines are close by and are not owned by Coca-Cola?

15. Compare the size of the welfare (deadweight) loss under monopoly in the case of perfect price discrimination and under the standard case of simple monopoly. Explain.

16. Use the accompanying diagram to answer a–c.

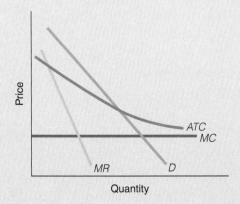

a. Indicate the efficient result on the graph.

b. Illustrate the profits or losses from the efficient result in (a).

c. Show the average cost-pricing solution. What profits are earned with that approach?

17. Governments around the world are allowing competition in the production of goods and services that have historically been considered natural monopolies. Competition has been introduced in industries such as the local telephone service and electricity provision. Why might the introduction of competition increase the efficiency of these industries?

18. The Mississippi Bridge Authority operates a toll bridge that crosses the river near St. Louis. Traffic over the bridge includes tourist traffic and commercial traffic. It also includes commuters who work in St. Louis but live on the Illinois side of the river.
    a. Would you expect demand for bridge use to differ at different times during the day? Why?
    b. How might costs differ in these time periods?
    c. What would be the effects of charging a higher toll to cross the bridge during busy times?

CHAPTER 14

Monopolistic Competition and Product Differentiation

In what kind of market do you think McDonald's, Dunkin' Donuts, and Starbucks compete? Obviously, these aren't the only firms out there selling coffee. Starbucks started with one coffeehouse in Seattle and now has stores in 50 countries. This market has elements of competition because anyone could open a new coffeehouse. Sounds like a competitive market, right? But are they really selling the same product? The products are also differentiated. McDonald's added espresso in order to compete in the Starbucks market, and Dunkin' Donuts spent millions to upgrade many of its stores. This is not like the market for wheat.

Each firm is unique in its atmosphere, location, and the quality of the products it serves. In fact, the market contains elements of both competition and monopoly. Restaurants, clothing stores, beauty salons, video stores, hardware stores, and coffeehouses have elements of both competitive and monopoly markets. Recall that the competitive model includes many buyers and sellers; coffeehouses can be found in almost every town in the country. You can even find Starbucks in grocery stores. In addition, the barriers to entry of owning an individual coffee shop are relatively low. However, monopolistically competitive firms sell a differentiated product, and thus each firm has an element of monopoly power. Each coffee store is different. It might be different because of its location or décor. It might be different because of its products. It might be different because of the service it provides. Monopolistically competitive markets are common in the real world. They are the topic of this chapter.

14.1 Monopolistic Competition

▶ What are the distinguishing features of monopolistic competition?

▶ How can a firm differentiate its product?

14.1a What Is Monopolistic Competition?

monopolistic competition

a market structure with many firms selling differentiated products

Monopolistic competition is a market structure where many producers of somewhat different products compete with one another. For example, a restaurant is a monopoly in the sense that it has a unique name, menu, quality of service, location, and so on, but it also has many competitors—others selling prepared meals. That is, monopolistic competition has features in common with both monopoly and perfect competition, even though this explanation may sound like an oxymoron—like "jumbo shrimp" or "civil war." As with monopoly, individual sellers in monopolistic competition believe that they have some market power. But monopolistic competition is probably closer to competition than monopoly. Entry into and exit out of the industry is unrestricted, and consequently, the industry has many independent sellers. In virtue of the relatively free entry of new firms, the long-run price and output behavior, and zero long-run economic profits, monopolistic competition is similar to perfect competition.

However, the monopolistically competitive firm produces a product that is different (that is, *differentiated* rather than identical or homogeneous) from others, which leads to some degree of monopoly power. In a sense, sellers in a monopolistically competitive market may be regarded as "monopolists" of their own particular brands. Unlike firms with a true monopoly, however, competition occurs among the many firms selling similar (but not identical) brands. For example, a buyer living in a city of moderate size and in the market for books, CDs, toothpaste, furniture, shampoo, video rentals, restaurants, eyeglasses, running shoes, movie theaters, supermarkets, and music lessons has many competing sellers from which to choose.

Restaurants can be very different. A restaurant that sells tacos and burritos competes with other Mexican restaurants, but it also competes with restaurants that sell burgers and fries. Monopolistic competition has some elements of competition (many sellers) and some elements of monopoly power (differentiated products).

© SUSAN LAW CAIN/SHUTTERSTOCK.COM

14.1b The Three Basic Characteristics of Monopolistic Competition

The theory of monopolistic competition is based on three characteristics: (1) product differentiation, (2) many sellers, and (3) free entry.

Product Differentiation

One characteristic of monopolistic competition is product differentiation—the accentuation of unique product qualities, real or perceived, to develop a specific product identity.

The significant feature of differentiation is the buyer's belief that various sellers' products are not the same, whether the products are actually different or not. Aspirin and some brands of over-the-counter cold medicines are examples of products that are similar or identical but have different brand names. Product differentiation leads to preferences among buyers dealing with or purchasing the products of particular sellers.

Physical Differences Physical differences constitute a primary source of product differentiation. For example, brands of ice cream (such as Dreyer's and Breyers), running shoes (such as Nike and Asics), or fast-food Mexican restaurants (such as Taco Bell and Del Taco) differ significantly in taste to many buyers.

Prestige Prestige considerations also differentiate products to a significant degree. Many people prefer to be seen using the currently popular brand, while others prefer the "off" brand. Prestige considerations are particularly important with gifts—Cuban cigars, Montblanc pens, beluga caviar, Godiva chocolates, Dom Perignon champagne, Rolex watches, and so on.

Location Location is a major differentiating factor in retailing. Shoppers are not willing to travel long distances to purchase similar items, which is one reason for the large number of convenience stores and service station mini-marts. Most buyers realize brands of gasoline do not differ significantly, which means the location of a gas station might influence their choice of gasoline. Location is also important for restaurants. Some restaurants can differentiate their products with beautiful views of the city lights, ocean, or mountains.

Service Service considerations are likewise significant for product differentiation. Speedy and friendly service or lenient return policies are important to many people. Likewise, speed and quality of service may significantly influence a person's choice of restaurants.

The Impact of Many Sellers

When many firms compete for the same customers, any particular firm has little control over or interest in what other firms do. That is, a restaurant may change prices or improve service without a retaliatory move on the part of other competing restaurants because there are so many rivals they tend to get lost in the crowd. That is, restaurants, drug stores, yogurt shops, and dry cleaners tend to act independently in metropolitan areas.

The Significance of Free Entry

Entry in monopolistic competition is relatively unrestricted in the sense that new firms may easily start the production of close substitutes for existing products, as happens with restaurants, hair salons, barber shops, and many forms of retail activity. Because of relatively free entry, economic profits tend to be eliminated in the long run, as is the case with perfect competition.

product differentiation
goods or services that are slightly different, or perceived to be different, from one another

How is monopolistic competition like monopoly? How is it like perfect competition?

economic content standards

In monopolistically competitive markets, sellers compete on the basis of price, product quality, customer service, product design and variety, and advertising. For instance, consider the price and nonprice competition in the restaurant market.

Costco's liberal return policy is legendary and differentiates its product from many others. Internet stories include attempts to return 10-year-old ping-pong tables and a woman who kept bringing back her fresh-cut flowers because they would lose their color after two weeks. Costco did have to change its return policy for electronics because customers would repeatedly turn in computers or televisions and upgrade to newer models—sometimes getting a better and less expensive television or computer.

SECTION QUIZ

1. Which of the following is *not* a source of product differentiation?

    a. Physical differences in products

    b. Differences in quantities that firms offer for sale

    c. Differences in service provided by firms

    d. Differences in location of sales outlets

2. Which of the following characteristics do monopolistic competition and perfect competition have in common?

    a. Individual firms believe that they can influence market price.

    b. Firms sell brand-name products.

    c. Firms are able to earn long-run economic profits.

    d. Competing firms can enter the industry easily.

3. Firms in monopolistically competitive industries cannot earn economic profits in the long run because

    a. government regulators, whose first interest is the public good, will impose regulations that limit economic profits.

    b. the additional costs of product differentiation will eliminate long-run economic profits.

    c. economic profits will attract competitors whose presence will eliminate profits in the long run.

    d. whenever one firm in the industry begins making economic profits, others will lower their prices, thus eliminating long-run economic profits.

4. Which of the following statements is true?

    a. Monopolistic competition is a mixture of monopoly and perfect competition.

    b. All firms in monopolistically competitive industries earn economic profits in the long run.

    c. Both (a) and (b) are true.

    d. None of the above is true.

---

1. How is monopolistic competition a mixture of monopoly and perfect competition?

2. Why is product differentiation necessary for monopolistic competition?

3. What are some common forms of product differentiation?

4. Why are many sellers necessary for monopolistic competition?

5. Why is free entry necessary for monopolistic competition?

Answers: 1. b   2. d   3. c   4. a

14.2 Price and Output Determination in Monopolistic Competition

▶ How are short-run economic profits and losses determined?

▶ Why is marginal revenue less than price?

▶ How is long-run equilibrium determined?

14.2a The Firm's Demand and Marginal Revenue Curve

Why does a monopolistically competitive firm have a downward-sloping demand curve?

Suppose the Coffee Bean decides to raise its price on caffé lattes from $2.75 to $3.00, as seen in Exhibit 1. The Coffee Bean is one of many places to get caffé lattes in town (Starbucks, Dunkin' Donuts, Peet's, and others). At the higher price, $3.00, a number of Coffee Bean customers will switch to other places in town for their caffé lattes—but not everyone. Some may not switch, perhaps because of the location, the ambience, the selection of other drinks, or the quality of the coffee. Because there are many substitutes and the fact that some will not change, the demand curve will be very elastic (flat) but not horizontal, as seen in Exhibit 1. That is, unlike the perfectly competitive firm, a monopolistically competitive firm faces a downward-sloping demand curve. The increase in price from $2.75 to $3.00 leads to a reduction in caffé lattes sold from 2,400 per month to 800 per month.

Let's continue our example with the Coffee Bean. In the table in Exhibit 2, we will show how a monopolistically competitive firm must cut its price to sell more and why its marginal revenue will therefore lie below its demand curve. For simplicity, we will use caffé lattes sold per hour. The first two columns in the table show the demand schedule. If the Coffee Bean charges $4.00 for a caffé latte, no one will buy it and will buy their caffé lattes at another store. If it charges $3.50, it will sell one caffé latte per hour. And if the Coffee Bean wants to sell two caffé lattes, it must lower the price to $3.00, and so on. If we were to graph these numbers, we would get a downward-sloping demand curve.

The third column presents the *total revenue*—the quantity sold (column 1) times the price (column 2). The fourth column shows the firm's *average revenue*—the amount of revenue the firm receives per unit sold. We compute average revenue by dividing total revenue (column 3) by output (column 1) or $AR = TR/q$. In the last column, we show the marginal revenue the firm receives for each additional caffé latte. We find this by looking at the change in total revenue when output changes by one unit. For example, when the Coffee Bean sells two caffé lattes, its total revenue is $6.00. Increasing output to three caffé lattes will increase total revenue to $7.50. Thus, the marginal revenue is $1.50, or $7.50 – $6.00.

It is important to notice in Exhibit 3 that the marginal revenue curve is below the demand curve. That is, the price on all units must fall if the firm increases its production; consequently, marginal revenue must be less than the price. This is true for all firms that face a downward-sloping demand curve. Recall from the discussion of monopoly that when the firm sells more output there are two effects: the output effect and the price effect. For example, in Exhibit 4, we see that if the Coffee Bean wants to sell four caffé lattes rather than three caffé lattes, it will have to lower its price on all four caffé lattes from $2.50 to $2.00. This is the *price effect*;

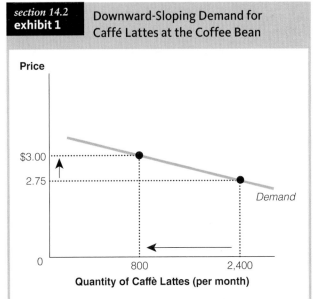

Downward-Sloping Demand for Caffé Lattes at the Coffee Bean

The Coffee Bean faces a downward-sloping demand curve. If the price of coffee increases at the Coffee Bean, some but not all of its customers will leave. In this case, an increase in its price from $2.75 to $3.00 leads to a reduction in caffé lattes sold from 2,400 per month to 800 per month.

What is the price effect of a change in price? What is the output effect of a change in the price?

Demand and Marginal Revenue for Caffé Lattes at the Coffee Bean

Caffé Lattes Sold (q)	Price (P)	Total Revenue (TR = P × q)	Average Revenue (AR = TR/q)	Marginal Revenue (MR = ΔTR/Δq)
0	$4.00	$ 0	—	
				$ 3.50
1	3.50	3.50	$3.50	
				2.50
2	3.00	6.00	3.00	
				1.50
3	2.50	7.50	2.50	
				0.50
4	2.00	8.00	2.00	
				−0.50
5	1.50	7.50	1.50	
				−1.50
6	1.00	6.00	1.00	

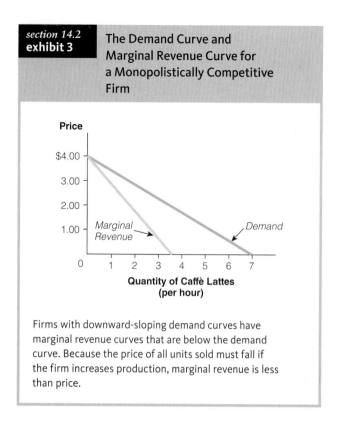

section 14.2
exhibit 3
The Demand Curve and Marginal Revenue Curve for a Monopolistically Competitive Firm

Firms with downward-sloping demand curves have marginal revenue curves that are below the demand curve. Because the price of all units sold must fall if the firm increases production, marginal revenue is less than price.

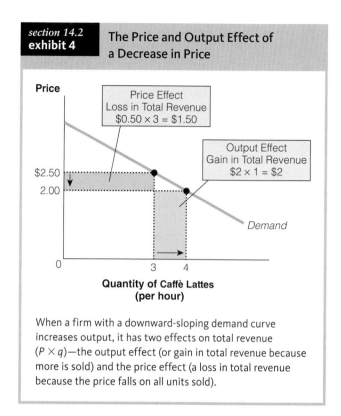

section 14.2
exhibit 4
The Price and Output Effect of a Decrease in Price

When a firm with a downward-sloping demand curve increases output, it has two effects on total revenue ($P \times q$)—the output effect (or gain in total revenue because more is sold) and the price effect (a loss in total revenue because the price falls on all units sold).

the lower price leads to a loss in total revenue ($0.50 \times 3 = 1.50). There is also an *output effect*; more output is sold when the Coffee Bean lowers its price ($2 \times 1 = 2). That is, more output is sold, which increases total revenue. It is the price effect that leads to lower revenue; consequently, marginal revenue is less than price for all firms that face a downward-sloping demand curve. Marginal revenue can become negative when the price effect on revenue is greater than the output effect. Recall there is no price effect in perfectly competitive markets because the firm can sell all it wants at the going market price.

14.2b Determining Short-Run Equilibrium

Because monopolistically competitive sellers are price makers rather than price takers, they do not regard price as a given by market conditions like perfectly competitive firms.

The cost and revenue curves of a typical seller are shown in Exhibit 5; the intersection of the marginal revenue and marginal cost curves indicates that the short-run profit-maximizing output will be q^*. Now by observing how much will be demanded at that output level, we find our profit-maximizing price, P^*. That is, at the equilibrium quantity, q^*, we go vertically to the demand curve and read the corresponding price on the vertical axis, P^*.

Three-Step Method for Monopolistic Competition

Let us return to the same three-step method we used in Chapters 12 and 13. Determining whether a firm is generating economic profits, economic losses, or zero economic profits at the profit-maximizing level of output, q^*, can be done in three easy steps:

1. Find where marginal revenues equal marginal costs and proceed straight down to the horizontal quantity axis to find q*, the profit-maximizing output level.
2. At q^*, go straight up to the demand curve then to the left to find the market price, P^*. Once you have identified P^* and q^*, you can find total revenue at the profit-maximizing output level because $TR = P \times q$.

3. The last step is to find total costs. Again, go straight up from q^* to the average total cost (ATC) curve, which reveals the average total cost *per unit*. If we multiply average total costs by the output level, we can find the total costs ($TC = ATC \times q$).

If total revenue is greater than total costs at q^*, the firm is generating total economic profits. And if total revenue is less than total costs at q^*, the firm is generating total economic losses.

Or, if we take the product price at P^* and subtract the average cost at q^*, this will give us per-unit profit. If we multiply this by output, we will arrive at total economic profit, that is, $(P^* - ATC) \times q^* = $ total profit.

Remember, the cost curves include implicit and explicit costs—that is, even at zero economic profits the firm is covering the total opportunity costs of its resources and earning a normal profit or rate of return.

14.2c Short-Run Profits and Losses in Monopolistic Competition

Exhibit 5(a) shows the equilibrium position of a monopolistically competitive firm. As we just discussed, the firm produces where $MC = MR$, or output q^*. At output q^* and price P^*, the firm's total revenue is equal to $P^* \times q^*$, or \$800. At output q^*, the firm's total cost is $ATC \times q^*$, or \$700. In Exhibit 5(a), we see that total revenue is greater than total cost so the firm has a total economic profit. That is, TR (\$800) $- TC$ (\$700) $= $ Total economic profit (\$100) or P^* (\$8) $- ATC$ (\$7) $\times q^*$ (100) $= $ \$100.

In Exhibit 5(b), at q^*, price is below average total cost, so the firm is minimizing its economic loss. At q^*, total cost (\$800) is greater than total revenue (\$700). So the firm incurs a total loss (\$100) or P^* (\$7) $- ATC$ (\$8) $\times q^*$ (100) $= $ Total economic losses ($-$\$100).

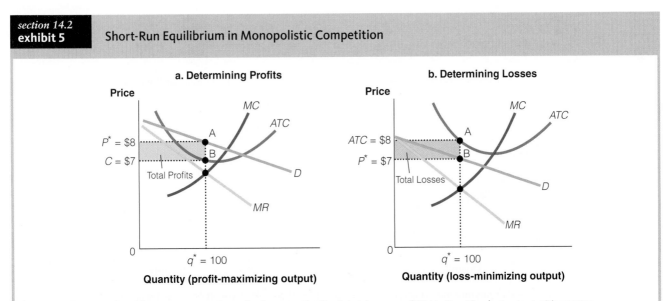

**section 14.2
exhibit 5**   **Short-Run Equilibrium in Monopolistic Competition**

a. Determining Profits

b. Determining Losses

In (a) the firm is making short-run economic profits because the firm's total revenue ($P^* \times q^* = $ \$800) at output q^* is greater than the firm's total cost ($ATC \times q^* = $ \$700). Because the firm's total revenue is greater than total cost, the firm has a total profit of \$100: $TR - TC = $ \$800 $-$ \$700. In (b) the firm is incurring a short-run economic loss because at q^*, price is below average total cost. At q^*, total cost ($ATC \times q^* = $ \$800) is greater than total revenue ($P^* \times q^* = $ \$700), so the firm incurs a total loss ($TR - TC = $ \$700 $-$ \$800 $= -$\$100).

14.2d Determining Long-Run Equilibrium

The short-run equilibrium situation, whether involving profits or losses, will probably not last long because entry and exit occur in the long run. If market entry and exit are sufficiently free, new firms will have an incentive to enter the market when there are economic profits and exit when there are economic losses.

What Happens to Economic Profits When Firms Enter the Industry?

In Exhibit 6(a), we see the market impact as new firms enter to take advantage of the economic profits. The result of this influx is more sellers of similar products, which means that each new firm will cut into the demand of the existing firms. That is, the demand curve for each of the existing firms will fall. With entry, not only will the firm's demand curve move inward but it also becomes relatively more elastic due to each firm's products having more substitutes (more choices for consumers). We see this situation in Exhibit 6(a) when demand shifts leftward from D_{SR} to D_{LR}. This decline in demand continues to occur until the average total cost (ATC) curve becomes tangent with the demand curve, and economic profits are reduced to zero.

What Happens to Losses When Some Firms Exit?

When firms are making economic losses, some firms will exit the industry. As some firms exit, it means fewer firms in the market, which increases the demand for the remaining firms' product, shifting their demand curves to the right, from D_{SR} to D_{LR}, as seen in Exhibit 6(b). When firms exit not only will the firm's demand curve move outward, but it also becomes relatively more inelastic due to each firm's products having fewer substitutes (less choices for consumers). The higher demand results in smaller losses for the existing firms until all losses finally disappear where the ATC curve is tangent to the demand curve.

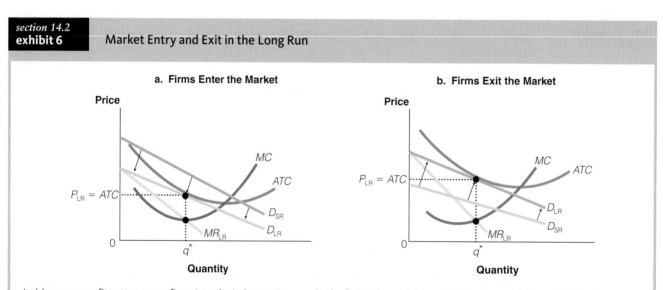

section 14.2
exhibit 6   Market Entry and Exit in the Long Run

a. Firms Enter the Market

b. Firms Exit the Market

In (a), excess profits attract new firms into the industry. As a result, the firm's share of the market declines and demand shifts down. Profits are eliminated when $P_{LR} = ATC$, that is, when the ATC curve is tangent to D_{LR}. In (b), some firms exit because of economic losses. Their exit increases the demand for existing firms, shifting D_{SR} to D_{LR}, where all losses have been eliminated.

14.2e **Achieving Long-Run Equilibrium**

The process of entry and exit will continue until all firms in the industry are making zero economic profits. When the market reaches this long-run equilibrium, no firms have an incentive to enter or exit.

Once entry and exit have driven profits to zero, the demand curve and average total cost curve will be tangent to each other, as seen in Exhibit 7. At the profit-maximizing output level, the firm earns zero economic profits.

In short, the monopolistically competitive producers are a lot like monopolists; they face a downward-sloping demand curve and set marginal revenue to marginal cost to determine the profit-maximizing output level. However, the difference is that at this profit-maximizing level of output the monopolistically competitive firm cannot make economic profits in the long run because the barriers to entry and exit in this market are assumed to be zero.

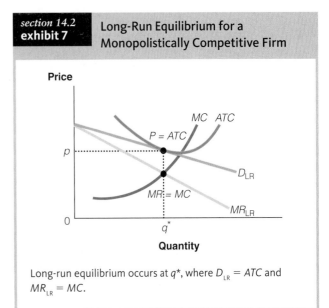

section 14.2 exhibit 7   Long-Run Equilibrium for a Monopolistically Competitive Firm

Long-run equilibrium occurs at q^*, where $D_{LR} = ATC$ and $MR_{LR} = MC$.

SECTION QUIZ

1. In monopolistic competition,

   a. firms face downward-sloping demand curves.

   b. firms have marginal revenue curves that are below the demand curve.

   c. the price on all units sold must fall if the firm increases production.

   d. all of the above are true.

2. A monopolistic competitive firm

   a. is making short-run economic profits when the equilibrium price is greater than average total costs at the equilibrium output.

   b. is minimizing its economic losses when equilibrium price is below average total cost at the equilibrium output.

   c. Both (a) and (b) are true.

   d. None of the above is true.

3. Which of the following is true of the monopolistically competitive firm in long-run equilibrium?

   a. Equilibrium price equals average total costs.

   b. Economic profits are zero.

   c. Incentives for firms to either enter or exit the industry have been eliminated.

   d. All of the above are true.

---

1. What is the short-run profit-maximizing policy of a monopolistically competitive firm?

2. How is the choice of whether to operate or shut down in the short run the same for a monopolistic competitor as for a perfectly competitive firm?

3. How is the long-run equilibrium of monopolistic competition like that of perfect competition?

4. How is the long-run equilibrium of monopolistic competition different from that of perfect competition?

Answers: 1. d   2. c   3. d

14.3 Monopolistic Competition versus Perfect Competition

▶ What are the differences and similarities between monopolistic competition and perfect competition?

▶ What is excess capacity?

▶ Why does the monopolistically competitive firm fail to meet productive efficiency?

▶ Why does the monopolistically competitive firm fail to meet allocative efficiency?

We have seen that both monopolistic competition and perfect competition have many buyers and sellers and relatively free entry. However, product differentiation enables a monopolistic competitor to have some influence over price. Consequently, a monopolistically competitive firm has a downward-sloping demand curve, but because of the large number of good substitutes for its product, the curve tends to be much more elastic than the demand curve for a monopolist.

Why don't monopolistically competitive firms achieve productive efficiency?

excess capacity

occurs when the firm produces below the level where average total cost is minimized

14.3a The Significance of Excess Capacity

Because in monopolistic competition the demand curve is downward sloping, its point of tangency with the *ATC* curve will not and cannot be at the lowest level of average cost. What does this statement mean? It means that even when long-run adjustments are complete, firms are not operating at a level that permits the lowest average cost of production—the efficient scale of the firm. The existing plant, even though optimal for the equilibrium volume of output, is not used to capacity; that is, excess capacity exists at that level of output. Excess capacity occurs when the firm produces below the level where average total cost is minimized.

14.3b Failing to Achieve Productive Efficiency

Unlike a perfectly competitive firm, a monopolistically competitive firm could increase output and lower its average total cost, as shown in Exhibit 1(a). However, any attempt to increase output to attain lower average cost would be unprofitable because the price reduction necessary to sell the greater output would cause marginal revenue to fall below the marginal cost of the increased output. As we can see in Exhibit 1(a), to the right of q^*, marginal cost is greater than marginal revenue. Consequently, in monopolistic competition, the tendency is for an industry to have too many firms, each producing a volume of output less than what would allow lowest cost. Economists call this tendency a failure to reach productive efficiency. For example, the market may have too many grocery stores or too many service stations, in the sense that if the total volume of business were concentrated in a smaller number of sellers, average cost, and thus price, could in principle be less.

14.3c Failing to Meet Allocative Efficiency, Too

Productive inefficiency is not the only problem with a monopolistically competitive firm. Exhibit 1(a) shows a firm that is not operating where price is equal to marginal costs. In the monopolistically competitive model, at the intersection of the *MC* and *MR* curves (q^*), we can clearly see that price is greater than marginal cost. Society is willing to pay more for the product (the price, P^*) than it costs society to produce it (*MC* at q^*). In this case, the firm is failing to reach allocative efficiency, where price equals marginal cost. Because the price is greater than the marginal cost, it would be profitable for the monopolistically competitive firm to sell to another customer. That is, trying to attract more customers is only profitable

section 14.3 **exhibit 1**	Comparing Long-Run Perfect Competition and Monopolistic Competition

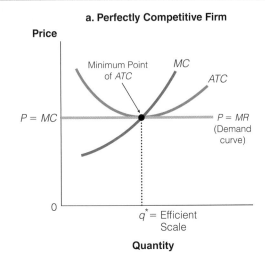

a. Perfectly Competitive Firm

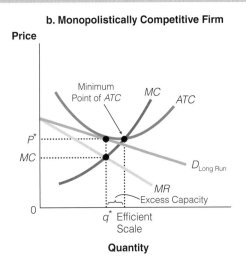

b. Monopolistically Competitive Firm

Comparing the differences between perfect competition and monopolistic competition, we see that the monopolistically competitive firm fails to meet both productive efficiency, minimizing costs in the long run, and allocative efficiency, producing output where $P = MC$.

if $P > MC$. If it were a perfectly competitive firm, it would not care because price is equal to marginal cost and the extra profit from another customer would be zero.

In short, monopolistically competitive firms are not producing at the minimum point of ATC, failing to meet productive efficiency, and not charging a price equal to marginal cost, failing to meet allocative efficiency. Note that in Exhibit 1(b), the perfectly competitive firm has reached both productive efficiency ($P = ATC$ at the minimum point on the ATC curve) and allocative efficiency ($P = MC$).

However, in defense of monopolistic competition, the higher average cost and the slightly higher price and lower output may simply be the price firms pay for differentiated products—variety. That is, just because monopolistically competitive firms have not met the conditions for productive and allocative efficiency, it does not necessarily mean that society is not better off.

Do monopolistically competitive firms achieve allocative efficiency?

14.3d What Are the Real Costs of Monopolistic Competition?

We just argued that perfect competition meets the tests of allocative and productive efficiency and that monopolistic competition does not. Can we "fix" a monopolistically competitive firm to look more like an efficient, perfectly competitive firm? One remedy might entail using government regulation, as in the case of a natural monopoly. However, this process would be costly because a monopolistically competitive firm makes no economic profits in the long run. Therefore, asking monopolistically competitive firms to equate price and marginal cost would lead to economic losses because long-run average total cost would be greater than price at $P = MC$. Consequently, the government would have to subsidize the firm. In addition, because there are so many monopolistically competitive firms, the administrative costs of regulation would be prohibitive. Regulation could also reduce the incentive these firms have to create what consumers want—differentiated products. So living with the inefficiencies in monopolistically competitive markets might be easier than coping with the difficulties entailed by regulations and the cost of the necessary subsidies.

We argued that the monopolistically competitive firm does not operate at the minimum point of the ATC curve while the perfectly competitive firm does. However, is this comparison fair? A monopolistic competition involves differentiated goods and services, while a perfect competition does not. In other words, the excess capacity that exists in monopolistic competition is the price we pay for product differentiation. Have you ever thought about the many restaurants, movies, and gasoline stations that have "excess capacity"? Can you imagine a world where all firms were working at full capacity? After all, choice is a good, and most of us value some choice.

In short, the inefficiency of monopolistic competition is a result of product differentiation. Because consumers value variety—the ability to choose from competing products and brands—the loss in efficiency must be weighed against the gain in increased product variety. The gains from product diversity can be large and may easily outweigh the inefficiency associated with a downward-sloping demand curve. Remember, firms differentiate their products to meet consumers' demand.

In addition, in most monopolistically competitive markets, many of the firms compete and products are substitutable. No single firm has substantial monopoly power. Consequently, the size of the deadweight loss will be small. Also, the firm's demand curve will be relatively elastic so the firm will be much closer to minimizing ATC than a monopoly.

Remember this little caveat: The theory of the firm is like a road map that does not detail every gully, creek, and hill but does give directions to get from one geographic point to another. Any particular theory of the firm may not tell precisely how an individual firm will operate, but it does provide valuable insight into the ways firms will tend to react to changing economic conditions such as entry, demand, and cost changes.

If the monopolistically competitive demand curve is relatively flat, is the size of the deadweight loss in this market smaller than that for monopoly?

SECTION QUIZ

1. In the long run, firms in monopolistic competition do not attain productive efficiency because they produce

   a. at a point where economic profits are positive.

   b. at a point where marginal revenue is less than marginal cost.

   c. at a point to the left of the low point of their long-run average total cost curve.

   d. where marginal cost is equal to long-run average total cost.

2. In the long run, firms in monopolistic competition do not attain allocative efficiency because they

   a. operate where price equals marginal cost.

   b. do not operate where price equals marginal cost.

   c. produce more output than society wants.

   d. charge prices that are less than production costs.

3. Compared to perfect competition, firms in monopolist competition in the long run produce

   a. less output at a lower cost.

   b. less output at a higher cost.

   c. more output at a lower cost.

   d. more output at a higher cost.

4. Both the competitive firm and the monopolistically competitive firm

   a. may earn short-run economic profits.

   b. will not earn economic profits in the long run.

   c. Both (a) and (b) are true.

   d. None of the above is true.

(continued)

SECTION QUIZ (cont.)

5. n the long run, monopolistically competitive firms

   a. fail to reach allocative efficiency (where $P = MC$).

   b. fail to reach productive efficiency, producing at output levels less than the efficient output.

   c. Both (a) and (b) are true.

   d. None of the above is true.

---

1. Why is a monopolistic competitor's demand curve relatively elastic (flat)?

2. Why do monopolistically competitive firms produce at less than the efficient scale of production?

3. Why do monopolistically competitive firms operate with excess capacity?

4. Why does the fact that price exceeds marginal cost in monopolistic competition lead to allocative inefficiency?

5. What is the price we pay for differentiated goods under monopolistic competition?

6. Why is the difference between the long-run equilibriums under perfect competition and monopolistic competition likely to be relatively small?

Answers: 1. c 2. b 3. b 4. c 5. c

Advertising   14.4

▶ Why do firms advertise?

▶ Is advertising good or bad from society's perspective?

▶ Can advertising increase demand?

14.4a **Why Do Firms Advertise?**

Advertising is an important nonprice method of competition that is commonly used in industries where the firm has market power. It would make little sense for a perfectly competitive firm to advertise its products. Recall that the perfectly competitive firm sells a homogeneous product and can sell all it wants at the market price—so why spend money to advertise to encourage consumers to buy more of its product? Why do some firms advertise? The reason is simple: By advertising, firms hope to increase the demand and create a less elastic demand curve for their products, thus enhancing revenues and profits. In short, this is how monopolistically competitive firms can differentiate their products to appeal to consumers. Advertising is part of our life, whether we are watching television, listening to the radio, reading a newspaper or magazine, or simply driving down the highway. Firms that sell highly differentiated consumer products such as soft drinks, toothpaste, razor blades, and breakfast cereals can spend between 10 and 20 percent of their revenue on advertising. However, firms that sell homogenous goods, such as wheat, rarely spend anything promoting their brands. The purpose of advertising is to sell more of the good at

Sometimes firms will try to convince consumers through advertising that their products are actually different. Dasani (Coca Cola) and Aquafina (Pepsi) are both bottled waters that consumers may think is bottled at the base of some pristine mountain range. In fact, both bottled waters fill up at the tap from the local water supply and then go through a rigorous filtering process that removes everything, even the natural minerals. Since many consumers believe tap water is unsafe, they purchase bottled water, even though most bottled waters are not federally regulated, as is tap water.

© ISTOCKPHOTO.COM/JFMDESIGN

USE WHAT YOU'VE LEARNED

Advertising

Q Why is it so important for monopolistically competitive firms to advertise?

A Owners of fast-food restaurants must compete with many other restaurants, so they often must advertise to demonstrate that their restaurant is different. Advertising may convince customers that a firm's products or services are better than others, which then may influence the shape and position of the demand curve for the products and potentially increase profits. Remember, monopolistically competitive firms are different from competitive firms because of their ability, to some extent, to set prices.

the going price. In perfect competition, the firm can sell all it wants at the going price. So perfectly competitive firms have no incentive to spend money on advertising. Only firms that have market power, and so charge a price above marginal cost, have an incentive to advertise in order to increase profits. Advertising to differentiate products is also important in oligopoly, as we will see in the next chapter.

14.4b Is Advertising "Good" or "Bad" from Society's Perspective?

What Is the Impact of Advertising on Society?

Isn't advertising wasteful to society?

This question elicits sharply different responses. Some have argued that advertising manipulates consumer tastes and wastes billions of dollars annually creating "needs" for trivial products. Critics argue that most advertising is psychological, trying to manipulate people's tastes, rather than informational. Advertising helps create a demonstration effect, whereby people have new urges to buy products previously unknown to them and perhaps creating a desire that may not have existed. Moreover, sometimes advertising is based on misleading claims, so people find themselves buying products that do not provide the satisfaction or results promised in the ads. Furthermore, increasing the perception of greater product differentiation and creating brand loyalty may make the demand curve for the product less elastic. Hence, a firm could charge a higher price over marginal cost, potentially leading to greater inefficiencies. Finally, advertising itself requires resources that raise average costs and increase prices.

© MAXIM BLINKOV/SHUTTERSTOCK.COM

If advertisers can convince potential customers there are really substantial differences between Burton and K2 snowboards, there are profits to be made.

On the other hand, who is to say that the purchase of any product is frivolous or unnecessary? If one believes that people are rational and should be permitted freedom of expression, the argument against advertising loses some of its force. In addition, advertisers might be focusing in on what consumer's want rather than what producers want to sell.

Furthermore, defenders of advertising argue that firms use advertising to provide important information about the price and availability of a product, the location and hours of store operation, and so on. For example, a real estate ad might state when a rental unit is available, the location, the price, the number of bedrooms and bathrooms, and proximity to mass transit, freeways, or schools. This information allows for customers to make better choices and allows markets to function more efficiently.

In addition, advertising allows consumers to be more aware of all the firms in the market and the differences in the prices they charge, which may reduce firms' market power. Advertising may also make it easier for firms to enter a market because it allows new entrants a means for attracting customers from existing firms.

Advertising as a Signal of Quality

An expensive ad on television or in the telephone book may *signal* to consumers that this product may come from a relatively large and successful company. The same is true when ads feature famous celebrities. Most people realize the celebrity does not know much about the product. However, the celebrity endorsement and expensive advertising may send a signal that this is a quality product.

Finally, a nationally recognized *brand name* will provide consumers with confidence about the quality of its product. It will also distinguish its product from others. For example, brand names such as Ritz-Carlton, Double Tree, or Motel 6 will provide the buyer with information about the quality of the accommodations more so than the No-Tell Motel. Or consider a national chain restaurant such as McDonald's or Burger King versus the Greasy Spoon Coffee Shop—consumers expect consistent quality from a chain restaurant. The chain name may also send a *signal* to the buyer that the company expects repeat business, and therefore it has an important reputation to uphold. This aspect may help it assume even greater quality in the consumers' eyes.

What If Advertising Increases Competition?

The idea that advertising reduces information costs leads to some interesting economic implications. For example, say that as a result of advertising, we know about more products that may be substitutes for the products we have been buying for years. That is, the more goods that are advertised, the more consumers are aware of "substitute" products, which leads to increasingly competitive markets. Studies in the eyeglass, toy, and drug industries have shown that advertising increases competition and leads to lower prices in these markets. In short, critics argue that advertising impedes competition, alters consumers' tastes, and may lead to "irrational" brand loyalty. But defenders believe it can increase competition and quality and often provides valuable product and service information.

SECTION QUIZ

1. If Rolf wants to use advertising to reduce the elasticity of demand for his chiropractic services, he must make sure the advertising

   a. clearly states the prices he charges.

   b. shows that he is producing a product like that of the other chiropractors in town.

   c. shows why his services are truly different from the other chiropractors in town.

   d. explains the hours and days that he is open for business.

2. Which of the following is (are) true about advertising?

   a. Expensive advertising may signal quality to consumers.

   b. A nationally recognized *brand name* will provide consumers with confidence about the quality of its product.

   c. Celebrity endorsements may send a signal that this is a quality product.

   d. All of the above are true.

(continued)

SECTION QUIZ (cont.)

3. Advertising

   a. is an important nonprice method of competition.

   b. is commonly used where firms have market power.

   c. makes no sense for a perfectly competitive firm.

   d. All of the above are true of advertising.

4. Advertising is intended to _____ a firm's demand curve and make it _____ elastic.

   a. increase; more

   b. increase; less

   c. decrease; more

   d. decrease; less

---

1. How can advertising make a firm's demand curve more inelastic?

2. What are the arguments made against advertising?

3. What are the arguments made for advertising?

Answers: 1. c 2. d 3. d 4. b

INTERACTIVE SUMMARY

Fill in the blanks:

1. Monopolistic competition is similar to both _____ and perfect competition. As in monopoly, firms have some control over market _____, but as in perfect competition, they face _____ from many other sellers.

2. Due to the free entry of new firms, long-run economic profits in monopolistic competition are _____.

3. Firms in monopolistic competition produce products that are _____ from those produced by other firms in the industry.

4. In monopolistic competition, firms use _____ names to gain some degree of control over price.

5. The theory of monopolistic competition is based on three characteristics: (1) product _____, (2) many _____, and (3) free _____.

6. Product differentiation is the accentuation of _____ product qualities to develop a product identity.

7. Monopolistic competitive sellers are price _____ and they do not regard price as given by the market. Because products in the industry are slightly different, each firm faces a(n) _____ -sloping demand curve.

8. In the short run, equilibrium output is determined where marginal revenue equals marginal _____. The price is set equal to the _____ the consumer will pay for this amount.

9. When price is greater than average total costs, the monopolistic competitive firm will make an economic _____.

10. Barriers to entry do not protect monopolistic competitive firms in the _____ run. Economic profits will _____ new firms to the industry. Similarly, firms will leave when there are economic _____.

11. Long-run equilibrium in a monopolistic competitive industry occurs when the firm experiences _____ economic profits or losses, which eliminates incentive for firms to _____ or _____ the industry.

12. Because it faces competition, a monopolistically competitive firm has a(n) _____ -sloping demand curve that tends to be more _____ than the demand curve for a monopolist.

13. Even in the long run, monopolistically competitive firms do not operate at levels that permit the full realization of _____ of scale.

14. Unlike a perfectly competitive firm in long-run equilibrium, a monopolistically competitive firm will produce with _____ capacity. The firm could lower average costs by increasing output, but this move would reduce _____.

15. In monopolistic competition the tendency is toward too _____ firms in the industry. Monopolistically competitive industries will not reach _____ efficiency because firms in the industry do not produce at the _____ per-unit cost.

16. In monopolistic competition, firms operate where price is _____ than marginal cost, which means that consumers are willing to pay _____ for the product than it costs society to produce it. In this case, the firm fails to reach _____ efficiency.

17. Although average costs and prices are higher under monopolistic competition than they are under perfect competition, society gets a benefit from monopolistic competition in the form of _____ products.

18. Advertising is an important type of _____ competition that firms use to _____ the demand for their products.

19. Advertising may not only increase the demand facing a firm, it may also make the demand facing the firm more _____ if it convinces buyers the product is truly different. A more inelastic demand curve means price changes will have relatively _____ effects on the quantity demanded of the product.

20. Critics of advertising assert that it _____ average total costs while manipulating consumers' tastes. However, if people are _____, this argument loses some of its force.

21. An important function of advertising is to lower the cost of acquiring _____ about the availability of substitutes and the _____ of products.

22. By making information about substitutes and prices less costly to acquire, advertising will increase the _____ in industries, which is good for consumers.

Answers: 1. monopoly; price; competition 2. zero 3. differentiated 4. brand 5. differentiation; sellers; entry 6. unique 7. makers; negatively 8. cost; maximum 9. profit 10. long; attract; losses 11. zero; enter; exit 12. downward; elastic 13. economies 14. excess; profits 15. many; productive; lowest 16. greater; more; allocative 17. differentiated 18. nonprice; increase 19. inelastic; smaller 20. raises; rational 21. information; prices 22. competition

monopolistic competition 394   product differentiation 395   excess capacity 402

SECTION QUIZ ANSWERS

14.1   Monopolistic Competition

1. How is monopolistic competition a mixture of monopoly and perfect competition?

Monopolistic competition is like monopoly in that sellers' actions can change the price. It is like competition in that it is characterized by competition from substitute products, many sellers, and relatively free entry.

2. Why is product differentiation necessary for monopolistic competition?

Product differentiation is the source of the monopoly power each monopolistically competitive seller (a monopolist of its own brand) has. If products were homogeneous, others' products would be perfect substitutes for the products of any particular firm, and such a firm would have no market power as a result.

3. What are some common forms of product differentiation?

Forms of product differentiation include physical differences, prestige differences, location differences, and service differences.

4. Why are many sellers necessary for monopolistic competition?

Many sellers are necessary in the monopolistic competition model because it means that a particular firm has little control over what other firms do; with only a few firms in an industry, they would begin to consider competitors as individuals (rather than only as a group) whose policies will be influenced by their own actions.

5. Why is free entry necessary for monopolistic competition?

Free entry is necessary in the monopolistic competition model because entry in this type of market is what tends to eliminate economic profits in the long run, as in perfect competition.

14.2   Price and Output Determination in Monopolistic Competition

1. What is the short-run profit-maximizing policy of a monopolistically competitive firm?

A monopolistic competitor maximizes its short-run profits by producing the quantity (and corresponding price along the demand curve) at which marginal revenue equals marginal cost.

2. How is the choice of whether to operate or shut down in the short run the same for a monopolistic competitor as for a perfectly competitive firm?

Because a firm will lose its fixed costs if it shuts down, it will shut down if price is expected to remain below average variable cost, regardless of market structure, because operating in that situation results in even greater losses than shutting down.

3. How is the long-run equilibrium of monopolistic competition like that of perfect competition?

The long-run equilibrium of monopolistic competition is like that of perfect competition in that firms enter when the industry makes short-run economic profits and exit when it makes short-run economic losses, which drives economic profits to zero in the long run.

4. How is the long-run equilibrium of monopolistic competition different from that of perfect competition?

For zero economic profits in long-run equilibrium at the same time each seller faces a downward-sloping demand curve, a firm's downward-sloping demand curve must be just tangent to its average cost curve (because that is the situation where a firm earns zero economic profits and that is the best the firm can do), resulting in costs greater than the minimum possible average cost. This same tangency to long-run cost curves characterizes the long-run zero economic profit equilibrium in perfect competition. Because firms' demand curves are horizontal in perfect competition, that tangency comes at the minimum point of firm average cost curves.

14.3   Monopolistic Competition versus Perfect Competition

1. Why is a monopolistic competitor's demand curve relatively elastic (flat)?

A monopolistic competitor has a downward-sloping demand curve because of product differentiation, but because of the large number of good substitutes for its product, its demand curve is very elastic.

2. Why do monopolistically competitive firms produce at less than the efficient scale of production?

Because monopolistically competitive firms have downward-sloping demand curves, their long-run zero-profit equilibrium tangency between demand and long-run average total cost must occur along the downward-sloping part of the long-run average total cost curve. Because this level of output does not allow the full realization of all economies of scale, it results in a less-than-efficient scale of production.

3. Why do monopolistically competitive firms operate with excess capacity?

Monopolistically competitive firms operate with excess capacity because the zero-profit tangency equilibrium occurs along the downward-sloping part of a firm's short-run average cost curve, so the firm's plant has the capacity to produce more output at lower average cost than it is actually producing.

4. Why does the fact that price exceeds marginal cost in monopolistic competition lead to allocative inefficiency?

The fact that price exceeds marginal cost in monopolistic competition leads to allocative inefficiency because some goods for which the marginal value (measured by willingness to pay along a demand curve) exceeds their marginal cost are not traded and the net gains that would have resulted from those trades are therefore lost. However, the degree of that inefficiency is relatively small because firms face a very elastic demand curve so the resulting output restriction is small.

5. What is the price we pay for differentiated goods under monopolistic competition?

Under monopolistic competition, excess capacity can be considered the price we pay for differentiated goods because it is the "cost" we pay for the value we get from the additional choices and variety offered by differentiated products.

6. Why is the difference between the long-run equilibriums under perfect competition and monopolistic competition likely to be relatively small?

Even though monopolistically competitive firms face downward-sloping demand curves, which is the cause of the excess capacity and higher than necessary costs

in these markets, those demand curves are likely to be highly elastic because of the large number of close substitutes. Therefore, the deviation from perfectly competitive results is likely to be relatively small.

14.4 Advertising

1. How can advertising make a firm's demand curve more inelastic?

Advertising is intended to increase a firm's demand curve by increasing consumer awareness of the firm's products and improving its image. It is intended to make its demand curve more inelastic by convincing buyers that its products are truly different (better) than alternatives (remember that the number of good substitutes is the primary determinant of a firm's elasticity of demand).

2. What are the arguments made against advertising?

Some people argue that advertising manipulates consumer tastes and creates artificial "needs" for unimportant products, taking resources away from more valuable uses.

3. What are the arguments made for advertising?

The essential argument for advertising is that it conveys valuable information to potential customers about the products and options available to them and the prices at which they are available, helping them to make choices that better match their situations and preferences. Advertising allows consumers to be more aware of all the firms in the market and the differences in the prices they charge. This may lead to firms having less market power. Advertising may also make it easier for firms to enter a market because it allows new entrants a means for attracting customers from existing firms.

PROBLEMS

1. Which of the following markets are perfectly competitive or monopolistically competitive? Why?
   a. Soy market
   b. Retail clothing stores
   c. Spago's Restaurant Beverly Hills

2. List three ways in which a grocery store might differentiate itself from its competitors.

3. What might make you choose one gas station over another?

4. If Frank's hot dog stand was profitable when he first opened, why should he expect those profits to fall over time?

5. Draw a graph showing a monopolistically competitive firm in a short-run equilibrium where it is earning positive economic profits. What must be true of price versus average total cost for such a firm? What will happen to the firm's demand curve as a result of the short-run profits?

6. Draw a graph showing a monopolistically competitive firm in a short-run equilibrium where it is earning economic losses. What must be true of price versus average total cost for such a firm? What will happen to the firm's demand curve as a result of the short-run losses?

7. How are monopolistically competitive firms and perfectly competitive firms similar? Why don't monopolistically competitive firms produce the same output in the long run as perfectly competitive firms, which face similar costs?

8. Can you explain why some restaurants are highly profitable while other restaurants in the same general area are going out of business?

9. Suppose that half the restaurants in a city are closed so that the remaining eateries can operate at full capacity. What "cost" might restaurant patrons incur as a result?

10. How is price related to marginal and average total cost for monopolistically competitive firms in the following situations?
    a. A short-run equilibrium where it is earning positive economic profits
    b. A short-run equilibrium where it is earning negative economic profits
    c. A short-run equilibrium where it is earning zero economic profits
    d. A long-run equilibrium

11. What is meant by the price of variety? Graph and explain.

12. How does Starbucks differentiate its product? Why does Starbucks stay open until late at night but a donut or bagel shop might close at noon?

13. How are monopolistically competitive firms and perfectly competitive firms similar? Why don't monopolistically competitive firms produce the same output in the long run as perfectly competitive firms, which face similar costs?

14. Why is advertising more important for the success of chains such as Toys "R" Us and Office Depot than for the corner barbershop?

15. Think of your favorite ads on television. Do you think that these ads have an effect on your spending? These ads are expensive; do you think they are a waste from society's standpoint?

16. Product differentiation is a hallmark of monopolistic competition, and the text lists four sources of such differentiation: physical differences, prestige, location, and service. How do firms in the industries listed here differentiate their products? How important is each of the four sources of differentiation in each case? Give the most important source of differentiation in each case.
    a. Fast-food restaurants
    b. Espresso shops/carts
    c. Hairstylists
    d. Soft drinks
    e. Wine

17. As you know, perfect competition and monopolistic competition differ in important ways. Show your understanding of these differences by listing the following terms under either "perfect competition" or "monopolistic competition."

		Perfect Competition	Monopolistic Competition
standardized product	productive efficiency	_____	_____
differentiated product	horizontal demand curve	_____	_____
allocative efficiency	downward-sloping demand curve	_____	_____
excess capacity	no control over price	_____	_____

18. In what way is the use of advertising another example of Adam Smith's "Invisible Hand," according to which entrepreneurs pursuing their own best interest make consumers better off?

19. How does advertising intend to shift demand? How does it intend to change the elasticity of demand?

Oligopoly and Strategic Behavior

Did you know that four companies—Apple, Dell, Hewlett-Packard, and Acer—account for more than 75 percent of all the laptops and desktops sold in the United States? This is what economists call a highly concentrated market. When a market is made up of a few sellers, it is called an oligopoly. Why are there so few competitors in industries such as computers, breakfast cereal, discount stores, and cigarettes? The answer is that barriers to entry are high, primarily due to economies of scale.

Oligopoly is a market structure where a few large firms dominate an industry. Other examples of oligopolistic markets

include commercial airlines, oil, automobiles, steel, breakfast cereals, and sports drinks. In all of these instances, the market is dominated by anywhere from a few to several big companies, although they may have many different brands (e.g., General Motors, General Foods, Apple Inc.). In this chapter, we will learn about the unique characteristics of firms in this industry.

15.1 Oligopoly

▶ What is oligopoly?

▶ What is mutual interdependence?

▶ Are economies of scale a major barrier to entry?

▶ Why is it so difficult for the oligopolist to determine its profit-maximizing price and output?

15.1a What Is Oligopoly?

Oligopolies exist, by definition, where relatively few firms control all or most of the production and sale of a product ("oligopoly" = few sellers). The products may be homogeneous (like oil or steel) or differentiated (like automobiles or breakfast cereals), but the barriers to entry are often high, which makes it difficult for firms to enter into the industry. Consequently, long-run economic profits may be earned by firms in the industry.

15.1b Mutual Interdependence

mutual interdependence
when a firm shapes its policy with an eye to the policies of competing firms

Oligopoly is characterized by **mutual interdependence** among firms; that is, each firm shapes its policy with an eye to the policies of competing firms. Oligopolists must strategize, much like good chess or bridge players who are constantly observing and anticipating the moves of their rivals. Oligopoly is likely to occur whenever the number of firms in an industry is so small that any change in output or price by one firm appreciably impacts the sales of competing firms. In this situation, it is almost inevitable that competitors will respond directly to these actions in determining their own policy.

15.1c Why Do Oligopolies Exist?

Primarily, oligopoly is a result of the relationship between the technological conditions of production and potential sales volume. For many products, a firm cannot obtain a reasonably low cost of production unless it is producing a large fraction of the market output. In other words, substantial economies of scale are present in oligopoly markets. Automobile and steel production are classic examples of this. Because of legal concerns such as patents, large start-up costs, and the presence of pronounced economies of scale, the barriers to entry are quite high in oligopoly.

15.1d Measuring Industry Concentration

How do you determine if an industry is an oligopoly?

The extent of oligopoly power in various industries can be measured by means of concentration ratios. A concentration ratio indicates the sales of the largest firms in the industry as a percentage of that industry's total sales. We can use four-firm or eight-firm concentration ratios; most often, concentration ratios are for the four largest firms.

The extent of oligopoly power is indicated by the four-firm concentration ratios for the United States shown in Exhibit 1. For example, in wireless telecommunications, the four largest firms, Verizon, AT&T, Sprint Nextel and T-Mobile have sales that are 94.7% of that

section 15.1 exhibit 1	Four-Firm Concentration Ratios, U.S. Industries				
Search Engines	**Arcade, Food & Entertainment Complexes**	**Wireless Telecommunications Carriers**	**Satellite TV Providers**	**Soda Production**	
Top four market share: 98.5%	Top four market share: 96.2%	Top four market share: 94.7%	Top four market share: 94.5%	Top four market share: 93.7%	
Major companies:	Major companies:	Major companies:	Major companies:	Major companies:	
Google: 64.1%	CEC (Chuck E Cheese) Entertainment Inc.: 52.2%	Verizon Wireless: 36.5%	DirecTV: 57.6%	The Coca-Cola Company: 41.2%	
Yahoo: 18.0%	Dave & Buster's: 35.0%	AT&T Inc.: 32.1%	Dish Network: 36.9%	PepsiCo: 33.6%	
Microsoft: 13.6%		Sprint Nextel Corporation: 15.4%		Dr Pepper Snapple Group: 15.4%	
		T-Mobile USA: 10.7%			

Sanitary Paper Product Manufacturing	**Food Service Contractors**	**Lighting & Bulb Manufacturing**	**Tire Manufacturing**	**Major Household Appliance Manufacturing**
Top four market share: 92.7%	Top four market share: 93.2%	Top four market share: 91.9%	Top four market share: 91.3%	Top four market share: 90.0%
Major companies:	Major companies:	Major companies:	Major companies:	Major companies:
Kimberly-Clark Corporation: 35.5%	Compass Group: 32.8%	General Electric Company: 32.9%	The Goodyear Tire & Rubber Company: 39%	Whirlpool Corporation: 43.8%
Proctor & Gamble: 30.0%	Aramark: 28.3%	Koninklijke Philips Electronics NV: 31.7%	Michelin North America: 28.2%	AB Electrolux: 20.7%
Georgia-Pacific: 27.2%	Sodexo: 25.6%	Siemens AG: 27.3%	Copper Tire & Rubber Company: 12.5%	General Electric Company: 17.1%
	Delaware North: 6.5%		Bridgestone: 11.6%	LG Electronics: 9.2%

SOURCE: *Highly Concentrated: Companies That Dominate Their Industries*, www.IBISworld.com, Special Report, February 2012.

industry's total sales. Concentration ratios of 70 to 100 percent are common in oligopolies. That is, a high concentration ratio means that a few sellers dominate the market.

Concentration ratios, however, are not a perfect guide to industry concentration. One problem is that they do not take into consideration foreign competition. For example, the U.S. auto industry is highly concentrated but faces stiff competition from foreign automobile producers. The same is true for motorcycles and bicycles.

15.1e **Economies of Scale as a Barrier to Entry**

Economies of large-scale production make operation on a small scale during a new firm's early years extremely unprofitable. A firm cannot

FLOTO & WARNER/GETTY IMAGES

Do you think economies of scale are important in this industry? Unlike home-cooked meals, few cars are "homemade." The barriers to entry in the auto industry are formidable. A new entrant would have to start out as a large producer (investing billions of dollars in plant, equipment, and advertising) to compete with existing firms, which have lower average total costs per unit because of economies of large-scale production.

section 15.1
exhibit 2 **Economies of Scale as a Barrier to Entry**

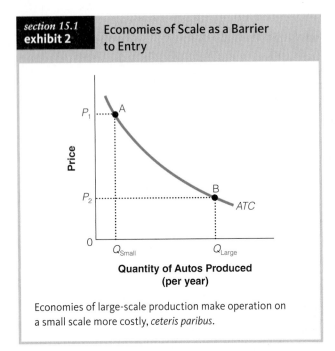

Economies of large-scale production make operation on a small scale more costly, *ceteris paribus*.

build up a large market overnight; in the interim, average total cost is so high that losses are heavy. Recognition of this fact discourages new firms from entering the market, as illustrated in Exhibit 2. We can see that if an automobile company produces quantity Q_{Large} rather than Q_{Small}, it will be able to produce cars at a significantly lower cost. If the average total cost to a potential entrant is equivalent to point A on the *ATC* curve and the price of automobiles is less than P_1, a new firm would be deterred from entering the industry.

15.1f Other Barriers to Entry

As in a monopoly, barriers to entry can also include government regulations and control over important inputs.

Firms sometimes can get government to impose barriers to entry. Many large firms will employ lobbyists to convince members of Congress to pass favorable legislation for the firm. Other government activities include granting patents, imposing tariffs (taxing foreign goods) and quotas (restricting the amount of foreign goods that can be legally imported), and restricting competition through government licensing. Occupational licensing (like that for doctors and dentists and roughly 300 hundred other occupations) restricts competition and raises wages for those in the protected industries. The justification usually cited for the laws is to ensure quality, but the increase in quality comes at a higher price.

Finally, the oligopolist might have control over an important input. As we discussed in Chapter 13, "Monopoly and Antitrust," De Beers at one time had control over most of the world's diamond mines. For many years, Alcoa, the world's largest aluminum producer, had control over the mineral bauxite, the raw material used to produce aluminum. Ocean Spray controls most of the high-quality cranberry bogs.

In short, the chemicals, electronics, and aluminum industries have possessed important barriers to entry because of patents or control over important inputs.

15.1g Equilibrium Price and Quantity in Oligopoly

It is difficult to predict how firms will react in situations of mutual interdependence. No firm knows what its demand curve looks like with any degree of certainty, and therefore it has a limited knowledge of its marginal revenue curve. To know anything about its demand curve, the firm must know how other firms will react to its prices and other policies. In the absence of additional assumptions, then, equating marginal revenue and expected marginal cost is relegated to guesswork. Thus, it is difficult for an oligopolist to determine its profit-maximizing price and output.

SECTION QUIZ

1. Which of the following is *not* a characteristic of oligopoly?

   a. A few firms control most of the production and sale of a product.

   b. Firms in the industry make price and output decisions with an eye to the decisions and policies of other firms in the industry.

   c. Competing firms can enter the industry easily.

   d. Substantial economies of scale are present in production.

2. Under oligopoly, a few large firms control most of the production and sale of a product because

   a. economies of scale make it difficult for small firms to compete.

   b. diseconomies of scale make it difficult for small firms to compete.

   c. average total costs rise as production expands.

   d. marginal costs rise as production expands.

3. In an oligopoly such as the U.S. domestic airline industry, a firm such as United Airlines would

   a. carefully anticipate Delta, JetBlue, and Southwest's likely responses before it raised or lowered fares.

   b. pretty much disregard Delta, JetBlue, and Southwest's likely responses when raising or lowering fares.

   c. charge the lowest fare possible in order to maximize market share.

   d. schedule as many flights to as many cities as possible without regard to what competitors do.

4. During the 1950s, many profitable manufacturing industries in the United States, such as steel, tires, and autos, were considered oligopolies. Why do you think such firms work hard to keep imports from other countries out of the U.S. market?

   a. Without import barriers, excess profits in the United States would attract foreign firms, break down existing price agreements, and reduce profits of U.S. firms.

   b. Without import barriers, foreign firms would be attracted to the United States and cause the cost in the industry to rise.

   c. Without import barriers, foreign firms would buy U.S. goods and resell them in the United States, causing profits to fall.

   d. Without import barriers, prices of goods would rise, so consumers would buy less of the products of these firms.

5. Which of the following are barriers to entry in oligopoly?

   a. Economies of scale

   b. Controlling an important input

   c. A patent

   d. All of the above

---

1. How can concentration ratios indicate the extent of oligopolies' power?

2. Why is oligopoly characterized by mutual interdependence?

3. Why do economies of scale result in few sellers in oligopoly models?

4. How do economies of scale result in barriers to entry in oligopoly models?

5. Why does an oligopolist have a difficult time finding its profit-maximizing price and output?

6. Why would an automobile manufacturer be more likely than the corner baker to be an oligopolist?

Answers: 1. c 2. a 3. a 4. a 5. d

15.2   Collusion and Cartels

▶ Why do firms collude?

▶ What is joint profit maximization?

▶ Why does collusion break down?

collusion
when firms act together to restrict competition

cartel
a collection of firms that agree on sales, pricing, and other decisions

joint profit maximization
determination of price based on the marginal revenue derived from the market demand schedule and marginal cost schedule of the firms in the industry

Why do firms collude?

15.2a Uncertainty and Pricing Decisions

Because each firm is interdependent, the behavior of an individual firm is difficult to predict. The firm is aware that if it changes the price, the quality, or the output, its rival is likely to react. In oligopoly, each firm can influence the price and its rival's behavior. Hence, the oligopolist's profit-maximizing decision is much more difficult than those in perfect competition or monopoly. The oligopolist who fails to accurately predict its rival behavior will lose profits.

15.2b Collusion

Because the actions and profits of oligopolists are so dominated by mutual interdependence, the temptation is great for firms to collude—to get together and agree to act jointly in pricing and other matters. If firms believe they can increase their profits by coordinating their actions, they will be tempted to collude. Collusion reduces uncertainty and increases the potential for economic profits. From society's point of view, collusion creates a situation in which goods very likely become overpriced and underproduced, with consumers losing out as the result of a misallocation of resources.

section 15.2
exhibit 1   Collusion in Oligopoly

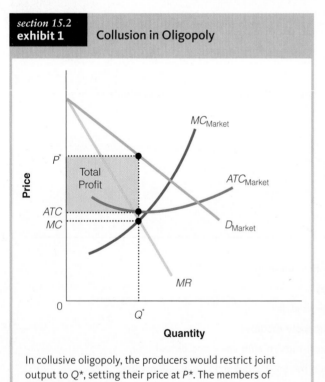

In collusive oligopoly, the producers would restrict joint output to Q^*, setting their price at P^*. The members of the collusive oligopoly would share the profits in the shaded area.

15.2c Joint Profit Maximization

Agreements between or among firms on sales, pricing, and other decisions are usually referred to as cartel agreements. A cartel is a collection of firms making an agreement.

Cartels may lead to what economists call joint profit maximization: Price is based on the marginal revenue function, which is derived from the product's total (or market) demand schedule and the various firms' marginal cost schedules, as shown in Exhibit 1. With outright agreements—necessarily secret because of antitrust laws (in the United States, at least)—firms that make up the market will attempt to estimate demand and cost schedules and then set optimum price and output levels accordingly.

Equilibrium price and quantity for a collusive oligopoly are determined according to the intersection of the marginal revenue curve (derived from the market demand curve) and the horizontal sum of the short-run marginal cost curves for the oligopolists. As shown in Exhibit 1, the resulting equilibrium quantity is Q^* and the equilibrium price is P^*. Collusion facilitates joint profit maximization for the oligopoly. If the oligopoly is maintained in the long run, it charges a higher price, produces less output, and fails to maximize social welfare, relative to perfect competition, because $P^* > MC$ at Q^*.

The manner in which total profits are shared among firms in the industry depends in part on the relative costs and sales of the various firms. Firms with low costs and large supply capabilities will obtain the largest profits because they have greater bargaining power. Sales, in turn, may depend in large measure on consumer preferences for various brands if there is product differentiation. With outright collusion, firms may agree on market shares and the division of profits. The division of total profits will depend on the relative bargaining strength of each firm, influenced by its relative financial strength, ability to inflict damage (through price wars) on other firms if an agreement is not reached, ability to withstand similar actions on the part of other firms, relative costs, consumer preferences, and bargaining skills.

ECS

economic content standards

Collusion among buyers or sellers reduces the level of competition in a market. Collusion is more difficult in markets with large numbers of buyers and sellers.

15.2d **Why Are Most Collusive Oligopolies Short Lived?**

Collusive oligopolies are potentially highly profitable for participants but detrimental to society. Fortunately, most strong collusive oligopolies are rather short lived, for two reasons. First, in the United States and in some other nations, collusive oligopolies are strictly illegal under antitrust laws. Second, for collusion to work, firms must agree to restrict output to a level that will support the profit-maximizing price. At that price, firms can earn positive economic profits. Yet a great temptation is for firms to cheat on the agreement of the collusive oligopoly, and because collusive agreements are illegal, the other parties have no way to punish the offender. Why do they have a strong incentive to cheat? Because any individual firm could lower its price slightly and thereby increase sales and profits, as long as it goes undetected. Undetected price cuts could bring in new customers, including rivals' customers. In addition, nonprice methods of defection include better credit terms, rebates, prompt delivery service, and so on.

The more firms in a cartel, the more difficult it is for all the firms to reach consensus. A successful cartel will block new firms from entering to keep economic profits high.

IN THE NEWS

The Crash of an Airline Collusion

Mr. Crandall: I think it's dumb as @#$% for !@#$%* sake, . . . to sit here and pound the @#$% out of each other and neither one of us making a #!@ !$&* dime. I mean, you know, @!#$, what the @#$!, is the point of it.

Mr. Putnam: Do you have a suggestion for me?

Mr. Crandall: Yes, I have a suggestion for you. Raise your @#$&!$% fares 20 percent. I'll raise mine the next morning. . . . You'll make more money and I will, too.

Mr. Putnam: We can't talk about pricing!

Mr. Crandall: Oh @#$% we can talk about any @#$%&*# thing we want to talk about.

consider this:

At the time of this conversation, Crandall was the president of American Airlines and Putnam was the president of Braniff Airlines. According to the Sherman Antitrust Act, it is illegal for corporate leaders to talk about and propose price fixing with their competitors. Putnam turned the tapes of this conversation over to the Justice Department. After reviewing the tapes, the Justice Department ruled that attempts to fix prices could monopolize the airline industry. American Airlines promised they would not engage in this type of activity again.

SOURCE: Staff, "American Air Accused of Bid to Fix Prices," *The Wall Street Journal,* February 24, 1983, pp. 2, 23.

GLOBAL WATCH

The OPEC Cartel

The most spectacularly successful example of a collusive oligopoly able to earn monopoly-type profits is the Organization of Petroleum Exporting Countries (OPEC) cartel. Although organized in 1960, it only became successful as a collusive oligopoly in 1973.

OPEC began acting as a cartel in part because of political concern over U.S. support for Israel. For 20 years before 1973, the price of crude oil had hovered around $2 a barrel. In 1973, OPEC members agreed to quadruple oil prices in nine months; later price increases pushed the cost of a barrel of oil to more than $20 OPEC's share of total world oil output had steadily increased, from around 20 percent of total world output in the early 1940s to about 70 percent by 1973, when OPEC became an effective cartel. Prices then stabilized, falling in real terms (adjusted for inflation) between 1973 and 1978 as OPEC sought the profit-maximizing price and politics remained relatively calm. By the early 1980s, however, prices were approaching $40 per barrel.

From the mid-1980s to the mid-1990s, OPEC oil prices hovered around $20 per barrel because of increases in non-OPEC production and the uncertain willingness of key suppliers (such as Saudi Arabia) to restrict supply. Recall that members in a cartel are trying to raise the price of oil through a coordinated effort at reducing the quantity produced. The problem is that collectively OPEC members would like to maintain a high price, but individually each country would like to increase its production to increase its profits. Many OPEC members have cheated on their agreements.

This means OPEC now controls 75 percent of the world's proven oil reserves (but it only produces about 40 percent of the crude oil each year), giving it some clout as a cartel. However, it is not just OPEC. High oil prices still emerge because of growing world demand and the political instability in the Middle East. By July 2006, oil prices had reached $78 per barrel. Between 2004 and 2008, oil prices rose sharply because of growing world demand (in part due to increased demand from the fast-growing economies of China and India) and political instability in the Middle East. In early 2008, oil hit a record high of around $140 a barrel, but by the end of 2008, in the midst of a worldwide recession, the price of oil fell below $40, despite OPEC's attempts to keep prices higher.

However, by 2011, with an increase in worldwide demand and fears of Middle East supply disruptions, oil increased to over $100 a barrel. But by mid-2011, prices fell back under $100 a barrel after member countries of the International Energy Agency said they would release 60 million barrels of oil from emergency stockpiles and on concern that the United States and European economies are weakening. In recent years, oil prices have been determined more by the forces of supply and demand and less by OPEC's artificial restriction of production. The losers: OPEC oil-producing nations; the winners: consumers around the world.

SECTION QUIZ

1. One of the reasons that collusive oligopolies are usually short lived is that
   a. they are unable to earn economic profits in the long run.
   b. they do not set prices where marginal cost equals marginal revenue.
   c. they set prices below long-run average total costs.
   d. parties to the collusion often cheat on one another.

2. In a collusive oligopoly, joint profits are maximized when a price is set based on
   a. its own demand and cost schedules.
   b. the market demand for the product and the summation of marginal costs of the various firms.
   c. the price followers' demand schedules and the price leader's marginal costs.
   d. the price leader's demand schedule and the price followers' marginal costs.

(continued)

3. Over the past 20 years, Dominator, Inc., a large firm in an oligopolistic industry, has changed prices a number of times. Each time it does so, the other firms in the industry follow suit. Dominator, Inc., is a

   a. monopoly.

   b. perfect competitor.

   c. price leader.

   d. price follower.

4. Most strong collusive oligopolies are rather short lived because

   a. collusive oligopolies are strictly illegal under U.S. antitrust laws.

   b. there is a great temptation for firms to cheat on the agreement of the collusive oligopoly.

   c. Both (a) and (b) are true.

   d. None of the above is true.

1. Why are collusive agreements typically unstable and short lived?

2. Why is the temptation to collude greater when the industry's demand curve is more inelastic?

Answers: 1. d 2. b 3. c 4. c

- -

Other Oligopoly Models   15.3

▶ What is price leadership?

▶ What happens to the oligopolists' profits if entry is easy?

▶ How can existing firms deter potential entrants?

15.3a Price Leadership

Over time, an implied understanding may develop in an oligopoly market that a large firm is the price leader, sending a signal to competitors, perhaps through a press release, that they have increased their prices. This approach is not outright collusion because no formal cartel arrangement or formal meetings are used to determine price and output, but this is what is called tacit collusion. Any competitor that goes along with the pricing decision of the price leader is called a price follower.

Price leadership is most likely to develop when one firm, the so-called dominant firm, produces a large portion of the total output. The dominant firm sets the price that maximizes its profits and the smaller firms, which would have little influence over price anyway, act as if they are perfect competitors—selling all they want at that price. In the past, a number of firms have been price leaders: U.S. Steel and Bethlehem Steel, RJ Reynolds (tobacco), General Motors (automobiles), Kellogg's (breakfast cereals), and Goodyear (tires). In the banking industry, various dominant banks have taken turns being the dominant firm in announcing changes in the prime interest rate—the interest rate that banks charge large corporate clients. Because the prime rate is widely cited in newspapers, it makes it easy for other banks to follow the lead and avoid frequent changes and competitive warfare.

price leader
a large firm in an oligopoly that unilaterally makes changes in its product prices that competitors tend to follow

price follower
a competitor in an oligopoly that goes along with the pricing decision of the price leader

price leadership
when a dominant firm that produces a large portion of the industry's output sets a price that maximizes its profits, and other firms follow

What is a price leader?

15.3b What Happens in the Long Run if Entry Is Easy?

Mutual interdependence is, in itself, no guarantee of economic profits, even if the firms in the industry succeed in maximizing joint profits. The extent to which economic profits disappear depends on the ease with which new firms can enter the industry. When entry is easy, excess profits attract newcomers. New firms may break down existing price agreements by undercutting prices in an attempt to establish themselves in the industry. In response, older firms may reduce prices to avoid excessive sales losses; as a result, the general level of prices will begin to approach average total cost.

15.3c How Do Oligopolists Deter Market Entry?

If most firms reach a scale of plant and firm size great enough to allow lowest-cost operation, their long-run positions will be similar to that shown in Exhibit 1. To simplify, we have drawn MC and ATC constant. The equilibrium, or profit-maximizing, price in an established oligopoly is represented by P^*. Typically, the rate of profit in these industries is high, which would encourage entry. However, empirical research indicates that oligopolists often initiate pricing policies that reduce the entry incentive for new firms. Established firms may deliberately hold prices below the maximum profit point at P^*, charging a price of, say, P_1. This lower than profit-maximizing price may discourage newcomers from entering. Because new firms would likely have higher costs than existing firms, the lower price may not be high enough to cover their costs. However, once the threat of entry subsides, the market price may return to the profit-maximizing price, P^*.

15.3d Antitrust and Mergers

In the beginning of this chapter, we introduced a method for determining an industry's market structure called a concentration ratio. However, the Justice Department and the Federal Trade Commission (FTC) both prefer to use a measure called the Herfindahl-Hirshman Index (HHI). The HHI is measured by taking the square for each firm's share of market sales summed over the firms in the industry. For example, if the industry has three firms and their market share is 50 percent, 30 percent, and 20 percent, respectively, the HHI would be:

$$HHI = 50^2 + 30^2 + 20^2 = 3,800$$

By squaring, the HHI produces a much larger number when industry is dominated by a few firms. According to the Justice Department, an HHI below 1,000 is very competitive, an HHI between 1,000 and 1,800 is somewhat competitive, and an HHI over 1,800 indicates an oligopoly. The HHI takes into account the relative size and distribution of the firms in a market. The HHI is lowest when a market consists of a large number of firms of relatively equal size. The HHI increases both as the number of firms in the market decreases and as the disparity in size between those firms increases.

A potential merger resulting in an HHI over 1,000 will receive close scrutiny. In 2007, for example, Whole Foods made a takeover bid for Wild Oats. Both were organic grocery stores. The FTC argued that the takeover would increase prices and limit competition in the organic food market. Whole Foods argued that it competes with many grocery stores that carry healthy food and organic products.

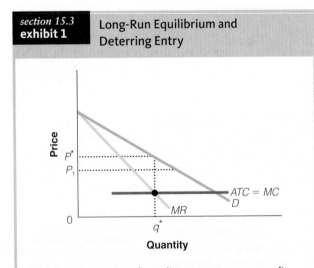

section 15.3 exhibit 1   Long-Run Equilibrium and Deterring Entry

With barriers to entry, oligopolists may earn excess profits in the long run. Theoretically, profit maximization occurs at P^* and q^* in the short run. Empirical work, however, suggests that oligopolists often actually charge a lower price than the short-run profit-maximizing price (such as P_1). This strategy discourages entry because newcomers may have costs higher than P_1.

The merger is still in appeal at the time of this writing. Another interesting case is the merger of Ticketmaster and Live Nation (see the In the News box).

Three Types of Mergers

There are three different types of mergers.

1. A *horizontal merger* combines firms that sell similar products; for example, if Motel 6 merges with Holiday Inn or GM merges with Chrysler.
2. A *vertical merger* combines firms at different stages of production; for example, Pepsi merged with Pizza Hut and Taco Bell. Similarly, a hotel chain may merge with a mattress company.
3. A *conglomerate merger* combines firms in different industries. For example, an automobile company might merge with a pharmaceutical company.

What is the difference between a horizontal merger and a vertical merger?

Since vertical mergers are not often a threat to competition, they are not usually subject to antitrust probes. They do not reduce competition in other markets. This is also true of conglomerate mergers—when an auto company merges with a pharmaceutical company, neither increases market share. Most of the problems occur with horizontal mergers. For example, an attempted merger between Office Depot and Staples was blocked.

15.3e **Antitrust and Pricing Strategies**

Most economists agree that price fixing should be illegal. However, there are antitrust laws that forbid other types of activities where the effects are not as obvious—predatory pricing, price discrimination, and tying.

Predatory Pricing

If the price is deliberately kept low (below average variable cost) to drive a competitor out of the market, it is called **predatory pricing**. However, both economists and the courts have a difficult time deciding whether or not the price is truly predatory or not. Even if the price is driven down below average variable cost (recall from Chapter 11, that when price is below *AVC* it is the shutdown point of a firm), the courts still have to determine whether the low price destroyed the rival and kept it out of business. And did the firm raise its price to the monopoly level once the rival had been driven out of the industry? Microsoft, American Airlines, and other companies have been accused of predatory pricing, but not convicted because it is so difficult to distinguish predatory pricing from vigorous competition.

predatory pricing
setting a price deliberately low in order to drive out competitors

15.3f **Price Discrimination**

Price discrimination, as we studied in Chapter 13, is a common pricing strategy for many businesses. It generally does not reduce competition unless it is part of a strategy to block entry or force a competitor out of the market; therefore, it is not normally challenged by antitrust authorities. However, it can be challenged under the Robinson-Patman Act, which places restrictions on allowable price discrimination.

15.3g **Tying**

Tie-in-sales *require* that a customer who buys one product (the tying good) must also buy another product (the tied good) that a customer needs to use the first product. Two companies that followed this practice were Xerox and IBM. When Xerox was the largest photocopier producer, they required companies that rented their machines to also buy paper from them. Similarly, IBM required that users of its computers buy IBM computer cards. IBM charged more for the computer cards than other firms would have charged.

IN THE NEWS

Ticketmaster and Live Nation Merger

Ticketmaster Entertainment and the world's largest concert promoter, Live Nation, completed a merger in January 2010. The new Live Nation Entertainment will own nearly 150 concert venues globally, sell over 140 million tickets a year, and promote over 20,000 concerts annually. The U.S. Justice Department required Ticketmaster to license its primary ticketing software to a competitor, sell off one ticketing unit, and agree to be barred from retaliating against venue owners who use a competing ticket service.

What is the purpose of the merger? According to Live Nation CEO Michael Rapino, "the idea here is merely to sell more tickets, more efficiently. As every industry observer knows, too many tickets go unsold and too many fans are frustrated with their ticket-buying experiences," he said, adding, "the better job we do of getting the right fan in the right

seat at the right time, the more money our clients are going to make."

SOURCE: Eliot Van Buskirk, "Live Nation, Ticketmaster Merger Risks Antitrust Scrutiny," *Wired*, February 10, 2009, http://www.wired.com/epicenter/2009/02/live-nation-tic/.

What is tying?

Antitrust authorities look for dominant firms that use types of pricing discrimination policies. For example, the Supreme Court ruled that studios could not force theaters to buy an entire package of films in order to get the rights to show a blockbuster movie. That is, tying a blockbuster movie together with a package of not-so-good B movies could allow studios to expand their market power. To economists, the "jury" is still out on whether various forms of price discrimination really impede competition.

USE WHAT YOU'VE LEARNED

Mutual Interdependence in Oligopoly

Q Suppose that Firm A is a member of a naive oligopoly, meaning that neither Firm A nor its competitors recognize the mutual interdependence that exists between them. Firm A decides to lower its price to capture a greater market share. What will happen to profits in this market in the long run?

A If an oligopolist believes that its rivals will not respond to pricing policies, it will expect to capture market share by reducing price. In response, rivals will cut prices as well, and if they do not understand the mutual interdependence among firms in oligopoly, they will attempt to undercut prices, as shown in Exhibit 2 in the movement from P_1 to P_2, and so on. This exchange would result in a price war, which could continue until economic profits were zero and price equaled average cost.

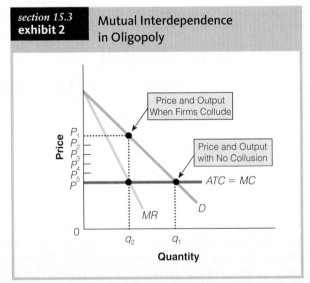

section 15.3 exhibit 2 — Mutual Interdependence in Oligopoly

15.3h **Is Oligopoly Efficient?**

Is oligopoly efficient from society's perspective? Does oligopoly meet the conditions for allocative efficiency, $P = MC$? Does oligopoly meet the condition for productive efficiency, $P = $ minimum ATC? Neither. Oligopolists often experience large economic profits year after year. This would imply that the price is greater than marginal cost and average total cost. So, unlike perfectly competitive markets, oligopoly fails to meet either allocative or productive efficiency.

However, oligopoly may be more competitive than what appears at first glance. One, there is a growing amount of foreign competition in the steel, automobile, and electronic industry, creating more competitive markets. Two, to the extent that limit pricing occurs, consumers may experience lower prices, as existing firms keep prices down to deter entry. And three, technological progress may be encouraged. Oligopolists will often sink their economic profits into research and development. This could lead to better products and improvements in production processes. That is, some of the inefficiencies of oligopoly may be offset by these other developments, which could lead to lower prices, better products, and lower costs of production over time.

SECTION QUIZ

1. Over the past 20 years, Dominator, Inc., a large firm in an oligopolistic industry, has changed prices a number of times. Each time it does so, the other firms in the industry follow suit. Dominator, Inc., is a

   a. monopoly.

   b. perfect competitor.

   c. price leader.

   d. price follower.

2. The Herfindahl-Hirshman Index (HHI) increases as the number of firms _____ or the disparity of firm sizes _____.

   a. increases; increases

   b. increases; decreases

   c. decreases; increases

   d. decreases; decreases

3. The Herfindahl-Hirshman Index (HHI) will increase the most in an industry when

   a. one large firm merges with another large firm.

   b. one large firm merges with a small firm.

   c. two small firms merge.

   d. a large firm separates into two firms.

4. Which kind of merger increases the HHI and thus triggers concerns about competitiveness?

   a. Horizontal mergers

   b. Vertical mergers

   c. Conglomerate mergers

   d. All of the above

---

1. What impact does easy entry have on the profitability of oligopolies?

2. Why are barriers to entry necessary for successful, ongoing collusion?

3. Why might oligopolists charge less than their short-run profit-maximizing price when threatened by entry?

(continued)

4. A group of colluding oligopolists incurs costs of $10 per unit, and their profit-maximizing price is $15. If they know that potential market entrants could produce at a cost of $12 per unit, what price are the colluders likely to charge?

5. Why is price leadership also called tacit collusion?

6. What two factors increase the Herfindahl-Hirshman Index (HHI)?

7. Why do horizontal mergers tend to concern antitrust authorities more than vertical or conglomerate mergers?

8. For someone to be engaged in predatory pricing, what must happen to prices after their predation? Why would potential entry undermine the strategy?

Answers: 1. c 2. c 3. a 4. a

15.4 | Game Theory and Strategic Behavior

▶ What is game theory?

▶ What are cooperative and noncooperative games?

▶ What is a dominant strategy?

▶ What is Nash equilibrium?

15.4a Some Strategies for Noncollusive Oligopolies

In some respects, noncollusive oligopoly resembles a military campaign or a poker game. Firms take certain actions not because they are necessarily advantageous in themselves but because they improve the position of the oligopolist relative to its competitors and may ultimately improve its financial position. For example, a firm may deliberately cut prices, sacrificing profits either to drive competitors out of business or to discourage them from undertaking actions contrary to the interests of other firms.

15.4b What Is Game Theory?

game theory
the study of strategic interactions among economic agents

Some economists have suggested that the entire approach to oligopoly equilibrium price and output should be recast. They replace the analysis that assumes that firms attempt to maximize profits with one that examines firm behavior in terms of a strategic game. This point of view, called game theory, stresses the tendency of various parties in such circumstances to act in a way that minimizes damage from opponents. This approach involves a set of alternative actions (with respect to price and output levels, for example); the action that would be taken in a particular case depends on the specific policies followed by each firm. The firm may try to figure out its competitors' most likely countermoves to its own policies and then formulate alternative defense measures.

Each firm will react to the price, quantity, and quality of rival firms. Because each firm is interdependent, each must observe the moves of its rivals.

15.4c Cooperative and Noncooperative Games

cooperative game
in this game, firms cooperate to increase their mutual payoff

Games, in interactions between oligopolists, can either be cooperative or noncooperative. An example of a cooperative game would be two firms that decide to collude in order to improve their profit-maximization position. However, as we discussed earlier, enforcement costs are usually too high to keep all firms from cheating on collusive agreements. Consequently, most games are **noncooperative games**, in which each firm sets its own price without consulting other firms. The primary difference between cooperative and noncooperative games is the contract. For example, players in a cooperative game can talk and set binding contracts, while those in noncooperative games are assumed to act independently, with no communication and no binding contracts. Because antitrust laws forbid firms to collude, we will assume that most strategic behavior in the marketplace is noncooperative.

15.4d The Prisoners' Dilemma

A firm's decision makers must map out a pricing strategy based on a wide range of information. They must also decide whether their strategy will be effective and whether it will be affected by competitors' actions. A strategy that will be optimal regardless of the opponents' actions is called a **dominant strategy**. A famous game that has a dominant strategy and demonstrates the basic problem confronting noncolluding oligopolists is known as the **prisoners' dilemma**.

Imagine that a bank robbery occurs and two suspects are caught. The suspects are placed in separate cells in the county jail and are not allowed to talk with each other. Four results are possible in this situation: both prisoners confess, neither confesses, Prisoner A confesses but Prisoner B doesn't, or Prisoner B confesses but Prisoner A doesn't. In Exhibit 1, we see the **payoff matrix**, which summarizes the possible outcomes from the various strategies. Looking at the payoff matrix, we can see that if each prisoner confesses to the crime, each will serve 6 years in jail. However, if neither confesses, each prisoner may only get one year because of insufficient evidence. Now, if Prisoner A confesses and Prisoner B does not, Prisoner A will go free (because of his cooperation with the authorities and his evidence) and Prisoner B will get 10 years. Alternatively, if Prisoner B confesses and Prisoner A does not, Prisoner B will go free and Prisoner A will get 10 years. As you can see, then, the prisoners have a dilemma. What should each prisoner do?

Looking at the payoff matrix, we can see that if Prisoner A confesses, it is in the best interest for Prisoner B to confess. If Prisoner A confesses, Prisoner B will get either 6 years or go free, depending on what Prisoner B does. However, Prisoner B knows the temptation to confess facing Prisoner A, so confessing is also the best strategy for Prisoner B. A confession would mean a lighter sentence for Prisoner B—6 years rather than 10 years.

It is clear that both would be better off confessing *if* they knew for sure that the other was going to remain silent because then they would go free. However, in each case, can the prisoner take the chance that the co-conspirator will not talk? The dominant strategy is the best strategy regardless of the strategy of others. In this case, the dominant strategy for Prisoner A is to confess because he would spend less time in jail regardless of whether Prisoner B confesses or remains silent. Confessing is also the dominant strategy for Prisoner B. That is, regardless of what Prisoner A does, Prisoner B can reduce his jail time by confessing. So, the prisoners know that confessing is the way to make the best of a bad situation. No matter what their counterpart does, the maximum sentence will be 6 years for each, and each understands the possibility of getting out free. In summary, when the prisoners follow their dominant strategy and confess, they will be worse off than if both had remained silent— hence, the "prisoners' dilemma."

That is, we see a conflict between group and individual rationality. When each prisoner independently pursues his or her own self-interest in this case, the two prisoners reach an outcome that is worse for both of them. Each prisoner knows that he will only have to serve one year if he can trust the other to not confess. But each also knows it is not in the best interest of the other to not confess. So each of the prisoners confesses.

noncooperative game

in this game, players do not cooperate but each pursues their individual self-interest

What is the difference between a cooperative and noncooperative game?

What is the prisoner's dilemma?

dominant strategy

strategy that will be optimal regardless of opponents' actions

prisoners' dilemma

a game in which pursuing dominant strategies results in non-cooperation and makes everyone worse off

payoff matrix

a summary of the possible outcomes of various strategies

A pitcher wants to throw a pitch that will surprise the batter. The batter knows that the pitcher wants to fool him. So what does the pitcher throw, knowing the batter expects the pitcher to fool him? Is this a game with strategic interaction?

STEPHEN MARKS/THE IMAGE BANK/GETTY IMAGES

section 15.4
exhibit 1   The Prisoners' Dilemma Payoff Matrix

		Prisoner B	
		Confesses	**Doesn't Confess**
Prisoner A	**Confesses**	6 years (A) — 6 years (B)	Goes free (A) — 10 years (B)
	Doesn't Confess	10 years (A) — Goes free (B)	1 year (A) — 1 year (B)

The sentence depends on the prisoner's decision to confess or remain silent and on the decision made by the other prisoner. When the prisoners follow their dominant strategy and confess, both will be worse off than if each had remained silent—hence, the "prisoners' dilemma."

What is a Nash equilibrium?

Firms in oligopoly often behave like the prisoners in the prisoners' dilemma, carefully anticipating the moves of their rivals in an uncertain environment. For example, should a firm cut its prices and try to gain more sales by luring customers away from its competitors? What if the firm keeps its price stable and competitors lower theirs? Or what if the firm and its competitors all lower their prices? What if all of the firms decide to raise their prices? Each of these situations will have vastly different implications for an oligopolist, so it must carefully watch and anticipate the moves of its competitors.

15.4e **Profits under Different Pricing Strategies**

To demonstrate how the prisoners' dilemma can shed light on oligopoly theory, let us consider the pricing strategy of two firms. In Exhibit 2, we present the payoff matrix—the possible profits that each firm would earn under different pricing strategies. Assume that each firm has total production costs of $1 per unit. When both firms set their price at $10 and each sells 1,000 units per week, then each earns a profit of $9,000 a week. If each firm sets its price at $9, each sells 1,100 units per week for a profit of $8,800 [($9 − $1) × 1,100]. However, what if one firm charges $10 and the other firm charges $9? The low-price firm increases its profits through additional sales. It now sells, say, 1,500 units for a profit of $12,000, while the high-price firm sells only 600 units per week for a profit of $5,400.

When the two firms each charge $9 per unit, they are said to have reached a Nash equilibrium (named after Nobel Prize–winning economist and mathematician John Nash). At a Nash equilibrium, each firm is said to be doing as well as it can *given the actions of its competitor*. For example, if each firm believes the other is going to charge $9, then the best strategy for both firms is to charge $9. In this scenario, if Firm A charges $9, the worst possible outcome is a profit of $8,800.

section 15.4
exhibit 2   The Profit Payoff Matrix

		Firm B's Pricing Strategy	
		Charge $10	**Charge $9**
Firm A's Pricing Strategy	**Charge $10**	(Firm A) $9,000 — (Firm B) $9,000	(Firm A) $5,400 — (Firm B) $12,000
	Charge $9	(Firm A) $12,000 — (Firm B) $5,400	(Firm A) $8,800 — (Firm B) $8,800

If both firms defect by lowering their prices from the level of joint profit maximization, both will be worse off than if they had colluded, but at least each will have minimized its potential loss if it cannot trust its competitor. This situation is the oligopolists' dilemma.

However, if Firm A prices at $10 and Firm B prices at $9, Firm A will have a profit of only $5,400. Hence, the choice that minimizes the risk of the worst scenario is $9. The same is true for Firm B; it too minimizes the risk of the worst scenario by choosing to price at the Nash equilibrium, $9. In this case, the Nash equilibrium is also the dominant strategy. The Nash equilibrium takes on particular importance because it is a self-enforcing equilibrium. That is, once this equilibrium is established, neither firm has an incentive to move.

In sum, we see that if the two firms were to collude and set their price at $10, it would be in their best interest. However, each firm has a strong incentive to lower its price to $9 if this pricing strategy goes undetected by its competitor. However, if both firms defect by lowering their prices from the level of joint profit maximization, both will be worse off than if they had colluded, but at least each will have minimized its potential loss if it cannot trust its competitor. This situation is the oligopolists' dilemma.

15.4f Advertising

Advertising can lead to a situation like the prisoners' dilemma. For example, perhaps the decision makers of a large firm are deciding whether to launch an advertising campaign against a rival firm. According to the payoff matrix in Exhibit 3, if neither company advertises, the two companies split the market, each making $100 million in profits. They also split the market if they both advertise, but their net profits are smaller, $75 million, because they would both incur advertising costs that are greater than any gains in additional revenues from advertising. However, if one advertises and the other does not, the company that advertises takes customers away from the rival. Profits for the company that advertises would be $125 million, and profits for the company that does not advertise would be $50 million.

The dominant strategy—the optimal strategy regardless of the rival's actions—is to advertise. In this game, both firms will choose to advertise, even though both would be better off if no one advertised. But one company can't take a chance and not advertise, because if its competitor then elects to advertise, the competitor could have a big year, primarily at the expense of the firm that doesn't advertise.

Arms Race

The arms race provides a classic example of the prisoners' dilemma. During the Cold War (mid-1940s to the early 1990s), the United States and the former Soviet Union were engaged in costly military expansion that hampered both economies. It exacted a greater toll on the

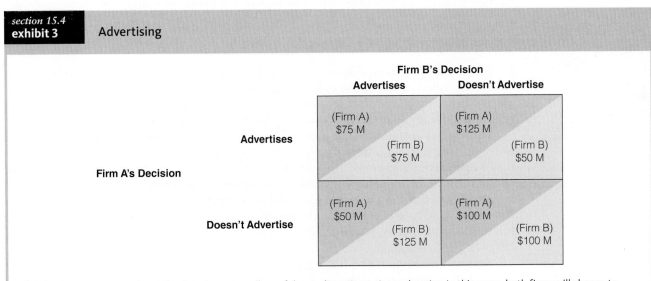

section 15.4 exhibit 3 Advertising

		Firm B's Decision	
		Advertises	**Doesn't Advertise**
Firm A's Decision	**Advertises**	(Firm A) $75 M / (Firm B) $75 M	(Firm A) $125 M / (Firm B) $50 M
	Doesn't Advertise	(Firm A) $50 M / (Firm B) $125 M	(Firm A) $100 M / (Firm B) $100 M

The dominant strategy—the optimal strategy regardless of the rival's actions—is to advertise. In this game, both firms will choose to advertise, even though both would be better off if no one advertised.

section 15.4 exhibit 4   Arms Race

		Country A	
		Spend More on Arms	**Spend Less on Arms**
Country B	**Spend More on Arms**	At risk (A) / At risk (B)	At risk (A) / Safe (B)
	Spend Less on Arms	Safe (A) / At risk (B)	Safe (A) / Safe (B)

For each country the dominant strategy is to build arms. Self-interest drives each participant into a noncooperative game that is worse for both.

Soviets because their economy was not as economically productive as the United States and may have ultimately led to the Soviets' decline. The United States' power was based on economic and military strength; the USSR's was based solely on military strength. Each country raced to produce more military goods than the other. Representatives from both sides would periodically meet to discuss arms reduction, but to no avail. Neither party was willing to risk losing its military superiority.

The dilemma was that each country wanted to achieve military superiority, and building more arms could make that possible, for a given level of arms spending by the other. Each would prefer less spending on the military but each rationally chose to spend more to avoid the risk of becoming militarily inferior. They were trapped in a spending war. Of course, negotiations to spend less would be the preferred outcome for both, if they could be assured the other party would not cheat.

As you can see in the payoff matrix in Exhibit 4, if Country A spends more money on arms, then Country B better do the same or risk military inferiority. If Country A chooses to spend less on arms, then Country B gains military superiority by not following. For each country, the dominant strategy is to build arms, which leads to an inferior outcome—a less safe world. This is similar to the collusion game we examined earlier where self-interest drives each participant to a noncooperative outcome that is worse for both parties.

15.4g **Repeated Games**

In the one-shot prisoners' dilemma game in Exhibit 1, we saw that the best strategy is to confess regardless of what your opponent does—your behavior does not influence the other player's behavior. In one-shot prisoners' dilemma games, self-interest prevents cooperative behavior and leads to an inferior joint outcome for the participants.

However, cooperation is not impossible because most oligopolistic interactions are not one-shot games. Instead, they are repeated games. Most firms assume that they will have repeat customers. For example, if a grocery store fails to provide fresh produce, customers can punish the store by shopping elsewhere in the future. These future consequences change the incentives from those in a one-shot game. All stores might have gained short-run profits from low-quality (and cost) produce, but all may offer high-quality produce because of the adverse future effects of offering lower-quality produce. In a repeated game, cooperation occurs as long as others continue to cooperate.

Suppose two firms are both going to be in business for many years. Several studies have shown that, in this type of situation, the best strategy is to do what your opponent did to you earlier. This type of response tends to elicit cooperation rather than competition. This form of strategic behavior is called a **tit-for-tat strategy**.

Why can a repeated game induce more cooperation than a one-shot game?

tit-for-tat strategy

strategy used in repeated games where one player follows the other player's move in the previous round; leads to greater cooperation

IN THE NEWS

The Game Theory of the Bar Scene Problem from *A Beautiful Mind*

The Problem

You and three male friends are at a bar trying to pick up women. Suddenly one blonde and four brunettes enter in a group. What's the individual strategy?

Here are the rules. Each of you wants to talk to the blonde. If more than one of you tries to talk to her, however, she will be put off and talk to no one. At that point it will also be too late to talk to a brunette, as no one likes being second choice. Assume anyone who starts out talking to a brunette will succeed.

The Movie

Nash suggests the group should cooperate. If everyone goes for the blonde, they block each other and no one wins. The brunettes will feel hurt as a second choice and categorically reject advances. Everyone loses.

But what if everyone goes for a brunette? Then each person will succeed, and everyone ends up with a good option.

It's a good thought, except for one question: what about the blonde?

The Equilibrium

The movie is directed so well that it sounds persuasive. But it's sadly incomplete. It misses the essence of noncooperative game theory.

A Nash equilibrium is a state where no one person can improve *given what others are doing*. This means you are picking the best possible action in response to others—the formal term is you are picking a *best response*.

As an example, let's analyze whether everyone going for a brunette is a Nash equilibrium. You are *given* that three of your friends go for brunettes. What is your best response?

You can either go for the brunette or the blonde. With your friends already going for brunettes, you have no competition to go for the blonde. The answer is clear that you would talk

DREAMWORKS/UNIVERSAL/THE KOBAL COLLECTION/REED, ELI

to the blonde. That's your best response. Incidentally, this is a Nash equilibrium. You are happy, and your friends cannot do better. If your friends try to talk to the blonde, they end up with nothing and give up talking to a brunette. So you see, when Nash told his friends to go for the brunettes in the movie, it really does sound like he was leaving the blonde for himself.

SOURCE: Presh Talwalkar, http://mindyourdecisions.com/blog/2008/03/10/game-theory-tuesdays-the-problem-from-a-beautiful-mind-buying-new-or-used/

A repeated game allows the firm to establish a reputation of cooperation. Cooperation may mean maintaining a high price or a certain advertising budget, provided that the other firm did the same in the previous round. In short, a firm has an incentive to cooperate now so there is greater cooperation in the future. However, if your opponent cheats, you cheat in the next round to punish your opponent for a lack of cooperation. You do what your opponent did in the previous round. In the tit-for-tat game, both firms will be better off if they stick to the plan rather than cheating—that is, failing to cooperate. Many cartels appear to employ the tit-for-tat strategy. In short, often the most effective strategy to promote cooperation is tit-for-tat.

15.4h Network Externalities

In our discussion of supply and demand (Chapter 4), we assumed that demand was a function of the price of the good (a change in quantity demanded) and the determinants of demand (the shifters that cause changes in demand). For example, the amount of ice cream we are

USE WHAT YOU'VE LEARNED

Nash at the Beach

Two ice cream vendors on the beach are selling identical ice cream at the same price. The demanders are uniformly distributed along the beach. To minimize transportation costs, each vendor might strategically set up at the 1/4-mile mark and 3/4-mile mark, each with an advantage of being halfway to its rival. However, the situation in Exhibit 5 is not a stable equilibrium because if vendor A thinks vendor B is going to stay put, then vendor A will move to the right, closer to vendor B, and capture three-fourths of the market, and vendor B will have the remaining one-fourth. Vendor B would then want to move to the left of vendor A. They would continue to leap-frog until they reached the center. That is, a Nash equilibrium will lead to both vendors locating in the middle—doing the best they can given what the competitor is doing.

Recall the discussion of the median voter model in Chapter 8, where the prediction was that the candidates will pick a political position in the middle of the distribution of voters. The ice cream vendor model helps us understand this phenomenon as well as why fast-food restaurants, car dealerships, and motels are often found in close proximity to each other.

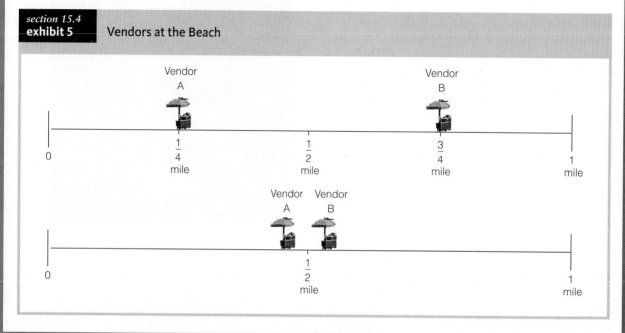

section 15.4
exhibit 5   Vendors at the Beach

---

network externality

when the number of other people purchasing the good influences quantity demanded

positive network externality

increase in a consumer's quantity demanded for a good because a greater number of other consumers are purchasing the good

negative network externality

increase in a consumer's demand for a good because fewer consumers are purchasing the same good

willing and able to buy is a function of the price of ice cream, the price of related goods (substitutes like yogurt and complements like hot fudge), income, the number of buyers, tastes, and expectations. However, we did not mention that for some goods, the quantity demanded depends on how many other people purchase the good. This factor is called a network externality. A positive network externality occurs when a consumer's quantity demanded for a good increases because a greater number of consumers purchase the same good. A negative network externality occurs if the consumer's quantity demanded for a good increases because fewer consumers are purchasing the same good. In other words, sometimes an individual's demand curve is influenced by the other people purchasing the good.

Positive Network Externalities

Many examples of network externalities can be found in the communications area, such as with fax machines, telephones, and the Internet. Imagine you had a telephone, but nobody else did; it would be relatively worthless without others with whom to talk. It is also true that if you were the only one to own a DVD player, it would make little sense for manufacturers to make DVDs and your DVD player would be of little value.

The software industry has many examples of positive network externalities. For example, it is a lot easier to coordinate work if all people are using the same software on their computers. It is also a lot easier (less costly) to get help if you need it because many people are familiar with the product, which may be a lot easier (less costly) than calling the support line for your software package. Another example is fax machines—others have to have one. In short, our demand increases as the number of users increases.

Another type of positive network externality is called the bandwagon effect, where a buyer wants the product because others own it. In recent years, we watched people get on the bandwagon in the toy industry with Cabbage Patch Dolls, Beanie Babies, American Girl dolls, Tickle Me Elmo, and Furbies, among others. It can happen in the clothing industry too (e.g., Tommy Bahama or Ugg boots).

bandwagon effect
a positive network externality in which a consumer's demand for a product increases because other consumers own it

Negative Network Externalities

Other goods and services are subject to negative network externalities, which may be a result of the snob effect. The snob effect is a negative network externality where a consumer wants to own a unique good. For example, a rare baseball card of Shoeless Joe Jackson, a Model T car (a tin lizzy), a Vincent Van Gogh painting, a Rolex watch, or an expensive sports car may qualify as snob goods where the quantity that a particular individual demanded of a good increases when fewer other people own it. Firms seek to achieve a snob effect through marketing and advertising, knowing that if they can create a less elastic demand curve for their product, they can raise prices.

Negative network externalities can arise from congestion too. For example, if you are a member of a health club, a negative network externality may occur because too many people are in the gym working out at the same time. Even though I may prefer a ski resort with shorter lift lines, others may view these goods as a positive externality and would increase their quantity demanded if more people were in the gym, on the beach, or at the ski slopes. Perhaps they do not want to work out alone, hang out on a lonely beach, or ride up on the chair lift by themselves. That is, whether it is a positive or negative network externality may depend on the consumer's tastes and preferences.

What is a negative network externality? What is a bandwagon effect?

Switching Costs

Along with the possible advantages of joining a larger network from capturing positive network externalities, you may also encounter costs if you leave—switching costs. For example, costs are associated with switching to new software. If you are well versed in Microsoft Word, it would be costly to switch to OpenOffice. Network externalities and switching costs are two of the reasons that eBay and Amazon.com have done so well. The first firm in a market, where everybody in its large customer base is familiar with the operation, gains huge advantage. Other potential competitors recognize this advantage and, as a result, are leery of entering into the business.

switching costs
the costs involved in changing from one product to another brand or in changing suppliers

In short, in industries that see significant positive network effects, oligopoly is likely to be present. That is, a small number of firms may be able to secure most of the market. Consumers tend to choose the products that everyone else is using. Thus, behavior may allow these firms to increase their output and achieve economics of scale that smaller firms cannot obtain. Hence, the smaller firms will go out of business or be bought out by larger firms.

SECTION QUIZ

1. In game theory
   a. there is not always a dominant strategy.
   b. a Nash equilibrium is a dominant strategy.
   c. collusion is an example of a cooperative game.
   d. all of the above are true.

2. In game theory
   a. cooperative strategies are more likely in repeated games than one-shot games.
   b. cooperative strategies are more likely in one-shot games than in repeated games.
   c. cooperative strategies are equally likely in one-shot and repeated games.
   d. we do not know whether cooperative strategies are more likely in one type of game or another.

3. In game theory
   a. a dominant strategy in a noncooperative game does not yield the same result as if players cooperate.
   b. a tit-for-tat strategy is a way to reward cooperation and punish noncooperation in a repeated game.
   c. in a Nash equilibrium, neither firm has an incentive to change behavior.
   d. all of the above are true.

4. Which of the following areas illustrates positive network externalities?
   a. Telephones
   b. Software
   c. Fax machines
   d. The Internet
   e. All of the above

---

1. How is noncollusive oligopoly like a military campaign or a poker game?
2. What is the difference between cooperative and noncooperative games?
3. How does the prisoners' dilemma illustrate a dominant strategy for noncolluding oligopolists?
4. What is a Nash equilibrium?
5. In the prisoners' dilemma, if each prisoner believed that the other prisoner would deny the crime, would each choose to deny the crime?
6. Why are repeated games more likely than one-shot games to lead to cooperative results?
7. How does a tit-for-tat strategy work?
8. Why would industries with substantial positive network externalities tend to be oligopolies?

Answers: 1. d   2. a   3. d   4. e

Fill in the blanks:

1. Oligopolies exist when only a(n) _____ firms control all or most of the production and sale of a product.

2. In oligopoly, products may be either homogeneous or _____.

3. In oligopoly, _____ to entry are often high, preventing competing firms from entering the market.

4. In oligopoly, firms can earn long-run _____ profits.

5. Oligopoly is characterized by mutual _____ among firms. Oligopolists must _____ because the number of firms in the industry is so small that changes in one firm's price of output will affect the sales of competing firms.

6. In oligopoly, barriers to entry in the form of large start-up costs, economies of scale, or _____ are usually present.

7. The economy of large-scale production _____ new firms from entering a market because high initial average total costs impose heavy losses on new entrants.

8. Mutual interdependence means that no firm knows with _____ what its demand curve looks like. The demand curve and the profit-maximizing price and output will depend on how others _____ to the firm's policies.

9. Because they are mutually interdependent, oligopolists are tempted to get together and agree to act jointly, or to _____, in order to reduce uncertainty and raise profits.

10. From society's point of view, collusion creates a situation where goods are priced too _____ and outputs too _____.

11. International agreements between firms regarding sales, pricing, and other decisions are called _____ agreements.

12. Although collusive oligopolies may be profitable for participants, they are often short lived because firms have a great temptation to _____ on their fellow colluders.

13. In oligopoly, an understanding may develop under which one large firm will play the role of price _____, sending signals to competitors that they have changed their prices.

14. Competitors that go along with the pricing decisions of a price leader are called price _____.

15. Collusive behavior is no guarantee of economic profits in the _____ run.

16. Without _____ to entry, new firms will be attracted by the economic profits earned when firms act to maximize joint profits.

17. New firms will lower _____ and break down existing pricing agreements. Price competition will result in prices approaching the level of average total _____.

18. Oligopolists may charge a price lower than the profit-maximizing price to _____ new firms from entering the market. This strategy will be effective when new firms face _____ costs than existing firms in the industry do.

19. In some respects, _____ oligopoly resembles a military campaign or poker game.

20. Oligopoly interdependence is often analyzed in terms of _____ theory.

21. Collusion is an example of a(n) _____ game.

22. In _____, each firm sets its policy without consulting other firms.

23. The primary difference between cooperative games and noncooperative games lies in the players' ability to make _____.

24. In game theory, a strategy that will be optimal regardless of your opponents' actions is called a _____ strategy.

25. In the traditional prisoners' dilemma, a(n) _____ matrix is used to illustrate the various possibilities and results for the two parties.

26. A(n) _____ equilibrium is reached in game theory when each firm is doing as well as it can, given the actions of its competitor.

27. A Nash equilibrium is _____ because once it is established, neither firm has an incentive to change behavior.

28. Repeated games are _____ likely to lead to cooperative results than one-shot games.

29. In a(n) _____ strategy, a game participant does whatever the other participant did during the previous play.

30. A(n) _____ externality occurs when a consumer's quantity demanded increases

because a greater number of consumers purchase the same good.

31. Positive network externalities are particularly common in the area of _____.

32. The _____ effect refers to the case where a buyer wants a product because others also own it.

33. Congestion can cause _____ network externalities by overcrowding.

34. Switching costs can give an advantage to the _____ firms in an industry.

Answers: 1. few 2. differentiated 3. barriers 4. economic 5. interdependence; strategize 6. patents 7. discourages 8. certainty; react 9. collude 10. high; low 11. cartel 12. cheat 13. leader 14. followers 15. long 16. barriers 17. prices; costs 18. discourage; higher 19. noncollusive 20. game 21. cooperative 22. noncooperative games 23. contracts 24. dominant 25. payoff 26. Nash 27. self-enforcing 28. more 29. tit-for-tat 30. positive network 31. communications 32. bandwagon 33. negative 34. first

KEY TERMS AND CONCEPTS

mutual interdependence 414
collusion 418
cartel 418
joint profit maximization 418
price leader 421
price follower 421
price leadership 421

predatory pricing 423
game theory 426
cooperative game 426
noncooperative game 427
dominant strategy 427
prisoners' dilemma 427
payoff matrix 427

tit-for-tat strategy 430
network externality 432
positive network externality 432
negative network externality 432
bandwagon effect 433
switching costs 433

SECTION QUIZ ANSWERS

15.1 Oligopoly

1. **How can concentration ratios indicate the extent of oligopolies' power?**
Concentration ratios indicate the fraction of total industry output produced by the largest firms in the industry, which is a guide to their ability to increase prices. However, they are imperfect indicators; for instance, they do not reflect foreign competition.

2. **Why is oligopoly characterized by mutual interdependence?**
Because an oligopoly includes few sellers, any change in output or price by one of them is likely to appreciably impact the sales of competing firms. Each of the sellers recognizes this fact, so what each firm should do to maximize its profits depends on what other firms do. Their choices and policies therefore reflect this mutual interdependence.

3. **Why do economies of scale result in few sellers in oligopoly models?**
Where substantial economies of scale are available relative to market demand, reasonably low costs of production cannot be obtained unless a firm produces a large fraction of the market output. If each firm, to produce at low costs, must supply a substantial fraction of the market, the industry has room for only a few firms to produce efficiently.

4. **How do economies of scale result in barriers to entry in oligopoly models?**
Low-cost entry must take place on a large scale in industries with substantial economies of scale. Therefore, existing firms could be profitable at their current prices and outputs without leading to entry. The great increase a large-scale entrant would cause in market output and the resulting decrease in market price could make that entrant unprofitable at those lower post-entry prices, even if current firms are profitable at current prices.

5. **Why does an oligopolist have a difficult time finding its profit-maximizing price and output?**
An oligopolist has a difficult time finding its profit-maximizing price and output because its demand curve is dramatically affected by the price and output policies of each of its rivals. This difficulty causes a great deal

of uncertainty about the location and shape of its demand and marginal revenue curves because they depend on what policies rivals actually adopt.

6. Why would an automobile manufacturer be more likely than the corner baker to be an oligopolist?
The automobile industry realizes substantial economies of scale relative to market demand, so lowercost automobile production can be obtained by a firm that produces a substantial fraction of the market output. As a result, the automobile industry only has room for relatively few efficient-scale producers. In contrast, the bakery industry does not have substantial economies of scale relative to market demand, so the industry has room for a large number of efficient-scale bakeries.

15.2 Collusion and Cartels

1. Why are collusive agreements typically unstable and short lived?
Collusive agreements are typically unstable and short lived because they are strictly illegal under antitrust laws in the United States and many other countries. Also, firms experience a great temptation to cheat on collusive agreements by increasing their output and decreasing prices, which undermines any collusive agreement.

2. Why is the temptation to collude greater when the industry's demand curve is more inelastic?
The more inelastic the demand curve, the greater the increase in profits from colluding to jointly restrict output below its current level and raise prices in the industry, and hence the greater the temptation to collude.

15.3 Other Oligopoly Models

1. What impact does easy entry have on the profitability of oligopolies?
Economic profits in oligopolistic industries will attract entrants, if entry is easy. Entrants may break down existing price agreements by cutting prices in an attempt to establish themselves in the industry, forcing existing firms to reduce their prices and suffer reduced market shares and thus undermining the profitability of the oligopoly.

2. Why are barriers to entry necessary for successful, ongoing collusion?
Because easy entry erodes economic profits where they are positive, barriers to entry are necessary for

oligopolists to continue to earn economic profits in the long run.

3. Why might oligopolists charge less than their short-run profit-maximizing price when threatened by entry?
When entry threatens to undermine the economic profits of an oligopolistic industry, firms in the industry may lower their prices below the level that would maximize their short-run profits in order to deter entry by making it less profitable.

4. A group of colluding oligopolists incurs costs of $10 per unit, and their profit-maximizing price is $15. If they know that potential market entrants could produce at a cost of $12 per unit, what price are the colluders likely to charge?
If the colluding oligopolists are afraid of attracting entrants who will expand market output and reduce market prices and the colluders' profits, they might price below their short-run profit-maximizing price in order to make it unprofitable for new entrants. In this case, colluding oligopolists might well charge $12 or just below rather than the $15 they would otherwise charge.

5. Why is price leadership also called tacit collusion?
Price leadership, where one (typically dominant) firm signals how it intends to change its price and other firms follow suit, does not involve explicit agreements to restrict output and raise price. However, it can potentially be used to coordinate firms' behavior to achieve the same ends.

6. What two factors increase the Herfindahl-Hirshman Index (HHI)?
The HHI increases as either the number of firms in an industry decreases or the disparity in firm sizes increases.

7. Why do horizontal mergers tend to concern antitrust authorities more than vertical or conglomerate mergers?
Only horizontal mergers between makers of similar products increase market shares in a particular market, triggering changes in the HHI.

8. For someone to be engaged in predatory pricing, what must happen to prices after the predation? Why would potential entry undermine the strategy?
To reap monetary profits after predatory pricing, a firm would have to raise its prices substantially afterward. Easy entry would tend to make such a price increase unprofitable, as it would attract new competitors.

15.4 Game Theory and Strategic Behavior

1. How is noncollusive oligopoly like a military campaign or a poker game?

Noncollusive oligopoly is like a military campaign, a poker game, or other strategic games in that firms take certain actions, not because they are necessarily advantageous in themselves but because they improve the position of the oligopolist relative to its competitors, with the intent of improving its ultimate position. Firm actions take into account the likely countermoves rivals will make in response to those actions.

2. What is the difference between cooperative and noncooperative games?

Noncooperative games are those where actions are taken independently, without consulting others; cooperative games are those where players can communicate and agree to binding contracts with each other.

3. How does the prisoners' dilemma illustrate a dominant strategy for noncolluding oligopolists?

The prisoners' dilemma illustrates a dominant strategy for noncolluding oligopolists because it is in each player's interest to make the same choice regardless of the choice of the other player. Where a strategy is optimal regardless of opponents' actions, that strategy will dominate (be chosen over) others.

4. What is a Nash equilibrium?

A Nash equilibrium is one where each firm is doing as well as it can, given the actions of its competitors. It is self-enforcing because once it is established, there is no incentive for any firm to change its policies or its actions.

5. In the prisoners' dilemma, if each prisoner believed that the other prisoner would deny the crime, would each choose to deny the crime?

The prisoners' dilemma illustrates a dominant strategy in which it is in the interest of each of the two prisoners to confess, regardless of whether the other prisoner confesses—Prisoner A gets a lighter sentence if he confesses (2 years) than if he does not (6 years) if Prisoner B confesses, but he also gets a lighter sentence if he confesses (6 months) than if he does not (1 year) when Prisoner B does not confess; and the same is true for Prisoner B. The result is that, given the payoff matrix, each prisoner will confess regardless of what he expects the other prisoner will do.

6. Why are repeated games more likely than one-shot games to lead to cooperative results?

While there are no adverse future consequences from "cheating" in a one-shot game, repeated games introduce these effects into the analysis by influencing the results of future games.

7. How does a tit-for-tat strategy work?

In the first round, you cooperate. Then, in each successive round, you do what the other player did in the previous round. This "rewards" the opponent's current cooperation and "punishes" any choice the opponent makes not to cooperate.

8. Why would industries with substantial positive network externalities tend to be oligopolies?

Consumers' demands are greater the larger the number of consumers. This could allow the more successful firms to grow and increase their output more, letting them achieve economies of scale that others cannot attain.

PROBLEMS

1. Which of the following markets are oligopolistic?
   a. Corn
   b. Funeral services
   c. Airline travel
   d. Hamburgers
   e. Oil
   f. Breakfast cereals

2. Which of the following are characteristic of oligopolistic industries?
   a. A large number of firms
   b. Few firms
   c. A high degree of product differentiation
   d. High barriers to entry
   e. Free entry and exit
   f. Mutual interdependence

3. Suppose Farmer Smith from Kansas and Farmer Jones from Missouri agree to restrict their combined output of wheat in an attempt to increase the price and profits. How likely do you think the Smith–Jones cartel is to succeed? Explain.

4. Explain how the joint profit-maximizing price of colluding firms under oligopoly is determined. How about output?

5. Explain how the long-run equilibrium under oligopoly differs from that of perfect competition.

6. Important differences exist between perfect competition and oligopoly. Show your understanding of these differences by listing the following terms under either "perfect competition" or "oligopoly."

		Perfect Competition	Oligopoly
allocative efficiency	large economies of scale	_____	_____
many small firms	productive efficiency	_____	_____
high barriers to entry	horizontal demand curve	_____	_____
few large firms	mutual interdependence	_____	_____
downward-sloping demand curve	no control over price	_____	_____

7. One of the world's most successful cartels has been the Central Selling Organization (CSO), which controls about three-quarters of the world's diamonds. This collusive oligopoly has kept diamond prices high by restricting supply. The CSO has also promoted the general consumption of diamonds through advertising and marketing. New supplies of diamonds have been found in Canada and Russia. These new mines, which are outside the direct control of the CSO, want to sell their diamonds on the open market.
   a. What would you predict will happen in the market for diamonds if these new mines do not cooperate with the cartel?
   b. What do you think will happen to CSO diamond advertising?

8. The U.S. Justice Department has been worried that the nation's four largest air carriers—Delta, Southwest, American, and United—use low prices to limit competition at the busiest airports. Predatory pricing exists when the dominant carrier at an airport matches the low prices of any new low-fare competitor and sells more low-fare seats. The major carrier holds these low prices until the new competition folds. The dominant carrier recovers any short-term losses with increased fares once the competition is eliminated.

   The government thinks that this pricing response is an anticompetitive strategy. The dominant carriers claim that this response is simply a part of competition. Which is it? How would each of the following pieces of information affect your decision as to whether it is an anticompetitive strategy or a competitive response? Check the appropriate column.

	Anticompetitive Strategy	Competitive Response
Large, unrecoverable start-up costs for new airlines.	_____	_____
Many airlines serve the airport.	_____	_____
Dominant airline drops price below average variable cost.	_____	_____
Dominant airline flights have excess capacity before the new airline enters the market.	_____	_____

9. What would the Herfindahl-Hirshman Index (HHI) be in each of the following situations?
   a. Ten firms, each with 10 percent of the market
   b. Four firms, each with 25 percent of the market
   c. Two firms, each with 50 percent of the market
   d. One firm with a monopoly in the market

10. Why would someone consider how broadly or narrowly the relevant market is considered to be so critical to the results when HHI values are used to evaluate mergers?

11. Assume there are initially 10 firms, each with a 10 percent market share.
    a. What is the initial HHI?
    b. What will the HHI become if two firms merge?
    c. What will the HHI become if three firms merge?

12. Answer questions a–c on HHI.
    a. What would the HHI be for an industry made up of one firm with 30 percent of the market, and 14 firms, each with 5 percent of the market?
    b. What would the HHI be if two of the firms with 5 percent of the market merge?
    c. What would the HHI be if the large (30 percent share) firm merged with one of the smaller (5 percent share) firms?

13. Are the following mergers horizontal, vertical, or conglomerate?
    a. *Newsweek* magazine and *Time* magazine
    b. Tyson Chicken and Popeye's Chicken restaurants
    c. CBS TV and Jerry Bruckheimer Productions (TV show producer)
    d. Alcoa and McDonald's
    e. Alcoa and an aluminum-siding company
    f. Sealy Mattress Company and Beautyrest Mattress Company
    g. a bakery and a sandwich chain

14. Two firms compete in the breakfast cereal industry producing Rice Krinkles and Wheat Krinkles cereal, respectively. Each manufacturer must decide whether to promote its product with a large or small advertising budget. The potential profits for these firms are as follows (in millions of dollars):

Firm A
Wheat Krinkles Cereal

		Large Advertising Budget	Small Advertising Budget
Firm B Rice Krinkles Cereal	**Large Advertising Budget**	(Firm A) $50 M — (Firm B) $50 M	(Firm A) $30 M — (Firm B) $100 M
	Small Advertising Budget	(Firm A) $140 M — (Firm B) $20 M	(Firm A) $150 M — (Firm B) $150 M

Describe the nature of the mutual interdependence between the two firms. Is a Nash equilibrium evident?

15. Suppose Pepsi is considering an ad campaign aimed at rival Coca-Cola. What is the dominant strategy if the payoff matrix is similar to the one shown in Exhibit 3 in Section 15.4?

16. Suppose your professor announces that each student in your large lecture class who receives the highest score (no matter how high) on the take-home final exam will get an A in the course. The professor points out that if the entire class colludes successfully everyone could get the same score. Is it likely that everyone in the class will get an A?

17. The following payoff matrix shows the possible sentences that two suspects, who are arrested on suspicion of car theft, could receive. The suspects are interrogated separately and are unable to communicate with one another:

		Suspect 2	
		Confess	**Don't Confess**
Suspect 1	**Confess**	(1) 6 years / (2) 6 years	(1) 1 year / (2) 10 years
	Don't Confess	(1) 10 years / (2) 1 year	(1) 2 years / (2) 2 years

For the information given in the payoff matrix above:

a. Is there a dominant strategy?

b. What is the dominant strategy? How do you know?

c. Is there a Nash equilibrium? How do you know?

18. Why are repeated games more likely than one-shot games to be cooperative?

19. Why might shirking on a team project in school be a dominant strategy, but not shirking on a team project at work?